W9-CBZ-485

Acclaim for
RON CHERNOW'S

THE WARBURGS

"Ron Chernow's blockbuster history traces the heart-rending saga of this German-Jewish banking family. . . . Despite his scrupulous documentation of sources, Chernow is never less than readable. A graceful and lucid writer, he offers old-fashioned narrative in the grand style."

—*New York Newsday*

"The history of a fascinating family. . . . What we learn about in this book is people. . . . Chernow is very good at bringing them to life. He has a sharp eye for detail. . . . One can open the book anywhere and enjoy it."

—*New Republic*

"Ron Chernow . . . has made the stories of these four brothers the cornerstones of a dark, though not quite tragic, family saga. [He is] a graceful writer with an eye for the telling anecdote. . . . The result is a book of considerable pathos and immediacy. . . . Through his portrait of this complex dynastic organism, he sheds interesing light on various larger historical themes."

—*Boston Sunday Globe*

"Excellent family history. . . . This chronicle of one of the most important banking families in history tells us much about the people. . . . A great, and lengthy, saga."

—*The Times* (London)

"The Warburgs stand revealed as a family more fortune-kissed, fated and fascinating even than the Kennedys, and . . . just as important . . . and now their story has been ably told."

—*New York Daily News*

RON CHERNOW

THE WARBURGS

Ron Chernow holds degrees in English literature from Yale and Cambridge. His articles on business, politics, and history have appeared in more than thirty national and regional publications. His celebrated first book, *The House of Morgan*, won the National Book Award for nonfiction. *The Warburgs* was awarded the Columbia Business School's 1993 George S. Eccles Prize for Excellence in Economic Writing, and was named a Notable Book by both *The New York Times* and the American Library Association. He lives in Brooklyn with his wife, Valerie, a sociologist.

Books by R O N   C H E R N O W

The House of Morgan
The Warburgs

THE
WARBURGS

THE
WARBURGS

*The Twentieth-Century Odyssey of a
Remarkable Jewish Family*

RON CHERNOW

VINTAGE BOOKS

A DIVISION OF RANDOM HOUSE, INC.

NEW YORK

FIRST VINTAGE BOOKS EDITION, AUGUST 1994

Copyright © 1993 by Ron Chernow
Family tree illustration copyright © 1993 by Anita Karl and Jim Kemp

All rights reserved under International and Pan-American Copyright
Conventions. Published in the United States by Vintage Books,
a division of Random House, Inc., New York, and simultaneously in Canada
by Random House of Canada Limited, Toronto. Originally published in hardcover
by Random House, Inc., New York, in 1993.

The Library of Congress has cataloged the Random House edition as follows:

Chernow, Ron.
The Warburgs/Ron Chernow.
p. cm.
Includes bibliographical references and index.
ISBN 0-679-41823-7
1. Warburg family. 2. Jewish bankers—Biography. 3. Jews—
Germany—Biography. 4. Jews—United States—Biography. I. Title.
DS115.C42   1993   943'.004924'00922—dc20
[B]   93-16599
Vintage ISBN: 0-679-74359-6

Book design by J. K. Lambert
Author photograph © Marion Ettlinger

Manufactured in the United States of America
10 9

To
VALERIE
and
MELANIE

"But the essential point which most non-Jews overlook and which forms the very crux of the Jewish tragedy, is that those Jews who are giving their energies and brains to the Germans are doing it in their capacities as Germans and are enriching Germany and not Jewry, which they are abandoning. . . . They must hide their Judaism in order to be allowed to place their brains and abilities at the disposal of the Germans. They are to no little extent responsible for German greatness. The tragedy of it all is that whereas we do not recognize them as Jews Madame Wagner does not recognize them as Germans, and so we stand there as the most exploited and misunderstood of people."

— CHAIM WEIZMANN to Lord Balfour,
December 12, 1914

"A non-German cannot possibly imagine the heartbreaking position of the German Jew. German Jew—you must place full emphasis on both words. You must understand them as the final product of a lengthy evolutionary process. His twofold love and his struggle on two fronts drive him close to the brink of despair."

— JAKOB WASSERMANN,
My Life as German and Jew

"When refugees meet and exchange stories about their escape from Hitler and their lives abroad, each has a unique story to tell, yet each story is like all the others: a life bravely made over but also a dream lost forever."

— PETER GAY,
The Jews of Germany:
A Historical Portrait

CONTENTS

Prelude.. *xv*

PART ONE
THE EMERGENCE OF THE WARBURGS

1. The Matriarch 3
2. The Imperial Theme 21

PART TWO
THE RISE OF THE MITTELWEG
WARBURGS

3. Meschugge Max............................. 35
4. Tragicomic Brothers 45
5. The Sage and the Serpents................... 57
6. Magic Mountain............................ 69
7. A Small Duchy in Westchester............... 85
8. The King of Steerage....................... 103
9. Secret Furies.............................. 113
10. Shy Warrior............................... 129
11. The Endangered German 141
12. Uptown, Downtown 157

13. Iron Cross................................. *171*

14. The Collapse.............................. *191*

PART THREE
THE FALL OF THE MITTELWEG
WARBURGS

15. Phantom Castle, Phantom Peace............. *209*

16. The Murder Exploding Detachment........... *219*

17. The Royal Couple *237*

18. A Season in Hell *255*

19. The Chemistry of Hate *267*

20. Warburg Redux............................ *279*

21. Capitalist Collectives *289*

22. A Stranger in Paradise *305*

23. Account X *321*

24. Blue Boys *335*

25. The Country Cousin *349*

26. Journey into Fear.......................... *365*

27. New Deal Noodles *383*

28. Beat the Devil............................. *399*

29. Unseen Menace *417*

30. The Closing Doors *429*

31. Partition *445*

32. The Twilight Dynasty *459*

33. Orphans of the Storm *471*

PART FOUR
THE WARTIME INTERREGNUM

34. Surreal Saviors............................ *489*

35. Deathwatch *501*

36. Little Man and Fat Boy..................... *513*

37. Charnel House *531*

PART FIVE
THE RETURN OF THE ALSTERUFER AND
MITTELWEG WARBURGS

38. The Upstart. 545

39. Our Aryan 565

40. Itinerant Preacher 579

41. Museum Pieces. 597

42. The Cousins Club. 609

43. My Viking. 623

44. Enemy of the City 641

45. The Quality of Mercy. 655

46. The European. 669

47. Fathers and Sons. 685

48. Forgotten Gravestone 697

49. A Town of Strangers. 709

Appendix 723

Acknowledgments. 726

Bibliography 729

Notes 740

Index 794

PRELUDE

The German Jews were a people shipwrecked by history. Arguably the most productive group of Jews in history, they were also, in many ways, the least typical. Few groups have been so admired for their achievements or so maligned for their attitudes. Persecuted by other Germans as too Jewish, they were often scorned by other Jews as too German. Their existence rested on a tenuous illusion of acceptance until the Nazis came along and tore that dream to tatters. People still puzzle over why these bright, industrious people were so blind to a mortal threat to their existence. In frustration, some Jews deny them the dignity of their tragedy.

This book attempts to clarify the mystery through the epic story of one of the world's most distinguished Jewish families: the Warburgs. No less than the Rothschilds, they were revered as Jewish royalty. A huge, charming, and gregarious clan with enormous *joie de vivre*, they may rank as the oldest, continuously active banking family in the world, tracing their ancestry to the sixteenth century. This ancient lineage permits a comprehensive look at Jewish evolution on German soil.

It is always dangerous to generalize about a clan as diverse and individualistic as the contradictory, opinionated Warburgs. But as a rule, one can say that they exhibited all the enterprise, daring, and philanthropy of the Jewish community in Germany. With their unfailing energy and high spirits, they adored music and literature, light verse and amateur theatricals, elegant parties and outrageous pranks. They financed German industry, influenced its politics, and enriched its culture. In fact, they excelled in so many areas—producing not only notable bankers, but eminent scholars, politicians, scientists, artists, musicians, philanthropists, socialites, and art patrons—as to rival such protean families as the Huxleys and Jameses. Their story exhibits the abundance of German-Jewish achievement and the eerily close fit of German and Jewish culture.

The Warburgs also displayed the shortcomings of German Jews. They could be snobbish, arrogant, and status-conscious, especially toward their Eastern European brethren. They were often rigid, authoritarian parents. Superpatriotic and steeped in German culture, they exhibited a fierce, sometimes uncritical, devotion to Germany until it was too late. Seemingly heedless of the darker side of the German psyche (although some family members were all too aware of it) and subservient to the state, they were generally ill equipped to deal with the tragedy that befell them. The Warburgs didn't love Germany wisely but too well.

Through the prism of their history, one sees all the forces that shaped the German Jews: their emancipation in Imperial Germany; their striking emergence in Weimar Germany; their persecution and expulsion in the Third Reich; and their stamina in America, England, Israel, and elsewhere. Few Jewish families so robustly exploited the opportunities open to them under the kaiser or suffered so grievously because of them. Because the Warburgs intermarried with the Schiffs and Loebs of New York, their story also traces the development of the German Jews abroad. Since part of the family returned to Germany after the war, their chronicle carries the story right up to the present.

The Warburgs owed much of their early success to Rothschild patronage and they later occupied an analogous place in Jewish charities. As the Rothschild star was dimming in the early twentieth century, the Warburg star shone most brightly. The contrast between the families is instructive. The power of the Rothschilds arose from the mysterious interplay between private banks and royal courts. The Warburgs, by contrast, were modern, proudly democratic, and closely allied with the new industrial classes. Viewing themselves as free, independent citizens of Hamburg, they identified with its ethos of social mobility, unfettered trade, and democratic politics.

Unlike other Jewish banking dynasties, the Warburgs never blended into the aristocracy and refused to be baptized or ennobled. They straddled two worlds, hovering between the Jewish community and gentile high society, accepted by both but never quite certain where they belonged. They tested the limits of tolerance in hitherto forbidden realms in politics, scholarship, and industry—all without surrendering their Jewish identity. As a result, they highlight in vivid form the baffling dilemmas faced by German Jews who wanted to retain their original identity and yet succeed in the larger society.

Whatever their hidden torment, the Warburgs negotiated their way through society with élan and a magnetic confidence. They escaped the physical and psychological ghettos that had penned in Jews. This was a new sort of Jewish family: glamorous, cosmopolitan, versatile, seductive, and almost perilously self-confident. Their story is more than just the tale of German

Jews, for it dramatizes the emergence of the Jewish people in the modern world. It also provides a panoramic view of Germany over the past century, the rise of the American Jewish community, and the creation of the state of Israel.

It is a tragic story of doubt beneath a veneer of self-assurance. Like other German Jews, the Warburgs struggled with an insoluble identity crisis, trying to solve the riddle of who they were. Their fragmented identity affected their business decisions, marriage choices, and political activities. They hoped these tensions would ebb with emancipation. Instead new freedoms only spawned new problems, including the powerful temptation of intermarriage and Christian envy. The Nazis would exploit the identity conflict among German Jews, which weakened their capacity to withstand assault.

If identity confusion was the source of psychological pain, it was also the crucible of creativity. They were assimilated enough to enter the upper echelons of society in Hamburg, New York, and London, but the Warburgs were never wholly accepted. This enabled them to combine an outsider's perspective with an insider's entrée. Often seeing things from a somewhat skewed angle, they tended to peer deeper into their times than their contemporaries.

As with other German Jews, the Warburgs displayed ambivalence about their religion. Long arrayed among the wealthy, paternalistic elders who governed the Jewish community, they had shed most of their spirituality by the time Hitler seized power. They were suspended between a religious past they had lost and a secular future they hadn't found. Rational in outlook, they sometimes felt embarrassed about a religion that seemed encrusted with musty superstition. They kept a wary, uneasy distance from things "too" Jewish, even though the values of Judaism permeated their lives, history, and culture.

Glandular optimists, the Warburgs tried to reconcile the contradictions of being Jewish and German, nationalist and internationalist, traditional and modern. They struggled to forge new syntheses in order to transcend these divisions. They wanted to square the circle, to make the world whole. But the world didn't allow them the luxury of this tolerant cosmopolitanism. In the end, they were forced to choose among clashing aspects of themselves. As with many German Jews, they discovered that it didn't matter how they defined themselves. In the end, Adolf Hitler would do it for them.

Brooklyn Heights
January 1993

The WARBURGS

Simon von Cassel
(D. 1566)

Jacob Samuel Warburg
after 1647 in Altona
(D. 1668)

Samuel
(D. 1595)

Moses Warburg
(D. 1701)

Jacob Simon
(D. 1636)

Samuel Warburg m. Rechel
(D. 1759)   Delbanco

Juspa-Joseph Warburg
(D. 1678)

Hela   Gumprich
Heckscher m. Marcus Warburg
                          (1727-1801)

Röschen Hausen m. Moses Marcus   Gerson
Abrahamson   Warburg   (1765-1826)
                (1763-1830)

Sara Warburg m. 1829 Abraham (Aby)
(1805-1884)   S. Warburg
                     (1798-1856)

Marianne Warburg   Rosa Warburg   Jenny Warburg
(1830-1882)   (1833-1908)   (1836-1894)
m.   m.   m.
Samuel Zagury   Paul Schiff   Michael Fürth
div. 1859   (1829-1893)   (1826-1900)

Malchen   Siegmund   Moritz M.
Warburg   Warburg   Warburg
(1831-1911)   (1835-1889)   (1838-1910)
m.   m. 1862   m. 1864
Adolph   Théophilie   Charlotte
Goldschmidt   Rosenberg   Oppenheim
(1810-1857)   (1840-1905)   (1842-1921)

© A.Karl/T.Kemp, 1993

continued on following pages

Siegmund Warburg m. 1862 Théophilie
(1835-1889)   Rosenberg
                               (1840-1905)

Mathilde Warburg   Anna Warburg   Rosa Warburg
(1863-1922)   (1866-1929)   (1870-1922)
m.   m. 1890   m. 1891
Marc Rosenberg   Martin   Alexandre
(1851-1930)   Blumenfeld   Baron de
                          (1855-1908)   Gunzburg
                                                (1863-1948)

Abraham S. Warburg   m. (1st) 1894   Olga L.
(1864-1933)   Leonino
                                     (1872-1895)

                     m. (2nd) 1897   Elly Simon
                                     (1873-1931)

Olga L. Warburg   Marianne   Karl S. A.
(1898-1965)   Warburg   (Charles)
m. 1919   (1901-)   Warburg
Friedrich   m. 1929   (1907-1972)
(Fritz)   Oscar H. L.   m. 1947
Lachmann   Goldschmidt   Luise Einstein
(1888-1938)   (1881-1960)   (1911-)

            Ellen J. Warburg   Ruth A. Warburg
            (1899-1940)   (1904-1967)
            m. 1920   m. 1930
            S. F. L. T. Plaut   Kurt M. Neu
            (1888-1948)   (1899-1982)

The Alsterufer WARBURGS

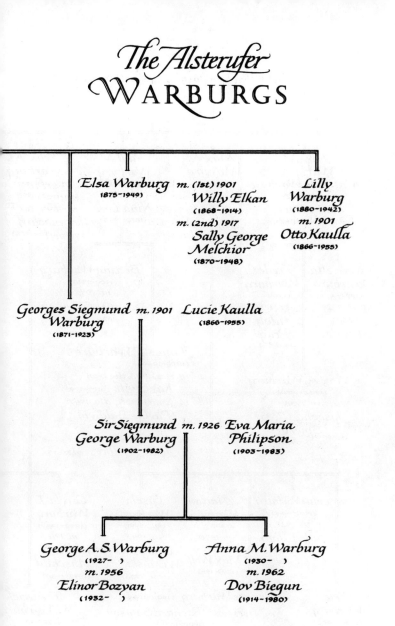

Elsa Warburg
(1875–1949)

m. (1st) 1901
Willy Elkan
(1868–1914)

m. (2nd) 1917
Sally George
Melchior
(1870–1948)

Lilly
Warburg
(1880–1942)

m. 1901
Otto Kaulla
(1866–1955)

Georges Siegmund
Warburg
(1871–1923)

m. 1901 Lucie Kaulla
(1866–1955)

Sir Siegmund
George Warburg
(1902–1982)

m. 1926 Eva Maria
Philipson
(1903–1983)

George A. S. Warburg
(1927–)
m. 1956
Elinor Bozyan
(1932–)

Anna M. Warburg
(1930–)
m. 1962
Dov Biegun
(1914–1980)

See following pages for
lineage of Moritz M. Warburg,
the Mittelweg Warburgs

Moritz M. Warburg m. 1864 Charlotte Oppenheim
(1838–1910) (1842–1921)

Aby M. Warburg (1866–1929)
m. 1897
Mary Hertz (1866–1934)

Max M. Warburg (1867–1946)
m. 1899
Alice Magnus (1873–1960)

Paul M. Warburg (1868–1932)
m. 1895
Nina Loeb (1870–1945)

Felix M. Warburg (1871–1937)
m. 1895
Frieda F. Schiff (1875–1958)

Marietta Warburg (1899–1973)
m. 1926
Peter Braden (1900–1975)

Frede C. Warburg (1904–)
m. 1938
Adolf Prag (1906–)

Bettina Warburg (1900–1990)
m. 1942
Samuel Grimson (1884–1955)

Max A. Warburg (1902–1974)
m. 1938
Josepha (Josi) Spiero (1903–1988)

James P. Warburg (1896–1969)
m. (1st) 1918, div. 1934
Kay Swift (1897–1993)
m. (2nd) 1935, div. 1947
Phyllis Baldwin (1903–1993)
m. (3rd) 1948
Joan Melber (1923–)

Lola Warburg (1901–1989)
m. 1921
Rudolf Hahn (1897–1964)

Anita Warburg (1908–)
m. 1940, div. 1950
Max Wolf (1899–1962)

Gisela Warburg (1912–1991)
m. 1943
Charles E. Wyzanski, Jr. (1906–1986)

Carola T. Warburg (1896–1987)
m. 1916
Walter N. Rothschild (1892–1960)

Eric Warburg (1900–1990)
m. 1946
Dorothea Thorsch (1912–)

Renate Warburg (1904–1984)
m. (1st) 1927 Richard Samson (1900–1943)
m. (2nd) 1940 Walter Strauss (1908–?)
m. (3rd) 1959 Sir William Calder (1881–1960)

Frederick M. Warburg (1897–1973)
m. 1946
Wilma L. Shannon (1903–1993)

The Mittelweg WARBURGS

Olga C. Warburg
(1873–1904)
m. 1898
Paul Kohn-Speyer
(1868–1942)

Fritz M. Warburg
(1879–1964)
m. 1908
Anna Beata Warburg
(1881–1966)

Louise Warburg
(1879–1973)
m. 1901
Julius Derenberg
(1873–1928)

Alfred P. Kohn-Speyer
(1899–1904)

Alice C. Kohn-Speyer
(1902–)
m. 1940
William H. Auerbach
(1892–1974)

Ingrid F. Warburg
(1910–)
m. 1941
Veniero Spinelli
(1909–1969)

Charlotte Esther (Noni) Warburg
(1922–)
m. 1945
Seco (Willy) Smulowicz (Shalmon)
(1910–1985)

Marian J. Kohn-Speyer
(1900–1988)
m. 1935
Ernest Sander
(1886–1981)

Edmund P. Kohn-Speyer
(1904–1985)
m. 1935
Alice Brown
(1904–)

Eva A. Warburg
(1912–)
m. 1946
Naftali Unger
(1909–1987)

Paul F. (Piggy) Warburg
(1904–1965)
m. (1st) 1926, div. 1934
Jean Stettheimer
(1906–)
m. (2nd) 1939, div. 1946
M. Constance Woodworth (D. 1983?)
m. (3rd) 1946 Barbara Tapper d'Almeida
(1907–)

Edward M. M. Warburg
(1908–1992)
m. 1939
Mary W. P. Currier
(1908–)

Walter J. Derenberg
(1903–1975)
m. 1949
Emily Hess
(1913–)

Gabriele C. Derenberg
(1914–)
m. 1952
David Schiff
(1912–1978)

Carl J. Derenberg
(1902–1977)
m. 1937
Hedwig J. Bollschweiler
(1908–1982)

Ruth Derenberg
(1906–)
m. 1928
César Domela-Nieuwenhuis
(1900–1992)

Gerald F. Warburg (1901–1971)
m. (1st) 1922 Marion Bab (1903–1982)
m. (2nd) 1933 Natica Nast (1905–1987)

Part One

THE
EMERGENCE
OF THE
WARBURGS

Sara Warburg.
(Warburg family, Hamburg)

CHAPTER 1

The Matriarch

Jews settled as far north as the Rhineland after the Romans destroyed the Temple in A.D. 70. Far from feeling alien, these winegrowers and craftsmen felt rooted in Germanic soil. But their pastoral idyll was shattered by the religious zealotry of the eleventh century. Butchered by the Crusaders, they were expelled from their farms and forced into moneylending. During the Black Death, roving flagellants cursed the Jews for supposedly causing the bubonic plague by poisoning wells. They were also periodically accused of draining blood from Christian children to bake unleavened Passover bread—the so-called blood libel. Like dark, disturbing figures from a grim fairy tale, the Jews would secretly linger on in the German psyche as ghouls tricked out in civilian clothes. This legacy would lie dormant, but never dead, in the culture.

The Warburgs sometimes claim to be Sephardic Jews and fancifully trace their genealogy back to medieval Italy. But the first certifiable ancestor appears in 1559, when Simon von Cassel moved from Hesse to the Westphalian town of Warburg, which was founded by Charlemagne. This picturesque walled town had four stone watchtowers that loomed over a maze of crooked cobbled streets, Romanesque churches, and half-timbered houses. The original Warburg house, built in 1537, still stands.

Imported by the Prince-Bishop of Paderborn, who granted him a *Schutzvertrag* or protective charter, Simon worked as a money changer and pawnbroker. Stymied by the Church prohibition against lending money at interest, noblemen conveniently recruited Court Jews to sin in their stead and stimulate trade. This created a rare historic case of a minority being segregated in a profitable job ghetto. Still a patchwork of three hundred kingdoms, city-states, principalities, and duchies, "Germany" needed Jewish money changers to exchange currencies among these polities. In the popular mind, Jewish bankers deftly exercised a sinister form of black magic, engendering an explosive mixture of envy and resentment.

Court Jews belonged to a special caste and occupied a paradoxical position. (The Warburgs were, strictly speaking, a minor species of Court Jews called *Schutzjuden* or "protected Jews.") However prosperous, they survived at the sovereign's sufferance and could be repudiated whenever debts grew too burdensome. They hung from a golden thread, suspended between gentiles above and Jews below. What anxious tremors fluttered beneath the comfortable air? For ten years, the *Schutzvertrag* guaranteed the religious freedom of Simon, his family, and servants. Yet they still paid a higher tax rate than that levied upon Christian residents. While Simon hosted the local synagogue in his home, Jewish corpses had to buried safely beyond the town walls in a special cemetery.

No innate cleverness about money pushed Jews toward finance. Barred from crafts by medieval guilds and from farming by local ordinances, they were shunted into trade or moneylending by default. In Warburg, they couldn't brew beer, sell shoes or clothing. Like many supposedly "Jewish traits," moneylending was artificially created by anti-Semitic barriers—even if anti-Semites later loudly decried "financial strangulation" by the Jews.

The Warburgs had settled in a tolerant town that didn't force them to listen to missionary preachers. They were never penned into ghettos at night or stigmatized by having to wear yellow badges, as in Frankfurt and other sixteenth-century cities. Because they were spared the psychic scars of early persecution, they would move about with extra self-assurance. Yet their background as protected Jews left them with a contradictory legacy. Dependent upon official patronage, Court Jews identified with authority figures who safeguarded their privileged status and they were always warily respectful of the state. More cultured and educated than ordinary Jews, they acted as community elders and felt deeply responsible for poor Jews. Simon's grandson, Jacob Simon Warburg, headed the Jewish community in the Paderborn bishopric, had the town synagogue in his home, and mediated between Jews and the prince. This ambiguous, hybrid status—neither totally Jewish nor gentile—contributed to the deeply schizoid Warburg character.

The town of Warburg was sacked during the Thirty Years' War, riled by religious fanaticism, and then struck by plague in 1666. The Peace of Westphalia of 1648 severed sea access for the small German states, starving inland trade. All this probably explains why, in 1668, Simon's great-grandson, Juspa-Joseph, moved north while retaining the name "von Warburg." (Before their nineteenth-century emancipation, German Jews couldn't take surnames, so sometimes adopted their hometown names.) Juspa-Joseph settled in Altona on the Elbe River, which flowed into the North Sea only seventy miles away. (He had been preceded by his son, Jacob Samuel, who moved there in 1647.) At the time, Jews couldn't live in Hamburg, even if they worked there, so they resided instead in Altona, a separate principality under relatively benign Danish rule. The Danes granted the Jews ample liberties, including the right to their own schools, cemetery, and synagogue.

Dropping his "von," Juspa-Joseph became plain Warburg. His northward move was momentous: This maritime setting endowed the Warburgs with a cosmopolitan air that must have been quite liberating after provincial inland Germany. On the Elbe, the Warburgs operated in a wide commercial world. Old merchant families launched rich argosies to prosperous port cities of the medieval Hanseatic League and this northern seaside world tied residents closely to London, Amsterdam, and other foreign cities as well. The Altona and Hamburg Jews forged strong links to their cities and, by 1668, the first Warburg was buried in an Altona cemetery.

In 1773, Juspa-Joseph's descendant, Gumprich Marcus, moved to neighboring Hamburg, a thriving city-republic with its own merchant flag, foreign consulates, and military defense. The Dutch-looking town was crosshatched with canals, lined with tall, slim houses, and topped by pointed gables. Special cannons boomed warning of high tides that periodically flooded the town. Europe's bounty passed through the harbor: fish bound for Scandinavia, wool for Flanders, fur from Russia. Like Bremen, Hamburg had elected councils and other quasi-democratic institutions missing in the backward, landlocked duchies. Not only would the Warburgs be anchored in this port city, but its tolerant civic culture would represent their Germany during the worst throes of nationalistic unreason. But although Hamburg had no ghetto, its Jews did remain fenced in by unseen barriers, assigned to certain streets. Even there, the Jews couldn't buy houses or own property but had to rent their lodgings from Christian citizens.

In 1798, Gumprich Marcus bequeathed his money-changing, pawnbroking firm to his two eldest sons, Moses Marcus and Gerson. They expanded it into a bank named M. M. Warburg & Co. which mostly brokered bills. The bank could not have been better located. Hamburg, renowned as a safe haven, profited from turbulence in neighboring countries. During the French

Revolution, noblemen stashed funds there for safekeeping and Amsterdam businessmen fled there to circumvent Napoleon's Continental Blockade. Hamburg jealously guarded its neutrality, since business was its secular religion. This single-minded devotion to material betterment would insulate it from political frenzy even as it created a certain smug, philistine complacency that would be the bane of some later Warburgs. If wealthy Hamburg burghers never reached for the sky, neither did they crawl in the mud.

The Warburg family often spawned contrasting types, and Moses Marcus and Gerson were the first such paired opposites. One embodied the family's solemn sense of duty and the other its free-spirited conviviality. With his thick shock of hair and cautious gaze, Moses Marcus was the steady, decisive brother, the Orthodox Jew and community leader, who subsidized publication of sacred Jewish works. He and his family lived above the Peterstrasse bank. The bald Gerson was a cheerful, uninhibited bachelor, irreverent and fun loving. When a relative visited Hamburg, Moses Marcus duly took him to synagogue, while Gerson spirited him off for a lively evening at the music hall.

For thirty years, the brothers squabbled bitterly. Before his death in 1801, the ailing Gumprich drafted a will to reconcile his sons. "Never part," he intoned. "Only through unity will you be strong and will your business flourish. . . . Mark my last words and admonitions."[1] Ignoring their dying father's injunction, the brothers fought on. At one point, they didn't speak for a year, if legend is to be believed. At the Hamburg stock exchange, they turned from each other in so rhythmic and reflexive a manner that people said it resembled a nimble square dance. Brokers would buy foreign exchange from one brother, then sell it to the other at a higher price. But in one area they agreed: Neither brother severed his Jewish roots, which was then unthinkable. When Moses Marcus and Gerson drew up their first partnership agreement in 1810, it was written in German with Hebrew lettering and dated 20 Sivan 5570 by the Jewish calendar.

From 1806 to 1814, Hamburg was occupied by Napoleon's troops and effectively annexed to France. For gentile residents, the occupation lacked redeeming features, since the new authorities levied heavy taxes and confiscated property owned in Hamburg by the British. The Jews, however, were in a quandary since the French Revolution had emancipated the Jews while Napoleon had liberated Italian ghettos. In fact, the otherwise brutal French reign proved something of a honeymoon for Hamburg Jews, who briefly enjoyed rights equal to other citizens and could buy houses and property in once-taboo streets.

In 1812, the French tried to extort five hundred thousand francs from the Jewish community by arresting Gerson and interning him with other wealthy Jews on the Lüneburg Heath. Relieved to be rid of Gerson, Moses Marcus stalled in paying his ransom and only capitulated under extreme duress from the Jewish community. By one account, he greeted his brother's release with the retort, "Why don't they keep him for good!"[2] Meanwhile, in prison, the sociable Gerson learned French and tried to drum up business with the military government.

Ultimately, the occupation damaged the Jewish community by fomenting in its wake a new nationalism heavily laden with Christian overtones. These nationalists glorified German peasants and the medieval past and were distinctly xenophobic and hostile to diversity—traits that would unfortunately persist in the culture. And when the French left, the Jews surrendered their newly won rights. In 1814, Moses Marcus joined a committee that futilely tried to perpetuate these fleeting freedoms acquired under French military rule. Instead, the Hamburg Jews experienced in 1819 the six-day pogrom of the so-called "Hep Hep" riots, instigated by exclusionary guilds that felt threatened by Jewish competition. In Frankfurt, mobs attacked the Rothschild house.

Gerson and Moses Marcus never called a truce in their private civil war. The friction between them surely sharpened when Gerson fell in love with Sara, the strikingly beautiful daughter of Moses Marcus.[3] She was only fourteen, and Moses Marcus must again have been outraged by the irresponsibility of his insouciant, devil-may-care brother who had found fresh ways to offend him.

When Gerson died in 1825, Moses Marcus faced a crisis that sporadically confronts every banking dynasty: he had no male heirs. With his sizable 250,000 Mark Banco fortune, he was ready to furnish a magnificent dowry for Sara: a partnership stake in the bank for any future son-in-law. Sara, a romantic young woman, must have been delighted to receive a marriage offer from her first cousin, Elias Simon Warburg, who had blue eyes, thin blond hair, and a handsome, sensitive, dignified face. But Moses Marcus and his wife, Rosa, thought they were too closely related. In 1829 they arranged for Sara to marry her queer-looking, slit-eyed second cousin, Aby Samuel Warburg, who thereby became a bank partner.[4] Aby seems the one man in Hamburg for whom the hot-blooded Sara felt no amorous attraction, and it must have been a jolting initiation into the hard realities of a banking family.

Such family liaisons were unavoidable in the small, claustrophobic Jewish community, especially in banking clans that sought suitable matches. To prevent the depletion of their precious working capital, the Rothschilds often married each other as well. And the pool from which Jewish banking families recruited prospects was tiny: Non-Jews were forbidden and most Jews were simply too poor. This chronic shortage of prospective partners made them search as far away as Russia, bringing marriage brokers into the scene. This tiny gene pool would intensify both the Warburg vivacity and gloom, yielding many marvels, oddities, and wonders. Wizards and dunces would issue from the same womb and the family would abound in eccentric geniuses. These semi-incestuous arrangements also yielded a dark legacy of manic-depression and schizophrenia that would haunt the Warburgs for generations.

In 1831, Moses Marcus died of a stroke while in synagogue, leaving the firm to Aby and the spurned suitor, Elias. It must have been a relief to Sara when Elias six years later left and formed his own firm.

By a fine coincidence, Sara and Aby bore the names of the original Jewish patriarch and matriarch, but were otherwise a classical mismatch: she was strong willed, smart, pious, and domineering, while he was timid, lazy, henpecked, and irreverent. He had an odd, distorted appearance, with a low forehead, pouchy eyelids that nearly obscured his eyeballs, and a long nose that ended in a wide mouth. His head was twisted about strangely on his neck. He was so small and jaundiced that boyhood friends dubbed him the "yellow dwarf."[5] Sara, in contrast, had been nicknamed the "Star of the Peterstrasse," and Heinrich Heine allegedly dedicated to her the poem "A Youth Loved a Maiden."[6] Besides her wide-ranging literary interests, she sang beautifully, attended theater and opera, and overshadowed her husband intellectually. Sara was a dynamo, Aby a pleasant dud.

Sara tried to rouse Aby to greater initiative, but the sallow little man cowered before her severity or else mocked her wryly. She educated their four daughters and two sons—Marianne (1830–81), Malchen (1831–1911), Rosa (1833–1908), Siegmund (1835–89), Jenny (1836–1894), and Moritz (1838–1910). The grooming of small children was a major outlet for stifled, frustrated wives in these arranged marriages. Yet Aby's abdication of authority irked her, and she chided him for lounging in his easy chair instead of disciplining the children. "Perhaps you, too, could rouse yourself for once," she taunted him. In response, he would jump up, smack some children at hand, then slump back in his seat.[7] Even at the bank he installed a comfortable swivel chair so that his passivity grew proverbial. Letters were brought to him as he lazed on a sofa. One night, Sara shook him awake. "Aby, the house is burning!" she whispered. Unfazed, Aby pawed skeptically at the wall. "It is not yet hot," he replied, then fell back to sleep.[8] As Sara and Aby accumulated six children, he couldn't quite keep track of them. One day, legend says, he found a filthy ragamuffin in the street and asked who the boy's father was. "Why, you are," said the surprised child.[9]

The frustrated Sara grew rigid, sharp of tongue, and autocratic in manner, demanding strict religious observance and forbidding her family from writing on Saturdays. The outward forms of piety sometimes seemed more important to Sara than their intrinsic meaning. Every Friday evening, clad in her best jewelry and most fetching hats, she presided like a sovereign over family dinners. The furniture, silver candlesticks, and glasses sparkled. The devout Sara wouldn't extinguish Sabbath candles. Instead, she put her pouting lips by the candles and recited a couplet that mentioned two Jewish holidays, Purim and Pesach. The hard "p" sounds blew the candles out, saving her from sin.

If Sara had the Warburg piety, Aby had the family humor and liked to poke fun at his godly wife. Once he told Sara that heaven, like a modern railroad car, was arranged with various classes. She would certainly occupy a first-class compartment, while he would settle into second-class. He pictured them traveling through eternity, separated by a low wall: "We can see each other, but we can't go to each other," he told her. "Up there that will be good enough for me."[10]

Like all tyrants, Sara required many small rituals of deference and even her children addressed her by the formal *"Sie."* If she was coming to lunch the next day, they had to inquire politely, "So mother, will we have the pleasure of seeing you tomorrow?" She would straighten and grandly answer, "The pleasure will be entirely mine."[11] Beneath these difficult, dowager airs, Sara was vain, insecure, and easily wounded. Once, she asked her little grandson Max whom he liked the most and he childishly stammered several names—his nanny, the milkman, a fruit delivery man, his parents—but omitted Sara. Later on, she said, "I have never forgotten this honest but stupid reply," and banished the boy forever from her affections.[12]

If Sara was imperious, her tyranny often betrayed a commendable sense of duty. Like other Warburg matriarchs, she had a strong, unremitting sense of noblesse oblige. Each summer, she and Aby rented one of three houses on the Alsterchaussee. One spring day, acting on a suspicious hunch, Sara asked Aby if he had forgotten to rent the summer house. "Of course not," he lied. When he found that all three houses were already rented, he grew petrified of Sara's wrath and secretly bought all three houses, renting out two. When Sara got wind of this, she asked, "Who lives in these other two houses?" An artist in one and a widow in the other, said Aby. "And you are taking rent from them?" she said, aghast. Refusing to take money from widows or artists, she made him go and return the money at once.[13]

Sara's children stood in awe of her and dreaded her disapproval. Through a marriage broker, she arranged for her eldest daughter, the plain, matronly Marianne, to marry a rich London Jew named Samuel Zagury, a man of Portuguese descent and dubious morals. The unscrupulous Zagury was a charlatan who squandered the dowry, seduced women, and engaged in disreputable business dealings.[14] Terrified of Sara's reaction, Marianne didn't tell her what had happened. After a telltale dearth of letters, Marianne's teenage

brother, Siegmund, went to London and retrieved her.[15] Not shirking responsibility, Sara went to London to negotiate with Zagury (characteristically, she
also took in plays and strolled in the parks) and engineered a formal annul-
ment of the marriage. It was no small fiasco, for Zagury fleeced the Warburgs
royally and the final settlement, not including exorbitant legal bills, stripped
the bank of a quarter of its capital.

While Aby had a good head for figures, liked hobnobbing with clients,
and had some talent for arbitrage—taking advantage of small price discrep-
ancies in different markets—Sara called the shots at the bank and proved
her father's real successor. The fires of youthful passion were cooled and
sublimated into stern business rigors, and Aby submitted the books to her
nightly. The bank's main business was now in foreign exchange and trade
bills. When the French abandoned Hamburg in 1814, the Warburgs and
other bankers replenished the local silver stock. These transactions brought
them into close contact with the Rothschilds, who excelled in metals trading. In a letter of August 4, 1814, the Warburgs displayed growing confidence and assured the Rothschilds that they could handle metal deliveries
as effectively as any house in Hamburg.[16] The Rothschilds had greatly profited from the Napoleonic Wars and were then infinitely more regal than the
Warburgs. So highly did M. M. Warburg & Co. value this connection that it
kept a special stock of stationery on hand for letters to all Rothschild affili-
ates. At one point, the bank even hired a man trained in magnificent penmanship to draft important letters to the Rothschilds.

Always a family of immense charm and masters at the art of business
seduction, the Warburgs cultivated this relationship through exquisite
courtesies. In 1838, they bought Meier Carl Rothschild a silver tray he
admired on a trip to Hamburg. In the 1840s, Willy Rothschild lived with Sara
and Aby, solving a dilemma posed by an absence of kosher food in Hamburg
hotels. In a shifting financial world, the Rothschilds, with all their royal
connections, seemed a secure bedrock. One night, as Aby tossed fitfully in bed,
Sara asked what was wrong. "Oh, God," he said, "I have given Rothschilds
an overdraft of 10,000 pounds and I'm worried about it." "Well, if that's all,
turn over and go to sleep," Sara said. "If Rothschild fails it will be quite all
right for you to go broke too."[17]

Even as the Warburgs emulated the Frankfurt Rothschilds, their own city
acquired new importance. The wars and revolutions that roiled Europe in
1848 also produced a human tide of emigrants who swarmed through Bremen and Hamburg en route to England and America. Both seaports constructed vast halls to house refugees awaiting transatlantic crossings, and this
large, transient population spurred the growth of the St. Pauli district, the
city's notorious red-light zone. Since Hamburg shipowners commanded a fleet

of four thousand seagoing vessels, the city became the crossroads of this profitable new human commerce.

Already a port of colorful vitality, Hamburg throbbed with new energy. The morning streets teemed with vendors in peasant costumes who hawked vegetables carried in yokes balanced on their shoulders. Everything seemed in motion: Dogs pulled fruit wagons, donkeys drew milk trucks, and flat-bottomed barges drifted through dark, greenish waterways, gliding under bridges so numerous that Hamburg was labeled the Venice of the North. In this marshy country, even elegant stores by the Alster Lake stood on oak posts driven deep into the soft terrain. The analogy with Venice went beyond omnipresent water; it was matched in the self-confident wealth of local burghers. Even casual visitors noted the ubiquitous signs of money—servants in red tailcoats delivering messages for merchant princes or pampered children en route to school outfitted in fancy velvet pants and lace collars.

The Hamburg Jews participated in the rising prosperity, with Jews and gentiles about equally represented in local banking and brokerage. Although until 1853 it was headquartered in the Neustadt, the petit bourgeois Jewish section, the Warburg bank flourished and the family seldom experienced discrimination. Yet, ugly undercurrents still flowed in the larger culture and occasionally surfaced. During the 1831 cholera epidemic in Berlin, the Jews were again accused of poisoning the wells. In 1842, an inflammatory tract claimed the discovery of an oven and old bones in a Nuremberg synagogue basement, supposedly the remains of grisly ritual murders committed by Jews against Christians. Each progressive wave of economic growth in Germany provoked a countermovement of virulent nationalism and intolerance among groups who felt threatened by change and this discontent always crystallized around the Jews.

When Sara and Aby celebrated their silver wedding anniversary in 1854, the infirm Aby was beset with worry. He fretted about the Zagury fiasco and the bank's slipping position with the Rothschilds. In 1855, his son Siegmund was apprenticing in London and Aby told him plaintively, "If you have the honour of seeing R. [Rothschild], you may tell him that we very much regret having to dispense entirely with his orders."[18] The following June, Aby wrote a will, canceled his summer trip, then ascended, at age fifty-eight, to his second-class train compartment in heaven where he would be safely apart from his wife. This left Sara doubly widowed, for she had to run both the family and the bank alone.

Sara was now a shrewd, worldly businesswoman, with red cheeks, a determined mouth, and jowly face. Her skin had turned to parchment, but she retained the bright, flashing eyes of girlhood. Assisted by a family friend, August Sanders, she courageously weathered her husband's death and ran the bank with several trusted clerks—a remarkable feat for a woman of her day. She enlisted her precocious elder son, Siegmund, who was now twenty-one and was given power-of-attorney in the bank; his younger brother, Moritz, eighteen, was too young for such responsibility.

These two brothers would reenact the furious conflicts of Moses Marcus and Gerson. Even as children, they looked like offspring of different families. Siegmund had a round nose and thick lips and was as swarthy as a little Ethiopian. Moritz had straight, delicate features and a clear complexion. Siegmund was smart, gruff, hard-driving, funny, and temperamental, while Moritz, a pampered dandy and engaging flirt, was languid and charming, the pretty boy in a queer-looking brood, and definitely Sara's favorite.

Soon after Aby's death, Sara was faced with one of the great crises in Warburg history, which she managed to convert into a famous triumph. The 1856 end of the Crimean War precipitated a steep deflation in commodity prices, which in 1857 toppled American banks and railroads. The panic spread to Scandinavia and then to Hamburg, where financial hysteria engulfed the stock exchange. The Warburgs and other local bankers had to redeem a flood of speculative bills they had endorsed and it looked as if many banks and trading firms would collapse. Sara's daughter, Rosa, had married Paul Schiff, who was managing director of the Credit-Anstalt, a Viennese bank recently formed by the Rothschilds. Paul not only put a vast amount of money at the Warburgs' disposal, but served as intermediary in talks to rescue the city.

To shore up local firms, the Hamburg Senate made an unsuccessful bid for a loan from Berlin, Paris, and other financial capitals. Then in November 1857, the Austrian finance minister dispatched Paul Schiff to Hamburg to investigate a possible rescue loan, with the upshot that Austria sent a train loaded with silver ingots to the Hanseatic City. The transaction was approved by Emperor Franz Josef I. The availability of this fabulous cargo for loans to leading banks—the so-called Silver Train of financial legend—quieted the chaos; six months later, the silver bars were returned to Vienna, and the Warburgs won enormous goodwill from the operation. This initiated a long history of Warburg involvement with the finances of the city-state and emphasized the value of the family's foreign contacts.

After this drama, the matriarchal Sara made Siegmund a partner in 1859 and Moritz in 1862. Although she soon ceded everyday control to the quick, decisive Siegmund, she yielded no royal prerogatives, and her wishes prevailed in all significant matters. She made Siegmund sign a partnership agreement that conceded her ultimate authority: "Although Herr Siegmund Warburg is empowered ordinarily to act according to his own judgment, he must nonetheless seek the opinion of Madame Warburg in matters of special importance, and to act in agreement with the latter."[19]

Every evening after the stock exchange closed, Siegmund and Moritz reported to Sara's house, where she grilled them on the day's affairs. If they didn't meet expectations, she probed. "Now explain yourselves. Siegmund, speak first."[20] Siegmund balked at her meddling, while Moritz was more sympathetic. It irked Sara that Siegmund sometimes skipped the daily briefings. There was something typically Jewish about this interplay between a strong, guiding mother and her talented, impressionable sons. Because many German Jewish businessmen engaged in overseas trade, they traveled frequently, leaving wives in charge of businesses in their absence and this made German Jewish women a particularly hardy breed. Honoring Sara's wishes, her sons closed the bank early on Fridays and avoided the stock exchange on the Sabbath. After spending Saturday afternoons closeted with Sara, they headed back to the bank after sunset.

The clashes between Siegmund and Moritz were only slightly less boisterous than those between Moses Marcus and Gerson. Siegmund was a prodigious, driving worker, often staying late into the evening, whereas Moritz was congenitally indolent. They argued daily and their rows grew so thunderous that the entire street echoed with the racket. At first, Siegmund demoted Moritz to back-office duty until a fellow banker teased him, "You are supposed to have such a very pleasant brother, do send him round to me some time."[21] This was as much a veiled reference to Siegmund's gruff temper as to Moritz's cordiality. Siegmund was prone to tactless candor, while Moritz had a light touch and pleasing geniality. A natural division of labor soon arose: Siegmund ran the bank while Moritz handled outside contacts.

Like his grandson of the same name, Siegmund Warburg had a perfectionist streak and passion for excellence, which showed up in the fine handwriting he demanded of employees. A stout, virile man with a broad, bearded face and flashing eyes, he rode vigorously on horseback each morning. Enterprising and dedicated to the firm's expansion, he had a reputation as a go-getter and risk-taker, quite unlike the conservative Moritz. It was Siegmund who elevated M. M. Warburg & Co. into the first rank of private banks. In 1863 the firm dropped its official title of *Geldwechsler* or money changers, assuming the far loftier designation of *Bankiers.* A tiny firm of ten employees, the bank sold bills of exchange, traded goods against government securities, and made loans. It had a messenger of heroic fidelity named Levien. While delivering bills one day, Levien keeled over from a cerebral hemorrhage. Yet "he clung to the briefcase with all his remaining strength and would not give up till another messenger whom he knew happened to pass and relieved him of it."[22] The bills safe, Levien claimed his heavenly reward after almost sixty years of Warburg service.

In 1865, Sara withdrew from the firm and moved to an impressive house at 49 Rothenbaumchaussee, but she continued to cast a proprietary eye on the bank for the next twenty years. Piloted by Siegmund, the firm moved to a prestigious location, 75 Ferdinandstrasse, in 1868. This was a prime corner spot slightly recessed from the squarish Inner Alster Lake and just a short stroll from the town hall and stock exchange. It stood hard by the headquarters of the great shipping and overseas trading concerns and signified a new Warburg centrality in Hamburg affairs. The Warburgs would steadily buy parcels adjoining this spot until they occupied the entire corner.

During the nineteenth century, Jewish emancipation occurred piecemeal in the various German states. In 1868, the last legal shackles were lifted from Hamburg Jews. From now on, they could marry gentiles, enter once-exclusionary guilds, and live anywhere they liked. After centuries of oppression, this sudden liberty would be the midwife of many wonders, a potent tonic to ambition, and help to transform a provincial banking house into a distinguished international firm. The Warburgs were buoyed by a fantastic sense of optimism, as stimulated by opportunity as they had long been toughened by obstacles. Instead of brooding over past injustice, Hamburg Jews responded with overwhelming and even slightly slavish gratitude for this long-awaited change. With the founding of the German Reich in 1871, Jews enjoyed civil rights throughout the new Empire.

The new freedom was at least partly illusory, for Jews were still blackballed from many positions in the military, civil service, universities, and judiciary. And citizenship brought fresh obligations, including compulsory service in the local militia. For the Jews, this wonderful moment was also fraught with distinct peril. Discrimination had acted as a preservative to their identity, while freedom threatened to corrode their unity and dilute their culture. Henceforth, they would try to be both Jewish and German at once—with initially happy but ultimately tragic results.

Both Siegmund and Moritz married in the 1860s and brought forth large broods that would capitalize on the new freedom with an almost rapturous joy and energy. Nobody rivaled the Warburgs in marrying well—both sons married rich, smart, socially ambitious women. In 1862, Sara dispatched Siegmund to Kiev to woo Théophilie Rosenberg, whose father owned vast forests. When her wealthy family vacationed in Germany each year, they had to travel by night, with the carriage curtains tightly drawn, to avoid brigands. As if he could only spare limited time from business for this transaction, the impatient Siegmund brusquely proposed to the twenty-two-year-old Théophilie. When she asked for time to consider, he refused. "No way, young lady. Either you decide at once or not at all."[23] She accepted. If Siegmund didn't exactly let love ripen on the vine, it may have been that the proposal was a formality in this brokered liaison. Théophilie's father had offered to fortify Warburg bank capital with a dowry of eighty thousand Mark Banco, which likely settled the matter expeditiously in advance.

The marriage spawned a byzantine network of connections that converted the Warburgs into a small-scale multinational corporation. Théophilie's older sister, the chic Anna, was married to Horace, Baron de Gunzburg, a cosmopolitan Russian with banks in St. Petersburg and Paris. Enriched by selling vodka to the Army during the Crimean War, the Gunzburgs belonged to a select group of Jews ennobled by the czar. For a time, Théophilie resided with her brother-in-law and sister in Paris, learning fluent French, becoming a francophile, and acquiring elegant airs in their splendid salon. Baron de Gunzburg befriended the French emperor and later advised the ill-fated Czar Nicholas II. Tightening the Russian tie, Siegmund and Théophilie's daughter married Anna's son.

The other fetching Rosenberg sisters married a rich Odessa banker, a Bavarian baron, and Budapest banker.

Such empire building by courtship was an efficient way to preserve and extend the capital of private family banks. In the last analysis, marriage brokers were perhaps the unacknowledged arbiters of financial power in nineteenth-century Europe. One should note, however, that these splendid marriages, so roundly toasted by the Warburgs, would later be transmogrified by the Nazis into the treacherous maneuvers of a worldwide conspiracy.

The fashionable Théophilie imported a French elegance into Hamburg. The preferred style of the local haute bourgeoisie was rich and substantial, but in a subdued, reserved way. Even the town's wealthiest merchants suspected frippery and courtly French manners. The Hamburg ethos was democratic and middle class—more that of a meritocracy than an aristocracy. Its bankers were businessmen, not court ornaments. So Théophilie was apt to strike her neighbors as haughty and affected and she returned the favor fully by looking down on their boorish provincial manners. She had thirteen children, six of whom died in infancy, and perhaps the strain of nonstop breeding cast a melancholy pall over her personality. The Warburgs would nickname her Théophilie with the Sour Face.

The heavy burdens that Siegmund shouldered as a young man had darkened his personality, giving him an incendiary temper and a somber air of premature age. His sister-in-law, Charlotte, noted his gloom. "Through the heavy, responsible position that he was burdened with in his younger years, there was in his facial expression and his entire being something serious and dignified that made his stocky figure seem older." While his underlying warmth was evident in his sudden and robust gusts of laughter, the sheer violence of his temper sometimes scared her.[24]

Yet compared to the dour Théophilie, Siegmund was well rounded and seemed almost lighthearted. He attended the opera weekly and sometimes launched into impromptu arias from *Carmen* over breakfast. Merging German and Jewish culture, he often joined his children for Weber songs after Saturday morning prayers. Sociable and funny, highly irreverent, he would fling his napkin facetiously across the table at Théophilie when she lapsed into one of her blue funks. She mostly left the children's education to French governesses. A strong-willed martinet, she demanded strict behavior, while Siegmund, with a keen eye for the absurd, roared with laughter at his children's pranks and loved it when his son, Aby S., locked his tutor in his room.

In the 1870s, Siegmund and Théophilie moved from their apartment above the Ferdinandstrasse bank to a pretty street called Alsterufer or "Alster shore." Their magnificent five-story house at Number 18 had belonged to the Prussian minister to Mexico. They now lived in Hamburg's most stately neighborhood, filled with senators, shippers, and aristocrats who built imposing villas far removed from the port's raucous bustle. Their house faced the gravel paths, meadows, and flower beds by the rambling Outer Alster Lake, affording them splendid views of swans, sailboats, rowing clubs, and lakeside cafés. On clear summer days, the lake had a sparkling clarity. On autumn and winter days, it had a melancholy beauty, often enveloped in a gray fog that softened the distant spires and muffled their chimes.

Siegmund and Moritz belonged to the last generation of Warburgs who followed Jewish custom strictly. Already in 1819, the Reform Temple in Hamburg had dabbled in more secular Judaism, dropping mention of the Messiah and a return to the Holy Land from its prayer book. The Warburgs still resisted such concessions to the surrounding culture. In his new home, Siegmund outfitted a private synagogue, complete with Torah scrolls and rows of pews. Each morning, wrapped in his prayer shawl, he prayed with the black leather tefillin strapped to his left arm and forehead. He forbade his children from eating nonkosher food at neighbors' homes or writing or working on Saturdays. As a leader of the Jewish community, he used his downstairs rooms for High Holy Day services and hired cantors for the occasion.

Having grown up in a circumscribed Jewish world, Siegmund remained a stickler for precise observance and had no use for the reformers. Once he rented a locomotive after missing a train to Karlsbad, fearing he might arrive after the Sabbath sundown. Another time, Siegmund and Théophilie took their son, Aby S., to a famous doctor in Cannstatt. To ensure kosher food, they hired a cook and rented an apartment for her. In later years, traveling to Genoa for his silver wedding anniversary, Siegmund brought his own ritual slaughterer along for kosher meat. If pious, he was never prudish. One day, Moritz informed him that a bank employee had fathered an illegitimate child. The fastidious Moritz wanted him fired, whereas the more red-blooded Siegmund dismissed the affair with a flippant remark: "I hope the mother is a pretty girl."[25]

Moritz was a handsome young man, hopelessly spoiled by an adoring mother. He grew up surrounded by four homely sisters and his good looks must have struck them as a small genetic miracle. After work, they gently slid off his shoes. At receptions, he wore gloves to avoid chafing his delicate skin when shaking hands. For his military service, he decided to lift a bugle and not a rifle, inviting a sergeant to his garden each Sunday for music lessons. He strode through life with well-fed serenity. Even in later years, his broad face was baby-smooth and never betrayed worry. He savored life's pleasures—good food, wine, cigars, music. A music aficionado, he kept leather-bound copies of his favorite *Lieder*. Regretting that Hamburg had no memorial to its native son, Brahms, he had a bust of him created for the music hall. Enamored of his own voice, Moritz made long-winded speeches at holiday dinners while carving the bird—until hungry guests prodded him to stop talking and resume cutting.

As a businessman, Moritz displayed a caution that braked Siegmund's periodic impetuosity. He displayed little of the gambler, preferring instead to sit on securities long-term rather than trade them, noting, "It is easier to make money with your behind than with your head."[26] Highly ethical, he carried a scrap of paper in his pocket for fifty years with the celebrated lines from *Othello:* "But he that filches from me my good name/Robs me of that which not enriches him/And makes me poor indeed."[27] While the Warburgs would certainly engage in their quota of subtle intrigues, they would remain scrupulously honest, and Moritz deserves much of the credit for this almost instinctive rectitude.

Nothing captures the man's vanity better than his rotating wigs. To dupe the world, he bought three of them. The first had long hair and suggested he needed a haircut. The second simulated freshly cut hair. The third was of an intermediate length. One grandson recalled that the day's wig stood ready at Moritz's bedside "on a contraption something like a modern lady's hatstand," so he could cover up his baldness as soon as he stepped from bed.[28] Sometimes, on cold evenings, he covered his sensitive scalp with a woollen cap. The pampered Moritz never even shaved himself. Instead, a young rascal named Gottschalk Sander—the Warburgs nicknamed him "The Messenger of the Gods"—came to the house every morning. As he wielded the blade, he pumped Moritz full of gossip. When Sander later developed a case of trembling hands, the Warburgs thought it time for a career change and secured work for him elsewhere.

Moritz's insistence upon Jewish observance prompted more rebellion than imitation among his children. All his chief philanthropic activities—founding a local orphanage, supporting the Jewish hospital and Talmud Torah school—revolved around Judaism. Serving on the board that governed the affairs of Hamburg's sixteen thousand Jews, he shrank from associating too much with Reform or baptized Jews. On Friday nights, he only invited non-smokers, since he didn't want to offend cigar-smoking guests by citing the Sabbath prohibition on lighting fires. When Moritz recited the Hebrew prayers, a butler would recirculate the men's hats on a tray so they could cover their heads. Late every Saturday afternoon, he sat with an unlit cigar in hand, suppressing, with placid heroism, an importunate craving for tobacco until the setting sun permitted him to smoke. Moritz was popular on one bank board because he always scraped off his nonkosher lobster and oysters onto a neighbor's plate.

With emancipation, religion increasingly clashed with the claims of worldly ambition. As Jews strayed further into the outside world, adherence to Jewish law became a terrible impediment to business success. Tracking down kosher restaurants in strange towns was often a bewildering and insoluble problem. For that reason, Moritz and Siegmund generally abstained from Scandinavian travel—no small sacrifice for a north German business—and Sara approved of this self-imposed travel ban. "Grandmother was afraid they would not eat kosher food there," Moritz's son explained.[29]

Whether doubtful of their enduring reality or still conditioned by ancient persecution, Moritz was reluctant to grasp the freedoms proffered by emancipation. The gates had swung open, but he hesitated to tiptoe too far outside the Jewish community, afraid of the repercussions. Shaped by millennia of persecution, the Jewish psyche didn't change overnight and Moritz had internalized too much caution to become venturesome. Once given the chance to buy a hereditary Prussian title for three million marks, he demurred with a knowing smirk: "I preferred to keep my kosher three million."[30] Moritz and Siegmund were still immured behind the old cultural walls.

The eminently practical Moritz accepted the way the world worked and never felt the youthful itch of idealism. As a young man, he observed, "That money compels deference in this world seems incongruous; but one cannot eat with philosophical phrases alone."[31] He wasn't one to marry a beautiful waif. In 1860, he went to Wiesbaden with Sara, who took the baths for her rheumatism. She posted him to a Rhenish musical festival where he met Charlotte Oppenheim and her cousin, Markus Goldschmidt, who came from an Orthodox Jewish family in Frankfurt. When Moritz, twenty-two, told his mother that he wanted to marry Charlotte, Sara brushed this aside. "Silly young man," she said.[32] But with her ravenous dowager's appetite for gossip, Sara must have known that Charlotte wanted to marry Markus and that the Oppenheims objected because they were cousins.[33] Did Sara's dismissive response to Moritz's statement mask a secret delight, even a hidden agenda?

In Charlotte Oppenheim, Sara found a daughter-in-law with drive and intelligence to match her own. Charlotte's father, Nathan, was a jewel and antique dealer in Frankfurt, a man of broad culture, who had cofounded the opera house, learned thirteen languages, and consumed the entire encyclopedia. Charlotte's mother, from the Goldschmidt banking clan, ran Nathan's jewelry business during his gem-buying trips abroad. The Oppenheims exhibited a cheerful work ethic and sense of community service that made them perfect counterparts of the Warburgs. Trained in piano and singing and able to spout long sections of Goethe by heart, Charlotte was a gifted bluestocking. Yet there was nothing vague or ethereal about this short, bustling woman, who was a compact little dynamo with big plans. She sat ramrod straight in her chair, her stiff spine and alert gaze capturing her resolute approach to life and domineering nature.

On June 12, 1864, Moritz and Charlotte were married and set up house in Hamburg, at Number 17 Mittelweg ("middle way"), just a few blocks from the Alsterufer home of Siegmund and Théophilie. Sara wasted no time showing her preference for the buxom Charlotte over the stylish Théophilie. On a July evening, Charlotte arrived in Hamburg and discovered that her new mother-in-law, with awesome energy, had set up an entire house for her. Agog, Charlotte wandered incredulously through the brilliantly lit rooms and up the stairways decked with welcoming flags. As she recalled, "The sight of the Hamburg maids dressed in brightly colored cotton dresses, white aprons and white caps with tulle ribbons was a perfect delight for me. . . . Our own bathroom. I would never have dreamt of such a thing in our home in Frankfurt." Sara had attended to everything. Opening a drawer in the breakfast room, Charlotte said, "I found a little 'account book,' stationery of all kinds, ink, pens—in short there was nothing missing. There was also a little pigeonhole for the household cash box."[34] Sara's faith in Charlotte was rewarded a thousandfold, for the Warburgs would be the embodiment of Charlotte's Oppenheim's spacious vision.

At this stage of her life, Charlotte was still gay and cheerful. She wrote poetry, often went to the theater and concerts, and was mildly surprised and faintly patronizing that Hamburg lacked an art gallery. She struggled with the local dialect and anglophile phlegm of the town, but in time she adapted and became Sara's protégée. She visited her mother-in-law every day after Sara's afternoon drive and darned clothes as they talked. Every evening, when Moritz came to render his report to Sara, Charlotte had already been there for hours.

The lazy Moritz was willingly dominated by the industrious Charlotte and entrusted her with running his home and educating his children. Years later, Dutch painter Jan Veth captured the contrast between them. Relaxed and idle, Moritz slouches with his cigar, staring out at the Elbe River. Charlotte only sat for the painting on the condition that she could write and she is shown busily penning her memoirs. Moritz has a "womanish" softness, Charlotte a "mannish" hardness. For the dreamy Moritz, life flows lazily by like the river while the puritanical Charlotte consumes each precious minute, writing.

Thus were the two branches of the Warburg family established. Alsterufer and Mittelweg would become Warburg shorthand for the competing sides. Alsterufer males would bear a middle initial "S." for Siegmund or Samuel, while Mittelweg males had an "M." for Moritz. For decades, the families would debate who had contributed most to Warburg renown—the Alsterufer or Mittelweg branches. Much of our story will revolve around their jousting, their alternating supremacy, their jealous rivalry. The Warburgs would not only compete brilliantly against their neighbors, but most furiously and mercilessly against themselves.

CHAPTER 2

The Imperial Theme

Just as most people are forever stamped by the culture of their adolescence, so German Jews were stamped by their emancipation during the reigns of Kaiser Wilhelm I and Wilhelm II. Their dawn was also Germany's and they were infected with its buoyant nationalism and cult of progress. The Warburgs' spectacular rise coincided with the tumultuous sequence of events that fused the German states into a single nation by 1871. Just as Germany belatedly scrambled to catch up with the Great Powers, so the Jews struggled to catch up within the surging new state. They happened to be liberated at a moment when the Fatherland teemed with economic opportunity, which permitted a spectacular debut for them.

In 1862, Otto von Bismarck started his long reign of iron and blood, infusing first Prussia and then all of Germany with a Spartan militarism that masked a blazing romanticism. The chancellor presented himself as a solitary heroic warrior, clad in cavalry boots, tunic, and spiked helmet. Much like a later chancellor, he was the lonely seer, bowed beneath the weight of German destiny. After a showdown with Denmark, he annexed the duchies of Schleswig and Holstein and in 1866 stunned Europe by defeating mighty Austria.

When Bismarck created the North German Confederation, he tried to coax

Hamburg into joining it. To overcome local objections, he embarked upon public works that connected the northern ports with Germany's interior by railway, and he also courted Jewish residents and extended Jewish freedoms. In Hamburg, he responded to Siegmund Warburg's proposal to create an "eternal cemetery." Under Jewish law, bodies were supposed to stay buried in the same spot until resurrection, whereas in Hamburg the Jewish graveyard was freshly dug up every hundred years. When Bismarck approved a new Jewish cemetery near Hamburg, Siegmund asked whether bodies could slumber there for eternity. "Certainly," replied Bismarck, "as far as it is in the power of the Prussian government to guarantee anything for all eternity."[1]

As Fritz Stern noted in his study of Bismarck's private banker, Gerson von Bleichröder, the chancellor betrayed a deep ambivalence toward Jews. Even though Bleichröder managed his estates, Bismarck repaid him by taking vicious swipes at Jews behind his back. For Bismarck, as for many gentile Germans, the Jew was a dirty secret, a useful catalyst to trade who was nonetheless feared and patronized socially. Opposing complete equality for Jews, Bismarck yet discouraged public displays of anti-Semitism.

Pursuing three wars in quick succession, Bismarck forged a military colossus under Prussian domination. The king of Prussia, Wilhelm, became the new German emperor. By 1871, Hamburg surrendered its long-standing autonomy to become an imperial state. The capstone of Bismarck's expansionary program was the Franco-Prussian War of 1870–71 in which he vanquished the French army and encircled and bombarded Paris for four months. In its aftermath, he extracted five billion francs in reparations from France and annexed Alsace and Lorraine. An intoxicated Germany awoke to sudden awareness of its strength, and a dangerous equation was drawn between power and conquest. The thrill of martial glory that infused the populace bound even reluctant liberals to Bismarck's despotism, breeding a reverence for authority and a warlike spirit that would later yield grim consequences.

—

The Franco-Prussian War drove a wedge between the already competitive Mittelweg and Alsterufer Warburgs, since Théophilie was a francophile and Charlotte was deeply nationalistic. This feud exacerbated the personal rivalry between the two women. Charlotte frequently mocked the haughty airs of her "French sister-in-law," while Théophilie sniffed at the "little provincial girl," as she dubbed Charlotte.[2] The real source of the quarrel, however, was Siegmund's unchallenged supremacy at the bank. It grated on Charlotte that Moritz had so little influence, and she goaded him to assert himself. As one Alsterufer Warburg described Charlotte's attitude: "She does not want to

Moritz Warburg smoking his cigar,
gazing at the Elbe River, while Charlotte Warburg
records her memoirs.
(Courtesy of Gabriele Schiff)

have a husband that is less well known than Théophilie's. Why does everybody talk about the powers and ability of Siegmund and not about her Moritz? Good natured and really quite modest, Moritz lets her talk. But in the end the continual nagging of Charlotte doesn't miss its mark."³ Under Charlotte's prodding, Moritz began to demand more say at the bank and quarreled more with Siegmund.

Gradually, the split assumed a political dimension. Having grown up in Frankfurt, which hosted the first federal parliament, Charlotte unashamedly exulted over the triumphs of the new German Empire. The Russian-born, francophile Théophilie, by contrast, envisioned her home as an international salon, free of stuffy German insularity. Charlotte supported Bismarck's French expedition, Théophilie opposed it. Emotions ran so high that the Mittelweg and Alsterufer Warburgs simply stopped speaking. To heal the breach, the two families jointly rented a large Dutch villa on the North Sea for the summer and began to talk again.

The Franco-Prussian War proved a powerful stimulant to the German economy—and, thus, to the fortunes of the Warburg family. Joint-stock banks sprang into being, and many boasted leading Jewish figures, such as Ludwig Bamberger at Deutsche Bank or Eugen Gutmann at Dresdner Bank. The financial needs of the new industrial enterprises outstripped the resources of private bankers, requiring public share flotations. At this juncture, the Warburgs began to underwrite securities, beginning their swift ascent into the world of *haute banque*. Siegmund patched up relations with the Rothschilds that had lapsed under his father. As a result, the Warburgs participated in the second loan that permitted France to pay reparations to Germany. This was a gigantic windfall for the bankers.

It was a giddy time, as businessmen fathomed the economic potential of a unified German economy. When France, with the help of the Paris Rothschilds, repaid its war debt within two years, the German economy was swamped with cash, setting off a speculative boom. Jewish entrepreneurs excelled in railroads, newspapers, electrical companies, and department stores. Because they wanted to cast off a blighted past, the Jews were natural modernizers and enterprising agents of an often vertiginous change. What stake did they have in clinging to a feudal past that had excluded them?

As bankers hawked shares of new companies, some unscrupulous promoters suckered investors into blatant stock scams. The Warburgs, who had avoided stock promotion, now shed their inhibitions and joined the fray. In 1870, M. M. Warburg & Co. helped to form the Commerz-und Disconto Bank, and Moritz joined the board. In Hamburg, the speculative frenzy was reflected in new villas built in the bucolic meadows by the Alster Lake. When flagrant excesses produced a stock market crash in 1873, the Warburgs suffered severe, but not crippling losses. As his son wrote, "Siegmund W. was badly depressed by the crash that followed, because losses persisted for so long a time."[4] Eventually, Siegmund grew philosophic, saying, "It was the Warburgs' good fortune that whenever we were about to get very rich something would happen and we became poor and had to start all over again."[5]

The 1873 bust proved a terrible setback for the recently emancipated Jews. Berlin banks were predominantly Jewish, and ruined investors scapegoated Jewish stock promoters for their misery. A converted Jewish railway mogul named Bethel Henry Strousberg was arrested for fraud and went bankrupt.

So even as this tumultuous decade provided opportunities for Jews, it exposed them to mounting attacks, for they were identified with the hectic, belated industrialism and booming urbanization of the early Empire. Already, more than half the German Jews were upper middle class and thrived under emancipation. They symbolized a modernity that many Germans found profoundly threatening and preferred to regard as a foreign graft, an alien presence, and not an organic development of their own society. When the Reichsbank was formed in 1875, broadsides branded it a Jewish conspiracy. One pamphlet said Jews were clustered in businesses that enjoyed large, easy profits, "namely in the banking business and in wholesale trade."[6] The term "anti-Semitism" first appeared in a Jewish newspaper in 1879 when Hamburg anarchist Wilhelm Marr injected the "Jewish Question" into German politics and launched his Anti-Semitic League. One should note that it was when Jews emerged from the ghetto—when they shed their beards and badges and became indistinguishable from other Germans—that the anti-Semitic movement first emerged. What disturbed the German Christians was the Jew as alter ego, not the Jew as Other.

In 1879, Sara rebuffed Bismarck in his request for the butter cakes—a famous Warburg tale. One day, a stockbroker and Bismarck hunting companion named Emil Vogt told Moritz that the chancellor wanted special butter cakes that were cooked for the Jewish Passover each year. Sara first agreed to supply them if her contribution remained anonymous; she would sign her annual gift, "From a patriot."[7] But in 1879, Adolf Stoecker, the court preacher, gave a venomous sermon against the Jews, arguing that "Israel must renounce its aim of becoming the master of Germany." Unless new restrictions stopped the Jews, "the cancer from which we suffer will grow."[8] When the opportunistic Bismarck failed to denounce Stoecker, Sara retaliated. "Then Bismarck will get no more butter cakes," she announced. When Vogt came to track down the missing cakes, Sara said tartly that Bismarck "should already know" why he hadn't gotten them.[9] He had met a will as imperious as his own.

Hamburg's Jewish community, if smaller than Berlin's, was also more secure, and its Jewish businessmen blended smoothly into the mercantile atmosphere. Berlin, as the home of the court and state bureaucracy and the feudal aristocrats and military caste, was rent by tension between rigid traditionalists and robust new capitalists. Hamburg, by contrast, warmed to the new industrial order, and its Jews didn't dislodge an entrenched Junker class. Here, the union of German and Jewish culture proved a potent and highly compatible mix. By the late 1870s, Siegmund was serving in the city council or *Bürgerschaft*.

Amid this setting of imperial pomp, Charlotte and Moritz Warburg prepared their five sons and two daughters for life in the new German Reich. After a shortage of male Warburg heirs, Charlotte rapidly provided four—Aby in 1866, Max in 1867, Paul in 1868, Felix in 1871, plus a daughter, Olga, in 1873. The twins, Fritz and Louise, arrived in 1879. The brothers, all with the middle initial M. for Moritz, formed a critical mass of energy and talent that would transform the Warburgs and lift them out of their provincial milieu. They had the traditional family yearning for success, but without the historic restraints and secret inhibitions. And there were five of them.

Charlotte trained her seven children with a cheerful but strict and didactic determination. Frustrated with Moritz, she sought fulfillment through her wondrous sons. At Mittelweg 17, she presided in a white lace cap, tied under her chin, and tight-fitting dresses that reflected her austere energy. To convey a Spartan rigor, she avoided soft chairs. Every afternoon, she reviewed the children's homework, correcting errors. Even when she was on holiday, she would scrutinize their homework by mail. On vacation in Ostend, she chided Aby for sending an essay on his best Viennese stationery. "Do you think your work would gain in my eyes for having a fine ship painted on top?" she asked.[10] Forging a team, she stressed not only the work ethic, but brotherly togetherness. She knew both how to stimulate and mitigate sibling rivalry. "My dear Max, do you remember to read aloud softly every day to yourself? Paul and Felix like listening when you read to them."[11] If Max had to memorize a poem for school, Charlotte made him pace the room, reciting it aloud for hours.

An evangelist of success, Charlotte papered the children's rooms with inspirational slogans. They would find doors marked "Carpe diem" or lift a desk top and behold, "See how beautiful it is, when brothers live in harmony with each other."[12] Although the daughters didn't receive as much education—Charlotte just assumed they would marry—they too were inculcated with the work ethic of this busy family. They were not allowed to read in the morning—a habit Charlotte deemed idle at that hour—and received only one new dress per season. She never told the children that Moritz was a rich banker, describing him as a "merchant," and she did everything possible to fight the corrupting indolence that comes with wealth. She also fought self-ishness. When the children were given little metal piggy banks, they had to set aside a tenth of their savings for charity in accordance with the Jewish practice of tithing.

Charlotte could be overbearing. Like Sara, she took pleasure in shaping people's lives and was an inveterate matchmaker. She would bring together young couples for dinner, push them out together for a twilight stroll, then bolt the French windows behind them until Nature's chemistry had achieved the desired effect. Charlotte demanded clockwork precision, even in charity. If a poor ward arrived late on Friday evening to receive alms, she grumbled impatiently, "Where is that *Schlemihl* then?"[13] As a granddaughter remarked, Charlotte had "an outlook on mankind decided by no whims, disciplined, measuring each emotion. I remember no superlatives in her speech."[14] A tidy housekeeper, she kept the cupboards locked and chided children for sitting in the wrong place. "Don't spoil the furniture," she would say.[15] Much of this rigidity must have stemmed, as with Sara, from thwarted creativity. Charlotte was a gifted woman who spoke several languages, wrote poetry, and published stories in the *Frankfurter Zeitung*. Indeed, Charlotte should have been the banker and Moritz the *Hausfrau*.

The constant stress on achievement produced lively but driven children with a great deal of bottled-up tension. Fortunately, Charlotte hired a warm, redheaded governess named Franziska Jahns, who had grown up in a Hamburg orphanage. This non-Jewish woman raised the children, giving her charges the uncritical love they needed—a fact Charlotte tacitly acknowledged by her jealousy. Not only was Franziska adored by the children, but her ecumenical presence would foster tolerance for almost forty years. To recite prayers with the children, she even learned Hebrew.

Moritz and Charlotte kept a kosher household, celebrated the Sabbath every Friday evening, and wouldn't let the children carry books on Saturday. (They hired non-Jewish servants known as "Sabbath boys" to perform this sin.) Moritz, who went to synagogue more than Charlotte, insisted that the children abide by Jewish custom. The boys hated the two dry pedants who taught them Hebrew and wouldn't accompany their father to the stale, airless synagogue in a small Mittelweg room. As children of the new German Empire, they found Moritz's religiosity old-fashioned and sometimes laughable. He was the last Warburg bathed in a Judaic atmosphere and they teased him with extraordinary irreverence—their way of coping with a father who seemed weak and chained to obsolete Jewish taboos. Moritz still carried pre-emancipation Germany, with all its outmoded prohibitions, in his head. Perhaps he succeeded more with his daughters. When Louise first ate ham, she was sure the skies would rebuke her with a clap of admonitory thunder.

Eventually, the five sons would jettison most Jewish customs. But if the Warburg sons lost much of their ancestral belief system, they would remain traditional and conscientious in discharging Jewish community duties. In this generation, Jewish identity wouldn't disappear but would be transformed into a Jewish-based philanthropy devoid of real spiritual content.

For all the stress on duty, Mittelweg 17 was never somber. The sociable Charlotte and Moritz were called "the couple that can't sit still" and constantly entertained people.[16] The children were also in perpetual motion. In the garden they had model trains, surrounded by a little cement wall. For special occasions, they put on amateur theatricals or recited sonnets. They had their own rowboat (named after Charlotte) for Alster Lake outings and abundantly possessed the Warburgian passion for music. The three boys formed a trio, with Paul on cello, Felix on violin, and Max on piano. Felix had a fine voice and would doggedly tramp through the snow for forty minutes to take violin lessons, foreshadowing his later involvement with the opera world.

A series of events in the 1870s introduced a touch of dread into this happy, self-assured family. In 1873, Aby, age six, contracted typhoid fever and was confined to bed. High-strung and imaginative, Aby already alternated between uproarious high spirits and fathomless gloom. As he lay in a fevered state, his mind swarmed with demonic images from an illustrated edition of Honoré de Balzac's *Petites misères de la vie conjugale*—precocious matter indeed for this bookish little boy. So delicate was his condition that doctors said nothing should disturb his equanimity. This gave Aby the chance to indulge his temper, which he brazenly used to manipulate others. Charlotte favored Aby, but she had already learned to fear his towering rages and impulses, and only Franziska Jahns could deal with him in these unreasonable moments.

Hardly had Aby recovered than another trauma followed. In 1875, Charlotte and her family took a cure at the Austrian resort of Bad Ischl. One day, while they visited a scenic mountain, Charlotte grew so listless that she had to be carried to the top in a stretcher. She developed a near-fatal case of typhus and was put to bed for an extended period. A Viennese doctor named Dr. Breuer, who attended the royal family, came to supervise Charlotte. Three times he nearly gave up hope. The nearby church had to curtail its bell-ringing to calm her nerves. All the while, nuns in strange hooded costumes paced the sick room. Charlotte's father came from Frankfurt to lead the children in Hebrew prayer, then treated them to forbidden sausages at a grocery shop. During the months that Charlotte was an invalid, the phobic, hypersensitive Aby found escape at the local library and disappeared into escapist tales of the American Indians. Never again would the world seem quite so safe or solid to him. Later, he often spoke of this childhood nightmare that had alerted him to the central fear of death and the unknown in all human societies.

For Charlotte, illness spread a shadow over her personality, dimming her humor and making her serious side more pronounced. She had lost her wonderful thick hair, which must have been painful for this plain little woman. The sickness also seemed to create a new distance with the solicitous Moritz, who confined serious discussions with Charlotte to late at night in bed.

Then another childbirth added to Charlotte's strain. The year was 1879. According to one version, after the delivery of a girl, Louise, she moaned, "Oh, so much pain for so little," only to have the doctor retort, "Don't worry, there's another one coming."[17] When Charlotte protested, "No thank you, I *won't* have another child," the doctor informed her, "You should have thought about that some time ago."[18] Then out popped a funny, puny twin brother, Fritz, who didn't resemble Louise at all and seemed a comical afterthought. Both twins had health problems and were constantly weighed by wet nurses. This agonizing double birth on top of the typhus drained Charlotte of her vivacity, and it never returned. Her grandchildren would remember her as a sober, humorless woman who gave them umbrellas and other practical gifts for presents. They never knew the lively young lady from Frankfurt.

The Mittelweg Warburg children were very unalike, yet they complemented each other so well that they collectively contained almost every conceivable talent and trait. Bound by an almost mystical sense of their destiny—what Jewish children had ever had such big dreams?—they grandly saw themselves reflected in the seven stars of the Big Dipper. When separated by travel, they gazed at the constellation and imagined that they could transmit secret messages to each other through the galaxy. Felix later used the Big Dipper as a personal emblem on gifts.

As the oldest, most brilliant, and most volatile child, Aby was the natural leader. He was already egotistical. As soon as the twins were born, he resented that he had to cede his billiard room to these intruders. For the rest of his life, he would mesmerize his siblings even as he exasperated them with his belligerent and insatiable demands. As a student, he was surpassed only by the third son, Paul, who was as quiet, sensitive, and self-effacing as Aby was flamboyant. Aby and Paul had Charlotte's focused ambition. The second and fourth sons, Max and Felix, inherited Moritz's charming, lighthearted, flirtatious manner. Olga was pretty, musical, and artistic and uniformly adored by all the brothers.

No visitor to the Mittelweg house would have guessed that the ingratiating but lackadaisical Max would someday head the bank and become a leader of the Jewish community in Germany. As the eldest son and a quicksilver wit, Aby was entitled to become the bank's senior partner. But he was already a voracious reader and disinclined to enter banking. His typhoid fever had caused Aby to miss a year in school, and for a time he attended the same grade as Max. One day, Aby, age thirteen, said to Max, age twelve, that he would renounce his bank partnership to Max if he would promise, in return, to buy him books for the rest of his life. Beneath the bantering tone, the conversation was deadly serious and Max consented after only a brief pause for reflection. "I told myself that when I was in the business I could, after all, always find the money to pay for the works of Schiller, Goethe, Lessing and perhaps also Klopstock, and so, unsuspecting, I gave him what I must now admit was a very large blank cheque."[19] They sealed the deal with a handshake. Later, Max said it was the only blank check he ever issued, and he had given it to one of the twentieth century's most passionate and incorrigible bibliophiles.

Max's partner in the bank would turn out to be the ugly, goggle-eyed little Fritz, who would always look like some strange foundling abandoned on the Warburg doorstep. He was mostly ignored by his four dashing older brothers. But his twin sister, Louise, retained a warm, motherly feeling toward him. Fritz was such a delicate child that on walks with Franziska Jahns, Louise would carry Fritz's coat. Charlotte never had much time for this often mischievous son, telling the other four, "Go see what Fritz is doing and tell him to stop it."[20]

One might note here, in passing, the extraordinary catalogue of psychosomatic ailments suffered by the Warburg children, from Paul's ulcers to Fritz's ear, nose, and throat problems. The strict upbringing and drive for success took their toll.

In vying with Théophilie, Charlotte wisely shifted the arena of competition from their husbands, where she could never win, to their sons, where she could never lose. The soft, indolent Moritz had fathered five prodigious sons and two sensitive daughters, while the aggressive, dynamic Siegmund brought forth two delicate, sickly boys and five strong daughters. His older son, Aby S. (not to be confused with Sara's husband or Moritz's oldest boy, Aby M.), was born two months prematurely and weighed only three pounds. Théophilie created an ersatz incubator. As Aby's sister recalled, Théophilie "wrapped him in cotton wool and made a small nestlike box for her tiny son on the warmest part of the stovepipe."[21] Because Aby S. lacked flexibility in his fingers, Théophilie had difficulty teaching him to write. Aby S. was handsome, but small, frail, and sickly. After boarding school in Karlsruhe, he apprenticed with Samuel Montagu in London and then returned to Hamburg to work in the family bank.

The younger brother was the thin, nervous Georges. Tormented by headaches, he was hard to educate and stuttered badly. At one point, doctors recommended a high-calorie diet, but Georges lacked the appetite and grew more dejected. Although good-natured and warm-hearted, Georges was high-strung and often difficult. As his sister Elsa recalled, Georges "had a temper too and was so furious that he threatened [once] to jump out of the window and was about to do so had I not been there to prevent it."[22] As a poor student who excelled only in history, Georges was sent to an agricultural school because it was less likely to tax his nervous system.

According to Théophilie's descendants, Charlotte gloated over her hard-charging team of superior sons. As Théophilie's granddaughter recalled, "In opposition to her own children who are very talented and whom she can't praise enough, she ridicules her nieces and especially the weakness and sickliness of Aby and Georges."[23] Clearly, in the next generation, the power balance would tilt rather drastically to the biologically blessed Mittelweg Warburgs, which caused consternation in the Alsterufer household.

While these children were growing up, Sara was still an unquestioned monarch who chaired many charities for the sick and poor. Even in her seventies, she fussed about her grooming and told Charlotte, "The older one gets the more importance one should attach to one's outward appearance."[24] Every afternoon, attended by driver and footman, she rode with her favorite daughter, the homely, divorced Marianne, and assorted grandchildren by the lake. One granddaughter recalled how Sara always exhorted her to "Sit straight child"—which was no easy matter, since the child's feet didn't touch the ground.[25] Sara's caustic tongue was still a widely feared instrument. When a taciturn bachelor joined her during a long, speechless ride, Sara bent over and whispered to him in parting, "What we've talked about is just between us."[26]

Ever since the Samuel Zagury scandal, Marianne had remained the self-effacing daughter, afraid to upset her neurotic and demanding mother. When she developed pains in the early 1880s, she kept the information to herself. By the time she spoke up, her illness was mortal, and she died in December 1882. Sara had never stopped blaming herself for the disastrous marriage of almost thirty years before. Now her grief was boundless and guilt ridden. Everybody would remember Sara's extraordinary dignity at this moment. That Friday evening, she refused to alter her weekly ritual or even refer to Marianne's death while the Sabbath lasted; she had to discharge her sacred duty. Gathering up her strength, she lit the candles and sang the psalms in her lovely soprano voice. All day Saturday, nobody mentioned Marianne. As Max recalled, "Grandmother lived with her God."[27] When the sun set on Saturday, Sara broke down and again gave way to inconsolable grief.

Like anything that she couldn't control, Sara feared death. In 1884, age seventy-nine, she died abruptly one morning—of a heart attack by one account, of a stroke while buttoning a shoe by another. The Hamburg papers said they had never seen so many mourners at a funeral. From Frankfurt, Baron Rothschild sent a special courier to lay floral decorations on Sara's casket. Afterward, Siegmund said Kaddish each morning in his synagogue at the Alsterufer. Refusing to disrupt his daily schedule, he wore his riding boots and spurs along with his prayer shawl—a fitting hybrid image of the German Jews in the early Empire. The second he was finished with his devotions, Siegmund flew out the door and went for his morning horseback ride.

Siegmund's robust constitution proved illusory. A few years after Sara's death, only in his early fifties, he grew ill. He and Théophilie began making constant trips to consult medical specialists, spending a year in Torquay, England, because of its mild climate, then the following year in Nice. Siegmund pondered his own mortality with equanimity. "I need not fear death," he said. "I have always obeyed the laws of the Jewish religion and when I die my children will have a safe future because my estate will be sufficient for all of them."[28] On May 13, 1889, he died of a heart attack at age fifty-four while staying at the Hotel Bellevue in Baden-Baden. He was buried in the eternal cemetery near Hamburg that he had helped to secure from Bismarck. The sturdy Théophilie would outlive Siegmund by sixteen years.

So at age fifty-one, the phlegmatic Moritz suddenly and implausibly headed M. M. Warburg & Co., assisted by his son Max, twenty-two, and his nephew Aby S., twenty-five. The bank was still a fairly modest affair, with twenty-three employees working by oil lamps, eating out of a kosher kitchen, and haggling over access to just one telephone. Far from creating a crisis, Siegmund's death would provide room for Moritz's exceptional sons to exercise their manifold talents. They would eclipse their father and surpass everything the Warburgs had accomplished up until that time. Born about the same time as the German Reich, they seemed to share its restless vigor and blind optimism. The Mittelweg Warburgs also flourished at a transitional moment in economic history, as regional firms expanded into national companies and increasingly exported or produced overseas. They would rise along with the explosive growth of the new global economy, as imperial governments and industrial titans required large-scale financing that only the private bankers of the day could provide. From the outset, the sons of Moritz Warburg seemed to have been born under a favorable combination of stars. How could they not be deeply, even perilously, endowed with hope?

Part Two

THE RISE
OF THE
MITTELWEG
WARBURGS

A strapping Max Warburg in the
uniform of his Bavarian light cavalry regiment.
(Courtesy of Anita Warburg)

CHAPTER 3

Meschugge Max

The Warburgs' fate was always intertwined with that of Hamburg, and they soared in tandem during the reign of the bombastic Kaiser Wilhelm II. When the first Wilhelm died in March 1888, his successor, Frederick III, was already afflicted with terminal throat cancer. During a ghastly three-month reign, the voiceless kaiser sucked on soothing ice cubes and communicated by notes. After he died in June, Wilhelm II, the twenty-nine-year-old grandson of Queen Victoria, became emperor. With his left arm shriveled from a difficult birth, this swaggering young man couldn't slice dinner meat and had trouble riding, a disability that likely fed his love of pomp and manly pursuits and produced a strong preference for the sea over land. In 1891, he declared, "our future is on the water," and Germany obligingly mobilized to build a massive fleet of battleships, reversing the traditional Prussian stress on infantry.

This was all extremely auspicious for seafaring Hamburg. In October 1888, in an early official act, Wilhelm II indicated his affections for the vibrant port when he laid the foundation stone for a new duty-free port in Hamburg, certifying the city's entry into the German Customs Union. As Germany's second biggest city, with more than half a million people, Hamburg was the gateway to the world. Its shippers, bankers, and brokers imported food while also spearheading a drive to conquer export markets. It was a marvelous decade for M. M. Warburg, which increasingly shared underwritings with the European banking aristocracy. It joined the Paris Rothschilds on a Dutch loan and Hambros of London on a Norwegian state loan.

Hamburg experienced electrifying growth that elevated it into a major world entrepôt. By the port, twenty thousand men razed picturesque old courtyards and sunless, narrow lanes to summon up the dazzling brick colossus of the *Speicherstadt*. It was a modern marvel of engineering, a warehouse city on the water, woven by an intricate network of bridges and canals. Each building had a water side where bundles of spice, coffee, and oriental rugs could be hoisted straight into open lofts. Photos show a city busily reinventing itself. Horse-drawn omnibuses raced along the streets, steamers plied the lake, and tall-masted ships packed the port. The port was a scene of hectic activity. In 1895, the aging Bismarck came to town and Bernhard von Bülow recorded his reaction: "He stopped when he set foot on the giant steamboat, looked at the ship for a long time, at the many steamers lying in the vicinity, at the docks and huge cranes, at the mighty picture presented by the harbor, and said at last, 'I am stirred and moved. Yes, this is a new age—a new world.' "[1] It wasn't really his world, though: In 1890, Bismarck had been swept aside by the brash young emperor.

Hamburg would always retain a dual personality. A rough, lawless place of swearing sailors, militant dockworkers, brutal bosses, and raffish whorehouses, it also had residential areas of surpassing refinement and elegant taste. Many burghers displaced by the *Speicherstadt* moved around the Alster lakes. Even the downtown business district kept a tranquil charm, the tapered lines of its verdigris church steeples sketching out a graceful silhouette. The boom sharpened social divisions, and the Warburgs and their neighbors had little direct contact with left-wing stevedores in the noisy, unruly tenements of the St. Pauli district.

Rushing to overtake other powers, Germany not only built new transatlantic ships, but expanded coal and steel production at a headlong pace. This belated industrial revolution—so accelerated, so compressed—generated both giddy excitement and a widespread sense of nervous exhaustion. It was hard enough for the Reich to forge a cohesive culture from its mosaic of constituent states, but it had to accomplish this even as railways, mills, mines, and factories transformed the country's face. A wise solution might have been to foster a culture receptive to diversity. Instead, Germany stressed monolithic conformity and engaged in an anxious, insecure, often escapist quest for a "pure" German identity, frequently finding it in a mythic past of virgin forests and mountains. Unfortunately, the Germans needed "outsiders" to define the still-elusive concept of "insiders," and the Jews nicely served the purpose.

Quite naturally, the Jewish community was more impressed by its gains in the new Germany than by the remaining areas of outright exclusion. Of the Warburg children, Max, the second son, was the most inflamed by the military pride and exalted rhetoric of the German Empire. He would be the Warburg most susceptible to the alluring vision that Jews could be fully absorbed into the mainstream of German society. His life would prove sadly emblematic of the fate that awaited superpatriotic Jews who attained prominence under the kaiser.

A poor student, Max only stayed in school to please Moritz and when he passed his *Abitur* in 1886 the family collectively exhaled with relief. As Max confessed, "actually, from age 16 to 18, I spent more time flirting than working."[2] Like other Warburg children, he rarely encountered anti-Semitism in school, and when it surfaced his best friend always trounced the culprits. Charlotte noted Max's engaging manner, his social skills. "Good old Max had friends in all circles," she said. "With his bright blue eyes under bushy eyebrows and his irresistible smile, he wins over everybody. Whatever he undertakes, he succeeds in doing."[3]

Photos show a slim, rakish young man. A great charmer, a fine dancer and rider, Max had a magnetic warmth and the power of quick decision. He gravitated to banking, but had a youthful need to associate it with some transcendent purpose. He wondered whether the banker "couldn't serve humanity, without squeezing it, and whether he couldn't turn the profit of the world to his own profit as well."[4] In 1887, Max apprenticed with the Frankfurt bank of I. Dreyfus, staying with his Oppenheim grandparents—a period memorable for his nonstop flirtation with cousins and other girls. In Frankfurt, he was exposed to the then superior culture of the Oppenheims and their artistic circle. Then he apprenticed with Wertheim & Gomperz in Amsterdam and scored his first business triumph by winning a correspondent relationship for M. M. Warburg with the Niederlandische Bank. Though he learned Dutch, he found Holland almost risibly tedious and seized every distraction, later saying, "Never have I so thoroughly examined a museum as I did the Rijksmuseum and the Mauritshuiz."[5]

Max was the first Warburg who assumed that his Judaism would present no stumbling block to his ambition. Some small warning voice that had whispered caution to his ancestors never spoke to him. Slightly deaf in one ear, he could have dodged military service, but he wanted to emulate those rich boys who got commissions in prestigious cavalry regiments. He was a superb rider who loved to drill and he knew he would look smart in uniform. Yet even the omnipotent Bleichröder had had to put forth strenuous exertion to get an army officer's commission for his son.

In October 1888, Max covered up his hearing defect and started military service with the 3rd Bavarian Light Cavalry Regiment in Munich, Bavaria being one of the few places with Jewish officers. Max's letters betray a deep admiration for military discipline and a growing patriotism, despite engrained anti-Semitism among the officers. In one paean to the Fatherland, he told Charlotte that whether it was a matter of social democracy or industrial enterprise, Germans tended to pursue things "with quite a different sort of effectiveness and thoroughness as in other lands."[6]

Within a year, the young chauvinist was appointed a noncommissioned officer and wrote Moritz a sixteen-page letter outlining in detail his plans to become a regular career officer. This was still a highly fanciful ambition for a Jewish boy, since Jews seldom rose beyond *Vize-Feldwebel* or sergeant of the reserve. (The Prussian Army lacked reserve officers until World War I.) Max awaited his father's reply with great hope. After a tense, painful wait, he received a one-line reply from the laconic Moritz that seemed to compress two thousand years of Jewish history into one word. "My dear Max, *meschugge* [crazy]. Your loving father."[7] If hurt and outraged, Max saw the wisdom of his father's advice when he was blackballed in secret ballot by the Bavarian officers. For all its folly, this early episode showed how fearless Max was in entering German society, if also how utterly doomed to disappointment. In his later stewardship at the bank, Max would often be likened to a general who instilled a spirit of joyful discipline and his confident, barrel-chested élan indeed suggested an imperial cavalry officer.

Moritz used his connection with the French Rothschilds to slip Max into a position as a secretary with Banque Impériale Ottomane in Paris in 1890. The city was plentifully supplied with fine wine and pretty women and it was a heady experience for the *bon vivant*. Max learned French by memorizing letters from old copybooks and sometimes attended Sorbonne lectures. By night, he caroused expensively. At the start of each month, Moritz sent a check to Max's rue de Teheran apartment. Since Max frittered away the funds before month's end, he crossed the Seine and stayed with a painter friend in the Latin Quarter until Moritz sent the next check. Max's sexual conquests must have been legion, for years later, riding down the Champs-Élysées with his wife, he would wave gaily at many women on the sidewalk.

Max did an obligatory stint at N. M. Rothschild & Sons in London, renting a flat near Park Lane and affecting a British manner. Given Hamburg's extensive trade links with Britain and anglophile culture, the fit was natural and easy. The status-conscious Warburgs were always close students of society, and to prepare for Rothschild gatherings Max pored over *Burke's Peerage*. After Paris, the City of London seemed staid and genteel. One day Baron Alfred de Rothschild reproached him for working too hard. "A gentleman is not to be found in the office before eleven and never stays beyond four."[8] Profiting from this advice, Max returned each weekend to Paris for revelry. When a friend spotted him there and reported this back in Hamburg, Moritz was incredulous, insisting, "That must have been a double, because my son is in London."[9] Moritz bet twenty marks that the *Doppelgänger* wasn't his son. Hastily Max confessed that he had indeed visited Paris—but on the most urgent of business purposes, of course.

This foreign idyll ended in 1892. Max was about to embark on a round-the-world trip with his London friend, Paul Kohn-Speyer, when news arrived that the Gunzburg bank in St. Petersburg had experienced a disastrous loss from the Lena Gold Fields in Siberia. When the bank stopped payment, this threatened a seven-million-mark loan that the Warburgs had outstanding to the Gunzburgs. Short-handed after Siegmund's death, Moritz summoned Max home to cope with the crisis. The Warburgs stood loyally by the Gunzburgs, strengthening the tie with their in-laws and even improving their own credit rating. Years later, the Gunzburgs lavishly and stylishly repaid the loan with a heap of gold coins.

For the Warburgs, troubles always arrived in battalions. In 1892, Max, a novice to the firm, struggled through a nightmarish summer. Because Hamburg was a seaport hosting a vast transient population, it was always susceptible to sudden epidemics. Tenement residents drank from the polluted Elbe River and sickness spread quickly. That summer, a virulent cholera epidemic ran through Hamburg, claiming eight thousand lives. The cholera bacillus could kill people in a day or two, since severe vomiting and diarrhea drained bodily fluids, and entire streets of inhabitants perished from contaminated water. At its height, the epidemic took a thousand lives daily and the terrified populace stopped shaking hands or even touching their own faces. Authorities sealed off the port and closed the schools. Whether for drinking or bathing, all water had to be boiled.

Unfazed, Max strolled confidently through this ghastly landscape of plagues and terrors, running the bank during the epidemic. All outgoing mail was disinfected. Although the thirty Warburg employees received two bottles of Hennessy cognac apiece to replace drinking water, several died. Since the Warburgs couldn't make people work, Max and two others toiled from seven in the morning until midnight. From his ground-floor window, he could watch municipal carts, piled high with fresh corpses, trundling by in the streets. He showed a characteristic faith in his own invincibility, a fearlessness both brave and foolhardy, an inborn certitude that he could outface danger. As a man of pure optimism, he typified German Jews under the kaiser. "I had the certain feeling that I was immune," he admitted.[10] Even after the plague ended, a mournful air lingered, as women shrouded their faces behind black veils and men walked the streets in mourning bands.

The cholera epidemic had unfortunate political repercussions, as anti-

Semites blamed it on the mass influx of Jewish emigrants. Agitators were quick to equate Jews with unhealthy foreigners, branding them an impure, unholy, alien element corrupting the body politic. The pestilence also gave isolationist German nationalists a chance to rebuke Hamburg for being overly influenced by outside economic interests. In time, the identification of Jews and inimical foreign trade would ripen in anti-Semitic literature and provide a theme with powerful nativist appeal. By the next year, the Anti-Semitic party claimed sixteen Reichstag seats.

Though only in his fifties, Moritz began to yield responsibility to Max, appointing him a partner in 1893. He thought Max would be a splendid businessman, if he could just muster the discipline. "If Max only arrives on time, he always gets the deal done," he observed.[11] Max soon began writing the annual reports. When the bank's chief clerk died that year, Moritz enlisted Paul, naming him a partner two years later. Moritz was extremely proud of his stable of thoroughbred sons—they must have seemed a gift of the gods—and his indolent, self-effacing nature encouraged his young prodigies to take charge quickly.

Paul was a thin, bony young man—"We Warburgs were built to be race-horses," he once said—who already showed a deep and ineradicable sadness in his warm, sensitive eyes.[12] As a boy, his intellectual feats even eclipsed those of Aby. Before his second birthday, he recited verse and sang songs with precise lyrics. As sickly and delicate as Max was red-blooded and impetuous, he was taunted by his older brothers. Felix's wife later recalled that "in his early years Aby and Max gave [Paul] what is nowadays called an 'inferiority complex' by refusing to play with him and telling him he was ugly and weak."[13] By early adulthood, the shy Paul suffered from a gastric ulcer and vague, nameless depression. Where Aby manipulated his ailments to indulge his wishes and expand his own personal power, Paul stoically bore life's crosses. If Aby's story would be one of a turbulent, narcissistic indulgence and exploration of self, Paul's would be characterized by an equally tenacious streak of disciplined self-denial.

Paul was a financial prodigy *malgré lui*, who made money without espe-cially caring about money. With his finely honed intelligence, he wanted to be a teacher or civil engineer, and early experience only confirmed a congeni-tal disdain for business that never entirely deserted him. He loathed his two-year stint with a Hamburg trading firm during which he laboriously stuck labels on merchandise bales at the docks. Then he trained at Samuel Montagu in London and the Banque Russe pour le Commerce Étranger in Paris. Because he had broken an elbow joint in school, he was excused from military service and took Max's place in the planned round-the-world tour. This carried him through Egypt, India, China, and Japan, ending with a transcontinental trip from Seattle to New York. Paul adored Japan's lyric beauty, recoiled at India's filth and squalor, and memorialized his trip in poems. He had an unusually fine sensibility for a young man starting a banking career.

Paul's entry into M. M. Warburg & Co. upset the pact between the Mittelweg and Alsterufer branches by which each side contributed one son as a partner. Théophilie had gotten her son, Aby S., admitted into the firm, but Paul tipped the balance toward transparent Mittelweg dominance. When Moritz had first broached this a few years earlier, Paul was enamored of Théophilie's cheerful daughter, Rosa. Moritz said not to worry, Paul would be her future son-in-law. "Théophilie got furious because according to her one thing had nothing to do with the other and apart from that she found it revolting that her daughter would marry her full cousin," said Théophilie's granddaughter.[14] When Moritz insisted that an expanding business required a third partner, Théophilie grudgingly sold part of her partnership stake to Paul.

Théophilie lived in grandiose fashion until the end. Even after Siegmund died, she stayed alone at the Alsterufer house, accompanied by a butler and four maids. In summer, she received relatives from Kiev and spent winters on the Riviera. A doughty, determined woman, she tried to combat her rheumatism by climbing the stairs of her house. When she died in 1905, Aby S. took over the Alsterufer house.

The Mittelweg Warburgs always thought Aby S. a dim-witted nonentity— "My uncle's oldest son was a dope," Fritz said flatly—who dedicated most of his time to family correspondence and Jewish community work.[15] Despite his handsome, aristocratic face and immaculate dress, he never shed the tiny appearance of a premature child. A charming melancholic, gentle and querulous, he later became severely diabetic, which made him temperamental. He chose wives of equal delicacy. In 1894, he married a frail, pretty Russian girl named Olga Lucie Leonine. A year after their marriage, Aby took her to a Freiburg doctor for special surgery so that she could bear children. After he returned to Hamburg, she developed complications and spent a terrible night of lonely suffering, afraid to disturb the nurse; three days later, she died. Aby S. never recovered. Even when he married Elly Simon two years later, he insisted that they name their first daughter Olga. He gave his first wife's jewelry and possessions to the little girl and retained a special affection for her.

During his decades at the bank, Aby S. was an invisible presence who seldom appears in official correspondence. He was more intelligent than the Mittelweg Warburgs made out, but sad and moody from his assorted maladies. As one grandson described the mood of his Alsterufer home, "It was most of the time a mood of sweet melancholy, drifting in like the gray mist on the wintry Alster."[16] Like a strict but loving nurse, his wife, Elly, tended him and traveled south with him to the Riviera for his health. Aby S. was pious and kept a kosher house and raised his children so strictly that they had to make appointments to see him. If they didn't finish their dinner, they would receive the same plate for breakfast.

Aby S. perpetuated French magnificence at the Alsterufer and had a special Louis XV salon. In his study he hung many French Impressionists and a Canaletto painting of the Grand Canal. The house contained rich red carpets, mahogany wainscoting, and furniture from Paris. An elevator gave it a passing resemblance to a small but elegant hotel. Footmen stood behind each place at dinner and the chief servant in this extravagant place even wore a tailcoat and white gloves. With unconscious pomposity, Aby S. once told his son, "Charles, please tell the butler to tell the maid to run my bath."[17] Aby S. was a stranger to ordinary life and seemed like a visitor from Mars on public outings. When his children got him to ride a public bus, he tried to tip the driver before disembarking. Later on, Aby S. bought an enormous red-brick weekend house on the coast at Travemünde, complete with lilac bushes, a tennis court, an open-air theater, and ponies for his son and four daughters.

Pretty much ignoring Aby S. at the bank, Max and Paul grew into a confident, unbeatable team. Paul was as thoughtful and prudent as Max was rash and dynamic. Where Paul was abundantly endowed with doubts, anxieties, and forebodings, Max was full of pep and a sometimes dangerously blind confidence. Paul seemed to carry the darkness of the Jewish past, while Max embodied the bright future. A story from their adolescence points up the contrast. One afternoon the brothers were reading together—Paul a weighty tome, Max a superficial novel. Abruptly Max snapped closed his book and said, "We must get dressed for Frau X's party." "Why should I go?" Paul replied. "I'm ugly, I have a bad figure, I am a bore, and I shall bore everyone." "I shan't be a bore," retorted the buoyant Max. "I shall be the life and soul of the party."[18]

Though Paul gladly ceded client relations to Max and stayed behind the scenes, he wasn't just a pliant, deferential subordinate, for his quiet intelligence commanded respect and Max listened attentively to his arguments. During their forty years of working together, Max treasured Paul as a pure, incorruptible, almost saintly, spirit. Of their early Hamburg days, Max said revealingly that Paul "always pushed me to the fore, not only without any envy, but pleased by every success that I had, even more than his own."[19] In a family with a boundless store of *amour-propre*, Paul conspicuously avoided all show of egotism.

From the outset, Max and Paul had a perfect, complementary camaraderie. They functioned so harmoniously that Moritz complained they failed to consult him, but in the end, he was happily upstaged by his sons. Max said his father "took particular pleasure in driving with these two ponies in tandem."[20] By 1895, Moritz had such implicit faith in his magical boys that he began to bow out of the firm. Maintaining its strength in foreign exchange and commercial bills, Max and Paul now issued securities for Scandinavian countries as Germany evolved from a capital importer to a banker for other countries. In his ceaseless travels, Max strengthened Warburg links with two legendary bankers, Louis Fränkel of the Stockholms Handelsbank (later Svenska Handelsbanken) in Stockholm and Otto R. Henriques of Copenhagen, whose firm served the king of Denmark.

Even as Max penetrated a broader political and business world than Moritz, he kept up his father's standing in the Jewish community. Max wasn't religious, but fully shared Moritz's sense of noblesse oblige. What distinguished the Warburgs was that they were quick to embrace the future yet remained true to tradition—opposing impulses that created strains. They subsidized the Jewish community but floated somewhere in the ether above it, much as in their early days as "protected Jews." It should be said that even as Bismarck enacted a wide range of social legislation in the 1880s, German Jews continued to maintain thousands of their own welfare agencies.

Meanwhile, anti-Semitism's potency was growing. In the 1890s, Hamburg newspapers sometimes told of meetings in dim, smoky basement halls at which strident, red-faced speakers decried "international Jewry" and called for stringent regulation of stock speculation or an end to Reichsbank dealings with private Jewish banks. In the Reichstag, too, the anti-Semitic bloc grew apace. Despite these menacing rumblings, German Jews felt secure in their position. They dismissed anti-Semitic agitators as a hysterical crackpot fringe and began to intermarry with Christians on a hitherto unimaginable scale. Jews began to identify more with German culture and less with their own religion. It was a measure of their confidence and success that they directed their philanthropy toward suffering Jews elsewhere. In 1891, for instance, Moritz participated in emergency efforts to end persecution against Russian Jews.

That German Jews would ever require such charitable aid would have seemed inconceivable in those palmy days when they were the most prosperous European Jewish community and perhaps the foremost success story in Diaspora history. Recalling an 1893 trip to Germany as a teenager, Chaim Weizmann remembered "the assimilated Jews of Germany, then in the high summer of their illusory security and mightily proud of it." Anti-Semitism existed but still in so subtle and shadowy a form that it could be easily overlooked. It seemed a confection of mad theories and ideological hocuspocus. Benefiting from hindsight, Weizmann noted how anti-Semitism "was eating deep into Germany in those days, a heavy, solid, bookish anti-Semitism far more deadly, in the long run, than the mob anti-Semitism of Russian city hooligans and the cynical exploitation of it practiced by Russian politicians and prelates. It worked itself into the texture of the national consciousness."[21] But this latent nastiness was still obscured by the new and brilliant glow of German Jewish success.

Tragicomic Brothers

Endowed with surplus sons for the bank, Charlotte and Moritz steered their fourth son, Felix, elsewhere. It was hard enough for Théophilie to swallow Paul's partnership; Felix would definitely have been *de trop*. So at sixteen, Felix went to learn the pearl and diamond business from grandfather Nathan Oppenheim in Frankfurt. Like Max, Felix was gay and affable, light-hearted and elegant, with bright, twinkling eyes. Also like Max, he was a mediocre student compared to Aby and Paul. He was free of the psychic shadows, the deep melancholy, that hung around other family members and had a lightness of soul, a buoyant spirit, that never deserted him.

During his six years in Frankfurt as a junior partner at N. M. Oppenheim & Company, Felix refined the social talents that would distinguish his philanthropy. He admired his witty, outgoing grandfather and adopted him as a role model. At Nathan's prompting, Felix studied French, Italian, and English and acquired a taste for painting and woodcuts. A ladies' man, he took girlfriends on excursions in a snazzy dogcart. Later on, he recounted the dubious business wisdom he imbibed from Nathan Oppenheim. "To sell a man pearls that you have got and that he wants, that is not business," Nathan said. "To sell a man pearls that you have not got and that he does not want, that is business."[1] On gem-buying trips, Nathan sat with arms tightly folded to foil pickpockets. In later years, at charity meetings, Felix would strike the same self-protective pose and would remain an expert on emeralds.

Even by Warburg standards, Felix was unusually responsive to music. At age ten, he had helped to drag a cumbersome cart loaded high with musical instruments around the Baltic resort of Travemünde. "I was so proud that I was permitted to help push the dirty thing that I felt like Beethoven," he said.[2] He thrilled to symphonic music under von Bülow's baton and gladly joined in as his class sang during walking tours of Hamburg. He played the violin, had a fine voice, and knew the scores of many operas, including Gilbert and Sullivan. Years later, he wistfully evoked his boyhood as a time when "Germany was beautiful and full of inspiration."[3] In Frankfurt, he associated with pupils at the conservatory. "It was there that I very frequently had the joy of listening and talking to Clara Schumann. . . . It was there that I met Brahms and it was in that neighborhood, for a good many weeks that I heard the daily practice of Rubenstein. It was there also that the gypsy songs—quartets—of Brahms came out first."[4] He puzzled over the romantic themes of Richard Wagner's new *Tristan und Isolde*, even though the composer had written a few years before that, "I regard the Jewish race as the born enemy of pure humanity and everything that is noble in it. . . ."[5] Even in later years, Felix could sing virtually every part in the Wagner repertoire.

The blithe Felix seemed an unlikely candidate to bolster the Warburg fortune and shore up its banking connections. Yet by marrying Jacob Schiff's daughter, Frieda, Felix provided the critical link with the opulent German-Jewish banking families of New York, a group celebrated in Stephen Birmingham's book, *Our Crowd*. The term came from the German phrase "*Unser Kreis*" (literally, "Our Circle") by which these families knowingly referred to each other.

A Frankfurt native and an Orthodox Jew (although he belonged to the Reform branch of American Judaism), Jacob Schiff came from a family that had befriended the Rothschilds and that counted six centuries of scholars, rabbis, and businessmen. Schiff visited the Warburgs frequently while managing the Deutsche Bank's Hamburg branch and once brought the boys a memorable toy fort. In 1873, Schiff accepted an invitation from Solomon Loeb to join the new banking house of Kuhn, Loeb in New York. Although he left Germany for good, Schiff never lost a thick, sometimes impenetrable German accent and a sentimental fondness for his homeland. In May 1875, Jacob Schiff married Therese Loeb, Solomon Loeb's daughter from his first marriage. With blue eyes, a short, dainty figure, and doll-like features, the sweet, yielding Therese would be dominated by Jacob and relegated to the role of affectionate pussycat.

A classic "Our Crowd" tableau.
From left: Jacob Schiff, Felix Warburg,
Solomon Loeb, and Frederick Warburg as a baby.
(Courtesy of Phyllis R. Farley)

Kuhn, Loeb emerged from a Cincinnati dry-goods and clothing concern started by German-Jewish immigrants. Cincinnati was then home to a large, bustling German population, mostly from Bavaria or north Germany. Many had come to America after the 1848 revolutionary upheavals in Germany and were known as "Forty-Eighters," though most had simply sought economic betterment. These largely Reform Jews tended to be antislavery and Republican in their politics. The Civil War was a boon to some, including Abraham Kuhn and his brother-in-law, Solomon Loeb, who made a fortune selling uniforms for Northern troops and opened their first New York store as an outlet for men's trousers. The color-blind Solomon seemed strangely placed in the textile trade. In 1867, flush with their wartime profits, Kuhn and Loeb inaugurated a New York banking house. Suddenly, these Cincinnati peddlers were strolling about in top hats on Nassau Street in lower Manhattan.

Stephen Birmingham has noted that wealth only deepened the mania for things German among these American success stories. "New York Jews began, in the 1870's, to say to each other, 'We are really more German than Jewish,' and were convinced that nineteenth-century Germany embodied the finest flowering of the arts, sciences, and technology."[6] They spoke German at home, cherished German music, and savored in their gilded exile the German culture they had left behind. These New York bankers often summered at German spas and scouted Germany for suitable wives.

The gentlemanly Jacob Schiff had the fierce, uncompromising energy of the self-made man and ventured into financial terrain then *terra incognita* for Jews: railroad financing. The most lucrative part of Wall Street, it was also the turf most jealously guarded by gentile banks. Despite Solomon Loeb's extreme discomfort with such daring, Schiff refused to yield, and Therese was caught in the crossfire between her imperious husband and her circumspect father. By 1877, Kuhn, Loeb won the Chicago & Northwestern Railroad as a client and by the 1880s Schiff had pushed his father-in-law into retirement. Solomon still reported to the office, but more to keep up appearances than to exercise any authority. The palace coup was now complete. By 1881, Schiff added the giant and prestigious Pennsylvania Railroad to the client roster and M. M. Warburg began to market Kuhn, Loeb's railroad securities in Germany.

When Felix met Schiff in 1894, the latter was already a prince on Wall Street, bested only by the great J. Pierpont Morgan—a truly astonishing feat for a self-made Jewish immigrant. Schiff was on intimate terms with two railroad barons, James J. Hill of the Great Northern railroad and Edward H. Harriman of the Illinois Central, and his masterful 1897 reorganization of the Union Pacific with Harriman would be a landmark financial operation. In time, Schiff's clients would come to include Westinghouse Electric, Western Union, U.S. Rubber, and American Smelting and Refining.

Who could conceive a sharper contrast than between Jacob Schiff and the young Felix Warburg? Schiff had a pointed, silver beard and blue eyes that could sparkle with amusement, but more often flashed with scorn or indignation. He knew how to harness every atom of his being to the task at hand. His life unfolding with clockwork precision, he used every instant profitably. Every morning, at exactly the same time, he inserted a flower in his buttonhole and strode smartly down Fifth Avenue in frock coat and top hat, short, spiffy, polished, his step nimble, his carriage erect, his passage so punctual that shopkeepers set their watch by him. On principle, he answered every letter on the day received. He had a little tablet listing the day's tasks which he methodically went through until the slate was wiped clean. Exemplary in charity, he never squandered time on frivolous entertainments. The puritanical Schiff never smoked, played cards, or engaged in sports. A sworn foe of waste, he saved string from packages and donated old newspapers to hospitals and prisons. Schiff lived according to clear, sharp principles whose truth was always self-evident to him. Trying to banish all unruly emotion from his life, he offered himself as a shining model to American Jews. Deeply ethical, he donated 10 percent of his income to charity. Sometimes he seemed to have more compassion for suffering in the abstract than in his immediate surroundings and he could be coldly dogmatic with his family, often inspiring more fear than affection.

Felix Warburg, in contrast, thrived on dances, parties, tennis, sailing, golf. He was the big Warburg spender, the notable dandy and rake, the brother least self-conscious about exhibiting wealth and having fun. Unlike Schiff, Felix could laugh at himself and see the absurdity even in serious situations. Perpetually lighthearted, he sincerely believed that life was meant to be enjoyed. That Felix would later inherit Jacob Schiff's philanthropic mantle is all the more remarkable in view of his easygoing, cavalier style and—from Schiff's standpoint—shockingly wanton youth.

Not surprisingly, Jacob Schiff wasn't thrilled when his sole daughter, Frieda, fell in love with the profligate Felix in Frankfurt in 1894. The year before, she had turned eighteen at a party at which Walter Damrosch stood in a tub and crooned a spoof of Wagner's Rhine Maidens. Convinced that his daughter was now dangerously eligible and attractive, the overly protective Schiff decided to remove her from harm's way and whisk her off to Europe. Even as a young woman, Frieda had a stately, aristocratic bearing, her hair drawn up in an elaborate pile on her head. Still very sheltered and unsophisticated, she also had a drily ironic wit. At fourteen, while mountain climbing at Chamonix, she fell and broke her collarbone. As she was being carted off to an nearby inn for emergency medical attention, she overheard a guide inquire, *"Est-ce qu'elle est morte?"*—"Is she dead?" From her stretcher Frieda sardonically assured him, *"Pas encore"*—"Not yet."[7]

Schiff was a strict, tyrannical father. When he was away, his only son,

Morti, had to write him daily in German. On one trip, Jacob admonished him, "I notice you always write every morning. I would prefer that you write late in the afternoon, because then you could assure me that you've been a good boy and no trouble to your mother."[8] Morti endured a boyhood of excruciating sermons and eternal punishment, as if he grew up with an Old Testament God right on the premises. When he later inherited the parental mansion on Fifth Avenue, he sighed, "It's wonderful to be the master of a house in which I have been spanked so often."[9] Even as a grown man Morti was dismissed from the table by his father for such minor infractions as tipping over a water glass.

Schiff adored his daughter and protected her virginity as if it were a sacred treasure. This meant subjecting her to a suffocating, hothouse life. He minutely scripted her existence, from the French and fencing lessons to attendance at the exclusive Brearley School, where she was one of the first Jewish girls. (Even in 1912, Bernard Baruch was crushed when his daughter was refused entrance to Brearley.) The hovering father made Frieda tense, insecure, and always afraid of upsetting Papa. A dutiful daughter, she inherited her father's parsimony, charity, intelligence, and seriousness. She even had his blunt, tactless manner, and never indulged in social lies. Frieda—as burdened with small cares and worries as Felix was blessedly free of them—would seem stiff and wooden amid the outrageous, almost vaudeville atmosphere of the Warburg family.

Stephen Birmingham notes that Schiff's concern for Frieda's innocence had a touch of hypocrisy, for she had arrived eight months after Jacob's marriage to Therese. He was stung when a friend gently teased him, "I want to congratulate you on the appropriate name you've given your baby—'*Früh-da,*'" or "there early" in German. Afraid of enduring an eternity of such unbearable jokes, Schiff demanded that Therese change the name, which she wouldn't do. He never spoke again to the man who had hazarded the dreadful pun.[10]

Frieda was naïve and Felix very worldly when they met in Frankfurt on May 5, 1894. Charlotte and Moritz were visiting the Oppenheims and were invited to a dinner given by the Dreyfus family for the Schiffs. Felix's roguish reputation preceded him. When Frieda asked her cousin, Otto Schiff, if any interesting young men would attend, he mentioned Felix. "He was, they assured me, the most attractive young man in Frankfurt," Frieda said.[11] When Felix sat next to her, the chemistry was potent. Later that evening, he burst into his parents' room and exclaimed, "I have met the girl I am going to marry."[12] When Frieda learned of this years later, she observed, "What nerve."[13]

The next morning, Moritz decided that he had better shuffle off and pay a courtesy call on Jacob Schiff. They had antithetical fears: Moritz was alarmed that his son had fallen for an American girl while Schiff dreaded Frieda's living in Germany. Despite profitable dealings between M. M. Warburg and Kuhn, Loeb, Schiff occupied a regal position in New York, while the Warburgs, despite their long pedigree, must have seemed provincial in comparison. For a patriarch of Schiff's unbending severity, Felix undoubtedly seemed flashy and flip and not sober enough for a top-drawer bank. Felix's apprenticeship in the jewelry business must have suggested to Schiff that he was being designated the family dunce. Before leaving Frankfurt, the Schiffs attended the horse races and when the grinning Felix again materialized, Jacob decided that Frieda wouldn't see him again during their stay.

After a Paris stay, the Schiff retinue visited the Warburgs en route to a Scandinavian cruise. Of that memorable dinner in Hamburg, Frieda wrote, "The charm of the Warburgs was deeply impressed on me that evening."[14] She seemed especially enchanted by Max. Funny and mercurial, the Warburgs had the warmth and wit for which Frieda had been starved. For a person raised in the claustrophobic Schiff household, the clowning brothers must have been irresistibly irreverent. As Frieda's daughter later said, "The Schiffs were never strong on humor. The Warburgs were."[15]

When the Schiffs went to Bad Gastein for mountain hikes and a cure, Felix coaxed Otto Schiff into going there on a walking tour with him. The power of love defeated Jacob Schiff's clumsy attempts to arbitrate Frieda's destiny. On a woodland lane, Felix waylaid his future bride. As they ambled through the gardens, he asked if she would like to spend her life in Germany. "With a wise premonition, I said I would never care to live there," recalled Frieda. "When I joined my mother, I must have looked quite pale, because she asked me what was wrong, and I made the classic remark: 'I *think* that fellow proposed.' "[16] Frieda's assent to Felix would prove a blessing for the Warburgs, ensuring a Wall Street connection for M. M. Warburg.

Upset by these unplanned developments, Jacob Schiff tried to reassert control over events. In his exact timetable for Frieda's development, he hadn't scheduled marriage for two more years. It especially irked him that he had planned this European trip precisely to forestall such spontaneous romance. Luckily for Felix, Jacob Schiff's best friend, Ernest Cassel (soon Sir Ernest), pleaded his case. Born in Cologne, Cassel had moved to England as a teenager, amassed a fortune with the house of Bischoffsheim and Goldschmidt, converted to Catholicism, and served as Kuhn, Loeb's foreign agent. An intimate friend and financial adviser to the Prince of Wales, the stout, bearded tycoon was jocularly known as Windsor Cassel. He was as sociable, sporty, and extravagant as Schiff was grimly austere. It was Cassel who had bravely leaped down the precipice at Chamonix to rescue Frieda, giving him moral authority in all matters concerning her. As an epicurean with luxurious tastes, Cassel must have had a natural sympathy with Felix. During a long walk, Cassel tried to reason with the furious Schiff. "Jacob, don't be silly. There's nothing wrong with the young man. He's attractive—he's healthy; he comes from a good family. If there is anything against him it may be that he's too young. Why not suggest to him that if he is serious after a year's time you will consider his proposal if he's still interested and comes to America."[17]

Schiff relented and decided to adopt the suggested one-year waiting period. To settle matters, he had a state visit with Charlotte and Moritz in the Belgian seaside spa of Ostend. In the course of two meals—one ended disastrously when Schiff was served nonkosher lobster and threw a fit—it was decided that for a year, Felix would write to Frieda from Germany. Schiff would open the letters, censor them, and read aloud appropriate portions to his daughter. Then he would reply to Felix on her behalf, allowing Frieda to scan the contents before the reply was sent. One day, when she expressed girlish delight that her father had finally switched to the informal *du* form, Schiff, with Scrooge-like rigidity, scratched out all the pronouns and verbs and reverted to the formal *Sie*.

When the year was up, Schiff kept his intentions secret but invited Felix to New York. A few days after his arrival, Schiff held a party and ended it by announcing that Felix and Frieda were engaged—welcome news that stunned the young couple as much as the guests. If Schiff bowed to reality, he was also restoring his imperial control, for he insisted that Felix (whose command of English was still tentative) move to New York and enroll as a Kuhn, Loeb partner under his watchful eye.

Petrified of water, Moritz was loath to chance the Atlantic Ocean and didn't attend the New York wedding in March 1895. Bidding farewell to Felix, he encouraged him to shun American custom and, especially, avoid iced drinks. Afraid he would fall in love with an American girl, Max refused to go, too, so Paul and sister Olga represented the family, a visit that would ultimately transform both their lives. Felix didn't know who would attend until Paul stepped down the gangway in New York. Felix cried, "I never expected you!" and Paul replied, "Don't you remember we made a vow that whenever either of us got married, the other would be there?"[18]

For the wedding, about 125 guests crowded into a tapestry-hung room of the Schiff mansion at 932 Fifth Avenue. An avalanche of gifts showered down on Felix and Frieda. Afraid of spoiling his children, Schiff was appalled when a splendid sixty-seven-piece silver set, including a forest of candlesticks, arrived from Ernest Cassel. The best man was Paul Warburg, while the maid of honor was Nina Loeb, a daughter from Solomon Loeb's second marriage and half sister to Jacob's wife, Therese.

Schiff was patently jealous of Felix. After a trip to Washington, D.C., the newlyweds returned to New York and stayed at the Plaza Hotel. When Jacob called on them, he could scarcely mouth the loathsome new name, Frieda *Warburg*. At dinner he didn't mask his blatantly competitive feelings toward Felix. When Frieda asked if he could do something, Jacob grunted in disgust. "Why do you ask me? You now have your husband to turn to."[19] When the young couple sailed to Italy for their honeymoon, Jacob insisted that they take along the Schiff maid, a veteran nag and shameless spy named Hermine Steinmetz. The redoubtable Steinmetz chided Frieda if she got a spot on her dress. Although Steinmetz tailed the young couple everywhere with the tenacity of an amateur sleuth, Frieda managed to become pregnant on the cruise. In later years, Felix loved to quip, "I spent my honeymoon with a German governess."[20]

When Felix and Frieda returned home, their life took on a preordained quality, as Jacob Schiff placed them in a stage set of his own careful devising. They moved into a house at 18 East 72nd Street that was fully staffed and furnished, and in 1897 Felix was admitted to a Kuhn, Loeb partnership. The patriotic Schiff believed that immigrants should speedily master the language and customs of the country and this probably explains why Felix was so quickly Americanized. With his charm and ebullience, Felix took to the American milieu with a chameleon adaptability, even though he was the first Warburg to leave Europe in at least fourteen generations.

Paul Warburg and Nina Loeb had already met in 1892 at the close of Paul's round-the-world tour. Their reunion as best man and maid of honor at Felix's wedding revived their intense mutual fascination. After the wedding, everybody noticed a magical glow in Nina Loeb. Her face was suddenly fuller, her cheeks were flushed, she seemed radiantly happy. Instead of joining her parents for their customary cure in Carlsbad, she accompanied Paul and Olga on the boat back to Europe. As they crossed the Atlantic, Paul proposed. Back in Hamburg, he awaited a wire from Nina, which invited him to join her in Carlsbad and make things official with her parents. When the favorable news came, Paul was at the bank and joyously flew down the stairs. He met Charlotte coming up the steps and breathlessly shouted, "I am engaged to Nina Loeb!" Instead of congratulating him, Charlotte reproved him: "And you break the news to me on the stairs?"[21]

In October 1895, Paul and Nina were wed at the Loeb summer home on the New Jersey shore, only half a year after Felix and Frieda, while the Warburgs in Hamburg threw a celebration the same day. To the tune of *Hansel and Gretel*, they wrote a song bemoaning that after Felix's marriage, the number of children in Hamburg had dipped from seven to six. Now they expected Paul and Nina to live in Germany and even the score. With "*Felix hin, Nina her/Sieben sind wir wie vorher!"* (With Felix there and Nina here, We're seven again as before!) they sang.[22]

It was ironic that Paul and Felix became the two "Our Crowd" brothers, because they were so antithetical, Felix wearing the comic and Paul the tragic mask. Paul's personality was mirrored in his fine, sensitive drawings of people. Done in a steady hand, they portrayed pensive people in somber, often solitary settings. Whereas Felix in early photographs radiates a self-confident air, an exhibitionist's winning ease, Paul has a shy, self-effacing stoop and a nervous glint in his eyes. Unlike the beaming Felix, Paul struggled to smile, as if clutched at by some inner constraint. As his son wrote, "His face was sad, but saddest when he smiled."[23] Everybody noted the contrast between the brothers. "Paul's mustache turned up, and he had a sad face," *The New Yorker*'s Geoffrey Hellman once wrote. "Felix's mustache turned down, and he had a happy face."[24]

When Paul and Nina married, they turned the family tree into a genealogical nightmare. Felix was Jacob Schiff's son-in-law and Paul now became Schiff's brother-in-law. This turned Paul into his brother's uncle. The situation was no less perplexing for Nina, who became the sister-in-law of her beloved niece, Frieda. Paul and Nina's two children were therefore first *and* second cousins to Frieda and Felix's five children.

As the youngest child from Solomon Loeb's second marriage—Frieda's mother, Therese, was the only child from the first—Nina was only five years older than her niece, Frieda. The Brearley girls were always highly amused when Frieda shouted up the stairwell, "Aunt Nina!" Sweet, gentle, and intuitive, Nina was Frieda's early mentor and confidante, a sort of wise, loving older sister, an intimate role she played with many women. Nina liked to tease Frieda affectionately, labeling her the family snob and aristocrat, but Frieda deferred to "Aunt Nina" in many things. Only later did this closeness give way to some suppressed rivalry and mutual carping.

Nina came from a family that resembled the Warburgs more than the Schiffs. The buxom, energetic Betty Loeb dominated husband Solomon the way Charlotte did Moritz. When Paul first met him, Solomon had keen blue eyes, a bald head, and two fluffy wings of white hair that stood out horizontally on either side. His white handlebar mustache drooped into side-whiskers and, as one Warburg commented, he had the erect bearing of an American colonel.[25] He dressed meticulously, had few interests besides business, and was a quiet, reserved figure.

Solomon hadn't exactly seemed marked out for riches. With his shoes strapped to his back, he had emigrated to America from Worms, Germany, after the 1848 revolution, growing so violently sick at sea that he pleaded with another passenger to pitch him overboard. He then joined a distant relative in the clothing firm of Kuhn, Netter in Cincinnati. After he married Abraham Kuhn's sister, Fanny, Abraham married Solomon's sister, Regina, and the tight-knit little firm was renamed Kuhn, Loeb. Fanny gave birth to a daughter, Therese (Jacob Schiff's wife), but then died during confinement for a second child.

As a widower with a six-year old child, Solomon toured Germany to find a wife and met Betty Gallenberg of Mannheim, a violinist's daughter training to become a concert pianist. To marry Solomon and move to America, she had to sacrifice her career. Like Charlotte Warburg, Betty Loeb transferred her oversize, thwarted ambitions to her four children and approached the art of mothering much as great generals approach major battles, drilling her little troops to perfection.

Betty Loeb always had a jolly, well-fed air, with a double-chinned face and lively eyes. Bright, sentimental, vivacious, she had a vast range of interests. It was Betty who got Solomon to move to New York from Cincinnati, which she found woefully philistine and provincial and nicknamed "Porkopolis." In New York she invited musicians to their Murray Hill home, read Émile Zola, and helped Lillian Wald to found the Henry Street Settlement and the Visiting Nurse Service. The Loebs were agnostics but belonged to Temple Emanu-El.

The Loebs had four children—Morris, Guta, James, and Nina—and Betty filled these four poor vessels to the brim with education and culture. The children formed a string quartet, with Nina on violin and James on cello. Solomon was tone-deaf and this only deepened his subservience to his wife. Betty had a Jewish mother's implicit faith that expensive lessons and tightly scheduled days of activity will produce healthy, wealthy, nonneurotic offspring. The four children endured a battery of tutors for sports, dance, riding, music, and languages. Betty was also a strong believer in heavy food, which she ladled out in monstrous portions that evidently overpowered visitors. "Guests, leaving her groaning boards, often had to lie down for several hours," reports Birmingham.[26]

Unlike Charlotte, Betty had to deal with a troubled, star-crossed group of children. Nina's ambition was to be a ballet dancer. But at age eleven, she fell from a goat cart in Central Park and broke her hip, which never properly mended. The surgeons applied a gruesome treatment: They put her in a cast and tried manfully to stretch her leg by heavy weights. For a year, she remained bedridden, reading a good deal. The would-be ballerina progressed from a wheelchair to clumsy steel leg braces. For the rest of her life, Nina had a lopsided walk and needed a cane and a built-up shoe. A game teenager with great physical courage, she tried to dance and ride horseback in the face of her terrible pain. At age eighteen, she even pathetically tried to do ballet for Betty.

As the youngest Loeb child and handicapped into the bargain, Nina received boundless sympathy and became very spoiled. She learned to use her weakness to get her way with people and evade responsibilities. Frieda spoke of Nina's "Madonna-like beauty," which may say more about Nina's sweet, luminous presence than her actual appearance. Nina had a gentle nature and a serene radiance that certainly bespoke inner loveliness. Because she was crippled, people were perhaps excessively quick to credit her facial beauty. When Paul met her, she was slender and dark-eyed but not, at least judging from photos, a beauty.[27] Paul was that rare young man who set little store by glamour and surface things. With his stoical, self-denying nature, Paul catered endlessly to Nina, who used her handicap to dominate and even manipulate him. As their daughter, Bettina, recalled, "She acted as though he were her possession. She was sick a lot and this made her center stage. She had to be waited upon. Father was always very solicitous. We all waited on my mother."[28] But she was also loving and highly protective of Paul's sensitivity.

Paul's and Felix's marriages guaranteed that the Warburgs would avoid the great strategic error of the Rothschilds, who had failed to build a major presence on a burgeoning Wall Street. Yet, however well they served Warburg interests, these twin 1895 marriages were prompted less by commercial calculation than by the wayward stirrings of desire. There is no evidence that they were arranged, and the Warburgs and Schiffs even had to conquer their qualms about them. These love matches would prove more beneficial to future Warburg prosperity than the family's shrewdest business calculations. The Warburgs had arrived in America on the eve of its industrial and financial preeminence. Representing Kuhn, Loeb in Germany, Max Warburg would acquire a new cachet in German banking and political circles. At this point, the Warburgs seemed to be fortune's favorites, for in the coming decades, Wall Street would prosper as Germany was beset by war, revolution, hyperinflation, depression, and, finally, the most unspeakable dictatorship. The New York tie would give the Hamburg bank a buffer against the blows that German history was about to mete out so liberally to bankers—and to Jewish bankers in particular.

CHAPTER 5

The Sage and the Serpents

If Paul's life was forever altered by Felix's wedding in March 1895, Aby's life was no less profoundly touched by Paul's wedding in October. A true nationalist steeped in high German culture, Aby didn't share the family's flourishing romance with the Anglo-Saxon world. In New York, he was repelled by what he saw as the brutal, vacuous materialism of America's East Coast and found the wedding festivities gaudily overdone. A business-obsessed America, he thought, had banished magic and poetry from its shores.

In Aby, the Warburg extremes of light and shadow, hilarity and tragedy, reason and madness contended for supreme mastery. He combined a madcap irreverence with a high-strung, often terrifying temperament and he admitted that his main trait was being easily annoyed.[1] The two sides of his nature seemed inseparable, mirth and sadness following each other in alternating waves. Later, his son speculated that Aby started out as a melancholic and gradually evolved into a choleric type.[2] Endowed with a certain Warburg clairvoyance that would become marked in his generation, he knew posterity would puzzle over his enigmatic personality and once observed, "I'm just cut out for a beautiful memory."[3] Asked on a questionnaire whom he would be if he could be somebody else, he replied, "Nobody else."[4]

In a photo of the thirteen-year-old Aby at the Realgymnasium Johanneum, he stands out among blond classmates for his dark coloring and facial expression. Extremely pleased with himself, he stares into the camera like a presumptuous young monarch. The princely gaze was something of a pose, for Aby was known not for lordly aplomb, but for temper tantrums. As we recall, he had been traumatized as a boy by his own illness and by Charlotte's near-fatal brush with typhus, which left him with a morbid fear of sickness. Even news reports of overseas epidemics could trigger full-blown anxiety attacks. During the 1892 cholera epidemic, he fled Hamburg and was criticized by his family for deserting Max.

Aby had an unforgettable appearance. A tiny, dapper man, prone to stoutness in later years, he had dark brown eyes that crinkled with merriment or blazed angrily. Like his brothers, he had a handlebar mustache and shaggy eyebrows. He was a whimsical fellow who could kick up his heels in outrageous dances. To small children, he was either magical or scary, a merry prankster or a dread disciplinarian, with brusque movements that seemed military and theatrical in their precision. He loved to joke in local dialects. As Kenneth Clark recalled, "He himself said that if he had been five inches taller . . . he would have become an actor, and I can believe it, for he had, to an uncanny degree, the gift of mimesis."[5] An overflowing fountain of aphorisms, witticisms, and anecdotes, he could be a tireless one-man show at a dinner party.

Like his brothers, Aby had a heightened sense of the absurd, and his taste for practical jokes took wickedly funny forms. Once, at a dinner party, Aby noticed that his pretty cousin, Elsa, was trapped beside a lisping bore. For the next five weeks, this lisping man telephoned Elsa and pestered her for a date despite her repeated and insistent refusals. Aby finally revealed himself as the culprit.[6]

Every great comedian requires a straight man, and Aby had several. One was Gottschalk Sander, Moritz's barber, who, as mentioned earlier, developed an unfortunate case of trembling hands. The Warburgs got Sander a job at a theater box-office in the Saint Pauli district, where he skimmed money and shortchanged Spanish sailors on exchange rates. When the tolerant Warburgs then made him a house servant at Siegmund's Alsterufer home, he would decorate the table with flowers stolen from the lakeside park. He also filched food from the breakfast table and Aby devised an ingenious revenge. One morning, he tiptoed into the breakfast room, deposited two soft-boiled eggs on the table, then stole out. A few minutes later, he walked into the room and seeing the eggs missing, squeezed Sander in a hearty embrace until broken eggs came streaming from the thief's pockets.[7]

The wit of the five Warburg brothers signaled a revolt against the stuffy

Aby Warburg, outfitted like
a European banker-cum-cowboy,
poses with a Pueblo Indian, 1896.
(Warburg Institute)

ways of their elders and their vestigial ghetto fears. It seemed the triumphant laughter of emancipation and enlightenment over confined superstition. This was seen in the endless teasing of Tante Malchen, the family's great figure of fun. The youngest and homeliest of Sara's four daughters, she grew into a dowdy, overweight woman with her gray hair parted beneath a bonnet and cap. For four years, she was married to a widower named Adolph Goldschmidt, who died of smallpox. Malchen never called him Adolph, but would just bark "Goldschmidt."

Tante Malchen's Jewish orthodoxy inspired the brothers to heights of zany mischief. Aby was the ringleader. Once, he and his brothers hid Tante Malchen's kosher veal roast. Then they marched into the dining room bearing a papier-mâché suckling pig, with an apple stuffed in its mouth. Another time, when she rang the bell for the next course, she discovered that her nephews had locked the maid in the pantry. Still another time, when Baron Mitsui visited the Warburgs, Aby told Tante Malchen that she had made a great impression upon the Japanese dignitary, who had asked him whether Malchen was "a painted Jewish war god."[8] Charlotte tried to suppress her laughter at these outrages perpetrated against her helpless sister-in-law. Then she, too, would burst out laughing, and an indignant Tante Malchen would throw up her hands, sighing, "Charlotte, you are the worst of them all!"[9]

The renegade Aby was determined to cast off the restrictions that bound German Jews, to test the limits of assimilation. He would struggle with forbidden feelings and subversive impulses. The whole drama of the contradictory German Jewish soul—pride and self-hate—was played out in his turbulent psyche. By adolescence, he not only had sold his banking birthright to brother Max, but had rejected all religious belief.

Aby decided to become an art historian—a choice that was highly controversial. He faced considerable family pressure to become a doctor, research chemist, or rabbi instead. As Max recalled, when Aby "visited his maternal relations in Frankfurt every single member of the family tried to dissuade him" from his chosen career.[10] Aby particularly resented the Jewish orthodoxy of his Frankfurt relatives. Once, at a wedding, an uncle kept quizzing him about Jewish customs, inquiring, "Tell me now, my son, what is the name of the ritual slaughtering knife?"[11] For Aby, this summed up a medieval, obscurantist Jewish world he wished to escape.

In Imperial Germany, Jews enjoyed less tolerance in the universities than in general society, and many professors were fiercely reactionary anti-Semites. As late as 1909, there were only twenty-five Jewish full professors in Germany. Since Napoleonic days, student fraternities had been hotbeds of anti-Jewish sentiment. When Aby went to study art history at the University of Bonn in 1886, he fought on the one hand to be liberated from his parents' orthodoxy, and on the other to gain acceptance in an academic world hostile to Jews. As he said, "as a Jew, I had a bitter two-front war."[12]

At first, he cooked for himself and lunched in a kosher household. Unfortunately, he was such an inept cook—he would pop open an umbrella to shield himself from flying bits of scrambled eggs—that he gave up the attempt to stay kosher; Charlotte and Moritz grew extremely upset. Instead of backing down, Aby, who was always fanatically principled, engaged in a pitched battle with his parents. He once said that he didn't live to be happy but to fight and would never compromise on religious matters.[13] He lectured Moritz, "Since I do not arrange my courses of study according to the quality of ritual restaurants but according to the quality of my teachers, I do not eat ritually."[14] Moritz and Aby viewed each other painfully, with mutual incomprehension: the father could only see the possibility for fulfillment within a Jewish context and the son outside of it. Aby was Charlotte's favorite son, whom she spoiled with packets of fancy food, clothing, cigars, and wine. Yet she, too, suspected that some shame about being Jewish lay behind Aby's obstinacy. "I am not at all ashamed to be a Jew," Aby defended himself, "and on the contrary I am trying to show others that representatives of my kind are well suited, in accordance with their talents, to insert themselves as useful links in the chain of present-day cultural and political developments. . . ."[15]

Everything in Aby's life suggested, at the least, a deep ambivalence about being Jewish. As a student at Bonn, Munich, and Strasbourg from 1886 to 1889, he ravenously absorbed German culture in the classroom, hastening his assimilation, but then encountered the baldest anti-Semitism in the street. In Strasbourg, in particular, he experienced abuse from the town guttersnipes and complained bitterly to Charlotte how he couldn't leave the house without someone hollering, "There goes the Jew." With heavy sarcasm, he noted that their "beloved German people" regarded Jews as interlopers with doubtful manners until they got to know them personally. Someday, Aby said, he would devote himself to solving the Jewish question so their descendants wouldn't suffer professional discrimination.[16] Aby always bristled at anti-Semitism, even as he tried to shake off his Jewish identity.

When Aby complained about abuse, Moritz was quick to sympathize and agreed that Germans often behaved like coarse upstarts. At the same time, he insisted that Hamburg was exempt from such vulgarity. He told Aby how anti-Semites had distributed broadsides on the streets only to have the mayor vigorously denounce them. He struck a typically Panglossian note: ". . . we are lucky here in Hamburg that it provides no soil for such nasty acts."[17] This sense of Hamburg as an exceptional situation, a shining refuge, would be a recurring theme in Warburg history.

Aby chose a field of study that paid tribute to his mercantile upbringing but did so in a very Christian context. He specialized in the art of Quattrocento Florence, which had been a tradition-bound city-state ruled by merchant princes—not unlike Hamburg. Early on, he reacted against the prevailing tendency to study only the formal properties of paintings, which turned the critic into a gifted aesthete, and he broke sharply from the connoisseur approach embodied by Bernard Berenson. He didn't think art history could be separated from the broader history of culture and ideas. Instead, he tried to reconstruct the social and economic world that had spawned Quattrocento art. To this end, he delved into arcane and unconventional records, such as business contracts of the Medici family.

In 1888, Aby studied in Florence and even did some freelance research on local museums for a revised Baedeker edition. Henceforth, Italy would be his second home, his special place. With his wonderful ear for language, he learned to speak Italian fluently. Short and dark, he was inordinately proud when people mistook him for an Italian. Afterward, people said his gestures and manners were expressive, delicate, and distinctly Florentine.

That December, Aby was pleased to escort through the Florence galleries a young Protestant woman named Mary Hertz. The daughter of a Hamburg senator, she had two brothers, Wilhelm and John, who had been Aby's fraternity brothers in Bonn. Aby and Mary had long chats before the cozy fireplace in the hotel where she stayed with her father. With an enthusiasm that surely alarmed Charlotte, Aby wrote, "Miss Hertz, who is an excellent painter, has such a surprising interest, simple and yet profound, in all artistic things that I really take pleasure in being a cicerone. . . ."[18] The first New Year's card that Aby received from Germany that year came from Mary.

Eight years would pass before Aby mustered the courage to marry Mary Hertz. During that time, he said, he was haunted by his parents' reaction. The German Jewish community was on the verge of an epidemic of intermarriage. By the early 1900s, every fourth Jew who married in Hamburg did so outside the faith. But there was no precedent among the Warburgs. Intermarriage was a great community taboo for a simple reason: The Jews were a tiny minority who would rapidly fade away if intermarriage became fashionable. The ban on such marriages before emancipation had, ironically, safeguarded the community. So a leading Jewish family, supposed to set an example, couldn't lightly allow its eldest son to break the former taboo.

Aby's situation was complicated by the fact that even as he flouted his family's sacred wishes, he relied on them for money. Just as Jewish merchants once supported the son who became a rabbi or talmudic scholar, so Aby wanted his family to bankroll his secular scholarship. Instead of making him humble, dependency made him importunate, a self-righteous enfant terrible demanding his due. A bullying tone often crept into his begging letters.

Starting in Florence, he began to shock his parents with his omnivorous appetite for books. After one five-hundred-mark binge, he wrote Moritz, "I now possess the nucleus of an exquisite library: this is the indispensable tool of my trade and I may well have to come to you two or three times with a similar request before I am able to supplement my library from my annual cheque. . . ."[19]

Aby took full advantage of the deal by which Max would become the banker and buy him books in return. Even as a boy, Aby was such an impassioned reader that he found it hard to focus on his homework. By age twenty, he bought books and even photographs with single-minded intensity, the collecting already showing incipient signs of an overmastering compulsion. As a bibliophile, Aby was terribly indulged by his family, much as when he was a sickly child. Later, the brothers would often resent the immoderate financial demands of the library, but they always accommodated his wishes. In 1890, Max told Aby not to concern himself with current troubles at the family bank. "The moment you start to look more closely into the firm you will inevitably be assailed by so many worries that they are bound at least to detract from your ability to work. What use is that to you? The way you want to live you will always be able to live thanks to a very wealthy father; the balance sheet will never need to worry you. . . ."[20]

Fortunately, Aby's work held promise of justifying the sacrifice. In late 1891, he completed a doctoral thesis on Sandro Botticelli, which deciphered the mythology of two of his paintings. A minor detail had arrested his attention: the flowing hair and drapery of classical figures in Renaissance art. Later celebrated for his aphorism, "The good Lord lives in the details," Aby already had a gift for disclosing large truths from incidental, overlooked features.[21] The wind whipping through hair and gowns made him question the orthodox view that classical art had introduced perfect poise into the Renaissance; Aby suspected more primitive forces at work. He began to see classical art less as a matter of serenity felt than of serenity achieved by conquering latent, disturbing forces. Much as Friedrich Nietzsche had spied the Dionysian side of classical drama, so Aby felt the secret tug of the pagan in its art. His dissertation was a great success, and he proudly mailed out a hundred copies to family, colleagues, and friends. It initiated his most enduring concern: the afterlife of classical art in the Renaissance.

The Jews had always been a bookish people, with some medieval Jews even picturing heaven as an enormous library. During his Botticelli research, Aby began to envision a unique sort of library. As he attempted to encompass the entire Renaissance worldview, he roamed freely across many disciplines, from psychology to philosophy, poetry to religion. Yet he had to visit one specialized library after another to get the rich synthesis he desired. As libraries grew, it became ever harder for scholars to browse in stacks and discover new material. Instead of combing library shelves, they had to submit request slips for known books, preventing happy, accidental discoveries. Aby now envisioned a library that would cut across disciplines, expose unexpected connections, and invite the scholar to rove its shelves, much like an intrepid explorer in a labyrinth. His student purchases already began to form the rudiments of such a dreamlike library.

After his dissertation, Aby took a last, abortive fling at a "practical" career and briefly studied medicine in Berlin. Then he did a year of military service with the horse artillery in Karlsruhe. Rising early to swab out horse stalls provided some needed respite from heavy mental labors. With his pint-sized body, Aby had trouble mounting the tall cavalry horses and in his first two days tumbled off his horse six times; he said he needed another three centimeters in his legs. Although the officers teased him, he was an ardent soldier and a good sport and wound up an *Unteroffizier* or sergeant. Aby was always deeply patriotic and enjoyed military uniforms as much as Max did.

Leaving the army in 1893 with his career plans still uncertain, Aby returned to Florence. With his army experience behind him, he fell prey to depression and anxiety. He was alternately merry and feverish, hopeful and despairing. Already he was so engrossed in art that others found it either riveting or exhausting to listen to his endless theorizing. When Felix and Frieda stopped in Genoa on their honeymoon, Aby took them to see some Leonardo da Vinci frescoes in a dimly lit cloister. Staring at the picture, Aby launched into a marathon lecture, only to turn around and find the newlyweds kissing instead of paying studious attention. He was irate. "You two are carrying on as if you had invented matrimony," he declared.[22] A prophet in search of disciples, Aby had no patience with dabblers and dilettantes and demanded a consuming dedication.

Aby developed a growing interest in ancient rites that had lingered on in the Renaissance, often in camouflaged forms. When stripped of its masks and with its symbols decoded, Aby spied at the bottom of European civilization surviving traces of an ancient barbarism. In the evolution of Western culture, he saw a conflict between rational and magical thinking that mirrored his own fragmented psyche. The streak of depression in the Warburg genes made him preternaturally alive to the darker tides that flowed in European culture.

To encounter pagan forces in their pure state and to observe how "primitive" man exorcised his demons, he decided to visit the Indians of the American Southwest after Paul's wedding in November 1895. He had first encountered these Indians in adventure books as a boy, when his mother lay ill with typhus. For Aby, it would be like a voyage to classical Greece—not the Greece of exquisite statues, but of orgiastic rites and Maenads dancing with snakes writhing in their hair. As Aby said, "two thousand years ago, in

Greece—the very country from which we derive our European culture—ritual practices were in vogue which surpass in their blatant monstrosity even the things we see among the Indians."²³

In all likelihood, Aby decided to attend Paul's wedding only because it coincided conveniently with this professional ambition. It would be his sole American trip and farthest voyage from Germany. He formed a close friendship with Nina's brother, Jim Loeb, who took him to Harvard to view the art collection and meet Charles Eliot Norton, professor of fine arts. In their aesthetic interests, collecting, worship of German culture, and later decline into madness, Aby and Jim Loeb would lead curiously parallel lives.

Aby's approach to art history had an affinity with archeology and ethnology. Having met a staff member of the Smithsonian Institution on the boat to New York, Aby went to Washington to review its Indian collections before setting out for the Southwest. The visit to the Pueblos would be a journey into his own psyche, a study of the contending forces shaping his life. He traveled alone by train to Chicago and Denver, ending up in Santa Fe and Albuquerque, New Mexico. Because he was twice associated by marriage with Kuhn, Loeb, he enjoyed a free pass on the Atchison, Topeka and Santa Fe railroad.

The Indians found the little German paleface no less strange and exotic than he found them. He spoke no Indian tongue; they spoke no German. He looked like a visitor from another world. In photos from the trip, he smiles out from beneath a small cowboy hat and colorful neckerchief, even as he wears a banker's suit with black vest and watch chain. He looks happy and relaxed, uncharacteristically so, as if temporarily released from the weighty burdens of European culture. For once, he didn't seem to be troubled by all the psychosomatic ailments that plagued him at home.

During one stage of his trip, he administered a fascinating test to children in a Hopi Indian school. He told them a German fairy tale that included a lightning storm, then asked them to draw the lightning. Twelve of the already Americanized children drew the lightning in naturalistic, zigzag fashion. Two of them, however, reverted to tribal custom and drew it as an arrow-headed snake, much as it appeared in their magic ceremonies. It was for Aby an instance of the persistence of tradition and myth beneath the veneer of modernization.

As spring approached, Aby traveled from Santa Fe and Albuquerque to the remote Indian reservations. A Jewish trader from Milan popped up and took him on extended trips. Together they braved snows and sandstorms and slept in tents. Once, a Catholic priest took him to a distant village so he could witness Indians in colorful tribal garb participating in a Mass. Held in native tongue, the entire service had to be translated for the priest.

Everything on the trip seemed a prelude to Aby's visit to two isolated Hopi towns. (The Hopis form part of the Pueblo tribe.) For two days, he rode in an open buggy beside a Mormon guide across a gorse-covered desert; for the last leg, an Irishman escorted him to the cliffside villages. The Indians allowed Aby to observe secret rites. He witnessed ceremonies in which hunters mimicked their prey, hoping to procure first by magic what they would subsequently procure in reality. Most importantly, he studied the snake-dance rituals that occurred every August when the Hopis invoked magic to ensure their harvest rains. They rounded up a hundred undulating serpents, dipped them in consecrated water, then stored them underground until the sixteen-day ceremony began. During those rites, the Indians hurled the live snakes at serpentine sand drawings of lightning. Through skillful handling, the Indians would cunningly induce the poisonous snakes to engage in ecstatic dances for days on end.

Aby felt that these rituals brought him closer to the pagan side of ancient Greece. In one ritual, the Indians switched from sacred liturgy to obscene parody and Aby saw a prototype of the chorus in Greek tragedy. "Anyone acquainted with ancient tragedy will recognize in this the dual nature of the tragic chorus and the satyr play."[24] His study showed him how magic distanced people from objects of fear, thus forming an intermediate stage on the road to a rational understanding of natural events. Yet he knew that such magic represented no final triumph over primordial fears. As he said, "there can be no assurance that the sap which nourishes it is, even to-day, not secretly drawn from the roots of bloody sacrificial cult."[25]

Before returning to the East Coast, Aby visited Pasadena and San Francisco and recoiled at the repellent scientific civilization that had gone from magic to a purely logical, hence sterile, explanation of events. It was hard for him to readjust to the banality of everyday life. Back in Hamburg, he donated native artifacts to the Ethnological Museum and gave a lecture embellished with snapshots to the Photographic Society. Max later said that Aby's trip to the American Southwest was his life's decisive event, and Aby agreed. "Without the study of their primitive civilization I never would have been able to find a larger basis for the Psychology of the Renaissance."[26]

Did Aby's Indian adventure harden his resolve to jettison his religious past, just as Western civilization had tried to transcend its pagan roots? As he came to regard Judaism as just another superstitious cult, he thought it cowardly and hypocritical to abide by its rituals. Both Aby's glory and downfall lay in his extraordinary fidelity to principle, even if it caused pain to others. Soon after returning to Hamburg in 1897, he finally summoned the courage to propose to Mary Hertz. It was the most difficult decision of his life.

Aside from religion, Mary was an ideal match. Her father was a patrician Hamburg shipper and senator and socially superior to the Warburgs; her mother came from the aristocratic Gossler family. A beautiful young woman with a round face, pale blond hair, and deep, gentle eyes, Mary looked very fetching in the boater hats and billowing sleeves of the Gay Nineties. She was a gifted painter and sculptress and as scornful of frauds and stuffed shirts as Aby. "When anyone tries to kiss my hand," she once said, "I get chills down my spine."[27]

Even in the hypercritical Warburg family, Mary would have no real detractors. As her son said, she had "the purest heart" he had ever known.[28] Only the saintly, rather innocent Mary could have put up with the stormy Aby and acted as a buffer to his chronic moods. Feeling intellectually inadequate beside him, she admired him greatly and offered him the rare gift of unconditional love. In later years, Aby paid tribute to Mary by calling her, "My wife, my best colleague, and my comrade."[29]

Objections to the marriage came mostly—but not exclusively—from the Warburg side. Mary's parents worried that Aby, still a gypsy scholar living off parental charity, lacked fixed career plans. The strong, loving Mary, who knew she was signing on for trouble, marched open-eyed into the marriage. On the eve of their engagement, Aby had a terrible panic attack, believing that their love had cooled. Already aware of his psychological instability, he shrank from inflicting his manic-depressive moods upon her. Mary brought him gently along with eloquent, faintly ironic reassurance: "If I want to step, with open eyes, into the trap of marrying a man whom I know will often torture me with his moods, that is my business, and none of his damn business."[30] She reminded him that despite his temporary depression, he was sound at bottom. Emotionally, Mary was deeper, purer, and more generous than Aby. In reply to her beautiful, personal letters, Aby would babble on about some Florentine fresco he had deciphered. If Aby had largeness of mind, Mary had equivalent largeness of soul.

Aby knew that his parents, especially Moritz, would be horrified if he ever married outside the faith. As Aby told Mary's family, Moritz had "in the sixty years of his life, against wind, weather, and passing currents, stood for the principle that Jews had their own ideals and shouldn't give them up."[31] Moritz indeed reacted with terrible anguish and pleaded with Aby to reconsider. He even offered to double his allowance if he desisted! Then, surprisingly, Moritz produced a compromise plan. He would consent to the mixed marriage if the children were brought up Jewish and the boys were circumcised. Aby would submit to no such conditions or any abridgement of his freedom. Discussing the proposal with John Hertz, Aby said he couldn't agree with Moritz that Jewish intellectual culture was superior to contemporary German culture.[32] Even though his more pragmatic brothers argued that Moritz just wanted a sop for his conscience, Aby remained obstinate. In the end, Senator Hertz couldn't consent to Moritz's proposal either, and it was dropped. When the engagement was made official in July, the pain overwhelmed Charlotte and Moritz.

Aby told his mother that Mary fit the pattern of ideal womanhood he had derived from Charlotte herself. Perhaps this helped reconcile Charlotte to the marriage. Taking a cure at Bad Homburg, she wrote to him saying that she had always had a large place in her heart for him—big enough for two children—and that Mary had now become her loving daughter. Moritz, however, was suffering unspeakably.[33]

Aby wrote to his father, saying he was gnawed by remorse every second, but had to stick to his principles. He promised his father that he would never convert away from Judaism, but could offer no guarantee for the children.[34] If hurtful, Aby's attitude was also pioneering and courageous, especially since he depended upon his father's largesse. Moritz sent Aby an elegiac reply, more in sorrow than in anger. "The thought that it was always the greatest joy for me to hold high the flag of noble Jewry and that I must see it, in time, at half mast from afar, is temporarily so overpowering that I can't describe it."[35]

For a time, Aby wasn't spoken of at the Alsterufer, as if he had ignobly died. In the end, Moritz and Charlotte accepted the match, but refused to attend the wedding of their apostate son. Out of respect for the Jewish community, Moritz asked that it not be held in Hamburg and it took place on October 8, 1897, at the suburban home of Mary's parents. Max and Olga attended for the Warburgs, suggesting that Aby's siblings had definite sympathy for his plight. In a conciliatory gesture, Moritz and Charlotte visited Mary and Aby on their honeymoon in Wiesbaden and then formally called on the Hertzes. Within a few weeks, Moritz had come around and was referring to Mary as his dear daughter. Indeed, her loving, patient attention to Aby for several decades would be prized by everyone in the Warburg family. Significantly, Aby and Mary installed themselves in Florence, not in Hamburg, and ended up staying there intermittently for the next five years. Like the Prodigal Son, Aby would always return home, but would never find it easy to stay for long or make his peace with its prosperous, mercantile culture.

CHAPTER 6

Magic Mountain

A s if to compensate the Warburgs for losing Felix to America, Paul and Nina set up house in Hamburg and stayed for seven years. They lived on a street called Grosse Fontenay near the Outer Alster Lake, a short walk from other family members. Their two children, James and Bettina, were born in Hamburg and had a bilingual, German-American upbringing, complete with English nanny and many transatlantic crossings. Though the most Spartan brother, Paul quickly catered to Nina's wishes. When he bought a fine horse and carriage to take his crippled bride around town, Charlotte accused him of being showy. The seven years spent under her mother-in-law's stern, cavilling eye must have been a trial for Nina, who was accustomed to being indulged.

Moritz did reserve the right to veto decisions and offer advice, but Max and Paul, still in their twenties, ran the Hamburg bank after 1895. With his manly gusto and luminous, engaging eyes, Max was a natural leader with a gift of easy command. Each morning, perched on a high stool before a slanting Victorian desk, he pored over newspapers and letters and shared incoming mail with partners. Then he made the rounds with a buoyant step, chatting with employees and quizzing them. He wanted the information fast and straight and he once asked to have a single word engraved on his tombstone: "Simplificator."[1] Born to rule, Max dominated the ten o'clock partners' meetings at the green baize table.

Max had a talent for attracting clients, and entertained a steady parade of visitors—businessmen, politicians, foreign bankers—as he branched out into a wider world of society than the cautious Moritz thought wise for a Jew. In 1897, Max, thirty, became a commercial judge, beginning his remarkable rise in the Hamburg power structure. Prone to sudden, sometimes fanciful, brainstorms, he needed a restraining influence and found it in Paul's prudence. If Paul idolized Max, he was also smarter and stubbornly asserted his judgment. Together, they would make M. M. Warburg & Co. the top private bank in Hamburg, a leader in acceptance credits, foreign exchange, and securities work.

In a family bedeviled by mental illness and psychosomatic maladies, Max had colossal energy, confident humor, and a hardy constitution. He could skewer people with a phrase, faintly praising one mediocre diplomat by saying, "But he sits so well at the table."[2] He was quick witted and inventive. Once a distraught employee telephoned Max on his wedding day to report that the bride's father, to block the event, had locked his daughter in the bathroom. Max telephoned the local fire department, which rescued the bride on a false alarm. He then informed the grateful young man that the one-hundred-mark fine for this abuse was his wedding gift.[3]

Only once did Max's robust metabolism falter. In 1896, he was exhausted from his early responsibility, and his doctors recommended a long sea voyage, which proved less than restorative. He journeyed to Capetown, contracted dysentery, lost forty pounds, and nearly died. In South Africa, he inspected tin mines and received a memorable audience with the queen of Swaziland. They sat on mattresses while the queen drank Max's gift of German beer and whooped uproariously at his remarks. He was puzzled by her uncontrollable mirth until his interpreter admitted he had invented Max's entire conversation.

While his son was in Africa, Moritz bought a country house that would turn into the Warburgs' ancestral home. Max and Paul had decided they would like to spend summers in the country. Often Max rode out on horseback to the fishing village of Blankenese, a charming place with dirt roads, houses clinging to the steep hillsides, and irregular lanes running down forested bluffs to the Elbe. This elevated land outside Hamburg provided spectacular views of the river and flat, distant orchards. One spot in Blankenese especially enchanted Max, a cool, shaded mountaintop glade of ancient forest and plunging ravines three hundred feet above the river. Moritz also fell in love with it, insisting that if the Warburgs ever got a summer house, it had to be there.

Olga and Paul Kohn-Speyer
strolling at the turn of the century.
(Warburg family, Hamburg)

The place was named Kösterberg, or Köster's Mountain, after the Hamburg auctioneer, H. J. Köster, who had built a house there in 1796. It had passed through several incarnations, first as a popular inn for Hamburg day-trippers, then as a residence for a wool merchant, Semper, and a banker, Bromberg. When Bromberg offered it to Moritz for an exorbitant one million marks, Moritz laughed at him. Then, while Max was in Africa, a suddenly chastened Bromberg approached Moritz at the stock exchange and anxiously asked for a bid. Evidently, he had returned early from a business trip to discover his wife in a tryst at Kösterberg. He couldn't bear the place a second longer and had to sell at once. Moritz paid just 240,000 marks, wiring Max in Madeira, "Kösterberg bought."[4]

With Felix in America and Paul destined to join him someday—Nina had only signed on for temporary duty in Hamburg—Moritz wanted a sprawling, comfortable place where the family could gather yearly. Kösterberg was a vast estate, with a coachhouse, stable, and gardens. One could wander for hours beneath its shady forest canopy in a magical stillness. In time, the children and twenty-one grandchildren of Moritz and Charlotte would assemble there each summer. For the Warburgs, Kösterberg would be their fortress, their shrine, their repository of memory.

Moritz and Charlotte occupied the former inn, an old eighteenth-century thatched-roof house. (In the early days, strangers would suddenly drift in and order beers.) From the way the long, steep-roofed building sat poised on the hilltop, it suggested a boat stranded by receding floodwaters and was dubbed Noah's Ark. Its balconies looked out on a broad, lovely bend in the Elbe, affording a view of ships steaming into Hamburg port. For all its magnificence, Kösterberg had a rough-hewn country grit. Because it had no lightning rods, the family had to sleep in blankets by the door during electrical storms. Tante Malchen's room was so leaky that she sometimes sat under an umbrella in bed. To go downtown, the men took a jangling, yellow carriage to the train station, pulled along sleepily by a fat black mare named Lola.

The Warburgs would all rotate through Noah's Ark. When Moritz and Charlotte constructed a large white house below it, Paul and Nina took up residence in the shiplike structure. Then they added a colonial-style house down the hill, yielding the Ark to Max; after Max came brother Fritz, then Max's son, Eric. It is the one house that has remained in Warburg hands for a century and has represented continuity for them.

Perhaps Kösterberg encouraged Max to think of marriage. The most virile, dashing Warburg boy, he attracted many young ladies. He was no crusader in terms of sexual equality. Taking a self-knowledge quiz as a teenager, he was asked to list his favorite historical heroines. "As soon as a woman emerges in history," he said, "I don't like her."[5] One might have predicted

Max would spend a lifetime philandering. Instead, he chose a young woman named Alice Magnus who faithfully served his royal splendor, and he repaid her with equal loyalty. As Frieda noted, "flirtatious Max, after he was married, never so much as took another woman out to lunch."[6]

Alice and Max became engaged in December 1898. Descended from the Altona Warburgs, Alice had grown up in Leipzig and Hamburg. Her mother, Lola—blond-haired, blue-eyed—was born in Odessa and served as a nurse in the Crimean War; her father, Hermann Magnus, was a furrier who died young. Lola and her nine children grew up as wards of the Altona Warburgs, receiving a monthly check from Pius Warburg. Alice's bitter childhood made her tense, insecure, and status conscious. Her favorite brother and sister died of diphtheria, to which she nearly succumbed, and an elder sister raised them strictly.

Alice was pretty and petite with thick wavy hair and a round, open face. She was very cultured. In her early twenties, she had lived in Vienna for three years with her relatives, the von Hornbostels. Aunt Helene was an opera singer and Alice got to know Brahms as a Sunday guest. She studied painting and drawing and savored Imperial Vienna. She developed such a talent for portraiture that in later years her superb rendering of Tante Malchen was praised by no less than Oskar Kokoschka on a Kösterberg visit.

She suppressed her early traumas and seldom referred to them. This made her tough and stoical in her habits, frugal behind her aristocratic air. She was smart but very rigid, quite unlike the more free-wheeling Max, whom she always chided for eating too much and smoking too many cigars. Her childhood status as poor relation made her a slave of fashion, and she was preoccupied with having faultless taste in furniture, clothes, and floral arrangements. She needed spotless elegance, wall-to-wall refinement. The early brush with diphtheria also left behind a notable obsession with cleanliness.

Max and Alice married after a three-month courtship and then honeymooned in Italy. In Warburg jargon, they took on the splendid composite name of "Malice," just as Paul and Nina became "Panina" and Felix and Frieda "Friedaflix." The success of the Malice match would mystify the Warburgs. Max was so charming and easygoing, Alice so stern and fastidious. The success probably derived from a perfect division of labor: Max ran the bank, Alice the household. He brought home the bread, she brought up the children and fed the guests. If the marriage was a bargain, each amply fulfilled the contract. In the early years, Alice had wit and laughter also and wasn't the cool customer she later became. Her disciplined, iron nature would, in fact, see Max through many crises.

Max married Alice just as he assumed responsibility in the larger community. He would be torn between his Jewish antecedents and the wider Christian sphere of politics and business he now entered. With more opportunities available to them, the Warburgs would feel more acutely the contradictory strains of being German and Jewish. As one historian said, "the Warburgs enjoyed a position in Hanseatic society markedly different from that of other members of the [Jewish] community. They were almost accepted as belonging to the ruling stratum of lawyers and merchants and had adapted the external circumstances of their life accordingly."[7]

For Max, Jewish leadership would be largely a matter of noblesse oblige. Alice never went to synagogue and used Yom Kippur to tidy up the linen closet. Only marginally more religious, Max attended synagogue on High Holy Days, but with a book secreted in his lap to pass the time during services. From respect for Moritz, Max and Alice kept a curious, dual household: a kosher one for Moritz's visits, a nonkosher one for daily use. If Moritz dropped by for breakfast, the servant girl was instructed to whisk away the ham before he could spot it.

Unlike the Bleichröders, Mendelssohns, and other august Jewish banking families, the Warburgs spurned titles or baptism, but still lived grandly. Max presided over so many charities that he was dubbed the "uncrowned King of Hamburg." Alice, meanwhile, orchestrated an elaborate social whirl flashier than anything Moritz and Charlotte would have tolerated as decent. In 1907, Malice moved to a large town house on Neue Rabenstrasse, where they had black-tie family dinners every night. Socially ambitious, they threw masked balls and elegant dinners and Alice dramatically advanced Max's career.

An exacting hostess, Alice kept a book in the kitchen that showed precisely what guests had eaten on previous visits, so they wouldn't be subjected to repeat menus. She designed an opulent setting of blue and yellow carpets, mirrored doors, a marble dining room, and chrome banisters. Butlers with white gloves and silver buttons greeted guests. In a salon furnished with Louis XVI pieces, Alice held teas for the ladies and poured from an exquisite gold and silver samovar. In her realm, Alice was imperious and omnipotent and Max couldn't touch her. Once, Albert Ballin, the shipping magnate, asked Malice's five-year-old daughter, Lola, who had the last word at home. "Father usually sees her point," was how Lola put it.[8]

On Easter Sunday, 1900, Alice gave birth to a son, Eric. In Max's quest for a second son, Alice then produced four daughters: Lola, Renate, Anita, and Gisela. After this last birth, Max cabled Friedaflix: "Alice has surprised the whole world and herself by producing another girl. Please begin to look for sons-in-law."[9] With comical symmetry Frieda and Felix had a daughter, followed by four sons.

The children were prisoners of Alice's immaculate settings. They couldn't use the front entrance, for Alice feared they would leave fingerprints on the polished banisters. With her usual rigor, she selected their clothes. In general, they lived apart from their parents. They breakfasted alone, lunched with mother, and had supper with nanny. They were not allowed to enter the kitchen, talk with servants, or dine with their parents until age sixteen. Among many rules governing their confined, regimented lives, they couldn't discuss food—this was impolite—and paid a fine into a box if they erred. Once when little Eric was asked for his birthday wish, he replied, "I would like this black vegetable again," because he had never heard the word "caviar" openly pronounced.[10] Believing water destroyed children's appetites, Alice allowed them one small glass in the morning and one at night. These extremely thirsty children would recall their childhood as a sub-Saharan drought.

No less than Betty Loeb, Alice packed her children full of costly lessons: gymnastics on Monday, violin on Thursday, French and English every day. These bankers' children had to record in a book every penny they spent. Amid plenty, they felt like orphans trapped in a Dickens novel. Each morning, emerging from their dark gray bedrooms with iron bedsteads, they had to bring milk to their two grandmothers.

Alice didn't bolster the children's confidence. She would tell them, "If people are nice to you, it's only because of your father."[11] At night Max would come home with a thick stack of correspondence and briefly stop by to visit the children in the nursery. "Did you do your good deed today?" he would ask, then fall asleep on the sofa.[12] These emotionally starved offspring received his love in small doses and lived for his fleeting visits or morning walks with them. Max could be a severe disciplinarian. When two of the children got poor grades, he sold off their beloved Swedish ponies. As a rule, however, he provided more affection than Alice, especially with his four adoring daughters.

The Warburgs expertly stimulated their children to achievement yet remained abysmally ignorant of child psychology. Basic childhood anxieties were alien territory. Every day, Alice picked up Eric at the Heinrich Hertz Realgymnasium. One day, he complained that other boys teased him about his American plus fours—fashionable knickerbockers of the time. The stoic Alice was perplexed. "Why should the comments of the other children concern you?" she inquired.[13] Eric was a delicate, blond boy, not terribly independent, and Malice did little to buck up his courage. He was drilled in the social graces and attended dance classes run by a man named Knoll who would appear as Knaack in Thomas Mann's *Tonio Kröger*. At age nine, Eric wore white gloves and asked little girls to dance in French. "*Madame,*" he would say, "*je me présente—mon nom est Eric Warburg.*"[14] As had happened with the children of Moritz and Charlotte, the nanny, Louise Kummerfeld, provided compensatory warmth to the orphaned children.

The children received confusing messages about religion. At school, Eric enjoyed the morning hymns and readings, especially from the New Testament. When he was seven or eight, Max took him one day, not to school, but to a large ugly brick building. "You see, we are Jews, and we are on our way to the synagogue," he told Eric en route. "The synagogue is for us what church is for the Christians."[15] The mystified Eric then entered a weird room full of men in shawls and skullcaps, swaying and mumbling indistinctly. He and Max stood behind Moritz and the chief rabbi as Eric tried to make sense of this buzzing, writhing congregation. He asked his father if these people were Arabs. Then, in a loud voice, he asked, "Do Jews really believe in Jesus Christ?"[16] Max removed Eric before he could cause further embarrassment. He decided the time had come for religious instruction. Eric was bar mitvahed in Hamburg in 1913, and Jacob Schiff came for the ceremony. Predictably, Eric's Jewish identity would always be rather vague and tentative.

The daughter who suffered most from Alice's parenting was the eldest, Lola. Small-boned and exquisite, she was Max's favorite, which probably aroused strong jealousy in Alice, who liked to pin labels on the children. Her nickname for Lola became "*dumme Lola*"—"stupid Lola."[17] Lola wasn't dumb, yet she spent her life trying to live down the stigmatizing name. Headstrong, she chafed under parental discipline and loathed having her hair curled nightly. Alice promised Lola this torment would end on her thirteenth birthday. But when Lola came downstairs on that day, with *uncurled* hair— before Alice had given permission—she was marched back upstairs and had them curled again. The other daughters received an adequate education. Renate and Gisela took their *Abitur*, while Anita attended the prestigious Salem school, but Lola had to make do with private tutors. The only books she received as a child were from shipping magnate Albert Ballin, who once gave her six volumes when she was sick.

None of the children had much conception of their wealth. They were schooled in humility and told never to give the impression of being rich. Once asked at a birthday party whether she was Jewish, Gisela refused to answer. When Alice asked why, Gisi stammered confusedly, "You always told us not to boast."[18] The Warburg children ventured into worlds sealed off to other Jews and always feared tokenism. Eric, Anita, and Gisi played hockey at the same sports club and tried to enroll their cousin. Told that the club wouldn't accept more Jews, they quit. Both in Hamburg and New York, the Warburgs were uniquely palatable to the Protestant elite, and this sometimes created an uncomfortable ambiguity about their place in the larger scheme of things.

—

The matchmaker for Max and Alice was apparently Max's sister Olga. Shy, gentle, and slightly downcast, Olga had Paul's sensitivity and looked like him.

In photos of Olga as a teenager, she gazes into the camera, wan and pensive, with a doomed, far-off look. A gifted pianist, she was adored by all her brothers. "Olga was strikingly sensitive, intelligent, witty, and had already distinguished herself through her good works as a 17-year-old girl," Max later wrote. "She was quite close to me later and finally became a confidante for the over-ambitious plans that I—especially after I returned from abroad—thoroughly discussed with her. I have met few women, who listened as well as Olga and with such intuitive female judgment."[19]

When Olga accompanied Paul to New York for Felix's wedding, she fell in love with Nina's brother, Jim Loeb. This passion would have tragic ramifications. The story would remain a dark family secret. As the nonconformist son of a banking dynasty, an aesthete devoted to art, archeology, and classical civilization, Jim found himself in the same situation as Aby Warburg but with a less accommodating family. After graduating from Harvard with Bernard Berenson in 1888, Jim wanted to accept an offer to teach at Harvard, work at the Boston Museum of Fine Arts, and study Egyptology in Europe. But even though Jim had no interest in banking and couldn't stand Jacob Schiff, Solomon Loeb insisted that he enter Kuhn, Loeb. Jim always assumed that Morti Schiff would inherit the firm's leadership.

Jim might have escaped Kuhn, Loeb if Solomon Loeb hadn't been rebuffed by his older son, Morris. As portrayed by Stephen Birmingham, Morris was an odd bird with a pathological tendency to hoard money. He stuffed thousand-dollar bills into his room's wallpaper—a habit that didn't augur especially well for a banking career. Morris also had phobias about mirrors and feared food poisoning. Although he became a distinguished chemistry professor at New York University, fate played a cruel prank on him. In 1912, he died of food poisoning, after eating a bad oyster at a chemical society convention. The fourth Loeb child, Guta, also led an unstable life. She married Isaac Newton Seligman, went through several nervous breakdowns, and spent much of her married life in sanatoriums.[20] Their daughter married Samuel Lewisohn, thus giving the Warburgs business ties to the influential Seligman and Lewisohn families.

As a young man, Jim Loeb had great charm and charisma. Handsome and heavyset, with a round, open face, he was funny and articulate, a fiery writer with fervent opinions. As a Kuhn, Loeb partner until 1901, he was so miserable he could scarcely function and his anguish aggravated his nervous ailments and severe depressions. He compensated by playing the cello and collecting Greek statues. In 1905, in his mother's memory, Jim, Panina, and Frank Damrosch founded the Institute of Musical Art, which later merged with the Juilliard Foundation to become the Juilliard School of Music.

The Loebs and Warburgs reacted vehemently against a match between Jim and Olga. It's unclear why. Perhaps Moritz and Charlotte didn't want to sacrifice a third child to New York. Perhaps they were disturbed by incipient signs of mental illness in Jim. Or maybe they suspected Jim would forego banking and they would have another expensive, acquisitive Aby on their hands. In her memoirs, Olga's cousin, Elsa, suggests that Jim didn't reciprocate Olga's love.[21] Family lore speculates that Olga and Jim were too closely related to marry—which isn't entirely convincing since they were no more blood relations than Paul and Nina.

One explanation is that Nina was profoundly alarmed by the proposed marriage. If Olga moved to New York, it became more likely that she and Paul would end up in Hamburg—a horrifying thought for her. The psychic repercussions went deeper, for Nina was infatuated with her brother, an adoration so intense that it struck people as unhealthy, even incestuous. Nina's daughter noted, "So deep was the love of these two for each other that most of their friends rather expected that neither of them would marry, so long as they had each other."[22] Nina never hid her extreme affection for Jim and automatically found fault with the women in his life. When Paul and Nina named their first child Jim, Nina wrote her brother that Paul had given her "a little Jim to make up for the big Jim I left behind me. . . ." She ended the letter by saying that her brother's beautiful head was "the pride of my life. . . ."[23] Where did that leave Paul?

Whatever the reasons for the stifled romance, it had extremely unfortunate consequences. The Warburgs encouraged Olga to marry Paul Kohn-Speyer, who had accompanied Paul around the world and headed the London firm of Brandeis, Goldschmidt, a major metal trading house. Olga acceded. Max knew the business advantages of such a match and later cited Paul Kohn-Speyer as the Hamburg bank's most important family member next to Paul and Felix.[24] After a Hamburg wedding in August 1898, Olga and her husband lived in a big corner house in Lennox Gardens in London. The following September they had their first child, Alfred.

For a person of Olga's pale delicacy, it is hard to imagine a less suitable husband than Paul Kohn-Speyer. Plain and balding with a little goatee and small round spectacles, he was cold, stern, humorless, and consumed by business. Born in Liverpool but educated in Frankfurt, he had left Germany to avoid military service. He tended to inspire more respect than affection in people. His fairness with friends was counterbalanced by a certain severity with his family. At work, he was a tyrant who brooked no opposition from his partner, Ernest Goldschmidt.

If Olga was pure poetry, Paul was all prose. The marriage must have magnified Jim Loeb's image to glowing, heroic proportions in Olga's mind, and she grew desperately unhappy in London. She poured out her heart in letters to her younger sister, Louise, in which the dark, rainy London weather became symbolic of her oppressive misery. The marriage was irremediably poisoned when Olga and her husband visited Germany in 1902. Pregnant for the third time, Olga suggested they leave their firstborn, Alfred, at Kösterberg and travel to Frankfurt. Paul agreed reluctantly. While they were away, little Alfred died of a sudden stomach illness and Max had the sad duty of going to inform them of this horrifying event.

Olga never recovered from the shock. To worsen matters, Paul Kohn-Speyer blamed her for the death. He would come home, march past her, then sullenly play with his model trains upstairs. After their fourth child, Edmund, was born in March 1904, Olga, exhausted from four births, slid into a deep postpartum depression. Paul Kohn-Speyer had little sensitivity to disturbed people.

Olga's close friend, Alice Hallgarten Franchetti, the daughter of a New York financier, came to tend her. Alice had been in love with both Paul and Max Warburg, but in the end she married a government official in Rome. Because her own mother had been mentally ill, Alice knew how to care for Olga and suggested that she consult a famous neurologist in Berne, Switzerland. In August 1904, they all went to see the doctor, staying at a luxurious hotel. The night before their appointment, Alice slept in one room with Olga, and Paul Kohn-Speyer stayed in an adjoining room—an arrangement that suggests the tense, uncertain state of their marriage.

During the night, Olga grew suicidal and tried to jump from the window. She struggled with Alice and finally managed to overpower her friend and leap from their third-story window into the river below.

A profound silence would surround Olga's suicide, deepened by guilt and sadness. When Max and Alice had a second daughter that December, they named her Olga Renate or "Olga reborn." The Warburgs felt they hadn't done enough to help Olga and would always welcome her children at Kösterberg. The episode darkened Charlotte's personality, so that her grandchildren would see only her somber sense of duty and not the joy that was eclipsed with Olga. It was all eerily analogous to Sara's reaction to Marianne's London misadventure with Samuel Zagury.

Paul Kohn-Speyer wouldn't talk about Olga or tell their three children what had happened, but he never went back to Lennox Gardens. Even the housekeeper was sworn to secrecy. For three years, Paul struggled to raise the children alone, before marrying Anna Leo-Wolf of Frankfurt, a cool, fashionable, rather standoffish woman. They had four more children. As we shall see, Olga's suicide would have ramifications decades later, when it would greatly embitter a major business dispute among the Warburgs.

Olga's death must have weighed on Jim Loeb's mind. With his parents' death, he came into a fortune and no longer had to endure the purgatory of Kuhn, Loeb. Yet this didn't free him. In 1905, he began treatment in a German sanatorium. As a student, Fritz Warburg, the youngest of the five brothers, had suffered from a hyperacid stomach and recuperated in the Binswanger Sanatorium in Jena. When Fritz steered Jim to Dr. Otto Binswanger, Jim didn't actually stay in the institute, but rented a nearby villa. When his depression lifted, Jim wanted to return to the United States, but was still tormented by epilepsy. The family sent Fritz to persuade him to try a Dr. Kroepelin in Munich, who had a special dietary treatment for epilepsy. It proved successful and Jim sent Fritz a beautiful black pearl in appreciation. Fritz always had qualms about the wisdom of his mission, for he believed that Dr. Kroepelin's cure had dulled Jim's flashing intelligence and created a truncated man. As Fritz said, "his mind became blunted, so that he really only thought of eating and drinking. He was still very amiable, but the entire quick-witted man was no longer there."[25]

Jim became increasingly introspective and never returned to New York; he remained a German expatriate for life. Recovering from the epilepsy treatment, he was tended by a redheaded nurse named Marie Antonie "Toni" Hambüchen, a doctor's widow. Unlike Olga, Jim found consolation for earlier romantic disappointments. In 1911, he moved to a vast, wooded estate called Hochried in the Bavarian town of Murnau, where he and Toni led a strange, reclusive existence. As Fritz recalled, "She nursed James Loeb and he then married her, to the great horror of my sister-in-law Nina, who was simply jealous. She idolized her brother. We always called them the Mutual Admiration Company. But she grinned and bore it."[26]

As a philanthropist and collector, Jim accomplished noteworthy deeds in his hermetic, self-imposed German exile. In 1910, he endowed the Loeb Classical Library, which during his lifetime produced 200 volumes of Greek and Latin literature in handy pocket editions, with English translations on the facing page. The next year, he financed the German Institute for Psychiatric Research in Munich. An avid collector of Greek antiquities, he also set up a ground-floor museum in his Munich town house and presided over musical performances there, with the audience seated on furniture from Versailles. He was the only family member who reversed the one-way migration from Germany to America, and he became a steadfast German patriot.

—

It was typical of the easygoing Fritz Warburg that he fondly recalled his stay in the Binswanger clinic as a happy interlude in which he gardened, puttered, and was spoiled rotten by nurses. He remained true to his motto, "One must suck honey from every blossom."[27] Although Fritz was always overshadowed by his four dazzling brothers, he savored life, treasuring small everyday transactions, the pleasures of a crowded tavern or café. His plodding pace gave him time to see and enjoy things that his busy, dynamic brothers missed. Earthy, warmhearted, and unpretentious, he evinced little of the snobbery of other Warburgs.

A funny-looking, goggle-eyed boy, Fritz seemed set apart from birth. Even his twin sister, Louise, who didn't resemble him, seemed stamped from another mold. Fritz's comical appearance, which cried out for a cartoonist's pen, only grew accentuated with time. He developed into a portly, lumbering gentleman with an unruly walrus mustache, protruding teeth, and eyes that bulged behind thick glasses. As torpid and sedentary as Max was brisk, Fritz was self-conscious about his appearance: Small children shrieked and fled in terror when they encountered him in a wood. Yet however painful these episodes must have been, he would throw back his head and laugh good-naturedly.

Thirteen years younger than Aby, Fritz didn't feel so keenly the Warburg imperative to have a spectacular career. In this extravagantly overachieving family, he could shelter behind his brothers's exploits and enjoy a benign neglect. Even during student days in Munich, Berlin, and Rostock, he showed modest ambition and snored his way through many classes. He associated with Jewish students, shunning those who chose baptism just to further their careers. Magnetically drawn to life's back alleys, lower depths, and illicit passageways, Fritz often seemed more preoccupied by the demimonde than the beau monde. He liked to regale companions with humorous anecdotes from Low German authors. In Berlin, he patronized a restaurant that used several back chambers to satisfy needs beyond the strictly culinary and he loved to joke about the versatile kitchen and waitress staff. In another marked departure from Warburg custom, Fritz enjoyed chatting in Yiddish and adored the *shtetl* lore of Eastern European Jews. Later, not surprisingly, he assumed many of Moritz's functions in the Hamburg Jewish community.

Fritz's life was often predetermined by events in his older brothers' lives. After completing legal studies in Berlin in 1902, he planned to practice law. Then Paul and Nina moved to New York, and Moritz had to recruit a second son for the bank. On the spot, Fritz had to renounce his legal career, doubtless an agonizing step for him, since he never had any special interest in banking. He trained in Frankfurt with the Disconto-Gesellschaft, then spent a year at M. M. Warburg. An apprenticeship in Paris was cut short by Olga's suicide. To help care for her three orphaned children, he moved into Paul Kohn-Speyer's house and worked at the metal firm of Brandeis, Goldschmidt. This proved invaluable, for Fritz afterward cofounded the Hamburg Metal Exchange and started a metals department at the Warburg bank.

By 1907, as the Warburg partner in charge of credit and personnel, Fritz was installed in a first-floor office next to Max, where he shuffled in late each morning and stayed late. He enjoyed being closeted with employees, hearing their stories and acquiring a comprehensive knowledge of the bank. He was intensely curious about people. Fond of graphology, he studied the handwriting of the M. M. Warburg employees and his daughters' friends. Fritz would never focus narrowly on money or power and regularly attended theater, cinema, and ballet.

The ugly Fritz married an extremely pretty distant relative. Blond and blue-eyed, Anna Beata Warburg stood a full head taller than Fritz. In yet another intermarriage, Anna was his second cousin, her father having left Hamburg decades earlier to escape the rigid orthodoxy of the Jewish community. He had married Ellen Josephson, who was descended from another Jewish banking family imported into Sweden by a seventeenth-century finance minister. (The Swedish actor, Erland Josephson, comes from the same family.) After reading an American book called *Patsy* about a crippled child, Anna Beata, fourteen, decided to devote herself to improving kindergartens, which were then little more than day-care centers with uneducated staffs. Like other Warburg women, she saw charitable work as a welcome escape from the drudgery of domestic life.

In 1896, Aby S. Warburg (Siegmund's son) visited Sweden and brought home the fifteen-year-old Anna to educate his children. She thus arrived in Hamburg as the poor relation, living as a governess at the luxurious Alsterufer residence and attending the progressive Fröbelseminar for kindergarten teachers. Fritz got to know her at the Alsterufer. As she prepared to return to Sweden in May 1908, he decided he had better propose quickly. Anna, more serious than the fun-loving Fritz, was taken aback and had to overcome worries about his profligacy. That year, they got married in Stockholm, with Paul coming from America for the wedding. On their honeymoon in Florence, Aby M. again played the voluble cicerone, as he escorted them through the galleries.

Anna never entirely shed a faint sense of shame and inferiority about having entered the family in the guise of a lowly governess. This gave her a detached, often critical, perspective on family matters. Her activist ideology clashed with her sudden wealth. As her daughter said, "My mother felt that wealth was a humiliating burden."[28] She felt self-conscious about being a rich woman who had to run a large house full of servants. As an educator and social worker, she knew nothing about managing a household or handling cooks. Family traditions that seemed sacrosanct or self-evident to others were persistently questioned by the iconoclastic Anna. Why was Aby exempt from earning money? Why did Max get a larger cut at the bank?

Anna Beata felt that Max's wife always studied her with a haughty, condescending eye. As the poor relations married to the two banking brothers, Anna and Alice were constantly compared—to Anna's detriment. As a hostess, who could compete with the overweening perfectionist Alice? It was a losing battle. So Anna and Fritz opted out of the whole family competition and cultivated a separate set of friends and interests. Yet they could never entirely shed a nagging feeling that they *should* keep up with Malice and their regal relatives.

A year after their marriage, Anna Beata joined the Fröbelseminar board and became involved in training people to run professional kindergartens. She and Fritz lived at Gross Fontenay 5, with an Alster Lake view, next door to where Paul and Nina had lived. Reacting against the massive, ornate, overstuffed furniture then voguish among Hamburg's prosperous burghers, Anna decorated the house with blue walls and light birch furniture.

It was a lively but troubled house: Fritz had a roving eye and often escaped to Berlin for assignations, and it was never a happy marriage. Contrary to what one might expect, Fritz and Anna weren't terrific parents. They traveled often, leaving the children with governesses. Fritz didn't know what to do with their three daughters—Ingrid, Eva, and Charlotte Esther—until the girls could sit and converse with him like little adults.

Fritz's twin sister, Louise, married Dr. Julius Derenberg, an ear, nose, and throat specialist. Louise was a warm, cheerful, and unaffected woman, who feared her mother but in many ways patterned herself after Charlotte. She read widely, kept a diary, and wrote poetry. Imbued with Charlotte's sense of duty, Louise threw herself into charitable work and helped to support seven or eight families. She would receive them in the dining room, tell them they had far too many children, and then give them money. Louise and Julius had four smart, sociable children—Carl, Walter, Ruth, and Gabriele—who grew up in an assimilated atmosphere with hardly any Jewish friends.

Raised in a protected home where money was a taboo subject, Louise was innocent of life's practicalities. When Dr. Derenberg courted her and she admired some beautiful furniture, Charlotte lectured her, "If you marry your little physician, you won't have that."[29] Nonetheless, Louise persisted. In another family, the bearded, intellectual Dr. Derenberg would have been regarded as a social ornament. A handsome bon vivant and music lover, he collected Japanese woodcuts and took an interest in Hinduism and Buddhism. As a serious botanist, he collected cacti and other desert plants in his greenhouse and even had a plant named for him in botany texts. Yet in the strict Warburg hierarchy of status, he wasn't a banker so he was demoted to a secondary position.

No less than Fritz and Anna Beata, Louise and Julius were made to feel the splendor and infinite superiority of the Malice household. The Warburgs measured themselves not only against the larger society but against each other. Having finally gained an opening in German high society, they were anxious to retain it, and this uncertain success intensified a status consciousness endemic among the German Jews. The snobbery was less a reflection of having arrived than a telltale index of some ultimate, underlying insecurity, a tacit fear that this newfound paradise might prove evanescent after all.

A Small Duchy in Westchester

N ina Loeb only agreed to live in Hamburg on a temporary basis, and Betty and Solomon Loeb continually clamored for her return. Nina's letters home bemoaned the cold, damp weather and the German pessimism, and she begged Paul to follow Felix's example and accept a Kuhn, Loeb partnership. A self-sacrificing spirit, Paul was caught between his loving, persistent wife and that master of persuasion, brother Max.

When news came that Betty Loeb was seriously ill in 1902, Paul agreed to move to New York. As he and Nina sailed west that summer, the plump, diabetic Betty struggled with gluttonous urges at the Loebs' Fishrock Camp in the Adirondacks. One day, as she reached for a forbidden wedge of pie, Solomon exclaimed, "Betty, don't!" She couldn't stop herself. "If it costs me ten years of my life," she declared, "I'll take a second helping of this excellent desert."[1] True to her prophecy, the rich food triggered an attack and she lay dead within twenty-four hours.[2] A year later Solomon died in bed from a heart attack.

Paul only moved to America under duress, having just become one of the first Jews elected to the Hamburg city-state council or *Bürgerschaft*. (Assigned to a low-prestige committee on chimney sweeps, he was kidded mercilessly about it by Max.) Max always said no brother had ever been a closer friend, and he and Moritz were despondent over Paul's departure. Max still exerted a magical and pervasive influence over his bashful younger brother. That Paul could resist Max's pressure to stay in Hamburg speaks eloquently of Nina's tenacity. In the end, Max conceded that Hamburg was too small a kingdom for the brothers' joint ambitions and felt it best that Paul had left. For all his idolatry of Max, Paul felt overworked and overshadowed by his brother.

Max and Moritz released Paul on the condition that he retain his Hamburg partnership, spending six months in New York and six months in Hamburg each year. In the end, they settled for his staying at Kösterberg in the summertime. For Paul, it was an emotionally charged departure. As his son said, before World War I Paul resided emotionally on both sides of the Atlantic.[3] Whereas Felix became a naturalized U.S. citizen by 1900, Paul waited until 1911, when his German citizenship became a political liability in his controversial crusade for a central bank.

Two things reconciled Max to Paul's loss. First, with the growing complexity of tax law and contracts, he thought it wise to hire a *Syndikus* or legal adviser for the firm, and chose an elegant, meticulous young Hamburg judge named Dr. Carl Melchior. For a private bank, this was a revolutionary act, and Moritz couldn't see how the man could possibly earn his keep. Yet Melchior, a humble man, deeply impressed Moritz and exhibited Paul's sterling qualities. Extremely lucid, precise, and of unquestioned integrity, he would play a role in German finance no less distinguished and unimpeachable than Paul's in America. By a nice symmetry, they would work together on German reparations.

Also sweetening the pill for Max was that Paul's joint Kuhn, Loeb–M. M. Warburg partnership magnified his firm's global power. The Kuhn, Loeb connection would elevate M. M. Warburg into being the foremost private bank in Hamburg, possibly in Germany. The two firms were now bolted together irrevocably by the telephone and teletype messages that passed daily between Paul and Max, making them privy to every notable development in American-European finance. "Even a house like Morgan was poorly informed about Europe in comparison to us," Max boasted.[4] By 1898, the fancy House of Bleichröder itself was grumbling that Max neglected them on Illinois Central bonds issued by Kuhn, Loeb and distributed by Warburgs.[5] After scoring a spectacular success in 1900 by placing German treasury bonds in America through Kuhn, Loeb—the money to go for Germany's expedition against the Boxer Rebellion—the Warburg bank participated in numberless government and railroad issues with Kuhn, Loeb. To crown its new eminence, M. M. Warburg was invited in 1905 to join the most august German financial committee, the Reich Loan Consortium.

Paul M. Warburg.
(Courtesy of Katharine Weber)

In New York, Nina and Paul rented a house at 3 East 82nd Street. Each morning, Paul walked downtown with Jacob Schiff, exchanging views all the while. Since he hated attracting attention, Paul felt uncomfortable with Schiff's grand, imposing manner and self-important airs. Paul's daughter said of these morning walks, "He hated the whole performance."⁶ Paul hid his feelings, however, and Schiff would always prefer him to the glad-handing, outgoing Felix, who wasn't always as deferential.

Paul arrived at Kuhn, Loeb right before the firm moved to a palatial twenty-two-story building at William and Pine streets. Wall Street was then rigidly split between "Yankee" banks tied to England and "Jewish" banks tied to Germany. For Kuhn, Loeb, the barrier was more porous. Among Jewish firms, it most nearly aped the style, manners, and success of the elite gentile firms, notably J. P. Morgan & Co. Its clients now included Royal Dutch Petroleum and Shell Transport and Trading as well as the Swedish, German, and Japanese governments. Through Sir Ernest Cassel, Schiff met British king Edward VII. In 1906, Paul and Max placed an issue of Pennsylvania Railroad notes in Paris, a coup for both firms, and Schiff fulsomely praised Paul: ". . . it will give you the feeling that you are really one of the four wheels which make the wagon go."⁷

Piloted by the imperial Schiff and assisted by the flamboyant Otto Kahn, Kuhn, Loeb didn't provide Paul with the same room for advancement as M. M. Warburg. He was a junior partner—talented, upcoming, but still junior. Speaking English with a British accent, he betrayed a double foreignness. (His children had to edit his essays for errors.) Unlike Felix or Max, Paul was introverted, with few intimate friends, and hardly anybody dared to call him by his first name. If warm and jovial at a family gathering, he could seem austere and cynically aloof in business circles. Peering over his glasses and studying the world skeptically, he didn't suffer fools gladly. In America, he was surrounded by an impenetrably lonely aura.

Paul was never at home in the Wall Street rough-and-tumble. Schiff had formed an alliance with railroad baron Edward H. Harriman, an unkempt little man of exceptional shrewdness and sizable ambition. In 1901, Schiff and Harriman teamed up with William Rockefeller and National City Bank in a boisterous battle to wrest control of the Northern Pacific railroad from Pierpont Morgan. Their titanic stock market duel for the road ultimately produced a truce between Morgan and Schiff, but at the price of a full-blown stock market crash caused by frantic, competitive bidding for the railroad's shares. Though Paul enjoyed working with Harriman, he didn't go for the gladiator tactics and generally didn't care for his work at Kuhn, Loeb.

It was a matter of happenstance that Paul became a great theoretician of central banking; he could have excelled at many things. Taking a scholarly approach to finance, he frowned upon the single-minded pursuit of money as crass and vulgar. As a resident insider equipped with an outsider's vision—a classic Warburg strength—he saw Wall Street's defects in a vivid, heightened way. He brought to America an encyclopedic knowledge of European central banks. By an uncanny coincidence, he arrived in America on the eve of a historic debate over whether the United States needed a central bank. The nation hadn't had one since Andrew Jackson spiked the charter for the Second Bank of the United States in 1836, and Paul's detailed knowledge would be a rare resource in the emerging, often ill-informed, debate.

From the time he started at Kuhn, Loeb, he was flabbergasted by the wild boom-and-bust swings on Wall Street, the weak, fragmented banking system, the giddy stock market gyrations. Soon after his arrival, panic convulsed the stock exchange, with interest rates on broker loans from banks soaring to a stratospheric 100 percent. "To a person trained under the central banking system of European countries," he confessed, "such conditions seemed bewildering and strange."[8] As a foreigner, he didn't accept such lunacy as inevitable. "I was not here for 3 weeks before I was trying to explain to myself the roots of the evil."[9] He thought it presumptuous, however, for a newcomer to lecture the natives and graciously remained silent.

In 1902, Schiff dined with President Theodore Roosevelt to discuss monetary reform. Schiff deplored the lack of an elastic currency, which meant that money became too tight in boom periods and too slack in bust. When Paul showed his senior partner an essay he had written advocating an American central bank, Schiff applauded the ideas, but was skeptical about their prospects in a country ferociously hostile to such schemes. The notion of a central bank was still highly controversial, and Schiff feared that if he wasn't discreet, Paul might get a reputation as a wild-eyed maverick. Although Schiff and others speculated vaguely about a central bank, only Paul, with his European training, had a clear grasp of the mechanics involved. Schiff advised him to show his essay, quite confidentially, to James A. Stillman, president of National City Bank.

After sending the memo, Paul looked up one day to see the president of Wall Street's largest bank looming above his desk. "How is the great international financier?" Stillman asked sarcastically, adding, "Warburg, don't you think the City Bank has done pretty well?" "Yes, Mr. Stillman, extraordinarily well," Paul replied. "Why not leave things alone?" Though shy, Paul wasn't meek and he bridled at this condescension. "Your bank is so big and powerful, Mr. Stillman, that when the next panic comes, you will wish your responsibilities were smaller." Suddenly defensive, Stillman snapped that American banking was more advanced than Europe's and didn't need to copy foreign models.[10] The exchange convinced Paul how premature it was to publicize his ideas, and he buried his essay in the drawer for four years. It is astonishing to think that Paul's seminal thoughts on the Federal Reserve System were jotted down within months of his arrival in America. Four years later, the essay so gleefully mocked by Stillman would be dusted off and published to famous effect.

—

Despite their strong family resemblance—both had bald pates, brown eyes, and thick, bristling mustaches—Paul and Felix were always defined in contrast to each other. Paul was known as "the sad Mr. Warburg" and Felix as "the happy Mr. Warburg."[11] The stereotype didn't credit Paul's wit or the gravity of Felix's philanthropy, yet it possessed a rough, serviceable truth. Paul could never be as close to Felix as he was to Max. He had internalized the reserve of Hamburg merchants, while Felix didn't hesitate to flaunt his wealth. As Paul's son noted, "He was often very much annoyed at his brother, Felix, who was quite gaily ostentatious in the way he lived and gave to various charities."[12] Nina and Paul, if charitable, gave anonymously and usually to individuals rather than organizations. Nevertheless, by any normal measure, Panina's living standard was inconceivably grand. When they traveled to Kösterberg, they took a valet-butler, a lady's maid, a nurse or governess, a cook, and one or two extra maids. Their town house at 3 East 82nd Street had electric elevators and Paul bought an electric hansom cab, with a driver posted above the passengers. Some of Paul's displeasure with Felix's consumption seems merited, but some probably reflects a repressed, self-conscious man's discomfort with a freer spirit.

The brothers differed in their attitude toward religion. Paul and Nina cast off religious orthodoxy and went to synagogue only on Rosh Hashanah and Yom Kippur. Like Aby, Paul refrained from any Jewish community involvement, incurring Moritz's displeasure. As Paul's son said, in his parents' household "a professional Jew . . . was another category for which we had no use."[13] It was a telling remark, since Felix and Frieda became emblems of institutional Jewish charity. Nina had been infused with some embarrassment about being Jewish. As Betty Loeb told her children, "When traveling on a train for short distances, never hurry for the exit when it reaches your stop. People will think you are a pushy Jew."[14]

Paul's children, Jimmy and Bettina, received scant religious instruction. Jimmy only learned he was Jewish in seventh grade and the shock never quite faded. "Religion was an empty space in my family background," he said.[15] Though "confirmed" (a word that replaced "bar mitzvah" in the Warburg lexicon) by Rabbi Judah Magnes, he found the instruction barren.[16] If Jimmy and Bettina ended up ambivalent, even hostile, toward their religious background, some of the blame can be traced to the dogmatic zeal of Jacob Schiff, who always lectured the Loebs that they weren't observant enough. He saturated his religion with a self-righteous, intolerant spirit. As Jimmy remembered, "I felt warmly about Grandfather Warburg's Friday evenings and loved the sound of Hebrew. On the other hand, I was repelled by the proselytizing religiosity of my New York uncle, Jacob Schiff."[17]

Felix and Frieda observed religious form less from true conviction than from respect for Jacob Schiff. Every Friday evening, they would pray together, light Sabbath candles, and hold hands in a family circle. Schiff led the prayers. The absence from the occasion of any sentient Schiff, Loeb, or Warburg in the greater metropolitan area constituted a serious breach of etiquette. Despite his later position in Jewish affairs, Felix was never observant and described his synagogue attendance as an "act de presence."[18] His grandchildren would note his peevish humor when he had to fast on Yom Kippur.

Schiff's strident moralism provoked a rebellion among Felix's children, who recited after each meal a prayer of grace that grandpa had written. No child was too young to be spared Schiff's stern precepts. Felix's youngest son, Edward, took the religious ceremonies more seriously than his impious older brothers. A nurse once suggested to him that he pluck a rose and present it to his grandfather. When the kind-hearted boy complied, Schiff sharply upbraided him. "Do you know what you have done?" Schiff asked. Little Edward stood baffled. "I know you did not mean it," said Schiff, "but just the same you killed something on the Sabbath, and so that you will remember this, I think it would be a good idea if you did not come down to meals with the grown-ups for the next two days."[19] This made Judaism seem a dreadful affair, a punishment dreamed up by an irrational sadist, and not a deep, joyful, affirmative experience.

For the first thirteen years of marriage, Friedaflix lived in a five-story town house at 18 East 72nd Street with an elevator and a squash court on the top floor. There the couple had five children: a girl, Carola, then four boys, Frederick, Gerald, Paul Felix, and Edward. These children grew up in a home bright with Father's banter, but somewhat counterbalanced by Mother's quite strict and definite ways. Suitably enough, Felix meant "happy" in Latin and he was nicknamed "Fizzie" from the sparkling Vichy Celestin soda water he loved and that seemed to sum up his effervescence. His quick smile lit his face like a light bulb. His friends referred to bright, cloudless days as "Felix weather."[20] A dandy, showman, and ladies' man, he approached life with a blithe, insouciant air quite unlike that of his wife.

Where Paul fretted about the corruption of wealth, Felix took a cheerfully hedonistic pleasure in costly objects. He loved cashmere coats, silk underwear—anything that caressed the senses. Like Max, he enjoyed dressing for dinner each evening. He wore beautifully tailored suits, a white carnation stuck in his buttonhole, and always smelled pleasantly of Pinaud's hair tonic or some other refreshing fragrance. Even his bald head shone as if polished daily. An avid sportsman, he loved to sail, swim, ride, dance, and play squash and tennis. A man of perpetual motion, he owned one of the first cars—a French De Dion Bouton—and by stamping his cane on the floor stimulated his chauffeur to accelerate to hair-raising speeds. Later, he owned a 102-foot schooner, the *Carol*, that featured polished brass, a crew of fifteen, and luncheons of lobster and squab. He never actually touched the wheel, but was always nattily attired in a yachting cap, blue blazer, and white flannels.

Felix had a consuming devotion to music. Sometimes he attended three concerts in an evening, mapping his itinerary so that he could catch a favorite piece on each program. The tone-deaf Frieda trailed along reluctantly or stayed at home; it is revealing that Felix's numerous lady friends were usually aspiring young opera singers. As a Kuhn, Loeb partner, Felix had special entree to New York's music world. In 1903, Jacob Schiff declined a Metropolitan Opera directorship in favor of partner Otto Kahn, who became the opera's chairman and effective owner four years later. After debuting at the Met, Enrico Caruso formed a close friendship with "Il Otto Kahn," as he called him.[21] In 1908, Kahn brought over La Scala's chief conductor, Arturo Toscanini. With Otto Kahn on hand, divas and opera scores no less than balance sheets and stock prospectuses floated in a mad swirl around Kuhn, Loeb, even if Schiff flinched when Kahn launched into extemporaneous arias. After he became involved with the Metropolitan Opera, Felix always sat behind the conductor, who would turn and bow to him before raising his baton. Once, Felix's secretary asked whether he wouldn't prefer a seat a few rows back. "Oh, no," he said, quite shocked. "I like to sit there and follow the score as the orchestra plays."[22]

In a family known for privacy and discretion, Felix was the only Warburg to build a mansion. In the panic year of 1907, he bought a lot on the north corner of 92nd Street and Fifth Avenue with a generous one hundred feet of frontage facing the Central Park Reservoir. This choice location was sandwiched between Andrew Carnegie's mansion a block south and brewer Jacob Ruppert's mansion a block north. An admirer of the Fletcher mansion at 79th Street and Fifth Avenue, Felix enlisted its architect, Charles P. H. Gilbert, to construct a mansion in French Gothic style. Made of Indiana limestone, with steep slate mansard roofs and ogee-arched windows with crocketed gables, this wonderfully gaudy edifice fit into the row of extravagant mansions that lined Fifth Avenue in the aftermath of the Gilded Age. But it was odd for a Jewish banker to choose a style so closely associated in the popular imagination with church architecture.

Jacob Schiff, who lived in a Beaux-Arts mansion a few blocks downtown at 932 Fifth Avenue, was aghast at the preposterous scale and Gothic style of the proposed house. "That's terribly conspicuous," he told Frieda, "and it will add to the social anti-Semitism in New York if a young couple build such an ornate house right on *Fifth Avenue*."[23] Schiff so abhorred the projected structure that, with a pained look, he averted his eyes as he passed the construction site each Sunday morning en route to the Montefiore Hospital, his pet charity. Unnerved by Father's displeasure, Frieda thought to herself, "Perhaps it's the fact that it's Gothic that upsets him so. Perhaps he'd like it better if we changed it to a Renaissance style."[24] She discussed such a radical change with Gilbert, but construction was already too far advanced, and the residential cathedral was carried through to completion.

Felix, a genial character, usually cajoled and humored his father-in-law into acquiescence. But with the Fifth Avenue house, Schiff drew a line in the sand. Felix told Frieda, "I just don't think I can go on working with your father under circumstances like these."[25] When Felix offered his resignation, Schiff shot back, "If you leave this company, I'll see to it that you never work anywhere in America again."[26] After Friedaflix occupied the building in October 1908, Schiff stopped by for a frosty one-hour visit in which he pointedly ignored the surroundings. The next day, he made peace, however, sending a housewarming present of $25,000. Ironically, the building that Schiff thought would stand as disgraceful testimony of Jewish ostentation would later house the Jewish Museum.

Outwardly, 1109 Fifth Avenue seemed about as playful as a basilica. Solemn, handsome, and airless, it was smothered beneath solid damask curtains, thick carpets, tapestries, giant chandeliers, massive woodwork, heavily upholstered furniture, and painted beam ceilings. An enormous oak staircase rose up five flights—the boys spat from the top floor into a spittoon at the base that never had a chance to dry, said Edward—and an elevator was also available. According to the 1910 census, the house deployed a small army of thirteen servants, ranging from a nurse to an engineer. After stepping through a lace-screened glass door, visitors were met by a squadron of liveried footmen. The mansion exhibited Felix's appreciation of precious objects, but none of his prankish high spirits or offhand manner.

The house came equipped with every comfort. Besides a dining room, the second floor featured a concert grand piano and an electric pipe organ, with a player attachment and numerous classical music and opera rolls. Felix loved to pump and sing along in full-throated style. Another second-floor room, bathed in deep red velvet, displayed Italian art gathered on trips to Rome. With its saints, Madonnas, and other Christian figures, this Red Room was often used for formal entertaining. An adjoining conservatory featured a

Madonna and Child attributed to Botticelli. Felix had few distinguished paintings, but he had two rooms full of superb etchings by Rembrandt, Dürer, and Cranach, installed between glass on special rotating pedestals so that both front and back could be viewed. The second-floor dining room, hung with tapestries, accommodated sixty for dinner. On the third floor, Frieda entertained friends for tea and Felix had an office overlooking Central Park. The fourth floor had the children's rooms and toy trains, while the fifth floor had a squash court where Felix volleyed against a pro each morning. The servants lived on the sixth floor.

This magnificent but overwhelming setting never quite gibed with the five bright, smart-alecky, irreverent children who traded barbs and quips at the table like fast-talking comedians in a madcap Marx Brothers movie. As Edward noted, "Father used to say had he had any idea what kind of family he was going to have he never would have built so formal a house."[27] More in the outrageous Warburg than the straitlaced Schiff mold, the children had a sense of humor that bespoke tacit rebellion against their German-Jewish heritage. Felix joined in. "Children should be obscene but not absurd," he said, and his crazy wit and puns set the tone.[28] Hesitant to discipline the children, he conceived of his fatherly role as something akin to a flamboyant social director on a fancy cruise ship. After breakfast, Felix was escorted down Fifth Avenue by his sons and they would all tip their hats, first left, then right, in perfect unison, as they walked.

As a young woman, Frieda had developed her father's partial deafness, which excluded her from the quick repartee. Especially in the early years, she took life seriously and tried futilely to instill a sense of economy in the children. She could be as carping with them as Felix was cavalier. She feared that the children would displease her father and this made her tense. To counter Felix's laissez-faire attitude, she became, by default, the family disciplinarian. "You always think your children are perfect," she would say.[29] Felix would retort, "Why is it that my children are so wonderful and yours seem to be so full of troubles?"[30] At the table, Felix and the children would clown *sotto voce* so Frieda couldn't hear the sharp-edged witticisms whizzing by. Sometimes the humor was at her expense and she ran crying from the room.

Trying to manage and regulate her children's lives, she came across as a taskmaster. As daughter Carola said, "she was too critical—her standards were very pedantic—she got much more loosened up later."[31] An anxious hostess, she insisted that the children appear formally before visitors and always selected their clothing. "Things were always laid out for us and we never questioned," said Edward.[32] The same held true for food. Sometimes, the children seemed like marionettes on a short string and even in the country the groom instructed them which way to ride. Frieda paid an emotional price for this strictness. The children warmed more to Felix and to affectionate relatives, such as Nina, than they did to her.

After their fourth child was born in 1904, Felix decided that his brood needed a house for summers and weekends. Until then, Friedaflix spent summers with the Schiffs at their fifty-acre house, "The Terraces," a stone house with opulent gardens on Rumson Road near Sea Bright, New Jersey. The Jersey shore was receptive to Jewish families—to a point. Though Schiff was a founder of the adjoining Rumson Country Club, he couldn't obtain membership for other family members. The same thing happened to Felix at the Sea Bright Tennis Club even after he donated tennis courts. Both Schiff and Felix resigned in pique and as a matter of principle from the two clubs.

The two commuted to Wall Street by ferry. Schiff reserved his own private cabin, something like an opera box, with its own outer porch for views and sea breezes. Starting in 1903, the Schiffs and Warburgs began to travel to Bar Harbor each August—every other August Frieda and Felix went to Kösterberg—when Maine was still alien territory for Jews. Since Jacob and Felix were railroad directors, their families traveled from Grand Central Station by private railroad car, a moveable feast of servants, horses, children, and grandchildren. The cars were sumptuous, with a kitchen and dining area on one side. The families slept in the upper and lower berths of brass beds, shielded from one another by curtains, and the children loved to watch the New England countryside flickering by the window.

This annual routine changed in 1904 when Felix bought thirty acres of property in White Plains, adjacent to the Century Country Club—an "Our Crowd" bastion—where his family spent many Sundays. The parcel didn't look promising to less sanguine eyes. When Nina's brother, Morris, saw this undeveloped property, he derided it as "Moneysunk."[33] But Felix kept buying additional land to square off the property, as he told Frieda. The original purchase would expand into a magnificent five-hundred-acre estate known as Woodlands. Felix liked to do things with panache, and this weekend hideaway was no modest country retreat. One visitor would describe it as "a tract of land as large as a duchy" in which the "Warburgs held state in considerable grandeur."[34]

This hilly, wooded part of Westchester then seemed remote from Manhattan, and the weekend trips were high adventure. The Warburgs drove up in a huge, custom-made Fiat that seated eleven and was equipped with rooftop luggage racks. In winter, they sat bundled up in furs and in summer donned sporty dusters. When they reached the main Woodlands gate, they still had another *mile and a half* to go before they pulled up before the main house. This gigantic Tudor affair had a central fieldstone tower with French Gothic windows reminiscent of 1109. Woodlands was rich, but also relaxed and rustic. When Frieda gave birth to Edward there, she simply sent a horse and buggy to fetch a doctor at White Plains Hospital.

So that Felix could have white carnations, he constructed an unusual greenhouse. It enclosed a tiled swimming pool, with exercise rings and trapezes dangling above the water. When Frieda lamented the lack of fresh milk for the children, Felix bought a prize herd of Guernsey cattle and named every cow after a different female family member. To teach the children American history, he laid out presidential benches along five miles of bridle path, each rough-hewn bench displaying the names and dates of another president. Friedaflix had a coach with four thoroughbred black show horses that won medals at Madison Square Garden. This particular hobby won Felix the nickname of the Black Prince. Woodlands also had tandem carriages, pair carriages, a pony for each child, and a polo field. Tennis became the family sport, and international stars from Forest Hills or the annual Rye Tennis Tournament often were seen on the grassy courts. All these lavish arrangements upset Jacob Schiff, who expressed his dismay by saying curtly, "I can't wait to have the children breathe the good sea air at Rumson Road."[35]

In many ways, Felix tried to convert Woodlands into an ersatz Kösterberg. He gave thirty acres to Panina, who built a Swiss chalet–style house there in 1912 that paid homage to Germany, and they named it "Fontenay" after the Hamburg street where they had lived. It featured a pretty outdoor study for Paul and rustic peasant furniture. When Nina grew wistful about the Elbe view from Kösterberg, Felix knocked down a whole stand of trees to open up a view of a golf pond at the neighboring Scarsdale Country Club. Because of Nina's handicap, Felix built a bridge over a gully on the property so that she could negotiate it in her wheelchair. Eventually Fontenay grew to eighty-four acres.

The Panina house was a five-minute stroll from the Friedaflix house, and every afternoon the two brothers played golf on their private Woodlands holes. Everybody was struck by the stark contrast of their homes. The Panina house was dark, quiet, cerebral, a cloistered place of contemplation; an ancient German butler answered the door. For all her warmth and civility, Nina shared some of Paul's depression and melancholy. The Friedaflix house, on the other hand, was brightly lit and swarmed with sprightly, laughing people. This contrast made a profound impression on Panina's children, James and Bettina, who yearned for the freedom next door. Felix dashed about like an overly enthusiastic teenager on the first day of summer camp. As he once wrote to his eldest son, Freddy, "I played *nine* holes of golf, swam, had a horseback ride with the children and rode the four—all before twelve o'clock. . . ."[36] For Felix, the transition to America seemed so easy and natural, while Paul would always retain something of a European formality and stiffness.

Felix belied the image of the philanthropist as a rich, complacent dilettante throwing sops at the poor. He was extraordinarily generous despite a constant fear that people wanted to con him—suspicion he expressed by a running gag. From his boyhood, Felix remembered that as the kaiser's car flashed by, its horn would sound a musical four-note chime. The kaiser's subjects supplied lyrics to this tune: "*Mit unserem Geld*"—"with our money"—they would sing. Sometimes, when approached for a donation, Felix hummed this ditty as his family laughed.[37]

If he was the most generous Warburg, Felix, as Schiff's son-in-law, was also the richest. Philanthropy saved him from being just a rich idler, giving him an identity he couldn't have found in business. After thirty years as a Kuhn, Loeb partner, Felix was still mystified by basic financial mechanisms. He once gave Edward some American Express checks he had already countersigned, unaware that his son then couldn't cash them. Later, he secured for Kuhn, Loeb a large securities issue from Kodak; it was his sole business coup.

Felix dedicated himself to philanthropy with a deep, sustained commitment. Inverting the natural order of things, he was a dilettante at work, but pursued his hobbies in earnest. At night, seated at a desk overlooking the Central Park Reservoir, one fist pressed to his forehead, he pored over charity reports. He ended up a philanthropic colossus, a one-man social welfare agency, to the point that even Schiff chided him, saying, "Felix, one can be over-generous, even in charity."[38]

On his desk, Felix kept a favorite quote, variously attributed to William Penn and Étienne de Grellet, that governed his good deeds. "I shall pass through this world but once. Any good thing therefore that I can do, any kindness I can show to any human being, let me do it now; let me not defer it nor neglect it, for I shall not pass this way again."[39] Where Schiff brought moralistic fervor to his vast charitable works, Felix did good deeds with a more spontaneous gaiety. If he couldn't do it with a smile, he said, he simply wouldn't do it. He never put on airs or assumed a tone of self-importance. Once asked why he donated so much, he replied, "I suppose that it is because of my confounded good nature."[40]

By the Civil War, America had only 150,000 Jews, many of them from Germany. But starting in 1881 with the Russian pogroms, an enormous tide of 600,000 Jews from Eastern Europe poured into Manhattan's Lower East Side by the century's end. Though they had little in common with these poor *Ostjuden*, Schiff and other German-Jewish leaders lobbied to keep the doors open to these impoverished masses. Already Americanized, the German-Jewish bankers stood atop the social heap while their eastern brethren came in steerage, panting and sweating at the bottom. Many German Jews were embarrassed by these tenement inmates, who seemed like crude, unpleasant reminders of their own past. Where the established uptown Jews tended to be highly conservative, the Lower East Side teemed with new ideas and social protest. Not only did the streets abound in pushcarts and peddlers, but in trade union organizers, muckraking pamphleteers, revolutionary orators, and millenial prophets.

The Russian and Polish Jews often found the German Jews arrogant, cold, and condescending. Defiantly proud, these poor Jews resented their assimilated brethren who tried to hide or transcend their Judaism and they often suspected their motives. In 1909, when Jacob Schiff and other leaders tried to introduce a *kehilla* or Jewish community structure under a dynamic Reform rabbi named Judah Magnes, the radical elements on the Lower East Side spied an insidious plot to pacify and subjugate them.

The German Jews were natural leaders in communal affairs, because they had the money to finance welfare schemes and the political alliances to effect them. There were no mass fund-raising organizations to elect democratic leaders, no pool of savings to tap. In those days, the people who provided the money dictated its use, plain and simple. No less than in Germany, the direction of Jewish affairs fell to a stratum of wealthy bankers who mingled in business and politics with the gentile establishment.

As a vocal critic of anti-Semitism, Jacob Schiff had a paternalistic but authentic regard for these newcomers. He subsidized a man named Adolph Benjamin who combatted the work of Christian missionaries in the slums. At the same time, he and other German Jews felt their own status in America threatened by any untoward publicity about the Jewish poor. In 1908, New York's police chief, Theodore Bingham, published an article entitled "Foreign Criminals in New York" which contended that Jews accounted for 50 percent of criminals in the city, although they comprised only a quarter of the population.[41] A survey that year also found that three quarters of the prostitutes hauled before the New York City Magistrate's Court were Jewish. Thus from a mix of fear, concern, and undeniable embarrassment, Schiff and other leaders tried to cure the abundant social ills among the Jewish immigrants.

Felix scorned the "silly layer cake" that separated the toplofty German Jews from the Russian shtetl Jews down below. "And the German Jews thought they had all the wisdom," he would say laughingly.[42] On the Lower East Side, he met the same desperate immigrants he had seen as a boy slumped over bundles at Hamburg's port, waiting to embark for America. Already in the 1890s, Felix toured the tenements and "saw parents at their machines, working until midnight so that their children might have the advantage of an easier life and education."[43] This glimpse into a very different Jewish reality became the impetus for his first charitable efforts. Frieda would be very much his companion in charitable work. Already in her early twenties, she had chaired the Building Committee of the YWHA and raised the money for a new building on Fifth Avenue and 110th Street.

Even before Felix moved to New York, Jacob Schiff and Betty Loeb had sponsored a young nurse named Lillian D. Wald, who came from a well-heeled, German-Jewish family in Rochester. She moved into the East Side slums, tending the poor for a pittance, and the rent for her Jefferson Street apartment was paid for by the Schiffs and Loebs. Thus began the Henry Street Settlement in 1893. Armed with more money from the Schiffs and Loebs, Wald merged three settlement operations into the Educational Alliance, which offered educational and recreational services for the poor; Felix later became a board member and it was his first major institutional affiliation. Schiff donated the money anonymously, only stipulating that Wald furnish him with a detailed monthly report. The left-wing Yiddish press attacked the Educational Alliance as a plot by uptown Jews to turn the slum dwellers into bourgeois Americans.

Wald also pioneered in sending nurses to the bedsides of the poor, a successful experiment that led to the Visiting Nurse Service of New York. For Felix and Frieda, Lillian Wald would be more than a friend and consultant—she was a direct human link with the lower end of the social ladder. She brought slum children to Woodlands for picnics on the polo field—Frieda would send down picnic lunches in a wheelbarrow—in what must have been sometimes awkward but moving confrontations of poor and rich Jews.

In the slums, Felix noted the squalor and absence of open-air playgrounds. On a block near Seward Park where a tenement had been razed, he and Lillian Wald cleared the ground, borrowed gym equipment from the Educational Alliance, pounded in a flagpole, and opened the East Side's first playground. For a generation of beleaguered Jewish immigrants, jammed into filthy, poorly ventilated tenements, Felix Warburg's name became mythical and synonymous with good deeds. He was the benevolent mystery man, operating unseen behind a maze of organizations. In a typical testimonial, comedian Eddie Cantor said, "As a young boy I was a recipient of Mr. Warburg's charity. He made it possible for me to enjoy a summer in the country, away from the filth and sidewalks of New York. What I know of helping my fellow men I have learned from this great Jewish leader. . . ."[44]

Through the Educational Alliance, Felix met another social activist, Julia Richman, who spurred his interest in educational reform. Felix was a very visceral man, and once again simple images of distress guided him. He was horrified by a visit to a dark, dingy school for truants on 19th Street where teachers meted out harsh punishment with rods and chains and made recalcitrant students sit in dunce caps—medieval forms of punishment. In 1902, Mayor Seth Low appointed Felix to the New York City Board of Education. Because he had been a mediocre student, he had to endure some family mirth. "Congratulations," Max telegrammed to Felix, "you will be relieved to learn that I have burned all your report cards."[45]

In his three years on the board, Felix pushed through lasting reforms. Inspired by Wald, he persuaded the board to assign nurses to public schools. He instituted special programs for mentally retarded children and eliminated the stigma against blind children by enabling those who read Braille to be placed in regular classes. Noting that young criminal offenders lacked follow-up from the courts, he recommended that social workers from the Educational Alliance check up on them periodically. This gave a fillip to the nascent probation movement and in 1907 Felix and Homer Folks were appointed to the first State Probation Commission in New York. Already, Felix's philanthropic interests were becoming so diverse as to defy easy summary.

This Jewish establishment reached its zenith during the lives of Jacob Schiff and then Felix Warburg. The same small group of German-Jewish bankers stood at the apex of a bewildering array of charities, whose names and duties might differ, but whose letterheads and sociological composition sounded suspiciously alike. As one observer said of the Schiff era, "hardly any enterprise of a Jewish philanthropic or educational nature was launched . . . without first consulting that dominant figure in the leadership of American Jewry."[46] When the commanding Schiff strode into a charity meeting, a respectful silence fell over the room; he was always first among equals.

The influence of these Jewish bankers grew in tandem with the prosperity of America. Just as Wall Street took over from London as the world's banker in the early twentieth century, so American Jews assumed responsibility from the Rothschilds and other European Jews for suffering Jews everywhere. The watershed event was probably the Kishinev pogrom of April 1903, in which the czarist government conspired. This massacre—ruled by blind mob fury— by the Romanian border near the Black Sea left forty-five Jews dead, more than five hundred injured, and two thousand families homeless. These numbers terrified a Jewish community whose senses weren't yet dulled by the unutterable horror of the Holocaust. From a selfish standpoint, American Jews feared that the massacre might stimulate an unwanted flood of destitute Russian Jewish immigrants to the United States, with an attendant backlash.

Jacob Schiff mobilized the American Jewish Community and got President Theodore Roosevelt to protest to Russia, which was Schiff's implacable foe. He unashamedly used his financial influence to thwart the czar at every turn. As he boasted to Lord Rothschild in 1904, "I pride myself that all the efforts, which at various times during the past four or five years have been made by Russia to gain the favor of the American market for its loans, I have been able to bring to naught."[47] At one point, Schiff pressed Teddy Roosevelt to conduct a Rough Rider assault, patterned after the American invasion of Cuba, against Russia.

In 1905, another set of deadly pogroms left two thousand Russian Jews dead, injured, or homeless. This led Jacob Schiff, Cyrus Adler, and others to create the American Jewish Committee a year later. It was the first group to coordinate the action of American Jews and the first American organization to support Jews worldwide. Drawn predominantly from the German-Jewish grandees, it reflected their stress upon assimilation and American patriotism instead of worldwide Zionist loyalty or anything that might smack of radicalism or "dual loyalty." Inevitably, they were accused by poor Jews of being latter-day "Court Jews," who wished to curry favor with the non-Jewish world.

Schiff and other Jewish merchant princes felt alarmed by Zionism because it claimed a universal Jewish loyalty while they were strenuously asserting their primary loyalty to America. They saw no necessary incompatibility in being both patriotic citizens and pious Jews. When Schiff and Felix financed the Jewish Theological Seminary of America to train teachers and rabbis, Schiff installed a bronze tablet in the main auditorium that contained, not a quote from Jewish scriptures, but one from Lincoln's Gettysburg Address. At a speech, he once said, "I am divided into three parts; I am an American, I am a German, and I am a Jew." Shmaryahu Levin, a Zionist, rose and asked Schiff if he divided himself horizontally or vertically and, if horizontally, which part did he leave for the Jewish people?[48]

Though not a Zionist, Schiff supported many projects in Palestine, including the Jewish Agricultural Experiment Station and the Hebrew Technical Institute in Haifa. He and Felix Warburg would regard Palestine as a spiritual home for Judaism rather than a future nation-state, but would be no less active or involved for all that. In 1906, Schiff warned in *The New York Times*, "It is quite evident that there is a serious break coming between those who wish to force the formation of a distinct Hebraic element in the United States, as distinct from those of us who desire to be American in attachment, thought and action. . . ."[49] Indeed, the break would be deep, bitter, and protracted. But it would be Felix, not Jacob Schiff, who would feel the full force of these contending factions within the world of Judaism and he would end up a tragic casualty of them.

Max Warburg proudly
holding his infant son, Eric, 1900.
(Warburg family, Hamburg)

The King of Steerage

Each afternoon in the early 1900s, Max Warburg sauntered around Hamburg's smaller downtown lake beside an ugly little man, who had a balding head, mustache, bulbous nose, and pince-nez. The man's shrewd, watchful eyes peered from behind heavy pouches. Smart, sarcastic, and irascible, he was no less funny and charming than Max himself. Walking in top hats, the two men reviewed politics and business as they proceeded to the stock exchange. They chatted so often by phone that they hooked up a special private line, despite the short distance between their offices.

This pint-sized figure of colossal energy was Albert Ballin, managing director of the Hamburg-American Line—always referred to by its acronym HAPAG—which he had boosted into the world's foremost shipping concern. Its lakeside palace, hard by the Warburg bank, was the hub of the shipping universe. Born in 1857 by the port into a lower-middle-class Jewish family, Ballin worked as a teenager in an emigration agency, lining up passengers for transport to America. By twenty-two, this business prodigy owned the agency and by twenty-nine he managed the HAPAG passenger department. In 1899, age forty-two, he emerged as the company's chief executive, presiding over a 175-ship armada that surpassed in size the merchant marine of any Continental power save Germany itself. This spectacular rise made Ballin one of the few Jews in the upper echelons of German shipping.

The steerage king revolutionized the business. Even before joining HAPAG, he had introduced cut-rate fares for emigrants that drove down the cost of Hamburg-to-New York travel from 120 to 80 marks. At HAPAG, he inaugurated direct weekly service from the Baltic to New York, set up freight service to the Orient, and dispatched liners to South America and Africa. He adopted the Hanseatic motto, "My field is the world."[1] Ballin made Hamburg a premier embarkation point for New World pilgrims, and probably more hopeful, petrified souls crossed the North Atlantic under his personal aegis than that of any other human being. To serve the swelling tide of passengers, he threw up enormous halls to house them, a veritable self-contained village of stores, churches, synagogues, and hospitals. This spared Hamburg contact with potentially contagious transients while passengers were shielded from venal local merchants. By undergoing medical inspections in Hamburg, travelers were also spared later trouble at Ellis Island. To keep his fleet busy when winter traffic slackened, Ballin dreamed up Mediterranean cruises. When he launched this luxury service in 1891, Kaiser Wilhelm II came aboard the cruise ship to confer his imperial blessing.

Ballin launched huge new ships, emblems of German might and global ambition, that dwarfed the Lilliputian people who lined the slipways at festive christenings. The scale of the enterprise was superhuman. Even at night, the shipyards echoed with hammers and presented gaslight vignettes of fumes arising from blacksmith fires. New machinery made possible ships of staggering capacity, permitting HAPAG to stow as many as 2,500 people at a time in steerage. The shipping concern also burgeoned into a major German employer, with over 20,000 people on its payroll by World War I. By 1910, Hamburg would be the world's second busiest port after New York.

It was Ballin who alerted Max to the opportunities open to enterprising Jewish businessmen in the Reich. Jewish financiers had a chance to serve as catalysts of the great new industrial ventures in the making. The prosperity of the late 1890s had caused religious barriers to recede, commencing the era of the so-called "German-Jewish symbiosis." During this tolerant, hopeful interlude, Ballin and Max exemplified the rapid advancement suddenly open to Jewish businessmen. Max knew Ballin was no choirboy, but a tough, cynical, wise-cracking boss and he even faulted Ballin's first biographer for omitting the man's "demonic, ruthless" side.[2] A convinced monarchist and uncompromising foe of trade unions and Social Democrats, Ballin practiced a bare-knuckled brand of management. During strikes, he imported English scabs whom he housed on boats on the Elbe, leading unions to denounce him as a "capitalist beast."[3] Max loved how Ballin fought bitterly, then forgave and forgot. Above Ballin's desk hung an English saying, "One damn thing after the other," which expressed their common joy in battle.[4] If both were suave and genial, Ballin had a more volatile temperament than Max and was certainly more prone to depression.

For twenty years, Max was the best friend and protégé of this titan of world shipping. With a Christian wife and an adopted daughter, Ballin adopted the Warburgs as his second family. While Paul lived in Hamburg, he and Ballin, who had back-to-back houses, would converse across the garden hedge. Ballin stood as godfather to Max's son and treated Max's four daughters with special avuncular warmth. Once, when Ballin moved into a new home, Max placed his children in separate rooms to recite greeting poems penned for the occasion. Max and Alice attended ship launchings, receiving privileged previews of new ships. Before launching the stupendous *Imperator*, Alice toured the ship and told Ballin she had never seen such tasteful beauty. When Max and Ballin inspected the ship, however, the new Ritz restaurant vibrated so badly that glasses on the table shook, and the demanding Ballin flew into a rage. The vibrations were only eliminated at great expense.[5]

Despite his success, Ballin worried that "the social ambitions of wealthy Jews only increased anti-Semitism," and his social world remained mostly Jewish.[6] He seldom went to synagogue and tapped Max as a conduit for contributions. Although he subsidized Jewish causes, Ballin stood aloof from the Jewish community and never tried to imitate Max's delicate balancing act. By working to reduce ticket prices to America, the two men helped to speed the tremendous exodus of European Jews to the New World before World War I.

In 1901, Kuhn, Loeb bought a few million HAPAG shares, and five years later M. M. Warburg joined the banking consortium that financed the firm. Aside from this profitable work, Ballin provided incomparable business contacts as he shepherded Max into the rarefied, exclusive, very snobbish world of German industrialists. At the time, a Jewish banker in Germany faced less discrimination with foreign bankers than with home-grown industrialists. Ballin brought Max into a sanctum hitherto closed to all but a handful of hand-picked Jews.

Under Moritz, M. M. Warburg had an ironclad policy of refusing seats on the supervisory boards or *Aufsichtsräte* of industrial companies. These board seats were pivotal positions and not the ceremonial posts of outside directors in Anglo-American business. German directors supervised managers, shared in profits, and stood liable for losses. In a momentous step, Ballin persuaded Max to drop Moritz's long-standing policy and take board seats. Perhaps more than any other single decision, this lured Max from the invisible Jewish ghetto and into new, unmapped, and unpredictable territory. And he would handle himself, not in the tentative or obsequious manner of Bismarck's banker, Gerson von Bleichröder, but with remarkable flair and self-confident poise. When he joined an elite dinner club, the Elektra, at the Chamber of Commerce, he was one of only two Jewish members.

Besides putting Max on HAPAG's board, Ballin requested that he sit on the board of Blohm & Voss, the top shipbuilder in Germany. Ballin feared that a financially troubled shipyard could weaken his company and he asked Max to advise them. Through such maneuvers, Max became a central factor in the rapidly expanding world of German shipping and trade. By the 1920s, he and his partners held seats on eighty or ninety company boards, closely integrating them into Germany's industrial elite on the eve of the Nazi takeover.

By the turn of the century, German Jews felt growing confidence about their place in society. When they formed the *Hilfsverein der Deutschen Juden* or the Aid Society of German Jews in 1901—Moritz was among its founders—its stated mission, again, was to alleviate Jewish suffering *abroad*. The Russian pogroms prompted Max's maiden involvement in Jewish charity as he assisted emigration to America. Before World War I, ninety thousand Russian Jews arrived in Germany, and native Jews feared this influx would upset their own tenuous place. German Jews tended to see the *Ostjuden* as an uncouth, beggarly rabble and wanted to push them further west. German Jews were always a strange compound of almost arrogant confidence and the most frightful insecurity.

It was probably through his association with Ballin that Max first became a target for anti-Semitic attacks. For instance, one 1912 cartoon in a Berlin anti-Semitic newspaper showed Ballin and a Jewish banker—evidently Max—in a conspiratorial chat. In his trademark pince-nez, Ballin sniggers greedily, "The soul of the German worker is our toy. It has no secrets from us. But our Jewish ideas are our secret that we can't allow any *goy* to get a glimpse into."[7]

Later, Max would note that when he began mingling with non-Jewish society in the early 1900s, he wasn't directly touched by anti-Semitism. Nevertheless, in hindsight, he saw that "the existence of this anti-Semitic current revealed itself in that one felt one's special position."[8] When a Zionist Congress met in Hamburg in 1909, Max boycotted it, believing it would abet anti-Semites who claimed that Jews were loyal to "international Jewry." Whenever Zionism reared its head, Max made ritual professions of his German patriotism—a reflex that became habitual with many fellow Jews. This constant reiteration of loyalty by the Jewish community would only embolden their tormentors, for it seemed to testify to underlying insecurity as well as genuine love of country.

Max and Ballin inevitably drew close to a kaiser enamored of the sea and intent upon expanding German naval power. As a true Hamburger, Max adored sailing and won many Elbe regattas in his boat, the *Alice*. His bank even financed whaling expeditions. At their initial encounter in 1891, the kaiser told Ballin, "Just bring our countrymen to sea and it will bear rich fruits both for the nation and your company."[9] Amid bunting and warships, the kaiser opened the Kiel Canal in June 1895, linking the Baltic and North seas and stimulating a romance with things maritime. In Wilhelm's mind, a first-rate merchant marine was inseparable from a strong navy, and he passed along equipment designs to HAPAG. He provided benevolent protection for the firm and was even rumored to be a large stockholder. As with any shipping firm, HAPAG vessels could be pressed into wartime service, and German police sometimes prodded emigrants to take German rather than British ships. In 1898, Ballin openly supported the naval buildup undertaken by Rear Admiral Alfred (later von) Tirpitz. "In the brutal struggle of nations for light and air, strength alone counts . . ." said Ballin.[10] Because the enemy chosen to justify this buildup was England, the naval race always placed the anglophile pair, Ballin and Max, in a tense, contradictory situation.

When the kaiser started a Regatta Week in Kiel each June, it became the sacred duty of German businessmen to sail with brawny vigor. By 1899, Ballin began to host the kaiser at an annual HAPAG dinner before the festivities. This royal patronage for the races was designed to spur popular support for a huge and expensive fleet. For Hamburg businessmen, who enjoyed privileged contact with the kaiser at these outings, the summer tradition was a tremendous boon.

Social direction of the event fell to Ballin, who orchestrated it like an impresario. He would float an enormous HAPAG liner into the Kiel Fjord to put up the kaiser's friends and retinue. HAPAG sometimes seemed an official arm of the Empire. A Ballin motto ran, "Everything for HAPAG, Ballin, Germany, Kaiser, Hamburg."[11] HAPAG ships had staterooms reserved for the kaiser, who sometimes chartered HAPAG liners for cruises. When Ballin negotiated an agreement with J. P. Morgan for a North Atlantic cartel, Wilhelm minutely reviewed the contract with Ballin.

Despite the fact that late Imperial Germany was the heyday of German-Jewish relations, the kaiser had uneasy social intercourse with the Jews. After 1905, he breakfasted every June at Ballin's Hamburg house, jokingly called Little Potsdam. Yet Kaiserin Augusta Victoria, who shunned Jews, didn't join her husband. For malicious Prussian aristocrats, men such as Ballin and Max Warburg only strengthened their impression that the Jews were acquiring far too much power.

Tragically, Max and other Jews drew close to the monarchy of the eve of its dissolution. Associating the kaiser with peace and prosperity, they grew nationalistic in their thinking. Max wasn't blind to the kaiser's quick resort to force or bluster to avenge an easily injured sense of honor. In July 1900, he composed a wistful, melancholy letter to his three-month-old son, Eric, lamenting how the world had become "a playground for self-deception and lies; the Kaiser is sending his troops to China, where his missionaries are supposed to proclaim the religion of love, and is swearing to avenge the assassination of his envoy in Peking."[12] At least in retrospect, Max accused Wilhelm of "Theatrical superficiality, impatience, an over-estimation of his own power in spite of the best intentions . . ."[13] He saw him as a weak, rash, impressionable blowhard who loved the sound of his own voice.

In 1903, only a decade after the green young banker had piloted the firm through the cholera epidemic, Max, age thirty-six, first met the kaiser. Brash and tactless, he nearly bungled the opportunity. Chancellor von Bülow thought the kaiser needed a lecture on financial reform and had Ballin bring Max to dine with the kaiser in Cuxhaven. When Ballin said he would have only ten minutes to lecture, Max refused to speak, saying the time was insufficient. His stubbornness bespoke extreme vanity and confidence, and he only submitted when Ballin got the allotted time expanded to thirty-two minutes.

Max rehearsed a twenty-five-minute speech and budgeted seven minutes for questions. The kaiser was a spoiled, peevish, and impetuous man who at once foiled Max's plans by blurting out: "The Russians will soon go bust."[14] Not yet a smooth courtier, Max retorted, "No, Your Majesty, the Russians aren't going bust."[15] He noted that Russia had recently taken a loan to retire an earlier one, not to enlarge its debt. Accustomed to sycophantic acquiescence, the kaiser fumed. "The Russians are too going bust," he thundered.[16] With a menacing lift of his eyebrows, the kaiser then spun about and walked out. "Thus my audience, which was supposed to last 32 minutes, ended after three minutes," Max said.[17]

It was revealing that Max, far from groveling, tried to impress the kaiser with his independent ways. When he got another chance to redeem himself, he nearly fumbled it again. During Kiel Week the next year, the kaiser proposed a toast to Max, saying he was ready for his long-postponed lecture on financial reform. In a surprisingly conciliatory gesture, Wilhelm confessed, "Incidentally, the Russians aren't going bankrupt." Instead of accepting this graciously, Max replied, "I already told you that then." The kaiser pounded his fist. "Must you always be right?"[18] Max apologized, then gave a successful talk on financial reform. Henceforth, Max met the kaiser every June.

This access exposed Max and Ballin to double jeopardy, for it attracted the wrath of anti-Semites and the scorn of Jews who feared assimilation. Chaim Weizmann would refer bitingly to "the usual type of *Kaiser-Juden* [Kaiser

Jews], like Albert Ballin or Max Warburg, more German than the Germans, obsequious, superpatriotic, eagerly anticipating the wishes and plans of the masters of Germany."[19]

To some extent, the *Kaiser-Juden* exaggerated their own influence at court. While Ballin and Max met the kaiser for Kiel Week, they were excluded from his inner social circle. Max's dealings with the kaiser can be too easily summarized in several anecdotes to suggest deep or lasting influence. Though Wilhelm consulted Ballin more than any other Jew, they only met six times a year—a notable advance for Jews, but hardly full acceptance. Max's tie to the kaiser never approached Bleichröder's labyrinthine relationship with Bismarck. Whenever Max thought he had finally persuaded the kaiser of a position, the next visitor would at once persuade him of the exact opposite.[20]

The kaiser's ambivalence toward Jews was typical of his compatriots. As a young man, he criticized Bismarck's relationship with Bleichröder, heaping invective upon Jewish journalists and politicians. Yet he later maintained relations with Jewish bankers and industrialists in the face of hostile whispers. He did this by redefining Court Jews as non-Jewish. As a Prussian official recalled, "Once midway in a diatribe by His Majesty against the Jews, Schmidt dared to remind him of his Semitic friends, Ballin and Franz Mendelssohn, whereupon William declared that he did not consider them to be Jews at all. And after his abdication, the kaiser even alleged that he had been unaware that Ballin had in fact been a Jew."[21] Ballin was consistently vetoed for cabinet positions and when offered the job of railway minister, he declined, telling Wilhelm that His Majesty seemed to forget he was a Jew.[22] Later, the kaiser said that in 1909 he would have named Ballin Bülow's successor as chancellor had it not been for Ballin's religion.[23]

Even this limited access of Jews to the kaiser provoked grumbling among anti-Semitic military officers and Prussian landholders. As old money, they resisted and feared the inroads of new money, rejecting liberated Jews as social upstarts. This anxious snobbery was paralleled by political feuds. Junker landlords wanted to prop up farm prices through import duties, while shipping companies and Jewish bankers in foreign trade strongly opposed protectionism.

Max loved to retail political gossip, hobnob with power brokers, and be privy to the mighty. Yet he was always a frustrated politician. Starting in 1903, he succeeded Paul in the Hamburg *Bürgerschaft*. At the time, local officials still resembled Rembrandt figures, wearing broad white ruffs and black robes with buckle shoes on official occasions. Max was a liberal member of a conservative party and his political positions were often similarly ambiguous. He wanted the *Bürgerschaft* to be elected, half by universal suffrage, half on the basis of professions—more meritocratic than the method in use, but still elitist. (During the 1906 suffrage debate, Aby ghosted Max's speech on the subject.) In national politics, Max encountered many more religious obstacles than in Hamburg. As a result, he operated more in the dim wings and unseen corridors of official Berlin, a style that would be seized upon and exploited by anti-Semites who didn't see that this low-profile approach was meant, ironically, to avert anti-Semitism.

Max so far conquered Moritz's aversion for political activity that by World War I, M. M. Warburg & Co. qualified as Germany's leading private bank in floating international loans. His partner Aby S. and the Alsterufer Warburgs feared this higher political profile would spark an anti-Semitic reaction. The more actively M. M. Warburg became engaged in German colonial adventures, the more its lending became subordinated to German foreign policy. As Max explained, "No one is so much dependent on his own government, as the so-called international banker. For no banker will conclude a loan transaction of any significance until he has been in touch with his own Foreign Office."[24]

The byzantine financial intrigues of the early 1900s bound Jewish bankers tightly to the state. The diatribes against Jewish bankers actually stood reality on its head, for they didn't exploit Germany so much as serve its imperial escapades to a fault. This very intimacy with the government would make it hard for them to react later on when persecution and terror came from the state itself.

The Kuhn, Loeb connection also implicated M. M. Warburg in more political work. Outraged by the pogroms against Russian Jews, Schiff made it a point of honor to finance Japan in its 1904–05 war against Russia and even paid for distribution of anti-czarist propaganda to Russian prisoners. In spring 1904, he shocked Japan's financial commissioner, Baron Korekiyo Takahashi, by volunteering to underwrite half the ten-million-pound loan sought by the Imperial Japanese Government in London and New York. This first of five major Kuhn, Loeb loans to Japan was approved by King Edward VII at a luncheon with Schiff and Sir Ernest Cassel.

When Japan was ready for a third loan in 1905, Schiff thought New York was saturated with Japanese bonds and asked Max to open a German market. To ensure that such a step conformed to German policy, Max remembered, "I did what every upstanding banker has to do in such cases, I went to the Foreign Ministry in Berlin."[25] The Krupp firm had warned the Foreign Office that Germany would lose munitions contracts if the third Japanese loan were placed entirely in New York and London. So Under-Secretary of State Arthur Zimmermann endorsed the move and authorized Max to negotiate with Japan. Before proceeding with his second Japanese loan, Max met the kaiser aboard his yacht to get his official imprimatur. This second issue was ten times oversubscribed, strengthening Japan's hand at the Portsmouth peace conference. That Max suddenly managed a major strategic transaction was a stunning achievement for a firm that just a few years earlier had been a provincial power.

Max owed this breakthrough to his brothers' presence at Kuhn, Loeb, but he had ably exploited the opportunity. He negotiated the first loan in London with Korekiyo Takahashi, later Japanese finance minister and prime minister. Takahashi never forgot the favor, later telling Max, if "I have distinguished myself in any way in my life, it is, to my great appreciation, due to your goodwill and friendship which you were kind enough to extend to me in old times."[26] After the war with Russia, Takahashi visited Hamburg, and in 1906 Schiff visited Japan. Schiff had a rare private lunch with the mikado at the Imperial Palace, where he was decorated with the Order of the Rising Sun. At one dinner, he sat beside Takahashi's teenage daughter, Wakiko, and casually invited her to New York, but Takahashi took the invitation quite literally. To Schiff's astonishment, Wakiko ended up going back with him and living with the Schiffs for three years.

The Japanese link produced several hilarious encounters for Max. When a Japanese delegation came to Hamburg, they stayed at the deluxe *Vier Jahreszeiten* hotel. By coincidence, Max and family were living there while their town house was being remodeled. The Japanese wanted to drop off their cards with the mayor and asked Max to accompany them. On the appointed day, he put on a round hat and trotted down the hotel steps, only to find them standing in the lobby in top hats. He dashed back up for a top hat. When he reappeared, the Japanese, having seen Max, had all switched to round hats. Max told them to freeze while he fetched his round hat and then they all proceeded in uniform garb to the mayor.

Because the House of Mitsui, an ancient Japanese dynasty, had opened a Hamburg branch, family members periodically dropped in on the Warburgs. Once Baron Mitsui came to dinner and, as he rambled on about labor relations in Japanese, Max mischievously leaned over and whispered to Charlotte that the baron wanted to know if Max's son, Eric, would marry his daughter.[27] On another visit, Baron Mitsui and his partner, Takuma Dan, asked how the Warburgs kept peace in the family. They told Max and Carl Melchior about battles inside the Mitsui clan and asked how to stop them. Max replied that the Warburgs quarreled as much as any family. He and Melchior suggested that Mitsui divide its operations into separate banking, shipping, insurance, and export companies, each supervised by a different family member who then reported to a central firm. In this way, Max took credit for suggesting to the Japanese the *zaibatsu* or conglomerate structure that would dominate their economy. In gratitude, Mitsui sent Max a wax Japanese general in a casket.[28]

At this point in Max's career, one is struck by the influence of three older mentors: Ballin, Schiff, and Louis Fränkel, who was mentioned earlier. This last was a self-made man who started his career in a cigar factory office and ended up head of the Stockholms Handelsbank, the major rival of the Wallenbergs' Stockholms Enskilda Bank. It was through Fränkel that M. M. Warburg raised loans in Germany for Denmark, Norway, Sweden, and Finland, completing its emergence as a global financial power.

Max brilliantly capitalized on opportunities, but also saw how much depended upon chance. He felt the full turbulence of his historic epoch and it gave him a certain saving modesty under the youthful swagger. He once advised a historian of the Warburg bank, "It should be shown—and I attach great value to this—how much the development of such a firm is governed by chance. . . . The description should be pervaded by a certain feeling of humility toward these forces."[29] The twilight of the Second Empire was Max's golden time, ripe with promise and seemingly free of peril. He operated under the assumption that Jewish progress was secure and irreversible. Indeed, from the vantage point of Wilhelmine Germany, it was hard to imagine that chance would soon turn so ruthlessly capricious in meting out untold hardship to Germany and its Jews.

CHAPTER 9

Secret Furies

Even as Max advised the kaiser, his older brother, Aby, remained a pariah in the Florentine exile he had occupied since his marriage to the non-Jewish Mary Hertz. Until 1904, he and Mary spent most of the year in Italy, returning to Hamburg for summers and once so that Aby could lecture on Leonardo da Vinci at the *Kunsthalle*. In Florence, Aby delivered speeches, studied the Renaissance, and participated in the German Art History Institute. Rejecting teaching offers at universities, he remained financially dependent upon his family. All the while, he had extended his talent for unraveling the mysterious symbolism of paintings by consulting arcane works, forgotten lore. He identified the figures on one Ghirlandajo fresco by examining contemporary coins and taxpayer rolls. Able to spot clues in the most unlikely places, he prized antiquarian books dismissed by others as heaps of worthless rubbish.

The marriage that had caused inexpressible pain for Aby, Mary, and their families had yielded, in fact, little unalloyed pleasure. As Aby's nephew noted, his "marriage to a charming and talented Christian patrician caused him deep and lasting grief."[1] Aby acknowledged the saintly virtues of the sweet, cheerful, self-sacrificing Mary whom he called, "My wife, my best colleague and comrade."[2] But their differences were deep and insurmountable. Where Aby was forever shut up with his books, Mary, a freer spirit, roamed through nature and painted *en plein air*. She especially loved to stand and sketch beautiful pastel landscapes in the heather around Hamburg. Each month, she drew upcoming events on a Kösterberg pillar and also created a marionette theater, with Alice as the resident costume designer.

That Mary revered Aby was comically illustrated in March, 1903, when Max and Alice celebrated their fifth wedding anniversary. They asked guests to produce skits of how family couples might appear twenty-five years later. Aby portrayed a bald, pot-bellied Max in Hamburg, talking to Paul in New York through a futuristic instrument that transmitted their voices and images. Then Malice played the future Mary and Aby. Mocking Aby's deep pedantry, Max sat at a desk, drafting an essay on why the Medici had blue spots in their white socks; he found the answer, of course, in the Flemish influence. Meanwhile, Alice, as Mary, fluttered adoringly around him, cooing at whatever inanity he mouthed. In closing, Max said he must make his essay so dense and convoluted that nobody would ever understand it.[3]

The main problem with the marriage lay in Aby's extreme self-absorption and mental instability. Already during the Florentine years (1897–1904), he felt tormented by chronic fears. One female visitor to Florence left a vivid, harrowing picture of his early marriage. When the woman and her fiancé first arrived, Aby and Mary seemed happy and united by shared artistic purpose. Aby studied while Mary painted, drew, embroidered. Then the high-strung Aby worked himself into a state of nervous exhaustion and grew distraught. Mary read to him and took dictation and this cheered and tranquilized him for a time. Then he plunged into even deeper despondency. Finally, like some wandering, restless apparition, he approached his startled visitors and said that if he were institutionalized, he hoped they would care for Mary. Aby was then thirty-three. Already, his mind alternated between delirium and lucidity. As he once noted in his diary, "Two days out of the carnival of my life—one merry, then fever attack, inclination to day-dreaming."[4] After he snapped out of the depression, the visitors were amazed that he could step back and analyze his behavior so clinically. He told the couple he planned to check into a Swiss clinic that spring—perhaps Kreuzlingen, to which he was later confined.[5] Among other things, he worried inconsolably about the damage he was doing to his young family.

The three children—Marietta, Max Adolph, and Frede—were never baptized, but they were brought up Protestant and sometimes attended church. In one diary entry, Aby noted with dismay that Marietta was considered a Jewess in school despite her vigorous protests. While his parents were alive, Aby, in a rare religious compromise, took the children to their Passover Seder

Mary and Aby Warburg at the time
of their controversial wedding, 1897.
(Warburg Institute)

each year. To salve his conscience, Aby would substitute German nursery rhymes or doggerel lyrics for the customary Hebrew songs. Ironically, it was the Protestant Mary who was appalled at this sacrilege committed against Jewish ritual.

For other Warburg children, Aby would be a magical little man who bubbled with jokes and dreamed up fabulous names for them. He would get down on his knees and enter their fantasy world. Sometimes, he could also be an angry authority figure who shook his cane at them for throwing stones at the chestnut trees. Aby's children would mostly see this disciplinarian side, the tough, demanding father, and he set for them the same inflexible standards as for himself. If they did something well, he gave them a backhanded compliment. "In the realm of the blind, the one-eyed man is king."[6] Prone to anxiety, he would stand fretfully by the window, flying into a tantrum if the children returned late from school. This compulsive man threw a fit if they wore the wrong color stockings. Mary wasn't a meticulously neat person and Aby constantly berated her for being such a poor housekeeper.

Immersed in his studies, Aby worked from morning to night and made time for the children only in passing. "While Aby is preparing his lectures," Max said with pardonable exaggeration, "the children aren't even allowed to pull the chain!"[7] Luckily, Mary loved children and shielded them from her husband's often mad and dictatorial whims. While Aby opposed Max Adolph's desire to be an artist, Mary encouraged it. Aby's thoughts were revolutionary, but his style would remain fiercely bourgeois.

In 1904, Mary and Aby returned to Hamburg, partly so Aby could gain some critical detachment for his study of Flemish influence in Florentine art. Aby said he was a Jew by birth, a Hamburger in his heart, a Florentine in spirit.[8] If he found family tradition burdensome, he also identified with it and told historian Percy Schramm, "Between the Prussian nobility and us old Jewish families, there is an underground connection. We don't live as we want, but as we should."[9] He was as proud of Hamburg's democratic merchant culture as he was dismayed by its thoroughgoing provinciality. As he investigated relations between Florentine artists and their rich patrons, the milieu reminded him of his own upbringing. As his assistant Gertrud Bing wrote, "One can almost say that in his works on Florence, Warburg wrote his own *Buddenbrooks*."[10] Aby hoped the Warburgs would recreate the glory of Quattrocento merchants, such as Francesco Sassetti, whose last will and testament he studied.

In his writings on art patrons, one can see Aby's conflicted attitude toward his family. He faulted those vain bourgeois benefactors who wanted painters to glorify their wealth and reproduce their magnificent jewels and robes. For Aby, such realism led to a static art that smothered passion and prevented the artist from creating symbolic, distanced forms. As he said of a Ghirlandaio fresco of the Tornabuoni family: "This is the kind of art a Renaissance banker's family likes, because they get a much better deal than do either religion or art."[11]

The practical reason behind Aby's return to Hamburg was that his growing library needed a permanent setting. Books were now the sum and substance of his life. If he traveled for a few days, he carried a suitcase crammed with obscure books. Even at the university, he had purchased books in a systematic way that suggested something more than a rich boy's hobby. As if on the family payroll, he asked his parents for a "raise." By 1900, his collecting went far beyond anything strictly required by his work.

That June, he broached the idea of a library to Max, shrewdly pitching it as a solid, blue-chip business investment: "I would not hesitate for a moment to enter my library as a financial asset in the accounts of the firm." Later, he exhorted Max to support his collecting as a form of family advertising no less laudable than Warburg support of the local Talmud Torah School.[12] In a favorite refrain, he would say that other rich families had their racing stables, while the Warburgs would have their library. Sensitive to the charge that capitalism was crassly destructive of German culture, Aby told Max, "we should demonstrate by our example that capitalism is also capable of intellectual achievements of a scope which would not be possible otherwise."[13]

In August 1901, Max and Aby vacationed together on the North Sea island of Helgoland, and Aby secured grudging assent for his library. When he asked Moritz the next year for money to buy two luxurious sets of books, Aby acknowledged that he was now preparing a library for posterity.[14] Moderation was foreign to Aby's passionate nature and the tempo of his collecting grew feverish. In 1903 alone he "increased his scholarly apparatus" by an astounding 516 books.[15] This scale of acquisition made it impossible to be a gypsy scholar, and in 1904 Aby hired a librarian to catalogue the growing mountain of books. Aby's brothers were apprehensive about bankrolling the library, and indeed it would be an oppressive and inescapable burden in their lives. By the time Aby and Mary moved into their first house on the Benediktstrasse, the books already covered a significant fraction of the living space, crowding out the inhabitants.

Whatever Aby's hopes for turning Hamburg into a model town for the rest of the Reich, it was still a cultural backwater. It had an art museum, three theaters, two large libraries, an opera, and a tradition of adult education. But most artists flocked to the rich imperial metropolis, Berlin, or the more avant-garde Munich, which was brimming with *Jugendstil* fervor, not to Hamburg. The Hanseatic City had no university, and its art museum lacked an outstanding collection of Old Masters.

Aby felt trapped among the dilettantes. As a lonely private scholar, he was pigeonholed as a brilliant oddball by most people, but he had resolute confidence in his own importance and originality. As he told a friend in 1907, "One day or other I shall send you a specimen of my method, which, I dare say, is new and therefore, perhaps, not as far acknowledged as I could expect."[16] Far from being monkish, however, he threw himself enthusiastically into civic activities, giving lectures on Botticelli, Leonardo da Vinci, and Dürer that drew capacity crowds of more than four hundred people. He organized a meeting on folklore, joined the board of the Ethnological Museum, and became active in the historical society. A staunch supporter of contemporary artists, he fought in 1906 for Hugo Lederer's controversial Bismarck monument, an enormous figure of stylized Viking solemnity that offended conventional local canons of realism.

To enrich Hamburg culture, Aby spearheaded a movement to found a local university. The issue generated heated debate, for merchants feared it would breed subversion and challenge the prevailing business ethic; perhaps for that very reason progressives and social democrats endorsed it. Aby converted Max into a partisan of the plan, and they participated in the 1907 creation of the *Wissenschaftliche Stiftung* or Academic Foundation, a university forerunner. The foundation brought scholars to Hamburg, offered lectures, and tried to forge links between scholarship and business. Max hoped Hamburg shipping lines would send scholars around the world, armed with introductory letters, to enhance the city's standing in world trade. The kaiser always opposed the university and associated the idea with Max.

For all his familial dependence, the dyspeptic Aby remained the dominant older brother. He had a hypnotic hold over his brothers, who were proud but also somewhat frightened and awed by him. Max said Aby could have been a fine banker, a view Aby himself shared. (One should note that Aby's library, with interminable bills and catalogues, was an elaborate business operation and that he used the same copybook method for letters as did M. M. Warburg & Co.) At least once weekly, he telephoned Max with a running commentary on events and frequently took a snooze on a sofa in Max's office. With seemingly psychic powers, he knew just when a client had upset his brother and often had eerily exact presentiments about stock market crashes and bankruptcies. "I hear the wings of the bankruptcy vultures rustling," he would inform Max.[17]

Max saw Aby as a walking encyclopedia who could never commit his ideas to paper. For years, Aby kept a bronze snail on his desk—his heraldic animal. He would scribble numberless tidbits and pithy, inscrutable fragments and never threw anything away. Between 1888 and 1903, he jotted down four hundred aphorisms. Max tried to wean Aby from this perfectionist madness and get him to publish. "If more books were read," Aby bridled, "then fewer would be written."[18] As a private scholar, he had the luxury of scoffing at those who had to rush into print prematurely. In his lifetime, he said, he cared only to be acknowledged by a small cluster of colleagues.

Aby was fantastically sensitive to any pressures to rush. Once, Max asked if he could receive visitors on short notice and Aby retorted that if people wanted to hear him, they had to wait weeks for him to prepare. He fulminated, "I am not one for improvisations."[19] Because of his lofty standards and self-indulgence, Aby would publish only a small handful of short studies in his lifetime and no masterwork. Such was the force of these writings, however, not to mention his extraordinary personal magnetism and the library's influence, that he left behind a cultural legacy wholly out of proportion to his skimpy corpus of published work.

It seems unlikely that Aby could have held a steady job. He was capable of brilliant, fitful bursts of energy, but not of steady, sustained work. In 1905, he tried without success to secure a position as lecturer at the University of Bonn. The next year, Bonn reversed itself and offered him a lectureship along with a post at the German Art History Institute in Florence. Aby agonized over the offer and spent two years in fruitless wrangling with the university. In the end, when Bonn gave him one last chance to submit his application, Aby thundered that he didn't want to be hurried. He remained a solitary scholar for life, complaining of the discrimination he suffered from the academic world, but also proudly defiant. As he told Max, "I am a scholarly private banker, whose credit is as good as that of the Reichsbank."[20]

Aby's physical and emotional health apparently deteriorated during this period. By 1905, he was suffering from diabetes and hay fever so debilitating that he had to cancel appointments during ragweed season. In 1907, he admitted to a physician that if people pressured him, he got nervous and couldn't produce; only in solitude could he develop his insights. Aby now slept just one to five hours a night, and his worried Dr. Wulff nearly forbid him to write at all.[21] The next month, Aby checked into a Rome hotel room, describing it as a surrogate sanatorium.[22]

Everything he studied ended up as another thinly veiled installment of his own continuing spiritual autobiography. His inner torment gave him a special purchase on the secret, clashing furies of Western art, because he felt them swirling around within himself. A great admirer of Nietzsche, he saw suffering and pain beneath classical beauty, the irrational elements that lurked, in disguised form, in classical, medieval, and Renaissance art. Aby became an apostle of reason, not because he thought people behaved rationally—he himself belied that notion—but because he feared they didn't. Yet in one fascinating letter of 1909 he showed some sympathy with the Dionysian side of life and even wondered whether Nietzsche's madness could have been cured had he submitted to pagan impulses. "I always regret—you may laugh at me—that the practice of the ancient, orgiastic ecstasy has been lost to us: if N. had been able, each quarter year, to be able to rave in an orderly, mysterious fashion—perhaps he might have become healthy and lived to a ripe old age, full of children, as a peaceful old merchant and paterfamilias. But where is my imagination leading me?"[23]

As Aby probed the atavistic impulses of modern civilization, he was drawn in 1907 to the study of astrology, which he saw as much more than dated mumbo-jumbo. Rather, it reflected the groping, fumbling way humanity had dealt with its existential helplessness in the cosmos before astronomy came along. He demonstrated how classical gods, in some medieval paintings, metamorphosed into astrological demons. He excitedly deciphered the Tarot cards, showing they weren't simply playing cards, but had been used to make astrological predictions. In December 1909, he told Felix that he had made his discoveries after buying fifteen hundred books on astrology the previous year.[24] These fearless forays into the occult had a way of leading to the edge of madness. Aby developed into a Faustian figure plumbing curious books and mastering esoteric documents. Unlike other rationalists, he felt the full, unsettling allure of superstition—perhaps this is why he forever stood on guard against unreason and the manipulation of emotion. In 1913, he carried on a fervent campaign against some astrological swindlers in Hamburg.

In April 1909, Aby and Mary moved to 114 Heilwigstrasse, where they remained for life. The move was dictated by the books, now spreading like some metastasizing science fiction monster. In the old house, books overflowed every room, grew into the lavatories; the ceilings couldn't support the weight any longer. The new house only temporarily solved the problem, for books, set in heavy oak bookcases, soon filled the basement billiard room, the hall, the drawing room, and the guest rooms on the first floor. Aby and family had to retreat to smaller rooms upstairs. (Though poor by Warburg standards, they always had maids and a butler.) To make room for more books, they moved the dining room from the ground floor to an upper floor. Aby's friend, Fritz Schumacher, the city building master, saw how the books stamped out any room for a reasonable family life. "The sensitive wife, who really had to have space for her own work as a gifted sculptress, took these primitive events upon herself with touching patience, but the growing children looked full of wrath at the triumphal march of the hated books."[25]

Aby's children also had to contend with his tyrannic moods and could never quite relax with the powderkeg Father. One moment, he could be a charming, sparkling personality, then he would suddenly feel betrayed by people and turn on them with a terrifying wrath. The children were exhausted by the unending mood swings. As Max Adolph later poetically described it: "We, his children, were living too near to the crater to visualize the majestic profile of the mountain at the time; but near enough to feel the earth tremble under our feet; to have an occasional dizzy glance down into the boiling crater; near enough to become afraid or nervous, and, when the nerves wore off, even worse: a bit callous."[26]

Max had asked Moritz to buy the adjacent property so that Aby could someday have a library next door, and Moritz reluctantly consented. For a long time, Max had urged Aby to build the library and thus separate his private and professional lives. Like a good Hamburg businessman, Max told Aby, he should leave his house daily and report to his office. But Aby wanted to be surrounded by his comforting books. When the library finally went up next door in the mid-1920s, he defeated its intent by joining it internally to his house behind their separate street facades.

At this point, the library was open only to a tiny circle of colleagues and art experts. In 1908 Aby hired his first research assistant, Dr. P. Hübner. The next year, he helped organize the International Art History Congress in Munich and began to gain recognition in the art world. Despite long, frustrating years of obscurity, he remained supremely confident, telling a disciple in 1909 that the goal of his library was "a new method of cultural science, whose basis is the 'read' image."[27] That is, Aby would penetrate the symbolic codes of paintings and not simply analyze their surface charms.

As a Jewish art scholar, Aby knew he was in a contradictory position. He saw himself as a futurist who stood uneasily between the stools of Zionism and assimilated Jewry.[28] In his work he often had to negotiate permission from the Vatican and other ecclesiastical authorities to examine art firsthand. He operated in a sphere of German life where anti-Semitism was particularly pervasive and virulent. Some scholars he admired—including the great Swiss historian Jakob Burckhardt—were openly hostile to Jews. Yet in 1909, Aby regretted that he couldn't be an executor of Burckhardt's estate, lamenting that "but there, as a Jew, I won't even be considered."[29] Emancipation had liberated Aby into a world rife with reactionary anti-Semites who denounced Judaism as backward and benighted. His decision to compete in this world was a courageous but also curious one.

Aby was always susceptible to Jewish self-shame and even self-hatred. As historian Hans Liebeschütz noted, he couldn't conquer his aversion to the ostentation of wealthy Hamburg Jews. He loathed elegant art books, which signified decadence to him. A warped idealism lay behind much late nineteenth-century anti-Semitism, which lamented the loss of a simpler precapitalist, rural past. Aby's hatred of the materialism in his own background gave him a secret, tormenting affinity with the enemy—a tension, among others, that would tear his soul apart. The occasional kernels of truth in anti-Semitic lies and distortions resonated in Aby's mind. Yet he was always extremely alert to any anti-Semitic slurs directed against him.

Aby's attitude toward organized religion hardened with time; he would no more attend a bar mitzvah than a church wedding, dismissing both as rank superstition. Though he had a talmudic section in his library, he used it to unravel obscure biblical references. In 1908, he was sent a questionnaire by the Hamburg Jewish community, which he returned blank and with a curt note: ". . . I am in no way subject to the Jewish Community, neither as member nor as object, rather I quite explicitly resigned from it and am to be regarded by it as a Dissident."[30]

While Aby might fancy himself a freethinker, the gentile world regarded him as a Jew. As with other German Jews, his Jewish identity pursued him like a shadow as he tried to escape it. With his prophetic antennae and gift for the zeitgeist, he sensed the anti-Semitic undercurrents of the time and had fewer illusions than Max. Like other sophisticated Jews, he was stunned by the Dreyfus affair. He followed it closely and told his mother that no war or epidemic could so disfigure a people as such mob rule.[31] In 1900, the old medieval charge that Jews committed ritual murders had again surfaced in a town near Danzig. Indignant over this, Aby tried to write an article about his generation of assimilated Jews, but he couldn't finish it.

———

As Aby drifted further from his Jewish roots, Moritz grew closer to God. While Charlotte wrote her memoirs, he devoted himself to Jewish causes. As leader of the Jewish community, he could be blandly imperious. Though never a Zionist, he favored Palestine development and led the Palestine Trading Society. The group was bleeding money when Moritz chaired its meeting in 1907. While ardent Zionists wanted to perpetuate it, Moritz had other plans. He allowed the Zionists to speak and remonstrate for one hour. Then, as one participant recalled, "he stood up and explained: The Assembly has decided that the Society will be liquidated. Universal astonishment. How come? The old Warburg, on the sly, had bought up a majority of shares and could pass any resolution that suited him."[32]

For years, Moritz chaired the local Jewish boys orphanage and supported the Jewish Hospital, helping it to build a nursing home. In 1908, on his seventieth birthday, Moritz and his sons endowed the Talmud Torah School with a brand-new building that cost 175,000 marks. Yet when Max's youngest daughter, Gisela, asked to go to the school, Max refused, alarmed that she might try to convert the entire family to Jewish orthodoxy.[33] For his part, Aby resented that the money wasn't being spent on his library and he wrote Felix a blistering letter, pointing out that "the courage to do something speculative in an intellectual connection—that is the greatest privilege of the private merchant!"[34]

On January 29, 1910, a few hours after Aby paid him a bedside visit, Moritz died gently in his sleep. Max was then running for the Hamburg *Bürgerschaft*. Having delivered a campaign address that night, he didn't get to bed until the wee hours. With her steely sense of ambition for her sons, Charlotte withheld the sad news from Max until the next morning.

The rich banker was buried in a plain coffin of unvarnished wood, the Jewish way of symbolizing that everybody has equal status before God. It pained Charlotte and the brothers that Aby would attend neither the funeral nor the memorial service, or recite the mourner's kaddish. When Max and Charlotte begged for some slight token of filial piety, Aby wouldn't budge: "I am after all in the eyes of others an unreliable customer, but in my own eyes a political opponent of clerical elementary schools such as the Talmud Torah School, and above all I am a 'Cherem' [banned] through my mixed marriage and as the father of non-denominational children whom I shall never lead to Judaism. . . . The Mourner's Kaddish is a matter for the eldest son: it signifies not only an external act, but at this public memorial service demonstrates acceptance of the moral inheritance. I will not make myself guilty of such public hypocrisy. No one is entitled to demand this of me." Aby said that Max had long ago assumed the Jewish responsibilities of the firstborn, "to my unclouded and grateful satisfaction."[35] In his diary, Aby bitterly equated religion with superstition.[36] For appearance sake, he agreed to be out of town or sick on the day of the funeral.[37]

Aby was as autocratic in his library as Max was in his bank. The year that Moritz died, he hired an assistant named Wilhelm Waetzoldt and was upset to learn after hiring him that the young man had just married. Aby assumed the right to intercede in the private decisions of his employees. With a later disciple, Carl Georg Heise, he demanded to see a picture of his wife, which he kept on view in the library for a month. "I must become familiar with her," he told his astonished pupil.[38] Once, a female candidate came to be interviewed for his art seminar. For a quarter hour, Aby paced back and forth in silence. Then, with his telepathic gifts, he suddenly burst out: "And what did your divorced husband do?" The startled woman admitted she had indeed been divorced.[39]

Waetzoldt didn't last long, but in 1911 he steered to Aby a twenty-year-old Austrian student named Fritz Saxl who shared the master's interest in astrology. While visiting Hamburg's *Kunsthalle*, Saxl came to the library and was struck by how the meticulous, demanding Warburg treated him as a fellow scholar, not as a youngster. Not that it was an equal relationship by any means. When Saxl began talking of his work, Aby quickly brushed it aside and expatiated on his own views. Saxl sat spellbound by the abundance of precise ideas that poured forth in a powerful rush. After finishing his doctoral thesis on Rembrandt in Vienna, Saxl went to work as Aby's assistant in 1913.

Saxl knew that working with Aby would be a rewarding but thankless task. The library was the looking-glass of Aby's mind, mirroring all his quirks and obsessions. As one disciple said, in his library, Warburg sat like the spider in its web.[40] When Saxl first saw it, it contained fifteen thousand volumes, mostly in German or Italian. It already contained sections on alchemy and numerology, as well as railway timetables, telephone books, lottery books, and old almanacs. This mad, wonderful mass of materials was expanding at a chaotic rate of about six hundred books a year.

Arranged according to no ordinary system, the books were projections of Aby's theories, tangible links in his chains of thought, their placement designed to show unexpected associations. He loved to handle books, ponder them, and rearrange them as his ideas evolved. As a pioneer of interdisciplinary study, Aby mocked the "border police" who kept academic subjects in hermetically sealed compartments. He was as much an ethnologist, social historian, or psychologist as he was an art historian.

From his desk, Aby enjoyed a view of the rear garden and Alster canal. He seldom went for a stroll and spent most of his time wandering in an inner labyrinth of arcane symbols and lore. Aby often stayed up nights, poring over booksellers' catalogues and jotting on index cards the titles of desired books. These cards came to occupy eighty boxes and Aby grew obsessive about their arrangement, too. As Saxl recalled, "Often one saw Warburg standing tired and distressed bent over his boxes with a packet of index cards, trying to find for each one the best place within the system; it looked like a waste of energy and one felt sorry."[41]

As Aby began to take private students, they became spectators of a magnificent, volatile showman. The portly little man would puff on a cigar, pace, drink tea, and lecture tirelessly until sweat stood on his forehead. There was something martial and imperious in his manner as he gestured with an emphatic wagging finger or exploded at an imprecise question. Despite a deep, personal interest in his students, he maintained a formal pedagogic distance. On one library shelf, he kept taboo books that he thought corrupted young minds—his *"Giftschrank"* or poison bookcase. Asked why he simply didn't ban these books, he said that one had to have the devil present to fight him with his own weapons.[42]

As Aby's career flourished before World War I, he emerged from his cocoon. After having labored in solitude, he enjoyed several spectacular lecture triumphs and the recognition brought a profound, if fleeting, joy. His first great intellectual breakthrough came during an Italian trip with his pupil, Carl Georg Heise, in 1910. When they stayed at the elegant Hotel Danieli in Venice, Aby wouldn't let Heise carry his red Baedeker about, lest they be taken for tourists, so Heise had to memorize the book instead. At the Palazzo Schifanoja in Ferrara, Aby studied frescoes whose enigmatic symbolism had puzzled scholars. For hours, he stood high on a scaffold, closely examining them, while Heise stood below. "Observers would have taken him for a detective rather than an art lover," said Heise.[43] When Heise briefly stared out the window at one point, Aby grew furious at this unforgivable inattention and hotly scolded him.

In 1912, Aby presented his detective work in Ferrara at an art history congress in Rome that he had helped to plan. He correctly predicted that this would be the last such congregation of scholars for a long time. It was fitting that Aby first blazed a trail in the scholastic firmament on the eve of the coming darkness. He declined to chair the conference, saying a Jew shouldn't preside over a world organization because that might be used to discredit it.[44]

Aby revealed the mysteries of the Palazzo Schifanoja frescoes by relating the symbols to their patron's horoscope. It was a dazzling display of erudition, exhibiting a mastery of astrology from Egypt to India. It also vindicated Aby's painstaking case-study approach, showing that works of art often carried secret cargoes of forgotten lore that could only be unearthed by scholars steeped in the period. By branching beyond the conventional bounds of art criticism, Aby had discovered the frescoes' hidden meaning. The Rome speech launched a new school of criticism, and Aby rushed bound copies to Paul and Felix. But the breakthrough provided no lasting satisfaction and only made Aby more resentful of his inferior status in Hamburg's merchant world. "How difficult it is to endure one's own futility in the Hamburg crepuscule," he wrote after the congress.[45] The city, he felt, slighted his contribution to local culture. Nevertheless, he was now committed to the bruising fight for a Hamburg University and had to stay. That year, he turned down a university chair offered in Halle. In February 1912, the Hamburg Senate made Aby an honorary professor in recognition of his work and for the moment he felt happy and vindicated.

———

Now forty-five, Aby would have no further chances to be freed from financial reliance upon his brothers. When Paul and Felix visited, Aby would arrange special classes and tours to explain his work to them. They were motivated by brotherly love, not family vanity, as they indulged Aby's perfectionism. This generosity may only have strengthened his autocratic nature. The book purchases became greater, the demands upon his brothers more importunate.

Aby's pleas wavered between blustering assertions of his own superior worth and abject beggary, an unfortunate situation that kept him in a state of perpetual adolescence.

Aby became more querulous in dealing with people. If somebody didn't acknowledge a book he sent or was slow to answer a letter, he grew indignant. He frequently upbraided book dealers for poor service and threatened to go elsewhere. Spoiled and brilliant, he even gave a tongue-lashing to the Hamburg school authorities over the stench in the ground-floor urinal of the city library. While Aby had a small coterie of devoted friends, whom he treasured, he was often at war with his native town. When Hugo Vogel painted three murals, meant to celebrate the history of Hamburg commerce, for the banquet room of the Town Hall, Aby led a vitriolic attack against them.

Right before World War I, Aby acted as a special consultant to HAPAG, a job that came through brother Max. Contemptuous of what he saw as the tacky decor of its ships, he hoped the line would give more artistic commissions to talented contemporary artists. Despite his Renaissance focus, Aby championed modern artists and adored Expressionist paintings. He even had a Franz Marc painting of colored horses in his house and loved to invent nonsensical stories to explain to visitors the vivid shades.

In June 1912, Aby learned that HAPAG planned to hang a large portrait of the kaiser in an admiral's uniform on the main stairway of the new steamship the *Imperator*, which would be the largest passenger ship in the world. Aby thought imperial dress more appropriate. He was also upset by the banal color photos and kitschy reproductions that hung in the salons and corridors. Albert Ballin allowed Aby to hire two painters, Kayser and Bruck, to do paintings for the *Imperator*'s dining room. When Ballin didn't like the finished product, he had the pictures removed, and Aby felt humiliated in the artists' eyes. He pleaded for a chance to make his case against the decision. Ballin graciously consented and even invited Aby on the *Imperator*'s test run. Instead of responding to this generous invitation, Aby refused to go, pleading hay fever, and his services were terminated. Perhaps because of this rift, Aby ranted about Ballin's despotic rule of the shipping empire. He thought Ballin needed the intoxicating stimulant of power and elegance, but that Max shouldn't be seduced by his mentor. "You're only a part of his entourage, which consists, in part, of men who are worth nothing and yet whom he doesn't want to do without."[46]

Picking up the smallest psychic rumblings, Aby's agitation increased with the war's approach. In earlier photos, he looked downcast and melancholy. By 1912, he angrily confronted the camera, his look restless and agitated. In late 1912, he gave a speech in Göttingen that left him exhausted and despondent. He complained of loneliness to Charlotte and told brother Fritz how depressed he was at the thought of returning to Hamburg, which he described as a "tavern of Philistine barflies."[47] His visits to the Waldpark Sanatorium in Baden-Baden became more frequent. The "cure" was then a fashionable ritual for the well-to-do, who drank the waters, dieted, and walked in beautiful natural settings. But given Aby's later history, it is hard not to see in these recurring visits to Baden-Baden an ominous preview of things to come. With the coming of the war, all of the demons that danced in the basement of Aby's psyche would come rushing to the surface.

Paul Warburg and daughter Bettina.
(Courtesy of Katharine Weber)

CHAPTER 10

Shy Warrior

Of the brothers, Paul seemed the least equipped to survive a long, turbulent crusade in the crucible of American politics. Washington struck him as even more wicked and faithless a place than Wall Street. He was gentle, unassuming, and reserved, with an old-fashioned, almost prudish faith in morality. The glad-handing camaraderie that smooths a political career didn't suit his quiet, scholarly demeanor. A self-conscious man who smiled but seldom laughed, he displayed his wit and revealed his emotions only to a small circle of intimates. His son described him as "Beloved of all, yet truly known by few."[1]

Yet other qualities did fit him for combat. A man of quiet intensity, he doggedly defended his beliefs, and when he spoke his words carried great authority. As journalist George F. Redmond noted, "He is the product of generations of gentle breeding, but if Paul Warburg is right, it is about as easy to move him as it would be for a gnat to push over the Woolworth Building."[2]

Paul was eager to escape from Wall Street. Making money held no charm for him, and the fortune he made at Kuhn, Loeb retired money as an issue anyway. Bearing an Atlas-like burden for the public weal—*that* appealed to his stoic nature no less than supporting a lovely, crippled wife. Of all of

Charlotte Warburg's children, Paul had most internalized the message of duty and sacrifice, taking as his personal motto: *In serviendo consumor.*[3]

This bashful man's crusade for an American central bank would be no less a personal than a political triumph. As *The Century* magazine said, "Paul M. Warburg is probably the mildest-mannered man that ever personally conducted a revolution. . . . He stepped forth armed simply with an idea. And he conquered. That is the amazing thing. A shy, sensitive man, he imposed his idea on a nation of a hundred million people."[4]

Intimately acquainted with European central banks, especially the Reichsbank, Paul didn't claim to originate new banking principles so much as import European practices.[5] As with Max in Hamburg, Paul meshed spectacularly with his historical moment. Once again, a Warburg succeeded because of his contradictory status. As a Jew in a gentile world, a German immigrant confronting a new country, Paul was able to spot flaws in American finance to which native bankers had been blinded by familiarity.

However technical in application, Paul's banking reforms were simple in principle. He wanted a central bank that issued a uniform national currency. Instead of bank notes based on government bonds, he favored an elastic currency, backed by gold and commercial paper as well, that would ebb and flow in quantity with the business cycle. During panics, the nation's twenty-two thousand banks adopted a *sauve qui peut* attitude. By selfishly hoarding reserves to protect themselves, they aggravated the general instability of the banking system. A central bank, Paul knew, could mobilize scattered reserves during crises, much as a fire department could pool water.

America also lacked what bankers term a discount policy. When banks took corporate IOUs, they were frozen in their portfolios and couldn't be resold as liquid assets. Paul wanted a central bank to rediscount commercial paper—that is, take it from local banks in emergencies and furnish them with liquid assets with which they could pay off depositors. He also wanted to dismantle a dangerous system whereby banks backed deposits with call loans and stock exchange collateral. During panics, they would sell stock abruptly to retrieve their collateral, leading to bloody crashes on Wall Street.

Such ideas may sound more common-sensical than controversial today. In the early twentieth century, however, debt-ridden farmers and populists dreaded that a Wall Street–dominated central bank would strangle them with high interest rates. Paul Warburg may have been a taciturn man, but in the tabloid press he formed part of a fearsome, glowering gallery of Robber Barons that included Jacob Schiff and Edward H. Harriman. After the 1907 panic, bankers were regarded as rogues, swindlers, and incompetents, and the age couldn't quite conceive of a scrupulous banker. Paul never functioned as a Wall Street stooge—he was too fiercely independent—but he was inevitably found guilty by association and denounced as respectable cover for grasping financiers.

Like Aby, Paul had a gift for prophecy, a special radar that detected social and political fragility. He spied hairline cracks in the facade of economic life that portended later collapse. Again like Aby, he viewed the world through a filter darkened by his own depression and saw problems perhaps hidden to happier souls. In 1906 he warned the Chamber of Commerce, "I do not like to play the role of Cassandra, but mark what I say. If this condition of affairs is not changed, and changed soon, we will get a panic in this country compared with which those which have preceded it will look like child's play."[6]

One night in 1907, Professor Edwin R. A. Seligman of Columbia University gathered distinguished economists and bankers in his home to debate reform. There, Paul made a stirring presentation. "You ought to write," Seligman told him. "You ought to publish." "Impossible," said Paul. "I can't write English yet—not well enough for publication." "The English can be arranged," Seligman said. "It's your duty to get your ideas before the country."[7]

This reluctant warrior was soon swept into battle. In 1907 panic swept New York's highly speculative trust banks, and a stampede of depositors emptied one bank after another. The stock exchange was temporarily shut as Pierpont Morgan orchestrated a rescue by government and bankers. The unfolding drama confirmed Paul's uneasy sense that American bankers didn't band together to combat trouble. He suggested that state clearing houses join in a national clearing house, but the major financial centers mistrusted each other too much for common action. Suddenly, James Stillman, president of National City Bank—who four years before had sneered at his central bank plan—now materialized at Paul's desk. "Well, where is your paper?" he asked. "Too late now, Mr. Stillman," Paul replied. "What has to be done cannot be done in a hurry. If reform is to be secured, it will take years of educational work to bring it about."[8]

Soon *The New York Times* asked Paul to write about bank reform. Digging into his desk, he dusted off the essay he had written soon after arriving in America. Entitled "Defects and Needs of Our Banking System" and published in the newspaper on November 12, 1907, it argued that the country needed to centralize reserves in emergencies. Obscure technical issues had taken on sudden urgency. "The appalling panic which we have experienced during the last few weeks will do more, I suppose, to bring home to the public the absolute necessity of a change in our present banking and currency system than all the efforts that have hitherto been made to warn the nation of the imminent danger," Paul said.[9] Reflecting the rampant paranoia about central banks in the heartland, nativist critics branded Paul's ideas "un-American," attacks that carried an ugly tinge when directed against a German-born, Jewish banker.

As he took his first tentative steps into politics, Paul remained a German citizen, spoke imperfect English, couldn't write idiomatically, and was still an M. M. Warburg partner. For this retiring man, public speaking was pure torture, yet he never relented. Soon he acquired a powerful ally: Senator Nelson W. Aldrich of Rhode Island, the czar of the Republican party and maestro of the smoke-filled rooms. Paul seemed a choirboy beside him, but they would form an effective, if unlikely, duo. Fearing his partisanship, Paul first encountered Aldrich with "a good deal of prejudice and suspicion." In time, he came to believe that Aldrich sincerely wanted banking reform to be his enduring political legacy.[10] At the same time, Aldrich was only slowly converted to the idea of an American central bank.

In December 1907, Paul first met Aldrich when the latter visited Kuhn, Loeb to ask how the Reichsbank issued treasury bills. Schiff didn't know and summoned Paul. By the time Aldrich left, an enthusiastic Paul mused, "There marches national bank currency and there goes currency reform."[11] Paul asked Schiff if he should write to Aldrich, explaining the dangers of allowing national banks to issue currency against government bonds. Afraid Aldrich might resent the pressure, Schiff said, "if you do, he will never look at you again."[12] Paul proceeded to ignore his brother-in-law's advice. On the last day of the year, while merrier souls got ready for New Year's Eve, Paul sent Aldrich a proposal for a uniform currency, showing how competitive hoarding of reserves produced calamity in banking crises.

By early 1908, Paul was giving speeches about how the Panic could have been averted. At the time, the Bank of England, the Reichsbank, and the Banque de France operated independently of government and their quasi-private character aroused alarm in America. Although a proponent of a strong central bank, Paul realized that any American counterpart would need popular constraints on its power.

On May 30, 1908, Congress enacted the Aldrich-Vreeland Currency Bill, which instantly thrust Paul into the hurly-burly of American politics, for the law mandated a National Monetary Commission to investigate foreign banking systems and file a report with Congress. The chairman would be Senator Nelson Aldrich. Lacking the requisite technical knowledge, the senator came to lean heavily upon Paul's expertise.

When Aldrich and other commission members sailed for Europe that summer, Schiff provided introductory letters to open doors in Berlin and later in Tokyo. In New York that fall, Aldrich held hearings at the Metropolitan Club and asked Paul to testify. Afterward, he drew him aside for an intimate tête-à-tête at a little table. Paul was thunderstruck to find that Aldrich had not only read his essays but now categorically endorsed a central bank. "Mr. Warburg," said Aldrich, "I like your ideas. I have only one fault to find with them." What was that? Paul asked. "You are too timid about it." Paul was flabbergasted: He said he thought he had been bold where weaker souls cowered. "Yes," said Aldrich, "but you say we cannot have a central bank, and I say we can." Bewildered and overjoyed, Paul left the club "elated."[13] One wonders whether Aldrich mentioned Paul's citizenship as a possible political handicap, for a month later he suddenly filed papers to become a citizen. Henceforth, Paul would closely advise the senator.

For political reasons, Paul vetoed the idea of a strong, centralized bank and tried to come up with a more palatable alternative, such as a central bank with branch offices. Responding to these same concerns, another reformer, Victor Morawetz, developed a plan for regional reserve banks. Paul supported this alternative so long as it provided a central mechanism for coordinating action in emergencies.

In November 1910, Aldrich, Paul, and four other experts sneaked off to discuss bank reform at a secret hideaway on Jekyll Island off the Georgia coast. With Democrats now in control of Congress and Progressives railing against Wall Street, the bankers had to travel incognito, lest they be accused of hatching a cabal. A favorite haunt of Wall Street tycoons, Jekyll Island was deserted in November and thus was a natural choice for a clandestine rendezvous.

In Jersey City, Paul and his coconspirators, outfitted as duck hunters, boarded a private railroad car. Never having shot a bird, Paul had to borrow a rifle to participate in the masquerade. The men traveled by night, with the blinds tightly drawn, and they called each other by their first names. (Hence, they were christened The First Name Club.) When they got off the train in Brunswick, Georgia, they spoke loudly and ostentatiously about sport. Apparently, they were rather amateurish actors, for the stationmaster knew at once who they were and said suspicious reporters had been snooping about. For a long time, the conspirators wouldn't admit the meeting had even occurred. Writing in 1928, Paul still abided by the oath of secrecy. "Though eighteen years have since gone by, I do not feel free to give a description of this most interesting conference concerning which Senator Aldrich pledged all participants to secrecy."[14]

During ten days at Jekyll Island, Paul's low-key but forceful personality stood out as the six men debated at a round table. When a cause engaged him, Paul was tenacious and he semihumorously dubbed himself a "fanatic" about bank reform. Aldrich wanted a central bank controlled by bankers. Bowing to political realities, however, Paul wanted to make concessions toward more public control. At one point, after a particularly testy exchange with Aldrich,

Henry Davison of the Morgan Bank ushered Paul from the room to calm him down. Paul was eager to launch a national education campaign and Aldrich had to damp his excessive ardor.

Frank Vanderlip of National City Bank described these strenuous days as the most stimulating intellectual experience of his life.[15] As a result of these talks, Aldrich announced the so-called Aldrich Plan in January 1911. By affixing his name to the bill, Paul thought that Aldrich had succeeded in conjuring up a Republican-banker plot, and the populist press pounced upon Paul's influence. A *Philadelphia American* headline blared, "Wall St. Banker, Not Aldrich, Drew Up Currency Plan." The subhead said, "New York Man Real Author of Scheme to Control Money."[16]

The term "central bank" was so politically loaded that the Aldrich scheme called for a National Reserve Association that would issue notes based on gold and commercial paper—a clear victory for Paul—and its board of directors would be dominated by bankers. At the same time, the system would disperse power by having regional reserve banks under separate boards.

For a political tyro, Paul was navigating in treacherous waters. For a foreigner and a Jew to play such an aggressive role—especially in matters of money—was daring and courageous. Jews were tolerated if they stayed in banking houses—that is, Jewish banking houses. Paul had now crossed an invisible line that exposed him to vituperative attack. That he acted as chief theoretician of the Aldrich Plan is somewhat less surprising than his vigorous public promotion of it. On March 21, 1911, he became a U.S. citizen just in time to chair a new National Citizens' League for the Promotion of a Sound Banking System. To veil its Wall Street auspices, the group set up headquarters in Chicago and promoted the general idea of monetary reform, not the Aldrich Plan per se.

Popular mistrust of the banking fraternity was at a high. A swelling chorus condemned the Wall Street Money Trust, which supposedly manipulated American finance. J. Pierpont Morgan was the archvillain, but Schiff and Kuhn, Loeb made the short list of enemies—the only important Jewish bankers included. Politicians were skittish about supporting any reform associated with these certified ogres of the populist press.

In January 1912, Paul joined twenty bankers and economists to win Teddy Roosevelt's support. Paul was impressed that Roosevelt was such a quick study. "It was fascinating to see him interrupt the speakers and drive straight for the important points," he said. "After a comparatively short, quick fire of searching questions, it seemed that he had obtained a perfectly clear picture of the problem involved."[17] When one economist doubted that America had men experienced enough to run a central bank, TR sat back and laughed: "Why not give Mr. Warburg the job? He would be the financial boss, and I would be the political boss, and we could run the country together."[18] The room burst into laughter. This friendly exchange proved misleading. TR's Progressive party opposed the Aldrich Plan and Paul keenly felt the betrayal, so much so that later, as his son said, Paul *"loathed Teddy Roosevelt . . . my father thought he was dreadful*—didn't trust him, thought he was a phony."[19] As his campaign went on, Paul would develop an air of chronic indignation. In many ways naïvely idealistic, he didn't have the thick rind or innate cynicism that would toughen him for the bruising business of politics.

When it was presented to the Democratic Congress in 1912, the Aldrich Plan fizzled, yet many of Paul's ideas would survive in the Federal Reserve Act. During the 1912 campaign, Woodrow Wilson largely dodged the issue. After his election, Paul was asked to develop a central bank blueprint compatible with the Democratic platform. On December 7, 1912, Paul gave Henry Morgenthau a plan specifically crafted to appeal to Democrats. It proposed twenty reserve banks, capped by a central board in Washington under government control. In late December, Wilson met with Congressman Carter Glass and endorsed a plan for a Federal Reserve Board that would supervise a system of regional reserve banks. It looked suspiciously familiar to Paul, who said sardonically, "President Wilson could not possibly have escaped a conclusion which so many other students of the problem had been forced to reach."[20]

In January 1913, Paul testified before the House Banking Committee, an occasion that brought him into direct conflict with his Washington nemesis, Carter Glass, a fiery former newspaper editor from Virginia. Paul was modest and reticent while Glass craved the limelight. Paul knew that Glass faced a delicate task. In fighting for a central bank, he had to champion a Republican plan yet clothe it in egalitarian Democratic rhetoric. From political necessity, Glass had to deny the large overlap of his ideas with Paul's. In testimony, Paul argued that the government should appoint a majority of the Washington board and the banking community the remainder. Glass and Wilson favored having all political appointees. Thus, they differed, not over the machinery, but over who would pull the levers. Glass wanted twelve to fifteen autonomous regional banks and faulted Paul's more centralized scheme as one of "central banks of the banks, by the banks and for the banks."[21] The two men weren't really that far apart and Glass used Paul as a foil to dramatize his own populist purity.

In late January 1913, Glass told Wilson that he had met with small-town Western bankers and they had "concluded that they could not carry out Mr. Warburg's purpose of 'battering the committee into a repudiation of the Democratic platform.'. . ."[22] The first draft of his central bank bill provided for at least fifteen regional banks, but also a Federal Reserve Commission in

Washington, with mostly public appointees. Again it departed from Paul's plan more in nuance than in essential outline.

Paul became involved in actually drafting the Federal Reserve Act through Wilson's closest adviser, Colonel House, who formed a back channel to Wall Street. In late April, President Wilson gave House the first digest of the secret Glass bill, which House handed to Paul for quick analysis. Glass later said Paul was hostile, whereas Paul preferred to style himself a sympathetic critic. To make them less provincial, Paul wanted to reduce the number of district reserve banks. House widely circulated Paul's unsigned critique within the administration. In late May, Paul sailed to Europe on a liner with House, who got his reactions to various draft bills, then approvingly wired them to Wilson. To placate the populists and Senator Robert L. Owen, chairman of the Senate Banking Committee, Wilson settled for a bill in June that provided for regional reserve banks, supervised by a Washington reserve board under presidential control. With all seven board members to be appointed by the President, Paul feared the new Reserve Board would be "hopelessly political."[23]

Even though the Glass-Owen bill was being debated in Washington, Paul stuck to his annual ritual of spending the summer in Europe and he kept up a correspondence with Colonel House. He already believed opponents were plagiarizing his ideas. "I have been in the international banking business for 27 years," he told House. "I have preached the gospel of reform on the lines now adopted at a time when Mr. Owen and Glass had not begun to study the alphabet of banking."[24] That his rivals had denied him credit would become a leitmotif in Paul's later years.

When he returned to the United States that fall, he met several times with Glass and discussed the banking bill at length with Senator Owen on a train from the capital to New York. Paul sometimes sounded a melodramatic note of alarm about the bill's defects. After meeting several senators in November, for instance, he complained to Sir Ernest Cassel, "I am mortified by the suicidal stubbornness with which sound suggestions have been swept aside so far."[25] Such hyperbole tended to divert attention from his basic sympathy for the measure and was later misconstrued as opposition.

On December 23, 1913, Wilson signed the Federal Reserve Act. Although he feared the prescribed minimum of eight reserve banks would make the system weak and unwieldy, Paul regarded the legislation as a spectacular triumph. "The passage of the Federal Reserve Act was a signal achievement and one for which the Democratic party could justly claim great credit," he wrote.[26] It embittered him that Glass and other belated converts portrayed the bankers as all opposed to the bill. For six years after the 1907 Panic, in fact, bankers had developed ideas that were then packaged into bills by Democratic politicians. In one critical respect, however, Paul's opponents were absolutely correct: He had dissented sharply on the issue of political control and feared White House domination of the new system.

The final act compromised on the seven-member Federal Reserve Board. It would include the treasury secretary, the comptroller of the currency, and five presidential appointees, of whom at least two would need banking experience. This last provision paved the way for Paul's own appointment to the board.

It is hard to parcel out credit for the Federal Reserve System, which went through such an extended gestation period. Many contemporaries cited Paul as its father. As *The New York Times* wrote, "In actual fact he had a more legitimate title to that distinction than any other American citizen."[27] Edwin R. A. Seligman, the Columbia University economist, said, "it may be stated without fear of contradiction that in its fundamental feats the Federal Reserve Act is the work of Mr. Warburg more than any other man in the country."[28] Paul had introduced the principle of mobilizing scattered reserves and the rediscount policy. In the late 1920s, Paul undertook a massive history of the Fed, in which he took withering exception to Glass's statement that the Federal Reserve Act bore no resemblance to the Aldrich Bill. Laying the two bills side by side, he showed they were "surprisingly akin."[29] The Aldrich Plan had provided for a more centralized system and greater banker control. Otherwise it was clearly a brother, though not an identical twin, of the Federal Reserve System.

This controversy over the Fed's authorship would pose a terrible dilemma for Paul. He hated show-offs and exhibitionists and especially detested the way Bernard Baruch paraded his political influence. Yet it grated upon his sense of injustice that he was denied credit. As his son said, "another man might either have asserted himself or let it go. He couldn't quite do either. He was an extremely just and gentle sort of man."[30] The issue dripped bitter poison into his mind.

Before enactment of the Federal Reserve Act, Paul had a cordial visit with Carter Glass at the Raleigh Hotel in Washington. Out of the blue, Glass shocked Paul by asking whether he would consider a seat on the new board. As Paul recalled, "I took the question more or less as a joke or, at the most, as a compliment, and told him that I did not think the President would be at all likely to submit the name of a man associated with one of the leading Wall Street firms."[31] Paul had a bit of time to grow accustomed to the idea. The day Wilson signed the bill, Paul wrote Glass a congratulatory letter. Then Glass reiterated, "I take leave to suggest that you might well give serious consideration to the rather personal question that I put to you in my room at the Raleigh when you were last here."[32] Paul foresaw the dilemma that would confront him: He might have to help administer a Fed whose flaws he had so persistently exposed. When Wilson offered Paul the post by letter, he accepted "by return of mail and without any reservation," as he said.[33] His appointment pacified a leery Wall Street.

In joining the Fed, Paul had to surrender lucrative partnerships at Kuhn, Loeb and M. M. Warburg as well as directorships at the B&O Railroad, Westinghouse Electric, and Wells Fargo Express. Aware of the prestige involved, Schiff also felt it part of his patriotic duty to let Paul go. Paul exchanged an income estimated at $500,000 a year for one pegged at $12,000. At the time he became a top American financial official, Paul had never even cast a vote: He became a citizen in 1911 and was in Europe on election day in 1912.

To the American public, he was a faceless figure. When one newspaper asked for his picture, he declined: "I have never yet had my picture in the newspapers and am rather proud of this record. Therefore you will pardon me for not breaking it now."[34] Paul's sense of public relations was faulty: He was behaving with the discretion appropriate for a private banker. Luckily, he had many more admirers than detractors. When one Midwest editor heard of Paul's nomination, he asked the head of a local bank, "We have just received a flash from Washington that a man named Paul M. Warburg is slated for the Federal Reserve Board. Who is he?" "Paul M. Warburg," said the bank president, "is the best-informed banker in the United States."[35]

If Wall Street hailed Paul as a paragon of banking, the populist press unleashed a torrent of violent criticism. As the *Philadelphia North American* said of Paul, "of all the financiers in the United States, there is none, we believe, whose nomination to the federal reserve board would be more offensive to the principle that credit should be freed from sinister influences. . . ."[36] Believing the new board had too many bankers, Senate Progressives seized on the chance to resurrect the Money Trust campaign against Kuhn, Loeb. The press zeroed in on Edward H. Harriman's railroad empire, with Schiff as his financial agent. Some papers saw a nefarious Kuhn, Loeb plot to overtake the house of Morgan, others a Warburg plot. As *The New York Times* reported, "The opponents of Mr. Warburg also say he is actively connected with the Hamburg banking house of Max Warburg," which would "give one of the powerful banking houses of Europe an unfair advantage."[37] At a time of tremendous xenophobia in America, the prejudice directed against Paul was often blatant. Congressman Joe Eagle said he opposed Paul's nomination because "he is a Jew, a German, a banker and an alien."[38] Under attack for the composite identity that had made him so uniquely valuable in American finance, Paul faced a typically Warburgian dilemma.

Board nominees required approval by the Senate Banking Committee. Paul agreed to testify if all nominees were treated alike. In early July 1914, three "popular" nominees sailed through without questioning, while Paul and Thomas D. Jones of International Harvester faced rougher sledding. Senator Joseph Bristow of Kansas commented acidly that Jones and Warburg, instead of being Fed nominees, should be "candidates for punishments for unlawful acts in violation of the Sherman law and other criminal statutes."[39] The committee voted against Jones and delayed Paul's confirmation, deciding to single him out for questioning. Stung by this patent bias, Paul dug in his heels and refused to appear, informing the committee pointedly that he wouldn't respond to humiliating, discriminatory behavior.[40] All of his native stubbornness flared up.

For the next four weeks, controversy stalled his nomination. Wilson, Treasury Secretary McAdoo, and Nebraska Senator Gilbert M. Hitchcock, acting chair of the Senate Banking Committee, pleaded with Paul to relent. The more insulted he felt, the more intransigent his dignity, which had lent him heroic stature in business circles, became. Paul telephoned McAdoo, bluntly stating that he wouldn't testify. On July 3, he wrote to Wilson and asked him to withdraw his name, saying the committee had placed upon his nomination "the stamp of suspicion and doubt."[41] Refusing to drop Paul's nomination, Wilson courageously converted it into a test of party loyalty. He felt he had to show the business community that the Democratic party wasn't hostile to it. As *The Wall Street Journal* said, "Not many bankers have had the distinction of having a President of the United States take up the cudgels in their behalf— and in a fight with the mighty Senate of the United States at that."[42] Paul's files show that Wilson prodded him to testify, telling him that "I could not in entire respect for the Senate request it to act upon your nomination in the present circumstances."[43]

The senators felt their own dignity offended, and a political stalemate ensued. In late July, Paul met with Senator Hitchcock on Long Island. Taking a conciliatory approach, Hitchcock said the committee meant no disrespect and had no plans to heckle him and reminded Paul that he wasn't a well-known personality. A small minuet of mutual apology ensued. Paul voluntarily gave Hitchcock answers to questions posed by the committee. Afterward, Paul told Wilson that he would meet with the committee behind closed doors. It would be a discussion, not a formal hearing, and without a stenographer present.[44]

Paul's appearance before the committee provided another lacerating lesson in Washington chicanery. He told the senators he wanted to "show that a Wall Street man does deserve the country's confidence in carrying on these things."[45] Senator Bristow remained unconvinced. For a day and a half, he grilled Paul so narrowly about Kuhn, Loeb that Paul snapped, "I think that my firm is not up as a nominee for membership of the Federal Reserve

Board."[46] Paul denied being a Rothschild agent in America, noting that August Belmont & Co. performed that service. He surprised the committee by saying that while he was a Republican, he had contributed to Wilson's campaign after Teddy Roosevelt entered the race. Brother Felix, he added, had supported Taft.

Paul acquitted himself ably and honorably, and the Banking Committee and full Senate confirmed his recommendation. Yet he was psychologically bloodied by the contest. Sensitive and a bit priggish, he was easily disillusioned. He felt superior to the congressmen who had tried to skewer him and derived no pleasure from his victory. When Colonel House said the controversy acquainted a wider public with his signal merits, Paul replied dryly, "While you may be right that the notoriety that I received may help me in some parts of the country, I sincerely wish it had never come to me. Personally I rather resented it."[47]

On August 10, 1914, Paul Warburg took the oath of office and began to serve on the Federal Reserve Board. One reason he had compromised about appearing before the committee was the outbreak of World War I on August 1. The issue of his German birth and recent citizenship—which had seemed so abstract and distant when first raised—would now haunt him for the next four years. The extraordinary good fortune that had catapulted him into early prominence would seem to abandon him without mercy. During his tenure in office, the Federal Reserve System—the financial instrument he had so carefully honed—would prove a weapon in the fight against his beloved Germany. By a terrible trick of fate, he and Max ascended to leading positions in American and German finance right on the eve of World War I.

The Endangered German

Max Warburg attained eminence in the heyday of imperial intrigue, when statesmen picked countries ripe for exploitation on unfurled maps and bankers served their will. Private bankers were ideal channels for such covert action because they didn't answer to shareholders or publish balance sheets. They also prized intelligence and operated with sphinxlike discretion that mimicked diplomatic activity. The involvement of Jewish bankers in often sub-rosa colonial activity fed popular fantasies that they ran a secret empire, when, in fact, they operated under the strict guidance of the German Foreign Office. Like other private bankers, Jewish bankers mixed business and politics in a way that made them liable to a later political backlash.

On the eve of World War I, Jewish bankers enjoyed such official favor as to make their later persecution the more perplexing to them. Some analysts have suggested that these Jews, still insecure at bottom, financed colonial expansion to certify their patriotism and to curry favor with the kaiser.[1] If so, their talents were abundantly exploited. Service to the imperial state lashed them to Germany's presumed mission in the world.

Max believed unhesitatingly that bankers should advance the overseas

interests of their governments. Noting how his British counterparts stimulated an economic rebound from the Boer War, he observed in his bank's
1904 report, "This shrewd merger of finance and politics didn't occur equally
well in Germany."[2] A liberal imperialist who thought Germany needed colonies to sustain a booming economy and population, he wished to extend
German power by peaceful settlement, not by military domination. A close
friend of Colonial Secretary Bernhard Dernburg, Max boasted that no German
bank more steadfastly supported colonial enterprises than his own.[3] At Dernburg's prompting, he cofounded the Colonial Institute in Hamburg to train
Germans to run the country's colonies. As an institute adviser, he stressed
that these pioneers must preserve their German identity in exotic settings. He
also helped to cofound—then twice rescued from bankruptcy—a Tropical
Hygiene Institute.

Max's colonial work strengthened his ebullient, enterprising presence in
official Berlin. If his judgment was later badly clouded by patriotism, we must
note that his early success was premised on government patronage. It was
during its period of colonial involvement that M. M. Warburg & Co. leaped
into the first rank of world banking, its balance sheet expanding from assets
of 46 million marks in 1900, to 127 million marks in 1914.

Germany was infused with a sense of manifest destiny about overseas
development. Bismarck had displayed only grudging interest in colonies,
regarding them as economic burdens that might spark friction with England
and France. In contrast, Wilhelm II wanted to compete for colonies and
bumptiously asserted German interests. With truculent pride and notable
self-pity, German leaders deplored the discrepancy between their robust domestic economy and the relative paucity of their overseas holdings. As late-
comers to imperial adventure, they tried to compensate by boldly exploiting
opportunities to make inroads against the French and British.

In 1904, Max joined a Deutsche Bank loan to the Imperial Ottoman Empire
to bankroll the Baghdad railway. The next year, the Foreign Office lured him
into tangled Liberian intrigue. After spurning loans from French and British
banks to avoid submission to their governments, Monrovia appealed to Germany. Working with Paul at Kuhn, Loeb, Max organized an international
loan for Liberia to thwart England and guarantee a market for German goods,
a loan so successful that most Liberian commerce ended up in German
hands.[4] By 1907, M. M. Warburg & Co. tied for first place in securities issues
among German banks, sharing top honors with the globe-straddling Deutsche Bank.

As the great powers jockeyed for influence in Asia and Africa, they formed
syndicates with other creditor countries to regulate the competition. The
elaborate cartel for China included Germany. By the late 1890s, HAPAG ran

Alice and Max Warburg
in their confident, pre-Nazi prime.
(Courtesy of Anita Warburg)

freight service there, and major Chinese ports swarmed with German merchants. In 1909, U.S. president William Howard Taft insisted that American banks join in financing Chinese railways. With Jacob Schiff and Paul Warburg participating in the American group, Max was recruited by the German Foreign Office to ensure German-American harmony. He later said, "We succeeded through our good offices, in constant contact with Washington and the Wilhelmstrasse, in achieving an understanding between America and Germany."[5] Max relished such a middleman role, which proved that international bankers could transcend national differences—a fond Warburg belief.

In 1909, he wooed a mysterious young man named Dr. Wilhelm Charles Regendanz, who fancied himself a budding German Cecil Rhodes. Bored with bureaucratic drudgery at the Colonial Office, Regendanz manufactured blueprints for German colonies in Africa. Dernburg told Max that this young man yearned for resolute action. Regendanz never thought small. In 1909, he wrote in his diary, "Must study maps to see where I can acquire a colony of my own."[6] Max offered him a job as a "legal adviser" at the bank, which was really window-dressing, for Regendanz would head a special department dedicated to colonial expeditions. The Colonial Office had slipped a trusted operative into a prestigious private bank.

Regendanz embroiled the bank in perhaps its most outlandish episode, a colonial affair that began as high drama and ended as deadly farce. In 1910, Max founded the Hamburg Morocco Society, with Carl Melchior as its chairman and Regendanz as chief executive. Its stated aim was to promote German mining in Morocco; its unspoken agenda was to challenge French predominance. About the same time, the Mannesmann Brothers created a new subsidiary, Morocco-Mannesmann, to exploit ore in southern Morocco.

Five years earlier, Wilhelm II had stepped off a HAPAG ship in Tangier and committed German prestige in North Africa, demanding that France follow an open-door policy for other powers. Starting with the 1906 Algeciras conference, France assumed police and budgetary powers in Morocco, while allowing other powers to intervene to safeguard their own interests. For several years, France and Germany warily coexisted. Then, in May 1911, France responded to local disturbances by seizing the Moroccan capital of Fez, which Germany branded a violation of the Algeciras pact. Intent upon teaching the French a lesson, the German Foreign Office decided to stake a strong claim to southern Morocco. It dispatched warships to Agadir, a dusty fishing village on the southern coast that had an old Portuguese castle overlooking a spacious bay. Berlin needed to concoct some pretext for this saber-rattling and preferred a commercial one to mask its political motives.

Instead of reacting with his typical bluster, the kaiser was actually squeamish about confronting France. When Max visited the Foreign Office on June 16, he received two requests: send Regendanz to southern Morocco and soften up the kaiser. "Should His Majesty the Kaiser inquire about Morocco while in Hamburg, so would it be in accord with the views of this office, if you should expressly underscore the importance of our economic interests in the south of the country," Baron Langwerth informed him.[7]

The alleged German interests in southern Morocco were speculative at best, nonexistent at worst. When Regendanz visited Under-Secretary of State Zimmermann on June 19, he provided him with geological reports of the Hamburg Morocco Society that conjured up rich veins of copper ore. Although an architect of German policy in Morocco, Regendanz hadn't actually visited the country, which freed his imagination from any factual encumbrance. He evoked not only storied mineral deposits, but a lush, fertile river valley near Agadir that was supposedly perfect for agricultural settlement. If this fecundity later proved apocryphal, it provided the German government with the "vital interests" it needed to send ships to protect. Max was now hip-deep in all the maneuvering. As the Foreign Office said, its policy relied on "very confidential information from Messrs. M. M. Warburg in Hamburg."[8]

There was a shortage of German nationals in southern Morocco to protect: to be more precise, there were none. Regendanz promised that he would land some threatened settlers on the scene by the time the warships arrived. In Hamburg, he drew up a magnificent appeal for help that could be issued by these threatened Germans and used to justify armed intervention. The Foreign Office could then appear to respond to private appeals, which it had secretly prepared in advance. Eleven firms with interests in the area, including the Hamburg Morocco Society, signed the appeal without even seeing its contents. The signatories claimed that their holdings were being assaulted by unruly natives and urgently requested help from Berlin.

While Regendanz was in Berlin, Max dined with the kaiser on June 19, meeting him again the next day. Unlike Regendanz, the kaiser had visited Morocco and was less than enthralled. His Majesty was too dovish for Regendanz's tastes, so the misguided young idealist kept the leader in the dark, believing the Agadir maneuver "urgently necessary for raising German prestige in foreign politics."[9] Max didn't mention Morocco, Regendanz noted triumphantly in his diary. "According to my request, Warburg had carefully avoided talking about Morocco with the Kaiser, who does not yet know."[10] Regendanz didn't entirely confide in Max either, fearing he lacked the warlike mettle to see the affair through to the bitter end.

In late June, Chancellor Bethmann Hollweg and Kiderlen of the Foreign Office went to secure Wilhelm's approval for the impending naval thrust. When they boarded his yacht, the *Hohenzollern*, cruising on the Lower Elbe, they learned that the kaiser had spoken vociferously against any Moroccan action. Suddenly faint-hearted, Bethmann asked Ballin if Max was on board: They needed a friend of the kaiser to prepare him. Max wasn't there, Ballin said, but could be summoned. "For the moment not necessary yet," Bethmann said, asking Ballin to see the kaiser instead.[11] When the kaiser reluctantly consented to the naval maneuver, a jubilant Kiderlen radioed from the yacht to Berlin: "Ships approved."[12] No less ecstatic, Regendanz cheered "Hurrah!" in his diary.[13]

The Hamburg group sent a mining engineer named Wilberg to Agadir, expressly to be threatened there by natives. Dubbed the "Endangered German" for his one-man impersonation of an entire besieged German colony, he was supposed to arrive in Agadir by July 1, 1911. Alas, it was a long, arduous trek. On the appointed day, Wilberg was still threading his way on horseback along narrow mountain passes. Sticking to its timetable anyway, Germany issued the Morocco letter, contending that Germans in Agadir had come under heavy fire. Berlin told the French they would avenge this indignity by sending a naval presence. When the German gunboat *Panther* appeared menacingly in Agadir bay, it couldn't find a bona-fide German to defend, not even the one dispatched for that sole purpose. The gunboat was joined by the battleship *Berlin.*

When Wilberg, distraught and exhausted, finally arrived in Agadir, he couldn't catch the attention of the two anchored ships. Running up and down the beach, he threw up his hands and shouted like a madman. The sailors aboard the *Berlin* spotted him, but dismissed him as a crazed Moroccan. Only when he finally stopped in despair, arms akimbo, staring forlornly to sea, did a German officer realize that he must be European, since Moroccans didn't strike that pose. On the evening of July 5th, the Germans sent a boat to collect this precious cargo: the Endangered German.

The German press reacted with hysteria to the supposed brutality inflicted upon German nationals. On July 21, David Lloyd George, Britain's chancellor of the exchequer, warned Germany of possible war, inflaming the German jingo press still further. The French withdrew their funds from Germany as war fever grew contagious across Europe. When negotiations ensued between France and Germany, Regendanz sent a guardedly hopeful note to the Foreign Office: "The whole of South-West Morocco is a very rich country."[14] At the same time, he admitted that the ore deposits *might* be, well, inaccessible. He seemed to be letting the Foreign Office—or perhaps himself—down gently.

That summer, Max sent Regendanz on a tour to survey the economic potential of southern Morocco. When he finally set foot on Moroccan soil in August, Regendanz didn't find the flourishing countryside of his dreams, but only a stony, arid desert. "I have doubts whether the settlement of German peasants can seriously be considered," he wrote.[15] No fabled wealth was in sight, just a lawless backwater full of camels and bandits. As he poked around Morocco in early September, the Berlin stock market crashed and banks were hit by runs. By the end of his tour, a chastened Regendanz was advising the Foreign Office against taking steps to win southern Morocco for Germany. He had based his strategy on a mirage. Abruptly, Germany lost interest in this place that aroused such shrill and passionate outrage in early summer.

The upshot was that Germany, in exchange for French predominance in Morocco, extracted a slice of the French Congo and extra land in the Cameroons. A disillusioned Albert Ballin confided to Max his relief that the whole "Morocco Comedy" was over.[16] Far from being called to account for his costly machinations, Regendanz was decorated by the kaiser. Everybody papered over the embarrassing episode. Henceforth, Regendanz renounced force in securing land and favored a conciliatory attitude toward England. But the damage had been done, and nationalist tensions were already inflamed. Noting that the Agadir crisis had brought Europe close to war, Max regarded the last-minute solution as nothing short of miraculous.[17]

It seems fitting that Moritz died right before Agadir, for he wouldn't have understood such banker dabbling in politics. He thought bankers should stick to business. Conceding such an attitude as proper in Moritz's day, Max argued that banking had irreparably changed. "Nowadays such a happy isolation of one's capacity for work—an aloofness from national and community political activity—is hardly possible. . . ."[18]

———

For the Warburgs, the prewar summers at Kösterberg were a magical, luminous time. As Moritz had hoped, Felix and Paul often returned, bringing growing retinues of nurses, valets, and maids. Later on, these faraway summers would seem slightly unreal in their naïve, sheltered happiness. The Warburgs had reached a ripeness of experience they would never regain. The brothers were all married, had children, and were embarked on upward career paths. The world wasn't yet rent by strife that would make life difficult for an international banking family that relied upon tolerance and easy intercourse among nations.

It seemed that the German Jews might at last achieve full integration into society. They found it hard to separate their happiness from the prosperity and martial glow of the Empire. One summer, the children were whisked off to watch a medal-bedecked kaiser review cavalry troops in his parade dress. Another time, Max got Felix invited to the test run of the *Imperator*, with the emperor himself on board for the gala event. The twenty-one German and American grandchildren of Charlotte and Moritz Warburg grew up surrounded by Imperial paraphernalia, and would remember the swords and funny spiked helmets of the Hamburg police.

From the Kösterberg bluff, the Warburgs enjoyed a ringside seat to the spectacular pageant of German naval power. Below on the Elbe, ships glided soundlessly by. The children were taught to identify the flags and markings of the vessels and they even knew the shipping lines from their distinctive foghorns. These passing ships connected them to a larger world. As Paul's son Jimmy wrote, "From our house, high on the hills overlooking the Elbe, I could watch an endless procession of ships of many nations going to or coming from almost every part of the world. . . . At the approach of the big Hamburg-American liners I would run up to the attic to dip the American flag, hoping for and sometimes getting a whistle-blast salute in reply from one of the captains who knew the family as frequent passengers."[19] The world's biggest vessels slid down the Hamburg slipways, capped by the 54,000-ton *Vaterland* in 1913, apostrophized as the largest moving object ever created by mankind.

Whether German or American, the large brood of grandchildren was stamped with a common identity. For sports, they all donned the same big blue linen shirts with white collars. The Aby S. daughters even had special clothing made up for Kösterberg visits: white batiste dresses with French lace collars. The cousins rode, swam, played tennis, or went hiking along the cool, tree-shaded footpaths. During the long summer evenings, Max taught the children to ride the ponies given by Albert Ballin. Kösterberg featured a crowded social calendar, with every occasion celebrated by poetry or amateur theatricals directed by professional theater directors retained by the Warburgs. The children would remember these busy summers as both sweetly poignant and terribly regimented. Like adorable puppets, they were posed for photographs in costumed *tableaux vivants* designed for the adults' pleasure.

Moritz had bought Kösterberg for its quiet, rustic charm. Soon after he died, Max built an imposing Renaissance villa in 1912, a red-brick mansion of surprising formality for a bucolic setting. It was designed by the French architect who did the *Imperator*'s dining room. Max needed a place to hold court. He not only mingled with Christian high society, but had inherited his father's leadership of the Talmud Torah school and the Jewish Orphanage. The curved back rooms of his villa had a panoramic Elbe view. Max and Alice could entertain up to forty-eight people for dinner. Each summer they recruited a chef and two under-cooks from a fine Berlin restaurant, often dining *al fresco* on the flagstone terrace. Alice would assemble floral displays in gigantic vases while an orchestra provided after-dinner dancing by moonlight.

Like Felix at Woodlands, Max converted Kösterberg into a self-sustaining farm, which grew vegetables and provided fresh milk for the children. He laughed that each liter of milk cost him about as much as a bottle of Mumm champagne.[20] No aspect of Kösterberg life gave him such pleasure as landscaping. He hired a landscape architect named Else Hoffa. She was one of Germany's first female gardeners and had trained at Sans Souci, the palace built by Frederick the Great near Potsdam. Max agreed to pay her a 10 percent "annoyance premium" if she never bothered him with worries.[21] She hired seventeen gardeners to tend lawns, flower beds, and greenhouses. Early each morning, Max would inspect the gardens with Fraulein Hoffa and one child. Down by the river, she created a series of terraces with a rose garden leading down to a natural amphitheater and a Roman Garden with tall topiary shrubs that framed river views. Surrounded by English box trees, the sunken theater had grassy bleachers with room for two hundred guests to watch family theatricals. After night performances, the audience would dance in the Roman Garden and then each couple would carry burning torches up along the parkland paths and return for more dancing on the terrace of the main house. Only for Charlotte was Kösterberg sometimes sad. Olga's suicide and Moritz's death filled the estate with ghosts for her. But she had her own, long-anticipated pleasure: Ever since girlhood she had wanted to see Rome. Now in her early seventies, she began taking daily Italian lessons and, in December 1913, took Felix's daughter, Carola, to Rome.

About the same time that Max built his aristocratic villa at Kösterberg, he tore down the old bank building on the Ferdinandstrasse, which dated from 1836. For several years he had been buying adjoining properties. On one side stood a fish store that on hot days broadcast dreadful smells, forcing the brokerage department to keep its windows shut in summer. Max tried every ruse to expel this fishmonger. "We went so far as to instigate one of our employees to marry the rather elderly proprietor of the fish shop, but despite working on both victims the marriage did not take place."[22] In 1906, Max got the property.

Begun in 1911, the new M. M. Warburg building was finished and occupied two years later. A grand neoclassical building, it resembled the Speyer Building on Pine Street in New York, itself modeled after the Florentine palazzo of Pandolfini. It made no real concession to Hanseatic taste. With its rusticated base, pediment-topped windows, and rooftop balusters, it resembled the impregnable financial fortresses of Wall Street and the City of London. A block from the Inner Alster, its front corner offices enjoyed lake views.

The new building reflected both Max's eminence and his confidence. Although the bank had 111 employees, the new building could house three times as many. The interior shone with polished mahogany doors and wainscoting, and the long, narrow corridors were decorated with glass-encased model ships. Everything about the building radiated a glow of success. Indeed, the Warburg partners—Max, Fritz, Aby S., and Paul in New York—now sat on nineteen corporate boards. Fritz described the period from 1900 to 1914 as the "happiest and most harmonious" in the bank's history.[23] For a large old Jewish family, it seemed almost too good to be true. As it turned out, perfection had been achieved right on the brink of war, chaos, hyperinflation, and new nationalistic trends in German life that would blight the Warburg paradise.

As a cosmopolitan banker engaged in international finance, Max Warburg feared the mounting xenophobia gripping Europe. Like most Hamburg businessmen, he wished to preserve close commercial relations with England. His annual reports from the early 1900s show a fatalistic disbelief in the surface calm. Max and Ballin hoped England and Germany would settle their differences and form an alliance, yet the jockeying for colonies and the naval arms race dangerously sharpened friction between them.

Max and Ballin were in a paradoxical position. Vocal supporters of peaceful relations with England, they also embodied Germany's global ambitions. Max saw that German expansionism heightened tensions, but he also believed that the Fatherland merited a new dispensation in world affairs. And Ballin was an ardent friend of England, but was painfully aware that his own commercial success was a major irritant in Anglo-German relations. When Britain's Cunard line launched the *Lusitania* and the *Mauretania*, Ballin retaliated with the prodigious *Imperator* and the *Vaterland*. Once, reflecting upon his anglophile reputation, he said, "I am the only German who may justly claim that he lived in a thirty years' war with England for the hegemony in the field of commercial shipping. During this time, if I may use a bold comparison, I have taken from the British one trench after another and I have attacked again and again, as soon as I could find the means for it."[24]

Max hoped to reconcile the roles of fervent patriot nationalist and enlightened internationalist—a very Warburgian dilemma. In 1907, he created a sensation by delivering a Bank Day speech about Germany's lack of financial preparedness for war. With the Reichstag vice-president sitting beside a beaming Moritz, Max noted that the Reich gold reserves in the Julius tower at Spandau would be depleted within the first weeks of war. Yet Max was no warmonger, and in 1908 an episode occurred that filled him with foreboding. In a strident *Daily Telegraph* interview, the kaiser said the German people were generally anti-British and that Germany needed a large fleet to regulate Far Eastern problems. Max and Ballin were so dismayed by this imperial-scale blunder that they lobbied Friedrich Naumann, a Reichstag reform leader, for curbs on the kaiser's power.

In June 1908, Max introduced Ballin to Sir Ernest Cassel, Jacob Schiff's London associate. Max, Ballin, and Cassel were a trio of like-minded souls who dreaded a European war and tried to unite England and Germany. Their exchanges were frank, sometimes brutally so. At their first meeting in 1908, Cassel bluntly warned Ballin that Germany's commercial ambitions would end in war. When Cassel said that England would one day ask Germany to stop its aggressive naval program, Ballin said that the Royal Navy had nothing to fear. But, in reality, having supported the naval buildup under Admiral Alfred von Tirpitz, Ballin now had growing misgivings about its wisdom. The following spring, he suggested to the kaiser during Kiel Week that he broach the idea of naval arms limitation talks with Cassel.

In May 1910, the dying King Edward VII summoned Cassel for a chat, rising to greet his guest despite his own weakness. In memory of his royal friend, Cassel created the King Edward VII Foundation to assist needy Germans in England and vice versa. It was chiefly designed to preserve the eroding relationship between England and Germany, and Cassel recruited Max as its treasurer.

An alarmed British Cabinet allowed Cassel to travel to Berlin for secret talks in January 1912 and the kaiser agreed to assay private talks with a British cabinet minister. A month later, Lord Haldane, Britain's war minister, accompanied Cassel to Berlin to discuss an end to Anglo-German naval competition. The stock exchange buzzed with rumors of this secret visit. Max told Ballin that unless he and Cassel wore fake beards and wigs they couldn't disguise their presence. The initiative came to naught.

In another last-ditch peace effort, Sir Ernest chartered the HAPAG steamer *Ypiranga*, inviting six leading English couples and six German couples (Max and Alice among them) to sail around Scandinavia. As they steamed, they desperately tried to devise measures to avert the coming bloodshed.

Max dreamed up new alliances to forestall war. He was a shrewd man who yet had a quixotic streak in politics and a sometimes naïve capacity for wishful thinking. At one moment he thought Germany and England could ally themselves with Scandinavia; at another moment, he pictured Romania, Austria-Hungary, and Germany forming "a firm bulwark against the Slavs."[25] At one point, he even believed that Germany, England, and France could reach an understanding in time.

Max's colonial exploits now shifted to advancing German interests while also trying to bolster the alliance with Britain. When the Colonial Office fretted over France's banking monopoly in Morocco, Max and Regendanz visited London in February 1914 to negotiate with Lord Milner for a German-English Bank in Morocco. The scheme would prove an instant casualty of the war.

Under a secret Anglo-German treaty negotiated in August 1913, the two countries divided Portuguese colonies, promising Portugal a large loan in return. This was colonialism at its most nakedly highhanded: England took southern Mozambique and northern Angola, while Germany got northern Mozambique and southern Angola. The resourceful Regendanz devised an Overseas Study Syndicate led by M. M. Warburg & Co., which met with Colonial Office members in attendance. At Max's suggestion, the group financed an expedition to Angola to lay out a railway connecting this region with German Southwest Africa.

In May 1914, Max performed his last, doomed masterpiece of colonial intrigue. A Dutchman in London named Pieter Vuyk bought up from British investors a majority of shares in the Nyasa Consolidated Ltd. This obscure transaction concealed an immense design. As Max's London representative, Vuyk acted under instructions from the German Foreign Office, and the purchase implemented part of the Anglo-German pact of the year before. For about 150,000 pounds, Vuyk bought more than 70,000 square miles of territory in Nyasaland or northern Mozambique. In this territory, nearly the size of England and about one third the size of Germany, the new owners assumed the right to police the country, levy taxes, and collect customs revenues. Despite its colossal size, this property had little immediate productive value. The entire territory contained but a single car, which could only drive endlessly up and back on a single mile of paved road.

Max now exercised a political influence out of proportion to his bank's capital. He had to enlist the larger Deutsche Bank and Berliner Handels-Gesellschaft to raise the 150,000 pounds for the Nyasaland deal—a loan surreptitiously repaid by Berlin. The whole sub-rosa affair confirmed Max's growing stature in the German Foreign Office. When war broke out, the British confiscated the Nyasa shares as enemy property.

Perhaps the dazzling success of his British dealings blinded Max to war's imminence. He felt England and Germany had brokered a new relationship. He was not alone in his false hopes. In May 1914, Max discussed the matter with German Chancellor Bethmann Hollweg, during a trial run of the *Vaterland*. A slightly bent figure with a melancholy, professorial face, the chancellor praised Anglo-German relations and insisted that England surely would remain neutral if Germany invaded Belgium.

In late June 1914, after a dinner with the Prussian envoy in Hamburg, Max sat alone for an hour with an edgy kaiser to thrash out events. He was shaken by Wilhelm's dark vision of the future, his anxiety that Russia would attack Germany by 1916. As Max said, "He complained that we had too few railways on the Western front against France; oppressed by his worries, he even wondered whether it might be better to strike first rather than wait. I did not in fact have the impression that he was thinking seriously of a preventive war, but his gloomy assessment of the situation caused me dismay."[26] To counter this, Max counseled patience and said Germany's position would strengthen with time.

The kaiser's confessional monologue showed how far Max had risen in just a decade. Yet pigheaded and surrounded by sycophants, Wilhelm was often deaf to the advice of knowledgeable businessmen. In his *Memoirs*, Prince von Bülow said that German decisions leading up to World War I were taken in "hermetically sealed rooms in the Foreign Office, without once consulting a diplomat of experience, or any intelligent businessman informed on international economics. Albert Ballin, Max Warburg, and others—all might have been asked."[27]

When Max returned home after seeing the kaiser, his children found him more dejected than they had ever seen him. His irrepressible sanguine spirits soon returned. That June, he again showed that congenital optimism that would be both his strength and his undoing. He made three trips to London to participate in a Rothschild loan to Brazil. On June 26, Max, in an optimistic outburst, told Sir Ernest Cassel, "I hear that a terrific love appears to have broken out between the Germans and the English, which let us hope will be a lasting one."[28]

Two days later, Ballin telephoned from the Kiel races to inform Max of the murder of the heir to the Austrian throne in Sarajevo. "That means world war," Max shot back.[29] He thought he didn't quite believe his own words, that he must somehow be exaggerating. Indeed, both Max and Ballin knew that war would shatter their world. One day, historian Gustav Mayer asked Ballin what would happen to HAPAG if war with England came. Ballin clapped his hand on Mayer's shoulder and said, "Dear Doctor, when the sky falls in, all the sparrows will be dead."[30]

All through a sultry July, Max held on to his belief that England would remain neutral in a war. Eight days before war was declared, Sir Edward Grey and Haldane assured Ballin in London that England would stay neutral if Germany waged war against France or Russia. Ballin passed this on to the kaiser, who later became bitter about this misleading report. It cost Ballin his high standing at court, and he regretfully concluded that his optimistic assessment had encouraged German rashness.

In late July, Max evacuated his London representative to Amsterdam to ensure continued cable connections with New York. To the end, he maintained a psychological resistance to the idea of war. A week before the war began, Carl Melchior arrived at work later than usual. The elegant, understated Melchior said simply, "I have had my army boots prepared; we are going to have war." At first Max thought he had heard wrong, then sprang from his chair and exploded in a volley of arguments as to why war was sheer madness. Melchior calmly replied, "I believe you are mistaken this time."[31]

At the end of July, war rumors shut the Hamburg Stock Exchange. On August 1st, Germany declared war against Russia. As large amounts of money were withdrawn from banks, it provoked a severe cash squeeze, and Max helped to sustain friendly stock exchange firms. He had been blind to the coming crisis, but when the war came, he reacted with sangfroid that made him a magnetic figure. One Hamburg businessman would remember him at this moment as "a hero; he stands like a rock amid the surf, and anyone who comes into contact with him feels the comforting calm that he radiates."[32] The next four years would test the limits of that heroic calm.

On August 4, Hamburg church bells pealed from the slim steeples that graced the city skyline. Great Britain had declared war against Germany. Ballin reacted with stunned disbelief. As dusk settled over the lakes and canals, throngs of young people massed in the downtown streets, chanting, "We want war!"[33] Max was infected by the initial euphoria and couldn't fathom the pessimism of Ballin, who looked old and haggard after a sleepless night. As Max later recalled, "We were too confident, so much so that Ballin again and again shook his head at us."[34] Unknown to Max, a series of events had begun that would plunge the Warburgs into a twenty-year tailspin from which they would not recover.

The casualties seemed remote, victory assured, to Hamburg citizens that August. Later that month, thousands of jubilant people, including Max's son, Eric, gathered before the *Rathaus* to cheer reports that the British Army was in headlong flight. To delirious roars, the entire Senate emerged on the balcony in tailcoats, while the mayor read aloud stirring battlefield news. Swept by emotion, the crowd called for the German flag to be raised and spontaneously began singing, *"Deutschland, Deutschland über alles."*[35] Max's partner, Aby S., was sure the war would end by Christmas.

The euphoria reflected a repressed anxiety seeking release. On August 6, Max and Ballin drove to Berlin to discuss financial preparations for war. About twenty times, jittery young soldiers stopped them at gunpoint and searched their car for spies. Rumors of enemy infiltration raced through Germany. "Panic ruled the entire country," said Max.[36] Yet he found the government so blandly confident of victory that the chancellor asked him what reparations Germany should extract from its defeated foes.[37] Max saw the military firmly in the saddle, setting the tone of policy and guiding popular opinion.

Mirroring the adults' enthusiasm, the Warburg children were tremendously excited by it all. Each evening, they gathered at the Kösterberg gate, impatiently waiting for Father to bring home war news gleaned from the bank's superior telegraphic connections to the outer world. Max stimulated their interest by installing a large battlefield map in their nursery. In this miniature war room, the children tracked troop movements with pins and kept a running journal of events. In time, they would visit wounded soldiers as parts of Kösterberg were pressed into hospital service. At Fritz's house, the nationalistic cook reprimanded his daughters for saying "good-bye" instead of using the martial farewell "God punish England!"[38]

The war had a drastic effect upon Hamburg, as an Allied blockade cut off international trade. The merchant fleet was laid up or confiscated in enemy ports. The government seized dozens of Ballin's ships, plating the glamorous cruise ships with heavy armor and mounting guns on them. The cavernous immigration halls and railroad cars were converted into hospitals.

The war drew Max still deeper into government service. Banking activity now revolved around war loans, and M. M. Warburg dealt more with state enterprises than private businesses. Once again, Jewish bankers were guided by the state's needs. At the start of hostilities, more than forty employees of M. M. Warburg & Co. enlisted, and Max often hired women to replace them. Carl Melchior entered the war in a Bavarian regiment. On August 9, he was severely wounded when he fell from a horse in Metz and was rushed to a military hospital. This providential event freed Melchior for government work, and he would become an influential figure in the wartime economy.

At first Max advised the government to declare a moratorium on debts. Soon regretting this, he proposed instead that new war-credit banks be set up to service German industry. Max, Fritz, and Melchior worked on statutes for the new Hamburg Bank of 1914, a financing model copied throughout Germany. Max also helped to set up marine insurance and war metal companies.[39]

Throughout the war, Max Warburg's head was at war with his heart. A visceral patriot who responded to rousing calls of wartime citizenship, he also acknowledged the harshness of German military rule. In 1915, he traveled to Belgium, a neutral country subjugated by Germany despite worldwide protest. In a charred landscape full of German flags and officers, Max felt the tremendous hatred of the Belgians toward his compatriots and heard numerous reports of German atrocities. As he reported home, the Belgians "tell many stories of murder, theft, looting, etc, that one simply cannot refute."[40] He was appalled at how brutally Germany stripped Belgium of machinery and raw materials and then carted them home. He greatly admired a German administrator named Dr. Hjalmar Schacht, who agreed that this callous plunder of Belgium must stop. When Germany balked at feeding the Belgians, Max supported the relief effort directed by Herbert Hoover, telling Schacht that Hoover's group was "really admirable."[41]

With two influential brothers in America, Max had a privileged place in German state councils. Early in the war, he declined an invitation to become

German ambassador to Washington, explaining that he would never head a branch office—a retort he later regretted as arrogant.[42] In all likelihood, he had Paul's interests in mind, for Paul, as a German-born American citizen, had already been tarred by vicious gossip in Washington, and Max's presence would have worsened matters. Max's refusal also set a contradictory pattern for him. He would court power, then step back, afraid of the abuse he might suffer as a Jew.

Attuned to American opinion by his Wall Street tie, Max knew the disaster that would befall Germany if the United States entered the war. In July 1915, the Warburg bank sent a telegram to the Imperial Navy Cabinet, warning about a mounting anti-German mood in America following the *Lusitania*'s sinking—a warning that upset the chancellor. Max was both respected and suspected as an American expert. On October 15, 1915, he received a visit at home from Admiral Henning von Holtzendorff, who wanted Max's opinion on the economic impact of intensified U-boat warfare. Max replied that Germany couldn't win the war by sinking enemy tonnage and that U-boat warfare would only draw America into the war. He urged the admiral not to underestimate America's war potential.[43] Max was asked to jot down his thoughts for the Admiralty's general staff, a memo that was rather cynically reviewed. As Max recognized, ". . . in their answer they insinuated in oblique form that my interests in America had dictated my conclusions."[44]

Not for the first time, the German-American composition of his family gave Max a truer picture of events abroad, but also made him vulnerable to attack from unfriendly nationalistic parties. The imperial honeymoon of the German Jews was about to end.

CHAPTER 12

Uptown, Downtown

Even though the United States didn't enter the world war until 1917, the outbreak of fighting in Europe ushered in an awkward, uncomfortable time of mixed loyalties for German-American families in New York. During their *fin-de-siècle* idyll, they had enjoyed a hybrid identity, summering in German spas and marrying Germans while indulging their American patriotism at home. Before August 1914, this was no contradiction, and presented no conflict. Frieda Schiff Warburg spoke English to her mother and German to her father. After the war began, she and Jacob Schiff were strolling in Bar Harbor one day, chatting in German, when Frieda noticed accusing stares. "Father," she whispered, "we can't do this anymore."[1] Henceforth, speaking German in public was strictly *verboten*.

Besides having relatives in the old country, these German Jews strongly identified with German culture. How could they reconcile their traditional love of German song and literature with Prussian troops on the march? As Peter Gay has written, it was believed in Allied countries during the war that "there were really two Germanies: the Germany of military swagger, abject submission to authority, aggressive foreign adventure, and obsessive preoccupation with form, and the Germany of lyrical poetry, Humanist philosophy, and pacific cosmopolitanism."[2] It was this latter Germany that "Our Crowd" had so wistfully cherished in exile.

The gentile side of Wall Street, reliant on British money, was staunchly anglophile, making Jewish bankers reluctant to voice their true feelings. As Jacob's Schiff's granddaughter recalled, "A German teacher who taught us on walks in the park stopped coming after 1914, when the war started . . . in our world there was much talk of *les Boches*, the Huns and such."[3] Metropolitan Opera impresario Otto Kahn of Kuhn, Loeb purged German operas from the repertory, while Schiff lifted restrictions he had placed on a large bequest to Cornell University intended to promote German culture.

The situation created frightful anguish for Paul Warburg, who had just attained his dream of joining the Federal Reserve Board. Whatever his inner sympathy for Germany—which he couldn't root out overnight—he became an American official of exemplary dedication, arriving at the Treasury building at eight o'clock each morning, staying until six, then poring over reports after dinner. He felt strong continuity with his public service in Hamburg. As he told *The New York Times*, ". . . certain persons said to me that they wondered how I could devote my time to a political office in Washington. To me it was the most natural thing to do. I was a member of the lower house in the free city and republic of Hamburg before I became an American citizen. I was educated to believe that it was the duty of a citizen to give his time and best thought to the welfare of the state. This is not only the German, it is the European view."[4]

When war broke out, Paul was widely regarded as having America's most fertile financial mind. He and Henry Davison of the Morgan bank had induced their friend Ben Strong of Bankers Trust to take the pivotal post of head of the New York Federal Reserve Bank. Strong and Paul were the only recruits to the brand-new system tutored in foreign banking methods. "Frankly stated, we were a lot of 'greenhorns' with no guide or compass," observed Strong.[5] This placed Paul in a critical position in August 1914. As European stock markets and banks shut down, he faced the giant task of modernizing American finance to cope with its sudden emergence as global banker.

One side of Paul brimmed with hope and delight about America's new prowess as the foremost creditor nation. Despite his brief citizenship, he gave speeches flavored with a robust Yankee optimism, proclaiming, "The American colossus is moving." At a 1916 speech in Buenos Aires, this German-born banker, speaking in Spanish, declared it doesn't "take any degree of bold prophecy to foretell what the outcome must be. The United States now is and from now on will be one of the world bankers."[6] Paul's work with the Fed ripened his patriotism, making him an eloquent booster of American economic potential. "It staggers the imagination to think what the future may

Official photo of Felix Warburg
as chairman of the Joint Distribution Committee.
(American Jewish Archives)

have in store for the development of American banking," he told Minnesota bankers in 1915.[7]

At times, his adopted American identity only thinly covered his German sentimentality. The European war made him heartsick. Even as he suffered malicious accusations of disloyalty, he was shaping the Fed into a potent instrument that might someday be used to prosecute war against his native country. He was a gentle man, totally unsuited for war. As his son said, "[The war's] savage brutality—quite apart from anxiety for his relatives in Germany—filled him with sadness and dismay."[8] He tried to resolve his conflicted feelings by taking a pacifist approach, favoring American neutrality and a negotiated peace. He wanted a world without victors and believed that a vengeful, jingoistic attitude by the Entente powers would only harden the attitudes of German militarists. Yet he couldn't entirely suppress a pro-German bias either, which colored his views and weakened his influence. He was increasingly at odds with the Wilson administration, which maintained official neutrality while tilting toward the Allies. As Paul's son noted, "When Wilson was a neutralist my father thought he was wonderful; when he began to be an interventionist he didn't think he was so wonderful."[9]

The war years were a time of profound social discomfort for Paul and Nina. Shy and withdrawn, they didn't relish the nonstop entertaining and social rounds required by official Washington. Yet they faithfully performed their social duties and threw large dinner parties, creating a glittering Washington salon visited by Agriculture Secretary David Houston, Interior Secretary Franklin Lane, Justice Oliver Wendell Holmes, and Benjamin Cardozo. They felt most relaxed with other young couples, including Assistant Navy Secretary Franklin D. Roosevelt and Eleanor. However fond of Franklin, Nina would sigh regretfully, "He's really a beautiful looking man, but he's so dumb."[10]

With anti-German sentiment everywhere in Washington, Paul and Nina introduced a protective distance from German-Jewish friends and relatives. "In New York, my mother spent time with all these relatives, stout women with too much jewelry and pearls," said her daughter. "In Washington, they had to get rid of a lot of their Jewish friends. My mother got a book about palmistry. To make new friends she read everybody's palm."[11] Nina suddenly showed a poorly timed loyalty to Germany. One New Jersey friend told her that the Hoboken ferries were crawling with German spies and that she should get rid of their loyal German servants. Instead, Nina took some old Kösterberg retainers down to Washington and openly entertained the German ambassador, Johann von Bernstorff. Otherwise, Nina was a good political wife and proved adept at tipping off Paul to hostile characters.

With Germany at war, Paul worried about Max with a pure, selfless love not shared by his family, who thought Max exploited his younger brother's idolatry. "During the war, father kept saying that we can't do this and that because we have to save money for Max," said Paul's daughter. "Then, when we went to Europe after the war, Max was building hothouses."[12] Paul later confided to Max that for all his putative neutrality, he had never really severed his emotional attachment to the old firm. "I myself have never lost the feeling of belonging to the firm, even when the partnership ended in 1914 and temporarily so many ramparts were erected between us, as only a wayward world can erect."[13]

Paul's agile mind devised reasons why the United States shouldn't go to war against Germany. By going to war, America would surrender its position as a "balance wheel" in world politics, able to mediate among nations. If war came, he warned Colonel House, Americans might briefly be buoyed by patriotic fervor. "But the longer the war lasts the clearer will it become that the suffering and the burdens of the war will be out of proportion to its causes, and the feeling will gradually gain the upper hand that, after all, we should have kept out of it."[14] Paul fancifully wanted Wilson to summon a conference with the Allies and demand that they spell out their peace demands. If these were punitive, he thought, the United States could then refrain from entering the war. It was a logician's impractical response to an irrational world.

At least publicly, Paul maintained that he endured no personal abuse as the highest German-born official in wartime Washington. "At no time have I had a single unpleasant or annoying remark passed in my presence."[15] Yet a nonstop whispering campaign was spreading innuendoes about him. The British ambassador in Washington, Sir Cecil Spring-Rice, told Sir Edward Grey that a Jewish conspiracy, masterminded by Kuhn, Loeb, had infiltrated the American government, and he gleefully cited Paul as the cat's-paw. "Since Morgan's death, the Jewish banks are supreme and they have captured the Treasury Department by the small expedient of financing the bills of the Secretary of the Treasury . . . and forcing upon him the appointment of the German, Warburg, and the Federal Reserve Board which he dominates."[16]

In Spring-Rice's superheated imagination, Jacob Schiff controlled *The New York Times* and was manipulating it to destroy Britain. When the British Treasury sent Messrs. Paish and Blackett to negotiate a Washington loan, Spring-Rice's inventive prose soared. Of Paul, he said, "He practically controls the financial policy of the Administration and Paish and Blackett had mainly to negotiate with him. Of course it was exactly like negotiating with Germany. Everything that was said was German property."[17]

Such smears circulated on the American side as well. Treasury Secretary McAdoo harbored a terrible antipathy toward Paul, who wanted the Fed to be independent of the Treasury Department's meddling. In retaliation, Mc-Adoo exploited the xenophobic mudslinging and tried to poison Woodrow Wilson's mind against Paul. In August 1915, McAdoo told Wilson that Paul "doesn't offer to inform the board of the conversations with Bernstorff and Albert . . . with each of whom he is very intimate—especially with Albert."[18] (Dr. Albert was the German financial attaché.) These accusations about Paul's loyalty really served as a proxy for a power struggle over leadership of the Fed.

Paul was undoubtedly in a position to affect policy toward Germany, especially after Wilson designated him vice-governor of the Federal Reserve Board in August 1916. That November, Paul helped to draft a Fed statement cautioning American investors against accumulating too many securities issued by warring nations. This effectively penalized France and England, since Germany hadn't issued Wall Street loans. Some contemporaries spied a subtle plot to undercut the Allies. Edward C. Grenfell, the senior Morgan partner in London, warned the British Treasury that the Fed maneuver was the work of "Warburg and other German sympathisers. . . ."[19] Paul cited a patriotic American concern for excessive exposure to risky securities, a view certainly consistent with his habitual financial conservatism and fears of wartime inflation. But what motives lay at the bottom of his mind remain a mystery.

———

Like Paul, Felix sympathized with Germany and championed American neutrality. When Paul joined the Fed in 1914, Felix took over his M. M. Warburg partnership, which he kept until the United States declared war in 1917. Handicapped with this political liability, he "leaned over backward in his American neutrality," said Frieda, to avoid even the appearance of favoring Germany.[20] Felix was less complicated than Paul, a lighter, more extroverted personality, who didn't brood about politics. He was full of New World optimism, while Paul seemed freighted with Old World *Weltschmerz*. Yet Felix was deeply saddened by the war and the bloodlust it aroused in America. As he wrote to Schiff one day, "As you have no doubt seen in the papers, yesterday afternoon the Stock Exchange became weak on rumors of approaching peace, such is the brutality of humanity nowadays."[21]

The war dislocation sped Felix's rise as the crown prince of Jewish philanthropy. As the financial center of gravity shifted to Wall Street, the war transformed New York into the hub of world Jewish charity. Aristocratic European Jews who had hitherto supervised Jewish philanthropy could no longer discharge that duty. From his solemn house on Fifth Avenue, implausibly adorned with Italian saints and Madonnas, Felix would be the last great benefactor of the Jewish masses, sustaining scores of charities. The Lower East Side tenements were now bursting with more than half a million Jews from Eastern Europe, many of whom required relief. Felix knew such dependency bred hostility and wished to see philanthropy democratized. He told Schiff, "There is no doubt about it that there is a tremendously strong feeling against the leaders who, on account of their prominence in Jewish affairs, took it upon themselves to speak for the people at large without consulting them."[22] Yet he happily enjoyed the prerogatives of wealth. And if Felix had an easy, sympathetic way with the *Ostjuden*—not true of many German Jews—he didn't hesitate to flaunt his power in charitable affairs to dominate organizations. One shouldn't picture Felix, for all his good nature, as a shrinking violet.

Felix once said that he devoted 75 percent of his day to charity and 25 percent to banking—surely overstating the banking portion. Aside from partners' meetings, he had little direct involvement in Kuhn, Loeb transactions, even as a senior partner. (He did have a shrewd eye for spotting talent, enlisting from a local Savarin restaurant a boy named George Bovenizer, who later made partner.) He probably turned to charity both to please Schiff and to compensate for his own boredom with banking. He was an inimitable mixture of pure hedonist and dedicated philanthropist. Right before the war, his charity work switched into a higher gear. As president of the Young Men's Hebrew Association from 1908 to 1916, he led the drive to create a national organization in 1913 and as an American Museum of Natural History trustee after 1910, he helped to set up its pension fund.

The need for overseas aid grew pressing during World War I as hundreds of thousands of terror-stricken Jews fled before advancing czarist troops in the Austro-Hungarian Empire. The seven million Jews stranded in the Russian-Polish Pale of Settlement desperately needed help as they were hounded from their homes, a calamity for Jews already imperiled by grinding poverty and persecution. Also in need of emergency aid were the nearly one hundred thousand Jews living in Palestine under Ottoman rule, a vulnerable group consisting mostly of elderly people, who had gone to die in the Holy Land, and idealistic young settlers working for a new agricultural society. When Turkey entered the war on Germany's side in October 1914, Allied ships cordoned off the Palestine coast, blocking fruit and vegetable exports from Jewish farmers. In Constantinople, American ambassador Henry Morgenthau appealed to American Jewry to relieve Jewish suffering in Palestine.

To ponder solutions to these multiple crises, Jacob Schiff, Felix Warburg, and other prominent German Jews met at Temple Emanu-El in October 1914. The Yiddish-speaking Orthodox Jews of Eastern Europe had already set up a war-relief committee. The German-Jewish leadership now created an umbrella group to coordinate all relief efforts. Acting on a suggestion from Felix's secretary, Harriet B. Lowenstein, they called it the American Jewish Joint Distribution Committee. Lawyer Louis Marshall would be president, and Schiff, declining to become treasurer, gave the fateful nod to Felix. Some delegates feared that Felix's allegedly pro-German sentiments would displease Allied opinion. Nevertheless, he soon graduated to chairman of the Joint Distribution Committee, a position he would retain until 1932, followed by five years as honorary chairman. The Orthodox Jews eventually dropped out, and the following spring the fiery rhetoricians and trade unionists of the Jewish Socialists entered the committee's capacious tent.

The Joint Distribution Committee was a momentous, unprecedented step for American Jews, who were contentiously divided between rich and poor, German and Russian, starchy Republicans and rabble-rousing Democrats. Historian Allan Nevins has summarized its significance: "A truly heroic effort! This Joint Distribution Committee represented much the largest cooperative enterprise and the most unselfish suppression of old animosities and jealousies in the history of New World Jews."[23] Uniting several strands of American Jewry, the Joint—as it was affectionately and lastingly dubbed—required consummate diplomatic skills. Intuitive, quick-witted, honest, and with a debonair diplomatic touch, Felix was tailor-made for such mediation. Hating political infighting, he knew how to create harmony, avert factional squabbles, and massage the tender egos of rich donors. In 1916, Schiff praised Felix's feat in raising millions of dollars for the eastern Jews, telling Max it was the more remarkable "especially because, as you know from experience, our varied co-religionists are always ready to attach the most varied conditions to their gifts and are quick to criticize."[24]

The Joint's leadership had a conspicuous overlap with that of the American Jewish Committee, which represented the rich, acculturated merchant families of German ancestry. Yet the Joint provided common ground for Jews who had formerly enjoyed little contact with the wealthy segment; the groups tended to circle each other warily. The immense psychological distance between downtown ghetto dwellers and uptown bankers was exposed when Felix held a dinner at 1109 Fifth Avenue to merge the various factions into the Joint. Unlike the seventy-five guests who arrived in dinner jackets, two Russian Jews wore business suits and telltale red ties. Felix decided to eavesdrop on these two, who stood admiring his Italian art. He heard one say, "When Communism comes and there's a division of property, I hope I draw this house." Felix chimed in: "When Communism does come, and there is a redistribution of goods, I hope that if you do get my house, you will also invite me to be your guest, because I have always enjoyed it."[25] He strode off in a huff.

For the most part, the Joint tried to channel money to local groups, rather than to operate its own programs. It steadfastly remained nonpolitical. It raised money at large fund-raisers, often in a highly emotional atmosphere. As one participant recalled after Rabbi Judah Magnes spoke at one rally, "A million dollars were contributed; and women tore their jewels from their hair and threw them to the speaker."[26] Despite its federation structure, the Joint still relied upon the largesse of a small circle of extremely rich men, including Felix and Julius Rosenwald of Sears, Roebuck.

The Joint got immediate results. By March 1915, it had loaded a coal ship, the *Vulcan,* with nine hundred tons of food and medicine bound for Palestine. Despite wartime danger in the Mediterranean, the ship received a special dispensation from England, Turkey, and Germany allowing it safe passage, and Woodrow Wilson pled for its safety. The Joint frequently operated under hazardous conditions. In 1915, it sent two workers to Poland in the Joint's khaki uniforms. Apparently mistaken for Polish soldiers, they were killed by the Russian Army.

The Joint became Felix Warburg's all-consuming passion, turning him into the most powerful man in the most powerful Jewish charity in the world. Herbert Agar left this tribute: "If one man can be given the chief credit for building a strong and lasting machine out of such unlikely material, it is Felix M. Warburg of New York. . . . Among his many gifts, of kindness and tact and charm, Felix Warburg had supremely the gift of persuading people to work together. He made his neighbors ashamed to be quarrelsome, ashamed to be jealous while there was great work to be done. Perhaps no one else could have welded harmoniously the Joint Distribution Committee."[27]

Felix knew that charities had to contend with two everlasting enemies: the pomposity and vanity of large donors and the inefficiency of their bureaucracies. It dismayed him that fund-raising siphoned off up to 60 percent of funds collected. To counter this, he created in 1917 the Federation of Jewish Philanthropies to solicit money for seventy-five Jewish charities in New York's five boroughs. With Felix serving as its first president until 1920, the Federation turned into the "Our Crowd" charity par excellence. By pooling their fund-raising resources, individual groups saved money and avoided divisive competition, a successful pattern copied by Jewish communities across America.

—

Throughout the war, a cloud hung over Kuhn, Loeb, dimming its Wall Street standing and clearing the way for financial domination by J. P. Morgan & Co. From the outset, the firm refrained from financial operations with Germany, but doubts about its patriotism lingered. Schiff would issue carefully hedged statements, deploring bloodshed and predicting an early end to the war. Like

Paul and Felix, he favored a negotiated settlement, exhorting Wilson to offer his good services as a mediator. *The New York Times* published an exchange between Schiff and former President Charles Eliot of Harvard in which Schiff advocated a negotiated peace.

Yet his early actions spurred rumors of secret German sympathies. Amid August 1914 reports that Japan planned to enter the war against Germany, Schiff cabled his friend, Baron Takahashi, that such a move could damage Japan's financial standing on Wall Street. When Russia sent a financial agent to New York to explore a war loan, Schiff, bane of the czarist regime, campaigned to thwart him. He personally subscribed to a German war loan through M. M. Warburg, eliciting personal thanks from German under secretary Zimmermann. Again in early 1915, "out of devotion to the old Fatherland," he secretly lent one million dollars to Germany from his own account, a move Max reported in high German government circles.[28] As Schiff wrote a friend in 1914, "My sympathies are naturally altogether with Germany, as I would think as little to side against my own country as I would against my own parents."[29]

Such behavior was consistent with Schiff's family ties, his hatred of Russia, and his reputation as Wall Street defender of Germany. Early in the war, Max unthinkingly assumed that Schiff would sacrifice all for the Fatherland. He was instructed by the German Foreign Office to woo Schiff with the prospect of a German-American alliance in the Far East that could block Japanese advances and protect China's commercial riches for the West.[30] Ballin and Max hoped that Schiff would provide all-important credits for German food imports and Max told him excitedly how the German military would recruit Jewish officers in future. "That at least will remain, out of the horror of this war, as a benefit for the entire nation, as I anyhow believe that many barriers must and will fall."[31] Schiff had to enlighten Max that pro-British sentiment on Wall Street eliminated any chance of placing German Treasury bills there.

Max and Schiff had always been such strange bedfellows that they were destined to clash at some point. Schiff was so strict, proper, and correct, Max so funny, irreverent, and debonair. During Max's first American trip in 1911, Schiff had held a breakfast for him, inviting forty business leaders. After Max spoke on the European scene, he sat down again next to Schiff, who leaned over and told him bluntly, "Too short and not optimistic enough."[32] Max respected Schiff's frankness, even when he didn't relish it. But probably nothing prepared him for the burst of candor that would suddenly erupt from Schiff during the war.

As the war progressed, Max regarded England in a far more malevolent light than he had in early 1914, the war bringing to the surface all his latent chauvinism. He now revealed a profound suspicion of English arrogance, faulting its imperial sway over the high seas. Stirred by a very German sense of grievance, he saw the war's roots not in a German-English arms race or commercial rivalry, but mainly in a British lust for power. "The more one studies the prewar history," he wrote Schiff, "the clearer it becomes that England, which rules the seas in so ruthless a manner, was and is determined to do everything to oppress Germany economically and politically. . . ."[33] He reviled England for its mercenary "shopkeeper's" spirit.[34] In an August 1915 speech, Max argued that Germany should demand sizable reparations after the war—a notable view given that Max was to become an archcritic of the Versailles Treaty.[35] He said that England would have to recognize Germany as an equal power that needed new borders to accommodate its growing population.

Schiff's attitude toward Germany shifted strikingly with the sinking of the *Lusitania* off the Irish coast on May 7, 1915. The massive ship carried 1,257 passengers, 128 of them U.S. citizens. Wall Street was aghast at the carnage, and pro-German sympathy was now perilously taboo. In a remarkable concession, the proud, unbending Schiff walked over to J. P. Morgan headquarters at 23 Wall Street to express his sympathy. Finding the anglophile J. P. Morgan, Jr., in the partners' room, Schiff deplored "this most unfortunate outrage." Instead of accepting this gesture gracefully, Morgan grunted in disbelief and stormed from the room. Later realizing his mistake, Morgan grabbed his hat and rushed to 52 William Street to apologize to Schiff. This started Schiff's conversion to the Allied cause.

The *Lusitania* outrage threw Max Warburg into terrible confusion and torment, for he believed Germany had the right to engage in torpedo attacks so long as England tried to intercept American food shipments to Germany. He fumed that Wilson didn't take a tougher line with England to ensure an even-handed policy. At the same time, he called the attack "barbaric."[36] Paul Warburg had similarly ambivalent emotions after the *Lusitania.* Repelled by the slaughter, he argued that American citizens shouldn't travel on ships of belligerent nations. Yet he thought German submarine warfare in the North Atlantic a justified response to Britain's blockade of Germany.

Friction on Wall Street between the Jewish and Yankee banks flared into trench warfare during the summer of 1915 when President Wilson revoked a ban on loans for belligerent governments. That September, the British and French sent over a financial delegation, headed by Lord Reading, to raise money. They negotiated a $500 million Anglo-French loan with J. P. Morgan & Co. Irate over Russian persecution of the Jews, Schiff told Lord Reading that Kuhn, Loeb would only participate in the loan if "not one cent of the proceeds of the loan would be given to Russia." Even more than the Rothschilds, Schiff was always relentless in thwarting the anti-Semitic czarist regime. Lord Read-

ing rejoined that "no government could accept conditions which discrim-
inated against one of its allies in war."[37] Kuhn, Loeb now had to decide
whether to join the Morgan syndicate or to abstain.

For Schiff, it was an excruciating moment as self-interest contended with
sentiment. As he told Max, England and France had already bought hundreds
of millions of dollars in American products. Kuhn, Loeb, as an American
house, had to act in American interests. It was now presented with the simple
question, "do you want, as one of the foremost American financial houses,
whose example will have a great influence, to encourage the interests of the
country, or will your sympathies for Germany make you place these interests
last."[38] With the question posed so starkly, Kuhn, Loeb couldn't straddle the
fence. Otto Kahn and Jacob's son, Morti, wanted to slough off the firm's
pro-German reputation while Felix wanted to boycott the Anglo-French loan.
Max and the German government prodded Schiff to boycott the loan. Max
shocked and enfuriated Schiff by asking if he, Max, could go to the German
newspapers and advertise that Kuhn, Loeb would refuse a dominant role in
the loan.[39]

This set the stage for the most dramatic partners' meeting in Kuhn, Loeb
history. Contrary to his usual steely aplomb, Schiff came to the meeting
somber and agitated, the clockwork perfection of his life having broken down.
Rising gravely, he said, "I have thought about this situation all night. Before
asking your opinions, I want to tell you that my mind is made up, unalterably.
I realize fully what is at stake for the firm of Kuhn, Loeb & Company in the
decision we are going to make. But come what may . . . I cannot stultify myself
by aiding those who, in bitter enmity, have tortured my people and will
continue to do so, whatever fine professions they may make in their hour of
need."[40] The other partners couldn't override the omnipotent Schiff. The next
day's headline baldly trumpeted the decision to the world: "Kuhn, Loeb,
German Bankers, Refuse to Aid Allies."[41]

It was a severe blow to the firm in London and Paris, where the news
ratified long-standing suspicions about Schiff. The firm's pro-Allied partners
went out of their way to defy the decision. The dandified Otto Kahn—German-born but a naturalized British subject who had briefly campaigned for
Parliament in 1913—carried on his own one-man blitzkrieg against his
native country. He personally bought a $100,000 piece of the Anglo-French
loan and Morti Schiff also contributed, defying his father. Kahn donated his
London villa, St. Dunstan's Lodge in Regent's Park, to house blind British
veterans and wrote anti-German screeds and articles, including one dropped
in quantity behind German lines.

Schiff's decision had bitterly ironic repercussions. Kuhn, Loeb was violently
assailed in Germany, with the press stressing Morti Schiff and Otto Kahn's

consultation with Lord Reading instead of Schiff's refusal. Stung, Schiff wrote Max a letter in November 1915 that disclosed his true views about the war. Far from being a blind worshipper, Schiff saw disturbing features in German society. After telling Max that he felt piety toward the land of his forefathers, he shocked him with a withering critique of a Germany that subordinated the individual to the state, allowed undue military influence, and lodged obstacles to human freedom at every turn. Where Max had railed against English naval domination, Schiff now told him that German domination of the seas would be far worse, a death blow for free trade. In closing, Schiff said he had been tortured by his decision on the Anglo-French loan and had based his refusal, in part, on his high regard for Max and Felix.[42]

In reply, Max feigned understanding, saying Kuhn, Loeb had to support American interests and couldn't damage its French and English connections. Then he went on to portray Germany as seen through his own rose-colored spectacles. He limned Germany as an earthly paradise, with "no illiterates, no poverty, in short the circumstances which are well known to you. . . . I know, at least in Europe, of no place where I feel freer than in Germany." He scoffed at the notion that the Allies fought for freedom and warned that if the United States threatened Britain's economic standing, England would unite with other countries and turn on her.[43]

Schiff could never really make up his mind about Germany. When the pro-Allied partners at Kuhn, Loeb scotched participation in a Belgian Treasury issue that might have aided the German occupying powers, Schiff personally subscribed to these bonds and got his partners to make an unpublicized five-million-dollar advance to the Reichsbank.[44] Then, to mend relations with Wall Street and replenish French foreign exchange reserves, Kuhn, Loeb provided loans to Paris, Bordeaux, Lyons, and Marseilles in late 1916, with Felix alone dissenting from the move. Both business and family ties between the Warburgs and the Schiffs had been premised on an assumption of continuing harmony between America and Germany. Now history had driven a stake through that alliance, and the breach would not fully heal for many decades.

Nina and Paul Warburg with their children,
Jimmy and Bettina, and a surprisingly photogenic
black dog, Washington, D.C., 1918.
(Courtesy of Katharine Weber)

CHAPTER 13

Iron Cross

Max Warburg had always regarded German history as a pageant of progressive advancement for his people. He predicted that the war would open opportunities in government and the military, that the sacrifices made by Jewish soldiers would be redeemed by a new postwar equality. Fighting side by side, Christian and Jewish Germans would seal a lasting fraternal bond.

Responding to the chauvinism stirred by war, Jews flocked to serve under an imperial flag emblazoned with an Iron Cross and eagle. In August 1914, Jewish groups issued impassioned calls to arms, urging the community to enlist and refute anti-Semitic libels about their questionable patriotism. Leading Jewish intellectuals in the German-speaking world published a petition applauding Germany's war aims. Jews responded with supreme loyalty. Of a total population of 550,000 Jews in Germany, almost 100,000 served in the German Army, 10,000 as volunteers. More than 12,000 perished for the Fatherland and 31,500 were decorated with the Iron Cross for bravery.

German Jews generally were excluded from the officer corps. Nevertheless, they performed nobly. The war managed both to arouse hopes and to dash them. Especially galling was the bigotry Jews often endured from their superiors. As American ambassador James W. Gerard noted, "The Jews here are almost on the edge of being pogrommed. There is a great prejudice against them, especially in naval and military circles, because they have been industrious and have made money."[1] Only the rare Jew obtained a commission in the standing army.

In June 1916, Max felt outraged when the War Ministry demanded a separate count of Jewish war participants. Having been decorated with the Iron Cross, he protested to the chancellor in the most irate language. The so-called *Judenzählung* or Jewish census arose from nasty, anti-Semitic insinuations from Reichstag deputies that the Jews were lazy shirkers weaseling away from combat duty. The War Ministry never released the census results. In March 1917, Max met with General von Stein, the war minister, and pleaded with him to issue a statement that Jews and Christians had fought with equal bravery. Von Stein, a parson's son, refused. Saying he prized Jewish achievements in many fields, he also cited the disrespectful frivolity of Heinrich Heine as an example of Jewish traits that frankly repelled him.[2]

However fervent his love for Germany, Max's indignation over anti-Semitism deepened during the war. "I don't accept that a German Christian loves the Fatherland more than a German Jew," he insisted in 1916.[3] Later that year, he made a controversial speech, reviewing 120 years of Jewish assimilation. He noted that Jewish rights granted by law had never been fully translated into practice and mentioned a shortage or absence of Jewish army officers, professors, judges, high-level bureaucrats, academics, and farmers. At best, Jews were tolerated, not fully accepted.

He tried to forge a synthesis between Jewish feelings and official policy, proving that one could be an authentic Jew and a proud German. German overpopulation, he stressed, sharpened economic rivalry between Jews and gentiles—a view that dovetailed nicely with his advocacy of overseas colonies. To explain anti-Semitism, he cited Christian fears of being overrun by poor, illiterate *Ostjuden* before the native Jews were assimilated.[4] Max's socioeconomic analysis was too pat, too facile, and turned a blind eye to the murky, irrational depths of Germany's political culture.

As the first Warburg who ventured into the world of German big business, Max overlooked unpleasant realities one moment, then awoke and saw them with penetrating clarity the next. In 1913, he wrote a revealing letter to Aby S., warning that they should not be misled by a lack of visible anti-Semitism in Hamburg since much latent anti-Semitism festered there. ". . . I notice it every time that, one way or another, I take an interest in neglected people."[5] Anti-Semitism under the kaiser, if often subtle, indirect, and easily overlooked, was nonetheless quite real.

To protect the Jewish community, Max counted upon the support of the Hamburg Senate, which was elected by the *Bürgerschaft*, not by popular vote.

These worthies had never chosen an unbaptized Jew for the Senate. As a *Bürgerschaft* member himself, Max steadfastly supported Jewish causes. In 1914, standing for a Senate seat, he was defeated by a slim margin of three votes. Almost universally, the press praised him as smart and able, attributing his defeat to anti-Semitism—a stinging rebuke for someone so unstintingly devoted to the war effort.[6]

Since the German Army allowed few Jewish officers, many prominent Jews entered wartime economic ministries. As the Allied blockade drove up food prices and provoked riots, secure food supplies became a top priority. Early on, Max suggested that food purveyors be placed under state supervision to prevent profiteering. Max, Ballin, and Melchior helped to organize the Imperial Purchasing Company, later called the Central Purchasing Company, to import food under government auspices.[7] The Warburg bank advanced payment and provided foreign exchange for such imports. In 1915, after Max proposed to Berlin that Germany court Romania with commercial contracts, the Foreign Office dispatched Melchior there, where he signed contracts for millions of tons of grain for Germany.

At the time, German Jewish patriotism didn't seem foolishly misplaced. As German troops swarmed into Polish territory formerly occupied by czarist Russia, they were greeted as saviors by Jewish inhabitants. While advancing Russian troops unleashed terrifying pogroms, Max worked to ensure that German occupation armies didn't punish Jews. Fretting over the long-suffering *Ostjuden*, richer German Jews still felt *they* were the invincible European Jews. Yet they worried that an influx of eastern Jews into Germany would subvert their own, still tenuous, standing. With their yarmulkes, black hats, shtetl folklore, and exuberant manner, eastern Jews stood out in German cities, embarrassing their elegant German brethren as ragtag reminders of a past that they wanted to forget and seeming to reinforce certain Christian stereotypes of Jews.

This status anxiety among German Jews produced a serious rift in wartime relief efforts. The Joint Distribution Committee in New York channeled large amounts of money to needy Polish Jews through M. M. Warburg & Co. By the time the United States entered the war, the bank was conduit for nineteen million marks in relief money. Many American Jews—especially Zionists such as Louis Brandeis—resented that this money was controlled by The Aid Society of German Jews in Berlin, of which Max was a member.[8] In letters to Felix, Brandeis accused the group of being pro-German and anti-Zionist and also complained that the Aid Society disseminated German propaganda in occupied territory to ingratiate itself with Berlin. The sorest point was that the Aid Society favored the *Grenzsperre*, a ban on emigration of Polish Jews into Germany.

After initial reluctance, Jacob Schiff sternly protested to Max Warburg.

Conceding that German Jews might be hurt by an influx of *Ostjuden*, he lectured that they were obligated to accept them. In high dudgeon, Schiff charged that German Jews were driven by "a purely selfish point of view which is entirely incomprehensible to American Jews generally and to me personally."[9] What if America had shut its doors to Russian, Polish, and Romanian Jews? Schiff asked rhetorically. It would surely have raised a hue and cry from European Jews.[10] On June 20, 1916, with Felix abstaining, the Joint voted to stop routing money through German-Jewish organizations. Max bitterly told Felix that the bank would only handle relief money distributed through the Aid Society. If bridling at the Joint's decision, Max understood that Felix, as chairman, was now powerless to stop it. As Max told him, "I know that you cannot help it, but are pushed by the dear Zionists."[11] Felix said the Zionists posited a deep cabal between the Warburg brothers: ". . . that Brother Max and I stick together is their firm conviction."[12]

In relief work, Max routinely cleared his moves with the German Foreign Office. "There was probably no German private banking firm that issued guarantees on behalf of the German Empire to as great an extent as we did," he wrote. "To that degree it is certainly true that we partially co-financed the war; especially in connection with purchases made in neutral foreign countries, where we had to give our guarantee."[13] The Reichsbank guaranteed so many Warburg loans that Max dreaded the prospect of Germany losing the war and the Reichsbank being unable to honor its numerous guarantees. If that happened, Max said, they might as well place an ad in the paper, saying, "M. M. Warburg & Co. stopped their payments on the field of honor."[14]

In 1917 Max was again thwarted in his bid for the Hamburg Senate. Competing against an undistinguished figure, he thought he had the contest wrapped up. The custom was for the victor to receive well-wishers in his home on election night. That Friday evening, Max raced home and debated whether to wear his tailcoat or tuxedo only to learn by phone that his opponent had won. Bravely, he made excuses, contending that the late hour had caused many members to depart before the vote, while other inebriated members had marked the ballot incorrectly. Aby, who wasn't fooled, reacted stormily. Max was soon cheering up those who came to console him. Never one to brood or bear a grudge, he searched for some redeeming feature and said his victory might only have incited anti-Semitic feeling. In the end, he and his family, including Charlotte, sat down to enjoy their usual Friday night dinner.[15]

—

For Aby Warburg, the war fulfilled his bleakest premonition of the triumph of madness over reason. The strain of the war shattered his ever delicate mental balance. Three weeks into the war, heeding his "prophetic belly," he gloomily predicted a German defeat. Early victories that sparked wild transports of joy in Hamburg only further depressed him. "We have triumphed to death," he said.[16]

The war's timing was tragic for him. In spring 1914, he had discussed his plans to turn his library into a research institute with his protégé, Fritz Saxl, but it proved a lovely, evanescent dream. When war broke out, Saxl was drafted by the Austrian army and plans for the institute were scrapped amid the general madness.

The usual tale of Aby's reaction to the war stresses his early pessimism and horror at bloodshed and conjures up a portrait of a sensitive, humane, reasonable soul. Unfortunately, Aby was intensely partisan, sometimes fanatically so, with an extremely slanted and one-sided view of events. He regretted the violation of Belgian neutrality, memorably saying that Germany now wore patent-leather shoes grotesquely spattered with bird shit.[17] Yet he vehemently defended German troops against accusations of civilian atrocities, saying they had been fired upon by snipers.[18] He was dismayed only by Allied barbarism against Germany. Even his early foreboding that Germany would lose was offset by countless, chauvinistic statements that it must and would win. In Aby's wartime correspondence, there is scarcely a cool, considered word to be found. He is less the apostle of reason than the embodiment of wartime belligerence.

During the war's first weeks, Aby wandered about in anguish, tortured by insomnia and gory, nocturnal visions. Each morning, he awoke with renewed disbelief that Europe was engaged in this mass act of suicide. Every death disturbed him. In January 1915, Aby S.'s grandson, Franz, died from an exploding shell on the Somme and Aby M. wrote his mother: "War swallows the best. We are stoking the furnace with pianos."[19] Feverish, restless, too old to fight and suffering from diabetes, the forty-nine-year-old Aby contributed to war charities, swapped news on street corners, and recorded battles in his diary. He wrote to Paul in Washington, hoping that Paul could counteract anti-German "slander" and get Americans to read German newspapers.[20]

Baffled by his own impotence, Aby decided to combat the Allies with the sole weapon at his disposal: his library. Everything must be subordinated to the war effort. Instead of chronicling art history—which he never entirely ceased to do—he began to catalogue the war, clipping eight or nine Hamburg and foreign newspapers daily. Soon file cabinets stuffed with clippings sprouted beside the bookshelves. Aby's student, Carl Georg Heise, pictured the library as a battlefield and Aby as its commanding officer. Eventually, Aby would accumulate some 25,000 excerpts from wartime news.

At first, this attempt to systematize the unspeakable gave the embattled

Aby an illusory sense of mastery over events. Then the effort grew so strenuous and massively exhausting that he had to dragoon the three children into
the effort and they hated copying out the extracts from the papers. When Aby
developed a sore shoulder, Mary had to serve as his secretary. Jim Loeb, who
spent the war in Germany, told Panina, "I have been trying to get Mary to
come here for a while, but I fear Aby will not let her off. Poor little woman;
she barely can call her soul her own!"[21]

Aby's wartime catalogue is often portrayed as a high-minded attempt to sift
fact from the fog of deceit. In fact, Aby was only enraged by supposed lies
directed against Germany and had no interest in discrediting home-grown
propaganda. He only saw his virtuous Germany unfairly maligned by a
malicious, uncomprehending world and blamed the press, not politicians or
generals, for the war. "Without the profligacy of the lying press, the war
might never have come about."[22] He envisaged a later war-crime trial in
which Germany would expose libels from the Allied press. Writing to busy
newspaper editors, Aby beseeched them to note down precisely the source of
anti-German statements. Only with such citations, he told an editor, "can the
material be reliably gathered for the 'Handbook of Lies' which must be written
after the war."[23] Editors must have been bemused by this strange, importunate little man who expected pedantic exactitude from harried war reporters.

Aby undertook one diplomatic mission. In 1914, Italy wavered whether to
side with Germany or defect to the Entente powers. Since Aby had lived in
Florence, spoke fluent Italian, and adored the country, he seemed an ideal
emissary for Germany. At a September 1914 meeting with Prince von
Bülow—soon to be named a special German ambassador to Italy—Aby offered to edit a new illustrated quarterly in Italian to keep Italy as a German
ally. The first issue of this *Rivista*, vetted by von Bülow himself, appeared in
October. In November and again in January 1915, Aby went to Italy to lobby
old friends and reported on his talks to von Bülow. He was so agitated that
his doctor only allowed him to make the second trip after he had rested for
eight days beforehand.

When Italy joined the Entente that spring, Aby felt deeply betrayed and
melodramatically likened Italy to a dear old friend stabbed to death by street
assassins. He insisted that the Italian government had acted in the face of
overwhelming popular goodwill toward Germany. As he told a former assistant, "It's a pity that one can't suddenly die from an attack of nausea. Incidentally, I will help to annihilate Italy, however and where I can. This bordello
must disappear."[24]

One cannot fathom Aby's venom without realizing that he viewed the war
as a struggle for supremacy between two highly unequal cultures. He saw
Germans as civilized and humanistic, Anglo-Saxons as venal barbarians.

Germany fought for freedom, and England, then America, for booty. He believed implicitly in the superiority of Germany and Italy, whom he pictured leading a European struggle for cultural dominance against the Far East. When Italy defected to the Allies, it blurred the clear-cut moral lines that had simplified the war for him and made it a holy cause. Good and evil were now frustratingly mixed up.

Despite the family ties to England and America, Aby thought that the two countries represented a rising new order of decadent, philistine materialism. As he told Paul, "Let them pay—that is the only maxim in which Anglo-Saxon culture believes. But there are ideological reactions and struggles for freedom that one can't suppress with gold and lies."[25] Aby so demonized Anglo-Saxons that he devised propaganda slogans for use by the German press that reflect a highly personal detestation. Contacting newspaper editors, he encouraged them to employ the slogan, "Britannia rules the slaves" instead of "Britannia rules the waves." The slaves were the United States and Italy. He suggested to one editor that an allegorical figure of Britannia be shown cracking a black and gold whip over an Italian *condottiere*.[26] To another editor he proposed that the United States should be referred to as the United Northern Slave States of America.[27] These mean-spirited gibes are the more remarkable when one realizes that Paul and Felix were sustaining Aby's cultural pursuits with American dollars.

In fairness, one must stress that Aby was already undergoing a slow-motion mental disintegration. His mind teemed with images of nightmarish intensity as he spoke of a planet streaming with blood, of a stormwind carrying off the delicate blossoms and leaves of German youth, of the wide, screaming mouth of heavy industry devouring the intellectual world. Upon first hearing rumors of peace in 1915, he grumbled, "The unchained beast must first drink up more blood."[28]

Aby's belief in German culture was echoed by Jim Loeb, now spending his ninth summer in southern Germany. Aby was delighted when Jim decided to ride out the war at his estate. Jim spent the war playing Beethoven and Brahms in the great hall of Hochried with its full organ. He thrilled to the mystical strains of Wagner and listened to friends reading aloud from Goethe's *Faust*. Like Aby, he was contemptuous of the Italians' betrayal, referring to them as "greasy traitors" while praising the Germans as "this uncomplaining, great heroic people."[29] Jim expanded his potato patch at Hochried to aid the war effort and gave a whopping one-hundred-thousand-mark donation to the War Relief Agency. No less than Aby, he clung to the view that Germany was fighting off the barbarian hordes.

—

The war thrust not only Max, Paul, and Felix into prominence, but even Fritz—the goggle-eyed younger brother with the walrus mustache. As chairman of the Hamburg Metal Exchange, he was tapped for the advisory board of the War Metals Company, which ensured a ready supply of raw materials for Germany.[30]

In 1915, Max traveled three times to Sweden at the behest of the Foreign Office and vainly attempted to get Foreign Minister Knut Wallenberg to abandon neutrality and fight with Germany. As soon as Wallenberg noted Sweden's extensive trade ties to England, the talks were frostily terminated. Max then advised the Foreign Office to send a commercial attaché to Sweden to foster trade, and Fritz was assigned to the Stockholm embassy as an economic adviser. He never received an official rank, giving him greater leeway to conduct barter deals.

Slated to stay in Stockholm for two weeks, Fritz ended up staying in Sweden with his family until the armistice. His friend Baron von Lucius, the head of the German legation, relied on him in business negotiations. No slouch, Fritz obtained a large loan for the Reichsbank and arranged a big swap of Swedish ore for the German coal that kept Swedish railroads running. He bartered German potash for Swedish lard, German coal for Swedish horses.

For Fritz and Anna Beata, the war years in Stockholm meant a pleasing respite from the eternal social domination of Malice. Anna, who came from the Swedish Warburgs, founded a Fröbel society there to promote progressive kindergarten work. She befriended Elsa Brändström, the daughter of the Swedish ambassador in Moscow, whose nursing work with German prisoners in Russia would earn her the title of the Swedish Florence Nightingale. Together, the women co-authored a children's book, *What Should We Do?*[31]

In July 1916 Fritz stumbled into the history books quite by accident. A Russian delegation was passing through Stockholm on its way home from financial talks in London, when a Count Olsufjew asked to meet a German from the economic sphere. Having sounded out the mood in France and England, he said offhand, he wanted to do the same for Germany. The casual request concealed a serious agenda. During talks at the Foreign Office in Berlin, Fritz had received instructions to follow up on such overtures, and von Lucius encouraged him to meet with the Russians.[32] (In Max's version, Fritz went only because von Lucius had left Stockholm the day before.[33]) Perhaps to give the German government some self-protective distance from the talks, Fritz claimed that he attended the Grand Hotel meeting with little official coaching and that he was astonished when the door opened and Alexander Protopopov, vice-president of the Russian Duma, strolled into the room. Suddenly Fritz was engaged in high-level, if discreetly unofficial talks, looking toward a separate peace between Germany and Russia.

In his opening remarks, Fritz was careful to stress that he was voicing his own views and not those of his government. He insisted that Germany had the stamina and resources to fight a protracted war, but that its real grievance lay with France and England, not Russia. He proposed a swap in which Germany would get Baltic territory and Russia parts of German-occupied Poland, followed by stepped-up trade between Russia and Germany.[34]

Again soft-pedaling the affair, Fritz later said that the conversation was improvised on both sides and that the German Foreign Office was skeptical of its success. In Russia, Protopopov faced a violently hostile reception. He made a presentation that seemed to impress the vacillating Czar Nicholas II. But when the secret talks became known, they were denounced by pro-British Russian liberals, and Protopopov, in self-defense, alleged that Fritz had initiated the talks. More a pawn than a master in this intricate chess game, Fritz was kept in the dark about parallel peace overtures that Germany was making toward Russia. Only after the war did an official correspondent inform him, "Your negotiations with Pr. and O. were only a link in a longer chain."[35] In November 1916, Germany announced an independent Poland and tried to recruit Polish volunteers, an inflammatory step that killed any chance for further peace talks with Russia.

When the Nazis later rewrote this history to suit their needs, the modest, unassuming Fritz was villainized for his "treacherous" part in the Protopopov affair. In 1925, Nazi publicist Theodor Fritsch insisted that Fritz had fumbled a sure chance for a separate peace in 1916. Such a peace, Fritsch declared, would have simultaneously assured German victory and spared Russia the Bolshevik Revolution. Fritsch asserted that any patriotic German diplomat could have successfully concluded the talks. So, in one deft stroke, the Nazis alleged that Fritz had wrecked Imperial Germany, advanced the Communist cause, and changed the entire course of European history.[36]

—

By 1916, the war that had sent cheering, delirious throngs into the *Rathaus* square in August 1914 had produced a dull feeling of oppression. With groceries scarce, the turnip formed the staple of the Hamburg diet. As food supplies dwindled, grim lines lengthened before stores. A third of the Hamburg population had to resort to huge public eating halls. The food shortages produced charges of rampant graft, resulting in strikes and police crackdowns. That September, women and students rioted, shouted "Down with the kaiser," and demanded an end to the war. As Max said of 1916, "Life took on a dreary, joyless heaviness."[37]

With the economy so dismal, Max fetched business from unlikely places. One day in 1917, he got a visit from Carl Hagenbeck, founder of the Hamburg zoo. With even humans scrounging and scavenging for food, it was prohibitively expensive for Hagenbeck to feed his beasts and he needed to borrow eight thousand marks. Max hesitated to lend money to sustain zoo animals in near-famine conditions and only agreed on the proviso that he take a mortgage on the rhinoceros. It was an inspired step: After the war, he sold the rhino to the Budapest zoo and recouped his money.

If Max fell prey to many delusions over the years, he foresaw with crystal clarity the folly of Germany's unrestricted U-boat warfare and accurately predicted that such a strategy would ensure America's entry into the war. In December 1916, Paul sent Max a letter through an intermediary that said the Allies had nearly exhausted the market for American loans but that U-boat warfare would foster sympathy and expand that market.[38] Having the benefit of Paul's wisdom, Max knew better than German military leaders exactly what U.S. entry would signify, but was often ostracized by officialdom. When Hamburg's Chamber of Commerce appealed to the kaiser in early January 1917 to start unrestricted submarine warfare, Max emphatically protested. But he could now voice his dissenting views only within a shrinking political circle.

He made two last attempts to modify policy. On January 20, 1917, he dined with Arndt von Holtzendorff, HAPAG's Berlin agent, and Karl Helfferich, the Imperial Treasury secretary, his most influential ally on the submarine question. As Max warmly argued the need to refrain from U-boat attacks, he could tell from Helfferich's skeptical expression that he had lost his last ally. German leaders didn't believe that America would wage war in retaliation. After Wilson sent his peace message to the U.S. Senate on January 22, Max implored the German Foreign Office to respond constructively and made a prophetic plea: "If it comes to war with America, we will boost the moral, financial and economic strength of Germany's enemies to such an extent that we can hope for nothing more in the future; that is my firm conviction. . . ."[39]

By chance, Max lunched at his club with Admiral von Holtzendorff and Arthur Zimmermann on January 31—the fateful day Germany announced the open U-boat campaign. Rather than finding his naval companions buoyant, he saw that they were subdued and depressed, as if secretly uncertain of their views. In early February, Wilson broke off diplomatic relations with Germany. During the next two months, even Paul Warburg argued that America should join the war if Germany didn't halt its misguided campaign of submarine terror. By April 6, 1917, the United States joined the war, as Max had predicted. For the German-American Warburg family, it was a disaster of unimaginable proportions and inexpressible grief.

Charlotte wrote a touching letter to Woodrow Wilson. Saying that there must be other mothers like her with sons on both sides of the ocean, she asked whether there was no chance of ending the war. Before the U.S. entry into the war, letters had still united the German and American Warburgs. Small and buxom but still energetic, Charlotte sat at her desk, a jar of boiled drinking water beside her, writing to her children in New York. She kept their return letters in a basket in the breakfast room and read them aloud whenever the entire family assembled. After April 1917, the Warburgs were cut off by an impenetrable wall. Occasionally, travelers brought smuggled letters from America, but these couriers were unreliable. One got scared and threw a packet of letters overboard on a transatlantic liner, causing Felix to throw up his hands in despair. "Such a *schlemiel!*"[40] For Max and Paul, who had corresponded so copiously, it was a strange, disorienting interlude. As if they had been Siamese twins, Max said he felt separated from his second self.[41] Felix now had to relinquish the M. M. Warburg partnership he had inherited from Paul in 1914.

The mood in New York now tended to anathematize all things German. Schools dropped German from their curricula and Beethoven's noble music vanished from the repertoire. For three years, "Our Crowd" had been grievously torn in their allegiance and suspected of subversive sympathies. War at least solved their identity crisis. Now they could invoke *force majeure* and support the Allies with stout hearts. Peace broke out at Kuhn, Loeb as partners courted the Allies. Suffering from heart trouble, Jacob Schiff adopted a strong anti-German posture. In March 1917, he told former Harvard president Eliot that because of the "ruthless and inhuman acts of the German Government, my attitude has undergone a thorough change, and I now only hope that before very long, Great Britain and France will be able to force a peace. . . ."[42] A year later, he was so incensed at Germany that he favored an all-out military victory that would "utterly and permanently do away with Germany's military establishment, which has proved the worse of the entire world."[43]

The czar's fall in early 1917 removed Schiff's last qualms about aiding the Allies. Foreseeing an end to state-sponsored anti-Semitism, he applauded the Menshevik revolution as "almost a miracle . . . almost greater than the freeing of our forefathers from Egyptian slavery."[44] Schiff advanced one million rubles to Alexander Kerensky's government—a loan he lost six months later when the Bolsheviks came to power. Later, the Nazis blamed Schiff and the Warburgs for having hatched the Bolshevik Revolution when they had merely supported the moderate Mensheviks. As noted earlier, Siegmund and Théophilie's daughter, Rosa, had married Baron de Gunzburg and they lived in a gorgeous St. Petersburg mansion near the czar's palace. On July 10, 1917, Felix greeted Baron de Gunzburg when he arrived in New York to enlist support for the Kerensky regime. After the Bolsheviks seized power, soldiers entered the de Gunzburgs' house and cleaned out their wine cellar. The baron was imprisoned and released only with difficulty. He and his family fled Russia and he ended up as a director of an Amsterdam bank.

Extremely blue after the United States severed relations with Germany, Felix told his son, "I am especially sorry that we are being brought into this mess as our chance to be the mediator and therefore the most influential power in the world has, I am afraid, been lost, and we become simply one of the many scrappers."[45] Once the United States was actually at war, Felix knew any further discussion was inappropriate and supported the war effort with his usual robust gusto. Like many German-born Jews, he was at pains to erase any residual suspicions of disloyalty and showed an exaggerated patriotism, wrapping himself in the red-white-and-blue. Felix became head of the USO, donating his small speedboat to the government's "Mosquito Fleet," and offering the YMHA building to the government as training quarters. He even had the steward at Woodlands stop feeding expensive lump sugar to the pampered horses.

Paul buried himself in war work, as the Fed and Treasury Department sold billions of dollars in Liberty Bonds. "The marketing of Liberty Loans and the procurement of capital for our infant war industries seemed his only concern," said his son.[46] Paul still tried to devise ways to end the conflict speedily. Like Max, he thought in terms of concessions that should be made to Germany, not *by* Germany. In August 1917, he told Colonel House that if only France would renounce claims to Alsace-Lorraine, reason would prevail in Germany and the military party would collapse. By virtue of his position, Paul found it harder than Felix to shake the stigma of being a pro-German sympathizer. One day in October, Supreme Court Justice Louis Brandeis ran into him on a Washington street. As Brandeis told his wife afterward, "He [Paul] is strong for peace now—'when America is at its might' & its word law with the Allies."[48]

For Paul and Felix, the war exposed a cultural chasm that separated them from their children. Like other immigrant parents, they had encouraged their children's assimilation into American society, then were pained and surprised when they succeeded. The generational shift was most striking with Paul's son, Jimmy. Where Paul was self-effacing, he spawned an expansive American son with a mile-wide rebellious streak, a taste for experimentation, and few inhibitions. Jimmy inhabited a brave new world of infinite possibility. Extremely handsome, loaded with brains and charm, he wanted to burst out of the family's Jewish ghetto. He struggled with an array of fugitive impulses that his father had mastered with formidable self-discipline.

Born in Germany, Jimmy and sister Bettina felt at home on two continents and became naturalized American citizens along with their father in 1911. Jimmy carried indelible memories of the military pomp of Imperial Germany. With a weakness for parades and uniforms, his childhood nurse would take him to see the kaiser whenever he visited Hamburg. Jimmy would always fancy himself an expert on Germany and muse about its fate in a very personal way.

Although Jimmy had immense respect—bordering on hero-worship—for his father, he also struggled with deep, unacknowledged resentment. He saw his father as saintly and noble, but also as repressed and limited in his sympathies for people. Jimmy located a psychological basis for his own stronger identification with America than Germany "because my mother was American and always considered it rather a sacrifice to live in Germany."[49]

In photos of this bespectacled adolescent during the war, he looks confident and foppish, a dapper rich boy with dimpled cheeks and a touch of boyish arrogance, his chin lifted in pride and defiance. As an editor of the Harvard *Crimson* his junior year—an exceptional achievement for a Jewish student—Jimmy showed how thoroughly Americanized he was. His sentimental ties to Germany dissolved early in the war as he seethed over the *Lusitania* incident and Germany's violation of Belgian neutrality. Feeling shame and anger at his German background, he contended that "the constant saber-rattling of the German Kaiser, the ruthlessly aggressive thrusting of the new German nation into the world arena . . . probably warrant the judgment that Germany contributed more than any other single nation to the outbreak of World War I."[50]

While Paul struggled with his sympathy for Germany, Jimmy fairly gloried in his pro-Allied sympathies. He came to the cause in a way calculated to hurt Paul. One day, Jimmy's classmate, Archie Roosevelt, invited him to breakfast with his famous father, who fulminated against the "skulking cowardice" of Wilson and the "evil wickedness" of the kaiser.[51] Jimmy had accepted, even though he knew Paul loathed Teddy Roosevelt. In the *Crimson*, Jimmy soon initiated a campaign for American "preparedness," then a code word for American entry into the war against Germany, and he wrote editorials favoring creation of a Harvard regiment. He later boasted, "we got practically the whole college enlisted."[52] Even in college, Jimmy delighted in controversial causes and displayed a flair for blistering polemics. In his crusade, he not only aroused the dismay of President A. Lawrence Lowell, but of his father. It is hard to imagine that Paul didn't perceive his son's behavior as a form of filial rebellion, or that Jimmy didn't intend it as such.

Graduating from Harvard in the spring of 1916 after just three years, Jimmy seemed destined for a Kuhn, Loeb career. In preparation, he worked as a clerk, track repairman, and brakeman on a freight train of the Baltimore

& Ohio railroad, a Kuhn, Loeb client. One day, he was approached by a friendly young director of the railroad, Averell Harriman, who recalled that his father and Paul had been great friends. The encounter began a long friendship.

Despite all appearances, however, Jimmy had more than banking in mind. Before the United States entered the war, Jimmy and some Harvard friends enrolled in the Curtiss Aviation School at Newport News, Virginia. They wanted to learn to fly so that they could enlist in the U.S. Naval Reserve Flying Corps when war came. The decision staggered Paul. Besides his love of Germany, Paul abhorred bloodshed and was flabbergasted by Jimmy's seeming lust for action. During a somber discussion, Paul told his son that he could understand responding to a draft, but that it escaped him why anybody would want to volunteer for "the horrible business of killing people."[53] Paul was devoid of the proverbial German love of uniforms or brass bands and thought people who rushed to enlist were just plain stupid. Nina calmed Paul down and got him to accede to Jimmy's action.

Concealing a vision problem, Jimmy enlisted and went to the naval air station at Hampton Roads, Virginia. The thought of his son dropping bombs on German relatives was so repugnant to Paul that it inspired one of his few devious acts. While Jimmy awaited an overseas assignment, Paul asked Navy Secretary Josephus Daniels to keep his son out of European combat. Daniels agreed. Jimmy's sister, Bettina, disputed this story, however, claiming that her brother's "faulty eyesight grounded him."[54] One wonders whether Paul disclosed the vision problem to sabotage his son's military stint. While waiting for combat duty, the versatile Ensign Warburg invented a magnetic compass for use in naval aircraft.

Jimmy only learned of his father's behind-the-scenes maneuver in the autumn of 1917 when he went to his parents to discuss his upcoming engagement to the non-Jewish Katharine Faulkner Swift. The issue of the war became intertwined with that of marrying Kay Swift. When Paul confessed what he had done, Jimmy felt more betrayed than ever in his life. "He did the one thing for which I've never forgiven him," Jimmy said.[55] Only with time would he see that he himself had been tactless and insensitive. "It was not until years later that I understand the anguish I must have caused my father by enlisting as a cadet naval aviator before the United States had declared war."[56]

Paul and Nina objected to Jimmy marrying Kay Swift on practical grounds. She was fresh and sparkling and they were both very fond of her. But Jimmy and Kay were barely out of their teens, and Jimmy seemed immature and unsettled. Also, the match was hardly standard "Our Crowd" stuff. The daughter of a music critic for the *New York World*, Kay at age eight had declared that her mission in life was to sing Brünnhilde at the Metropolitan Opera House. She was a talented scholarship student at the Institute of Musical Art and the New England Conservatory of Music. After her father died in 1914, Kay and her British mother, Ellen, lived in shabby-genteel poverty on Manhattan's Upper West Side. Kay supported them by playing piano and giving lessons.

At a time when Warburg women only ventured outside the home to perform charity work, Kay was an independent career woman who played chamber music with two other attractively gowned women in The Edith Rubel Trio. Latching on to this trio, Margaret Lewishon invited them to her father's camp on Upper Saranac Lake, where Kay met Bettina. She introduced Kay to her brother, the handsome young naval flyer. Before long Kay's trio was playing Woodlands concerts.

Kay's mother was as relentless in urging Kay to marry Jimmy as Paul and Nina were reluctant.[57] In a vision, she said, her dead husband had spoken to her, saying Kay should marry the rich twenty-one-year-old man. Jimmy later would say he had gotten married because of a ghost. Paul loathed this domineering mother. "I am a butterfly of gentleness and sweetness and harm-less-ness as compared to this daughter-eating woman," he told Bettina.[58]

Since his parents objected to Kay Swift, Jimmy proposed the day after he learned about Paul's betrayal with the Navy secretary. On June 1, 1918, he married her "in a spirit of revolt against parental authority."[59] The standoff over Jimmy's marriage to Kay Swift recapitulated the fight over his enlistment. Once again, Paul was stubbornly opposed and only gradually persuaded by Nina. But Paul and Nina couldn't stop the marriage. They had set up a trust fund for Jimmy with a hefty annual income of $4,000 a year that he could draw on from his twenty-first birthday in August 1917 and Jimmy instantly took advantage of this date to declare his independence.

This intermarriage stunned the American Warburgs. Jacob Schiff sent Jimmy a telegram that reads like a parody of his often callous, self-centered dogmatism: "I wish you joy to your happiness but cannot refrain from telling you that I am deeply disturbed by your action in marrying out of the faith in view of its probable effect upon my own progeny."[60] This may have prompted Schiff's stern policy of disinheriting heirs who married outside the faith, which would shape and distort the lives of his grandsons. Finding Kay Swift very sweet and gifted, Felix took a more relaxed, worldly, view of the match, telling one correspondent "while my father naturally would have strongly objected to his grandchild marrying a girl of the Christian faith, nowadays these things will happen."[61] He and Frieda weren't nearly so complacent when they faced the identical situation.

Felix did agree with Paul with regard to the war: Neither was thrilled by his sons firing upon their German cousins. Dropping his customary paternal banter, Felix virtually forbid his oldest son, Freddy, from rushing off to war. A year younger than Jimmy, Freddy also went to Middlesex and Harvard and wrote for the *Crimson*. He was an athletic, sociable, funny young man, with a sharp, caustic wit. By the summer of 1917, Frederick, twenty, was finishing his military training at Harvard, selling Liberty Bonds, and itching to see action. Noting that Freddy had two years left at Harvard, Felix lectured him that "they seem to you so superfluous that you are willing to throw them away for the sake of watching the murder on the other side. . . . I am determined that until you are twenty-one you will not join the aggressive forces."[62] A year later, however, traveling down to Camp Lee in Virginia, Felix proudly watched Freddy drill his crackerjack company, which acquired the unlikely moniker of "The Warburg Shock Troops."[63]

———

For the American Warburgs, the real casualty of the war was not the uni- forming of sons but the sad dénouement to Paul's spectacular career at the Fed. During the war, he had battled two suspicions: that he was a secret agent of "Kaiser Billy" and that he was in cahoots with Wall Street to reduce the number of reserve districts to strengthen the central board. An unswerving defender of Fed independence, he engaged in a running battle with Treasury Secretary William G. McAdoo, who was chairman of the Fed. (Not until the 1930s was the Treasury secretary dropped from the board.) By June 1916, political feuding reached such a pitch that Paul met with Woodrow Wilson for twenty minutes to discuss the problems. Paul felt the meeting eliminated any lingering suspicions and left the White House with "the confident feeling that no doubt remained in the President's mind with regard to the sincerity of my motives and the honesty of my convictions."[64] On August 10, 1916, Wilson made Paul first vice-governor of a board until then composed of equal members.

But Wilson failed to reappoint Paul in August 1918. This was the shatter- ing event of Paul's life. He felt his own tender child brutally snatched from his hands. The standard explanation for Paul's downfall spotlights his German birth, which made his position untenable in wartime Washington. Paul him- self contested this. As he wrote cryptically a decade later, "Suffice it to state that it was not—as is generally assumed—my German birth that was the real cause of my withdrawal. While we were at war that phase of the question was only used as a blind by a senator opposed to my reappointment."[65]

Paul's papers, indeed, reveal a far more convoluted Washington drama. The government was then raising billions of dollars in Liberty Loans, an operation that threatened to crowd private industrial borrowers from capital markets. Paul suggested forming a Capital Issues Committee to review industrial borrowing needs. If the committee found that needy strategic companies were being denied access to the marketplace, the War Finance Corporation would step in and provide the money.

At first, the Capital Issues Committee functioned as a voluntary body, with Paul its acting head. When a draft bill proposed incorporating the committee into the War Finance Corporation, Paul marched to Capitol Hill with his old nemesis, Treasury Secretary McAdoo, to testify for the measure. Though Congress suspected them of plotting together, Paul knew that, in reality, they were often at "dagger's ends."[66] As the Capital Issues Committee was originally conceived, McAdoo would have had sole authority to appoint members. To embarrass and harass him, Senator Henry Cabot Lodge asked McAdoo if he didn't think it suitable to have the president name the committee members, with Senate consent. "There was, of course, nothing to do for McAdoo but to consent very readily and graciously to this request," recalled Paul.[67]

Seated beside McAdoo, Paul watched this seemingly innocuous episode unfold with sheer horror. He knew that Lodge's superficially trivial ploy had just ruined his career, for Senate consent would now expose him to the poisonous darts of Senator Robert L. Owen, whom he thought behind the move. In the wartime situation, if Paul remained on the Fed he would have to be on the Capital Issues Committee, for the two bodies would act jointly in many matters. And committee membership would now subject him to Senate scrutiny at a highly inauspicious time. In the xenophobic climate, his German birth could easily be exploited by Senator Owen. Glumly Paul saw that "if my name were presented to the Senate, opposition would be aroused and the easy plea that it was a dangerous thing to place the right practically to pass upon the weal and woe of the country's financial industries in the hand of one who had such close blood relations with the leading men in the enemy's country."[68]

Paul shrank from creating political discord when America could least afford it. Many newspapers were already trying to hound him from the Fed by sowing doubts about him. As one newspaper wrote with more passion than accuracy, "The fact that Mr. Warburg is said to have a brother who is now the head of one of the largest banks in Berlin and he is said to have another brother who is the head of the German secret service in a north European country are other reasons why the wisdom of appointing him to positions of great influence in the war administration is doubted."[69] In early April, amid much family dissension—Jimmy pleaded with him to take a principled stand for reappointment—Paul decided that the whispering campaign must be silenced. This could only occur if he offered to resign when his term expired in August. He thought this necessary but not fair. "During a period of war people act as in a fever and reasoning is impossible," he wrote McAdoo.[70] What mattered, he said, was to refute any insinuations of disloyalty and "leave no doubt in the people's mind that the Administration has full confidence in an American citizen even though his cradle stood in Hamburg and even though his brothers are said to be influential friends of the Kaiser (I wish they were influential; many a thing would have remained undone in that case!)."[71]

To settle the matter, Paul told Colonel House that he would frame a letter to the president offering his resignation in such a manner that Wilson would feel free to make the right decision. The critical paragraph of his May 27, 1914, letter ran as follows:

"Much to my regret, Mr. President, it has become increasingly evident that should you choose to renominate me this might precipitate a harmful fight which, in the interest of the country, I wish to do anything in my power to avoid. . . . On the other hand, if for reasons of your own, you should decide not to renominate me it is likely to be construed by many as an acceptance by you of a point of view which I am certain you would not wish to sanction. In these circumstances, I deem it my duty to state to you myself that it is my firm belief that the interest of the country will best be served if my name be not considered by you in this connection."[72]

There's no doubt at all that Paul hoped Wilson would courageously defy his detractors and reappoint him. But the same president who had shown such brave resolution during Paul's 1914 confirmation battle would now strike Paul as cravenly evasive. With Paul stretched on the rack, Wilson waited an unconscionable time to reply. In mid-July, when he still hadn't heard and reporters got wind of his May letter, Paul broke down and contacted Joe Tumulty at the White House, asking why his letter hadn't been answered. After checking, Tumulty told Paul that Wilson wouldn't disclose the reasons for his delay. On August 3rd, Tumulty told Paul that Wilson was waiting to consult with McAdoo, who wouldn't return to Washington until August 9—the expiration date of Paul's term. So Paul waited ten weeks for a reply.

When it finally came on August 9, 1918, it was the dreaded death sentence. And Wilson didn't especially sweeten the pill.

"My dear Mr. Warburg: I hope that my delay in replying to your letter . . . has not given you any impression of indifference on my part or any lack of appreciation of the fine personal and patriotic feelings which made that letter one of the most admirable and gratifying I have received during these troubled times." He blamed the delay on McAdoo's absence. "Your retirement from the board is a serious loss to the public service. I consent to it only because I read between the lines of your generous letter that you will yourself feel more at ease if you are left free to serve in other ways.

"I know that your colleagues on the Board have not only enjoyed their association with you, but have also felt that your counsel has been indispensable in these first formative years of the new system which has served at the most critical period of the nation's financial history to steady and assure every financial process, and that their regret is as great as my own that it is in your judgment best now for you to turn to other methods of service. . . ."[73]

Paul griped at the letter as belated and niggardly in its praise. Thus ended the extraordinary crusade that had swept up the young, uncertain banker ten years before. His Washington career expired with stunning abruptness. The letters pouring in from his friends showed little awareness that he had wanted Wilson to refuse his resignation. Most applauded his noble, self-sacrificing stand; only a handful of more intimate and knowing friends disparaged Wilson's move as false and sanctimonious.

The press reacted with enormous sympathy. Editorial commentary was almost worshipful, praising Paul's statesmanlike resignation and asserting that nobody had done more to assure the lasting success of the new Fed. As several papers noted, Paul had been such a respected and knowledgeable figure that, as far as the outside world was concerned, Paul *had* been the Board. As *The New York Times* said, "The prestige and authority which the board now enjoys as a balance wheel in American banking during wartime is largely due to him."[74] Some newspapers noted the divergent treatment of Paul and Max. While Paul was banished from Washington, Max never encountered similar imputations of treachery in Berlin about his tie with Paul.

It was with profound sorrow that Paul cleaned out his desk in Washington. In government he had found his true *métier* and now had lost it. He and Nina set off for the Pacific Coast via the Canadian Rockies so that Paul could enjoy his "first loafing in four years," as he phrased it.[75] Although his salary had been much lower in Washington than on Wall Street, he had no interest in returning to Kuhn, Loeb despite encouragement from Felix. As he told Colonel House, "My mind is not bent on making money—certainly not in these times. . . ."[76] While he already contemplated writing an authoritative history of the Fed's founding, he said he would rather be making history than recording it.

For the rest of his life, Paul would be wistful. He went from a singularly favored life to a tragic fall. Like other incorruptible young idealists, he reacted to keen disappointment by becoming cynical and pessimistic. He and Nina returned to their house at 17 East 80th Street. For a time, he flirted with becoming a consultant. But he knew the United States would emerge from the war as a global power and he already mulled over plans for restoring German-American ties.

Paul's Washington career underscores a fundamental tension in the old European banking dynasties. They specialized in international business and planted family members in different financial capitals. This internationalism only worked well in an age of peace, free trade, and unfettered capital flows, such as existed before World War I. Between the world wars, the Warburgs' country-spanning alliances would be harshly challenged in a savage new era of nationalism, protectionism, exchange controls, and hateful racial ideologies. Before long, Max would face the same dilemma in Germany that Paul had in America, as it was alleged that his true allegiance resided, not with the Fatherland, but with shadowy Jewish interests abroad. Far from being seen as advantageous to Germany, the Warburg connections would breed an injurious new mythology.

CHAPTER 14

The Collapse

Fate, with perfect cruelty, had positioned the German-American War-burgs on opposing sides of the Great War. Yet even as it became a private civil war, setting brother against brother and cousin against cousin, the family maintained a touching fidelity that transcended politics. In February 1917, Max's son Eric wrote to his pro-Allied cousin Jimmy about the hardships of the frigid Hamburg winter. In a bitter cold snap, the Alster had frozen over, blocking coal barges and forcing the authorities to commandeer freight trains, horses, and carriages to haul coal. In the harsh winter weather the poor huddled in public warming halls. Bicycles disappeared with the confiscation of rubber, and even bandages were made of paper. Fresh food was extremely scarce.

Eric, sixteen, told Jimmy that his hour of military service fast approached and that he could see recruits drilling in the schoolyard below. With the government frequently raiding the teaching corps for soldiers, classes operated on reduced schedules. Eric bid a poignant farewell to his American cousin, who had so avidly exhorted his Harvard classmates to fight Germany. "Now America has also broken off diplomatic relations and I fear that means war, for American life will perish because of it. I won't write more about this.

Our personal friendship shouldn't be impaired by politics! *Auf Wiedersehen* in peace!"[1]

A happy boy who had grown up surrounded by adoring sisters and female cousins, Eric was short and blond, frail and slightly lazy. At one point, Alice had secretly visited his school and asked that he be kept back for half a year to correct his laziness. With no time to help Eric in school, Max shipped him off to Uncle Aby, who would listen to his essays, take out an enormous pen and scrawl scathing comments in the margins. But despite these strict tutorials, Eric always retained great affection for Aby's warm merriment. Eric had inherited only his father's superficial traits. Charming and gregarious, with a sly twinkle in his eyes and a sunny nature, he lacked Max's deep, driving ambition. Eric was dominated by his father, who decreed that his son must enter the bank. The family mocked how Eric began sentences, "Well, as my father says. . . ." Max would unashamedly open Eric's love letters. This regimented upbringing would produce a young man with a powerful wanderlust and a craving for freedom and adventure.

Already an ardent patriot in Max's mold, the teenage Eric worked with his aunt, Dora Magnus, at the Hamburg War Aid society.[2] Foreseeing that he would be drafted in 1918, Max tried to toughen up the boy with manual labor. On April 15, 1917, his seventeenth birthday, Eric and three classmates boarded a train for east Mecklenburg to perform volunteer farm work on an estate. Before he left, Alice solemnly instructed him to kiss the hand of the landowner's wife. When Eric and his friends arrived, the large, brisk chatelaine rushed to the coach door to greet them. When Eric kissed her hand, she cuffed the poor boy's forehead with "tremendous fists," as Eric remembered, leaving a large red bruise.[3] (In later years, Eric would be careful to take both her hands at once.) Eric and his friends performed brutal harvesting labor while also supervising older Polish laborers. During ten-hour days, they squatted on their knees and grubbed up sugar beets, then slept in a barn hayloft swarming with mice and rats.

In spring 1918, Eric volunteered for the Prussian Field Artillery Regiment in Berlin, receiving a memorable martial farewell from Uncle Aby.[4] When Eric announced his departure, Aby unearthed his old pearl-handled revolver and a gigantic saber, broad and curved as a pirate's. Aby insisted that such a dashing sword was *de rigueur* for a proper young soldier. Eric protested—to no avail. En route to his barracks, he ditched the saber in a streetcar rather than risk the mockery of fellow recruits.

Aby's hair and mustache were now speckled with gray. He strolled about town with a troubled air, moody and restless, a self-described "tortured neurasthenic."[5] Finding wartime Hamburg desolate, he thought vaguely of taking a teaching position elsewhere. People noticed that he was impossibly

Aby Warburg and his son,
Max Adolph, August 14, 1925.
(Warburg Institute)

touchy and irascible. After visiting Kösterberg, Jim Loeb told Nina, "Aby is growing more intolerable as he grows older . . . and a womanish squeamishness, coupled with direct boorishness of behavior" made him "more a source of irritation than joy to us. . . ."[6]

Ever the dark mirror of the historical moment, Aby's psyche reflected Germany's deteriorating situation. The prospect that the coarse, grubby Anglo-Saxon culture might prevail tormented him. The whole universe seemed disordered, a grisly projection of his apocalyptic nightmares. Aby's friends saw him spinning out of control during the war. As city planner Fritz Schumacher said, "With Warburg one could see, full of care, a growing pessimism, which uncontrollably seized his mind."[7]

From the early days of conflict, Aby periodically checked into the Waldpark Sanatorium in Baden-Baden as he grew morbidly afraid of illness. He had a running, mirthless gag that he was off to the repair shop and would emerge brightly lacquered. But his mood swings sharpened. He worked with blazing intensity then descended into a state of anxious jitters that rendered him unfit for work. The doctors prescribed evermore potent medicines to counteract this progressive depression. Before entering the Waldpark Sanatorium in September, 1917, Aby drew up a last will and testament. Again displaying his deep streak of Jewish self-hate, he asked to be buried not with the Warburgs, but with his non-Jewish Hertz in-laws.

As Aby slid into madness during the war, his dependency upon his family expressed itself in growing anger. He always had lived in childlike dependence upon his brothers, who had indulged him with a stupendous two hundred thousand marks by 1917. Yet he rewarded their generosity with increasingly truculent demands for money. As his illness advanced, Aby's rage at them became ungovernable—perhaps an inverted form of guilt. He bitterly attacked Paul and Felix for not making more Loeb and Schiff money available for his library. Aby was a complicated man and this indignation by no means reflected the full range of his feelings toward his brothers. He expressed great warmth for Paul and his achievements, and Felix often had a soothing effect on him.

During the war, Aby seemed preoccupied with his Jewish identity, or lack of it. Irate over Anglo-Saxon propaganda, he embarked on a study of political pamphleteering during previous eras of turbulence in Germany, concentrating on the Reformation and Martin Luther. He increased his purchase and reading of books on religion. For most Jews, it was hard to see beyond Luther's anti-Semitism, his portrayal of Jews as demonic creatures, miserable vermin and vampires. Luther thought Jews had "enslaved" Christians through usury and well-poisoning as well as by draining blood from Christian children for use in secret rituals. In flaming, violent language, Luther thundered that Jewish schools, prayer books, and synagogues should be torched; Jewish homes destroyed; and their inhabitants hounded from the land. In 1935, the Nazis would rush out a popular new edition of his inflammatory pamphlet, *On Jews and Their Lies*.

And how did Aby view Luther? As "one of the great liberators of mankind, a heroic figure fighting for enlightenment and the emancipation of faith from the shackles of a narrow dogma," in the words of E.H. Gombrich.[8] He was drawn to the noble Luther who had emancipated Europe from the primitive magic of astrological thinking by stressing free will. The Warburgs evidently were distressed by Aby's fascination with Luther, for he felt obliged to defend his interest to Fritz's wife in 1917. He pointed out that his admiration for Luther dated from adolescence. Praising him as intellectually fearless, Aby stated that Luther had helped to free him from a Jewish orthodoxy that had tried to enslave him.[9]

If Aby was heartened by Luther's triumph over superstition, the study of his era also transported him to a time of baleful omens and dark doomsday prophecies. His mind seethed with images of black magic, the occult, astrology. These irrational arts must have leaked corrosive acid into his unconscious mind even as his conscious mind celebrated Luther's rationalism. It required the assistance of Fritz Saxl—back in Hamburg after serving as an Austrian artillery officer in Italy—for Aby to prepare his April 1918 speech on prophecy in the age of Luther.

Aby wanted to see the more backward Jewish culture subordinated to advanced German culture. In one interesting 1915 episode, this Aby (M.) protested to his cousin, Aby. S., about the latter's posting of a death notice for a Jew in the newspaper. Aby M. was indignant that the ad didn't carry the Iron Cross in the upper left-hand corner. "That is no sign of faith," he said of the Iron Cross, "but an honorary symbol under which all of Germany (finally!) unites." Aby ended the letter by bluntly demanding that his cousin, in future, be sure to sign his name Aby *S.* Warburg.[10]

Aby M. supported the war unreservedly to the end and believed that Germany's cultural superiority guaranteed the country's triumph. He and Mary invested in German Treasury bills and bought some more for the children. He grew more vindictive toward Germany's foes, saying, "Without punishing the Italians, the war will have no appropriate finale!"[11] Aby was revolted when America declared war. Even though Paul and Felix were American citizens, Aby lashed out at America as a "pimp of the war fury" and said "this new enemy perhaps brings us to the highest degree of loathing."[12] In his September 1917 will, he specified that his library, now nineteen thousand volumes strong, should definitely remain on German soil, ideally forming the basis of a cultural institute at the projected University of Hamburg. Aby saw his world of high German culture being devoured by the war, which he viewed as "a bloody, endlessly dripping propeller. . . ."[13]

Leonardo-like, Aby fantasized about strange, exotic weaponry that might magically turn the tide of battle. In 1916, he tried to sell people on a science-fiction weapon he had devised on paper that would shoot out streams of electrical sparks at captive balloons that floated above London for defensive purposes.[14] Toward the war's close, he envisioned a massive Allied air attack against Hamburg. One day, he rushed breathless into Gustav Hillard's office and began unfolding blueprints for a futuristic air-defense system, complete with shelters and observation towers.

Recalling the episode years later, Hillard credited Aby's clairvoyance: "Such an attack was then a technical Utopia and for such a defense all the defense batteries of the German Army wouldn't have sufficed. Exactly a quarter-century later the destruction of the city was accomplished in the form of Warburg's vision."[15] It was not the last time that Aby's imagination would seem to have a special foretaste of future devastation.

——

When Germany's unrestricted U-boat warfare brought America into the war, strengthening the Entente, Max Warburg felt a joyless satisfaction in the precise fulfillment of his prediction. For all of Germany's military braggadocio, he knew the war was lost and thought it should have been ended sooner. But popular fury against the enemy had now been screwed to such a pitch that German politicians feared speaking the bitter truth. "Our opponents couldn't imagine that statesmen could be such fools as to persist in a senseless war, always hoping for something that had long been hopeless," Max wrote.[16]

After the American envoy at the Hague, Garret, intimated that he might be willing to talk with an influential German, Max was recruited for a last, fruitless peace mission in March 1918. Having American brothers, Max seemed well suited for the job. The new chancellor, Count Georg von Hertling, summoned Max to Berlin and asked him to sound out Garret on peace terms. Max traveled to the Hague with Dr. Kurt Hahn, a brilliant, mercurial, Oxford-educated man, who had monitored the British press for the German Foreign Office. In the Hague, they ended up playing an elaborate guessing game for several days. Sensing reluctance on the American side, Max hesitated to take the initiative while Garret, in turn, waited for Max to make the first move. They never met and Max returned quite dispirited from Holland. Later, when General Erich Ludendorff accused him of trafficking with the enemy, Max pointed out that Count Hertling had sent him.

In June 1918, Max made a speech on postwar economic policy before 175 Reichstag deputies visiting Hamburg and thus established himself as an expert on the mark's postwar value and German foreign debt. At breakfast afterward, he sat beside the chairman of the Social Democratic party, Friedrich Ebert, whom he found charming, smart, and resourceful in tough situations.

The kaiser spent the summer of 1918 shut up in a fool's paradise, insisting upon total victory over England, while the public was likewise deceived about Germany's real prospects. Max had seen Wilhelm II only once during the war, when he came to the Hamburg *Rathaus* and asked Max about the proposed University of Hamburg. When Max said that he'd had other cares during the war, the kaiser took offence. In early September, General Ludendorff asked Ballin if he would go to Kassel and impress upon His Majesty the gravity of the situation. Like Max, Ballin was haunted by visions of doom and foresaw a bloody, possibly Bolshevik, revolution in Germany following defeat. Berlin's uncompromising attitude toward a negotiated peace guaranteed harsh exactions from the victorious Allies. Ballin thought the kaiserin and Wilhelm's advisers were screening the leader from unpleasant facts to protect his fragile nerves. Unfortunately, Ballin's power had waned at court. When he arrived, he didn't see Wilhelm alone, much less get to issue his warning.

Max emerged as a pallbearer in the funeral for the German Empire, an involvement that came through Prince Max von Baden, a friend and frequent Kösterberg visitor, whom Max had met through Red Cross work. A genial, humane man who traveled with Ralph Waldo Emerson's essays in his pocket, the prince was a progressive figure for his time. During the war, he proposed military reforms and constitutional changes that would have reduced the kaiser to a figurehead and augmented Reichstag powers. Max and the prince agreed on the futility of U-boat warfare and both men wanted to renounce postwar designs on Belgium.

Prince Max replaced Hertling as chancellor. Before this happened, however, the prince asked Max Warburg to meet with Friedrich Ebert and sound out the Social Democrats' position. Max invited Ebert to his room at the Hotel Adlon and told him that Hertling's credit was destroyed at home and abroad. He asked whether Ebert would support Prince Max as chancellor. Ebert fidgeted at the idea of having a prince occupy that position. Max then asked whether he and his party would assume the difficult task of governing Germany. When Ebert balked, Max stressed the value of a peaceful transition under Prince Max.[17] No less than Max, Ebert feared a revolution that might lurch in an unforeseeable direction and he agreed to support Prince Max to achieve a safe, gradual transition. The next day, Ebert told the Reichstag, "I spoke yesterday with one of the Hamburg businessmen, who told me that Hertling no longer enjoys any trust here or abroad."[18]

The hobgoblins of hatred were manifestly abroad when Prince Max consulted Max Warburg at Dessau on September 23, 1918. Early war euphoria had turned to a severe and punitive disenchantment with German leaders. The overwhelming rage threatened to unleash pent-up anti-Semitism amid a clamorous public search for scapegoats. Asked to form a government, Prince Max offered Max the job of finance minister. Ordinarily, this would have represented a dreamlike culmination of his career, but Max spurned the offer at this perilous moment. "In my answer I said without hesitation that I had gladly placed myself at his disposal, but that I knew the Germans and knew that they would never, ever, accept a Jewish finance minister."[19] Max explained that he had an extra liability, for the Social Democrats would dismiss him as a front man for the capitalist bosses. He would serve instead as an adviser.

The two men had a melancholy chat that Max felt was more an end than a beginning. For all his admiration of the prince, Max thought he had come too late and was too weak and inexperienced for this extremely precarious moment. When Max said that he would have to persuade the kaiser to abdicate, the prince, a liberal monarchist, grew flustered. "But that is just what I mean to avoid," he said.[20] Max Warburg knew that Germany would demand a martyr in defeat and that the kaiser couldn't escape popular retribution.

Gradually the full dimensions of the debacle dawned upon a shocked, disabused German populace. Although Max and the prince had scoffed at Germany's military boasts and bluffs, they now found it necessary to combat a military pessimism so ingrained that it bordered on panic. Von Hindenburg and his exhausted, frightened comrades wanted to petition for an immediate armistice. Even though this initiative came from the High Command, Max presciently warned Prince Max that he and the civil government would later be blamed for such a hasty step. Believing that Germany's bargaining position would be weakened by precipitate surrender, Max grimly joked that it was better to send the generals across with a white flag.[21]

Contrary to the later Nazi legend that the German Army was "stabbed in the back" by Jews and spineless politicians, both Prince Max and Max Warburg favored holding out for a few weeks to strengthen Germany's hand. The prince's private secretary, Kurt Hahn, even thought that peaceful impulses might break out in England if Germany held fast. To combat the military's insistence that President Wilson would respond leniently to an armistice request, Prince Max "decided to call Max Warburg to my aid in order to combat the illusion that America would show itself conciliatory if only we humiliated ourselves. Warburg, as one of our best experts on America, had often been consulted by military and political authorities."[22]

During a Crown Council meeting on October 2, Prince Max and Hindenburg presented contradictory prognoses to the emperor. Hindenburg said the army couldn't withstand even another forty-eight hours of combat. Prince Max deplored this self-destructive haste, which the Americans would only construe as weakness. He cited his recent talk with Max Warburg. "The best Americans," Max had said, "were gentlemen, but there were all the self-opinioned individuals who knew nothing of Europe. If Germany humiliated herself now, not the good type, but the bad, would be masters of the situation."[23]

The next day, Max Warburg met General Erich Ludendorff at the Hotel Adlon. Highly agitated, Ludendorff insisted that Germany immediately declare bankruptcy. Max thought Ludendorff had lost his nerve. Prince Max arranged another meeting at the hotel between Max and Colonel Hans von Haeften, Ludendorff's deputy in Berlin. Max told him, "I know it seems strange that I, as a civilian, should be relying on the military, urging them to fight on, when my only son is being trained and is ready to fight in the trenches, but I beseech you not to give up now!"[24] Coincidentally Eric was then bathing in his father's hotel suite. Marching with his company back to their barracks and passing the Brandenburg Gate, Eric had managed to secure a two-hour leave to see his father. When Colonel von Haeften asked Max if he could wash up, he startled Eric in the bathtub. Dripping, Eric sprang from the tub and, stark naked, saluted the colonel with correct military form.

The military ignored calls for delay. On October 5, Prince Max signed an armistice request, which Max Warburg considered a fatal blunder. On October 23, the United States issued a note, stating its refusal to deal with "military masters and the monarchical autocrats of Germany" and warning that, if necessary, it would demand surrender instead of peace negotiations. Enraged, Max Warburg pleaded with Prince Max for a tough, defiant response to Wilson's note. "I am absolutely sure of the American mentality," he told the prince. "We ought to turn upon them, and not at any price allow ourselves to be trodden on any longer. There must be something included in the note, which warns the enemy against the resolution of a people driven to despair."[25] The tone prefigured the assertive nationalism that Max would exhibit at Versailles.

Despite the prospect of certain defeat in late October, the admirals prepared to send the Kiel fleet into a suicidal naval engagement. On November 3, 1918, this inhuman order sparked a sailor uprising that soon spread to the army and workers, then emerged as a full-blown revolution. The first news of the Kiel uprising appeared in the Hamburg newspapers on the morning of November 5th and to instant effect. The harbor workers, always a radical, disaffected group, were ripe for insurrection. Exempt from military service, they had been browbeaten, overworked, and threatened with being packed off to the trenches if they protested. By noon, a wildcat strike in one shipyard gave way to more strikes and calls for a general strike. Workers seized a torpedo boat in the harbor, mounting a heavy gun in its bow, then occupied the train station and the Elbe tunnel. Hamburg had always been a labor and Socialist stronghold, albeit firmly controlled by local merchants. On November 6, the power structure was suddenly inverted, as the Workers' and Soldiers' Council took control. In the ensuing general strike, political prisoners were freed and workers surged through the streets, bearing red strips on their arms and streaming bright red flags from their cars. The first glimmers of counterrevolution appeared as anonymous sniper fire killed several workers.

As adviser to the Senate finance committee, Max Warburg would play a central role in this unfolding drama. However sympathetic to reform, he dreaded the radical upheaval that now overwhelmed the city. In the momentary chaos, Hamburg found itself with two clashing governments. At the Chamber of Commerce, Max argued for contacts between the old guard and the rebel government to discuss city-state finances. Hamburg Treasury notes held by M. M. Warburg and other banks would soon expire and had to be renewed, giving the creditors immediate leverage. When Hamburg ran short of cash, the policemen couldn't be paid. Soon Max and two other businessmen were summoned by the chieftain of the Workers' and Soldiers' Council, Dr. Heinrich Laufenburg.

When Laufenburg brought up the Treasury bills, Max said the bankers would roll them over only at the behest of the Senate finance committee and after closely auditing Hamburg's expenses. Laufenburg read the riot act to Max. "You still don't seem to be clear as to who it is who will decide the matter," he said. Max retorted, "I'm aware of existing conditions. It lies within your power not to pay off the Treasury bills. If nevertheless you would like them renewed, then you must allow me to name the conditions under which my friends and I will undertake that renewal."[26] Growing hot under the collar, Laufenburg told Max to take twenty-four hours to reflect. When Max said he didn't need more time, he was unceremoniously dismissed on the spot.

———

Albert Ballin and his mighty HAPAG fleet were prime revolutionary targets. A convinced monarchist, Ballin loathed leftists of every stripe but saw the need of reform to salvage remnants of the ancien régime. He had quaintly pictured a new postwar order overseen by reasonable businessmen, not by these ragged, shouting masses who poured through the streets hoisting banners. On November 8, members of the Workers' and Soldiers' Council stormed the HAPAG bastion facing the Inner Alster and took over the company boardroom. Although Ballin refused to budge from his desk, he couldn't dislodge the protesters and told one visitor, with his wry, cynical humor, "The people should for once have a decent room to hold a meeting."[27]

After a generation of near omnipotence in global shipping, Ballin saw his world rapidly disintegrating. The victorious Allies were certain to plunder his company. Hoping to cripple Germany's military potential, they would demand any ships not already sunk or seized. The busy port of Hamburg would fall silent. Ballin feared that only a short step would separate liberal democracy from outright socialism. The HAPAG seamen and their Social Democratic champions would now be at the helm.

As the war approached its end, the morose Ballin was in an uneasy, overwrought state. Nervous, bad tempered, he saw the world refracted through a dark prism. As he wrote a friend, "How terribly stupid is this life in normal times, and how insupportable it becomes in this murderous war."[28] That autumn, when Ballin saw Eric in uniform striding down the street before HAPAG headquarters, he burst into tears, fearing his class would prove the last sacrificial lambs of war. A chronic insomniac, Ballin sedated himself with ever larger quantities of veronal and opiates to sleep and tried to soothe his nerves with long country weekends or stays at a sanatorium in Bad Kissingen.

The final indignity came on the afternoon of November 8, when the revolutionaries in the HAPAG boardroom threatened to arrest or beat him. That afternoon, Ballin also learned the kaiser would abdicate the next day. The destruction of the political and economic underpinnings of his world was now complete. He left the building and walked home through the dusk only to be received at the gate by his upset wife, who had received menacing telephone calls that her husband would soon be jailed.

Overcome, Ballin took a large dose of sleeping pills—whether to calm or kill himself remains a mystery. When he collapsed, his doctor was immediately called. He and a servant carried the comatose Ballin to a Mittelweg clinic where they tried to pump his stomach, but the drugs produced a bleeding ulcer and Ballin's heart gave way from the hemorrhaging. Max phoned the clinic, but didn't get there before Ballin died at one o'clock in the afternoon on November 9, 1918—the day the Empire ended.

For Max Warburg, it would always be an article of unquestioned faith that Ballin had not committed suicide. He told people that Ballin's doctor had personally assured him that his friend had died of a stroke. This begged the obvious question of whether he had purposely taken pills that triggered the stroke. Perhaps Max found it too frightening to think that his mentor, who had tutored him so loyally and filled him with such manly confidence, could have succumbed to despair. He had drawn strength from Ballin's example as a Jewish businessman who had risen to the summit of German society. Historians, though, would almost universally lean to the suicide theory of Ballin's death.

The final scene of Germany's wartime drama played itself out swiftly. After

Wilhelm II fled to Holland aboard the royal train, a republic was proclaimed from the Reichstag balcony, with Friedrich Ebert its leader. Max Warburg felt that, in some small measure, he had helped to nudge Ebert forward. On November 11, France dictated peace terms to Germany in the Forest of Compiègne, and battlefields fell silent after four years of carnage.

After the frenzied cheering and ritual assurances of victory, Germans felt dazed by sudden defeat. For a nation schooled in almost reflexive obedience to authority, the humiliation shook a fundamental public faith in military, industrial, and political leaders. A wide vacuum of belief thus opened, providing room for radical new ideologies of left and right to take root. They would have a potent allure to those battered, crippled, tattered veterans who now began drifting back into cities short of jobs, food, and coal.

German Jews watched the kaiser's abdication with profoundly mixed feelings. Although full acceptance had eluded them, they had been favored children of the Empire. On the other hand, the war had defeated their hopes for major gains and revealed the hidden limits of Christian trust. The end of the Empire left a deep residue of uncertainty, for the kaiser's rejection was far more decisive than affirmation of the new Republic. As Max later told Colonel House, "The revolution in Germany too was a collapse of the old order after nearly five years' war exhaustion, rather than the conscious pursuance of new thoughts. Only after the collapse people began to conscientiously work for the new era."[29]

In retrospect, it is clear that the crumbling edifice of Empire released a deadly effluvium that would smother and finally choke the Jews. Max still retained access to many politicians, but his instincts told him to move gingerly now and he didn't try to convert influence into real power. Max and Alice refused invitations from Ebert, as Max explained, "because I didn't want to create the reputation for Ebert that he was dependent on the Jewish side."[30]

When Ballin's funeral was held in a Hamburg suburb on November 13, the revolutionary ardor briefly ceased and the old order enjoyed a last moment of pageantry. Hundreds of mourners strode gravely behind Ballin's coffin, which was wrapped in a blue-and-white HAPAG insignia. In an oration extolling Ballin, Max said it was hard to imagine German expansion of the past thirty years without him. Max had counted on Ballin's support in the reconstruction ahead. In his last diary entry, Ballin had written, "From Stinnes came word that both Centre Party and Social Democrats had agreed that I should conduct the peace negotiations. I replied that I would not shirk it, but that I would gladly see somebody else doing it."[31] Max and Carl Melchior would succeed Ballin in that role.

The day before the funeral, the Workers' and Soldiers' Council voted to dissolve the Hamburg Senate and City Council. The old regime decamped and the new regime moved into the *Rathaus*, running up the red flag. The city's fiscal situation deteriorated, with foreign creditors balking at lending more money. On November 16, Dr. Laufenburg, chairman of the Council Government, invited Max and other business dignitaries to lunch at City Hall. They ate at a long table lined with heavily armed revolutionary sailors, taking turns drinking from a communal soup tureen. As a heavy rain fell, Max heard chants rising up from an angry crowd outside. Before negotiations began, he stood at the window beside Senator Werner von Melle, the tireless champion of a Hamburg university. Though Max was assisting him in the project, he had found von Melle a monomaniacal bore on the subject. Now as Max pondered the momentous breakdown of German society, von Melle whispered, "I think that this new turn of events isn't at all a bad thing for the university."[32] When Max burst out laughing it snapped some of the gathering tension.

In the end, Max and other bankers preserved the Senate finance committee's role as custodian of Hamburg's credit.[33] The big Hamburg, Berlin, and Frankfurt banks were about to secure a large American credit and Max pointed out that if the Workers' and Soldiers' Council sent their own representatives to the negotiations, Hamburg might be excluded. Taking the hint, the Revolutionary Council announced two days later that it would temporarily revive the Senate and City Council. There would also be a new business-dominated Economic Advisory Council to oversee Hamburg finances along with the militant council. This subtle counterrevolution signaled the quiet persistence of traditional forces amid all the left-wing posturing and sloganeering. The revolutionaries made little headway with the food and fuel shortages and the growing ranks of jobless workers. On March 26, 1919, the City Council—henceforth to be elected in free, secret elections—regained its old powers from the revolutionary Council. The red flag of revolution was lowered from the *Rathaus* as if it had all been a brief holiday of make-believe.

———

Like Ballin, Aby Warburg's mental balance teetered along with the Empire, and his strained nerves finally snapped from the accumulated tension and exhaustion. His breakdown, curiously, paralleled the one suffered by Thomas Mann's Faustus after World War I. For four years, Aby had labored at his newspaper index, as if this colossal, systematic drudgery might keep the demons at bay. He never wavered in his belief in Germany's sacred cause. Commiserating with Eric in 1918, Aby said he understood the hardship of war, then added, "If our youth don't stand up, how should we protect ourselves against the enslavement, the real extermination by the Entente?"[34] Though a freethinker, Aby was a typical German Jew in his gratitude toward the kaiser. As his later assistant, Gertrud Bing, wrote, "He never forgot that Imperial Germany treated the Jews well and even later on he didn't like to hear people criticize it."[35]

By September 1918, Aby had to stop seeing people or even reading newspapers, lest they stimulate dreadful new forebodings. Then, in October, all his terrible premonitions came true with Germany's defeat, and the threads that had tenuously kept his mind together suddenly burst apart. A keen observer of this unraveling was Aby's pupil, Carl Georg Heise. During the revolutionary turmoil of that fall, as Aby stood poised on a knife edge of madness, Mary asked Heise to come to the Heilwigstrasse house to deal with her husband. Heise found a gaunt Aby wandering through the rooms, muttering to himself and gesturing theatrically. "His brain worked feverishly and unchecked, everything was exaggerated and thereby distorted," said Heise. However wild, Aby's words had their own coded logic.

Consumed by guilt and shame, Aby drew Heise into a corner to make a terrible confession. While talking with a university professor, Aby said, he had told the man "At the bottom of my soul I am a Christian!"[36] He was appalled by his own admission. Now he flagellated himself as a loathsome coward, who hadn't paid due homage to his religion and family and couldn't be seen in public. When he made Heise swear to keep his revelation a secret, his disciple agreed. "He thereupon immediately screamed it out loud, so that the neighbors could hear it through the open windows," said Heise.[37] Aby grew so violent that Heise feared for his own safety and took shelter behind protective objects. "His voice was terrible. Hoarsely shouting, it now grew shrill, now sank back in an exhausted whisper."[38]

It is remarkable that Aby felt so profoundly guilty about his desertion of Judaism. Apparently, he had never renounced his heritage with a clear conscience and the iconoclasm had taken a terrible toll. He had long occupied a lonely no-man's land, neither a true Jew nor a gentile, but some unique amalgam of both. He was the Warburg dilemma incarnate. Where did a rational sophisticated Jew belong in the modern world? In July 1918, his brother-in-law, Wilhelm Hertz, invited Aby and Mary to a family gathering along with two anti-Semitic guests. Afterward, Aby hotly told Wilhelm never to invite them again with such people around.[39] At the same time, his impatience with Zionism grew. Even after Britain issued the Balfour Declaration, supporting a Jewish homeland in Palestine, Aby denounced Zionism as hopelessly mystical and romantic.[40] The semiassimilated, intermediate world of bourgeois comfort inhabited by Max and other German Jews also had no appeal for him.

As the offspring of a prominent Jewish family who had entered the heavily anti-Semitic world of German art history, Aby was always in an extremely awkward position. At moments, he blamed his family for his being Jewish. "It was as though he hated *being* a Warburg and yet, at the same time, couldn't escape from the fact that he *was* a Warburg," said a family member.[41] He often criticized the Jewish community yet feared giving comfort to anti-Semites. To complicate matters further, he depended upon his Jewish family for money to study Christian art in chapels and basilicas. All these contradictions must have had terrible internal reverberations for such a mentally unstable man.

Aby's slow-motion breakdown shattered his family. The wartime pictures of Aby, Mary, and the three children are enveloped in a heavy, stifling gloom. Aby looks fidgety and troubled, while Mary has a downcast, sorrowing Madonna's gaze. Max Adolph stares dreamily into the far distance, while the younger daughter, Frede, seems aloof, as if holding herself apart from the pull of an emotional vortex. The eldest daughter, Marietta, looks tearful, beautiful, tragic.

Aby's children watched him with fearful admiration. In his self-absorption, he felt neglected by them and would chide them, "You are not nearly curious enough for my liking."[42] Max Adolph was a pale, gentle, artistic teenager who pondered with compassion the enigma of his contradictory father. "This physically fear-ridden man was mentally the most fearless man I have known," he said.[43] Max Adolph was unwell during the war and greatly affected by his father's slippage into madness. By October 1918, Aby was even considering taking Max Adolph to Switzerland, possibly to the Kreuzlingen clinic.[44] That month, as the German war machine fell apart, madness staked its final claim on Aby. Always excitable, he now grew preternaturally so and talked incessantly. Perceiving danger and annihilation everywhere, he blamed himself. As E. H. Gombrich has written, "The two preoccupations of his scholarly life, the expression of passion and the reaction to fear, were gripping him in the form of terrible tantrums and phobias, obsessions and delusions which ultimately made him a danger to himself and his surroundings. . . ."[45]

On an early-morning walk with his lovely cousin, Elsa, Aby grew so upset that she telephoned the doctor when they got home. At first, nobody knew what to do except to restrain Aby. The next day, he was placed in an isolation cell at a local clinic. He would always blame his family and friends for having shut him up like a wild animal for several weeks of sheer terror. Aby's nervous breakdown was soon followed by another.

His starry-eyed, idealistic son, Max Adolph, reacted in a powerful manner. He was walking along a cliff's edge, when he had a mystical experience. He apprehended the immensity of the universe, the cosmic unity of all things.[46] As he later wrote, "Strangely enough, when I was 16 years old, my father's and my fatherland's sudden terrible breakdown sparked off in me, like a flash, this very vision; this flash was kindled by the fire of Herakleitos of Ephesos, as far as my immature mind could grasp him."[47] He said the vision's intensity never entirely faded and prevented him forever after—for reasons he never articulated—from applying himself for very long to any single field in life. Perhaps earthly life seemed to him afterward an insignificant way station on an eternal journey.

For a time, Aby tried to return home and resume work. His teenage daughter, Marietta, had trained as a nurse. In a terrible misstep, the family had her care for her deteriorating father, an experience that scarred her for life. In his last hours of freedom, Aby knew that the madhouse awaited him and that he might never emerge again. Luckily, the young Fritz Saxl was on hand to take over the library. After his release from the army, Saxl had mounted an antiwar exhibition called "No More Wars," under Austrian government auspices. Until the very end, Aby continued to work, using every spare moment, and he wouldn't cede any authority to Saxl until he left Hamburg.

Aby ended up at the Kreuzlingen sanatorium on Lake Constance in Switzerland, run by psychoanalyst Ludwig Binswanger. The Binswangers had already treated Fritz Warburg and Jim Loeb. Confined in a closed wing, sealed off from the outer world, Aby would allow only a small handful of relatives and colleagues to visit him. He lived in a strange twilight existence of alternating madness and lucidity. In his early days of confinement, he was joined by Max Adolph, whose nervous breakdown the doctors treated with a newfangled therapy in which patients lay in baths of tepid water to quiet their nerves. Unfortunately, as he tried to relax, Max Adolph could hear his father's tortured screams at the end of the corridor.[48]

Before his confinement, Aby had suffered such agony that friends and relatives hoped he would find solace in the sanatorium. His friend, Percy Schramm, was reminded of the ancient saying that the gods offer madness as a gift of grace.[49] The future seemed murky. As Aby's cousin, Elsa, wrote in a May 1919 letter: ". . . I think constantly of Aby M. To part from this world may not be so terrible, but what hurts is that he had to suffer so much this last year and that we do not know what will be the end of it."[50]

Ironically Aby departed from Hamburg at a moment of triumph for him. Spouting the slogan, "Education hurts nothing," he had long struggled to persuade local business leaders to start a university.[51] In April 1919, the City Council approved creation of the University of Hamburg, which the kaiser had opposed as a potential nursery of subversive thought. With the monarchy and military discredited by war, a weary citizenry searched for fresh answers, and hordes of returning veterans required education. So the world of the intellect thrived in Hamburg even as its main apostle fell prey to the madness he had so long feared and so heroically resisted.

Part Three

THE FALL
OF THE
MITTELWEG
WARBURGS

Carl Melchior.
(Warburg family, Hamburg)

Phantom Castle, Phantom Peace

In early 1919, Germany wasn't yet at peace; hostilities merely shifted from the western front to domestic streets. The Weimar Republic was born amid high hopes and the blackest despair. Led by President Friedrich Ebert, the Social Democrats assumed office with a program to construct a welfare state and alleviate the misery of the demobilized soldiers. This ambitious agenda would clash with an urgent need for fiscal austerity, impaling the Republic on the horns of an insoluble dilemma.

The most determined foes of the new regime were the Spartacists, a Marxist splinter group that aimed at a Soviet-style republic. It was headed by Karl Liebknecht and Rosa Luxemburg, the latter the daughter of a wealthy timber man who was descended from a line of rabbis. Targeting rich local merchants for protest, the Hamburg Spartacists, according to Warburg family legend, marched on Aby's house before he entered the sanatorium. "Ten or fifteen of them went to his house," recalled his niece. "He said to them, 'Gentlemen, first let's have a glass of wine.' They sat at his dining room table and stayed the whole night, roaring with laughter."[1]

The Spartacists were opposed by the illegal, paramilitary *Freikorps*. Later used to circumvent the military limits imposed on Germany at Versailles, these marauding mercenaries—many of them footloose, embittered, unemployed veterans—were financed by right-wing business groups. To counter the Spartacists, the Weimar government tossed its own weary troops into pitched battles. Max's son, Eric, first saw combat in this vicious internal war. Before Christmas 1918, he and his regiment stormed the Berlin Castle, occupied by a mutinous naval division; eight gunners died in an abortive effort. Eric's unit ejected Spartacists from other buildings. On January 15, 1919, Luxemburg and Liebknecht were both assassinated in Berlin.

Eric was a young monarchist who prayed for the kaiser's restoration. On Wilhelm's birthday, he wrote his father, "God grant that we may yet have the monarchical form of government, which is the only correct one for Germany."[2] His exposure to Berlin bloodshed and Communist takeovers of banks and universities confirmed his already deep-seated conservatism. As Spartacist terror spread, he deplored governmental weakness. "Against these people, there is only one method: fight, fight, and fight yet again."[3] When Eric worked for a Berlin bank after being demobilized, he was nearly beaten up for opposing a strike.

In March 1919, after twelve hundred people had died, martial law was declared in Berlin. Strikes and revolutionary councils sprang up with the improvised speed of street theater. The mark plunged, beginning a bottomless spiral, for nobody could assign a value to the currency until German reparations were set. This started the financial ruin of middle-class Germans who had invested their savings in war bonds. Though the fighting was over, the Allied blockade still cut off imports of food and fertilizer. Even the fishing fleet was grounded, and black markets flourished to cope with the shortages.

As a constitutional assembly met in Weimar, the government struggled to get its bearings. For the Versailles peace conference, it had to rely upon private experts to represent Germany, the financial intricacies of reparations pushing Jewish bankers to the fore at a perilous juncture. As early as November 16, 1918, Max Warburg had received a telegram, inviting him to represent the German Treasury as a delegate. The government hoped that with his American brothers, Max might convince the Allies to settle for reasonable reparations. But he knew that in the rancorous postwar atmosphere, he should tread cautiously. He explained that a Jew shouldn't undertake the mission, "for without doubt, if the conditions of the Entente were dreadfully hard . . . the consequence would surely be anti-Semitic attacks."[4] Instead of using private bankers, Max suggested that the Treasury dispatch Finance Ministry officials to Versailles. The government insisted, however, that private bankers had the negotiating skills and foreign stature and that the victorious Allies would feel more comfortable dealing with them.

Max recommended as a delegate his legal counsel, the lucid, incorruptible

Carl Melchior, who had seen wartime government service in Romania and Russia. In 1917, Melchior had replaced Felix as an M. M. Warburg partner, the first nonfamily partner in the bank's 120-year history. (His brother married Aby S.'s sister, Elsa, after Carl became a partner.) State Secretary Schiffer told Max, "At least go as the chairman of the finance delegation!"[5] Max recommended Melchior as chairman, saying he would gladly serve under him on the finance committee. Since Melchior was younger than Max, not to mention subordinate at the bank, an astounded Schiffer asked, "You don't mean to say that you're willing to work under Dr. Melchior as chairman?" Max replied, "Under nobody more willingly than him."[6] Indeed, he would serve under Melchior on the finance committee, while Melchior also served on the main delegation under Foreign Minister Count Brockdorff-Rantzau.

For Max to advance Melchior's name was an inspired move, for his junior partner would distinguish himself at Versailles. Yet one wonders whether Max was entirely candid with Schiffer in declining the finance chairmanship for himself. After all, as a Jew and Warburg partner, Melchior was no less vulnerable to anti-Semitic smears than Max. Perhaps Max feared the repercussions for Paul's career if he adopted a high profile at Versailles. In any event, in Melchior Max created a unique go-between to the political world. For fourteen years, Melchior would play a role at every major reparations conference, giving Max wide yet unofficial influence. And in business, Melchior would provide a consistently thoughtful foil to Max's often excessive exuberance.

Pictures of Carl Melchior show an elegant, polished bachelor, with close-cropped silver hair, an erect bearing and air of imperturbable calm. His round, mournful eyes seemed to deliberate upon tragic possibilities. With innate courtesy and self-control, he seldom showed strong emotion. "He was a very dignified man with a stillness and quietness about him," said his niece.[7] While people noted that he looked younger than his years, he also carried some unspoken burden of sadness that made him seem prematurely aged.

Melchior had replaced Paul as the bank's resident sage, and they came to occupy somewhat analogous places in German and American finance. Both men of enormous wisdom, dignity, and integrity, they were filled with gloomy foreboding. With his big ego and gambler's daring, Max seemed to like people of modest, unassuming brilliance. Melchior's love of literature, painting, and art—he collected German Expressionist painters and terra-cotta figurines from the Middle East—appealed to Max. Not surprisingly, Max said he and Melchior became like brothers.[8] Once he told Ballin that he had never had a colleague of such clear, steady vision. "I estimate him appreciably higher than myself, which, given my own lack of modesty, will say a great deal."[9]

Melchior was an unwavering German patriot who liked to quote Friedrich

List, "In the background of all my thoughts stands Germany."[10] Yet in a period of intense national suspicions, he would win universal praise for his honest dealings and rare objectivity. As John Maynard Keynes said, Melchior "upheld the dignity of defeat."[11] The friendship between Melchior and Keynes started in a French railway car in January 1919 when they discussed a proposal to get food to Germany in exchange for surrender of the German merchant marine. Keynes recalled, "Melchior spoke always deliberately but without pause, in a way which gave one an extraordinary impression that he was truthful."[12] In a tavern back room, Melchior had the somber task of negotiating away the German merchant fleet.

In March, Keynes and Melchior met again at the Belgian resort of Spa. The ship surrender deal hit a serious snag when the Allies tried to remove the German crews. In this incendiary atmosphere Keynes and Melchior discovered a personal bond. Keynes remembered Melchior: "Staring heavy-lidded, helpless, looking, as I had seen him before, like an honourable animal in pain."[13] They began their own informal talks. Keynes said Germany would only get food for ships and advised a conciliatory posture. In reply, Melchior "spoke with the passionate pessimism of a Jew. German honour and organisation and morality were crumbling; he saw no light anywhere; he expected Germany to collapse and civilisation to grow dim; we must do what we could; but dark forces were passing over us."[14] Later on in Brussels, they concluded a deal whereby Britain swapped food for German ships.

At first Max Warburg seemed slow to fathom the full meaning of German defeat. As his nephew, Hans Blumenfeld, wrote, "In December 1918 I had run into Max Warburg at the door of the family bank. . . . He believed in the full restoration of prewar Germany in a postwar world."[15] By late March 1919, Max and Melchior were meeting with the financial delegation in Berlin. While they expected harsh terms at Versailles, the actual reparation figures dwarfed their direst estimates. In New York, Felix saw Max headed for sure disaster. "For him to go to Versailles, where he has had so many jolly dinner parties, as a supplicant for his country is a changed role indeed," Felix wrote. "It can make very little difference what their opinions and their desires are—they will have to sign what is placed before them, perhaps under protest, if they are permitted to voice it. Whatever they sign, they will be blamed for afterwards."[16]

When Max and his fellow delegates went to the peace conference, they had to travel past the cratered battlefields of northern France. Since nearly one and a half million of their compatriots had died in the war, the French thirsted for revenge. When the German finance delegates were taken to the Château de Villette near Compiègne, they at first had no idea of the identity of their plush prison. They had fine and abundant food, washed down by vintage wines. Like guests staying in a luxury hotel, they played golf and lawn games. All the while, they stood under the unceasing surveillance of two hundred heavily armed soldiers. They couldn't use the telephone or receive visitors and inhabited a castle seeded with listening devices and spying servants. Max figured out their whereabouts when a butler confided that he worked for Baron Stern of Paris, a banker who had entertained Max at his balls during Max's Paris apprenticeship. Gradually, the guards relaxed the tight security when they saw that the delegates weren't plotting escape.

At the first plenary session of financial experts on April 4, Max perceived the intransigence of their Allied opponents. He approached Thomas W. Lamont, a partner of J. P. Morgan & Co. and a member of the Reparations Commission. With faith in Wilson's idealism, Max nonetheless had grave doubts about the American president's political skills, party backing, and European expertise. He suggested to Lamont that he meet with Wilson and Colonel House to lay the groundwork for a reasonable settlement—a stillborn overture. Lamont liked Max and spoke to him because he regretted the high-handed treatment of the Germans. Yet even he believed that Max was making inflammatory predictions about German collapse to induce a lenient settlement.

Max's letters home to Alice leave no doubt that he was genuinely alarmed by the deteriorating situation. He feared that a "wave of bolshevism" would engulf Germany and then all of Europe. On April 5, he and Melchior took a guarded stroll through the Compiègne forest, savoring its violets, primroses, and wild strawberries. The contrast between the sylvan beauty and the dreary political prospect struck Max forcibly. Usually a figure of almost glandular optimism, Max grew panicky about German prospects. When a short-lived Soviet Republic was declared in Munich on April 7, he wrote Alice, "The world is mad! So what is to be feared is complete collapse there which will drag down the rest of the world...."[17] On April 15, "Easter Riots" broke out in Hamburg, as rampaging mobs cleaned out stores and prompted martial law. During this surreal period, Max and his fellow captive delegates golfed on the lawn of the sleepily beautiful castle.

After a meeting on April 16, Max buttonholed Lamont and they spoke briefly in furtive whispers. Though Max warned of mounting German unrest, Lamont said he couldn't arrange a meeting with Wilson. The newspapers had previewed astronomical estimates of Allied reparation demands, and Max warned that no German delegation would sign such a document. Lamont offered no comfort, noting that the Allies were united and that American feeling toward Germany was exceedingly bitter.[18]

Lamont agreed to circulate to Wilson and House a memo Max had prepared. This ill-advised document throbbed with an intemperate sense of nationalistic grievance. Max couldn't suppress his belief that Germany was, in truth, the injured party. Instead of admitting German guilt, he wanted a neutral arbitration court to decide the matter and railed against the Allied "crime" of starving Germany by a blockade. He tactlessly stated that the death rate among the eight hundred thousand German prisoners in France exceeded the wartime killing and that Germany's food need should now assume paramount importance. "Time is wasted with useless discussions about the question of responsibility for the outbreak of the war."

Endorsing the League of Nations, Max yet resisted the idea that Germany required political reform and he reiterated the paean to German democracy that he had urged upon Jacob Schiff during the war. He insisted that "it has to be borne in mind, that even before the war Germany had the most democratic electoral system in the world, more democratic than the British system." Lamont found this assertion so astonishing that he jotted in the margin no fewer than four question marks. As to the notorious passivity of the German populace, Max saw this not as a vice, but as wise acquiescence to a perfect state: "The German people were under the impression that their administration was good and honest and therefore it did not worry much about politics."

In a manner that must have infuriated the Allies, Max equated German suffering with that of France and Belgium. "Certainly France and Belgium have suffered visibly the most in this war. But the question remains open, whether the sufferings of the totality of the German people on account of the terrible privations they had to endure were not at least equally severe." He dismissed any future threat from German militarism, saying it would only return if reawakened by Entente militarism. In a final gratuitous swipe, he said it wasn't Allied military cunning, but sheer superiority in soldiers and war materiel "and the raw weapon of starvation" that had produced Allied victory.[19]

Thus in one stroke, Max had confirmed every stereotype of the whining, unrepentant, self-pitying German. In passing the memo along to Bernard Baruch, Lamont commented, "The nerve that these boches have is something terrible. I think you will agree with me that they are utterly lacking in insight into the real situation."[20]

On the eve of the German delegation's move to Versailles, Max wrote Eric in a philosophic vein, trying to peer beyond the troubled present. Noting turmoil at home, he observed that revolutions, at the beginning, always smash beautiful monuments, but that one shouldn't despair. In an image that strikingly foreshadowed his Pollyanna views of 1933, he wrote, "We may regard that as a mere token of a temporary political fever. It will pass away."[21]

At four-thirty the next morning, Max, Melchior, et al., were roused from bed and taken to Versailles. Their train entered a station ringed by French troops. Max got into the backseat of a car that would take them to the hotel, but, as a little dig, he was ordered into the jump seat by his "overseer," a Lieutenant Henry. At the Hotel des Reservoirs, the German delegates were greeted by soldiers brandishing fixed bayonets. This hotel, too, was honeycombed with spies and listening devices. The Germans found they could leak positions to the press simply by leaving notes strewn about on tables. "After the golden cage of the Château de Villette," Max wrote Alice, "the hotel seems quite uncomfortable."[22]

At Versailles, the Germans were subjected to many petty indignities and denied permission to stroll after lunch. A police prefect told them, with heavy sarcasm, "Your wishes have been anticipated by the French authorities. Follow me." Marched down to the Bassin de Neptune behind the château, they were given a narrow space of sixteen meters by four meters for pacing. As the others grew indignant, Max advised calm. "Isn't it better to leave ill alone?"[23] Later on, they could roam freely in the park.

On May 7, the Allies presented their terms. When Clemenceau rose to deliver his speech, Count Brockdorff-Rantzau asked Max and Melchior whether he should remain seated. They advised against any discourtesy. The count, ignoring them, was roundly criticized for rudeness. The Germans were shocked by the exorbitant Allied demands, which stipulated that Germany would lose 13 percent of its prewar territory, including Alsace-Lorraine and parts of East Prussia. Germany would have to yield its colonies, overseas investment, and much of its merchant navy. The Rhineland would be occupied, the German army reduced. The controversial "war-guilt clause" made Germany acknowledge that it was the aggressor responsible for the war.

The Germans had until May 17 to reply, a period Max described as the most depressing of his life. Within two days, the financial delegates had concluded they could never sign such a document and debated whether to leave. Only the confusion in Berlin deterred them. Max felt trapped in a nightmarish phantasmagoria in which high-sounding rhetoric of world community masked base, sadistic motives of punishment. Max unburdened himself to Alice: "But to announce a new world era, to speak of loving kindness and justice, and then to set out on an expedition of world banditry, to plant the seed of new conflict and murder faith in a better time to come, that surely is to commit a sin of world proportions, and to see that done with one's own eyes fills one with horror and with dread."[24] The comment is notable for its grasp of the magnitude of the Allied blunder, yet also shows how quickly Max shifted blame away from Germany.

Under duress, the German delegates formulated counterproposals. Max was stunned when the usually conservative Melchior suggested that they offer a stupendous one hundred billion gold marks. Melchior thought it better to make a reasonable offer, however steep for Germany, than an unrealistically low one which would be rejected out of hand. After Melchior cited that figure, Max couldn't sleep the whole night. A member of the French finance ministry asked Max what would happen when Germany finally caved in to French demands. "We'll go bankrupt," Max said. "And France?" "France will go bankrupt the day after we do." The Frenchman was so flabbergasted by this remark that he demanded Max's removal from the delegation. *"Celui-ci est trop impertinent."*[25]

The one hundred billion gold mark offer was rejected by the Allies as too paltry. Nevertheless, in Nazi propaganda, that figure would stick to both Max and Melchior like a burr. The Germans warned that stiffer terms would be rejected. When Keynes left Versailles, Melchior said to Max that he must have concluded that the Allies were imposing impossible demands. Departing for home to set the matter before their government, the Germans suffered one final humiliation. As they got into their car, a mob jeered them and pelted them with rocks. Melchior caught one in the neck, but wasn't seriously injured. Max's cousin, Dr. Hans Meyer, got a glass splinter in his eye that he removed. One secretary was hit in the head by a stone and suffered a cerebral hemorrhage.

The Allies had hoped that German businessmen would be more amenable to a large reparations bill—a major miscalculation—and placed especial faith in Melchior. Woodrow Wilson thought that if only the case were patiently explained to Carl Melchior or Max Warburg, the Germans would see the light. Instead Max lobbied Colonel House for leniency. Contrary to Allied hopes, Max and Melchior remained dogged foes of the peace treaty.

The German financial delegates took a special train to Weimar and, en route, drew up a report for the government. Engaged in intensive discussion, the busy delegates moved from one compartment to the next and scarcely noticed the landscape flickering by. By the time they arrived in Weimar on June 18, they had unanimously decided to recommend rejection of the treaty, with Melchior taking a major hand in writing up the report.

Weimar proved a scene of tragicomic confusion that foreshadowed the Republic's fate. The delegates were greeted at the castle vestibule by a shuffling, pipe-smoking man in slippers, who proved to be not the porter, but the Reichstag president, Fehrenbach. As they waited for interminable Cabinet meetings to end, the financial experts never even had a chance to defend their recommendation to reject the ruinous treaty. On June 20, when the Cabinet resigned, Max wrote to President Ebert, tendering his resignation. He said he thought it best if the government had advisers who were in agreement with its policies.

The new Cabinet consented to the Allied terms, and on June 28, 1919, a new German delegation signed the infamous treaty in the Hall of Mirrors at Versailles. For all his vehement opposition to the treaty, Max knew that Germany could reject it only at its peril. "Whatever one chose, one chose hell," he said. "It was simply a question, which hell promised to be of shorter duration."[26] Max believed that Versailles had encumbered the German democratic parties with an unpopular treaty while allowing right-wing parties to feed freely off the misfortune.[27] Besides coping with the Versailles stigma, Max also had to defend his November 1918 conduct with Prince Max in the waning days of war. In 1919, Hindenburg alleged that the German Army had been "stabbed in the back" by the politicians. Soon the Nazis would seize upon the issue of Versailles and the "November criminals" and Max would suffer, quite unjustly, from his blameless association with both controversial episodes.

After a nearly four-month absence, Max returned to Hamburg that June at a time of mayhem. The local citizenry was in an uproar over charges that a local meat packer, Herr Heil, had adulterated jellied meats with animal parts. On June 24, waving dog heads, dead rats, cow tails, and other parts that supposedly flavored his meats, protesters rolled Herr Heil to the Alster Lake on a wheelbarrow and dumped him in. After the military commandant ordered a crackdown, riots broke out and exchanges of machine-gun fire and grenades left dozens of soldiers and demonstrators dead. By June 27, with martial law declared, nearly ten thousand soldiers blanketed Hamburg.

The Versailles Treaty produced a search for homegrown culprits. In the Jews, right-wing zealots found a vulnerable domestic group whom they could use as a proxy for those foreigners whom they couldn't touch. In 1919 Adolf Hitler began to proselytize among angry veterans in Munich beer halls. At Berlin University, Eric Warburg heard Albert Einstein deliver lectures on relativity amid repeated heckling from anti-Semitic students.

Max was shocked to discover that the *Schutz-und-Trutz-Bündnis*—the Defensive and Offensive Alliance—was distributing yellow leaflets at the stock exchange, blaming him for the "Warburg Jewish Peace" and the one hundred billion gold mark offer.[28] One pamphlet warned, "The American Jew Baruch is Wilson's financial expert. . . . The father of the 100 billion offer is the big, Hamburg-based banker, Max M. Warburg. . . . Away with the rule of this international power, foreign to our national traditions. . . ."[29]

Max was stunned at being blamed for a treaty he had so indignantly rejected. At this first postwar appearance of anti-Semitic bile, he was heartened by the sympathy he received and he grew feisty and combative. "On the stock exchange everybody condoled with me," he told Alice, noting that one person distributing broadsides was beaten up. Of the one hundred billion mark offer, he said, "Well, they are not getting even that now. They have surprises awaiting them."[30]

On July 31, 1919, the Weimar Assembly adopted a constitution. Germany was now a democratic republic, restoring the 1848 black, red, and gold flag. These new legal forms immediately had to contend with extremist violence. A Spartacist revolt in Hamburg was squelched as assassinations spread across Germany. In many respects, the Weimar government was less radical than alleged by the right. It didn't alter many significant power relationships, allowing the Junker-industrialist coalition to retain its old influence. It also failed to prosecute right-wing murders with the same vigor as left-wing ones, reflecting its reliance on the military and the persistence of Wilhelmine judges.

For all his imperial nostalgia, Max Warburg would be a steadfast champion of the new republic, if skeptical of its comprehensive welfare state policies. In late 1918, he made an unorthodox move by joining the Deutsche Volkspartei (DVP) or German People's party, whose most notable personality was Gustav Stresemann. Max felt at home in this conservative party, which stressed tax cuts and less state interference with business, but it also had an anti-Semitic wing that Max needed to check. He also assumed a position on the central committee of the historically anti-Semitic Reichsbank.[31]

In general, the Weimar Republic would fulfill Jewish hopes of greater civil equality, ushering in an explosion of Jewish cultural, political, and economic achievement. Jews would advance in the arts, universities, upper civil service, business, and mass media. Unbaptized Jews were finally elected to the Hamburg Senate. It was a golden age for German Jews, but one already shadowed by a sense of latent menace.

Unfortunately, the last barriers to Jewish integration fell on the eve of Nazism. Emancipation was completed right before its wholesale repeal, leading to great psychic confusion. For the Warburgs, the war's end had started a long, dizzying downward trajectory. The family that had seemed Fortune's favorites would now seem captives of a malevolent fate. The brilliant marriages, the transatlantic success, the ubiquitous political influence—all the family's erstwhile achievements—would now begin to work against them in the hands of industrious Nazis, isolationists, and hard-core xenophobes.

CHAPTER 16

The Murder Exploding Detachment

Separated by war and a news blackout, the Warburgs didn't heal their transatlantic wartime breach until June 1919. While Max was away at Versailles, Charlotte was startled to receive through an intermediary a letter from Felix. Elated by this note, which seemed to flutter from the sky, she told the responsible gentleman, "Many thanks for passing along the letter, which shows me, after a long time, the handwriting of my beloved son Felix. Thank goodness, he assures me that all goes well with my children and grandchildren abroad."[1] Charlotte would die of a heart attack two years later, having seen her sons surpass her most immoderate ambitions.

After Germany signed the peace treaty in 1919, a backlog of musty mail also tumbled in on the amazed American Warburgs. Vacationing in Bar Harbor, Jacob Schiff suddenly got faded letters from Max Warburg, some waylaid by English censors in 1915. One letter from Max sent congratulations to Felix's daughter, Carola, upon her 1916 engagement to Walter Rothschild. By the time this reached America, Carola and Walter had a two-year-old daughter. Max had enclosed a snapshot of his five children—all were now considerably taller. Hoping to bury their old feud, Schiff acknowledged Max's patriotism, but told him it would perhaps be best to avoid the war issue. "I am sure you will agree with me that it will be better if we do not enter upon any discussion of these events."[2]

In political exile ever since leaving Washington, Paul was eager to start afresh and forget that "stupid struggle between nations."[3] Under Fed rules, he couldn't return to private banking for three years. After his bruising, disillusioning Washington stint, his melancholy was deeper, his pessimism more engrained. He contemplated his next step from the comfort of the six-story limestone mansion he and Nina occupied at 17 East 80th Street. Designed by Cass Gilbert, it had sixty-five rooms and twenty-five thousand square feet of space. Paul might mock Felix's extravagance, but he was no pauper. His house had a squash court and a pipe organ and an interior of heavily upholstered comfort. The sofas had velvet cushions set in massive frames of polished wood. In a rich candelabra glow, Dutch Old Masters hung from the walls in ornate gold frames.

It grated on Paul that German-born Americans had been suspected of wartime treachery and that even their mother tongue remained taboo. During a Friday soirée at the Schiffs in 1919, he watched with cynical amusement as an entertainer sang German *Lieder*—in English. Afterward, he told daughter Bettina, now at Bryn Mawr, "This business of taking a German's mind and work as *koscher*, but his poor language as *treife* [unkosher], is more than I can stomach."[4] Paul took pride in his German background, but seemed self-conscious about his religion. In January 1920, he wrote Bettina, "Last night at the theatre there was a crowd of coreligionists dressed (or undressed) as a theatre party—I felt sore and ashamed to look at them, and blessed my stars that you were at Bryn Mawr!"[5]

Once again Paul could advocate better American-German relations, free of any political encumbrance. Flush with cash from booming exports to Europe, America had emerged as the world's supreme financial power. The Liberty Bonds had spawned a vast new market of American investors, who were ripe for the first time to buy foreign bonds. Paul hoped this trend would help to resurrect central Europe.

Like Max, Paul often seemed blind to the Pandora's box of fears, hatreds, and resentments opened by Germany's defeat. He naïvely believed Germany cleansed of militaristic tendencies. In late 1918, he told Colonel House that "we must treat Germany as we did Russia when freed from the yoke of the Czar—as a new friend, a chastened being that has sinned much and has suffered more. . . . I am not worrying about Germany, I think the chastening defeat will bring about a healthy rejuvenation."[6] Yet he knew the Versailles Treaty threatened to polarize German politics and subvert the fragile Weimar democracy.

For Germany, Paul envisioned a middle path between sharp-elbowed capi-

Max Warburg in the 1920s.
(Warburg family, Hamburg)

talism and totalitarian Bolshevism. In March 1919—before he visited Europe—Paul ardently told Morti Schiff, "Every bit of news that we get from Germany gives a clear indication that the military spirit has been broken, and that they do not care what happens to their army and navy in the future; that they want peace and a chance to vindicate themselves before the eyes of the world."[7] Unlike Paul, Morti had just been in Germany and had seen unsettling attitudes persisting behind the shifting masks of monarchy and the Republic. Cautioning Paul against soothing illusions, Morti said he had found no regret whatever among Germans "for murder of women and children, for rape and outrage; for wanton and unnecessary pillage and destruction. . . ."[8] A subtle anglophile shift at Kuhn, Loeb—not to mention his dislike of Morti Schiff—made Paul reluctant to return to the old firm, which he feared would thwart his desire to aid Germany and brother Max. Already he mulled over a scheme to restore their business relationship.

In early August 1919, Paul sailed to Europe, hoping to repair the torn fabric of the past. He told Alice, "The main thing is to see mother and you all again and talk over the future—and forget about the past."[9] In Saint Moritz, Paul was reunited with Max who was trying to arrange German trade finance with Swiss banks. The two brothers discussed their postwar business relationship. Stripped of official position and fretting over an isolationist America, Paul would now serve as a sort of free-lance statesman. In Europe, he was recruited into an effort by bankers and private citizens to end the stalemate over postwar economic issues and counter virulent nationalism. His friend, Dr. Gerard Vissering, governor of the Netherlands Bank, invited him to an Amsterdam meeting in October to discuss reparations and other economic issues.[10]

With Amsterdam a devil's nest of espionage, the group met privately in Dr. Vissering's mansion. Keynes would vividly remember this emotional talk, set against a somber, steady drizzle. He had also invited Carl Melchior. After the stifling secrecy of Versailles, it was a great luxury for these German, English, and American experts to enjoy candid discussions about economic matters. Keynes stated that Germany was the key to solving the global debt problem. With fervor, Paul replied, "If people in Germany could only get a germ of hope that their situation is seriously considered by the other countries, it would do a lot of good."[11] Keynes thought England dangerously oblivious to Continental affairs. To alert world opinion to impending trouble, he proposed an appeal to the new League of Nations, which would hold its first sitting in January 1920.

Paul and Keynes drafted the appeal, which warned that excessive reparations would cripple German productive capacity and harm creditors as well as debtors. Paul wanted to spread this message through an advertising campaign. Much as in his early Fed crusade, he displayed a messianic fire, a homiletic style. However restrained in demeanor, he was extremely passionate and forthright in his judgments. After Amsterdam, he told John W. Davis, the U.S. ambassador in London, "Let us get back to peace; let us forget hatred; let us stop destroying and let us begin to construct!"[12] Again, he was a man captured by a mission.

After one session, Paul walked through Amsterdam with Keynes and Melchior. They ended up at Keynes's hotel room, where he read aloud from his manuscript of *The Economic Consequences of the Peace*, with its acerbic portrayals of Allied statesmen at Versailles. "I noted its effect on the two Jews," Keynes wrote. "Warburg, for personal reasons, hated the President [Wilson] and felt a chuckling delight at his discomfiture; he laughed and giggled and thought it an awfully good hit. But Melchior, as I read, grew ever more solemn, until at the end he appeared almost to be in tears."[13]

On January 15, 1920, the appeal authored by Keynes and Paul Warburg and signed by many luminaries was issued to the press. Herbert Hoover, William Howard Taft, and J. P. Morgan, Jr., cosigned the American version with Paul. They stated that burdensome reparations could foster revolution in Germany and Austria as popular revulsion against unjust debt bred an ugly, desperate mood. The affected governments would print money to pacify the populace, generating inflation.[14] This prescient document had no effect, as Hoover had warned Paul. Indeed, the U.S. Treasury Department thought its dire predictions overblown and resented Paul's involvement as possibly conveying an impression of official American favor. In April 1921, the Allies set the reparations tab at a stupendous 132 billion gold marks or $33 billion.

Paul developed a heavily tragic sense of politics as he saw emotions producing disasters that reason had clearly foreseen. As he later said of these postwar days, "madness ran its course" instead of timely diplomacy. During a German trip in 1920, his pessimism grew as he saw shabby scientists sweeping the streets. Equipped with the acute Warburg antennae for the zeitgeist, he saw further danger in the offing. As he wrote, "Europe at present is like a big steamer sunk by a torpedo. It is idle to discuss to-day what kind of Ritz restaurant or social hall she should have when she is afloat again."[15]

In economics, Paul's prophetic powers were as unerring as Aby's in the cultural sphere, and he initiated a new phase as an embattled Cassandra. Whether from his Jewish background, personal sensitivity, or outsider status as an immigrant, he had a coldly detached vision of things. His Washington defeat had only sharpened his loathing for political folly and ineptitude. For the past five years, he thought, the world had consumed more than it produced, creating inflationary pressures. Now governments were printing money instead of submitting to needed austerity. "The world lives in a fool's paradise based upon fictitious wealth, rash promises, and mad illusions," he said.[16] "We must beware of booms based on false prosperity which has its roots in inflated credits and prices."[17] Indeed, global inflation crested in 1920, followed by a severe slump—the first confirmation of Paul's grim prophecies.

There was a moralistic dimension to his predictions. Paul saw wartime sacrifice giving way to intoxicated self-indulgence—a theme he would sound up to the 1929 crash. He criticized America's selfish retreat from global responsibility and the materialistic frivolity of the Jazz Age. He thought America morally obligated to assist European recovery by reducing German reparations and war debts owed to America by its Allies. Paul took on the stoic, unbending tone of a prophet who knew the world was weak, selfish, and deaf to his warnings.

In April 1921, Paul, encouraged by Max, launched the International Acceptance Bank in New York. The IAB's blue-ribbon shareholders ranged from Kuhn, Loeb to the London Rothschilds. Paul, Felix, and M. M. Warburg also held large blocks of stock. Bank was a misnomer for the IAB, which didn't take deposits. It specialized in a form of trade finance called banker's acceptances, which had long existed in Europe, but only became possible in America under the Fed. An acceptance was a short-term credit extended by a bank to a customer. With these credits, Paul hoped to rebuild a shattered Germany and by July he was financing German grain imports. Since the Nazis later accused Jewish bankers of sabotaging the economy, it is worth noting that Paul and Max acted as a critical conduit of Wall Street money at a time when credit was scarce. Already in 1920, the Warburgs pulled off a big transatlantic deal for the German electrical company, AEG, selling a quarter of its new loan issue to the Guggenheims.

Perhaps Paul's most compelling motive in forming the IAB was to help Max and the Hamburg firm. The IAB gave unique advantages to M. M. Warburg, which served as its European agent and executed much of its European business. Bolstered by the New York connection, Max participated in share issues for Friedrich Krupp and Daimler Motors in 1921. In the end, this Wall Street link would prove a mixed blessing, for the cautious Paul funneled money to Max that only fed his ebullient speculative instincts. But in the early 1920s, the New York connection buoyed the Hamburg bank while other banks struggled to recuperate from the war.

—

Pictures of Max Warburg from the early 1920s show a barrel-chested figure with powerful, squared shoulders and a buccaneer's charm. He radiates a sense of massive willpower and native optimism. In early 1920, he seemed mildly hopeful even as new extremist voices were heard. It was, after all, at this time, February 1920, that a small workers' party, started in a Munich tavern a year before, was restyled the National Socialist German Workers' Party. Its leader, Adolf Hitler, blasted the Versailles Treaty and called for an end to Jewish citizenship. He railed against Jewish financiers who had allegedly delivered Germany to the "thralldom of interest payments."[18] This faint drumbeat would grow much louder.

For a man comfortable with the middle ground, Max was alarmed by the polarized politics of Weimar Germany and he would try repeatedly to orchestrate coalitions of his conservative DVP with Social Democrats and other liberal parties to shore up the center. On March 13, 1920, the new Republic's fragility became evident when a naval brigade, headed by Dr. Wolfgang Kapp, marched on Berlin in an aborted putsch. At first, government troops wouldn't fire on the rebels, and Max feared the military would side with them. The putsch was eventually put down thanks to the combined strength of the Social Democratic party and the trade unions. But for overseas investors, the Kapp putsch reinforced uneasiness about German stability.

At the Spa conference in July 1920, the reparations issue dovetailed with resurgent anti-Semitism. France threatened to seize the Ruhr if Germany didn't deliver two million tons of coal yearly. Hugo Stinnes, the German coal baron, preached defiance. While he acknowledged that this might create chaos, perhaps even a fleeting bout of Bolshevism, he thought that Germany could then blame the Allies. Max didn't feel quite so cavalier. Melchior, a Spa delegate, reluctantly submitted to Allied reparations demands. When another courageous Jewish delegate, Walther Rathenau, said Germany had no choice but to submit, Stinnes published a letter interpreting German acquiescence, not as a grim, unpleasant necessity, but as a form of Jewish guile. In chilling anticipation of Nazi propaganda, he claimed to detect a pattern of racial voting in the German delegation: "Because of a foreign psyche, a number of representatives at Spa have broken the German resistance against shameful demands."[19]

As the year progressed, Max slid into growing pessimism, especially about Germany's currency. Several factors were contributing to inflation. The government had financed the war through loans, not taxes, thus providing an incentive to repay in debased coin. Committed to a lavish social welfare agenda, Weimar politicians were powerfully tempted to print money. And as the mark dipped in value, it made imports more expensive. The Warburgs saw friends auctioning off family heirlooms to pay bills or yanking their children from expensive private schools.

A lethal gloom settled over Hamburg. The train station was crowded with slovenly men who marched daily to the harbor to seek nonexistent work. The Warburgs themselves had trouble supporting pet charities. As chairman of the Jewish Hospital, Fritz kept it alive through monthly checks from Paul. "The disintegration of Germany is becoming evident on all sides," Max wrote in the bank's 1920 annual report. "There is a silent poverty that is developing. . . ."[20] The gathering inflation forced postponement of a historical volume commemorating the bank's 125th anniversary.

With mounting postwar anti-Semitism, Jews were reluctant to seize political opportunities available in Weimar Germany. Melchior declined offers to become German reconstruction minister and head of the Economics Ministry and Max also resisted highly tempting offers. In June 1921, he dined in a Berlin club with Walther Rathenau, the Jewish reconstruction minister. As Max said afterward, "He pestered me to enter the Cabinet, as Finance Minister or Minister of the Foreign Office, but I reassured him that I would stay by my last."[21] Max again believed he had a double liability, for the left would attack him as a banker, the right as a Jew.

The inflation exacerbated social tensions in Germany, producing a handful of winners and legions of embittered losers. Uneducated people fantasized that Jewish bankers orchestrated this complex monetary phenomenon for their gain. Disproportionately represented in private banking, well-to-do Jews were generally better equipped to deal with inflation, while elderly people on pensions and depositors with small bank accounts fared worst. People ravaged by inflation resentfully watched financiers shuffle money into foreign currencies or tangible assets to preserve their capital.

Max moved about with a fearfulness at odds with his native ebullience. When Matthias Erzberger, the finance minister and a Catholic moderate, was murdered by two former officers in August 1921, bloodthirsty supporters rejoiced in the streets. Alarmed, Max decided to hold the October wedding of his eldest daughter, Lola, at Mittelweg 17 instead of at the local synagogue. He rejected another offer to become the German ambassador to the United States, trying to reduce his political visibility.[22]

With his Wall Street connections, Max was courted by Berlin and the Foreign Office prodded him to travel to New York to lobby for an international loan. Agreeing that only such a loan could prop up the plunging German currency, he pursued this theme with Colonel House at the American embassy in Berlin in June 1921. He told House not to be fooled by Germany's surface calm and evoked a nation exhausted by war, terror, hunger, and revolution.[23] Max still thought America could urge moderation upon France.

Already the new republic coped with endless Cabinet shuffles and a doomed air of perpetual crisis. Germany couldn't seem to regain its balance. By early 1922, the mark had dipped to 4 percent of its prewar value, thinning the Warburg fortune. In January 1922, Chancellor Josef Wirth invited Melchior to join a team drawing up plans for an April reparations conference in Genoa.

With Hugo Stinnes angling to head the delegation, Max and Melchior scented trouble ahead. When Wirth asked Max to attend with Melchior, he refused and instructed Melchior on how to avoid being scapegoated. "I consider it *de facto* incorrect for our firm to be too strongly represented at this conference. . . ." he said. "I should like only to ask in advance that you immediately leave the room if in connection with an international loan there is a demand for financial supervision of Germany."[24]

While Max navigated warily through these treacherous waters, a Jewish friend abandoned all such restraint: Walther Rathenau. Rathenau's father had founded the foremost German electrical concern, AEG, a prime Warburg client, and Walther succeeded him. He was a curious compound of visionary economist, utopian philosopher, and down-to-earth pragmatist. A cultured, gifted linguist, he inveighed against the machine civilization that had spawned his family's wealth. In a 1912 book, he proposed that three hundred men controlled Europe's economic destiny—an assertion later perverted by the Nazis into the myth that three hundred *Jewish bankers* controlled Europe. Rathenau thought anti-Semitism would wane in Germany as a new technocratic class overtook the effete aristocratic order.

The dapper Rathenau, with his trim Van Dyke beard, frequently visited Kösterberg. On one visit, he laid out a plan to redesign the gardens into a French park, with terraces descending to the Elbe River. Max had reservations about Rathenau, having sparred with him over the War Metal Society. He found Rathenau highly literate and a superb orator, but also a vain, insufferable windbag who once droned on through an entire dinner while Max and Alice stared in stupefied silence. Max saw himself as a simplifier and Rathenau as someone who tended to confuse complexity with profundity.

For Chaim Weizmann, Rathenau typified those acculturated German Jews who "seemed to have no idea that they were sitting on a volcano. . . ."[25] Where Max shunned the political limelight because of anti-Semitism, Rathenau sought it out. After the 1920 Spa conference, he became a lightning rod for Nazi attacks. Indeed, the party faithful chanted a couplet, "Shoot down that Walther Rathenau / That cursed, Goddamned Jewish sow."[26]

In January 1922, Rathenau was named foreign minister, the highest position to which any Jew had ever risen, yet he stood in a precarious spot. At Genoa, he imperiled his own security with a pro-Soviet speech that inflamed the Nazis. When Max lunched with him afterward, Rathenau suddenly seemed to have aged. He told Max, "That very day in Genoa I said to myself: at this moment Max Warburg is saying to Melchior: 'What an ass Rathenau is making of himself!' " Max admitted he had made similar remarks, but phrased more diplomatically.[27]

When Rathenau again pushed Max to join the Cabinet, the latter said it would tempt fate to have two Jewish Cabinet members—one was controversial enough. Hamburg had been shaken by right-wing bomb explosions as violence edged closer to home. As if to illustrate Max's point, Rathenau lowered his voice, saying gravely, "You cannot imagine how many threatening letters I receive." They discussed ways to combat anti-Semitism.[28]

Despite these threats, Rathenau didn't take the basic precaution of having bodyguards. Four weeks later, on June 24, 1922, he was riding to work along the Königsallee in Berlin, when two young leather-jacketed thugs drove up beside him and forced his car to the curb. One sprayed Rathenau with a submachine gun, while the other tossed a grenade into the car, blowing him from his seat. One assassin was killed by police and the other killed himself. Years later, the Nazis erected a monument to these heroic young martyrs. When other conspirators were later interrogated, it turned out they had consumed the anti-Semitic forgery, *The Protocols of the Elders of Zion,* and believed that Rathenau had conspired with fellow Jews to dominate the world.

For the Jewish community, Rathenau's murder embodied their worst fears. Even the most powerful, apparently, weren't immune to the deadly subterranean currents that swirled just below the surface of German society. Max saw the ghosts of Versailles haunting Germany, as he had predicted. "The assassination puts Germany to shame because it reveals once more the increasing savagery of German morals," he wrote to Paul. "One feels the coming storm, the consequence of that disintegration which daily increases here. . . . It may well be that this murder will give the signal for further disturbances."[29]

Max was more prophetic than he knew, for the Rathenau murder was the first of a dozen planned by a group called the Murder Exploding Detachment. The target list included Berlin newspaper editor Theodor Wolff—and Max Warburg. They had chosen a dramatic setting to slay Max: at his inaugural speech at Hamburg's Overseas Club on June 27. Fortunately, the Hamburg police chief tipped Max off to the plot and advised him to avoid public appearances, vary his schedule, shun restaurants, and stay away from his beloved Kösterberg. After several warnings, Max heeded the advice and moved into the temporarily vacant apartment of his sister-in-law. Alice wasn't allowed to accompany him and it would be an agonizing time for her.

The Hamburg police assigned a congenial young police lieutenant, whom Max later referred to as "P.," to the banker." Max and this protector lived as intimately as lovers. P. slept by Max, ate with him, strolled with him. "I became thoroughly acquainted with the life of a man who is pursued by his own shadow," said Max.[30] The sociable Max tried to befriend P. The first night, they tried playing chess, although P.'s poor game soon ended this experiment. The next morning, Max was flabbergasted to find two strange men in the breakfast room. "Aha," he thought, "there you are!"[31] In fact, they were housepainters, not assassins. Max didn't think it smart to hole up in a building surrounded by painters' scaffolding, so he and P. moved to his cousin's house. That night, his cousin, afraid of disturbing Max asleep in the bedroom, stepped on a chair to loosen a light bulb instead of flipping a noisy switch. When she fell with a crash, P. dashed into the room, flashing a pistol with dramatic derring-do. After nervous giggles, they all went back to sleep. Meanwhile, the other Warburg partners traveled to work in bombproof cars with bars and grates over the windows, accompanied by a police escort.

After several days of nervous antics, the Hamburg police told Max they couldn't vouch for his safety. He decided to spend several weeks in Amsterdam with Alice. With his monograms already on his linen, Max assumed the name Max Werner. Because tip-hungry local porters knew the red-and-yellow Warburg trunks, Malice swapped them for a blue-and-white set. After a few weeks, Max was ready to return to Hamburg. Alice fought down her fears and returned with him. Although a tough, proud woman, she nonetheless followed Max's lead in major matters despite her terrible, continuing anxiety about his safety. When they got home, the children were startled to see them. Why had they returned so soon? Max explained that Holland was so boring, he decided he would rather take his chances on Germany. In Hamburg, he was greeted by an outpouring of sympathy. The Senate thanked him for his tireless efforts for the city, and the Jewish community wired congratulations to which Max replied, "the attacks brought about because of my Judaism have only brought me closer to it."[32]

That September, Max took a two-month trip to America for security reasons and to appeal for lower reparations. After Rathenau's murder, he withdrew into the political shadows. Before boarding the liner to New York, he and Alice took a steamer to Cuxhaven. For the last time, Max was accompanied by the faithful P. With a severe wartime head injury, P. was under strict doctors' orders to abstain from alcohol, but nevertheless joined Max in a farewell cocktail. By the time P. got back to Hamburg, the forbidden cocktail had triggered deranged behavior. He began to fire at fellow police officers and was subsequently shut up in an asylum.

Max later found out that the friendly young police lieutenant had, in fact, been a Nazi spy. A well-drilled Nazi cell existed in the Hamburg police department. (When the first Storm Troopers unit was formed in November 1922, it was headed by a Hamburg police clerk.) Far from guarding Max, P. had kept his Nazi comrades closely posted on his movements and Max would have been an easy murder target had he not fled to Amsterdam.

After docking in New York, Malice stayed with Friedaflix at 1109 Fifth Avenue, a sentimental reunion made more poignant by Max's brush with death. For the rest of his life, Felix would fret about his brother's safety. Indignant over the plot, Felix tried to persuade *The New York Times* to write an editorial, arguing that "the German militarists, after having gotten the German people into disrepute by disregarding the rights of others, are now trying to wash their hands by blaming the Jews for Germany's misfortune."[33] Felix found many culprits for Germany's troubles: the Allies for failing to buttress the Weimar regime, Weimar politicians for their weak vacillation, the militarists for having created the situation in the first place. Felix said that six months earlier Rathenau had told a London friend of his "that he knew that he was to be the next; that he was not afraid of traveling outside of Germany, but he was doomed in Germany, but that he did not talk about it out of consideration for his old mother."[34]

Felix and Frieda scheduled many outings for Max, including musical revues and his first football game. After the cheerless atmosphere in Germany, Max found America bright and hopeful. The brothers recaptured their old sense of fun with a hilarious golf game at Woodlands. As Felix described it, "Paul taking every shot terribly seriously and mourning over every bad shot, Max making fun of every bad shot—and he makes only bad ones—and your poor lame father beating them all hollow, to the great amusement of the multitude."[35]

Afterward, Paul and Max went to Washington, Paul arranging meetings for his brother with Secretary Hoover at Commerce, Hughes at State, and Mellon at Treasury. These talks boosted Max's hopes that a conference of experts might be convened to reduce reparations. Paul circulated a private memo describing the "danse macabre" of the reichsmark, with hyperinflation already wiping out the savings of an alienated German middle class. "Those of them who are unable to become workers of some sort are, literally, starving, freezing, and dying."[36] It was a frustrating time for the Warburgs. Paul saw America sunk in an "intellectual coma" and warned Washington that "we are surrounding ourselves with a wall and moat of cynicism and selfish materialism. . . ."[37] When Max sailed back to Germany aboard the *Aquitania* in November, Paul and Felix asked him to stay longer, but Max thought he must return to the wheel of his ship in Hamburg.[38]

By the time he returned, the mark was in an alarming free fall. The French accused the Germans of engineering this drop to sabotage reparations, a viewpoint Max and Melchior sharply contested. A new government was headed by Wilhelm Cuno, Ballin's successor at HAPAG. The Nazis claimed Max had "installed" Cuno; Max actually had been dismayed to learn of the appointment while steaming back across the Atlantic.[39] The new chancellor pleaded with France for a reparations moratorium. Instead, France declared Germany in default on some timber deliveries.

The upshot was that on January 11, 1923, sixty thousand French and Belgian soldiers took over the Ruhr to enforce payment, by force if necessary. When the Cuno government called for passive resistance in the Ruhr, the French decided to operate the local coal mines and iron foundries themselves. Max applauded Germany's tough, morale-boosting resistance. When American lawyer John Foster Dulles discussed the Ruhr with Max and Chancellor Cuno aboard the SS *Albert Ballin*, Max defended the "spontaneous resistance of the population against violence."[40] At the same time, Max feared its economic consequences. To sustain striking workers, Berlin had to make support payments that would further fuel inflation. In February, Max warned Cuno that the burden of supporting the defiant Ruhr workers would complete Germany's ruin. Everything now hastened the upward spiral of prices. Germany printed money to pay Ruhr workers while France put seized reichsmarks back into circulation, swelling the money supply.

At M. M. Warburg, inflation created a frenetic tempo that clashed with the Victorian formality. As soon as employees were paid, they crossed the street to the Karstadt department store and spent the money before prices rose. The cheaper mark created a bonanza for foreign investors who bought German properties at bargain prices, arousing resentment against the bankers who executed these deals. M. M. Warburg switched much of its capital into foreign currencies. With black humor, Max joked that the staff in 1923 spent its time scribbling zeroes in ledgers. From 1921 to 1922 alone, the firm's balance sheet exploded from 1.6 to 37 billion marks! Inflation fed speculation, with clerks constantly chalking up new prices on the foreign-exchange blackboard and the bank had to lower the curtains when HAPAG employees across the street spied on them through binoculars. Hamburg's docks teemed with people trying to buy foreign currency from disembarking sailors.

The rush from devalued paper into gold and other commodities drove prices up further. Max thought of buying a farm to hedge against inflation. "The Mark completely ceased to deserve the appellation 'currency'; it became simply an illusion," he said. "Worthless scraps of paper, each nominally representing one million Marks and stuffed into huge sacks, dominated the market. Amid the torrent of events cascading down one after another, the firm's arrangements whirled in confusion."[41] To deal with the hyperinflation, Max helped to organize a makeshift affair called the Hamburg Bank of 1923, which issued emergency currency backed by gold. Paul's International Acceptance Bank granted its first dollar credit to the 1923 emergency bank.

In this frenetic atmosphere, M. M. Warburg & Co. celebrated its 125th anniversary on January 6, 1923. The party, held at the Alsterufer home of Aby S., had been intended as a big, expansive affair, like a farmer's wedding, with every employee invited. But the vast paperwork produced by inflation had swollen employee ranks from about two hundred to five hundred, so only those with twenty-five years of service attended. Merry speeches alternated with muted words of thanksgiving. As Max said of the participants, "They were all inspired by a feeling of gratitude that we had somehow struggled onward through all these periods of misfortune."[42]

The most remarkable speech was given by a precocious newcomer, twenty-year-old Siegmund Warburg, grandson of the first Siegmund and a nephew of Aby S., who defined tradition as "the spirit of a particular atmosphere, which has arisen where one generation after another has worked with a similar purpose."[43] To sustain this tradition, he stressed the need for fairness, loyalty, reserve in personal life, and a German way of thinking. Closing with a paradox, he said traditions die when people cling to them too strongly or hanker too willfully after the new. This sort of epigram would become his trademark.

However chastened by war and inflation, the Warburgs retained a faith in Germany's future. Every now and then, they got jitters. Returning from a ski holiday that month, Eric stopped to hear Hitler speak in a Munich beer hall. Afterward, he wrote to his cousin, saying that the man was surely mad. But if the Allies didn't soften the Versailles Treaty, if they insisted upon extracting the last ounce of revenge, this deranged man, with the hoarse voice, would someday rule Germany.[44]

That summer, the mark spun out of control. In mid-June, a dollar equaled one hundred thousand marks, a month later two hundred thousand marks. By late July, the dollar rose to one million marks, by late August ten million marks, by September one hundred million marks. In November, the dollar fetched twelve trillion marks on the black market. In October, it cost a few trillion marks to post a letter. With bread prices tripling hourly, people dashed about frantically with big wads of devalued paper stuffed into their pockets. The printing of money was the only profitable activity left, as 1,783 presses stamped out worthless paper. It took 30 plants just to produce the sea of paper.

As Germany lurched toward civil war, Cuno fell in August 1923 and was replaced by Max's hero, Gustav Stresemann, who immediately declared martial law. Strike-torn Hamburg was a war zone, with bullets flying everywhere and mobs pillaging food stores. In late October, Communists seized seventeen police stations and blocked railway lines. The police struck back, patrolling in armored cars mounted with machine guns, and they cleared Communist strongholds by hurling grenades into buildings.

The next bold adventure came from the political right. In early November, Hitler, Hermann Göring, and Ludendorff essayed their bloody Munich Beer Hall Putsch, which was swiftly crushed. Hitler used the subsequent trial to issue electrifying tirades against the Jews and to emerge as a national figure. In the Munich court, he said he had acted to prevent a Jewish financier from mortgaging the German railway to gain an international loan to Germany—a possible reference to Max or Melchior. After his employees overheard violent threats made against him in the street, Max fled Hamburg for twenty-four hours. To guard against future trouble, the Warburgs began to create investment companies in America, Britain, and Holland. Sentenced to five years in prison, Hitler ended up serving an extraordinarily lenient sentence of less than nine months in Landsberg prison. There he ate well, put on weight, and began to compose *Mein Kampf*.

On November 12, 1923, following the Hitler putsch, the government named Dr. Hjalmar Schacht to a special post to stabilize the German currency. He oversaw the issue of a new currency, the rentenmark, issued in restricted quantities and backed by mortgages on German real estate, gold, and foreign exchange. As the first rentenmark banknotes circulated on November 15, the printing presses stopped making the old money. Max predicted the rentenmark would fail, tempting France to introduce the franc in occupied territory. Instead, good new money drove out bad old money.

When the Reichsbank president, Rudolf Havenstein, died on November 19, a competition to succeed him arose between the reactionary Karl Helfferich and Dr. Hjalmar Schacht. Max was a member of the Reichsbank's Central Committee, which met beneath tall oil portraits of the three kaisers while messengers in blue livery with gilt buttons scuttled in and out. Despite Max's presence, the Reichsbank remained anti-Semitic in its hiring policy. Max supported Schacht less from enthusiasm than from fear of Helfferich. In the end, he was spared the necessity of voting for Schacht because he had to sail to New York.

Dr. Schacht indeed became the Reichsbank's president on December 22, 1923, and won global renown for slaying inflation by the following summer. This averted further deterioration of the political situation, which was taking an anti-Semitic turn.

There were some hideous previews of the future. In November 1923, a pogrom against the *Ostjuden* occurred in Berlin. As the *Vossiche Zeitung* reported, "Howling mobs in all the streets. Looting is going on under cover of darkness. . . . On all sides, the same cry: 'Kill the Jews!' "[46] In 1923, the police still bothered to clear the streets instead of simply watching, as they would do later. Returning to Hamburg before Christmas 1923, Max so feared an outbreak of mob violence against the bank that he gained permission from the police to issue firearms to eight employees. Max often described his bank as a fortress, and for once the image had a ring of literal truth.

The subsequent Warburg story is inseparable from that of Dr. Schacht, who would serve as their sometime patron and protector under the Third Reich. Schacht's father, who had worked in a New York brewery, so admired a local newspaper editor that he named his son Hjalmar Horace Greeley Schacht. At school, Hjalmar studied Hebrew and took his doctorate in political economics before working at the Dresdner and Danat bank. A starchy, arrogant figure, Dr. Schacht outwardly looked the proper old-school banker, with his wire-rimmed round spectacles, mustache, and bowler hat. Beneath the respectable facade, however, he was a shrewd opportunist with a slightly mad gleam in his eye. With the benefit of hindsight, Max noted his chameleon quality, his brazen opportunism. He could "change course with great energy and ruthlessness and . . . sacrifice the principles which he had just seemed to uphold. The deciding element in his character was his powerful instinct of self-preservation. He could not bear to be out of power for any length of time."[47] Max wasn't quite so censorious at the time and later exaggerated his early doubts about Schacht. As Paul's son, Jimmy, recalled, "For some reason which I find difficult to explain, I disliked and distrusted the German wizard of finance, while my father and uncle Max both admired and trusted him."[48]

Later on, Max would pin more hopes on Schacht than upon anybody else. If, in the grimmest days of the 1930s, he could indulge the belief that the Warburgs still enjoyed some sacred place in the German scheme of things, it was partly due to his special relationship with Dr. Schacht.

—

In the early 1920s, anti-Semitic assaults against the Warburgs solidified into a sweeping theory that tied them to a conspiracy with other Jewish bankers. The major source material was *The Protocols of the Elders of Zion*, an infamous forgery perpetrated by the Okhrana, the czarist secret police. This devious work sought to strengthen czarist despotism by playing upon fear of Jewish revolutionaries. The book recounts secret speeches supposedly delivered by a group of Jewish elders to a cabal of coconspirators, outlining a plan for world domination. (It actually reworked a pamphlet written by Maurice Joly in 1864 that ascribed maniacal ambitions to Napoleon III.) An English translation circulated in Washington and Germany after the war. In 1919–20, it was handed out to White Russian troops to discredit the Bolshevik Revolution as a global Jewish plot. The Warburgs were putative masterminds on the banking side.

In early 1920, Henry Ford laid his hands on a London copy and greatly amplified its themes. That May, his Michigan newspaper, the *Dearborn Independent*, ran a front-page article, "The International Jew: The World's Problem," which launched seven years of invective. As the isolationist Ford pondered the failure of his wartime peace campaign, he identified the Warburgs and other Jewish bankers as the warmongers who had thwarted him. That the Warburgs had opposed the war and suffered from it financially didn't seem to faze him. The *Protocols* allowed Ford to attack both Communists and Wall Street financiers by showing a hidden affinity between them.

To the benighted, the *Dearborn Independent* had to explain exactly why conservative, Republican Jewish bankers would aid Bolshevism. The paper noted Schiff's animus toward Russia and financing of Japan, turning this into an insidious German-Japanese plot to undermine Russia. Max Warburg was alleged bagman of the conspiracy who gave money to Leon Trotsky. Not content to cite actual Jewish participants in the Bolshevik Revolution, the *Dearborn Independent* found them crouching behind every rock. According to the newspaper, Kerensky's real name was Adler, and Lenin's children spoke Yiddish to each other. Noting that Rothschild in English meant "Redshield," the paper said this was why Bolsheviks were called "Reds." Ford had a field day with Paul Warburg, who linked the Jewish banking cabal to the Federal Reserve Board that Ford so despised. Of Ford's charges, perhaps the most damaging was that Paul and Max had jointly concocted the Versailles Treaty—even though Paul hadn't gone and Max hadn't signed the document. The *Dearborn Independent* wrote, "As has been recounted in the press the world over, the brother from America and the brother from Germany both met at Paris as government representatives in determining the peace. There were so many Jews in the German delegation that it was known by the term 'kosher,' also as 'the Warburg delegation.' "[49]

The Warburgs held special attractions for conspiracy theorists. Because they had intermarried with many banking families, their family tree could be portrayed as the dangling and poisonous tentacles of a strangling monster. As citizens of different countries, they could be made to typify "international Jewry"—treacherous, rootless, forming a Fifth Column in every country. And since the brothers were politically active in their respective countries, they could be depicted as treasonous foreign agents.

When the American Jewish Committee learned that Ford and the Ku Klux Klan bankrolled anti-Semitic propaganda in Germany, they debated what action to take. Should Paul bring a libel suit? Should they boycott Ford products? Or try for a congressional probe? In the end, they decided not to dignify Ford's efforts with a response. Nobody knew whether a counterattack would fan the flames of prejudice or blow them out. Jacob Schiff endorsed silence. "If we get into a controversy we shall light a fire, which no one can foretell how it will be extinguished."[50] The timidity was short-sighted: Ford didn't apologize for his anti-Jewish statements until 1927, even though the *Times* of London exposed the *Protocols* as a forgery in 1921.

In 1921, Max sued Nazi publicist Theodor Fritsch for publishing a German edition of Ford's *The International Jew*. It contained a bogus letter from Berlin banker Carl Fürstenberg, telling his Bolshevik comrades that they should transfer their money to a special account at M. M. Warburg & Co. Winning the lawsuit, Max got a recantation printed in several papers. The next year, he discussed with Felix and the American Jewish Committee how to curb growing worldwide anti-Semitism. They feared that if they mounted a global campaign against slander, they might only play into the hands of their enemies, who would cite this as proof of the Jewish conspiracy. So Max argued in favor of quiet legal action. At the 1922 meeting, Felix said that in inflation-ridden Germany even anti-Semites "are worrying more about their daily bread than about the Jews."[51]

The hyperinflation, in fact, gave an incalculable boost to anti-Semitism. The Nazis claimed that the inflation profiteers were all Jews, profiting from the common people's misery. Ideologue Alfred Rosenberg declared that a Nazi government would expropriate banks and stock exchanges. Playing on hoary Shylock images, Bavarian engineer Gottfried Feder blamed Germany's ill on "stock-market capitalism" and "world usury capitalism" and demanded an end to the "thralldom of interest payments."[52] The hyperinflation enshrined the Jewish banker as the most Machiavellian of Jews in the Nazi bestiary.

On February 22, 1923, the Nazi newspaper, the *Völkischer Beobachter*, attacked Paul, Felix, and Max. With droll humor, Max described the edition as having "a portrait of me which was not at all bad and which carried the superscription, 'Banking Jew and Labor Leader.' "[53] Knowing a Munich court would never defend Jewish bankers, he decided against trying a libel action.

About the same time, brother Fritz was questioned by parliamentary committees about his World War I talks with Protopopov, which now led to anti-Semitic theories of a Jewish wartime sellout.

History was being steadily rewritten, with even relatively obscure Jews suddenly cast into leading roles, their minor, fumbling actions now elevated to cunning acts of high treason. Deeds that once had redounded to the Warburgs' glory were being systematically transmogrified into the stealthy machinations of a subtle demonic international conspiracy.

CHAPTER 17

The Royal Couple

A man of stern willpower, Jacob Schiff made few concessions to age in his last years. During the 1919 summer, he took eight-hour hikes at Bar Harbor, refusing to admit the least fatigue afterward. He kept up a magnificent pose of perfect health and never allowed a nurse in the house. Now and then, he grew wistful. In January 1920, he told Max that he looked forward to seeing his beloved German haunts again, but added, "I must live more in the past than the future. . . ."[1] A month later, he attended the twenty-fifth wedding anniversary of the Friedaflix match he had so fiercely opposed. At 1109 Fifth stood a big silver-coated oak tree, embellished with silver acorns that popped open to disclose snapshots of his grandchildren.

During his last week of life, Schiff reported to the office daily. On September 22, 1920, too weak to attend Yom Kippur services, he insisted upon fasting at home. The next day, when he arrived at Sea Bright, the chauffeur extended a helpful hand, but Schiff stiffly brushed it aside and entered his house unaided. Very deaf, strict, indomitable, he concealed his illness even from senior partners at Kuhn, Loeb.

At the Sabbath's close on September 25, Jacob Schiff, age seventy-three, died with his wife, Frieda, and Morti at his side. His obituary was the headline story in *The New York Times*. As he lay in state, surrounded by purple asters and abundant floral arrangements, veiled women and men in black arm bands paid their last respects. Despite his cold, exacting nature, Schiff had affected many people, and his Temple Emanu-El funeral had a cathartic power. Polish and Russian Jews paid tribute to the king of the German Jews. Hundreds, perhaps thousands, of *Ostjuden* tramped up Fifth Avenue from the Lower East Side slums just to stand outside the synagogue, and Jacob's niece would recall, "Hundreds of immigrants in those hats, trying to get in and not being able to, standing out there, silent."[2] They trailed the funeral cortege past stores closed in tribute, then passed over the Queensboro Bridge to Brooklyn's Salem Fields where Governor Al Smith and Mayor John Hylan attended the burial.

Schiff's death marked a watershed for the American Warburgs and "Our Crowd." Leadership at Kuhn, Loeb passed to Schiff's socialite son, Mortimer, marking a transition from an ambitious founding generation to far more complacent and sociable successors. Few would have predicted that Schiff's bon vivant son-in-law would ably assume his philanthropic mantle. Felix would preside over Jewish charity with a touch as light and genial as Schiff's had been ponderous. In fifteen years after Schiff's death, Felix and Frieda would personally dispense thirteen million dollars, sometimes a million dollars at a shot. Frieda never quite escaped her father's shadow. As Felix dealt with Schiff's estate, he told his son, "the responsibility for dear Mumpy [*sic*] to reach a decision, when she has always been protected to such an extent, is not so easy. . . ."[3]

Schiff's passage began a major shift in the ethos of the American Warburgs, since he had enforced the old-time religion. "Conformism more than faith compelled our family's religious observance," Felix's youngest son, Edward, said.[4] Nobody could match Schiff's severe belief in the sanctity of Jewish life. But if anything, his self-righteous zealotry backfired, producing a posthumous revolt against his piety. He had made devotion seem dreadful, not joyous, and his descendants would rush to trade his Old World darkness for Jazz Age buoyancy.

Schiff left a taxable estate of thirty-five million dollars with taut strings attached, so that his rigid hand reached beyond the grave. He set up trust funds for his grandchildren that allowed them to draw income until age forty and, capital *and* income after that. There was a catch, however: If they married outside the faith, they forfeited their fortune. Felix defended Schiff's decision: "He and many others have felt that intermarriage brings problems, and in our case probably the lowering of standards of pride and usefulness to those who need us most, and it is for that reason that Grandpa and I always felt so strongly on the subject."[5] This created an agonizing dilemma for Felix's

From left: Felix Warburg, Vera Weizmann,
Frieda Warburg, and Chaim Weizmann at a Boston
conference for the United Palestine Appeal, 1928.
(American Jewish Archives)

sons, who felt progressively more distant from their Jewish roots. The eldest, Freddy, would be nearly fifty before he married, while Gerald and Paul Felix entered into unhappy first marriages to Jewish wives.

Felix now assumed a loftier position among the Warburgs, but it resulted from more than the inheritance. Before the war, a rough parity had existed between the American and German Warburgs in terms of wealth. Kösterberg and Woodlands were, arguably, estates of equivalent grandeur. Now German defeat and inflation had reduced the fortune of the Hamburg clan and somewhat humbled it. When Felix and Frieda traveled to Kösterberg in the 1920s, trailing heaps of luggage and teams of servants, their lives would seem inconceivably grand. With Aby locked in a sanatorium, Paul chased from Washington, and Max and Fritz plagued by zealous anti-Semites, Felix would seem the lucky brother. This suited his sunny nature just fine.

Felix was the last family grandee and enjoyed his wealth free of guilt and with a spirit of infectious fun. When his chauffeurs rocketed down Fifth Avenue on the wrong side of the street, friendly local cops just waved them through the intersections. Legions of servants and tradesmen always fluttered around Felix, keeping him well groomed and debonair. Once late for an appointment, Felix asked his barber if he could cut his hair without removing his collar. "Mr. Warburg," the man replied, "I've been cutting your hair for twenty years. I could cut it with your hat on."[6] Each morning the local florist sent Felix a fresh white carnation.

Friedaflix entertained on a scale that, by today's standards, seems absurdly extravagant. It wasn't uncommon for them to have seventy-five people for dinner. When daughter Carola married Walter Rothschild in 1916, nine hundred people tramped through 1109 Fifth Avenue to eat and drink. Attired in a blue velvet suit with silver buttons, Edward held aloft the enormous train of his sister's gown. Carola had huge blue eyes, a handsome, square-jawed face, and a husky voice thickened by cigarettes. She had great sex appeal and an easy way with men gained from being an attractive young woman who grew up surrounded by an adoring father and many brothers. Endowed with Felix's grace, she was also a good listener and the trusted confidante of many Warburgs. Felix spoiled her silly. By the time she married Walter, she had twenty-two pieces of costly jewelry, including a floral brooch with sixteen diamonds and a necklace with twenty-eight rubies.[7] For her wedding present, Carola got a Woodlands house, surrounded by thirty acres of real estate.

Of the five children, Carola was the only one who married just once and to a Jew. Walter was a genial man with a big, infectious grin. His father ran the A&S department store in Brooklyn. Unrelated to the banking Rothschilds, he joked that he belonged to the Brooklyn Rothschilds. Frieda had an awkward first meeting with Walter's family in that alien borough. When she declared, "The only other time I ever was in Brooklyn was at a funeral," the Rothschilds whooped with laughter and things improved at once.[8]

Much to Frieda's horror, Felix insisted upon a constant whirl of concerts and dances at 1109. With his boyish zest, he flitted from one activity to the next, merging the roles of social director and paterfamilias. A quicksilver sort of man, always needing variety, he taught his children to dance and instructed them in tennis and other sports. Born to wealth, Felix's descendants would be the socialite Warburgs, far more preoccupied with café society, country clubs, and the Social Register than their cousins.

Felix often bemoaned his children's frivolity. "Old and young are trying to have a good time through their own stomachs and pockets, and do not care a hang for the rest. My own children are very nice and agreeable as children go, but not much of an exception in regard to the life they lead."[9] Regretting that they ignored Warburg traditions of public service, he tried to teach them that deep friendships aren't formed at golf or cards, but through shared work. About Freddy, who worked at M. M. Warburg and Kuhn, Loeb after Harvard, Felix said in 1923, "if he is awake at night, it is more on account of dances than on account of initiating any new revolutionary ideas."[10] Of his third son, Paul Felix, he sighed affectionately, ". . . he avoids books and knowledge as a captain tries to avoid fog."[11] A deep love lay behind all the exasperation and Felix was a warm, doting father. But his letters are veined with an unmistakable sense of disappointment that his children weren't developing more serious interests.

Felix's sons had trouble finding their niche in the world, in part because they never needed to work. The deeper explanation lay in their contradictory upbringing. Felix tried to impart discipline while raising them in an elephantine Fifth Avenue mansion and a Westchester estate of several hundred acres. At Woodlands, he and Frieda acted like English gentry, playing polo and tennis and giving their children English-sounding names. As a businessman, Felix provided a poor role model, having used Kuhn, Loeb as a base for extracurricular activities. After Schiff's death in 1920, Felix even wanted to resign from the firm and had to be persuaded to stay by Morti Schiff. Felix had little abiding interest in banking, but he discouraged his sons from branching out in other professional directions and this arrested them in a kind of psychological limbo.

Their education at Middlesex and Harvard converted Felix's sons into fraternity jocks, keener on parties and sports than Jewish charity. Carola went to the Brearley School, which had only a tiny percentage of Jewish girls. Felix's sons ran around to football games in raccoon coats given by Grandma Schiff. (When Frieda tried to withhold Paul Felix's raccoon coat until his grades improved, Grandma Schiff indulged him instead.) Felix saw no tension between the education he provided his children and the reactions he expected. The Warburg boys grew up with few Jewish friends and socialized mostly with non-Jewish girls. So even as Felix pleaded for Jewish tradition, American institutions of his own choosing subtly undid all his work.

The children were also exposed to ambivalent attitudes toward Judaism. Frieda had faith, but not her father's deep religiosity, and Felix was more a cultural than a spiritual Jew. On Yom Kippur, Felix would fast, but stroll about in a bad temper, while Frieda abstained to appease her father's hovering ghost. Almost without realizing it, Frieda and Felix took on the trappings of wealthy, WASP society. They talked of their sons being confirmed, not bar mitzvahed, and of their going to Sunday school, not Talmud Torah.

Curiously, in the 1920s the American Warburgs encountered more anti-Semitism than their German relatives even as they seemed to blend into an all-American milieu. The Hamburg family coped with Nazi agitators and murder plots, but this was the menace of the unseen mob. Frieda and Felix had difficulty booking certain hotels as Jews. Carola later instructed her daughter not to apply for certain debutante dances, lest she be spurned as a Jew.

Felix wanted his sons to furnish proof that American Jews were true-blue patriots, telling Frederick that "unless the Jews become the best citizens of the country to which they have sworn allegiance, neither their happiness nor their safety can be assured."[12] When Felix learned that a man named Levy wanted to sell Thomas Jefferson's home, Monticello, at an exorbitant price for a national shrine, he sent Judge Jonah A. Goldstein to negotiate with him. As Goldstein recalled, Felix "didn't like the fact that a man named Levy was trying to make money out of a national shrine and he thought that would affect the relationship between Jews and people down south and in other parts of the country."[13] Citing a nameless donor, Goldstein offered Levy $250,000 in top-grade securities to donate Monticello to the U.S. government. Levy died before negotiations were completed, and Monticello was finally bought through a foundation. "But Warburg was willing to give that big money without his identity being known solely because he didn't want to have a Jew named Levy trying to cash in on the title to the Jefferson home," said Goldstein.[14] Such actions tacitly answered unspoken accusations that Jews were grasping and disloyal.

The final contradiction in the Friedaflix home concerned their marriage, a happy match filled with strange undercurrents. As mentioned, Frieda became partially deaf, like Jacob, after Edward's birth and couldn't hear the *sotto voce* wisecracks that passed between Felix and the children. This relegated her to an inferior position and made her the hapless butt of many gags at table. Felix always shone and twinkled to Frieda's detriment. He seemed full of gaiety while she lacked humor. Felix loved the *Carol*, while Frieda hated sailing. The partly deaf Frieda didn't share the Warburg love of music. And while Felix dealt with their sons in a droll, bantering style and wrote affectionate poems to Carola, Frieda *worked* at being a good mother. When her children were at school, she wrote to them daily and never abandoned the strict sense of duty she had inherited from Father. Frieda assumed the hard part of parenting, while Felix blithely and, one suspects, somewhat irresponsibly enjoyed himself.

For all his talk of duty, Felix had a weakness for pretty women and exploited the usual Victorian double standard: He ran around while Frieda stayed at home, the dutiful wife. Vivacious and fun loving, he squired mistresses openly about town. "He had lots of ladies," said his niece. "He said they weren't mistresses, but he took them to the opera with orchids on their front."[15] The grandchildren were puzzled to find Frieda absent from the *Carol*, but Irene Wyle, Hulda Lashanka, or some other lady friend present. Small wonder that Frieda learned to loathe the love boat.

Felix had distinctive tastes in women, favoring aspiring opera singers with substantial, well-sculpted bosoms and Wagnerian girth. He promoted their careers through auditions with Otto Kahn. It became a joke at 1109 that when Felix went off to "ride his bicycle," he was cycling off to a rendezvous. After a time, the boys noisily teased: "Are you going out to ride your bicycle, Father?"[16] Frieda was straitlaced but pragmatic and bowed to painful realities. Whatever her suffering, she tolerated the mistresses. Her old-fashioned, self-sacrificing attitude saved the marriage and perhaps made it a happy, if highly unequal, one. But it presented the children with a picture of Felix as a happy hedonist. They were exposed to a lot more than the legendary philanthropist and perhaps imitated Father more closely than he cared to admit.

———

The search for an identity would be a long and arduous one for Felix's children, draining away enormous psychic energy. Perhaps it was easiest for Freddy, the eldest, who was bright, jovial, and quick-witted. At one point, he bolted to Lehman Brothers when Kuhn, Loeb refused to make him a partner straight off; otherwise he spent his life at the family firm. Things were far less simple for the second son, the high-strung, outrageously funny Gerald. Slim, handsome, debonair, with piercing eyes and wavy black hair, he had an aristocratic air and a constant, boyish crush on some lady. He loved to ride and play tennis, fitting the Woodlands style of English gentry. Beneath the surface contentment, however, lay a complex, fearful, and insecure young man. As his brother noted, "He wouldn't fly in airplanes, he hated islands, he suffered paralyzing stage fright, not to mention claustrophobia."[17]

Surprisingly, Gerald's musical passion was often a source of friction, not harmony, with his father, who was a director of the Metropolitan Opera and the Philharmonic Society. Felix subscribed to so many concert series that they kept him busy nearly one hundred evenings each year. At the Metropolitan Opera, the conductor, Bodansky, would bow to him before taking up the baton. If the bassoonist missed a note, Felix and Bodansky would turn in unison and glare at the culprit. For chamber music concerts at 1109, the Warburgs set up rows of gilt chairs in the music room. The four Stradivarius instruments owned by Felix sometimes figured in these concerts. At one musical evening in 1924, Felix invited three friends to bring their "Strads" "so it seemed as if Stradivarii were being made in Hoboken in a baker's shop," Felix said.[18] As he got older, Gerry played Felix's Stradivarius cello that dated from 1725, La Belle Blonde.

At an early age, Gerald was given Jim Loeb's half-sized childhood cello, but was also told that it was harebrained to become a professional musician and that artists were wild, Bohemian wastrels. While Gerald was at Middlesex, Felix encouraged him to play his cello and piano, though he feared Gerald might choose a musical career. At 1109, Gerald would sit at the concert grand piano and tap out jazz, Gershwin, or Cole Porter tunes. Sometimes Felix sang Schumann *Lieder* in his pleasant baritone while Gerald accompanied him. "There was always a double message about music," said Gerald's daughter. "Music making as an amateur was fine, but it was *déclassé* to do it as a professional."[19]

Already at Middlesex, Gerry experienced terrible conflict, trying to be a gentleman and good sport but also an artist. (He once combined both roles famously, playing ragtime on an upright piano on the lawn outside while a fire burned in a dorm. Later, he said he fiddled while Rome burned.) Gerry longed to go to a conservatory, but Felix insisted he go to Harvard. Defying his father, Gerry worked hard at flunking out of Harvard—he walked out of one exam—and was disappointed to get a Gentleman's "C" freshman year when he had striven mightily to fail. After his brief stay at Harvard, Gerry spent some time at the Institute of Musical Art.

Having saturated the boy with music, Felix was upset that his gifted son wanted to be a professional cellist. To settle matters, Felix took him to audition before violinist Franz Kneisel. After Gerry played, Felix said, "Has the boy got talent?" "Talent he's got," said Kneisel, "as long as he's ready to starve for it." "That," Felix retorted, "is the only thing I can't provide."[20] Felix was only persuaded to support Gerry's ambition by Kay Swift, Jimmy's wife, herself a professional pianist. She said Gerry had talent, even if he probably lacked drive.[21] Frieda supported Gerry's ambitions, but Felix never overcame his feeling that gentlemen should confine music to the amateur sphere.

During his Harvard year, Gerry had fallen in love with a non-Jewish New England girl. As a result, Felix decided to send him to study cello in Vienna with a Professor Buxbaum. There Gerald shortly met his first wife, the beautiful Viennese Marion Bab. Though born Jewish, she had been raised as a Protestant by her parents because of Austrian anti-Semitism. When she married Gerald in 1922—Felix had to call upon his connections to find a rabbi willing to marry them—she reconverted back to Judaism. With so much anti-Semitic agitation in Vienna, Felix advised Gerald not to ride around in a big car, for the natives "would find out in no time that this is a rich, Jewish, American boy. . . . As you no doubt know, there are riots every day in the attempt to keep Jewish students out of the universities. . . ."[22]

At first, it seemed the Warburg name might assist Gerald's career. He and Buxbaum played concerts in Austria and Germany, with Felix subsidizing their quartet. In late 1924, when they played Hamburg, Uncle Max told someone in his office to buy the remaining seats in the concert hall. The man was supposed to go at the last minute, but instead went straight to the hall and purchased several *hundred* tickets. That night, when Gerry stepped on stage, he faced an audience papered almost entirely with M. M. Warburg staff, who applauded with lusty abandon. Backstage after the concert, a flushed, excited Gerry told Max that he and Buxbaum were so pleased that they planned to visit Hamburg again. Max, alarmed, had to confess what had happened, and Gerry said his father had done the same in the past. Max deducted the concert from Felix's Hamburg account and never invited Gerry to play again.[23]

Although Gerry would become a top American cellist, the family patronage hurt him, even after he made his debut at Carnegie Hall as a soloist with the New York Philharmonic Symphony Orchestra. (As a financial angel of the orchestra, Felix packed the house for the concert.) People felt they didn't need to support a rich kid by buying tickets to see him or putting him on a program. The beautiful Stradivarius provoked publicity, but distracted newspaper attention from the player. Gerry was also an anxious performer, who did best in private. Before concerts, he was sick with fear and afterward emotionally spent. Gerry would always believe that he had never achieved his just desserts as a musician. The privileged birth, which would have provided an entrée in any other career, proved an insuperable handicap in this one.

———

Many of Felix's acquaintances saw him as a charming, gregarious playboy, yet he reigned over a maze of time-consuming charities. Before his death,

Schiff recognized Felix's new maturity, observing with admiration how he "had really grown very considerably and is doing wonderful work."[24] No longer the snazzy young rake with the dogcart, Felix could pontificate as gloomily about the world as Paul. "One is afraid to open the paper in the morning, fearing that some new, outrageous self-seeking effort is bringing additional misery to millions," he said in 1923. Max would later note how Felix evolved from a serene, cheerful lover of music and art to "a serious-minded philanthropist who devoted almost all of his spare time to helping others."[25]

Felix didn't really like his Kuhn, Loeb partners and happily escaped into "pipe dreams," as he dubbed his philanthropy. At work, he had a special cabinet installed to track his fifty-seven charities; a leather flap would flip open to produce file cards on each. "I am like Heinz's pickles," he said. "I belong to fifty-seven varieties of committees."[26] He loved the work and said that if he couldn't do charity with a smile, he wouldn't do it. A very smart, well-read woman, Frieda also came into her own, serving as president of the Young Women's Hebrew Association and making a substantial donation to Lillian Wald's Visiting Nurse Service in her father's honor.

In the 1920s, Felix and Frieda Warburg held court as the King and Queen of American Jewry. Every Jew with a crazy scheme or pet hope gravitated to 1109 Fifth Avenue, which conjured up images of a bottomless store of wealth. Cyrus Adler has left an evocative image of how Felix was besieged everywhere by dreamers, crusaders, and opportunists. "When he crossed the ocean, his cabin was a sort of center, and I have seen him in hotels in London and Paris, where his ante-room or little parlor almost looked like a public office."[27] Never a great intellect, Felix was extremely intuitive and had a fingertip feel for the most worthy supplicants.

With 1.64 million Jews, New York City now boasted the world's largest Jewish community, and the Joint Distribution Committee was undisputed colossus of overseas aid. Postwar changes in Europe had isolated many Jews in new nation-states carved from the old, collapsed empires and the Joint sped relief to poor Jews in Poland, Romania, Austria, and Hungary, setting up bread lines and soup kitchens. In 1919, Felix lobbied the State Department and Red Cross to get a one-hundred-million-dollar food appropriation for Poland, which was experiencing dreadful pogroms. In 1921, he made a European tour that convinced the Joint to undertake sweeping economic reconstruction work in Jewish communities.

The group's executive committee met at Felix's office at 52 William Street or in the Rembrandt Room of his mansion, named for the etchings on display. From around the world Jews journeyed there to plead their cause. As chairman, Felix received a panoramic view of Jewish suffering. He employed multilingual stenographers, but even they were stymied when Yiddish writer Sholem Asch visited Kuhn, Loeb. Launching into a rapid, idiomatic Yiddish, he overwhelmed the poor stenographer, who appealed to Felix. "What shall I do," she whispered, "I can't understand a word." "Never mind," Felix replied, "I'll tell you later." The impassioned Asch bellowed on for nearly an hour, wringing his hands, tearing his hair, and nearly bursting into tears at one point. When it was over, the bemused stenographer nervously inquired, "What did he say?" and Felix retorted, "Just say Sholem Asch says the Jews in Poland need help."[28]

In 1923, Felix met a man from this Eastern European world who would bewitch, enchant, perplex, and infuriate him for almost fifteen years. This Pied Piper was no colorful shtetl character, babbling in Yiddish, but a shrewd, elegant, worldly man with a doctorate in chemistry: Chaim Weizmann. Now a British subject, he smoked expensive cigars, wore Savile Row suits, and had butlers and chauffeurs at his Addison Crescent home in London. With his tony wife, Vera, he negotiated his way with ease through European salons and ministries. Weizmann was perfectly suited to woo the Warburgs, for he shared their urbane, confident style, if not their ideology.

Before World War I, Zionism lacked urgency for many Jews. In 1882, Baron Edmond de Rothschild set up the first colony in Palestine, and in 1897 Theodor Herzl created the World Zionist Organization. Apart from small agricultural villages, the Jews in Palestine then consisted mostly of pious, elderly people, who went to study and die on holy soil. The world war destroyed the income sources of these colonists. On November 2, 1917, Britain released the Balfour Declaration, saying that, "His Majesty's Government view with favour the establishment in Palestine of a National Home for the Jewish people. . . ."[29] A month later, General Edmund Allenby captured Jerusalem and emancipated it from four hundred years of Turkish rule. Among other things, Britain wished to cultivate Jewish bankers on Wall Street. The British mandate over Palestine was officially incorporated into the Versailles Treaty.

Even though the Arab population greatly dwarfed the Jewish population, the Arabs took fright at the abrupt influx of Jewish refugees from postwar pogroms in the Ukraine and elsewhere. In 1921, they rioted, forcing the British High Commissioner to limit Jewish immigration. The next year, the League of Nations ratified the British mandate and endorsed a future Jewish national home west of the Jordan River. Despite these conspicuous feats, the Zionist movement was stalled for lack of money and was nearly bankrupt by 1923.

Zionism had to work as an economic proposition and not just as a romantic ideology. With the movement strapped for cash, it couldn't buy more land to attract more pioneers. Unemployment soared to depression levels and teachers and officials went unpaid. Despite this discouraging situation, lush images of irrigated deserts, drained swamps, and planted trees continued to tantalize Weizmann's mind. To realize his dreams, however, he needed to divert to Zionism some American Jewish money then flowing to European Jews.

When he decided to woo the rich, American non-Zionists, Weizmann must have done so with some reluctance, for he scorned them as autocrats who patronized the unkempt, ill-bred Jews of Eastern Europe; they might not understand his burning vision of a Jewish state. For German Jews comfortably ensconced on Park Avenue, Palestine seemed a dusty outpost best suited for colonial investment or modest social experimentation. For East European Jews in the Lower East Side slums, by contrast, it was the heady stuff of millennial dreams. Although they had exercised their power benevolently, the conservative "Our Crowd" bankers didn't want to yield power to Zionists, who often struck them as raw, boisterous upstarts. For these Jewish bankers and lawyers who solemnly asserted their patriotic credentials, the Zionist movement raised the dread specter of dual loyalty which they forever tried to lay to rest. They feared Zionism would only give flesh to the anti-Semitic mythology of a monolithic international Jewry, which commanded the unspoken loyalty of Jews everywhere. As Schiff had written, "But speaking as an American, I cannot for a moment concede that one can be at the same time a true American and an honest adherent of the Zionist movement."[30] Schiff gave generously to Palestine, but was careful to label himself a "cultural and religious Zionist," not a "political Zionist." Only in 1919 did he warm to a Jewish homeland as the best way to absorb the Jewish masses threatened by the Bolshevik Revolution.

The Warburgs weren't enthused by a Jewish state. Immensely wealthy, on excellent terms with business and political leaders in Germany and America, they had operated successfully in the precarious gray zone between the Jewish and gentile worlds. For all the anti-Semitism they faced, they seemed to be living proof that Jews could advance in their home countries. Max Warburg stubbornly resisted Zionism, lest it reinforce Nazi fantasies of a Jewish Fifth Column. So many people tried to recruit him to Zionism that he established a set policy of giving each advocate a half hour to make his case. He rather narrowly regarded Zionism as a colonial venture and an unprofitable one at that. When publicist Ernst Feder solicited his views on Palestine in 1927, Max brushed the subject aside, saying he already had major interests in Cameroon, Togo, and the Dutch West Indies and that Palestine couldn't possibly match the lucrative return on these holdings. Noting the prominence of German Zionists in the movement, he quipped that both Jews and Germans were bad politicians and together they would be catastrophic.[31]

Ancestral home in the Westphalian town of Warburg. Its size shows that the Warburgs were already a family of some wealth and prominence in the sixteenth century. (Courtesy of Anita Warburg)

The amazingly homely family of Sara and Aby Warburg. The swarthy boy to Sara's left is Siegmund, while her pampered favorite, Moritz, leans close to her. (Private collection of E. G. Lachman)

Sara's house at Rothenbaumchaussee 49, where she closely quizzed Siegmund and Moritz each night. (Private collection of E. G. Lachman)

A careworn Siegmund
Warburg, who bore the
weight of the bank from
his early years.
(Courtesy of Elsbeth
Oppenheimer)

Siegmund's fashionable
wife, Théophilie Warburg,
known locally as "Théo-
philie with the Sour Face."
(Courtesy of Elsbeth
Oppenheimer)

Alsterufer 18, home of
the first Siegmund and
Aby S. Warburg.
(Private collection of
E. G. Lachman)

A lyrical, melancholy view of the Alster Lake from the Alsterufer 18 mansion.
(Private collection of E. G. Lachman)

Charlotte Warburg often smiled in early photos before her daughter, Olga, committed suicide. (Courtesy of Alice C. Auerbach)

Moritz Warburg, probably wearing the toupee that showed him with freshly cut hair. (Courtesy of Alice C. Auerbach)

Five Warburg children with their beloved governess, Franziska Jahns. From left: Felix, Max, Olga, Paul, and Aby. (Warburg family, Hamburg)

Jacob Schiff and his doting,
solicitous wife, Therese.
(Courtesy of Carol Rothschild
Noyes)

Jacob Schiff with a curious, alert Bettina Warburg.
(Courtesy of Katharine Weber)

A companion photo to the family men pictured at the beginning of chapter four.
From left: Frieda Warburg, Betty Loeb, Therese Schiff, and Carola Warburg as a baby.
(Courtesy of Phyllis R. Farley)

An uncharacteristically subdued **Felix Warburg with Frieda and three children,** from left: **Carola, Frederick, and Gerald.** (Warburg family, Hamburg)

The main house at Woodlands. (From the collection of Mr. and Mrs. Edward M. M. Warburg)

Moritz with four of his sons, taken before his death in 1910. From left: Paul, Aby, Max, with Felix standing. Notice Aby's easy air of dominance. (Private collection of E. G. Lachman)

Always incorrigible clowns, the "Famous Five" sons kneel in mock adoration before Charlotte and Moritz Warburg. (Warburg family. Hamburg)

Nina Warburg with daughter Bettina.
(Courtesy of Katharine Weber)

Jimmy Warburg, looking every inch the
young genius, and sister Bettina as
teenagers. (Courtesy of Katharine Weber)

Picnic scene: Paul in shirtsleeves in middle, Nina in hat on right, her brother Jim Loeb
on his knees, Bettina in foreground, Jimmy faintly poking up in rear.
(Courtesy of Katharine Weber)

This rare photo shows an urbane Aby, looking like a banker, and an earthy Max, looking like a seaman. (Courtesy of Anita Warburg)

A dusky Aby, age thirteen, stands out among his blond classmates with his coloring and amused expression. (Warburg family, Hamburg)

Aby, at right, perched on his steed in his regiment. Because of his tiny stature, he had trouble mounting the tall horses. (Warburg family, Hamburg)

One summer vacation in Denmark, Mary and Aby created a book of ABCs, with drawings by Mary. Here, Aby kicks up his heels in a hilarious pose.

This drawing of Aby and Max illustrates the letter V and says, loosely, "The bird nests are too far away for the care of the worried fathers."

This drawing for the letter Y says, "Uncle Aby angrily sees his Mary swimming far out."
(All three drawings, courtesy of Frede and Adolf Prag)

Mary Warburg and her three children about the time that Aby left the Swiss asylum. The terrible strain of those years is written in Mary's face. (Maria Christina Warburg [Mills])

Marietta and her husband, Peter Braden, who spent World War II inside Nazi Germany. (Maria Christina Warburg [Mills])

The famous reading room at the Warburg library, whose elliptical shape held mystic meanings for Aby. (Warburg Institute)

From a platform at lower left, Aby Warburg salutes construction workers during topping-out ceremony of the Warburg library, October 1, 1925. (Warburg Institute)

Exterior of Warburg library, 1926. One can discern the letters KBW— *Kulturwissenschaftliche Bibliothek Warburg*—above the ground-floor windows. (Warburg Institute)

Gertrud Bing, Aby Warburg, and Franz Alber in Aby's hotel suite in Rome, 1929.
At the right one can make out collage panels for his projected picture atlas, *Mnemosyne*.
(Warburg Institute)

A crestfallen Aby Warburg
after emerging from the
asylum, circa 1925.
(Warburg Institute)

Lushly abundant archway at Kösterberg, with hanging ferns. (Courtesy of Anita Warburg)

An opulent stairway leading down to the open-air theater at Kösterberg.
(Courtesy of Anita Warburg)

Anita Warburg stars in a play by the Hindu writer, Tagore, at the open-air theater of Kösterberg. Three professional directors helped with these amateur theatricals. (Courtesy of Anita Warburg)

The grassy bleachers in the open-air theater seated up to 250 guests who afterward danced alfresco in the adjoining Roman Garden. (Courtesy of Anita Warburg)

The four daughters of Max and Alice Warburg. From left: Gisela, Lola, Anita, and Renate.
(Courtesy of Anita Warburg)

Lola Hahn-Warburg with Benita on lap and Oscar by her side, 1927.
(Courtesy of Lucie Kaye)

After facing the loyalty issue in Washington, Paul steered away from Zionism and mostly avoided Jewish organizations. When the German-born sociologist Arthur Ruppin tried to convert him to the cause in 1923, Paul replied testily: "Even if you were right in your explanations about the importance of Palestine and the destiny of the Jews, I couldn't join you, because as an American I don't *want* to be convinced by you."[32]

Felix was the most excited about Palestine. To some extent, he approached the subject as a banker searching for sound, prudent investments and demanded studies to gauge how many settlers could be absorbed economically. In January 1923, he wrote breathlessly that the "pioneer stock . . . is going to make Palestine into a second California . . . perhaps."[33] In time, Palestine would also kindle his imagination as a possible incubator for a Jewish cultural Renaissance. Outright statehood would remain another matter.

When Chaim Weizmann arrived in New York in spring 1923, he believed only two men could break down the resistance of wealthy, assimilated American Jews to Zionism: lawyer Louis Marshall, head of the American Jewish Committee, and Felix. Perhaps no fund-raiser has stalked a donor more assiduously than Weizmann did Felix. When he got a surprise luncheon invitation to 52 William Street, Weizmann at once accepted. (Vera saw it as a snub that he wasn't invited to 1109 Fifth.) "Enthroned in one of the more palatial rooms of that palatial building, I found an extremely affable and charming gentleman, very much the *grand seigneur*, but all kindness," recalled Weizmann.[34]

Felix made an extended speech about money being squandered in Palestine. For every dollar raised in America, he said, only one penny ended up in the Mideast. Weizmann stared at him flabbergasted. "A more fantastic rigmarole, I have, to be honest, never heard from a responsible quarter: bolshevism, immorality, waste of money, inaction, inefficiency, all of it based on nothing more than hearsay."[35] Bursting with impatience, Weizmann turned the tables. "What if things were the other way round?" he asked Felix. "Suppose I came to you with a collection of all the tittle-tattle and backstairs gossip that circulates, I have no doubt, about Kuhn, Loeb and Company? What would you do?"[36] Felix answered, "I should probably ask you to leave." Weizmann replied, "I can hardly ask you to leave, for I am your guest."[37] To get over this bramble patch, Felix offered to contribute ten thousand dollars to Palestinian development, but Weizmann wouldn't let him off the hook so easily. The only way to make amends, he insisted, was for Felix to see Palestine with his own eyes. To Weizmann's amazement, Felix replied, "Your suggestion is the right one. I will talk it over with my wife, and if possible go to Palestine at once."[38]

Felix retained grave reservations about Zionism, preferring to earmark money for specific Palestine projects and avoid the maelstrom of Zionist politics. He already worried about what he saw as a bellicose, arrogant tone that Zionists adopted in dealing with the Arab question. And conditioned by the genteel charity world, he couldn't abide the bitter, often vituperative partisanship of Zionist politicians, who frequently dispensed with the amenities.

Nevertheless, as his American tour ended, Weizmann bubbled with enthusiasm. American Jews had opened their checkbooks, he told Vera, and for the first time in Zionist history the deficits had vanished. Ecstatic over the American funds, Weizmann said that Zionists in the near future would have all "the millions that are required for the setting up of Palestine. . . . All the Jews, beginning with Marshall and Warburg and down to the East End, talk about nothing else but the height to which the matter has been raised. . . ."[39] When Felix telephoned on the eve of his departure to congratulate him on his triumphant journey, Weizmann was delighted. He rated his conquest of Felix, Marshall, et al. as the financial equivalent of the Balfour Declaration.[40]

Felix and Weizmann would go through countless cycles of enthusiasm and recriminations. For all his conviviality, Felix could be temperamental. When presented with a disagreeable thought, he would turn bright red and exclaim "Nonsense!"[41] But he and Weizmann were always held by a strong social bond that included their wives. After his exhausting trips to small-town America, the sophisticated Weizmann enjoyed repairing to the stately comfort of 1109 Fifth Avenue or Woodlands. He found many American Zionists dull and unsociable while the Warburgs were always scintillating company.[42] Weizmann's spellbinding power over women included Frieda. As Vera later wrote, "My husband liked beautiful women, but they had to have brains as well, which she had in abundance."[43] Frieda said of Weizmann's first lunch at 1109, "I had not felt warmly toward Dr. Weizmann up to that time, but he came and, like Caesar, he conquered me at once."[44] Frieda was a woman of strong and definite views, and her budding enthusiasm for Palestine swayed Felix.

When they visited Palestine, Weizmann hovered in the background, leaving nothing to chance. He forewarned the Warburgs' Zionist host, British Lieutenant Colonel Frederick H. Kisch, that if Felix were impressed by Palestine "he would be ready to be very helpful, and his help means a great deal."[45] Another resident worked his magic: Rabbi Judah Magnes. The former rabbi of New York's Temple Emanu-El, a handsome man with deeply burnished skin, was a great baseball fan and long-standing Warburg intimate. He had officiated over Carola's wedding and Freddy's and Jimmy's bar mitzvahs. Despite Felix's personal support, Magnes's wartime pacifism and radical sympathies for the Bolshevik Revolution had strained his relations with the German-Jewish elders. In the early 1920s, he had relocated to Palestine with his family. An exponent of Arab-Jewish reconciliation, Magnes guided Felix and Frieda around Palestine and would profoundly shape their views about its future.

As Weizmann predicted, the Warburgs were enthralled. Where Felix had expected wretched people looking for handouts, he encountered proud, doughty settlers. On his first morning, an elderly farmer approached and gave him the year's first fruits and vegetables. "I was delighted," Felix said. "My first contact with Palestine convinced me that the attitude I had previously held was wrong."[46] One wonders to what extent Weizmann orchestrated these scenes as the trip moved through a succession of poetically staged vignettes. The Warburgs approached Jerusalem amid a glowing sunset. The next day, they visited Mount Scopus and saw the beginning of the Hebrew University, which would become a favorite charity. As they stared at the Dead Sea, Nazareth, and the Valley of the Jordan, Magnes conjured up the university that would soon rise on the Scopus ridge. When the Warburgs visited a stone quarry, they talked to Russian Jews who seemed ablaze with a sense of mission. "Their eyes sparkled with fire, knowing that some of the stones on which they worked would be part of the Einstein Institute," said Felix.[47]

By the end, the two Fifth Avenue sophisticates had fallen completely under the enchantment of the arid, ancient country. "You probably think I am foolish," Frieda told Felix, "but I want to own some of this soil." They bought an orange grove and gave Magnes a five-hundred-thousand-dollar check for an Institute of Jewish Studies at the Hebrew University.[48] This first major endowment permitted the university to open by 1925. Although not converted to Zionism, they were seduced by the idea of a Jewish cultural flowering in the Holy Land. Kisch watched with fascination as Frieda partly shed her father's prejudice against Zionism. "Mrs. Warburg told me that she and her husband felt themselves a hundred per cent American and could not enter into the spirit of our life, although they were lost in admiration for what they saw around them."[49]

The trip was a triumph for Weizmann's cunning. An elated Felix sent him a postcard, saying, "I have seen what is being done and I feel like throwing myself on the ground and kissing every inch of the soil."[50] When next in New York, Weizmann must have quietly gloated over his success. Of Felix, he said, "I have seldom witnessed a more complete conversion."[51] Yet rather than showing open jubilation, Weizmann reacted with coy circumspection. When Felix asked about this apparent lack of enthusiasm, Weizmann said it would take more than one visit to understand Palestine. "I am sure you will go again, and yet again—and not merely as a tourist; and in the end we shall understand each other."[52] Despite Felix's ardor, Weizmann knew Palestine now simply ranked as one among his fifty-seven charities and he wanted much, much more.

Felix would serve as a critical intermediary between Zionists and non-Zionists. Under their mandate, the British gave the World Zionist Organization the power to create a Jewish Agency for Palestine. With Felix's help, Weizmann would enlarge the Jewish Agency to include rich non-Zionists. In 1925, Felix contributed fifty thousand dollars to the Palestine Foundation Fund for agricultural work. He also joined Louis Marshall and Herbert Lehman in setting up the Palestine Economic Corporation to channel investment money into commercial and agricultural projects and Felix became its honorary chairman. For all of Felix's generosity, however, Weizmann often sounded a peevish, disgruntled note when talking about Felix. "He is full of good intentions," he said, "but his 'practical plans' are usually hopeless. It is true he does not insist on these plans, but it takes a good deal of polite conversation to talk him out of them."[53]

—

The Hebrew University would be both a shared passion and flash point of controversy between Felix and Weizmann. As early as 1907, Weizmann had selected the Mount Scopus site and already in 1918, with Turkish guns still roaring in the distance, had laid its foundation stones. For Jews excluded from Russian schools and barred from many academic posts in Germany and America, higher education was a priority issue. Academic anti-Semitism was still so pervasive in America that people would say of Jewish candidates, "His only chance in the academic world . . . was to have Felix Warburg endow a chair for him."[54]

The Hebrew University was intended as a repository of Jewish wisdom, a citadel of intellectual respectability. It was a vision that engaged the passions of Felix, Weizmann, Albert Einstein, Baron Edmond de Rothschild, and a distant Warburg relative, Professor Otto Warburg. A friend of Theodor Herzl and a famous botanist at the University of Berlin, Otto Warburg had headed the World Zionist Organization. After moving to Palestine, he set up an agricultural research station at Rehovoth. He would head the botanical department of the Hebrew University, donating to it his outstanding collection of tropical plants.

On April 1, 1925, Lord Arthur Balfour presided over the opening ceremonies for the Hebrew University, a moving event in a natural amphitheater. The solemn occasion concealed a furious dispute raging about the university's direction. That September, the Board of Governors, largely at Felix's prompting, chose Judah Magnes as chancellor. Chaim Weizmann became president and Albert Einstein chairman of the Academic Council. The Magnes choice was a clear victory for Felix, who idealistically envisioned the university as a seat of Jewish learning, not as a breeding ground for

Zionism. The more hardheaded Weizmann scoffed at this as romantic hogwash and wanted the university to train doctors and scientists for the coming Jewish state.

Late that year, Felix complained that Weizmann was introducing politics into the university, swamping the Board of Governors with Zionists "to turn the university into an international debating society."[55] Relations between Felix and Weizmann further cooled as the latter faulted the Joint for diverting money to Poland, not Palestine. But every time that Felix lost patience with Weizmann and threatened to cut off donations, Weizmann managed to lure him back into the fold with all the masterful eloquence at his disposal.

In university affairs, Einstein proved an even more formidable foe than Weizmann. He was a frequent guest at 1109 Fifth Avenue and sailed with Felix aboard the *Carol*. On one voyage, he stared with hypnotic fascination at a table tilted at a strange angle, held by center weights down below. Felix treated Einstein to his own version of relativity: "Everything is relative except relatives, and they, alas, are constant."[56] A cynical critic of the rich grandees of Jewish charity, Einstein heatedly opposed Magnes as chancellor and wanted a distinguished scholar as academic head of the university.

Einstein was the matchless ornament of the enterprise but could be a terrible prima donna. In 1928, he told Weizmann that he would resign if Magnes didn't stop "sabotaging" the naming of an academic head. "For if this state of affairs continues the University will not only become a laughing stock in a matter of several years but it will also, indirectly, do serious damage in the eyes of the world, to Palestine and to all those who work for it."[57] He tartly ended this protest to Weizmann: "Kindly show this letter to Mr. Felix Warburg."[58] He also complained to Felix directly: "Pretend that a small stock corporation operating from Jerusalem under the management of a Mr. X, would be making transactions and investments which you consider impractical and absurd, and doing all this in your name and on your responsibility. Would you put up with such a state of affairs?"[59]

The feud was temporarily settled in June 1928 when a Professor Selig Brodetsky was named academic head. Even Magnes himself sometimes chafed at the inordinate power of his patron, Felix M. Warburg. Once he wrote in his diary: "F. M. W. and his family are among the finest and noblest of human beings. They are inherently good and have a real sense of service to others. But just because they are rare among their kind they are called upon to assume burdens which they cannot carry."[60] He listed the stupendous range of Warburg responsibilities, then wondered: "how is it possible for one family, or the small group revolving about that family to breathe 'soul' into these institutions, each one of which requires deep understanding and constant personal attention?"[61] The question would linger for another decade or so before it was answered by a radical democratiza-tion of power in Jewish affairs. As the Zionist movement gained strength, it would, among other things, terminate the reign of the Warburgs, Schiffs, Rothschilds, and other banking mandarins who had so long governed, un-challenged, the Jewish community.

A Season in Hell

I t was ironic that Aby Warburg's fame spread most rapidly while he was immured in the Binswanger sanatorium on Lake Constance. For all his fiery originality, before the war he had been mostly known only to a small group of cognoscenti. Often veering off into obscurity, Aby never catered to popular taste. Tortured by perfectionist madness, he didn't publish even one book. As he once lamented, "Month of torment, despairing anxiety about work which still has to be done."[1] He scribbled tens of thousands of notes, cryptic fragments that foreshadowed large works that never materialized. As his assistant Gertrud Bing said, "All over his writings there are traces of wreckage: projects not carried out, promises of articles never written, and ideas which were never developed."[2] His final legacy would be a score of compressed, hermetic essays, written in a German of formidable density that would defy easy translation. Yet his influence would be enormous.

Aby needed a vigorous disciple, a popularizer, and found one in Fritz Saxl, the able young Austrian who took charge of the twenty-thousand-volume library. The shy Saxl was the antithesis of Aby. He was a man of little small talk, while his mentor was a spectacular fountain of words. Where Aby brooded over decisions, Saxl acted with such intuitive dispatch that Aby dubbed him "Saxl *à vapeur*" or "Saxl, Full Steam Ahead."[3] Cordial and generous with colleagues, Saxl found Aby's authoritarian manner maddening and never quite forgave Aby for making him drop his early research on Rembrandt. Saxl's students would report about him a similar heavy-handedness.

By 1920, the Warburgs, despairing that Aby would ever emerge from his Swiss asylum, named Saxl the library's acting director, with Gertrud Bing his deputy. Max and Fritz sat on the library board. Working wonders, Saxl turned this private, inbred library into an outstanding public research institution. Taking the books stacked on shelves or heaped, higgledy-piggledy, around the library, he produced the first systematic catalogue. He gathered scholars from various disciplines, held seminars, offered lectures, and then published them. Saxl knew how to appeal to the public without cheapening the institution's mission.

By making books prohibitively expensive, Germany's inflation hurt many private scholars who subsisted on family inheritances. When Max and Fritz could no longer buy books, they turned to Paul and Felix, whose dollars enabled Saxl to continue buying books uninterrupted. This, in turn, helped to attract top scholars. Both American brothers found Aby's work rather arcane and probably supported it more from fraternal love than any great conviction of its ultimate worth. Ironically, despite Aby's contempt for Anglo-Saxon culture, it was American money that saved his library in the 1920s, then English money in the 1930s.

Giving a great fillip to the Warburg library was the founding of Hamburg University, a cause so dear to Aby's heart. On August 19, 1921, he was named an honorary professor in absentia. Soon students began to filter over to the Heilwigstrasse. Jewish scholars found a new openness in the Weimar universities. Among the prominent Jewish scholars appointed to chairs in Hamburg were Erwin Panofsky in art history and Ernst Cassirer in philosophy. Saxl wooed both for seminars and research. Although Panofsky and Cassirer had only an informal association with the library, they ended up doing a lot of writing, teaching, and lecturing there. Much of the creative output of Weimar scholarship would come from such private research institutions.

After arriving as a university lecturer in 1920, Panofsky toured the library with Saxl, and it struck him with the force of a revelation. The rows of books seemed limitless, rising to fill every nook in the house. "The everlasting train of books seemed to lie there unperceived, as by a whiff of magic, which lay upon them like a magical spell."[4] When Panofsky later met Aby for the first time, the man made no less striking an impression. Panofsky called Aby a mixture "of brilliant wit and dark melancholy, the keenest rational criticism

Aby Warburg, circa 1925.
(Warburg Institute)

and most empathetic readiness to help," marked by an "enormous tension between the rational and the irrational."[5] Like Aby, Panofsky sought to unlock the content and symbolism of paintings, which he thought a deeper means of engagement with the work of art than through connoisseurship and formal analysis. He began to conduct seminars at the Warburg library in 1921.

The neo-Kantian philosopher Ernst Cassirer arrived in Hamburg in 1919. (At first, he and his wife, Toni, had balked at coming after receiving news that right-wing students were handing out anti-Semitic leaflets urging a boycott of Jewish professors.) Cassirer's first glimpse of the library thoroughly captivated him, too. He told Saxl that he was afraid to return, lest he meander forever through this enchanted labyrinth of books. For her husband, Toni said, Aby's library was like a mine shaft glowing with buried treasure.[6] Cassirer would end up as the Warburg library's most prolific author.

Even as these scholars did honor to him, Aby walked along the shadow line of madness. He complained that the sinister demons he had investigated in art history had now taken their revenge and conquered him. Incarcerated in the closed wing at Kreuzlingen, he filled diaries with indecipherable jottings. When Carl Georg Heise visited him, Aby gave him a book of Jakob Burckhardt's essays with this dedication: "in gratitude for his visit to the inferno at Kreuzlingen."[7] It was indeed a Dantesque journey for Aby. When Heise arrived, he was led into a garden where he heard frightful screams coming from the building. When they met, Aby said, "Did you just hear a lion roar? Imagine, that was me!"[8] Aby talked distractedly, insisting that his wife, Mary, stood in grave danger in Hamburg and that Heise must protect her. Heise had to swear to send Aby a coded telegram, reporting on the status of these threats.

The Warburgs were extremely attentive to Aby. Max always made sure to arrive exactly on time so as not to unnerve his older brother. Patient and long-suffering as always, Mary wrote daily and visited often, while also raising their three children. Sometimes stormy encounters occurred with family members. As Frieda recalled, "Mary and his other brothers and sister made him more nervous, and Felix was the only person who could calm him down."[9] At one point, Aby asked to see Max's nine-year-old daughter, Gisela, who was his favorite niece, and Alice took her to Switzerland. When the little girl arrived, Aby stood on the stairway beside a large male nurse. "This is the man who poisons me every night," Aby informed Gisela.[10] Since he feared people would steal his notes, his pockets were bristling with papers. When they dined, Aby heaped gargantuan portions on his plate, then only nibbled a tiny bit. The little girl saw that he was prey to strange compulsions and private rituals. In buttoning his collar, he thought it very important which way the button went in. Aby was a compassionate man who knew, even in madness, that he had upset his niece. That night, he called Alice at her hotel to say, "Tell my Gisela that not everything I said was true."[11]

During Aby's time in Switzerland, his illness gave him a two- or three-hour reprieve each afternoon in which he could think clearly and receive visitors. The fearful clouds that gathered around him momentarily dispersed and his remarkable powers of self-analysis resurfaced. Even in the grip of some compulsion, he often recognized the absurdity of his behavior. He knew that his hands were clean and that he kept washing them needlessly. He was both trapped within himself and able to stand apart from himself—his old split personality in grotesquely magnified form. He didn't want sedation, which would dull his mental powers. He exchanged letters with Saxl, who sent him lists of new books, and stayed abreast of Hamburg matters. Every Easter, Saxl spent weeks at a nearby hotel and walked twice daily along the lake to see Aby. In some cases, the mental illness heightened Aby's power to penetrate imagery. As Gertrud Bing said, "[Saxl] spent his days at the hospital taking down at Warburg's dictation ever more poignantly worded interpretations of remembered facts and pictures . . . and these he would later write out in his own room."[12]

Aby always spoke gratefully about the clinic director, the remarkable Swiss psychiatrist Ludwig Binswanger. As Max said, "I believe that it was in large part not only the doctor Binswanger, but the human being Binswanger and his wife who brought him [Aby] back to life."[13] Binswanger was the scion of a distinguished psychiatric family. His father, Robert, had directed the Kreuzlingen clinic before him, and Uncle Otto taught psychiatry at Jena. (In fact, Aby apparently went to the Jena clinic before permanently transferring to Kreuzlingen in April 1921.) Ludwig himself had studied with C. G. Jung and formed a lasting friendship with Sigmund Freud. If Binswanger was, loosely speaking, a disciple of Freud and formed part of his Viennese circle at one point, they disagreed about many things. Binswanger used psychoanalysis as the foundation of every patient's treatment, but rarely relied upon it exclusively.[14] Instead, he pioneered an eclectic therapy called "existence analysis" in which he examined the total person in his social surroundings, drawing upon anthropology no less than psychotherapy.[15]

Versed in many disciplines, Binswanger was an ideal therapist for the multifaceted Aby. One is tempted to say that Binswanger took the same broadly eclectic approach to people that Aby did to paintings. They got on famously. With boastful accuracy, Aby told Binswanger, "You won't get many patients of my intelligence who also know that they are ill."[16] While Aby contended that psychoanalysis met little success with him, we know that it figured prominently in his treatment. For instance, Binswanger and Aby agreed on the importance of Aby's nursemaid to his emotional development.[17] We also know that Aby avoided discussing the Oedipus myth with colleagues because it had such a troubling resonance for him.

Many observers have commented upon the parallels between the thought of Aby Warburg and Sigmund Freud: their common fascination with psychological symbolism, the struggle of rational against pagan impulses, the sublimation of primitive urges into art, and the need for liberation from repressed fears. As one Aby Warburg scholar observes: "It shows clearly the complexity of Warburg's existence, that in his influence as a scholar he can be placed near Freud and at the same time he could have been his patient."[18]

Interestingly enough, Freud took a personal interest in Aby's case. On November 3, 1921, he wrote to Binswanger: "You currently have in your fine institution . . . a Professor Warburg of Hamburg, a man in whom I take a great interest, as much for his clear-sighted works, as for the fact that he is the cousin of my most intimate lady friend (a former patient). May I inquire what is happening with him and whether you concede any chance that he will again be capable of work?"[19] The reference to the female friend may refer to Helene Schiff, the daughter of Aby and Sara's daughter, Rosa, who married Viennese banker Paul Schiff. Family lore claims that Helene was in love with Freud and was one of his patients.

At times, Binswanger contended that Aby's madness would fade away if only he lived long enough.[20] But now the doctor gave Freud a prognosis of unqualified gloom. Since childhood, he noted, Aby had been ruled by obsessive fears and compulsive behavior. The 1918 breakdown, in his view, marked a transition from neurotic to psychotic behavior, with muscular tension that hadn't yet subsided. He gave an interesting description of Aby's dual personality. Usually mad in the morning, Aby was often calm enough to have tea with him or make excursions in the afternoon. "He is apparently interested in everything, has excellent judgment about people and the world, his memory is outstanding; nevertheless, one succeeds only for a short time in getting him to focus on scholarly topics." Binswanger ended the letter on a gloomy note, saying Aby would probably never conquer his madness or work creatively again.[21] Thanking Binswanger for the information, Freud never renewed the inquiry.

Aby would always stress his own powers of self-regeneration rather than the treatment he received. By spring 1923, he was starting to exorcise his private demons and thought he might go home. Saxl gained Binswanger's permission to conduct an extraordinary test of Aby's fitness to leave: Binswanger agreed that if Aby could prepare and deliver a competent lecture to the inmates, he could go. Clinic doctors doubted Aby could succeed.

For his subject, Aby reached into his own remote past and that of Western civilization. He decided to talk about the Serpent Ritual of the Pueblo Indians, which he had studied in the American Southwest nearly thirty years before. It was a splendid choice for reasons both profound and mundane. A colorful yarn accessible to a lay audience, it was apt to give confined people a pleasing sense of mental travel. And the theme held special meaning for Aby, who believed that the terrors of mental illness had given him special insight into mankind's conquest of its own primitive fears. This same process had led to the creation of art that created a consoling and objectifying distance from that terror. Aby might be a lonely tormented genius, but he also saw himself as Everyman. Weeks before the lecture, he wrote in his diary, "Sometimes it looks to me as if, in my role as psychohistorian, I tried to diagnose the schizophrenia of Western civilization for its images in an autobiographical reflex."[22] In lecture notes, he wrote, "All mankind is eternally and at all times schizophrenic."[23]

As was his wont, Aby worked on the speech in an all-consuming frenzy and completed it in a few weeks. In April 1923, he delivered it before an audience of inmates, guests, and staff doctors. Entitled, "Reminiscences from a Journey to the Pueblo Indians," it would, for a long time, be his only study available in English. In traveling to the Southwest, Aby explained, he had hoped to observe the transition from lower to higher forms of paganism, mirroring what had happened in ancient Greece. "Two thousand years ago in Greece— the very country from which we derive our European culture—there were certain ritual practices in vogue which surpassed in their blatant monstrosity the things we see among the Indians."[24]

Aby confessed that he hadn't spoken the Indian tongues or even seen the snake dance ritual firsthand, but he had discussed it at length with the Pueblos. Dreading famine, the Indians tried to avert it through symbolic manipulation of the rain-producing lightning. The zigzag pattern of the slithering snake's body made it a natural emblem for lightning. By gathering serpents from the desert and dancing with them, the Pueblos tried to master the lightning symbolically. This formed a key transitional stage in the cultural progression from magic to higher logic.

The lecture contained a surprising finale, for Aby didn't take a simplistic, progressive view of history. He pointed out that science and technology had superseded the old myths that had once interpreted natural phenomena for humanity. However, he saw new threats arising from this. He flashed a photo he had taken in San Francisco showing a top-hatted man striding down the street, with electric wires strung above him and a building with a pseudo-classical rotunda in the background. "In this copper-snake, invented by Edison, he [modern man] has wrested the lightning from nature. . . . The modern Prometheus and the modern Icarus, [Benjamin] Franklin and the

Wright Brothers who invented the aeroplane, are those fateful destroyers of our sense of distance who threaten to lead the world back into chaos. Telegraph and telephone are destroying the cosmos."[25] These technological forces, Aby contended, had destroyed the space needed for the healthy contemplation of natural phenomena. Symbols were good, he thought, because they permitted mankind to meditate upon the universe in tranquility.[26]

The lecture was a stunning success, and the doubting doctors marveled at Aby's triumph. He had elevated his suffering not just into a tool of personal enlightenment, but into an aid and source of solace to fellow sufferers. Self-absorbed for so long, he had now acknowledged his common humanity. On his lecture draft, he wrote, "The images and words are intended as a help for those who come after me in their attempt to achieve insight and thus to dispel the tragic tension between instinctive magic and analytic logic. They are the confessions of an (incurable) schizoid, deposited in the archives of mental healers."[27]

It would be another fifteen months before Aby left Kreuzlingen for good. In early 1924, he still wavered and the doctors themselves remained uncertain. To persuade Aby to resume work in Hamburg, Saxl dispatched Ernst Cassirer to see him, thinking Cassirer the sort of steady soul who could stiffen Aby's resolve. Before Cassirer's visit in January 1924, Aby spent days in a fit of nervous expectation, preparing and scrawling numberless questions. When Cassirer arrived, Aby panicked and kept him waiting a half hour. Suddenly, he wanted every object to be cleared from his desk top. Doubtless from nerves, he had relapsed into the old fetishism in which these objects possessed malevolent powers. All in all, it was a successful visit, but Aby still wavered between clarity and strange, mystical babble. Afterward, Cassirer strolled with Aby, who leaned on Mary's arm. At one point, Aby, pointing to a room, declared, "Look, Cassirer, that's where they keep my wife a prisoner up there."[28]

One day in August 1924, a small, anxious man left the Kreuzlingen clinic. If his eyes were darker and indescribably sad, he was also more gentle and serene, radiating a calm power, a new philosophic detachment, the air of arrogant authority and explosive temper having disappeared. Aby's departure represented a tremendous triumph of human willpower over paralyzing fears, and he justly took pride in it. As his son said, "like Münchhausen, he used to say, in that great classic yarn, he had pulled himself out of the swamp by his own pigtail."[29] Dubbing himself a *revenant* or "ghost," he spoke of his second life and signed one letter "Warburg redux." As Fritz Saxl said, "He had the feeling, and inspired it in others, that he was a soldier come home after a victorious battle, a battle for life against the forces of darkness and hell."[30] Aby described his return to normal life as a miracle and it would continue to surprise him almost daily.[31] He had overcome his inner conflict with tremendous perseverance, putting his struggle to creative use at the same time.

By an astonishing coincidence, the literary sensation of 1924 was Thomas Mann's *The Magic Mountain*, which sold fifty thousand copies that year. In the book, Hans Castorp visits his cousin in a Swiss sanatorium, contracts tuberculosis, then spends seven years there (versus six for Aby). For Mann, the sanatorium serves as an image of prewar Europe sliding into irreversible despair and death, while for Aby it had proven a temporary place of healing and renewal.

Secluded for six years, Aby had missed whole chapters of history: the revolution, Versailles, the Rathenau murder, and hyperinflation. Except for the war, he had experienced only the optimism of late Imperial Germany. Now Weimar Germany had caught up with his prophetic soul. This time of chaos and disintegration opened up compartments of the human mind that had been sealed shut in quieter times. There was a new vogue for things that had long obsessed Aby, especially the irrational and mystic sides of life. Expressionist art—dark, pessimistic, with violent colors, disjointed figures and a nocturnal air of doom—dominated painting and drama. The pagan underpinnings of civilization burst forth. Yet the temper of the time often glorified what Aby had most feared. The Surrealists, for example, tried to tap the uncensored mind as a pure spring of creativity. Peter Gay has spoken of the "revolt against reason" in Weimar Germany and the "love affair with death" that "loomed so large over the German mind."[32] The Warburg library, with its meticulous scholarship, would resist the fads of irrationality that thrived in the 1920s. At the same time, the surge of interest in esoteric subjects, ranging from ethnology to astrology, inevitably fostered curiosity about Aby's recondite research.

When Aby reached Hamburg, he announced his arrival by sending Ludwig Binswanger a picture postcard of Hamburg's harbor. It must have been dreamlike but disconcerting to find his private library—his retreat from the world—now turned into a public institution. And where he had been a somewhat obscure scholar before his forced retirement, he now headed a theoretical school and was admired by such luminaries as Cassirer and Panofsky. Aby walked into a library that was newer and bigger, having expanded in directions no longer strictly dictated by his own thought patterns. Staring at a sudden bulge in books, he sighed with horror, "My poor Renaissance!"[33]

As an honorary professor at the university, Aby was soon teaching attentive seminar students, though he continued to suffer from spasms and nervous ailments and had to intersperse his work with rest cures. On April 25, 1925, he delivered his maiden speech at the Warburg library. Regretfully,

Ludwig Binswanger declined the invitation, telling Aby that for him the lecture would have been more than a reunion, but "a sort of official end of your existence as a sick man."[34] Binswanger often said that he missed Aby from both a human and intellectual standpoint and he would frequently use his patient's trenchant witticisms in his own professional speeches.

For his lecture on astrology, Aby had to stand for nearly two hours and improvised from hand-held notes. Max wryly told Binswanger that two hours on astrology was perhaps too much of a good thing, but that Aby had at least demonstrated he was up to the demands of his work.[35] Mary expressed amazement at his stamina and said that he wound up in a stronger state than his listeners.[36] Such self-reinforcing flights of energy and invention had always been characteristic of Aby.

Friction was bound to develop between Aby and Fritz Saxl, who had assembled his own staff and flourished in the absence of his autocratic mentor. Aby was quick to perceive threats to his authority. With a touch of black humor, he said his colleagues "couldn't get accustomed to the fact that I wasn't dead, but was back and alive."[37] Indeed, the institute proved too small for both men. By 1926 Aby dispatched Saxl to England to study astrological manuscripts, a move also dictated by their romantic competition over Gertrud Bing.

Even while Aby was at Kreuzlingen, his brothers had contemplated a separate library building on the adjoining site at 116 Heilwigstrasse. They hoped this might both draw Aby back to Hamburg and give Mary some breathing space. As usual, their house was bursting at the seams with books. Thirty thousand volumes crept up the staircase and billowed into every corner. Pantry and billiard room bulged with books, shelves sagged dangerously, and halls and landings were congested. The accretion never ended and more books kept arriving every day.

In 1924, Aby awarded the contract for an adjoining Warburg Library to architect Fritz Schumacher, who then passed on the project to Gerhard Langmaack. Managing to foil his brothers' plan for a separate library, Aby had the two buildings internally fused behind separate facades, producing combined shelf space for 120,000 books. On August 25, the foundation stone was laid. Soon trucks rumbled through the neighborhood, carting steel and concrete slabs to protect the books. Safes arrived to house rare books and a fire alarm system was installed. At one point, Aby lectured on the library's purpose to the carpenters and suppliers. To avoid publicity, the library would possess an austere front of patterned brick with the initials KBW or *Kulturwissenschaftliche Bibliothek Warburg* (The Warburg Library of Cultural Science) in *Jugendstil* lettering. The interior was ingenious. During their Kreuzlingen chat, Ernst Cassirer had extolled the ellipse as a central creative figure of the universe.

Aby knew it traced the course of the orbiting planets and insisted upon an elliptical lecture room for the library. The reading room also had curving walls and tall rows of books illuminated by a huge circular skylight.

The library was a family endeavor, the brothers contributing 188,000 reichsmarks to its completion. Because of Aby's finicky demands, the structure cost four times its original estimated price. Aby had an iron balustrade from Sara's old house brought over. Max donated a former bank elevator and brother Fritz a candelabra from the stairway. At the May 1926 dedication, visitors passed beneath the word *Mnemosyne*—the Greek goddess of memory—which was emblazoned above the front entrance.[38] Above the door of the lecture hall, Aby put a photographic blowup of a fresco detail, showing a criminal bursting from his ropes and escaping with his life—an image pregnant with autobiographical meaning. Erwin Panofsky gave the inaugural lecture. In a delightful talk, Max likened the library to a Warburg bank branch that would deal with cosmic instead of earthly pursuits.

Aby gave the mayor a tour of the new institution, taking him to an upper floor of the library which had a circular terrace with a view of the willow-lined Alster Canal out back. Aby told the *Bürgermeister* that this terrace was the library's most important feature, for here refreshing yoghurt would be served. At this joyous moment, Aby came up with a joke that was, in his typical fashion, oddly ghoulish and premonitory. He said that Hamburg might someday be destroyed and he pictured a chat, years later, between two elderly ladies: "Warburg? Yes, who *was* that Warburg? No idea. Oh, yeah, Warburg, he was the small man in the Heilwigstrasse who served yoghurt."[39]

After the opening, Aby lectured on Rembrandt's painting of the Conspiracy of Claudius Civilis. Instead of studying this from a photo, Aby had had an enormous copy painted and hung in the library stairway. Struggling with asthma, he spoke at first in a quiet, labored manner and the audience feared he wouldn't finish. Then, he gained strength and wound up mesmerizing his audience. The Warburgs were still slaves to Aby's whims and family attendance was compulsory at such events. Aby was irate when Alice didn't bring his niece Gisela to one long evening lecture. "She can sleep after I'm dead to her heart's content," he complained.[40]

The library developed a devoted following of scholars, students, and guests, whom Aby—with a nod to Kreuzlingen—referred to as his institute's "patients." Those who visited the reading room discovered a marvelous but forbidding maze of books, laid out with their own quirky arrangement. By design, there was no catalogue to steer them through this maze, forcing them to browse and discover connections with their own eyes and hands. For the serious scholar, it was a place always packed with delightful surprises. All the curious interconnections of Aby's theories were reflected in the idiosyncratic placement of the books. At last, near the end of his life, Aby saw his fantasy projected into vivid reality. The solitary figure, after years hidden away in a sanatorium, had suddenly become a celebrated public man.

The Chemistry of Hate

Like all German Jews, Max Warburg lived with an insoluble dilemma. If he flexed his muscles, he confirmed Nazi fantasies of Jewish power; if he displayed excessive caution, he invited opponents to trample him with impunity. Dubbed the "Uncrowned King of Hamburg," he wore that crown uneasily. Despite their central role on reparations, Max and Melchior continued to shrink from overt political action. "Whatever we championed would at once have been represented as in the interests of international Jewry," said Max.[1]

Despite the Warburgs' caution, the anti-Semitic barrage against them only intensified. The more Max was accused of evil machinations, the more marginal his true power became. In 1923, he decided to adopt a more aggressive attitude toward press libels. He still trusted that the German state would combat the Nazi menace, an abiding faith in legal forms that was predictable, if misplaced. Unlike Eastern European Jews, German Jews regarded the state as their protector from anti-Semitic predators—and none more so than the Warburgs, who had benefited from state patronage as both Court Jews and private bankers. In fact, the courts of Weimar Germany would prove far more tolerant of extremism from the right than from the left.

By 1924, the Nazi party formed a small Reichstag bloc, and their propaganda featured a comprehensive critique of the modern world. Many Germans felt disoriented by their belated passage into modernity, the pace of industrialization and urbanization seeming to them chaotic and frightening. Wartime defeat and the discredited monarchy had left a vacuum in which a thousand ideologies flourished. Active in the stock exchange and mass marketing, department stores and promotion, theater and advertising, the Jews of Weimar Germany seemed to personify this exciting but also upsetting new world. They not only advanced in the professions, but became integral to the arts. With Jews suddenly prominent in so many areas, the Nazis could hold them responsible for every novelty from industrial consolidation to financial speculation to avant-garde thought.

In this atmosphere, it no longer sufficed to charge the Warburgs with isolated acts of betrayal. Now every random fact of their existence had to be closely spun into a fantastic conspiracy. The family's business-cum-marriage links seemed especially productive soil to the paranoid Nazi mind. Felix's love for Frieda or Paul's for Nina became incriminating steps in the family's march toward world mastery. The theory was infinitely elastic, weaving every thread of Warburg history into a lurid tapestry. The Nazis didn't worry about internal contradictions. The Warburgs were secret stooges both of Wall Street *and* Russian revolutionaries. Some left-wing agitators even accused Max of financing the Nazi party itself. The point was not to be accurate but to breed suspicion and confusion.

As anti-Semites exploited the Weimar press freedom, the mouthpiece for slander against the Warburgs remained Leipzig pamphleteer Theodor Fritsch, founder of the Hammer publishing house.[2] Fritsch gave his calumny a pseudoscholarly gloss. He tried to dust off the old myth that Jews engaged in ritual murder—the blood libel that thirsty Jews needed Christian blood to celebrate Passover. He claimed to have spent years poring over rabbinical writings from the Talmud to the Cabala. By deciphering Hebrew passages opaque to other gentiles, he alleged, he had learned that Jews were allowed to trick gentiles in business, kill their bosses, and expropriate non-Jewish wealth. No lie was too preposterous or fantastic. As early as 1915 Fritsch began to pay modest fines and serve brief sentences for libel. In 1922, the Reichstag rebuked him for breaking a pact to refrain from attacks on Max Warburg. This only whetted his appetite, however, and so he ghosted a book called *Spanish Summer*, published under a pen name in Switzerland, that resumed his anti-Warburg diatribes.

In 1923, Fritsch produced two venomous Hammer broadsides that finally forced Max to sue him. In one, "The Secret Kaiser," Fritsch portrayed him as the master wire-puller of German politics and "Chief of Staff of World Jewry,"

Felix and Max Warburg on the Kösterberg terrace.
(Courtesy of Anita Warburg)

who had installed Wilhelm Cuno as German chancellor in 1922.[3] Fritsch called Max the country's richest man, controlling fifty foreign and domestic banks. (He only controlled one.) After outlining Max's links to the Schiffs and Loebs, Fritsch charged that American Jewish bankers had instigated the war to profit from it, thus exactly inverting the reality that the "Our Crowd" bankers had been the least warlike on Wall Street—out of love for Germany. In another article, Fritsch asked, "Who is Responsible for the Defeat?" and answered, predictably, that it was a Jewish cabal led by the Warburg bank. "The men of the Golden International alone bear the responsibility for the dreadful events of the last ten years," Fritsch enlightened his readers.[4]

In August 1923, both Max and Melchior filed a suit against Fritsch, which was delayed after Fritsch became a Reichstag member and gained some political immunity. On June 28, 1924, two Social Democrats took up the cudgels for Max in the Reichstag and denounced Fritsch. The trial against Fritsch finally convened that December. It was a fascinating case, for under the judicial system of the day, Max could confront Fritsch directly and he handled himself with quick wit and cool self-assurance. Fritsch, in turn, previewed the entire stockpile of Nazi rhetoric against the Warburgs. The Nazis delighted in such trials to exhibit their inflammatory oratory. But the trial provided only a shadowy preview of the 1930s, because the Jewish victim still felt secure enough to engage in a certain amount of irony.

In his opening statement Max gave a heartfelt affirmation of his German loyalty. "What Herr Fritsch thinks of me personally, I don't care, but I have a name to defend that has existed for centuries in Germany and especially in Hamburg. I cannot admit that because my activity, by chance, has occurred more in the public sphere than that of my forefathers, that it should be spattered with mud. Already in the years 1870/71, members of my family volunteered and died, just as they did in the years 1914–1918. We are not surpassed in our love of the *Vaterland* and our service to the *Vaterland* by any Christian."[5] Max adduced facts that undercut Fritsch's demonology, pointing out that prewar Germany lacked Jewish officers or government ministers; that the Reichsbank hadn't employed Jews even in lowly positions; and that the majority of M. M. Warburg clients were Christian. He could only laugh ruefully at Fritsch's rigmarole of charges.

In reply, Fritsch tried to give a veneer of respectability, even high-mindedness, to his verbal savagery. "I should like to explain again . . . that my attacks aren't directed against the plaintiffs as people, but rather to combat a universal principle, the Jewish system, which is, naturally, represented by people. . . . I stress that I have no objections to Herr Warburg as a person. It's possible that he's the most honorable man. My attacks are only directed against him to the extent that, as a member of international high finance, he is responsible for certain facts. . . .''[6] One of Fritsch's lawyers presented his client as an idealist under siege, driven by undying love of the *Volk*, while his other lawyer saw the trial as a small but noble chapter in the two-thousand-year-old struggle by Aryans to throw off the yoke of Jewish subjugation.

Throughout the trial, Max treated Fritsch in an urbane, mocking style, as if humoring a lunatic. After Fritsch's opening comments, Max interjected, "I don't know, whether at this moment, I can now say a word for Jewish international finance."[7] The dry wit played well against Fritsch's crackpot tenacity. In his ramblings, Fritsch told how the Jew was always a Jew first and hence a suspect national of any country. Citing the Warburgs as part of a secret Jewish world government, Fritsch noted how they served governments in an advisory role to mask their influence. There was a slight grain of truth contained in this distortion, for Max Warburg had indeed avoided office and favored advisory positions. But he had done so precisely to avoid such anti-Semitic slurs!

Fritsch also blamed Max, Melchior, and their Jewish confederates for enriching themselves during the war by profiteering and sending tainted food to the front. Max retorted that he and other bankers had, in fact, lost 80 or even 90 percent of their capital during the war and hyperinflation. It was more difficult for Max and Melchior to dispute that they had offered to pay one hundred billion marks at Versailles. They explained that Germany had to make an offer and that it was a sensible one. They also recounted their train journey to Weimar to persuade the German government to reject the treaty.

Turning his attention to Paul Warburg, Fritsch branded the Federal Reserve Board a stratagem of Jewish bankers to consolidate their world financial power. "The Federal Reserve Board is ostensibly a state institution, when in truth it is completely in Jewish hands," Fritsch stated.[8] Max noted wearily that Paul had sacrificed a millionaire's salary to take the job and had almost all Christian supporters in his crusade for the Fed. "Now it is simply explained, because my brother had the idea and the rare fortune to see the idea he fought for recognized, the Federal Reserve Board must be under Jewish influence."[9] Fritsch couldn't believe that any Jew would undertake a cause for selfless reasons. Pretending to quote talmudic law, he said that Jews could only *appear* to help non-Jews, but were actually mandated by their religion to harm them.[10] Having spent the war under suspicion of concealed German sympathies, Paul Warburg was now cruelly portrayed as nemesis of the German people. Fritsch lumped together Paul (the "Finance Dictator") and Bernard Baruch (the "Economics Dictator") as the two Hebrews who had conspired to destroy Germany.

Part of the strength of Nazi ideology was that it was both vague and all-inclusive, an elastic garment that could clothe hate of any size or shape.

To exploit disenchantment with capitalism and fear of socialism, the party linked Jews, Wall Street, and the Russian Revolution in one improbable whole, thus maximizing Nazis' appeal to populists of both left and right.

In 1924, the Nazis were still gadflies—more pests than mortal threats—and the trial had moments of gruesome carnival humor. At one point, the judge read passages in which Fritsch described his experience in a wartime Turkish sick bay. A young doctor, with a foreign accent, had supposedly told him that he had been trained at the behest of Max Warburg. Each year, evidently, the Warburgs trained about five hundred young Jewish conspirators from Poland and elsewhere as businessmen, bankers, lawyers, and diplomats and then slipped them into various countries as a Fifth Column. Max facetiously responded to this hocus-pocus: "If I had trained young people for foreign service, I would have had Germans trained first," he said.[11]

Fritsch had the cheek to chide Max's behavior after the Rathenau assassination. By furnishing him with a private bodyguard, Fritsch alleged, the Hamburg police had shown how much more they valued a Jewish Warburg life and he accused Max of cowardice for changing his residence each night to elude the assassins. Max saw that Fritsch was just trying to make him appear nervous and ridiculous.[12]

The verdict was a sham that only emboldened the Nazis and invited them to court further libel suits. Although the judge declared that Fritsch hadn't provided a shred of proof to support his allegations, he sentenced him to only three months in jail. Remarkably, he ruled that Fritsch had not acted with malice, but had erred in good faith! Upon appeal, the mild three-month sentence was reduced to a thousand-mark fine. It was a stunning example of how the old imperial judges had made the Weimar Republic a paradise for publicity-mongering extremists.

Fritsch quickly published a transcript of the trial entitled "My Battle with the House of Warburg—An Episode in the Fight against World Capital," complete with fresh slander against Jewish figures.[13] He distributed a copy to every Reichstag member. In the following years, he would reiterate his charges against Max Warburg, sometimes in the guise of a general indictment of world Judaism, without naming Max. Other times, he put caution aside and revived the charge that Fritz had torpedoed the Stockholm negotiations with Protopopov in World War I.

The Fritsch story has an interesting coda. By 1927, Felix, Louis Marshall, and the American Jewish Committee had convinced Henry Ford that the *Protocols of the Elders of Zion* were patent forgeries. Ford, as mentioned, had used the *Protocols* as the basis for his book, *The International Jew.* Not only did Ford apologize to the Jews and retract the book, but he wrote to Fritsch, asking him to recall the German edition. Deaf to these pleas, Fritsch published *The International Jew* right until the Nazi seizure of power in 1933.

In 1924, with its currency stabilized, Germany entered a brief, misleading period of economic normality. Extremism began to ebb and the Social Democrats gained in strength. Paul called 1924 the year when the war ended and reconstruction began.[14] M. M. Warburg & Co. now occupied its handsome new neoclassical palazzo on the Ferdinandstrasse, but no longer needed so much space. With inflation over and the "liberation from Lilliputian accounts, from scribbling zeroes," as Max said, the staff shrank from 535 to 358 employees in just a year.[15] The new headquarters was elegantly equipped with mahogany telephone booths in corner offices to assure private calls from partners to clients. There was also a *Geheimdienst* or secret service, secretarial rooms that were off-limits to visitors and that handled mail only partners could see. If a "Z" was affixed to the end of a letter, it had to be destroyed after reading. Such discretion was standard procedure in private banks yet fed an impression that the Jews must be steeped in dark dealings.

The mood brightened further in Germany when the Allies reduced reparations at the 1924 Dawes conference in London, but economic relief came at a steep political price. In exchange for lower payments, the Allies took as security a first mortgage on German government revenues from taxes on beer, tobacco, and other items and gained some control over the Reichsbank and German railways. An agent general was appointed to gauge Germany's capacity to pay reparations. As a sweetener for Berlin, the Dawes plan envisioned an international loan of unprecedented size that would ultimately allow Germany to pay reparations with borrowed money, thus starting the fatal carousel of global lending that would spin dizzily for a decade then collapse.

After the Reichstag adopted the Dawes scheme amid fierce controversy, J. P. Morgan and Company mounted a giant loan for Germany. Melchior had been a German delegate in London and so the plan was predictably denounced by the Nazis as the latest maneuver by Jewish capital to enslave Germany. This theory encountered one snag: the House of Morgan was notoriously anti-Semitic. This didn't deter the Nazis, who revealed that J. P. Morgan's original name was Morgenstern! Even General Charles Dawes, the Chicago banker, was hiding Jewish roots. As the new Julius Streicher publication, *Der Stürmer*, informed the faithful, "His name is Davidsohn. He is a fullblooded Jew."[16]

The Dawes Plan had a profound impact upon Weimar Germany, as French troops evacuated the Ruhr and the rentenmark was replaced by the reichsmark. The Warburgs welcomed the Dawes Plan and the hopeful mood it induced after years of defeatism. Paul predicted, correctly, that Germany would now shed its outcast status in global financial markets. A brief honeymoon ensued as short-term foreign loans from America and England flooded into a Germany only recently boycotted by foreign bankers. "Every Tom, Dick and Harry began going to Europe, discovering borrowers and throwing loans at their heads," recalled Paul's son, Jimmy.[17]

With Germany the major debtor of the 1920s and America the major creditor, the Warburgs again occupied a pivotal place in transatlantic finance—probably the last time the stars were perfectly aligned for them. Paul's International Acceptance Bank (IAB) organized the American and Continental Corporation to extend medium-term credits to European—especially German—industry. Paul and Max funneled foreign money into Hamburg state loans and helped to rebuild the German merchant marine, confiscated at war's end. As one Hamburg official later said, "Max Warburg must get the credit, beyond anyone else, for the re-emergence of an important German merchant fleet."[18] Paul's IAB gave credit to HAPAG, while Max courted Averell Harriman, pressing him to form a joint venture with Ballin's old firm. Under the deal struck, Harriman would initially provide American ships, while HAPAG would offer route structures and port facilities. The venture got HAPAG up and running again, but was fiercely criticized by Americans who alleged that HAPAG ships had harbored spies and saboteurs during the war.

Paul had advised Dr. Schacht on how to tame inflation and had been involved in the Dawes loan. As a reward, the IAB became the American agent for the Reichsbank and its Gold Discount Bank subsidiary, providing the latter with a twenty-five-million-dollar credit that strengthened Germany at a critical juncture. Max was now appointed to the prestigious *Generalrat*, the Reichsbank advisory board, a position he would hold until Hitler's advent.

The Wall Street money that revived Germany also carried hidden perils for the Warburgs. The family was associated with America, which was both feared and admired in Weimar Germany. As the pattern of the glossy new consumer society, America appealed to chic urban sophisticates. For other Germans, however, America epitomized the soulless, technocratic society that would supposedly stifle the true organic "German" spirit. That an American agent general, S. Parker Gilbert, governed Germany's economic destiny only added to their hostility. So the Warburg's American connection helped the Nazis to vilify the family as an "alien" and "cosmopolitan" force that owed its real allegiance to groups outside of Germany.

Foreign credit was a drug that fostered a short but artificial prosperity in Germany and Max later referred to the *Scheinblüte* or "illusory boom" of 1925. The foreign money, he feared, only masked underlying economic problems, such as high German taxes and the bloated Weimar bureaucracy. Repeatedly voicing grave doubts about the debt accumulation, he was himself swept up in the boomlet and committed fatal misjudgments. Unlike Paul, he wasn't a cautious, sober man holding out against the frenzied crowd, but a red-blooded buccaneer. Max took money routed from New York by Paul and recycled it into a giant loan to the Karstadt department store, plus a stake in a hotel chain. Both ventures would end disastrously.

In 1925, Max was deeply saddened by the sudden death of Friedrich Ebert and the election of Paul von Hindenburg as president. He worried about the world's reaction to having a military man as head of state. Later in the year, Dr. Schacht invited Hindenburg to a Reichsbank dinner. As Max watched the aging marshal lumber heavily along the corridor, with furrowed brow and melancholy expression, he felt he was watching a man risen from the dead. It all seemed a frightful throwback to the past.[19]

Capping the events of mid-decade was the signing of the Treaty of Locarno in 1925, which paved the way for German admission to the League of Nations the next year. Carl Melchior was appointed the sole German member of the League's Finance Committee, which further embellished M. M. Warburg's reputation. Germany's status as an international pariah now seemed behind it. Max's hero, Gustav Stresemann, even briefly toyed with the idea that Germany could again become a great power.

Awash with foreign money, German industry embarked on a merger wave that produced huge trusts and cartels. Daimler and Benz merged. The new United Steel Works arose, second only in size to U.S. Steel. In 1925, six large chemical corporations formed the most massive trust, I. G. Farben, which ranked as Europe's largest corporation. It would produce the bulk of dyes, pharmaceuticals, photographic film, nitrogen, and magnesium made in Germany. Though a staunch free marketeer, Max favored industrial mergers and executed several of them, including that of two North Sea fishing concerns. As so often in the past, Jewish financiers were catalysts of changes that embittered the losers. They aided the department store trend, for instance, which hurt small shopkeepers, who later joined Nazi cadres in disproportionate numbers.

Max added a board seat on I. G. Farben to twenty-six others he now held. (By 1928, the Warburg partners collectively held eighty-seven director seats.) Since the Nazis would later employ I. G. Farben carbon monoxide to murder mental patients and also exploit its synthetic fuels, it is odd to recall that in the 1920s the firm was regularly pegged a "Jewish business" in anti-Semitic literature. In fact, it was Max's presence on its board that occasioned the initial feud between the combine and Nazi agitators.

His adversary was a short, stocky man with a trim Hitler moustache named Dr. Robert Ley. The holder of a doctorate in food chemistry, he worked as a chemist at Bayer pharmaceuticals. Inspired by accounts of Hitler's 1924

Munich trial, Ley commenced a double life. A sober chemist by day, he spent his evenings standing on tables in the beer gardens of Cologne and Aachen, drunkenly preaching hate. He and his thuggish bodyguards often ended the evening by trading blows with Communist hecklers. Dr. Schacht saw Ley this way: "He was a notorious drunkard, given to every kind of erotic excess, and without the slightest sense of responsibility."[20] His enemies in the Nazi party tried to thwart him by claiming he was half-Jewish. Nevertheless, in 1925 Hitler signed an order making him the Rhineland *Gauleiter*, or regional leader.

When Bayer merged with five other firms to form I. G. Farben, the Nazi rabble-rouser suddenly found himself working for a certified "Jewish combine." Ley must have seen the advantages in this and he didn't muzzle his views. In 1927, he railed against Max and his brothers in speeches. No matter how much Max tried to sidestep political activity, he couldn't evade this propaganda whirlwind. He was a fighter by nature and, as with Theodor Fritsch, didn't intend to take this quietly. He appealed to Hermann Bücher, who sat on Farben's economic advisory board and persuaded Farben's management to issue an ultimatum: either Ley would refrain from future Nazi activity or he would resign.

During a *Gauleiter* meeting in Weimar on November 27, 1927, Ley discussed the matter with Hitler, showing him the letter Bücher had circulated to management. Max Warburg was in a no-win situation. If Ley opposed him and won, it would be a great Nazi victory; if he lost, it would only expose the tentacles of Jewish power. Hitler advised Ley to stand firm and said he should ask I. G. Farben what right they had to make such a demand upon him. The talk stiffened Ley's resolve to become a Nazi martyr, and a month later, he wrote to Hitler, "What good is the most wonderful and secure job, if Germany perishes?"[21] An unrepentant Ley thus defied the Farben management: "I take it as my duty as a National-Socialist leader to attack every parasitic enemy of the *Volk*. If the Jewish supervisory board chairman Warburg can prove that I am wrong, I will be silent. Otherwise not."[22]

Farben dismissed Ley but continued to pay him a monthly stipend so he wouldn't defect to a competitor. With the money, he founded a Nazi paper in the Rhineland. The episode helped Ley's slimy career, elevating him into that pantheon of Nazi heroes who had suffered for the *Volk*. The Nazi press exploded in an orgy of abuse against I. G. Farben, which was now unmasked for all time as a tool of "money-mighty Jews."[23] Hitler later rewarded Ley by making him head of the German Labor Front, the largest organization in the Nazi party.

The Nazis held their first Nuremberg party rally in 1927. They now began to win their first recruits among respectable elements, including reactionary military officers, beleaguered Prussian landowners, and a smattering of industrial barons. Even in Hamburg, which prided itself on its freedom from right-wing intolerance, the Nazis made their first halting inroads. In 1926, speaking at the city's elegant lakeside hotel, the Atlantic, Hitler was cheered by shippers, industrialists, and aristocrats. Soon Brownshirts marched on Sundays through working-class neighborhoods by the port, and Josef Goebbels came to Altona to address a mass rally.

Even as the Nazi movement gathered force, the Warburgs' power in Jewish communal affairs reached its peak. In November 1928, the newspaper of the local Jewish community ran a one-hundredth-anniversary issue, which lauded M. M. Warburg & Co. as the city's foremost bank. As throughout Jewish history, financial power translated into philanthropic influence. The Weimar welfare state hadn't entirely superseded the self-governing structures of the Jewish community. That same year, Aby. S. Warburg—Max's partner and cousin—joined the board of the Central Association of German Citizens of Jewish Faith (*Centralverein*), then fighting anti-Semitism.[24] Max, now sixty-one, became executive director of the influential *Hilfsverein der deutschen Juden*, the Aid Society of German Jews. It would have been a weighty responsibility at any time. On the eve of the darkest turn in Jewish history, it would place Max Warburg in a leadership position that would force him to make excruciating decisions among unpalatable options.

The Jews in Weimar Germany had been successful enough to lend some credence to Nazi propaganda and arouse gentile envy and resentment. But they were neither numerous nor powerful enough to pose any real threat to the Nazis. Weimar had set them up as the perfect scapegoat, blessed with the appearance, but not the reality, of overwhelming power.

Aby Warburg in Florence, 1927.
(Warburg Institute)

CHAPTER 20

Warburg Redux

As the oldest and youngest of the Famous Five brothers, Aby and Fritz represented opposing sides of the split Warburg personality. Whether facetious or arrogant, Aby was an apostle of high culture, an archperfectionist, closeted with his books and pondering abstruse matters. He had jettisoned Jewish culture in favor of classical European culture. Fritz, however, embraced the Jewish community, both as a partner and personnel director of M. M. Warburg, and as chairman of the Jewish Hospital in Hamburg after the war. Unlike Aby, he was earthy and unassuming, a worldly man who liked street life and casual café conversation.

After Charlotte's death, Fritz and Anna Beata moved into her Mittelweg house where they had a large library and an electric piano. They became the Jewish conscience of the clan, maintaining the traditional Friday evening gatherings and bringing in a tutor to teach Hebrew and Jewish history to their three daughters. Aided by the American brothers, Fritz and Anna Beata maintained their style of life despite the hyperinflation. Always guilty about their wealth, Anna Beata was disturbed that they enjoyed comfort at such a dreary time for many Germans. "We're unfortunately too rich," she would say.[1] It pained her to invite friends to Kösterberg, and she dressed her daughters plainly so as not to flaunt their wealth.

Of all the Warburgs, Fritz most savored the artistic experimentation of the Weimar years. Max's tastes were more philistine: he liked slapstick and broad comedy in film and theater. Fritz had very catholic, sophisticated taste and would rush off to Berlin to catch the latest Max Reinhardt production. His unhappy marriage to Anna Beata also made him a familiar denizen of the St. Pauli district, where he seemed to charm the demimonde. The ladies in Hamburg's red-light zone would lean from their windows and squeal excited greetings to "Uncle Fritz." He once shocked Jimmy's wife, Kay, by taking her to a local night spot where naked women rode around the bar on horseback, waiting for male customers to leap up into the saddle and ride off with them. Felix's son, Eddie, experienced a similar surprise when Fritz took a field hockey team from the Salem school to a late-night restaurant in the St. Pauli district. As the young athletes sipped hot soup, they witnessed another form of sport being practiced inside curtained booths. Perhaps some underlying self-consciousness about his queer appearance drew Fritz to this world of easy and anonymous pleasures.

Aby never delved into this raw side of life, never opened himself up to the quotidian world; he cared about exceptional people, not ordinary ones. His high-minded self-absorption only deepened after his emergence from Kreuzlingen. In 1925, Mary sketched a drawing that suggested the impassable chasm between them. Aby sits bent over a book, sadly lost in thought, while through the window, one can see Mary in the distance, climbing a mountain with a jaunty, energetic step. The picture tells a tragic tale of the dreamer and the doer, introvert and extrovert. While Aby struggled with his demons in Switzerland, Mary had brought up three children, managed the house, and found solace in painting and sculpture. And she did it with a remarkable absence of complaint or self-pity.

Carl Georg Heise speculated that Aby's return to Hamburg sprang from a premonition that he wouldn't live long and that he wanted to be near his family.[2] If so, lost love proved hard to recapture. Aby might want to start afresh, but the children were scarred from his lengthy struggle. The dreamy Max Adolph loved his father's warmth and admired his oratorical power to enchant and educate. He saw Aby as a prophetic spirit like Martin Luther, Karl Marx, or Friedrich Neitzsche, a titanic force of nature. Yet he also feared him. As he wrote, "Aby Warburg was a volcano. . . . Every volcano is an uncanny stranger to its nearest surroundings, however many scraps and fragments of their top formation the lava may contain. The next akin [sic] are rarely its nearest relatives in spirit."[3]

Emotionally sapped by his illness, the children found it hard to give full credit to Aby for his extraordinary achievement in escaping from the sanato-

rium. A certain compassion and sensitivity had been burned out of them.
"And this blunting of our nerve ends earned us bitter epithets from his lips,
when apparently we failed to appreciate his return from the hell of his illness;
the miracle of living with a 'revenant' not from the dead but from the mad,"
said Max Adolph.[4]

Aby was an imperious German father who showed less tolerance for his
wayward son than Moritz had shown for him. Thwarting Max Adolph's
ambition to become a painter, Aby shipped him off to a strict boarding school
and made him read classics at various universities. In 1927, Max Adolph took
a doctorate in philosophy from Berlin University and his dissertation on Plato
impressed Aby with its intellectual power. As dynastic in his library as Max
in the bank, Aby wanted Max Adolph to succeed him as director of the
Warburg Library. In 1926, Aby took him on a Swedish pilgrimage to see
Rembrandt's *Claudius Civilis*, which he then had copied at great expense.
Sensitive, eager to please, Max Adolph suppressed his own wishes.

In his final years, Aby's acquaintances spied a new serenity and sweetness
in him. Toni Cassirer said all traces of sickness effectively vanished, yet this
seems a gross overstatement.[5] Aby knew he had received a reprieve from the
gods and, far from being bitter about lost time, was deeply grateful for this last
chance to work. Upstairs at home, he worked under a drawing of Nietzsche
after his breakdown that had special meaning for him.

In photos of Aby from the late 1920s, one sees a man with so many faces
that he seems to possess multiple personalities. At moments, he resembles a
portly, smiling Buddha. At other times he appears a broken figure with dark
rings under his eyes, crushed by the burden of his scholarship and ravaged
by the recent asylum terror. He still suffered from fits of rage and delusions
and his demons never abandoned him. He couldn't entirely banish the
mumbo-jumbo that his rational mind so fervently resisted. For instance, his
desk-top objects held a fetishistic significance for him and Aby grew agitated
if visitors fiddled idly with them. Politely but firmly, he would advise visitors
to leave everything in place, fearing that any loose play with these imple-
ments might realign his stars and unleash tides of cosmic evil. Many of Aby's
late scholarly interests—his fascination with airplanes, for instance—reflect
these cosmic obsessions.

The sovereign remedy for Aby was work. He felt like some undaunted
explorer who had penetrated a remote, dangerous region and brought back
a captured cargo of precious knowledge. As his mental powers revived, he
returned with excitement to his prewar interests, even to a boyhood enthusiasm for postage stamps. Like semeologists of a later day, his intellectual
empire widened to encompass such everyday cultural artifacts as stamps,
coins, photos, posters, and advertisements, which he analyzed with the same

intensity he once reserved for art works. A critic at large, he snapped at the "childish" advertising for HAPAG liners and waged a campaign against a cigarette firm with a brand called Nestor, deploring this profanation of the Greek classics. He even threatened to direct the full financial power of M. M. Warburg against the impious company.

This impossible genius had attained cult status and enjoyed the patient tolerance granted to lovable, original, important cranks. By late 1925, he was teaching his first seminars at the Warburg Library. On December 20, 1926, he escorted Foreign Minister Gustav Stresemann through the library, treating him to a disquisition on stamps. As they walked around, Aby made it clear who ruled in *this* little world. He showed Stresemann how much one could deduce about a country's politics from studying its stamps and even gave Stresemann a reproachful lecture on scholarly precision. Presenting some contemporary German stamps that featured Goethe's head, Aby said, "Herr Chancellor, will you please read the inscription here, if you can." Smiling, Stresemann read, "Johann Wolfgang Goethe." Aby retorted, "Incorrectly read, Herr Chancellor. Just look here, doesn't it say, Joh period, Wolfg period, Goethe? And that is just the entire misfortune with our Weimar Republic, that everything is abbreviated and therefore too short."⁶ Aby had an irrational hatred of abbreviations.

However debilitated by illness, Aby still had spurts of superhuman energy and demanded that audiences sit through lectures that droned on for hours. Felix's son, Eddie, would remember suffering through a five-hour marathon on "Why the King of England Sits in the Position of Neptune on the Pound Note."⁷ To enter Aby's world was to submit unequivocally to his tyranny. The first time a future assistant, Klaus Berger, visited the library, Aby expatiated for nearly five hours on the library's aims. "Without disruption, without a pause. I felt as if I were nailed to the seat, before a great firework."⁸ In 1927, Max sent two government officials with some surplus time on their hands to see the library. After a four-hour monologue by Aby, the flabbergasted men stumbled out the front door, dazed but uplifted. One confessed to the other, "This afternoon, my life acquired more depth than in the previous forty-eight years."⁹ Intellectual luminaries also beat a path to Aby's door. He corresponded with Thomas Mann about Babylonian astrology, a subject that concerned the latter for a new book, presumably *Joseph and His Brothers.*

In his last years, Aby returned to his pioneering work on cosmological symbols in Renaissance art. Cheered by Hamburg's decision to create a planetarium in the water tower of the city park, he began work on a novel exhibition about astronomy and astrology that he would later donate to the planetarium along with a small study library. Assembling an imaginative collage of 150 pieces, he demonstrated how humanity had progressed along a rising curve from superstition to scientific certitude. For the section on modern cosmology, Aby enlisted the aid of Einstein, who toured the library and afterward wrote Aby, "It was especially interesting for me to see how little expenditure it requires to lead credulous humanity around by the nose."[10] Aby was pleased by the accolades that tumbled in upon him. The planetarium, with his exhibition, opened on April 15, 1930, after his death.

At the end, Aby, in his early sixties, focused his energies on the problems that had preoccupied him for a lifetime. With intimations of mortality, he wanted to employ every spare minute constructively and told Max, "One must arrange one's life, as if one lived forever, but be ready every day to die."[11] When Aby sat for a painting by Mary, he was impossibly skittish, as if he needed to be in constant motion. In a pleasant return to scenes past, he made peace with Italy, which had so deeply wounded him in 1915. Both in 1928 and 1929, he made extensive trips there with his assistant, Dr. Gertrud Bing, whom Kenneth Clark would praise for her "nun-like" devotion to Aby.[12]

Fritz Saxl had recruited Bing to work at the library and he and Aby vied for her favor. Since Saxl was married, Aby became enraged whenever his young rival expressed the slightest interest in divorce. Bing was cool, smart, slim, and ambitious. She had short hair, dark eyebrows, and no-nonsense glasses that sharpened a look of keen intelligence. In one photo with Aby, she looks very self-possessed and emancipated, as if she knew her worth. Having fallen under Aby's spell, she was slavishly loyal to him and followed his wishes without protest. She likened him to an Old Testament prophet in eloquence and wrath and felt that something in his gaze stared straight through her.[13] She was the great romance of his life and enhanced the mental ardor of his two culminating trips to Italy.

During this period of miraculous rebirth, Aby's relations with Mary were cordial but distant. She either didn't know about the affair with Bing—the Warburgs thought her amazingly naïve—or chose to look the other way. The failed marriage strengthened Mary's dedication to her own art. She was tolerant of Aby's endless travels with Gertrud; the 1929 trip alone lasted much of the year. It is heartbreaking to read the letters she exchanged with Aby in his absence. He would babble on about his scholarly escapades with "Bingia," as he styled his traveling companion. Or he would grow indignant about books or papers tardily forwarded from Hamburg. But of inquiries about Mary, her life, her work—we hear hardly a word. When he wrote her from a Rome hotel at Christmas 1928, he said nothing more than "Merry Christmas" and that she should give the children whatever presents they wanted.[14] Until the end, Aby never lost the mutually reinforcing egotism of the genius and of the pampered, spoiled eldest son.

Asking nothing for herself, Mary seemed glad that her husband had survived the asylum and approved of his decisions to extend his journey. In 1928 and 1929, she met Aby and Bing when Aby returned to his old "repair shop," the Heinsheimer clinic in Baden-Baden, for cures. In fact, the Warburgs felt grateful to Bing for taking care of Aby. With this sickly, older man, she probably acted more as a nursemaid than a mistress. He was so exhausted on their travels that he often had to cancel appointments for days on end and consult doctors. In 1928, when Aby briefly considered his first American trip since the 1890s—a project vetoed by Dr. Binswanger—his brothers made it a precondition that Gertrud accompany him.

Aby's last Italian trips were gigantic scholarly sweeps through churches, palaces, and universities. He traveled heavily laden with books. It was a final chance to study essential works of art and Aby was thrilled by the warm reception he received from librarians and curators who remembered him from earlier days. Both Stresemann and Konstantin von Neurath, the German ambassador to Rome, helped to open doors. Reverting to his earlier political beliefs, Aby showed von Neurath how the antique cultures of the Mediterranean had influenced Germany and how this necessitated closer North-South links.[15]

The capstone of Aby's career was to be the "picture atlas" he planned to publish under the title *Mnemosyne,* his library's motto. It was intended as a summary statement of his interdisciplinary approach to Western culture, with special emphasis on the influence of classical art in the Renaissance. He took panels and packed them with collages of imagery that showed unexpected relations among symbols over time. Onto some forty screens, he crowded fifteen hundred images that included paintings, drawings, engravings, and woodcuts as well as stamps, coins, photographs, and posters. As if shaping his theories with his hands as well as his mind, he constantly reworked their arrangement, much as he had the organization of his books. He was writing a history of the Western mind in pictorial design. Once again, Aby saw the story of Western civilization paralleling that of his own psyche.[16] This mosaic would remain incomplete, though largely finished, at his death.

On January 19, 1929, Aby presented fragments of his picture atlas at a lecture in Rome, flashing through 250 pictures in a two-and-one-half-hour tour de force. He was boyishly excited by the plaudits he received. The lecture not only exhibited Aby's brilliance, but his courage, his stamina. During the first ten minutes, he suffered a mild heart spasm, but then developed such steam that the institute director had to hint that Aby was exceeding his allotted time—an affront Aby wouldn't forget. For future speeches, Aby needed a doctor in attendance. Often he started out slowly, struggling for breath, then ended up roaring and gesticulating and exhausting his audience.

During lectures, Aby liked to fasten his gaze on a single listener and often planted a friend in the front row for that express purpose. For his speech in Rome, he eyed a young man named Kenneth Clark, who found the experience a revelation. Under Aby's influence, Clark abandoned the connoisseur's approach to art to plunge into symbolic studies. Aby's method so intrigued him that he rejected an invitation to assist Bernard Berenson in Florence and left this stunning tribute to Aby: "Warburg was without doubt the most original thinker on art-history of our time, and entirely changed the course of art-historical studies."[17]

Despite his weak heart and diabetes (he took insulin), Aby pressed ahead with his plans. By a marvelous coincidence, this expert on symbols was present in Rome for the signing of the Lateran Treaty, which reconciled the Vatican with the Italian state. Holding up small binoculars, Aby stood in St. Peter's Square with two hundred thousand other spectators as the Pope delivered his blessing. Upset by the blatantly Fascist symbolism, he studied closely a film of Benito Mussolini signing the treaty. "I was astounded by the pretty Caesarean malice of the play of his lips," he wrote Mary.[18]

It seems poetically just that idyllic scenes graced the last months of Aby's tortured life. In Naples, he and Bing stayed at the Excelsior Hotel, which had a view of the blue sea and smoking Vesuvius. They breakfasted with Berenson at I Tatti, even though the latter disliked German Jews. As Berenson once observed, "They may have Jewish noses and souls but their minds are super-German and that to me and not their Jewishness makes them a public danger."[19] While consulting with Berenson about the Fogg Museum at Harvard—Berenson planned to donate his villa and library to the university—Felix urged him to meet with Aby, and this may have been the origin of their breakfast. In any event, Aby and Bing admired the setting and Berenson's grandiose library before they motored up through Verona and Mantua and left Italy forever.

In his last days in Hamburg, Aby wasn't free of the lifelong quarrels that had bedeviled him. The university had hoped to create an archeology professorship for him, which he thought might lift his oppressive work burden. When it didn't materialize in the spring of 1929, he grew furious and told the head of the Kunsthalle that if he were healthy and ten years younger, he would consider moving his library to Rome.[20] He never entirely made peace with the cultural backwater that was his ancestral town.

Aby's relations with his brothers also never lost a certain uneasy edge. Whatever money they gave, Aby wanted more and even solicited Frieda for funds. As Jimmy Warburg recalled, "The money for the library came in annual donations, sometimes accompanied by audible groans, from his brothers in the banking business. Aby had no compunctions about assessing them for what he considered the only worthwhile product of their mundane endeavors."[21] If his brothers protested, Aby flatly predicted that his library would outlast M. M. Warburg & Co. He couldn't stop his compulsive book collecting and in 1929 pushed his bed away from the walls to make room for more shelves.[22]

On August 21, 1929, the five brothers posed for a last photo at a board meeting of the library. The gray-haired Max sat in the middle, still virile and confident. Fritz looked cheerful, but off balance, peripheral. Two months away from the stock market crash he had predicted, Paul seemed downcast. Felix alone seemed radiant, with a broad, beaming smile. Sad and wistful, Aby sat to the side, his hair and mustache white. At the last minute, this historian of symbols cupped his hands and held them up toward his brothers in a begging posture. It was a poignant jest. The brothers had delivered on their promise to support him, but at considerable cost. Aby's ceaseless demands had always carried a tacit criticism of their business lives. So it was proper and fitting that he offered them this final laugh at his own expense.

Very aware of world events, Aby still bombarded Max and Eric with telephone calls, expressing stern judgments about contemporary events. Ever a student of the zeitgeist, a lightning rod for charged particles in the air, Aby saw the coming threats to civilized discourse and heard the jackboots marching. He believed his library could be an antidote to the menace. On the morning of October 26, 1929, he grew apoplectic on the phone while discussing the plebiscite for the new Young Plan on reparations, then under sharp Nazi attack. Yet his anger soon subsided and when his family doctor, Heinrich Embden, called that afternoon, he sang out gaily, "All is well above the collar."[23] Aby, age sixty-three, ventured no claims for the body below.

That evening, Gertrud Bing stayed for dinner after work, as she did once a week, and Mary retreated to her studio on the top floor in a remote corner of the roomy house. Aby and Bing were having a lively exchange when Gertrud suddenly heard Mary calling "Aby!" Aby scoffed, saying that Mary would not do that and that she was too far away for her voice to be heard. Unconvinced, Bing went upstairs to investigate and found Mary working in her studio. She told Bing that she hadn't called Aby; later, she admitted she had heard Aby calling "Mary!" and had dismissed it as implausible. Wife and mistress then returned to the dining room and found Aby dead from a heart attack on the floor. The historian of symbols died in a way that imaged his strange triangular relationship with these two women.

The next morning, the two found the last entry in Aby's diary, a line of verse praising the "late-ripening apple tree" in his garden.[24] He had identified with this old tree, which seemed dead and then suddenly put forth white blossoms again. To preserve Aby's memory, Mary had photographs taken of his head so she could sculpt a posthumous bust. Even in death, Aby refused to feign piety. Although Jews believed that dead bodies should be buried and remain untouched until the Messiah's advent, Aby left instructions for his cremation.

The Warburgs summoned Fritz Saxl back from London to take charge of the sixty-five-thousand-volume library. Max advised Gertrud Bing to start collecting reminiscences for a future biography, but her emotional involvement with the subject would always prevent its completion.[25] Much of Aby's influence stemmed from his personality, not his small output of published work. He therefore required talented disciples far more than other original thinkers; he found them in Saxl and Bing. They brought out the first two volumes of Aby's collected writings in 1932, right before Hitler took power, but much of his writing would remain unpublished or untranslated.

When Aby died, the newspapers recognized him as a major figure. His was a reputation purchased at the price of great personal pain. One obituary described him as "unrelenting against compromise and half-measures, a fighter, a judge courageous and severe, a servant of scholarship. So powerful was his personality that he will live on as an inspiring example."[26] Indeed, as the years passed, his reputation grew enormously. As art scholarship turned to "deconstructing" myth and symbolism, he was hailed as a progenitor of one of the century's most influential critical schools. George Steiner would call him "one of the seminal figures in modern culture," who created "nothing less than a new model of the Renaissance and of the relations of the secular West to its antique well-springs."[27] His posthumous reputation is now firmly established. John Russell of *The New York Times* has said that many qualified observers now consider Aby "the greatest single influence on the development of art historical studies in this century."[28]

In the end, the gods proved kind to Aby Warburg. He died two days after the start of the 1929 Wall Street crash, which would shatter the false prosperity of the 1920s and usher in a world as murky and ominous as anything in Aby's most tormented dreams. By December, the Warburg library was struggling financially, and Felix pledged fifty thousand dollars a year for it to survive. Aby had promised lavish subsidies to attract scholars and the brothers once again made good on their promises.

It is unbearable to contemplate the anguish Aby would have suffered in Nazi Germany, with its book-burnings and glorified rites of pagan brutality.

He got out just in time, before his beloved German culture gave way to barbarism. The year after his death, the Nazis ran the Bauhaus out of Weimar. Before long, they would reject the cultural contributions of an entire generation of Jewish scholars. In the end, Aby Warburg had won his struggle with the forces of unreason. Germany, alas, had not.

CHAPTER 21

Capitalist Collectives

Felix Warburg's growing eminence in the 1920s was perhaps the most implausible success story among the Famous Five brothers. Long patronized as the family flyweight, dismissed as not bright enough for the Hamburg bank, he had steadily risen in stature in the charity sphere after Jacob Schiff's death. Scion of a rich family and married to a smart heiress, he had the rare good fortune to convert his natural goodness into a career.

The times abounded in opportunities for New York Jews to aid their overseas brethren as the American economy hummed along and much of Europe languished. On June 17, 1924, Felix and other dignitaries gathered for a highly unusual luncheon presentation at the Kuhn, Loeb offices at 52 William Street. Dr. Joseph Rosen, a prominent agronomist with the Joint Distribution Committee, unrolled a huge, colored map of the Ukraine and the Crimea. The purple tracts, Rosen explained, designated current Jewish farm colonies. Blue sections indicated areas abandoned or seized from pre-Revolution landowners and now offered free by the Soviet government for Jewish agricultural settlements. Red tracts, which had always been state owned, also formed part of a unique Soviet offer now on the table.

Jews in Biblical times had worked as shepherds, farmers, and vintners, but they had become highly urbanized in the modern world, shunted into trading, peddling, or moneylending. Confined to the Pale of Settlement under the czar, the Russian Jews hadn't been allowed to buy or manage land beyond their tumbledown shtetls. A czarist plan to resettle them on the land had turned into a wretched hoax, hobbling its recipients with myriad rules. So the map unfurled by Rosen tantalized these Jewish leaders with a sense of limitless possibility.

After the Revolution, the Bolsheviks dropped the policy of state anti-Semitism, but most Jews didn't fit into the new prescribed categories of proletarians and peasants, and Jewish traders and artisans were maligned as "anti-social" or "class enemies." So the Soviets sympathized with any program that would convert them into "productive" laborers on the land, especially if it meant a massive influx of American dollars and modern agricultural technology.

A stalwart Republican—Frieda was the family Democrat—Felix had no more relish for the Bolsheviks than for the reactionary Romanoffs. During the 1920s, he and Herbert Lehman provided large loans to David Dubinsky so he could purge Communists from the International Ladies Garment Workers Union. Felix dreaded the glib Jews-equal-Bolshevism equation that was gaining currency in anti-Semitic circles and that featured in recent Nazi diatribes against Max and Fritz. Stories filtering back from the workers' paradise made him recoil: "No private property permitted, no trading permitted, the houses belonging to the Government, and nobody permitted to have more than his daily portion of bread. . . ." he told his sons, aghast.[1] At first Felix wouldn't sign an agreement with a Soviet government dedicated to Marxist principles.

As famine and civil strife convulsed the postwar Pale, threatening nearly three million Soviet Jews, Felix and the Joint couldn't ignore their urgent plight and worked intimately with Herbert Hoover and his American Relief Administration. Tens of thousands of Jews were being murdered by marauding bandits. Entire villages were wiped out in fierce fighting between Soviets and Poles. Then, in 1921, Soviet crops failed, a disaster so colossal that the Joint set up soup kitchens there, and even the U.S. Congress sent corn to alleviate the situation.

Among the Hoover relief aides grappling with the crisis was Dr. Joseph A. Rosen, nicknamed "the famine angel of Russia." After being jailed in Siberia for his Menshevik views, Rosen emigrated to the United States in 1903. He never entirely shed his Socialist sympathies, which helped to make him palatable to the Soviet government. On a field trip to the famine district, Rosen contracted typhus and nearly died. In 1922, he worked out an agreement with the Soviets to create loan co-ops and training schools for Jews and began to advocate an enormous colonization project. A successful experiment that

Felix Warburg in his favorite yachting cap.
(Warburg family, Hamburg)

resettled five hundred families on the land stimulated the appetites of both the Soviet government and the Joint for further action.

This set the stage for the dramatic June 1924 luncheon at Kuhn, Loeb. The Ukraine government stood ready to transfer two hundred thousand acres for Jewish farm resettlement, with Rosen foreseeing another one and a half million arable acres available in the Crimea. The Joint was being offered the equivalent of a small state. "It is the best black soil of Russia," said Rosen. "There are no more fertile lands anywhere in the United States."[2] In summary, he declared, "I don't see any other project of such importance and value, a possibility that will never repeat itself."[3]

Rosen inflamed the imagination of these Jewish luminaries. Emotional and volatile, Felix was quick to catch fire and then radiate an infectious enthusiasm for a new project. "I absolutely agree with Mr. [James N.] Rosenberg's statement in regard to the desirability of giving this experiment a fair trial," he said. Because these conservative bankers and lawyers felt jittery about cooperating with Bolsheviks, Felix added, "I am not afraid that this action could in any way be misconstrued and used against the Jews in Russia, whatever the future may bring."[4]

A month later, after securing the State Department's imprimatur, the Joint created the American Jewish Joint Agricultural Corporation—the so-called "Agro-Joint"—with an initial four-hundred-thousand-dollar appropriation and Rosen as its president. Herbert Hoover would hail this audacious venture as "one of the outstanding pieces of human engineering in the world."[5] It would progress under the most unlikely auspices, with Felix finally coaxing Julius Rosenwald of Sears, Roebuck, and John D. Rockefeller, Jr., into making huge gifts to agricultural cooperatives deep in the Soviet Union.

The saga of the Soviet Jewish farm settlements is a forgotten chapter of history. The project spoke to a long-standing Jewish dream of escaping from job restrictions imposed upon European Jews since medieval times. Farming held an ancient attraction for Jewish urbanites. Chaim Weizmann envisioned agriculture as forming the heart of Jewish life in Palestine. Baron Maurice de Hirsch and the Rothschilds had sponsored agricultural colonies in the nineteenth century. As bankers who were dismayed by invidious clichés about Jewish cleverness with money, the Warburgs favored Jews entering the full spectrum of employment. Felix also had a rich man's sentimental faith in manual labor and urged young Jews to consider fields other than finance. In the Soviet Union, Dr. Rosen saw a great historic experiment under way. "Since the Diaspora, for twenty centuries we Jews have been pushed from pillar to post. We have never been given a decent chance to settle on the soil. . . . The accusation is always leveled against us that we are exploiters and profiteers, lawyers, bankers, etc. It has remained for Russia . . . to give Jews the first opportunity in modern history—indeed the first opportunity in two thousand years—to prove that the accusation always leveled against us is a lie."[6]

At first, the Agro-Joint contributed the bulk of funds; the Soviets made a minor contribution. The land often lacked water, and the Soviets were glad to have American plutocrats drilling expensive wells. Some ten thousand whitewashed houses with red tile roofs sprouted across the Soviet steppes. The scale of Agro-Joint colonization was awesome. In a dozen years, it transplanted more than a quarter-million Soviet Jews to 215 colonies spread over two and a half million acres of land. They rode a thousand American-made tractors and tended twenty thousand cows, twenty-five thousand chickens, and even eighty-five hundred pigs. In time, four hundred vocational schools also sprang up to teach Jews metal, woodworking, printing, and other trades.

Some colonies had a Zionist bent and saw themselves as way stations on the road to Palestine. The bulk of Zionists, however, regarded the colonies as a dangerous distraction. Weizmann derided the "Babbitts" for diverting precious funds from Palestine and feeding Utopian fantasies that Jews could find a home in Soviet Russia.[7] He saw the large sums being spent as dollars disappearing down a bottomless drain. In 1925, Dr. Stephen S. Wise presented a lengthy indictment against the Agro-Joint, denigrating Felix et al. as disloyal Americans and Soviet dupes who lured Jewish settlers to colonies only to expose them to future butchery. Louis Marshall recalled, "Dr. Wise, in a speech made at Springfield, Massachusetts, said that one Bialik [Chaim Nachman Bialik, a poet] was worth more than a thousand Felix Warburgs, amid a tumultuous applause from the audience. . . ."[8] Even moderate critics argued that the Agro-Joint would only benefit a tiny percentage of Jews and that the Soviets would ultimately renege on the deal.

Nevertheless, for Felix the Soviet colonies brought out the sort of joyful, pioneering zest that Zionists felt for Palestine. Now in his mid-fifties and moving into semiretirement, Felix often seemed a more old-fashioned fellow. It annoyed him that young people spoke slang, not the beautiful formal speech of old, and he regretted how motion pictures were replacing leisurely reading. This yearning for a simpler age of innocence made him a ripe convert for the romantic Soviet settlements.

In 1927, Felix, fifty-seven, and Frieda, fifty-three, took an around-the-world trip. Unable to detach himself totally from his fifty-seven charities, he instructed his secretary, Alice R. Emanuel, to keep him liberally supplied with news. When Alice returned from vacation, the news-starved Felix sent a two-word cable: "Please gossip."[9] On the boat, Felix, in a wistful mood, jotted down reminiscences. Recalling how he and other Warburg children once pretended to communicate through the Big Dipper, he entitled his memoir, "Under the Seven Stars."

Leaving Frieda in Japan, Felix traveled to the Soviet Union and toured forty

Agro-Joint colonies with Dr. Rosen, Dr. Bernhard Kahn, and James Becker. Felix kept a diary while Becker shot a thousand feet of film. At first, they traveled by private railroad car. Entering more remote regions, they climbed into two chauffeured limousines for long overland rides to settlements. Their shiny cars were increasingly caked and spattered with mud as they drove across treeless plateaus of rich black soil covered with wild grass and weeds. After driving for hours, the whitewashed Agro-Joint houses would suddenly come into view and hundreds of sunburnt people would pour from the fields to greet the legendary Jewish leader from New York. The group visited a settlement named Felix Warburg No. 4 and 5, and Felix also laid the cornerstone for a high school that bore his name.

For a pampered man accustomed to luxury, he responded to these threadbare outposts with the glad-handing gusto of a politician on the hustings and his curiosity seemed insatiable. He watched horses pulling ploughs through the bountiful earth and surveyed machine shops, medical dispensaries, vineyards, tile factories, flour mills, and cooperative workshops. Suddenly he was like a modern Prospero, standing before a world he had conjured into being. In one colony, he met a Mr. Shapiro, the old caretaker of Baron de Gunzburg's properties. In community rooms and schools across the Crimea and the Ukraine, Jewish settlers flocked to hear this elegant, effusive man applaud their efforts in a German accent. For the rest of his life, Felix would carry unforgettable memories of peasants stooped over crops, as in Millet paintings, and of moonlit trains speeding across the steppes.

Jews had always wondered how they would look and act if liberated from the historical accidents that shaped them. In these Soviet villages, Felix saw a healthy contrast to the jaded urban sophisticates he had known, Jewish and Christian. Of the women, he said, "They do not mind getting wrinkles, no foolish lipsticks or youthful short flapper costumes."[10] The men seemed noble and weatherbeaten—proof that Jews could be good farmers. "Why should they not be so?" he asked. "It is the historic occupation of the Jew."[11] Indeed, the colonies thrived even though most of the farmers lacked experience.

Elated by his two-week trip, Felix said it had been "thrilling, inspiring, reassuring, encouraging and made one feel grateful for the privilege of being connected with this enterprise and its workers."[12] When he met Soviet leader Alexei Rykov in Moscow, Felix not only praised the colonies, but solicited extra government help. They worked out a plan for the Agro-Joint and the Soviets to raise together twenty million dollars for the settlements in a fifty-fifty split. Parroting the capitalist line to please Felix, the Soviets assured him that Agro-Joint farmers could set their own, higher prices for better produce and could buy their own animals with their earnings. In fact, some Agro-Joint colonies were extremely collectivist, a fact the Joint conveniently preferred to overlook.

A week later, Felix was debriefed by the U.S. embassy in Berlin and sounded decidedly more pessimistic about Bolshevist Russia than in his glowing reports to the Joint. "He states that buildings, plants and machinery are deteriorating, no provision being made for repairs or up-keep," an embassy official told Washington. Felix had evidently undertaken free-lance diplomacy in Moscow, telling Rykov that U.S.–Soviet relations could only improve if the Soviet Union honored foreign debts and ceased anti-American propaganda. Rykov said they were ready to honor debts dating back to the Kerensky government.

Back in New York, Felix championed the Agro-Joint colonies with indefatigable energy—an ironic fate indeed for the son-in-law of Jacob Schiff, historic scourge of the Soviets. To market Soviet bonds for the venture, the Joint set up the American Society for Jewish Farm Settlements in Russia, Inc., an operation that made some curious political bedfellows. To appease the Zionists, the Joint raised the money from rich individuals, not its own funds. Julius Rosenwald subscribed five million dollars, Felix one million, John D. Rockefeller, Jr., five hundred thousand, and Paul Warburg fifty thousand. Felix served as honorary president. These donors had to endure the caustic wit of Dr. Stephen Wise, who sneered, "Millions, including a very large sum from Warburg, are poured into Russia; Palestine gets investigations."[13] The Zionists delighted in noting that Russia, historic bane of the Jews, was now being rewarded. Yet Felix also ranked among the largest American donors to Palestine and saw no contradiction in subsidizing the Soviet colonies as well.

Sometimes Dr. Rosen seemed blind to distasteful realities of the workers' paradise. When a critic objected that the Soviets would betray the Jews, Joseph Rosen reacted in high dudgeon, asserting that nearly 90 percent of the Soviet people were peasants whose lives were better after the Revolution. Felix could also duck some ugly truths. When asked about the persecution of rabbis under the Bolsheviks, he deplored it, but was quick to note that the Soviet government was improving the economic lot of the Jews.[14]

In the last analysis, it was impossible for these capitalist islands to survive in a socialist sea. Stalin was extremely anti-Semitic and by the late 1920s had purged Jews from high positions. In late 1929 Communist party ideologists (including Jewish ones) denounced the foreign bourgeois organizations behind the Agro-Joint, as the great wave of forced collectivization got under way. In January 1930, the Joint Office in Berlin sent a confidential cable to New York that resonated with horror: "Stalin group complete control adopted decidedly left wing policy." It described the ruthless extermination of Kulaks, or rich peasants, and the brutal collectivization of millions of poor ones.[15] Before long, Jewish colonies were forced to accept as much as 50 percent non-Jewish workers, destroying their rationale for being.

Felix was terribly shocked by events, and Rosen struggled to prevent him from losing heart. In 1930, Max warned his brother that the colonies couldn't withstand Stalinist policy and that the dream had expired.[16] Agro-Joint autonomy was whittled away by ideological assault. Where it once built individual houses, it now had to create houses with communal arrangements and state agronomists superseded those from the Joint. Many Jews who had welcomed the colonies as havens from state interference began to abandon them. As many Jews drifted off to work in factories and became approved proletarians, the very need for the colonies seemed to disappear. By 1932, the Soviets began a program to dismantle the Agro-Joint project in stages.

As the settlements evolved into a bizarre hybrid of Park Avenue charity and Marxist agriculture, some Agro-Joint staffers evolved into Soviet fellow-travelers. In the mid-1930s, the group sent Evelyn Morrissey to spend four weeks in the Soviet Union. She wrote a book about her travels in which she seemed bewitched by the country and gushed about the marble pillars, wide platforms, and leather seats of the Moscow subway. She solemnly visited Lenin's tomb and stared agog at Moscow construction sites. She concluded: "We have read much of forced and prison labor conditions and its horrors, but here in these golden fields of sunflowers we cannot visualize what it means."[17]

Until the very end, Felix was reluctant to surrender the Agro-Joint experiment. In 1937, its factories and workshops were absorbed into local Soviet agencies. A few years later, the State Department informed the Joint that the Soviets had confiscated its funds and shot many Jews.[18] Hundreds of Agro-Joint agronomists were evidently imprisoned or vanished. In 1940, the last assets were transferred to the Soviet government. However worthy and ambitious, the experiment had backfired and vindicated the warnings of the Zionists. Whether from confusion, embarrassment, or disappointment, the episode was buried, forgotten, obliterated. Most people don't know it ever happened or that in the 1920s American capitalists had briefly been the largest landlords in the Soviet Union.

—

Zionist displeasure over the Soviet misadventure was exacerbated by a severe economic downturn in Palestine in the late 1920s. Weizmann repeatedly complained to Felix about high unemployment in Tel Aviv and the costly dole needed to cope with it. In 1927, the Zionist enterprise itself seemed in peril as more Jews left Palestine than arrived. When Felix donated fifty thousand dollars to cushion unemployment, Weizmann responded with extreme gratitude. That year, Felix also participated in the Survey Committee, which worked to establish spending priorities for Palestine.

Weizmann felt confident that he had implanted in Felix and Frieda an enduring interest in a Jewish homeland. Now he started to court the German

Warburgs. German Jews generally felt threatened by the Zionist movement. Max mocked his brother's flights of enthusiasm about Palestine and faulted his handsome bequest to the Hebrew University. Like other German Jews, Max dreaded the dual loyalty charge and stressed that his principal fidelity rested with Germany, not Palestine. He viewed Palestine as a possible sanctuary to restore the Jewish spirit, a cultural gift to mankind, but not as a refuge for stateless people.

Hence, when Weizmann wooed Max in Berlin in 1928, he proceeded in low-key style. "It is admitted on all sides in Germany that any favourable attitude on his part would be of enormous value in German Jewish circles," Weizmann told Felix.[19] Later, Weizmann would grumble that Max had "never been friendly" to the Zionist cause.[20] During their two-hour talk in Berlin, they were joined by Max's daughter, Gisela. The sixteen-year-old Gisi was a skinny, idealistic teenager, petite and blue-eyed, who hungered for religious involvement. She said she felt like a fool when she sat in synagogue and didn't know Hebrew.[21] A principled girl, she once learned that a friend's parents had excluded Jewish girls from a dance. She approached the girl and said they would stay friends, but she would never set foot in her house again.[22] Max found his youngest daughter's passionate idealism praiseworthy, if occasionally excessive.

Gisi sat rapt during the two-hour talk. Max frequently contradicted Weizmann and came across as an unyielding German nationalist. After the meeting, Gisi went into the bathroom and burst into tears. When Max asked why she was crying, she said bluntly: "Because Mr. Weizmann was so much more convincing than you were." Of her conversion to Zionism by Weizmann, Gisi said, "He picked me like a ripe apple."[23] Weizmann reciprocated Gisi's admiration and predicted that she would someday be his secretary. In alarm, Max and Alice packed Gisi off to a rugged Zionist camp, hoping a summer of shoveling manure and menial tasks would cure her. The tactic boomeranged and she was soon sending letters to Weizmann in Hebrew. After leaving school, she worked for Youth Aliyah, which trained adolescents for rural life in a future Jewish state.

A more fateful encounter occurred between Weizmann and Max's exquisitely beautiful eldest daughter, Lola Hahn-Warburg. While her sisters Renate and Gisi took their *Abitur* and Anita attended the Salem school, "Stupid Lola," as her mother called her, received private instruction and a strict Victorian upbringing. Lola found bright, fiery, intellectual men irresistible and they fully repaid the compliment. Max said that a father of daughters was nothing but a cannon to shoot down boys, and with Lola his cannon had to boom away. When she fell in love with a Viennese banker in Hamburg, Max had the young man transferred back to Austria. When Max prodded his feisty daughter to marry a suitable Swiss banker, she retorted, "If you want to merge with that particular bank, why don't you do so outright instead of using me."[24]

In 1921, Lola had married Rudolf Hahn, who came from a powerful Jewish industrial family associated with the Warburgs. Rudo was then apprenticing in the foreign exchange department of M. M. Warburg. With her stubborn, independent streak, Lola took the hyphenated name of Hahn-Warburg. Rudo's older brother, Kurt, had been secretary to Prince Max of Baden and the founder of the progressive Salem school. From an emotional (but not sexual) standpoint, Lola's marriage to Rudo would be a ménage à trois. Lola was forever spellbound by the charismatic Kurt, who sparkled beside the stolid, manly, sports-minded Rudo. Years later, when Kurt told Lola that he had picked her as Rudo's wife the first instant he saw her at a ball, Lola shot back, "Why didn't you ask me yourself?"[25]

By the time she met Weizmann, Lola had blossomed into a glamorous Berlin hostess, with an enigmatic, Mona Lisa smile. A woman of fine-boned beauty, she combined great willpower with physical fragility. Even as a young woman, she had a slight hand tremor so that people at parties would hold straws to her mouth and feed her cocktails. "She had an intense way of establishing contact with people," said a friend. "She asked penetrating, interesting questions and always maintained a lively interest."[26] Fiercely principled, a born fighter, she wanted to be more than a social lioness. As a *Hilfsverein* member, she had already helped to rescue Jewish children stranded in Poland.

In the late 1920s, Berlin Jews were swept up in a vogue for the Habimah theater troupe, the first Hebrew theater. Started in Moscow and influenced by Konstantin Stanislavsky, its eclectic repertoire ran the gamut from Shakespeare to Sholom Aleichem. When it got to Berlin in 1927, it was nearly bankrupt. Along with two other rich boosters, Margot Klausner and Wilfrid Israel, Lola became the group's financial backer, soliciting funds in Berlin drawing rooms. She learned Chaim Weizmann was in Berlin and went to his hotel to ask for a donation. He refused to divert money from his Zionist work, but Lola evidently made a strong impression on him.

The mutual attraction was foreordained. Weizmann was a mesmerizing orator and committed to a noble crusade—a sure recipe to entice Lola. Weizmann and his wife, the elegant, snobbish Vera, had briefly separated in 1925. Although they were reunited the next year, Weizmann pursued romances with other women, and Lola was certainly among the most important of these liaisons. After the cool, rather remote Vera, Lola must have seemed hot-blooded indeed. Of this affair, we shall say more later. We should note that Weizmann was also aware that Lola might convert Max to Zionism. As he told Felix after meeting with Max, "I have great hope that his daughter, Lola, will continue the good work. . . ."[27]

Adopting a tactic he had used with Felix, Weizmann persuaded Max that he couldn't judge Zionism fairly from afar. So Max decided to make his first trek to Palestine. In April 1929, he and Alice, along with Gisi and Anita, met Felix and Frieda in Genoa. Proceeding to Jerusalem, they were met by Weizmann, who had been extremely sick and defied his doctor's orders to stay in bed, so important did he deem the Warburg trip. Staying at the American School for Oriental Research, the group observed excavations at the Wailing Wall next door. Every morning, cars would arrive to whisk them to kibbutzim or historic shrines, all accompanied by the hypnotic, running commentary of Chaim Weizmann. The place exerted its spell on the Warburgs. "Nobody had told us how beautiful the country was," said Anita.[28] Gisi wrote to Aby that Palestinian Jews were the world's best, tough and self-sacrificing, "with blond, strong, Hebrew-speaking farmers' children."[29]

Everywhere Felix was received as a great patron and Max was impressed by his social skills; he hadn't appreciated before the amazing rapport his brother had developed with people of varied backgrounds. Previously blasé about Palestine, Max marveled at the land reclamation and the draining of malaria-infested swamps and at how downtrodden Jews from the Pale were turned into dignified, self-reliant figures. He grew enthusiastic about the Holy Land as a laboratory for a more humane capitalism—a quixotic turn typical of Max. "Both brain and brawn are being developed," he told a Berlin meeting. "When the farm laborer returns to his home from the fields, he finds a well-stocked library at his disposal, where he not only can read the latest literature on agricultural subjects or on Palestine, but can obtain a knowledge of things outside his immediate scope and horizon."[30] Max helped to start an economics archive in Palestine. He believed Palestinian Jews could only prosper in harmony with their Arab neighbors and opposed tariffs that might segregate the Jewish economy from the Mideast marketplace.

To ensure a steady cash flow for the Hebrew University, Weizmann contrived a little plot. Before the Warburgs arrived, Weizmann told F. H. Kisch to propose to Felix that he buy coastal land for an orange plantation, with its revenues earmarked for the university. "It should be pointed out to him that there are 70,000 or 80,000 dunams of land available on the coast useful for orange plantations, in a pivotal position, the most valuable land in Palestine, yielding a good return. . . ."[31] Indeed, Felix bought a lovely orange grove on the main highway to Jaffa and had an architect draw up plans for a house, hoping to spend a month there each year. After Palestine, Felix and Frieda vacationed in Cannes with Chaim and Vera Weizmann. This perhaps represented the high-water mark in the highly mutable relationship between the Warburgs and Weizmann. Back in New York, Frieda began taking Hebrew lessons, frugally scribbling her exercises on the backs of envelopes.

When Theodor Herzl first launched the Zionist movement in the 1890s, he had expected affluent Jews to bankroll it. Yet from the outset, the poorer masses had provided the foot soldiers and the emotional impetus for the movement. Now rich German and American financiers seemed ready to fulfill the role Herzl envisaged. The occasion for this rapprochement was a Zurich meeting in the summer of 1929, when Zionists and non-Zionists created a comprehensive Jewish Agency, the administrative body for world Jewry provided under the British Mandate. Before the meeting, Felix and Weizmann retreated to Louis Marshall's house in Saranac Lake, New York, to thrash out a compromise plan. Zionists and non-Zionists would split the Agency seats fifty-fifty in a so-called "pact of glory." Under this mutually beneficial arrangement, Weizmann would get the non-Zionist money needed to solve Palestine's economic problems, while non-Zionists welcomed an opportunity to develop Palestine without being obligated to create a Jewish state.

Wariness existed on both sides. Some hard-core Zionists dismissed the pact as a simple sellout for money. When they grumbled that the new recruits would dilute the movement's purity, Weizmann assured them that Zionists would retain the upper hand. When non-Zionists wondered whether they were being tricked into supporting a Jewish state, Felix countered that their role had nothing to do with Jewish nationalism. Afterward, Weizmann rhapsodically thanked Felix for his help: "It would not have been possible but for your kind magnanimous soul and Mr. Marshall's broadminded desire to see things through."[32]

When the Jewish Agency met at Zurich's Tonhalle in August 1929, it proved a grand moment of amity and concord for Jews everywhere. Besides Felix and Louis Marshall, a cavalcade of Jewish dignitaries entered the hall, including Albert Einstein, Léon Blum, Sir Herbert Samuel, and Lord Melchett. The Jewish elite was joined by many poor Jews who came on foot. As one participant said, "Dress ranged from Oriental-looking caftans to the most modern western styles."[33] The Warburgs were well represented. Felix's daughter, Carola, dropped off the children with Frieda and came along with her father while Weizmann persuaded Lola to come. Max turned down an invitation from Felix to participate in the Jewish Agency, yet convinced other German Jews that their involvement in no way impugned their German loyalty. "They are assisting in an heroic work without doing their native Germany the least slight or harm," he maintained.[34]

Cheered by a standing ovation, Weizmann spoke in Hebrew and English, but mostly in German. He extended an olive branch to non-Zionists. "We never wanted Palestine for the Zionists; we wanted it for the Jews. . . . The Balfour Declaration is addressed to the whole of Jewry."[35] The meeting represented a personal triumph for Weizmann's legerdemain. He was elected president of the Jewish Agency and Felix became chairman of the Administrative

Committee. For a fleeting moment, the political infighting ceased, dissolved in a spirit of fraternity.

As a rule, Felix Warburg steered clear of Jewish politics, preferring to mediate among warring groups. In charity work, he always pleaded for the common cause against factional agendas. As Carola said, "Father was never one who was very much interested in political action and maneuvering. He rather preferred to have men of good will sit around a table and come to a consensus and agreement."[36] Here, however, Felix brought an inappropriate standard to the bruising world of Jewish politics: Zionism was a tough-minded movement, not a global philanthropy, and the great conciliator would find himself pestered by conflicts that couldn't be healed by soothing words or compromise. In the struggle for Palestine, people weren't sane or moderate, but uncompromising. Felix's work in the Jewish Agency would therefore be his life's most exasperating experience, for he never entirely understood the nature of the beast.

While the Jewish community celebrated the pact of glory, it was received with equivalent dread by the Arabs. In late August 1929, a minor altercation between Jews and Arabs at the Wailing Wall flared up into a confrontation. Seizing on statements made by Zionists in Zurich, the grand mufti of Jerusalem warned of Jewish genocide against Arabs and issued a plea for Holy War against Jewish settlers. Sword-wielding Arab mobs rushed into the Jewish quarters of Jerusalem and Hebron, massacring 133 Jews and wounding three hundred others. There were only a few hundred British police in Palestine, and their first response seemed slow and half-hearted. The belated crackdown by British troops imported from Egypt proved bloody, leaving 116 Arab dead and 230 wounded.

On September 11, the Jewish Agency suffered another terrible setback. Louis Marshall died from pancreatic disease, leaving Felix as undisputed head of American non-Zionists. (That year, he also joined the executive committee of the American Jewish Committee.) Then the crash on Wall Street dealt a staggering blow to short-lived hopes that Zionism had surmounted its chronic financial crisis.

Far from discouraging Jews, the Palestinian riots prompted a huge outpouring of support. Felix and Lord Melchett headed a worldwide call for help and appealed to British prime minister Ramsay MacDonald. Felix and Frieda contributed two hundred thousand dollars to pay Jewish teachers, and Felix also organized the Palestine Emergency Fund, which raised more than five million dollars to repair riot damage. This money reposed in the Broadway National Bank and Trust Company in New York since its chairman, David Brown, took part in the relief effort. Felix was extremely dubious about the safety of this bank and, as we shall see, his hunch would prove sound.

To disburse this money, Felix drafted a Harvard instructor named Maurice Hexter as his personal emissary, "his ear phone and mouthpiece," in Palestine. Hexter, hesitating, consulted Harvard president Lowell, who said, "Dr. Hexter, the University owes Felix Warburg and his father-in-law so much for their generous gifts that we feel we can't refuse anything he asks of us."[37] One morning in September 1929, Hexter went to Kuhn, Loeb and was provided with a ten-thousand-dollar letter of credit. At a farewell dinner at 1109 Fifth Avenue that evening, Hexter found a mysterious manila envelope slipped under his plate and marked "To be opened on the boat." Overcome by curiosity, Hexter opened the envelope in the car that took him to the midnight departure of the *Île de France.* He found a second ten-thousand-dollar letter of credit, with a note from Felix describing it for expenses that "you might be embarrassed to put on the other letter of credit."[38] Hexter would have many such experiences of Felix's generosity. On his sixtieth birthday in 1931, Felix gave him a gift of six thousand dollars, causing Hexter to wonder, "Who else gives presents on *his* birthday?"[39]

In Palestine, Hexter carried a gun and had a guard/chauffeur to drive the fancy but overly conspicuous Packard that Felix bought him. Whatever the threat, Hexter typed out a weekly report for Felix on Saturday mornings. For security reasons, he would take a four-hour train trip to Cairo if he needed to telephone.

The conflict between Jews who favored compromise with the Arabs and hard-line Zionists tore at the temporary unity reached in Zurich. As Albert Einstein told Weizmann, "If we don't find a way to cooperate with the Arabs, then we have learned nothing from the Via Dolorosa of two thousand years, and deserve our fate."[40] Tutored by Judah Magnes, the Warburgs were extremely sensitive to the Arab plight. Even before Zurich, Felix supported unofficial talks between Rabbi Magnes and Harry St. John Philby, a colorful adventurer and adviser to King Ibn Saud of Arabia. Their goal was to create a legislative council, with Arabs and Jews represented in proportion to their population; in exchange, the Arabs would recognize the Balfour Declaration. Magnes was severely reprimanded by the Zionists for these extracurricular talks. Years later, while crossing a Zurich bridge, Weizmann blurted out testily to Felix's son, "I don't see why you Warburgs think that Magnes is so sacrosanct."[41]

The Warburgs were badly shaken by the 1929 riots, which they believed underscored the futility of any Jewish state that uprooted Arabs. Max feared a self-sustaining cycle of Jewish-Arab reprisals. "We're all convinced that the development of Palestine, as we wish it, is only possible, if Arabs and Jews live peacefully together," he told Felix.[42] The Arab backlash reinforced a Warburg preference for a cultural homeland instead of a Jewish state. Writing to a cousin, Felix alluded to the awakened Arab masses, concluding, "I am therefore convinced that we must honestly and officially give up the idea of a Jewish nation, but I hope that we can succeed in establishing our 'national home' there. . . ."[43] Felix thought Weizmann paid lip-service to the Arab issue, but dodged it. When Hexter asked Felix if relief money could be used to arm Jewish settlers, "He said no, very firmly," according to Hexter.[44]

The 1929 Arab riots created a split in the British government over Zionism, and the following spring the British temporarily limited Jewish immigration to Palestine. As his colonial secretary, Ramsay MacDonald had named the socialist, anti-Zionist Lord Passfield, a.k.a. Sidney Webb, who ordered an investigation of the Arab disturbances. Felix had an encouraging talk with Ramsay MacDonald at Chequers and even with Lord Passfield.

That summer, Felix and Max took the waters at Baden-Baden and discussed the Mideast situation. Max was very worried about Lola, who was now having an affair with Weizmann and had visited Palestine with him. He had warned her that Weizmann was really after the Warburg money for the Zionist movement. Hexter recalled that Max at Baden-Baden "confided to me that he was worried about the free-and-easy ways of one of his daughters, Lola. . . . Lola was reputed to have a long affair with Chaim Weizmann, whose wife, Vera, had long become accustomed to his 'flirtations.' "[45]

In October 1930, the Zionists were stunned when the Passfield White Paper advocated drastic restrictions on Jewish immigration and land purchases in Palestine. The Arabs were correspondingly overjoyed, since the British document seemed to repudiate the Balfour Declaration. Weizmann thought Zionism was dead. Because the Jewish Agency hadn't been consulted, Weizmann, Lord Melchett, and Felix resigned their posts in protest. Felix felt personally betrayed by Passfield, who had promised him that Jewish emigration to Palestine would continue. "I have asked people to believe the intentions of the British government," he told the press. "I have helped to bring about the agency. I have invested more than $1,000,000 in Palestine, hoping that others would do likewise. Through me, the Jewish people were misled."[46] The Zionist intrigue and British duplicity took their toll on Felix, who was unaccustomed to all the squabbling in the Zionist movement. As he told Magnes that fall, "I am blue, overworked, ugly, green and hard to live with just now."[47] So vital was Felix to the cause that his resignation nearly crippled the Jewish Agency finances, which were already seriously hurt by the 1929 crash. As the depression set in, Felix had to limit himself to gifts of about fifty thousand dollars.

Felix strenuously lobbied in London to reverse the British policy. In February 1931, Ramsay MacDonald sent a letter to Weizmann that reinterpreted and, in effect, renounced the Passfield White Paper. Though some Zionists scoffed, it was a significant victory, for it reopened the gates of Palestine on the eve of the Nazi takeover in Germany, which would send forth a massive stream of wandering Jews into a world that effectively barred them. Soon the slender strip of land by the Mediterranean would acquire an importance unforeseen by even the most zealous Zionists.

CHAPTER 22

A Stranger in Paradise

P aul Warburg was never in step with the Roaring Twenties, its isolation-ism and speculation, its sensuality and frothy escapism. It was too gaudy an age for a man of such sober judgments who never bought the moonshine rhetoric that America had entered a New Era of perpetual prosper-ity. Paul adhered to old-fashioned banker's wisdom that in prosperous times one should meditate upon past crises. In the 1920s, he played the ancient Jewish role of the martyred prophet shunned for his fearless truth-telling. When Paul strode into the Century Country Club one day in 1928, a member exclaimed, "Here comes old Gloomy Gus!" a gibe that summed up his uncom-fortable situation.[1] Paul had an innate sense of tragedy that was quite foreign to the exuberant American spirit.

Like Felix, Paul indulged a nostalgia for things old, beautiful, and sanctified by time. He still warmed to Brahms and Bach, not the new dance bands. He bought a beautiful collection of manuscripts called the Locker-Lampson Album that contained letters from Voltaire, Mozart, Rembrandt, Swift, and many other historic figures. In painting, he preferred Old Masters, works of richness and depth, and rejected modern art as crudely shallow. For Paul, the Jazz Age was a decadent time that had cast off the old, established values at its peril.

If sober in style, Paul was never a narrow financial man. "He was a real Renaissance man," said Benjamin Buttenwieser of Kuhn, Loeb, "for not only did he know as much or more about banking as anybody in the world, but also he had wide knowledge of literature, history, economics, music and art."[2] He also showed an open-mindedness foreign to the image of the stodgy banker. As chairman of the International Acceptance Bank, he donated generously to the Juilliard School of Music; sustained the Loeb Classical Library when his brother-in-law fell ill; befriended Booker T. Washington and served as treasurer of Tuskegee College; and protested the arrest of birth control advocate Margaret Sanger. Generous but discreet in charity, Panina believed Friedaflix a bit too showy in their gifts.

While he harvested the distinctions of an illustrious career, receiving honorary degrees from Heidelberg, New York University, and Occidental College, Paul never recovered from the blow Woodrow Wilson had dealt him in 1918. As Jimmy later said of his father in a poem, "He could forgive betrayal, boast or threat/ He could forgive but never would forget."[3] Paul viewed the world through skeptical eyes and the resigned melancholy of a man who knew his best accomplishments lay behind him. In a typical mood of sad whimsy, he joked to daughter Bettina of being in a "reminiscing gaga mood" and complained of being tired and bored.[4] For all their love, Paul and Nina didn't buoy each other. Nina had developed into a stout, matronly woman, with gray hair parted down the middle, and a soft, open, jowly face. Her dark brown eyes still had an electric sparkle, but she suffered from heart palpitations and occasional depression and Paul often seemed downcast as well. By the late 1920s, he was also in poor health.

With Bettina, Paul exhibited the warmth and charm too often edited out of his public personality. Behind the austere image of banker rectitude, he could show a playful side, scribbling puns to her and funny poetry. To care-worn Paul, Bettina seemed the precious bluebird of Youth. They had a secret, flirtatious relationship, with a fair amount of baby talk. When Paul gave her a bracelet in 1926, he wrote couplets that ended, "It pleases me quite fearful-lee/To chain said daughter's heart—to me!"[5] In their relationship Paul even hazarded Yiddish humor. Once, commenting on his hopeless golf, he asked, "must I go and swing a stick like a *goy?*"[6] Even Paul's most intimate friends never heard this voice.

Paul exhorted Bettina to enjoy life and savor youth instead of emulating his own work addiction. He was that rare Jewish father who advocated a more relaxed approach to life. "The whole story goes by much too quickly, and then one is old, bald, and philosophic," he warned.[7] Bowed by duty, Paul told Bettina that he had wasted half his life in needless worry. These homilies had

From left: Joe Cook, Dave Chasen,
Kay Swift, and Jimmy Warburg in a
rehearsal for Fine & Dandy, *1930.*
(New York Public Library)

their effect upon Bettina and Jimmy, who would try to combine intellectual accomplishments with a busy social calendar.

It pained Paul to see the speculative bandwagon proceed on Wall Street, especially when the central bank he had helped to forge wouldn't prick the speculative bubble. From 1921 to 1926, Paul sat on the advisory council of the Federal Reserve Board, sometimes as vice-president, giving him a ringside seat but small influence. Once again, his prophecies about the Fed were chillingly correct. From the outset, he had warned that the body lacked the necessary insulation from political pressure. The U.S. Treasury secretary served as board chairman and the president needed Senate approval to reappoint members. Hence, the board was packed with presidential cronies, not banking experts, producing a bias toward easy money and indulging speculation. An unchecked vogue for consumer credit also stimulated artificial demand, masking a global glut of products.

In the late 1920s, Paul compiled his monumental, two-volume history of the Fed. He wrote it to refute what he saw as the exaggerated claims for himself made by Senator Carter Glass in his book, *An Adventure in Constructive Finance*. Even though Paul had praised Glass's contribution to the Fed, he felt Glass overstated things. A stickler for facts—there was a pedantic streak in Paul—he was dismayed by the host of claimants now sporting the title "Father of the Fed." "I really don't know who was the baby's father," he said, "but, judging from the number of men who claim the honor, all I can say is that its mother must have been a most immoral woman."[8] In 1927, when Paul and Nina went to Pasadena for a three-month rest, staying in a charming cottage, Paul dictated a portion of his tome each afternoon. During a second Pasadena stay a year later, he finished it. It was published in April 1930.

In the book, Paul laid out, side-by-side, sections of the Aldrich Plan and the Federal Reserve Act. With the scrupulosity of a talmudic scholar, he showed how the banker plan he had largely crafted at Jekyll Island had provided the technical rudiments for the reserve system. In recounting the Fed's genesis, Paul stressed the banking fundamentals, not the final political crafting of the bill, which perhaps accounted for a different slant from Glass. It is telling that the self-effacing Paul spent so much time in this self-vindication. As Jimmy explained: "My father was a very quiet man, and people who didn't know him well said he was an extremely modest man, which wasn't strictly true . . . he definitely wanted recognition for what he did, and rarely got his due because he was so diffident."[9]

Beyond recognition, Paul wanted to publish his book in time to promote debate about the Fed's role during the stock market boom. In 1927, the Fed cut interest rates and spurred financial markets, but then failed to reverse course in late 1928 and 1929 despite signs of a dangerous overheating on Wall Street. Instead of flowing into productive investment, surplus corporate funds fueled the stock exchange frenzy. The Warburgs especially worried about this trend because the bull market diverted investment capital from Germany and the rest of Europe.

In light of this uncertain foreign outlook, Paul and Jimmy executed a well-timed, cautionary maneuver in 1928. The International Acceptance Bank had issued foreign credits without a saving cushion of domestic deposits. Sensing trouble ahead and no less concerned than Paul by the massive overhang of global debt, Jimmy prevailed upon his father to merge the IAB with a solid domestic institution. In late 1928, the IAB was absorbed by America's oldest bank, the Bank of the Manhattan Company. Dating back to 1799, it had a large branch system with abundant deposits. The safer, more rounded institution that emerged helped the IAB weather the 1929 crisis. Paul and Jimmy joined the board of the Bank of the Manhattan (itself later merged into Chase Manhattan) while Jimmy became president of its new securities affiliate, the International Manhattan Company, in March 1929. Since Jimmy had originated European securities issues for Kuhn, Loeb, he was well versed in the political situation there.

The Bank of the Manhattan wanted to have a European foothold. In September 1929, M. M. Warburg established an Amsterdam bank called Warburg & Company that helped to implement this wish. This first outpost beyond German borders ended a 131-year precedent of operating only domestically and it had the pleasant effect of reuniting the family. Max was chairman, Paul and Fritz deputy chairmen, and Eric and a new Hamburg partner, Dr. Ernst Spiegelberg, were to lead the venture. The Amsterdam bank would provide the Warburgs with a critical financial lifeline outside Germany on the eve of the Third Reich.

Paul later contended that scarcely a day passed in 1929 when he didn't fret about the Wall Street madness. It disturbed him that stocks were now valued, not by past earnings or current worth, but by uninformed guesswork about future prospects. As a Jew, a naturalized citizen, and eternal outsider, he seemed immune to the euphoria that affected others. He warned Frieda's brother, Morti, about the coming debacle and convinced him to shift some of his personal wealth into cash. (Morti still ended up sacrificing half his wealth after 1929.) Paul's advice emboldened Morti to overrule Otto Kahn and shift Kuhn, Loeb capital from risky stock exchange loans into safe municipal bonds, sparing the firm the worst of the crash. Thanks to Paul, the Warburgs generally endured the crash better than other rich families. Felix fully shared Paul's fright about the market.

In March 1929, Paul publicized his prophecy at a time when Wall Street considered such pessimism traitorous. As in 1907, he felt duty-bound to act, even though he knew he would be crucified. As he said, "It is a desperately unpopular undertaking to dare to sound a discordant note of warning in an atmosphere of cheer, even though one might be able to forecast with certainty that the ice, on which the mad dance was going on, was bound to break."[10] Paul issued his warning in the annual report of the International Acceptance Bank of March 7, 1929. He thought it politic to warn Washington of this thunderbolt and alerted Treasury Under Secretary Ogden Mills the day before. He told Mills that Washington had chosen to let speculation run its course, "which means to leave the gamblers in control until a crash will bring speculation to an end. . . ."[11] He sent a copy of the report to Treasury Secretary Andrew W. Mellon, whom he faulted for sacrificing economic prudence to political expediency. Other financiers saw the coming calamity, Paul knew, but feared the abuse that would greet any public expressions of concern.

Paul's report was a spectacular act of prescience in which he foresaw both the crash and the Depression. He staked his prestige outright and didn't mince words. After deploring that America's savings were being siphoned off into speculation, he drew the policy choices starkly for the Fed: It could either yield to speculators or curb them. "If a stock-exchange debauch is quickly arrested by prompt and determined action, it is not too much to hope that a shrinkage of inflated stock prices may be brought about without seriously affecting the wider circle of general business. If orgies of unrestrained speculation are permitted to spread too far, however, the ultimate collapse is certain not only to affect the speculators themselves, but also to bring about a general depression involving the entire country."[12] It was one of the great calls in American financial history.

In follow-up newspaper interviews, Paul conceded that higher interest rates might cause a painful liquidation of shares. If the Fed didn't act, however, it would require more agonizing future remedies. Paul's warning set off a temporary sinking spell in the market and stirred apprehension in Washington. On March 14, Mellon suddenly told the press that bonds presented a good buying opportunity but that stocks were "too high in price to be good buys."[13] It was a cup of water thrown on a bonfire.

As Paul suspected, his report was regarded as sacrilege in financial circles. People whispered that he was selling the market short. Jeered at board meetings, he was accused of "sandbagging American prosperity."[14] Just as Aby had had simultaneous intimations of personal and universal doom, so Paul's premonition of a crash coincided with a heightened awareness of his own mortality. In late June, he made out a will that contained a touching farewell note to Nina.

When the New York Fed finally hiked interest rates in August 1929, Paul thought it had acted at least half a year too late. He seemed so enervated by worry that Max urged him to take two weeks of rest. When the crash came, Paul didn't gloat or experience *Schadenfreude*. Saddened by a sense of human futility, he wondered why people had been too greedy to avert certain doom. His sole consolation was that the banking system, backed by the Fed, survived the crash without a major loss of depositor confidence. The Warburgs saw firsthand legions of ruined investors. On two occasions, Jimmy watched distraught investors leap from upper-story windows, and Felix was besieged by desperate men. He did save several of them. Ironically, the 1929 crash, in a roundabout way, would claim Paul as a victim, too, for it set in motion a sequence of events that would topple the German banking system and force Paul to squander his fortune to save the family honor.

Even as Paul bemoaned Wall Street gambling, he was oddly tolerant toward Max, who had expanded too rapidly with American credits Paul had placed at his disposal. Max treated the fortunes of Paul and Felix as a backup bank reserve. Even before the crash, Jimmy warned his father that this imaginary safety net only tempted Max into risky ventures. He also thought Max didn't direct enough business to them in New York. "I tried to make it clear without being too explicit that my father bore a large share of the blame for the overextension of the Hamburg firm's engagements," Jimmy said.[15]

Why did Paul let down his guard? From the time he was a boy, Paul had revered Max, admiring his spirit and charm. Max took an easy joy in life that the chronically depressed Paul must have envied. Another important factor made Paul and Felix defer to him. Max believed—and his brothers concurred—that he had maintained the family firm while they went off to make a mint in America. This gave Max some moral leverage in soliciting their help. Paul felt so keenly the need to help Max that he resented it whenever Jimmy urged restraint. We must also remember that the Famous Five had drawn tremendous strength from a solidarity rarely found among such ambitious, competitive brothers.

Max confessed that he didn't foresee the meaning of the crash for Germany. Dependent upon foreign, especially American, credit in the 1920s, the German economy was endangered by its withdrawal. Its stock markets plunged, its cities scrounged for cash, and Berlin turned to a bank consortium that included M. M. Warburg for an advance. The crash would be a turning point for Max and start an unending sequence of misfortunes. By coincidence, it came during a month that also saw the death of Aby and of Gustav Stresemann, the German foreign minister, a personal hero whom Max regarded as the last politician who might have checked Germany's decline. He thought the moderate Stresemann had been worn down by petty political infighting. Troubles, as always, arrived in battalions.

—

Panina had two strapping, Americanized children—Jimmy and Bettina—
who were as sociable, spirited, and daring as their parents were cautious and
shy. Born in Hamburg, they yet had an American sense of opportunity.
Angry, rebellious, they had more fire and intelligence than Felix's children.
Brother and sister would turn their back on Jewish tradition as passé, although both would invoke a liberal, egalitarian tradition rooted in Judaic
thought. Among children of the Famous Five, Bettina and Jimmy would
distance themselves most from a sometimes claustrophobic family.

As a child, Bettina had dark, shiny hair that had made her look like a young
Apache. She developed into an emancipated young woman with an athletic
figure and photogenic smile. She reacted against an upbringing so pampered
that her governess brushed her teeth. Going to the other extreme, she developed a strong will, an indomitable craving for independence, and would never
tell Nina where she was going. She had a highly unusual résumé for a young
Jewish woman. After Brearley, she went to Bryn Mawr, the first young
woman in the family to go away to college. Like Jimmy, she gloried in her
audacious nonconformity.

Affected by the schizophrenia of her favorite uncles, Aby and Jim Loeb, she
became a psychiatrist despite her parents' dismay and took pride in her
trail-blazing career. At the time, psychiatry was considered suitable only for
muscular males who could handle hefty patients in padded cells. Bettina went
to the Cornell University Medical Center, followed by the National Hospital for
Nervous Diseases in London. She was liberated in both her social and professional life. As she recalled of her London sojourn, "All eyes were popping out
of the Bloomsbury boardinghouse windows when that American in evening
dress was called for and returned at shocking hours by gentlemen in large
automobiles."[16] Back in the United States, she worked at the Boston Psycho-
pathic Hospital, Harvard's pathology lab, and at various mental hospitals
before starting a private practice at the New York Psychoanalytic Institute.

Bettina always flaunted her iconoclasm and defiance toward her stuffy
upbringing. As she later said, "Nice Jewish girls 'came out.' They did not go
to college, only 'bluestockings' did that, and they specialized in being unattractive. Girls brought up in big houses with lots of servants certainly didn't
go to Medical School, coming home reeking of formaldehyde from the anat-
omy lab. Neither did they—oh supreme frightening horror—learn to catch
babies in Harlem."[17] (This was apparently how she referred to delivering
babies.) Bettina adored her father, but not Nina, whom she saw as outwardly
sweet and generous but always demanding something in return; everything
came with strings attached so that Nina could stay in control. Jimmy also

thought his mother frequently behaved in a spoiled, manipulative manner beneath her lovely surface.

The identification with her father gave a clinical, rational cast to Bettina's mind. Destined to became a prominent psychoanalyst, she would display a cool, abstract, unsentimental approach to life. A doctrinaire Freudian, she would issue *ex cathedra* pronouncements, giving people the uncomfortable sense that she secretly analyzed them. She cast a cold eye on her family. Later, she drew a chart in which she divided them into psychiatric categories, showing how the Loebs were long on manic-depressives and the Warburgs on schizophrenics. Yet a coquettish side also lay underneath, a by-product of her relationship with her father. In the midst of hardheaded talk with men, Bettina could suddenly flash a girlish, boldly inviting smile.

By modeling herself after men, Bettina competed with Jimmy more than a sister ordinarily would have with a handsome older brother. She seemed both fascinated and infuriated by him. Even as a little girl, she had a large doll named Paul that she would dress up every day in the clothes that Jimmy wore. Bettina knew Jimmy hated this but she kept on doing it. The incident would capture their lifelong ambivalence toward each other. It also expressed Bettina's adoration of her father.

When Frieda and Nina played that eternal game of Jewish mothers called "Who has the most brilliant son?" Nina fielded one of the foremost candidates of modern times. She pushed her son Jimmy relentlessly: If he got 99 percent on a test, she asked why he hadn't scored 100. For the American Warburgs, the educational system was the most potent agent of assimilation, melting the old German-Jewish bonds. Frieda, Nina, and their daughters joined a tiny handful of Jewish girls at the Brearley School. Along with Felix's sons, Jimmy attended the Middlesex School near Concord, Massachusetts. Located hard by the first battlefield of the American Revolution, it took only a small number of Jewish boys. Middlesex had been founded by Boston patricians and financed with money from the WASP investment bank of Lee, Higginson; it became a feeder school for Harvard. Studying in a town identified with Emerson, Thoreau, and Hawthorne made a lasting impression on Jimmy. "No boy can go to Middlesex without absorbing both American history and a certain amount of American culture," he said.[18]

At Middlesex, Jimmy achieved grades so astronomical that other boys bet on them in pools. A special Greek class was arranged to keep him busy. Middlesex students came mostly from several Christian denominations, and Sunday attendance at chapel was compulsory. The strict but liberal headmaster, Robert Winsor, was a Unitarian. Jimmy went to Middlesex after being bar mitzvahed by Rabbi Judah Magnes and, predictably, felt self-conscious about his religion. Like other Warburg children, he associated Judaism with the burning and sometimes rigid religiosity of Jacob Schiff. In the Unitarian faith, Jimmy professed to find an ethical code consistent with the wisdom he had absorbed from Rabbi Magnes.

Jimmy would always feel terribly ambivalent about being Jewish and he absorbed contradictory messages from his parents. As a schoolboy in New York, Jimmy signed his initials, JW, on school papers. One day, a sadistic older classmate inserted an E between the two letters. When Jimmy turned to Nina to explain such taunting, she responded in a way that betrayed anxiety instead of pride about being Jewish. She conceded that some people disliked Jews. "She said that because of this, a Jewish boy should always be very careful not to push himself forward," Jimmy later wrote. "This puzzled me. It seemed like accepting some sort of second-class status."[19] Far from being meek, as Nina recommended, Jimmy would be defiantly assertive.

By sending their sons to Middlesex, Friedaflix and Panina virtually guaranteed that they would socialize with non-Jews and marry outside the faith. Nonetheless, they were then dismayed when this happened. When Felix and Frieda deplored their children's estrangement from their German-Jewish roots, Freddy, the eldest, retorted: "If you wanted us to stay locked in the Jewish community and be active solely in all their communal activities, you should have sent us to Horace Mann and Columbia instead of Middlesex and Harvard. Why should it surprise you that Bunker Hill means more to us than the days of the Old Testament?"[20]

Jimmy would stray farthest and most determinedly from the fold. At Harvard, he excelled at everything, exchanging letters in Greek and Latin with uncle Jim Loeb and graduating *magna cum laude* in classics. After his marriage to the musical, non-Jewish Kay Swift, Jimmy clerked for the Metropolitan Bank of Washington and worked for the First National Bank of Boston, whose original charter petitioners included John Hancock. After his wartime feud with his father, he needed distance from Paul. Jimmy became an expert on textile financing for the Boston bank. Always a prolific writer, he cranked out booklets on financing wool, cotton, hides, and leather. He felt marked out for big things and approached life with a brash, instinctive confidence. In 1921, the new commerce secretary, Herbert Hoover, called him to Washington and asked if he would become assistant secretary of commerce—a junior Cabinet post for a twenty-five-year-old! Amazingly, Jimmy balked, asking what his duties would be. "Helping me," said Hoover. "But what do you do?" Jimmy pursued. "You'll find out if you take the job," replied Hoover irritably.

At once, Jimmy conceived a distaste for Hoover and the proposal. He discussed the offer with his father. Still smarting over his Washington comeuppance, Paul advised, "Don't you touch that. Washington is a place that destroys people. You stay out of there."[21] Jimmy wrote to Hoover and declined the invitation. Later, he would be understandably puzzled by his own behavior. The incident set a pattern, the first of many occasions when Jimmy, from sheer hubris, would fritter away opportunities. The gods had so generously endowed him with talent that he lacked normal human caution about spurning offers. His supreme confidence could shade off into arrogance, blinding him to the limits of his own powers and fortune's fickle nature.

In writing to Hoover, Jimmy mentioned that he wanted to join his father's new bank. One suspects that Paul made an attractive offer to counter Hoover's. In late 1921, Jimmy and Kay moved to Riverside Drive so Jimmy could enter the IAB as a junior officer. For Jimmy, the overwhelming reason for becoming a banker was so that he could work beside his extraordinary father. A loving son, he respected Paul's brilliance and his principled concern for world affairs. He enjoyed listening to him discourse about Keynes, Versailles, and the plight of Germany. Banking for Paul was never a sterile pursuit of money, but a very human activity saturated with political and social concerns.

Jimmy had deeply divided feelings about his father and this made him feel guilty. He didn't always see his father as a gentle, unassuming saint. We must recall that Jimmy worked with his father for years. On the job, Paul could be sharp and exacting, correcting his son with a suppressed pique that gave an edge to his words. Paul was a strict father and very sensitive to slights. One day after work, while riding uptown and chatting with his father, Jimmy turned to watch a fire engine go by. For twenty blocks, Paul kept a frigid silence until Jimmy finally asked what was wrong. "Well, if you can't listen to what I'm saying there's no point in my talking," his father shot back.[22]

As with Felix and his sons, a generational gap divided Paul from Jimmy. Paul was straitlaced, puritanical, and family-minded, while Jimmy had a wild, libertine streak. He wanted to venture beyond the "Our Crowd" ghetto of banking, Jewish philanthropy, and wealthy Jewish friends to dabble in art, high society, and sexual experimentation. The strain of generational change first appeared when Jimmy wrote serious poetry in college. Poetry had long been a Warburg pastime but only as an amateur exercise for family gatherings, with light verse the preferred, gentlemanly style. Nina didn't want Jimmy to publish his poetry. The idea of it seemed ostentatious to her. When the *Atlantic Monthly* published his first sonnet, Jimmy didn't tell her and when she heard about it from someone else, she was hurt. His parents' cultural rigidity bothered Jimmy. A fresh, irreverent young man, he reflected the swinging, unconstrained spirit of the 1920s. He came to see his father as a priggish man of somewhat limited sympathies, who could be unforgiving toward those who didn't share his values.

Jimmy was the first American Warburg to flee the family, with its byzantine feuds and warring wings. His life was restless and unsettled. As he yearned for excitement, it did not take him long to make his first forays into the high life. As a young banking star, he was amassing a small fortune and had the money and style to lead an elegant life. In the mid-1920s, he bought and adjoined two town houses on East Seventieth Street, which he staffed with five servants; a chauffeur drove his three daughters to school. One day in 1924, Jimmy and Kay were riding horseback in Greenwich, Connecticut, when they came to a lovely, maple-shaded colonial house named Bydale. It had an old barn, a stone water tower, and a windmill. At the time, Connecticut was very Christian. Nevertheless, Jimmy and Kay bought Bydale and decorated it with Early American furniture, adding a tennis court, swimming pool, and stables. Eventually Jimmy increased the original twenty-five acres to eighty-two acres. He liked to ride one of his seven horses along the bridle paths before breakfast.

This tycoon-cum-country squire life was only part of the story. Jimmy and Kay decorated their East Seventieth Street town house in sleek black and white and threw parties as wild and glamorous as the setting, with lots of heavy drinking and urbane people lounging by two back-to-back grand pianos. They were among the social darlings of the era, with Kay—vain, childish, witty, delightful—the beautiful flapper who reliably taught guests how to do the Charleston. She and Jimmy knew everybody: Fred and Adele Astaire, the *New Yorker* crowd at the Algonquin Round Table, Beatrice Lillie, Ring Lardner, Marshall Field, Averell Harriman, Dick Rodgers, Larry Hart, Robert E. Sherwood, Marc Connelly, and, most memorably, the Gershwin brothers. Jimmy was suddenly leading a double life. The sober banker by day, he played late-night poker with Harold Ross, Herbert Bayard Swope, and other literary figures. If Nina frowned on his poetry, well, Jimmy was spurred on by Franklin P. Adams, who had befriended Kay's father.

After the prudish Panina world, Jimmy faced constant temptation and often submitted to it. Women were smitten by him and he had a long list of conquests. Kay was a dazzling, effervescent personality. Encouraged by the prevailing social license, Kay and Jimmy had an open marriage and neither lacked for willing partners. It is hard not to see Jimmy's behavior as a rebellion against Paul. Paul was so repressed that he thought one-piece female bathing suits indecent when they came into vogue after the war. His father, Jimmy said, believed "that a man should be grateful to his wife for fulfilling a carnal requirement, the existence of which was, on the whole, regrettable."[23] In one poem, Jimmy wrote of Paul's "strong distrust/ Of the experiments of reckless youth," which signaled Paul's attitude toward his *bon vivant* son.[24]

This sexual license formed part of a larger revolt by Jimmy against his Jewish ancestry. The problem didn't stem from Kay, who had many Jewish show-biz friends. Two of her three husbands would be Jewish. By contrast, Jimmy would have three non-Jewish wives and he gravitated to places such as Greenwich that had a WASP image. For all the surface glitter, the three Warburg girls—April, Andrea, and Kay—grew up in a cold, empty environment, for Jimmy and Kay were absorbed by their social lives. Jimmy avoided talk of religion with his daughters. One day at Brearley, at age eleven or twelve, Andrea learned from Florence Straus, another "Our Crowd" girl, that she was Jewish. She was stunned by this information.[25]

In 1925, an irresistible but disruptive figure entered this rather fragile family circle: George Gershwin. The first time that Kay saw him performing his own music at a rehearsal, she thought how much this lithe, agile man resembled his music. Kay's partner from the Edith Rubel Trio, cellist Marie Rosanoff, brought George and Ira along to a Warburg party. Kay was captivated by George's vibrant personality and electrifying keyboard style. He made a memorable exit. Springing abruptly from the piano, he said, "I have to go to Europe," then vanished.[26] In late December, Kay met him again at a party in conductor Walter Damrosch's apartment to celebrate the premiere of *Concerto*.

Soon Gershwin was a frequent visitor at the Warburgs' East Seventieth Street town house and even composed the *Spanish Prelude* there. Kay's musical tastes began to shift. Before, she had been snobbish about show tunes. "I liked blues, spirituals, fast music, but not musical comedy."[27] Under Gershwin's tutelage, she became an enthusiast for popular music and began writing songs. In 1927 Dick Rodgers hired her as a rehearsal pianist for *A Connecticut Yankee* and this completed the transition. Kay, in turn, helped Gershwin with counterpoint and orchestration.

Gershwin was a magnetic figure for a musical woman, and with Jimmy often away on business, the situation was ripe for mischief. As one Gershwin biographer notes, ". . . the Warburgs were an enlightened couple who often went their separate ways without overt frictions or jealousies. Whether seeing Kay in their customary Manhattan haunts or horseback riding with her at the Warburg farm in Connecticut, Gershwin did not have to contend with a righteously indignant or jealous husband."[28] For all his affected worldliness, Jimmy had been a sheltered boy with scant knowledge of Bohemian circles. He was a man about town, not a true free spirit, and was in way over his head. Kay and George began visiting galleries, concerts, and parties together. She became his secretary, proofread his scores, and joined him for duets. Parts of some important Gershwin scores exist in her hand. An unsuspecting observer would have assumed they were married, for Kay would insert a fresh flower in George's lapel before concerts, then wait backstage to applaud him lovingly afterward. Possibly in homage to her, Gerschwin named his November 1926 musical *Oh, Kay.*

Later Jimmy was very bitter about the affair, but he didn't put his foot down soon enough. With George and Kay already inseparable, Jimmy proved remarkably obliging. The night before Gershwin's departure for his last European trip in March 1928, Jimmy and Kay threw a bon voyage party and the carousing went on until five in the morning. Jimmy agreed to give Gershwin a guesthouse at their Greenwich farm where he could compose parts of *An American in Paris* and ride horseback with Kay. When Jimmy was away, George cropped up at breakfast in a bathrobe. After the premiere of *An American in Paris* at Carnegie Hall that December, George and Kay left the concert hall together to celebrate, with George buying her two bracelets on 57th Street.

Jimmy was accustomed to being the unrivaled lady-killer, and the sparkling Gershwin must have been punishing competition. Jimmy was in a painful quandary. Kay had provided him with escape from everything he found stifling—banking, Judaism, puritanism, the claustrophobic Warburgs—yet he felt devalued and peripheral in her world. How could he elevate his status in their rarefied artistic circles?

Only the versatile Jimmy could have answered the question as he did. Capitalizing on his poetic gifts, this precocious young banker became lyricist for Kay's show tunes. As he explained, the decision came about partly "because her interest was contagious and partly because I feared that our lives might otherwise drift apart."[29] Since Paul couldn't understand his son's desire to write lyrics, Jimmy wrote under the stage name Paul James, while his wife used her maiden name, Kay Swift. Libby Holman crooned one of their torch songs, "Can't We Be Friends?" in the *Little Show* of 1920.

This set the stage for Kay and Jimmy's collaboration on a musical comedy, *Fine & Dandy,* starring Joe Cook. When the show's producers went bust right before opening night, Jimmy convinced his friends Marshall Field and Averell Harriman to throw in money with him to save the show. (The three had invested in a Soviet manganese venture together some years before.) The play ran for more than 250 performances, yielding two hit songs, "Fine & Dandy" and "Can This Be Love?" which would pay royalties for three decades. As a Broadway musical composed by a woman, it was an important first in theater history.

But the show's success didn't solve the Warburgs' marital problems. If anything, this new phase accentuated the strain on Jimmy as he tried to resolve his identity crisis not by choosing a single identity, but by simultaneously adopting several. On an ocean crossing in 1930, he showed his verse to Alfred Knopf, who published it in a thin volume, *And Then What?* Then came a second volume, *Shoes and Ships and Sealing Wax*, again under the name Paul James. Jimmy knew, however, that he was fighting a losing competition against Kay's artistic friends. "It was particularly exhausting for a lyric writer whose banking career demanded that he get to his office at nine in the morning when most of the theatrical world was still in bed."[30]

The tensions only grew in the weird triangular relationship of Jimmy, Kay, and George Gershwin. When Gershwin conducted the opening of his antiwar operetta, *Strike Up the Band*, on January 14, 1930, Kay sat behind him in the first row. Two of the Warburg daughters liked to do a little song-and-dance routine to "I've Got a Crush on You," and when he came to that point in the overture, Gershwin turned to Kay and whispered, "April and Andy." Afterward, Kay and Jimmy hosted a party at their apartment to which Gershwin brought Sergei Prokofiev. Jimmy had to watch as Gershwin exulted in the ecstatic reviews read aloud to guests.

By this point, Jimmy and Kay's marriage was probably doomed. They were clever children playing with firecrackers that were bound to explode in their faces. But they didn't see how soon it would occur or that the 1929 crash would claim them, too, as indirect victims. For the thunderous collapse of stocks on Wall Street would have profound financial repercussions in Hamburg, demanding Jimmy's extended absence from home just when his marriage could least afford it.

The "Famous Five" brothers pose for a
last photo at the Warburg library, August 21, 1929.
At the last moment, Aby cupped his hands to
symbolize his lifelong supplication.
(Warburg Institute)

Account X

On his business trips to Germany in the 1920s, Jimmy Warburg experienced confused feelings toward his native country. Sometimes taken aback by his nostalgia for childhood scenes, he was also appalled by the street fights that enfeebled the Weimar Republic. In 1929, he heard Adolf Hitler speak at a Bremen rally and saw a crowd transfixed by his shrill gibberish. "Just watching the effect he had on people while talking what to me seemed like sheer nonsense, I had a goose-pimply feeling that this was a phenomenon that wasn't as unimportant as it might seem."[1] When he tried to coax uncles Fritz and Max into reading *Mein Kampf*, they dismissed it as a heap of idiot scribblings.

Capitalizing on the agricultural depression, the Nazis began making inroads among indebted farmers in the late 1920s. Hamburg merchants still found it hard to fathom the potential Nazi threat. When Rudolf Hess came to town in 1929, he asked a local Nazi to scout up some interested business leaders, but the man could only muster five or six souls. That summer, a Nazi major informed Hitler that only three of two hundred leading Hamburg personalities favored their party. Business leaders worried about the socialist content of a National Socialist party that mingled extremists of Left and Right, while they tended to dismiss its anti-Semitism as a mere propaganda ploy to lure a crackpot fringe.

Nineteen twenty-nine was a banner year for M. M. Warburg & Co., which now ranked as the largest and most prestigious private bank in Germany, giving Max preeminence in the Jewish community. To some outside observers, he seemed a naïve superpatriot, striding blindfolded into the future. That year, Norman Bentwich visited Kösterberg and would recall being "entertained by Max Warburg at his pleasance on the Elbe. The leader of German Jewry at that time had no misgivings. . . ."[2] The portrait was overdrawn, for Max had vague but persistent forebodings. Reluctantly he stayed in the conservative German People's Party (DVP) to keep its anti-Semitic wing in check. The electoral decline of such centrist parties would set the stage for the drift to authoritarian extremes in the early 1930s.

As since the end of the war, Max hesitated to assert his power or enlist the influence of the overseas Jewish community to combat anti-Semitism. He was always on the defensive, always afraid of playing into the hands of the enemy. He had kept some distance from both Friedrich Ebert and Gustav Stresemann so they wouldn't be tainted by association with a prominent Jew. As he told Felix in 1929, "We must, under all circumstances, avoid an international battle against anti-Semitism, since we will otherwise naturally be accused of mixing foreign elements in domestic German relations. . . ."[3] There was a cruel irony here: To disprove Nazi propaganda, German Jews were isolating and weakening themselves. This same tendency made them chary of Zionism. In 1930, several hundred Jewish leaders signed an ad asserting their German loyalty and rejecting a Jewish homeland: "We regard ourselves, along with the overwhelming majority of German Jews, as members of the German, not of the Jewish, people."[4] The more insecure they felt, the more avidly German Jews would rush to prove their patriotic credentials.

A staunch supporter of the Weimar Republic, Max feared that intemperate criticism of the young republic was eroding its legitimacy. He endorsed a tepid form of social democracy and believed that German business should recognize unions, pay higher wages, and assist impoverished workers. While at Baden-Baden in 1930, he learned from caddies and chauffeurs that they couldn't find winter work, so he wrote to government officials, advocating relief work instead of the dole. Conservative at the core, Max mostly worried about Bolshevism, deficit spending, high taxes, and excessive indulgence of unions. Nevertheless, a quixotic, eccentric streak often made his views extremely inconsistent and unpredictable.

In 1929, the Nazis reaped a propaganda bonanza from the Young Conference in Paris. The German delegation was led by Reichsbank president Dr. Hjalmar Schacht. His deputy was Max's distinguished partner, Carl Melchior.

With his trim mustache, cultured manner, and deep sad eyes, Carl Melchior symbolized the best in German public service. For ten years, he had tried to reduce reparations through well-reasoned argument. While Dr. Schacht blustered, Melchior maintained his unruffled calm and held informal talks with the other side. After the conference, Melchior's health broke down from overwork and his doctors warned him against overexertion. Yet he remained active on the reparations issue. Henceforth, he often wore dark glasses, shunned young people, and brooded about his health, all the while despairing that reason would save the political situation.

The Young agreement abolished Allied controls over German banks and railroads and provided for a reduced, but extremely long, reparations schedule through 1988. In the future, payments would be channeled through a Bank for International Settlements in Basel, with the ubiquitous Melchior named to its administrative board.

Instead of acknowledging that the Young Plan improved matters, the Nazis branded it a fresh insult to German honor and organized a campaign to reject it. Agitators fulminated against "Three generations of forced labor!"[5] Doubtless thinking of Melchior, they dubbed it "a Jewish machination" and "a product of the Jewish spirit."[6] Ruhr industrialists joined the chorus of denunciation. Even though he signed the document, Dr. Schacht then turned against it and, to court the extreme Right, issued bombastic attacks from his country estate. To explain this reversal, he blamed cosmetic changes made in the Young Plan at the Hague in January 1930. Feeling shaken and betrayed, Melchior saw the bare-faced opportunism in Schacht's *volte-face*.

When Schacht threatened to resign from the Reichsbank over the Young Plan, Max decided to call his bluff. As a member of the Reichsbank Advisory Council, he had a meeting convened to consider Schacht's behavior. "I moved that the resignation which he had threatened be accepted," Max wrote. "Of course, Schacht knew that I was the power behind his dismissal."[7] The council unanimously accepted Schacht's resignation and Max resisted a move to have Melchior succeed him. Instead, on behalf of the council, he telephoned Dr. Hans Luther and asked him to become the next president. The incident is worth noting since it not only made Schacht heroic to the Nazis but perhaps gave Schacht a concealed motive for later revenge against Max.

The Wall Street crash ushered in the sort of depressed economy in which extremism thrives. German exports fell, foreign credit dried up, and unemployment more than doubled in a year. Meanwhile, the massive short-term debt run up in the 1920s began to fall due. In 1930, the Weimar Republic died the death of a thousand lashes as the new chancellor, Heinrich Brüning, began to govern by presidential decree. A quiet Catholic conservative and financial expert, Brüning would end up crippling the young democracy with his resort to emergency measures. While claiming a bogus respect for democratic forms, the Nazis pushed political conflict into the streets, and the Brownshirts chanted, "Possession of the streets is the key to power in the State."[8] Profiting from agitation over the Young Plan, Hitler emerged again as a national figure.

In elections that September, the Nazis scored their first stunning electoral success. In 1928, the party had polled a scant 810,000 votes. Now, just two years later, it received 6.4 million votes, swelling its Reichstag representation from 12 to 107 seats and dwarfing substantial Communist gains. It was a terrifying portent for German Jews, especially the bankers. After the election, Goebbels said the Nazis would expropriate banks, a view taken up by the enlarged Nazi contingent in the Reichstag. German stocks plunged as spooked foreign creditors pulled their money from Germany.

German Jews wondered if the Nazi victory was a fleeting aberration or prelude to a nightmare. The American Warburgs always had a clearer picture of the situation than their German relatives. After the 1930 elections, Jimmy returned to New York and told his father that Hitler was a madman who would try to conquer Europe. "He thought I was out of my mind," said Jimmy.[9] Over lunch, Jimmy repeated the prophecy to Albert Wiggin, head of the Chase Bank, who afterward wisecracked to Paul, "You ought to put your son away somewhere and not let him scare people like that."[10] That November, Felix warned an eminent group of American Jews about the Nazi menace, but they, too, thought Hitler would fade away before long.[11]

Max was staggered that so many Germans would heed the rhetoric of these coarse, uneducated anti-Semites. "Their knowledge is small;" he told Paul, "they possess great energy, but it is partly the energy of the hopeless and the desperate."[12] Having watched their agitators give speeches on buses and trains, Max knew that the Nazis had well-drilled recruits. Nevertheless, he thought the phenomenon would be short-lived and likened events to the wave of anti-Semitism that passed over France during the Dreyfus Affair.[13] Carl Melchior thought the Nazi demagogy might be curbed if they participated in a coalition government, whereas Max shied away from this risky course.

Max's wife, Alice, was so profoundly disconcerted by the 1930 elections that she made Max promise to curtail his political and business activities. On October 3, 1930, he signed a statement that said: "I hereby give to my beloved wife—Alice, born Magnus—my assurance, that on the basis of the recent agitated election period I have decided to arrange my life in future in a freer fashion. I promise, gradually, to give up my honorary posts, to withdraw increasingly from public life, to shorten my work time, to spare more time for longer trips and to dedicate myself more to my family."[14] Max signed this pledge to pacify Alice but he was incapable of honoring it. As the episode shows, the German Jews weren't cavalier about the Nazis. Rather, they would hesitate, procrastinate, and rationalize inaction for far too long.

The Nazis appealed to the petite bourgeoisie—disgruntled shopkeepers, teachers, lower-level civil servants—and had less appeal to the Hamburg patricians. Twice in 1930, when Hitler visited Hamburg, Max noted that he had to soften his anti-Semitic rhetoric to cater to local tastes. That September, Hitler assured HAPAG chief Wilhelm Cuno that the Nazis didn't want to persecute the Jews, but just to reduce their political predominance. Cuno was so pleased by this "moderate" Hitler that he arranged for him to address the Hamburg National Club, where the latter avoided anti-Semitic themes and stressed the benefits of Eastern conquest. In another Nazi breakthrough in business circles, Emil Georg von Stauss of Deutsche Bank invited Dr. Schacht to a private dinner at Hermann Göring's home in January 1931. Hitler knew the value of having a respectable financier in the party ranks.

The Depression nearly killed off the Warburg bank before Hitler had a chance to do so. Everything conspired against the firm: capital flight after the Nazi victory, the wholesale liquidation of German securities by Americans, and the plunge in German share prices. This made the bank increasingly vulnerable to some shaky commercial loans made in the 1920s, especially a large one to the Rudolf Karstadt department store.

In October 1930, Max sailed to New York to discuss the elections and the economic crisis with his brothers. Even though Paul and Felix didn't accept Jimmy's scenario about Hitler, they were frightened by the Nazis and dubious about M. M. Warburg's economic future. They suggested that Max end the bank's 132-year independent existence and merge it with a larger bank. This was anathema to Max. "To this I could not agree," he wrote. "Inspired by my basic individualism in all economic matters, I desired to continue the firm as an independent private enterprise. I was unwilling to furl my sails."[15]

The sheer exuberance that had served him so well in a growing, optimistic Imperial Germany would shackle Max with false hopes in a disintegrating Weimar. As ever, he had a hypnotic hold on his brothers, especially Paul, and made such a brilliant sales pitch that Paul and Felix poured more of their own money into the firm. In February 1931, Paul put up an astounding two million dollars, while Felix chipped in another quarter million. Troubled by the German outlook, the American brothers also pumped capital into the new Amsterdam operation, Warburg & Company. This cash infusion bought time for Max, for during the next year the firm would lose 80 percent of its foreign and 50 percent of its domestic deposits.

The most serious threat came from Karstadt. Warburg credit had accelerated the store's expansion and Fritz sat on its supervisory board. The Warburgs invited Carola's husband, Walter Rothschild, to come and file a report on Karstadt. As the genial head of the A&S department store in Brooklyn, he seemed the ideal person to appraise the situation. After he arrived, Walter strolled around the corner to the department store then returned with surprising speed. "Karstadt is going to go bankrupt," he said with Delphic conviction. Amazed, Max asked how could he tell so quickly? "Any department store that sells pillows on the ground floor is going to fail."[16] Walter further noted that department stores suffered disproportionate harm in economic crises. Petrified, Eric told his father that he wanted to flee the sinking ship, but Max termed desertion out of the question.[17]

In early 1931, fear seized the banks of central Europe. In March, Germany announced plans for an Austrian-German custom union that would violate the Versailles Treaty and French investors withdrew huge amounts from both countries. The colossal Credit-Anstalt of Vienna, which was associated with the Rothschilds and controlled nearly three fourths of Austrian banking, suffered a severe blow. The government had forced it to absorb a failing agricultural bank and now it was hit by an outflow of French money. As a board member, Max rushed to Vienna in May to lunch with Baron Louis von Rothschild, the bank's president. He arrived in time to witness the depositor run at close range. He was staggered that the bank's managers had so profoundly lost their way and kept directors in the dark. "They had been drowned in the details of the day and lost all vision of the whole."[18] In London, Jimmy told Anthony de Rothschild that if his family ever needed help, they could count on the Warburgs—a stunning reversal of their nineteenth-century roles.[19]

With Germany and Austria interwoven by financial ties, the Credit-Anstalt debacle destroyed depositor confidence in German banks. Karstadt flirted with bankruptcy. On June 16, 1931, North German Wool failed, triggering a financial crisis as it dragged down German creditors, most notably the huge Danat Bank on July 11. Financial panic seized all of Germany. To halt depositor runs, the government declared a bank holiday and German stock exchanges shut down until September. Max faulted the Reichsbank for having acted gingerly to stem the fear and he regretted his patronage of the unimaginative Dr. Luther. The government issued a blizzard of emergency decrees, but nothing could assuage the universal anxiety.

Max had been writing to New York about bright spots and silver linings in the dismal scene. After the Credit-Anstalt, Paul and Felix sent Jimmy to Germany to investigate M. M. Warburg. Felix worried that if Paul went, Max would only charm him again and lead them all down the primrose path.

This mission would woefully complicate Jimmy's relationship with Max, who had long been his favorite uncle and role model. Jimmy liked Max's *savoir-faire*, preferring his red-blooded swagger to his father's eternal caution. Max worked hard, played hard; earned much, spent much—a formula Jimmy would adopt. Yet Jimmy also shared Paul's qualms about Max as a businessman and criticized his breakneck expansion. Jimmy would spend much of the year in Germany, sifting through the wreckage. In earlier times, he had loved the old-fashioned bank, just now switching to typewriters and still reluctant to add new-fangled adding machines. Having proudly served as a trusted go-between for Max and Paul, he was now given a gravedigger's duty. "In a strange sort of way I was forced to become the protector of both my father and his brother. It goes without saying that this was not a happy relationship."[20]

In Hamburg in June, Jimmy was shocked at Max's cheerful and blithe complacence. And Paul had worried that Max might become suicidal! Jimmy thought the Hamburg bank a terminal case and tried to persuade Paul and Felix that all further rescue efforts were futile. Even as the unsuspecting Warburgs celebrated Max's sixty-fourth birthday at Kösterberg, Jimmy delivered a death sentence for his firm, writing privately to Paul:

"It's really not a matter that any one but you and Felix can decide. So far as my interest in your fortune is concerned, go as far as you like. I don't mind starting at scratch again, but don't please be under any misapprehension as to what you are doing if you do it. The only safe way to regard such a job is to consider the money lost. My own inclination at the moment, cruel though it may sound, is to let them bust if they have to, and help the family afterwards rather than go practically bust yourself in trying to save the situation. . . . Sorry to give you this so brutally, but it is a matter of time, and besides there isn't much I can say to make it less brutal."[21]

Paul was suffering a shinglelike back condition that he attributed to tension over Max. Felix balked at saving Max, grumbling that their older brother only approached him at "milking time." He submitted at the insistence of Frieda, who was nonetheless furious with Max for putting them in such a situation. Nina, distraught, described the situation as a nightmare. Only Paul—ever faithful, ever loyal to Max—never wavered, even though he was keenly disappointed that Max had chosen the rescue option.

Writing to Jimmy, Paul acknowledged the financial sacrifice involved in saving Max. Then he went on: "Still, it is the right thing to do. What good does money do us if we lose our good name and desert those we love—even though they acted like idiots." The letter breathed a fine, selfless spirit of love for Max. "I do not like—and never did—to hit a man when he is down, and particularly not when I love him as dearly and pity him from the bottom of my heart. On the other hand, I am truly incensed and I believe that we must be severe, or things will drift along as they did in the past. . . . But what a terrible end [for Max] after so brave a fight and a life so full of generosity and devotion."²² Just as Nazi propaganda was pounding the theme of Jewish greed, Paul and Felix showed an exemplary indifference to money in a matter of family honor.

To his credit, Jimmy responded with gallantry when presented with this *fait accompli.* "I must say you and Felix are a great pair of brothers to have," he wrote to his father. "In your shoes I would have done the same thing, but I honestly couldn't have advised you to do it, because so far as the money is concerned, I think it's thrown out of the window in a lost cause. As I said in my memo, I don't believe that Max is capable of changing himself to the extent that would be required to give the business any kind of a chance. Nevertheless, this way we ought to be sure of a decent funeral with full military honors. . . ."²³ Ending on a brave note, he said he and Kay were still young and healthy and could survive on his reduced salary.

Beyond the $2.25 million given in February, Paul and Felix extended another $1 million in July. They also assumed $2.5 million in obligations Max owed to the IAB and the Bank of the Manhattan Trust and guaranteed another $1.3 million in syndicate participations. In October, the two brothers split a further $1.78 million advance to M. M. Warburg, bringing the total to almost $9 million. Paul's contribution represented more than half his entire fortune. As corporate conduit for these loans, the American Warburgs created something called the Kara Corporation. Although this entity effectively owned the Hamburg bank, Paul and Felix transferred control back to Max and his partners, asking only for interest on their loan. They accepted junior status among creditors—that is, if bankruptcy came, they would be the last to be paid.

Later on, Jimmy repeatedly told the story of how he had convinced the American Warburgs to save M. M. Warburg. He allowed this fallacious legend to circulate and enjoyed some family glory as a result. As he wrote, posing as the modest hero, "Later, when Max got into trouble, it was my lot to insist that he be given the extremely costly help required to keep the old family firm afloat."²⁴ Eric always believed that Jimmy had persuaded Paul and Felix, quite against their will, to shore up the bank. Yet Jimmy had advocated killing the bank and never completely forgave Max for demanding such a sacrifice. The need for this rescue created a certain coolness between the German and American branches of the family.

In his autobiography, Jimmy also narrated a dramatic tale of how he put together a scheme to rescue the Danat Bank and the German banking system. What he omitted to say was that it camouflaged a scheme to save Uncle Max. At a family war council in July, Paul and Felix decided that they wouldn't contribute further bail-out money *unless* M. M. Warburg merged with a stronger institution. In that event, they would provide the "dowry" for the marriage.

At this point, Jimmy had a brainstorm. President Hoover had just declared a moratorium on reparations. American banks also agreed to extend their short-term credits to Germany, starting the so-called Standstill Agreement. This left many American firms with idle deposits sitting in German banks. A superb salesman, Jimmy convinced these firms to convert twelve and a half million dollars of such deposits into capital to bolster the Danat Bank. Danat would sell its retail deposits and branch network to the Dresdner Bank, then merge its wholesale operation with M. M. Warburg. As Jimmy informed the Danat Bank, the American banks would only participate "with the stipulation that our Hamburg friends, M. M. Warburg & Co., be induced to bring the greater part of their personnel and their business."[25] The new institution would be at least partly piloted by Warburg partners. An elaborate face-saving exercise for Uncle Max, it would let him go bust with dignity intact.

The soundings that Jimmy and his cousin, Siegmund (Aby S.'s nephew, now an M. M. Warburg partner) took in Berlin suggested that Chancellor Brüning would be pleased by the plan, which might restore confidence in the banks. In late August, Max, Siegmund, and Jimmy laid the plan before Brüning, who listened attentively. They presented an impressive list of blue-chip firms prepared to participate: General Electric; General Motors; IT&T; International Harvester; Kuhn, Loeb; and Hambros Bank. "As he listened," recalled Jimmy, "the eyes behind his spectacles filled with tears. Finally he said, 'Gentlemen, this is like manna from heaven. I should like you to talk about this to [Reichsbank president] Luther without delay.'"[26] Overjoyed, Brüning told them that unless significant Reichstag opposition developed, the plan could be enacted in three days.[27]

A snag developed over a secret, ten-million-mark asset at Danat that was inscrutably labeled "Account X" on the books. Bank officials wouldn't disclose its nature and Brüning promised to probe the matter. For a week, the chancellor dodged the Warburgs until Jimmy, exasperated, said the American offer would expire in forty-eight hours unless they heard from Brüning. The chancellor invited him in that afternoon, but didn't ask him to sit down. Again with tears in his eyes, he expressed gratitude, but, without elaborating, said he had to decline the American offer. Only years later did the Warburgs learn the mystery behind Account X, which represented a bad loan to President Hindenburg's spendthrift son, Oskar. Rather than expose this scandal, Brüning rebuffed the rescue plan. Two years later, Hitler would blackmail Oskar about his tax evasion and other financial improprieties.[28] The whole affair was an agonizing lesson in political cowardice for Jimmy. "It was now more than ever clear to me that Hitler's accession to power was only a matter of time. . . . Had the banking collapse been prevented, it would have cut one leg out from under the Nazi drive for power."[29]

The strenuous summer of worry took its toll on Paul, who had to skip his usual vacation. When England went off the gold standard in September, he thought the world had been seized by financial madness. Governments were abandoning sacred rules that had governed global finance for generations. Frieda dated Paul's irreversible illness from that news. "I have studied finance and economics and international trade all my life, and now, after these recent events, I have come to the conclusion that I know nothing whatever about any of them," Paul was supposed to have said in his last days.[30] An economic fatalist, he believed busts could only be prevented by dampening the preceding booms. Thanks to syndicates, cartels, and protectionism, the world had built and produced too much. Both Paul and Jimmy blamed the twin burdens of reparations and Allied war debt for the artificial prosperity of the 1920s and the subsequent Depression. Until his last days, Paul pleaded for a lightening of German reparations.

Suffering fatigue and eyestrain, Paul heeded doctors' orders and took a rest at White Sulphur Springs in West Virginia. When Paul met him at the dock in November, Jimmy saw from his drawn face that his father was a broken man. Jimmy and Bettina found something listless about Paul, his vital spark extinguished. In December, he had a stroke, though his family thought he would recover. Then he developed pneumonia and lay in a coma for weeks. On December 10, Jimmy succeeded him as president of the International Acceptance Bank. "During his lucid moments he spoke to me about many things but never once mentioned his brother Max or the Hamburg firm," said Jimmy of his father's last days. "I am convinced that what had destroyed his will to go on living was that Max, for whom he had throughout his life felt a younger brother's slave-like devotion, had let him down."[31]

When Paul died on January 24, 1932, at his East Eightieth Street home, Felix, Nina, Jimmy, Kay, and Bettina congregated at his bedside. As Jimmy said, this Cassandra died "with his world tumbling about his ears."[32] Perhaps the most gifted financier of his day, he was buried at Sleepy Hollow Cemetery above the Hudson River.

There would be acrimonious disputes among the Warburgs as to whether Max had inadvertently hastened Paul's death. Jimmy believed Max had abused his brother's generosity. As he told Max's daughter, "I am not the only one who felt sure that he [Paul] simply did not want to go on living when his idol turned out to have feet of clay; it was not just my 'assumption.' "[33] Bettina always spoke sarcastically about Max, whom she thought hid a selfish agenda behind grandiose pronouncements. She nicknamed him "Maxie the Taxi," saying, "Max expected you to do everything, not for him, but allegedly for the firm. He was too clever to be autocratic."[34] In explaining Paul's death, Max emphasized his worries over the frenzied finance of the 1920s. On the threshold of the Third Reich, he had lost a wise counselor and irreplaceable confidant.

With Paul's death, the public saw that he had pursued public service to the detriment of his personal fortune. At first, *The New York Times* estimated his worth at fifty million dollars and hinted that the real amount might be double or triple that. In fact, his estate came to two and a half million dollars—about half of what he had spent for brother Max. On his deathbed, Paul made Jimmy and Bettina promise to support Nina in her accustomed style. In a farewell note to Nina, he wrote: "Whatever may happen to this miserable heap of bones of mine, my love will always remain with you and shield you from loneliness. . . . I believe in the story of the blue bird. As long as people think of those that have departed, so long do they live."[35]

Felix commissioned Malvina Hoffman to sculpt Paul's head, and she struggled with the assignment for a long time. Then one morning, she telephoned Felix and said, "Paul came to my studio last night and sat for the sculpture." Felix went to the studio and, sure enough, this lady of the mystical bent had completed the head.[36]

Jimmy memorialized his father in a series of highly personal poems that reveal the libertine son's sense of guilt before the revered but straitlaced father. He dwelled on Paul's power to avoid temptation, to stick to the straight and narrow path. He couldn't seem to praise his father without flagellating himself. As he wrote:

> How many words of counsel, ripe and sage,
> Have fallen from your kindly lips and lain,
> Unheeded in the dust,
> When I was arrogant and vain
> And scornful of the wise and just?[37]

This season of death and financial crisis forever alienated Jimmy from his family. Twice in 1932, Felix sent Jimmy back to Hamburg to straighten out the firm, and the two operated in a more bare-knuckled style than while Paul was alive. Over Max's objections, they devised numerous schemes to salvage the bank in some shrunken form. The American Warburgs always suspected that their German relatives lived extravagantly and Jimmy oversaw an austerity drive, subjecting his older uncles to an inquisition about their spending habits. It was a degrading routine: Max and Fritz had to justify sending their daughters, Gisela and Ingrid, to Oxford. Eric and Max assured Jimmy they needed their spas and sailing trips to cope with these tense times.

Jimmy and Felix saw the Warburg bank as consumed by turf battles. In a stunning vote of no confidence—one Paul would never have countenanced—Max was stripped of his supervisory role and prohibited from leading board meetings. Because Jimmy thought Fritz lazy and inept, he banned him outright from meetings and decreed that he couldn't interfere with business in any way.³⁸ It was a brutal business. Jimmy found an ally in Siegmund, the other young prodigy, who liked Jimmy's brash intelligence and fully shared his doubts about Max's ability.

In late 1931, M. M. Warburg formed a joint venture with one of the few major banks that had weathered the year well: the Berliner Handels-Gesell-schaft, associated with the Fürstenberg family. The venture was supposed to initiate closer links, but it never led to full fusion. From the Jimmy-Felix correspondence, it seems clear that they wanted to give M. M. Warburg a dignified funeral, not to resurrect it. Felix wouldn't issue a blanket guarantee that it would survive and referred scornfully to Max's "palace" on the Fer-dinandstrasse, which he thought had saddled the firm with high overhead. Jimmy sold many of M. M. Warburg's investments in central Europe and attempted to relegate Max to a humbler future role. Max resented the joint venture with the Berliner Handels-Gesellschaft, which forced him to play the junior partner. As Jimmy told Felix, "The relationship with the Handels-Gesellschaft has worked out excellently—due very largely to Siegmund's persistency, and more or less over Max's dead body."³⁹ This tension between Siegmund and Max began to intensify a feud that would eventually turn the whole Warburg empire topsy-turvy.

In a similarly unsentimental fashion, Jimmy wanted to shutter Warburg & Co., the Amsterdam affiliate. Endowed with better instincts, Felix suspected it might someday offer a convenient escape route for the family. "It might be advisable to keep it alive just in case Hitlerism makes living for the family so outrageously disagreeable that it might want to have another pied-à-terre to move to."⁴⁰ Jimmy agreed with Felix's political fears; by the time he left Germany in spring 1932, he thought nothing could stem the Nazi tide or protect the Warburgs. "When I said good-bye to my uncle Max and my Hamburg friends, I did so with a feeling of sad foreboding. I knew that a chapter in European history had ended."⁴¹

The Hamburg experience left Jimmy estranged from his relatives there and fed up with family intrigue and infighting. As intermediary in an unpleasant tug-of-war, he had been put into the unfair position of having to dictate policy to his older relatives. Before Paul died, Jimmy told him that he wished to break away from the IAB, and Paul urged him to go to Kuhn, Loeb instead. This missed the point: Jimmy wanted to escape the whole maze of family complica-tions and renounce his place as scion of a famous banking dynasty. "I am perfectly frank to state that I have had my belly full of family businesses and would not of my own choice and free will leave one family business in order to embark upon another."⁴² He said he didn't share the feeling of martyrdom that had compelled Felix's sons, Freddy and Paul Felix, to enter banking. Indeed, after Paul's death, Jimmy brushed aside Felix's offer to join Kuhn,

Loeb and he would finally discard all ambition to be a banker. Henceforth, he would be the family renegade, moving apart from the other Warburgs.

It must have embittered Jimmy that his protracted stays in Hamburg had provided an opening for Kay's affair with George Gershwin to flourish. Staying at Bydale, the Warburg farm in Connecticut, Gershwin wrote and dictated sections of *Porgy and Bess* to Kay, who jotted down half the original score. He became a fixture around the place. Referring to this decades later, Jimmy still seemed to smart: "I liked Gershwin but resented the way in which our whole life was taken over by this completely self-centered but charming genius. . . ."[43] Gershwin didn't take ordinary precautions to conceal the affair. In 1932, Random House published *George Gershwin's Song Book*, with a dedication from George to Kay. To be cuckolded in public by a celebrity was more than a man of Jimmy Warburg's ego could bear. The affair also had a very deleterious impact upon the three Warburg daughters, who were openly exposed to it at Bydale. One of the three came upon George and Kay *in flagrante delicto* and was shattered by the experience.

While definitely not the marrying sort, Gershwin contemplated marriage with Kay and solicited friends' views about the wisdom of such a course. Perhaps Gershwin was deterred by the three daughters (he had strained relations with April, the eldest, who saw what was going on) or by Kay not being Jewish. Maybe he feared marrying a divorcée. Gershwin once said, "Why should I limit myself to only one woman when I can have as many women as I want?"[44] When Jimmy confronted Gershwin and told him to go ahead and marry Kay if he liked, the composer fled in panic from the offer.[45]

The situation became still more tangled when the three members of this love triangle ended up involved with the same psychoanalyst: Gregory Zilboorg, a neighbor of Jimmy and Kay on East Seventieth Street. Bettina, who had trained with Zilboorg, referred Kay to him because she was in a muddle about the Gershwin affair. A flamboyant refugee from the Russian Revolution, Zilboorg was a short, dark Svengali-like figure in glasses who mesmerized the Warburgs until adoration turned to disenchantment. His colorful past cloaked him in a mysterious aura. He had been secretary to the labor minister of Kerensky's cabinet, was a Cordon Bleu chef, a photographer, a polyglot fluent in more than eight languages, a medical doctor, and the author of a major history of psychiatry. With showmanship and exceptional intelligence, he created a following that ranged from Lillian Hellmann to Marshall Field. A fine diagnostician and brilliant talker, he would, on occasion, reduce patients to tears, extract their innermost secrets, and use them for purposes of control.

Psychoanalysis was still new and daring in America, with a spice of the forbidden about it, so the venturesome, avant-garde young Warburgs were drawn to it. But far from finding clarity with Zilboorg, Kay ended up being seduced by him on the analytic couch during sessions. According to Kay's granddaughter, this was much more a matter of selfish manipulation by Zilboorg than of any romantic attraction on Kay's part. When she broached the subject of divorcing Jimmy, Zilboorg warned her against taking such a step. If she persisted in this, he threatened to poison the minds of Jimmy and Gershwin against her—both of whom he knew—so that neither would have anything to do with her.[46] In the end, Kay was not to be dissuaded and called his bluff. In late 1934, she went to Nevada to get a divorce from Jimmy. But though Kay dropped Zilboorg, Jimmy and Gershwin decided to go into therapy with him.

Kay never married Gershwin, which didn't surprise friends of the composer. When Kay and Gershwin once entered a nightclub, Oscar Levant quipped, "Ah, here comes George Gershwin with the future Miss Kay Swift."[49] In 1935, she was still his constant companion, presiding over an opening-night party for *Porgy and Bess* at Condé Nast's Park Avenue penthouse apartment. When Gershwin went to Hollywood the following year, he and Kay had a tearful farewell at Newark Airport. They never saw each other again, though Gershwin kept abreast of her doings. He died of a brain tumor in July 1937. Kay subsequently married twice—first to a rodeo star and then to a radio announcer—but always kept alive the sacred flame of Gershwin's memory and music. Scholars would seek her out to discover how Gershwin had played particular passages.

One side of Jimmy felt extremely bitter and humiliated by the breakup with Kay. Another side thought she'd simply gone haywire and he assigned to her the royalties of the songs they had coauthored. For Jimmy, the world that had crackled with such promising life and energy suddenly exploded. In marrying Kay and traveling in her artistic circles, he had ventured from the family, flouted tradition, and dabbled in a dangerous new kind of life. He had stepped outside the Jewish social ghetto only to find that the glittering world beyond bristled with secret dangers of which he, for all his sophisticated pose, had been innocently unaware.

CHAPTER 24

Blue Boys

The New York Warburgs were a twice-emancipated family. Their ancestors had been invigorated by the broad opportunities open to Jews in Imperial Germany. Now, in the 1920s and 1930s, they experienced a second burst of freedom as they advanced into the upper echelon of American society, adopting the graces and manners of WASP aristocracy. This new freedom was giddy but perplexing. Rich and cultured, the Warburgs gained access to parties and clubs that excluded other Jews, placing them in a terrible bind by exposing them to the temptation of being token Jews in a Christian world. To be the first Jew in a club or school could be seen either as courageous pioneering or as shameful collusion with the enemy.

The offspring of Felix Warburg in particular felt a fragmented identity and sometimes seemed exhausted by a Hamlet-like search for their true nature. Compared to the generation of the Famous Five brothers, Felix's four sons would seem less rounded, less complete, lacking the energy and drive of their ancestors. They would carry the historic ambivalence of German Jews toward Judaism to the logical conclusion of intermarriage and a diluted religious identity. If they did obligatory stints in Jewish fund-raising, it remained peripheral to their lives. (Felix's youngest son, Edward, was the clear exception.)

Gradually the American Warburgs would drop the public leadership role that had been reflexive in the family since the sixteenth century. Ironically, the American Warburgs would shed much of their Judaism, while the persecuted German side of the family would preserve it better.

The Jazz Age had a potent effect upon the young Warburgs, who craved adventure and wrote off "Our Crowd" as old hat. Seduced by wealth, they traveled in affluent Protestant circles where their religion was a hindrance. To some extent, this transition was characteristic of this generation of "Our Crowd." Mortimer Schiff had French racing stables and a house in Palm Beach where he entertained Averell Harriman and Joseph Kennedy. The Schiffs and the Kahns entered the Social Register before the Warburgs. But the Warburgs seemed, if anything, even more socially ambitious, as if determined to prove that they could go anywhere and do anything.

Warburg men had abided, with a few exceptions, such as Aby, by a code of conduct that began to break down. Under that code, they had chosen practical careers in banking or business to serve the family interests; after hours, they could indulge in the extracurricular pleasures of wealth. They could travel in gentile society so long as they contributed to Jewish causes. They could engage in the arts, but only as patrons or connoisseurs. They could have mistresses, if marital concord were preserved. They could date non-Jews, so long as they didn't foolishly fall in love. And they could participate in sports in amateur gentlemanly style.

Felix had perfectly executed that balancing act, preserving the best of Europe while cheerfully adapting to America. Having so gracefully straddled the German-American and Jewish-gentile divides, he didn't understand why his children wrestled with these conflicts. He never realized that his children were products of his own contradictory impulses. He wanted his sons to be red-blooded, well-rounded, all-American kids who went to Middlesex and Harvard and played tennis and touch football. Then he wondered why they lacked an overriding interest in Jewish philanthropy. With his children, Felix could never sort out the confused promptings of his own heart.

Each of Felix's children inherited a piece of him, so that, collectively, they added up to a rough portrait of him. They had his lively, witty manner, his engaging personality, his splendid sense of fun, but not his steadfast commitment to social causes and a wider political world. They had the Warburg wind in their sails without the ballast. They inherited the sort of great wealth that weakens ambition and shifts priorities to leisure pursuits. Jacob Schiff's widow, Therese, spoiled her grandchildren terribly, leaving them, when she died in 1933, an estate of $4.6 million, plus a trust fund that had started out with $6 million in 1910. No longer needing to make money, the young Warburgs learned to thumb their noses at whomever they liked.

Carola Warburg Rothschild.
(Courtesy of Carol Rothschild Noyes)

Felix's eldest daughter, Carola, most readily took up her assigned place in the Warburg universe. She was everybody's favorite, and her home featured good talk and ready cocktails even during Prohibition. Felix doted upon her, saying, "She is like a thoroughbred horse, and has to be ridden with a light hand."[1] In marrying the rich, Princeton-educated Walter Rothschild, she found an easygoing man who negotiated his way handily through the often prickly Warburg clan. As head of the A&S department store, Walter didn't need to worry about status competition.

Inheriting her parents' anglophile tastes, Carola loved horses, dogs, country living. She devoted time to several hospitals, the Girl Scouts, the Federation of Jewish Philanthropies, a maternity center, and other Warburg causes and, in many ways, she modeled herself after Frieda. Yet her Jewish activities were more a matter of family pride and homage to the past. When asked if she were a practicing Jew, Carola sighed, "Well, I was married by a rabbi. . . ."[2] Her three children would marry five times in total, all outside the faith.

Carola's brothers found the Warburg legacy and wealth more problematic. They were trapped between a heritage that seemed perfected and a future that seemed forbidden. They could never quite find the center of their lives. In business, they were too well-heeled to be aggressive, too pampered to be industrious. Felix didn't allow them to apply their energies in new ways or stake out a fresh identity. This posed more problems for the sensitive, artistic, pair, Gerry and Eddie, than for the sporty, outgoing Freddy and Paul Felix or "Piggy."

Bowing to family duty, Freddy, the eldest, spent virtually his entire career at Kuhn, Loeb. His rugged face, with its broad, balding forehead and bumpy chin, expressed a pugnacious personality. Freddy had a dry, acerbic wit that deflated pomposity. At his teasing best, he could be funny and delightful, a bubbling stream of quips; at his worst, he could be caustic, even hurtful.

As a great sports fan, Freddy brought international stars to the Woodlands tennis courts. Left to his own devices, he might have edited a sports magazine. Nobody doubted Freddy's banking ability, but he lacked the fire of his uncles. In the 1930s, he bought a horse farm and stud in Middleburg, Virginia, and cultivated the role of a country gentleman, hunting foxes and raising horses. He had numerous charities—Middlesex School, Harvard, the Boy Scouts, and Smith College—but few with Jewish connections. Some family members think Freddy remained a bachelor until his late forties because of the clause in Schiff's will disinheriting those who married outside the faith. Others think he was just having too much fun to settle down. Whatever the case, he was almost fifty before he married the feisty Wilma Shannon in 1946.

The third Warburg son, Paul Felix—invariably known by his nickname, Piggy—was cut from the same cloth. A gay blade and raconteur, a delightful fellow who always had a ready quip on his lips, he was the family clown. One summer in Paris, he returned to the Ritz after an all-night binge and stumbled into his parents' room by accident, throwing his cane at a shape hulking in his bed. It turned out to be Frieda, who straightened up and said, "Your father will speak to you about this in the morning."[3] Most of the time, she roared at his screwball antics, though she disapproved of his philandering.

Although Piggy never graduated from college, Felix had great affection for this incorrigible, madcap boy. When he left school, Felix got him a humble job with the B&O Railroad in Baltimore and used to write him letters that began "Dear Railroad Magnate." While working on the railroad, Piggy met another rich young man who persuaded him to invest in his new business and Felix reacted angrily. "I love you dearly," he told his son, "but if you're so irresponsible with money as all that, I'm going to put you on an allowance." The friend was William F. Paley and the investment was the nascent CBS.[4]

Piggy did outrageous things in a way that usually caused delight, not offense. While skiing at Sun Valley once, he collided with Mrs. Nelson Rockefeller, whom he had never met. As the two sprawled, dazed, in the snow, Piggy turned and said, "Excuse me, Mrs. Rockefeller, I'm Piggy Warburg and I promise to marry you in the morning."[5] Later serving as special assistant to Ambassador Averell Harriman in London, Piggy startled the British royals on a receiving line when he was asked how long he had known his female companion. "Oh, about forty seconds," he replied.[6]

Piggy worked under uncle Paul at the IAB and then served as a vice-president at the Bank of the Manhattan; later he worked at Bache & Company and Carl M. Loeb, Rhoades & Company. As a ubiquitous figure in café society, he drummed up business among celebrities. He knew many figures in the film world and eventually bagged the accounts of Sylvia Sidney, Dolores del Rio, Eddie Cantor, Miriam Hopkins, and even Babe Ruth. In 1926, he married the first of three wives: Jean Stettheimer, a very pretty, sociable Jewish woman from San Mateo, California, who loved horses and the outdoors and whose father owned a textile company. The marriage lasted eight years and yielded two attractive daughters. Piggy would be active in the Federation of Jewish Philanthropies, but most deeply involved in *Project Hope*, the hospital ship that later brought American medicine to Third World countries.

Interestingly, Felix had smoother relations with his two jock-and-banker sons than with the aesthetic Gerald and Edward. However roguish in his private life, Felix was a conventional, bourgeois father and Gerald and Edward learned that the Warburg children enjoyed only an illusory freedom. They grew up with enough wealth to do anything, but were hemmed in by secret rules that prevented them from parlaying their interests into successful, sustained careers.

At first, Felix didn't consider a musical career suitable for Gerald, but by the late 1920s he had relented. If Gerry was to be a professional cellist, Felix would see that he succeeded. At his son's prompting, he bequeathed to him his four Stradivarius instruments so that Gerry could form the Stradivarius Quartet. Felix insisted upon selecting the other musicians even though Gerry longed for independence. To make his son a star soloist, Felix had arranged for his Carnegie Hall debut with the New York Philharmonic Symphony Orchestra under Walter Damrosch. This pushed Gerry into the spotlight prematurely when he needed more training. Despite a beautiful sound and delicate phrasing, Gerry was handicapped by technical gaps in his background and Felix's aid prevented him from developing the necessary discipline and self-confidence. Gerry also never knew whether he was being invited to play for his talent or to curry Warburg patronage.

Gerry grew up no less confused about religion. As organist for daily chapel at Middlesex, he was exposed to the music's religious content, which perhaps seeped into his mind. Baffled by his own contradictions, Gerry called himself a Unitarian, but could never bring himself to sing Christmas carols. On High Holy Days, he sat, unseen, in shirtsleeves in the choir loft of Temple Emanu-El, playing Kol Nidre. As a confirmed assimilationist, Gerry thought it best to mix people of different backgrounds.

Gerry was the first to defy the family taboo against divorce. While he wanted to flee his German-Jewish background, his beautiful Viennese wife, Marion, enjoyed the elegant Woodlands life. Having shopped with bags of worthless money in postwar Austria, she wanted the security against which her husband rebelled. If sweet and charming, Gerald was also flighty and moody and didn't provide Marion with much stability. She began to doubt whether he had the talent to become a famous musician. Already beset by enough doubts, Gerry couldn't contend with a skeptical wife.

Marion had become a pet of the Warburgs. When she and Gerry decided to get divorced in 1933, Felix and Frieda were thunderstruck and reacted in a way that implicitly blamed Gerry. Felix not only hired and paid for Marion's lawyer, but encouraged a generous settlement that strapped Gerry for years. Marion would receive large alimony payments for life, regardless of whether she remarried. Gerry, very upright and correct in such matters, submitted to these terms. Felix and Frieda would remain close with Marion.

The notion of divorce was shocking for Jewish parents in 1933; the identity of Gerry's second wife added to the blow. Hard on the heels of the divorce, Gerry married Natica Nast, the daughter of *Vogue* publisher Condé Nast. Natica was German Methodist on one side, French Catholic on the other, and was raised a Catholic. A tasteful young woman, a good rider, she often served as her father's hostess; as a teenager she had modeled wedding veils in *Vogue*.

When the wedding took place in Grandpa Nast's living room, with Freddy as the best man, Frieda and Felix stayed away, much as Charlotte and Moritz had boycotted Aby's wedding. They scheduled an out-of-town trip and sent a telegram instead. Frieda and Felix favored Jewish marriages—Frieda would say, "The best way was Jewish"—but were never rigid moralists who banished wayward children. Once they had formally registered their objection to the new ways, they would restore family harmony.

Even before the wedding, Frieda had written to Natica, saying that she understood Natica was beautiful and gracious and regretting that, under the circumstances, they couldn't meet. Grandma Schiff gave Natica a ring to ease the tension. After the wedding, Gerry and Natica were invited to lunch with Felix and Frieda. Afterward, Frieda asked Natica to take a stroll in the garden while the guests speculated about this tête-à-tête. The two women returned locked in intimate talk. Frieda had evidently decided that the time had come to make peace within the family and move on. She said to Natica, "My dear, you're so nice, you must be Jewish."[7]

The match between Gerry and Natica was a sensible one. He played his cello while she wrote and painted and they were enormously devoted to each other. To escape Woodlands, they moved to the heavily WASP North Shore of Long Island. When they joined the Creek Club, which banned Jews, Natica became the member of record. Natica didn't regard this as tokenism or as submitting to prejudice, but as pioneering, an assimilationist idea very congenial to Gerald, who would never resolve his conflicted feelings toward Judaism. When his daughter, Geraldine, became one of the few Friedaflix grandchildren to marry a Jew, Gerry was disappointed.[8]

The match to Condé Nast's daughter didn't assist Gerald's career, which already suffered from a perception that he didn't exactly need the work. But although Gerry never fulfilled his dream of becoming a distinguished cellist, he nonetheless had an interesting, diverse career, becoming a founder and conductor of the Brooklyn Symphony Orchestra; a vice-president of the City Center of Music and Drama; and a trustee of the Mannes School. He gave children's concerts, did a series on Beethoven for public television in New York, and made recordings with the London Royal Philharmonic. He would generously—and anonymously—lend his Stradivarius instruments to young musicians for auditions and competitions.

It sometimes seemed that the fame of Gerry's instruments fared better than his own. From Felix, he had inherited La Belle Blonde Stradivarius, later swapping it with the Havemeyer family for the 1711 Duport Stradivarius, considered by some the greatest of all Stradivarius instruments. (Gerry sweetened the swap with cash to even the exchange.) It had been played in performance with both Beethoven and Chopin themselves and supposedly bore scars from Napoleon's spurs. One night, Gerry invited Mstislav Rostropovich to sample the cello at a postconcert supper. The great cellist savored its rich sound. After Gerry's death, Natica sold it to Rostropovich for a substantial price and he treasured the splendid instrument. When Gerry's daughter went backstage to say hello, Rostropovich patted the instrument and said, "That's Gerry's soul singing in there."[9]

With his youngest son Edward, Felix again experienced a failure of vision. Edward was short, blue-eyed, and sensitive. A newspaper once described him as "a slender young man with the eyes of a dreamer."[10] His nickname was "Peeper," since he had reminded his German governess of a *Piepmatz*, or little bird. Always Frieda's favorite, he showed great compassion for his mother and often did sweet, thoughtful favors for her. Even their political views gibed: Eddie and Frieda were the house Democrats and Eddie escorted Frieda on trips to Palestine in the 1930s. Wanting to be accepted by his macho older brothers, he ended up being ribbed instead as mother's little darling. This introduced doubt and insecurity that Eddie would strive to cover up.

A superb raconteur and inveterate punster, Eddie had a droll, sly, humor that sneaked up and exploded upon the listener. He responded to the avant-garde arts of the day, but Felix wanted him to be a proper Victorian gentleman. On Eddie's twenty-first birthday in 1929, Felix warned against self-pity. "Avoid that always—but pity others with all the noblesse oblige that station requires."[11] This was the voice of another era. Felix also exhorted Eddie to steer clear of the Social Register crowd into which his children were drifting. "I have avoided the money-mad crowd who only know that measure of success and for that Piping Rock country club crowd I have not much time to spare."[12]

By the time Eddie entered Harvard, he was a short, handsome, dapper young man. As a freshman, he befriended Lincoln Kirstein, whose father ran Filene's department store in Boston and knew his A&S counterpart, Walter Rothschild. (Kirstein's father helped to form Federated Department Stores aboard Walter's yacht.) Along with John Walker III, Eddie and Lincoln rented space above the Harvard Co-op in 1928 and launched an enterprise called the Harvard Society for Contemporary Art. Started right before the Museum of Modern Art (MOMA) in New York, it brought many European modernist works to American shores.

The three young men reacted against the polite, tasteful art esteemed by their affluent families in favor of fresh, bold, rebellious, free-flowing modern works. Art historian Nicholas Fox Weber speculates that as Jewish outsiders at Harvard, Eddie and Kirstein were especially receptive to this art. "Kirstein and Warburg embraced modernism in part because, knowing that they were out of the mainstream anyway, they elected to foster rather than mitigate their sense of difference."[13]

Borrowing pictures from the Rockefellers and other wealthy families, they exhibited works by Picasso, Braque, Matisse, Derain, Brancusi, and many European artists still considered controversial in some American quarters. There was a daring show on recent Parisian art and another on "Modern German Art" that flew in the face of anti-German sentiment. Eddie and his father proved financial mainstays of the venture. This extended Felix's work with Paul Sachs, who came from another "Our Crowd" family and ran the Fogg Art Museum. Felix was such a munificent benefactor of the Fogg that Frieda often pressed Eddie to find out why Felix never got an honorary degree.

On January 26, 1930, Eddie went to Back Bay station to pick up Alexander Calder, who was supposed to bring seventeen pieces for exhibition. Instead, as he dismounted from the train, Calder greeted Eddie with three rolls of wire wound around his arm. Back in Eddie's room, Calder changed into pajamas and began twisting the wire into whimsical shapes. Within forty-eight hours, he had brought forth more figures for his famous circus. Glancing at a photo on Eddie's desk, Calder whipped off a caricature of Felix, with a Star of David at its base. To signify Felix's trademark carnation, Calder slid a test tube through the buttonhole. (Eddie bought that and two other Calders with his allowance money!) On January 31, Calder staged the first public performance of his circus at the gallery above the Harvard Co-op.

One might have thought that Eddie would respond to Uncle Aby's work. Quite the contrary. On a visit to Hamburg in the summer of 1929, he apparently found Aby an insupportable bore who lectured for hours on remote topics. Eddie liked the spontaneity of modern art, while Aby's approach seemed stuffily pedantic. The German trip, however, had one momentous result. Having turned twenty-one in June, Eddie had inherited money from Grandpa Schiff. A friend who worked in a Berlin gallery showed him Picasso's *Blue Boy*. This downcast, pensive figure enchanted the young Harvard undergraduate who plunked down seven thousand dollars for it. On the trip home, he worried about Felix's reaction and decided to reduce the amount he had paid by half. When Eddie told the customs officer that he had paid thirty-five hundred dollars for the painting, the man gasped. "You bought a $3,500 picture? You mean you actually paid that for this? Sonny, I'm going down the dock, and when I come back, you change that figure to $1,000."[14] Piggy was there to add comedy to the scene. "Thanks," he told the customs officer. "You see, we find it cheaper to let him do this than to keep him at Bloomingdales [Westchester Hospital]."[15]

At 1109 Fifth Avenue, Eddie had converted the fifth-floor squash court into an art gallery, which enjoyed an outlaw existence. Instead of trying to understand the Picasso, Felix and Frieda dismissed it as obscene and revolting and demanded its removal to the fifth floor. Felix had only grudging respect for Eddie's precocity in the art world. As he wrote to him about the Harvard gallery, "In regard to your art exhibit and salesroom, I have no objections to the matter in principle, unless it would be that it would detract from your work. If it teaches you business methods, there will be no harm done."[16] Felix talked about the gallery as if it were a small boy's lemonade stand, not a serious artistic commitment.

Money opened doors for Eddie but also sowed inner confusion. After graduating from Harvard, he discussed a teaching post with Georgiana Goddard King of the Bryn Mawr art department, who explained that she lacked the necessary budget to hire him. "But if I were to receive a check from some anonymous donor for a thousand dollars," she said slyly, "that could go for your salary." "Shall I write the check now?" Eddie asked. "There's no hurry," she said.[17] The episode recalled Gerry's everlasting dilemma as to whether he was a performer or a patron in disguise.

While teaching at Bryn Mawr, Eddie, age twenty-four, was named a trustee of the new MOMA, making him and Nelson Rockefeller the youngest trustees. In 1933, Eddie moved to New York and worked as a volunteer at MOMA, helping to found its film department and serving as its treasurer. Another young adviser to the museum, architect Philip Johnson, redesigned Eddie's apartment at 37 Beekman Place. Done in the international style that Johnson would make famous, the apartment had pigskin furniture, sleek black and white lacquered surfaces, fishnet curtains, and a glass wall. It was hard for Felix to savor this style, but he tried to be a good sport. When he visited the apartment, he already had a heart condition, yet climbed the three flights of the brownstone and perched nervously on a metallic, modernist chair. As he bent forward to dial the telephone, the chair collapsed under him and he crashed to the floor, bruising his jaw. "That's what I like about modern art," Felix said. "It's so functional."[18] Frieda was similarly uneasy with avant-garde art. As a patron of Gaston Lachaise, Eddie donated one of the sculptor's billowing ladies to the museum. The stout Frieda saw the work, implausibly, as a wicked piece of fun at her expense. "All I can say, Edward," she told him curtly, "is that I think this is a personal insult."[19]

Although Eddie had never even seen a ballet, he wound up as the financial angel of the American Ballet, the forerunner of the New York City Ballet. On European trips, Kirstein had become acquainted with Serge Diaghilev's Russian Ballet and its choreographer, George Balanchine. America still lacked a national ballet company and it seemed an exotic art form to most Americans. Martha Graham and Denishawn pretty much exhausted the roster of serious dance. In late summer 1933, Lincoln Kirstein, just back from Europe, raced up to see Eddie at Woodlands. As they wandered through the woods, Kirstein said he had convinced George Balanchine to start an American ballet school and company. Eddie agreed to split the cost of bringing over Balanchine and his business manager, Vladimir Dimitriev, to discuss the venture. On October 17, Eddie and Kirstein met the two Russians at the pier and squired them around town, taking them to Radio City Music Hall and the RCA Building.

The trip was a success, and the fledgling School of American Ballet soon opened in a studio at Fifty-Ninth Street and Madison Avenue. Balanchine set to work on an ethereal new ballet, *Serenade,* set to Tchaikovsky music. To offset this gossamer work, Eddie thought they should hazard an American subject and suggested that Balanchine try a spoof on a Harvard-Yale football game, complete with flappers and students in raccoon coats. The result was *Alma Mater,* with the book by Eddie himself. Gershwin declined to write the music but suggested Kay Swift, and the ballet evolved into a very Warburgian endeavor. John Held, Jr., a *New Yorker* cartoonist, did the sets.

Eddie was disappointed when Balanchine refused to see a real football game, which didn't augur well for the project. Friedaflix couldn't figure out this new phase of Eddie's life. For his twenty-sixth birthday in June 1934, Eddie asked if the new dance troupe could perform at Woodlands. His parents agreed not just to ballet but to a buffet for two hundred guests. The ballet crowd that swarmed through Woodlands that June night was a far cry from the usual staid guests. "My poor parents had no idea what hit them," admitted Eddie.[20] A platform was set up on the lawn, spotlights were installed on the roof, a piano was tucked in the bushes. While dancers changed in the swimming pool, the audience waited on lawn cushions. Then the dancers appeared for *Serenade,* lifting their arms to the heavens—which responded with a sudden gust of rain. (Balanchine had altered the opening stiff-arm lift, which reminded Eddie of the Nazi salute.) The guests agreed to return the next night. This didn't stop Eddie from running about in a dither the next morning. In a tizzy, he asked, "Where's Lincoln?" and brother Freddy answered, "Booth shot him."[21] The next night, the heavens cooperated and the audience was enthralled. Unfortunately, *Alma Mater,* Balanchine's first stab at Americana, proved a flop. It fared far better in December at its first public performance in Hartford. George Gershwin sat in the audience and afterward called Kay Swift in Nevada to express his admiration.

As financial backer and business manager of the budding American Ballet, Eddie helped to pilot it through an extended financial crisis. He has left a memorable vignette of the company's first Manhattan season at the Adelphi Theater in 1935. "Lincoln and I sat in the empty house with our hands cupped, covering our eyes. By the third performance, there were about 5 members of the ballet company's family in the audience."[22] Embarking on a cross-country tour, the company went bankrupt in Scranton when the tour manager absconded with the receipts, sticking Eddie with steep bills. The disaster-prone company teamed up with the Metropolitan Opera for the

1935–36 season. Henceforth, Eddie was only sporadically involved, most notably in 1937, when he commissioned Stravinsky to write a new score, *Jeu de Cartes*, for a Stravinsky Festival.

Eddie grew tired of the ballet prima donnas. He also had a nagging sense that Lincoln leaned on him for money, whereas they had split the costs evenly in earlier days. Having felt that people exploited his father's generosity, Eddie was sensitive on that score. Disillusioned with the avant-garde, Eddie parted company with Kirstein. Kirstein would still be with Balanchine when the New York City Ballet was formed in 1948 and he remained a director of the company for decades. Bruised and bitter, Eddie didn't attend another ballet for forty years.

Eddie got only limited praise from his father for his path-breaking work in art and ballet. Felix sympathized with his financial travails, but never quite considered this grown-up business. Sometimes Felix could be lightly mocking, other times damning. At one point, he likened Eddie's patronage of the ballet to running a house of ill repute.[23] He simply couldn't concede that a career in the arts was a legitimate way for a male Warburg to spend his life.

Despite his zany, inspiring moments in art and ballet, Eddie realized that he was trying to please others, not himself. "I was a timid guy wanting very much to be included," he said. "And wanting to be part of the gang. The gang that I wanted to be part of was the young enthusiastic art followers and collectors."[24] He was still little brother trying to please and impress his mocking older brothers. At bottom, it didn't sit well with him that he had strayed so far from family traditions. By the late 1930s, his life would undergo a radical shift.

Meanwhile, Eddie succumbed to the craze for psychoanalysis that infected the American Warburgs. Bettina referred him to Gregory Zilboorg for analysis along with Kay Swift. Felix and Frieda were mystified by all this hocus-pocus and, as it turned out, they were absolutely correct. Eddie went to Zilboorg every day for more than twenty years. Instead of fostering autonomy, Zilboorg kept Eddie in a highly profitable state of dependence.[25] Zilboorg mingled his professional and social life in an unethical manner. In late 1935, when Eddie and George Gershwin visited Mexico and dined with David Siqueiros and Diego Rivera, Zilboorg went along with them. Fearing a hostile reception from the Mexican radical artists, the conservative Zilboorg packed a gun.

In her biography of psychoanalyst Karen Horney, Susan Quinn points out that by 1934 questions were being raised about Zilboorg's ethics in connection with bookstore funds at the New York Psychoanalytic Institute. One public relations executive complained to the institute in 1940 that he was financially exploited by Zilboorg, who had asked him to help pay his taxes; Zilboorg had taken five thousand dollars from the man for doubling as his business consultant.²⁶ Before his death, Eddie Warburg told similar bitter tales of making loans to Zilboorg and sometimes being asked to pay Zilboorg's taxes.²⁷ When Eddie once mentioned that he was buying a mink coat for his wife, Zilboorg got him to buy one for his wife as well.²⁸

What angered Eddie was not Bettina's initial referral to Zilboorg, for he believed that she had acted in good faith and honestly erred. But Bettina, evidently, learned that Zilboorg was a rascal long before the rest of the family and never alerted them to the danger. By the time she did, it was too late and the damage had been done. Kay and Jimmy had gotten out of analysis after a brief time, but Eddie didn't and he never forgave Bettina.²⁹ Gregory Zilboorg finally died in the late 1950s.

*The magnificent Stockholm wedding
of Siegmund and Eva Warburg, November 18, 1926,
with two bridesmaids from Eva's family.
(Private collection)*

CHAPTER 25

The Country Cousin

To represent the fifth Warburg generation in the Hamburg bank, destiny chose two second cousins so totally unlike, so visibly mismatched, that they seem to step forth from a family feud as conceived by Thomas Mann. Max's son, Eric, was like someone born amid a perpetual party. Fair-haired, sociable, fun-loving, he was a good-natured young man, a born diplomat, but not particularly serious. His cousin, Siegmund—grandson of the first Siegmund, son of Georges, nephew of Aby S.—was a dark, brooding young man of great charm and smoldering moods. With a massive intellect, he delivered blunt judgments on a world that often struck him as weak and errant. Eric was casual, modest, and relaxed, and never took himself too seriously. Siegmund carried great hopes and a powerful sense of ambition. Yet both were steeped in Warburg history and tradition and neither yielded to the other in his reverence for the family name.

As the crown prince in Hamburg, Eric was inevitably likened to his father and found wanting. Yet Max groomed him to head the bank, which was a blow to the talented, precociously wise Siegmund. Whenever Eric daydreamed about becoming a farmer, military officer, diplomat, or shipowner, Max directed his thoughts back to banking. Eric knew that, in the end, his career choice was a foregone conclusion. Awed by his autocratic father and always seeking his approval, Eric only slowly developed self-confidence. He talked of his father reverently but feared him. "When he was younger, Eric was very shy and didn't believe in himself as much," said his sister Anita.[1]

Max talked about Eric with the wry humor reserved for the lovable but slightly ne'er-do-well son. Their relationship was friendly and correct, but seldom warm, and Max appreciated Eric more with the passage of time. Offsetting the remote father was the warmth of four worshipful sisters and numerous cousins. Eric developed a shy, flirtatious manner with women that lasted a lifetime. Once again, the genes skipped a generation, for Eric was in the mold of grandfather Moritz, genial and charming and endowed more with social than business gifts.

After Eric's military service, Max sent him to apprentice with banks in Berlin, Frankfurt, and then London, where hostility still lingered toward Germany. Eric couldn't read a German paper on the London underground without attracting unwelcome attention. During his year there, Eric trained at the metal trading house of Brandeis, Goldschmidt, run by his uncle Paul Kohn-Speyer (husband of Aunt Olga, who committed suicide). He enjoyed hunts at the Kohn-Speyer estate in Surrey, but proved too blithe a spirit for his strict uncle. At lunch one day, Eric was joking with the secretaries and trying to impress them. He bet he could vault over several low partitions that separated the work areas. Taking a running start, he flew over the hurdles and landed smack on Paul Kohn-Speyer's desk—who walked in at that very moment and sent Eric packing. He then moved to N. M. Rothschild and was a frequent visitor at the Southampton estate of Baron Lionel de Rothschild. By this point, the Rothschilds and the Warburgs regularly traded trainees.

In 1923, Eric sailed for New York, planning to spend a year in America. At Ellis Island, a seemingly trivial event occurred that would profoundly affect the Warburgs in the future. By chance, an immigration officer placed a stamp in Eric's passport that gave him residence status. In the future, he merely had to renew this visa at six-month intervals to maintain his status. Interpreting this as an omen, Eric would keep returning to America so that in 1938 he managed to obtain U.S. citizenship in a week while hordes of German Jews futilely struggled to get in.

Always an admirer of Uncle Paul, Eric worked at the International Acceptance Bank and trained with Piggy. Several times weekly, he and his uncle saw John Foster Dulles of Sullivan & Cromwell, who performed legal work for the bank. Living at Woodlands, Eric took ski trips to New England and joined Felix for summer sails to Maine. He had a chameleon's adaptability in foreign countries that made him seem at home everywhere. After his puritanical German upbringing, Eric loved his exuberant, irreverent American cousins, who teased him mercilessly. Still timid about sex, he liked the swinging style of cousin Freddy's bachelor group. At parties, ogling a pretty young woman, he would whisper, "Freddy, that one's a peach. Please present me."[2] He was especially close to Paul's daughter, Bettina. Their relationship evidently took a romantic turn when they traveled to Spain together one year. It was not the only such liaison between the German and American cousins.

In 1924, Eric set off on a train tour of the United States with his oldest Hamburg friend, Wolfgang Rittmeister. Equipped with introductory letters, they received friendly receptions everywhere. Paul provided Eric with a letter to the president of the First National Bank of Portland, Oregon, who offered Eric a job in the foreign department. Delighted by the Oregon greenery—the rainy climate reminded him of Hamburg—he sold his return train ticket and worked at the bank. He rode horses, fell in love, and tooled about in an old Chevrolet Max bought him. It was a welcome respite from Hamburg, where every step in his life seemed predetermined by his father.

When Max grew alarmed that the crown prince might abdicate and stay in Oregon, he ordered him home. Eric wouldn't leave and suggested that his father train the brighter Siegmund as the future senior partner. (In later years, Eric would laughingly claim credit for Siegmund's success.) Instead, at Max's behest, Paul laid down the law to his nephew. "My dear boy," he wrote, "there are those so unable to help themselves that they can only get out of a bath when they have pulled a plug. Others can't bring themselves even to pull the plug. So I am going to pull the plug for you. Come back to New York."[3] Thus ended Eric's western adventure. Back in New York, he worked for the American and Continental Corporation, the IAB subsidiary that was granting credits to Europe.

Returning to Hamburg in 1926, Eric moved into the original Kösterberg house called Noah's Ark. He and Wolfgang Rittmeister bought an old Danish customs cruiser, which they converted into a fast, seaworthy yacht called the *Kong Bele*. It would be Eric's form of escape, his floating sanctuary, during the Third Reich. A social butterfly, Eric often sailed with his aristocratic companions and had few Jewish friends. Like Max, he identified with Judaism for its social and ethical values, not for its spiritual essence. In the late 1920s, Eric fell in love with a non-Jewish girl named Beatrice Blohm whose father came from an old Hamburg merchant family in the Venezuelan trade. Max was ready to let Eric marry her, but Alice firmly opposed it. Apparently, Malice had to break up other affairs as well, and Eric would remain a bachelor until the late 1940s.

Eric was conscientious at work, but not strongly motivated. At noon each day, he trooped to the stock exchange and watched the traders shouting at each other. Specializing in Scandinavia, he got to know the Wallenbergs and the other influential families. Already Eric gravitated toward charity work, serving as treasurer of Aby's library. Despite lukewarm enthusiasm for banking, Eric advanced at M. M. Warburg with the magic speed of the heir apparent. In January 1927, less than a year after returning from America, he was named *Einzelprokurist*, or a holder of the power of attorney. Siegmund wouldn't attain this distinction for two more years and never forgot the snub from Uncle Max. It converted him into a lifelong militant on the subject of nepotism.

With some conspicuous exceptions, such as Paul and Jimmy, Warburg boys tended to fall into one of two patterns: they were either weak sons cowed by strong fathers or strong sons emboldened by weak fathers. Siegmund fell into the second category. His father, Georges, was something of a family misfit. Even as his celebrated cousins attained dazzling success, Georges led a troubled life. He was a poor student who suffered from dreadful headaches, hiccups, and a crippling stutter that he only cured with difficulty. Kind, warm-hearted, spontaneous, he also had an ungovernable temper.[4] The thin, excitable Georges grew so gaunt that the doctors had to recommend a high-calorie diet.

When a doctor blamed steam heat for Georges's headaches, Théophilie dispatched him to a coal-heated school near Stuttgart. An avid reader, Georges excelled in history, but doctors thought a historian's career too strenuous for him and urged a tranquil life as a gentleman farmer. So Théophilie bought him an estate, Uhenfels, in the Swabian Alps near Urach, not far from Stuttgart, which had been owned by the royal marshal of the king of Württemberg. Set in a beautiful rocky spot with soaring vistas, the house sat on a steeply wooded hillside fed by streams and overlooking a small valley. Uhenfels was a curious blend of the rich and rustic. A place of Spartan comforts often snowbound in winter, it had unheated hallways, lacked running water, and was lit by kerosene lamps. Instead of renting out the tiny storybook castle, Georges saved it for the overflow from family visits. This pastoral corner of Germany was the antithesis of bustling Hamburg and gave Siegmund an entirely different upbringing from his cousins.

In December 1901, Georges married Lucie Kaulla, the daughter of a Stuttgart lawyer. They met through Otto Kaulla, who married Georges's sister, Lilly, earlier in the year. The following September, Lucie gave birth in Tübingen to their sole child, the receptacle of their dreams, Siegmund George. The infant's grandfather of the same name had died thirteen years before and thirteen would be this Siegmund's lucky number.

In southwest Germany, Kaulla was a name to conjure with, surpassing that of Warburg in prestige. As Court Jews to German and Austrian courts, the family was ennobled and intermarried with other banking clans. During the Napoleonic Wars, they provided credit, horses, and other commodities to the Kingdom of Württemberg and even shared a salt monopoly with the prince. They cofounded the Württemburgische Hofbank, the outstanding regional bank. The Kaullas belonged more to the grand world of the court than to the Jewish community.

At the turn of the century, Lucie seemed destined for life as an old maid and didn't marry until age thirty-five. A short, quiet, tidy woman who was quite well educated, she often dressed in black. She was modest, slow-moving, and conscientious in everything she did. Weak and sickly, Georges was five years her junior. Lucie had been a delicate child, too, and was considered too frail to marry. Georges and Lucie would be totally devoted to each other, achieving a collective strength that neither could have managed alone.

Lucie's fragility covered an iron tenacity. (Perhaps inherited from her mother, who at age eighty startled a burglar by hollering, "Get out of my house at once!"[5]) Lucie was very musical, played the piano, and composed waltzes, marches, and minuets. Like many German Jews, she had absorbed classical culture from Goethe to Beethoven and was highly patriotic. Her ideals, values, and biases were passed on to her son. Lucie appreciated smart people and lacked interest in high society with its superficial striving. Totally unsnobbish, she schooled Siegmund to disdain the frippery he would find rife among his Hamburg relatives. Instead she inculcated in him a deeply puritanical sense of service, and he always retained something of his mother's critical reserve toward splendid people.

Lucie had signed on for a loving but trying marriage. Her poetry and music hadn't exactly prepared her for running a large, backward estate, with fields, orchards, stables, and eighty-four hundred sheep. Every day Georges strode the fields and ably managed the books, yet he squabbled with the estate steward, forcing Lucie to arbitrate. The first fifteen years of their marriage were reasonably happy. Georges served as the town's deputy mayor and presided over Social Democratic rallies, buying kegs of beer to woo thirsty voters.

The war shattered this life. During this bleak time of extreme poverty, starving Swabian peasants scrounged for food at Uhenfels while the Warburgs tended wounded soldiers. Extremely patriotic, Georges invested his fortune of six million gold marks in war bonds that depreciated to virtual worthlessness in the postwar inflation. The teenage Siegmund supported the war and engaged in heated arguments with his skeptical father. This boyhood chauvinism would leave him with a permanent mistrust of patriotism, planting the seeds of the future world citizen.

In 1916 Georges's mental state worsened. His headaches intensified, his temper flared more readily, he exhibited symptoms of severe manic-depression. He had a disturbed look in his eye. Later, Siegmund scarcely talked about his father, as if the memories were too painful, though he always kept a photo of Georges by his bed. "My father was of the most spontaneous and warm-hearted nature, but the more his suffering increased, the more difficult it became to protect him from deep depressions and shattering agitation," he said.[6] Henceforth, Lucie both nursed her husband and cared for the estate, which she did in stoical, uncomplaining style. To avoid jarring Georges's nerves, she made the ultimate sacrifice: she ceased playing her beloved piano.

A photo of Siegmund during the war shows a serious little boy in knicker-bockers, with a faraway look in his eyes. He had little contact with other local children. To fill this solitude, he read an enormous amount, and books piled up in his corner room. He grew accustomed to creating imaginary worlds and extravagant dreams. He attended the Humanistisches Gymnasium in Reutlingen and enjoyed the classical languages, but he hated absences from home. So that he could stay home with Lucie and read, he learned how to fake illness by manipulating the thermometer, and Lucie turned a blind eye to her son's trick. He had a far more positive experience at the Evangelisches Seminar in Urach, where he was the first Jewish student to be admitted since its 1479 founding. In photos with classmates, Siegmund stands out as a slight, dark boy surrounded by tall blond young men. Already he seemed marked out as someone apart from the crowd. He earned excellent grades and wanted to become a teacher.

The supreme influence upon Siegmund's life was Lucie. She was his all-purpose sage, his inexhaustible fountain of epigrams. Their relationship was deepened by the isolated estate; the troubled, infirm father; Siegmund's status as an only child; his extraordinary precocity; and his unusual sensitivity to adult concerns. One suspects that Siegmund's career was first conceived in Lucie's mind, just as Charlotte and Sara had implanted ambition in their sons. Lucie passed on to him her own perfectionism. She had been taught to prepare for things meticulously, execute them thoroughly, and then criticize her own performance. It was a chess master's approach to life, with chance reduced to a minimum by premeditation and postmortems. Treated like a little adult, Siegmund had no governess or sibling to offset Lucie's training.

A true daughter of the Enlightenment, Lucie believed in reason, discipline, and willpower. She repeated to Siegmund a maxim she learned from her father: "My child, when you must choose between two different paths, ask yourself which is the harder one for you, and once you are clear about it, choose the harder path; this will prove to be the right one."[7] That path had to be pursued with unflinching toughness, whatever the pain. Contrary to what one might expect, Siegmund found nothing grim about this upbringing. "I think the general view of people—that puritanism is something necessarily depressing, dark, shadowy—is wrong."[8]

To be sure, Lucie had a wry, subtle sense of humor and a quiet *joie de vivre*, but otherwise everything about Siegmund's childhood seemed serious and weighty. He always carried the unspoken sorrows of this solitary boyhood, giving him a melancholy cast. In later years, he would lack small talk, easy chatter—the everyday currency of social intercourse. Lucie trained Siegmund, formed his work habits, and reasoned with him about everything. For five years, she helped him with his homework in a loving but unsparing manner. If he made a tiny error, he had to rewrite the entire page. "She would repeat the criticism of something I'd done, again and again, until she was certain I would not forget it," said Siegmund.[9] To improve his memory, he had to learn poems by rote and sometimes cried when he couldn't reproduce them just as Lucie wished. Siegmund must have been very secure in his mother's love that he wasn't crushed by this rigorous training.

Lucie instilled in him such a reverence for the higher life of the mind as to unsuit him for more mundane pleasures. When Siegmund was eight, he returned home with a chocolate bar that he had bought with his allowance money and Lucie reprimanded him for not spending it on something worthwhile. (By no coincidence, Siegmund would always struggle with a craving for forbidden chocolates.) When he left for his first dancing lesson, Lucie said, "If you see an ugly girl standing alone you should go and ask her to dance."[10] These sentiments were noble, but asked a lot of a young boy. Lucie's world was cerebral, controlled. Everything seemed to unfold under the aspect of eternity.

In her religion, Lucie was a prototypical German Jew, imbued with a sense of Jewish tradition shorn of mysticism. Her Judaism was an amalgam of rationalist philosophy and German classical culture. To Siegmund, she often quoted Schiller's lines: "Which religion do I profess? None of those you name. And why none? From religious conviction."[11] At age fifteen, she had received a Jewish prayer book in German dedicated with a motto from Plato. She emphasized ethical obligations, often saying that happiness arose from duties fulfilled. Until Siegmund was thirteen, she joined him for bedside prayers each night, even if entertaining dinner guests. On the eve of his bar mitzvah (when he gave his speech in Latin) she told him that, henceforth, he must pray alone. "When you pray, the most important thing is to think very hard about all the wrong things you have done during the day. And if you cannot think of at least five or six or seven things you have done wrong, then something is wrong with you."[12] Discipline and self-criticism were stressed, not compromise or forgiveness. One can see here the clear overlap of German and Jewish culture, with their similar exaggerated regard for work and achievement.

Siegmund's relationship with Lucie set the pattern for others in his life. She so adored her son that it made him accustomed to unqualified loyalty and an absence of strong dissent from people. He would later transfer these often highly unrealistic demands to the world at large. Lucie also left him with extremely high standards, both for himself and others, that a messy, disorganized, and fallible world would always frustrate.

Though exiled from Hamburg, Georges was an avid student of Warburg history and knew the family tree intimately. He tutored Siegmund about how his industrious grandfather Siegmund built up M. M. Warburg & Co. while the lazy, spoiled Moritz attended to Sara. After Paul became a partner with Max, the Alsterufer Warburgs felt entitled to a second partnership to even the scales. To this end, Georges was given the right to enter the firm with his brother, Aby S. Because he had waived that right, he and the other Alsterufer Warburgs thought Siegmund entitled to a partnership.

In 1919, Siegmund was seventeen and in a quandary about his future when uncle Max took things in hand. He knew Siegmund was smarter than Eric and already saw in him flashes of his grandfather. "What do you want to do now?" Max asked. Siegmund said he wished to study history and philosophy, then go into politics. Max, scapegoated for Versailles, must have been dubious. He pretended to agree with Siegmund while pushing him in another direction. "I think that's an excellent idea," he replied. "But what I think you should do in addition is work for a few years in our old banking firm, because it may be very useful for you to know a little about business."[13]

Still green and bashful, Siegmund was flattered by Max's attention and very impressed by his charm and flair. While Georges wanted his son to inherit his estate, he realized that Siegmund looked beyond the Swabian Alps, so encouraged him to train in Hamburg. In 1920, Siegmund moved into the Alsterufer house of uncle Aby S. His entrance into the Hamburg bank foreclosed other careers—teaching, politics, philosophy—that would always tease him with a sense of phantom might-have-beens. The Alsterufer Warburgs at once feared that the Mittelwegs might try to steal Siegmund to their side. "Intrigues against Siegmund to move to Mittelweg and out of Alsterufer," his cousin Olga recorded in her diary in October, 1921.[14]

That year, Georges suffered the first of several strokes that forced Lucie to attend to him night and day. She handled him with great solicitude, sharing his happiness while shielding him from care. In October 1923—right at the peak of the inflation—Georges died at fifty-two and was buried on the estate. In his will, he left a special bequest enabling every child in the village, at some point, to take a four-day Swiss holiday. This made him a sainted figure in local memory.

Georges's death left a distraught Lucie terribly burdened, and Max promised he would take care of Siegmund. Lucie began a long, bittersweet widowhood. While still managing the estate, she returned to the piano for the first time in years. Twice weekly, she took lessons in Stuttgart and resumed composing and playing Beethoven and Bach. In her musical compositions, Siegmund thought he detected a buried yearning for happiness beyond earthly cares. Georges's death only deepened the already intense bond between mother and son.

With his father dead and the family fortune wasted by inflation, Siegmund, twenty-one, assumed premature responsibility. He would always be stooped under one burden or another, lending a somber air to his elegance. Georges's death sharpened his sense of the Mittelweg-Alsterufer rivalry. Two weeks after his father's passing, Siegmund told Aby S.'s son, Karl, that the death reminded him of their family legacy and how few male heirs they had in their branch.[15] He was the only son bright and able enough to assert the Alsterufer honor at the bank.

Siegmund's experience in the Hamburg family would leave him scarred and embittered. At the bank, he worked extremely hard but didn't advance as fast as he hoped. He stood far above his peers there. His cousin, Karl, had been slow in school and was often rebuked by Max for his sluggish, perfunctory manner. Eric, though bright, was distracted by his busy social affairs and often absent. Siegmund felt himself a star deprived of his rightful place in the Warburg firmament because he came from the wrong side of the family. For the first (but hardly the last) time, Siegmund knew the stifled resentment of the gifted outsider who feels excluded by well-born insiders.

Siegmund must have envied Eric, with his many friends and doting sisters. Even as Siegmund bore the yoke of early responsibility, Eric courted adventure and romance in Hamburg and America. Competitive and bright, Siegmund saw his Hamburg relatives coasting on their names and Eric, in particular, seemed to embody the vanity of inherited wealth. Siegmund would always be sensitive to Eric's frivolous, social-climbing side, but less sensitive to his sterling qualities, his personal generosity, devotion to charity, and good nature.

Siegmund faced ostracism from the Mittelweg family. Having grown up in rustic Swabia, he was the country bumpkin from a remote, slow-paced region. He was teased as a bookworm and a mother's boy who was always writing to Lucie. He suddenly encountered *raffinée* cousins who dressed stylishly, wrote poems, and threw fancy parties. He was well worked over by the Mittelweg snobs and gossips. "We treated him like dirt," conceded Aby M.'s daughter, Frede. "He wasn't from Hamburg and we were young and foolish."[16] Not all Warburgs felt repentant about their early treatment of Siegmund. "He was conceited and very bright," said Bettina. "He and Eric were neck and neck all the time in the firm. Siegmund felt he was from the inferior branch of the family and brighter than Eric. But Eric was papa's son and in the saddle."[17] Max fed Siegmund's bitterness through blatant favoritism. At day's end, he would call in Eric and confide in him about business matters. Eric believed this partiality bred envy in Siegmund, who was extremely sensitive to slights.

Siegmund reacted to condescension by putting on airs and adopting a superior pose, wrapping himself in a moody, Byronic aura of mystery. Like most loners, he nursed his wounds and hid his emotions, awaiting his chance for vindication, even revenge. At the bank, he had many friends who found him a keen listener and warm, stimulating companion. And he wasn't shunned by all Mittelweg Warburgs. He was a great favorite of Louise Derenberg (Fritz's twin sister) and her husband. Their daughter, Gabriele, liked to chat with this brainy, attractive cousin. In the mid-1920s, when Siegmund stayed with Louise's family, she taught the rustic relative how to tie a tuxedo tie.

Whatever his inner bruises, Siegmund found many role models in Hamburg. In the early years, he loved Max's swagger and would later adopt many of his sayings and methods in London. At first he found Carl Melchior cool and forbidding, then developed an enormous admiration for him. He saw Melchior as an Erasmus-like figure who pursued truth and mastered his emotions. Siegmund would mimic the way Melchior reviewed all options in a discussion before advancing his position, or the way Melchior wrote brief cryptic rejection letters to minimize the offence given.

In 1925, Siegmund apprenticed at N. M. Rothschild & Sons in London, auditing courses in currency theory and other subjects at Cambridge University. As he roamed about the quadrangles, he drank in the magnificent architecture and fragrant greenery. Foreshadowing things to come, he wrote home, "My love for Germany hasn't diminished here, but I admire many things and one quickly feels at home here."[18] Again an outsider, he didn't join a college, claiming they were all ruled by cliques. In London, Siegmund already betrayed a knack for latching on to exceptional people, including a young German banker named Hermann Abs, apprenticing with Guaranty Trust. The two young men went to the theater and concerts together, forming an important intellectual friendship.

Back in Hamburg, Siegmund fell in love with a spectacularly beautiful young Swedish woman named Eva Maria Philipson, a distant relative. Eva had instinctive elegance. After the rough-hewn Uhenfels, she must have seemed a vision from paradise. Her exceedingly handsome father, Mauritz, headed the Svenska Handelsbanken, a rival to the Wallenbergs' Enskilda Bank. He was a strong, forbidding man, a domineering father, and a tough negotiator. Though Jewish, Mr. Philipson was the first in his family to marry outside the faith. Raised as a Protestant, Eva knew the Bible intimately.

Eva was born into a family that favored a cloistered life for young girls, had a strict, repressive childhood, and stood at the mercy of a horrible governess. She was so regularly reprimanded by her parents that one day at the dining table she looked up at a painting on the wall and told her irritated parents, "Grandpa isn't cross with me." Her strict father discouraged her interest in nursing and dance and her mother always dressed her in fashionable sailor suits that she hated. Eva's brother was a Nordic giant, enormously tall and good-looking. The Philipsons believed Eva should know foreign languages and rotated her through England and France. In the mid-1920s, she was sent to Hamburg, partly to learn German and partly to protect her from the murky enchantments of Paris. Hamburg seemed a safe refuge, and she stayed with Fritz and Anna Beata, who came from the Swedish Warburgs.

When Fritz took her to the bank one day, she was at first delighted. Then he led her to a desk, handed her copy to type, and left the room. Suddenly realizing she had been involuntarily drafted as a secretary, she burst into tears. When another secretary asked what was wrong, she said, "I have a terrible cold."[19] The young men in the bank fiercely vied for Eva and all work stopped when she entered a room. Eva and Siegmund fell in love instantly. She was attracted by his dark good looks, his dazzling intelligence. His passionate intensity must have been irresistible after her severely formal upbringing. She had been taught to swim, sail, and sew, but not to read. For Siegmund, Eva was the stuff of boyish fantasy, stylish, *soignée*, but also bright. She had fashion-plate good looks and a serious, if still untutored, interest in politics and ideas.

Fearing his catty cousins, Eva insisted they keep the love affair and the engagement secret. One day, she was traveling on a train with her parents when she screwed up her courage and announced, "I'm engaged." She knew her parents would be shocked and they jumped in amazement. To denigrate Siegmund's conquest, the Mittelweg Warburgs grudgingly said they felt sorry for Eva. But Siegmund was an extremely eligible young man and Eva felt very lucky to beat out the stiff competition. Some Warburgs did see Eva as a bit of fluff and no match for her deep-thinking fiancé.

But Eva was more than pretty decoration for Siegmund. As the more worldly partner from a high-society background, she had a maternal tenderness toward this young man who still had a country roughness. For all her feminine charm, Eva was tough-minded in dealing with people and less likely than Siegmund to be swayed or blinded by emotion. With Siegmund prone to swing from excessive enthusiasm to equally unwarranted pessimism, Eva provided emotional stability. She was the gyroscope that kept him on a steady course. Near the end of his life, Siegmund alluded to this difference: "My wife says that in certain dealings with human beings I am a baby."[20]

Siegmund and Eva went to Swabia to announce their engagement to Lucie.

Though Siegmund wasn't an observant Jew, Eva converted to Judaism to satisfy the Warburgs and, on the eve of their wedding, went to a *mikveh* or ritual bath in Stuttgart.

On November 8, 1926, Eva and Siegmund were married in the Golden Hall of the Grand Hotel in Stockholm in a huge society affair attended by the Wallenbergs, the Fränkels, and the Swedish banking elite. About two hundred guests were present, with a contingent of more than forty people from Hamburg. Three people officiated over the ceremony: the mayor of Stockholm flanked by the chief rabbi of Stockholm and the Philipson family pastor. At this tense affair, the Jews sat on one side of the aisle, the Christians on the other. Notable among the guests were several dashing young men in brilliant blue military uniforms reputed to be disappointed suitors.

The wedding pictures convey sadness behind the glitter. Siegmund liked simplicity and he and Eva seem smothered and oppressed by all the pomp. The photos also show that Siegmund was now a mature, sophisticated young man. He was already highly moody and had a fearsome temper. Next to his cubbyhole at the Grand Hotel, one reception clerk pinned a note with the warning, "If he rings, you must RUN" to answer. Following the Stockholm wedding, Siegmund and Eva had a small, private Jewish ceremony in Germany.

After their marriage, at Max's direction, Siegmund began an apprenticeship in the United States. In 1927, the newlyweds sailed for Boston, where Siegmund worked for the accounting firm of Lybrand Ross Brothers & Montgomery. Their first child, George, was born in Boston. Siegmund loved the American lust for enterprise and freedom from tradition, yet also deplored the cultural homogeneity and standardization. Shocked by his own ignorance of American history, he drew up a reading list and spent a lot of time closeted with his books. Playing Pygmalion, he had Eva read the books, too.

Before leaving the United States, Siegmund worked with Paul at the IAB and Felix at Kuhn, Loeb in late 1927 and early 1928. In remarkable letters that Siegmund wrote to Eva's father, it is apparent that he developed a quick distaste for his American relations—which they would richly repay over the years. While he found the Friedaflix children nice and lively, they struck him as indifferent to matters of the spirit and he said that among the Americans he met, he liked his own family least. As with American Jews generally, he thought the New York Warburgs were parvenus ashamed of their roots and trying too hard to be Americanized.

Siegmund observed the friction between Paul and Morti Schiff and reflected that they were better off in separate firms.[21] Though he found Paul hypersensitive, Siegmund was otherwise overcome with admiration for his fine, subtle humanity. He found Jimmy a gifted but frightful bluffer who preferred debating to doing things, got into too many fights with people (especially Uncle

Max), and was an unreliable friend. As would happen again in the 1950s, Siegmund saw Kuhn, Loeb as a fading star. For all its strength in the railroad and steel industries, he thought the firm dangerously overloaded with vain, snobbish partners who preferred their hobbies to hard work. It was a prescient insight.

With his international seasoning and exquisite wife, Siegmund perhaps felt that he had exorcised past hardship. He was a rising young man, who enjoyed his food, wine, and cigars and liked sporty, dapper clothing. Yet there had already been a reminder of fate's malevolence. This misfortune came from a freak accident. Siegmund had a cousin, the smiling, bespectacled Albert Kaulla, who was like a brother to him. One Christmas at Uhenfels, Albert had accidentally swallowed a thumbtack that did no immediate harm but couldn't be located by X-rays. The family hoped that someday it would naturally be expelled. Then while Albert trained at M. M. Warburg the thumbtack reappeared, piercing his lung as he exercised one morning. On February 15, 1927, he died at age twenty-two. A distraught Siegmund swore to Lilly and Otto Kaulla that he would try to replace Albert and be a son to them.[22] When his own son, George, was born seven months later, Siegmund gave him the middle name of Albert.

Then a flaw appeared in the crystalline perfection of the marriage. On November 1930, Eva, age twenty-seven, gave birth to a daughter, Anna, in Hamburg. When the nurse brought Anna to Eva for breast-feeding, she was disturbed by a spot on Eva's breast. It was diagnosed as cancer and the breast was removed. Eva's dignified reaction to this disfigurement showed her inner strength and lack of self-pity. It also started a lifelong struggle with cancer.

Around this time, Siegmund saw the limits of his prospects at M. M. Warburg. Eric might be agreeable, but Siegmund had no respect for him as a banker. In January 1929, Eric became a partner along with Dr. Ernst Spiegelberg, while Siegmund only graduated to *Einzelprokurist*, or a holder of the power of attorney, along with Dr. Hans Meyer. Siegmund didn't become a partner until 1930.

Now Siegmund began to create distance between himself and Max. For a long time, Siegmund had chided his uncle for not opening a Berlin branch. Max was afraid of offending banking friends and only kept a pied-à-terre there to conduct political talks and entertain clients. Regarding this as foolish obstinacy, Siegmund began to think of Max as a dilettante strategist. He also suspected that the Emperor Maximilian, as he dubbed him, was afraid that he wouldn't be able to control everything that went on in a Berlin office. Siegmund saw Berlin as a place where he could run his own show and enjoy a sophisticated political and cultural milieu. Unlike other Warburgs, Siegmund found Hamburg hopelessly provincial.

Siegmund aroused Max's fury by siding with Jimmy over the need to merge with the powerful Berliner Handels-Gesellschaft. When Max finally agreed to open a Berlin branch in 1931, Siegmund was appointed manager, thus opening his escape route from the Hamburg bank. Apparently he took full advantage of his freedom to the point where Max confronted him, chiding him for keeping him in the dark about his doings and insisting that he file a weekly report on his activities.

Siegmund would always be steeped in the intellectual world of Weimar Germany. He had intense respect for his Uncle Aby. He also admired Walther Rathenau and Gustav Stresemann, regretting they didn't inspire the same hero-worship as the militaristic Hindenburg and Ludendorff. He had a penchant for the bold, sweeping, rather grandiose historical theories that flourished amid the turbulence and decay. He liked strong, unsentimental ideas that provoked thought and shocked the complacent. Devouring Spengler, he was infected by the deep cultural pessimism of the 1920s, which suited his melancholic nature. The notion of global decay, of apocalyptic change, seemed to appeal to him. He responded to Hegel's view of history as a vast progression of dialectical change. Such theories, which viewed the petty affairs of men from a godlike perspective, suited his pose of intellectual superiority. Fortified by Spengler and Hegel, he floated above the fray.

Another important influence was Nietzsche, especially *Beyond Good and Evil*. The philosopher's contempt for the weak, mediocre conformists of modern Europe struck a deep chord in Siegmund, who had found examples in his own Hamburg family. Siegmund liked the notion that Providence supplied a special dispensation to superior men. He was always interested in the exceptional individual who wished to sweep away the dead encumbrances of the past and start a new order.

In 1930, Siegmund gave a funeral oration for his uncle, Marc Rosenberg, a charismatic art historian and a dashing freethinker. Siegmund's speech displayed his flair for theatrics and powerful imagery. He lauded Rosenberg as a lonely visionary, dedicated to high ideals. Rosenberg could well sneer at the cheap applause of the vulgar crowd, for he was the Nietzschean *Übermensch.* "Lightning and thunder could flash from his eyes, the lightning of vision and the thunder of indignation, an unholy thunderstorm that, far beyond good and evil, tried to crush everything petty and ugly. . . ."[23] For Siegmund, Rosenberg represented a dying breed of true aristocrats, who fought the solitary fight for truth. "He had the most difficult courage that exists, the courage of loneliness and independence."[24] The hyperbole reflected a tendency toward hero-worship that never entirely deserted Siegmund, who, in personal letters and speeches, was often carried away by the mood of the moment.

Another revered figure was Stefan Zweig, who had become a pacifist during the war and lived in Austria. By 1923, Siegmund, twenty-one, was corresponding with the famous writer, having sent him a fan letter about his biography of Romain Rolland. As with Rosenberg, Siegmund admired qualities in Zweig that seemed to mirror his own. He liked his refusal to take easy, crowd-pleasing positions, the way he spurned the superficial pleasures of radio and sports. Like Rosenberg, Zweig relished books and ancient beauty while rejecting soft, corrupt, bourgeois pleasures. Siegmund shared Zweig's pessimistic view that the world might pass through a dark, collectivist period of state bureaucracies before returning to a time of individual freedom. This dark interlude would be filled with gloom, barbarism, and intolerance.

The move to Berlin gave Siegmund a front-row seat for the disintegrating Weimar Republic. Sharply critical of the Young Plan, he joked that it would lead to ever "younger" plans until the whole reparations farce ended.[25] When the Credit-Anstalt collapsed, he saw that the fixed stars could indeed fall from the heavens. As he later said, "It was fantastic. People everywhere had said it couldn't happen. Well, it did happen."[26] Heading a Berlin office of about ten people, Siegmund dipped into politics and wrote political pamphlets. He later said only Hitler's advent ended his career in politics.[27] Siegmund liked to shake things up and often expressed shocking political opinions. In 1930, he told historian Alfred Vagts that a German war against Russia would solve internal German problems and crises.[28]

In the Warburg debate over Hitler's future, Siegmund would later symbolize the pessimistic, far-sighted view of events. Yet before 1933, he was far less alarmed than Uncle Max and, in fact, conspicuously blind to the threat. In 1930, he told his cousin Karl that he didn't share the resentment toward the Nazis common in their circles. The anti-Semitism aside, he saw redeeming qualities in the party. "The Nazis are doubtless in part dreadfully primitive in human and political terms," he wrote. "On the other hand, one finds among a large part of them valuable, typically German strengths, which are indeed incredible in a political connection, but show strong feeling for social and national duties. . . ." He regretted that the ranters had given anti-Semitism a central party role.[29] With his Hegelian vision, Siegmund seemed philosophically resigned to the growing radicalism of late Weimar Germany, arguing that it was a transitional part of the ebb and flow of history.

Like Carl Melchior, Siegmund succumbed to the delusion that if the Nazis entered the cabinet, they would behave more responsibly. "I have no doubt that the Nazis, once they are in the government . . . would hardly commit any more stupidities than most other governments."[30] This is worth stressing, for Siegmund was later withering in his mockery of Uncle Max's belief that the Nazi fever would pass. Yet in December 1931, Siegmund urgently told Jimmy that Germany needed shock treatment and that the longer the Nazis were banned from government, the more power they would wield when they entered it. A certain amount of anti-Semitism, he conceded, would accompany this move. "But I don't believe that any deeply invasive measures in this direction will be taken and that, in any event, only during a short, transitional period, because the best and most capable followers of the Hitler movement won't go along with such demagogic trains of thought."[31] If Siegmund was later caustic about those misled by false hopes, it probably stemmed, in part, from embarrassment about his own youthful myopia.

CHAPTER 26

Journey into Fear

The worst casualty of the global depression, the Germany of 1932 was fertile ground for demagogues, as unemployment soared to almost 30 percent of the work force. In Hamburg, knots of children gathered before open windows, singing hymns so that strangers would toss down coins. The fleet of mothballed ships grew daily in the harbor. This abject misery made the populace ripe for irrational diatribes against Jewish bankers, enabling the Nazis to give a leftish veneer to their propaganda and feed off populist resentment of the rich.

Their screeds extended to corporations with close ties to Jewish banks, such as the chemical giant I. G. Farben, which had ten Jews, including Max Warburg, on its boards. In June 1931, the Nazi press branded the concern a tool of the "Jew Warburg."[1] With malicious humor, I. G. Farben was restyled "Isidore G. Farber."[2] Afraid that its state-backed synthetic fuel program might run into political obstacles, the firm dispatched two operatives to meet with Hitler in June 1932. Already envisioning the Volkswagen and the Autobahn, Hitler recognized the importance of synthetic fuel and muted subsequent attacks on the firm. That year, Max left the Farben supervisory board.

For Max, the progressively more strident anti-Semitism provoked an emotional mix of anger and dismay. He thought the Nazi fever would fade as prosperity returned, that the intolerance was just a passing phase. In the meantime, he fulminated against a cowardly middle class that groveled before Hitler and was aghast that Germany should repay its loyal Jewish citizens with such ingratitude. The *Vaterland* had "left the ranks of civilized nations and lined up with the ranks of pogrom nations. Nothing has so depressed me as a German in recent years as this anti-Semitic propaganda. . . ."[3] When he resigned from the German People's Party in 1932, he ruefully joked that Germany only had parties one could leave, none that one could join.[4] Max had long cudgeled his brain for ways to reconcile German and Jewish tradition, but this exercise now seemed futile. For the Warburgs, the stars had darkened.

The Nazis triumphed at a time when German Jews were sloughing off their Jewish identity. Hitler caught them off balance, leaning the wrong way. In 1932, the rate of intermarriage among Jews reached an astounding 60 percent.[5] With just a modicum of patience, the Nazis could have solved the entire "Jewish Problem" through sheer inaction. The Holocaust originated in a country where the Jewish population was highly acculturated, lending the violence a bitter, fratricidal edge. In the Soviet Union, gentiles looked down on downtrodden Jews, but in Germany, they envied them, even though Jews comprised less than 1 percent of the population. It wasn't their alien quality so much as their familiarity, their uncomfortable resemblance to other Germans, that enabled Hitler to tap fears of "racial pollution." His stress on biological purity would have made no sense if Jews hadn't mingled so intimately with non-Jews.

For a well-connected Hamburg banker, the enemy could seem curiously faceless. Max dealt mostly with upper-crust industrial leaders, who largely opposed Hitler in the early days. Wealthy Germans derided National Socialists as contemptible boors and dreaded their alleged socialism. More contact with small businessmen might have spared Max many illusions. Only at Bad Harzburg in October 1931 did major industrialists of the Ruhr and Rhineland flirt openly with the Nazis; Dr. Schacht, steel magnate Fritz Thyssen, and other businessmen joined with them in declaring a national front against Bolshevism.

The Warburgs did fight the Nazis. Eric joined a group called the Circle of Young Hamburgers, which fought against the polarization of the late Weimar period.[6] In September 1931, they waged a successful campaign against the Nazis in local elections. Backing a centrist coalition, they distributed brochures that deplored both Left and Right extremism. They didn't focus on anti-Semitism but on Nazi protectionism, which threatened Hamburg's foreign trade. In an imaginative brochure entitled "Keep the Gate Open," the

Eric Warburg, Lola Hahn-Warburg, and her son, Oscar,
at Lola's Wannsee house in the 1920s.
(Courtesy of Anita Warburg)

Circle depicted a man valiantly pushing open the trade gates as Nazis and Communists tried to slam them shut.

In late 1931, Hamburg's Jews were shaken by a series of cemetery desecrations, and community leaders sought an ecumenical protest. Aby S. Warburg was assigned to appeal to the Protestant Church and he wrote to his friend, chief pastor Dr. Heinz Beckmann, suggesting that Jews unite with Christian leaders in a newspaper ad to protest these abominations. Beckmann declined in a mealy-mouthed reply. "If I may express my personal opinion, I don't expect much in these turbulent days from public statements. It is much more important that each man and woman, in the circles in which they can have an effect, should fully express their views repeatedly."[7] This letter foreshadowed the cowardice of many German pastors in protesting Nazi atrocities.

The economic crisis destroyed the republic's legitimacy, radicalized the masses, and destroyed the appeal of moderate parties to the middle class. By 1932, the ceremony of law disintegrated as street fights between Nazi and Communist thugs became daily events in Berlin. Communists would raid shops, then the Storm Troopers of the SA would show up as saviors of the shopkeepers. Many Hamburg stores sported swastika flags during Reichstag elections that summer, as fear gripped the seaport. As Christabel Bielenberg wrote, "I knew it to be advisable to refrain from taking a stroll through certain parts of Hamburg on a Sunday, because the Monday morning newspapers nearly always carried an obituary of an over-ardent politician, or of some innocent bystander, who found themselves taking part in a political demonstration over the weekend."[8]

The Warburgs hovered above the level of Brownshirt beatings, street taunts, and blatant humiliation. Yet they saw the abyss yawning before them. "The world grows blacker and blacker," Max wrote Jimmy in April 1932. "One always believes that it can't get any blacker, but then there are new surprises and you are amazed that you're still standing on your own two feet."[9]

In late May, Max was surprised when Brüning fell, succeeded by the centrist Franz von Papen. The strongman in the new cabinet was the defense minister, General Kurt von Schleicher, an authoritarian figure who had headed the political bureau of the Reichswehr. Both the chancellor and defense minister thought they could neutralize Hitler and manipulate him for their own purposes. The Warburgs didn't foresee that the von Papen government would destroy the last foundations of the republic and produce a deadly political vacuum. Siegmund applauded the changes, praising von Schleicher as courageous and decisive and von Papen as smart and decent.[10] Max hailed the new regime for its tough stand toward labor.[11] Only Felix spied a conspiratorial pattern, viewing Brüning as victim of a plot masterminded by industrialists who wanted to abolish the welfare state.[12]

As the Warburgs discussed collective action in case of a Nazi victory, they faced the old dilemma of asserting their power and risking a backlash, or lowering their profile and emasculating themselves. Most of the time, they opted for caution. When discussing Nazi attacks against the Jewish deputy police commissioner of Berlin, Bernhard Weiss, Max argued: "Wouldn't it be better, if they [the Jews] kept in the background, in any event politically, in these times and didn't assume responsibilities they couldn't discharge?"[13]

In late July 1932, the Nazis scored stunning election gains. Capturing 13.7 million votes and 230 out of 608 Reichstag seats, they established themselves as the nation's largest party. Carl Melchior was appalled that respectable politicians now trafficked with men who "have committed murder in the usual sense of the Penal Code and thus should have been condemned to death even by a regular tribunal."[14] Though the murderers had momentum on their side, they suffered a temporary setback in the November elections, losing two million votes. We should note that on the eve of the Third Reich, a majority of Germans still opposed Hitler. Unfortunately, the opposition was badly splintered, Weimar's failures having discredited gradualist, reform politics. The constitutional sphere seemed irrelevant as four hundred thousand SA and SS thugs poured into the streets, giving "democracy" a paramilitary flavor.

What is striking in these waning Weimar days is how frequently the Warburgs were governed by hope and not fear. In their papers, the nearness of the impending nightmare isn't evident. In September 1932, Siegmund cabled Jimmy that the new government shouldn't create alarm: "On the contrary, probable that energetic, stable political development assured for next few months."[15] In December, Max told Felix that all was not bleak because Hindenburg had decided not to appoint Hitler as chancellor.[16] In a speech at the Rotary Club, Max lauded the year's "upward movement" and the "return to an even and calm development in politics and the economy."[17] Proximity blinded the German Warburgs, while distance aided their American relatives.

When Eric telephoned from London on January 30, 1933, he learned that Adolf Hitler had just become chancellor and declared that they should "give him enough rope to hang himself."[18] The Warburgs would nurse such forlorn hopes for years. At once, swastikas bloomed in Hamburg, as Jews were insulted by bands of newly emboldened Nazis. Throwing up barricades, the Communists tried a general strike, but the SA and SS cleared the streets.

For Max, Hitler's advent didn't express popular anger so much as high-level machinations. Unable to adjust to these grisly new realities—to see that history had turned a corner suddenly—he still placed his faith in the common sense of the German people. "I considered it absolutely inconceivable that this man [Hitler] could ever become sole ruler of one of the most creative, competent, industrious and powerful of peoples," he later confessed.[19] The events of early 1933 struck him as fleeting madness. Indeed, modern German history provided no precedent for such total, systematic barbarism. The gradual, stealthy pace of change helped to lull its targets. The strangler, by design, would tighten his grip slowly, then release it, then slowly tighten it again. "We always thought we had reached the all-time low," said Max's daughter, Gisela. "Then the Nazis would ingeniously invent something else."[20]

In retrospect, Max Warburg's actions over the next five years would seem blind, daring, foolhardy, and courageous all at once. He had strong powers of self-deception and one feels exasperated with his incurable hopefulness even as one admires his dogged courage in the face of incalculable danger. The glandular optimism, the sense of invincibility, that had lifted him to the apex of the German business world would now be his undoing. We should note that Max's views often reflected those of other Jewish leaders. After Hitler came to power, a major Jewish organization, the Centralverein, announced confidently, "We are thoroughly able to hold our own and to fight successfully against the attacks made by Mr. Hitler and his followers."[21]

As patrons of a rich array of local institutions, it seemed inconceivable to the Warburgs that they could ever be driven from Hamburg. In this tolerant, cosmopolitan city, the Nazi triumph didn't seem foreordained. The Warburgs believed in Hamburg's general freedom from anti-Semitism, although other Hamburg Jews saw the local variety as just more subtle and insidious. Not only did the aristocrats who lived by the Alster Lake have a snobbish contempt for the Nazis, but the left-wing dockworkers of "Red Hamburg" made it a stronghold for Social Democrats and Communists. In the Reichstag vote of March 5, 1933, these two parties got 44.5 percent of the Hamburg vote, surpassing the Nazis. Nationwide, however, the Nazis received 44 percent of the votes—their peak performance before the complete dismantling of democratic government.

In Hamburg, the party moved swiftly to suppress local dissent and consolidate their power. On March 8, when the Hamburg *Bürgerschaft* voted in a new senate, menacing Storm Troopers lined the chamber walls and excluded Social Democrats and Communists. Instead of the local *Gauleiter*, the Nazis installed as mayor the patrician Carl Vincent Krogmann who came from an old shipping family. Krogmann once said that he supported the Nazis because they seemed the only alternative to a dictatorship based on bayonets! After the new Nazi-dominated senate voted him in, Krogmann appeared on the *Rathaus* balcony amid resounding church bells, with the swastika flag flying overhead and jubilant throngs cheering below. Believing Krogmann a conciliatory figure, Max approved the choice. As Emil Helfferich, who participated in the selection process, said, "Krogmann with his unwavering single-mindedness deceived many who had expected him to be a compromiser, including Max Warburg."[22]

Less than a week later, Krogmann sent Baron von Schröder to see Max. The baron cordially explained that Max shouldn't take it amiss if the mayor didn't consult him as much in future about financial matters affecting the city. He said that Krogmann needed to refute charges in Nazi party circles that Max, "being the financial dictator of Hamburg, had insisted that he [Krogmann] be elected to his office and that he was really burgomaster" by Max's grace. Max replied that he understood and that Krogmann shouldn't worry.[23] Four days later, in a radio speech, Krogmann pandered to hatred of Jewish bankers, saying Hamburg must develop banks independent of Berlin banks and foreign connections—a clear swipe at M. M. Warburg.[24] Before long, the Nazis purged Jewish officials from the civil service, including Leo Lippmann, who had served Hamburg for decades. Upon hearing this, a shaken Max said, "Death rides fast."[25]

Despite these events, Max whistled in the dark, seeing Nazi ideology as a blend of good and bad ideas. Perhaps the evil elements could be purged, he thought, leaving the good. As with Siegmund, German Jews weren't entirely immune to the Nazis' ringing, nationalistic appeals, even if they abhorred the anti-Semitism. On March 19, Max told Jimmy that he hoped peace and order would soon prevail in Germany. Of the Nazis, he said, "It is a pity that this movement, which has so much good in it, is encumbered by so much rubbish and that the anti-Semitism makes it impossible to line up in formation with this movement."[26] Max fooled himself into believing that Dr. Schacht and non-Jewish friends would furnish political protection.

The Warburg women generally seemed less deluded, perhaps because they heard fewer promises from business associates who proved faithless in the end. Tough and unsentimental, Max's wife, Alice, thought it futile to stay in Germany and pleaded with her husband to leave. But Max said he must defend his firm and the Jewish community and so Alice stood loyally by his side. When Max urged Eric to leave for the United States, he refused to budge. "I didn't want—as the only son—to see my father in a German concentration camp while I was living on Park Avenue in New York."[27] Eric did, however, make trips to America over the next five years to renew his American residency status.

Stymied by Max's stubbornness, Felix used every stratagem to get him to leave. He saw that Max kept offering his love to a Germany that only reciprocated with hatred—the plight of so many German Jews. As someone who had idealized German culture, Felix was traumatized, too, by the Nazi takeover. Angry and perplexed, he walked around muttering, "I am so ashamed that this has happened."[28] Upset by events, he spent much of February and

March 1933 at home with a heart spasm. As he told Chaim Weizmann that April, "In regard to the madness of Germany, no words can express the disgust that everybody feels that that beautiful country should have gotten into such rotten hands. . . . My own people . . . still whip themselves into a hopefulness and the same old patriotism which had made them bring all kinds of sacrifices without receiving any reward. . . ."[29]

Constantly worried about his Hamburg relatives, Felix was often starved for information. Max likely kept him in the dark for several reasons. He doubtless feared the censor, didn't wish to worry Felix, and knew Felix opposed his decision to stay. The upshot was that Felix operated in a vacuum when he could have used news of Nazi oppression to lobby Washington.

Once the Nazis had cleansed Germany of opposition parties and ended parliamentary government, they turned their attention to the Jews. By mid-March, the rank-and-file were storming department stores and demanding a boycott of Jewish businesses. As much to guide as to incite these volatile emotions, Hitler and Goebbels championed the idea of a boycott. In a March 27 radio broadcast, the government announced that on the morning of April 1st, at the stroke of ten, SA and SS members would take up positions outside Jewish stores and warn the public not to enter. This offense was portrayed as a defensive measure against "Jewish atrocity propaganda abroad."[30] To add further terror, Göring told Jewish community leaders that they would be held responsible for any anti-German propaganda appearing abroad. Eager to create jobs through exports, Hitler wanted to minimize adverse publicity overseas.

In reacting to the boycott, a split was immediately apparent between foreign Jewish groups who wished to fight and German Jews who wished to negotiate. The latter feared that foreign protest would only seem to confirm the notion of a world Jewish conspiracy inimical to Germany. They also knew that they and not their vocal brethren abroad would feel the stinging lash of reprisals. As a result of their tenuous absorption into German life, the Jewish community had always preferred diplomacy and negotiation to public confrontation.

Overseas Jews labored under no such need to appease the Nazis. The day that the boycott was announced, twenty thousand people crowded into a Madison Square Garden rally in New York to condemn the treatment of German Jews, while another thirty-five thousand milled about outside. When a counterboycott of German exports was launched, it posed an excruciating dilemma for the American Jewish Committee. Started by the Jews of German ancestry, the committee feared exposing relatives to reprisals. At the same time, they had to respond to the spontaneous anguish of American Jewry. In the end, the committee opposed the boycott of German goods and tried to halt the Madison Square Garden rally, urging speakers to cancel their appearances. A fatal division sapped "international Jewry" even as the Nazi press claimed that it operated with a single, implacable will.

Max and Eric typified those Germans Jews who thought the foreign boycott of German products would backfire. On March 29, Eric sent a breathless cable to Friedaflix that the April 1 boycott would be carried out against Jewish firms "if atrocities news and unfriendly propaganda in foreign press mass meetings etc. does not stop immediately."[31] After Felix read this cable to the president of the American Jewish Committee, Cyrus Adler, the group issued a statement that repudiated any boycott of German goods and branded advocates of such a position "irresponsible."[32]

Felix was trapped in a quandary. At heart, he sided with the boycott, telling one friend how German youth were becoming so imbued with hatred that the masses would only turn against Hitler if they felt "that their pocketbooks are attacked by their own foolishness. . . ."[33] Yet family loyalty tugged the other way. Instead of an outright boycott of German products, he compromised and favored voluntary refusal to buy them. He told Eric that the real problem lay with the German government and not with American Jews. "Resentment so widespread no individual efforts to stem it likely available unless government changes attitude," he cabled. "Will continue to discourage mass meetings and unfounded atrocity stories."[34]

In hindsight, it is easy enough to see through the false promises and bluffs of Nazi leaders. Yet at the time, German Jews were lost in a mad tangle of speculation that obscured the uniform malevolence of their opponents. "Hitler is a very weak man," Dr. Bernhard Kahn, European director of the Joint Distribution Committee, said the day before the boycott. "He is in the hands of Göring and Goebbels. . . . We must strengthen his hand. . . ."[35] Within days, Kahn was chased from Berlin because of his ties to American Jews and he relocated in Paris. In July, the Joint would spearhead a one-million-dollar fund-raising campaign for German Jews, with Felix as honorary chairman.

April 1st proved the day of terror the Nazis had envisioned. People marched through Hamburg with signs proclaiming, "Germans don't buy from Jews." In many cities, Nazi hooligans hurled stink bombs into Jewish stores, scattered merchandise, and intimidated shoppers. Jewish private banks were largely exempt from this organized intimidation. When the boycott officially ended on April 4, German Jews felt great relief and Max thought they had survived the worst of Hitler.[36]

Because of haunting newsreel images of goose-stepping soldiers and Nuremberg rallies, we forget that some semblance of normality remained for well-to-do Jews in large cities in 1933. The Warburgs had to deal with ostracism, not outright terror. When Max walked to work each morning, he no longer tipped his hat, since people crossed the street when they saw him coming. Indeed, it became dangerous for an "Aryan" to chat or walk with him in the street. Family members were kicked out of chess clubs and swimming pools. An eerie isolation descended upon the Warburgs' private lives. They received fewer dinner invitations and, when they did, the guest list had been scrupulously screened by anxious hosts afraid of inviting party spies. The family servants remained faithful, providing some comfort in the fortress-like isolation.

If the Warburg family experienced, at worst, creeping menace in Hamburg, they didn't fare so well elsewhere. For years, Jim Loeb and his wife, Toni, had led a reclusive life at his Murnau estate of Hochried. A remarkable benefactor of German culture, Jim had built a new wing of the Murnau hospital in 1932 and was named an honorary citizen of the town. He bequeathed to a Munich museum the most important antiquity collection ever donated by a private individual in Bavaria and devoted enormous sums for a Munich psychiatric research center under Dr. Binswanger. These gifts would receive no thanks.

Two days before Hitler took power, Toni suddenly died. Upset by her death and the political situation, Jim Loeb suffered a fatal heart attack on May 27, 1933. Then (or possibly at a later date) the Nazis wouldn't let Jim and Toni's ashes be buried at Hochried. In a courageous act, the Count and Countess Resseguier secretly buried the ashes behind a sculpture near the Hochried gate. In a final indignity, the Nazis seized the Munich research building from Dr. Binswanger, deleted the name Loeb from the stone, and turned it into a center for Nazi theories of racial superiority.

The month Jim Loeb died, Hitler asked Dr. Robert Ley to merge German trade unions into one big Nazi labor organization named the Labor Front. Ley, we recall, was the drunken I. G. Farben chemist who had attacked Max in the 1920s and sacrificed his job in consequence. From a palatial government building, Ley would now manage a vast treasury to indoctrinate German workers and control a private army of blue-uniformed henchmen. As creator of the holiday group "Strength Through Joy," he would even subject German workers to Nazi brainwashing in their leisure activities.

On June 9, the Warburgs were stunned by news of the double suicide of Moritz Oppenheim—Charlotte's brother—and his wife, Käthie, in Frankfurt. Moritz had worked in the family jewelry business and become an important patron of German science. He had subsidized a Helgoland aquarium and endowed a chair in theoretical physics at the University of Frankfurt. As a donor to the university's observatory, he even had a small planet, "Mauritius," named after him. He and his elegant Viennese wife had a cultured home, featuring music every Sunday afternoon.

The story of Moritz and Käthie highlights the Jewish suffering that an-

tedated the gas chambers. After the Nazis took power, the elderly couple—
Moritz was eighty-five, Käthie almost eighty—grew increasingly despondent.
When their only son, Paul, emigrated to Brussels, their solitude deepened.
They decided to die with the same harmony as they had lived. For the
Warburg brothers, who associated the Frankfurt Oppenheims with carefree,
youthful days, it seemed a terrifying omen. "How it all happened is mysteri-
ous to me," Felix wrote, "but no doubt the Hitler Regime made life for them
a plague and they were yearning for the end of their days."[37]

One paradox of the Warburg story is that while the family figured prominently in a mad farrago of Nazi allegations, M. M. Warburg & Co. enjoyed a
relatively privileged place in the Third Reich. The same Jewish bankers who
starred in the pages of *Der Stürmer* enjoyed, in practice, a certain immunity
from attack. However fierce the Nazi rhetoric against them, they were ac-
corded more privileges than almost any other Jewish group, as the Nazis
happily exploited the financial power that they so eagerly denounced. They
got away with this because private banks operated in an elite universe foreign
to the street hoodlums and small shopkeepers who comprised the party
faithful. With eighteen million reichsmarks of capital, M. M. Warburg & Co.
was probably the largest and most eminent private bank in Germany, rivaled
only by Mendelssohn & Co. in Berlin.[38]

That Germany benefited from Jewish bankers who allegedly plundered the
Volk was one of Nazism's dirty secrets. The bankers had something Germany
desperately needed. A lot of foreign trade floated through Hamburg on Warburg credits and the Nazis were short of foreign exchange needed to rearm
Germany. And without strong exports, Hitler couldn't create rapid job growth
needed to buttress his regime. Thus, he granted a special dispensation to the
very people he most reviled. If this belied the party worldview about the Jews,
it never seemed to disturb the committed.

Another factor giving Jewish bankers some immunity from attack was their
international connections. The Warburgs were a showcase family well
known abroad. "The Nazis were very interested in portraying Germany as
okay in the outside world," said Max's daughter, Gisela. "Goebbels knew that
the Warburgs had a lot of relations in the U.S."[39] Again the bankers were
saved by aspects of their work otherwise used to arouse paranoia.

The atmosphere of M. M. Warburg & Co. after 1933 was an implausible
blend of the frightening and the mundane. Max would evoke the mortuary
gloom of the ancestral bank, with grandfather clocks ticking away as a
shrinking staff tried to fill empty hours. The mail dried up and fewer clients
stopped by in person. The number of clients plummeted in 1933 from 5,241

to 1,875 and the firm was expelled from many securities syndicates. Max stubbornly kept up daily visits to the stock exchange. But where friends once crowded around him, he now stood alone or with his employees. He was shadowed by the secret police, who photographed people approaching him at the exchange or visiting the bank. For a man once dubbed the uncrowned king of Hamburg, it was all a nightmarish reversal.

M. M. Warburg's slowdown didn't entirely result from the Nazis. The moratorium on repayment of German loans froze international capital flows. When the Reichsbank clamped more controls on capital movements, it handicapped the Warburgs, who specialized in foreign trade. Also, the bank still suffered from the 1931 debacle, which required cost-cutting. Among the many factors holding Max in Germany was doubtless his desire to regain the eminence he had enjoyed before 1931. The Nazis had deprived him of a chance to restore his glory.

If business at the Warburg bank was never nearly so moribund as Max made out, it had much to do with the patronage of Dr. Hjalmar Schacht. Assigned to deliver Hitler's economic boom, he had to transmit to the *Führer* the unpleasant news that Germany needed these devilish Jewish bankers. Schacht had not only been a key emissary to big business at a time when industrialists still feared the Nazis, but also gave some financial legitimacy to a party that attracted a large number of monetary quacks. Hitler prized Schacht as a respectable figure who could hoodwink foreign financiers. In 1931 Hitler said of him, "He *is*, in fact, enormously skilled and enjoys great respect, even among the foreign, and especially among the Jewish-American international bankers. And that is why I, too, think highly of him."[40] Hitler bragged that Schacht was the only "Aryan" who could outswindle the Jews.[41] In a totalitarian state where every human body seemed expendable, Dr. Schacht alone enjoyed special freedoms, and this would even extend to protesting the abuse of Jewish businessmen.

This old-school banker, with his pinstripes, cigars, and wire-rimmed glasses, never joined the party and regarded many Nazis as coarse ruffians. Later disclaiming knowledge of the Final Solution, he would yet mastermind the German economic revival that made Hitler omnipotent. On February 20, 1933, at a meeting of business leaders at his home, Göring predicted that the March 5 elections would be "the last for the next five years, probably even for the next hundred years."[42] Once the crowd was warmed up, Dr. Schacht stepped forth, raised three million marks for the Nazis, then administered the fund himself. This opportunist fancied himself the one sane man who could moderate Nazi excesses from within. Watching Hitler deliver his first radio address in 1933, he said he thought it might be "possible to guide this man into the path of righteousness."[43] When the *Führer* said the Jews could continue working as before, Dr. Schacht professed to believe him. Max would hear these specious promises from Schacht's own lips.

When Hitler demanded the resignation of Dr. Luther, the head of the Reichsbank, in March 1933, he proposed Dr. Schacht in his stead. As a member of the Reichsbank advisory board since 1924, Max participated in the vote. He and two other Jewish bankers on the eight-member council were caught in a touchy position. Max thought Schacht a smart, opportunistic blowhard who overestimated his talents; Max also had never forgiven his cynical betrayal of Carl Melchior after the 1929 Young conference. Nevertheless, he voted for Schacht at the March 16 meeting, telling Jimmy afterward, "Under current conditions, I consider it objectively correct that Schacht get this post, for his personal influence over the government is so important that mistakes, which he will unquestionably make, will be offset. I voted for him *de plein coeur* and am glad that Luther himself did the same."[44] Max joined two other Jewish bankers in appending his signature to the March 17 appointment document signed by Hitler and Hindenburg. The advisory board was dissolved in October 1933.

If Max's business life hung from a thread after 1933, it was Dr. Schacht who could wield the shears, for he held life-and-death power over private banks. Since the 1931 crisis, the Reichsbank enjoyed dictatorial control over foreign exchange—the lifeblood of any international bank. Schacht could obliterate the 135-year history of M. M. Warburg in one stroke. Recognizing this, Max told Jimmy that everything depended upon "what Schacht plans to do in general with private banks and bankers and in particular, how a private Jewish bank can do business in future."[45]

For Max, Schacht's appointment promised some small rationality in financial affairs instead of weird Nazi experiments or a vicious purge of Jewish bankers. His relationship with Schacht at first duped Max into a sense of security. It gave him high-level access to the Nazi bureaucracy of a sort enjoyed by few Jews. Max felt he should use this influence for the Jewish community, which, in turn, bolstered his importance in the community. For Jews who felt bereft of any court of appeals in a Germany gone mad, Max Warburg, with his government contacts, could render unique service. He had an open door to Schacht and periodically discussed with him topics of mutual concern.

Jimmy and Felix thought Max was manipulated by the wily Schacht. As Jimmy later said, "My uncle, Max Warburg . . . always claimed that Schacht was doing the best he could to protect the Jews. I never believed him. I think [Schacht] talked out of one side of his face to people who were anti-Semitic and out of the other side of his face to people who were pro-Semitic, but I have no proof of that."[46] Yet at moments Schacht bucked the Nazis at great personal risk. In the rogues gallery of the Third Reich, he is the hardest person to bring into moral focus, for he exhibited both patent hypocrisy and unquestionable courage. If Max proved gullible, he had some reason to trust Schacht.

Being ignorant of financial matters, Hitler granted Schacht unusual autonomy in Nazi officialdom. Once asked whether Hitler had financial ideas, Schacht boasted, "Yes, he had one idea and a very good one. It was, leave it to Schacht."[47] As his policies lifted Germany from the Depression, Schacht enjoyed immunity from party criticism. In May 1933, he shielded the bankers' trade association from party meddling and it confirmed Max and two other Jews as board members.

The most startling proof of Schacht's freedom from party strictures was seen in the Reich Loan Consortium, the august bank syndicate that marketed German government issues. Of fifty member banks when the Nazis seized power, a third were Jewish, and Schacht resisted the party's efforts to expel some of them. Gradually almost all Jewish banks were pruned and only three managed to stay until 1938, including M. M. Warburg & Co. Membership in this body provided the Warburg bank with protection and permitted leading industrial firms to continue doing business with it safely. If M. M. Warburg enjoyed the imprimatur of the Reich Loan Consortium, how could it be considered a traitorous firm?

Besides Schacht, several businessmen tried to guide Hitler toward economic sanity, and he was only too pleased to exploit their naïveté. In early 1932, Hitler dispatched Wilhelm Keppler, the owner of a small chemical factory, to court Hamburg business chieftains. He recruited Emil Helfferich, Carl Vincent Krogmann, and others into a select group of economic advisers to Hitler.

For a time, this Keppler Circle provided a bridge between the business world and the Nazis, and Hitler responded enthusiastically when the group accepted Dr. Schacht. Hitler assured them that he was the soul of moderation on economic matters. "I'm no doctrinaire," he told them. "I'm a politician and no economist. I rely upon your better judgment and wide experience."[48] Drawn heavily from the Hamburg trading world, the group endorsed lower tariffs and an end to exchange controls. Hitler let them frolic in this fool's paradise as long as it suited his purpose.

Few Jewish businessmen had better access to the Keppler Circle than the Warburgs. Emil Helfferich, a silver-haired man with round spectacles and a white, Old Testament beard, worked around the corner from the Warburg bank, doing business with the Dutch West Indies. The Warburgs had financed and even invested in some of his colonial enterprises. Eric later described Helfferich as a cunning, insincere opportunist, but no Nazi.[49]

When Hitler took power, the Warburg partners held 108 seats on corporate boards, reflecting the close ties between German banks and industry. As they were expelled from boards and lost customers through subtle Nazi pressures, the Warburgs turned to the Keppler Circle. In May 1933, Max and Eric met with the group at the Berlin branch of the Kommerzbank. Infuriated by all the snubs and rebuffs, Max asked, point-blank, which board seats should be abandoned and which kept. Discomfited by this bluntness, Helfferich said the matter should be decided on a case-by-case basis and vaguely told Max to yield seats where the pressure was most intense. Eric never forgot the pained expression of his father, who craved clarity in this wilderness of fear and innuendo. That July, Hitler appointed Keppler as his personal economic adviser. The following year, in a telltale shift, the Keppler Circle was supplanted by the Himmler Circle.

Some Warburgs, notably Jimmy, thought Max should resign from boards instead of waiting to be booted out, but he refused to go quietly or surrender his economic power. In his 1933 annual report, he told colleagues that they should defend the bank as a fortress and that "no Board seat that is taken from us should be regarded as definitely lost and every opportunity should be seized to regain these positions, even if success may yet be far off."[50] This combative attitude coincided with his belief in the transitory nature of the Nazis.

The manner in which Max was hounded from corporate boards ranged from the absurdly correct to the wantonly cruel. At a May 1933 board meeting of the German Atlantic Telegraph Company, the commissar of the ministry of the post, Herr Kunert, explained that the ministry wanted Jewish board members to resign. With a nod to Max and others, Kunert insisted no offense was meant. "There was no objection personally to the Jewish gentlemen in question. On the contrary, their services in the rebuilding of the company were highly esteemed. But these were new times, against which no one could prevail."[51] Max expressed astonishment that the ministry of the post could propose something of such dubious legality. Even a forceful protest from Averell Harriman—who had, at Max's behest, financed a transatlantic cable for the company in 1921—couldn't save his seat.

With the telegraph company, Max at least had a high-level executioner. Not so with the Hamburg Economic Service. Though a founder of this institute, Max learned of his dismissal from a junior employee, a total stranger, who stopped by to tell him that he had to resign. A few years earlier, Max had received the gold medal from the Hamburg Chamber of Commerce. Now he learned in a tritely polite, hypocritical letter that he had just been expelled. The Philharmonic Society, the Board of Higher Education, and other organizations shunted him aside. To justify these decisions, these groups hid behind the all-purpose euphemism that retaining Max was "*untragbar*" or "insupportable." During 1933, Warburg partners experienced only one act of heroism. When Max was evicted from the Kiel Institute for Seafaring and World Economics, two board members resigned in protest. Such courage was generally conspicuous by its absence.

For sheer pathos, nothing approached Max's departure from the Hamburg-American Line. In the world slump, the company relied upon government subsidies to survive, making it especially susceptible to pressure. The Nazis wasted no time in putting out revisionist histories that denigrated the Jewish Albert Ballin. Apparently the decision to banish Max from its board came straight from Mayor Krogmann.[52] The farewell scene would become the stuff of legend. To camouflage his expulsion, the board retired two non-Jewish members, Max von Schinckel and banker Rudolph von Schröder, at the same time. Their departure was "celebrated" at a breakfast meeting on a gray, drizzling Thursday morning in spring 1933. In a second-floor conference room, overlooking the Inner Alster Lake, the HAPAG board sat at a large, oval table spruced up with flowers. White-jacketed stewards lined the wall and attended to guests. The elegant setting clashed with the vicious nature of the occasion. Beneath the fake festive touches, the atmosphere was somber, the clatter of spoons magnified by the silence. Once the stewards cleared the table, they left the room.

The Nazi party monitored the meeting through the presence of Count Rödern, the commissar for shipping. It fell to Max von Schinckel to speak first and he delivered a poignant if halting speech about his years with the company. Overcome with emotion, wiping tears from his eyes, the stooped, despondent figure suddenly broke off and walked out of the room. An awkward silence ensued. The quick-witted Max Warburg sprang to his feet and added what he thought von Schinckel would have said. At the same time, he broadened it into a valedictory for himself and Rudolph von Schröder.

When Max resumed his seat between Count Rödern and another board member, he heard them whispering behind his back as to who should reply. To spare them this decision, Max stood, tapped his glass, and delivered a farewell address to himself that began, "My dear gentlemen, dear Mr. Warburg!"[53] The speech that followed was laced with suppressed anger and delivered in lightly mocking style. Addressing an imaginary Max Warburg, he said, "To our great regret, we have learned that you have decided to leave the board of the company and consider this decision irrevocable."[54] Max proceeded to catalogue his long service to the company. He told how he had smoothed over rough times between Ballin and the board. He told of his wartime service and how he helped to rescue HAPAG from its postwar crisis. Twice the Warburg bank had provided critical financing when less loyal banks refused. "We have never forgotten you for this," Max concluded. "And now I would like to wish you, dear Mr. Warburg, a calm old age, good luck and many blessings to your family. We know that you, as you have already explained, will always place your advice at our disposal, whenever we shall request it."[55] Max sat down in dead silence at last broken by irrelevant bluster from Count Rödern about buying an estate and becoming a farmer. Emil Helfferich would head the new, nazified board.

Several versions of Max's speech appeared in the European press and his grace under pressure cheered Jews everywhere. When the story popped up in America, Felix, to protect Max, denied that such an event had ever occurred, while acknowledging the bitter irony that HAPAG had been "Aryanized."[56] "The steamship line which a brave Jew, Albert Ballin, built up with all his patriotism and energy, now flies the Nazis' swastika on the yardarm. And what irony of fate that the ship called after Albert Ballin should be so decorated."[57]

In later years, Max hesitated to repeat these tales of rude dismissals, because they paled to petty slights after the Holocaust. Yet they hurt deeply enough. Also, things would get much worse. In 1933, the Nazis didn't sweep Warburg partners wholesale from company boards. By year's end, the bank had lost only 18 of 108 board seats—making dismissals the exception, not the rule. The willingness of German companies to retain Warburg partners was, in many ways, more remarkable than the minority that capitulated to pressure. It suggests that German big business didn't gleefully join in the witch-hunt against Jews, or at least valued Jewish banking connections.

Wherever possible, the Warburgs tried to insert a non-Jewish Warburg employee when they vacated a seat in order to retain the business connection. The usual substitute was Dr. Rudolf Brinckmann, who was then an office manager with full power of attorney. With mirthless humor, the Warburgs called the faithful Brinckmann "their Aryan" and he evidently replaced Max on HAPAG and many other boards.[58] Despite their strident megaphone denunciations of Jewish bankers, the Nazis again proved unexpectedly accommodating. If hypocrisy is the tribute that vice pays to virtue, then the Nazis certainly had their own left-handed way of showing respect for the sinister Jewish moneymen.

*James M. Cox and Jimmy Warburg sail for the ill-fated
World Economic Conference in London, June 1933.
(Wide World)*

New Deal Noodles

D espite his father's death and his frayed marriage to Kay Swift, Jimmy Warburg retained a golden boy's luster in 1933. This young mandarin of high finance boasted an array of impressive titles. As president of the International Acceptance Bank and the International Manhattan Company and vice-chairman of the Bank of the Manhattan, Jimmy was, at thirty-six, probably the youngest chief executive on Wall Street. His good looks and brains had produced supreme self-confidence. As Herbert Feis recalled, "Warburg was experienced in the banking world and shimmering bright, but almost too quick and self-assured."[1] A close observer might have speculated that this smart, polished young man was poised for great deeds—or else headed for a great fall. The one impossible thing was for Jimmy Warburg to stroll quietly down the byways of life.

After Paul's death, Jimmy had to rebuild the fortune frittered away in the 1931 rescue. Luckily, he had an amazing knack for making money. Managing his father's estate, he shifted funds from municipal bonds into common stocks right at the 1932 market bottom, a well-timed move which guaranteed a comfortable future for his family, Bettina, and Nina. By this point, Jimmy wanted to renounce banking and escape the velvet trap of the Warburg family. His description of Woodlands life sums up his feelings about the whole clan: "a rather dull though luxurious life on a family anthill."[2] But he couldn't escape the Warburgs yet. M. M. Warburg still owed the American Warburgs and the Bank of the Manhattan considerable money from 1931, and Jimmy felt obligated to see the drearily interminable matter through.

In late 1932, the Bank of the Manhattan decided to drop its securities affiliate, the International Manhattan Company. As president of the subsidiary, Jimmy cast about for opportunities beyond finance. The cascading bank failures didn't augur well for a career on the Street. In early 1932, Jimmy wrote Siegmund a highly prophetic letter that foresaw the shutdown of America's banks, concluding that "until that happens and people realize that when it has happened they are still not dead, the tide of fear cannot be turned."[3] He was still a fairly conservative young man—if already possessing a broad streak of iconoclasm—and condemned the 1932 Republican platform for abandoning individualism, which he thought would pave the way for paternalism, even dictatorship.

After Franklin D. Roosevelt was elected, Jimmy, as a precocious young banker, was consulted about the banking crisis by a Roosevelt Brain Trust short on Wall Street friends. Numerous ties knitted the Warburgs and Roosevelts. The president-elect and Eleanor had socialized with Panina during the war and FDR had admired Paul's work at the Fed. "I always felt that his work of absolute impartiality was largely instrumental in making the success of the Board in the war years," Roosevelt said.[4] FDR's son, Jimmy, Jr., had roomed with Eddie Warburg at Harvard freshman year, while Freddy had befriended Curtis Dall, who married FDR's daughter Anna. The Dalls lived in a Woodlands cottage while Curtis and Freddy worked together at Lehman Brothers. So if the Warburgs remained rock-ribbed Republicans—and if Frieda's vote for FDR scandalized Felix—they weren't exiled to the political wilderness in 1933.

Early in the year, Jimmy Roosevelt and Professor Raymond Moley lunched at Jimmy Warburg's bank to discuss economic policy. Finding Moley evasive on major issues, Warburg saw that the Brain Trust remained fuzzy on financial strategy. A few days later, Moley informed Jimmy that FDR had picked him as one of three experts to sketch an agenda for the upcoming World Economic Conference. In a meeting with economic advisers Rex Tugwell and Charles Taussig, Jimmy tried to figure out whether the inscrutable Roosevelt would abide by his campaign pledge of a sound dollar and balanced budget or try to cure the Depression through inflationary nostrums.

In February 1933, Jimmy joined a dozen other prospective advisers for a meeting with the president-elect at his Sixty-Fifth Street home. When FDR was wheeled into the drawing room, he shone with a sun-god radiance for

Jimmy: "I vividly remember my first impression of F.D.R.'s massive shoulders surmounted by his remarkably fine head, the gay smile with which he greeted his guests, and the somewhat incongruous, old-fashioned pince-nez eyeglasses that seemed to sit a little uncertainly on his nose."[5] As he flipped through the guest list, FDR's face lit up when he ran across Jimmy's name. He saluted Paul's fine work at the Fed and stunning 1929 prediction. "Ray Moley tells me that you are the white sheep of Wall Street," Roosevelt said. Jimmy retorted that the title belonged to his father and that white sheep didn't necessarily beget white lambs. Roosevelt laughed, saying, "Anyway, I want you to work with Ray Moley on the banking and currency situations."[6]

In his inaugural speech, FDR signaled that bankers no longer stood on the sacred pedestal they had occupied in the 1920s. "The money changers have fled from their high seats in the temple of our civilization," he said.[7] The bankers of the Jazz Age would become "banksters" in the New Deal, and before long it was regarded as apostasy on Wall Street to have any association with FDR. After Roosevelt declared a holiday that shuttered America's eighteen thousand banks, Moley brought Jimmy down to Washington to shape policy and restore confidence before banks reopened. Evidently, Jimmy made an excellent impression on Roosevelt, who even queried his advisers about naming him to the Federal Reserve Board. Then, on Friday morning, March 17, Jimmy awoke to a bushel of congratulatory telegrams. To his amazement, *The New York Times* headline said, "James P. Warburg To Be Woodin's Aide," followed by the subhead, "He Is Reported Choice of Treasury Head to Fill Position of Under-Secretary."[8] This was all news to Jimmy.

An adoring fan of her brilliant son, Nina appeared at his apartment and urged him to take the post. Such a step posed financial obstacles for Jimmy. Paul had left much of his estate in Bank of the Manhattan shares. If Jimmy took a government post, he would have to unload this bank stock when no real buyers existed, and the resulting loss would thin an already reduced inheritance. With two homes, three daughters, a wife, and a mother to support, Jimmy also didn't know whether he could afford the steep salary cut that accompanied public service. Finally, as the sole Wall Street renegade in Washington, he might have to defend unpalatable policies. Regarding Wall Street as enemy territory, the Brain Trust refused to consult its gray eminences.

The upshot was that this wayward son of Wall Street decided to work for the New Deal for six months in an unofficial, unsalaried capacity. A few days later, he explained the bank stock pickle to Roosevelt, who suggested that Jimmy serve without a title. As *The New Yorker* later said, Jimmy was "virtually the sole link between the old Wall Street tradition and the federal government."[9] Jimmy tried to insert his friend Averell Harriman of Brown Brothers into the New Deal, telling Roosevelt that he should name him U.S. ambassador to Germany, to no avail.

Jimmy would cherish his Washington foray as the most stimulating adventure of his career. As with Paul, it left him with a lasting if unrequited love of public service. In a difficult transition, Jimmy went from blistering family battles to punishing political squabbles. At first, he marveled at the "creative chaos" in Washington that had wiped away national gloom.[10] Spending the business week at the Carlton Hotel, then returning to New York on weekends, he suffered another forced separation from Kay. Jimmy was put into the position of being a certified class traitor, as the sensational Pecora hearings in the Senate probed Wall Street activities of the 1920s and held bankers up to public obloquy. In late March, Roosevelt mentioned to Jimmy that counsel Ferdinand Pecora was turning his guns against private banks, including Kuhn, Loeb, and he said "this with a wicked twinkle at me," Jimmy noted.[11]

Jimmy was no hidebound conservative. He advised FDR to cheapen the dollar to stimulate exports and wasn't averse to the deficit spending championed by Keynes. Yet as the son of Mister Sound Money, he felt uneasy in an administration marked by sometimes amateur experimentation in the monetary sphere. He winced at this slapstick side of the New Deal, with its arcane disputes and skirmishing factions. FDR wanted to honor Paul Warburg's memory but not his policies. Jimmy thought the president and Moley had only a primitive grasp of money issues and certainly lacked the expertise to manage a currency. "The really frightening thing about this was that none of these fellows knew anything about it and were just gaily tinkering with this whole mechanism." Jimmy confessed, "My sacred cows were being slaughtered."[12] Before long, he defined his task as simply one of spiking the most harmful experiments.

By April, Roosevelt felt himself under extreme pressure to take radical measures to end misery among the farmers. Slumping commodity prices and rampant foreclosures had produced a quasi-revolutionary ferment in the farm belt. To prop up prices, Jimmy advocated devaluing the dollar in relation to gold and other currencies, while maintaining a link between gold and the dollar. For Jimmy, the gold standard was the only solid base upon which to anchor the financial edifice.

In mid-April, FDR summoned his economic advisers and, with surprising joviality, announced that the United States would jettison the gold standard. In other words, paper currency could no longer be redeemed for gold. When the president dropped this bombshell on his advisers, the mood of the meeting turned ugly. Sympathetically, FDR read aloud the Thomas amendment to the proposed farm bill, which would permit the government to print greenbacks and take other monetary measures to aid recovery. To his consternation, Jimmy saw Roosevelt resorting to inflationary measures as a deceptively simple way to solve the Depression. "At the risk of being impudent, I went so far as to say that I considered the passage of such a bill completely hare-brained and irresponsible."[13]

For private bankers of that era, scrapping the gold standard seemed as strange and forbidding as urging the planets to stray from their orbits. In September 1931, Paul had grown sick when he learned that England had gone off gold. Upon leaving the White House, Lewis Douglas, the conservative budget director, turned to Jimmy and said, "Well, this is the end of western civilization." "I don't think it's quite that," Jimmy answered.[14] But he did fear that such nationalism would damage the global economy. In this respect, Jimmy was the true son of a Jewish banking dynasty, for he always favored global coordination and harmony over any naked assertion of national interests.

—

Jimmy found himself at the center of a gathering debate as to how FDR should respond to Hitler, who also came to power in early 1933. Some Jewish leaders would fault the Warburgs for failing to alert FDR to the danger. Supreme Court Justice Louis Brandeis noted Felix's initial reluctance to act. As he told Rabbi Stephen Wise in 1933, "Warburg, [Paul] Baerwald (of the Joint Distribution Committee) and others who have relatives in Germany dare not say anything publicly."[15] This charge was baldly twisted by Wise who never missed a chance to knock the Warburgs. In a 1936 letter to Albert Einstein, he wrote: "When I saw Brandeis, he told me that the President would have acted in March 1933, if it had not been for the Warburg family." Wise added, "You see, Professor Einstein, how these great philanthropists are our deadliest enemies and a fatal curse to the security and honor of the Jewish people."[16] We should note that Brandeis and Wise were both Zionist leaders with an implacable ideological antipathy to the Warburgs.

Were these charges valid? It is hard to make a monolithic statement about the Warburgs, who were a large, diverse, and eternally squabbling brood. In general, one can say that the charge had some validity in early 1933, but very little after that. For information about Germany, Jimmy relied upon Max and Eric who, as mentioned, tried to appease the Nazis at the time of the April boycott. On March 22, Jimmy described a report he had received from Eric through an intermediary: "The reports we were receiving here were grossly exaggerated, and that all the families were well and un-worried and that all the protest meetings and the American publicity were doing more harm than good."[17] Having previously criticized his Hamburg relatives for complacency about Hitler, Jimmy now chose, unaccountably, to accept their interpretation of events.

At first, Jimmy parroted the official State Department line that Nazi treatment of the Jews was a matter of internal German policy. In writing to Felix's son, Freddy, he even introduced a note of dubiety about the "horror stories" from Germany: "A protest against barbaric atrocities, *assuming their existence,* is one thing, but a protest against an economic boycott—while that is perhaps a more reprehensible thing in itself—is a horse of a different water. . . ."[18] (my italics) After discussing the German situation with Jimmy in May, Felix Frankfurter thought he was advising FDR to appease Hitler—an allegation Jimmy later hotly disputed, insisting he had favored a very tough policy.[19]

Certainly, one can say that as Jimmy acquired more information, he abruptly changed his position. On May 2 he lunched with James McDonald, a New York lawyer just back from Germany. A member of *The New York Times* staff and president of the Foreign Policy Association, the silver-haired McDonald gave Jimmy a radically different glimpse of events inside Germany. McDonald was horrified by a talk with Hitler, who told him, "I've got my heel on the necks of the Jews and will soon have them so they can't move."[20] McDonald predicted that German Jews would retrogress to medieval ghetto status and that Hitler would trigger a European war. "He said that if he were Max he would certainly not keep his family in Germany today," Jimmy wrote in his diary. "All in all, the picture he paints is far worse than anything I have heard yet."[21]

Appeasement accusations also swirled around Felix. In August, *The New Republic* claimed that he had dissuaded Roosevelt from protesting Jewish persecution, arguing that this would hurt German Jews, and Walter Winchell repeated the charge in his column. As noted, Felix had reluctantly bowed to the wishes of Max and Eric and opposed a formal boycott of German goods. Yet he clearly sounded the alarm in private meetings and was singularly free of illusions about the Nazis. Felix lobbied to get the toughtalking James McDonald appointed the new U.S. ambassador to Germany instead of historian William E. Dodd, who believed the Jews dominated German economic life.[22] As soon as Dodd was appointed, Felix told Dodd about the suicide of his Oppenheim relatives.[23] Along with Irving Lehman, Felix lobbied Roosevelt for a far more receptive policy toward German-Jewish refugees. As he reported with disappointment in October, "So far all the vague promises have not materialized into any action."[24] Felix was assuredly not twiddling his thumbs.

That autumn, the Joint Distribution Committee turned to the League of Nations for help with Jewish refugees from Germany. When Germany threatened to veto such an action, the League set up a special commission outside normal channels to negotiate with the Nazis. Felix and Frieda touted McDonald to head the new High Commission for Refugees from Germany and helped to secure FDR's support. The group had to be privately funded, so the Joint contributed to its work and Felix personally supplemented McDonald's low salary. McDonald found Felix a notable exception to non-Zionist Jewish leaders who seemed blind to the Nazi menace. In January 1934, the two men made an impassioned plea for action to Jewish businessmen assembled in the London New Court offices of Lionel de Rothschild. McDonald fervently warned that the six hundred thousand German Jews were in peril. "Warburg, respected and loved through the world for his philanthropies, followed with a plea for immediate action," McDonald recalled of this futile exercise with the British.[25] "Their stony silence told us that they were not to be stampeded by two 'American alarmists.' "[26]

Felix dedicated enormous time to saving German Jews. Acting in part upon suggestions from James G. McDonald, he spearheaded a three-million-dollar effort by the Joint to resettle Jews in Palestine and in 1934 helped to set up the Refugee Economic Corporation to spur development there. He also created the Emigré Charitable Fund to train, finance, and resettle Jewish refugees from Germany.[27] During this time, Felix was also honorary president of the Palestine Economic Corporation.

The main problem during the Roosevelt administration was not the laggard response of the Jewish leadership, but the political isolationism of Depression America. Roosevelt knew about events in Germany but chose not to intervene. On June 16, 1933, FDR told Ambassador Dodd, "The German authorities are treating the Jews shamefully, and the Jews in this country are greatly excited. But this is also not a government affair."[28] Struggling with massive unemployment, Roosevelt feared a political backlash if he admitted desperate European refugees. FDR wasn't anti-Semitic and recruited many Jewish aides. Yet radio priest Father Coughlin and other demagogues were inflaming anti-Semitism, making it an inauspicious time to admit Jews. An inward-looking America didn't want to absorb a tide of German-Jewish refugees. By law, a maximum of twenty-five thousand could be admitted each year, but the actual number fell far short of that, and the process was slow and cumbersome. The problem in Washington was never one of information but of political will.

—

In May 1933, Jimmy renewed his acquaintance with Dr. Schacht, whom he had hated ever since their dealings in the 1920s when the International Acceptance Bank was the American agent bank for the Reichsbank. Before Schacht came to Washington, Jimmy advised Roosevelt that Schacht was a "slippery character."[29] He lived up to this warning. To ingratiate himself with Hitler, Schacht had contrived an insolent plan to stop payment on one billion dollars in German debt owed to American investors. To give the appearance that Washington tacitly blessed this step, Schacht wanted to announce the decision following his Washington talks. Hitler loved the sheer gall of it and Schacht promised that he could dupe the Americans.

Jimmy blamed the Depression on German reparations and other war-related debt and advocated debt reduction as the only sensible policy. That spring, he even floated something called the Warburg Plan to lighten the Allied debt load. But he opposed the cynical, unilateral debt repudiation contemplated by Dr. Schacht with its misleading air of U.S. approval. Since Germany had been a major recipient of Wall Street largess in the 1920s, a total cessation of payments was no small matter.

On May 8, a curious meeting occurred in Washington at the German embassy, which had been financed partly with a loan from Paul Warburg in earlier days. Jimmy sat opposite the new German ambassador, Dr. Luther, and Dr. Schacht, his successor at the Reichsbank. Having just heard horror stories from James McDonald, Jimmy aggressively pressed the Jewish question. Schacht reacted with a brazen denial of any problem. As Jimmy noted, Schacht had "said that he himself is anything but anti-Semitic and that he thought the whole thing was already over its crest and would boil down to a fairly sensible basis pretty soon. He cited the fact that he was keeping Max on the board of the Reichsbank and that he [Max] had also just been re-elected as one of the six governors of the Clearing House."[30] Schacht hinted that he privately disagreed with some of Hitler's policies, but couldn't say so aloud.

Meeting with Secretary of State Cordell Hull, Schacht delivered a bombastic speech, saying that Germany would suspend debt payments the next day, but wanted to consult with Roosevelt first. To protect Roosevelt from this trap, Jimmy went to the White House and suggested that FDR direct a calculated insult at Schacht. He proposed that a White House aide call Dr. Schacht and cancel his appointment with FDR for the next day, citing a meeting with the Chinese minister. Roosevelt thought the arrogant Schacht needed such a comeuppance and this also appealed to his sense of mischief.

The next day, making a deliberately insulting pun, Hull handed Schacht a note saying that the U.S. was "profoundly shocked" by Germany's debt decision. In his high stiff collar and rimless glasses, Schacht was made to stand in embarrassment for three minutes while Hull calmly scanned some papers. Having assured Hitler that all was proceeding smoothly, Schacht now saw that the Americans wouldn't fall for his little charade. He would have to wait to announce his debt default. On his way back to Germany, Schacht told members of the American Jewish Committee in New York that he would plead with the Nazis to treat the Jews leniently. In an amusing coda to Schacht's visit, Roosevelt said to Jimmy one day, "You know, Jimmy, it would serve that fellow Hitler right if I sent a Jew to Berlin as my ambassador. How would you like the job?"[31]

After the Schacht visit, Jimmy focused on monetary preparations for the World Economic Conference, which would open in London on June 12. Strenuously resisting having Bernard Baruch and Joseph P. Kennedy on the American delegation, Jimmy said he wouldn't go if FDR picked these Wall Street speculators to pay off political debts. After Versailles, the Warburgs had learned to be gun-shy about global conferences. Jimmy's diary shows that he opposed Baruch from fear that anti-Semites might brand the American team an "international Jewish delegation."[32] Still smarting from Versailles, Max declined Jimmy's social invitation to meet him in London to discuss Germany. Noting the vicious libel that he and Paul had secretly negotiated at Versailles, Max said that he didn't want to give "any opportunity to the observation that a Warburg also participated in the negotiations on the German side."[33] They agreed to meet in Paris or Amsterdam.

The Nazi propaganda had now washed up on American shores. In June 1933, the Jewish War Veterans slipped an observer into a rally of seven hundred people in Queens, New York, held in a swastika-draped garden restaurant. The spy reported brisk sales of Theodor Fritsch's book, *My Fight with the House of Warburg.*[34] A Nazi newspaper in New York, *Das Neue Deutschland* or "New Germany," ran a philippic against the Warburgs that September, trotting out the old canard about Paul and Max scheming at Versailles.[35]

Even as Jimmy fled his Jewish identity, he was cast as an archconspirator in the international Jewish cabal. A Dutch publishing house produced a book entitled *The Resources of National Socialism: Three Conversations with Hitler* by J. G. Schoup, which made the absurd claim that Jewish capitalists had secretly bankrolled Hitler to preserve their German investments against a Bolshevik revolution. It was written in the form of secret confessions by a Sidney Warburg who was clearly patterned after Jimmy. This odious potboiler claimed that after the 1929 crash, Jewish bankers sent Sidney to Europe to deliver $8.5 million directly to Hitler and his followers. Alerted to the book by a Warburg partner in Amsterdam, Jimmy notified the publisher that it was a forgery and he got it withdrawn. But it would pop up in various forms for many years.

In the spring of 1933, Jimmy was still dazzled by Roosevelt and convinced he would go down as a great American president. The London conference would make him revise his opinion. The monetary group was headed by

James M. Cox, who delegated currency questions to Jimmy, giving him a major role. Before leaving for London, Jimmy presented a series of resolutions to Roosevelt who approved them—a bit too readily, it seemed. If Jimmy felt flattered, he also feared that this quick response betokened a lack of serious commitment.

London was initially full of memorable moments. At a reception one night, Jimmy smiled at what seemed a familiar face standing by the wall. "You've made a mistake," the man said, stepping forward. "You either think I'm Lord Hailsham, the worst War Minister we've ever had, or Bennett of Canada. We all look like pink pigs, but I'm Winston Churchill."[36] Then out of office, Churchill had just completed his life of the Duke of Marlborough. This chance encounter ended with supper at Churchill's club, a recitation of the great man's career, and late-night brandy at his house. Jimmy would consider it the most fascinating night of his life.

At first the negotiations seem to thrive. Jimmy and Cox worked out an agreement to stabilize currencies and end the destructive spiral of competitive devaluations. When they cabled details to Roosevelt, they received no reply and assumed this meant approval. Then Jimmy received a message from Raymond Moley that changed his life: "Tell him [Warburg] it's dead and bind up the wounds."[37] This foreshadowed Roosevelt's message of July 3, 1933, in which he railed against the currency stabilization proposal as based on the "old fetishes of so-called international bankers. . . ."[38] Belatedly, FDR had realized that currency stabilization might clash with his goal of stimulating higher farm prices. Economic nationalism had won out. It fell to Jimmy to convey this message to Prime Minister Ramsay MacDonald, who feared his political leadership would collapse with the failed conference. "This knocks the whole thing into a cocked hat," he told Jimmy, who had a young man's keen susceptibility to disappointment.[39]

Feeling betrayed by Roosevelt and spying a Machiavellian streak in the man, Jimmy reacted emotionally. On July 6, he submitted his letter of resignation to delegation chairman Cordell Hull and said of the president, "I do not feel that I can interpret his mind at a distance of 3,000 miles . . . we are entering upon waters for which I have no charts and in which I therefore feel myself an utterly incompetent pilot."[40]

Before returning to Washington, Jimmy met Siegmund, Max, and Alice in Amsterdam on July 8. The German Warburgs told of the terror reign at home, their candor suggesting the degree to which they muzzled their views inside Germany. They told of Jews hounded from schools and professions, of blind Jews evicted from special institutions. "The internal situation is a great deal worse than it looks from the outside," Jimmy wrote. "A cold pogrom is going on, not only against the Jews but against all people with other political convictions than those of the Nazis."[41] Jimmy's growing militancy, alas, coincided with the decline of his Washington influence.

Max told Jimmy that M. M. Warburg's business hadn't been severely hurt by events, although Jimmy thought it only a matter of time.[42] He urged Max to leave Germany or at least spend more time away. Max and Alice didn't know they were bracing for a sustained, hellish period. As Jimmy told his diary, "He and Alice are quite remarkable and feel that they want to give their country a few more months of grace before they definitely turn their backs upon it; also, Max feels that he can do and, in fact, is doing a lot to help various Jews who are in distress."[43] Weeks later, Felix and Jimmy revived the idea of Max selling his German assets to the Berliner Handels-Gesellschaft and moving with his foreign assets to Warburg & Company in Amsterdam.

On his way home, Jimmy met with John Maynard Keynes. They tried to devise a managed currency scheme strong enough to pacify New Deal radicals, but weak enough to avoid great damage. Keynes warned Jimmy that Roosevelt had fallen under the spell of a monetary crank from Cornell University named George Warren, who had previously devised formulas to get chickens to lay more eggs. On the boat home, Jimmy read Warren's work and agreed that it was "rubbish."[44] For Jimmy, FDR was fast losing his halo.

When he entered FDR's office for a lunch on July 24th, Jimmy found George Warren and James Harvey Rogers of Yale going out. After the professors left, Jimmy and FDR ate lunch off the president's desk. Jimmy was a cocksure young man who behaved like a young prince entitled to take liberties with the king. "I told him [Roosevelt] that his message of July 2nd had been most unfortunate both in substance and in tone. This caused him to get quite angry and he said that I should have seen the American press comment, which had been universally favorable."[45] At first, Roosevelt claimed that he hadn't seen Jimmy's cable from London. When Jimmy unearthed it, the president admitted he had glanced at it, but hadn't given it much thought. Very good in tense situations, Roosevelt defused Jimmy's anger at the lunch by treating him as an errant son and adopting his usual bantering tone about monetary matters.[46]

Though Jimmy met with Warren and Rogers in New York at FDR's request and found them more reasonable than expected, he was dubious about their plan to raise farm prices by boosting gold prices. Roosevelt then invited Warren, the farm economist, and Jimmy, the slick young banker, to thrash things out at Hyde Park. They sat through a meal overseen by the stern, formidable Sara Delano Roosevelt, FDR's mother, who reminded Jimmy of Grandma Charlotte. Contesting Warren, Jimmy made a vigorous speech that recovery required confidence in the dollar. As they left, Warren said to Jimmy,

"Well, I guess you ruined my plan." But Jimmy knew that in the money sphere, FDR was a sucker for snake oil peddlers. "On the contrary," Jimmy replied. "You have won."[47] Warren's plan to use inflation to end the Depression seemed to awaken every conservative fiber in Jimmy's body.

Roosevelt was eager to try the Warren voodoo. He began to raise gold prices, creating inflationary jitters that sent the dollar skidding. On September 20, Jimmy made a pitch against further devaluation, contending that inflation would harm workers, people on fixed incomes, and small businessmen. This time FDR was more sarcastic, his voice acquiring a rougher edge. "If we don't keep the price of wheat and cotton moving up, I shall have marching farmers," he said.[48] The president and his young adviser were at a crossroads. Certain that Roosevelt was being dangerously irresponsible, Jimmy disclosed that he would launch an anti-inflation campaign along with banks and insurance companies and FDR warned him not to do it. When Jimmy left the White House, he assumed it was for good.

On October 21, Jimmy listened to FDR's fireside chat from a friend's home in Chicago. When FDR endorsed the Warren program, Jimmy felt as if he had absorbed a body blow. Before long, FDR, Henry Morgenthau, and Jesse Jones set new gold prices each morning as the president had breakfast in his bedroom. Sometimes they pitched coins to determine the price. This capricious approach to fiscal policy sent the dollar crashing, without delivering the desired rise in farm prices.

Returning to the Bank of the Manhattan, Jimmy rallied businessmen against inflationary policy. He recruited Bob Lovett of Brown Brothers, Harriman, and John Schiff into a lobbying campaign. Swept up in a crusade, Jimmy could be impetuous and strangely heedless of the consequences. Only later did he see that he had defected to the diehard Roosevelt haters and not to the concerned Democrats. He sometimes drew extreme analogies between FDR and European fascist leaders. "Mussolini was essentially a gangster and Roosevelt was essentially a humanitarian," he said. "But in their approach to an economic crisis, they were willing to make some of the same compromises."[49]

By January 1934, FDR had abandoned his fling with George Warren, freezing gold at thirty-five dollars an ounce. In a peace overture, Roosevelt invited Jimmy for a pleasant evening at the White House along with William Bullitt. FDR praised the agile way Jimmy had deflected vicious attacks from Father Coughlin. But the rebellious impulse never slept for long in Jimmy, and he now decided to broaden his attacks against the New Deal. He decided to lecture the president on how to run the country, the first of several misadventures that would make him persona non grata at the White House.

In 1934, Alfred Knopf published Jimmy's withering polemic against the

New Deal, *The Money Muddle*, which he had written on a Caribbean cruise. As the first such critique by a former administration insider, it generated enormous attention and became a best-seller. On May 2, Jimmy sent FDR an advance copy, contending that it wasn't meant to be hostile to the New Deal. Roosevelt didn't buy this, as shown in his reply several weeks later:

> Dear Jimmy—
> I have been reading *The Money Muddle* with plenty of interest.
> Some day I hope you will bring out a second edition—but will you let an old friend make a special request of you before you do it? Please get yourself an obviously second-hand Ford car; put on your oldest clothes and start west for the Pacific Coast, undertaking beforehand not to speak on the entire trip with any banker or business executive (except gas station owners), and to put up at no hotel where you have to pay more than $1.50 a night. After you get to the Coast go south and come back via the southern tier of States. . . .
> When you have returned re-write *The Money Muddle* and I will guarantee that it will run into many more editions!
> After the above insulting 'advice to a young man'—do nevertheless run down and see me some day.[50]
>
> > Always sincerely,
> > Franklin D. Roosevelt

Jimmy was stunned by this rebuke, which called him a spoiled rich kid out of touch with reality—not exactly the way he liked to see himself.

—

Jimmy's sudden drift to the political Right was accelerated by changes in his personal life. By late 1934, he insisted upon an end to the marriage to Kay Swift, who got a Reno divorce. In later years, Kay would grow wistful about Jimmy, but he wouldn't reciprocate the nostalgia. He blamed her for the busted marriage and wrote her out of the family history. He insisted upon having custody of the children. During his brief period as a bachelor, Jimmy had his eldest daughter April serve as hostess and preside over dinner parties, raising her to an adult eminence. When Jimmy married Phyllis Baldwin in April 1935, it shattered April, who was suddenly demoted to a child again. Jimmy retained custody of Andrea and little Kay, but April ended up staying with her mother.

Each of Jimmy's three wives reflected another facet of his fragmented identity. After Kay's show-business world, Jimmy now went for high society, marrying a tall, thin, soignée WASP from an old-money background. A liberal Republican from a conservative family, Phyllis Baldwin shocked her family by marrying a Jew. She was bright, had trained as a political econo-mist, and was politically active in Manhattan's "silk-stocking" district; her brother was a congressman. Through Phyllis, Jimmy entered the Social Regis-ter and moved further from his German-Jewish background. He had no Jewish friends, sent his kids to Sunday school, and kept a Christmas tree at holiday time. When two of his three daughters married Jewish men, he was offended.

If somewhat cool and repressed after the blithe Kay Swift, Phyllis took Andrea and Kay to dances and other activities and proved a better mother than their self-absorbed parents. Jimmy increasingly felt competitive with the independent, self-assertive Phyllis and began to call her shrewish. Prone to depression, Phyllis entered analysis with the ubiquitous Zilboorg and stayed with him for many years. Jimmy was never very good around psychological problems, and the childless marriage ended up an unhappy one.

The marriage into the Baldwin family hardened Jimmy's conservatism and he began to attend Liberty League dinners. In many ways, Phyllis was more tolerant than Jimmy, who sometimes had a crude taste for ethnic humor. Yet the country-club world of the Baldwins didn't discourage Jimmy's vendetta against Roosevelt. In late 1934, he published a book, *It's Up to Us*, that drew an analogy between the New Deal and the totalitarian states in Europe. Jimmy was now slipping into the worst sort of reactionary hyperbole against FDR.

In 1935, he published *Hell Bent for Election*, a tract that introduced the phrase "soak the rich" into the lexicon. His thesis was that Roosevelt had enacted the Socialist party's platform, not the Democrat's. It was a foolish blunder. In intemperate, hyperbolic language, he conjured up a picture of Franklin Roosevelt as a power-hungry dictator who fooled himself and the people. "I think Mr. Roosevelt has a definite liking for the devious as opposed to the direct," Jimmy wrote.[51] He accused the president of egregious igno-rance in economic matters and summed up by saying that "barring an extreme radical or an extreme reactionary, almost anyone would be better than Mr. Roosevelt. . . ."[52] The book sold more than one million copies and became a bible for Roosevelt foes. It again took Jimmy time to realize that the effort was unworthy of him. As he said later, the book "was about as nasty an attack as anybody could produce."[53]

In 1936, Jimmy and Phyllis collaborated on a thin book, *New Deal Noodles*, that took alphabet letters and made barbed rhymes about government fig-ures. FDR was portrayed as a vain, smiling charlatan, leading the country into a benignly misguided dictatorship. The ridicule was laid on pretty thick. "The whole New Deal is full of hickies/One of these is Mr. Ickes, Who Plays his little pranks and quirks/ Under the head of Public Works."[54] Rexford

Tugwell fared no better: "T stands for Tugwell, and dear T.V.A./T stands for the Taxes we'll all have to pay."[55] With bile left to spare, Jimmy published a sequel to his best-seller called *Still Hell Bent* that described FDR's policies as "a strange mixture of Socialist and Fascist principles."[56]

When the Republicans nominated Governor Alfred M. Landon of Kansas for president in 1936, Jimmy realized he had bet on the wrong horse. Landon seemed an economic nationalist, while Roosevelt edged toward international cooperation. On October 13, Jimmy swallowed hard and wrote a mea culpa letter to Cordell Hull, saying he would vote for Roosevelt. "I was flayed by the Republican press and received only a chilly welcome from the Democrats, which, I thought, was precisely what I deserved."[57] A fallen angel, he didn't reenter politics until after World War II and then as a professional maverick, not a Washington insider.

It is hard to reconcile this Roosevelt-hating Jimmy Warburg with the super-liberal pamphleteer of later years. Some demon tended to drive him to extremes, making him find fault with authority figures and assert his own superior wisdom. He liked to flirt with disaster, to seek the dangerous path. He had, inexplicably, squandered a special relationship with the president in a feud that had taken on a distinctly personal tone. In psychoanalysis with Zilboorg, Jimmy realized that FDR had replaced his dead father. Along with reverence, he had transferred much of his underlying rage and a strong need to strike out against paternal authority. This psychic tension was compounded when Roosevelt scrapped the gold standard and committed other financial sins that would have shocked Paul, giving Jimmy "an uncomfortable feeling of having taken part in the desecration of my father's life work, even though my conscious reason informed me that these reforms were urgently necessary." The explosive finale of Jimmy's work with Roosevelt shows how wide and deep was his self-destructive streak, the result of suppressed anger that he turned both against others and himself.

Chastened by his Washington experience, Jimmy resigned as vice-chairman of the Bank of the Manhattan in 1935. The Warburgs remained major bank shareholders and Jimmy stayed on the board. He then made the wise decision to strike out as a lone venture capitalist. In 1937, he heard about interesting experiments being made in Cambridge, Massachusetts, by a young Harvard dropout named Edwin H. Land, who had devised a way to filter out headlight glare by passing light through sheets of polaroid material. Jimmy gathered a crew of bankers, including Averell Harriman, the Rockefellers, and Kuhn, Loeb to sponsor the new Polaroid Corporation. For his efforts, Jimmy got a substantial block of stock, with options to buy more in future. When Land got his great brainstorm for instant photography in 1943, Jimmy made his second fortune. Much like his father, Jimmy was uncannily good in business, but it didn't seem to matter to him. Instead he craved the rough-and-tumble of a political world that had now learned to perceive him as a volatile personality who could never fit into the polite conformity of official Washington.

Beat the Devil

O nce a breezy, fun-loving young man, Max Warburg at sixty-six was far more somber and introspective. In his Kösterberg studio, which resembled an Italian monk's cell, he dreamed forlornly of reconciling Zionists and non-Zionists, Jews and other Germans. Until this time, he had engaged in philanthropic Judaism, attending High Holy Days at the synagogue, covering the deficit of the Hamburg Jewish community, chairing the Jewish orphanage, and sitting on the board of the Talmud Torah school. Now he hoped to fashion a new Judaism that might transcend divisions and heal a troubled world. It would prove a sad, dispiriting exercise amid the jackbooted madness of 1933.

Writing to philosopher Martin Buber, Max said they needed a Judaism suited to modern times. The question, of course, was where it would be practiced. Still anti-Zionist, Max envisioned Palestine as a sanctuary for persecuted Jews and a seat of Jewish learning, not as a sovereign Jewish state. But even as Palestine loomed somewhat larger in his vision, he tried to devise new syntheses of German and Jewish culture. While German Jews should support Palestine, he said, they mustn't lessen their devotion to the Fatherland.[1]

From the time Hitler seized power, Max was of two minds and led a schizoid existence. One side of him exhorted Jews to stay and fight, accusing those who left of cowardice. This same man, however, was pivotal in many schemes to promote a Jewish exodus. He tried to develop a new set of reflexes without discarding the old ones and never escaped this contradiction. In many ways, Jewish financiers were the least well suited to deal with the situation, not only because they bore the brunt of much Nazi propaganda, but because they had long reposed their trust in the state and couldn't adjust to an adversarial situation.

If Max emerged as central to emigration schemes, it was because money was often the major snag for Jews hoping to flee. Many countries asked for financial guarantees before receiving Jews, which was a considerable hurdle because of German exchange controls. In 1931, the Brüning government had imposed a 25 percent flight tax on capital shifted abroad and under the Nazis, these extortionate taxes steadily rose, making the decision to leave excruciating. As private bankers, the Warburgs could sometimes offer means to help Jews extricate money from Germany.

After 1932, German citizens could only convert blocked marks into other currencies at a steep discount that would skim off 96 percent of the amount in question by the end of the decade. Jewish leaders racked their brains for ways to secure more favorable exchange rates. At this point, the Nazis were encouraging a Jewish exodus, which they thought might spread anti-Semitism abroad, especially if the refugees were poor. They also sought ways to counter the worldwide Jewish boycott of German goods and boost exports. The upshot was the so-called Haavara agreement (*haavara* means "transfer" in Hebrew) of August 1933, negotiated between Palestine Jews, backed by the Jewish Agency, and the Nazi government. In the end, this devil's pact may have spared fifty-two thousand Jewish souls from the crematoria.

Under the Haavara agreement, departing Jews would deposit their marks in blocked accounts in Germany. A year later, they would receive an equivalent amount in Palestine pounds. The hitch was that the Jews had to use those blocked marks to buy German machinery, pipe, fertilizer, etc. The Jewish immigrant was repaid with the proceeds when German goods were resold in Palestine. It was a mutually beneficial, if bizarre, business: Goods from Nazi Germany were helping to build Jewish Palestine, while Palestinian Jews created German jobs.

To supervise this transfer agreement, German Jews set up the Palestine Trust Company (Paltreu), and M. M. Warburg & Co. acted as conduit for three fourths of the money. The Palestinian end was handled by the Anglo-Palestine Bank, later called Bank Leumi. Considerable sums of money flowed through this pipeline—almost 140 million reichsmarks by the outbreak of

Siegmund and Eva Warburg.
(Private collection)

World War II—and it provided steady business for the Warburg bank in a grim season.

Naturally, many Jews were appalled by a deal that strengthened the Nazi economy, and even the Joint Distribution Committee shied away from such a controversial project. That eternal Warburg nemesis, Rabbi Stephen S. Wise, thundered: "There is something worse than entering Zion with bowed heads, and that is with unclean hands!"[2] In hindsight, it seems hard to credit the purist position of never negotiating with the Nazis under any circumstance, although the outrage was certainly understandable at the time.

Until 1936, Palestine was the prime destination for the German Jews, and Chaim Weizmann thought it the only defensible destination. "Everything else is a palliative, a half-measure, and merely postponing the evil day," he told Felix.[3] Felix doubted that Britain would issue enough immigration certificates to make Palestine more than a partial solution. He worried that the Zionists were raising false hopes and that a sudden, mass influx of Jews would provoke Arab wrath. As Palestine became the focus of German-Jewish emigration, it grew harder to talk about saving Hitler's victims without dredging up the divisive Zionism issue.

Trying to beat the devil, Max wanted to take the Haavara concept and elevate it to a grandiose plane. He daydreamed about a giant transfer bank that might permit a third of German Jews to depart for a country of their choice. That summer, he explored this concept with Dr. Schacht in Berlin. Max privately told Jewish leaders that they should exploit Nazi fantasies of infinite Jewish wealth and have overseas Jews ransom out their German brethren. Max had a recurring pipe dream that through some masterstroke of financial ingenuity, he could solve the whole problem and broker a big deal with the German government.

Though the Jewish community in Germany numbered little more than half a million people, they were well organized and operated many charities. The Aid Society of German Jews (*Hilfsverein*) had been started in the early 1900s to speed the passage of persecuted Russian Jews to America after pogroms in the Pale. Max was at first its vice-president, then, during the Third Reich, its chairman. With Hitler's rise, self-preservation superseded noblesse oblige as the group's raison d'être, and it emerged as the foremost group advising Jews who wished to go elsewhere than Palestine.

The German Jews weren't passive sheep submitting to Nazi terror. After the Nazi boycott of Jewish stores in April, Max, Melchior, and other Jewish leaders created in Berlin the Central Committee for Help and Reconstruction (*Zentralausschuss*), which helped fleeing Jews with advice, loans, and job training. It placed twenty thousand Jewish children in special German schools for retraining and resettlement work. The Warburgs were indispensable members of the group, which was partly financed by the Joint in New York. Because it was an American institution, the Joint also afforded some legal protection to German-Jewish philanthropy. To emphasize their American ties, the Warburgs invited the American consulate general in Hamburg to rent vacant space on the second floor of M. M. Warburg during the Third Reich.

By late summer 1933, German Jews were demanding strong leadership and besieged Max with requests for action. In August, he received a fervent plea from Jewish leaders in Cologne, asking him to become the new Moses. "We urgently appeal to you in the name of German Jewry: don't shut your ears to the cry of distress. Take up the burden that we present to you."[4] Some weeks later, Max joined with other non-Zionist leaders in Essen to create a group that could speak to the Nazi government on behalf of all Jews: the Reich Representation of German Jews (*Reichsvertretung*). It would oversee emigration to Palestine and elsewhere and provide Jewish schools, training, and welfare. Once again, Max was a central figure. As historian Yehuda Bauer has written, he not only initiated the group but took "a decisive part in setting up its leadership" and was "to a great extent the arbiter of its policies."[5] At the founding meeting, Max declined to be chairman, believing the Nazis might exploit his close association with Weimar politicians. Instead he persuaded Berlin Rabbi Leo Baeck to become president, with lawyer Otto Hirsch as vice-chairman. Later, Max would believe Baeck had been too peaceful a man to enforce harmony among headstrong personalities.

———

In all these activities, Max was sustained by the dignified example of Carl Melchior. When the Nazis seized power, a gravely pessimistic Melchior trooped into Max's office with a simple request. For most of Melchior's life, he hadn't been especially concerned with Jewish matters. He had waged a fruit-less campaign to free Germany from reparations only to be reviled as a blackguard Jew. Having discharged his debt to his country, he now wished to dedicate his time elsewhere. "From now to the end of my life, I would like to fight for the civil rights of the Jews, which have been cancelled in Germany."[6] Max examined the thin, worn face of his old friend, with the veins popping from his temples. "There was visible the *escalier du mort*," Max said. He tried to dissuade Melchior from this strenuous task, but the latter insisted, "It is a service I owe." As a bachelor, Melchior felt he was better positioned than Max for hazardous duty. "I do not cling to life. After all, I have been in the trenches now for twenty years."[7]

In March 1933, Melchior resigned as a German representative to the Bank for International Settlements before Schacht pushed him out and stepped down as chairman of the Beiersdorf supervisory board.[8] He didn't regard the

Nazis as amenable to reason. Rather he scented such pent-up violence in the air that he thought it only made sense to negotiate the exit of Jews from Germany.[9] Melchior's health declined and he suffered almost daily heart spasms. Late in the year, he married his long-standing mistress, Marie de Molènes. Twenty years younger than Melchior and from a noble French family, she was a writer of romantic novels. When she suddenly got pregnant after many years with Carl, he wanted to legitimate the child. Melchior labored under a powerful premonition of doom. In December, fearing possible arrest by the Gestapo, he gave his power of attorney to Dr. Kurt Sieveking. A few days later, on December 30, 1933, he died of a stroke from angina. As Max said ruefully, "He died in harness."[10]

In a touch of the macabre, Max's partner, Aby S., died of a stroke the same day as Melchior, and the Warburg bank was abruptly stripped of two of its seven partners. Aby S. had been a harmless, retiring man with little involvement in the firm, who had devoted most of his time to family and religious matters. On the board of the Jewish community, he was active in the early 1930s in contesting anti-Semitism. In 1934, Aby S.'s son, Karl, wanted to leave for England and was terrorized into selling the Alsterufer house for a distress sale price of 120,000 reichsmarks. He had been warned that Aryans could no longer be tenants in Jewish-owned buildings and received threats from the building department that he would have to paint the house's exterior. When the sale money was finally remitted to Barclays Bank in 1939, it amounted to exactly 82.5 pounds under the confiscatory exchange rates.[11]

Max learned of the death of his two partners while sailing back to Germany aboard the *Olympic*. He had gone to New York with a secret agenda. With many American banks still possessing frozen credits in Germany, he wondered whether they could tap this blocked money to create an American bank in Berlin that would buy M. M. Warburg and the Berliner Handels-Gesellschaft—a reprise of Jimmy's 1931 idea. Such an American bank, Max thought, would enjoy extra legal armor in protecting Jewish clients. The project, unfortunately, never came to pass.

———

In 1933, the demonic images that had tormented Aby M. Warburg were projected into gruesome reality. Aby had hoped that art and culture would curb unreason. Instead, the Nazis hunted down artists and intellectuals as state enemies. When the Gestapo shuttered the avant-garde Bauhaus in July, Eddie Warburg brought painter Josef Albers and his wife to America, guaranteeing Josef's salary at Black Mountain College in North Carolina. Jewish museum directors were hounded from their posts and Aby's pupil, Carl Georg Heise, was expelled from Hamburg's art museum. For the centennial of its native son, Brahms, Hamburg banned the young Jewish pianist, Rudolf Serkin. Even the local statue of Heinrich Heine was put away in a shed.

Far from guarding free expression, the German universities served as hothouses of intolerance. On May 10, 1933, students hurled books by Mann, Einstein, Proust, and Freud on a pyre outside the Berlin Opera House, followed five days later by an SS bonfire of books near Altona. The Nazis severed the "Jewish" Warburg Library from Hamburg University and decreed that it was unlawful to visit this contaminated venue. Already strapped by the Depression and weakened by drastic economies, the library effectively ground to a halt.

Hamburg's university had been a showcase for Jewish scholarship in Weimar Germany, and Max had received an honorary doctorate for his founding efforts. In 1929 Ernst Cassirer rose to become its rector—the first Jew to achieve that distinction in Germany. Now in April 1933, Jewish professors were "cleansed" from its faculty. Teaching in New York that spring, Panofsky got a cable advising him of his dismissal, and Cassirer was likewise driven out. The head of the Warburg Library, Fritz Saxl, resigned as honorary professor. Max stayed on the university's board, insisting that German scholarship should return to its old thorough independence.[12]

For the Warburgs, the idea of uprooting and relocating the library was heavily freighted with symbolism: It was like severing the family tap-root in Germany. As Gertrud Bing said, "To Max Warburg the idea that the Institute should leave its native soil was at first distasteful. . . ."[13] Mary and her children at first also resisted the move. Pessimistic about the library's future, Saxl had to fight against family illusions. At first, the library was saved by a legal loophole. Felix and Paul's estate owned 60 percent of the library, which enabled George Messersmith, the American consul general in Berlin, to release a statement declaring portions of it to be American property. This provided temporary immunity from attack. If the library had been German property, it would have fallen under "monument protection" regulations that would have made later transfer impossible.

For the Warburgs, the issue of Aby's books mirrored the larger debate about how to respond to Hitler. Felix wanted both his brothers and Aby's books to leave, and was disturbed by their endless dithering. In August, he told a friend, "I personally am very anxious to have the books transferred, but the Hamburg people still feel that this insanity of Hitler is curable."[14] Felix rebuffed an offer to house the books at the Germanic Museum at Harvard, stating that "with Hohenzollern and Hitler tendencies in the air," he preferred having the books at New York University, where Panofsky was teaching.[15] Holland wanted the wandering library, and Italy offered to put it into a Roman palazzo, but "going to Italy seemed like getting out of the frying pan into the fire," commented Eric.[16] These destinations suffered a common flaw: They would only have accepted the books as a gift, which would have saddled the Warburgs, under German tax law, with an insupportable burden. The British, however, understood that for tax and political reasons, the transfer had to be in the form of a temporary loan.

In July 1933, Professor W. G. Constable of the Courtauld Institute and Dr. C. S. Gibson of Guy's Hospital visited Hamburg to reconnoiter. In October came another prestigious scout: Sir Denison Ross, head of the Royal School of Oriental Languages. Back in London, Sir Denison assembled a committee under Lord Lee of Fareham, a former first lord of the admiralty and chairman of the Courtauld Institute. Having received an emergency call from Fritz Saxl, Kenneth Clark, head of the National Gallery, extolled the Warburg Library to Lord Lee. The Warburgs agreed to send the library to the University of London as a three-year loan without a permanent endowment. For three years, the American Warburgs would supply forty thousand gold marks and the German Warburgs ten thousand gold marks per annum. The committee also got a three-year financial pledge from Samuel Courtauld and found suitable quarters on the ground floor of Thames House near Parliament. On October 28, 1933, the British sent a formal invitation to Max to lend them the library. Now the Warburgs turned nervously to the German government for the all-important permissions.

Responsibility in the matter rested with the Hamburg government, not Berlin. Some hard-core Nazis wanted to plunder the library for their "cultural centers," while bureaucratic admirers of Aby wanted to keep the library. For seven weeks, Max conducted tense, delicate negotiations with Dr. W. von Kleinschmit, director of the Authority for Church and Artistic Matters in Hamburg. The Nazis had ambivalent reactions to the transfer. They saw a chance to persuade the British of how reasonable they were, but feared accusations of hypocrisy from their followers. How to have it both ways?

In the end, Kleinschmit told Max that he would impose a total news blackout about the transfer. He pointedly warned, "I now loyally also expect from you that you will use all your influence to prevent the foreign press from publishing anything regarding the transfer of the Library to England."[17] He said he expected the library to return in three years. In a minor concession, the Warburgs agreed to leave behind two fragments of Aby's corpus: two thousand books related to World War I and the panels created for the Hamburg planetarium.

The Warburgs now moved swiftly to ship out the library. Workers stripped the edifice of eighty thousand books and thousands of photos and slides. The entire library—including iron shelves, cameras, and bookbinding devices— was packed into 531 boxes by hand-picked anti-Nazi movers. As they performed this bittersweet task, Mary set out cups of tea for them on the trestles and planks. The mountain of boxes was then loaded onto two small ships, the *Hermia* and the *Jessica*, moored down by the Elbe docks. Freighted with their precious cargo, they steamed down the river and across the North Sea, then docked in the Thames. Saxl, Bing, and other refugee scholars fled to London as well. As Saxl said wryly, "Some scholars like Petrarch or Erasmus have always been fond of traveling, but traveling adventures are not so common in the lives of learned institutions."[18]

The timing of the move was providential. Two weeks later, jurisdiction over such matters passed to Goebbel's Propaganda Ministry. In 1934, the *Völkischer Beobachter* ran a scathing, full-page review of a bibliography published by the Warburg institute, showing how even scholarly work could be ransacked for propaganda purposes. And even if Aby's books had survived the fanatical bonfires of 1933, they might have perished in the wartime aerial pounding of Hamburg. The hollowed-out shell of the Warburg Library stood as a ghostly reminder of the creative force of Jewish scholars in Weimar Germany. As one observer put it, the building, with the word "Mnemosyne" over the door, "became the empty sham of a beautiful memory."[19]

After the boats removed the books that had been both the bane and joy of her life with Aby, Mary Warburg developed cancer. In her self-sacrificing, uncomplaining way, she didn't mention her pains to the doctors at first. She died almost exactly one year after the books left for London.

Right before Mary died, Felix said that she and her children could sell the library building and keep the money. In exchange, he was given authority over the final disposal of Aby's books.[20] This became a matter of some moment as the deadline for the three-year "loan" to London approached its expiration date. Samuel Courtauld had provided three thousand pounds per annum for the library on the condition that it stay in England at the end of the three years. Now Felix had a sudden brainstorm. Why not bring over Saxl and the books from London, have Panofsky give seminars, and recreate the Warburg Library in Paul's vacant mansion at 17 East Eightieth Street? Felix was prepared to donate five hundred thousand dollars for a joint memorial to Paul and Aby.

This idea petrified the German Warburgs, who had been evasive with the Nazi authorities about the library's ultimate fate. In July 1935, Felix had a stormy session with Eric in New York and tried to figure out why the Hamburg family was so intransigent. Eric finally revealed that the *Völkischer Beobachter* had made an incendiary political issue of the Warburg Library, portraying it as a nefarious family plot to make money by selling "non-Aryan" books to education institutions. Felix was stunned and expressed astonishment that he had only learned of this after prodding Eric: "I told him what I have told him over and over again—that I wanted all the news and all the truth about the things in which I was interested and not predigested stuff and this thing I should have heard long before his accidental coming over," Felix told Max afterward.[21]

A memo in the M. M. Warburg file shows how perilous the book issue had become. Eric wanted to reassure von Kleinschmit that the original three-year loan to England would be extended from five to twenty years, since Germany then enjoyed better relations with England than with America. "A broaching of this question can therefore be of *great* trouble for us in Germany," the memo warned about a possible transfer to America.[22] Also, the English might feel double-crossed if they lost the books, which could inspire anti-Semitism in London. Finally, the memo contended that Paul had never been a special fan of Aby's work and that it made no sense to commemorate them jointly.[23] Eric secretly enlisted his cousins Bettina and Edward to foil Felix's plan.

In late 1935, various schemes were floated to reconcile the feuding Warburgs. Panofsky advanced the notion of having a Warburg sister institute in America that might exchange students and scholars with London. Eric proposed a diplomatic settlement: forty-two thousand books would go to New York, ten thousand back to Hamburg, and thirty thousand would remain in London. Gertrud Bing rightly objected that this division would destroy the library's raison d'être.[24] Backed by Aby's son, Max Adolph, Max urged Felix to relent, saying that any attempt to dislodge the books would have frightful consequences for them in Germany, since the Nazis would never believe that the Hamburg Warburgs lacked ultimate authority over the library.[25]

It seems peculiar that Felix persisted despite such warnings. Eric even warned him that he might be thrown into a concentration camp if the books sailed to New York.[26] Felix sounded out the American ambassador in Berlin, William E. Dodd, about whether the library could travel to New York. In response, the State Department drew up a report that should have dispelled Felix's illusions on the subject. It stressed that the library had been transferred without publicity, but that a shift to New York would generate press coverage and anti-German protest in New York. The library, in short, should stay in England. Across the report, Felix scrawled one word: "Rubbish."[27] Felix must have thought Max instigated this document.

In late 1936, Felix capitulated when it became clear that, at the very least, Berlin's reaction was a terrible imponderable. In the end, Samuel Courtauld gave the Warburg Institute a seven-year financial reprieve and the University of London provided space in the Imperial Institute buildings. Thus the "temporary loan" of the library to London began to take on the trappings of an irreversible move. The Anglo-Saxon culture that had struck Aby as such a lethal menace to mankind during World War I had ended up safeguarding his own legacy.

—

In Warburg iconography, Max would symbolize those German Jews who thought it best to stay in Germany and tilt lances with the devil, while Siegmund would symbolize those who thought such a course wrong and futile. As mentioned, Siegmund had at first been sanguine about the Nazis. If he experienced a radical conversion, it probably had something to do with geography. Managing the M. M. Warburg office in Berlin, he and Eva saw *The Three-Penny Opera* and socialized more with political activists, intellectuals, and other undesirables targeted by the Nazis. Because Hitler saw Berlin as infested with his enemies, its citizens heard more stories of midnight disappearances than people elsewhere. Siegmund wasn't lulled by the optimism that came with the territory in Hamburg.

Gravitating to rebels and iconoclasts, Siegmund struck up a close friendship with the black sheep of another famous family, Edmund Stinnes. Like the Krupps and Thyssens, the Stinnes family had helped to develop the German coal and steel industry. Hugo Stinnes, we recall, had injected the "Jewish question" into the debate over reparations policy. His younger son, Hugo, Jr., became a convinced Nazi. Edmund became an equally impassioned foe of Hitler. With a doctorate in chemistry, he owned a chain of gas stations when Hitler came to power. He not only had many Jewish friends but a half-Jewish wife, which introduced an element of fear into his life.

In 1933, Edmund Stinnes met Hitler to discuss the German economy. He left aghast. "He felt that Hitler was completely off-the-wall—screaming, nonsensical, irrational," said his daughter.[28] To worsen matters, Edmund's business companion at the meeting was captivated by Hitler. As Edmund's closest Jewish friend, Siegmund would certainly have heard all about this encounter.

Siegmund had to cope with many forms of stress and again shouldered premature burdens. In 1933, his uncle, Otto Kaulla, a retired Stuttgart judge, was roughed up by Nazi hooligans. And Siegmund worried constantly about his fragile mother, Lucie, who struggled with the giant, thankless task of running the Uhenfels estate in southwest Germany. Amid his other concerns, Siegmund had to scrutinize her contracts for manure, feed, and the purchase of horses. In 1932, he learned that the estate's longtime steward, Otto Sauter, had secretly run up crushing debts. When confronted, Sauter got abusive and sent Siegmund a threatening letter, saying he and his wife would no longer tolerate such treatment. He brazenly asked "in what manner you wish to pay us off."[29] Lucie was flabbergasted to discover the magnitude of Sauter's loans. Siegmund tried to pacify the blackmailer with flattering letters, but the strategy didn't work.

When Hitler came to power, Siegmund said he had never seen his mother so indignant.[30] She was appalled that Germans had succumbed to such irrationality. The Nazis and the economic disaster on her estate sapped her physical and emotional strength. Siegmund had a Stuttgart lawyer, Dr. Peters, who kept him posted on events. In May 1933, Dr. Peters told Siegmund that tension between his mother and Sauter had acquired such animosity that she was contemplating legal action. At a Stuttgart hotel, Lucie poured out her heart to Peters, saying she felt abandoned by her son. "Frau W. then told me that her son had lost all interest in Uhenfels."[31] Dr. Peters believed Lucie's shattered nerves needed rest. Though Sauter resigned, the new manager turned out to be a Nazi, providing more trials for the beleaguered Lucie. She must have then suffered some kind of breakdown, for she spent two months in 1935 and eight months in 1936 at the Sanatorium Hochberg in Urach. Given his devotion to his mother, Siegmund must have experienced terrible worry.

Siegmund later tended to glorify his decision to flee Germany as an impulsive act of clairvoyance, yet it was intermingled with many personal and business considerations. In March 1933, Siegmund went for a chat with Baron Konstantin von Neurath, the German foreign minister. A career diplomat, descended from a noble Swabian family, the conservative baron had been a neighbor of Siegmund's and an avuncular figure in his life. Widely regarded as an opportunist and mediocrity, he was used as window-dressing to deceive governments abroad about Nazi intentions. With high respect for Siegmund's intelligence, he valued the impressions that the young banker gleaned on trips abroad. When Siegmund entered his office, von Neurath greeted him cordially and asked if he had come to report on a foreign trip.

"On the contrary, Herr Minister. I've come to report on some happenings right here in Berlin which worry me a great deal. . . . Do you know that people are arrested in the middle of the night and sent to prison without any judicial procedure?"[32] The smile left von Neurath's face. The SS had arrested Jewish and Catholic friends of Siegmund under special warrants called *Schutzhaftbefehle*. Created for the purpose of protective custody during the Weimar years, the Nazis had converted them into terrifying instruments of preventive detention.

Von Neurath confessed to having heard such reports and admitted they were "most unpleasant," but waved them away as the inevitable, messy aftermath of a revolution.[33] Siegmund wouldn't let him off the hook so easily. "It's brutal injustice," he said. "Despotism."[34] Squirming, von Neurath regretted such things. "But after all, what can I do?" he replied.[35] Siegmund pointed out that because the Nazis had never formally abrogated the Weimar Constitution, President von Hindenburg still had emergency power to dismiss any chancellor who violated the constitution. If Hindenburg fired Hitler, Siegmund argued, the Reichswehr would back him. "And it is well known, Herr Minister, that you have the ear of the President."[36]

The baron, who didn't belong to the Nazi party until several years later, then made a chilling remark that forever altered Siegmund's life. "I have to tell you, my young friend, that I myself am considered politically unreliable and must be very careful. Sorry, but there is nothing I can do. Good luck, and good-bye."[37] Siegmund later characterized this admission as a "hint of fate." Thunderstruck, he went to his office and phoned Eva in a panic, saying, "If the Foreign Minister himself has a bad conscience and is afraid, I have no doubt what will happen here to all of us sooner or later."[38] Not long afterward, Siegmund had a visit from Edmund Stinnes, who had been tipped off to an impending law that would forbid all family members from leaving Germany at the same time. About to travel to America, Siegmund feared that Eva and the children might be trapped inside Germany. "If you don't get out tonight," he told Eva, "I'm not going to America." On the spot she began to pack, planning to take the children to Sweden at once. Siegmund and Eva later gave their furniture to Edmund Stinnes for safekeeping.

Having surrendered her Swedish citizenship, Eva was petrified, since she knew it would be no easy matter to regain it. Yet her father, as head of the powerful Svenska Handelsbanken, arranged for her to see a high official who assisted her in retrieving her nationality. Because Eva's mother had cancer, Sweden became a natural destination and she stayed there with the two children for a year. Her mother died in November 1933, three years after Eva herself contracted breast cancer.

Siegmund would allow the impression to linger that the von Neurath talk had actually occurred in March 1934—not 1933—and that he had thereupon immediately left for London with his family.[39] The chronology was far more complicated. Siegmund was in the thick of reorganizing the Karstadt department store. With Eva and the children safely settled in Sweden, Siegmund sailed for New York in April and was met by Jimmy at the Brooklyn docks. On the eve of his departure from New York, the Warburgs threw a dinner for him that was marred by a panicky call. Siegmund's Berlin assistant, Roesler, had traveled to Prague to call in safety. "He urged Siegmund not to come home . . . that the bolshevistic part of the Nazis was getting stronger by the minute. . . ."[40] The Warburgs mulled over Siegmund's next step, agreeing that he should stop in England and make sure, as Jimmy said, "that if he went back into Germany that he could get out again because it is essential for M.M.W. to have someone outside the country."[41]

Jimmy's comment hints at an unfolding Warburg strategy after Hitler rose to power. Max decided to shift the center of gravity to foreign fields, setting up small outposts in various countries to service Jewish clients as they fled Germany. "The German Jewish refugees in England, among whom there were many of our former Hamburg customers, began to reestablish their businesses there and asked us to supply credit," Max said.[42] At the Amsterdam meeting following the London economic conference, Jimmy had proposed forming a new company in Amsterdam with the Berliner Handels-Gesellschaft to be called the Dutch International Corporation. This financial holding company would provide an escape route for family members, enable the Warburgs to assist Jews to transfer money abroad, and help retain clients who had left. In June 1934, the deal was sealed in a fifty-fifty split between Warburg & Company and the Fürstenbergs of the Berliner Handels-Gesellschaft, and Siegmund personally conducted the negotiations with Hans Fürstenberg.[43] Eva's family, the Philipsons, and the Wallenbergs also took small stakes in the venture, according to Hans Fürstenberg.[44]

For years, Max had wondered whether to create a London office, only to be deterred by fear of offending the Rothschilds. Now Hitler removed any chance that the Rothschilds might misinterpret such a move, since many German-Jewish banks were dispatching young representatives to London. By August 1933, lawyers in London had drawn up papers for a new firm, and Max went to London to brief Lionel de Rothschild and the Barings. In September and October, Siegmund stayed at Brown's Hotel to assist with the preparations. There were two companies under way. One was the Merchants and General Investment Corporation, to be wholly owned by Warburg & Co. of Amsterdam and Paul Kohn-Speyer. As Max told Felix in October 1933, "First and foremost Siegmund and Eric will manage the new company in London."[45] The ambitious Siegmund must have recoiled at the idea of sharing leadership with his cousin. The other entity was The New Trading Company, which was controlled by the Dutch International Company, an entity owned by a cluster of Dutch banks, including Warburg & Co. in Amsterdam, plus banks owned by Hans Furstenberg, Edmund Stinnes, and Albert Voegler. Siegmund was only marginally involved with Merchants and would adopt New Trading as his primary vehicle.

Relations between Max and the temperamental Siegmund sharply deteriorated that year. In August, Max reprimanded him, "You left yesterday without saying good-bye, which caused great offense."[46] They were bound to clash. Both were empire-builders with charm, daring, vision, and a strong autocratic streak. Even in the 1920s, Siegmund felt ambivalent toward Max, finding him inventive but superficial and impressionable. In many ways, he preferred the more humane Fritz. Gradually, the conviction ripened in Siegmund that Max was a *faux bonhomme*, a name-dropper, his friend on the surface, but a tough and ruthless character underneath.

Having spent two years wading through the Karstadt wreckage, Siegmund must have foreseen a sorry future for M. M. Warburg. Even if the bank thrived in a post-Hitler era, he would have to share power with Eric. So when Siegmund had his blinding flash of insight with von Neurath and decided to emigrate, he could afford the courage of his clairvoyance. Max, in turn, must have felt betrayed by Siegmund's unilateral decision. In January 1934, Siegmund completed the massive Karstadt reorganization, freeing him to leave.

In early May 1934, Siegmund had a heated debate with Uncle Max that summed up the excruciating choices faced by German Jews. Max had always been a fighter. When people asked whether their sons should go into business, he retorted, "Is your son a fighter—a fighter by nature?"[47] He told Siegmund that Nazism was a transitory sickness and accused him of running away from the problem. Siegmund said that by staying in Hamburg, Max was raising false hopes and misleading people who didn't have the Warburg money and resources to protect them. "Most of my family said, 'You are mad, you are crazy, you are defeatist,' " Siegmund recalled of his decision to leave.[48]

On May 31, 1934, Siegmund immigrated to London. Only thirty-one, he carried many scars and postponed dreams into exile. He rejected joining Kuhn, Loeb, deciding he was too European to become a Yankee and probably knowing that he could more easily run his own show in London. In Britain, Jews had enjoyed freedom and prosperity since the early nineteenth century, and the City of London had always been guardedly receptive to them.

Later on, Siegmund liked to portray himself as a threadbare immigrant who lost everything in Germany and started afresh in London. As a *New Yorker* profile put it, "Although Siegmund George Warburg is a member of an old and powerful banking family on the Continent, he started just about from scratch when he and his wife arrived in England from Nazi Germany as refugees in 1934. His total worth at that time was less than five thousand pounds."[49]

It doesn't detract from Siegmund's stunning achievement to state that he started life in London with signal advantages and a host of impressive connections. He and his family first lived in a mock-Georgian house in Westminster—not exactly a shabby part of town—and they had a butler and cook. Siegmund called on Montagu Norman, governor of the Bank of England, and they discussed a good school for Siegmund's son, George.[50] The Rothschilds and other City worthies received Siegmund, not as a lone, obscure refugee, but as ambassador of the distinguished banking house of M. M. Warburg & Co. (After arriving in London, Siegmund remained a Warburg partner in Hamburg and Amsterdam, retaining personal liability there.) Submitting a naturalization petition in 1934, Siegmund was sponsored by the barons of British finance—the Rothschilds, the Hambros, the Barings, and Lord Bearsted of M. Samuel. New Trading's bills were countersigned by N. M. Rothschild, giving the nascent firm the finest interest rates.[51] Siegmund's most important contact was perhaps Paul Kohn-Speyer, the chairman of Brandeis, Goldschmidt, who had married Olga Warburg. Paul Kohn-Speyer provided

Siegmund with small offices at his own headquarters on King William Street. He also took a small share in New Trading and financed many of Siegmund's early transactions.

Once Siegmund had recuperated from a bout of jaundice, the New Trading Company was launched with four people on October 3, 1934. Siegmund liked to suggest that the company was his sole creation, but the little firm was created as much *for* Siegmund as *by* him and formed part of a broader Warburg plan to follow clients abroad. It started with modest capital of 120,000 pounds. Half of the share capital was held by the Dutch banks grouped under the umbrella of the Dutch International Corporation in Amsterdam. The very name "New Trading" betrayed its origins, since many Dutch and German banks were called trading companies in homage to their origins as overseas trading banks. To the more literal British, it seemed an odd and confusing name. In early 1935, Max told Hans Fürstenberg that the Warburgs would trim their investment in Dutch International, but boost their New Trading stake, citing Siegmund's intense work for the latter as making that move logical.[52]

To penetrate the inbred world of the City, the Warburgs needed to furnish New Trading with a high-class British board. In searching for people who were socially top-drawer, the M. M. Warburg partners touted Harry Lucas as the best possible manager, with Siegmund as his "adviser."[53] There seems little doubt that Max intended to control both Siegmund and New Trading. In August 1934, his partner, Ernst Spiegelberg, told him that if they instructed Siegmund clearly about the London setup, "I believe that we can steer the London boat quite according to our wishes."[54] But the strong-willed Siegmund hadn't fled Germany to serve as a foot soldier again for Max.

Holding a quarter of the share capital, the new manager, Harry Lucas, brought just the right tony profile to New Trading. An old Etonian who was also Jewish, he had trained at Rothschilds and managed the National Discount Company. The son of a fabulously wealthy Goldsmid heiress, he enticed his cousin, Dick Jessel, into becoming a New Trading investor. Jessel's mother was also a Goldsmid sister, and his grandfather had been the Master of the Rolls. So Lucas and Jessel put Siegmund in the very midst of the Jewish nobility of England, giving his tiny firm a cachet out of all proportion to its size. Tall, thin, and very charming, Lucas waltzed in at ten o'clock each morning and never equaled Siegmund's industry. But he tutored Siegmund in the manners and mores of the City and did the hiring for the firm.

The rest of the British facade was equally illustrious and branched out beyond the Jewish community. Sir Andrew McFadyean, a former high civil servant, would become chairman of New Trading. Closely associated with the Liberal party and a former private secretary to Prime Minister Stanley Baldwin, he had met Siegmund through his work on the Reparations Commission in Berlin. Sir Kenelm Lee Guinness of the brewing family, an ex-racing car driver who had started a spark plug company, also joined the board. Other luminaries included Gerald Coke of Rio Tinto and the self-made Sir Louis Sterling, the head of EMI.

In recounting his London start, Siegmund was wont to edit out his Hamburg relatives, as if he had sprung, full-blown, out of nowhere. It is hard to imagine that Siegmund could have assembled the distinguished London board without the Warburg and Fürstenberg money and connections. Nonetheless, the credit for building up the firm must go entirely to Siegmund. Despite the stigma of being an immigrant with a thick Swabian accent, he developed New Trading with a tremendous fighting spirit. His desire to succeed was perhaps a disguised form of revenge against fate, a determination not to let the Nazis ruin his life. Often exhausted and even sick from overwork, he had to resist Eva's pleas to take a vacation.

One of Siegmund's secrets was that he never sought refuge in false pride. He was scrappy, opportunistic, and unorthodox in finding clients. Having seen the German banking collapse firsthand, he focused on fee-based business with limited risk. To create the modern Denham film laboratories for producer Alexander Korda he assembled an investor group and interested the giant Prudential insurance company. It turned out that Korda overstated the potential of his new studios and disaster loomed. Siegmund grew so upset that he became ill, lost his voice, and couldn't even talk on the telephone. He feared the Korda fiasco would ruin his reputation and by dint of hard work arranged a last-minute rescue along with Henry Grunfeld. "From that moment on," he said, "I had established my reputation with the Pru."[55] (Other sources speculate that it was Pearl Assurance.) As a result of the debacle, however, New Trading sacrificed the support of two key financial angels, the German Brettauer brothers, who had, in one stroke, nearly doubled the firm's capital.

Siegmund spent an enormous amount of time helping to extricate Jewish families and their money from Nazi Germany, often through barter or blocked-mark deals. He was active in refugee organizations. In 1934, Violet Bonham Carter, the daughter of former Prime Minister Herbert H. Asquith, spoke in the Royal Albert Hall about the plight of German-Jewish children. As a result of this speech, Siegmund became acquainted with her and won the friendship of a blue-ribbon family.[56]

By a wonderful coincidence, Siegmund ended up in the same city as his friend and literary idol, Stefan Zweig, who was driven into exile by the Nazis in 1934. He assisted Zweig in converting his blocked marks at M. M. Warburg in Hamburg into pounds sterling at Warburg & Company in Amsterdam.[57]

The two discussed publishing a monthly journal written by German-Jewish refugees, and Siegmund referred Zweig to Uncle Felix for funding. It proved a pleasant daydream of the sort that momentarily diverts those who have irretrievably lost their homeland.

Siegmund and Zweig often mused about the myopia of a world that turned a blind eye to the Nazi peril overshadowing Europe. Uncle Max might retain hope, but Siegmund's pessimism now hardened into absolute conviction. As he told Zweig in 1935, "I believe that the Hitler Regime in Germany still sits, as before, firmly in the saddle while the outside world has accepted it completely (with curious speed and ease . . .)."[58] Siegmund was never fooled by the periodic tactical lulls in Hitler's aggressive rhetoric. When Hitler entered the Rhineland in 1936, he thought war was inevitable. And when the Japanese invaded China in 1937, he told Zweig that it was but a small installment of the tremendous disaster that would engulf Europe within a year or two.[59]

CHAPTER 29

Unseen Menace

Of Malice's four daughters, only Lola and Gisela stayed in Germany throughout the terror of the 1930s, and both showed their father's tough, pugnacious spirit in fighting for the Jewish community. During the Weimar years, the four daughters with the Italianate names—Lola, Renate, Anita, Gisela—made an impressive transition from conventional female roles to political and social activism. The tremendous energy channeled into family and firm by Sara and Charlotte now burst out in a dozen new directions, as Warburg women experimented with new forms of freedom in the 1920s. The strict, puritanical upbringing of the Warburg daughters produced a devotion to good causes, but also a taste for the romantic, the taboo, and the unorthodox.

The oldest and youngest daughters, Lola and Gisela, shared Max's view that cutting and running from Germany was cowardice. The Third Reich hastened Lola's metamorphosis from society hostess to ardent Zionist and activist. Frieda chided the exquisite, blue-eyed Lola as a vain hypochondriac, a " 'glamour girl,' very conscious of her charm" in the Berlin salons of the 1920s. But with Hitler's rise, Frieda said, "when [Lola] could no longer indulge in expensive cures, she took up social work in the Zionist field."[1] Lola took up social causes in the 1930s when she was still a magnetic figure of delicate beauty and alluring manner, with a deep theatrical voice. She and her industrialist husband, Rudolf Hahn, lived in the Berlin suburb of Wannsee, where the Final Solution would be plotted years later. The turbulent times brought out a passionate, combative tenacity in Lola, a fighting spirit not unlike that of her father, whom she adored. She was a compound of gossamer beauty and iron will, Mona Lisa with a field marshal's soul.

As already mentioned, Lola, in marrying Rudo, had entered into a strange, triangular relationship with his brother, Kurt, the founder and headmaster of the Salem school. Rudo was a big, hearty outdoorsman who liked to hunt, garden, and sail in yachting regattas. "[Lola] said she always felt safe with Rudo," said a friend.[2] Where Rudo was earthy, Kurt was brilliantly mercurial, and Lola worshipped his mind. Many Warburgs thought that the bachelor Kurt was either asexual or a repressed homosexual, which, if so, probably enabled Lola to achieve great intimacy with him without arousing the jealousy of his brother.

As occurred with Chaim Weizmann, Kurt slaked Lola's thirst for intellectual stimulation. Aware of her lack of education, she avidly listened to Kurt spouting his pioneering theories of education and became his devoted pupil. As with all causes she advocated, Lola gave herself unreservedly to Kurt and catered to his personal needs. From early brain surgery, he suffered from an excruciating sensitivity to sunlight and wore thick, gogglelike glasses. Lola helped him to select the wide-brimmed hats that became his trademark and she kept the curtains drawn for him. (He even had Venetian blinds installed in his car.) Kurt fully reciprocated the fascination and always said that Lola would have been a wonderful Salem student.

When Kurt and Prince Max of Baden started Salem on Lake Constance after World War I, they had envisioned it as a training ground for a new generation of German leaders, and many civil servants and aristocrats sent their children there. The school was housed in an old Cistercian monastery, donated by the prince, and it enforced a Spartan, disciplined style. As part of its mission, the school hoped to instill democratic principles in its students. Clearly, a crusader such as Kurt couldn't coexist with Nazism, and when Hitler praised some SS men who murdered a young Communist in 1932, Kurt wrote to the Salem parents, informing them that Nazi and Salem principles were incompatible. If they disagreed, parents were encouraged to withdraw their children from the school. Kurt gambled everything on a matter of principle, and most Salem parents supported him.

In March 1933, the Nazis arrested Kurt and forbid further contact between him and his students. Lola frantically cast about for ways to get him released. She even went to a fashionable Berlin analyst who had treated Rudolf Hess

Lola Hahn-Warburg
with her children, Benita and Oscar.
(Courtesy of Lucie Kaye)

in the hope of learning something about that Nazi that might help. After vigorous protests from British Prime Minister Ramsay MacDonald, Kurt was released. A veteran anglophile—Salem was patterned after a British public school—he emigrated to Scotland, where he founded the Gordonstoun School. Among the boys following him was Philip Mountbatten, who became head boy at Gordonstoun. Both Prince Philip and Prince Charles would number among the Gordonstoun alumni, later providing Lola with a coveted link to the British royal family.

Lola suffered a second misfortune in 1933. On a sweltering summer day, Rudo was about to take their children, Oscar, ten, and Benita, six, for a horseback ride when Oscar sagged mysteriously in the heat. It turned out he had polio, possibly contracted from the swampy land around the Hahns' weekend house outside Berlin. Unfortunately, it wasn't properly diagnosed for two weeks. When the doctors said that Oscar should be isolated and quarantined in a hospital, Lola insisted that he be treated by their Jewish doctor. When this proved impossible, she stayed at home with Oscar. She threw herself into this medical ordeal with awesome stamina and searched for the best medical advice. Max and Alice ordered a special bed from Switzerland that rose like a hospital bed. For six and a half weeks, Lola slept beside Oscar and cared for him. A woman who thrived in a crisis, she found extra reserves of energy. With characteristic faith in her own judgment, she administered morphine to Oscar in a way that she knew would relieve his pain without producing addiction. Lola would say she had given birth to Oscar twice.[3]

The golden girl of the 1920s was now often tired and worn from helping her crippled child. Every night, she and Oscar would pray together. He was an active and high-spirited little boy, and this made it harder for him to accept his handicap. With almost fanatical perseverance, Lola tried to persuade him that he could live normally. Equipped with crutches and special shoes, Oscar slowly learned to walk. Even with the irons biting deep into his flesh, he moved about with tremendous determination. Despite many initial failures, Lola got him to play table tennis until he could beat other people and she encouraged him to develop his upper body muscles. When Rudo went shooting, Oscar went too, and while at Gordonstoun, he went sailing. Standing on crutches, Oscar was bar mitzvahed in July 1936 and was only frustrated that he couldn't dance at the celebration.

With Oscar, Lola exhibited superhuman bravery. One day, in a case of mistaken identity, the Gestapo appeared at the door and asked to search the house. In a flash, Lola said they could enter only on one condition. In one room, she explained, they would see a little boy on crutches. "I will tell him that you are all insurance men so as not to upset him." When the Gestapo poked their heads into his room, Oscar greeted the "insurance men" and waved his crutches.[4] Many Warburgs believe Lola became so obsessed with

Oscar as to neglect her daughter, Benita. Some anecdotal evidence supports this. One day, Benita was bitten by a bee but at first said nothing. When the child was asked why she hadn't spoken up sooner, she said she didn't think anyone would care.⁵ Benita herself said she never felt neglected.⁶

In the end, Lola's devotion to Oscar curbed her affair with Chaim Weizmann, which persisted after Hitler came to power. Weizmann's letters from the early 1930s are sprinkled with references to trysts with Lola in St. Moritz, Zurich, and Palestine. He didn't seem to hide these assignations from his wife. Lola shared his passion for Palestine, even though it is hard to picture her opting for the rugged life there. She had the irresistible appeal of a gorgeous woman who enjoyed dedicating herself to visionary men. Weizmann anointed her with affectionate names, calling her Loli or dearest Lol.

To this confidante, Weizmann unbuttoned his feelings in melancholic letters that revealed his secret worries. He bewailed his fatigue, depression, and disappointments. After moving to Palestine, he was dismayed by its gold rush atmosphere. "Some days I could cry from fatigue and heartache," he told her in 1934.⁷ What he couldn't say publicly as a Zionist leader he often confided to Lola. "It seems to me that I'm the oldest Jew in the world, perhaps 2,000 years, with all the miseries and failing and hopelessness loaded on him. . . ."⁸ He didn't mince words about non-Zionists in the Jewish Agency, including Felix, berating them for their superficiality and frivolity.

Weizmann sympathized with Lola over Kurt Hahn's arrest and her struggle with Oscar. "That you have to carry the burden of two and sometimes three families is unjust, but the world is construed absurdly," he wrote.⁹ Oscar's polio came at a critical juncture in their love affair. Before she died, Lola told friends that she and Weizmann had discussed divorcing their spouses and went off to Switzerland with such thoughts in mind. Then Oscar wrote to Lola, saying how much he missed her. She knew then she could never leave Rudo. The affair with Weizmann petered out, apparently, by the time Lola and Rudo fled to London in 1938.¹⁰

Despite her enormous domestic burdens, Lola made a noteworthy contribution to Jewish welfare work in Nazi Germany along with her youngest sister, Gisi, who also lived in Berlin. A skillful organizer and fund-raiser, Lola copied her father's methods. She worked closely with Wilfrid Israel, whose family owned the large, voguish Berlin department store of N. Israel. A dapper, discreet homosexual, Israel counted artists and intellectuals among his friends and served as the original for the Bernhard Landauer character in Christopher Isherwood's novel, *Goodbye to Berlin.* During the Nazi years, he was Max Warburg's secret emissary, assigned to sensitive missions to Britain. Like Max, he thought wealthy Jews had a special obligation to stay in Germany and resist the Nazis.

In 1932, Wilfrid Israel talked to the poet and teacher, Recha Freier, about ways to counter the corrosive despair among Jewish youth. When the Nazis banned Jewish students from most universities, the need for action grew urgent. So Israel and Freier joined forces with Henrietta Szold, Lola, and others to create Youth Aliyah, which would train and send Jewish teenagers to Palestine. (*Aliyah* means "ascent" or "emigration" in Hebrew.) Besides instructing young Jews in crafts and agriculture, it also taught them Hebrew. Lola acted as liaison between the organization and other Jewish groups. Youth Aliyah would help thousands of teenagers resettle in Palestine by World War II. Some students were trained at Kösterberg in gardening, fishing, and seamanship.

Starting in 1935, the skinny, blond, blue-eyed Gisi was a spark plug of the Youth Aliyah office in Berlin. For two years, she had worked at M. M. Warburg and then attended lectures at Oxford before Henrietta Szold, the founder of Hadassah (the American Women's Zionist Organization), recruited her for Palestine work. During a 1935 Palestine visit, she cabled home that she wanted to stay but Max cabled back: "Understand wish but beg you to come home."[11] Gisi obeyed. The Warburg answer to Joan of Arc, she was an inspirational speaker at fund-raisers and unselfishly devoted to Youth Aliyah. "I like to know that Hitler's victims are being turned into democratic fighters for freedom," she told one audience.[12] Often she had the weighty task of selecting those applicants to be trained for Palestine.

At one point, while her boss underwent an operation, Gisi temporarily served as director of Youth Aliyah in Berlin. It occurred just as the British drastically cut back on immigration certificates for Palestine. To maintain morale, Youth Aliyah sent out a circular to Jewish teenagers, urging them to study Hebrew in the meantime. During this period, Gisi was summoned to the dread Gestapo headquarters on the Prinz Albrechtstrasse. She knew that many people who had entered the building never emerged from its torture chambers. For thirty minutes, Gestapo interrogators searched for a blue file. When they found it, they began asking her, unexpectedly, to translate Hebrew words. It gradually dawned on Gisi that a Youth Aliyah clerk, by some grotesque mistake, had mailed a Nazi *Gauleiter* the literature urging Jewish teenagers to study Hebrew. The recipient took it as an offensive joke. Gisi patiently explained that it was an accident, with no insult intended. "If you engage in other such jokes," she was told, "your outfit will be closed."[13] After her release, she went back to the Youth Aliyah office. Once the initial wave of terror passed, she began to contemplate the comic spectacle of a Nazi official breaking open the Youth Aliyah envelope. "I had a hysterical laughing fit in the office, thinking of that *Gauleiter* opening his mail, telling him to learn Hebrew." She said she had never laughed so hard in her life.[14]

It was typical of Gisi to maintain her good humor and equanimity in difficult moments. When Hitler decided to force Jews to adopt Jewish-sounding first names if they didn't already have them, Gisi applauded the move in the Youth Aliyah office. "Hitler has saved us thousands of marks," she said, because they could shorten cables to the last name alone and thus save money. Max was bewildered that his daughter could joke about such matters. "That is the strangest humor I ever heard," he told her.[15]

———

Two of Max's daughters, Renate and Anita, were spared much of the Third Reich. In the 1920s, Renate may have seemed the most colorful daughter, if a shade eccentric and naïvely susceptible to the exotic fads of the Weimar years. With her spunk and verve, she seemed a lot like Max. This versatile young woman studied Latin and Greek, wrote poetry, played the piano, became an expert in antique organs, and painted well enough to sell her work. In 1927, she married Dr. Richard Samson, son of the Warburg family lawyer and anything but your typical Jewish doctor. Through a Berlin guru, he had become an adherent of a mystic Indian sect that believed in vegetarianism and practiced sex only during full moons. Becoming involved in the cult too, Renate had to wear all white. About fifty devotees followed the guru's dictates, even when he told them to dig for gold at a certain spot outside Berlin. After the Nazis came to power, Anita learned from Somerset Maugham's niece that the maharajah of Indore was seeking a personal physician and local hospital director. Though sixty doctors had already been interviewed, Dr. Samson got the post and not only took Renate and their son, but brought a team of German physicians with him.

With their son, Mattanja, the Samsons lived with the maharajah in fairy-tale magnificence, dwelling in a mansion staffed by thirteen servants and with a pet cobra in the garden. Chafing under lunar limits imposed upon her sex life, the red-blooded Renate fell in love with Walter Strauss, a doctor her husband recruited from Germany. She divorced Samson and married Strauss who was a fine doctor, very musical, and a good sportsman, but without Renate's joie de vivre. He proved a disastrous, disloyal husband. They moved to Glasgow, had a spastic daughter, and later divorced. In her last years, Renate would marry an eminent archeologist, Sir William Calder, who would die within a year after their marriage.

Anita, the third daughter, was pretty, spirited, and very sociable. After attending Salem, she studied violin with the first violinist of the Berlin Philharmonic. Then she turned to sculpture in 1928 after Max shipped her off to Florence to break up a love affair. In time, she also drew and designed textiles and ceramics. Dubious about the future of German Jews, she left for London in 1935 after Siegmund assured Max that he would guarantee her financial security. Soon after arriving in London, Anita had an expensive pearl necklace appraised and insured by Lloyd's of London. By a freakish coincidence, it was stolen within days. Teams of suspicious insurance inspectors fanned out, convinced the theft had been staged. When they concluded that it was legitimate, Anita received enough money to support herself for two years.

Anita imagined that she could act as a bridge between England and newly arrived refugees from Germany. Working with the Jewish Refugee Committee, she supervised exhibitions for refugee artists. In 1940, she married the non-Jewish Max Wolf, son of a Swiss mayor, and a courageous correspondent for the *Manchester Guardian*. For three years, he had worked underground in Germany, his cover story being that he was writing for a film magazine. Putting his life at risk, he sneaked out the minutes of the Reichstag trial in the bottom of a bag of fruit.

The extremely colorful Malice daughters were much more like Max than Alice. Funny, vivacious, and enthusiastic, they were totally committed to social causes. Anita and Renate had their mother's artistic talents, but not her remote temperament. They came to terms with Alice only with difficulty. Lola found it hard to confess her resentment of the mother who had brutally tagged her "stupid Lola." She would refer to her "beloved mother" but there was always something forced and labored about it. The distance from their mother certainly added to the daughters' adoration of Max. Their identification with Father doubtless fed their emancipated outlook on life and their desire to seek fulfillment outside the home in unconventional ways.

———

Fritz Warburg and his twin sister, Louise Derenberg, were less nationalistic than their older brothers, and their families were consequently less sanguine about the plight of German Jewry. Louise's son, Walter, was a patent lawyer who could no longer practice or publish articles. Desperate to leave in 1933, he told Felix he couldn't imagine exposing children to such fanatic hatred.[16] His sister, Ruth, was married to a leftish Dutch avant-garde artist, César Domela, who had befriended Mondrian, Klee, Kandinsky, and other artists now denigrated as degenerate by the Nazis. The Domelas left after the Reichstag burning in 1933 and would survive World War II in occupied Paris. Ruth's sister, Gabriele, worked at a home for delinquent girls in Frankfurt and as a social worker for the Hamburg Jewish community before fleeing to England in 1936. The Derenberg children would harbor bitterness toward Max for encouraging their mother to stay in Germany. In the end, it was César Domela's Dutch citizenship, not Max's connections, that would rescue Louise.

Fritz never shared Max's certitude that Nazism, like a bad dream, would vanish in time. "He wasn't as nationalistic a German as Max," said his daughter. "He was more realistic about it because he talked to more people. But he didn't think it could happen to him."[17] Indeed, Fritz and Anna Beata didn't frequent the elegant dinner parties attended by Max and Alice and so perhaps had a more sober view of things. After 1933, Fritz headed the Jewish community in Hamburg, attending to the perpetual financial crisis of the local Jewish hospital. He also chaired an adult education committee that tried to keep a flicker of civilization alive amid the general bestiality. After having given her career to the Fröbel kindergarten association, Anna Beata was kicked off its board and set up her own Jewish kindergarten. When her daughter, Eva, was dismissed from her teaching job at a kindergarten amid a good deal of anti-Semitic abuse, she, too, started her own day nursery. Fritz's family hadn't been religious, but they now had to study Jewish history and lore to teach the Orthodox Jewish children who flocked to them. Eva was converted to Zionism and began to keep kosher at Kösterberg.

In 1933, Ingrid and Eva were already young women, but Fritz's third daughter, Charlotte Esther ("Noni")) was just eleven and experienced National Socialism through more innocent eyes. At night, she dreamed that Nazis hid in the Kösterberg park and were about to come and snatch her away. Each morning, when the chauffeur drove her to school, she looked out the window and saw anti-Warburg graffiti scratched on the walls. Hurt and bewildered when teachers and students began to tease her about her wealth, she made the driver drop her a block from her school, so other children wouldn't see the rich Jewish girl embarking from a fancy, chauffeur-driven car.[18] After a time, the Nazis purged the old liberal teachers and brought in a new corps of conformists who made the children salute the swastika flag each morning. When the headmaster banished Jewish students in 1935, Noni was sent to the Eerde school in Ommen, Holland. Started by English Quakers the previous year to serve, inter alia, as a refuge for persecuted Jewish children, it received financial aid from Eric Warburg. Aby M.'s son, Max Adolph, went there to teach.

By a pleasing biological joke, the prettiest of the three sisters, Ingrid, most resembled the homely Fritz. With her darkly exotic good looks and statuesque carriage, she reminded everybody of the Egyptian queen Nefertiti. Ingrid would later describe her early years at Kösterberg as an earthly paradise, with the family house shaded by towering beech trees that Fritz called his "elephants." It was a place where the dahlias seemed to bloom forever and the apples and pears hung heavy on the trees. "One believed in a progressive development of Germany in economics and politics and the Jewish Warburg family, with its far-flung family and professional connections abroad, would doubtless be a part of that development."[19] Ingrid often stayed with Lola in

Berlin, attending Max Reinhardt productions and viewing the art of Käthe Kollwitz and George Grosz.

Fritz and Anna Beata gave Ingrid a good education, sending her to Salem and then to the University of Heidelberg. In 1932, she and Gisi studied English at Somerville College at Oxford. This year would acquire a powerful retrospective glow. Ingrid met Chaim Weizmann, who warned of the fate about to overtake German Jews. She also befriended Isaiah Berlin and Fritz Schumacher, the nephew of the well-known Hamburg architect and later famous as the "small-is-beautiful" economist. Most of all, she was smitten by a German Rhodes scholar at Balliol College named Adam von Trott zu Solz, who was destined to become a storied member of the German Resistance.

Tall, handsome, and urbane, Adam would flit temptingly through Ingrid's daydreams for a lifetime. He had blue-blooded antecedents. His father was a Prussian culture minister and his grandfather an ambassador under Bismarck. On his mother's side, he was descended from John Jay, the first chief justice of the U.S. Supreme Court. A thoughtful and principled young man, Adam starkly saw the horrors ahead in Germany, yet was imbued with a patrician sense of state service. In 1933 he returned to Germany, determined to fight the Nazis from within. This decision disappointed and confused many Oxford friends, who saw any government service in Nazi Germany as prima facie evidence of betrayed idealism.

After her time at Oxford, Fritz urged Ingrid to resume her education at Hamburg University. She studied English, German, and philosophy and wrote a dissertation on the English Puritan Lucy Hutchinson. Ingrid was grateful for being rooted, one last time, in German culture before it was rudely snatched away.[20] Fritz also encouraged her to immerse herself in the Jewish philosophy of Martin Buber and the plays and novels of Sholem Asch. This simultaneous dedication to German and Jewish culture summed up the entire tragic dilemma of the Warburgs.

In the twilight reality of 1933, the terror had an eerie way of intruding from the shadows then disappearing—as if nothing had happened. On a vivid day that spring, Ingrid was out strolling with a young lawyer named Peter Bielenberg. (The Warburgs would introduce Peter to Adam and the two became blood brothers in the Resistance.) They crossed the lovely Lombardsbrücke that separated the two lakes in downtown Hamburg. The bridge had pretty Victorian lamps, with garland-wreathed cherubs at the base. Ingrid and Peter suddenly saw a commotion ahead. Two short men ran by them in terror, clutching briefcases, pursued by two husky, winded SA men. Instinctively, Peter made a move to stop the SA men, but Ingrid—with a self-protective instinct—squeezed his arm. "Peter," she said, "are you mad?"[21] Ingrid's gaze made him stop. When they turned again, the crowd that parted for the frantic chase scene had regathered. They again formed part of a large group of pedestrians enjoying the sunshine. The lake shone, the unpleasant incident had ceased, the curtain had closed over the hideous reality. The two hunted men were probably trade unionists. In early May 1933, Hitler disbanded the unions and raided their offices. The trade-union offices in Hamburg were in the Hotel Atlantic, beside the Lombardsbrücke.

Increasingly, Kösterberg seemed a sanctuary from a world governed by madness. As Ingrid said of the 1933 summer she and her family spent there, "More than ever, Kösterberg was like a tranquil island."[22] With its consoling shade and beauty and ancient trees, the estate embodied the wealth and culture the Warburgs had enjoyed for generations. That summer, fresh from his Oxford exams, Adam von Trott visited Kösterberg and tried to convince Fritz that the Warburg wealth wouldn't immunize the family from persecution. When Adam insisted that no Jewish family was safe, Fritz didn't believe him.

The love affair between Adam and Ingrid was doomed to be a casualty of circumstance. While serving his legal apprenticeship, Adam came under strong pressure to join the Nazi party. One morning in December 1933, as the mist rose from the Elbe below, Ingrid wrote a long, anguished letter to Adam, saying that their friendship couldn't survive his entry into the party even if it was meant to camouflage his political dissent. "Because it is humanly impossible that you should belong to a group for whom an important position is repugnance for my group."[23] This by no means ended Ingrid's affection for Adam and she rendered important help to him in his Resistance work in coming years.

In February 1934, Adam von Trott committed an error in judgment that would later haunt his efforts to win foreign support for the Resistance. The *Manchester Guardian* ran a series about the persecution of Hessian Jews, and Adam sent the paper a letter that denied any problem and sounded suspiciously like a Nazi whitewash. He wrote that Jews encountered no discrimination in Hessian courts, nor were Jewish merchants penalized by the Nazi boycott. "Again and again I have spoken to active storm troopers who feel themselves pledged to the race doctrine of their leaders but would never consider themselves justified to execute it with methods of violence, and who turn with indignation from the suggestion of atrocities being committed in their presence."[24] The letter was a grievous lapse of judgment.

For Ingrid and other Warburgs, the Nazi threat first appeared as a sudden chill in the air, not a knock at the door. At the university, students drifted silently away from her. One day, a student approached her and apologized that in future he couldn't greet her anymore or he might have to forfeit his scholarship.[25] Another day, Ingrid climbed up a ladder at the university library to fetch a book. Losing her balance, she crashed to the floor and blacked out momentarily. When she awoke, she saw that the students still sat at their desks, pretending not to notice. Nobody had risen to help her. While driving back to Kösterberg, she realized that her arm was broken. "The shock over the behavior of my fellow students was greater than the pain."[26]

For the Warburgs, the Hitler years were often such an incongruous mix of banal, quotidian reality suddenly tinged with horrible, sadistic touches. When Ingrid took her oral exams at the university, two professors concealed Nazi badges behind their lapels as they quizzed her about Plato.[27] When she passed the test and became one of the last Jews to graduate in 1936, her parents decided to reward her with a trip to Uncle Felix in New York. Before going, she made a poignant farewell trip through Franconia and Bavaria with some friends bound for Palestine. While the landscape was peaceful and lovely, anti-Semitism shattered the tranquility at every stop. Many towns had warning signs at their entrance saying, "Jews enter this town at their own risk."[28] As they rolled through a Germany bedecked with swastikas and throbbing with a palpable hatred, Ingrid and her friends sang German and Hebrew songs, including the Hatikvah, the Jewish anthem, saying good-bye to the Fatherland in their own way.

The Closing Doors

For Max Warburg, the final illusions of influence began to yield to the reality of a country drenched in violence and bloodshed. Each hope was dashed by some terrible new setback. On June 28, 1934, Max met with Franz von Papen to protest the treatment of Jews, and the vice-chancellor was charming, if noncommittal. When Max said Jews could leave Germany in orderly fashion if the government cooperated, von Papen agreed to ponder the matter. Two days later came the "Night of the Long Knives." Ernst Röhm, the SA chieftain, and hundreds of Storm Troopers were massacred in a gruesome power struggle that established Himmler's dominance. For Max, it was all doubly devastating because the murder victims included von Papen aides whom he had met with forty-eight hours before.

That September, the Nazi weekly, *Der Stürmer*, launched a searing attack against the Warburgs, complete with a photo of Max captioned, "Representative in Versailles, Financial Backer of Social Democracy."[1] The article raked over the moldy lies about Paul and Max being at Versailles and said an American Warburg had attended a world Jewish Congress to strengthen the boycott of German goods. As if one could quote Scripture to the devil, Max insisted that his lawyer, Dr. Hermann Samson, write a formal protest letter to the Gestapo! Dr. Samson duly wrote, pointing out that Max had belonged to the conservative German People's Party and sat on the right side of the aisle in the Hamburg *Bürgerschaft*. How could such a man be accused of aiding Social Democracy?[2]

A few weeks later, Max and Alice sailed to New York. Their spirits were refreshed by these periodic trips abroad. They still held to the belief that fate had unpacked all the horrors that could possibly befall them. As Felix wrote, "Brother Max and Alice and Anita arrived looking remarkably well and they are courageous and anxious to do things for others." Then he added, with a note of exasperation, "On what their optimism is based, I haven't been able to find out, outside of the fact that they feel things cannot go on as they are now."[3]

In 1935, Malice returned to America to lobby for aid to German Jews. Even in New York, Max was shadowed by the Gestapo, and his speeches to Jewish groups were monitored. Sticking to the official line of the German-Jewish leadership, he pleaded for an end to the organized boycott of German goods. Communist groups assailed him with anti-Semitic propaganda dressed up as progressive thought. The Communist *Daily Worker* told its readers that Max came to the United States representing the Nazi government and was "rewarded handsomely" by being named an "Honorary Aryan."[4] Echoing the old Sidney Warburg canard, the Yiddish paper *Freiheit* made the hurtful charge that Felix, a member of the Jewish bourgeoisie, had given the Nazis a seven-million-dollar loan in 1933.[5]

The libel of the "Honorary Aryan" circulated so widely that Felix felt obligated to respond in a letter to Samuel Untermyer, a distinguished Jewish lawyer. He evoked the humiliations that Max had suffered, the expulsions from corporate boards. But he knew the real uneasiness resided with Max's access to Dr. Schacht and other Nazi officials. As he explained to Untermyer, Max believed that "so long as he has some sort of contact with people such as Schacht, he owes it to his co-religionists to make some effort (probably mostly unsuccessful) to get some relief for the people who cannot leave and cannot get their funds out. It is a great source of anxiety and sorrow for me to have him over there and I have made every effort to tempt him to leave the country, but he feels that he is too old to expatriate himself and that it may be of some use to his co-religionists for him to be there. He doesn't care what happens to him personally."[6]

In this perilous time, Max still had his old powerful presence, the barrel chest and firm jaw, but heavy pouches hung from his eyes and his expression seemed beleaguered. His lack of concern for his own safety was partly bluff. "He was afraid every day what might happen to him," said his daughter. "He was really risking an awful lot."[7] As a thick pall settled over the Warburgs,

Max and Felix Warburg conferring
at the Hotel Bellevue in Baden-Baden, 1930s.
(Courtesy of Anita Warburg)

Alice sometimes retreated into a world of private melancholy. When she was distraught, she sat alone in the corner of a beautiful room that she had designed in green satin with Italian furniture. This setting seemed to comfort her. Eric later said he felt that during this time he had one foot in the concentration camp.

Starting in the spring of 1935, reports reached Felix that Max was slipping into fathomless despair. Everything he believed in was now being twisted and debased. After meeting Max in Paris, Dr. Bernhard Kahn told Felix, "He, too, has lost all the optimism he still had a few months ago and sees no way out but the emigration of Jews from Germany within a period of 10 to 15 years."[8] Max, who had once been proof against depression, now couldn't slough it off. Eric entreated him to flee, but Max thought it unconscionable for community leaders to depart. He also thought his wealth and power would shield him. One day, he and Eric were walking by the Inner Alster Lake when Max pointed to the M. M. Warburg building. "See that building there," he said. "That is more than a building. That is our fortress. *It* will protect *us*."[9]

Despair gave Max the gallant, giddy pugnacity of the hopelessly defeated. After spending an evening with him in May 1935, Rabbi Morris Lazaron likened Max to a "lion at bay." He sent Felix this telling vignette: "We had quite an argument the other evening at his [Max's] home in Hamburg. Erich took the position it was useless to fight. Your brother [i.e., Max] was magnificent! 'We have nothing further to lose,' he said. 'If we are degraded to second-class citizens, if these laws go through it is only a question of time when we shall all be forced out. They are using us now because we can help. I'm for fighting.' "[10]

In his confused, unsettled state, Max urged Jews to stay and fight while also making clandestine overtures to have them admitted into Syria, Cyprus, Turkey, Egypt, and Latin America. He helped to start the Paraná Project, which settled a small number of German Jews as coffee planters in the Brazilian jungle. He explored prospects for Jewish settlers on a coffee farm that he partly owned in Guatemala. All the while, he couldn't shed his dream of Jewish assimilation in Germany amid its universal negation. Even for ordinary Germans, it was agonizing enough to sacrifice the wealth, position, and friendships accumulated over a lifetime. For the Warburgs it meant renouncing a banking empire built up over almost 140 years. It seemed inconceivable that their centuries of faithful service to Germany could end so suddenly, so ignominiously. In 1935, Adam von Trott and a friend visited Ingrid at Kösterberg and again urged Fritz to flee with his family. "My father didn't take their warnings seriously and referred repeatedly to the long-standing and profound connection of the Warburgs with Hamburg and Germany," Ingrid recalled.[11]

Max had identified so implicitly with Germany's destiny that to abandon the Fatherland was tantamount to repudiating his fundamental being. No matter how despondent he became, he still had no inkling of how bad things would become. When Mussolini attacked Ethiopia in October 1935, Max told his grandson Oscar, "You must really follow the military developments in this war carefully, because it will be the last war in your lifetime."[12] At the Berlin bar mitzvah of Felix Meyer, an Alsterufer Warburg, in early 1937, Max proposed this toast to the Jewish boy: "Always remember that you are a German."[13]

Until this point, Max had tried the path of reason, attempting to persuade Nazi officials that by stripping Jews of wealth, they deterred them from leaving. If the path of appeasement seemed hopelessly sterile, we must recall that Jewish leaders operated in a totalitarian atmosphere of constant surveillance. Even when Max chaired the Aid Society of German Jews (*Hilfsverein*), he was watched by police and had to delete risky passages from speeches. That April, he was extremely upset when Berlin insisted that the group change its name to the Aid Society of Jews in Germany, implying that a German Jew was a contradiction in terms. Even though he became a vice-chairman of the Reich Representation in 1936, Max later admitted that the group had been too polite in contesting Hitler. "Again and again, though unsuccessfully, I sought to substitute flaming words for the polite documents of Privy Councillors."[14]

Max's split personality perhaps mirrored the contradictory position of his firm, which was in a grim but not entirely desperate state. As small Jewish banks were hounded from the provinces, it created an advantage for large, metropolitan Jewish banks, such as M. M. Warburg, which picked up clients. As one scholar noted, "In the course of the Nazi period, the bank had acquired more and more Jewish customers and had become the preferred bank of the Jewish economic sector."[15] M. M. Warburg ensured confidentiality to harried Jewish businessmen of a sort a non-Jewish bank could never match. The bank aided them with foreign exchange; negotiated the sale of Jewish businesses to "Aryans"; and sold German assets for foreign companies. Hence, while the volume of its credit business contracted, the number of Warburg clients actually *rose* in 1935 from 1,875 to 2,183, and the bank booked more than one million reichsmarks in profit. The bank wasn't thriving amid the crisis, but it certainly kept afloat.

German industry defied the Nazi fanatics and continued to do business with the Warburgs. In the mid-1930s, the bank lost some major clients, including Daimler-Benz and the Maxhütte of Friedrich Flick, but, astonishingly, these were the exception, not the rule. In 1935, the bank surrendered just four of seventy-two supervisory seats on corporate boards—a startling fact that confirms Max's repeated contention that anti-Semitism was all too real but far from universal among the German economic elite. Unfortunately, this only helped to deceive him about the strength and durability of the Nazi appeal among less lofty Germans.

—

It was never clear whether Max's relationship with Dr. Schacht was finally his salvation or misfortune. As Schacht's wizardry revitalized the economy— unemployment plunged from 6 million to 2.6 million in Hitler's first two years in power—it made the *Führer* heroic to the masses. It also gave Schacht a seemingly impregnable position in economic affairs. In July 1934, he met with Hitler in Bayreuth, where the *Führer* drank in inspiration at the Wagner festival. Hitler asked if Schacht would head the Economics Ministry as well as the Reichsbank. "Before I take office I should like to know how you wish me to deal with the Jewish question?" Schacht asked. "In economic matters, the Jews can carry on exactly as they have done up to now," Hitler said with a straight face.[16] Henceforth, Dr. Schacht would preside over the Reichsbank in the morning, then stroll over to the Economics Ministry on Unter den Linden for the afternoon.

In 1935, he still retained jurisdiction over the treatment of Jewish enterprises. That May, he added a fancy new title, "Plenipotentiary for the War Economy," his mission to reconcile economic growth with rearmament. Because a foreign exchange shortage could hurt rearmament, Schacht needed to maintain links with bankers abroad and thus acquired a vested interest in protecting Jewish bankers.

Foreign exchange was also much on the mind of Jewish bankers. Because of punitive exchange rates and the flight capital tax, Jewish emigration entailed a sudden, massive loss of this wealth. Even with Paltreu, Jews going to Palestine in 1935 relinquished 25 percent of their wealth; to settle elsewhere meant a loss of 78 percent. During the first eight months of 1935, Max met with Schacht ten times and many of these meetings must have revolved around foreign exchange. For instance, Max tried to negotiate the best rate possible for the Joint Distribution Committee, which had to convert dollars into marks to maintain its work in Germany.[17] This open door to Dr. Schacht clearly bred a misleading sense of security in Max and other Jewish bankers. In March 1935, U.S. Ambassador William E. Dodd dined at the home of Hans Fürstenberg. Max was also a guest. In his diary, Dodd noted the faith that these Jewish bankers reposed in the Reichsbank chief: "There were other guests claiming to be friends of Dr. Schacht, as they indicated more than once."[18]

An adept double-talker, Dr. Schacht walked a fine line between Jewish businessmen and Nazi stalwarts. Opinionated, conceited, he thought he could beat Hitler at his own game, simultaneously knocking economic sense into the *Führer's* head while protecting the Jews and placating foreign opinion. Sometimes he was quite vocal about the mistreatment of Jews. On July 15, 1935, Nazi thugs went on a spree on Berlin's fashionable Kurfürstendamm, ransacking Jewish shops. In a radio speech, Dr. Schacht condemned the violence and said Jews should be free to engage in business. Goebbels made the press censor this speech. In an extraordinary move, Schacht then had the Reichsbank publish ten thousand copies of the speech and display them at its branches across Germany. A quarter-million copies were printed. At times, when Schacht reopened Jewish businesses, it created a furor among Nazi activists. He wasn't motivated by humanitarian love of Jews. In internal Nazi counsels, he argued that persecuting Jews only hurt his effort to obtain raw materials and foreign exchange for arms and public works.

On September 15, 1935, the Nuremberg Laws repealed the entire history of Jewish emancipation and transported the community back to the Middle Ages. These decrees stripped Jews of citizenship, deprived them of the vote, and barred them from public office. Nor could Jews and people of "German blood" marry or have sexual intercourse. (In Hamburg, a Jewish brothel was set up to service clients without running afoul of the law.) Henceforth, the Warburgs were living on borrowed time. As Eric said, "Those were years of standing by lost posts, full of abominations and human disappointments."[19]

The German Jewish elders now tried to experiment, finally, with militant action. Max convinced the Reich Representation to attempt a mass protest on Yom Kippur. In synagogues across Germany, speakers would simultaneously speak out in protest. "And since I would have thought myself cowardly had I caused it to be read by others while I took no share, I decided to deliver it in the synagogue of the Jewish Orphan Asylum," Max said.[20] In doing this, Max and others would risk deportation to concentration camps. The Reich Representation amateurishly bungled the action by mailing out all eight hundred fliers at once. This tipped off the Gestapo, which confiscated them, banned the protest, and arrested two leaders of the Reich Representation, Dr. Leo Baeck and Dr. Otto Hirsch. Shifting position, the Reich Representation now began to advocate a mass exodus of Jews from Germany.

A few days later, Max was summoned by Dr. Schacht, who played him for a fool. Schacht professed satisfaction with the Nuremberg Laws and denied that they diminished the status of the Jews. They only assigned a *different* value to them, he noted. The laws' purpose, Schacht continued, was to restore tranquility to economic life. After speaking with high officials, Schacht was certain this was their sincere intention. In future, Jewish businesses would no longer be disturbed.

Belatedly, the scales fell from Max's eyes. He saw that Schacht's real agenda at the meeting was to get him to muzzle criticism of the Nazis by Samuel

Untermyer, a group of American Jews organizing a boycott of German goods, and the *Manchester Guardian*, an unsparing critic of Hitler. Max suddenly tired of being blackmailed by Schacht and told him he refused to protest the American boycott or counter criticism abroad. Thus ended Max's efforts to appease the Nazis, although not his relationship with Schacht.[21]

After the Nuremberg Laws, Max unveiled new strategies to deal with the darkening situation. He came up with a plan for a world peace conference that would provide a cover for a global rescue effort for German Jews. Instead of attacking the Nazis' anti-Semitism, he would inveigh against their militarism and worshipful devotion to the state. With the Nazis preaching the need for *Lebensraum* (living space) for Germany's growing population, Max intended to argue that such population pressure could be relieved by allowing unrestricted Jewish emigration.[22]

By the end of 1935, about 100,000 Jews had left Germany in three years while 450,000 dangerously temporized. Now, as the timetable of doom markedly accelerated, tens of thousands of Jews desperately wanted to get out. The Aid Society of Jews in Germany collated reports from four hundred worldwide correspondents, describing local job markets and helping Jews with visas, ships, loans, and resettlement. As the group's chairman, Max Warburg still dreamed of a liquidation or transfer bank that would permit a vast exodus of Jews. He broached the idea to Schacht of having overseas Jews ransom German Jews, partly by buying German goods. Nazi officialdom knew of these talks and let them continue unofficially. Part of Max's plan was to expand the Haavara concept of having Jews deposit marks in Germany, then receive an equivalent sum in foreign currency. To finance the scheme, he would raise an enormous loan from overseas Jews that would be collateralized by property left behind in Germany by emigrating Jews.

Max regarded this scheme as his master plan to free German Jews from bondage. On November 7, 1935, Jewish leaders met in London under the aegis of the Central British Fund at the Rothschild offices in New Court. First they listened to a plan presented by Simon Marks to settle German Jews in Palestine alone. Then, speaking for non-Zionists, Lionel de Rothschild described Max's plan for a bank with three million pounds in capital to be used for emigration to all countries, not just Palestine. James G. McDonald reported glowingly to Felix. "For Lionel he showed an almost amazing enthusiasm . . . he was anxious that this should be the major program, and that the Palestine scheme should be subordinated to it or made a part of it."[23]

In combatting the Nazis, perhaps the most harmful factor was the simple disunity of world Jewry during the emergency. The issue of mass emigration from Germany exacerbated latent tensions between Zionists and non-Zionists just when Jews could least afford it. Chaim Weizmann was offended by his exclusion from the London meeting, which buttressed his suspicion that treacherous non-Zionists favored destinations other than Palestine.[24] Weizmann had defended the Haavara agreement but didn't trust Max's new Liquidation Bank and was disappointed to learn that Palestine would get only 20 percent of funds earmarked under the scheme.[25] As he told Simon Marks, "The recent utterances of our friend Max Warburg (who for some reason best known to himself now poses as an expert on Jewish and Palestine matters), and the arrogance with which his brother [Felix] approaches any subject connected with Palestine, about which he really knows little and understands still less, are portents indicating the dangerous tendency to which I refer."[26] Weizmann milked the Warburgs for money but then didn't want to listen to their views.

The Rothschilds converted the leading British Jew, Sir Herbert Samuel, to Max's plan. A Liberal member of Parliament and former Cabinet member, son of the founder of the Samuel Montagu merchant bank, he had spoken for the anti-German boycott in Parliament. Samuel accurately feared that American Jews and trade unionists would never accept a plan premised on increased imports from Germany. In January 1936, having made discreet soundings at the Foreign Office, he, Lord Bearsted, and Simon Marks got ready to sail to New York to promote a transfer plan. They came equipped with two versions, one for general emigration, along the lines Max proposed, the other slanted to Palestine. The objective was to rescue as many as 168,000 German Jews in four years, with two thirds of the money to come from American Jews and one third from British Jews.[27]

The Nazis were skittish about cutting a deal with Jewish bankers and didn't want to answer embarrassing questions. So the whole operation hinged on secrecy. Then, on January 6, 1936—a week before the British trio sailed—*The New York Times* ran a front-page article headlined, "World Jewry to Be Asked to Finance Great Exodus of German Co-Religionists."[28] The article named the three Englishmen and said the projected migration of German Jews would be the biggest since the seventeenth-century Huguenots. As the article baldly stated, the project was based upon "conditions designed to restore economic and financial prosperity to the German Reich." The alternative, of course, was further repression for trapped Jews. Once again, it was a Hobson's choice. Either Jews could aid their German brethren and the Third Reich or spurn the Nazis and leave the German Jews to their own devices.[29] As Norman Bentwich lamented, "The choice was between satisfying the emotion of the Jewish masses outside Germany and facing the economic realities of Jewry inside Germany; and German Jewry was the loser."[30]

The newspaper publicity scotched the Warburg Plan. Some American Jews simply shrank from aiding the German economy, while others thought it would mark a terrible precedent. Would fiendish governments, in future, deliberately persecute Jews in order to have them ransomed by rich Jews overseas? The three British leaders journeyed to New York anyway. They succeeded in setting up a Council for German Jewry, with Felix, Paul Baerwald, and Rabbi Stephen Wise as the American representatives, but the transfer plan seemed stillborn.

Never easily dissuaded, Max prevailed upon a divided Reich Representation to submit a new plan to the Economics Ministry on January 27, 1936. He spent days in Berlin lobbying, pleading for a moratorium against attacks on Jewish business and for an orderly departure of the Jews. Two days before Hitler sent troops into the demilitarized Rhineland in March 1936, Dr. Bernhard Kahn told Felix that long-running talks about the Warburg Plan between Max and Schacht were deadlocked.[31] Despite sympathy for his scheme, Schacht had already confided in Max about his own political troubles. He had undertaken a campaign against Goebbels's diversion of hard currency for foreign propaganda, which spawned a legion of new enemies for him.[32]

In despair, Max manufactured one last, all-encompassing dream. In London, Sir Osmond d'Avigdor Goldsmid presided over a small, charitable foundation that, he told Max, could provide seed money for the Liquidation Bank. At the time, he didn't realize that the foundation's charter made this impossible. In the meantime, Max rejoiced to think that he had found the needed money. Despair gave way to a powerful reverie. Max envisaged the liberation of 120,000 Jews—in fact, half of all German Jews under age 45.[33] Back in London, he seemed cheerfully confident that he would pin down 500,000 pounds in commitments for his transfer bank.[34]

In fact, the foundation had a mere 125,000 pounds in capital—woefully short of what Max needed—and already had extensive commitments to provide cheap credit to small Jewish businesses in Eastern Europe. With naïveté odd in a banker, Max had believed that Sir Osmond would simply pledge the capital *en toto* to his bank. Dr. Bernhard Kahn went to disabuse him. He described the deflation of Max's hopes: "I must confess that it has seldom been my lot to have a more painful conversation with Mr. Warburg. When I explained the situation to Mr. Warburg . . . [he] was extremely disappointed. It seems that this possibility of the Foundation giving all of its funds for the purposes of the proposed bank was the last great chance which he saw for the establishment of that institution."[35] Max bitterly reproached the "hundred percent retreat" of Sir Osmond.[36]

Siegmund was involved enough in Max's scheme to draw fire from the Zionist press in America.[37] In spring 1936, he spent several weeks with Friedaflix at 1109 Fifth Avenue. Siegmund delighted in Felix's open, generous nature, and Felix liked his nephew's straightforward manner. Because Siegmund wasn't a joiner or organization man, Felix drafted him as the ideal liaison between the Joint and the foremost British Jews. From a business standpoint, this gave Siegmund entrée into the upper echelons of the clubby world of high finance in Britain. Both Felix and Siegmund thought Max's talks with Schacht were a farce and that the Nazis exploited Schacht as respectable cover for their crimes. Felix remembered the soothing but empty words he had heard in the Soviet Union from Rykov during his Agro-Joint trip. As he told Hans Fürstenberg, "They are evidently doing to Schacht what I saw Stalin do to Rykov—put him where he can be consulted, giving him a title, but keeping him, so to say, a physical and mental prisoner."[38]

Even after his overpowering disappointment with Sir Osmond d'Avigdor Goldsmid, Max's imagination still minted elaborate transfer schemes, some of which he implemented. He created a London bank called the International Trade and Investment Agency that transposed the Haavara concept to a global plane. Just as Paltreu transferred money to Palestine through the purchase of German goods, so the new Altreu would do the same for destinations other than Palestine.

The American Warburgs also set up their own ingenious network to spring Jews trapped in Germany. Bettina Warburg sat on a committee of the American Psychoanalytic Association that obtained visas and jobs for Jewish psychiatrists and analysts. Since the Nazis branded psychoanalysis a Jewish science, there was an urgent need to assist these people. Bettina tapped a ready source of funds. With exchange controls in place, M. M. Warburg hadn't been able to remit interest payments on the 1931 loan that Paul and Felix made to rescue the bank. This Kara Corporation money was idly accumulating in Germany. Bettina instructed Eric to use it for two- to three-hundred-reichsmark advances each to psychiatrists and others who lacked the means to emigrate. The recipients were also provided with three thousand dollars to pay for visa applications in America on the proviso that they later replenish the revolving fund. In this way, Bettina and Eric quietly saved 154 people, many prominent in the psychiatric world. Bettina never publicized this heroic work and before her death destroyed all documents related to the effort, save a simple list of beneficiaries.[39]

———

The Warburgs' special influence during the Third Reich depended upon their matchless access to government officials, a situation threatened on February 10, 1936, when the Gestapo, under Heinrich Himmler, emerged as supreme police organ of the Third Reich. It soon promulgated rules designed to isolate Jews by outlawing meetings between Jewish leaders and Nazi officials that were not initiated by the government. Max suggested that the Joint send an

American to Germany who might function as a go-between for the Jews with the Nazi bureaucracy.

Dr. Bernhard Kahn in Paris was dubious, believing such an American would quickly be immobilized in Germany. Nevertheless, Felix and Paul Baerwald crafted a plan that would stay secret until 1960. A former Pennsylvania labor secretary named Peter Glick volunteered to serve as the German liaison. When Felix and Baerwald learned Glick had five children, they rejected him for such a hazardous assignment. Peter suggested his brother David instead. A Pittsburgh lawyer fluent in German, David Glick was prepared to assume the extreme risks associated with the mission. He knew that as soon as he arrived in Berlin, he would be taken in for questioning by the secret police. "I suggested to Messieurs Warburg and Baerwald that my first objective should be to meet with Mr. Himmler, who was the chief and Head of the Gestapo."[40]

In April, Glick stopped in London for a confidential briefing with Max and other German Jews, then proceeded to the Esplanade Hotel in Berlin. He met with U.S. Consul General George S. Messersmith, who telephoned Himmler to arrange an interview. A few days later, Glick and Messersmith's assistant, Raymond H. Geist, entered Gestapo headquarters at No. 8 Prinz Albrechtstrasse, passing beneath a sign that said, "Entry Here Forbidden to Jews."[41]

Geist assured Himmler that nobody knew of Glick's visit. Their purpose, they explained, was to help Jews leave Germany. At this point, the Nazis preferred expulsion to extermination, and even found some common ground with Zionists who admonished Jews to flee to Palestine. Himmler summoned his chief lieutenant, Reinhard Heydrich, who escorted the visitors to see one of the more bizarre specimens lodged in the Gestapo bureaucracy. Dr. Karl Haselbacher was the top man for Jewish Questions. With curious, clerklike precision, Haselbacher kept a meticulous card file with the names, addresses, occupations, and activities of thousands of German Jews. Without further ado, he gave Glick his phone number and a list of leading Jews in large cities. It was an implausible scene—the Gestapo furnishing a complete mailing list to expedite the escape of German Jews! To their astonishment, Glick and Geist flew easily through the interviews.

Later, Glick marveled that William Shirer and other seasoned journalists in Berlin never got wind of his existence. Max monitored his activities and sent such positive reports to Felix that the Joint renewed his contract for a second year. Returning to Germany in 1937, however, he was harassed by Gestapo officers. This secret Jewish emissary then secured a letter that he could flash to Secret Police anywhere in Germany, indicating that he had official support. Glick's mission lasted until mid-1938.

At this point, Himmler and Heydrich had less quarrel with the Zionists than with the patriotic, acculturated Jews who pleaded with people to stay.[42] If Max Warburg showed folly in urging Jews to dig in their heels, he also showed tremendous courage by bucking official policy. The Gestapo actually forbade Jews from making any public references about staying in Germany. In speeches, Max always professed to favor emigration. In private, he exhorted Jews to stay.

This contradictory situation was highlighted at an unforgettable speech Max gave to a joint meeting of the B'nai B'rith lodges in Hamburg in 1936. The Gestapo eavesdropped on such Jewish gatherings and reviewed speakers' notes in advance. While a Gestapo observer listened intently, Max approvingly surveyed the immigration prospects in different countries. As people milled about in the social hour afterward, Max noticed that his Nazi auditor had left. He then committed an act of exceptional courage as recounted by historian Hans Liebeschütz:

"Max Warburg called the members back for a final word which proved to be a complete retraction of his speech. He emphasized his belief that German Jewry would survive the storm, if they remained in the country. The majority of the assembly was probably more astonished than persuaded, but everybody must have been deeply impressed by the speaker's courage. An uncautious word by one of the hundred or more men present could bring the heretic statement to the knowledge of the men in power."[43] By risking his life and laying himself at the mercy of the audience, Max not only exhibited great courage, but exemplary trust in the Hamburg Jewish community.

For many German Jews, the Warburgs were heroes who eased their way out of Germany by providing money, training, or foreign currency at advantageous rates. Others, however, would feel bitter toward Max Warburg as a man who, by urging them to stay, had played god with their lives. That Max made strong, emotional appeals for people to stay is certain. Whether people were actually swayed is more difficult to say. For instance, in 1936, Hans Liebeschütz's wife, Rahel, consulted a lawyer named Dr. Fritz Fenthol about emigration. When Max learned of this visit, he invited Rahel to Kösterberg and bluntly warned that she couldn't use his services for emigration. As she recalled this emotional episode, " 'You know that I am the God of the Jews,' as [Max] described his immense prestige in the community with this inappropriate expression, 'but I can't fulfill my duties for the Jews if you run away from me.'"[44] On a more conciliatory note, Max ended by saying he might be able to convert Rahel's money at a rate superior to the official one. When she then sent a friend to the Warburg bank, he asked to speak with Dr. Rudolf Brinckmann, the office manager. Instead the friend was shepherded to Max's office where, Rahel assumed, he got the same speech she had heard.

The story of Max Warburg shows the extent to which the German Jewish psyche was damaged by the Nazi terror. This ebullient, self-confident man, who had so long felt invincible, fell prey to inner fears and insecurities. In April 1936, he made a sadly revealing speech to the Aid Society in which he told how Jews were conservative and clung to their soil. He noted that, for sentimental reasons, some departing Jews packed tiny bags of German soil in their suitcases. He told prospective emigrants that in their newly adopted countries, they should steer clear of politics; scatter themselves evenly through the provinces; and not congregate noticeably in big cities. "The more quietly the Jewish immigrant lives in his new homeland, the easier it will be for him to establish a foundation for himself."[45] It was a weary prescription for eternal, second-class citizenship.

———

As host to the Olympic Games in August 1936, the Germans wanted to spotlight for Berlin tourists the serene prosperity of the new Germany, and so the Jews experienced some temporary relief. Demonstrations ceased and the more obnoxious placards, such as "No admittance to Jews and dogs," were taken down.[46] But, as Felix warned a correspondent, the surface calm was deceptive and "underneath there is cruelty and humiliation everywhere."[47]

In his unremitting efforts to get Max to leave, Felix kept suggesting travel and urged him to accept a long-standing invitation from his old friend Korekiyo Takahashi to visit Japan. After the Russo-Japanese War, Takahashi had served as prime minister and finance minister. In 1936, Max and Alice finally accepted Takahashi's invitation. They had never seen Japan and it seemed an appropriate moment for a rest. On the eve of the trip came news that the eighty-year-old Takahashi had been murdered by military fanatics. For Malice, it was as if no true exit existed from their nightmare.

The Warburgs constantly grappled with the paradox of being mercilessly pummeled in the press yet spared in the flesh. They were at once the most and least privileged of German Jews. To celebrate the annual Nuremberg rally in 1936, the *Stürmer* devoted almost an entire issue to *The Protocols of the Elders of Zion*. Max's photo was juxtaposed with that of Karl Marx and the Nazis blamed the Warburgs for both capitalism and communism. All of Europe was swamped with this nonsense. In November 1936, the official organ of the Italian Fascist party, *Fascista Regime*, claimed that Felix Warburg and Kuhn, Loeb had bankrolled Lenin, Trotsky, and the entire Bolshevik Revolution.[48]

And what punishment did the Nazis mete out to these malefactors? Despite the grim backdrop, M. M. Warburg turned a profit in 1936. Nobody was more amazed than Siegmund who traveled freely (if perilously) in and out of Germany before he had a "J" for "Jew" stamped in his passport. As late as July 23, 1936, he told Felix, "M.M.W. & Co. are still remarkably untouched by the

Nazi situation and the business is doing very well."[49] With Felix at least, Siegmund tended to be full of praise for Max. "Under these circumstances," he said, "it is particularly admirable how Uncle Max keeps his balance and even his sense of humour."[50]

What sort of business could a Jewish bank do in 1936? After the Nuremberg Laws, the bank employed eight attorneys to guide Jewish businesses through the labyrinth of racial laws, as they transferred money or sold businesses. M. M. Warburg booked fees for managing the Paltreu accounts, which also provided the firm with low-interest deposits.[51] The bank also remained a member of the prestigious loan consortia for Hamburg and Reich debt. Most remarkably of all, it quietly performed business for elite firms of German industry. In 1936, for instance, the bank still disbursed interest payments to bondholders for Friedrich Krupp A. G. of Essen. At the same time, Max was forced off the board of North Sea Fisheries, which he had helped to found, and the company rechristened two boats that had been named the *Carl Melchior* and the *Max Warburg*. One must understand this peculiar, surreal, and maddeningly illogical reality to appreciate the extreme perplexity felt by the Warburgs in trying to figure out their future.

In his memoirs, Max shied away from the fact that his bank remained profitable in 1936. He preferred to dwell on the monotony and ostracism. Some of this reticence doubtless came from embarrassment at having done business with firms, such as Krupp, that later profited from the war effort, or from guilt at having earned money while other Jews faced terror. But Max's suffering was real enough and only seemed slight in the light of later heinous crimes. As he wrote, "In Hamburg conditions were not quite as vile as in some other territories. Yet Jewish life was unendurable. Especially dreadful was the knowledge that again and again both Jews and non-Jews disappeared forever in prisons and concentration camps. One knew they were tortured even to death and one was powerless to give them any aid. No one who has not experienced it can even imagine the National Socialist terror. Horror and despair overwhelmed us. I was convinced now that all was lost. But I could not yet bear to admit it to myself, my family, or my employees. In the increasing agony of my spirit what sustained me was the feeling that I must do my duty toward my fellow Jews by helping them to a dignified mode of emigration."[52] Max omitted mentioning his efforts to get Jews to stay.

Helping the Warburgs and other wealthy Jewish families to endure the Third Reich was the fact that they often had supportive employees and domestic help, who served as a buffer against the surrounding hate. The Warburgs were exceedingly lucky in this regard. For nearly ten years, Eric's Kösterberg house had been tended by a young woman named Minna Wethling. Then the Nuremberg Laws made it illegal for Jews to employ as domestics gentile German women under forty-five. Regretfully Eric let Minna go and hired an Austrian named Kathi Schwärz who came from Hitler's birthplace, Braunau. A staunch anti-Nazi, she had gone to school with the *Führer*, who was called "Crazy Adolf" by his chums. When she went to register in Blankenese, she said "*Guten Morgen*" to the officials who reprimanded her for not greeting them with "*Heil Hitler.*" They made her wait half an hour. When they asked where she was born, she then berated *them* for not recognizing the name of the *Führer's* birthplace.

A brave, kindly woman, Kathi entered into a weird marriage of convenience. After the 1934 "Night of the Long Knives" came a crackdown on homosexuality, which had been rampant in the SA. To protect him from a concentration camp, Kathi married a homosexual who briefly worked as the Warburgs' butler. Kathi had faint contempt for the man and his sporadic alcoholic binges, but stood by him.

Eric would joke that in those cheerless days he had three strikes against him, any one of which could have landed him in a concentration camp: one, he was Jewish; two, his housekeeper was anti-Nazi; and three, his big black Newfoundland dog, Teddy, didn't like uniforms and tended to snap at people who wore them.[53]

Partition

Now in his sixties and semiretired, Felix, with his speckled gray mustache, looked like a courtly European aristocrat. He wore pince-nez set in a tortoiseshell frame that dangled from a ribbon. He had heart trouble, diabetes, and arthritis so severe that he couldn't grasp his squash racket and had to abandon the game. Despite his maladies, he never lost his spruce, natty appearance or quick smile. When he went yachting aboard the *Carol*, he was as dandified as ever in crisp blazer with pocket handkerchief and white flannel pants.

As he survived one Kuhn, Loeb partner after another, Felix found himself, much to his surprise, the grand old man of the firm. "I was never born to be a banker," he confessed. "I buried nine partners and now end up as the sole survivor of this big firm, with nothing but young people about me."[1] He pulled off his one big deal. He was friends with the musician Leopold Godowsky who, along with his brother-in-law Leopold Mannes, had invented a practical technique for color photography. Kuhn, Loeb negotiated on their behalf with Eastman Kodak, which bought the process and introduced it as "Kodachrome."

The growing threat in Germany often dimmed even Felix's sunny nature.

The world's troubles seemed to flow across his desk as he was deluged by letters from German Jews, many of them strangers, pleading for money and affidavits. These heartrending letters forced him to exercise godlike powers. In general, he resolved this excruciating dilemma by providing help if he had some link to the supplicant. If not, he referred the person to relief agencies.

Though situated in New York, Felix was featured in the Nazi bestiary of Jewish financial demons. The *Stürmer*, having fully acquainted its readers with Max, now added Felix to the roster. It published a photo of him with New York governor Herbert Lehman and the Joint's Paul Baerwald above the caption, "Chief Jewish agitators against Germany at a conference in New York."[2] The photo was a fabrication. Felix spurned invitations to meet German officials in New York, lest he seem to condone Nazi policy. At the same time, when Wilhelm Furtwängler, the conductor and German chauvinist, visited New York, Felix defended his right to play, saying he was being made a scapegoat by Jewish protesters. Germany preoccupied Felix. He felt bereft of his birthright and spoke movingly of the desecrated beauties of his German youth.

Now honorary chairman of the Joint, Felix had the satisfaction of heading the foreign group with the most extensive program inside Germany. In 1936, it covered school costs for sixty thousand Jewish children banned from state schools, subsidized thousands of Jewish shopkeepers, trained and transported youth to Palestine, and retrained older people. Quite unlike Max, Felix preached that the terrors of exile paled beside the extreme danger of lingering in Germany. He especially feared that the elderly would "have to go into their graves without even having the assurance that these very graves will remain unmolested by hoodlums in their blind rage."[3]

As Jews mobbed American consular offices in Germany, the State Department assigned extra personnel to handle the throngs. Felix and Governor Herbert Lehman repeatedly pressed FDR to issue more visas. In November 1935, they petitioned him to boost the number of German Jews admitted annually from twenty-five hundred to a still modest five thousand. This still fell far short of the twenty-six thousand who could be legally and theoretically admitted each year. As the governor told FDR, "Mr. Warburg and those associated with him in caring for the unfortunate refugees are very desirous of having the very stringent regulation with regard to the immigration quota from Germany liberalized to some extent by the State Department."[4] Lehman sent the president a long, despairing letter about the situation in Germany that James G. McDonald had written to Felix. But the president didn't care to take such a controversial public stand, and Felix grew despondent as vague promises turned into windy rhetoric. To its everlasting shame, the United States would accept only 157,000 German Jews from 1933 to 1942—about the same number of Jews admitted in the single year of 1906.[5]

An ailing Felix Warburg attends a dinner
for conductor Walter Damrosch, January 1937.
(Wide World)

When convenient, the president would invoke the Warburgs to mask his own cowardice in confronting the nativists and isolationists. In January 1936, Rabbi Stephen Wise, after visiting the White House, told Einstein, "Unfortunately, and I tell it to you with sorrow . . . his [FDR's] first word was 'Max Warburg wrote to me lately that things were so bad in Germany . . . there was nothing that could be done.' " Wise continued, "You see how this bears out our theory that Max Warburg and his kind do not really desire to help. This is doing exactly what the Nazi government would wish him to do."[6] Wise always loathed Park Avenue, non-Zionist Jews and often denounced the dictatorship of 52 William Street (Kuhn, Loeb headquarters) and its "satellite oligarchy," the American Jewish Committee.[7] His charge seems heavily colored by ideology. The Roosevelt Library at Hyde Park can locate no such letter from Max.[8] Why didn't Roosevelt mention to Wise instead the November plea from Felix and Lehman?

The plight of the German Jews aggravated tensions between Zionists and non-Zionists. Afraid of another Diaspora, Zionists saw Palestine as the sole legitimate destination for Jews escaping from Germany. Felix didn't neglect Palestine. In 1934, he had spearheaded the Joint's three-million-dollar effort to resettle Jews there as honorary president of the Palestine Economic Corporation. If a solid, sober Republican at home, Felix fantasized about a classless society in Palestine, purged of human frailty. His Utopian vision of Jewish farmers and artisans settling there was oddly reminiscent of the dreams he had once projected onto the Agro-Joint in Russia.

In the last analysis, Felix was less concerned with *where* German Jews emigrated than *whether* they emigrated. In 1935, the Joint Distribution Committee used approximately a third of the money it allocated for German-Jewish relocation in Palestine. That year, Felix chaired the drive to create the ten-million-dollar Refugee Economic Corporation and became its first president. The group provided loans to Jews moving *anywhere.* Weizmann, aghast, suspected that affluent non-Zionists had again betrayed an unspoken bias against Palestine. He later told Felix, "All the results in other countries, with the possible exception of North America, are ridiculously small in comparison with what Palestine can do for German Jewry, and what it has already done."[9] Felix wearied of those who seemed to place ideology above the simple, inescapable matter of saving lives.

Relations between Felix and Weizmann deteriorated from other disputes as well. Weizmann had gotten Israel Sieff of Britain's Marks and Spencer to establish a scientific institute in Palestine in memory of his teenage son, who had committed suicide. As president of the Hebrew University, Weizmann pictured the Sieff Institute as a wing of the university. Felix and others alleged that Weizmann ran the Sieff lab as his personal fiefdom, diverting money to it rightly destined for the university, and this assault on his integrity deeply angered Weizmann.

Nevertheless, in February 1935, Friedaflix sailed with Chaim and Vera from Genoa to Palestine. The sixty-four-year-old Felix now traveled with a heart doctor in tow. When they steamed into Haifa harbor, the Holy Land worked its old magic upon Felix. He toured his one-hundred-acre orange grove near Rehovoth and was delighted to hear German spoken along with Hebrew. Yet he was disheartened by Tel Aviv's helter-skelter growth, a housing and land shortage, and flagrant inequalities among Jewish settlers. Most of all, he feared flaring tensions with the Arabs, as more than sixty thousand Jews arrived that year. Amid fears that Arabs might try to kidnap them, guards were posted along the roads that Felix and Frieda traveled. The trip confirmed Felix's view that German Jews should be widely dispersed to many countries, while Weizmann thought this would merely complete Hitler's dirty work by scattering Jews to the earth's four corners.[10]

In September 1935, Weizmann had resumed the presidency of the World Jewish Organization and the Jewish Agency. For some time, Felix had suspected that behind a facade of cooperation with rich non-Zionists, the Zionists ran the Jewish Agency through the Executive Committee. This seemed to violate the parity agreed to in the 1929 "pact of glory," and Felix felt betrayed.[11] He found the committee chairman, David Ben-Gurion—a socialist from Russian Poland—arrogant, ruthless, and dishonest. Once again, Felix brought genteel expectations to the rough-and-tumble of Jewish politics. As he told Weizmann, "You see I am not a politician but a practical businessman, and in business partners are not treated quite so roughly as this."[12] On some level, he never jettisoned the idea that Zionism was a charity and that large donors should run the show. He expected the Executive Committee to report to him and other non-Zionists on the Administrative Committee then abide by their wishes.

These arcane organizational disputes mattered intensely as the question of Jewish statehood arose suddenly on the historical agenda. For years, Weizmann had told Felix that their disagreements concerned only trivial details. Whenever the term "Jewish State" arose and Felix winced, Weizmann patiently explained that the term was being used figuratively. Indeed, Weizmann was ejected from the Zionist leadership in the early 1930s as too moderate on the statehood issue, which he then considered a wonderful but distant dream. For Weizmann, the Zionist state could only emerge after a protracted interim phase of infrastructure development.

Hitler speeded up the timetable of Zionism in a way nobody could have foreseen. As Weizmann said, the world for Jews was "divided into places where they cannot live and places where they may not enter."[13] Barred elsewhere, Jews poured into Palestine, and more emigrated there in the three years after Hitler's rise than in the previous twelve combined. There was now an overwhelming need for a state.

For skittish Arabs, the influx evoked the specter that Jews might soon form a majority in Palestine. In April 1936, this produced anti-Jewish rioting by Palestinian Arabs. Forming the Arab Higher Committee under the grand mufti, they launched a general strike. For the non-Zionist Warburgs, who had imagined Palestine as a peaceful oasis, this was a shocking turn. Paradise became a bloodstained battlefield. Felix thought Zionist bombast about a Jewish state had thrown matches on a tinderbox. Weizmann asked Felix for money for self-defense groups to protect Jewish settlers and told hair-raising stories of butchered women and children. Felix wouldn't budge, warning Weizmann, "you know how strongly we feel that we never wanted and always objected to arming on both sides, and I am afraid we must stick to that decision."[14]

To ease Arab-Jewish tensions, the high commissioner proposed a Legislative Council with both sides represented. Supporting this initiative, Felix even offered to finance a Peace Garden in Palestine where Jews and Arabs might meet in amity. Irate at his advocacy of a Legislative Council, Weizmann believed this would only doom the Jews to eternal minority status and eviscerate Zionism. "The soul goes out of our work if we are reduced here to the same minority position as anywhere else," he said.[15] He thought Felix was duped by Arab moderates whose views didn't reflect the more extreme views of the masses.

Among Jewish businessmen, Felix proselytized for pacifism, telling Simon Marks that it was better to disarm Arab and Jew alike "than to make a shooting gallery out of Palestine."[16] He saw Arab-Jewish relations slipping into an unending revenge cycle and cautioned Sir Herbert Samuel, "all this big talk about Jewish Nation and Arab disdain can only mean bloody heads and misfortune."[17]

In truth, events were now rendering obsolete the position of the wealthy non-Zionist benefactors. In the 1920s, they could set up a farm or school in Palestine as a straightforward charitable act, whereas every donation was now enmeshed in partisan politics. Weizmann prodded Felix to replace Baron Edmond de Rothschild and finance pro-Jewish propaganda in the Mideast. Felix balked, citing his current expenses in combatting anti-Nazi activities in the United States.[18] He wouldn't cross the line into political activism.

To mollify the Arabs, Britain curtailed immigration certificates. The last door clanged shut for German Jews just as life in Germany grew intolerable. Although Palestine had been the major mecca for emigration, a far smaller percentage of German Jews emigrated to Palestine in 1937 than in 1933. The

Reichsbank also issued new rules making it harder to transfer money to Palestine, persuading Max that Palestine had reached the limits of its absorptive capacity. As he said, "For the time being, Palestine is the most expensive colony that has ever been created in the world."[19]

To study the Mideast uprising, the British government appointed the Peel Commission in May 1936. As it held hearings in Palestine, a critical realignment occurred in Jewish politics. In closed session, the commission broached to Weizmann the idea of partitioning Palestine, which Weizmann thought the Jews could only reject at their peril. It even occurred to him that the Palestinian Arabs might prefer having a Jewish state—*if* they had one of their own as well.

As statehood gained ground, Felix felt hoodwinked by the Zionists. With a Jewish state now within reach, Zionists no longer had to truckle to their wealthy non-Zionist patrons. Felix was deeply depressed to learn that at one Zionist gathering somebody had said that the presence of Felix Warburg in Jewish philanthropy was a calamity.[20] After his enormous contributions to Palestine, Felix was dismayed by such ingratitude.

In March 1937, he gathered up several black notebooks of memoranda and went to London for a meeting of the Zionist Organization in Great Russell Street. So long dismissed as the pleasant, carefree Warburg brother, he now carried with him the entire burden of the non-Zionist wing of the Jewish Agency. His London days were minutely budgeted to deal with different causes, and desperate people from across Europe flocked to consult him. As associate Dr. Maurice J. Karpf recalled, "It was almost as if a King had come on a visit, and the people came to do him homage and seek his help."[21]

Weizmann was ready for Felix to vent his bile against the Zionists. Instead of reacting sympathetically, he bad-mouthed Felix as a nuisance. "He is coming over with a cargo full of grievances and complaints and he is becoming more and more peevish and primadonnish as time goes on," Weizmann griped to Lola. "God only knows why!"[22] It irritated him that Felix dwelled on the issue of Executive Committee power. "Frankly," he told Lola, "I have no slightest interest in all these 'problems' which are of no importance in my estimation but to which he seems to attach such undue value."[23] Suddenly, Weizmann forgot that Felix and his ilk had saved the Zionist movement from bankruptcy in the 1920s.

Whether he liked it or not, Weizmann had to deal with Felix's displeasure at the March 24, 1937, meeting. Famous for his fresh carnation and bright, flashing smile, Felix arrived in a somber mood. He reviewed the pact by which Zionists and non-Zionists had split power fifty-fifty in the Jewish Agency. He described how Zionists had subverted that pact while he kept quiet. "But I have held my horses as long as I could. . . . It is not fair. We have worked hard, we have given millions . . . your American friends are leaving the ship because you continually ask them to pay fare without admitting them to the dining room. . . . It cannot go on. We refuse to remain in an uncalled-for minority. . . . This may be my swan song. If so, I regret it, but what I say here, I mean."[24] Like Aby, Paul, and Max before him, Felix was chastened by history. This was a different man from the jaunty, blithe socialite. As Maurice Karpf remembered, "His eyes were filled with tears, his chin quivered, and his voice broke. He had to stop."[25]

Eloquently, Weizmann rebutted him. He noted that non-Zionists were an amorphous group of individuals, while the Zionist movement had to answer to its members. Driven by historical imperatives, it couldn't always observe the niceties. "We have the unpleasant business of having to make friends and we cannot choose our bedfellows. We do this not for our glory, but for the cause." Then Weizmann voiced the tacit resentment that had always lurked below the surface. "Fortunately for you, Mr. Warburg, your position is different. Your constituency is different. We are life and death in this thing and your people are not."[26] For rich non-Zionists, Palestine indeed represented a dream; for the Zionists, it meant survival. Nonetheless, Felix extracted a pledge from the Agency Executive that the old fifty-fifty formula of 1929 would be honored.

On July 7, 1937, the Peel Commission recommended sharp cuts in Jewish immigration. Calling the post–World War I British Mandate unworkable, it proposed a three-way partition of Palestine into separate Arab and Jewish states, with a British Mandatory zone in between. The Zionists were upset with the tiny strip of land designated as their state, while for Felix this small patch of ground confirmed his worst fears. He thought Jewish settlers would quickly cover the narrow space, producing one of two unpleasant outcomes. Either they would have to curb Jewish immigration—defeating the entire idea of a Jewish sanctuary—or risk creating uncontrollable population pressures that would, in the end, provoke strife with their Arab neighbors. Also convinced that such a state would be an economic fiasco, Felix said it would come yearly to Kuhn, Loeb, begging for loans. Instead of statehood, Felix favored having three unarmed provinces, one Jewish, under the same British Mandate.

Even before the Peel report, Felix and others in the American Jewish Committee held secret talks with the Arabs to negotiate a settlement. They explored a deal by which the Arabs would agree to a sizable jump in the Jewish population so long as it never exceeded the Arab population. As Felix cabled Max, the American non-Zionists believed that "partition is a definite declaration of impossibility of Arabs and Jews living together."[27] Weizmann bluntly rejected these negotiations and questioned whether the participating

Arabs spoke with the blessings of the mufti or the masses. He couldn't accede to a formula that again condemned the Jews to minority status.

With these matters debated against the backdrop of Nazi Germany, passions ran high. Both sides thought their solution would allow the largest influx of Jewish refugees. Felix thought that while a deal with the Arabs might consign Jews to minority status, it would also relieve Arab anxiety and save lives by permitting a prompt increase in Jewish settlement. No less fervently, Zionists believed that Hitler had shown the overwhelming need, now and forever, for a Jewish state. Palliatives would no longer suffice.

In late July, Felix met with Irving Lehman, Cyrus Adler, and other Jewish leaders in Woods Hole, Massachusetts, to discuss whether Felix should attend the August meeting of the Jewish Agency Council in Zurich. It was decided that he should go "so that I may not be charged with being a deserter at this serious moment," Felix explained.[28] In poor health, he defied his doctors' advice to skip Zurich—a fact he kept from his colleagues. Even before sailing, he was besieged with cables, telegrams, and telephone calls that drained his strength. Many people noted that Felix had suddenly aged. He seemed tired and without the old elastic step.

By the time he arrived at the Zurich Tonhalle, many non-Zionists had defected to the Zionist side on partition. Haggard from lack of sleep, Felix was the first speaker in the General Debate on August 18. Some would remember his speech as poised and dignified, but the content was bitterly accusatory. Felix recounted the glorious founding of the Jewish Agency in that same Tonhalle years before. "Since those days we have tried to turn into reality a dream of beauty and true help; this is now about to be cruelly reduced." Still clinging to the old Warburgian dream of universal brotherhood and acceptance, he noted that America had shown how people of diverse religions could live together. He also stressed that American Jews had funneled millions of dollars to Palestine and that non-Zionists had donated much more than Zionists. Then he came to the nub of his speech: "We believe that the plan submitted to us should not be pursued any further *without first making a serious effort to obtain an understanding from Jews and Arabs in Palestine.*" After evoking a rather farfetched vision of the ideal Palestine being a second Switzerland, he concluded with a warning: "If this Council's efforts will be directed merely towards the establishment of a Jewish State and not the simultaneous fulfillment of responsibilities towards its neighbors, we won't be able to go along with you. . . ."[29]

When Magnes presented a non-Zionist resolution for an Arab-Jewish state, the audience grew surly. Interrupted by heckling, Magnes said, "What is the Jewish State that is being offered? It is a Jewish State which, in my opinion, will lead to war, to war with the Arabs."[30] Weizmann tried to placate Felix, while the feisty Ben-Gurion scorned halfway measures. Weizmann engineered a compromise by which five non-Zionists would sit with seven Zionists on the Executive Committee of the Jewish Agency. This was all public relations. The reality was that partition was approved, albeit reluctantly, with the Executive authorized to negotiate for a Jewish state with Britain. After the Arabs rejected the plan, it came to naught. That same month, a new British White Paper further curbed emigration to Palestine.

After the Tonhalle meeting, Felix and Maurice Hexter strolled back to their hotel together. "I remember walking home with him to the Baur-au-Lac, a broken man," recalled Hexter. "It was only then that the bitter antagonism which [Felix] carried to the end emerged. . . ."[31] Felix was now a broken man with glimmers of his own mortality. At one point he mentioned to Hexter that he was the last surviving founder of the Palestine Survey Committee of the 1920s. "When is my turn coming?" he asked.[32] He handed Hexter two closed manila envelopes, both addressed to friends, and asked him to deliver them if he died.

Suffering from fatigue, Felix met his daughter, Carola, in London and they sailed back to New York aboard the *Berengaria*. By coincidence, Ben-Gurion was on the same boat. Felix waved and went to speak with him. At first, he couldn't resist some sarcasm about Ben-Gurion's behavior in Zurich, but the two ended up having a pleasant journey. Ben-Gurion softened somewhat his opinion of Felix and saw that he wasn't a haughty grandee. "I saw before me a man who undeniably loves Eretz Israel," he said. "He has a wholly Jewish heart, but he is a petty man and narrow-minded. . . . Surrounded as he is by sycophants and servants, it is difficult for him to come to terms with a people's democratic movement and even more difficult for him to understand it."[33] This view paralleled Weizmann's impression of Felix. For his part, Felix didn't modify his view of Ben-Gurion, whom he regarded as a fanatical propagandist lacking in statesmanlike calm or judgment.[34]

The clash between Felix and Ben-Gurion went far beyond personalities. Ben-Gurion believed that Felix and other rich, charitable Jews felt threatened by a Jewish state, which would supplant the old elite. A Jewish state, said Ben-Gurion, would jeopardize their "property, status, rights, and influence."[35] This reflected a long-standing resentment felt by poorer Jews against those aristocratic leaders who had pleaded their cause in European ministries. The Zionist movement was, in part, a populist revolt against Jewish banking royalty. As Weizmann exulted, "The Warburgs and the Rothschilds and their methods have gone for ever."[36] At the same time, the rise of the welfare state meant that responsibilities once borne by wealthy Jewish elders were now assumed by secular officials.

Felix was so angry with Weizmann that the Warburgs thought the two men would never talk again. In a last-ditch effort in late September, Felix summoned an emergency meeting of Jewish leaders at Briarcliff Lodge overlooking the Hudson River where he made an impassioned plea to repudiate Weizmann and partition and pushed his plan for Swiss-style cantons in Palestine. Weizmann and Ben-Gurion rightly believed that Felix felt threatened by a Jewish state, which, he now said, would disenfranchise world Jewry and would be governed solely by those "who live in Palestine, vote in Palestine and belong to its government."[37] Though Felix got the executive committee of the Joint to condemn partition, the larger battle had been lost.

A few weeks after the conference, on October 18, 1937, Felix suffered a heart attack. The pain, he joked, was nothing compared to what Weizmann had inflicted upon him.[38] Torn apart by the partition dispute and worried about Max and his family in Germany, Felix had labored under a double strain. Frieda blamed both factors for his heart attack. Two days later, he died at age sixty-six, with Frieda and his five children by his bedside. He was honored with a large funeral at Temple Emanu-El at which his sons carried the coffin. Scores of financial and political luminaries—including John McCloy, Sidney Weinberg of Goldman, Sachs, and George Brownell of Davis Polk—attended the service. Felix was buried in Salem Fields Cemetery in Brooklyn.

Frieda reacted to Felix's death with the same self-effacing dignity she had shown throughout their marriage. Even as he lay dying, she telephoned one mistress—she apparently knew the number by heart—and said, "Hulda, I think you'd better come."[39] On less intimate terms with the other women, Frieda asked Edward to help. "Now, Edward," she said awkwardly, "there are certain things I can't do."[40] She mentioned several opera singers that Felix had escorted over the years. Stoic about the double standard of her day, Frieda told Edward that she didn't feel jealous but grateful to Felix's mistresses, who had apparently given him something that she could not.[41] It was a remarkably tolerant view, to put it mildly, and couldn't have captured all of her true feelings. Despite Felix's philandering, she would always remember him with great love and joy.

Felix's death shattered Max, who now believed he had hastened the death of both of his American brothers. In his bank's report for 1937, he said of Felix: "Across the last years of his life fell a large shadow of concern for his family in Germany, and in particular, I must say, for me."[42] The words must have been painful to write. Perhaps from feelings of guilt, Max considered leaving Germany and even visited New York with Alice, but then returned to Hamburg.

Felix was the last of a disappearing breed and an irreplaceable figure in Jewish charity. Nobody had equivalent style, prestige, or stature. As *The New*

York Times observed, "Never has there been shown in our time a finer sense of the obligations of wealth than he put into his daily deeds of human sympathy."[43] Felix and Frieda had distributed thirteen million dollars to two hundred causes over the past fifteen years. Henceforth, Jewish philanthropy would shift from the paternalism of individual Jewish bankers to fund-raising bureaucracies, administered by professional staffs. As Felix predicted, the Jewish state would reduce the relative power of Diaspora Jews who had superintended the welfare of their communities.

In his will, Felix had one last posthumous chance to exhibit his generosity. Thirty-five house servants, ranging from gardeners to chauffeurs, got bequests between one hundred and ten thousand dollars. Each of 125 Kuhn, Loeb employees got a check of two hundred to two thousand dollars, depending upon their length of service. The bulk of the money went to Felix's five children, who divided the estate equally. Following an old-fashioned custom, Felix left ethical wills, advising each child as to the best charitable work to pursue.

Shortly after Felix died, Frieda summoned her children for a meeting. She took Felix's pet charities and parceled out responsibility for them among her children. Carola took health care; Freddy education for black children; Gerry music and the arts; Piggy civic duties; and Eddie Jewish philanthropy.

Felix died at a moment when Eddie had grown disillusioned with his fast, forbidden, Bohemian world of art and ballet and wanted to return to his roots. Having already visited Palestine several times, he picked the Joint as his chief project and headed its 1938 fund-raising drive in New York and became its vice-chairman. For a time, Felix was succeeded as chairman by Paul Baerwald, a shy, modest, hard-working partner of Lazard Frères. Eddie would succeed him, carrying the Warburg banner into the post–World War II era. Already in 1938, Eddie assembled a committee to coordinate Joint activities around the world.

Ironically, he would reign over the Joint while married to a Christian divorcée, Mary Whelan Currier, a pretty fashion editor for *Vogue*. Warburg sons now married stylishly slim American women, not the stout German ladies of old. Eddie and Mary were married in December 1939 in the apartment of her boss, Condé Nast. When Eddie stalled in introducing Mary to his mother, Frieda knew it. "I deeply resent the fact that I should have been the last one in the family to meet Mary," she told Eddie. Her agile son retorted, "Yes, I know; but Ma, you don't meet the champion until the finals."[44] Frieda knew she had lost the battle to preserve her family's Jewish identity. Instead of fighting it, she chose to retain her children's love over rigid adherence to doctrine. Resigned to her fate, Frieda laid out her best jewelry on two card tables and asked Eddie to pick a ring and brooch for Mary. "Mary is not going to sneak into the family," she stated. Frieda did everything to make Mary feel welcome, even telling her privately that in marrying a Jewish man, she might now face certain restrictions, such as booking hotels. Mary replied that she didn't like hotels anyway.[45]

On the eve of the wedding, Frieda gathered the family one last time in the large, tapestry-hung dining room at 1109 Fifth Avenue. It was a farewell to the ornate mansion as well as to Eddie's bachelorhood. Everybody wore evening clothes and ceremoniously toasted the newlyweds. Freddy, the family wag, wrote a poem for the occasion, notable for its sophisticated wit and hard, cutting edge. It warned Mary not to expect fidelity from any Warburg male: "Some stay married months, some weeks/But all in all their record reeks. . . . The Boys, except for Uncle Max/Are apt to be a wee bit lax. . . ."[46]

Frieda hadn't really ventured outside the "Our Crowd" world of wealth and comfort. After Felix died, she took her first faltering steps alone. She jousted with Weizmann, warning him in 1938 that a small Jewish state would destroy twenty years of effort in Palestine.[47] The Zionists resisted vigorously her effort to replace Felix in the Jewish Agency. She became honorary president of the American Friends of the Hebrew University and honorary chair of the Joint's women's division. Despite being the daughter of Jacob Schiff and the widow of Felix Warburg, she wasn't sure of her own religious beliefs. After her brother, Morti, died, she had moaned to Dr. Magnes, "Judah, give me faith."[48] Yet she remained strongly bound to Jewish tradition. After reading a book by Rabbi Morris Lazaron called *Common Ground*, she wrote to thank him. "To be a good American, a loyal Jew, coupled with the spiritual uplift which Palestine has given me personally have often been confusing problems to me; and you have given me a better balanced point of view."[49] She remained true to the Panglossian Schiff-Loeb-Warburg conviction that one could simultaneously be true to one's religion, one's country, and oneself.

Lola and Max Warburg at her Wannsee home.
(Warburg family, Hamburg)

CHAPTER 32

The Twilight Dynasty

ven as Max helped people to flee and supervised preparation of an instructional booklet for emigrants, he tried to comfort those who stayed behind. He was a guiding spirit behind the Hamburg chapter of the Jewish Culture League (*Der Jüdische Kulturbund*), which sought to divert the community with cultural activities ranging from film to cabaret. It provided work nationwide for seventeen hundred Jewish actors, entertainers, and musicians hounded from their jobs. On January 9, 1938, in a last, misplaced expression of faith in the future of German Jewry, Max hammered in the *mezzuzah* to dedicate a new Jewish Community Center in Hamburg. With Jews banned from libraries, theaters, and social clubs, they were imprisoned in their homes, and Max hoped this center would buck up their courage. He made a substantial contribution to the complex, which contained a theater, restaurant, and two-hundred-seat lecture hall. The restaurant was also suitable for weddings and other festivities. This macabre place foreshadowed a nonexistent future and, appalled by the poor timing, many Hamburg Jews refused to contribute.

In his inaugural speech at the center, Max said bravely, "We are responsible for the minds and spirits of our people, which are not to be crushed by the miseries and anxieties of every day."[1] His words bore no connection to the bleak reality. He described the new center as life-affirming—which required quite a stretch of the imagination. With Nazi monitors sitting in, he peppered his speech with patriotic touches. "Our exclusion from many fields of activity makes it impossible for us today to work for the country in which we were born and which we are ready to serve."[2] The major thrust of his talk was that Jews needed to reaffirm their religion against its savage negation. Regardless of whether a German Jew was observant or not, he concluded, "today he is a Jew, with all the emotional barriers, all the problems and cares, which the times inflict upon him!"[3] The speech received extended applause.

Even as Max oversaw plans for the cultural center, Goebbels dispatched a goon squad through German museums to cull the most blatant examples of "Bolshevik-Jewish" art for display at a special Munich "horror show." When the "Degenerate Art" exhibition opened there in July 1937, it featured paintings by Beckmann, Chagall, Kandinsky, Kokoschka, Nolde, Grosz, and other artists reputedly perverted by the Jewish spirit. By the following spring, the Nazis had "cleansed" German museums of this "Jewish garbage," confiscating sixteen thousand works.

This crusade against modern art suggested to Eric Warburg a novel rescue plan. M. M. Warburg & Co. owed money to the Norske Creditbank in Oslo that it couldn't repay because of the moratorium on foreign debt payments. Eric asked the Reich Economics Ministry whether the Warburg bank "as a German bank could pay back its foreign debts to an evil foreign bank with 'degenerate art.' They thought it a brilliant idea."[4] So, as if embarked on a furtive mission, he went to a cellar window of the Hamburg art museum, bought on the cheap several paintings by the Norwegian Expressionist Edvard Munch, then sent them to Oslo plastered with the permission stamps of the Third Reich.

———

All illusions would soon be over. The clock was now approaching midnight. Max had hitched his star to Dr. Schacht's, a strategy that had at first paid off handsomely, enabling him to survive in a charmed sphere, protected by invisible barriers, if surrounded by enemies. But by 1936, this strategy miscarried as Schacht's own power waned. The blustery, opinionated central banker caused offense on several fronts. He repeatedly grumbled to Hitler that Goebbels, Himmler, and other Nazis siphoned off foreign exchange for their own use. And for all his elastic morals, Dr. Schacht hewed to an old-fashioned banker's faith in sound finance. Instead of favoring autarky, he wanted Germany to bolster its foreign exchange reserves through exports. He also thought economic growth had reached a point where further arms spending would be inflationary. For a long time, he violated his own principles and advanced rearmament through his Mefo-bills, barter deals, and exchange controls. But Hitler grew tired of his warnings about inflation. In consequence, Schacht slowly shed his strange glow of political immunity, and Hitler began to brush aside this pigheaded man who had outlived his usefulness.

First Hitler gave supervision of foreign exchange and raw material matters to Schacht's archrival, Göring, in April 1936. That same year, he unveiled a four-year plan to rearm Germany and again assigned the supervisory role to Göring. Right next door to Schacht's Economics Ministry, Göring erected his own private bureaucracy, the Office for Raw and Synthetic Materials, manned by a staff of five hundred. It would become the tutelary spirit behind German war preparations and promulgate a militaristic policy of autarky instead of free trade.

As Schacht's power dipped, the Warburgs knew they might soon forfeit their government patronage. As Felix told the Joint in April 1937, "We had a few friends over there who were in high positions, but who are now losing their power."[5] On cue, German businesses took a tougher line with Jewish bankers. Word filtered down from Berlin that companies should purge their boards of Jews or lose government contracts; many were stampeded into dropping Jewish firms. The number of M. M. Warburg clients now skidded from almost 3,000 in 1936 to about 2,200 in 1937. Between 1936 and 1938, Warburg partners lost eighty board seats, which left them with a meager eighteen. Siegmund was expelled from two boards in 1937: the Hotel Atlantic (Hitler's favorite haunt in Hamburg) and the Cameroun Railroad Company. In many cases, the Warburgs slipped in a substitute. Most often it was Dr. Rudolf Brinckmann, the highest-ranking non-Jewish employee, for whom this produced a stunning, overnight elevation in status—a fact the Warburgs would pointedly bring up later. Another substitute was Dr. Kurt Sieveking, who came from a distinguished legal family. In 1936, as a way of expressing solidarity with the Jews, he surrendered a lucrative law practice and took a job with M. M. Warburg. He was later a mayor of Hamburg.

It rankled party zealots that Dr. Schacht had kept the Warburg bank in the Reich Loan Consortium, the august body that marketed government debt. By 1937, M. M. Warburg was one of just three Jewish banks left in the group; when the bank had joined the Consortium in 1905, one third of the fifty member banks had Jewish owners. Even though M. M. Warburg got a minute 1.5 percent sliver of consortium issues, the mere fact of its membership mattered greatly. "[Dr. Schacht] knew the importance in the matter of loan flotations of at least our firm and that of Mendelssohn," said Max.[6] The cachet was of immense practical value, for it signified that the firm still enjoyed some official favor. If bullied by Nazis, industrial companies could cite the Reich Loan Consortium as their justification for doing business with the Warburgs.

So long as Dr. Schacht clung to power, Max believed he could survive. He often said that he wanted his firm to be the last one out of Germany, not the first. If his firm were liquidated, he feared that it would throw Jewish employees on the street and so dismay the entire Jewish community that it would flee—in retrospect, the optimal solution.

Max Warburg's destiny was determined on August 11, 1937, when Dr. Schacht met with Hitler on a sun-drenched terrace on the Obersalzberg. Schacht's boisterous rows with Göring now threatened to disrupt the whole rearmament program. After Schacht adjourned with Hitler into his study, a furious dialogue ensued. The windows were open and guests on the terrace heard the two men raging at each other. Schacht was one of the few officials who dared to holler at Hitler. He now tendered his resignation, citing irreconcilable differences with Göring. When Hitler insisted that he reconsider, Schacht only said he would think about it. From then on, Schacht's power eroded, and on September 5, 1937, he took a leave of absence from the Economics Ministry. The Ministry of Justice promulgated new rules that made it illegal for Nazi party members and government employees to patronize Jewish shops. The last Jewish war veterans were booted from the Reichsbank staff.

That September, Dr. Schacht asked Max to visit him in Berlin. The somber central banker said, "I'm sorry, Mr. Warburg, but I can't keep your firm in the [Reich Loan] Consortium any longer." Max was jolted from his trance. At once he knew that he had lost his protective cover. "Then we'll have to liquidate the firm," Max said. Schacht replied that he had expected that.[7] As Max recalled, "We said goodbye after, for thirty years, we had in all possible ways worked together."[8]

Back in Hamburg, Max found the city awash with rumors that M. M. Warburg *wanted* to liquidate—rumors he thought fanned by the Nazis. Along with Felix's death in October, these events had a crushing impact upon him. When Schacht yielded the Economics Ministry to Göring in December (while keeping the Reichsbank presidency), the new nazified ministry told Max he had to transfer his bank to Aryans. Schacht's downfall was a general disaster for Jewish bankers and businessmen, for his successors drastically curtailed the raw material and foreign exchange quotas that were essential for many Jewish firms.

Schacht's downfall came amid a huge wave of so-called Aryanizations that transformed the German economy. The Warburg bank, in fact, negotiated forced sales for many Jewish businesses, a ghoulish activity that became a staple of its work by 1937. As distinguished names in Jewish banking disappeared—Gebrüder Arnhold, S. Bleichröder, J. Dreyfus & Co., and nearly two hundred other private banks—their clients shifted to the Warburgs. As Max noted, "We more and more became the confidential bankers of the Jewish business world."[9] With many large Aryan banks financing these takeovers, Jewish businessmen trusted M. M. Warburg to broker their deals and the partners scoured the world for foreign firms that might purchase Jewish businesses with blocked mark accounts.

These involuntary sales to predatory Aryans were conducted in an extremely tense atmosphere. Many Jewish businessmen awaited entry visas elsewhere and didn't know whether they would escape. They sold their shares based on original cost, not market value, and received nothing for goodwill, which led to staggering capital losses of as much as 70 percent. The notaries handling these contracts needed to get approval from the local Nazi office. If the party thought the terms too generous, they were sent back for further negotiation. Once this legal extortion was completed, businessmen had to pay the 25 percent Flight Capital Tax. After more duties and punitive exchange rates, Jews might get 10–20 percent of the remaining pittance out of Germany. By the end, most Jewish businessmen were battered and broke. Outright theft might have been kinder. The Nazis rationalized these coercive moves by saying that the Jews had built their businesses through trickery and cheating. As German firms profited from the Aryanization drive, it implicated them more deeply in Nazi machinations, which would finally culminate with their exploitation of slave labor during the Holocaust.

A fierce Aryanization battle raged over the pipe and blast furnace company controlled by the family of Lola's husband, Rudolf Hahn, and his brother, Kurt. As Göring tried to expel Jewish owners from industries of strategic importance, especially in mining and metals, he found an enthusiastic supporter in Friedrich Flick, later a convicted war criminal. With a crude steel empire that by 1932 rivaled that of Krupp, Flick had lavishly subsidized Heinrich Himmler and the SS. By 1937, he sat atop the largest privately owned iron and steel combine in Germany.

In searching for pig iron to feed his steel mills, Flick had long eyed a company known as Lübeck Blast Furnace (*Hochofenwerk Lübeck*). The largest firm in Thomas Mann's native city, Lübeck, it provided gas and electricity. This conglomerate also owned a sprawling complex of blast furnaces on the Baltic Sea, a cement factory, a coking plant, and a copper foundry. Its owners were mostly Jewish: the Hahn Works (*Hahnsche Werke*), the Berlin metals trading house of Rawack & Grünfeld, and M. M. Warburg. This investment constituted the Warburgs' only large-scale industrial participation, and Max was a managing director, Eric apprenticed there, and Fritz sat on its supervisory board.

Early in the Third Reich, Lübeck Blast Furnace was forced to name several unwanted Aryans to its boards. One of them, a Nazi official named Dr. Werner Daitz, quietly notified the military in 1935 that the company had 90 percent Jewish or foreign ownership. Under the guise of national security, Daitz and Flick conspired to take over the firm. At first, the Hahns and the Warburgs stood firm, and Flick didn't press the issue for he knew time would only make his Jewish prey more pliant.

Before 1937, most Aryanizations were undertaken by small-time Nazi opportunists. Now large industrialists saw they could buy major businesses cheaply and receive government support to extract giveaway terms. Spurred on by Göring, Flick resumed his assault on Lübeck Blast Furnaces in a campaign later dubbed "a form of industrial piracy" by one Nuremberg prosecutor.[10] Instead of bidding directly for the firm, Flick stalked the weakest of the three owners: Rawack & Grünfeld.

To terrify the Jewish owners, Flick drew upon the services of Alfred Rohde, who had managed his operations in Upper Silesia. Terror formed an indispensable part of Aryanization campaigns because the Nazis at first feared that formal confiscation of Jewish property might trigger legal reprisals abroad, including the attachment of German assets. So the owners had to be psychologically stampeded into selling. Rohde went to see Dr. Ernst Spiegelberg, an M. M. Warburg partner and the bank's Berlin representative after Siegmund fled. The meeting curiously intermingled civility and blackmail. Speaking as a supposed "old friend," Rohde advised Spiegelberg to do his best to have Rawack & Grünfeld sold to Flick quickly. "Otherwise the entire group will get into trouble," said Rohde.[11] Rohde hinted that R&G had violated German foreign currency rules and "this matter has already been investigated by the responsible government authorities."[12] In November, Flick told Spiegelberg that high authorities were pestering him to deal with the Lübeck "problem."[13]

With Schacht's downfall, Spiegelberg knew that Flick wasn't bluffing. To expedite matters, Flick turned to Göring's Four-Year Plan office. The head of its iron and steel division, Herr Oldewage, invited Spiegelberg to his office and informed him that the German General Staff wanted to see R&G Aryanized. For this chat, Oldewage set curious ground rules, permitting Spiegelberg only to answer "yes" or "no." Spiegelberg wouldn't abide by those terms. Finally, Oldewage said that R&G would lose its license to import ore from Scandinavia and the Soviet Union until Flick got his majority of shares. This was equivalent to a death sentence for the company, and Oldewage noted that Spiegelberg was "strongly impressed" by this threat.[14] In internal memos, the Flick people gloated over the alarm created in the Hahns and Warburgs by menacing speeches issuing from the Nazi brass. By mid-November, Flick had amassed 25 percent of R&G's shares. A few weeks later, Spiegelberg negotiated the final sale to Flick, who agreed that M. M. Warburg would remain R&G's banker. He also said that Dr. Fritz Warburg would remain head of the supervisory board or would be succeeded by Dr. Rudolf Brinckmann.

Flick now proceeded to his real target: Lübeck Blast Furnace. Backed by Göring, Flick applied pressure far more flagrantly than he had with Rawack & Grünfeld. This time, Flick bought just half the target company—the bare minimum needed—to save on cash. He no longer needed to waste even a penny. As Rudolf Hahn later testified at Nuremberg about Flick, "He threatened us with arrest and internment in a concentration camp."[15]

In January 1938, Friedrich Flick bought, at a 50 percent distress-sale discount, the shares in Lübeck Blast Furnace owned by the Hahns and M. M. Warburg, with the remaining shares sold to Mannesmann. In these transactions, the Hahns took payment in foreign currency, payable in London, which would allow Rudolf and Lola to resume life abroad.[16] At Nuremberg, Telford Taylor contended that this rapacity only stimulated Flick's appetite for further plunder of Jewish businesses. "The acquisition of the blast furnaces opened wide Flick's eyes to the interesting and profitable possibilities of 'Aryanization,' " said Taylor.[17]

Rudolf and Lola had stayed in Germany from many motives. Like Max, they had thought it cowardice to desert the Jewish community. They also suffered from the upper-class Jewish mythology that they were somehow immune to the abuse being meted out to poorer Jews. They never imagined it could happen to them.

For five years, Lola had worked with Youth Aliyah in Berlin and placed hundreds of German-Jewish children in foreign homes. Along with Weizmann, she lobbied Britain to boost the quota for Jewish children admitted to Palestine. She knew she stood in growing danger in Berlin. After Fritz's daughter Ingrid made a speech in Sweden relating horror stories about Nazi treatment of Jews, Lola was summoned to Gestapo headquarters. Though she escaped harm, she now knew that the Gestapo tracked her activities. She also learned that her name appeared on a Nazi blacklist of vocal Zionists. As if Lola needed more trouble, she was also suffering from a kidney ailment.

The upshot was that in September 1938, Rudo and Lola decided to leave Germany and fly to London. In part, they managed to get out by selling their Berlin home to a Nazi *Gauleiter*. With Kurt now running the Gordonstoun school in Scotland—the Salem school would be evacuated to Wales during the war—England arose as a natural destination. Lola made a typically theatrical exit from Berlin. "She looked like a film star," said her sister. "Everybody was crying. Lola's arms were full of flowers."[18] At the airport, she was thoroughly searched by a guard who asked her name. When she said Warburg, the guard apologized. "Well, if you had told us that before, we wouldn't have bothered you."[19] The Hahns, however, were treated to one last indignity. After the plane took off, they were approached by an unexpected passenger: Otto Steinbrinck, Flick's lawyer, who was on a business trip to London. He couldn't resist a last sadistic jab: "You're lucky that you were still able to get out at all," he told the Hahns.[20]

—

With M. M. Warburg evicted from the Reich Loan Consortium, Max hunted for friendly parties to buy his bank. The negotiations took place amid a stifling, intolerable gloom. In mid-March 1938, Hitler triumphantly entered Vienna to celebrate the *Anschluss* with Austria. After breaking into the Rothschild mansion, SS men emerged bearing silver, paintings, and other spoils. Baron Louis Rothschild was arrested and held hostage until his family sold off their properties at scandalously low prices. The Nazis carted off masses of Jews to the Dachau and Buchenwald concentration camps in an orgy of anti-Semitic excess. One of Max's Viennese cousins, Richard Rosenbacher, leaped to his death from the third-floor window of his home. Jews in Vienna were committing suicide at the rate of two hundred per day.

Returning from Austria, Hitler addressed a huge throng before the Hamburg *Rathaus*. The *Führer* also christened a new ship the *Robert Ley*, honoring Max's old nemesis from the 1920s. The pace of Aryanizations quickened, as a quarter of the remaining forty thousand Jewish businesses underwent forced sales during the next year. This destroyed the last vestiges of the Jewish economic power that had figured so largely in Nazi cosmology.

For a Jewish bank, the choices were simple. It could liquidate; sell out to an Aryan bank; or be Aryanized—that is, the Jewish partners could sell their stakes to non-Jews and preserve the firm. It was fully consistent with Max's beliefs that he chose Aryanization, which kept alive the slim chance of someday returning to Germany. At first, the Warburgs hoped to bring in 51 percent non-Jewish partners and keep a minority stake for themselves. But on January 4, 1938, Göring issued a decree that classified those firms with even one-quarter Jewish ownership as subject to Aryanization. A wholesale transfer of the firm now became inevitable.

Negotiations took place at the Berlin office of M. M. Warburg under the close scrutiny of the Reich Economics Ministry. On March 19, 1938, Dr. Gustab Schlotterer of the Foreign Economics department was told to keep M. M. Warburg intact to safeguard its foreign-exchange credits and overseas connections for the Third Reich.[21] This government policy dovetailed with the Warburgs' own wishes, for it permitted a moderately friendlier Aryanization to occur. Friendly was an extremely relative term in this terrifying atmosphere, and the Warburgs always viewed it as a de facto expropriation. As

Max said, "In outer form 'Aryanization' was not supposed to be confiscation; in final result it was exactly that. It was accomplished in the form of an agreement, which was placed before one to sign with the threat 'If you do not agree, then. . . .'"[22]

The Warburg bank was no worthless corpse. Visiting Hamburg in January 1938, Siegmund, who still moved in and out of Germany with remarkable ease, was again astounded by the brisk pace of business.[23] M. M. Warburg even turned a profit in 1938 as it benefited from a lengthening list of desperate Jews who transferred their assets there. It proved the value of a private bank that could ensure a high degree of confidentiality.

The Aryanization of M. M. Warburg would be the biggest of a private bank. To complete the transfer, the bank was converted into a new limited partnership. To the family's dismay, the Hamburg government, still wishing to capitalize upon the renown of the Jewish bank, insisted that it retain the M. M. Warburg name. The purchase price of 11.6 million reichsmarks was pure eyewash since the buyers paid nothing for goodwill. Of 6.4 million marks actually paid to the Warburg partners, the partners left a "silent participation" of 3 million in the bank. They wanted the bank to have sufficient operating capital, even though they had no voting rights.[24] Of 3.4 million marks left, the Reich Flight Capital Tax took away a quarter, or 850,000 marks. The Warburgs then had to pay one million marks in bare-faced tribute for Third Reich approval of the Aryanization. Of 1.55 million marks remaining, the Nazi exchange rates confiscated another 90 percent, leaving 155,000 marks of the original 6.4 million.[25] The silent participation was later converted into a bank balance and then confiscated outright by the Nazis at the outbreak of the war.

At first, Fritz and Max planned to stay in Hamburg, tending to their charities and overseeing the bank's transfer. Max, in particular, still couldn't sever his emotional ties to Germany or admit that his kaleidoscopic journey through the Third Reich had come to a sudden end. He and Fritz negotiated an unusual arrangement with the authorities by which they received the right of dual residence, allowing them to enter and leave the Third Reich unimpeded and retain a private secretary's office in Hamburg.[26] Max told Jimmy that this passport matter was so important to the partners that the Aryanization plan hinged on it.[27]

The Nazis wanted to bar foreigners from the Aryanized bank and prohibited the Warburgs from selling stakes to overseas firms. This torpedoed a Wallenberg plan to buy shares for their Enskilda Bank in Stockholm.[28] The new head of the bank would be the Warburgs' all-purpose Aryan and general manager, Dr. Rudolf Brinckmann, a man who shall figure largely in our story. He had a broad face with tufty eyebrows and a rather Oriental cast. Born in Turkey and of Turkish-Greek extraction, he had emigrated to Germany as a teenager, studied law and economics, and learned six languages. After working for E. Ladenburg in Frankfurt and Deutsche Bank in Constantinople, he was hired by M. M. Warburg in 1920. He had fully inhabited the Warburg universe. Not only had he rotated through every department at the bank, but had even worked with Paul at the IAB in the 1920s. He didn't become a partner until 1938 even though he occupied many corporate board seats vacated under duress by Warburg partners.

The other new chieftain was Paul Wirtz, a Hamburg exporter with a long, pointed nose and piercing eyes. From an old local family, he was former head of the Anglo-Chilean Nitrate Syndicate in London. He took the position with M. M. Warburg out of a feeling of Hanseatic duty. Both Brinckmann and Wirtz were not only longtime Warburg associates, but staunch anti-Nazis. Although the Warburgs picked Brinckmann and Wirtz, they had no written agreement from them as to what would ever happen if the Nazis fell from power. It was assumed, however, that these custodians would loyally return the bank to the Warburgs.

The partnership stakes were scattered among eleven investors so that no single group could seize control. Large stakes went to the partially state-run *Bank für Deutsche Industrie Obligationen* in Berlin, the *Industriekreditbank* in Düsseldorf, and that Warburg ally for several years, the Berliner Handels-Gesellschaft. Both the electrical giant, Siemens (through Siemens & Halske and Siemens-Schukert) and the Good Hope Steel Company (*Gutehoffnungshütte*) also took shares. There was a further sprinkling of old-line Hamburg and Bremen trading firms in the shipping, coffee, and Latin American trade.

On May 30, 1938, Max Warburg reported as usual to the handsome neoclassical palazzo he had built on the Ferdinandstrasse. He assembled the bank's two hundred employees in the canteen, a room of dark wood paneling with a view of the slim verdigris spire of St. Jacob's church. For forty-six years, Max had ruled the bank with his own characteristic mix of charm and autocratic paternalism. Today, not trusting his own emotions, he smiled wanly as he greeted the staff.

His youngest daughter, Gisi, came for the farewell ceremony. She still worked for Youth Aliyah in Berlin, where the phones were now tapped and things had grown impossibly tense. When she arrived at the bank, she came upon a grotesque scene. The Nazi party had just delivered a gigantic oil painting of Hitler, to be hung in Max's office after the portraits of all Jewish partners were removed. Staring gloomily at the picture, the concierge wouldn't touch it. "They'll have to get another fool to hang it up," he told Gisi.[29]

Age seventy-one, Max wanted to leave in dignity and prove that the Nazis hadn't extinguished his spirit. Having forgotten his trademark white carnation, he asked Gisi to fetch a fresh one for his lapel. An almost legendary figure among Hamburg Jews, he now seemed all too mortal and fallible. He had wanted Eric, as a member of the fifth generation, to deliver the speech, but his son was in New York on business. So Max read aloud a communiqué that would appear in the press the next day, announcing that he, Fritz, Eric, and Dr. Spiegelberg were leaving the bank. Max explained that they had weighed two options: either abolish the bank outright or (and he never actually mouthed the hated word) Aryanize it by transferring control to friendly, non-Jewish hands. "We chose the second path because we did not wish this firm, which has been our life's work up till today, to be destroyed. Above all, we did not wish your community, in which you grew close in decades of work, to disintegrate."[30]

With great pride and ineffable sadness, Max introduced the two men who would henceforth steer the firm. Dr. Brinckmann delivered a paean to the bank's tradition. "I promise you that the tradition of trust and the spirit of camaraderie and helpfulness, which we have always upheld in this house, will be preserved in future."[31] Paul Wirtz promised to be a fatherly figure. A grateful Max extolled both as wise, fair, and far-sighted men.

Aside from a notable lack of bitterness, what made Max's valedictory address so remarkable was its hopefulness. It tacitly foresaw a post-Hitler Germany in which the Jews and M. M. Warburg & Co. would again flourish. Far from being elegiac, it was positive, forward-looking, as if Max were just going into a temporary exile. In retrospect, the speech seems prophetic and escapist in about equal measure.

Max tried to condense all his accumulated banking wisdom into his talk. He urged the staff, in his absence, to pay close attention to each transaction, to provide professional service of uniform excellence, to spread risk and assist troubled clients, and to be constantly alert for adverse events. Warmly thanking the staff, he noted that he might never walk through the office again. "We wish you success in your work," he said in closing, "for the benefit of the Hanseatic city of Hamburg and for the benefit of Germany!"[32] This final apostrophe to the Fatherland, just when it had so sorely betrayed him, was vintage Max. Thus ended centuries of continuous Warburg activity in Germany.

Many employees stood misty-eyed as they listened. By the end, dozens wept in an emotional outpouring as they surged forward to shake Max's hand. He later said he felt as if he stood before his own coffin, for they sobbed as if it had been his funeral. The image was apt, for expulsion for Max Warburg was death-in-life. The Warburgs' fairy-tale existence had been blown away as if it had never existed.

After shaking every hand, Max returned to his office and signed a last message to the staff, urging them to preserve the bank's spirit. Then he left the building that had been a monument to his effort and never returned, even though he didn't sail to New York until late summer. Fritz and Anna Beata soon departed for Sweden. In the weeks that followed, Max received many expressions of sympathy from business friends.

Meanwhile, the campaign against Jewish businessmen went forward unmercifully. On June 20, the Economics Ministry banished Jews from stock and commodity exchanges and two weeks later prohibited them from serving as agents or brokers, completing the rout of the Jewish financier. Increasingly that summer, the Gestapo shipped off "asocial" Jews to concentration camps.

Outside Germany, press reports of the Aryanization produced an electrifying effect. As *The Times* of London said, "The transformation of M. M. Warburg and Co. is one of the more spectacular incidents of the present energetic drive against Jewish influence and participation in financial and business activity in the Reich."[33] The paper noted that financial circles estimated the bank's capital at forty million marks, while it had changed hands at only twelve million marks. In other words, even at this fictitious official price, the Warburgs had surrendered a fortune; at the actual price, they were effectively wiped out. It was ironic that the firm that had saved the capital of so many Jews had forgotten, in the end, to save itself.

In their final days in Germany, the Warburgs lingered on in a ghostly limbo. Though evicted from the bank, Max didn't know when he would leave, having obtained the special right to dual residence. The Warburgs maintained a superficial aura of comfort that couldn't disguise their enormous sadness. On July 15, 1938, a woman named Bertha Ehrenberg visited Kösterberg and in her diary poetically captured the Warburgs' despair. She arrived in a lovely twilight, against which the Warburgs seemed spectral figures, relics of a dead world:

"Everything in that twilit evening was so remote and as if already forgotten by the world. Enormous, unreal trees, such as those that only in Hamburg or England take root in the landscape, afforded glimpses of a distance in which the broad, still river flowed toward the horizon opposite. Everything was quiet and almost unreal—another world—and in this quiet and remoteness I met the men whom I had met years before at the height of their power, their influence, their prestige intact. They sat there together, the Warburgs, Erich, Hans Meyer from Paris, Spiegelberg and Liebmann, once the heads of the bank, now stripped of their rights, denounced as 'rogues' and 'scum,' their estate no longer cheerful and the only thoughts in their minds, how to get out of this captivity. . . . Outwardly everything calm and friendly and cheerful, 'composed,' but I sensed intensely the dreadful and tragic tension which lay over these uprooted, obliterated people."[34]

Orphans of the Storm

The bond between Max and Eric deepened during their final uncertain days in Germany. Eric had been his father's confidant, providing emotional support, while harboring a pessimistic outlook. He believed that the Nazis, through the *Autobahnen* and public-works projects, had inspired unwavering mass enthusiasm. While he had friends in the Resistance—three would be executed before the war ended—he thought Hitler too tightly guarded for an assassination attempt, which might only provoke brutal reprisals. If more realistic than his father, Eric shared the Warburg feeling of immunity to extreme danger and didn't sufficiently credit the Nazis' warlike intentions.

Eric was better suited to the smooth arts of diplomacy than to the rough-and-tumble of confrontation. In the early 1930s, he was active in the Anglo-German Association, the Friends of the United States, and other groups that promoted international harmony. He passed through the Third Reich with his own cheerful resilience. "I do not envy him his life," Eddie Warburg said of him in 1938, "but I do envy him his real nobility of character which enables him to carry on with such grace and charm."[1]

In part, Eric weathered the persecution through travel, including twice-yearly trips to America to establish residency there. In 1936, he traveled aboard the zeppelin *Hindenburg*, which spectacularly exploded the next year. He often sailed to Scandinavia aboard the *Kong Bele* with Gisi, aristocratic girlfriends, and Alain de Rothschild. In the summer of 1938, Eric made a memorable last trip that showed that the boat no longer protected him from harassment. He was about to sail one day when the Gestapo swarmed aboard. Under strict foreign exchange rules, nobody in Germany could carry more than ten marks aboard a ship. With dread, Eric realized that he had a *verboten* twenty-mark note stashed in his pocket. While the Gestapo slashed open everything from sails to food cans, Eric squeezed the note into a tiny ball then popped it overboard. As secret police prowled the decks, Eric prayed that the crumpled, bobbing bill wouldn't suddenly unfold and declare his crime. By this point, he was already preparing to depart for America and planned to leave his boat behind in a Danish harbor.

For the Warburgs, it was a summer of atrocious news and tender farewells. The Nazis now required all Jews to carry special identity cards with the middle name "Israel" added to male names and "Sara" to female names in official documents. Yet the Warburgs still found people who preserved a semblance of civility amid the darkness. When Eric said good-bye to a family friend, Cäcilie von Klinggräff, she led him to an enormous boulder on her property, dragged there by twenty horses from the Pinnow-Chemnitz border at the end of World War I. On this boulder were inscribed two Biblical words to commemorate the missing soldiers: "We wait." These words, the old woman said, now applied to Eric.[2]

The Warburgs were buoyed by these people who resisted Nazi propaganda and represented the good, enduring side of German culture. For instance, on the day Hitler seized power, Max's close friend, Paul Reusch, head of the Good Hope Steel Company, had installed a stone bench in his park bearing the Greek motto that whoever made a pact with tyrants would perish.[3] The Warburgs never believed that the human spark entirely died among the German people, and this gave them hope of a renewal someday.

The family began shutting down Kösterberg. The authorities informed them that they had to keep one house full of furniture, but could ship the rest elsewhere. The half-Jewish Warburg gardener, Else Hoffa, selected the best pieces, then crammed all the worst junk into one house. Later, she went to England and became chief gardener for an English lord. In late August 1938, Max, Alice, and Gisela sailed to New York, expecting to return in late autumn. Even amid unspeakable crimes, Max couldn't cut the emotional cord with Germany. Fritz, who had remained in Germany from loyalty to Max, said his brother's "attachment to Hamburg and Germany was still so strong, that he by no means ruled out a return to Germany 'after Hitler.' "[4] In New York, Max planned to attend a conference on refugee aid and appeal to the Joint for

Alexandra Danilova in Swan Lake, circa 1938.
(Private collection of Alexandra Danilova)

extra money for German-Jewish emigration. He had no idea that his trip would lengthen into permanent exile or that he would never set eyes on Germany again.

In Berlin, Gisi had distributed money for exit permits and she didn't want to emigrate as long as distraught Jews were still trapped there. Since her passport had been taken away, Max got her another by telling Hamburg officials that she wanted to raise money abroad for Jewish emigration—an idea that still attracted the Nazis. "I was the only German Jewess who cried when she got her passport because I didn't want to leave," she said.[5]

On August 23, 1938, Eric left Kösterberg and his trusty Newfoundland dog, Teddy, without knowing whether he would see Germany again. He made a short trip to Stockholm to say good-bye to Fritz and Anna Beata then traveled to New York. On September 29, 1938, he became a naturalized citizen after only ten days in America, thanks to the residence stamp having been placed in his passport in the 1920s. Since Max and Alice were now in New York on a visitors' visa, that accident saved their lives.

While they were in New York, *Der Stürmer* heaped more calumnies on the family in a vicious tirade entitled, "The Jewish Warburgs in the World War." The readers again learned that Paul had forged the Federal Reserve Board expressly to wage war against Germany and that he and Max had headed their respective war staffs. "They led them in the interest of their money and in the interest of the Jewish race." The paper blamed the Warburgs for killing thirteen million non-Jews in the war. Felix was posthumously dragged in as a stealthy intermediary. "Very probably he played the most dangerous role of the three Warburgs," the author speculated. He resurrected the shade of Jacob Schiff, reporting him boasting to the New York Stock Exchange during the war, "The war will turn out, as it will, but we Jews have won the entire world." Not only did Schiff mastermind the Russian Revolution, but Kuhn, Loeb was rewarded with exclusive rights to sell the Romanoff jewels.[6] This violent rhetoric, of course, projected the sadistic impulses of the Nazis themselves.

In early November, a seventeen-year-old Jewish student murdered a German diplomat in Paris, Ernst vom Rath, to avenge the deportation of his parents and other Polish Jews. This unleashed *Kristallnacht* on the night of November 9, 1938, a dress rehearsal for the Final Solution. The SS herded twenty thousand Jews into concentration camps. Among the hundreds of synagogues burned was Hamburg's Grindelhof, built partly at the behest of Moritz Warburg with large sums from Felix. In general, the pogrom wasn't popular in Hamburg. "The Nazis sent troops there from Berlin," recalled Gisela, "because they were afraid the locals wouldn't destroy enough synagogues."[7] Even though ninety-one Jews were killed, the Nazis demanded that the Jews pay one billion marks in damages for Rath's death and another 250 million marks to repair streetlamps and storefronts! It was now that Himmler began to organize the bureaucratic machinery that would annihilate Jews instead of simply expelling them.

The night of shattered glass ended Max's hopes. Frieda watched him absorb the dreadful news. "I remember how . . . he turned to his son, Eric, in my sitting-room and said, 'Now it's finished. Will you get us into Canada, so that we can re-enter on a quota?' "[8] Dr. Kurt Sieveking cabled from Hamburg, warning Max that he faced imprisonment if he set foot on German soil. *Kristallnacht* made Max realize that he and his family were now castaways, indefinitely marooned in America.

Eric took Max and Alice to Toronto so that they could re-enter the United States as parents of an American citizen under a preferential quota. It was a fantastic stroke of luck for them, since the United States sifted through three hundred thousand applications and FDR still refused to loosen the restrictive quota system. Deeply grateful to Eric, Max teased him that it was the one time he had made himself useful. He wished to become a U.S. citizen, he said, so he could convert Eric into a second-generation American.[9]

Gisi, twenty-six, couldn't accept that she could no longer fight in Berlin, that the struggle had ended in defeat. "I was homesick for Germany, for the trench spirit in Youth Aliyah," she said.[10] She was about to return to Germany when *Kristallnacht* occurred. To relieve her frustrated energies, she made a transcontinental fund-raising trip for Youth Aliyah.

With *Kristallnacht*, the terror struck more directly at well-to-do Jews left in Germany. The Gestapo rounded up affluent Jews to extort money from them. Some seven hundred Jews were crowded into a Gestapo detention center at Fuhlsbüttel, outside Hamburg, including Fritz Warburg. As longtime chairman of the Jewish Hospital, he had returned from Stockholm a few days earlier to deal with the hospital's grave financial straits. Founded in 1839 by Salomon Heine (the poet's uncle) it was a pet Warburg charity, which the Nazis for years had tried to shut down. As Jews evacuated Germany, the hospital labored under heavy debts and needed constant Warburg bailouts. By late September 1938, the medical situation grew dire, as the government ousted Jewish doctors from general practice. Informed that authorities planned to cast out hospital patients in a week, Fritz returned to Hamburg to bargain for an extension. He was grabbed at the airport on his way back to Sweden.

Always a sickly, wheezing, torpid man, Fritz fainted at the Fuhlsbüttel prison after standing for ten hours in a packed cell. At first, he shared a single room with seven other people. When the others were all released within days, Fritz knew the Nazis meditated special plans for him. Luckily, Fritz was warm and garrulous and got on famously with the turnkey, who asked if he could bring him a companion. Fritz mentioned a Dr. Cohn, then shaving the heads of some old prisoners. The obliging turnkey then strode through the prison, shouting in a stentorian voice, "Dr. Cohn, please, as company for Dr. Warburg!"[11] Henceforth, the turnkey brought Fritz a new cellmate each day. As a Jewish community leader, Fritz felt obligated to keep up morale and he regaled the other inmates with entertaining stories or tales of the prophets. To distract them, he also analyzed their handwriting and formed such close friendships that he later sent many prisoners "Care" packages from Sweden.

During his prison months, Fritz remained in the agonizing position of being detained with his passport revoked. He escaped from Germany through the intercession of Baron Cornelius von Berenberg-Gossler, who came from an old-line Christian banking house in Hamburg. In mid-April, the baron secured an appointment at Gestapo headquarters in Berlin with a man named Wolff, adjutant to Police Chief Himmler. While the baron sat there, Wolff discussed Fritz's case with Himmler's lieutenant, Reinhard Heydrich. Berenberg-Gossler formed the distinct impression that the Nazis planned to exploit Fritz as a pawn in the event of an international incident. The Gestapo proposed a deal: They would let Fritz go if he ransomed a large number of poor Jews into Sweden. A week later, the baron told Wolff that Fritz would furnish the wherewithal for one hundred Jewish children and poor adults to depart. After more cloak-and-dagger meetings, the Gestapo informed Fritz on May 6, 1939, that he could claim his passport. After a curious delay of three days— he unaccountably dawdled—Fritz and Anna left for Sweden on May 10.

They found it miraculous to be back in their Stockholm flat. "Yes, it's really true, we're really here," Anna wrote her daughter. "I still can hardly believe it, but it's beau-u-u-ti-ful!"[12] She praised Fritz's unselfish courage during the crisis. Anna Beata felt they had done enough for the community inside Germany and could now, with a clear conscience, help from abroad. The Jewish Hospital turned out to be beyond redemption. The Jewish population was shrinking and gentile patients dared not enter. The hospital couldn't continue this way and the Hamburg government took it over. During the Final Solution, the Nazis would use it for military sick bays. When they admitted Jewish patients, they would poison them with sleeping pills.

Like Aby, but quite unlike his other brothers, Fritz was never drawn to the speed, dash, and dynamism of America. Since his wife was Swedish, they adopted Stockholm as their new home. An avid conversationalist, Fritz relished the café and street life and the rich selection of movie theaters and Jewish lectures. Not only did Anna Beata resume her kindergarten work, but their daughter, Eva, brought along to Sweden her kindergarten children. Keen to emigrate to Palestine, Eva stayed in Sweden at the express wish of

Henrietta Szold of Youth Aliyah and became the group's Swedish representative. In the end, she joined her pupils in Israel.

Although Max and Fritz escaped with families intact, they had made no provision for their sister, Louise, Dr. Derenberg's widow. Max claimed that Louise couldn't overcome her attachment to Germany and her friends. Louise's children, however, felt that Max encouraged her to stay, but then neglected his brotherly duty. After *Kristallnacht*, it fell to César Domela—the Dutch, avant-garde artist who had married Louise's daughter, Ruth—to slip into Germany and bring out his mother-in-law. In his concern for the general weal, Max sometimes had a funny way of overlooking specific cases close at hand. There was some bitterness among Louise's children that Max had urged his sister to stay in Germany while knowing that he himself had the option of someday entering the United States through Eric.

———

The Warburgs, who had been rooted to Germany for centuries, now returned to the wandering, nomadic life of Diaspora Jews. Whether in England, Sweden, or America, they were again strangers and sojourners in the land. They didn't lapse into brooding or self-pity but hit the ground running. They had lost wealth, power, and position, but not their brains, talents, connections, and self-confidence. Like royalty in exile, they still felt responsible for German Jews.

By stirring the conscience of the British government, *Kristallnacht* at least ended up saving thousands of Jewish children. A central catalyst was Lola Hahn-Warburg, who continued to evolve from beguiling society hostess into a dedicated political activist. Max warned people, "The first time that you meet my daughter, she will behave like a lady, the next time she will get on your nerves with her noble social matters."[13] Still contending with a new language and homeland, she threw herself into refugee activities, working in a building near Russell Square with sister Anita. In late November 1938, she accompanied a delegation to the Home Office to plead for persecuted German-Jewish children. Lola provided moving anecdotes of their suffering. That night, Sir Samuel Hoare, the Home Secretary, told the House of Commons that the British government would waive the usual visa requirements for these children and admit them without passports. From the British standpoint, this reflected compassionate statesmanship and practical politics. By receiving more Jews into Britain, the government hoped to lighten the dangerous population pressures building up in Palestine.

By December, the first children began to arrive in England from Germany, Austria, and Czechoslovakia. They came clutching a single suitcase and ten marks apiece. Many were orphans or had parents in concentration camps. In

London, some experienced fresh indignities as prospective foster parents fussed over selections. "It was like a cattle market," said Gisi. "The blond and blue-eyed little darlings were taken. The Jewish-looking ones were not."[14] Suicides occurred among the more seriously depressed children.

Heading the welfare section of this Refugee Children's Movement, as it was eventually called, Lola received the most intractable cases. Strong-willed, domineering, but with a warmly magical attraction for young people, she was perfect for the job. She had an instinct for dealing with troubled youth. One day, a delinquent barged into her office. As she recalled, "When I was behind my desk, he jumped up suddenly, took out a knife and cut the telephone wire. Then he opened the window and started climbing out on the ledge. I tried to remain very calm. I said to him, 'I'm very unwell. I have bad kidney trouble. It is so cold in here with the window open. Will you please come back into the office?'"[15] The boy responded. Lola ended up driving him to the hospital then placing him in a special home. Another time, a young girl was struck mute by mental illness. Lola kept bringing her flowers in the hospital and sitting quietly by her. Years later, the former patient, now a healthy young woman, tracked her down and said, "I shall never forget your visits."[16] People became passionately attached to Lola and accepted her overbearing side as part of the package.

At first, it was hard for Lola to operate in a world where the Warburg name didn't command instant respect or even recognition. She had to cope with the hostility that often greeted German accents—an excruciating experience for victims of Nazi oppression. (These chilly relations led Lola's sister, Anita, to help Jewish refugees to find volunteer work with British citizens through the All Nations Volunteer League, which secured six thousand posts.) In one North Wales town, Lola's accent was deemed so sinister that she attracted an unwanted police escort. She succeeded in her work despite these impediments. The Children's Transport movement was a magnificent achievement that had snatched ten thousand children from the gas chambers by the time it ended in August 1939. It rescued one third of all Jewish children who escaped the Nazis. Half the Jewish children in Germany were never to emerge again.

—

The Austrian *Anschluss* heightened pressure on the Roosevelt administration to offer a haven for Jewish refugees. To deal with at least the cosmetics of the problem, Roosevelt convened an international conference on refugees in the French resort town of Evian on Lake Geneva in July 1938. Attended by representatives of thirty-two countries, this conference was long on noble resolutions but short on deeds. Its one notable achievement was to create the

Inter-Governmental Committee on Political Refugees. Headquartered in London, it would be directed by George Rublee, an American lawyer, with strong backing from Lord Bearsted and Anthony de Rothschild. Rublee found FDR less than ecstatic about the whole venture. "My guess is that the President went along with the idea because he may have thought that some sort of a gesture was necessary to assuage the indignation excited by the persecution of the Jews, but without any real hope of success in improving the lot of the Jews in Germany."[17]

Rublee's activities ended up revolving around a plan offered by Dr. Schacht to ransom the German Jews. It was an intellectual cousin of the plan peddled by Max Warburg for years. Schacht's plan foresaw a sizable confiscation of Jewish property, whereas Max's plan was designed to preserve Jewish wealth. Negotiations occurred at the end of Schacht's Reichsbank reign. In September 1938, he had secretly plotted with General Ludwig Beck and others to seize Hitler in the Reich Chancellery and bring him before a state tribunal. Both Beck and Schacht thought Germany fatally unprepared for the war that Hitler contemplated against the Western powers. When Neville Chamberlain and Édouard Daladier agreed to attend the Munich Conference, the crestfallen conspirators grew dejected and abandoned their scheme.

On his way to America in September 1938, Max met with Rublee and Lord Winterton at the British Foreign Office. He said the German government would consider a deal permitting a mass exodus of Jews in exchange for a boost in German exports. He also alluded to a recent visit to the Foreign Office in Berlin in which he had expounded a plan to export fifty thousand Jews a year.[18] Hence, Rublee wasn't surprised when Berlin sent out feelers about just such a plan in October, with Schacht the moving force. Schacht wanted to impound a quarter of all remaining Jewish assets in Germany as collateral for a large dollar loan that Jews abroad would extend to the Nazis. The collateral would finance German exports to pay off the loan. Over a three-year period, the fund would resettle 150,000 Jews and superintend the departure of 400,000 people from Germany and Austria.

That November, when *Kristallnacht* threatened to derail these negotiations, Schacht shrewdly turned adversity to advantage. He openly denounced the November atrocities, telling his Reichsbank staff, "I only hope that none of our office boys took part, then for such people there is no room at the Reichsbank."[19] Schacht said that if Jews couldn't safely conduct business in Germany, the government should help them to leave. According to Schacht, Hitler was sufficiently upset by foreign reaction to *Kristallnacht* to inquire, "Have you any suggestions?"[20] Schacht won Hitler's and Göring's consent to pursue his transfer scheme in London, though he steered clear of Joachim von Ribbentrop and the Foreign Office.

Under camouflage of talks with the Bank of England, Schacht pursued his plan in London that December. He insisted that while awaiting their liberation, Jews still in Germany would be protected and elderly Jews allowed to die peacefully on German soil. Lord Winterton and Rublee reacted favorably to the plan and agreed to consult with financial experts, as well as eminent British and American Jews.

The political reaction recapitulated the controversy aroused by Max's earlier plans. Chamberlain and Lord Halifax opposed any plan that might fortify the Nazi economy while FDR derided it as ransom for hostages.[21] British and American Jews were again reluctant to submit to patent blackmail. They also objected to the proposed committee, which might seem to substantiate Nazi fantasies of a world Jewish cabal. Once again, the Jews, far from ruling the universe, hesitated to flex their muscles for fear of provoking a backlash. As Siegmund noted after a meeting with Lionel and Anthony de Rothschild, they shrank from any Anglo-American Jewish political bureau because "one can endanger his English citizenship, if one becomes too strongly active in Jewish world actions."[22] After Kristallnacht, nobody wanted to grant to Nazi Germany loans secured by seized Jewish assets.

While Max supported the Schacht negotiations, Siegmund cast a more dubious eye over the affair. With great ardor, he had thrown himself into refugee work. He would get distraught calls from people trapped in Germany then run around trying to raise money for them. Often he ended up helping them from his own pocket. He tried to coax German and Austrian refugees into setting up a job-training program and lobbied for expanded refugee camps. Checking his business ambitions for the moment, he subordinated everything to aiding German Jews. At one point, he was busily preparing applications for sixty refugees trying to enter Peru, Brazil, and other countries.[23] Exhausted much of the time, he seldom arrived home before ten-thirty at night.

Moving in and out of Germany on business, Siegmund exposed himself to great danger and was never entirely sure that the Nazis would let him return to England. He was extremely worried about political developments in Germany. On August 16, 1937, he penned an eloquent letter that was to be read by Eva in the event of his death. Full of lofty exhortations to have faith in the final triumph of goodness, it also contained characteristic, sardonic touches on how to raise George and Anna. He asked Eva to provide for them "a quiet, peaceful, natural growing-up, free from the fuss of social to-do, breaking records and sport, free also from small-minded 'time killing' activity such as the restless driving-around of cars, sightseeing and all other ways of 'passing the time' (what a dreadful expression)." He paid tribute to their marriage but also honestly alluded to their difficulties, telling her, "please do not ever forget that at all times of our life together I have loved you so very dearly, as dearly as any human being can love another. And when we have come under a cloud, as intense people are wont to do, and our love has been overcast for a while, it has always come back into the light stronger than ever."

—

During this period, the marriage had indeed come under a cloud. An avid ballet-goer, Siegmund met Alexandra Danilova, a celebrated star of Diaghilev's Ballets Russes, on a transatlantic liner. A product of the Imperial Theater School in St. Petersburg, she had left Russia with George Balanchine and lived with him as his common-law wife in the 1920s. When Siegmund met her, Danilova was in her early thirties, dancing with the Ballet Russe de Monte Carlo. She had an almond-shaped face with beautifully sculpted eyelids that made her a pensive Madonna in repose. So long and faultless were her legs that Lloyd's of London would insure them for $500,000 in the 1940s. She had star qualities that must have won Siegmund: She hated fuss and pomposity; was stoically impatient with whining; had awesome discipline as a dancer; and conducted herself with a natural, unaffected dignity. She was Siegmund Warburg's counterpart in the ballet world.

Siegmund approached her on the ship with characteristic premeditation, first inviting Danilova's friend to dinner, then asking her to introduce him to the prima ballerina. Smitten, he wooed Danilova with the prodigious charm at his command. By the time they docked in Europe, they had arranged a rendezvous in Berlin, where she was scheduled to dance.

"Siegmund helped me to get into a beautiful hotel in Unter den Linden," Danilova recalled. "He said, 'You must stay in this hotel. It's the best and I will see to it that you get in there. I was very thankful."[24] At a later date, Siegmund would be rigidly circumspect, but in this liaison he seemed heedless. In Berlin, he not only openly attended Danilova's performances, but squired her to the opera and took her to dinner at a cousin's apartment. With breathtaking devotion, he gave her an antique ruby ring, trimmed with tiny diamonds, that he told her had belonged to the Hapsburg dynasty. Later he added a blue sapphire brooch that she would always keep locked in her bank vault.

Enchanted with Danilova, Siegmund betrayed none of his volcanic temper or fickle, arbitrary moods. He was infinitely tender. "He was very nice to me, very warm and kind. He treated me with respect. He was easy to talk to and be with. Maybe it was easy for him to be with me because whatever he spoke I would know. He loved the ballet and he admired me as a dancer and a woman."[25]

For Siegmund, Danilova must have brought laughter and brightness into a refugee life darkened by misfortune and dislocation. As for Danilova, she was touched and flattered by Siegmund's gallantry and fell in love with him. Since they both had peripatetic lives—international bankers and prima ballerinas had that much in common—their itineraries frequently crossed in the coming year. They had many trysts, including a stay together at the George V in Paris; three days in Hollywood (Danilova insisting they travel there separately for discretion's sake), and frequent visits at Danilova's flat on Shepherd Market in Mayfair. To make sure no gossip circulated, she didn't tell a soul about the romance for more than fifty-five years.

Nonetheless reports ran through the City about Siegmund's rapt, faithful attendance at Covent Garden. Whether word filtered back to Eva through family channels or whether Siegmund finally admitted to his amorous escapade is unclear. Whatever the case, Eva decided that she didn't intend to be a tolerant, two-timed wife. She suddenly took both children to Paris and forced Siegmund to make a choice. Fortified by her personal inheritance from the Philipsons, she didn't have to truckle to him. Her family alibi was that George and Anna were catching colds in the London damp and needed a change of climate.

While Eva was in Paris, Siegmund visited New York and was summoned by Frieda, who told him that she was extremely fond of Eva and that he should do everything in his power to keep her. (Since Frieda tolerated Felix's flings, it suggests the gravity of Siegmund's plight.) During his time with Danilova, Siegmund had sidestepped all talk of family. "He never talked about his children or his wife," said Danilova, whose second marriage to an Italian engineer, Giuseppe Massera, had by now ended. "He never spoke about them and I didn't ask."[26] Warburg legend claims that Siegmund even considered divorcing Eva, although Danilova contends that she and Siegmund never discussed marriage.

Danilova knew the affair would end someday, ballerinas not being considered respectable mates for up-and-coming young bankers. She was also a supremely dedicated dancer, wedded to her career, and would never have renounced touring. Nevertheless, things were still rosy with Siegmund when Danilova got an unexpected letter. "He said that he couldn't see me anymore. It was a very sort of official letter—like you say somebody's service is finished. A banker's letter."[27] The letter was conspicuously devoid of warmth or explanation, as if Siegmund needed to telegraph, with coldly irrevocable finality, that the affair was over. When Danilova wrote, asking to have lunch one more time, Siegmund never replied. It was said that when Eva returned from Paris, her dark hair had prematurely turned white.

Siegmund must have experienced tremendous struggle before sacrificing the alluring Danilova. This exquisite dancer was quite unlike anyone he had encountered even in *his* vast experience. An ambitious man, Siegmund must have known that divorce and remarriage to a ballet dancer would have tarred him, if not with a scandalous image, with an unwanted Bohemian one. Whatever the bargain he struck with Eva or with himself, Siegmund adhered to it, with iron fortitude, for his entire life. He did everything he needed to do to save his family.

Amazingly, Siegmund and Danilova never set eyes on each other again, even though she spent the postwar years in New York, later teaching at the School of American Ballet with Balanchine. Sometimes she wondered whether Siegmund had ever again come silently, anonymously, to see her perform. The circumstances behind his final letter would remain a lifetime mystery. She never had the consolation of an explanation nor anyone to grieve with. Of the family tempest stirred by the romance, she knew nothing. Like Siegmund, she had an uncommon capacity for keeping secrets. Even when she published her memoirs in 1988, she toyed with disclosing the episode, but stuck to her three husbands and her career. Siegmund would have appreciated such willpower.

More than fifty-five years later, Danilova would look back upon the aborted love affair philosophically, recalling it with sweet nostalgia instead of bitterness. "I was very hurt," she said. "But I keep my big mouth shut. I never told anybody. He probably respected that from me. Maybe our romance was an escape for him to a completely different world. I was like a beautiful garden full of flowers for him. Maybe it was his caprice. Together we had fun which he probably needed. I understand that I had to take this out of my heart and not tell anybody, not even my girlfriends. I still remember *avec tendresse* the time that we get together and I understand later, how big he was. So I had to respect his wishes."[28] When told, as an old woman, of the reasons behind Siegmund's letter, she expressed sympathy for Eva, saying she had been smart to force her husband to make a clean break. Either from guilt or discomfort, Siegmund emphatically refused to attend ballet in later years. He locked the experience away in some private compartment of fondly remembered but doubtless painful experience.

———

Constantly worried about his mother, Siegmund pleaded with Lucie to abandon Uhenfels, now run by a Nazi superintendent, and come to London. But Lucie prided herself on her autonomy and still felt surrounded by decent people. She didn't understand why she had to leave and, to Siegmund's dismay, was stubborn about staying. "She said, 'Everybody in the village knows me,'" recalled Siegmund's cousin. "She felt protected and she also provided work to a lot of people."[29] But after *Kristallnacht* she no longer felt safe. In December 1938, Siegmund and Lucie sold Uhenfels for 150,000 reichsmarks—a substantial sum that couldn't be extricated from Germany. As with other German Jews, the effective confiscation of her property made Lucie less attached to material things. After Siegmund fetched her in Paris and brought her to London, she lived with Siegmund and Eva much of the time; otherwise, she stayed in hotels, pensions, and other transient residences, refusing to own real estate again. The experience also made Siegmund more cerebral, less materialistic. Each year in the 1930s, he and his family moved to another apartment. Siegmund often told Eva that, at worst, they would spend their lives in a two-bedroom apartment.[30] He had a taste for fine items but didn't need them.

Outraged by British passivity toward the Nazis, Siegmund condemned Chamberlain for fondling the Nazi gangsters. He attributed this to misplaced guilt over Versailles and the anti-Bolshevist sentiment so shrewdly exploited by Hitler.[31] After the *Anschluss*, he applauded the tougher tone taken by England and even began to fear warmongering in some British quarters.[32] Persuaded that the salvation of German Jews far outstripped the resources of private philanthropy, he called for bold, decisive action by both the British and American governments.[33]

The Schacht mission to London disturbed Siegmund because it seemed more appeasement that would simply make the Nazis sneer at the weak, pliant Western democracies. "It makes no sense to appease the German government with friendly words," he wrote, "when sharp remarks, such as those that Roosevelt recently made, are much more effective. . . ."[34] It is unclear whether Max knew that Siegmund was trying to undermine the Schacht mission with timely warnings to key individuals. After meeting with Schacht in December, Lord Bearsted turned for an opinion to Siegmund, who warned that Schacht was considered suspect by the Nazis and was hence poorly positioned to conduct serious negotiations. As one who despised Schacht, Siegmund scoffed at any humanitarian motives behind his mission, asserting that "his activity in this matter above all serves the foreign ex-change balance of Germany and thereby improves his own personal position with the Nazi government."[35] Siegmund interpreted the Schacht plan as another Nazi ruse to relax tensions before unleashing fresh and more violent assaults.

On January 2, 1939, Hitler called Schacht to the Obersalzberg for a report on the London talks. By this point, the *Führer* had lost patience with the niceties of neoclassical economics as well as Schacht's constant moaning about the inflationary repercussions of the Göring rearmament plan. "You don't fit into the National Socialist picture," Hitler told Schacht.[36] On January 20, Schacht was cashiered from the Reichsbank, ending his bizarre marriage of convenience with the Third Reich.

This didn't end the ransom talks. Göring assigned Helmuth Wohltat of the Economics Ministry to continue negotiating with Rublee in Berlin. In February 1939, Rublee resigned his post. Various secret talks apparently persisted through May, with the quiet backing of the Warburgs and Kuhn, Loeb, but they came to naught.[37]

As if still magnetically drawn back to Germany, Max and Alice crossed the Atlantic on the *Queen Mary* in July 1939. They took the waters in Vittel, France, smack amid the Maginot Line. Meanwhile, Eric sailed from Denmark to other parts of Scandinavia with friends and seemed to have a young lady on each Baltic island. The group seemed oblivious of impending war. Once again, Siegmund was prescient, convinced by spring that war was inevitable.[38] That July, he and his associate, Harry Lucas, had a hand in a statement issued by Chamberlain in the House of Commons, which supported increased spending for refugees.[39] Another British director of New Trading, Sir Andrew McFadyean, had protested to the Italian government the expulsion of German and Austrian Jewish refugees earlier in the year.

Max was mystified by the Hitler-Stalin nonaggression pact in August 1939 and further stunned by the onset of war. Luckily, Eric got his parents off the Continent by the last train and Channel boat back to England before hostilities broke out. He was standing in the American embassy in London when Neville Chamberlain declared war against Germany. After the first air-raid alarm, he strolled over to St. James's Palace where the guards had suddenly traded their bearskin hats and ornamental uniforms for somber khakis. Eric suspected that this war would end the old aristocratic order left behind by the first war. He and his parents sailed to New York on separate crossings, aboard ships brightly illuminated to alert German attackers that they were neutral. Having driven them from Germany, the Nazis let the Warburgs cross the Atlantic in safety.

From the outset, Siegmund yearned to aid the war effort. Right after the Nazi invasion of Poland, he offered to introduce Stefan Zweig into the proper Whitehall circles so he could write propaganda leaflets to be dropped over Germany. As he told the author, "I think at the moment the Authorities would not only welcome large leaflets to be dropped by aeroplanes but also smaller leaflets which might be included in articles smuggled from Holland and Switzerland into Germany."[40] Zweig declined the invitation, saying any clever journalist could do as well.

Two months later, Siegmund made a trip to France and Switzerland that he mysteriously described to Zweig as the most interesting of his life.[41] It would prove the final act of the convoluted Warburg drama with Dr. Schacht, who feared that the still limited war could widen into a worldwide catastrophe. Schacht sought out German businessman Gero von Schultz Gaevernitz, the brother-in-law of Siegmund's close friend, Edmund Stinnes, and told him that he desperately needed to speak to President Roosevelt. He intended to ask Roosevelt to demand an end to the war while guaranteeing Germany's 1914 borders (minus Alsace-Lorraine); there would also be a popular vote taken in Austria, under League of Nations supervision, over whether the country should remain with Germany. Still in touch with several generals of the Resistance, Schacht thought that if Hitler rebuffed Roosevelt's offer, it would then strengthen their resolve to act. What he most needed, he said, was British support for his safe passage through Gibraltar en route to Washington. He had cooked up an idea for a lecture tour that might camouflage such an American mission.

Gero von Gaevernitz promptly went to Switzerland and sent a telegram to Siegmund, inviting him for a visit. Within a day, Siegmund wired back, "Arrive tomorrow Zurich, Hotel Neues Schloss." Siegmund must have known something momentous was afoot. To Gaevernitz's amazement, Siegmund arrived with a distinguished British civil servant. After hearing the account of Schacht's proposed journey, the British civil servant said that only the prime minister or the Cabinet could approve such a sensitive mission. After the two men returned to London, Siegmund had to send Gaevernitz a one-word telegram: "No."[42] It later turned out that the British lacked the necessary trust in Schacht, who had shopped similar proposals before the war. The previous winter, Siegmund himself had warned the British that the Nazis deemed Schacht unreliable. In the current circumstances, this should have been a powerful recommendation. Instead, the British government managed to complete its perfect record of ignoring overtures from authentic members of the German Resistance. American secretary of state Cordell Hull then repeated the error in Washington.

Part Four

THE WARTIME INTERREGNUM

Eric Warburg sailing with Countess
Marion Dönhoff, later the publisher of Die Zeit.
(Warburg family, Hamburg)

CHAPTER 34

Surreal Saviors

During his new life in New York, Eric lived at first with Frieda and his cousins at 1109 Fifth Avenue and sat on endless refugee resettlement committees, including one that brought three thousand German and Austrian doctors to America. With Siegmund settled in London, it was no accident that Eric planted his flag in the other capital of Anglo-American banking. The financial world would always seem too small to encompass these two striving Warburgs. In 1938, Eric started E. M. Warburg & Co. at 52 William Street in the Kuhn, Loeb building. After the sumptuous Warburg bank in Hamburg, this new firm was a humble start-up, with minimal capital and scarcely more than some desks. To show he was still active and unbowed, Max took an office there and reported to work daily. The erstwhile emperor of Hamburg finance was now confined to a little eyrie in a Manhattan office building. Eric felt duty-bound to hire former workers from Hamburg, giving his firm the sadly forlorn flavor of a refugee enclave for transplanted employees and clients.

However modest the lives of these exiled Warburgs, they had the inestimable advantage of an illustrious name and myriad connections. Even during the war, Eric provided an office for Baron Robert de Rothschild (father of his friend Alain) who worked beneath an Oskar Kokoschka painting that Eric had salvaged from Kösterberg. He was cast in a pundit's role by a Wall Street famished for educated guesses about German war strategy. In early April 1940, Thomas W. Lamont, senior partner of the Morgan bank, invited him to an elegant black-tie soirée and posed this after-dinner question: "Eric, you really know the Germans, what do you think will be the next move?" Through the cigar haze, Eric said that Hitler would do something unexpected. "Well, speculate!" Lamont encouraged him. Eric guessed that the Nazis would employ their U-boats to seize the Norwegian coast. A few days later, the Nazis made him a prophet. Amazed by this bull's-eye prediction, Lamont telephoned and asked, "Well, Eric, what's going to be the next move?"[1]

However traumatic, the expulsion from Hamburg provided a small measure of psychic relief for Eric. He had shown little real flair for business and always walked in the gigantic shadow of his father. Now the political scene provided scope for his latent diplomatic skills. When Stalin invaded Finland in December 1939, the Finnish ambassador in Washington appealed to Lewis Strauss, a Kuhn, Loeb partner who had once assisted Herbert Hoover. (He would chair the Atomic Energy Commission after the war.) Strauss hatched a scheme with the New Deal's Ben Cohen to aid the Finns with money from America's Export-Import Bank. They got Donald C. Swatland of the Cravath law firm to create a new corporate entity called the Finnish-American Trading Corporation, with offices at 52 William Street. As chief of this entity, Eric shipped everything from Ford trucks to Idaho peas to fighter planes to Finland. This war matériel had to cross a submarine-infested Baltic Sea. In the end, the aid proved futile and by March 1940 the Finns sued for an armistice.

Of German ancestry, Jimmy Warburg also considered himself an expert on European events and betrayed a deep emotional commitment to stopping Hitler. He had long been disturbed by American isolationism and Roosevelt's appeasement policy. On a Canadian steamer during the summer of 1937, he told Senator Robert A. Taft that Hitler's march into the Rhineland was only the prelude to an all-out campaign of European conquest. The senator brushed this aside, saying, "After all, the Versailles Treaty was unjust, and the Rhineland is a part of Germany."[2]

Those who had not experienced Nazism firsthand found it hard to credit the fervent rhetoric of those who had. At New York's Economic Club in March 1939, Jimmy debated Senator Burton K. Wheeler of Montana and lawyer John Foster Dulles. Never one to mince words, Jimmy said that the only way to avert war was for the United States to warn the Axis powers that any threats against England or France were threats against America. Wheeler scoffed at the notion that war would come or that, if it did, the United States should enter. Jimmy always thought Dulles a pompous stuffed shirt, a view amply confirmed when Dulles intoned, "Only hysteria entertains the idea that Germany, Italy or Japan contemplate war upon us."[3] Not without a touch of admiration, Dulles described the Axis powers as the "dynamic have-not nations" whose legitimate demands must be met. As soon as Germany invaded Poland that September, Jimmy believed that only American intervention could stop the Nazi juggernaut.

Frustrated with American myopia, eager to educate the public, Jimmy knew he had to heal the old breach with FDR. After the Nazis marched into Paris, Jimmy stopped by the White House and asked for a sheet of writing paper. In a personal note to Roosevelt, he explained that he had come to Washington to visit his former commanding officer, now at the State Department. "Being that near I could not resist the temptation to come across the street and do something I have long wanted to do, and that is to say to you, 'I was wrong and I'm sorry.' "[4] Obviously, Jimmy could have written from New York, but the spontaneous gesture added drama and underscored his sincerity. Two days later, Roosevelt replied in a gracious spirit. "Thank you for that letter of June nineteenth, so generous in tone and magnanimous in spirit. There is no statute of limitations on good will and I want you to know that I accept wholeheartedly everything you say, and appreciate, more than I can tell you, having you say it as you did."[5]

Ever since Paul's death, Jimmy had steadily shifted the spotlight of his attention from financial issues to foreign affairs, as if slowly casting off his Wall Street background. The war in Europe helped smooth things over between him and Roosevelt, because it assigned a lower priority to domestic issues that had divided them. In June 1940, Lewis Douglas, the former budget director, invited Jimmy and other friends to a dinner to brainstorm about how America might aid England and even enter the war. This influential group eventually expanded to include John McCloy, Dean Acheson, Frank Polk, and Allen Dulles. Because it usually met at the Century Association in New York, it took the nickname the Century Group. It provided Roosevelt with the theoretical legal foundation for the deal by which the United States gave Britain fifty destroyers in exchange for the use of British bases in the Western Hemisphere.

When Jimmy endorsed Roosevelt over Wendell Wilkie in the presidential race that autumn, it marked his fleeting return to political favor in the Washington establishment—the last time that he would enjoy insider status for another twenty years. When the president invited him to the White House, Jimmy found his old mentor cheerful, if somewhat aged. As he walked in, Roosevelt kidded him about repentant sinners, but didn't prolong the gibe. He ended up confiding to Jimmy his concern that the war was fast depleting the British Treasury.

After the election, Roosevelt made clear to the public that American exports to Britain might dry up without financial aid. Acutely aware that loans to the Allies had burdened world finance with exorbitant debts after World War I, Jimmy favored outright grants to England rather than a repeat of the earlier charade. He also thought America should begin to mobilize for war, a theme he stated in an open letter to Congress in December 1940. Unwilling to shrink from the hurly-burly of debate, Jimmy published a provocative book, *Our War and Our Peace*, that again sounded the theme that the United States could avoid entanglement in the European war only at its peril. He waged a vigorous campaign for congressional passage of FDR's Lend-Lease Bill, which he defended in a radio symposium. "The more we are able to do quickly—now—the less we shall have to do in the end," he said. The United States was "not helping enough to insure a defeat of the gangsters, but helping quite enough to put us next on the list of victims."[6]

After Lend-Lease was enacted, Jimmy participated in the founding of the Fight for Freedom Committee, which endorsed American entry into the war. He raised money and placed newspaper ads for the group, which numbered Eddie Warburg among its sponsors. The committee's bête noire was Charles Lindbergh and his isolationist America First movement. The chairman of the Fight for Freedom Committee, Bishop Hobson of Cincinnati, asked Jimmy to debate Lindbergh in Madison Square Garden before a nationwide radio audience. Some committee members feared that Jimmy, as scion of a Jewish banking dynasty, was a poor choice to joust with Lindbergh, who might scare up the old anti-Semitic hobgoblins of undue Jewish influence—a concern Jimmy shared. Bishop Hobson dismissed this as irrelevant. In the end, instead of dodging the issue, Jimmy faced it squarely: "Jew or Gentile, an American can say only this to Charles Lindbergh: 'Your second non-stop flight has taken you to a strange destination.' "[7] Whether Lindbergh loved or hated the Nazis didn't really matter, Jimmy contended, for his sweeping pronouncements weakened Allied confidence and stiffened German resolve.

As had happened to his father in the first world war, Jimmy became the target of intensely xenophobic, anti-Semitic attacks as America debated entry into the war. Senator Bennett C. Clark of Missouri tried to discredit him by fanning nativist resentment. Interviewed by the *Chicago Tribune*, he said of the Fight for Freedom Committee, "The great radio spokesman of the group is Mr. James P. Warburg, an international banker of great repute, a man who was not even born in the United States. He was fortunate in being brought to this country from Germany in his youth."[8] In a phrase drawn from the moldy stock of anti-Semitic smears, he branded Jimmy a "huckster of other men's blood" and said he spent the previous war working for a railroad and a Washington bank.

The senator didn't know the anguish Jimmy had caused his father by wanting to go to war against Germany. Jimmy explained that he had gone to Newport News, Virginia, to learn to fly in the hope of being recruited into the U.S. Naval Reserve Flying Corps. He had finally risen to a lieutenant's rank. "Is your cause so weak," Jimmy asked the senator, "that you must resort to lies and slander in order to blacken the character of those whose arguments you cannot meet?"[9] Acknowledging the senator's mistakes, the *Chicago Tribune* printed a front-page correction. A few weeks later, Jimmy wrote to his friend James V. Forrestal, the under secretary of the Navy, and asked if he could return to active duty. "I'm not looking for a prestige job but for a chance to do my bit wherever I usefully can to fix 'Uncle Adolf.' "[10]

As always in Jewish history, once the anti-Semitic demons were released they were hard to recall. Jimmy reaped a harvest of hate mail, including a letter from one *Tribune* reader who said that Senator Clark might repent his statements, but the reader didn't. "You are a jew monger. A jew war maker. You have upset the whole world. Your god dates back to the golden calf."[11] This missive sounded mannerly compared to the threat from a nameless "American mother" in Skokie, Illinois, who bluntly warned Jimmy that if any of her three sons had to go to war, then "you have attended your last social affair."[12] It was, of course, horribly ironic that Jimmy, who had tried so hard to distance himself from Judaism and blend into the gentile world, was the victim of such unbridled malice. As the Warburgs had repeatedly learned, every time they tried to renounce their Jewish identity, the world was happy to remind them of it. With the outbreak of European hostilities, there was no sudden burst of generosity in America to receive German Jewish refugees and only another twenty-one thousand were admitted during the war.

———

As with so many German Warburgs, Ingrid ended up staying in New York far longer than she had dreamed. After graduating from Hamburg University in 1936, Fritz's exquisite daughter, who so resembled an Egyptian queen, made a six-week trip from Hamburg to stay with Friedaflix in New York. (Fritz gave sage parting advice: "Never drink water with ice!"[13]) She returned to Hamburg briefly the following summer and experienced the funereal grace of Kösterberg. As she told her friend Adam von Trott, "The beauty of Kösterberg and its people has acquired something painful during these last few years."[14]

Now impoverished immigrants, the German Warburgs were suddenly thrown together with the super-rich, partygoing American Warburgs, producing many strange clashes and contrasts. Some of the German refugees found their American cousins snobbish and standoffish, wallowing in luxury. Staying at 1109 Fifth Avenue, Ingrid got to observe all the comic foibles of

Friedaflix. Frieda provided Ingrid with credit at many stores, while displaying Jacob Schiff's frugal rigidity. One day, as Ingrid stuck a stamp on a letter that was a penny too much, Frieda bristled with horror. "Darling you must never do that! What do you think, that we have become rich?"[15] Felix, on the other hand, was a smiling Lord Bountiful. One Saturday morning, he tried to coax Ingrid into a playful day at Woodlands. She refused, saying she had to raise three hundred dollars for a school for refugee children. Taking out his wallet, Felix tossed three hundred dollars in crisp bills on the bed. "Sometimes, one has to do things for their sheer pleasure and not think about it too much," he declared. "Now you can come with me."[16]

When Felix received an invitation to speak in Rochester that winter of 1936–37, he suddenly thought of a wonderful stand-in: "Why not Ingrid? She's just come from Germany."[17] Soon Ingrid was drafted to speak for the Joint and rendered firsthand accounts of Third Reich atrocities in 220 American cities. These talks had an unexpected impact upon Ingrid, who was young, passionate, and overflowing with a generous but naïve fervor. While telling of Nazi terror, she saw that American Jews inhabited a more ghettoized world than had their Hamburg counterparts before Hitler. Visiting Frieda in Palm Beach, she noticed that Frieda's grandchildren couldn't get into the local country club, a form of exclusion that seemed to affect American Jews everywhere. She spoke in Jewish social clubs set up to provide an alternative to discriminatory WASP clubs. And she was dismayed by the checkbook philanthropy of newly rich Jews who donated money to certify their status then felt absolved of any need for further political action. The cross-country journeys helped to radicalize Ingrid.

With a quixotic craving for action, Ingrid dreaded being some genteel society lady, raising money in well-upholstered drawing rooms. She was the rebel spawned by every rich family. She sought to generalize the Warburg philanthropic impulse into broader political goals. At first, her political activism seemed to flow logically from her heritage, but then it acquired a strong momentum and transported her far beyond it. Like other members of persecuted groups, she envisioned a world in which religious and national divisions would be subordinated to new universal beliefs. If the Third Reich drove some Jews back to their religion, it encouraged others to fantasize about classless societies and Utopian ventures and Ingrid drifted deep into socialist causes. She could be vocal and dogmatic in expounding her views. Once she lectured her aunt a bit too loudly and Frieda put her in place: "Ingrid, I am not a hall."[18]

In the late 1930s, Ingrid still hoped to return someday to a redeemed, purified Germany. As with Eric, her association with Resistance figures bolstered her faith in a post-Hitler Germany. Also important was her romantic admiration for Adam von Trott. Trott, we recall, was the former Rhodes scholar and son of a Prussian civil servant who had returned to practice law in Germany after Oxford. A handsome aristocrat and valiant crusader, Trott believed that Nazi foes should stay in Germany and fight the evil from within. Ebullient and talkative, Trott was now committed to a somber course as he tried to rise up in the German Foreign Office to strike a deadly blow against Hitler. Trusting to the common sense of the German people, he thought that the German officer corps, with its honorable, conservative traditions, would act to avert a suicidal war.

In March 1937, when Trott stopped in New York en route to a Rhodes fellowship in China, Ingrid met him at the pier. She arranged for him to discuss the German Resistance with her new friend, Eleanor Roosevelt. (The first lady—ugly duckling in a dashing family—reminded Ingrid of her father.) As he tried to alert influential foreigners to the existence of a legitimate German opposition, Trott was plagued by questions about his own authenticity. How could a true Resistance member travel as a member of the information section of the Foreign Office? Such apprehension was reinforced by memories of the ill-advised letter Trott sent to the *Manchester Guardian* in 1934, denying the persecution of German Jews.

Drawn mostly from old nobility and high military ranks, the German Resistance was never a broad-based, populist movement, and its members' stature worked against them. Composed of a loose network of small groups, it lacked a coherent political philosophy aside from the urgent desire to overthrow Hitler. The most important component was probably the Kreisau Circle, so named since its members met in Silesia at the Kreisau estate of Count Helmuth von Moltke who, like his friend Trott, was a former Rhodes scholar. For many outside Germany, it seemed unthinkable that such highly placed figures could be bent on subversion. After having been duped repeatedly by Hitler, Western governments were wary of being deceived again.

In June 1939, Trott bravely disclosed the nature of his sub-rosa work to Neville Chamberlain, Lord Halifax, and others in London. They stared at him blankly. It was hard to accept at face value a conspirator whose fare was being paid by the German Foreign Office. And when Trott pleaded that England should keep the door open for negotiation with Germany, it sounded like a fresh appeal to appease Hitler. When Trott came to New York that October—the war had now started—he had several Warburgs vouch for his sincerity. Eric told him, "Mr. von Trott, something must be done about Germany," and Trott replied, "You, Mr. Warburg, do it here, and I will do it in Germany."[19]

Adam went to Ingrid's small apartment at 25 West Fifty-Fourth Street, which was decorated with a blue sofa and other relics salvaged from Hamburg. The Oxford Adonis now seemed tired and older, his hair thinning, his manner beleaguered. Officially, Adam was to represent the German Foreign Office at a conference of the Institute of Pacific Relations. In reality, he planned to make covert contact with FDR as a member of the Kreisau Circle. Ingrid saw that Adam's commitment to Resistance work was now irrevocable and that he was prepared to pay the steepest price. Nonetheless, he encountered ingrained suspicion at a time when people equated Germans with Nazis. Ingrid and Adam walked across Central Park to see Frieda, who chatted amiably enough with Adam. But afterward Frieda scolded Ingrid, "How dare you bring a German in my house!"[20] For three months, Adam's movements were tracked by FBI agents, as well as the Gestapo and British intelligence. Nobody was quite sure what game he played or whether he could be trusted.

Ingrid introduced Adam to left-wing refugee activists associated with the Resistance group *Neu Beginnen*. She also wangled an invitation for him to have tea with Eleanor Roosevelt and her friends. The first lady seemed oblivious of the extraordinary peril involved in Trott's mission and introduced him airily by saying, "This is Adam von Trott, a friend of ours, who will tell you about the German underground movement."[21] Afraid of alienating FDR, Trott handled this amazing gaffe with aplomb.

While Trott met with Treasury Secretary Henry Morgenthau, Supreme Court Justice Felix Frankfurter, and State Department officials, the president evaded him. Trott conveyed the message that Britain and France should openly repudiate any wish to wage a war of extermination against Germany. This would undercut Hitler's paranoid ranting and erode his support. Throughout the war, many Warburgs believed that the Allied policy of unconditional surrender only stifled opposition in Germany and reawakened fears of another Versailles, whereas publication of generous peace terms might actually have fomented resistance to Hitler.

Having received warnings about Trott from England, Felix Frankfurter poisoned Roosevelt's mind against him. After J. Edgar Hoover supplemented this with FBI reports on Trott's movements, the president saw only a potential security breach. "For heaven's sake," he told Frankfurter. "Surely you did not let your Trott friend get trotted out of the country without having him searched by Edgar Hoover. Think of the battleship plans and other secrets he may be carrying back."[22] It didn't dawn on Roosevelt that Trott might be a bona fide Resistance figure.

Meanwhile, to Ingrid's eternal regret, Trott returned to Germany and married Clarita Tiefenbacher, the daughter of a Hamburg lawyer. Henceforth, Trott and other Resistance members, spurned by the outside world, would operate alone. Ingrid later said that because of her knowledge of this small band of courageous anti-Nazis, she couldn't assign universal guilt to all

Germans. In the end, Adam would make a believer of the skeptics by entering the conspiracy to kill Hitler and paying the ultimate price.

Engaged in many causes, including schools for refugee students and orphans, Ingrid would be best known for her work with the Emergency Rescue Committee (ERC), which was formed in her apartment after France fell to the Nazis in June 1940. Millions of people made a chaotic exit from the occupied north to the southern zone, which was under control of the Vichy government. Many European anti-Fascists who had taken refuge in France now found themselves trapped. The ERC was set up to obtain emergency visas, affidavits, and money for these stranded Nazi opponents. Eleanor Roosevelt helped the group bypass the bureaucracy in obtaining visas for leading anti-Fascists.

Ingrid's apartment overlooked the garden of the Museum of Modern Art, which provided the names of many endangered artists. Thomas Mann and others submitted lists of authors. As executive assistant to the ERC chairman, Frank Kingdon, Ingrid took part in the struggle to save Marc Chagall, Walter Mehring, André Masson, and Franz Werfel, while other ERC members aided André Breton, Max Ernst, and Heinrich and Golo Mann. On an earlier visit to Stockholm to see her parents, Ingrid had brought back across an Atlantic swarming with U-boats the stepdaughter of Carl Zuckmayer, the playwright. Cynics in the Warburg family observed that Ingrid always managed to save the celebrities and leave the less glamorous cases to others.

Ingrid often welcomed rescued artists at the New York piers, and many incongruous scenes unfolded as the exotic leaders of central Europe's avant-garde washed up on American shores. She especially remembered the Surrealists' wives, who stepped off the ship in sandals with colorful, handmade necklaces and green-lacquered fingernails. There were a fair number of prima donnas. When Nina threw a luncheon for Franz Werfel, his wife, Alma Mahler, gave a rather theatrical description of her escape from Europe. She told how she had picked pebbles from her sandals with her poor little pooch in her arms, as if she had made a barefoot trek all across Spain.

The ERC was often flying blind in tracking down threatened artists and intellectuals amid the alarums of war. In July 1940, the group decided on a daring operation in Ingrid's apartment: They would send their own hand-picked underground agent to Marseilles. They chose Harvard-educated Varian Fry, a fastidious young man with horn-rimmed glasses and a literary background. A former editor of *The New Republic* and author of many foreign-policy books, he ran the publishing program at the Foreign Policy Association. A month later, when he left for Lisbon in a Brooks Brothers suit, he carried a letter of recommendation from Eleanor Roosevelt and refugee lists drawn up by the Museum of Modern Art and the New School for Social Research.

Even though nothing in his background had prepared him for intrigue, Fry worked miracles in Marseilles. Shadowed by the Gestapo, he worked in a feverishly oppressive atmosphere of suicides, nervous breakdowns, and desperate entreaties for help. He secured forged papers; set up clandestine convoys to take refugees into Spain on foot; and helped prisoners escape from internment camps and evade the Vichy police. The overwhelming pressure brought out heroic qualities in Fry. "I've almost become a monomaniac as far as my work is concerned," he wrote home. "I think of nothing else, dream of nothing else, speak of nothing else."[23] In the end, Varian Fry saved several hundred anti-Nazi refugees from almost certain death. Uneasy about Fry's illegal maneuvers, the well-bred Joint steered clear of his work, but it had its own Scarlet Pimpernel, Wilfrid Israel, who distributed certificates to Palestine while working in Iberia. (Israel, we recall, was an intimate of Lola's from Berlin days and Max's secret intermediary with British Jews.) The Joint would help ten thousand French Jews to escape through Lisbon.

After losing Adam von Trott, Ingrid was ripe for another memorable crusader. One day, an Italian friend brought a free-spirited Italian leftist named Veniero Spinelli to an ERC meeting. A funny, colorful character with a checkered past, he had been jailed in Italy as a Communist organizer, fought against Franco in the Spanish Civil War, and then entered the Foreign Legion to escape arrest by the Fascists. When he showed up in Ingrid's apartment, he still wore the tattered uniform of the Foreign Legion. For a woman eager to reject her bourgeois upbringing and dive headlong into revolutionary politics, the roguish, irreverent Spinelli had a storybook perfection.

It turned out that Veniero came from a highborn family of Bourbon nobility. But as a socialist agitator, he couldn't afford to be addressed as "Marchese" and dropped the title. Frieda thought this a shame—it was what most appealed to her about him. "But darling," Frieda gently prodded Ingrid, "why doesn't Veniero use his title? You know, it is important even here."[24] Many saw Veniero as a self-centered opportunist who wanted to underwrite revolutionary fantasies with Warburg money. He unfortunately chose a moment when the fabled Warburg gold was turning to dust.

Ingrid steadfastly ignored hints of family displeasure about Veniero's character. In January 1941, he issued an ultimatum: either Ingrid would marry him immediately or not at all. She consented and bought two platinum rings once she realized that Veniero had overlooked this bourgeois custom. They had a private civil wedding, followed by an awkward reception for family and friends. Veniero asked Ingrid if he could make a speech. "Please, you'd better not," she cautioned.[25] Suddenly the family liberal, Nina drew the bridegroom aside and said, "Veniero, please tell me which side you fought for in Spain. You can tell me, but better not tell the others."[26] Nina gave him the armchair in which Paul had drawn up plans for the Federal Reserve—a curious gift indeed for this scourge of the status quo. Max made a wistful speech about the united Europe that would emerge after Hitler's defeat. Then he kissed Ingrid and shook Veniero's hand with the plea, "Stop the revolution!"[27]

At first, Veniero entered the U.S. Army to fight in Italy, then deserted in protest over American insistence on unconditional surrender. Meanwhile, Ingrid had two children by the itinerant agitator, who would disappear for long stretches to fight in Italy then unexpectedly reappear in New York. At one point, he materalized to announce that he needed a thousand dollars to publish a pamphlet on Italian autonomy. To oblige him, Ingrid pawned her ruby-and-diamond bracelet. These sudden appeals for money for political causes would form a leitmotif with Veniero. Many Warburgs thought that Veniero was abusing Ingrid and tried to dissuade her from continuing the marriage. Lola went on a special mission to reason with her, but to no avail.

When Ingrid met Veniero, her life turned a corner and was never the same again. It created a radical discontinuity between her aristocratic past and proletarian future. After the war, the Spinellis lived in a working-class section of Rome and had five children in all, bringing them up as Catholics. Despite Veniero's revolutionary talk, his sense of comradeship didn't extend to shared child-rearing and kitchen duty. Veniero never really held a fixed job and worked as a full-time political activist, adopting causes and periodically disappearing. In Stockholm, Fritz and Anna Beata worried incessantly about Ingrid and their Italian grandchildren. At one point, Ingrid stayed with them and Fritz talked vaguely about getting Veniero a job in a bank. After Adam von Trott and the breathless early years fighting Fascism in New York, the rest of Ingrid's life would seem something of an anticlimax. She stayed married to Veniero and brought up five lovely, interesting children. But she never recaptured the high sense of beauty and purpose that had animated her time with Adam and the Emergency Rescue Committee.

*Mittelweg 17, home of the Warburg
Secretariat in the bleak days after 1938.
(Warburg family, Hamburg)*

Deathwatch

E ven as the Warburgs sounded the alarm about the German menace in America and Britain, the Nazis exploited their good name in foreign banking circles. Until 1941, the authorities insisted that the Aryanized firm retain the M. M. Warburg name so regularly denounced by *Der Stürmer*. The new owners, of course, favored keeping the old name, which added value to their purchase, and Brinckmann later told Siegmund he had only changed the name under intense political pressure.[1] Most Warburgs, however, found it profoundly upsetting that a bank in Nazi Germany, over which they no longer exercised control, still bore their name. Many Jewish employees followed them into exile, but six stayed and perished in the camps.

After the war, the Warburgs, at least in public, would idealize Rudolf Brinckmann as a man who had resisted the Nazis and piloted the firm through the dark years. Did Brinckmann deserve these encomia? Evidence can be marshaled on both sides. Brinckmann did bravely withstand pressure to contribute to Nazi causes, such as the Karl Kaufmann Foundation. (Kaufmann was the *Gauleiter* of Hamburg.) On the other hand, he caved in to demands to hire extra Nazis and to purge the staff of Jews within a specified period. Every staff member had to join Dr. Robert Ley's German Labor Front.[2]

In fairness to Brinckmann, it is hard to imagine any employer who could have flouted such demands. After May 1938, the bank also had to conform to general banking practice under the Third Reich. For instance, it had to report all deposits to the authorities in two categories: Aryan and non-Aryan.

Oral testimony from Warburg employees presents a mixed picture of Nazi meddling at the bank. In 1933, not a single employee belonged to the party, and the staff refused to elect the in-house labor council required by new legislation. By the time a Herr Glücksmann joined the bank in 1936 in a clerical position, however, he already felt surrounded by Nazis: ". . . and the other colleagues who sat in the room were all party comrades. . . . Everything was 'Heil Hitler' from the first day on."[3] Either because this was hidden from them or because they chose to look the other way, the Warburgs never spoke about such infiltration. One suspects that a dual reality had emerged: one when the Jewish bosses were around, another in their absence.

After the 1938 Aryanization, the house Nazis who had formerly concealed their insignias behind their lapels began to brandish them openly. That December, Max's secretary, Martha Beyer, returned from abroad and was shaken by Brownshirt penetration of the bank. "We had had the impression that the Warburg firm was an oasis in this brown tide and when I returned and saw the different old colleagues again, wearing the party insignia— which one didn't expect at all—I was very shaken."[4] Fear seized the staff. Beyer suspected that the man seconded by the Industriekreditbank (now a one-fourth owner) was a hard-core Nazi spy.[5] Nonetheless, M. M. Warburg enjoyed some immunity from party harassment. At one point, the staff was summoned to a nearby cellar and had to suffer through dreary speeches exhorting them to join the party, but it proved an isolated episode. For a time, an SS man was assigned to the bank and was supposed to review everything. In fact, he interfered little and when he was drafted into the army, he wasn't replaced.[6]

Once the Warburgs were gone, Dr. Kurt Sieveking still negotiated several Aryanizations from the Berlin office, including that of the fashionable N. Israel department store. At the same time, Brinckmann and Adolf van Biema campaigned to win back Aryan clients that had dropped the Warburg bank from political pressure. They traveled to Essen to regain the Krupp account and wrote numerous letters inviting companies to resume business with M. M. Warburg, reminding them that the reasons for their original decision no longer applied. The letters all ended "Heil Hitler" or "German greetings," the Nazi salute.[7] Brinckmann made a concerted effort to recoup lost corporate board seats and membership on the local Reichsbank committee.

The Nazis quickly reneged on the 1938 deal made with the Warburgs. The former partners had left behind about three million reichsmarks as a silent participation. Within six months, the *Gau*'s economic adviser told the bank to deduct 500,000 of that and the remainder was converted into an interest-bearing bank account. On March 27, 1941, the government decreed that all business names must be Aryanized. Remarkably, Nazi bureaucrats at the Economics Ministry, the Four-Year Plan office, and the Reichsbank wanted to exempt M. M. Warburg. Their request was spurned and on October 27, 1941, the bank was finally christened "Brinckmann, Wirtz & Co."[8] The government also confiscated the Warburgs' silent participation and took over Kösterberg, thus completing the pauperization of one of the mightiest families in Germany.

Not all Warburg assets in Germany had remained in the firm. In October 1938, Max and Fritz set up a Secretariat with a twofold mission: to manage the Warburg blocked mark estates and to provide money and advice to needy emigrants. To supervise this office, they chose Robert Solmitz, who also assumed their places on Jewish charity boards.

The Secretariat was headquartered at Mittelweg 17, the old house that once belonged to Charlotte and Moritz, then to Fritz and Anna Beata. Hamburg Jews called it the Oasis, with good reason, for it provided relief from their barren and dangerous existence.

In December 1938, Himmler took away Jewish drivers' licenses, curtailing mobility. After September 1939, Jews couldn't walk the streets after eight o'clock in the evening, were banned from public transport, and could shop only one hour per day. They were liable to be pressed into forced-labor brigades. The two hundred thousand desperate Jews left in Germany—about 60 percent had now escaped—were thrown back on their own resources and had to band together.

At Mittelweg 17, the stranded Hamburg Jews cherished the older, better German culture that had sustained them. The Secretariat tried to keep local artists busy. Well-known actors read aloud from Rilke or Goethe, while pianists and violinists gave concerts in the first-floor library. Later on, their serenades were interrupted by air raids; the audience then descended to a large cellar shelter where the Jewish caretaker, Baer, lived with his wife and three small children. The head of the Jewish Community, Dr. Max Plaut, moved his office into the building, which seemed to gather people like a rescue boat picking up dazed survivors from a shipwreck.

The Warburg Secretariat gave many desperate people hope as well as seed money for emigration. The revolving fund set up by Eric and Bettina still provided small advances through M. M. Warburg & Co. In a setting of constant intrigue, Dr. Plaut conducted almost daily negotiations with the Gestapo to spring people from prison. Once they were released, he and Solmitz rushed them out of Germany, for delay could mean a sudden detour to a concentration camp.

Solmitz and Plaut frequently dealt with a Herr Göttsche, who headed the Gestapo's Jewish department for Hamburg. Solmitz said Göttsche was one of the few Gestapo officials with a particle of conscience; perhaps for that reason, Göttsche committed suicide at the close of the war. At a time when emigrating Jews couldn't return to Germany, Solmitz traveled freely back and forth to Stockholm to consult with Fritz. This freedom was illusory, however, for the Gestapo told Solmitz that if he didn't return, his wife would be shot. When Solmitz had trouble reentering Germany after one trip, Herr Göttsche furnished him with a highly unusual I.D. that said, "Robert Israel Solmitz travels in the interest of the German Reich."[9] Whether this privilege resulted from Gestapo policy or money extorted from the Warburg Secretariat, one can only speculate.

The Gestapo was certainly titillated by the idea of plundering Warburg wealth. This became clear after Germany conquered Poland and considered creating a vast Jewish settlement area near Lublin. One day, Göttsche called in Solmitz and Dr. Plaut and unveiled a secret plan, drafted in Himmler's office, that carried the code name "The Hamburg Plan." It envisioned a reservation state in Poland for European Jews, where they would be sent to govern themselves. Göttsche shamelessly appealed to his listeners' vanity and lust for power, promising Dr. Plaut that he might be president of the new state and Solmitz the finance minister. The head of the Hamburg Talmud Torah school, said Göttsche, would be minister of arts and education.

Having waved this before their eyes, Göttsche got down to the crux of the matter. "Naturally the implementation of the project would have to be financed by the Jews themselves," he said. "The Warburgs are considered very suitable for that. If they only wanted to do it, the Warburgs in America could raise the necessary money to found such a reservation state."[10] Göttsche told Solmitz to consult Fritz in Stockholm, who could convey the suggestion to Max in New York. Solmitz promptly went to confer with Fritz for a few days.

Fritz dictated a response, couched in guarded terms. Though he pretended he hadn't heard from New York, his reply clearly shows that he had consulted with Max and the Joint. He said that he found the idea of a Jewish state in Poland an extremely interesting one, but that such large sums could only be mustered by the Joint Distribution Committee. And the Joint was upset by the disappearance of one of its representatives, whom the Germans had yanked off a ship bound for Stockholm.[11]

When Solmitz read this to Göttsche in Hamburg, the latter jumped up and sent a message to the Gestapo in Berlin, which responded to the Joint's complaint with lightning speed. A few days later, Göttsche told Solmitz that the Joint's representative had been traced to a camp for foreign prisoners, Stalag II. The Joint official (who must have been startled by this miraculous event) was promptly released and sent to America. On March 23, 1940, word of the reservation plan leaked into the press, along with speculation that it would be an extermination center in disguise. With that, Göring and Himmler decided to scrap the plan.

Meanwhile, the chances of escape dwindled for those Jews left in Germany. A sinister milestone came in late 1939 when the first gas chamber was constructed in Brandenburg. Deportations in Hamburg began in 1940, when Jews were rounded up and deported from a pretty, grassy triangle on the Moorweidenplatz. The first shipment contained mentally ill Jews, plucked from institutions; the sane and healthy soon followed. In September 1941, the Nazis revived the old medieval stigma, forcing Jews to wear a black star of David on a yellow background, with the word "Jew" inscribed across the middle. A month later, the massive deportations to the camps began. Of twenty-four thousand Jews living in Hamburg when Hitler took power, six thousand would head east to the death camps and never return. Most went to Theresienstadt, the "model" concentration camp set up to fool Jews and foreign visitors, but many also went to Auschwitz and Riga.

By 1941, life for Jews had grown intolerable in Hamburg. They were herded into dingy, ramshackle quarters with each person assigned just five square yards of living space. In the spring of 1941, the Warburg Secretariat went out of existence, its headquarters expropriated for a Nazi party business operation. Solmitz and his wife fled through occupied France and Spain and entered the United States via Portugal. The valiant secretaries who had worked with him, plus the entire family of caretaker Baer, ended up being butchered.

The Warburgs of Hamburg were spared the ghastly world of the ovens and crematoria, but their distant relatives, the Altona Warburgs, boasted no such luck. For a long time, the two clans had been locked in a fierce cultural and financial rivalry. A literate, musical family, the Altona Warburgs had entertained Brahms at their home and felt superior, in many ways, to their Hamburg relatives. Many had been baptized—which always remained taboo among the Hamburg branch. Then, after more than a century of business, the Altona banking house of W. S. Warburg merged with the North German Bank of Hamburg in the early 1900s, as the Altona Warburgs fell into decline. The grandfather of Max's wife, Alice, had founded W. S. Warburg in 1804.

The W. S. Warburg manager, Albert Warburg, had died right after World War I. The hyperinflation had chopped down his estate to 1 percent of its value. Albert's widow, Gerta, began to sell off art while their daughter, Betty, worked as a doctor in Hamburg. To local residents, it seemed absurd that a lady named Warburg should work for a living, and to the Hamburg Warburgs this would have seemed decidedly vulgar.

Gertrud Wenzel has written a touching memoir of her grandmother Gerta and aunt Betty. Already in her eighties, Gerta had money stashed away in England and could have escaped in the 1930s, but was too wedded to her adored Germany. "She loved the German nation. She had been a part of it for sixty years. She persuaded herself that the madness of the Thirties could not last."[12] One night after *Kristallnacht,* Dr. Betty Warburg was visiting a sick child when sadistic teenagers pounced on her and beat her face with sticks. She grew frightened and withdrew into her room. "Only late at night would she leave the house for a walk, armed with a stick, much too weak and frightened to use it in her defense."[13] Gertrud's parents held on in Altona, her mother knitting in fear by the window and her father spending his days sitting down by the pier.

Possibly from proud memories of the old rivalry, these Altona Warburgs never appealed to the Hamburg Warburgs, so far as one can tell. On May 8, 1940, Gerta and Betty belatedly crossed the border into Holland, only to be followed by the Nazis two days later. They ended up in the gas chamber at Sobibor. Gertrud's parents remained in Altona, convinced that a compassionate world would never allow the Nazis to implement their monstrous rhetoric. They were martyrs to their innocence.

—

The final act of the Warburg drama in Europe was enacted on the Keizersgracht in Amsterdam, where the family had set up Warburg & Company in 1929. After 1933, this lone Warburg outpost beyond German borders proved a providential place to sell blocked marks and assist Jews to transfer money out of Germany. In 1936, to shield the Amsterdam bank from increasingly onerous Nazi regulations of foreign exchange and tax matters, the Warburgs had loosened the ties between Warburg & Co. and M. M. Warburg. Siegmund and Hans Meyer, a Warburg cousin, became sole Amsterdam partners, withdrawing from the Hamburg firm. At the time of the 1938 Aryanization in Hamburg, the Nazis fleeced the Warburgs of more than a million Dutch guldens as the steep price for keeping the Amsterdam bank.[14]

Max's wish to preserve the Amsterdam firm aggravated relations between the American and German Warburgs. In the 1931 bailout, Paul and Felix had set up the Kara Corporation to grant a seven-million-dollar loan to M. M. Warburg. After their deaths, Jimmy headed Kara. Extremely fatalistic about the European outlook and tired of forever indulging Uncle Max, Jimmy and his American cousins wanted to shutter Warburg & Company in Amsterdam, which was wholly owned by the Kara Corporation. They thought that the existence of two Warburg banks in Europe—one under Nazi supervision in Hamburg, another under Warburg control in Amsterdam—created a misleading equation between them and gave the Aryanized Hamburg firm an aura of family approval. As a result, they agreed, only with the deepest reluctance, to maintain the Dutch bank.[15]

Knowing that the $7 million loan was gone forever (but not forgotten), the American Warburgs slashed the debt owed by their German relatives to $1.44 million. This last figure equaled the total value of assets held by the German Warburgs outside Germany. Jimmy adamantly insisted that heirs of the Hamburg partners shouldn't receive money that their fathers still owed to the Kara Corporation.[16]

On May 10, 1940, Jimmy's forebodings were spectacularly confirmed when the Germans invaded Holland, trapping Warburg employees and relatives in Amsterdam. Having been neutral in World War I, Holland had seemed a promising sanctuary in case of war, and Jews had flocked there from many parts of Europe. In New York, Eric and Max felt powerless as they contemplated the prospect that fourteen relatives and coworkers might be consigned to concentration camps. The story of what happened next exists in several, slightly contradictory, versions, but the general outline seems clear.

A few weeks after the Nazi invasion, Helmuth Wohltat was appointed the German *Kommissar* for Dutch banks. Having negotiated the ransom plan with George Rublee in Berlin, he knew the Warburg partners well. In a sympathetic manner, he notified the Warburgs that he would soon be forced to place Warburg & Company under German supervision. He admonished them that, as Jews, they couldn't remain partners and should leave at once. He further advised them to transfer control of the Amsterdam bank into reliable hands.[17] Both Wohltat in Holland and the Reich Economics Ministry wanted to transfer the Warburg bank to a German bank and urged Rudolf Brinckmann to take over Warburg & Co. in Amsterdam. Brinckmann—by now the Aryan for all seasons—at first hesitated to assume the burden of a second Aryanized bank.

Stuck in another blind alley, the Warburgs still had some bargaining power left. In taking over Holland, the Nazis were at pains to prove that they had no plans for formal annexation of the country. To this end, they tried to maintain some facade of legality, however transparently fraudulent. In negotiating the fate of Warburg & Co, the Warburgs insisted upon safe passage from the country for all relatives and employees as part of any deal.

The mysterious agent of fate in this volatile situation was a Berlin lawyer, Dr. Fritz Fenthol, who specialized in smuggling people from Germany through behind-the-scenes negotiation. His top-notch government connections enabled him to merchandise human lives. Depending upon which Warburg you ask, Fenthol was either a courageous intermediary with the Nazis, saving threatened Jews, or a base trader in human souls who exploited people's misery for profit. Whatever the truth of this complex individual, he carried on a thriving trade in Nazi-occupied Europe.

Fenthol had one vulnerable point, and potentially a fatal one: He had a Jewish wife stuck away in Switzerland. Some Warburgs believe that in 1940 Fenthol suddenly invented a mission to Japan due to rising Nazi suspicions about his wife. If that is so, his sudden appearance in New York must have occurred en route to the Far East. He confidentially informed Max and Eric that *The New York Times* was about to publish an exposé that would ruin his business and possibly end with his imprisonment. Presumably, the reporter planned to disclose the existence of Fenthol's Jewish wife. Eric later claimed that he contacted friends at the *Times* and got the Fenthol story spiked. When Fenthol then returned in tears and asked how he could repay this great favor, Eric coyly replied that there was one favor he could ask, but that it lay beyond Fenthol's powers. What was that? Fenthol asked and Eric told him about the fourteen people pinned down in Holland.[18] Furnished with their names and addresses, Fenthol returned to Germany via Japan and the Trans-Siberian railroad and got in touch with Rudolf Brinckmann. Fenthol must have served as intermediary in the subsequent negotiations with the Nazis before fleeing to Brazil in March 1941.

Brinckmann told the Berlin authorities that he would take control of Warburg & Co. in Amsterdam *if* they guaranteed safe passage from Holland for the fourteen Jews. Some family members say that the American Warburgs had to hand over a sizable bribe to the Gestapo to grease the deal, with one million dollars the most commonly cited figure.[19] It is unclear whether Fenthol was bagman for the payoff. It is known that the Nazis operated a shakedown racket by which Jews outside Europe paid ransom to free those trapped in Holland. "It appears that the Dutch Warburgs and several other wealthy families took this way out of Holland," notes one scholar.[20] The Amsterdam bank placed under Brinckmann's nominal control was renamed Kommanditaire Vennootschap M. M. Warburg & Co. and run by a trusted clerk, L. Bysterus Heemskerk. He tried to act as a caretaker, doing as little new business as possible so as not to aid the Nazi war effort.

Warburg & Co. must have been worth a good deal to the German government, for in March 1941 these fourteen Warburg employees and family members received an unusual send-off from Nazi-occupied Holland. With Brinckmann waving farewell on the platform, the fourteen boarded a regularly scheduled train with a special SS-escort assigned both to watch and protect them. Accompanied by other Warburgs on the train as a result of a separate deal, they traveled across occupied France, unoccupied France, Spain, and Portugal. By one account, the Warburg contingent kept the doors locked during the trip so that Nazi guards couldn't enter their compartment. Right before they crossed the French border, an SS man told one person in the Warburg party, "We are supposed to accompany you to San Sebastián, but I have a girlfriend in Hendaye. Would you permit me to leave you in Hendaye?" "I think we can handle ourselves," the Warburg relation answered dryly.[21] In Lisbon, the party boarded a ship to Cuba and entered the United States with visas secured by the American Warburgs. Several would work as employees of E. M. Warburg & Co. on Wall Street in one of the more elaborate cases of corporate relocation on record.

One Warburg was excluded from the train: Olga Lachmann, the eldest daughter of Aby S. She had Dutch nationality since 1920, having lived in the Hague with her two children, Grace and Eddy. Olga would claim that Max had deliberately banned her from the train because of a bitter feud they had in the 1930s over the disposition of her father's estate. She would base this charge on postwar discussions with Heemskerk, who claimed to have seen telegrams that passed between the Warburgs in New York and the SS police or *Sicherheitsdienst* in Berlin. There is no way to verify this grave charge or even to say whether Max had final say over the list of passengers. Passage, after all, was paid for by the American Warburgs, who may have had the last word. Miraculously, Olga and her children survived the war in Holland.

———

As the Warburg train rolled out of Amsterdam in 1941, it also left behind Max Adolph Warburg, Aby and Mary's son, who had taught at the Quaker Eerde school in Ommen in northeast Holland. A splendid refuge, the school was situated in a castle with parquet floors and marble staircases. This enchanted little educational kingdom was bound by a moat. Max Adolph not only taught art, history, and classical languages, but, with a nod to his father, created a frieze of constellations for the main salon and designed the cover of the school magazine.

Like many sons of strong, tyrannical fathers, Max Adolph was starry-eyed, gentle, and sensitive and cherished Eerde as a place where children of all nations could learn under ideal conditions. As a classical scholar, Max Adolph shared Aby's delight in untangling myths and decoding symbols. In 1934, he received a teacher's diploma from Hamburg University for a Latin paper analyzing the representation of the Goddess Fortuna in the arts and literature—a quintessential Aby Warburg topic. Like his father, too, Max Adolph was a marvelously imaginative lecturer. Yet he lacked Aby's colossal, almost demonic, drive. He was casual, even boyish, and free of great ambition.

Brought up as a Lutheran, Max Adolph became a Quaker during his Eerde stay. He married Josepha Spiero, who had two children from a previous marriage. While her son was sent to safety in America in 1939, the protection of her Jewish daughter, Heilwig, would become a full-time preoccupation for Max Adolph and Josi. They also had their own little girl with the charming name of Lux. On May 10, 1940, the Germans jolted their fairy-tale realm of Eerde. As Josi recalled, "we woke up in the castle because the windowpanes were rattling so strangely—until we understood that they were blowing up bridges, that it meant us, and that now everything, everything was lost."[22]

Though the Dutch helped to protect many Jews, the SS campaign in Holland was one of special severity. Max and Josi thought they had found an escape hatch from the horror when the Fine Arts Department of New York University—which had been eager to house the Warburg library—offered Max Adolph an assistant professor's post. It seems likely that the Warburgs in New York had a hand in this offer. The couple then made countless trips to the passport office in Amsterdam to fill out endless forms. Their passports had "J" for Jews stamped on them. At the passport office, Josi perceived that "one of the gangsters there was a little more human than the others" and she charmed him into bestowing upon them "Half Aryan" status.[23] When the Nazis blocked them from traveling to America, they had to figure out how to survive the war in Holland.

Josi had plenty of spirit. As her daughter said, "She was cocky, strong, beautiful, bossy, and really the first woman my father knew."[24] She proved resourceful under pressure, as did the more delicate Max Adolph, who had suffered a nervous breakdown with his father after World War I. The German occupation seemed to free him temporarily from his private fears and gave him the large courage of a transcendent cause. He said that in Nazi-occupied Holland evil became so palpable that people forgot the daily little demons.[25] "It was the best time of his life," said their daughter, Lux, whom they christened Maria Christina to put out of harm's way. "He was needed as a teacher and a father and he had to find hiding places for his wife's daughter from her first marriage."[26]

By the summer of 1942, the Germans began the systematic purge that would kill off three quarters of the Jewish population. Aided by Max and Josi, the Jewish children at Eerde began escaping into the forest. To avoid pursuit, they would stage fake suicides by leaving their shoes and a farewell note by a stream.

The hunt only intensified. On April 1, 1943, the Dutch newspapers announced that the province in which Eerde was located must be cleansed of Jews. Three months later, Josi gave birth to a frail, cross-eyed little girl named Iris, who turned out to have Down's syndrome. This child adored the imaginative Max Adolph much as children were once charmed by Aby. By year's end, the Nazis shut down Eerde, intending to turn it into a school for the Hitler Youth.

These terrible events strengthened Max Adolph. During the next two years, he and Josi found twenty-two separate hiding places for Heilwig, who had false identification papers. Much of the time they communicated with her by coded messages. Faced with gnawing poverty, Max Adolph led a primitive life, digging potatoes and chopping trees to sustain his family. He kept the cultural flame burning by delivering secret lectures on art history—a small defense of rationality amid omnipresent barbarism that would have pleased Aby.

By September 1944, the Allies landed in Holland, but liberated the south first and only slowly fought their way northward. That winter, Max and Josi sat in nightly agony behind blackout curtains in their farmhouse, listening to British planes buzzing overhead. Their house, not far from the assembly place for V-1 and V-2 rockets, was mercilessly bombarded by the Allies. One night, bombs rained down, and a terrified Josi grabbed the sleeping Iris from her crib. "I carried her in my arms and Warburg and I ran under falling timbers, crashing windows and dropping bricks—down the stairs and out of the house. We jumped into a foxhole on the road, and when there was a pause in the bombing, we went from one hole to the other. Under a hail of bullets and crashing bombs I threw myself into the snow, covering the dirty, fearfully crying Iris with my body."[27] They subsequently had to abandon this house with its smashed windows and a hole punched through its roof.

On April 10, 1945, Canadian troops liberated Ommen, and two days later, Max Adolph and Josi brought Heilwig out of hiding. At first, Max Adolph wanted to teach in Hamburg and reeducate the Germans, but couldn't get a position there. He never lost his admiration for German discipline and culture. In the end, he and his family moved to England in 1947, settling in Dulwich near Fritz Saxl and Gertrud Bing. Fiercely anti-German, Josi thought it her proudest moment when she received her British naturalization papers. By contrast, Max Adolph would find the British indecisive and wishy-washy and often said, "Life is too short to be English."[28]

So strong and gallant during the war, Max Adolph broke down when they got to England. Once in the Promised Land, with the pressure off, he could no longer keep the old demons at bay. He taught art history at the progressive Dartington Hall while Josi worked there as the head housekeeper. Waves of depression made teaching difficult, and Max Adolph bounced from school to school. Over the years, suffering from severe manic-depression, he underwent psychoanalysis and electric-shock treatment. At one point, Lola got him posh psychiatric help but he drifted in and out of institutions for life. A small syndicate of relatives, including Eric, Fritz, Lola, Frieda, Freddy, and Max Adolph's brothers-in-law, gave him generous financial support. His dream was to lecture at the Warburg Institute in London. When he finally stood up to deliver a lecture about his father, he stared at the audience and announced that he couldn't do it. His life was blighted by unlucky genes and the dislocations of war and persecution. As Max Adolph once stated mordantly on an application form, "My life so far has been rich and varied, but obviously not a success story from *Reader's Digest.*"[29]

In 1937, Max Adolph's younger sister, Frede, had published in German a doctoral dissertation on Dr. Samuel Johnson's "Lives of the Poets," which she completed at Hamburg University. Remarkably, at that late date, Frede was still treated civilly by her teachers because she was Aby Warburg's daughter. A year later, she married another German refugee, Adolf Prag, and spent the rest of her life in England, where Prag became a master of the Westminster School and they had three children. Very aware of Aby and Max Adolph's psychological problems, Adolf Prag would gamely shield Frede from ever succumbing to a similar fate.

One Warburg spent the entire war in Nazi Germany: Max Adolph's older sister, Marietta, who as a young woman had nursed Aby during his breakdown. In 1926, she married Dr. Peter Braden, a specialist in childhood diseases, who sometimes worked as a doctor for the Warburg bank. Braden was extremely bright and articulate, a diabetic, but also headstrong and irascible. He had several friends in the German Resistance—most of them later murdered—and had been dismissed from his Mannheim clinic for his political activities. Although anti-Nazi, Braden kept dithering about whether to stay in Germany and lost the chance to leave. Both he and Marietta, ignorant of foreign languages, were afraid to trust their luck and venture abroad.

Even though Peter was "full Aryan" and Marietta "half Aryan," it is still hard to believe that a Warburg daughter lived unmolested in wartime Germany. Peter worked in a hospital while Marietta did part-time social work. They never knew whether Marietta's ancestry would suddenly be exploited, so they had a hideout ready in a nearby well. They had a house in a Hamburg suburb, where they survived the war intact. Some Warburgs would describe them as living in relative comfort, while others would claim that Marietta suffered grievously from rheumatism and arthritis pains and nearly starved as she gave food to her diabetic husband. There were many such cases of Jews who eked out a subterranean life in Germany during the war, usually married to an Aryan. Through Marietta, the Warburgs maintained their record of at least four centuries of continuous existence in Germany, as if the family could never really let go of the place.

Little Man and Fat Boy

Settled in a comfortable apartment on Park Avenue and spending summers with Frieda at Woodlands, Max and Alice lived like impoverished royalty in exile during World War II. The splendor of the American Warburgs contrasted vividly with the fallen state of their German relations. Malice found it hard to take root in new soil and they sometimes seemed to live from packed suitcases. At times, Max was charming, a ham actor with slapstick humor, the old twinkle back in his eye. At other moments, he was gruff, bitter, a defeated warrior. He now had silver hair and a noticeable embonpoint. During meals at Woodlands, he sat on the opposite side of the table from Alice, hiding behind the huge floral arrangement so she wouldn't carp at his overeating. He took long walks, delighted in W. C. Fields movies, and shot an occasional golf game with his wife.

If some Warburgs saw Max as a broken, tragic figure, he insisted that he wasn't discouraged. He had the good fortune to serve on the Executive Committee of the Joint, which remained in a position to aid European Jewry until American entry into the war. Starting in 1939, Eddie Warburg cochaired the Joint and secured German government approval to aid Jews in occupied territories.[1] Max worried about anti-Semitism in America and submitted blueprints for new strategic directions. He sent a lengthy memo to Eddie stating that "All Jews outside Palestine ought never [to] be politically active, but should rather interest themselves only in cultural and economic things"—advice he had long preached but never practiced.[2] At meetings, Max seemed to fumble when he spoke and lacked the easy air of authority he had worn in Germany. The "uncrowned king of Hamburg" had the tentative, uncertain manner of an immigrant.

To keep up his spirits, Max reported daily to 52 William Street and sat on the advisory board of E. M. Warburg & Company, which mostly invested money for Hamburg and Amsterdam refugees. With his motto "*Semper Avante*"—"always ahead"—he had idle dreams of someday re-creating his empire in America. Ever the organization man, Max founded several organizations to assist refugees, including Help & Reconstruction—which still taught English *and* German to Jewish kindergarten children—and the American Federation of Jews from Central Europe.

Like other immigrants, Max and Alice felt grateful to America and toured its scenic spots with virgin wonder. When Nina accompanied them to Upper Saranac Lake in the Adirondacks, Max seemed enthralled: ". . . I have never been more impressed by the beauty of this country, as well as the climate and the entire atmosphere, than by this part of the world. . . ."[3] Chastened by Hitler, he shed the grandiosity he had sometimes flaunted during his giddy days of early success, when the progress of German Jewry seemed so triumphant, so irrevocable.

Max struggled with guilt over the trouble he had caused Paul and Felix, the money he had squandered in the 1920s and early 1930s. Although Frieda felt strongly that Max had speeded Felix's death, she was never bitter and made things warmly inviting for Malice at Woodlands. Indignant over Nazi atrocities, Frieda privately ventilated anti-German sentiments that might have shocked Max. After one restless night, she confided to Edward that she had suppressed an important fact about his life. "For heaven's sake, Ma, you aren't about to tell me at this late date that I'm illegitimate?" "Well, actually, it's along that line," Frieda replied. "Edward, did you know that you were the only one of the children who was made in Germany?"[4] Once, Edward took Frieda and Max to the Sleepy Hollow Cemetery, where Paul rested amid beds of ivy and myrtle sprigs. The grave site released such a flood of powerful emotion in Max that his grief seemed almost beyond endurance. "He was all in tears and practically bellowing," Edward said. "He was tremendously upset."[5]

With his health declining, Max turned to the consolations of philosophy. His Job-like experience in Imperial, Weimar, and Nazi Germany had taught him stern lessons about the impermanence of wealth, the vanity of worldly

Lieutenant Colonel Eric Warburg bids farewell
to Hermann Göring after over twenty hours
of interrogation in Augsburg, Germany, May 1945.
(Warburg family, Hamburg)

aspirations. After visiting Palestine in 1929, he had commissioned an artist to sketch Moses gazing at the Promised Land that he would never enter. In the picture, Moses sits on an angular boulder, a thin, elongated figure with a pointed white beard, his eyes calmly lifted toward Heaven. Max identified with the picture, which he hung above his New York workplace. Shortly after Germany invaded Poland, he inscribed on its back: "The events of the war and the revolutionary time in Germany only made it ever clearer to me that every possession is vanity. I didn't want to chain my destiny too much to Kösterberg, which we all so dearly loved."[6] In late 1941, when he and Fritz lost their German citizenship and residual partnership stakes in Hamburg, Max wrote a moving birthday note to his daughter Anita. His last illusions were now in shreds. "The firm M.M.W. & Co. Hamburg is cancelled, my mark fortune is confiscated (I'm sorry for all those who could be helped by us!). I hope the Amsterdam firm will be cancelled too, so that we can start here a new M.M.W. & Co. *in time*. I am *ausgebürgert* [expatriated]. All that clarifies the situation. . . ."[7]

Long a prince of philanthropy, Max now beseeched others for help. He began writing to poor relations whom he had once helped, trying to cadge money. On December 17, 1942, the man vilified by the Nazis as the omnipotent mastermind of world finance had to take a $12,500 loan from Nina Warburg. A week later, in what must have been a daunting blow to his pride, Max accompanied Jimmy to a law office to close the books on the Kara Corporation, the corporate vehicle for the 1931 bailout loan, now a worthless shell. Jimmy transferred to Uncle Max all the Kara assets for a one-dollar bill.[8] It must have been a bitter moment for both men as they signed.

Max spent much of the war writing his memoirs in German. With a generous advance from Macmillan, he planned to finish the book within a year, but it became a taxing, Sisyphean task. Max filled up reams of paper and suffered through interminable drafts, as teams of scholars and friends were enlisted to doctor the sprawling manuscript. In the end, Jimmy, Gisi, and Hans Meyer teamed up in a little cabal to persuade Max to cancel the book, and he duly returned the advance in 1945.[9] In the early 1950s, Eric privately published a posthumous, severely abridged version. Among other things, the Warburgs hesitated to publish the story of Max's salad days in Germany at a time rife with anti-German sentiment.

Why Max's agony over this book? The problem was partly literary. Max's spontaneous charm disappeared in formal composition. If his tongue raced, his pen faltered. And there were deeper psychological problems. Because his ego had been so sorely bruised during the 1930s, he sought to recapture a vanished glory. This led to a bloated, self-aggrandizing style in which he boasted of even trivial contacts with government officials. To salve his wounded pride, he told stories of famous statesmen foolishly ignoring his sage advice and this created the impression of an arrogant, self-important man.

Too voluble in many places, the manuscript was excessively reticent in others. Max was justly indignant about the abuse he had suffered after 1933. But as the final shadow fell over European Jewry in World War II, he knew that a horrifying new standard of abuse was emerging. In the lethal year of 1942 alone, the Nazis exterminated two and a half million Jews. As Max wrote, "When, in order to compose this book, I reread my contemporary memoranda of the time of the National Socialist regime in Germany, it seemed to me that all I suffered in those days in hurt, humiliation, loss of opportunities for usefulness, and fortune, was insignificant and unworthy of mention compared to the unspeakable persecution which, more dreadful from year to year, has filled the world with horror."[10] He conspicuously evaded many subjects: his urging Jews to stay and fight; his opposition to the anti-German boycott; his various transfer schemes. In the end, Max couldn't gaze deep into his own conscience and coldly tote up the moral balance sheet. He was in too weak a state to admit error.

As for Warburg bank history, he skipped over Karstadt and other lending disasters. Some of this was understandable. Hitler had plucked away his chance to resurrect the Hamburg bank after the 1931 disaster and he needed to clutch at some wisp of self-respect. Unfortunately, in this psychologically fragile state, he asked Jimmy to review the manuscript. Eric once reproached Jimmy for sprinkling his observations with too much paprika and the latter, indeed, could never tone down his criticism. Now he took dead aim at Max:

"As to the history of M. M. Warburg & Co., I hate to say this, but I find it shockingly hypocritical and inaccurate. The reader is led to believe that you and your partners conducted an extremely successful business in difficult circumstances, that you observed sound principles of banking, did not speculate, did not overextend yourselves, and knew at all times just where you stood. The reader would very likely believe you required a modest amount of help from your American brothers, and *that* only when circumstances beyond your control made the going especially tough. The facts, as you and I know, were unfortunately quite different. I am not sure that it would be a good idea to tell the true story of M. M. Warburg & Co.; certainly it would be painful to do so; but at least the true story is far more dramatic than the one you tell . . ."[11] Jimmy, if right, delivered the truth in a bald and brutal style. He told Max to write a book about political events in which he had participated.

In unpublished conclusions to his memoirs, Max showed that he had never fully dislodged Germany from his heart. He admitted that the Third Reich revealed flaws in Germany's political culture, stemming from the undemocratic nature of the original member states in Bismarck's Reich. He also condemned excessive power vested in the military hierarchy. "Germany was a bureaucratic and military state without statesmanlike thinking."[12] Yet he vigorously denied that all Germans were Nazis. He refused to see Germany as irredeemably evil, a stain on the European map, but rather as a human compound of good and bad impulses. When he brooded over Germany's postwar destiny, it was less as an embittered exile than as a loyal, if keenly disappointed, German. Sure that Nazism would collapse, he believed the Jews would have a central role in rebuilding the postwar world, thus anticipating the postwar attitudes of Eric, Siegmund, and even Jimmy.

The hardheaded banker flirted with fanciful schemes for world federalism and regional groupings to supersede nation-states. He seemed a dreamy old man taking refuge in simplistic visions. Periodically, he circulated plans for a postwar order to Wall Street bankers. In one memo sent to Thomas W. Lamont, senior partner at the Morgan bank, Max called for a stronger League of Nations with a Department of Migration to redistribute the world's population on a more rational basis.[13] He still viewed Palestine as a place of cultural rebirth, open to all religions and governed as an international trusteeship. Max never overcame his sense that Weizmann betrayed the Warburgs and he resented that the Jewish Agency presumed to speak for Jews worldwide. In 1942, he spurned an invitation to see Weizmann, labeling him "a dangerously good orator and a most unreliable partner."[14] Despite the Third Reich, Max still believed Jews could be good assimilated citizens around the world. "The task of the Jews in all lands is to remain true to Judaism and simultaneously to be good citizens of the country in which they live; and adapt their customs to that country."[15]

While Max never renounced his romance with Germany, Alice was determined never to set foot in Germany again. If suffering made Max softheaded and dreamy, it had made her tough and flinty. Whether playing bridge with Frieda or painting at Woodlands, she wore a craggy, no-nonsense expression. Still faithful to Max, she headed the women's division of his Help & Reconstruction. She was a stoic woman of tremendous pride who scorned pity. Once during the war, Nina and Frieda decided to buy her a fur coat and Alice reared up, saying, "When I need a fur coat, Max will buy it for me."[16] She couldn't quite fathom that her family's wealth and standing had faded, miragelike. One day in Lola's house in London, Alice spilled some water and absently rang the bell, waiting for servants to come. Lola had to remind her that they had no servants.[17] In New York, Alice continued to shop lavishly, buying expensive high-fashion items from Bendel's, and she thought it awful when Frieda bought plain print dresses from Bloomingdale's.

Alice sometimes seemed dazed, shell-shocked, by the expulsion from Eden. On two trips to New York, Siegmund perceived the pathos of Alice's abstractions: "Aunt Alice seems to be quite well," he told Fritz, "but one has not the impression that she has any feeling for what is going on in the world; she lives, so to speak, mechanically in the present but in reality in the past."[18] Another time, he wrote, "Aunt Alice is remarkably self-controlled, but so much so that I find it sometimes rather *unheimlich* [eerie]."[19] In 1944, Max and Alice, age seventy-seven and seventy-one, scored 100 percent on their citizenship exams and became naturalized American citizens.

—

Exile loosened family bonds and dissolved the old Hamburg culture. Max could no longer veto inappropriate suitors for his daughters and lamented that he had been so cavalier about their religious upbringing. In London, Anita had married outside the faith to journalist Max Wolf. Max was upset but he knew that in a world gone mad, he could no longer control such matters. Gisela still worked for Hadassah, touring the country, frequently discussing Palestine with Frieda. In 1943, she married a young federal court judge, Charles E. Wyzanski, Jr., in a fancy Woodlands wedding. Charles, thirty-seven, was an overseer of Harvard College who had already argued nine cases before the Supreme Court. Max was thrilled to have this *Wunderkind* son-in-law. Charles ended up suffering from manic-depression, confronting Gisi with a problem already too prevalent in her own family.

The Warburgs avidly digested war news. Still haunted by the punitive Allied behavior at Versailles, they were dismayed when Churchill and Roosevelt called for unconditional surrender of the Axis powers at the Casablanca conference in January 1943, reversing an earlier pledge to seek a just, not a vengeful, peace. (As a captain in the Army Specialist Corps, Frieda's son, Paul Felix, worked on Casablanca arrangements.) They hoped for an equitable settlement, not a war of extinction. When the decisive battle of Stalingrad ended in February 1943, Veniero Spinelli asked Max, "Mr. Warburg, you must, no doubt, be happy today?" "Why?" asked Max. "Hitler has lost the battle of Stalingrad," retorted Spinelli. "No," said Max, "that's no reason for joy, for the last chance for Germany to obtain a just peace has now been wasted."[20]

Many Warburgs believed the Casablanca declaration would produce a fight-to-the-death mentality in Germany, eliminating any hope of a German opposition. Indeed, it caused profound dismay among Resistance members. Jimmy Warburg thought the doctrine played straight into Goebbels's hands and submitted a memo to FDR to this effect. Belatedly, Ingrid Warburg's faith in Adam von Trott was rather grimly vindicated. On July 20, 1944, Count Claus Schenk von Stauffenberg planted a bomb under the table at Hitler's war headquarters in East Prussia. Singed and shaken by the blast, Hitler nonetheless walked away intact and immediately ordered reprisals. Both a friend of Stauffenberg and his foreign-policy adviser, Trott was one of almost five thousand people arrested and murdered in revenge. He was hanged from a meat hook at Plötzensee jail on August 26, 1944. Realizing that her suspicions had been sadly misplaced, Frieda apologized to Ingrid: "You were right, my darling."[21] In the massive sweep following the plot, the Gestapo imprisoned Dr. Hjalmar Schacht, Hitler himself drafting the arrest order. The central banker who thought he could outwit the Führer finally fell victim to his own overweening pride and self-delusion.

—

Not surprisingly, several Warburgs wound up in Anglo-American intelligence work. As international bankers, they possessed the language fluency, intimate knowledge of foreign countries, strategic cunning, and necessary sense of discretion. They were also fiercely motivated to defeat Hitler. At first, the war promised to complete Jimmy's rehabilitation in official Washington. In August 1941, he became a special assistant to Colonel William J. Donovan, who would spearhead anti-Nazi propaganda efforts as Coordinator of Information. After Pearl Harbor, Jimmy worked in the Office of War Information (OWI), headed by journalist Elmer Davis, which was responsible for defining the propaganda line in various countries.

In the summer of 1942, Jimmy joined the first wave of propaganda specialists dispatched to London, serving as deputy director of the overseas branch. Enjoying top-secret security clearance and installed on the top floor of Claridge's, he worked on the North African and Normandy invasions. During his OWI tenure, two events occurred that shocked and embittered him, foreshadowing his disenchantment with postwar U.S. policy. These battles served as catalysts for his metamorphosis from conservative, anti-New Deal scourge of the 1930s to ultraliberal pamphleteer and outspoken policy maverick of the 1950s.

The first episode concerned the North African invasion in November 1942. Jimmy took part in a diversionary maneuver designed to trick Germany into thinking the Allies planned to invade Norway. Operation Torch crews were also slated to seize radio stations and newspapers in North Africa for propaganda broadcasts. But after the Allies landed along the Algerian and Moroccan coasts and quickly established control of the region, Admiral J. F. Darlan, a subordinate of Marshal Philippe Pétain, wouldn't agree to a formal armistice. Darlan was a reactionary figure who had visited Berchtesgaden the year before, trying to pique Hitler's interest in Franco-German cooperation in North Africa. The Allies now decided to cultivate Darlan as an alternative to the Vichy government and negotiated the Clark-Darlan agreement to secure his military cooperation. The deal acknowledged Darlan as head of French North Africa and gave him control of broadcast outlets taken over by Torch teams. This legitimated the existing government in Algiers, enabling Darlan to execute anti-Jewish laws. Like General Charles de Gaulle, Jimmy was scandalized by the betrayal of Allied ideals for short-term expediency and circulated strong internal denunciations of the pact. Incapable of tactical compromise, Jimmy gave way to unsparing opinions that always made him a disruptive force.

This principled, headstrong streak again surfaced during a heated row over OWI broadcasts that followed Mussolini's fall as Italian prime minister in July 1943. Marshal Pietro Badoglio, chief of the Italian General Staff, formed a new, non-Fascist government, but one that still claimed loyalty to the Axis. Assuming that the United States would reject the Duce's collaborators instead of grooming them as successors, Jimmy and his colleagues on the airwaves called King Victor Emmanuel a "moronic little King" and Marshal Badoglio "a high-ranking Fascist."[22] The Roosevelt administration, in fact, wanted to negotiate with these Mussolini sympathizers and repudiated the London broadcasts. Right-wing opponents of the OWI waged a witch-hunt, denouncing supposed Communist influence in the agency. In February 1944, Jimmy tendered his resignation rather than upset OWI's workings. He felt victimized by an internal power play and an abrupt reversal in American policy. Though disillusioned, he wrote speeches for labor leader Sidney Hillman in support of FDR's reelection that year.

These experiences again confirmed that Jimmy suffered from the curse of early success. As a banker, everything had proceeded smoothly for him. But in his rocky political life, he repeatedly acted with impulsive confidence and got into trouble. He was always being squeezed by bureaucratic battles or undermined by slippery ideological shifts. For all his fine idealism, he had a tendency to shoot himself in the foot, as if some self-destructive streak prevented him from rising to the high level of his natural talents. Politics would be his nemesis, his obsession, his fickle, tormenting mistress. After his OWI service, Jimmy would be a Washington pariah, a renegade from the Establishment that had once so warmly embraced him. The golden boy of the Warburg family was too smart, too cocksure by half, too uncompromising to fit into any corporate or bureaucratic setting in a predictably imperfect world.

—

While his parents adjusted to the American scene with some difficulty, Eric Warburg exhibited his chameleon quality for blending into many backgrounds. A short, cheerful man with little apparent shadow in his nature, he seemed happy and hopeful even at the most implausible moments. Max had pounded into him the maxim "carpe diem," which Eric took to heart. Like many domineering fathers, Max never strengthened his son's confidence or delegated power to him. Only in World War II did Eric shake off his father's enormous psychological weight. Now he would show a spontaneous flair for quiet, behind-the-scenes diplomacy and intelligence work. By offering scope for his talents, the war would be a happy period for him, a moment of internal liberation. Where wartime service would precipitate Jimmy's break with the Establishment, it would secure Eric's entrée in both Washington and Whitehall, where he collected powerful friends who would help to advance his postwar career.

Genial and mild-mannered, Eric never pretended to be a deep thinker, had no vast talent as a banker, and didn't take himself too seriously. He liked to sail and socialize with his wellborn friends. Yet he was imbued with Max's German nationalism and shared his concern for Germany's future. Unlike other German Jews, Eric never stopped thinking of himself as German, even as he fought tooth-and-nail against the Nazis.

When the Japanese bombed Pearl Harbor, Eric believed the Axis powers had committed a fatal blunder and itched for a chance to fight. Felix's sons—Frederick, Paul Felix, and Edward—joined the U.S. Army. Rebuffed by the Red Cross, Eric volunteered for the U.S. Army Air Force Intelligence. The American military urgently needed people steeped in the German language, politics, and geography and so in the early summer of 1942, Eric was shipped to Florida for an officer-training course.

Although the twelve hundred future officers were housed in Palm Beach hotels, the experience was anything but luxurious, since Florida suffered through its hottest summer in thirty years. The feet of the trainees blistered as they marched on hot pavements, and twenty or thirty officers regularly fainted on daily parade. At night, the wilted recruits slept in hotel rooms with windows sealed and blackened for security reasons. Eric thrived in this steamy hell, as his native talent for deftly handling delicate situations came into play. He overcame his shyness about public speaking and liked the Americans he met, especially Warner Marshall, a cousin of General George C. Marshall.

At the end of his Florida stint, Eric went before a board of generals to receive his officer's commission. As a veteran of the Prussian field artillery, he enjoyed clicking his heels smartly. As a practical joke, Warner Marshall told him to snap his heels for the generals. Eric was incredulous, but Marshall assured him he was serious. So when Eric entered the room, he clicked his heels rather ostentatiously. Agog, the commanding general asked where he had served in the armed forces. Trilling his r's, Eric crisply replied, "Prussian Guard, Field Artillery." The generals squirmed. Luckily, Eric had a chance to explain the circumstances of his departure from Germany. Dismissed with best wishes, he left with one last, snappy heel click.[23] Apparently, his superiors saw the comic incongruity of having Eric in their ranks. One day he asked in his heavy accent, "What do I say if I'm taken prisoner?" and his superior replied, "Well, say that you're from Milwaukee."[24]

Eric attended an intelligence school in Harrisburg, Pennsylvania, run by the Army Air Forces. He endured a grueling daily program of lectures and gymnastics. Even at meals, the young officers sat at tables where only German, Italian, or Japanese was spoken. Long the insouciant socialite, Eric was pleased and slightly surprised by his sudden utility in the war. The new captain wrote proudly to Alice, "According to the results of the last week your son must be considered a military genius, anyhow in the eyes of the school for they gave him the *highest mark possible* on a strategic problem involving many hours of blood and sweat and tears."[25]

Eager for combat, Eric was distraught when he was assigned instead to teach at Harrisburg. Refusing to spend the war in Pennsylvania, he protested to his friend, Brigadier General George Brownell, who retorted, "You are in the army, and you damned well do what you are being told. Is that quite clear?"[26] Nevertheless, Eric lobbied in Washington to reverse the decision and two weeks later was roaring off in a bomber to England. With his brisk Prussian manner and British-accented English, he became a liaison officer between Army Air Force and the Royal Air Force and trained at a secret interrogation center in Buckinghamshire, where British agents grilled captured Germans. They accumulated voluminous files on the German armed forces, compiling sixty thousand documents on Luftwaffe personnel alone.

Eric landed with Allied forces in North Africa and found himself in east Algeria. (Piggy also wound up in Algeria as an aide to Robert Murphy and General Dwight D. Eisenhower.) To inform the family of his whereabouts and bypass censors, Eric referred to a Kokoschka painting of the region owned by the Warburgs. This exotic spot of remote snowy peaks, desert, camel caravans, and lemon trees formed an unlikely setting for a Passover Seder in April 1943. Sitting beneath a picture of Pétain, Eric and seventy other Jewish soldiers sat in a stifling schoolroom, passing a bottle of wine and singing off-key. Eric, who had never worked with such fervor, coasted on a wave of enthusiasm. In a family haunted by angst and crippled by depression, he seemed almost abnormally well adjusted.

The surrender of Germany's Afrika Korps in May proved highly emotional. It stirred Eric to see thousands of his quondam compatriots trudging in defeat along dusty roads. The prisoners were gathered into camps without fences since they were surrounded by forbidding desert; escapees simply perished in the desert. Eric helped to run one prison camp for German prisoners at the Cap

Bon peninsula in Tunisia. For his charges, he obtained proper food and medicine, actions that anticipated his postwar tolerance toward Germany.

After the Allies invaded Sicily in July 1943, Eric went to investigate Luftwaffe positions. But Eric, who was about five foot six, was so weakened by dysentery that he weighed less than ninety pounds. To recuperate, he flew to London, where Lola and Anita took him to a German refugee doctor. Then he flew to Washington for a two-week stint at the Pentagon while convalescing at Freddy's horse farm in Virginia.

During this period, Eric influenced two critical military judgments. In 1942, the town of Lübeck was subjected to fierce aerial bombardment that destroyed many patrician homes celebrated in *Buddenbrooks* and damaged two majestic Gothic churches. The following year, the Royal Air Force intended to go back and flatten the town. Eric tried to dissuade the head of the British Bomber Command, Sir Arthur Harris—later dubbed "Bomber Harris" for his role in carpet-bombing Dresden—from this second bombing mission, arguing that Lübeck had no strategic but major cultural significance. After the bombing of London and Coventry, Harris retorted, he would freely bomb any German target.

Eric then tried another tack. He got in touch with Carl Burckhardt, president of the International Red Cross in Geneva, who informed the British government that all letters and parcels sent to British prisoners of war in Germany were routed through Lübeck. Based on this information, Eric contended, the second Lübeck bombing was canceled.[27] After the war, Eric would receive the Golden Ducat medal of the Lübeck Senate and always be hailed in the press as the "Savior of Lübeck."

While resting at Freddy's farm, Eric also had a dramatic encounter at the Pentagon with his friend Warner Marshall. As a planning staff member, Marshall was involved in framing postwar plans for Germany, which would be on the agenda at the forthcoming Teheran summit of Churchill, Stalin, and Roosevelt. After passing through infinite checkpoints at the Pentagon, Eric was taken into a room that contained a map concealed behind a curtain. This map sketched the proposed American, British, and Soviet occupation zones. When the curtain was drawn back, Eric saw, to his consternation, that both Hamburg and Schleswig-Holstein lay in the Soviet zone, with the Elbe River serving as a border.

Several generals asked Eric to comment on this provisional division and he responded in purely strategic terms. If the Kiel Canal ended up in the Soviet zone, he explained, the Soviets would control the Baltic Sea. He also made a case for retaining Hamburg by noting that America would need a postwar seaport to handle troops stationed in Germany. When the generals cited Antwerp, Rotterdam, Le Havre, and Cherbourg, Eric argued for something closer. "Which harbor should we grab?" he was asked. Eric, natu-rally, said, "The best harbor is Hamburg. But if the British won't let you grab Hamburg, try to get Bremen, if necessary by creating an enclave of Bremen territory which would be American held."²⁸ Eric never knew whether the generals heeded his arguments, but the Soviets got neither the canal nor Hamburg. The East-West partition was shifted just east of Ham-burg, thus preserving the slim chance of a Warburg revival in Germany someday.

Promoted to major, Eric got the prestige assignment of preparing an intelli-gence unit for the D-day landing in Normandy. After wading ashore near Isigny, he camped on the beach in a pup tent and bumped into his pint-sized cousin, Eddie, who wandered about in a steel helmet. Eddie wasn't fashioned for the martial arts, and Eric thought he looked ludicrous. "During the landing, I lost my shaving brush," Eddie said. Having appropriated a fashion-able badger shaving brush from a captured Luftwaffe pilot, Eric handed it to the little chairman of the Joint Distribution Committee.²⁹

For reasons of statecraft, the Allies decided that the Free French should march into Paris alone on the first day of Liberation. For intelligence pur-poses, however, a tiny contingent of British and American officers, including Eric, accompanied Major General Philippe Leclerc on August 25, 1944. Ig-noring instructions to clear the streets, delirious Parisians swamped the liber-ators with hugs, kisses, flowers. Parents held their children aloft to be blessed "as if we were saints," recalled Eric. He later estimated that he had kissed seven hundred women during this effusive welcome on the Champs-Élysées. "It might have been fun with twenty of them, but not more," he said.³⁰

Even as euphoria infected Paris, Eric tried to halt reprisals being meted out to Germans. He drove in his jeep to the Hotel Majestic, now a detention center for seven hundred German prisoners. After misinterpreting random shots of joy fired into the air, the French guards had marched out four German officers, killed two, and lined up ten more for execution. Eric told his compan-ion, a Royal Air Force officer named Eric Dagset, that they couldn't witness such atrocities without protest. Dagset feared that the vengeful French might react violently to any interference. When the French guards swiped Eric's Tommy gun, he saw an opportunity to slow down the killings. He summoned the French deputy commander and threatened him with a court-martial if his Tommy gun was not returned. He also insisted that, for intelligence reasons, the ten Germans be interrogated before execution, a dilatory tactic that saved their lives.³¹

Eric rediscovered tattered remnants of his prewar world. He rang the doorbell at 23 Avenue Marigny, home of Baron Robert de Rothschild, and an old butler in livery named Felix answered the door. He had guarded the residence against Nazi looters after the Rothschilds fled. Exhausted by D-day and the Liberation, Eric was now suffering from pneumonia. Felix nursed him in a four-poster bed beside a cheering wood fire. Eric shared the house with Lord Victor Rothschild, a British cousin then commanding a squad defusing bombs. The Paris police received keys to the palace of Baron Maurice de Rothschild in the Rue Faubourg St. Honoré, which had been used by Nazi officers during the Occupation. Retrieving the keys, Eric and Felix explored a mansion stripped bare of everything except for oil paintings of Hitler, Göring, and Goebbels. Göring had helped himself to several Rothschild paintings.

The Warburgs' charitable instincts immediately surfaced in Paris. While Eric interrogated Luftwaffe officers at the Petit Palais, Eddie—who always dubbed Eric his fourth brother—arrived in Paris to crank up operations of the Joint Distribution Committee, Paris having been prewar center of the Joint's European activities. Now a lieutenant in helmet and field jacket, Eddie went to the agency's neglected, run-down office on the Rue de Teheran and discovered only a deaf old caretaker on the premises. The Nazis had incinerated ninety thousand French Jews, a quarter of the total population. About ten thousand Jews had survived the war in Paris, many concocting false passports and camouflage identities, and they were now close to starving.

By his first night there, Eddie had ten soup kitchens up and running on the Paris streets. Eric prevailed upon Victor Rothschild to deliver a message to London, instructing the Joint in New York to authorize sixty-five thousand dollars in emergency borrowing to feed refugees. Read aloud at a fund-raiser in New York, Eddie's cable quickly raised the full amount. Other Warburgs appeared on the scene. Eddie's older brother, Piggy, brought in the secret files from North Africa to a newly reopened American embassy.

Eric performed a service that would be thankfully remembered by the French Rothschilds. Baron Robert asked Eric to locate his sons, Alain and Elie, both captured French officers, and Eric traced them to a POW camp near Lübeck. It turned out that Eric had unwittingly saved Alain's life. During one battle, Alain wore a pair of Zeiss binoculars around his neck that Eric had given him, and they absorbed shrapnel that would otherwise have pierced his heart. Writing to his pregnant wife from the prison camp, Alain suggested that if the child were a boy he should be named Eric, which in fact occurred. Later on, this son would be a senior figure in the Rothschilds' Paris firm and sit on the advisory board of the Warburg bank in Hamburg.[32]

In the spring of 1945, Eric sent a truck and driver to fetch the Rothschild brothers, who had spent five years in captivity. Eric was stunned when a shaken Alain balked at returning to Paris. "I've lost my mother, my father, my wife and my sister are in America," he explained. "I don't have anybody to whom I can return in Paris. Shouldn't I stay with you who are closest to me?"[33] A few days later, Eric gently coaxed him into flying back to Paris with him and starting over again.

—

Toward the war's end, Eric again grappled with the perennially troubled Warburg library. After war broke out, Aby's books had been evacuated to two spots outside London, while the staff soldiered on in South Kensington. To foster preservation, Warburg staffers photographed historic London buildings, such as the British Museum or 10 Downing Street, in case they were demolished during the blitz. Even this rump operation was disbanded when the Warburg librarian, Hans Meier, was killed by a bomb.

When financial guarantees for the Warburg library expired in 1943, Aby's books again faced a grave fiscal crisis. Fritz Saxl rebuffed an invitation from the Library of Congress in Washington to adopt the Institute, believing they had a moral obligation to remain in Britain. Also, a spot check showed that the British Museum didn't have 30 percent of the books in the Warburg Institute, confirming the library's local value. On behalf of the Warburg family, Eric negotiated an agreement in November 1944 whereby the Institute was formally transferred and incorporated into the University of London. The *Manchester Guardian* noted the irony of this coup. "The nation's greatest Christmas present this year comes from Germany."[34] Eventually, the library would be housed in a building on Woburn Square and two Warburgs would always sit on the board of trustees. Having twice escaped organized German violence, Aby's books now came to a safe resting place.

—

As interrogation chief for the Ninth U.S. Air Force, Eric had a bumper crop of captured German officers to quiz that spring. Many Luftwaffe pilots had been heavily indoctrinated by the Nazis and Eric had to break them without applying torture. To convince the Germans that their situation was hopeless, he would show them films of English air battles. If necessary, he played rougher. When he discovered that one recalcitrant officer had thirty-five letters from his mistress, he said coolly, "These letters will be returned to your wife through the International Red Cross." The man blanched. "It is not enough that we will probably lose the war, and I will lose my job as a professional officer. Now you will destroy the last thing that I have—my family life." Eric handed him one letter for each honest answer he gave until all thirty-five were tidily returned.[35]

This work gave Eric a panoramic view of a German military caste thoroughly corrupted by Nazism. As he noted, they realized that "while they were in a technical sense 'doing their duty,' they had allowed political gangsters to lead their country straight into disaster."[36] The whole rogues' gallery marched past him. Count Edwin von Rothkirch, who led German troops into Vienna in 1938, struck Eric as a Junker caricature. When he saluted another German officer, he wearily lifted two fingers to his cap, letting a beribboned monocle tumble from his eye. Eric also interrogated Franz Halder, the former chief of staff arrested in the 1944 plot against Hitler. As they walked in the woods for hours, Halder briefed Eric on Hitler. "Hate was the man's predominant characteristic," he said, "and a passion for destruction, accounts of which caused him intense pleasure."[37] Not every German was repentant. Eric debriefed Göring's aide, Oberst Walther von Brauchitsch, who said of the Allied victory, "This time you won it." Eric noted the stress laid on the first two words.[38]

Eric was often quick to forgive the German military and some old, slumbering admiration for the officers corps, especially its more aristocrat members, emerged. Eric spent weeks interrogating the tall, professorial General Alexander von Falkenhausen, the former military governor of Belgium. Eric believed that while he had deported prisoners to death camps, he had opposed the deportation of forced labor to the extent possible, thus saving hundreds of lives in Belgium. Eric also persuaded the Americans (but not the British) that Falkenhausen qualified as a member of the German Resistance. Though imprisoned for his role in the July 20, 1944, plot, Falkenhausen himself disclaimed any such identity. In Eric's view, he refused to hide behind a shield, even one he had justly earned. After the war, Eric protested to Allen Dulles when Falkenhausen was detained in a prison camp. In March 1951, a Belgian military court sentenced him to twelve years hard labor, a conviction reversed on appeal. Because of Falkenhausen's age and poor health, Eric welcomed the reversal. Years later, Freddy Warburg asked John J. McCloy, then high commissioner of Germany, about the early postwar years. "Was my cousin Eric during that time of any use to you?" "Yes, he really was, with one exception," said McCloy. "Which was the exception?" asked Freddy. "The case of General von Falkenhausen," said McCloy.[39]

When Hermann Göring was captured by U.S. troops on May 6, 1945, the Allies wanted to pump him for information that might be usefully applied against Japan. With exquisite irony, this critical task was assigned to Eric, who arrived in Augsburg for the assignment in early May 1945. Göring's economic bureaucracy had spearheaded the Aryanization of M. M. Warburg, and now fate, with a commendably poetic sense of style, created a fine opportunity for revenge. Eric would call it "the grand finale" of his wartime work.

He spent more than twenty hours with Göring. At first, leaning on a cane, the 250-pound Göring shuffled in dressed in a blue shirt and gray sweater.

Later, in his grandiose thespian manner, he switched to a gray uniform with gaudy epaulets of pure gold. Good with accents, Eric introduced himself as a Mister Vikstrom, the name of a Swedish-American officer whose family had known Göring's Swedish first wife. Eric and Göring had met at parties in Sweden in the 1920s. Although Göring marveled at the excellent, very upper-class German of his interlocutor, he never recognized Eric. To disguise the interrogation and give it a more conversational flavor, Eric memorized, in batches, more than five hundred questions designed to reconstruct Luftwaffe tactics and strategy since the Battle of Britain. As the interrogation proceeded, a sergeant in the corner took notes.

Eric handled Göring with elaborate mock courtesy and knew just how to exploit the field marshal's insufferable vanity. Even before they reviewed Luftwaffe history, starting with German sorties in the Spanish Civil War, Göring confided, "I do not want to complain but I have been quartered in a house over there with three other prisoners of war who are nothing more than generals." He noted the Reich's gracious treatment of Pétain. "And he was after all only a marshal, I am the Reichsmarschall!" roared Göring, thumping his chest. Eric discovered he had only to call him "Herr Reichsmarschall" to manipulate him with ease.[40]

In Göring's confused ramblings about the Third Reich—it was hard for Eric and his fellow officers to keep Göring focused on any subject for long—several themes recurred. He professed that he had defended the government against Nazi penetration and blamed Hitler's bungling for every Luftwaffe setback. Having once boasted that no enemy bomber would ever fly over German soil, Göring confessed amazement at the range of Allied planes. As for strategic bombing of Germany, he said the raids against synthetic-fuel plants had inflicted the most damage. "Without fuel, nobody can conduct a war."[41] Göring dwelled on the Soviet menace, as if even now, the Nazis could prey on fears of Communism to strike a deal with the West.

Of course, Göring washed his hands of any responsibility for the Holocaust. Banging the table, he said, "I never signed a death sentence or sent anyone to a concentration camp. Never, never, never!—except, of course, when it was a case of necessity."[42] He had abhorred the anti-Jewish campaign, he said. "Of course Jewish influence had grown too strong, but I never approved the methods used to deal with it, and they cannot be excused."[43] He produced stubs of checks that his wife had allegedly sent to a Jewish tailor at Theresienstadt, confiding, "Theresienstadt was not as bad as it was reputed to be."[44] Describing a Jewish work detail he had seen at an East Prussian airport, he implied that far from being slave laborers, they were a bunch of pampered loafers. In his summary report, Eric warned that Göring was far from deranged. "In fact, he must be considered a very 'shrewd customer,' a great

actor and professional liar who most likely made some mental reservations. . . ."[45]

The parting scene between Eric and Göring again displayed the latter's
comic-opera pomposity. Göring was to be flown to Luxembourg in a Piper Cub
and he appeared at the Augsburg airport in a white raincoat and cap that
reminded Eric of a Berlin traffic cop on a rainy day. He took one frowning look
at the little plane, said it looked unreliable, and refused to board it. Two
hundred American officers and soldiers eavesdropped as Eric massaged the
field marshal's vanity one last time. "Herr Reichsmarschall," said Eric, "we
guarantee your safe arrival."[46] Satisfied, Göring squeezed his capacious body
through the tiny door.

The Göring interrogation taxed Eric both physically and emotionally. As he
wrote to Freddy, "I am still exhausted from 20 hours with the fat boy."[47] Yet
he described the interrogation as the most extraordinary two days of his life.
He sent one of Göring's uniforms to George A. Brownell who then strutted
around the Pentagon in the Luftwaffe uniform to general merriment.

Because of the lax security in his cell, Eric wasn't particularly surprised
when Göring cheated the hangman by swallowing a poison capsule. The
Warburgs had now outlasted one of their chief tormentors. After the war,
they would have the satisfaction of surviving many others.

Charnel House

I n the autumn of 1944, Eric set foot on German territory for the first time since 1938, as the Allies carried the ground war to the Fatherland. On a damp, gray October day, he entered Aachen to observe firsthand the Third Reich's ghastly legacy of gutted, skeletal buildings and dazed survivors. Eric described it as a dead city that conveyed a sense of "great coldness, tiredness and infinite exhaustion like in 1918."[1] He recorded ghoulish images: limbs protruding from rubble; a tailor's dummy still sporting undershorts; stray, ravenous animals. The Nazi overlords had fled these charred ruins, leaving behind a wretched populace who inspired in Eric both compassion and disgust. "Of course they share the responsibility of what happened to this poor Europe very fully, for they probably 'heiled' when things went their way and they kept silent when they should have rebelled at a time when they still could have."[2] Eric and his men claimed as their headquarters one of only twenty roofed houses left in Aachen. In the cellar, huddled with children, they found several frightened nuns whom they recruited as their cooks.

By spring 1945, the British advanced toward Hamburg while American troops swept north toward Berlin. As they maneuvered to encircle the Ruhr, two wings of General Eisenhower's army were united at the ancient Westphalian town of Warburg. Three days after the armistice, Eric entered Hamburg. What a dreamlike moment as this German-Jewish refugee—now a conquering American lieutenant colonel—rode into town. "It was an extraordinary feeling to drive over the big—incidentally quite undestroyed—Elbe bridges after all these long years," he wrote home.[3]

When Eric had last seen Hamburg it was a thriving, elegant city. Within minutes, the appalling devastation overwhelmed him. Whole neighborhoods had been scorched by firestorms, erased from the map. As he targeted German industrial centers, Bomber Harris had zeroed in on Hamburg for its shipbuilding and aircraft production and raw-material imports. Starting in July 1943, the town had been pounded by saturation bombing, and more than half of it had simply disappeared. The toll of destruction numbed the mind: 118,000 people dead, 60,000 disabled, 295,000 houses destroyed, 3,000 ships sunk in the harbor's watery grave. The city lay paralyzed beneath 43 million cubic meters of rubble.

The Hanseatic city, which had prided itself on its tolerance, had been turned into a charnel house. In the nearby Fuhlsbüttel and Neuengamme concentration camps, 50,000 Jews, Communists, social democrats, Gypsies, homosexuals, and Resistance fighters had perished. At the end, it seemed some might survive, and they were packed onto two ships in Lübeck Bay. Then British aircraft strafed the ships, burning or drowning seven thousand persecuted souls on the brink of deliverance. Only six hundred Jews survived the war in Hamburg, mostly those in mixed marriages.

As Eric sped through the city, vistas of ruin unfolded before him. Once gracious, picturesque houses were reduced to hollow structures lining the canals. The proud tower of the *Rathaus*, which had defined the skyline, had burned down. The Blohm and Voss slipways, launch sites for the dazzling HAPAG liners, stood destroyed. Eric had lost Hamburg twice: once in 1938 and now again. He later wrote, "Four years of war hadn't depressed me as much as the sight of that bomb-lashed city, where I had known every nook and cranny, even without street signs, which were now for the most part gone."[4]

Notwithstanding the ferocious bombing, Hamburg held some hope of regeneration. An astonished Eric found, still intact, the old Mittelweg house of Moritz and Charlotte, which had been used by the Warburg Secretariat as a refuge for trapped Jews. Aby's former house and adjoining library building had also escaped serious damage. Despite all the destruction, Hamburg had retained its shape and silhouette. However ghostly and disfigured, it was recognizably the same place, especially in residential sections by the lake. The same could not be said of the Altona and St. Pauli factory districts, which had taken frightful punishment.

Concentration camp orphans on the steps of Max Warburg's
former villa Kösterberg, May 1946.
(Courtesy of George Schwab)

Then the biggest surprise appeared. Eric drove to the small downtown lake, the Inner Alster, which had been covered with camouflage during the war. The neighborhood east of the lake showed extensive wreckage, and only one building seemed unscathed. "The bank building, like a miracle, is standing like a fortress in a mass of surrounding rubble," Eric wrote home excitedly.[5] The preservation of the Ferdinandstrasse building was a minor miracle, tarnished by a vicious whispering campaign in town that alleged, "That's typically Jewish. They [the Warburgs] got them not to shoot the building."[6] In fact, the building had taken a direct hit in March 1941, when a bomb whistled down the marble stairwell and struck a metal plate above the bank vault, unleashing a choking cloud into a crowded air-raid shelter. So many bombs exploded around the bank that employees joked that their main wartime business was sweeping glass. The Berlin office that Siegmund had run was demolished in an air raid.

Eric learned that Brinckmann and Wirtz, along with other Hamburg bankers, had been placed under house arrest by British authorities. Through a friendly American liaison officer, Major Spivak, Eric had already provided Brinckmann with privileges enjoyed by no other local banker. Spivak got Brinckmann groceries, fetched his car from Bremen, and even posted an "off-limits" sign around his house. When Eric drove out in his jeep to see him, the grateful Brinckmann emerged from his doorway and greeted him with tears in his eyes. For Eric and other Warburgs, Brinckmann momentarily seemed a hero who had saved the bank while managing to minimize cooperation with the Nazis.

Did Brinckmann deserve such high praise? The employees of the bank would later agree that Paul Wirtz had remained politically clean. But Brinckmann's record wasn't spotless, nor could it possibly have been in Nazi Germany. Some of his wartime business likely had military significance. One annual report from the war years contains a cryptic reference to a shipping deal guaranteed by the Reich. Brinckmann had friends among Greek shipping moguls, and bank employees visited Greece during the war.[7] One former employee said that British occupation authorities fired several bank employees who were Nazi party members—an assertion Brinckmann denied.[8] For several years, the British Trading with the Enemy Department would probe an unspecified Brinckmann transaction.[9] The Turkish-born Brinckmann had also visited Teheran during the war to foster trade. So while Brinckmann never collaborated outright with the Nazis and clearly didn't sympathize with them, an odor of suspicion clung to him.

Eric knew nothing of this history as he embraced Brinckmann in May 1945. After their reunion, Eric went to English Brigadier General Armitage to request that the military field hospital be removed from Kösterberg so displaced persons could be housed there. Armitage asked who attended the estate during the war. "The General Management Company, which is located at Brinckmann, Wirtz & Co.," Eric replied. He was startled by the general's rejoinder. "Oh, Brinckmann, Wirtz are a bad lot, they threw out the Warburgs." Eric, introducing himself, explained that Brinckmann and Wirtz had behaved quite respectably.[10] After a tussle, he prevailed upon the British to lift Brinckmann's house arrest and let him, Wirtz, and their new associate, Hermann Schilling, return to the bank within three days—weeks ahead of their counterparts at other banks. But Eric wouldn't see Kösterberg until September.

It must have been eerily moving for Eric to reenter the beautiful neoclassical bank, now a spectral place denuded of its cherished artifacts and mementoes. Only three paintings adorned the vacant corridors: an oil portrait of Hitler, a Bismarck picture, and an English hunting scene. In a touching gesture, Brinckmann said to Eric, "Here is your desk. Let us begin again."[11] Eric reminded him, delicately, that the Warburgs were no longer partners and that he still served in the American Army. For seven years, it had seemed inconceivable that the Warburgs might start afresh in Germany. "But the hope was nevertheless always there," Eric confessed.[12]

To his immense credit, Brinckmann did ask Eric point-blank whether the Warburg partners wished to return and retake control of the bank.[13] He also wrote to Max, saying he had but one wish—to place the old firm back in his hands.[14] This clearly appealed to Max, but he was now old and ailing. The timing of the offer proved unfortunate in other ways. Like most Jews, Eric reeled as the full magnitude of the Holocaust was revealed. Germany seemed a mournful place of tears and ashes. What Jew would rush back? It furthermore appeared that decades would pass before a ruined Germany ever returned to normality. Eric also wanted to know more about the financial controls on banks.[15] Finally, there were political considerations. Hamburg now lay just thirty miles from the Soviet zone and was severed from its lucrative trade links along the lower Elbe River. Eric fretted about a Soviet invasion. In fact, through channels, he had urged General Eisenhower to keep the populous states of Thuringia, Saxony, Western Saxony, Magdeburg, and West Mecklenburg instead of West Berlin, which he feared would simply become a mousetrap.[16]

Yet Eric was also impressed by the speed with which industrious Germans were cleaning up their cities and he never ruled out the possibility of return. As he told his father, "It is too early to make any decision with regard to the future there (return). I personally think it's out on a 'for good' basis but I think that if those in control *really welcome it*, some liaison might be worked out later."[17] Clearly, the prospect tantalized him, and John J. McCloy would later give him the official seal of approval he wanted.

Meanwhile, Eric directed food parcels to Brinckmann, Wirtz and fostered a resumption of business. Evidently through Eric's aid, Brinckmann sat on a Denazification Tribunal—no small political advantage for a postwar German banker. Distressed by his problems with occupation authorities, Brinckmann felt inordinately grateful to Eric for his help. In general, one can say that Brinckmann behaved as the loyal, decent caretaker figure the Warburgs had pictured when they chose him in 1938. When Eric gave him a handwritten letter from Max, Brinckmann "was deeply touched by again seeing Father's handwriting after all these years and was quite humble after having been somehow depressed and restless before," Eric told his parents.[18]

Before leaving Hamburg, Eric performed an act of family piety. For his father's sake, he wanted to make sure that the graves of Charlotte and Moritz and Sara and Aby had not been desecrated. While searching for them, he found himself, by accident, not in the Hamburg cemetery, but in the ancient Altona Jewish cemetery, which contained Alice's Warburg ancestors. To build barracks, the Germans had leveled the grounds and pushed aside gravestones, and heartless locals now swiped gravestones to use as doorsteps. Eric strung up barbed wire around the cemetery and began to restore the gravestones. It turned out that the Warburg burial sites in Hamburg were intact; Eric's grandparents and great-grandparents had slept undisturbed throughout the Third Reich. Eric was also reunited with the one Warburg who had spent the war in Germany: Aby's eldest daughter and his cousin, Marietta, who had married the Christian Peter Braden. Finding her thin and underfed, Eric procured Care packages for the Bradens and many other old friends.

Eric had the rank and mobility to get a bird's-eye view of a defeated Germany. He flew down to Bavaria, swept over a shattered Nuremberg, then glided by Hitler's Berghof, tucked away in solemn Alpine splendor on the Obersalzberg. Eric got out to inspect the hollow remains of Hitler's retreat, reflected on the dreadful Munich tragicomedy of 1938, pondered the lofty mountain peaks. Events had moved with disorienting speed. As Eric told Freddy, "we drove down the steep mountain road where a few days before the gangsters were still racing with their big Mercedes cars. . . ."[19]

Later, riding in Mussolini's personal bulletproof car, Eric and his chauffeur went to Hochried, Jim Loeb's estate in Murnau, now occupied by the U.S. Army. Soldiers were amusing themselves by taking target practice with Jim's collection of antique Egyptian glass. His books and ashes had been preserved by his friends, the Count and Countess Resseguier, who had defended the property against SS encroachment. When Eric entered the house, he was startled to see a portrait of old Solomon Loeb staring at him from above the fireplace.

In Berlin that September, Eric found Rudolf and Lola's Wannsee house still standing in an expanse of debris.

An uproarious Felix Warburg in Cortina, Italy, August 1922. His teenage son, Eddie, took this high-spirited picture that was dubbed "Greeting the Dawn." (American Jewish Archives)

A somber Max Warburg seated beside Gisela and Charles Wyzanski at their July 1943 wedding. A uniformed Eddie Warburg stands behind the newlyweds. (Courtesy of Katharine Weber)

Anita Warburg. (Courtesy of Anita Warburg)

Gisela Wyzanski. (Courtesy of Anita Warburg)

Gisela and Charles Wyzanski in later years. (Warburg family, Hamburg)

Felix Warburg chairs the Joint Distribution Committee, August 16, 1918. Jacob Schiff, lower right, grudgingly yields center stage to Felix. By this point, the Joint had raised $12 million for Jews in war-stricken Europe. (American Jewish Archives)

The Warburg mansion at 1109 Fifth Avenue, circa 1920, today home of the Jewish Museum. Jacob Schiff found the Gothic architecture unforgivably *goyisch*. (The Jewish Museum)

Frieda Schiff Warburg. (Warburg family, Hamburg)

Lola Hahn-Warburg with her lover, Chaim Weizmann. Note how they kept a protective distance from each other in case the photo fell into mischievous hands. (Private collection)

Prince Philip visits Lola and Rudolf Hahn at their Burnside home in England. Observe how the regal Lola marches one step ahead of the prince. (Warburg family, Hamburg)

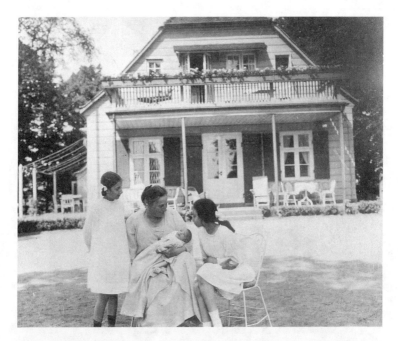

Anna Beata Warburg and her three daughters in front of Noah's Ark at Kösterberg. The ship-like silhouette of the house is visible from this angle. (Courtesy of Tamar Nussey)

Anna and her Swedish mother.
(Courtesy of Tamar Nussey)

Fritz and Anna Beata Warburg around the time of their marriage. (Courtesy of Tamar Nussey)

A portly old Fritz Warburg in Stockholm, circa 1950, with grandchildren, Tamar, left, and Benjamin. (Courtesy of Tamar Nussey)

Ingrid Warburg Spinelli.
(Warburg family, Hamburg)

Veniero Spinelli.
(Warburg family, Hamburg)

A fascinated Siegmund studies his colorful grandfather, Max Kaulla. (Private collection)

Lucie, Georges, and the lordly infant, Siegmund. Notice that Lucie's gaze is much stronger and steadier than her husband's. (St. Paul's Girls' School)

Siegmund clutches his teddy bear. (St. Paul's Girls' School)

Siegmund, in rear, exhibits thespian talent in a family spoof of *Carmen* in the park of Aby. S.'s house at Travemünde, July 1928. He poses with his cousins. (Private collection of E. G. Lachman)

Siegmund and Eva Warburg with her Philipson mother, brother, and father. The photo suggests Mauritz Philipson's commanding nature. (Private collection)

Portrait of Siegmund Warburg done for his wedding, November 8, 1926. The photographer admirably captured his penetrating eyes. (Private collection)

Bridal picture of the exquisite Eva Warburg, November 8, 1926. (Private collection)

Siegmund, Eva, George, and Anna at The Hyde, Little Missenden, August 1938. (Private collection)

Lucie Warburg visiting Siegmund at Selsdon Court, near Croydon, 1934. Siegmund sometimes got pudgy and took fasting cures. (Private collection)

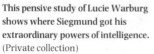

This pensive study of Lucie Warburg shows where Siegmund got his extraordinary powers of intelligence. (Private collection)

Lucie shelters from the sun, probably in Travemünde. (Private collection)

Bettina Warburg.
(Courtesy of Katharine Weber)

Nina Warburg in her roly-poly later years.
(Courtesy of Katharine Weber)

Bettina and Jimmy Warburg, who never resolved an intense love-hate relationship.
(Courtesy of Katharine Weber)

Piggy Warburg and the second of his three beautiful wives, Constance Woodworth, in the Road to Mandalay Club before their January 1939 wedding. (Wide World)

Gerald Warburg.
(Courtesy of Anita Warburg)

Frederick Warburg at the time he received a distinguished service award from the Boy Scouts, May 1963. (Wide World)

Ace kibbitzer Eddie Warburg gets a belly laugh from Golda Meir.
(From the collection of Mr. and Mrs. Edward M. M. Warburg)

Eddie sits flanked by Eleanor Roosevelt and a stony-faced Golda Meir.
(From the collection of Mr. and Mrs. Edward M. M. Warburg)

Eric Warburg as a dapper young man.
(Warburg family, Warburg)

Eric in Palm Beach, Florida, in an officer
training program, 1942. Twenty to thirty
men collapsed daily in the semitropical
heat. (Courtesy of Anita Warburg)

Max Warburg and daughter Renate at Woodlands during World War II. Observe Max's
sudden paunch, hearing aid, and chastened expression. (Warburg family, Hamburg)

Eric Warburg meets with John J. McCloy. (Warburg family, Hamburg)

Inside the Hamburg bank, Eric pauses beneath a portrait of Paul Warburg. (Warburg family, Hamburg)

Eric's son, Max, one of the few Mittelweg Warburgs ever blessed with hair. Today he heads the house of M. M. Warburg & Co. (Bent Weber)

Dorothea and Eric Warburg with their children at Hunt Cottage, White Plains, in the early 1950s. From left: Erica, Max, and Marie. (Courtesy of Anita Warburg)

However indignant at the Nazis, Eric was moved by the almost prehistoric misery to which starving Germans had been reduced. Some people were too weak to stand or hold a cane or lift a light parcel. As Eric told Nina, "I am the last who forgets what the Nazis have done and of the indescribable guilt of theirs. But I seriously doubt that this is the answer and one day there will be a feeling of deep shame upon us in the West that this is the better world we have been fighting for. . . ."[20]

Even before his Hamburg homecoming, Eric had heard about the death camps and their legions of cadaverous inmates. After studying some of the first snapshots from the camps in early May, he wrote, "And the faces of these human beings who have gone through a golgotha compared to which a soldier's death seems like triumph, speak their own eternal words. And although these saints—50–70 pounds of bones—were perhaps for some time with their thoughts no more on this world, I am sure they would ask us if they could, never to forget."[21] When Eric showed the photos to one captured German officer, the man wept, telling Eric that he knew the Germans had lost the war, but only now did he realize that they had lost their honor.[22] In 1933 there had been more than half a million Jews in Germany and about 170,000 of them had died in the camps.

From afar, Eric participated in efforts to evacuate Theresienstadt near Prague, where tens of thousands of Jews had died. He obtained a list of Theresienstadt survivors which he forwarded to the Joint. The chief rabbi of Berlin, Dr. Leo Baeck, had been among the Jewish leaders sent there. He had spurned all invitations to leave for America, saying, "As long as one Jew remains in Germany, my place is with him."[23] Eric dispatched a lieutenant to Baeck with orders to reunite him with his daughter in England. But this figure of exceptional nobility preferred to be the last to leave the camp. Even as the occupying Soviets goaded Jewish inmates to take revenge on Nazi guards, Baeck preached forgiveness: "Don't touch them, ignore them. It's not our task to repay one injustice with another."[24] This attitude deeply affected Eric.

Eric's refusal to engage in any revenge against the Germans also had historical roots. He thought of the impassioned letters his father had written from Versailles and how the Jews had ultimately been victimized by the vengeful spirit shown by the Allies. Throughout the war, he had talked of the need to avoid repeating that error. He hoped Max's memoirs would appear around the time of the armistice, reminding the victors of the hazards of vengeance.

In Lüneburg, Eric witnessed a memorable scene of justice being handed out to the Germans. Robed, bewigged British judges presided over a trial of forty offenders from Bergen-Belsen and-Auschwitz. Sitting with sordid, brutish faces, the Nazis wore large numbers for identification. Eric was thrown into emotional turmoil, torn between a desire to punish these men and to let normal justice proceed. To calm his nerves and sort out his feelings, he sat in the old Lüneburg church, which had the organ once played by J. S. Bach. Convinced of the need to rehabilitate and not punish Germany, he was upset by the broad-based denazification campaign that stigmatized so many people. "I would be much harsher with several hundreds of thousands of Germans who are real stinkers, if necessary more, but the rest must have a hard chance, but a chance," he insisted.[25]

Eric would always be disturbed by the facile equation of Germans with Nazis. At Allen Dulles's behest, he spent time with members of the German Resistance at Wiesbaden that summer, to make them feel less isolated, and in coming years he provided financial help to their families. As wartime head of the Swiss office of the Office of Strategic Services, Dulles had been in charge of American intelligence for Germany. He had trained Eric in mail drops and other intelligence methods. Having collected information on Hitler's opponents, Dulles wrote a postwar book about the German Resistance, and Eric assisted him with the research, bringing him into intimate contact with many brave figures and reminding him of German traditions other than National Socialism.

Eric devoutly believed that Germany must reform itself and he feared the imposition of outside morality. Repeatedly he warned Washington that the denazification program was netting too many little people. When Dulles asked for his thoughts, Eric argued for swift justice against Nazi bigwigs. "Otherwise, the Nazi criminals would use the floodlight of the courtroom not for the first time in order to fully exploit such a stage and which many of them are only too anxious to do."[26] Fearful of the Soviet Union, Eric wanted to push the political agenda beyond the Third Reich toward economic renewal. It worried him that most Germans believed America would go home while the Soviets would stay.[27]

As an American colonel, Eric declined to participate in the Nuremberg trials that began in November 1945, believing the Germans should judge themselves. He also spurned an offer from John McCloy to participate in the Control Commission for Germany. Instead he functioned as a watchdog to ensure that the Nuremberg trials were conducted fairly.

We might note two events of special Warburg interest. On October 25, 1945, Dr. Robert Ley, former Nazi nemesis of Max Warburg, committed suicide in his Nuremberg cell. Trying to hang himself by a towel, he choked to death instead. Dr. Hjalmar Schacht proved as arrogantly self-righteous on the witness stand as at the Reichsbank. Thirty-two prisons had not managed to dent his vanity. Able to point to his role in various anti-Hitler plots, he was acquitted by the court. A German denazification tribunal sentenced him to eight years in a labor camp. Dr. Schacht was finally acquitted on appeal and set free in September 1948.

—

Eric was a man of composite identity who felt American, German, and Jewish in turn. His Jewish identity was certainly the weaker part of his nature and he took actions in 1945 that would have been viscerally impossible for many Jews. He feared the Soviets would waylay many luminaries of German science; already, they were carting off rocket technology from Peenemünde. After alerting his dozing superiors to the scientific threat, Eric was authorized to requisition the Hotel Wittelsbacher Hof in Bad Kissingen. Working against time, he assembled a convoy of jeeps and trucks and rounded up German scientists and their families, housing them at the hotel. In a three-week period, he evacuated to the three Western zones about 160 scientists, including atomic researchers and V-2 rocket experts, a goodly number of whom ended up in the American space program. One of them was Wernher von Braun, who would visit Eric regularly after the war.

This unquestionable triumph for Western security inevitably meant the rescue of many scientists tainted by Nazi associations. The V-2 rocket had not only killed thousands of British civilians, but twenty-five thousand concentration camp inmates had perished in the hellish underground tunnels that assembled it. Eric's own files contain a report that in the Nordhausen tunnels 150 slave laborers died every day producing the giant rockets. In Germany's atomic program, female inmates from Sachsenhausen were pressed into service to handle radioactive uranium plates. Eric himself would later secure reparations for victims of slave labor programs. Yet, as an intelligence officer in 1945, he showed no regrets about rescuing the scientists. If Eric had a strong sense of Jewish ethics, he didn't have a Jewish nervous system.

Eric was equally forgiving of the brilliant but weird Otto Warburg, one of Germany's most distinguished biochemists. (Not to be confused with Otto Warburg, the botanist and Zionist mentioned earlier.) A cold, rigid bachelor, selfishly devoted to his work, Otto was descended from Simon von Cassel and hence was a distant relative of the Hamburg Warburgs. His father, Emil—a distinguished physicist and friend of Einstein—was a baptized Jew while his mother was a Christian. As a youthful prodigy Otto got a doctorate in chemistry and a medical degree. When he served in the Prussian Horse Guards in World War I, Einstein persuaded him that he was too promising a scientist to risk his life, and Otto, having won an Iron Cross, duly returned to Berlin.

Eric enjoyed collecting people. By the time he first befriended Otto in 1933, the latter had already won the 1931 Nobel Prize for physiology and medicine for his work on respiratory enzymes. The Rockefeller Foundation had built Otto his own Institute for Cell Physiology at the Kaiser Wilhelm Institute (later the Max Planck Institute) in the Berlin suburb of Dahlem. The solitary Otto was oblivious of political realities. When he visited Kösterberg after Hitler seized power, he didn't know that Germany had left the League of Nations. Eric found Otto vain and pompous, but also witty, charming, and bristling with original insights. Whenever Otto telephoned in the 1930s, he asked Eric, "You don't smoke, young man?" and "You ride every day, young man?" Eric would reassure him on both counts.[28] Throughout the 1930s, Eric supplied Otto with everything from books to riding breeches.

The Nazis didn't bother Otto, who treasured the seclusion of his Berlin lab. At one point, he discussed with Max and Eric taking a post in a British university, "but imagine if I had to talk with the other Professors, and above all with their wives!" he said.[29] In April 1933, when the Interior Ministry expelled all Jewish scientists from the Kaiser Wilhelm Institute, Otto and other directors were spared. In 1937, Max Warburg was chased from the Kaiser Wilhelm board—which was, by then, performing nasty racial research masquerading as science—but Otto remained.

Otto's survival in Nazi Germany aroused considerable controversy in the scientific community. In 1935, Hitler had a polyp removed from his vocal cords. Afterward, he dreaded that he would develop cancer and hoped Otto might devise a cure. Indeed, during his career, Otto would make notable strides in cancer research, showing the carcinogenic nature of food additives and cigarette smoke and demonstrating how cancer cells are destroyed by radiation. He became so obsessed with environmental carcinogens that he would not eat store-bought bread and had his own organic garden to produce fruits and vegetables. Otto displayed a certain arrogant idealism during the Third Reich. Outspokenly critical of the Nazis, he retained a Hungarian Jew, Erwin Haas, as his technician until 1938. When the Gestapo challenged Haas, Otto replied that he thought the anti-Jewish laws applied solely to German Jews!

In 1941, Otto lost his post briefly because of his Jewish ancestry, but a few weeks later received a personal order from Hitler's Chancellery to resume work on his cancer research. Otto's Reichswehr friends got Göring to take a second look at his genealogy, which produced a convenient finding that Otto was just one-quarter Jewish. Otto was content to profit from this sleazy maneuvering. As Otto's biographer, Hans Krebs, later wrote, "Warburg's willingness to let his Jewish blood be diluted in this way, and thus to make a pact with the Nazis, incensed colleagues outside Germany."[30]

In 1944, Otto won a second Nobel Prize for his enzyme work, but Hitler decreed that Germans couldn't accept Nobel Prizes. Because he had narrowly missed winning in the late 1920s, had won in 1931, and had won but couldn't accept the award in 1944. Otto entered that rarefied circle of scientists who have been considered three times for the Nobel Prize. He justified his decision to stay in Nazi Germany by claiming that he was performing extremely important cancer research that would save lives and that he couldn't transfer his research operation abroad.

At war's end, Otto didn't shrink from instructing the advancing Soviets about his own importance. "Do you know who I am?" he said. "The famous Nobel prize winner, Professor Otto Warburg from Berlin."[31] Once the Soviets let American troops into Berlin, Eric scouted out Otto, who remained in hiding. In a dramatic reunion, Otto walked out of a dark underground passage. For a few seconds, he actually exhibited human emotion, telling Eric tearfully, "I always knew the war would really be over only when *you* stood before me."[32] Then Otto reverted to his workaholic self, telling Eric that he needed forty liters of petrol to pick up scientific instruments. When Eric said this was forbidden, Otto scoffed. "I couldn't care less; all I want is the 40 liters of petrol."[33] Eric obliged him. Until Otto died in 1970, Eric showed great solicitude for him. In his last letter to Eric, Otto wrote, "I shall get the third Nobel Prize for us, because in one or two years we shall have resolved the problem of cancer."[34]

———

In this season of bittersweet wonders, Eric returned to the hilltop pleasance that had symbolized beauty and civility for the Warburgs: Kösterberg. He had a moving reunion with the redoubtable Braunau farm girl, Kathi Schwärz, whom he had recruited as a housekeeper for Noah's Ark after the Nuremberg Laws. While German officers occupied Kösterberg and swam in the pool, she had safeguarded the premises from abuse. She would fearlessly lecture *Wehrmacht* officers who threw their boots on the furniture. "You'd jolly well better behave here as you do at home," she told them.[35] (They stripped the place of its furniture anyhow.) Eric was also amazed to find his old Newfoundland dog, Teddy, who was now blind and unable to recognize his long-absent master. With his innate dislike of uniforms, Teddy had been the bane of Nazi officers.

Touring the grounds, Eric saw the dreadful changes wrought by war. Because of the property's height, the Germans had mounted antiaircraft guns and radar atop the two water towers. A bomb had chipped off a corner of Noah's Ark. The Nazis had turned Kösterberg into a military hospital specializing in jaw injuries, with Malice's villa converted into surgical wards and Max's studio serving as the operating room. Fritz and Anna's house had been a sick bay for wounded soldiers. The military had thrown up dozens of barracks across the lawns, leaving the grounds rank and unweeded; the

Roman terrace was converted into a potato patch. Wehrmacht cars had flattened the rhododendron bushes. Despite these grotesque transformations, Eric could already picture the place pruned, tidied up, restored. "Altogether Kösterberg is as beautiful as ever and I am sure that the mess can be cleaned up very easily," he wrote to Bettina and Nina.[36]

For the time being, it was a moot point as to whether the Warburgs would ever inhabit Kösterberg again. Encouraged by British authorities, Eric pressed ahead with plans to resettle children from concentration camps on the estate. Aided by the Joint and the Jewish Agency, Eric created a center for orphans from Bergen-Belsen, Theresienstadt, and elsewhere. The estate that had recently hosted German officers suddenly swarmed with 100 to 150 German, Czech, Polish, and Hungarian Jewish children.

The lice-infested children who came to Kösterberg found it hard to adjust to normal life. Still plagued by nightmares of the camps, many refused to take showers for weeks. At Kösterberg, they learned foreign languages and job skills that would prepare them for life abroad. Ironically, this former residence of a leading non-Zionist Jewish family became a nursery of Zionist militancy. "Everybody wanted to go to Palestine," said one of the children. "You were almost looked upon as a traitor if you didn't. We were training for the Irgun—the Jewish underground. We saw the British as no better than the Nazis."[37] Hundreds of children would rotate through Kösterberg before the program ended in the late 1940s.

In August 1945, Eric went by train to Sweden and at the Stockholm train station set eyes on Fritz and Anna for the first time in six years. Now in their mid-sixties, they had helped many German refugees during the war years. Two of their daughters planned to move to Palestine. With Max sick and Alice worried that her son would contract disease in the German rubble, Eric didn't dawdle and returned to New York in September, sailing from Bremen on a Liberty Ship with six hundred other soldiers.

The Colonel Eric Warburg who sailed across the Atlantic that September was a far more accomplished, self-assured man than the socialite of earlier days. For his wartime service, he would receive the American Legion of Merit medal, the Order of the British Empire, and the French Croix de Guerre. Delighted and slightly astonished by this sudden blossoming, Max still wanted Eric to resume banking as soon as possible—a field in which his son was never born to excel. So Eric returned to the same dilemma he had faced in prewar days. In war, he had shown surprising leadership gifts. When peace broke out, he had to step down from the pantheon of war heroes and resume the role of an ordinary mortal.

Part Five

THE RETURN OF THE ALSTERUFER AND MITTELWEG WARBURGS

Siegmund Warburg and his son, George,
in officer training corps uniform, Deerhaddn, 1941.
(Private collection)

CHAPTER 38

The Upstart

On April 18, 1939, Siegmund Warburg had become a naturalized British citizen, giving him a measure of wartime security and protection. But he knew all the terrible fears and apprehensions of a Jew who had escaped from Germany. Early in the war, his New Trading Company had managed a Cash-and-Carry syndicate with the Rothschilds, Hambros, and other banks to finance American imports. In German propaganda broadcasts, William Joyce—dubbed "Lord Haw-Haw" from his sneering tone—had denounced German-Jewish perpetrators behind the operation. As Britain braced for invasion in the summer of 1940, Siegmund decided he wouldn't be taken alive by the Nazis and got an arsenic capsule from a friendly doctor, to whom he remained profoundly indebted. After the war, Siegmund's name would have appeared on a Nazi blacklist of the first people to be rounded up if Germany invaded England, except for a clerical error, which put his son George's name on the list instead.

Grateful to be in England, Siegmund and Eva never spoke German to their two children, and Lucie operated in English from the time she arrived. Siegmund regretted that he couldn't appreciate English poetry as much as German poetry. Yet he steeped himself in Churchill histories and Charles Dickens novels and, in a typical bit of hyperbole, declared that reading Anthony Trollope surpassed a university education. He collected wartime speeches and clippings, with a view to possibly writing a book about the war. Roused by Churchill's fiery exhortations, he rated them the finest public utterances since the ancient Greeks.[1] Like other scholarly projects in Siegmund's life, the war book came to naught. However much he immersed himself in British culture, Siegmund would always remain, in mind and manner, a product of Weimar Germany—its cultural pessimism, its sweeping, dialectical generalizations, its mystical yearnings for close friendships, its fear of the dark forces of history.

Both as a German refugee and a Jew, Siegmund was extremely sensitive to slights. One morning, he took a train into the City from his house near Great Missenden and inadvertently gave in the wrong ticket at the end. The ticket collector didn't care for people with German accents and asked him to pay a fine. Siegmund thought he had made an honest mistake and, after Nazi Germany, didn't care to be bullied. While his friends and lawyers at Slaughter & May advised him to pay the fine and forget the petty insult, he refused to knuckle under to pressure. He retained a tough lawyer and successfully contested the fine, yet often talked later about the fear he felt in opposing the state.

Even if never entirely at home in England, Siegmund was greatly impressed by the cheerful resilience of the British, the quiet heroism of ordinary people. Their plain, stoic, no-nonsense manner pleased the German puritanism he had imbibed from his mother. After a "doodlebug" attack on London in 1944, he marveled at the uncomplaining reaction of his staff, telling a correspondent, "It is significant that when I came the other morning to the office our liftman told me that he had been bombed out the night before, but he was just as punctual for his morning duty as on every previous occasion, and he was just as jolly as usual."[2]

Like many refugees, Siegmund and Eva were struck by the often kindly treatment they received from the British. After going to great pains to retrieve her Swedish citizenship in 1933, Eva was reluctant to renounce it again, but being a Swedish national entailed certain wartime hardships. Once she had to pick up Siegmund at the train station after curfew hours and phoned the police to ask for permission. The officer said slyly, "Well, madam, I can't give you permission, but I won't see you."

Lucie, now an old woman in her seventies, spent her days writing letters and playing the piano. But she still qualified as an enemy alien. Periodically this elderly lady had to answer police questionnaires about whether she owned a motorcycle or harbored any dangerous weapons.

Even when he later grew rich, Siegmund never lived lavishly and didn't try to ape aristocratic London bankers, with their posh clubs and country houses.

Driven neither by greed nor social climbing, he could display a monkish austerity. Because of petrol rationing during the war and the bombing of train lines, Siegmund and his family gave up their Great Missenden house in 1942 and stayed in a pretty suburban apartment in Roehampton Lane, with a splendid park view. This modesty suited Siegmund just fine. As he told a friend, "it accords with my passionate wish to simplify life as far as possible which I think is one of our chief duties as far as personal life is now concerned."[3]

If Siegmund prided himself on a fiercely logical mind, it operated amid a welter of turbulent emotions. Whether assessing events or people, he could be wildly impulsive or uncannily correct. Early in the war, he was plunged into an agony of doubt about the Allies' chances to defeat Hitler only to reverse position sharply after Germany invaded the Soviet Union in June 1941. A few days later, he sent a sweeping, rather cold-blooded, Hegelian analysis to Stefan Zweig, saying that the war, however horrible, was an agent of social advancement. "It confirms me in the opinion that basically it is really a good destiny due to which increasingly larger and larger parts of the world have to go through the purgatory of war and destruction in order to arrive at a cleaner and saner state of things. This is exemplified in this country where the war has created a much stronger spirit of comradeship and sacrifice."[4]

Perhaps building on the intermediary role he had played between Dr. Schacht and the British government in the autumn of 1939, Siegmund engaged in intelligence work with the Ministry of Economic Warfare. His British partner, Harry Lucas, was deeply involved in Ministry work and Harry's brother-in-law, John Noble, worked to decode enemy messages. Jewish refugees were a valuable intelligence resource. Siegmund was apparently consulted by the government for his comprehensive knowledge of German business and politics and also helped to obtain supplies in various countries.

———

Siegmund often sounded stoically philosophic about having to start his life over again in England. He liked to quote his grandfather Siegmund, who said, "It has been the Warburgs' good fortune that whenever we were about to get very rich, something happened to make us poor and we had to start all over again."[5] At his New Trading Company, Siegmund gathered around him a group of first-rate German and Austrian refugees, who had also fallen far below their former lofty perch in the world. This sharpened their drive for success and enabled them to prevail against monumental odds. Far from being defeated by fate, these German Jews would exhibit fantastic enterprise and be rewarded with commensurate success.

A later executive would coin the term "uncles" for these founding fathers of what would evolve into S. G. Warburg & Company. The term was oddly revealing, for it implied that the tiny firm of two dozen people was a surrogate family for these political castaways. It also hinted at the cautious, fussy, pedantic, somewhat secretive style of these men. Siegmund, significantly, was never an uncle, but the paterfamilias, floating above the fray.

Though Siegmund was always the star of the show, he needed his supporting cast of uncles. Many people would come to regard him as the foremost global banker of the late twentieth century, but he didn't excel in basic financial techniques. His genius never lay in crafting a deal, restructuring a balance sheet, or appraising shifting financial markets. He always had teams of minions to do that. Siegmund was the master salesman, long-term strategist, and reigning administrative deity rolled into one. If a maestro who couldn't play every instrument, he knew how to coax topflight performances from his team of virtuosi. He understood intuitively the fears and insecurities of his fellow refugees, making them feel special and important. They feared, honored, and respected him. A man of warmth and extraordinary charm, he could also be a ruthless autocrat who knew every managerial trick to inspire, terrify, cajole, goad, and manipulate his staff. He was, at once, a seductive and unsettling presence.

The nuts-and-bolts operation fell to Siegmund's chief executive, Henry Grunfeld, whom many would regard as the brains of the firm and the smartest banker in London. For almost fifty years, he and Siegmund were as inseparable as Siamese twins. Feeling he owed his worldly success to Siegmund, Grunfeld worshipped him. Siegmund found Grunfeld a bit dour and Prussian, but revered his talents. Henry was the technician who would execute his wishes without ever challenging his ultimate authority. They developed a telepathic sense of each other's thoughts. If Siegmund suddenly shifted gears with a client in mid-conversation, Grunfeld would pick up the signal and follow suit without a word being spoken between them.

While Siegmund attracted, indeed encouraged, a certain mystique, Grunfeld avoided the limelight and lacked the king-sized ego that usually goes with superior intelligence. He shunned the travel in which Siegmund gloried and led a private life. Before his death, Siegmund told him, "You couldn't have done it without me and I couldn't have done it without you."[6]

Both men had a very Germanic sense of discipline and exactitude. In Siegmund it was coated with charm, while in Grunfeld it stood out more nakedly. Where Siegmund had a melancholy elegance, Grunfeld looked and acted all business. His narrow, thin-lipped face, steely spectacles, and austere mien reflected his bladelike mind. Presented with a complex problem, he could ferret out the hidden flaws and devise a pure, elegant solution. Where Siegmund had a guileless, almost childlike credulity at certain moments,

Grunfeld was a thoroughgoing skeptic. Nobody could palm off damaged goods on Uncle Henry, and Siegmund seldom made a major step without having Grunfeld scrutinize it.

While Grunfeld hadn't known Siegmund in Germany—he hadn't even realized the Warburgs were Jewish—these two agnostics had parallel backgrounds. The Grunfelds had been a prominent Jewish family with steel and chemical interests in Upper Silesia for three generations. (This was the same family of Rawack & Grünfeld mentioned earlier in connection with Friedrich Flick.) With similar educational backgrounds, both Henry and Siegmund had been young businessmen, burdened by early hardship, their families having surrendered fortunes to inflation and the Third Reich. They were bound by a common desire to recreate their former status. As Grunfeld said, "We both had the burning ambition and determination to get back to the position which we had in Germany and to show to the world and to ourselves that we could do it."[7] Because neither had much capital to contribute to the firm, they had to build up their shareholdings through options.

In comparing their later attitudes toward Germany, Grunfeld would always stress that Siegmund had left Germany voluntarily, whereas he had fled from persecution. In spring 1934, the Gestapo arrested Grunfeld in Berlin, and held him for fifty-four hours. As they dragged him from one prison to another, his terrified wife couldn't determine his whereabouts. Grunfeld only got out because he was an Honorary Spanish Consul in that part of Germany. At this critical juncture, he was shocked by the cowardice and indifference of supposed friends, a lesson that stayed with him. When released by the Gestapo, Grunfeld was advised by a friendly judge to go underground and he lived with his family in the Black Forest. After the Night of the Long Knives butchery, he left Germany. His father was financially plundered by the Nazis, and the family fortune was whittled away by the Flight Capital Tax, punishing exchange rates, and Aryanization. Many members of his family were killed during the Third Reich.

In 1935, three people told Grunfeld about the Dutch International Corporation's London venture and said that Siegmund needed somebody with industrial experience to match his financial knowledge. All three intermediaries later became Nazis and died in the war—an irony not lost upon the superstitious Siegmund and Grunfeld. During his last overnight trip to Berlin in 1937, Grunfeld was returning to the airport when Heinrich Himmler pulled up beside his taxi in a Mercedes—a baleful omen. It would be Grunfeld's last glimpse of Berlin. Unable to banish memories of his 1934 arrest, Grunfeld never set foot in the city after the war. The arrest also left a lasting aversion to frivolity—perhaps explaining why he and Siegmund never posed for photos.

The third member of this early triumvirate was Eric Korner, the head of the investment department. A country doctor's son born in a village outside Vienna, Korner was an assimilated Jew and former cavalry officer. His first encounter with Siegmund occurred in Berlin in the 1930s, when they met for a six o'clock morning walk, the two competing to show which one rose earlier. While working in his Berlin bank, Korner was arrested by the Nazis, which would produce an embarrassing postwar incident.

Unlike the other uncles, Korner was funny, tough, outgoing, flamboyant, brash, and mischievous. "I like my desserts and my clients to be rich," he once said in his extremely thick Austrian accent.[8] The accent was so impenetrable that his British colleagues thought he once said "Venezuela Day" when he was trying to ask "When is Labor Day?" Another time, he inquired about a mysterious company called Kelly Cigars—that turned out to be Tennessee Gas, fantastically enriched by an Austrian accent.[9]

Like the other uncles, Korner was a cultured man who loved opera and symphonic music and collected illuminated manuscripts. Endowed with a vast range of European contacts, Korner would later be able to raise millions of dollars with a few telephone calls. If Grunfeld dryly stuck to the facts, Korner, the firm's stock-exchange man, knew how to embroider a sales pitch. After the war, he was trying to sell shares in the London Rubber Company to the church commissioners. When asked what the company made, he covered the telephone receiver and urgently asked a subordinate, who said they manufactured condoms. Aghast, Korner asked what else they made? Garden gloves, said the young man. "They're the world's largest garden glove company," Korner told the church commissioners briskly and closed the sale.[10]

During World War II, Siegmund and the uncles suffered comparative isolation in the City of London. Though a naturalized British citizen, Siegmund was legally obligated to note his German origins on the company letterhead by appending to his name "(formerly German)." The uncles ruefully referred to themselves as the "natives," mocking how they thought the British stereotyped them. The City viewed them as queer birds indeed but treated them with occasional kindness as well as condescension. When New Trading suffered bomb damage at one point, Rex Benson of Robert Benson (later incorporated into Kleinwort Benson) provided temporary space for the natives in his office. N. M. Rothschild remained the fairy godmother of New Trading and sometimes sent them unwanted business. Until well into the 1950s, N. M. Rothschild was always the first firm to receive the annual financial statement of Siegmund's firm.

Like other stranded Jews, the uncles were shocked by the hostility that greeted anyone with a German accent during the war. They were sometimes perceived less as Nazi victims than as risky German partisans. Declared an enemy alien on the war's third day, Grunfeld had to surrender his car and required permission to travel for the duration. Struggling with a heavy German accent and carrying a German passport, he constantly had to allay suspicions as he tried to drum up business in war factories. It was an insane situation that would have defeated all but the hardiest souls.

After Germany overran Holland in 1940, Britain interned German Jews as enemy aliens and crowded more than thirty thousand into camps outside Liverpool or on the Isle of Man. Because Jews were often seized between eight and nine o'clock in the morning, Grunfeld would wander around Hyde Park at six in the morning to avoid arrest. Eric Korner, not so lucky, spent several months shut up on the Isle of Man.[11] By no coincidence, Siegmund and the uncles would remain haunted, secretive in style, and alert for enemies. They had known the fear of the midnight knock on the door in Germany, then had encountered suspicion in England.

Unexpectedly, the war Germanized the New Trading Company, as British staff members were swept into the armed forces. Employees took turns on the roof at 82 King William Street, doing duty as fire wardens. When air raids started and bombs dropped around the building, the edgy Germans were the first to fling themselves to the floor. New Trading built a basement bunker for alerts, but after a time people got blasé and didn't go downstairs. A wartime ban constrained the uncles from speaking or writing German in the office. One day, after BBC radio announced that German aircraft were dropping bombs at random, the uncles stood squinting over a map, trying to locate the town of Random.[12] Attempting to function in a foreign tongue, these refugees developed an English that was, syntactically, pure German. Henry Grunfeld would be celebrated for his famous exhortation, "Then into action we must swing" and his dismissive reference to "All that sky in the pie."[13] Even Siegmund continued to write letters about "having" people for lunch until his secretary gently noted that he sounded as if he were devouring his guests. At first, George Warburg screened his father's letters for Germanic howlers at home then later arbitrated disputes at the office over English usage. Siegmund never shed his strong Swabian accent. Later he admitted that he could have learned to speak without one, "but I didn't, because I would have sounded ridiculous."[14]

In many ways, exile simplified life for the uncles. After the Third Reich, they didn't care for the trappings of power and only wanted wealth that was portable. It would take time before they bought houses in England or felt rooted. Siegmund epitomized these contradictory men, for he combined a renowned name and old-money tastes with the creative spark of the self-made businessman. Seldom has an ambitious underdog stepped into the fray with such a fine pedigree. From the outset, he and his colleagues exhibited a Spartan style and worked extraordinarily long hours—something the privileged sons of the City could never match. At first, they observed Jewish holidays, but when they noticed gentile competitors still working, they began to skip the observance. Every Saturday, a secretary took four hours of dictation from Siegmund at home and on Sundays he telephoned the uncles, reviewing the week's business. Many nights, Siegmund took clients out to dinner. The Warburg wives would always feel widowed by the firm.

At work, Siegmund introduced methods he had learned at M. M. Warburg in the 1920s and, psychologically, stepped into the role of Uncle Max. Every morning, when the uncles and other executives arrived at eight or eight-thirty, they sat around a table and perused each other's mail before the nine-fifteen meeting. Letters were summarized and abstracts circulated to all directors. Outgoing mail had to be read and initialed by a colleague—a time-honored German practice. To avert bureaucratic segmentation and debilitating turf wars, Siegmund gave the firm an open, free-flowing feeling. To foster a group feeling, he rotated people among departments and created talented generalists. Among other things, this wedded clients to the firm instead of to any single director. It also concentrated power in Siegmund's hands and prevented the emergence of rivals to his authority.

Siegmund's disciplined upbringing instilled in him an exaggerated need for order, which was probably intensified by the chaos of his early adult life in Germany. A perfectionist by nature, Siegmund couldn't tolerate tiny errors in letters and threw fits over misplaced commas. He dreaded the dry rot of mediocrity, the spreading miasma of sloth. This concern for detail extended to matters of dress. Equipped with legendary powers of observation, Siegmund would chide a secretary for a spot on her blouse or a bit of exposed petticoat. He became the arbiter of office style; one time when his secretary wore a fashionable scarf tucked into a sweater, Siegmund asked her, in a funny, quizzical, understated way, whether she had a sore throat.[15]

Although a man of beautiful manners and punctilious etiquette, Siegmund struggled to control his emotions. He was a prototypical German Jew—exacting, disciplined, hypercritical, industrious—and pushed himself and others relentlessly. Aside from social evenings spent playing gin rummy or bridge, he didn't want to squander a second. He had already given up too much time to the Nazis. He seldom read newspapers, relying instead on summaries prepared at the office. Aside from walking and stair-climbing, he never exercised and disapproved of athletics. Before the war, he borrowed a big green Ford from Gero von Gaevernitz, but otherwise never had a car or learned to drive and always took hired cars. (After one catastrophic driving lesson, the petrified instructor told Siegmund he was dangerous.) Even while riding in the car to work, he would read or dictate letters to his secretary, often clearing up the backlog of mail by the time he arrived at the office.

Siegmund's lack of interest in small talk or carefree leisure activities produced an extraordinary human being, but also a driven one with a lot of bottled-up tension. Already in New Trading days, he could be a martinet who flung file holders and telephone directories when people didn't behave exactly as he wished. (After his outbursts, he said he felt sick but also better.) He personalized work relationships to an unusual degree. Frequently elated after hiring somebody, he would then grow disenchanted and the idealization could abruptly curdle into disgust. Sometimes he seemed to have a separate little psychodrama going on with each employee. Behind the polished erudition, Siegmund was an extremely sensitive, vulnerable, and lonely man. When people disappointed him, he could break down and weep. Like Eva, Grunfeld was more even-tempered and tried to shield Siegmund from the volatile extremes of his own titanic emotions.

After two world wars, hyperinflation, the 1931 banking collapse, and Adolf Hitler, Siegmund could never scrub past disasters from his mind. A chronic worrier, he gloomily foresaw postwar America sunk in a deep economic morass and chided America's religious faith "in the automatic effects of unbridled private enterprise and competition if only laissez-faire economics are allowed to run their course."[16] Still leftish in outlook, he predicted that Soviet living standards would overtake those of England and possibly America. He thought the Soviet Union would dominate central Europe after the war, but didn't seem to mind, praising the country's "shrewd political leadership" and "efficient handling of her military and industrial affairs."[17] Impressed by Soviet might, Siegmund began taking private lessons in Russian.[18] He often argued with his tutor, insisting that Russian grammar was illogical and to blame for his errors. As with so many of his views, Siegmund would radically revise his opinion of the Soviet Union and become something of a cold warrior in the 1950s.

———

As immigrants, the uncles had to hustle and innovate to capture clients from established houses. They had no false pride. Henry Grunfeld would gleefully recall snaring a fifty-pound retainer in Paris. At a time when London bankers seldom spoke foreign languages, New Trading lured British clients by catering to their foreign needs. Siegmund followed Uncle Max's practice of providing high-quality, personal service to every client, large or small. He often told trainees that they never knew whom their client might be dining with that night.

A striking case of this wisely democratic strategy involved publisher Fredric

Warburg, a descendant of the Swedish Warburgs, who bought Martin Secker's foundering publishing house in 1936. (He is not to be confused with Felix's son, Frederick.) When Victor Gollancz refused to publish George Orwell's *Homage to Catalonia,* Fredric snapped it up. Offended by this leftward turn, Secker left the publishing house and financial disaster beckoned. Fredric's aunt steered him to Siegmund for a five-thousand-pound loan. As he said, Siegmund "took as much trouble over my miserable 5,000-pound investment as he could have done over the millions in the aluminium affair."[19] Siegmund planted a refugee editor from the *Frankfurter Zeitung* on the board and he himself nominally headed Secker & Warburg at one point during the war.

It was a paradox that the premier financier of his age would always remain queasy about being a lender. Even in later years, the Warburg bank would be known as the most conservative in London, rarely lending against real estate or shipping. However stodgy banking might seem in London, the uncles deemed it risky stuff and fretted over each loan. Grunfeld had sat on the board of a failed bank in 1931 and remembered the *Schadenfreude* with which rival banks watched his institution sink below the waves.

While Grunfeld excelled in banking, Siegmund found it boring and adhered to the ancient banker's dictim that "Lending is to cover overhead."[20] His experiences in Germany had taught him the need for a diversified income stream from financial services and long-term investments. The will-o'-the-wisp that teased him was to develop a fee-based business—that is, to pour high-priced, confidential wisdom into the ears of chief executives instead of making loans or taking positions. His role model was André Meyer of Lazard Frères. Once, on a flight to New York, Siegmund anxiously prepared for a meeting and suddenly blurted out to his companion, "There's only one man in the world that I am totally afraid of and intimidated by and that's André Meyer." But despite his monstrous temperament, Meyer was also a man of financial acumen, and Siegmund closely studied his moves.

Siegmund would always prefer strategic corporate planning to humdrum short-term lending, for it allowed greater scope for his imagination. In the early days, he often served as a bridge between small industrial companies that were short of capital and large institutional investors. Often he represented those investors on small company boards and in the 1940s parlayed this into nonexecutive chairmanship of a plywood manufacturer, a dredge builder, and a chemical engineering firm.

The boldest such industrial foray came in the 1940s with S. G. Warburg's purchase of the metals trading house of Brandeis-Goldschmidt, long headed by the Napoleonic Paul Kohn-Speyer. This step would unleash a family feud venomous even by Warburg standards.

Because the battle involved a clash of personalities, we must review some family history. Olga Warburg, sister of the Famous Five brothers, had married Paul Kohn-Speyer and then committed suicide after the birth of their fourth child, Edmund, who grew up close to his Warburg relations. Paul Kohn-Speyer subsequently married Anna Leo-Wolf. Eddy was dark and Semitic-looking while Anna was blond and coolly fashionable. She and Eddy conceived an intense dislike for each other. When Anna first set eyes upon the three-year-old Edmund, she burst out laughing at the queer child.[21] Paul and Anna Kohn-Speyer had another set of pretty blond children, and for a long time the children thought they all issued from the same marriage. In time, Olga's memory faded and Paul didn't talk about her.

As Olga's children grew older, they learned of their separate parentage, but remained ignorant of their mother's suicide. On a trip to New York in the 1930s, Eddy' sister, Alice, learned the true story of Olga from Frieda and Nina. During the war, Alice disclosed to Eddy the secret of their mother's suicide. Although shattered, he was relieved to know the truth.[22] If he had known earlier, Alice speculated, he might not have regarded his stepmother as an interloper.[23]

Paul and Anna Kohn-Speyer behaved like British gentry, celebrating Christmas and contributing to the local church. They lived on a 154-acre estate in Surrey called Old Quarry Hall that was nicknamed Old Quarrel Hall by the Warburgs. Run by two dozen servants, the estate had tennis courts, espaliered fruit trees, a working farm, several cottages, and a dairy. When Paul sent Eddy to a prep school in Kent run by two Anglican priests, the boy didn't even know he was Jewish. When the Great War broke out, the bilingual Kohn-Speyer children stopped speaking German. As a Jew with a hyphenated German name, Eddy faced double jeopardy in a jingoistic school rife with anti-Semitism. He read law at Balliol College, Oxford, became a barrister, and trained at M. M. Warburg in the 1920s. After his loveless childhood, Eddy treasured the lively Warburgs and regarded Eric as more a brother than a cousin. The Warburgs knew Eddy was highly flawed and erratic. Bright, clever, and amusing, he could also be brash and tactless, showing flashes of irreverence that either charmed or infuriated people. As Eric told people, "Insult Eddy before he insults you."

In 1929, Eddy interned with the National Lead Company in New York. When he asked to head the New York office of Brandeis, Goldschmidt, his father insisted upon having a Christian at the helm instead.[24] To cope with his strained relationship with his father, Eddy consulted his cousin Bettina, now a psychoanalyst, who advised that his relationship with his father might improve if they worked together. It wasn't an inspired insight. Paul Kohn-Speyer was a rigid, humorless perfectionist while Eddy was undisciplined with an incorrigible delight in naughty pranks. They frequently argued in the office.

The question of succession at Brandeis-Goldschmidt was a momentous one. Paul Kohn-Speyer was the Copper King whose firm brokered the output of many mines and surpassed in trading volume all copper dealers on the London Metal Exchange. The firm also had strength in tin, nickel, and lead. Paul Kohn-Speyer had scant regard for Eddy's business ability and groomed as successor Cecil Goldschmidt, son of his deceased partner. When Cecil Goldschmidt died young in 1934, it reopened the successor question.

Out of friendship for Max Warburg, Paul Kohn-Speyer had provided desk space, telephones, and an office at Brandeis-Goldschmidt when Siegmund arrived in London and he also financed many of his early transactions. Paul Kohn-Speyer regarded Siegmund's business ability so highly that he appointed him an executor of his estate. Toward the end of his life, Kohn-Speyer apparently believed that Siegmund had taken advantage of the Brandeis, Goldschmidt connection to build up his own business.[25]

The Kohn-Speyer children claim that as soon as Paul died in 1942, Siegmund began to ingratiate himself with the widow Anna, who came to rely implicitly upon his judgment.[26] The Warburgs thought Siegmund unfairly exerted his charms with the elegant Anna and gossiped about it. In April 1943, Eric warned his father, "Lola writes that Siegmund is playing as Executor his old Jew Süss game with Aunt Anna versus Eddy. If true: a rather nasty role!"[27] To appreciate the venom behind Eric's gibe, one must understand the allusion to Lion Feuchtwanger's 1925 novel about Joseph Süsskind Oppenheimer, the unscrupulous Jewish financial adviser to the Duke of Württemberg. Jud Süss, as he was known, had exploited state monopolies, been arrested for subversion, exhibited in an iron cage, then hanged for high treason. The story became a staple of anti-Semitic narratives in the 1930s.

After Paul Kohn-Speyer's death, the family had to pay heavy death duties and Siegmund later claimed that Anna had begged him to take Brandeis-Goldschmidt off her hands. It took Siegmund four years to accomplish that feat. On May 22, 1946, the London papers announced that Brandeis, Goldschmidt & Co. had been converted into a limited partnership with authorized capital of five hundred thousand pounds. Rio Tinto bought the controlling stake, and S. G. Warburg & Co., presumably to show confidence in the deal, took a minority interest; a few years later, Warburgs bought out the entire company. Siegmund always felt skittish and snobbish about the unpredictable trading business—it seemed a crazy arena where mob psychology ruled—but Grunfeld was experienced in metals and he later acted as chairman of Brandeis, Goldschmidt.

After spending the war as an intelligence officer in the Royal Air Force,

Eddy worked with the Control Commission in Germany, drawing up laws for the postwar occupation. On the day he was demobilized, the Brandeis, Goldschmidt sale was closed.[28] "Eddy said that if he was there at the time, he could have prevented the sale of Brandeis, Goldschmidt," said a coworker of Paul Kohn-Speyer. "He felt that it had been done behind his back. It must have been especially painful since he had been fighting while other people were making money."[29] What rankled, too, was that his father had given Siegmund his start in England. The Brandeis, Goldschmidt sale struck Eddy as base ingratitude. He got a three-thousand-pound severance check and was disinherited from his family firm. The only assets he managed to salvage were some badly bombed copper plants that Brandeis, Goldschmidt owned with National Lead in Germany.

Eddy fervently believed that Siegmund had taken advantage of the Kohn-Speyers' distress and the postwar situation to obtain the firm at a giveaway price. At the time, industry rumor said the sale price of Brandeis-Goldschmidt didn't even cover estate taxes for Paul Kohn-Speyer. For many reasons, it is extremely difficult to judge the validity of Eddy's weighty accusations against Siegmund. The price issue is a vexed one because the wartime market was dormant. As suppliers of a strategic metal, copper firms operated under government controls and could only make a fixed percentage on trades. Even after the war, metals firms were closely regulated, making it hard to price their worth.

In addition, the value of a trading house lay less in quantifiable assets than in the realm of reputation and managerial skills. Paul Kohn-Speyer had been a legendary trader, but also an autocrat and one-man show. He left behind a number of mediocrities, including a head bookkeeper who turned out to be an embezzler. After Paul Kohn-Speyer's death, the house needed to be rebuilt from scratch. It is, finally, impossible to establish the essential facts of the case since S. G. Warburg & Co. executives contend that no Brandeis, Goldschmidt files exist from before 1953.

Paul Kohn-Speyer had effectively vetoed his son as a possible successor, and it was widely acknowledged that Edmund was inept and unpopular with the firm's executives. With justice, Siegmund saw Edmund as a contrary, disruptive, mixed-up fellow who could sabotage the smooth working of any firm. By common consent, Siegmund and Henry Grunfeld did an outstanding job with Brandeis, Goldschmidt, improving its management and running it far better than Edmund could have done. Right after the war, with the metal exchange still shut down, Warburgs used idle Brandeis, Goldschmidt capital for financial ventures. Even in the early 1960s Brandeis still functioned as a major moneymaker for S. G. Warburg, earning more than Siegmund's celebrated exploits in the Euromarkets.

From a business standpoint, the takeover was a smart move for Siegmund, even if he begrudged the time that Brandeis demanded from Henry Grunfeld. But it meant inflicting severe pain upon the son of the man who had given him his London start. It took a certain intestinal fortitude to expel Edmund Kohn-Speyer from the firm associated with his father. Siegmund looked upon himself as a man of high ethical standards, and the words "courage" and "integrity" often figured in his vocabulary. He frequently quoted his mother as saying that one had to take the right path, however tough. This gave him honesty, but also a certain unbending severity in pursuing his goals. Like the young man so enamored of Nietzsche, he always felt he had the higher sense of mission on his side.

Certainly, no single act in Siegmund's career aroused more animosity among the Warburgs, who were doubtless happy to find a reason to taunt and malign their successful and often defiant cousin. Bettina Warburg never stopped seething about the incident, saying of Siegmund: "He had a horrible character. He did Eddy Kohn-Speyer out of his father's business."[30] She clung to a more extreme view of Siegmund than most Warburgs. Yet the Mittelweg Warburgs, despite enormous respect for Siegmund's success, would come to view him as a man of many masks, hidden agendas, ulterior motives. Even as he emerged as the most famous Warburg, he would remain the family black sheep, if popular among his Alsterufer relatives.

The story of Eddy Kohn-Speyer's subsequent life is a sad one. After the Brandeis, Goldschmidt sale, he became a deeply depressed person, something of a misfit. In the drab atmosphere of 1946 Britain, he couldn't find work and had to become a gentleman farmer. Several times in the 1950s, the Warburgs tried to make peace between Siegmund and Eddy, but both men were hardened in their self-righteous indignation. As Fritz wrote, "Siegmund Warburg is a red flag for Eddy, because he feels so badly treated."[31] Siegmund fancied himself the injured party, because "he feels that Eddy behaved too nastily toward [him] to become again involved in any negotiations with him," as Ernst Spiegelberg said.[32]

Till the end of his days, even when old and nearly blind, Eddy would buttonhole people and pour out his woeful tale of Brandeis, Goldschmidt. He nursed such an obsessive hatred of Siegmund that he wrote poisonous, obscene letters to Eva, warning her against Siegmund. He would tell people that if killing were legal, he would take a gun and shoot Siegmund.[33] On his seventieth birthday, Eric invited the family to Kösterberg. At once Siegmund asked if Eddy would attend and declined when he learned that his nemesis would be there. When Eddy arrived at the house, he asked if Siegmund was there and grimly quipped, "I brought my shotgun along."

—

As World War II ended, it became clear that fate had handed Siegmund a rare opportunity. The Holocaust had interrupted the preordained order of succession in the Warburg kingdom, allowing a new claimant to the throne. Not only had the Nazis swept away M. M. Warburg, but Max was now old and infirm, suffering from a bad heart and high blood sugar. If Siegmund acted swiftly, he could seize the Warburg name and initiative. For sheer brains and ambition, he had always felt, with justice, far superior to his Mittelweg relatives and he resented having to beg for scraps from Uncle Max's table. Now in his mid-forties, Siegmund was ready to start life anew. With the war over, a German name for a London firm was no longer an impediment.

Max automatically assumed that *he* would guide the postwar plans to refurbish the Warburg name. During the war, Eric periodically stopped in London and noted the awesome strides being made by Siegmund. After one dinner in December 1943, Siegmund and Eric talked late into the evening about New Trading's future. Afterward, Eric, in alarm, told his father, "They are very active and I hope not too much so if peace should appear one day around the corner."[34] While in London in September 1944, Eric discovered that Siegmund planned to establish an Amsterdam pied-à-terre for New Trading after the war—without Eric or Max. This was a highly significant step, for the Warburgs regarded Amsterdam as the most strategic spot to spearhead their reentry into Europe.[35] When Eric asked him to elaborate on his plans, Siegmund grew tight-lipped. "You have to add to that the New Trading's expansive trend and my cousin's personal ambitions and you have the picture, namely that they will under all circumstances create themselves such a pied à terre," Eric wrote.[36] To brake his cousin's expansion, Eric pleaded with Siegmund to consult them before undertaking any plans in places where the Warburgs had operated before the war.

Siegmund resented the insinuation that Max and Eric had some monopoly on the family name, which struck him as appalling hubris. No less proud of the Warburg name than they, he considered himself the best qualified to carry the banner forward and he didn't intend to take a back seat to Eric again. All along, Siegmund had felt sharply conflicted emotions toward Uncle Max, who had started out as beloved uncle and surrogate father, then become the domineering boss partial to his son. Now Siegmund increasingly disparaged Max as pompous and arrogant, and with an inflated sense of his wisdom. Toward Eric, Siegmund had never felt warmly, finding him charming and amusing, but also a lightweight snob who lacked courage, guts, and drive.

In Hamburg, Max had been a giant presence in the financial world, Siegmund a nonentity, a country cousin from the wrong side of the family. Now as he began to fathom the scope of Siegmund's ambitions, Max derided him as an upstart who had forgotten his place in the Warburg universe. Max thought it absurd that his nephew should arise as the heir to and custodian of the august Warburg name.

One can only imagine what old scores were being settled here. Many Warburgs believe Siegmund sought vindication, not just for himself, but for the entire humiliated Alsterufer branch, which had suffered such ridicule from the Mittelweg clan. "Siegmund felt very strongly that he was going to get that particular branch back into the mainstream," said his cousin, Ruth Fleck. "He adored his father and wanted to set the record straight."[37] Siegmund had regarded the Mittelweg Warburgs as weakened and corrupted by money while he had worked himself to the bone. His revolt against Max was the ultimate revenge of the poor relation. His ascent would indeed represent a startling comeback for the Alsterufer Warburgs, a throwback to the glory days of his grandfather Siegmund.

Siegmund denied that the rechristening of New Trading as S. G. Warburg & Co. in early 1946 had anything to do with Max or Eric. To be sure, custom demanded that a London merchant bank be named after its founder and principal figure, but, as Max and Eric pointed out, Siegmund wasn't an important shareholder in New Trading. Siegmund cited a leading figure at the Bank of England who had urged him, "Siegmund, if you are going to start a new banking house, it must be with your name and nothing else."[38] His correspondence suggests that the timing of the name change related to Eric's return from Germany to New York in late 1945. In early September, Max insisted that Eric stop in London to hold an emergency meeting with Siegmund about the name change. Both Max and Eric were disturbed by some of Siegmund's shareholders, whom they saw as unsavory.[39] (Since Siegmund's major backers included Edmund Stinnes, the Petschek family from Czechoslovakia, and other highly reputable business figures, it is unclear to whom this refers.) Back in New York, Eric held long talks about the future with Max, who was ailing but still alert. Max kept dwelling on the theme that the Hamburg firm should rise again under the Warburg name.[40]

On November 19, 1945, Siegmund told his cousin Charles (formerly Karl), "Eric has recently been released from the American Forces and he has now discussions with his father as to the future setup in which he will work. For your personal information I am not quite without apprehensions in this respect, because I understand that Uncle Max and his son are both very much taken by the idea to revive the old M.M.W. & Co. firm which in my opinion would be most premature at this moment *to say the least*."[41] If the name M. M. Warburg & Co. were revived in Europe, Siegmund couldn't use the Warburg name without creating confusion. There was now a powerful temptation to seize the name, but he had to act quickly and decisively.

For two months, Siegmund dithered over the name change. As a veteran of the 1931 banking crisis, he was extremely reluctant to see his name on the door of a bank and suggested the name Mercury instead. For six consecutive weekends, he and Henry Grunfeld wandered around Putney Heath and Wimbledon Common, Grunfeld trying to persuade Siegmund that New Trading was a misleading name for a bank and that Siegmund's name was the right and proper one. Siegmund feared the responsibility of such a step, as well as the sizable potential for failure. On January 14, 1946, Siegmund wrote his cousin Charles that they had just decided to baptize the firm S. G. Warburg & Co.[42]

Max and Eric engaged in a long, acrimonious correspondence with Siegmund in an attempt to deter him from using the name. Deeply resentful, Max began to snigger at Siegmund's company as the Jew Trading Company. Max and Eric felt that Siegmund had started in London with support from M. M. Warburg and Paul Kohn-Speyer and that he had now double-crossed both of them. Max jeered that the new-fangled S. G. Warburg & Company would never amount to anything. "Every one of my personal friends thought it was right," Siegmund said of the name change. "Only some members of my more distant family thought it was wrong."[43]

On January 29, 1946, *The Times* of London ran a minute three-line notice on the bottom of page seven. It said in its entirety: "The name of the New Trading Company has been changed to S. G. Warburg and Company. Since its formation the firm has developed into a house of industrial and merchant bankers and it is felt that the original name is no longer appropriate. There will be no variation in the management and activities of the company."[44] The little firm had thirty employees, with total share capital of just 233,000 pounds. The announcement in no way foreshadowed its prosperous future. Siegmund was always the first to say that he never dreamed it would become a leading London house. "I thought we could find a little niche where we could do things the others wouldn't do."[45]

Max had lived to see the Warburg name revived, but under quite different auspices from those he had expected. After Siegmund changed the name, Max suffered a heart attack in February 1946. He lingered on feebly, robbed of his old vitality and resigned to his fate. He suffered from memory lapses and found it hard to concentrate. Despite their past differences, Jimmy came to Max's sickbed, preferring to remember the good early days when he had preferred Max to his own father. Max's confused mind combed through the past, returning to Ballin and Melchior, the first world war and Versailles, the bright times with his three dead brothers. Flabbergasted to learn of the six million Jews who had died in the gas chambers, he insisted, one last time, that Nazism was a passing disease in Germany and that people should remember the good that had come from German culture.

Max's mind frequently turned to Aby. Right after the war, he cherished a vivid reminiscence of Aby, which Carl Georg Heise had written in an air-raid shelter during Berlin bombing raids. Max's own perishable world of power and wealth now lay in ruins while Aby's books and ideas had endured. To Eric, Max confessed that he had underestimated Aby, whose mad, nocturnal visions had been lit by such lightning flashes of truth. "He used to say: Your firm will be bankrupt at a time when my library will flourish. . . . How many times, when we had discussions, didn't I tell him that he was an idiot! But after all I think he came nearest to the truth."[46] With similar humility and candor, Max told Fritz Saxl that most of his own work had been destroyed but that Aby's library had survived as a family legacy.[47]

Eric always swore his father would have returned to Hamburg whereas his sisters were equally adamant that he would never have gone back. In his last days, Max succumbed to nostalgia and talked in his delirium about the coachman readying the horses to take him back to Kösterberg. He died on December 26, 1946, at age seventy-nine. More than one thousand people jammed the funeral at the Park Avenue synagogue. Afterward, Max was reunited with Paul at the Sleepy Hollow Cemetery. His death was a tremendous blow for Alice, who had stood steadfast by her husband's side through two world wars, an assassination plot, and years of persecution.

By an uncanny coincidence, Paul Wirtz died two days after Max so that a joint memorial service was held for them at Brinckmann, Wirtz in Hamburg. An openly moved Rudolf Brinckmann gave a thoughtful speech of remembrance then joined the now-tiny Jewish community in Hamburg for a service at a local synagogue.

Max's death was exceedingly strange for Fritz, who had been overshadowed for so long by his four flamboyant brothers. "Of course, I have suddenly become much older through Max's death," he wrote. "So long as he 'ruled,' even with a weakening hand, I could still feel like the younger brother."[48] With his gray walrus mustache, Fritz still lumbered slowly through life, yet he had outlived in his plodding way his more dynamic brothers. Grumbling about high Swedish taxes, he otherwise seemed to enjoy Stockholm. He and Anna helped many Jews during the war and cared for a Finnish refugee child. In the basement of their apartment building, Fritz indulged an old passion and set up a graphology institute.

Like Max, Fritz felt the mysterious pull of a Germany that now survived only in memory. Drinking sherry and eating herring at the Restaurant Metropol, he would reminisce about the past and suddenly find himself sliding from Swedish into a quick, colloquial German. Fritz never discounted the possibility of moving back to Hamburg after the war. He didn't assume all Germans were Nazis and feared the victorious Allies would punish rather than rehabilitate his former countrymen.

Once young men of such infinite verve and promise, the Warburg brothers were all humbled in the end. For all his pep and resilience, Max had lost his wealth, his standing, and his invincible dream of Jewish assimilation into German life. He was left with a handful of memories, vague hopes, and wounded pride. If still a flawed and very fallible human being, he was a weightier and deeper man than the dashing, devil-may-care young man who had yearned to be a German cavalry officer. Like his brothers, he had been rounded and humanized by suffering, if also embittered. He died without knowing whether or not he was the last Warburg to practice banking on German soil.

*Rudolf Brinckmann and Eric Warburg
in a Hamburg restaurant, 1958.
(Warburg family, Hamburg)*

Our Aryan

A t the end of World War II, Hamburg was a patchwork of bomb debris that would take years to clear. Military jeeps negotiated rubble-strewn streets. The former Gateway of Germany had sacrificed its fleet, its overseas trade, its vital links to the outer world. As food rations dwindled to one thousand calories per person per day, tuberculosis and other ailments spread. To deal with the housing shortage, people lived in cylindrical huts of corrugated metal with small doors and two windows punched out in front. Inside the neoclassical Brinckmann, Wirtz palazzo, employees struggled with a lack of heat. Pushing their desks into one large room around an old iron stove, they worked in hats and coats while messengers rubbed their hands by the stove. The grimness of the war years had not ended.

When the Warburgs considered returning to Germany, these material deterrents paled beside the mournful psychological ones. As for all Jewish families, Germany was now a taboo place peopled by ghosts. One day, occupation authorities sent the Warburgs a Torah shrine and curtain salvaged from Theresienstadt. What Jew could move beyond such memories? The two hundred thousand Jews still in Germany were mostly displaced people, eager to depart for Palestine or elsewhere. It seemed that Hitler had won and that the

Jewish community in Germany would shortly be extinct. Around the world Jews boycotted Volkswagens and other German products—much as in 1933—and wouldn't set foot in the pariah state.

However attenuated his Jewish identity, Eric Warburg felt these sentiments and spurned Brinckmann's invitation to return to both Hamburg and the bank. During the war, he had emerged as a personage in his own right, which only made the readjustment to civilian life more difficult. Forgetting his own youth, Max mocked his desire for a military career, saying, "A Jewish general we've never had."[1] As for so many veterans, real life must have seemed anticlimactic to Eric as he returned to the tiny refugee firm he had founded at 52 William Street. Cheerful, affable, optimistic, Eric—unlike Siegmund—didn't have the fierce entrepreneurial energy to found an empire. Although always twinkling with bright ideas, he tended to lack the follow-through and staying power to see them implemented.

The E. M. Warburg employees were Hamburg and Amsterdam expatriates speaking a garbled mishmash of German and English. They were generally perplexed by American securities markets. Like a figure from another era, Eric strolled about Wall Street, making formal courtesy calls on banks. He advised Jewish immigrants and German businessmen interested in establishing contacts in the American market. Eric was a bright man, but more conventional in his thinking than Siegmund, who responded to innovation with enthusiasm.

With his life disrupted, first by the Nazis, then by the war, Eric found himself an eligible, footloose bachelor in his mid-forties. After living with Frieda, he took a small apartment in a brownstone on East 52nd Street. Max and Alice wanted Eric to make the sort of match that would have been suitable in Imperial Germany, but that seemed anachronistic in postwar New York. During one of Eric's leaves in 1945, Alice invited to tea a young lady named Dorothea Thorsch, then working for the Dutch Red Cross. She greatly admired Eric in his spanking khaki uniform and he immediately saw her as a prospective wife.

Tall, slim, with an aristocratic manner, Dorothea came from an eminent Austrian banking family that had been on good terms with the Warburgs. Her father, Alphons Thorsch, had headed a private bank second in prestige in Vienna only to that of the Rothschilds. Dorothea had grown up in an opulent mansion with frescoed ceilings. When Eric met her, she was saddened by the recent loss of her father. To cheer her up, he invited her on a ski trip to New Hampshire with his friends Lloyd and Ellen Garrison. After the dark war years, Eric seemed like pure sunlight to her. "He was a person who was unable to hate," she said. "He was very constructive—always seeing the positive in life."[2] With Eric's long history as a ladies' man, Max and Alice pressed him to wrap things up quickly. On Valentine's Day 1946, the couple were married after an eighteen-day engagement. At first, they shared Eric's one-bedroom apartment, with its convertible sofa and wobbly bookshelves—a steep descent from Kösterberg. As they added three children—Max, Marie, and Erica—Frieda invited them to live at Woodlands at Hunt Cottage, a Colonial frame house that dated from before the American Revolution.

Dorothea came alive with Eric (although she had to cope with the captious Alice) but she had signed on for a stranger destiny than she knew. Eric harbored nostalgia for Hamburg, while Dorothea, as both a practical and emotional matter, never wished to see Austria or Germany again. Scenting trouble, she and her parents had left Vienna for Switzerland in February 1938. Following the *Anschluss*, the Nazis ransacked the Thorsch household; a haughty officer told the servants, "Please tell the lady of the house that she has very good taste."[3] Noticing empty jewel boxes, the soldiers threatened the housekeeper with a concentration camp if she didn't disclose the whereabouts of the jewels. Under duress, the woman admitted that Dorothea's sister, Eva, had removed them. Eva was arrested and thrown into a tiny cell with five drugged people. For three weeks, she listened to shrieking people being tortured upstairs before the Thorsch family obtained her release through bribes. When Eva's train arrived at the Swiss border, Dorothea saw her sister seated at one window and instantly realized from her blank expression that she was permanently scarred. The Thorsch family ended up on property they owned on Canada's west coast.

Dorothea never liked Brinckmann, but felt guilty about an episode that occurred soon after she and Eric moved to Hunt Cottage. The stocky Brinckmann visited in an outfit that Dorothea found tasteless: knickerbockers, a yellow pullover, and suspenders. At one point, he took her aside and asked if she would like to return to Germany. "Not at all," she said in horror. "I don't want to go back to your country when you're starving."[4] Dorothea thought that the canny Brinckmann interpreted this as a sign that Eric would never return to Germany. Such hints may have given free rein to forbidden fantasies that had secretly flitted through Brinckmann's mind. Very upset by Dorothea's remark, Eric told her afterward that she had ruined everything. It seems unlikely that Dorothea's comment had the impact she imagined, but the episode certainly revealed Eric's early inclination to return to Germany and, equally, Dorothea's settled aversion to doing so.

As an old-fashioned merchant banker, Eric didn't want to have responsibility for a Hamburg firm while residing in New York. Germany seemed neither habitable nor profitable. When Brinckmann urged restoration of the M. M. Warburg name in 1946, Eric, hesitant to open old wounds, refused.[5] That year, scattered anti-Semitic outbreaks occurred in Germany, including cemetery desecrations, as some Germans again pounced on the Jews as the authors of all their misery. Scavenging for food and shelter, ordinary Germans weren't preoccupied by the Holocaust and didn't particularly care to be reminded of such unpleasantness. In July 1946, forty Jews were killed in pogroms in Poland.

As innocent beneficiary of a historical accident, Brinckmann stood in an odd position. The 1938 Aryanization had given this Turkish immigrant entrée to the German establishment. After the war, he acquired sudden prominence as the senior partner of a major private bank. The man the Warburgs once nicknamed "Our Aryan" hadn't stolen the bank or tried to keep it unfairly and he had discharged his duty faithfully in 1945. Henceforth, he could feel he had done the right thing and indulge the tempting daydream that temporary stewardship might turn into permanent control. In future years, the Brinckmanns and the Warburgs would be quick to spy hypocrisy in each other's position. When the bank didn't seem profitable in the first postwar years, Brinckmann volunteered to return it. As business picked up, he changed his mind. Eric would be accused of the same thing in reverse.

Not only did Eric's New York business languish but he was strapped with heavy responsibility. In his will, Max had divided his estate into six equal parts—two for Eric and one apiece for his four daughters. In exchange for the extra share, Eric assumed responsibility for his sisters. Gisela and Lola were settled comfortably enough, but Anita and Renate were not and Eric worried about their financial predicament. As Siegmund noted after a 1947 trip to New York, "I find Eric rather aged and one has the feeling that he is rather worried about lots of things."[6]

After the armistice, nobody suspected that Germany would rise again from the ashes or that an economic miracle would shortly revitalize German business. In 1946, Brinckmann, Wirtz posted a small loss but then began to boom. Private cars once again sprouted in Hamburg alongside military jeeps. It must have incensed Eric that while E. M. Warburg & Co. had a payroll with a dozen employees, Brinckmann, Wirtz—the ancestral Warburg bank—had well over a hundred. And a spirit of restitution, spiritual no less than financial, was suddenly in the air. In 1947, the Hamburg Senate renamed a street in the family's old lakeside neighborhood Warburgstrasse. Eric's return trips to Hamburg lengthened. By 1947 local firms prepared to resume import-export business forbidden by the Trading with the Enemy Act. In April, an advisory council in the British zone drafted a bill for restitution to Jewish victims of the Nazis. Hounded out in the 1930s, Jewish businessmen began to return to Germany to negotiate the restoration of shares in their old firms.

After the 1946 flaps over Brandeis, Goldschmidt and the christening of S. G. Warburg & Co., one might have thought Eric and Siegmund would drift apart, but they were bound by common family problems. They had to collaborate to recover Warburg money invested in tea and rubber plantations in the Dutch East Indies. These Dutch colonial interests had become "enemy property" after Germany invaded Holland, and it took the Warburgs years to retrieve their money from the Indonesian government.[7] Eric and Siegmund were like quarreling convicts in an old prison melodrama, who find themselves chained together at the ankles after their escape. On a psychological level, each had something the other wanted. Eric admired Siegmund's dark, magnetic intelligence, his daring and decision. Siegmund must have envied Eric his light, spontaneous charm and social ease, not to mention his comfortable childhood. Fate had lashed them together in an intricate love-hate relationship.

The battle over the Hamburg bank would, at first, cause them to join forces. In retrospect, it seems amusing that Eric should have invited Siegmund into the fray. Eric wanted Brinckmann to restore a 30 percent share of the bank to the Warburgs and he needed Siegmund's steely will to toughen his own resolve. In early 1947, Siegmund met with Brinckmann in Zurich to thrash out a restitution plan for the former Warburg partners. At once, they entered a thicket of thorny legal, financial, and ethical questions. At this point, Siegmund still revered Brinckmann for his anti-Nazi attitude, telling Eric that "Rio" has "acquired an attitude of philosophical detachment and mature wisdom which is quite remarkable—Brinckmann more so than any other man I met in recent years."[8] Because the Warburgs viewed Brinckmann as a savior, not a scourge, they were eager to strike a friendly agreement and not resort to pressure from occupation authorities.

In his talks with Siegmund, Brinckmann elaborated his own revisionist history and brazenly denied that the 1938 transfer had constituted a true Aryanization. Noting Max's brush with bankruptcy in 1931, he said the firm had mostly crumbled away (*abgebröckelt*) by 1938. When Siegmund replied that the old partners were never paid for goodwill, Brinckmann denied that the bank had any goodwill left in 1938 and claimed he had saved the remnants of a failed institution. He waved away the 150-year history of the firm as a petty matter of no account. Touting his own contribution, Brinckmann suggested a 10 percent instead of a 30 percent restitution. Siegmund was tactful but firm. "I said that whilst he and Wirtz had without any doubt been motivated by the highest considerations at the time of the Aryanisation of the firm and even thereafter, the way in which the Aryanisation had taken place had been largely influenced by Nazis pressures and Nazi habits."[9] In an interesting aside, Brinckmann revealed that the bank derived important income from his directorships at Beiersdorf, HAPAG, and other seats he had assumed when the Warburgs were pushed off those boards in the 1930s.

Rudolf Brinckmann had been created as a Warburg front man in the Third Reich, but now, with his new, suddenly inflated sense of self-importance, he refused to admit it.

A caustic perspective on Brinckmann was provided by former Warburg partner Ernst Spiegelberg, now working for Siegmund in New York. Spiegelberg noted the remarkable fact that Brinckmann had not paid a single mark to take over one of Germany's leading private banks! What, he asked tartly, had happened to the one million reichsmarks in hidden reserves left behind with the old assets?[10] In Spiegelberg's view, Brinckmann had grown giddy and drunk with power from the praise Eric heaped upon him after the war. Arguing for speedy reparations, he told Fritz, "I don't believe that time will work to our advantage, if we wait. The human conscience tends to weaken rather than to sharpen."[11]

It had never been easy to deal with Brinckmann, who was a strong, cold, and humorless man. His very face was fearsome, with its dark, beetling eyebrows and sloping, slightly Oriental eyes. Brinckmann had fought so much with his partner, Wirtz, that the latter had threatened to quit. Thrifty, industrious, Brinckmann was a solid but unimaginative banker. One strongly suspects that an element of class revenge lay behind his obduracy. What old resentment lurked in the mind of this longtime Warburg retainer, who used to flirt with Max's daughters at parties? How could Brinckmann have respected Eric after watching Max bully and demean his poor son for many years?

After Wirtz's death, Eric knew that Brinckmann needed help and urged him to appoint another partner. Brinckmann chose Hermann Schilling, formerly of the Prussian State Bank in Berlin. Eric got wind of unfavorable news about Schilling, but by the time he told Brinckmann, it was too late, and in 1947 Schilling became the second partner. Schilling boasted of his involvement with the German Resistance. He had worked with Dr. Johannes von Popitz, the Prussian finance minister, who was arrested and executed after the 1944 plot against Hitler. Spiegelberg suspected this was a fig leaf for Schilling's earlier support of the Nazis.[12] But Eric credited Schilling's story and passed along the latter's memo on the July 20 bomb plot to Allen Dulles for his book on the German Resistance.[13] Schilling was a very dynamic but difficult man, whom one employee likened to a Prussian thunderstorm.[14] His advent greatly complicated matters, for he emerged as an implacable foe of Eric's return to the firm.

In May 1948, the British military government in Hamburg announced a restitution law for the recovery of stolen Jewish property. A month later Economics Minister Ludwig Erhard replaced the old reichsmark with the stable deutschmark. This currency reform ended the black market, triggering an economic boom that doubled the gross national product in a year and wiped away German gloom. The stage was set for a robust revival, as well as for the final showdown between Brinckmann and the Warburgs.

While Fritz wanted the British authorities to prod Brinckmann into restoring the old M. M. Warburg name, Eric and Siegmund preferred a gentlemanly approach.[15] Siegmund even allayed suspicions about Brinckmann raised by Britain's Trading with the Enemy Branch, which investigated Brinckmann's wartime takeover of Warburg & Co. in Amsterdam. Siegmund told British authorities that "Brinckmann had always been an extremely loyal and straight character, that he had been consistently anti-Nazi, and that as far as Nazi pressures had allowed him he had been considerate and faithful to the various members of the Warburg family."[16] Siegmund and Eric assisted Brinckmann in reactivating many foreign contacts for the bank.

The Warburgs so trusted Brinckmann that when they sat down to work out a restitution deal in 1949, Eric didn't consult a lawyer or tax adviser. Rather, negotiating for himself, Fritz, Siegmund, and Spiegelberg, he treated Brinckmann as an honorable man. Under the final agreement, the Warburg group got 25 percent of the firm and eighty thousand deutsche marks in reparations, settling claims under the new law and compensating the Warburgs for goodwill and hidden reserves. (Siegmund put his portion straight into S. G. Warburg & Co.) The old partners also received a critical option: They could increase their stake to a controlling 50 percent during a five-year period, starting October 1, 1948.[17] Significantly, the Warburg group didn't have the money to exercise the 50 percent option, which would have averted the whole marathon battle that followed. Eric made two other extremely damaging mistakes. He didn't insist upon the name change as part of the restitution package and didn't ensure that he could someday return as a general partner.

With E. M. Warburg & Co. as its New York representative, Brinckmann, Wirtz became the first German bank to restore an American connection—no small matter in a reawakening Germany hungry for raw materials. Because Volkswagen needed Pennsylvania coal to operate, it became the bank's number one client—even as Jews worldwide shunned its products. For all of Brinckmann's overweening vanity, few foreign banks knew the Brinckmann, Wirtz name and the staff constantly had to explain that they were the old M. M. Warburg in disguise.[18]

In the early postwar years, the new German democracy was still fragile. Sometimes in Hamburg the Soviet Army seemed just over the hill. When Brinckmann and Schilling grew alarmed during the grim winter of the 1948–1949 Berlin Blockade, Eric advised them to imitate wealthy Germans and purchase a fully-stocked, seaworthy ship for a quick getaway in case of trouble. In a Hamburg canal, Eric's old pal, Wolfgang Rittmeister, found a rusting hulk called the *Atalanta*, which had been damaged by Soviet bombs in the Baltic. The bank bought and refurbished the three-masted schooner, which became one of the first German yachts seen in England after the war. It was later used not to evacuate employees, but to entertain hundreds of prominent guests, including Chancellor Helmut Schmidt.[19]

With the restitution law, the Warburgs found themselves reliving unpleasant events, including the rancorous battles with Friedrich Flick from the 1930s. Instead of resisting reparations for Lübeck Blast Furnace, Flick saw advantages in cooperation. He needed money to comply with a new law passed for conversion of the iron and steel industry. Through his associate, Alfred Rhode, Flick proposed to Spiegelberg that the Warburgs and the Hahns might want to pump additional capital into his firm in exchange for restoration of their shares. Spiegelberg, in turn, proposed that Flick might wish to revive the dormant account of Lübeck Blast Furnace at Brinckmann, Wirtz.[20] Indeed, in 1950 Brinckmann, Wirtz floated a large bond issue to help Flick modernize the iron and steel operations of his Maximilianshütte, creating a curious community of interest between persecuted Jewish bankers and a notorious convicted war criminal.

To regain their lost place in the world, Eric and Siegmund found themselves in a paradoxical position: They possessed a competitive advantage mostly through their German connections. On postwar trips to Germany, they saw the economic miracle taking shape long before their Anglo-American competitors. They retained links with many German businessmen who were only too eager to tap Warburg money and assuage their residual guilt at the same time.

Not having lost family members in the Holocaust, the Warburgs didn't have insuperable mental obstacles about doing business with Germany. When news of the death camps first reached London, Siegmund attended a solidarity service at a synagogue—the only time he went in those years—but he didn't suffer actual family losses. In 1945, a suicide wave swept London as Jewish families learned of lost relatives. At New Trading, Henry Grunfeld and Eric Korner had many relatives who had died. (Interestingly, both refused to demand postwar reparations, believing life too short for legal action.) A postwar uncle in the investment department, the Austrian Charles Sharp (born Karl Spitz), lost his mother's Hungarian relatives in the Holocaust and refused to go back to Austria. He never sought restitution for his old house in Vienna, which would have meant dealing with the Austrians. Another uncle, thin, gaunt, meticulous Ernest Thalmann, a former Berlin banker, also never returned to Germany.

Siegmund respected the reluctance of some uncles to visit postwar Germany, but felt no such scruples himself. As Charles Sharp recalled, "Siegmund Warburg had no qualms to travel to Germany after the war and to contact and be contacted by former personal and business friends. He would meet even those who had prominent positions under the Nazis, though he did so in the first place for business reasons."[21] Siegmund refurbished these contacts even as the provincial British banks dozed. He envisioned London as the hub of a new United States of Europe—a visionary position that won him few plaudits at the time. "All I got was a shaking of heads from such people as Mr. Anthony Eden, who was a friend of mine, and Ernest Bevin, who was not a friend of mine," Siegmund said.[22]

With his strong Swabian accent, Siegmund remained very German in his thoroughness, attention to detail, sense of duty, and hard work. His desire to reestablish the Warburg name in Germany exercised a romantic claim on his imagination. He regarded Germany as the land of Goethe and Heine as well as a breeding ground for Hitler and Göring. Where Henry Grunfeld disliked the subservience and exaggerated respect for authority common in German banks, Siegmund seemed more forgiving. A few years after the war, he attended an alumni reunion at his old *Gymnasium* and enjoyed returning to the Swabian Alps of his boyhood where he still felt "at home."[23] After the war, Uhenfels was broken up, its little castle bought by a Stuttgart jeweler and its house and farm taken over by the local municipality. Soviet prisoners of war had been dumped in the burial grove of Siegmund's father and he had the bodies removed. Siegmund always retained a distinct partiality for southern Germany and faulted Bismarck for having forged a German Reich. From 1949 to 1959, Siegmund's friend and old Swabian neighbor, Theodor Heuss, was West German president.

Siegmund didn't believe in collective guilt, whether of Germans, Bolsheviks, or Jews, and grew furious at loose talk that all Germans were Nazis. He grew irate with one Kuhn, Loeb partner who, as he said, "used to make every single German responsible for every crime committed under the Hitler regime!"[24] Like Eric, Siegmund tended to blame the cowardice of the German middle class for Nazism. "Siegmund knew that not all Germans were Nazis because he knew many minor aristocrats who were against Hitler," said his friend Dr. Carl H. Goldman.[25]

In December 1949, Siegmund made his first trip back to Hamburg, having recuperated from a small operation in Germany that summer. From the affecting moment when his train crossed the Elbe bridge, he marveled at how well the city had survived, how fast it was being rebuilt. Staying at his old haunt, the Hotel Atlantic, he sauntered through the streets nostalgically, poking his head into bookstores, and had poignant reunions at Brinckmann, Wirtz. As he wrote Uncle Fritz, in Germany "the mixture of good and bad and of light and shade has at all times been great and is to-day greater still."[26] When he and Eric dined at their favorite restaurant, the Ehmcke, sitting beneath portraits of Bismarck and Moltke, Siegmund discerned at once that Eric was back in his element. "I was rather struck to find him so much happier in Hamburg than at any of the other places where I had met him during the last few years."[27]

For other Warburgs, the idea of visiting Germany was a vexed matter. Most stayed away for years. Carola wouldn't set foot there, and Gerald wouldn't play his cello there. Of course, the family couldn't resist the odd twinge of sentimentality. From the vantage point of postwar exile, the memory of Kösterberg had an unreal shimmer. After the war, Eric's sister Anita helped to organize a search bureau in London under the aegis of the British Red Cross. Heading a staff of sixty people, she reunited thirty thousand stateless families in central Europe. After her divorce from Max Wolf, she would end up in New York, a single woman, taking care of Alice and starting again, working in the gift department of a department store and in a Madison Avenue specialty shop.

When she returned to Kösterberg right after the war, Anita felt like a ghost, an intruder. As she drove up the drive, a new tenant, the director of the Hamburg museum, the Kunsthalle, shouted from upstairs, "Please remove the car. We don't allow people to park their cars here."[28] Things were soon straightened out and there were tearful reunions. But Anita could never forget the so-called friends who didn't know the Warburgs after 1933 or only entered the bank by the side entrance. And there were still painful surprises to reckon with. When Anita entered the military officers club in Hamburg, she discovered vases and a Roman fountain swiped from Kösterberg by Nazi brass, which she had restored to the estate.

In 1949, Gisi got a letter from her former nanny and wept at the thought that she would never see her again. Her husband, Charles Wyzanski, suggested that she return to Hamburg, not to see Germany, but to see her nanny. Upon arriving, Gisi was met by the nanny and the old Warburg chauffeur, and they all burst out crying together. Driving through a city still clogged with rubble, they went to the Brinckmann, Wirtz building where the veteran employees showered Gisi with two dozen red roses.[29] But she felt that postwar Hamburg was just the simulacrum of a dear place she had once known. She often talked of the Warburg love affair with Germany and likened their disappointment to the excruciating pain of being spurned by one's lover.[30]

Instead of selling or renting the large Kösterberg houses of Max and Fritz, Eric decided to donate them for charity. In August 1949, Eric took Baroness Louise Sophie Knigge, vice-president of the German Red Cross, to see the two houses, which she thought perfect for meetings and a new project for mothers with small children. To win the acquiescence of Fritz and Anna, Eric wanted to christen the place with a Swedish name, so it was called the Elsa Brändström House. Elsa Brändström, of course, was the daughter of a Swedish ambassador to the Soviet Union, who had been shocked by the savage treatment of POWs during the first world war and ended up a Florence Nightingale, saving tens of thousands of lives. When Hitler asked her to head the German Red Cross, she replied in one word: "Never." As a close friend of Fritz and Anna, she was the perfect person to be memorialized at Kösterberg.

Keeping open the option of returning to Germany, Eric set aside for his own use the original building, Noah's Ark. Already he was in the thick of efforts to rehabilitate Germany and bind it closely to the West. Along with Allen Dulles and Reinhold Niebuhr, he had formed the American Committee to Aid Survivors of the German Resistance. Countess Marion Dönhoff, a Prussian aristocrat who aided the Resistance and later became publisher of *Die Zeit*, helped to screen the recipients for CARE parcels. Eric lobbied for an American-German chamber of commerce to promote West German exports to America. Alarmed by a possible Soviet invasion, he suggested to Allen Dulles that the American government begin contingency planning for the creation of a German government-in-exile, should the worst come.[31]

Like other Warburgs, Eric was horrified by the Morgenthau Plan to deindustrialize Germany. Its intention was to eliminate Germany's capacity to make war, reducing it to a pastoral state. When a diluted version was adopted at war's end, Eric considered composing a polemic against it, much as Keynes had done with the reparations issue after Versailles. The plan enacted in 1946 went beyond aircraft and ammunition factories to encompass everything from synthetic oil to tractor plants.

In Hamburg, Eric saw, firsthand, the dismantling program being directed by the occupation government. German shipyards could only repair ships, not build them, and this threatened the city's future as a maritime center. As a former builder of U-boats, Blohm & Voss was a prime target for political retribution. In July 1949, occupation authorities began blowing up the cement slipways that had launched the gigantic HAPAG liners. Thousands of people lost their jobs, as dynamite explosions went on for sixty consecutive days. Newspaper photos showed a wilderness of broken cement slabs at the port. At a time of widespread unemployment, Hamburg's industrial base was being sabotaged, breeding resentment against the Allies and hobbling German recovery.

A few days after signing his August 1949 agreement with Brinckmann, Eric dined alone with John J. McCloy, the new American high commissioner for Germany, at his villa outside Frankfurt. A short, balding, affable man, McCloy enjoyed hobnobbing with the rich and powerful, and his career had long been intertwined with the Warburgs. His mother, a hairdresser, used to do Frieda's hair during summers at Bar Harbor. When McCloy joined the Cravath law firm in 1924, he performed legal work for Felix and Freddy at Kuhn, Loeb and for Paul at the International Acceptance Bank. Freddy often invited him to play tennis at Woodlands or ride at his horse farm in Virginia; he even helped persuade McCloy to head the World Bank in 1947.[32] Because he was so close to Freddy, Eric had known McCloy since the 1920s.

In the Jewish community, McCloy would remain a controversial figure because of his wartime record. As assistant secretary of war in 1943, he had opposed bombing raids against the railway lines that transported Jews to Auschwitz and other death camps, believing it more efficacious to pursue military targets and end the war quickly. It was also thought that any railway disruptions from bombing would only be temporary. Winston Churchill, who dissented vigorously from this view, was isolated on the issue. From misplaced fear that Jews would be killed, some Jewish groups had even concurred in the policy of not bombing the rail lines. Eric always supported McCloy on the issue and felt later attacks on him were malicious and unjustified.

McCloy was also taken to task for his lenient treatment of Nuremberg war criminals in 1951, most notably when he granted clemency to Alfried Krupp and eight other Krupp directors convicted for exploiting slave labor from the camps. McCloy thought the real culprit was the senile Gustav Krupp, not his playboy son Alfried, and said he had acted merely to bring the Krupp sentence in line with those of Friedrich Flick and I. G. Farben executives. Telford Taylor, the American chief prosecutor at Nuremberg, vigorously disputed that Alfried was just a junior figure. At moments, McCloy was also heroic to Jewish groups. Responding to a personal appeal from Eddie Warburg and the Joint Distribution Committee, he passed a "General Claims Law" to compensate Nazi victims soon after his arrival in Germany.[33]

When he dined with McCloy in August 1949, Eric advocated West German participation in European defense and closer scrutiny of war crime judgments obtained by unfair interrogation. But the opinion that enraged McCloy was when Eric pleaded for an immediate halt to the dismantling program. In internal Washington debates, McCloy had given qualified support to the Morgenthau Plan. Now he told Eric that, in antiquity, defeated German tribes had to smash their swords and spears. Eric nimbly replied that they weren't talking about swords but plowshares—machines that could be applied to peaceful purposes. If McCloy persisted with dismantling, Eric warned, it would poison German relations with the Allies, foster nationalism, and possibly drive Germany toward Communism.[34] McCloy was so irate that he nearly asked Eric to leave the room. By the end of the dinner, however, McCloy had cooled off and asked Eric to produce a list of plants he might save from demolition. He gave Eric forty-eight hours to provide names.

On August 27, Eric addressed a letter to McCloy containing the requested list. To rally the support of German unions and politicians, Eric proposed that McCloy save ten steel, synthetic gas, and synthetic rubber plants. He never published the list of firms, but his papers show that they included the steel works of August Thyssen and the Krupp synthetic gas works.[35] McCloy managed to save these facilities.

This intervention with McCloy coincided with, and perhaps accelerated, a significant turn in American policy. When Eric's close friend, Marion Dönhoff, told the new chancellor, Konrad Adenauer, about Eric's talk with McCloy on dismantling, he simply couldn't believe it.[36] But by November, Adenauer had won agreement from U.S. Secretary of State Dean Acheson that dismantling would end in critical economic sectors, including certain forms of ship construction. Germany, in return, agreed to stay demilitarized and remain vigilant against any recurrence of Nazi thinking. Responding to cold war pressures, the Allies had decided to recruit their former enemies as their new friends. Adenauer would bring Germany into NATO and the European Community and firmly anchor his country to the West. As denazification gave way to amnesty, many personalities from the Third Reich were rehabilitated. Of 177 Nazis convicted at Nuremberg, only 12 were sentenced to death in the end.[37]

By urging Eric to move back to Hamburg, McCloy gave official sanction and high moral purpose to an agonizing personal decision. Eric thought he had shown McCloy and his wife, Ellen, that it was dangerous to impute guilt to all Germans and that even prominent Jews could advocate forgiveness toward Germany. It was a view that would make Eric controversial in the Jewish community. In a letter to McCloy decades later, Eric recalled, "When you came to Germany as High Commissioner, you and Ellen, after those dreadful years of the Nazi rule, the Holocaust, soon found out that there was also another Germany, the brave forces of the internal German resistance, many of whom had given their lives in the fight against the tyranny."[38]

By the late 1940s, Eric's German identity was again welling up from the depths. He was reverting to an older and wiser version of the debonair young man he had been before the Third Reich, the Holocaust, and the world war. The more he visited Germany, the more time seemed to rub away the superficial American persona, revealing underneath the youth who had so admired the German military and aristocracy. He was moving forward, as it were, into the past.

Jimmy Warburg.
(Warburg family, Hamburg)

Itinerant Preacher

Jimmy Warburg didn't have to deal with the apocalyptic upheavals experienced by his cousins Eric and Siegmund, but he had suffered his own political exile. Having started out in the upper reaches of Washington and Wall Street, he had operated in the world of the possible and doable. He tried on careers the way other men tried on suits, but succeeded too quickly and then blundered badly. He lacked patience for the sordid compromises of politics. Too headstrong and mercurial to fit into any establishment, he described himself to a friend as "one whose function in life seems to be to swim upstream against the currents of prevailing prejudice and opinion."[1]

In the postwar years, a messianic streak surfaced in Jimmy as he shifted into a fringe political world. Reversing the customary course of things, with age he became a liberal dreamer who advocated idealistic causes. In a rite of self-purification, he cut himself off from the banking world and resigned from corporate boards. He stayed on the Polaroid board, however, making a mint from Edwin H. Land's invention of instant photography for black-and-white and then for color film. Jimmy said his role at Polaroid was to shoot down the more impractical ideas that streamed from Land's fertile mind.

Freed from financial worry by Polaroid and several other shrewd investments, Jimmy could indulge his preferred maverick role of producing unsparing, irreverent opinions that would provoke and even scandalize Washington. He became a freelance crusader, a wandering troubadour of Democratic liberalism, an "itinerant preacher" of a new foreign policy, as he told Adlai Stevenson.[2] When Jimmy won the Gandhi Peace Prize in 1962, Stevenson would hail him as a "public citizen extraordinary" who worked "in the great tradition of the 18th-century pamphleteers. . . ."[3] Jimmy published reams of policy tracts, set a record by publishing more than fifty letters in *The New York Times* after 1949, spoke at rallies, organized protests, and testified at congressional hearings. By the end, he would publish more than thirty books, as if he were a solo movement, a one-man ministry of state. For the World Federalists, he crisscrossed America, preaching free trade and nuclear disarmament enforced by a global police. For Jimmy, who no longer had to answer to anybody, it was an ideal life.

He seemed perennially out of step with his time. First ostracized by Wall Street for his New Deal flirtation, he was then ostracized by the New Deal for reverting to Wall Street dogma. Now his liberal side emerged just as America slid into the somnolent conservatism of the late 1940s and 1950s. As a dissident and gadfly, he kept an uneasy relationship with friends who still prowled the halls of power. Clinging to the manners of the Washington insider, Jimmy wanted to have it both ways—to issue controversial opinions yet socialize with the mighty. He had a suave, insouciant way of pressing ideas upon friends such as Dean Acheson, but they backed off from him as too combative and independent and felt threatened by his alarmist, often messianic views.

Jimmy was estranged from most Warburgs and regarded the Friedaflix clan as particularly shallow. His tensely competitive relationship with sister Bettina worsened when Jimmy saddled her with responsibility for Nina, who often seemed depressed in her last years. The wartime absences took a toll on Jimmy's childless marriage to the independent-minded Phyllis Baldwin. For twelve years, she had cared for his children, but she wanted to be more than Mrs. James P. Warburg. When the marriage ended, Jimmy wondered whether he was too self-sufficient ever to be happily married.

After two failed marriages and an explosively uneven career, Jimmy, fifty-two, tried to start afresh. In 1947, he was scouting about for a new secretary when his daughter, Kay, suggested a twenty-five-year-old friend named Joan Melber, who had graduated from Simmons College and worked for a radio commentator. In Joan, Jimmy found the sort of bottomless adoration only an admiring younger woman can bestow. In September 1948, they got married by a minister in Bronxville and spent part of their honeymoon at the first World Federalist conference in Luxembourg. With no Warburgs left in Hamburg, they skipped Germany, but visited Fritz and Anna Beata in Stockholm.

Though twice Joan's age, Jimmy didn't think it fair to deprive her of children, and they had two sons and two daughters. Still trying to escape his past, Jimmy didn't tell the new set of small children about the previous ones until it came out by accident—an extremely painful revelation for all concerned. The ever-censorious Bettina chided her brother for being an overly strict father, preoccupied with his sons. "It was he who set the standards for the children and constantly set them too high, making himself the ultimate authority, which they resented but could not openly oppose."[4] To mark a final break with his rambunctious early life, Jimmy moved full-time to Connecticut around 1950. He turned the town house on East Seventieth Street, which had witnessed the glamorous Gershwin parties, into a small apartment house, keeping the top floor as his pied-à-terre. He was finally an authentic family man.

—

Even as he parted company with other Warburgs, Jimmy evinced a very Warburgian concern for Germany. Toward the end of the war, he issued a scathing critique of the Morgenthau Plan and opposed the partition of Germany, its surrender of eastern territory, or anything that suggested a victor's peace. Soon after the war, he spent three months in the occupation zones, writing a series of articles for the *Chicago Sun* syndicate. At the time, civilians couldn't travel in Germany, and Jimmy enlisted the aid of John J. McCloy and Dean Acheson, who favored the project. The series established him as a leading voice on Germany and when he returned Edward R. Murrow telephoned and invited him to do a half-hour CBS radio broadcast on the subject.

In Germany, Jimmy was shocked by the economic devastation. "Everywhere, the people had a gray, haunted look. Most were living on a near-starvation diet."[5] He was appalled by the general evasion of responsibility for Hitler and found virtually no acknowledgment of guilt. "The Germans were sorry for themselves and seemed to feel that they had been in no way responsible for what the Nazi regime had done."[6] People kept telling Jimmy, "But I was only a little man. What could I do?"[7] The Germans cast themselves as innocent victims, dwelling on Allied raids against them instead of their bombing of London, Coventry, Rotterdam, and Warsaw. In a 1946 study by the U.S. Military Government in Germany, more than a third of Germans polled still styled themselves a superior race and thought Hitler's treatment of the Jews justified.[8] A few years later, Jimmy was thunderstruck when Adenauer confessed to the Bundestag that 134 of 383 employees in his Foreign Ministry had formerly belonged to the Nazi party.[9]

While alert to persisting Nazi tendencies, Jimmy also produced a balanced analysis of German society at a time when objectivity was still extremely difficult. Like Siegmund and Eric, he deplored any wholesale condemnation of

Germans. "Is it correct to say that militarism, brutality, and aggression flow in the bloodstream of a German 'race'?" For Jimmy, such racial theorizing smacked of Hitlerism. He thought hate and authoritarianism latent in all political cultures. In Germany they had been fed by an exaggerated nationalism and unquestioning obedience to authority. He shared Eric's view that Germans should judge themselves and that the occupation should be brief. Yet he also wanted to see large numbers of Nazis, SS, and Gestapo members rounded up and prosecuted as war criminals and was irate at the squalid political compromise entailed in pardoning high-ranking Nazis.

As often in the past, Jimmy ended up frustrated in his prescriptions for postwar Germany. In October 1949, the Soviets created the German Democratic Republic and the next year President Harry S Truman called for rearming West Germany and incorporating it into NATO. Jimmy managed to work out a position on Germany that infuriated just about everybody. He angered some by supporting a reunified Germany and others by arguing that Germany should remain neutral and unarmed instead of being drawn into NATO. He won Einstein's support for a neutral, demilitarized Germany. Where Jimmy had hoped that his birthplace would be purged of evil elements and provide a laboratory for social change, he saw his fond dreams falling victim to anti-Communist hysteria in America, as cold war imperatives superseded justice. As he told Milton Eisenhower, "I have been a persistent and outspoken, though rather lonely critic of a policy which has led . . . to the dangerous business of making a wholly unregenerate and unreliable West Germany the keystone in the arch of Western defense."[10]

Throughout the 1950s, Jimmy remained a lonely soldier of lost causes as he proselytized for an alternative foreign policy. He was outraged by the cold war zealotry that led to witch-hunting campaigns against his friend Joseph Barnes and others. Starting with the 1952 presidential campaign, Jimmy was a foreign-policy adviser and speechwriter to Adlai Stevenson. He kept trying to get Stevenson to attack cold war shibboleths and the bipartisan foreign-policy consensus of the 1950s. Though Stevenson admired Jimmy and enjoyed his comic rhymed couplets, he generally ducked his controversial advice and focused on domestic issues. By 1954, Jimmy was suffering from a heart condition and angina and gave up tennis and other strenuous activities, although he worked for Stevenson again in the 1956 campaign. As he cranked out endless books and position papers and issued his urgent appeals to reason, he remained peripheral to the real political action of the decade. Jimmy had ended up the way he was destined to: as a king without a court.

—

Unlike Jimmy, Eric thought a neutral Germany would simply invite Soviet domination of the country. The antithesis of his cousin, Eric was a consummate insider, who enjoyed attending meetings of the Council on Foreign Relations and other elite organizations. In the early 1950s, he remained an Air Force Intelligence Reserve officer, lecturing at the CIA and training a future generation of interrogators.

Despite his fears of Soviet intentions, Eric increasingly leaned to going back to Hamburg. In 1951, he competed with Siegmund for a Kuhn, Loeb partnership and lost out. Aside from Siegmund's superior talents, Kuhn, Loeb preferred his British connections to Eric's German ones. Because he was so close to the second-richest partner, Freddy Warburg, Eric was crestfallen that he had still lost out in the competition. The setback made him face squarely the lackluster performance of E. M. Warburg & Co. and he turned his attention more to Hamburg. Starting in 1952, Eric and Dorothea began spending summers at Kösterberg with their three children.

Outwardly respectful to Brinckmann—Eric called him Senior—Siegmund and Eric saw a new vanity emerging in the former office manager. In June 1950, with Warburg help, Brinckmann was named to the management advisory board of the Bank for International Settlements. Suddenly fancying himself a financial statesman, Brinckmann enjoyed strutting about at international monetary conferences and he traveled so much that Eric, behind his back, dubbed him John Foster Brinckmann. Brinckmann discovered a new sense of self-importance, as his identity became entangled with the Brinckmann, Wirtz name.

As Eric began spending part of the year in Germany, Siegmund warned him against sharing a partnership with the autocratic Brinckmann, whose one-quarter stake matched that of the combined Warburg group. Siegmund no longer saw Brinckmann as a brave anti-Nazi, but as a pompous, vain, pig-headed man. As he told Eric, "During the last few years, I've found Brinckmann extraordinarily arrogant and egotistical, but during my last discussion in Hamburg I found that his arrogance and his egotism had gradually reached a point where they are scarcely bearable any longer."[11] Since Brinckmann knew Eric would shrink from working in a bank named Brinckmann, Wirtz, the issue of Eric's return elevated the touchy name question to the top of the agenda.

Eric indeed felt demeaned working in a bank that still had the Aryanized name. No less romantic than Siegmund, Eric would convert restoration of the M. M. Warburg name into a sacred crusade. As the Warburgs began to challenge the legitimacy of the Aryanized name, Brinckmann must have felt rudely cheated of his miraculous gift. In the rubble of 1945, Eric had turned down his offer to return the bank. Now, with the German economic miracle under way, Eric was back on his doorstep. Brinckmann decided that an ethical statute of limitations had elapsed, that he now had a fair moral claim to the business, a view upheld by several shareholders, who insisted that

Brinckmann oppose any further concessions to the Warburgs.[12] He was spared the need to wage the battle alone when his new partner, Hermann Schilling, developed a fanatical opposition to Eric's return. This allowed Brinckmann to pose as the Warburg savior, a statesman above the hurly-burly, while Schilling did the dirty work.

More than Siegmund, Eric dreaded unpleasantness. Both in business and society, he excelled in persuasion, not confrontation. To win over Schilling, he drew up a memo, outlining his position. Then he went to discuss it in a friendly manner with Schilling, who was vacationing in Bad Kissingen. During their talk, Eric noted that Hermann Abs was settling the German foreign debt in London, which would set the stage for an economic rebound. It seemed a fitting moment to restore the M. M. Warburg name, Eric said. Expressing no sharp dissent, Schilling asked for time to reflect upon the memo.

What Schilling did next scandalized Eric. Without informing Eric or Brinckmann, he took the memo and convened a secret meeting of the bank's shareholders—at least, those upset by Eric's prospective return. On October 20, 1952, this rump group circulated, sub rosa, a manifesto that reached Eric in a roundabout manner. The document must have reawakened Eric's every unspoken anxiety about latent anti-Semitism in Germany. It stated bluntly that in earlier years, when the shareholders wanted the Warburg name, the Warburgs had refused. Now, it continued, "it seems quite doubtful whether the old name still represents 'goodwill' and the Warburg family therefore must expect that their business associates won't make further sacrifices."[13] Suddenly, the Brinckmann name was a sterling asset, the Warburg name a dreadful liability. "Today, the bank, under its current name, has achieved worldwide prestige through the tireless efforts of its partners."[14]

What made this memo so offensive was its palpably anti-Semitic flavor. At moments, it had the gloating, sniggering tone of the most vicious *Der Stürmer* diatribes. "For the limited partners, the achievements to date have already meant a considerable sacrifice—*unlike for the Warburg family*—in terms of the heavy damage to their wealth that they have already suffered during the war and its aftermath."[15] When he read this, Eric told Brinckmann, in horror, that the author apparently didn't know that the Nazis had stolen the Warburg money and that they had no wealth left to suffer wartime damages. He caught the nauseating whiff of Nazism. Referring to the phrase "unlike for the Warburg family," he said that the author "apparently believes that he either still lives in the Third Reich, where such a comment seemed necessary and appropriate, or else he still has such an attitude today."[16] Having recently arranged a very large line of credit for Brinckmann, Wirtz with N. M. Rothschild in London, Eric keenly felt the ingratitude of this mutiny.

Brinckmann maintained innocence of the secret meeting and said that he personally favored restoring the name—but of course, he added helplessly, his hands were tied. Had he covertly instigated Schilling and his cabal? Siegmund and Spiegelberg thought Brinckmann played a mischievous game, while Eric and Fritz reserved their anger for Schilling and tended to exonerate "Rio." As Eric told Fritz, "as to loyalty, good will, and a feeling for tradition, in spite of all the failings familiar to us, there can be no doubt about Rio."[17] Brinckmann reminded Eric that he had offered to restore the name in 1945, but that Max had found the moment inauspicious.[18] Brinckmann also warned that if he ever left the bank, it would be lost to the Warburgs forever.[19] In this way, Brinckmann kept suggesting that he was saving the Warburgs from a more ignominious fate.

The October 20, 1952, revolt was the opening shot of a protracted battle between the Warburgs and the shareholders from the "friendly" 1938 Aryanization. It would look a lot less friendly in retrospect as things began to get bloody. Fritz despised Schilling, whom he thought ignorant of the firm's venerable history. Schilling warned Fritz that if he were forced out of the firm, it would cost several million marks.[20] Having thus far refrained from legal pressure, Eric had a lawyer explore measures to force restoration of the old name.[21] Taking off the kid gloves, in turn, Schilling told this lawyer that unless Eric left Hamburg right away, he would summon a shareholders' meeting, precipitate a break with the Warburgs, and buy them out.[22] Doubtless enjoying this circus, Brinckmann threw up his hands with Eric, saying he had tried, in vain, to reason with Schilling.[23] Schilling kept saying he wouldn't resign or let Eric back into the firm.[24] He grew so venomous that the Warburgs wondered whether Eric, even in victory, could ever share the same office with this foe. The revolt scuttled a tentative agreement to restore the M. M. Warburg name.

Brinckmann also squabbled with Schilling, whom he used to block the Warburgs, while using the Warburgs to block Schilling. In this mad, surreal fracas of warring personalities, Brinckmann wouldn't let the Warburgs speak directly to the bank's shareholders, portraying the latter "as the black men, while in reality he himself was the most petty of them all," Ernst Spiegelberg noted. "And now his true nature and the loyalty he wears for show toward the Warburgs is of the greatest help to him in his previously launched battle against Schilling."[25] Meanwhile, Spiegelberg thought Brinckmann, who had two sons, was hatching plans to erect his own banking dynasty on the ruins of the Warburg fortune.[26]

Schilling's wrath and Brinckmann's guile encouraged Eric to invite Siegmund deeper into the melee. It would be another instance of Eric inviting Siegmund into a situation and then regretting it. Siegmund's post-restitution stake in the Hamburg bank was small: 9 percent of the one-quarter Warburg share versus 56 percent for Eric and Max's estate and 25 percent for Fritz. Nonetheless, Siegmund would henceforth play a role out of proportion to his investment. Eric revered his cousin's ability. He needed the tactical genius of Siegmund, who was a match for the toughest and craftiest adversary. While Eric was often indecisive, Siegmund had the settled convictions that could sustain him through long, rough battles. When it came to Warburg family honor, Eric and Siegmund were of a piece. Later on, *Time* magazine contrasted the two but noted their common desire: to "restore all the past glory to a many-faceted clan. . . ."[27] After the humiliating October 20 revolt, Siegmund displayed genuine compassion for his embattled Mittelweg relatives. "These last few weeks must have been absolute hell, particularly for you and Eric," he wrote to Fritz.[28]

The problem with tapping Siegmund's talents was that it encouraged his designs on the Hamburg firm. However often he categorically denied any wish to take over Brinckmann, Wirtz, Eric never trusted him. Even as they fought Brinckmann and Schilling, Eric never knew whether Siegmund was helping him or manipulating him as a cat's-paw. If he and Siegmund pushed Brinckmann aside, would Siegmund then push him aside? Siegmund's associates today confess that Siegmund indeed saw Brinckmann, Wirtz as a superb potential vehicle for his reentry into Germany—that Eric wasn't just paranoid. As one S. G. Warburg & Co. executive admitted, "If Siegmund and Eric had succeeded, Hamburg would have become effectively a subsidiary of London. The 'child' firm would have become father to the father." Eric and Siegmund might scorn each other, but in the last analysis they needed each other and didn't hesitate to use each other. Their alliance would exacerbate tensions in their relationship. Siegmund would feel that Eric hadn't acted with sufficient courage and decision, while Eric would feel that he had merely functioned as a tool in the hands of his overbearing cousin.

Adding another layer of complexity to this psychodrama was the fact that Siegmund trusted Schilling, while Eric trusted Brinckmann. The Warburgs warned Schilling that he shouldn't try to drive a wedge between them.[29] A disgusted Fritz thought the Warburgs should just sell out and walk away.[30] But the whole affair had now become a question of principle, something far beyond legal wrangling or commercial calculation. It came down to the effrontery of two people, Brinckmann and Schilling, who dared to elevate their real but short-lived achievements above the 150-year efforts of the Warburg family.

The fatal blow to the Warburg group was a sudden feud that erupted between Eric and Siegmund. In June 1953, Siegmund met with Schilling to mediate his dispute with Eric. Eric expected Siegmund to read the riot act to

Schilling, to probe his Third Reich behavior and demand justice for the Warburgs. Instead, Siegmund came away with a positive impression of Schilling and blamed the duplicitous Brinckmann.[31] Eric felt deeply betrayed by Siegmund's kid-glove approach. In a rage, he questioned Siegmund's motives in not abiding by their agreement. Siegmund, in turn, became angry and said he was only involved, not from any personal agenda, but from family sentiment. Siegmund always made much of the fact that Eric dealt too gingerly with the Hamburg situation, yet it was Eric in 1953 who favored a confrontational approach, while Siegmund urged tactical patience.

Had Siegmund acted in good faith or sabotaged a situation that would have put Eric back in control? We'll never know. What is certain is that Siegmund now refused to exercise the option, saying he no longer fit into the Warburg group and asking to withdraw from all matters related to Brinckmann, Wirtz & Co.[32] Disgusted by the whole rowdy spectacle, Fritz decided against exercising the option. And Eric lacked the money to do so alone. So the Warburgs let the 1953 deadline elapse without exercising their option to boost their stake to 50 percent, which would have ended the marathon feud. By squandering this opportunity, the Warburgs also strengthened Brinckmann, who could now savor their lack of internal cohesion.

—

As the German economy thrived, the Hamburg bank posted impressive profits. Visiting Germany in early 1954, Siegmund wondered at the "monstrous industriousness of the people," the tonic effect of low wages and tax incentives. Hugely attracted to the aggressive Deutsche Bank, he noted nonetheless that German businessmen automatically assumed he was allied with Brinckmann, Wirtz. So he couldn't drop a proprietary regard for the Hamburg bank.

Everywhere Siegmund heard that Schilling was the proficient, hard-working partner, while the vainglorious Brinckmann gallivanted about the world, neglecting business.[33] He kept warning Eric that instead of being fooled by Brinckmann's "sentimental words," they should hitch their fortunes to Schilling. Early on, Siegmund spotted Brinckmann's dynastic ambitions, noting that he wanted a partnership for his son Christian as a precondition for naming any additional partners.[34] Repeatedly warning him against Rio's obstinacy, Siegmund advised Eric against moving back to Hamburg and said it was easier to take the fortress from without than within.[35] The final member of the Warburg group, Ernst Spiegelberg, also warned Eric that he could never be happy working with Brinckmann in a place called Brinckmann, Wirtz & Co.[36]

Despite all these valid reservations, Eric yearned to return to Hamburg. His Wall Street business was sluggish while Hamburg was active. In 1954 he told

Brinckmann that he was willing to move back and become a full-time resident partner. But so long as Schilling remained, Eric couldn't implement his plan. Then, in September 1956, something unexpected happened: Schilling, weary of the long tussle with Brinckmann and Eric, decided to quit. So on October 1, 1956, Eric became a full-time partner in a firm still bearing the odious Brinckmann, Wirtz name. Brinckmann, shameless, told Eric that he should be grateful to be accepted back into the firm as a partner.[37] It is unclear whether Eric realized that Brinckmann despised him as both a person and banker.[38]

After his tiny Wall Street office, Eric felt at home again at the Ferdinand-strasse bank, with its mahogany wainscoting and brass doorknobs. He arrived early, worked late, and won back many old clients. He performed many acts of homage. Hanging family portraits and engravings on the walls, he wrote explanatory legends beneath each one. Nothing pleased him more than to give visitors historic tours of the bank and he became the repository of Warburg lore and legend. The marble stairwell at the entrance had a plaque listing employees who died in World War I. Eric was the sole employee to have fought on the Allied side in World War II. Soon after returning, he put up a plaque listing the six Jewish employees and one Resistance fighter murdered by the Nazis, as well as people who had died in prison camps or in air raids on Hamburg. There would be no tablet commemorating those employees who died as German soldiers.

From the outset, Eric suggested that the firm be renamed "Brinckmann, Warburg & Co." or "Warburg, Brinckmann & Co." In his glowering, moody style, Brinckmann bristled every time Eric broached the subject, saying the topic should be postponed to an appropriate moment. The bank, he claimed, would lose enough customers with Schilling's departure and couldn't risk a name change as well. Then he cited a possible loss of Arab business if the Jewish name were restored.[39] Then he said that the time for the name change had passed, that it should have been done within six to eight years after the war, if at all.[40]

After balking, Brinckmann accepted a third partner, Dr. Friedrich Priess, a former judge. Because of Brinckmann's intransigence on the name issue, Eric brought Siegmund onto the Finance Committee in late 1957. The Warburgs even sent Kurt Hahn to confront Brinckmann in a blistering 1959 exchange. (It was Eric who had brought Hahn back to the Salem school after the war.) Hahn said he had heard "ugly talk" to the effect that Brinckmann refused to restore the Warburg name because of "latent fear" of the Nazis. Of course, Hahn added quickly, he himself didn't believe such slanderous talk, but that was the rumor. Brinckmann exploded at the insinuation, conveniently blaming Schilling for opposition to Eric and repeating how he himself had brought the bank its postwar renown. Proposing that the name become M. M. Warburg, Brinckmann & Co., Hahn confided to Brinckmann, "Eric Warburg has lost caste by entering the firm before this debt of honour had been paid."[42] When Brinckmann contended that other shareholders would never accept the name change, Hahn said that Brinckmann could have his way in the matter.[43]

In returning to Hamburg, Eric had to deal with the shocked incredulity of his own family. To many of them, it seemed he had failed to learn the historic lesson about the folly of German-Jewish assimilation. The American Warburgs were especially horrified by this apparent sacrilege. As for the German-born Warburgs, some thought Eric returned too soon, while others were stunned that he returned at all. Some Jewish *Angst* was absent in Eric. A pragmatic man, he didn't see Germany as a haunted place full of sinister memories. Although he had seen many atrocities up close, he didn't succumb to the paralyzing horror that understandably afflicted other Jews. Nor did Siegmund, for that matter.

It is striking that the Warburg men were far more willing to make peace with postwar Germany than were the women. In part, a businessman's practicality came into play. The men wanted to do business with postwar Germany and found it expedient to forgive, if not to forget. Siegmund and Eric also had the advantage of having dealt with many industrialists in the 1930s who weren't Nazis. They found it hard to demonize Germans as a whole or believe in some irremediable taint in their culture. Because he had military and aristocratic friends who had worked in the Resistance, Eric could find a circle of people who were socially congenial and politically clean. For Eric—unlike for most Jews—there was another Germany to which he could return.

Whether from guilt or genuine conviction, Eric exalted his return into a larger statement of German-Jewish reconciliation. "After the Holocaust, it seemed more important than ever that Jewish people should return, even if only a few, to Central Europe, considering that it was here they had truly contributed greatly in cultural, scientific and in commercial fields."[44] He didn't feel that the Jews could write off an entire nation. A traditional man, he had never relinquished his past. A 1955 *New Yorker* article described him conducting "an investment-banking business downtown in a hive of family portraits and early prints of the town of Warburg."[45] For all his equanimity, exile in New York must have been bruising to Eric's pride. How could one be heir to a noble tradition and rely upon family largess? The Warburg name might be honored in Hamburg, but it carried little weight on Wall Street in the early postwar years.

When Eric decided to return to Hamburg, Dorothea was confused and perplexed. They had created a bilingual, bicultural home and had even hired a German governess to teach the children German folk songs. But after the

Kösterberg summers, they had always returned to the protective air of Woodlands. For Dorothea, the Nazi terror was indelibly engraved upon her memory. She had seen that people, once given license to kill, turn it into a blood sport. She could never again share Eric's easy trust in people. When he presented his decision as a *fait accompli*, he didn't know whether Dorothea and the children would join him. She didn't want to take the three children from school and transplant them to Hamburg. Marie was then thirteen, Max twelve, and Erica eight. So at first, Eric lived alone at Kösterberg and spent summers there with his family, winter vacations with them in America, and he saw them at other times of the year.[46] Between 1956 and 1960, Eric spent about six or seven months per year in Hamburg.

After Frieda's death in 1958, her children donated Hunt Cottage and Woodlands to the White Plains Board of Education while the Warburgs built a new house in New Canaan, Connecticut. Eric still wasn't sure he wanted his children to go to school in Germany and wondered whether he would best Brinckmann in their contest. Dorothea, likewise, didn't know if Eric's move was permanent. In the end, their family life hinged upon Dorothea's willingness to follow Eric. In 1960, in a tremendous act of self-sacrifice, Dorothea swallowed her fears and took her family to a Germany still visibly scarred by the war.

After the rich, sleepy America of the 1950s, it was hard for the children to adapt. As small children, they had first visited Germany in 1952 when milk was still delivered in aluminum containers by horse and carriage and Hamburg was strewn with weeds and rubble. "I remember riding the bus or the train and seeing many invalids or people with badly burned and disfigured faces," said Eric's eldest daughter, Marie.[47] While Eric exposed the children to members of the German Resistance, they realized these were exceptional cases. As Marie said, "it was unquestionably difficult to actually begin to consider Germany our new home, and to live in a society in which most adults over the age of forty had either been active supporters of National Socialism or at best followers."[48]

School was a great adjustment for the children, especially for the free-wheeling, rebellious Max, who grew homesick for the more relaxed atmosphere of American schools. He disliked the military academy style of Salem under Kurt Hahn and was transferred to Louisenlund in Schleswig. After taking religious training in Bremen, he was bar mitzvahed in Hamburg—the first Warburg boy to have done this in thirty years.

In their high school history classes, the children had to deal with the wide spectrum of postwar German responses to the Third Reich. Marie's history teacher engaged in candid soul-searching and showed the class a film on the Holocaust. On the other hand, Max's teacher was so afraid to venture anywhere near the 1930s that he safely ended his course with

Bismarck. Eric's infectious optimism helped to carry the family through many rough patches.

The Warburgs joined a tiny band of about fifty-five Jews who returned to Hamburg. Some of them were doctors and lawyers who couldn't get professional licensing in exile.[49] From 1955 to 1959 about six thousand Jews returned to Germany, mostly from Israel or Latin America, swelling the Jewish population to twenty-one thousand compared to a half million in 1933.[50] Several hundred Iranian Jews settled in Hamburg, which had a thriving trade in Oriental rugs. The Warburg case was an extremely rare example of a prominent Jewish family returning voluntarily from an Anglo-Saxon country. Encountering the disapproval of the world Jewish community, returning Jews would often pretend that their return was temporary. Eager to exorcise the past, both West and East Germany welcomed this redemptive return flow of former Jewish citizens.

Eric and his family moved into Noah's Ark, the old eighteenth-century house at Kösterberg with the sloping roof, creaking floors, and Elbe vistas. With Paul's house soon to be demolished and Max's and Fritz's villas being used by the German Red Cross, it was the one house left. Otherwise the gracious atmosphere of stately trees, rolling lawns, and rhododendron bushes remained intact. Eric's childhood friend, Wolfgang Rittmeister, lived next door and they sailed again on the Baltic in the *Kong Bele*. (Wolfgang's brother, John, a courageous psychiatrist, had been shot by Nazi thugs in 1943.) Kathi Schwärz, the farmer's daughter who had protected the estate from *Wehrmacht* officers, again served Eric his morning orange juice and brought up the three Warburg children. She would die in Eric's arms in 1968. Eric delighted in reviving his father's customs—such as taking a different child for a walk each morning or placing a spoon over a glass when somebody repeated an oft-told tale.

In searching to recapture the obliterated past, Eric introduced his three children to a world he had known as a boy. Like him, they took sailing lessons on the Alster Lake. In time, all three developed a dual German-American identity and felt comfortable in both countries. Nobody dared subject the Warburg children to anti-Semitic comments, although they had to contend with some painful, self-serving misconceptions about the 1930s that classmates had absorbed from their parents. Because Eric and Dorothea didn't want the children always to feel apart as Jews, they celebrated both Hanukkah and Christmas at Kösterberg. Earlier at Hunt Cottage, Alice had been mortified to see a Christmas tree standing in a side room.[51]

Several things eased Eric's transition back to German life. As a Jew eager to foster reconciliation, he was treated as a conquering hero and even subjected to a certain amount of sycophancy. Germany needed Jews willing to forgive, and not many Jews cared to oblige. Eric's status, which had declined in New York, rose in Germany. Hamburg had never warmed to the *Führer* as much as other places and there was correspondingly less neo-Nazism lingering after the war. Kurt Sieveking—the lawyer who had bravely joined M. M. Warburg in 1936—became a postwar mayor, as did Max Brauer, who had bravely jumped from a window of Altona City Hall in 1933 and fled to America. Eric worked out a deal by which he gave the city the Roman Garden at the base of Kösterberg. In exchange he received ten lucrative permits to build houses on the hilltop and the sale of these permits enabled Eric to rebuild his depleted capital.

Eric returned to Hamburg when former Nazi overlords were still in evidence. At parties, Eric would ignore the former Nazis or sidle away from them. With his bustling energy and Old World gallantry, he learned how to thread his way through this social mine field. Some former friends, ashamed of their behavior under Hitler, came to apologize and Eric generally forgave them. For a Jew in postwar Germany, acceptance could be as unsettling as rejection, for he never knew whether he was being used by a friendly German to cleanse a guilty conscience or even to cover up past crimes.

Eric's Viennese wife often found the situation far more unsettling. Not being from Hamburg, she couldn't tell the good people from the bad and so was more suspicious than Eric. She remembered the Nazi period too vividly to fall into easy social intercourse and always bridled at the anti-American sentiment. At one party, a man tried to ingratiate himself and lapsed too quickly into the familiar *"du"* form. When he tried to intertwine their arms and drink a toast with her, Dorothea instinctively recoiled. "How do I know what you were doing during the war?" she asked. An uncomfortable hush silenced the room. The man then candidly confessed that he hadn't been a hero during the Third Reich.[52]

Eric and Dorothea felt that they had a full social life and enjoyed the company of German aristocrats who had found Hitler vulgar and boorish. But many Warburg relatives doubted the idyllic portrait they sketched, seeing Eric and Dorothea as socially isolated, while pretending all was fine. Among Warburgs in America, stories would circulate of Eric trying to climb into the upper ranks of Hamburg merchant society while being derided as "Eric Warburg, the Jew" behind his back. One senses that Eric acquired a psychological investment in the basic decency of many Germans, while some relatives had an equal investment in their view of Germans as incorrigibly evil. Eric worked hard to promote German-Jewish reconciliation and closer American-German ties. As treasurer of the American Council on Germany, he kept John McCloy posted on events and often spoke to him every week on the phone.

Eric never missed a chance to remind Hamburg of the Warburg contribution. Most people didn't know that a celebrated Warburg library had ever existed in Weimar Germany. On a gray, windy day in October 1958, Eric presented the Kunsthalle with a bust of Aby that Mary had sculpted after his death, based on photographs of his corpse. (Aby said he would only sit for a life-size equestrian statue.) In a therapeutic ceremony, a Hamburg senator, Dr. Hans Biermann-Ratjen, recalled attending a charity meeting at M. M. Warburg with Max in the 1930s while Brownshirts marched in the street below. He expressed gratitude for Eric's healing gesture: "What we see here is no German self-abasement but a catharsis."[53]

Never observant Jews, Eric and Dorothea only attended synagogue on High Holy Days. They stood aloof from the rug-trading Iranians who now comprised the bulk of the local Jewish community and Eric's remoteness caused grumbling. In 1958, he joined with Protestant and Catholic clergy to lay the ground for a new local synagogue on the twentieth anniversary of *Kristallnacht*. As chairman of Hamburg's Jewish Hospital—with Fritz the honorary chairman—Eric revived the 120-year Warburg connection with the institution, heading a drive for a new facility. Nicknamed the Fox Terrier by his family, Eric was a dogged fund-raiser and didn't hesitate to exploit his name. People often found it easier to give than to argue with Eric. He also contributed to the Institute for the History of German Jews and the Friends of the Hebrew University.[54]

Eric had a low-profile style, an aversion to publicity. Having passed through the Third Reich, he didn't wish to say anything that could be exploited by the malicious. In the early 1950s, he published an abbreviated and sanitized version of Max's memoirs. The volume was cryptic about the Third Reich whereas during World War II Eric had exhorted his father, "you must be very detailed and specific from 1933 on. . . ."[55] Eric steadfastly resisted the efforts of historians to write a book about the family, even though he gathered voluminous materials to that end. Having made the decision to return to Hamburg, he didn't care to open the Pandora's box of the past except where an important matter of principle was at stake.

Outwardly, Eric was always reassuring about German-Jewish relations. When Jewish groups visited Germany, he would state authoritatively that anti-Semitism was extinct. In private he wasn't nearly so sanguine. He often complained that German schoolchildren weren't taught enough about the unattractive past and worried about the manic-depressive nature of German political culture, which he saw as prone to alternating euphoria and dejection. "We must see to it," he said, "that we never again fall too low, but also that we don't rise too high."[56]

Indeed, Eric was always apprehensive about extremism. He scanned the press for the slightest breath of anti-Semitism, then pounced on the offending editor. Already in the late 1940s, the Warburgs had dealt with a spate of newspaper stories and books dredging up the old "Sidney Warburg" canard that the Warburg family had bankrolled Hitler. According to American Jewish Committee documents, Ludendorff's widow, Mathilde, was especially active in perpetuating this nonsense.[57] A 1948 Swiss book called *Spanish Summer* said that Jimmy Warburg personally delivered the last payments to Hitler in February 1933. The author, Severin Reinhardt, conjured up another *Elders of Zion* Jewish conspiracy. He alleged that Kuhn, Loeb controlled J. P. Morgan & Company (which would have come as welcome news to Kuhn, Loeb) and that Jacob Schiff and Morgan partner Tom Lamont had financed the Bolshevik Revolution.[58]

With the Sidney Warburg story, it was Eric who protested to the newspapers and obtained formal retractions. Jimmy contemplated a libel suit, then decided that publicity would only serve the neo-Nazi cause. Instead he privately brought the matter to the attention of American, British, and French authorities and wrote an affidavit reviewing the entire history of the Sidney Warburg hoax.[59]

In the 1950s, Zionist groups largely lost interest in Germany but the American Jewish Committee did not. Before returning to Brinckmann, Wirtz in 1956, Eric had joined the AJC's Foreign Affairs Committee. Once in Germany, he served as their media watchdog, surveying the press for signs of resurgent bias. In 1956, the German interior minister seized nine thousand copies of an anti-Semitic pamphlet called "The Bank Conspiracy of Jekyll Island" in which Paul was again chastised for creating the Fed to further Jewish power. Eric was heartened when Bonn dealt promptly with the matter.[60]

But the neo-Nazi movement never entirely died out in Germany. In 1953, the British high commissioner arrested seven former Nazis—including Hamburg *Gauleiter* Karl Kaufmann—for infiltrating conservative political parties in Germany. A report issued by American authorities in Germany that year stated, "The majority of the Germans believe that there was more good than evil in National Socialism."[61] Three years later, the Nazi party was outlawed along with the Communists, but in the late 1950s, vandals again scrawled swastikas on German synagogue walls.

If anything, Eric was overly sensitive to references to Jewish wealth or power. He protested a 1957 *Der Spiegel* article which mentioned Jews involved in developing the hydrogen bomb. The article made no special point of their religion. While admitting the article lacked malice, Eric still warned the AJC, "The Hitlers of tomorrow, however, can only too easily interpret it again as 'the most sinister influence.' "[62] That same year, Eric grew indignant about a profile of Sir Ernest Oppenheimer in *Der Spiegel*, which described the monopoly power of the South African diamond mogul. Again, Eric told the AJC that the article wasn't overtly anti-Semitic. "However, by a very slight twist all this is excellent material for a future 'Stürmer.' . . ."[63] In 1959, *Stern* published a letter about financial sources of the Nazi movement, citing the Sidney Warburg fabrication. In a stinging letter to the editor, Eric warned that the book had been the subject of legal proceedings and could be again.[64] Behind a soothing facade of German-Jewish amity and reconciliation, he maintained eternal vigilance on the issue. Eric was never quite as certain that the volcano was extinct as he publicly professed. There was always a little quiver of doubt.

*Nina, Alice, and Frieda Warburg at
the Fishrock camp in the Adirondacks.
(Courtesy of Katharine Weber)*

Museum Pieces

In 1941, Frieda Schiff Warburg had a heart attack, which was delicately styled a "breakdown" by the family. It began a slow deterioration of her health. Despite frequent nausea, she soldiered on, grateful that she and Felix had traveled in better days. When first widowed, she lived at 1109 Fifth Avenue with refugee relatives: first Ingrid, then Max and Alice and Gisela and Eric. For a long time, she lived with her eldest son, Freddy, the last child to marry. Every day they breakfasted in silence, with Freddy reading the sports section and Frieda studying the obituaries. Their most spirited exchange came the day Babe Ruth died, when their interests memorably dovetailed. Till the end of her life, Frieda kept abreast of world events, devouring books and newspapers.

The cavernous mansion seemed vacant without Felix and the sociable, laughing children. When Frieda moved into a duplex apartment at 1 East Eighty-Eighth Street, she couldn't bear to see the old house razed. In 1944, on the seventy-third anniversary of Felix's birth, she bequeathed the Gothic structure that her father feared would precipitate Manhattan pogroms to the Jewish Theological Seminary of America for its Jewish Museum. It was a logical recipient, Felix having served as a director and founder of the museum in 1904. In a Music Room ceremony, Frieda, her voice thickening with emotion, handed the deed over to Rabbi Louis Finkelstein. "This house is so full of precious memories and giving it away is not easy."[1] Three years passed before the museum opened to the public in May 1947 and a nervous Frieda stepped again into its ghost-ridden foyer. At once, she breathed easy. "I must confess that the first time I entered 1109 after it had been transformed into the Jewish Museum was a very poignant moment. But I discovered to my joy that, instead of depressing me, it gave me a wonderful feeling of happiness."[2]

On January 21, 1945, Frieda had suffered a great loss with Nina's death. With her Louisa May Alcott hairdo, Nina had entertained guests at lovely English teas during the war. If downcast in later years, she at least suffered in style and went about in a chauffeured Rolls-Royce; even in death Paul spoiled her. Before she joined him in the Sleepy Hollow Cemetery, she provided for a Paul Warburg chair in economics at Harvard, later occupied by John Kenneth Galbraith.

Frieda jealously guarded Felix's memory. In his 1949 autobiography, Chaim Weizmann portrayed Felix as an obstinate, misinformed philanthropist and Frieda fired off a blistering letter of protest. Gradually she emerged as a figure in her own right with a decided activist bent. She led a Hadassah fund-raising drive to build a Jerusalem hospital and established a foundation to aid Israeli immigrants. Socially, she strayed beyond the confines of Our Crowd and showed more of Felix's versatility.

From her father, Frieda had inherited a strong superego that had lent a stiff edge to her personality. Now she loosened up and showed more humor, playing bridge, enjoying her grandchildren, hazarding jokes in speeches, and chain-smoking with remarkable abandon. She delighted in the racy exploits of her niece Dorothy Schiff, publisher of *The New York Post*, who was as emancipated as Frieda had been sheltered. At the same time, Frieda kept her father's bluntness and never hesitated, for instance, to tell people they were too fat. No less punctual than Jacob Schiff, she would direct an icy glare at visitors who came late. As frugal as ever, she loved to buy clothes from catalogues and excitedly informed friends of her bargain purchases.

In her final years, Frieda traded the Woodlands manor for a smaller house on the estate, Meadow Farm, where her widowed mother had lived. Even as she became a semi-invalid, the regal Frieda held court in bed. She demanded old-fashioned formality, with children always "presented" to her. "The grandchildren were brought in dressed up at teatime and made nice noises," said Piggy's daughter, Felicia. "We ate wonderful little tea sandwiches. She always had people around."[3] When bored or irritated with the discussion, she turned off her hearing aid. After the morning mail arrived in a leather box, she dedicated herself to her extensive correspondence. Attended by Otto the butler and Hilde the maid, Frieda wintered at Eden Road in Palm Beach and was thoroughly the *grande dame* as she stared at the world through a lorgnette. Reclining on a couch, she dictated her reminiscences into a tape recorder, which Eddie spun into a charming little volume.

At Meadow Farm, Frieda often stretched out on a chaise longue in pale silks and lace. Several times a week, Dr. Herman Tarnower came to take her blood pressure and Frieda smoothed his way into "Our Crowd." Allergic to digitalis, she needed close monitoring and Dr. Tarnower showed up so regularly at midday that Eddie anointed him Doctor Lunch Hour. Years later, as the best-selling "Scarsdale Diet Doctor" of tabloid notoriety, Dr. Tarnower was shot by his disgruntled lover, Jean Harris, the headmistress of an exclusive girls' school. Frieda could be a dangerous patient. She was so addicted to cigarettes that even when the doctors placed her in an oxygen tent, she would push it aside to light up, creating a general fear of explosion.

The great sadness of Frieda's last years was the rash of intermarriage among her children. When Freddy married outside the faith in 1946, all four sons had non-Jewish wives. More of her grandchildren would end up celebrating Christmas than Hanukkah. It was a stunning development for the royal family of American Jewry, as was the epidemic divorce rate among the Friedaflix grandchildren. Some of the intermarriage resulted simply from demographics: The Warburgs found many more partners of their educational and socioeconomic level among non-Jews. Yet it also suggested, if not a purposeful flight from the Jewish past, a notable eagerness to blend inconspicuously into WASP society. It marked the climax of a steady progression away from faith in the Warburg family and among German Jews generally, as the doubts of one generation hardened into denial in the next.

For Frieda, Judaism represented a rich ethical tradition and she showed little interest in prayer or ceremony. Yet she went to synagogue on High Holy Days and it upset her that her grandchildren celebrated Christmas. Frieda, however, learned to accept even unwelcome changes in an adaptable, loving spirit. A fiercely loyal woman, she choked down her feelings for the sake of family cohesion. In the end, family brought her more solace and comfort than religion. In 1956, age eighty, Frieda wrote, "There have been times when I yearned for the ability to lose myself in deep religious faith, and, although I have observed many of the forms, I must admit that the most meaningful experience to me has been the sense of family (*Familiengefühl*) which has grown and flourished in our household."[4]

If Frieda lightened up in later years, Alice Warburg never shed her rigidity. Suffering did not soften her personality; in fact, it made it even more brittle. Unlike Eric, Alice refused to forget the Third Reich and at first wouldn't set foot in Hamburg. Fearing Eric might try to waylay her to Germany, she decided to boycott Europe. Only when Eric swore that he would never try to steer her back did she visit Lola and Renate in England. Old German sentiment welled up only once. When Chancellor Adenauer made his first official trip to America, Eric took his mother to hear him speak in German. At the end, she suddenly rose up from her aisle seat and made her way to the lectern. Extending her hand to Adenauer, she said, "Mr. Chancellor, that is the first time in many years that I am once again proud of a German!"[5]

Nobody thought Alice could survive Max's loss but she had her own plucky energy and proudly stoic humor. With Russian toughness in her soul, she never lost her martinet manner. With her cane, she would tap imperiously on Madison Avenue store windows to criticize the floral decorations. Taking refuge in art, she set up her easel *en plein air* and painted landscapes at Woodlands, in Scotland, and in the French Alps. Small, precise, elegant, she clung to small rituals of fashion, as if outer order might translate into inner peace. Eric left this telling image of her at Max's grave: "Watching her stand high above the Hudson River at Father's grave on his anniversary days, one cannot help but wonder if the flowers which she arranges for him again and again with endless pain in always varying ensembles do not give to her something similar to a prayer."[6]

Every Sunday, Alice brought caviar to Frieda at Woodlands. The two aging dowagers would converse on the balcony of the indoor pool, sitting beneath potted palms and watching their grandchildren splashing below. They had sixty years of turbulent, eventful history to share. On September 14, 1958, Frieda died in her sleep at Meadow Farm. Alice was in Europe at the time and ailing and her children pleaded with her to skip the funeral. "Friedel would have gone," she said with crisp resolution and she went.[7] On December 7, 1960, Alice Magnus Warburg, age eighty-seven, also went to her grave.

Before she died, Frieda had decided to deed the large house and 150 Woodlands acres to the local school district. Suburbanization had set in locally, and Paul's old house, Fontenay, had been torn down to make room for a real estate development. The imposing Woodlands entrance now yielded to a shopping center, and the main house became a school administration building. The Warburg wood was chopped down for a high school. Despite decades of active philanthropy, Frieda's estate was still valued at $9.1 million. Having made several munificent gifts in the 1950s, she pledged in her will another third of her money to pet Warburg charities, including the beloved Joint, the Federation of Jewish Philanthropies, and the Hebrew University.

After Frieda's death, the Warburgs suddenly seemed more scattered and anonymous. "It was sad that with her death, the cohesive force in the family became splintered," Edward wrote. "From then on, while we all remained close, the family broke up into its several component parts."[8] Over the previous century, the tight-knit Hamburg family had been dispersed to many countries and then split up within their adopted lands. But the Hamburg bank had endowed them with shared purpose and interests, drawing them into a partnership both real and figurative. They had also been united by suffering, the recurring bouts of anti-Semitism reminding them of their common ancestry.

Now the American family bonds were dissolved by enormous wealth and success. The American Warburgs proved the possibility of successful acculturation, but at the expense of their religious identity. With their good looks and great charm, they found a welcome place in many blue-ribbon families. Piggy's daughter, Felicia, married Robert Sarnoff, son of the chairman of RCA and NBC; she later married Franklin Roosevelt, Jr. Eddie's daughter, Daphne, would marry Michael Astor.

It was Carola who held together the Warburg family. She kept up many charitable alliances, and her afternoon tea table was the Warburg clubhouse. She nearly ended up married to Lord Mountbatten after Edwina Mountbatten—the granddaughter of Sir Ernest Cassel—and Walter Rothschild both died in the 1960s. "Dickie" and Edwina had been frequent Woodlands guests and one of their daughters spent the war with Carola. In later years, Dickie stayed with Carola whenever he visited New York; they shared ice-cream sodas, Rockefeller Center, and the Rockettes. For his seventieth birthday, Carola gave him a swimming pool and Dickie invited her over to use it. "He was famous for his courage but just on a personal basis he was so stimulating, attractive and so very thoughtful," said Carola.[9] If they had met twenty years earlier, Mountbatten mused, they might have married. Now he felt it too late for anything beyond an affectionate friendship.

Henceforth, the Warburgs would resemble other modern families, leading separate lives, seeing one another at the random, intermittent collisions of wedding and funerals. They had lost the tradition that welded them together. Judaism had been the focal point for Warburg charitable and political involvement, tying them to transcendent causes and steering them away from the pursuit of pleasure that comes to dominate many rich families. The American Warburgs found it harder to maintain the disciplined sense of duty amid material splendor that had been the historic hallmark of the family. And the fabled fortune was chopped ever finer by inheritance. In many ways, the withering of Jewish identity completed the process of assimilation that had started in late nineteenth-century Germany. Once emptied of spiritual content, Judaism became a series of onerous obligations. For a socially ambitious family, mingling with fancy gentile society, it was a barrier to social advancement, an unwanted burden from a darker past.

Ironically, within a generation, discrimination against American Jews would largely cease in housing, schools, clubs, and corporations. In fact, by century's end, the American Jewish experience would seem to prove that Jews *could* be a successful minority, even as the German-Jewish experience seemed to prove the reverse. The Nazi experience itself had worked to strengthen the group identity of the American Jewish community.

The Warburgs retained their Jewish charitable interests, less from conviction than from homage to the past. Their ambivalence was seen in their attitudes toward Israel. Before World War II, the American Jewish community had been embroiled in feuds between Zionists and non-Zionists. Then the Holocaust convinced nearly all Jews of the need for a sovereign state. The American Warburgs were proud and jubilant when Israel declared its independence on May 14, 1948, and won President Truman's blessing. Felix's nemesis, David Ben-Gurion, became prime minister, Weizmann took the ceremonial post of president, and James G. McDonald was named first U.S. ambassador. Some sixty thousand German Jews ended up in Israel and became important factors in the country's life. In many ways, the European socialism represented by Ben-Gurion and other early leaders pleased the Warburgs more than the conservative nationalism that later predominated, for the socialists at least embodied the Utopian, idealistic vision of Israel that had animated Felix, Frieda, and Rabbi Judah Magnes.

First as cochairman of the Joint starting in 1939, then chairman from early 1941—a tenure interrupted only by his war service—Eddie headed the organization until 1965, carrying on Warburg tradition in Jewish philanthropy. Right after the war, he toured Jewish communities across Europe for the Joint and was decorated by Belgium and Italy for his work in helping to evacuate five hundred thousand Jews from displaced-persons camps. During the 1947 United Nations vote to partition Palestine, Weizmann delightedly accepted Eddie's help, exulting that Felix's son "has come very close to the Zionist ideology."[10] Eddie led an emergency fund-raising drive to house Holocaust survivors in Palestine and another to evacuate Jews from Arab countries after the 1948 Arab-Israeli war worsened their plight. In the 1950s, he also became the sole Jew on the New York State Board of Regents.

For years before the war, the Joint had vied with the United Palestine Appeal (UPA) for charity dollars, the Joint being favored by the fat cats of Jewish philanthropy and the UPA by the Zionist masses. After *Kristallnacht*, the two groups decided to stop bickering and merge their fund-raising into the United Jewish Appeal with Eddie leading its first fund drive in 1939. From 1950 to 1955 Eddie served as its president, helping to raise one billion dollars for the UJA, which became the principal source of American money for Israel. (Frieda would contribute up to $500,000 per year.) He also recruited Nelson Rockefeller for the nonsectarian side of the campaign.

By the 1950s, the world of American Jewry had been radically transformed by prospering Russian and Polish Jews. The former pushcart peddlers from the Lower East Side now owned small businesses and sent their children to college to become doctors and lawyers. As professional charity staffs tapped this new pool of wealth, they no longer needed to rely upon the German-born banker and merchant princes. The old Jewish power structure had been based on a lopsided distribution of wealth between German Jews and their poor Eastern European brethren. Now the astonishing growth of the American Jewish middle class reduced the role of the Jewish banking families. The state of Israel also turned the whole power structure topsy-turvy.

Given this situation, it is to Eddie Warburg's credit that he maintained the Warburg presence in the Jewish charity universe. As a gregarious fund-raiser, he exhibited a schmaltzy side that appealed to the *Ostjuden* and brought out a warm side of his own nature. Whether in New York or Florida, he pressed the flesh in a way that would have horrified the starchy old German-Jewish elders. Eddie's influence never rivaled that of Felix, but at a time when Israel relied upon American Jewish goodwill, he occupied a pivotal position. The American Jewish community was now the world's largest, and New York City was its thriving hub. Eddie visited Israel more than thirty times, becoming a tireless booster of its image as a democratic island. On trips, he often acted as cicerone for wealthy donors, introducing them to Abba Eban, David Ben-Gurion, Golda Meir, Yitzhak Rabin, or his close friend, the Austrian-born mayor of Jerusalem, Teddy Kollek.

In the 1950s, the Jewish Agency, the quasi-governmental body that handled immigration to Israel, received as much as two thirds of its budget from the United Jewish Appeal. Anything that threatened the UJA therefore had major implications for a Jewish state predicated on gathering Jews worldwide. As Eddie helped to funnel massive amounts of money to Israel, he had to counter a stinging attack from his cousin, Jimmy Warburg. Jimmy always claimed to have no problem about religion and professed contempt for Jews who changed their name to hide their identities. "I have never pretended not to be a Jew; I've always declared myself as a Jew, but I am always a little puzzled to know why I do, except from a sense of loyalty and of not wanting to be a renegade."[11] This was much more high-minded than he actually felt. He elsewhere admitted that, "Religion was an empty space in my family background."[12] By no accident had he married three non-Jewish women and moved to the WASP enclave of Greenwich, Connecticut, when it wasn't hospitable to Jews.

For Jimmy, Judaism represented a set of universal moral principles and he thought a good Jew was a world citizen. Never endorsing Zionism, he faulted American Zionists during the 1930s for focusing on German-Jewish emigration to Palestine as the sole legitimate solution to the problem. Having been bar mitzvahed and taught Hebrew by Rabbi Magnes, Jimmy supported his appeal for a binational Arab-Jewish state, a fanciful notion that had intrigued Felix too. He recognized that the West's shameful failure to absorb persecuted Jews in the 1930s and 1940s made Israel an absolute necessity, but he worried that American support of Israel would alienate the Arabs. To Adlai Stevenson, he touted an even-handed Mideast policy, condemning both Arab terror raids against Israel and Israeli reprisals against Arab villages.

Jimmy fearlessly criticized Israeli policy at a time when American Jews reflexively rallied around Israel, treating its policies as sacrosanct. In the historic mold of Max and Felix, he saw the need for a sanctuary for persecuted Jews. At the same time, he hotly disputed Zionist ideology that urged *all* Jews to move to Israel. Under the 1950 Law of Return, Israel recognized the right of every Jew in the world to settle there. In Jimmy's view, this would engender frightful population pressures and ultimately an expansionist Israeli state. Where most American Jews approached Israel warily, Jimmy waded in with both feet, saying in June 1958 that, "The treatment of the Israeli Arabs as second-class citizens is not only morally indefensible but stultifies the Israeli Government's professed desire to see justice done to the refugees."[13] Israeli policy, he insisted, was debated with more candor in Israel than in American Jewish circles. "If an American Jew deprecates the growing influence of the Orthodox theocracy in Israel, or the chauvinistic worldwide nationalism of Zionist leadership, or the treatment of the Arab minority in Israel, he is likely to be denounced as a renegade, if not as an anti-Semite."[14]

Once again, Jimmy courted controversy with his own personal brand of courage and perversity. He didn't hedge his views or modulate his language. In incendiary language, he inveighed against the United Jewish Appeal, lashing out at the leadership long symbolized by the Schiffs and Warburgs. It wasn't lost on the Warburgs that Eddie had been five-time national chair of the UJA. Jimmy committed the unpardonable sin of criticizing Israel in public. On November 27, 1959, he delivered an inflammatory speech to Congregation Mishkan Israel in New Haven that caused an uproar. He conceded the need for a haven from anti-Semitism, but said, "It is quite another thing to create a new chauvinistic nationalism and a state based in part upon medieval theocratic bigotry and in part upon the Nazi-exploited myth of the existence of a Jewish race."[15] Jimmy warmly supported charitable work in Israel, but blasted the United Jewish Appeal for contributing charitable funds to propaganda activities that encouraged emigration to Israel. He also charged the UJA with aiding particular Israeli political parties, including the nationalist Herut Party, later the Likud Party associated with Menachem Begin. It is interesting that Jimmy's position echoed Felix's last speech at Briarcliff Lodge in 1937, when he said that if a Jewish state were established, he would urge friends to contribute only through nonpolitical channels.[16]

With the New Haven speech, Jimmy achieved the status of a certified Traitor to His Religion, having broken the tacit code that American Jews could only dissent privately from Israeli policy. The UJA trotted out Senator Jacob Javits of New York to defend the organization and Jimmy was tagged an enemy of Israel and an Arab propagandist in various quarters.[17] While he suffered unfair abuse, he had also expressed his views in a way calculated to antagonize his opponents. Still the angry young man, he needed to rile authority figures and later conceded that in attacking the UJA, he hadn't sufficiently emphasized his support for Israel.[18]

After the New Haven speech, Eddie stopped talking to Jimmy. In the end, Jimmy won the fight. Afraid of losing its tax-exempt status, the UJA began to segregate political from charitable contributions in 1961. That year, when Jimmy underwent a cancer operation, Eddie sent him an ivory walrus as a peace overture. The rift was healed, but the damage was done. The episode confirmed Jimmy's status as a black sheep of the American Warburgs.

———

No less than her brother, Bettina defied convention and broke from the Warburg mold. She, too, had prided herself on her distance from the Warburgs and her repudiation of their conservative, monied past. Even when Bettina finally married in her early forties it caused a row. Nina had been a patroness of Malvina Hoffman, a talented sculptor who had studied with Auguste Rodin. In the 1920s, Malvina had married a gentle, effeminate Englishman named Samuel Grimson, a concert violinist who had been gassed in the trenches during World War I. While on a twenty-four-hour leave to see the Cremona violins during the war, his hands were crushed in a truck accident, ending his career. Afterward, he collected antique instruments and paintings and invented a color-television tube.

When Nina gave Malvina and Sam a cottage at Woodlands, Bettina, age twelve, set her sights on Sam right away. Malvina may have been either lesbian or bisexual—according to which Warburg you talk to—and that, in turn, may have encouraged Bettina to think she could succeed with this older man. When Bettina snatched Sam away from Malvina after an extended romance and married him in 1942, there was a noisy ruckus among the Warburgs, many of whom took Malvina's side. Starting with her marriage to Sam Grimson (who died in 1955), Bettina either played the role of daughter to a much older man—reenacting her relationship with Paul—or mother to a much younger man.

Not surprisingly, Jimmy griped about Sam, and Bettina's baby talk with him drove Jimmy wild. Bettina, in turn, was hypercritical of Jimmy's three wives. Brother and sister circled each other like scorpions, never able to let go. Raised in a gloomy, puritanical household, they savored forbidden fruits and thought they had the power to do anything. Bettina became involved with psychoanalysis when it was daringly avant-garde and she developed into a doctrinaire Freudian. Extremely bright, she was also rigid and prone to stick reductive labels on people. She had no scruples about contacting analysts who were treating younger Warburgs to offer her own diagnosis and to reveal family secrets. Like Jimmy, she was smart, headstrong, and extremely willful. At the same time, she had a flirtatious, girlish side that would suddenly peep out beneath the stern professional air.

For all their competitiveness, Bettina was asked to read and criticize Jimmy's writings in manuscript. Once, when Jimmy couldn't make a foreign-policy trip to Iran, he suggested that she take his place. This began an infatuation with Iran that lasted until the shah's overthrow dashed Bettina's dreams. She spent years working to modernize the Iranian medical system, helping to complete the Shiraz Medical Center and acting as a roving psychiatrist. The younger Warburg women were stunned that Bettina developed such admiration for Iran, not just because of her Jewish background, but because of the subservient role of women in Islamic culture. Bettina brushed aside objections, saying Westerners didn't understand the Moslem world.[19] As early as 1960, Eric warned her that the shah's repressive government would produce popular revulsion. Bettina preferred to believe that such bogus rumors were fanned by regime opponents. Her love of Iran forms a striking parallel with Jimmy's apostasy on Israel. To the extent that Bettina cared at all about Israel, it involved Palestinian justice and the need for Arab-Jewish reconciliation. Besides her Iranian work, she also donated enormous time and money to Native American projects. Bettina was a woman of exceptional generosity, who quietly paid for the college education of at least two dozen students over the years without any fanfare. (She called them "Grimson Scholars.") But, like Jimmy, she always had to lead the parade and never fit easily into a traditional family setting.

———

During the war, Fritz had considered but rejected moving to Israel, saying he was too old to adopt the Hebrew language. Unlike Felix and Max, he hadn't visited prewar Palestine and disagreed with the Zionist view that all Jews belonged in Israel. As he observed to a friend, "The 2,000-year-old history of exile cannot be undone and a portion of the most valuable Jewish traits has arisen from the experience of exile."[20] A world citizen, Fritz relished Ortega y Gasset's view of the Jew as an itinerant cosmopolite, the yeast of many cultures.

Fritz nursed no grudge against postwar Germany, which he hoped would be integrated into a pan-European community. If left to his own devices, he would have moved back to Hamburg, but Anna Beata preferred Sweden. Fritz returned often to Hamburg, staying in a hotel and working to rebuild the Jewish Hospital—the same charitable interest that had led to his 1938 imprisonment.

On summer vacations, he and Anna Beata returned to the Black Forest and met Ingrid and her five Italian children there. A few times, Fritz and Anna visited Italy and toured the Vatican and Roman museums. They worried constantly about Ingrid, whose husband, Veniero, seemed to pursue his political dreams more assiduously than he did a steady income. To help their chronically cash-strapped daughter, Fritz and Anna reduced their own living standard.[21] Bowing to Veniero's wishes, Ingrid raised their five children as Catholics, to which Fritz and Anna acquiesced. The most Jewish of the Famous Five brothers ended up paying to educate Ingrid's Italian children in Catholic schools.

Each year Fritz and Anna visited their two daughters who had moved to Israel. Eva continued her work with young children, which had been interrupted by Hitler. In 1947, she appealed to Eleanor Roosevelt for aid in getting seventeen hundred Jewish orphans interned on Cyprus into Palestine, and Mrs. Roosevelt relayed her letter to President Truman. In Israel, Eva took care of fifty children on a kibbutz, while her sister Charlotte Esther (Noni) worked with deaf and blind children. Eventually, with one daughter in Italy and two in Israel, it became a strain for Fritz and Anna to remain in Sweden. After Fritz had a stroke in the 1950s, he and Anna Beata moved to Israel despite Fritz's earlier resolutions.

Even before they arrived, Anna and Fritz wondered how they would fit their cumbersome old Mittelweg furniture and pictures into the tiny rooms of a kibbutz bungalow. Indeed, in Israel, they would seem like exotic refugees from a forgotten world. It was late in the day for them to make such a transition. This was especially true of Fritz, who, for all his affection for Jewish folklore, was a classic denizen of European cafés, restaurants, and movie theaters. He missed his old friends and longed for a telephone.

Now lame on one side and suffering from back trouble, Fritz always had a nurse in attendance. Both his hair and walrus mustache had turned white. For long hours, gazing out from glum, pouchy eyes, he sat on a white rocking chair rescued from the Kösterberg terrace. Always sedentary, he now seemed virtually immobile. As Eric reported, "Poor Fritz is really still mentally all there but he can hardly move and he feels like Napoleon on St. Helena."[22] Fritz, uprooted, avidly sought news about the Hamburg bank and Kösterberg. On October 13, 1964, he died at the Nezer Sereni kibbutz, age eighty-five. Anna Beata followed him two years later. Fritz's twin sister, Louise—the last surviving child of Charlotte and Moritz Warburg—died in 1974 at age ninety-four. Seventy years had passed since her beautiful sister Olga had thrown herself from the window of a Swiss hotel room. It was remarkable that among the seven children of this nationalistic German family, only Aby had died on German soil. When Fritz died, it was still unclear whether the Warburgs would take root in Germany again or whether the great saga had ended.

The Cousins Club

S iegmund Warburg had the sparkle and audacity of the gifted entrepre-
neur, but these qualities had to struggle against a deep-seated pessimism.
Since he viewed the world through a dark lens, he forever saw the stable
political universe about to crumble into chaos. In the early postwar years, he
again pictured Western economies slouching toward Armageddon. After a
New York visit in 1947, he told Fritz, "A real depression in the United States
is just around the corner."[1] A few years later, he warned "be prepared for an
international inflation wave . . . which may be on a scale comparable to the
German inflation wave of 1921/2 (though not 1923!).''[2] At first he despaired
of American global leadership, then was heartened by the Marshall Plan and
Jimmy Warburg's activism for it. Admiring of the Soviet Union during the
war, he had come to regard it as the chief bogeyman. "There is, I think, too
much easygoing optimism in the air throughout the whole Western world
and I am afraid there is therefore a relaxation of effort on the Western side
towards the cold war which is by no means over yet."[3] Turning conservative,
Siegmund rooted for a Tory victory over Labour in 1950.[4]

He was forever jittery about his firm. In 1953 S. G. Warburg & Co. moved
to more spacious quarters at 9–13, King William Street—a move that another

boss might have celebrated, but which aroused superstitious fear in Sieg-mund. As he told Fritz, "I have a *cauchemar* about too big an organisational basis for a private banking house."⁵ Still fearing excessive reliance on bank-ing, Siegmund steered S. G. Warburg & Co. into diverse businesses. With this in mind, he decided to create a holding company and bought a shell company called Central Wagon Company. When the Labour government nationalized the railroads, it stripped Central Wagon of its assets and this enabled Sieg-mund to use its stock exchange listing for his new holding company. The customary name would have been S. G. Warburg Holdings, but Siegmund again thought it tempting fate to put his name on a listed company with a banking component. The new vehicle was baptized Mercury Securities in-stead.

The common wisdom about Siegmund Warburg is that he ruled his firm not by ownership, but by sheer force of personality. In fact, before the Central Wagon deal was finalized, he formed another private holding company called Warburg Continuation. Endowed with slender capital, it took control of S. G. Warburg & Company by subscribing to a new class of shares that had voting rights, but not equity rights, over the operating company. Siegmund took 52 percent of Warburg Continuation and parceled it out in four equal pieces among himself, Eva, and their two children, with the remaining 48 percent divided among the directors. So it was something of an illusion that Mercury Securities controlled the Warburg bank. Without fuss or publicity, this ar-rangement lasted for twenty years.

Siegmund wanted to revive Warburg glory on Wall Street and in Germany and resurrect an international capital market moribund since the 1920s. S. G. Warburg would be London's most cosmopolitan bank, with its domestic and foreign activities interfused. But for all his brains, charm, and famous name, Siegmund faced an insuperable hurdle: He was an international banker in a provincial postwar City straitjacketed by exchange controls and bound by an insular outlook. World finance was now centered upon New York and conducted in dollars.

By 1946 Siegmund was bustling about Wall Street, trying to drum up business. The next year, he set up American European Associates, drafting Dr. Ernst Spiegelberg, his former Hamburg partner, to head it. Traveling on the *Queen Mary*, staying at the Drake Hotel, and working from a Bank of the Manhattan office, Siegmund began to trail a cloud of mystery behind him. He started to project his mythic persona of the brilliantly mercurial banker who stayed in discreet hotels on several continents and advised powerful clients in intimate chats. His capacity for work was awesome. Aboard the *Queen Mary*, his secretary typed away in her cabin and they worked either Saturday or Sunday. As he had in the 1920s, Siegmund felt at home in New York,

Sitting in an Alpine setting, Siegmund Warburg
is caught, red-handed, reading a newspaper.
(Private collection)

enjoying its zest and vitality. Thanks to Hitler, he now had relatives galore there and once said that he had counted seventy-two of them, if widows and divorced wives were included.⁶

In London, Siegmund was fast becoming a legend, but he was patronized in the smug world of postwar Wall Street. This snobbery would be, in many ways, more insidious than the brittle upper-crust condescension he dealt with in London. In New York, people called him "Siggy" Warburg, a diminutive that made him cringe. Indeed, his tiny firm in London still had only a few dozen people and more second-tier clients than blue-chip companies on its roster. He was fussy about whom he dealt with, but the upper-bracket firms eluded him.

Siegmund made the fateful but highly questionable decision of trying to restore the fame of Kuhn, Loeb, which he considered a "Warburg firm." Paul and Felix had been partners and Felix's son, Freddy, remained a general partner. When Siegmund had trained there in the 1920s, Kuhn, Loeb had been so regal that its letterhead simply announced "William and Pine Streets." In the 1950s it still shared preeminence with Morgan Stanley, but precariously so. For over a century, it had financed railroads, steel mills, and shipping firms, and had contributed to the growth of the auto, film, and aviation industries. It also served as agent bank for many foreign governments. For Siegmund, its client list must have shimmered like the stuff of fantasy: Bethlehem Steel, Eastern Airlines, Westinghouse Electric, Western Union, Polaroid Corporation. He spied a chance to revitalize a Warburg house and simultaneously catapult his London firm to the top of world finance. It was an implausible daydream that would tease, torment, and tantalize him for a decade.

As Siegmund had already foreseen in his apprenticeship days, Kuhn, Loeb had become a rich, sleepy place run by sedate partners who banked fat, easy domestic profits. They assumed business would come to them. Once led by aggressive immigrants, the firm had settled into a state of exaggerated gentility, with a formal, airless, almost mortuary atmosphere. In the reception area, beneath pictures of Felix Warburg and Jacob Schiff, two black men took visitors' hats. The secretaries were called Miss and men by their last names. The firm served only sherry at lunch, which featured lots of jejune chatter about French wines and European hotels. The style was still so discreet that a young employee could be fired after lunch if heard discussing a client's business at a restaurant.

John Schiff, Jacob's grandson and the chief partner, and his adviser, Sir William Wiseman, knew the firm risked stagnation. A shrewd cloak-and-dagger figure, Wiseman had been the chief British spy master in America during World War I and then became a Kuhn, Loeb partner. He spotted

Siegmund as a rising London star and told Schiff that Siegmund could be the spark to recharge Kuhn, Loeb's battery. In 1951, Schiff wooed Siegmund with a fantastically tempting offer: He could become senior partner of Kuhn, Loeb if he moved to New York and made it his principal activity. But Siegmund had an immigrant's fondness for England and owed much to the Bank of England, the Rothschilds, other friendly British firms, and the industrious uncles. So he declined, later explaining that "having built up my firm in England, I felt very deeply attached to England and I wouldn't dream of moving my domicile from London."[7]

Instead, Siegmund became a normal Kuhn, Loeb partner, spending half the year in New York and sharing his New York earnings with his London firm. Since the New York Stock Exchange forbade officers of foreign banks from becoming partners in member firms, Siegmund started out in late 1952 as an "executive director" and didn't officially become a partner until 1956. In reality, he enjoyed a partner's authority all along. As one associate said, "His views on the New York Stock Exchange, from his experience as a partner in Kuhn, Loeb, produced invective of a style and force which could rival Swift."[8]

Siegmund was extremely excited about the prestigious Kuhn, Loeb connection and instructed his London secretaries to address letters to American businessmen as "Mr." but to Kuhn, Loeb partners as "Esquire." His relatives were dubious about his prospects. Knowing how he set himself up for disappointments, Eva warned that the Kuhn, Loeb partners were rich and self-satisfied and that he was taking on a losing battle. But Siegmund liked a challenge and was excessively confident of his own powers of persuasion.

John Schiff hoped Siegmund would develop transatlantic business, bring European clients to Kuhn, Loeb, and serve the firm's clients in Europe. He put Siegmund on the executive committee, a stunning feat that made him the sole European banker with such standing in a top-drawer Wall Street house. Henceforth, S. G. Warburg & Co. and Kuhn, Loeb would represent each other in London and New York.

During his stormy Kuhn, Loeb tenure, Siegmund faced the same predicament that had stymied him in Hamburg and London. He was again the capable outsider, the brilliant upstart, baffled and derided by threatened insiders. This maddened him, making him more determined to succeed. For Siegmund, Kuhn, Loeb was the sort of haphazard outfit that brought out his moralistic contempt for waste.

With his penetrating vision, Siegmund at once spotted the firm's flaws. In 1954, he prepared a memo charting Kuhn, Loeb's real, if still imperceptible, decline. In London, Siegmund had created a free-flowing collegial atmosphere. Anticipating Japanese methods, he would form teams for each client and have green recruits working beside senior directors. In contrast, Siegmund noted that the ossified Kuhn, Loeb had gone from Jacob Schiff's dicta-torship to separate baronies. Too lazy to chase new business, the firm coasted on its past. "On the one hand," he told John Schiff, "there is too much free play for dilettantism without sufficient appreciation of the importance of professional work."[9] Siegmund was shocked at how Kuhn, Loeb moved by inertia. "The firm has apparently no long-range plan, other than to hang on to existing clients and to try—by no particular or definite method—to get new ones. Its organization, at best, is rudimentary and unintegrated. . . ."[10] For Siegmund, if the people, corporate structure, and culture were right, the rest would fall into place.

Siegmund's critique was prescient. Unfortunately, his efforts to galvanize Kuhn, Loeb became ensnared in the issue of his own personal ambitions. It was widely feared that Siegmund wanted to dominate or take over Kuhn, Loeb and run it from London. No sooner did he join the executive committee in 1953 than he lobbied to be its chairman.[11] In the 1954 memo, Siegmund urged Schiff to appoint him managing director, spawning mistrust.[12] A few weeks later, Siegmund told Schiff defensively, "your remark yesterday about the question of powers gave me the impression that you thought I wanted to have dictatorial powers."[13] Siegmund had a clear-sighted view of Kuhn, Loeb's problems but his thrusting style, superior intelligence, and sometimes overbearing manner unsettled the leery Americans.

Critical of the firm's fragmented structure, Siegmund generated many sweeping blueprints to concentrate power in a small leadership group that always seemed to include himself. He thought piecemeal solutions a form of cowardly evasion. The model he invoked was the close teamwork and profes-sionalism of his London firm. But Siegmund's Prussian sense of hierarchy collided with the anarchic culture of an American partnership. When he tried to end turf wars at Kuhn, Loeb by having partners share the morning mail—imitating the uncles in London—it created an uproar. Siegmund also disliked the American mentality that people who produced the most should be paid the most, which he thought undercut the necessary team spirit.

Siegmund was now a personage in his own right, a powerful presence when he entered a room. With a melancholy, world-weary aura, sallow complexion, and saturnine smile, he was an enigmatic figure. He seemed a magician who might suddenly pull a scarf from his sleeve or a chess master who might spring an unexpected move. Still striking with his jet-black hair and piercing eyes, he wore well-tailored, double-breasted suits of dark blue or gray. The wheels of his mind always turned. A mesmerizing orator, he spoke softly, but with such cogent, precisely chosen words that people leaned for-ward and sat riveted. He had a knack for delivering remarks that seemed spontaneous but were premeditated down to the opening pleasantries. Siegmund was so artful that people at a meeting could never spot his precise agenda, which often came wrapped in a carefully spun tissue of secondary or tertiary concerns.

Like a cloistered scholar, he paced the Kuhn, Loeb halls, his hands clasped behind him, his back increasingly hunched. Enormous tension was bottled up inside him. In fact, his famous charm seemed to spring from a lifelong struggle to tame his strong emotions. Sometimes his nervous shoulder tic gave a telltale twitch when he asked a loaded question. His eyes were cool, steady, watchful, and all-seeing. If he stopped to chat with a young associate, clapping a hand on his shoulder, his eyes would scan the work on the employee's desk. Phenomenally diligent, he often started at eight-forty-five while the American partners ambled in at ten. Throughout his life, Siegmund had minutely budgeted days, but never seemed in a hurry. He was always available if problems arose and he knew how to make twenty guests per day feel they were currently his top priority.

But instead of seeing Siegmund's strength and drive, many Kuhn, Loeb partners saw an overweening and egotistical upstart. They didn't warm to the Old World erudition that enchanted others. For many in the flippant Kuhn, Loeb crowd, Siegmund's book chatter sounded pretentious. When he cultivated Lehman Brothers partners for new business, his detractors yawned. They didn't respond to Siegmund's view of the banker as a combination of guru, confidant, and management consultant. At the time, Wall Street bankers condescended to their more threadbare British counterparts and this certainly extended to Siegmund.

The hidebound Kuhn, Loeb partners didn't see the world changing around them. Recruited in the Depression, they were inward-looking and unsettled by Siegmund's international bent. After all, if foreign business superseded domestic, their own place in the firm might be devalued. It irritated Siegmund that they couldn't see Europe reawakening. As a German Jew who had suffered the consequences of Versailles, he wanted to revive Germany and Austria and sedulously cultivated contacts while other bankers wrote off central Europe altogether. When Hermann Abs negotiated German debt in London in the early 1950s, he was still under a cloud, having been the most prominent German banker during the Nazi regime. Siegmund defended his friend Abs against critics and won Abs's eternal gratitude. Having fled Germany, Siegmund would now become a major figure in its rehabilitation.

Siegmund took pride in Kuhn, Loeb's Jewish antecedents, but opposed ethnic exclusivity. He would say, "You know, Kuhn, Loeb will always be recognized as a Jewish firm, but shouldn't be exclusively so."[14] This Jewish refugee steered Daimler-Benz and Bayer to Kuhn, Loeb at a time when German companies hungered for American capital yet faced hostility. In 1960,

Siegmund arranged a London share quotation for the August Thyssen steel combine—the first listing of a German stock since the war. Since Fritz Thyssen had been an early business supporter of Hitler, Siegmund's action occasioned grumbling in London's Jewish community. S. G. Warburg & Co. also introduced Farbenfabriken Bayer and Hoechst on the London Stock Exchange, as well as the Discount Bank of Israel.

Though Siegmund was never complacent about a potential Nazi revival, he thought prosperity and close Western ties the best way to forestall that. This was clearly seen in his advocacy of the European Coal and Steel Community (ECSC), a precursor of the European Community. For a century, Germany and France had sparred over the coal and steel of the Saar and Ruhr. To bind the two countries in amity, the French foreign minister, Robert Schuman, devised a plan in 1950 for a supranational coal and steel authority, hoping that such a visionary step would make war "not only unthinkable but materially impossible."[15] As a friend and admirer of Schuman and Adenauer, Siegmund believed the ECSC would submerge German nationalism in a European identity. For a German refugee who had lived through the breakdown of European civilization, it was an exciting venture.

The leading theorist of European integration, Jean Monnet, was friends with Donald Swatland of Cravath, Swaine—the lawyers for Kuhn, Loeb. When the ECSC searched for New York financing, Swatland directed it to Kuhn, Loeb. Because he was a European partner in an American firm, Siegmund was a major attraction for the ECSC, and Swatland would regard him, André Meyer, and Jean Monnet as their era's three leading figures in international finance.

To sell the issue, Siegmund organized a road show of American steel, coal, and banking executives to study the ECSC firsthand. He had to conquer glib cynicism that provincial Americans couldn't understand such a security. Most individual American investors vividly recalled the foreign debt defaults of the 1930s and shied away from the issue, forcing Siegmund to lobby insurance companies. He cleverly piqued the interest of a reluctant Metropolitan Life by likening the ECSC to New York's Port Authority. Siegmund had an unsurpassed talent for selling issues by dramatizing their larger political dimensions. People felt they were purchasing a piece of history. Though mostly placed in Europe, Siegmund managed to sell 10 percent of the ECSC issue on Wall Street. This landmark transaction deal was the first long-term postwar dollar loan for a European institution sold in America. The ECSC would be Kuhn, Loeb's foremost institutional client. Siegmund also brought in the European Investment Bank.

Siegmund also lured the Republic of Austria. "Uncle" Eric Korner enjoyed a virtual lock on the country, which he nursed back to financial respectability. He made a bundle for S. G. Warburg by figuring out which defaulted Austrian and German bonds would be redeemed. In Vienna, Korner enjoyed unequalled stature. He delighted in sitting in the chairman's seat at the Credit-Anstalt. "He loved the Vienna Opera, the Salzburg festival, staying in the Imperial Hotel in Vienna and attending concerts conducted by Karajan or Boehm, both having been undiluted Nazis," recalled fellow uncle Charles Sharp.[16] The appreciative Austrians later decorated him with the Order of Merit. Again, a Jewish refugee helped to revive his former country, poignantly refuting miserable old Nazi myths. On one trip to Germany, Korner was walking through the Dresdner Bank when he spotted the man who had turned him in to the Gestapo in the 1930s. Briefly, he considered telling his host, the bank's senior director, but then decided to let sleeping dogs lie.

If Siegmund's deals stood out as milestones, they didn't shake Kuhn, Loeb's lethargy. The prevailing attitude was summed up in a letter Freddy wrote Eric in 1958, "We have been very busy with Siegmund's ventures in Europe but now that he is back in London peace seems to be descending upon us."[17] What should have been an edge for Siegmund—his family link—worked against him. Siegmund had an entrepreneurial flare long extinguished among the American Warburgs and Schiffs, who were preoccupied with sports, charity, and society. The "Our Crowd" bankers knew that Siegmund came from the wrong side of the family and looked down their noses at him.

Holding most of Kuhn, Loeb's capital, John Schiff had a caretaker attitude toward the firm. He wanted to preserve his fortune without making waves. Tall and silver-haired, with a perennial tan, Schiff was called the "Most Handsome Man on Wall Street" and had the style of an English gentleman. His father, Morti, had died young in 1931, leaving behind an estate of twenty-nine million dollars, a thousand-acre estate in Oyster Bay, and the Kuhn, Loeb leadership. John married Edith Baker, the gentile daughter of banker George F. Baker, entered the Social Register, joined exclusive clubs, and aped the pastimes of British gentry, including polo and fox hunting. Like many in "Our Crowd," he jettisoned his Jewish ancestry. Unlike his ultraliberal sister, Dorothy, John was a rock-ribbed Republican who spent the 1930s grumbling about "that man" in the White House.

Schiff admired Siegmund's verve and welcomed his enthusiasm. At least on an abstract level, he liked the idea that Siegmund would restore the firm's historic overseas strength. But Schiff was a weak man who shrank from the skirmishing that any reform efforts provoked, and Siegmund was infuriated by his lack of follow-through. Every time Siegmund thought he had convinced Schiff of something, somebody would come along and undo all his work.

Often that person was Freddy Warburg, Felix's eldest son and John's first cousin. Freddy was as easygoing as Siegmund was intense and they cordially hated each other. Freddy disliked anything too earnest and found Siegmund ponderous. As Sir William Wiseman warned Siegmund, he suffered "in the first place from a great handicap of family opposition."[18] Shrewd and funny, Freddy like the effortless, amateur pleasures of life. He could toss off clever poems and limericks. People would laugh so hard at Freddy that it sometimes bothered Frieda.

A veteran prankster with a devilish sense of humor, Freddy shared many bachelor escapades with Eric. Freddy once accompanied Eric to a debutante ball in New York when the latter's English was still tentative. Spying a lovely girl, Eric asked Freddy how to address her mother. Following Freddy's instructions, Eric approached the mother, clicked his heels, and said, "Madame, I would very much like to screw your daughter."[19] Freddy's humor could be less than endearing. Returning to Harvard for his twenty-fifth reunion, he addressed the class as follows: "It's interesting that you classmates haven't changed a bit. But what are you doing with these middle-aged women?"[20]

Everybody at Kuhn, Loeb retailed Freddy's witticisms. "What a cruel thing to force anybody to be in his own company," he once observed. Of Long Island dinner parties, he complained, "You are liable to be seated next to some unknown girl who, when you toss her the ball conversationally, will promptly put it into her pocket."[21] Perhaps his most memorable retort was in response to a question about how many people worked at Kuhn, Loeb. "About half," Freddy said after a pause.[22] After Felix died, Freddy had succeeded him as trustee of the American Museum of Natural History and helped to create the Felix M. Warburg Memorial Hall. As work on this exhibition space dragged on, Freddy sent the museum a note, saying drily that he had thought the hall was in remembrance of his father, not of him.[23] Freddy would later have a rollicking funeral at Temple Emanu-el, with a long parade of friends recounting hilarious Freddy stories.

Although Freddy had Passover Seders and attended synagogue on High Holy Days with Frieda, he had a faint Jewish identity, was never a Zionist, and didn't wish to visit Israel. From homage to Felix, he raised money for the Federation of Jewish Philanthropies, but devoted more time to the Boy Scouts, sports, and Middlesex School. In 1946, he married a tall, funny, formidably blunt lady named Wilma Shannon. On Jewish holidays, he was always in a quandary about whether to work or not. If he stayed out, he felt hypocritical; if he went in, he felt guilty. All the same, he didn't deny his Jewishness. One day, he refused to take a call from Clarence Dillon because the Dillons had changed their name from Lapowski, supposedly to conceal their Jewish ancestry—an unpardonable sin in Freddy's eyes.[24]

As a businessman, Freddy was definitely an underachiever, preferring to play tennis or ride at his horse farm in Middleburg, Virginia, where he accumulated a thousand acres. He bought Connecticut property with John J. McCloy and spent many weekends there. Freddy exemplified the American Warburgs, who had taken on the sedate style of old money, while their German relatives again had to hustle for a living. Like John Schiff, Freddy was too wealthy to exert himself and preferred to keep the status quo at Kuhn, Loeb. He was never terribly energetic, but he was a great door-opener. Through his friendship with pilot Eddie Rickenbacker, Kuhn, Loeb got the Eastern Airlines account and Freddy also got the firm into the big Ford Motor underwriting of the 1950s.

John Schiff trusted his cousin and confided in him. Beneath his nonchalant air, Freddy was shrewdly alert and always had Schiff's ear. Sharing the disdain for Siegmund prevalent among many American Warburgs, Freddy became his unyielding foe. He found Siegmund too smart, too competitive, and too eager to assert control and he resented his efforts to be one of the family. The American Warburgs patronized Siegmund and mocked his nervous gestures, such as his unconscious habit of wringing his hands. Once, when Siegmund's name arose at a dinner party, Piggy exclaimed, "Siegmund Warburg is a horse's ass!"[25]

Having apprenticed at M. M. Warburg, Freddy was close to Eric and saw the Warburg family feuds through his eyes. When Rudolf Brinckmann visited Kuhn, Loeb, Freddy called him "Brinckie" and treated him with a sardonic, back-slapping familiarity; Brinckmann cringed with each slap.[26] When Eric invited Siegmund on the Brinckmann, Wirtz finance committee, Freddy voiced strong disapproval. "This I would warn you against because after he has 'settled' in you will find yourself indebted to him and that isn't good," he told Eric.[27]

Siegmund was always fond of Frieda. Instead of delighting Freddy, this annoyed him. Ever since the 1920s, Siegmund had taken a derisory view of Felix's children who richly repaid his disdain. One day, Siegmund stopped by Freddy's office and said, "Do you realize that tomorrow is your mother's birthday?" Freddy said sardonically, "Listen, Siegmund, when I need you to tell me that tomorrow is my mother's birthday, I'll ring for you."[28] Both men could be petty and vindictive with each other. Siegmund was once aghast to find Freddy with his arm around a woman in his office. The American Warburgs, in turn, saw hypocrisy in the puritanical Siegmund, since Frieda had learned about his affair with Alexandra Danilova in the 1930s.

In dealing with Kuhn, Loeb, Siegmund couldn't escape family feuds. Freddy had been bitter about the failure of the German Warburgs to repay the 1931 bailout loan, which he held against Siegmund.[29] Eric had also given Freddy an earful about the Brandeis, Goldschmidt affair. One day in 1958, Freddy dredged up this ancient history and threw it in Siegmund's face. To make matters worse, he cited *Eric* as its source—Eric who had just put Siegmund on the Brinckmann, Wirtz finance committee to help with the name change! At once, Siegmund sent off a blunt note to Eric:

"As far as I could understand his sweeping indictments Fred W expressed the opinion that when I started my London activities through New Trading that was entirely based on general and financial support by MMW & Co. and that subsequently I 'took over' [*sic* Fred W] New Trading, simultaneously eliminating MMW & Co. Fred W amplified this statement by pointing out that I had likewise 'taken over' Brandeis Goldschmidt, depriving Eddie Kohn-Speyer of his position there. With these and similar remarks Fred W tried to demonstrate the dishonest and dishonorable manner in which I had acted." Siegmund told Eric that he couldn't believe Eric had ever made such statements and demanded a prompt response.[30]

Through Freddy's outburst, Siegmund had probably learned Eric's true feelings toward him. Bound by mutual need if sometimes separated by mutual disgust, Siegmund and Eric were never honest with each other because they couldn't afford to alienate each other. Eric now beat a quick retreat and retracted his statements. Within three days, he wrote to Siegmund:

"What you write regarding a conversation between you and Fred W. is therefore altogether incomprehensible to me—on general grounds and consequently regarding particular remarks, two of which you specifically mention. M.M.W. & Co. never had any interest to speak of in New Trading; the difficulty of making use of Eddie K. S. in any kind of business is a topic which I remember that we discussed in years gone by, and always agreed upon! In closing I can assure you that I have but one wish: namely that the basis of real mutual trust which has steadily grown between us should never be destroyed."[31] Both Eric and Siegmund deplored falseness in the other, yet each had stored up so many grievances against the other that candor would only have created paralysis in their dealings.

—

In the mid-1950s, Kuhn, Loeb left its historic building at 52 William Street and moved into more anonymous quarters at 30 Wall Street. Trying to be modern, the firm got rid of its grandfather clocks and other relics, but seemed to lose its *élan vital* as well. By 1957, Siegmund was deeply frustrated by his lack of apparent progress at Kuhn, Loeb, which he likened to a 1910 Rolls-Royce. Aside from a few deals, he told Schiff, "I have wasted my efforts; my working capacity in the firm has been reduced through lack of professional surroundings and in some cases through clear obstruction and procrastination."[32] Siegmund wanted to replace the separate fiefdoms with a central structure to coordinate services to clients, merging the department that hunted new business with the one that distributed securities. Business opportunities were slipping away from lack of internal communication. To eliminate opposition, he also proposed a new rule that would shunt Kuhn, Loeb partners older than sixty into a nonexecutive role.

In a great breakthrough, Siegmund got John Schiff to name J. Richardson Dilworth as a managing partner who would integrate the business of *all* departments. In the bright, extremely gracious Dilworth, Siegmund found a kindred spirit who thought the firm would either change or wither. Siegmund functioned as his "charlady," hovering over his work. Dilworth believed so implicitly in Siegmund's mission that it didn't bother him if Siegmund wanted to incorporate Kuhn, Loeb into S. G. Warburg & Company. He felt the patient needed radical surgery and Siegmund was just the man to wield the knife.[33]

It was a doomed effort. Suspicious partners saw Dilworth as a stalking horse for Siegmund. One particularly hostile partner, Henry Necarsulmer, constantly warned Schiff that Siegmund was pulling the wool over his eyes while plotting to take over Kuhn, Loeb.[34] When Siegmund was in London, his Kuhn, Loeb enemies took out their aggression on the unaided Dilworth. By spring 1958, despairing of any real change at Kuhn, Loeb, Dilworth left to manage the Rockefeller family money.

In time, this Rockefeller connection would yield momentous benefits for Siegmund, who at once told London subordinates to treat Dilworth with special care. For the moment, however, he was distraught over Dilworth's departure. Siegmund should have left at this point, but reinvigorating Kuhn, Loeb had become an *idée fixe* for him, much as had the name change for Eric in Hamburg. He couldn't resist Kuhn, Loeb's alluring client list and historic Warburg associations. Having restored the family's luster in Europe, he was convinced he could save it on Wall Street.

Each Sunday, Siegmund spent hours on the phone with Schiff, trying to arouse him to decisive action. In Churchillian tones, he warned about the "appeasement of arbitrary attitudes and undisciplined habits which have been allowed to creep in and grow over a long period of time. . . . Appeasement leads in the end always to disaster, and the right course is not temporizing, but speedy action. . . ."[35] It was for naught.

From Montego Bay, Sir William Wiseman watched the mounting conflict between Siegmund and his partners. Even though he had recruited Siegmund, he now told John Schiff that Siegmund and his reform scheme could only succeed if Schiff fired three or four intransigent partners and gave Siegmund unlimited control. "In the first place you wouldn't do this," said Wiseman, "also it might be a great mistake."[36] Siegmund was the perfect person to found a firm and stamp it with his own personality. What he couldn't do was submit to the culture of an existing firm with its own mix of personalities and history. He was too strong a figure to submit to compromise or an auxiliary role. He also had a rare capacity to arouse full-blown paranoid fantasies among less secure colleagues.

What Siegmund didn't know was that he was on the brink of two break-throughs in London that would lift him into the upper echelon of world finance. He had entered Kuhn, Loeb as a figure of subordinate status, hoping to bask in the reflected glory of the old firm. Now he was about to become a star in his own right. After the battle for British Aluminium and the rise of the Euromarkets, he wouldn't need Kuhn, Loeb anymore. During the 1960s, S. G. Warburg would steadily rise while Kuhn, Loeb would drift, falter, then finally disappear.

My Viking

E ven as Siegmund Warburg became the storied financier, he never lost his extreme attachment to his mother. Arriving in England in 1939 at seventy-three, Lucie shared her son's admiration for British gentleness and fairness. Sure of Hitler's defeat, she endured the wartime bombing with surprising aplomb. Even in old age, she displayed a quiet *joie de vivre* that masked an iron core. Despite arthritis that made her hands clawlike, she played her grand piano two hours daily. For much of the war and after, she lived with Siegmund and Eva—a trial for her patient daughter-in-law, who never complained but was sorely tested. Lucie never quite adjusted to Siegmund's being married and, to Eva's mortification, would appear at bedtime to serve hot chocolate to her son.

Lucie and Siegmund spoke virtually every day and his devotion to her seemed unlimited. With their shared values, attitudes, and humor—they even had a remarkably similar handwriting—they enjoyed an easy rapport. However hostile Siegmund might feel toward some Warburg relatives, his love of the Kaullas was spontaneous and unalloyed.

Lucie spent her last years in a nursing home in Holland Park. In spring 1954, while Siegmund was at Kuhn, Loeb, Lucie fell in her room and broke several ribs. It speaks much of her consideration for her son that this eighty-eight-year-old woman made everyone swear not to tell Siegmund, lest he curtail his trip. By early 1955, she was suffering frightful asthma attacks, yet never lost her humor. About to visit New York, Siegmund remarked, "You really should come with me in the plane to America." "I would gladly do that," Lucie answered facetiously, "if I didn't have so many business obligations here."[1]

Lucie Warburg died on October 25, 1955, at age eighty-nine. That day, she was overheard playing Beethoven's Appassionata sonata—music as turbulent and bravely triumphant as her life. Siegmund was overcome with grief. For more than fifty years, they had been welded together by common solitude, suffering, and problems. Lucie had been the linchpin of his life, his career's cornerstone. To his staff Siegmund preached her principles of disciplined self-criticism. As he said, she had endowed him with a complete set of standards and objectives.[2]

No less ascetic than Siegmund, Lucie didn't want a funeral and was cremated in privacy. Though Siegmund lived for another twenty-seven years, her influence always remained with him. He had a death mask made of Lucie, converting remembrance into a sacred duty. Soon after she died, he wrote an affecting memoir about her in German. Each year, the S. G. Warburg & Co. staff dreaded the anniversary of her death, for Siegmund would arrive in a black and inconsolable mood. The smallest misstep could trigger him off. Because Lucie had served as both father and mother, he never came to terms with her death. In later years, when people visited Siegmund in Switzerland, they would notice the painting of Lucie prominently hanging in his study.

The solitary boyhood and the stern but doting mother had combined to produce a self-centered man. Brought up as the center of the universe, Siegmund grew accustomed to the role and kept it until the end. From Lucie he learned to transmit love with a kind of didactic severity, mingling the roles of father and instructor. This didn't bode well for marriage.

Many people suspect that Eva Warburg lived a life of quiet desperation, suffocating in the immense social enterprise of being Siegmund's wife. This overstates the matter, but it certainly had an element of truth. This shy, private woman was a magnificent actress and a fathomless mystery to the outer world. She seemed quiet around her husband and often sat apart when Siegmund talked business with visitors. She never spoke a word out of turn. She had a silken strength, a cool, lovely Swedish impenetrability. Exceedingly gentle and feminine, she confided in few people and struck many as aloof. "You could be close to Eva, but you couldn't touch her," said Siegmund's cousin, Elsbeth Oppenheimer.[3] Beneath her soft radiance, she had an inner toughness that Siegmund valued and he fondly dubbed her "my Viking."

Eva and Siegmund Warburg in the flowers.
(Private collection)

Siegmund chose a wife who catered to his minutely exacting tastes and could endure his constant absence from home. Eva looked and behaved like a duchess (without the supercilious air) and turned the act of pouring tea into exquisite stagecraft. A fine lady with no petty instincts, she was shocked by the catty gossip of the English society women when she arrived in London. She was never affected or haughty and when people stopped by their table at the Savoy Grill, Eva would rise with Siegmund to greet them—at a time when other women remained seated. Eva had natural class.

In the early 1950s, Siegmund and Eva moved from Roehampton Lane to a penthouse flat at 95, Eaton Square. Stanley Baldwin had lived two doors down and Neville Chamberlain across the square. The move to Belgravia signified that these Jewish refugees had *arrived*. With a natural gift for decorating, Eva created a faultless stage setting for Siegmund's career. On Saturday afternoons, they shopped for antiques, buying the old silver, Old Masters, modern paintings, and eighteenth-century English furniture that would set just the right tone of subdued elegance.

As a banker, Siegmund's style was to erase the barriers between business and pleasure. "You cannot be someone's banker until you are their friend," he would say.[4] Another time, he commented, only half in jest, that he never attended a meeting where business was discussed. By fusing home and office, Siegmund had to subordinate Eva to the massive requirements of his career. Over time, Siegmund's business and social calendar would expand to fill his waking hours, removing any chance for a relaxed or natural private life.

From Eva, Siegmund demanded superhuman precision as they entertained an endless stream of bankers, politicians, clients, and trainees. Everything had to be planned, with nothing left to chance. With her slight, hesitating voice and rather British manner, Eva could uniquely deliver that perfection. Many visitors marveled at the clockwork precision at Eaton Square, with a butler in black tie brought in from the office to serve dishes from silver platters. If Siegmund wished to appear casually elegant, he might slip into black patent leather pumps. Evenings ended with port and cigars for the men. Eva played her role beautifully and Siegmund called her his greatest career asset.[5]

On the surface at least, it often seemed that Eva was reduced to a splendid ornament with little chance to develop her own personality. Their marriage revolved around his life, not hers. Siegmund even had to approve her dresses. Because he hated polka dots, she didn't wear polka dots. And she was always turned out immaculately, as Siegmund required. With another man, Eva might have experimented—might even have been a bit of a rebel—but Siegmund froze her into a formal social role. She came from a generation of women who took their cue from the men and she felt it her task in life to help her husband. As a girl, she had received tough training, which made the transition to being Siegmund's wife less jarring than it might otherwise have been. She also took for granted the terrific pace of his work, which she had grown accustomed to in Hamburg and Berlin.

The relationship that started so romantically in Hamburg had been tested by many trials: Eva's early cancer, the flight to Sweden and London, the death of Eva's mother, the breakdown of Siegmund's mother, the Danilova affair, the London blitz, the adjustment to a new country, etc. Their bark had weathered rough seas. In the late 1930s, Siegmund often didn't arrive home until late at night. After the war he spent more than half the year on the road, so that Eva had to adapt her life to his extended absences.

In 1948, Eva, forty-five, developed cancer in her remaining breast. Siegmund didn't see how she could cope with its loss and wouldn't let her have surgery. This ultrarational man then did something strange: He took Eva to an unconventional doctor who rubbed ointment on the breast and the cancer, implausibly, went into remission. The fear of cancer haunted their lives although Eva, with her extraordinary self-discipline, never voiced that fear. Whenever she fell ill, Siegmund was beside himself with worry. His friend, Dr. Goldman, who treated Eva for cancer in the 1960s, recalled, "He was frightfully worried about her, but in an almost impersonal way. Siegmund adored his wife, but he didn't understand her. She was very interested in clothes, fashion, and decorating. Their relationship was cordial but distant."[6] One should note that there was always a certain coolness between Dr. Goldman and Eva. But other people had a similar sense of a curious distance, a forced ceremony, between the couple.

At bottom, Eva was far more than a pretty decoration. She was shrewd and worldly while Siegmund retained a touch of naïveté. If he breakfasted in New York with his secretary, it didn't dawn on him that people might gossip. Eva warned Siegmund against putting people on a pedestal only to set himself up for later disappointment. She mothered Siegmund and constantly advised her exhausted husband to take vacations. When he traveled, she would pull aside aides at the airport to tell them what Siegmund needed. She always felt protective toward him. Siegmund greatly respected her judgment and would often pull her out of the kitchen to eavesdrop on a long-distance business call so that she could offer her advice afterward. They shared many values, including the need for punctuality and reliability.

The marriage had a strong Pygmalion streak. If Siegmund read a book, Eva had to read it. If he liked erudite books, he assumed this gave her equal contentment. They had shared pleasures, ranging from bridge to country walks, and each year went on what Siegmund called a "fasting cure" together so he could lose weight. But with Siegmund chained to his ambition, Eva never demanded parity. He also paid little heed to his in-laws. Not fond of the Philipsons, he seldom went to Sweden, even on business. When he did, the trips were short, carefully orchestrated, and didn't include Eva.

Eva had great difficulty in expressing herself and tended to swallow her anger. She had many unexpressed regrets. As someone who enjoyed ceremony, she would have gladly celebrated the Sabbath, but Siegmund shunned any traditions that lacked logic. He was allergic to organized religion, which played no real part in their lives. Eva might want to linger over dinner and talk, but Siegmund would bolt down his food and go back to his briefcase. Siegmund was such a scintillating talker that Henry Kissinger and other luminaries would fly across the Atlantic just to lunch with him. Yet, after Siegmund's death, Eva lamented that they had never just sat and talked after dinner.

Siegmund read late at night and had a separate bedroom from Eva. Even when they traveled, he took a room with two beds—one for sleep, the other to set out his books and business papers. A creature of habit, with a manic need for order, he arranged everything down to the last detail. If he had apples in his hotel icebox, he neatly lined them up in red, green, and yellow parallel rows. Similarly at work, he had yellow folders for mail, blue for notes, orange for stock-exchange lists, etc. In his closet, he had three versions of each blue and gray suit—one for summer, one for winter, one for medium weight.

At times, Eva revolted. When she packed his suitcase for trips, he demanded that every pen and pencil be lined up. Once Siegmund raised a terrible ruckus when she omitted an item. Indignant, Eva swore she would never pack his suitcase again and made good on her promise. In later years, she wouldn't go with him to New York, fearing she would be dragooned into nonstop dinners. Perhaps resenting this, Siegmund didn't let her come to New York in the 1960s when she once wanted to visit some friends. He sent a sanctimonious telex from New York, saying he didn't wish his "dear one" to "overstimulate" herself by traveling there.[7] One senses that, in the end, Eva struck a bargain: She would give part of herself to Siegmund's career, but the rest she would keep to herself. This may explain the private, aloof air people noticed about her. One side of her felt relieved by Siegmund's frequent absences, which gave her a little time to herself. Life with Siegmund was alternately exhilarating and oppressive.

Complicating the marriage was Siegmund's relations with George and Anna, who experienced the predictable problems that come from having a strict, workaholic German father with authoritarian tendencies. As with everything, Siegmund formed precise pictures in his mind of how his children should behave then refused to modify that image. Both children were British in style: polite, understated, modest, private, and rather inscrutable. They didn't have their father's fierce ambition and were much more like Eva. This meant Siegmund was somewhat isolated in his own family. Eva, meanwhile, walked a delicate tightrope. As a good mother, she had to protect the children from Siegmund's excesses without setting him off. She learned to invite Anna's friends over only when Siegmund was away and it wouldn't conflict with his schedule. When she defended the children against Siegmund's wrath, he would arrive at the office in a terrible state of agitation, asking the uncles rhetorically how Eva could possibly take George or Anna's side?

Siegmund adored Anna, who didn't bear the dynastic burden of being a son in a banking family. She was a fine, modest young woman with little self-confidence. She was so shy that she trembled in young men's arms when they danced. Yet, underneath, she was imaginative and strong-minded. Very bright, she went to St. Paul's Girls' School and to Oxford University. In true Max Warburg fashion, Siegmund blocked Anna's wish to marry an Indian cartoonist for *The Observer* and arranged for her to work at the Weizmann Institute. Whether by chance or secret rebellion, Anna fell in love with men who seemed the antithesis of Siegmund.

At Christmas 1959, Anna had visited Israel with her parents and decided to live there. In 1962, age thirty-one, Anna married a real estate developer, Dov Biegun, who was nearly twenty years her senior. They had met while Dov was visiting Israel and decided to settle there. In some respects, Dov was a prototypical Eastern European Jew. Raised in a shtetl rich in Jewish folklore, he remembered mounted Cossacks bursting into his house and whipping his grandfather. After studying economics in Prague, he ended up in the British Army during the war, performing intelligence work in Norway. All but one of his sisters had died in the Holocaust. A zealous Zionist, he participated in dangerous underground work in the period immediately preceding Israel's creation.

Dov was a talented, cosmopolitan man who knew fourteen languages and was a superb storyteller. But by Siegmund's standards, he was rough, crude, and engaged in business that definitely wasn't *haute banque.* Though Siegmund opposed the match, Anna persisted and she and Dov had one daughter. Dov—who called Siegmund "the Chief"—used to joke with Anna that Siegmund's ideal wedding would contain two people: "You and him." Siegmund was forever dispatching lieutenants to help Dov with commercial deals that never seemed to pan out.

Siegmund had a more troubled relationship with his son, George, who was tall, blue-eyed, sensitive, and self-effacing. His facial structure resembled Siegmund's, but otherwise he looked like Eva's brother. His gentle, courteous manner owed something to Eva, something to his proper British education. During the war, when George attended Westminster School, Siegmund saw with delight a British gentleman in the making. "I am very pleased with the development of George who is a keen and gentle young man," he told a friend, adding that his son had "a lot of the reserved gentleman in him."[8] The fiery, obsessive German father and the quiet, soft-spoken son would stare at each other across a deep cultural chasm. Of her shy son, Eva would say, "George is a wonderful young man. But when he goes out to meet people, I have to tell him in advance, 'Now George, be charming.' "[9]

Perhaps because he experienced little frivolity as a boy, Siegmund adopted a serious attitude toward his son. On George's twenty-first birthday, Siegmund gave him a life insurance policy—with George expected to pay the premiums himself.[10] As a young man, George fantasized about joining his father's firm and for five years trained as an accountant in preparation. In 1954, Siegmund brought him into S. G. Warburg & Co. under the tutelage of Frank Smith, who worked with medium-sized British companies. George was terrific with numbers and enjoyed the clients, but Siegmund pictured him as a big international banker. Wanting George to follow in his own footsteps, he tried to inspire him, telling him the firm needed new ideas. In the end, it upset Siegmund that he and Eva hadn't spawned another superman, but only a bright, pleasant, polite young man of above-average intelligence and verbal gifts—not a world-historical figure.

Siegmund was tough with George, criticizing him sharply if he failed to write a proper letter, as he did with all the young men. Sometimes he gave him especially difficult accounts. George felt the full burden of paternal expectation. He and Siegmund had mismatched sensibilities. Siegmund demanded dawn-to-dusk elegance, while George was informal, loved folk and modern art, and didn't try to impress people. One Monday morning in the 1960s, Siegmund arrived at work aghast: He had seen George wandering through the London streets on Saturday in casual clothes! George liked the free spirit of London in the sixties, while Siegmund jeered at the student demonstrators as Rebels Without a Cause. Both father and son were stubborn and refused to yield ground to each other.

Another son might have rebelled or have capitulated to all of Siegmund's wishes. Instead, George tried to please his father while quietly asserting his own autonomy. Siegmund opposed George's wish to marry Ellie Bozyan, a non-Jewish woman of Armenian extraction whose father was a professor at the Yale Music School and the university organist. Short, cheerful, warm, and friendly, Ellie was very musical and encouraged George's Bohemian bent. She wasn't the *soignée* fashion-plate blonde with old-money antecedents that Siegmund had in mind for George and she was certainly too American and emancipated for his tastes. Ernst Spiegelberg was courageous enough to intercede with Siegmund and put in a good word for Ellie. In return he suffered a permanent demotion in his standing with Siegmund.

In the end, George refused to bow to Siegmund's will. By announcing his engagement right after Lucie's death he wounded his father. In 1956 George married Ellie in a simple, nondenominational service outside the summer home of Ellie's parents in Newport, Rhode Island. Siegmund, Eva, and Anna attended. At Eva's suggestion, they invited the nanny who had taken care of George in Boston nearly thirty years before and she brought along her policeman husband. Siegmund and Eva were delighted to see this woman again and were struck by how the intervening decade had been so tranquil for her, so turbulent for them.

At the office, Siegmund gave George many chances and wanted his son to succeed, but George's heart wasn't in the business. He didn't always function as a smoothly oiled machine. At one S. G. Warburg–Kuhn, Loeb summit meeting in the early 1960s, George was put in charge of arrangements. He was supposed to see to it that the tables were set up in faultless S. G. Warburg style—every pencil sharpened, every pad aligned. Instead, he didn't show up and went with Ellie to a concert. When the participants arrived, nothing was ready—a huge embarrassment to Siegmund, who muffled his anger. Then John Schiff innocently asked where George was and Siegmund erupted in a tantrum so intense that he actually foamed at the mouth. An embarrassing moment ensued before a quick-witted Kuhn, Loeb partner suggested that they adjourn to caucus. Siegmund disappeared into an adjoining room with Henry Grunfeld, who tried to calm him down.[11] Siegmund never said anything to his son and nobody else ever dared to mention it to George.

Siegmund would have been upset by the insinuation that he was an autocratic parent and professed astonishment at the notion that his son might legitimately have a psychological complex about having a strong father. He simply thought he knew what was best for his children and acted accordingly. But such a powerhouse of a man—such a freight train of energy—would have overwhelmed any son. In 1963, George left S. G. Warburg & Co. to set up his own financial-advisory firm called Wainside. The day he left, he said a great weight had been lifted from his shoulders. Siegmund thought George's departure a terrible mistake and interpreted it as an unforgivable act of disloyalty.

The departure dashed Siegmund's hopes for establishing a new Warburg dynasty in London. He tried to be philosophic about it. Echoing the speech Uncle Max had made at the May 1938 Aryanization, he said the firm was a living entity that transcended its current occupants, and that S. G. Warburg & Co. was his child as much as any human child.[12] It was a terrible irony that Siegmund, who cared so deeply about family honor and waged such a lengthy crusade to revivify the Warburg name, had nobody to inherit the firm. By universal agreement, he had failed as a father. For all his extraordinary intelligence, he was never introspective or privy to the secret workings of his own mind and always suffered from some fateful shortage of self-knowledge. Because he didn't fully understand himself and hadn't known a normal family life as a child, he didn't know how to act when things went awry. He dwelled only on how others had disappointed him, never the reverse.

After George left, Siegmund made random efforts to recruit other Warburgs into the firm to perpetrate the name. On one Paris visit, he invited Eddy Lachman—a grandson of Aby S., who had spent the war in Holland with his mother, Olga—to lunch at an elegant Parisian hotel. Already, on a previous visit, Siegmund had suggested to Eddy that he change his name to Warburg. Now Siegmund carried his plan a step further. "During lunch Siegmund asked me why I wouldn't join him at the bank. I immediately shot back that I was a journalist and not a banker. 'Oh,' he answered, 'that you can learn in six months.' I was a bit aghast. Then I thought how unkind such a proposition was towards my cousin George, with whom I had played." Eddy remembered the unhappy experience of relatives who had worked for Siegmund and was grateful when Eva rescued him. "Eva, sensing my embarrassment, remarked that nepotism in business never worked."[13]

—

Perhaps it was his disappointment with people that made Siegmund so passionate about books. Entranced by them from boyhood, he got an unadulterated joy from reading that he didn't get from business. As Eva noted, "If Siegmund is engrossed in a book, you could put him in a chair in Piccadilly Circus and he wouldn't lift his head from the page."[14] At the dentist, Siegmund would take his novocaine injection, then sit in the chair reading Plato, oblivious of everything else. Like a perennial graduate student, he read, absorbed, annotated, and internalized books. An amazingly speedy reader, he could put away six books in a weekend. On trips, he always lugged in his suitcase a huge edition of Burton E. Stevenson's *The Home Book of Quotations.*

Reading in several languages, he went through Stendhal, Tolstoy, Shakespeare, Goethe, and Trollope. How many London bankers read Greek and Latin classics for pleasure? How many had waded through Thomas Mann's *Doctor Faustus* three times? How many could recite by heart the last page of *Tonio Kröger?* He once said, "The four most important things to me are first, human beings; second, books; third, the sun; and fourth, music."[15] In London, he seldom had the third and despite his fondness for Bach, Mozart, Beethoven, Schumann, and Handel and frequent trips to the Glyndebourne Opera, his musical appreciation trailed behind his love of books. Even Siegmund conceded his love of books sometimes surpassed his interest in people: "And I find it even sometimes more interesting to meet other people in books than in person."[16]

Every Monday morning, Siegmund would arrive with three or four book reviews marked off from the Sunday paper. His three secretaries would promptly purchase the books and assemble pertinent reviews up front. His motto from Samuel Butler was then stamped in each book: "Progress in Thinking is Progress Toward Simplicity." Siegmund would note important passages and mark their page numbers in pencil up front. He always carried, in a soft leather case hand-sewn by Eva, a rubber eraser for corrections. The vast majority of his books dealt with history, biography, philosophy, or literature, with only a smattering of books on economics—an odd omission for a legendary financier. He preferred to read about totalitarianism or sexual motivation than about corporate bonds. If one read all of George Bernard Shaw, he sometimes said, that would be an education in itself.

In the end, Siegmund accumulated about four thousand closely read books. It was a very Jewish love of books. No less than Uncle Aby, Siegmund took pride in his library and was annoyed if someone rearranged it. But though an ardent bibliophile, he only went once to the Warburg Institute and declined offers to serve on the board, probably from fear that he would be pumped for money. His careful distancing from the Institute also stemmed from its association with Eric and the Mittelweg Warburgs.

Siegmund enjoyed conversing about books. The top corporate people, he said, preferred literary talk to dull chatter about debentures. Very often, after a meeting, a surprised client would receive a hand-delivered parcel of books that Siegmund had mentioned. To judge their interests or test their intellectual subtlety, he asked young job seekers in interviews what they had read lately. A learned discourse about Thomas Mann or August Strindberg could more easily land a job than sound economic reflections. When a young prospective recruit named Martin Gordon told Siegmund he was studying classical languages and literature at Oxford, Siegmund exclaimed, "I'm *so* glad you are not studying economics!"[17] Some cynics thought Siegmund's book talk a magnificent cover, a sure-fire sales pitch designed to lure clients seeking that coveted touch of "class." If so, it was a masterful strategy, for it allowed Siegmund to create a seamless unity between his banking career and his all-consuming hobby.

Siegmund read purposefully, culling epigrams that appealed to him and could be used in conversation. Starting in the 1930s, he had secretaries type out memorable extracts and added aphorisms of his own coinage to the pile. Eventually he accumulated more than two thousand quotations. Stuffed into a drawer, they would form part of a commonplace book that would occupy Siegmund in his last years.

How could a man of infinite appointments have time for this stupendous personal culture? The answer is that Siegmund never wasted a second. In stores, he would point his umbrella at clothes and say, "I'll take three of those." When he bought glasses, the optometrist would bring frames to his office. Siegmund would try them on and not even bother to look at himself in the mirror. Though he helped to introduce commercial television in Britain, he scarcely ever watched it and didn't listen to radio or attend movies. He never traveled without a book; if he had a few minutes to spare in a taxi or airport, he would open a book and read.

In general, Siegmund skipped the small and large social niceties of life, although he liked a cozy evening at home playing bridge or gin rummy. Unless absolutely required, he didn't attend cocktail parties or International Monetary Fund meetings and never joined the gentlemen's clubs that form the backdrop of London business. He declined invitations to most weddings, bar mitzvahs, and other such celebrations. He had no small talk. If he sat next to a bright, gorgeous woman at a dinner, he would chat delightedly all evening; but if seated next to an attractive vacant woman, he would stare into space. As a rule, he attended no dinner party with more than ten people, convinced it would lack serious talk. When Harold Wilson invited him to dine at 10 Downing Street, he asked, before accepting, how many people would attend. As he once grumbled, "these big parties, where there are 100 people, this is modern barbarism."[18]

Siegmund reflected a cult of simplicity common among the intellectual heroes of his boyhood. He mocked the money-mad crowd. "If orange juice were as expensive as champagne," he said, "people would serve it at elaborate parties."[19] For this banker, greed was the most shameful sin. He complained that many financial people had an "erotic relationship to money" and cited André Meyer as a prime offender.[20] Siegmund likened such mercenary tendencies to necrophilia.[21] A monkish side of him hated all material striving. In 1949, he visited Paul Ziegler at his monastery. Originally Jewish, Ziegler was an old friend who had converted to Catholicism and become a Benedictine monk and Siegmund came away highly impressed by his regulated life.[22]

Siegmund's head seemed too large for his body, and the symbolism was appropriate, since he was an entirely cerebral person. He was so unmechanical that Eva filled his fountain pens. This discomfort with the physical universe probably contributed to his withering, merciless views on sports. In his hatred of skiing he was nearly pathological. People went skiing, he said, to overcome inferiority complexes, but it made them instead moral cowards by consuming their courage on the slopes. At dinner parties, to general merriment, Siegmund delighted in mimicking the frenzied faces of skiers careering down the slopes. More than one S. G. Warburg person who broke a leg skiing invented a story about having been in a traffic accident.

This contempt for sports may also have stemmed from Siegmund's own physical shortcomings. He suffered from a curvature of the spine that degenerated into a slight but noticeable humpback. (In later years, a doctor thought Siegmund had a shadow on his lung because the hump so distorted an X-ray.) Because of this deformity, Siegmund walked with a stoop. When fitted for suits, he straightened up and they never perfectly fit him. Self-conscious about the hump, he seldom removed his jacket; many people who knew Siegmund for decades never saw him in shirtsleeves. Both psychologically and sartorially, Siegmund was a tightly buttoned-up person. To be sporty, he donned a beret but that was absolutely the extent of his liberties.

Siegmund's preoccupation with clothing of conservative taste was partly professional. He thought a banker should present just the right image, which meant approved shades of black, blue, and gray. Any shade of green or brown struck him as a shocking lapse of taste, although he occasionally made grudging exceptions. When Robin Jessel began working for him, Siegmund summoned him one day. "Robin, I see you have on a brown suit. But I see you are wearing black shoes. Harry Lucas always said that it was okay in the City if you had on a brown suit if you also wore black shoes."[23] At Kuhn, Loeb, he once called in a young executive to tell him that his suit wasn't right, that it was getting shiny, and that he might consider purchasing another.

Siegmund had an unerring eye for telltale details and was fascinated by the character clues hidden in neckties. Never a believer in fashion statements, he said, "If you notice the tie a man's wearing, it's too loud."[24] He learned more about clients from their clothing than their balance sheets. One day in the 1960s, he brought some German and American executives together to discuss a deal he had been pondering for some time. In the middle of lunch, Siegmund's mood changed and he suddenly, inexplicably, cooled off on the deal. At a later postmortem, his puzzled staff asked what had gone wrong. Apparently, the American chief executive had hiked up the sleeve of his suit, disclosing shirt cuffs with monogrammed initials. With gleeful derision, Siegmund asked, "Did you see the man's cuffs?" He thought it an appalling example of nouveau-riche vanity that forever altered his opinion of the man. Doing deals with the man was now *infra dig*.

In his relations with people, Siegmund would "read" them and track their development, as if they were interesting characters in a novel. If he wanted to hire somebody, he would pursue them relentlessly for years. He had an uncanny ability to blend people from fancy and mundane backgrounds. At a time when the City hired young Tories with public school and Oxbridge backgrounds, Siegmund opted for offbeat characters. He hired a young Reuters correspondent named Ian Fraser who decided to leave the press agency and enter merchant banking when his advancement was blocked. Despite his total ignorance of banking, Siegmund hired him because of his fluency in German and knowledge of Germany. When he offered to hire a Canadian diplomat named Tony Griffin, the latter demurred, explaining that he had no banking experience and was a poor mathematician. "My dear friend," Siegmund replied, "I want you precisely for the fact that you're a diplomat and not a mathematician."[25] He would hire people for his own distinctively quirky reasons. When a young solicitor named Bernard Kelly showed him a list of his legal accomplishments, Siegmund seemed surprisingly impressed. Kelly protested that the deeds listed were routine things, like wills and estates. Siegmund smiled and said, "Yes, but I like that you made up the list."[26]

As a lifelong student of human nature, Siegmund was often attracted to people who were rebellious, even controversial. In the 1950s, he hired a man named Christopher Burney, a British spy captured in France during the war who had been imprisoned in Buchenwald for over a year. After the war, Burney wrote a book about his experiences called *The Dungeon Democracy* that outraged the Jewish community. Although he condemned German barbarism, he didn't glorify the Jewish inmates either and showed how badly they had behaved under inhuman conditions: "They were annoying in the extreme by their obsequiousness, even to the S.S., and even among themselves they behaved more like animals than men, fighting and even robbing the dead and dying of their clothing."[27] Some reviewers found the book tasteless, while others saw it as remarkably brave and candid.

Something about Burney piqued Siegmund's curiosity. A born contrarian, Siegmund was often drawn to people who took unpopular stands. "Siegmund took Burney in as a trainee in the 1950s," recalled John Libby of Kuhn, Loeb. "One day Siegmund said to him, 'I don't think you're happy here' and suggested a walking tour for 30 days."[28] Siegmund made him a manager in the British and French Bank and when that didn't work out, got him another job. Siegmund didn't prolong the world war. In the 1950s, he hired as a trainee the son of the former head of I. G. Farben, the industrial conglomerate that, among other things, had manufactured gas for the camps.

Siegmund knew thousands of people, yet the inner man remained veiled. As Lord Roll noted, "This created a certain aura of mystery round him and led to his becoming a near-legend in his lifetime."[29] Although Siegmund and Henry Grunfeld worked together for forty-seven years, they never posed together for a picture. Photos never graced S. G. Warburg reports or brochures, which were printed on plain paper. No firm was more reticent. Siegmund liked to quote his Kaulla grandfather on the three degrees of secrecy. In the first, a man swears to keep something secret, but tells his wife. In the second, he doesn't tell his wife. In the third stage, he doesn't remember the secret himself three years later. Siegmund inhabited the third stage.[30]

Like many people who stayed clear of the newspapers, Siegmund created a mystique by omission. He only gave a few interviews during his lifetime and then only on the proviso that he meticulously edit and "correct" them before publication. He never submitted to spontaneous self-exposure and maintained complete control over his public image. When he granted an interview to the *Sunday Telegraph* in 1970, it was such a novelty that the paper trumpeted, "Sir Siegmund Warburg speaks."[31] He enjoyed his reputation as a man of infinite contacts, a canny sphinx, a confidant of industrial titans.

Siegmund condemned psychoanalysis as symptomatic of personal weakness and was puzzled why somebody as smart as Jimmy Warburg took it seriously. Yet Freudian theory permeated his thinking—for instance, his belief that gossip compensated for sexual inadequacy—and he had his own ersatz therapy.[32] With a powerful strain of hypochondria, Siegmund often stopped at the doctor on his way to work and constantly fretted about his health. He always had a ruling doctor or guru. One Warburg director suggested that he try a distinguished London physician named Dr. Carl Heinz Goldman, a German-Jewish refugee who started a one-man practice after the war. When Siegmund entered his office, he addressed the doctor in Latin and was startled when he replied in perfect Latin. It was like a homecoming, the first exchange establishing that they had the same classical *Gymnasium* education in Germany. This forged a strong bond between them. Sometimes, however, Siegmund spoke in a Swabian dialect that even Dr. Goldman couldn't understand.

At first, Dr. Goldman ministered to Siegmund's body, treating him for diabetes and tension-related headaches and giving him placebo injections of vitamin B_{12}. Siegmund, brightening after these visits, christened Dr. Goldman the *"Zaubermeister,"* or "Miracle Man." After a time, the visits expanded into wide-ranging historical discussions about Bismarck's error in creating the German Reich or Hitler's clever exploitation of public-works projects to build mass support. A man with an air of oracular wisdom, Dr. Goldman also had a worldly side and liked to discuss financial ventures with Siegmund.

In time, Dr. Goldman tended to Siegmund's sorrows as well as bodily aches. To discuss emotional problems directly was very hard for Siegmund, which meant that his anger sprayed out in a thousand indirect and inappropriate ways. There was a frightening spot of vulnerability inside him that produced great pain. When despondent about his wife, family, or colleagues, he began to spill out his problems to Dr. Goldman in what sounded suspiciously like Freud's "talking cure." "Siegmund was a deeply unhappy and lonely man," said Dr. Goldman. "He was often plagued by suspicion and contempt of other human beings. He was a hard critic of his colleagues and didn't get on with anybody. He had a fear of office intrigues and came to me to unload his worries. He was completely egocentric and fundamentally conceited. He thought most other people were fools."[33]

Extremely sentimental, Siegmund would often shower friends with gifts and fulsome, flowery letters of affection. Dr. Goldman was touched by Siegmund's tokens of esteem: the hundred blue plums he later sent from Switzerland, finely wrapped in tissue paper, or the complete *Encyclopædia Britannica* that arrived one day. After they once discussed the psychology of debtors and creditors, Siegmund got so carried away with enthusiasm that he invited Goldman to join the S. G. Warburg board. The doctor declined, knowing he would lose his independence. At the same time, Siegmund never showed much interest in Dr. Goldman's personal feelings. "He deeply affected me because he was so brilliant and so lonely," said the doctor.

Siegmund's other intimate friendship was with the S. G. Warburg graphologist, Mrs. Theodora Dreifuss. Handwriting analysis was far more popular in Germany and Austria than in England and was a long-standing Warburgian pastime. Max had converted Moritz to graphology after sending a client's handwriting to an expert and getting back a detailed, accurate report.[34] An amateur graphologist, Fritz often analyzed handwritings in the M. M. Warburg mail. Even Henry Grunfeld was a believer, having ferreted out an embezzler in his prewar German firm through graphology.

In the 1950s, Siegmund started to use graphology to screen job applicants at S. G. Warburg & Co., hoping to weed out people who were depressed or devious and spot those who were especially creative and reliable. Graphology revealed things ordinarily concealed from view. But in postwar London, it seemed an arcane procedure that added to the image of S. G. Warburg as a very strange, alien firm. After applicants wrote a few lines in a fountain pen, their handwriting, age, and sex were passed along to a graphologist. This diagnostic tool was taken seriously at Warburg. In one case a person rejected at his first interview was called back and hired on the strength of his graphology test.

Once concerned about the emotional state of an associate, Siegmund sent a specimen of his handwriting to Theodora Dreifuss, a Swiss graphologist and psychologist who was a distant relative on the Warburg side. Her analysis stunned Siegmund: She seemed to know more about the man from his handwriting than Siegmund did after years of daily conversation. Siegmund began to use her regularly, and after a time no important person was hired at S. G. Warburg & Co. without her approval. The analyses Theodora mailed to London were often astounding in their scope and precision. To further her work, Siegmund in 1963 endowed from his own pocket the European Foundation of Graphological Science and Application, creating a chair in graphology at the University of Zurich.

Educated in psychology, Theodora Dreifuss was an imposing woman, proud, stimulating, funny, perceptive, and sometimes gruff. She was one of the few people who could tease Siegmund or disagree with him and get away with it. She tried to wean him away from a constant need to convert people to his point of view. In her strength, self-confidence, and fierce intelligence, she was his counterpart and once boasted of her analyses, "I've never been wrong." There was an almost universal impression at S. G. Warburg that Siegmund and Theodora were lovers. In letters, he struck the warmest tone with her and often spent spare weekends with her in Zurich. Siegmund's fascination with graphology extended beyond office use, and he sent Theodora letters from politicians he knew. He liked to have a secret knowledge of people's weaknesses, a sense of what made them tick, a competitive edge in understanding them. And he liked to keep Theodora busy.

Whether or not they were lovers, Theodora occupied a place in Siegmund's life analogous to that of Dr. Goldman, and he took personal problems to her. Often, Dr. Goldman would go to Zurich, too, so that they formed a little trio. In later years, Siegmund even had daydreams about the three of them starting a consulting firm together with his chief secretary, Doris Wasserman. It was a characteristic Siegmund pipe dream. Even as he became a grand personage, he yearned to withdraw into a life of simple pleasures. He looked back wistfully to the tough, early days when his London business was still small. He had no sooner succeeded than he began to dream of starting again and escaping from the extraordinary machine he had created.

Siegmund Warburg making a
quite definite point in negotiations.
(Courtesy of Peter Spira)

Enemy of the City

Siegmund Warburg's virtues and vices were closely allied. The qualities that made him a trying person—his perfectionism, hair-trigger temper, and high expectations—made him a matchless banker. To his adoring but fearful troops at 9–13, King William Street, he conveyed constant dissatisfaction, making people strive to perform better. They stretched themselves for Siegmund, believing they worked directly for him and taking pride in it. Like some omnipresent deity, he would telephone even lowly subordinates to offer profuse praise or scathing criticism. He read outgoing mail and pounced on errors. Subordinates felt this all-seeing man knew their innermost weaknesses. Because they feared his reproach and revered his intelligence, they struggled to please him, giving him a powerful grip on them. The constant monitoring of everybody's work allowed Siegmund to identify talented newcomers.

This boss had a long list of pet grievances. He didn't like diminutives, abbreviations, or people who chatted with clients in the corridor. He was tough on smokers long before such militancy was fashionable. Like schoolboys sneaking behind the headmaster's back, even senior executives puffed away on the sly. When uncle Ernest Thalmann—a bright, rather delicate man who respected but feared Siegmund—heard him shuffling down the hall, he would slide open a desk drawer, squash his cigarette in a hidden ashtray, then close it. One day, Siegmund shuffled into Thalmann's office and saw wisps of smoke issuing from a slit. "My dear Ernest," he said with wry amusement, "I think your desk is on fire."

A marvelous actor, Siegmund would stage fake tantrums then slyly wink at his associates, saying, "Well, I think that had the right effect, don't you?"[1] Sometimes he whispered in German to Grunfeld, "Should I get angry?"[2] He adroitly used his temper to keep people nervous, off balance, uncomfortable, working at maximum capacity. Pleased when one secretary said a boss had to be a bit disliked to be respected, he exhorted soft-spoken executives to shout more. It was not unusual for Siegmund to materialize in a laggard department and start to rave like the wrath of god, "We're not a second-rate firm. We're not a third-rate firm. We're a tenth-rate firm!" Then he would storm out, leaving his startled subordinates sitting there, agape, wondering what had just happened.

Sometimes the histrionics were in earnest. Siegmund liked to scream, bang his fists, and slam doors. Occasionally, if a colleague's telephone line was busy, he hurled the phone violently at the wall then buzzed for a porter to retrieve it. He might do this several times in an hour. One day, after a flaming row, Siegmund burst from his office and flung his cup across the hallway, nearly hitting the poor lady pushing the tea trolley. Afterward, he apologized to the shaken woman.[3] Telephone-throwing became de rigueur at Warburgs. One recruit remembers approaching the building his first day and seeing a lonely telephone swinging high on a cord from an upper-story window.

Sometimes Siegmund's outbursts were calculated and spontaneous at the same time. His Alsterufer relative, Eddy Lachman, records this story of having lunch with Siegmund and Eva in Paris:

"When the lunch was over Siegmund went to the garderobe where he had checked his umbrella. Eva and I stood some distance away. The check-in girl handed him a wrong umbrella and with French aggressiveness kept insisting that it was his. Siegmund started to roar like a wounded lion. Eva and I—knowing what was bound to happen—retreated into the most obscure corner of the lobby trying to look as if we had nothing to do with the offended man at the garderobe. Siegmund kept on shouting and protesting. Within seconds he was encircled by all the gold-uniformed porters, flunkies, and assistant managers in striped pants that the hotel could muster, as they were obviously afraid that some terrible accident might happen. The public formed a wide ring of curious onlookers around the scene that lasted quite a few minutes. In the end—after the head manager had penetrated into the wildly gesticulating mob and had found Siegmund's own umbrella—he came to us in our corner, quietly happy, totally satisfied, smiling broadly as if nothing had happened. The storm was over."[4]

At S. G. Warburg & Co., the working day lasted well into the evening, winning it the nickname of "the night club."[5] It was known as a two-coat firm—one coat you wore, the other you left on your seat if you slipped out. Siegmund worked harder than anybody. At eight-fifteen in the morning he was already in the back of his chauffeured car, dictating to his secretary. When he rode home with Henry Grunfeld in the evening, they reviewed the day's events. One evening, wandering through the office at six-thirty, Siegmund was dismayed to find empty desks. The next morning he fired off a memo, expressing regret that people left so early.[6] Shrewd at office psychology, he would stop by certain departments at seven every evening, training people to linger. When London suffered a blackout in the early 1970s, the S. G. Warburg staff beavered on by candlelight.

People found Siegmund's persistent demands terrifying, joyous, outrageous, uplifting. Many wives resented that he had stolen their husbands. When one wife fretted that her husband always explored deals that never reached fruition, Siegmund smiled. "Well, when I start a hundred deals, I can get two. But that doesn't mean I can do fifty to get one."[7] He went to extraordinary lengths to cultivate clients. Once, trying to impress Courtauld, the textile concern, he told a blue-uniformed messenger to hop on a motorcycle and—without paying attention to traffic lights—deliver a package personally to the chairman. "He used to say, 'We must do things with style,' " said his colleague, Arthur Winspear. "We must achieve the results. And the profit-and-loss account will follow."[8]

Although Siegmund denied it, S. G. Warburg hosted two separate lunches every day: one at 12:30 (ending promptly at 1:25) and a second at 1:30. At the less important 12:30 lunch, Siegmund would stop by to chat before presiding over the 1:30 affair. Although served in style, the fare was never rich or fancy. Siegmund agonized over place settings for lunch. Instead of talking about cricket, the firm brought in staff experts to make constructive suggestions so that no client left empty-handed. Siegmund taught his staff not just to advise but to listen to clients, to study and heed their needs. At other firms, if the person in charge of an account went on holiday, the account shut down. At Warburgs, somebody always returned the client's call. Siegmund demanded that incoming letters be answered the same day. With a punctilious regard for the amenities, he never failed to send birthday or condolence cards to clients.

In the early 1960s, the firm moved to a nondescript office building at 30, Gresham Street, posting no nameplate outside. Siegmund worried about overly rapid growth. "Oh God," he thought, "it's a bigger office, it's a more sumptuous office, a more pretentious office. I'm very afraid of provoking the gods."[9] Despite its antique clocks and fine prints, the office displayed what Siegmund termed "dignified austerity." After Nazi Germany, Siegmund and Grunfeld never shed their fears of sudden catastrophe and kept the style lean and sober. When one director wished to buy a Rolls-Royce, Siegmund talked him out of it as unbecoming. Even as the firm grew rich, it remained extremely frugal, using standard-issue furniture and serving midday coffee from plastic cups. Visitors, in contrast, drank from china cups and were received in rooms outfitted with beautiful furniture.

The firm's frugality could be comical. When a young director named Peter Spira sent a telegram from New York ending, "Best regards, Peter," Grunfeld was riled by this extraneous verbiage and suggested he end the telegram "Spira." (Siegmund ended his "Siegmund.") Another time, Spira ordered cold lobster from Harrod's for a directors' meeting. The next morning, Grunfeld summoned him. "You were outrageously extravagant for the dinner last night. You had five courses." "Five courses?" asked Spira. "Yes, you had a starter, lobster, cheese, fruit, and coffee—five courses," said Grunfeld.[10] For fifty years, Siegmund and Grunfeld carried passport photos showing them at age thirty because it seemed a waste of time and money to update them.

This sense of economy extended to words. Siegmund banned "in order to" as an extravagant substitute for "to." He loathed the expression "in point of fact" and immediately suspected of dishonesty anybody who began a sentence, "Frankly." He inveighed against "a diarrhea of words and constipation of ideas" and rivaled Hemingway in his passion for brevity. The secret of letter writing, Siegmund said, was to picture the desired answer then write a letter to produce it. Siegmund's own letters were models of understated elegance.

Even though there was no official chain of command and people could freely approach any executive, the uncles had a very German sense of hierarchy. They gave the impression of people at war. Indeed they *were* at war, still fighting the Nazis and seeing to it that Hitler didn't ruin their lives. The organizational structure was awesome. Each incoming letter was opened, summarized, then circulated to all directors before the nine-fifteen morning meeting. This Jesuitical firm even had strict rules about ending letters. For those in high standing, letters were signed, "Yours ever." More than one associate of Siegmund's grew pale with fear upon losing the coveted "Yours ever," reflecting a demotion in standing.[11]

These rules earned Siegmund the sobriquet of the "Headmaster" even as they produced work of exceptional polish. The Bank of England said the best-written memos came from S. G. Warburg. Siegmund stressed the importance of Warburg memos becoming the basis of deal discussions, enabling the firm to define the agenda. He also thought that ideas committed to paper acquired precision and could furnish evidence for later use. In 1972, when

Rothschilds tried to exclude S. G. Warburg from a Eurobond issue for an American client, Siegmund dispatched a young associate, Richard Lutyens, to the archives to unearth the memorandum of a verbal agreement he had made with Rothschilds fifteen years before. It was there, just as Siegmund predicted.[12]

Having lived through many upheavals, these German and Austrian refugees had an exaggerated need for order. The same systems that ensured top performance served as instruments of control. S. G. Warburg's success rested on a paradox: The firm was headed by a mostly benevolent tyrant who preached a teamwork ethic. Siegmund shunned the star system in favor of esprit de corps. The firm spent inordinate time keeping people informed. As Sir David Scholey later said, "We never use the first person singular, such as talking about *my* client or *my* proposition."[13] At least two Warburg people were present at all client meetings. Despite this intense group culture, Siegmund saw the firm as his own personality writ large and would never yield his prerogatives on major issues of personnel, strategy, and client relations.

After Weimar Germany, Siegmund didn't want to be blindsided by unpleasant surprises and liked to map out contingencies in advance. The two most taboo expressions at his firm were "Let's cross that bridge when we come to it," and "There's no point crying over spilt milk." Before takeover contests, Siegmund set up offensive and defensive teams to simulate all permutations of battle. People had to know their fall-back positions if their strategy misfired. He insisted upon postmortems to avoid future repetition of errors. Siegmund quoted Lucie as saying that if you were disappointed, you either became bitter and poorer or profited from it and became richer.[14] Or that a mistake was only a mistake if one didn't learn from it.[15] Or there was no bad weather, only inappropriate clothing. Banking for Siegmund involved perpetual self-criticism. At one point, he assigned a person to record all mistakes made and the remedies applied.

By 1957, Siegmund had crafted the splendid fighting machine that would soon dominate London finance, but he still had second-rate clients. He now ran a miniconglomerate. Besides Brandeis, Goldschmidt, he controlled the rubber merchants Hecht, Levis and Kahn, an ad agency, a firm of insurance brokers, and a property-development company. Most of these ventures prospered, although S. G. Warburg skirted reputational ruin with a copper refiner called Elkington. The Warburg-appointed manager engaged in sober hedging operations on the metals exchange, but when the price went the wrong way, he kept increasing his stake and ended up speculating wildly to cover his losses. It took Henry Grunfeld several hours to extract a confession from the man. A rescue operation was then mounted so that neither shareholders nor the S. G. Warburg image suffered.

To complete restoration of the Warburg name, Siegmund wanted to enter the front ranks of London merchant banks. To do so, he had to penetrate the august Accepting Houses Committee, whose seventeen member firms stood at the summit of London finance. With special backing from the Bank of England, their trade bills were discounted at the finest interest rates. Twice a year, the group met at the Bank of England, and the meetings were chaired by the governor himself. Many venerable member firms—Baring, Rothschild, and Schroder—traced their ancestry back to the early nineteenth century. The Committee was the very quintessence of *haute banque*.

In 1957 a member bank came up for sale for the first time in fifty years. Although the least prestigious member, Seligman Brothers provided the entrance ticket Siegmund wanted. Originally from Darmstadt, Germany, the Seligmans had emigrated to America, founded a distinguished house on Wall Street, then planted family partnerships in London and Paris. While not practicing Jews, they were socially prominent and on good terms with many substantial Jewish families. When two Seligman senior partners died in the 1950s, their firm was strapped for cash and managerial talent and needed to merge to survive.

As Siegmund negotiated with the Seligmans, it wasn't crystal-clear that S. G. Warburg would inherit its Accepting Houses cachet after a merger. So Geoffrey Seligman went to secure the regal blessing of C. F. Cobbold, the Bank of England governor, who nodded and said approvingly of Siegmund, "No rough elbows." Cobbold actually thought Siegmund something of an upstart, but respected him. Siegmund insisted that the merged firm bear *his* name. After hesitating, the Seligmans agreed that the letterhead would read, "S. G. Warburg & Company (incorporating Seligman Brothers)." This merger with a member of the venerable Accepting Houses Committee was an astonishing milestone for a firm launched just a decade before.

When the merger took place in May 1957, S. G. Warburg employed about eighty people and Seligman forty people. In retrospect, it seems the Seligmans were swallowed by Warburgs, not merged, and it was never an easy fit. Siegmund would have preferred Seligman Brothers without the Seligmans, but he needed them to retain their clients. Reginald Seligman was a clubman who liked to ski and fox hunt and was destined to clash with Siegmund. He left after a brief period. The funny, easygoing Spencer Seligman stayed but never ascended into the top ranks.

It was Cambridge-educated Geoffrey Seligman—formal, urbane—who experienced the greatest success and the keenest frustration. At first, Siegmund treated him courteously and placed him in an office with the aristocratic Lord Bridgeman so he would feel at home. But while Siegmund adorned Geoffrey with suitably high titles, he never admitted him to the inner sanctum of uncles. Seligman worked exceptionally hard, bringing in lucrative British clients such as Maxwell Joseph of Grand Metropolitan. In America, where he had Seligman and Lewisohn relatives, Geoffrey tended to such major clients as Textron and Cummins Engine. And he deferred to Siegmund. Yet Siegmund lorded it over Geoffrey, lest anyone think Seligmans had taken over Warburgs. Many associates suspect that Geoffrey expected far more from the merger and that the outcome must have quietly rankled. "Siegmund was always very hard on Geoffrey Seligman," Dr. Goldman confirmed. "He thought he was too social and went to too many parties."[16]

Once his bank absorbed Seligman Brothers, Siegmund was in a unique position. He now had establishment credentials. But in the dull, provincial City of the 1950s, he again faced condescension from insiders as he had in Hamburg, or at Kuhn, Loeb. People snickered at S. G. Warburg & Co. as "bond-washers" who made small profits by turning over securities that went X-dividend. Siegmund was again cast in the role of arriviste and enfant terrible.

For all his love of Britain, Siegmund deplored the tolerance of mediocrity he found in postwar London. Once, Siegmund and Eva entered a men's shop and Siegmund asked for a particular article. When the sales clerk replied brightly that they were out of stock, Siegmund exploded and made a scene. "How can you say that with such pleasure?" He found such complacency in the bowler-hatted City, too. (Hardly anybody at Warburgs wore bowler hats or carried furled umbrellas.) He thought the British upper class feared excellence and exertion and took refuge in an effete, snobbish gentility, behaving with an arrogance it no longer merited.

Siegmund's entire career seemed but a preamble to the British Aluminium battle that rocked London in late 1958. This fight would spotlight his tactical daring, his scorn for the smug scions of inherited wealth, his courage to gamble all for the sake of ambition, and his refusal to compromise in matters of principle. At the end, the British Olympians would be forced to acknowledge him as a peer, a new Prince of the City.

Siegmund entered the fray through Kuhn, Loeb, which advised American Metal Climax. In 1957, the American firm began to acquire shares in British Aluminium. When Siegmund went to plead for an American Metal Climax role, he was stiffly rebuffed by the British Aluminium (BA) board. So he knew he was dealing with an exclusive, inbred company that didn't welcome intruders.

Kuhn, Loeb also advised Reynolds Metals, which now decided to make a run at BA instead of American Metal Climax. Such a possibility was first broached in 1957 during a poolside talk in Jamaica between Sir William Wiseman—Siegmund's Kuhn, Loeb mentor—and Richard Reynolds. At the time, BA's stock was grossly undervalued, selling at a price about equal to the cost of a new plant it had built in Canada. Siegmund loved to shake up dozing firms. When Wiseman told him of Reynolds's desire to control British Aluminium, he saw a potential business conquest on a scale that had thus far eluded him.[17] Operating with astounding agility and stealth, Siegmund and Kuhn, Loeb amassed one million BA shares in New York and London before BA management noticed anything amiss. Even in the spring of 1958, the company still couldn't identify the predator buying up its shares.

Siegmund knew BA would create a brouhaha about a Yankee invasion of British industry. So he arranged a joint venture between Reynolds and a Midlands engineering group, Tube Investments Ltd. (TI), which was advised by Helbert Wagg. If they succeeded in buying British Aluminium, the British firm would have a 51 percent stake and the American firm a 49 percent stake. This should have laid the national-interest issue to rest, but it didn't.

In September 1958, Siegmund and Grunfeld worked out their strategy with Richard Reynolds and Sir Ivan Stedeford, the chairman of TI. Within weeks, they planned to inform British Aluminium that they controlled about 10 percent of its outstanding stock. Kuhn, Loeb; S. G. Warburg & Co.; and their friends held another 3 percent, while American Metal Climax retained its old 7 percent stake. Siegmund didn't contemplate a hostile takeover and braced for perhaps a year or two of protracted talks. He thought a judicious mixture of force and tact, thrust and retreat, could secure board representation for Reynolds/TI by peaceful means.[18] Instead, it would turn into the century's bloodiest financial row in London and leave behind a trail of bruised feelings and recriminations for years.

To understand this venomous fight, one must comprehend the sociology of the combatants. BA executives fancied themselves the industry's aristocrats. The chairman, Lord Portal, was a decorated wartime chief of air staff. Managing director Geoffrey Cunliffe was son of a former Bank of England governor. When BA got wind of trouble, it summoned Olaf Hambro and Lord Kindersley of Lazard Brothers to mount a defense. Both bankers sat on the Court of the Bank of England and were close friends of Cobbold. For these gentlemen, Siegmund committed several mortal sins at once. He was an arriviste conducting a hostile takeover against a blue-ribbon British firm for an American client. Lord Portal repeatedly warned that the honor of Great Britain was threatened by the ragtag Reynolds rabble. In June 1958, he had begun to negotiate a deal with Alcoa, which he considered BA's American counterpart. He sniffed at Reynolds Metals as an aggressive interloper, which reflected the way his City advisers perceived S. G. Warburg & Company.

The Aluminium War was thus a clash between those born to power and those who felt themselves entitled to more power based on superior drive and intelligence. Siegmund's main ally was the tall, silver-haired Lionel Fraser, the chairman of Helbert Wagg. A self-made man and butler's son, he admired and identified with Siegmund and served as something of a mentor to him. "Lionel felt that anybody who had started from nothing and achieved eminence was on a par with him," said his partner Michael Verey.[19] Sir Ivan Stedeford of TI was also self-made. And Siegmund was the offspring of a great dynasty who had started over in a foreign country. He would dwell on the bigotry turned against him during the Aluminium War. "They were up in arms against me," he recalled. "First of all, I was a newcomer in the City. Secondly, I was not an English newcomer, but a German newcomer—a Jewish newcomer, a fellow who has not been educated in British schools, a fellow who speaks with a foreign accent, all that sort of thing."[20]

Hostile takeovers were then unusual in the sedate City, where most deals were quietly negotiated in wood-paneled parlors before burning coal fires. If a merchant banker made an unfriendly bid, he was supposed to notify the chairman of the merchant bank advising the target firm. Siegmund violated this genteel code, which shocked the City. One day, the tall, mustachioed Hugh Kindersley of Lazards ran into Siegmund on the street and asked point-blank if he were buying British Aluminium shares. Siegmund said his firm was only buying BA stock for an investment account—neglecting to mention that it was for another metals company. When Kindersley found out Siegmund had lied to him, he flew into a rage. As a rule, Siegmund didn't tolerate falsehoods, but he made a distinction between lying and allowing someone to misinterpret a literal truth. He would wryly remark that it was sometimes acceptable "to lie the truth." In any event, the issue of the "lie" helped to convert the conflict into an extremely ugly, personalized affair. All the City firms had to declare their loyalties, much like friends taking sides in an especially bitter divorce.

———

In November 1958, the Reynolds/Tube group twice visited the posh BA headquarters on St. James's Square and informed Lord Portal of their stake. Offering to pay the equivalent of a hefty seventy-eight shillings per share, they proposed "an association of interests."[21] Lord Portal rebuked them haughtily and indicated that he was negotiating with another group. On Friday afternoon, November 28, the two sides had another frosty exchange at which Lord Portal rose and said grandly, "Excuse me, my bankers will take over." He started to leave when Ivan Stedeford shot back, "If you leave, Lord Portal, I'll leave." With that, Lord Portal sat back down.[22] It turned out that BA had negotiated to sell Alcoa a one-third stake for a stingy sixty shillings a share—a deal apparently hatched via André Meyer.[23] With extraordinary arrogance—and in a dreadful tactical blunder—Lord Portal refused to put the superior Reynolds/TI offer before the British Aluminium shareholders.

Capitalizing on BA's misstep, the Reynolds/TI team left the meeting and hastily set up a press conference. It was late Friday afternoon and Grunfeld knew the British bankers would soon be rushing off to their country houses. So he called a press conference for seven-thirty that evening in a surprise attack. Sir Ivan disclosed the secret negotiations between BA and Alcoa. He also pointed out that the national sovereignty issue was a red herring, since the British TI would hold a 51 percent stake in BA if their bid succeeded. When the press sought a reply from Lord Portal, he had already left for the weekend, affording a public-relations bonanza for Warburgs. Next to the smooth Warburg effort, Lord Portal seemed pompously gauche when he spurned the superior Reynolds/Tube bid as giving away "a powerful empire for the price of a small kingdom."[24]

Siegmund made one last failed peace mission to see his opposite numbers at Lazards and Hambros, but it was clear a grudge battle of monumental proportions was shaping up. As *The New Statesman* described the animosity directed toward S. G. Warburg & Company: "This bank is regarded as an interloper in the City. Its founder has built it up . . . by pursuing the vigorous tactics which other banks pursued in the time of their first barons."[25]

As the uproar grew, letters appeared in the *Times* assailing Siegmund's patriotism. At one point, Siegmund told Joe McConnell of Reynolds that a leading banker wished to see them. When they arrived, the man said Prime Minister Harold Macmillan had personally asked him to pass along a request that Reynolds cease and negotiate an amicable settlement.[26]

Bypassing negotiations, Siegmund appealed directly to shareholders and the press. Financial power was now shifting from the old financial barons to institutional investors, who owned at least one third of the BA shares. These portfolio managers were outraged by Lord Portal's cheek in describing the sixty-shilling Alcoa offer as somehow preferable to the seventy-eight shilling Reynolds/TI offer. They saw the establishment acting to safeguard its interests rather than to protect BA shareholders.

Siegmund wasn't entirely an embattled underdog in the Aluminium War and enlisted some powerful allies. Sir George Bolton, a maverick Bank of England director, had urged him to breathe life into backward British Aluminium management, an attitude shared by some colleagues in Threadneedle Street.[27] Although most of the City lined up against him, he knew Barings, Rothschilds, and Kleinworts sided with him. When Barings offered him an acceptance credit to signal its support in the heat of battle, Siegmund was jubilant. He called Barings the "finest of all the City houses" and said its senior partner, Sir Edward Reid, "went out of his way to indicate sympathy and support in various ways."[28]

By Christmas 1958, BA and the City were ready to fight back with all the firepower at their disposal. On New Year's Eve, amid rousing patriotic appeals, fourteen of the top seventeen London merchant banks announced a bid to buy BA shares at eighty-two shillings—four shillings more than the rival bid—to stop the Yankee carpetbaggers. Those accepting the bid would only get eighty-two shillings for half their shares and had to hold their remaining shares for three months. An awed *Times* of London said the consortium represented "an array of City institutions on a scale never before seen in a take-over battle."²⁹ Siegmund Warburg, refugee, now faced twenty-seven indignant men with titles, all lined up behind British Aluminium. Besides Hambro and Lazard Brothers, he also had to contend with Morgan Grenfell, Samuel Montagu, and a host of other influential firms. Siegmund was shocked that the City had ganged up on him in this way for such self-serving reasons. Once again, his opponents misplayed their hand, for their new eighty-two-shilling offer made a mockery of Lord Portal's earlier acceptance of just sixty shillings from Alcoa. Lazards and Hambros hoped the Bank of England would negotiate a peace and call a truce and Siegmund was duly summoned by a telephone call from the governor's secretary. In a manner that Siegmund found patronizing, Cobbold told him to desist, saying such things were simply not done in the City. Siegmund replied that his firm had a commitment to its clients and wasn't prepared to change its course of action. He returned to his office in a fury, outraged at the barefaced cheek of the consortium in instigating Cobbold to take such an unprecedented step.

Ultimately, each side blamed the other for rejecting the peace overture. In the end, Siegmund, fearless, kept buying shares in the open market at a furious pace. As German refugees, he and the uncles didn't feel bound by the club rules that ordinarily inhibited bare-knuckled competition. Incensed at how the establishment was bucking him, Siegmund warmed to the fight, determined to win at all costs. He now staked everything on victory, for defeat would leave him vulnerable to a legion of enemies.

On January 4, Reynolds/TI hiked its offer to eighty-five shillings. Siegmund excitedly sensed they were on the verge of victory, and portfolio managers rushed to cash in their shares. Though he knew he was fighting the battle of his life, he remained composed. He had the calm resolution and zest for battle of great generals who can inspire the troops. As Eric Roll noted, Siegmund could be cool in a crisis and enjoyed the sporting element of battle.³⁰ He liked the rapid tempo of takeovers, with their new developments every hour. It also gave him a chance to *épater le bourgeois*—than which nothing gave him more pleasure.

By January, 6, 1959, Reynolds/TI announced that it had achieved majority control of British Aluminium stock. Siegmund Warburg had defied the British establishment and won. It had been an article of faith that hostile takeovers didn't happen to major British firms. Siegmund had smashed that myth with one terrific blow.

This feat gave him worldwide fame. The fifty-six-year-old sphinx emerged to appear in media photos. He didn't crow about his triumph but he clearly knew its significance. *Business Week* showed the victor with a crooked, self-satisfied grin.[31] He appeared sure of himself and faintly amused by all the fuss. In a bit of attitudinizing, Siegmund wondered aloud whether he should retire to read history and philosophy or write a book or two.[32]

At first, he encountered tremendous ill-will in the City. People crossed the street when they saw him coming. Lord Kindersley blustered, "I will never speak to that fellow again."[33] When Kindersley attended a reception at the Austrian Embassy, he saw Siegmund, turned around, and walked out.[34] Jimmy Warburg was friends with Kindersley, and the Aluminium War sealed his dislike of Siegmund. To try to heal the breach, Lord Brand of Lazards—known as Mr. Establishment—invited Siegmund for a black-tie dinner that proved an uncomfortable affair. Hostility would linger between their two firms for years. Another consortium participant, Morgan Grenfell, would refuse to do business with Warburgs for fifteen years.

Slowly people realized that they needed Siegmund Warburg and couldn't afford his wrath. Three months after the Aluminium War, he was approached by a friend of Olaf Hambro, who said, "Olaf feels so sad that this old friendship between him and you doesn't exist anymore." Siegmund denied hard feelings, saying Olaf had been like a grandfather to him. "Oh, then you would be prepared to see him again?" He would be delighted, Siegmund said. An emotional reunion occurred in the partners' room at Hambros, Olaf embracing Siegmund and exclaiming, "Siegmund, haven't we been *awful fools?*"[35] Yet Olaf never accepted the stock market as the arbiter of corporate fate and made peace with Siegmund mostly as a matter of business necessity.

The Aluminium War was a watershed for S. G. Warburg & Co., giving it an exalted place in corporate finance, as executives took notice of Siegmund's masterstroke. It was also a watershed for the City, which had come to prefer style and ceremony to competence and conviction. When somebody asked Henry Grunfeld how Warburgs won the BA battle, he said simply, "We just didn't make any mistakes and the other side did."[36] Before Siegmund came along, mergers were negotiated on the backs of envelopes. Now merchant banks set up professional corporate finance teams to stop the Warburg juggernaut. Young turks at other merchant banks wanted to imitate Siegmund. In the coming decade, the entire City would take on the disciplined, fighting spirit of S. G. Warburg. Corporate battles would henceforth be fought in the open and not behind closed doors. One man had indeed made an amazing difference.

Despite Siegmund's undoubted triumph, the affair exposed some shortcomings of hostile takeovers that would bedevil Anglo-American finance for decades. The famous victory may have been a net loss for the companies involved. Some observers believe the need to win evinced by Siegmund and his clients superseded the economic logic of the deal. However thrilled by Siegmund's victory, Reynolds had paid a very high price. In 1957, BA shares had traded for as low as thirty-six shillings then had risen as high as eighty-five shillings during the battle. Noted Michael Verey, who advised TI for Helbert Wagg: "It didn't emerge for years that the fight was a very expensive one for the client. In fact, Siegmund gave Reynolds poor advice. British Aluminium was not worth it at that price."[37]

The high purchase price made Reynolds/TI reluctant to spend money on the company. "Both TI and Reynolds realized that they had overpaid," said Ronald Utiger, a later British Aluminium chairman. "BA had a considerable need for investment. But Reynolds and TI made it clear that having paid what they had paid, they weren't willing to put more into the company. The takeover was a tremendous strategic mistake. They couldn't exploit possibilities in Australia and elsewhere that required capital. Alcoa, without question, would have seen the potential and could have provided the financial and technical background to go forward in these ventures."[38] This revisionist view, of course, enjoys the benefit of hindsight.

Meanwhile, battle-hardened S. G. Warburg troops emerged supreme in the rough-and-tumble art of takeovers. During the 1960s, the firm seemed virtually invincible, whether on offense or defense. In Henry Grunfeld and Frank Smith, Siegmund had the two reigning masters at crafting bids. He could now fulfill his dream of having a low-overhead bank that booked big fees as financial consultants instead of through lending money.

This winning aura attracted many clients. In July 1959, Siegmund advised Roy Thomson, the Toronto barber's son who owned a chain of Canadian newspapers, in his purchase of the *Sunday Times*. Siegmund, who seldom read newspapers, already had as a client Cecil King, the tabloid press baron of the *Daily Mirror*, who had been turned down by older, stodgier merchant banks. Advised by Siegmund, King would become Britain's largest newspaper publisher. When King and Thomson vied for Odhams Press in the early 1960s, Siegmund advised Thomson that he would represent King, the client with seniority. Thomson was taken aback, but after he lost, he returned to Warburgs in an extraordinary gesture of confidence.

After the Aluminium War, a partner at a rival bank confided to Siegmund, "No company director whose shares are publicly quoted can sleep well from now on, because he must always wake up in the middle of the night and wonder who will make a raid on the company."[39] Siegmund, who hated inept entrenched managers, rejoiced at that remark. At the same time, he had found a charm in the very gentle, leisurely British style that he was helping to end. In a 1970 interview, Siegmund admitted that he had often asked himself whether "there is not a strong grain of wisdom behind an inclination in this country to resist the modern urge for ruthless efficiency at the cost of human values."[40] Either the Janus-faced Siegmund was storming the twenty-first century or waxing sentimental about the nineteenth.

On the strength of the Seligman merger and the Aluminium War, Siegmund had succeeded in resurrecting the Warburg name from the ruins of the Third Reich. Nobody had ever entered the clubby London elite so quickly. With this staggering achievement, Siegmund recapitulated an old Warburg story of fighting back from adversity. He also demonstrated the perseverance of the German Jews in exile. Once again, the Jewish banker had been an agent of new ideas, threatening the status quo but invigorating the scene. Many would trace an absence of creative sparkle in postwar German finance to the annihilation of the Jews. In expelling people such as Siegmund Warburg, the Nazis had severely hurt the Germany they presumed to save and had conferred a priceless gift upon their British enemies.

CHAPTER 45

The Quality of Mercy

Now in his early sixties, Eric had the balding Warburg head, prominent forehead, deep-set eyes, and tufty, beetling brows. Despite his battle royal with Brinckmann, he was a cheerful man of great vitality who moved quickly as he barreled down the hallway of the Hamburg bank. Unlike Siegmund, he didn't seem to carry the scars of a dark, turbulent history. Nothing gratified him more than to show visiting Warburgs his rich trove of memorabilia at the bank and at Kösterberg. A sense of tradition sustained him in his struggle to recapture the bank.

Reflecting the eternal ambivalence of the German Jew, Eric Warburg alternately demanded justice and granted forgiveness in postwar Germany. After returning to Hamburg, he emerged as a gray eminence of German-Jewish reconciliation and hence a figure of considerable symbolic weight. When eternally skeptical Jewish visitors later quizzed Chancellor Helmut Schmidt about whether anti-Semitism persisted in Germany, he would lift the telephone and have his sailing partner, Eric, reassure the wary visitors. Never as sanguine in private as in public, Eric nonetheless still viewed Nazism as an extinct volcano.

Each year, Eric lunched with Count von Rothkirch, the languid, monocled general who had led German troops into Vienna in 1938 and whom he had debriefed at war's end. He made peace missions to other old *Wehrmacht* officers. During the North African campaign, Eric had tracked down a Lieutenant Almenröder, whom the French had shut up in an old, rat-infested fortress. After the war, Almenröder became a Catholic priest in a cloister near Munich. Thirty years after their wartime meeting, Eric sought him out to return a confiscated pocket knife. The two men talked animatedly for three hours. Such visits expressed Eric's reverence for the military caste and his strong need to settle past differences. If Siegmund was an iconoclast by nature, Eric was a staunch traditionalist, who wished to return to the well-worn paths of his pre-Hitler life.

Emotionally it was always dangerous business to revisit the Nazi past. In 1945, Eric's deputy had interrogated a short, stocky lieutenant general named Fritz Bayerlein, who had been Rommel's tank chief in North Africa. After the war, Bayerlein entered the Persian rug business, which brought him to Hamburg each year. Eager to make amends, he always paid a visit to Eric. In 1967, right after the Six-Day War, he burst into Eric's office, unfurling a military map of the Sinai peninsula. For two hours, he babbled on with gusto about Israel's blitzkrieg tactics. "You must confess," he said, "the boys have learned a lot from us." Usually a model of tact, Eric replied, "Indeed, Mr. Bayerlein, the few who weren't gassed probably learned their lesson."[1]

Though Eric encountered little, if any, overt anti-Semitism, he found moral stupidity of the sort that had, in the past, shaded into full-blown Nazism. He had generously given model ships to a nearby church in Blankenese. One Sunday, he strolled by the church and, hearing the choir singing, decided to drop in to listen. The text of the pastor's sermon was the crucifixion of Christ by the Jews. Governing his temper with difficulty, Eric sat down and wrote the pastor a calm letter, pointing out that the Romans, not the Jews, had murdered Christ. The pastor not only accepted the correction but later asked Eric for an introductory letter when he visited Israel. Eric taught forgiveness to the Christians.

Among Eric's competing parts—German, Jewish, and American—the German side came to predominate as he again surrendered to his old imperial love of the aristocracy and military. His memoirs would be a faintly embarrassing cavalcade of "vons" and generals he had known. Yet his Jewish side was never wholly extinguished. In the face of adversity, he could fight stubbornly for his principles. In 1952, the Conference on Jewish Material Claims against Germany, representing twenty-four organizations of Holocaust survivors, concluded a reparations agreement with Konrad Adenauer. Between 1953 and 1965, Germany agreed to pay Israel more than seven hundred million dollars and the Claims Conference more than one hundred million.

Eric Warburg.
(Courtesy of Anita Warburg)

While the East Germans disclaimed responsibility for the Holocaust and refused to pay a cent—they were supposedly all anti-Fascist "freedom fighters"—West Germany would devote about 5 percent of its annual federal budget to compensate Jewish victims. It was a pittance beside the suffering, but an important symbolic gesture. Germany would end up as Israel's second-most important trading partner after the United States. This mutually advantageous relationship gave Germany global respectability and Israel economic aid.

The 1953 agreement also provided for an indemnification law to compensate individual Jews for loss of life, health, careers, or retirement benefits. No provision was made, however, for the 150,000 concentration camp inmates exploited as forced labor. They had endured filth, beatings, and starvation, often in nightmarish underground plants. During the war, German companies could order slave labor by phone and the victims would be promptly shipped off by rail. Afterward, German executives sheltered behind the flimsy excuse that they had merely served as agents of the Third Reich. They often pleaded ignorance of the atrocities carried out in their own installations.

When the Claims Conference sought reparations from the successor firms to Krupp, Flick, Siemens, Rheinmetall, and I. G. Farben, Eric functioned as a pivotal figure, and the conference used Brinckmann, Wirtz to transfer payments. Afraid of opening the door to unending lawsuits, most German companies reacted in an extremely defensive, bureaucratic style. To extract payments from niggardly, unrepentant companies required massive research. Before approaching Krupp, Benjamin B. Ferencz of the Claims Conference compiled evidence showing that Alfried Krupp had known about the slave labor. In 1943, Krupp officials inspected naked prisoners at Auschwitz and some executives even handed out assignments to concentration camp inmates at a Krupp munitions factory.[2] When Ferencz presented a lengthy brief about this to Alfried's top aide, Berthold Beitz, Beitz blanched and exclaimed, "Blackmail!"[3]

After this unpromising start, the conference enlisted the help of John J. McCloy, now chairman of the Chase Manhattan Bank in New York. With his controversial pardon of Alfried, McCloy feared that any concession he helped to elicit on reparations might look like a belated payoff. Nevertheless, McCloy dined with Krupp at his mountaintop villa in Essen in mid-1959. When Krupp resisted McCloy's plea to settle with the conference, Ferencz sued Krupp in New York, demanding ten thousand dollars per slave worker.

Enter Eric. It offended his sense of justice that a billion-dollar outfit could just shrug off responsibility. Since Krupp was a Brinckmann, Wirtz client, Eric approached Beitz in a uniquely ambiguous role: He was both a Jew asking for justice and a friendly German businessman offering timely advice. Before the conference filed suit in New York, Eric showed Beitz damaging documents that confirmed Alfried's knowledge of the slave labor and advised Beitz to avoid bad publicity by settling.[4] Certainly Eric's role turned up the moral pressure on Krupp. With Krupp's blessing, Beitz flew to America and offered to pay $2.38 million. The final sum came to a meager $500 per victim, but at least there was a grudging admission of wrongdoing.[5]

Other cases were far more uncomfortable for Eric. Siemens Bauunion had employed about eight thousand camp prisoners at underground arms factories.[6] While the firm later alleged that it was coerced into using slave labor, a 1945 internal company report suggested otherwise.[7] Meeting with Siemens leadership, Eric disclosed that the conference had possession of the damaging 1945 report, which induced the firm to settle.[8]

The reparations work led straight to that Warburg bogeyman of the 1930s, Friedrich Flick, who had waded hip-deep in the horror. As Himmler's friend and patron, he had toured concentration camps with the SS chief himself.[9] The Nobel dynamite company, 80 percent owned by Flick, had written an especially grisly chapter of Nazi history. It had commandeered women from Auschwitz to insert explosives into bombs and grenades. Their errors were often repaid with instant death.[10] After the war, Flick was sentenced to seven years in jail for exploiting slave labor and funding the SS, until McCloy commuted his prison term in 1951. Flick then resumed his business career, acquired control of more than three hundred companies, and became the richest man in Germany. So much for earthly justice.

When it came to callous arrogance, Flick had no peer and he blustered that "nothing will convince us that we are war criminals."[11] When Eric was tapped by the conference to approach Flick, he found himself negotiating with Flick's representative, a man for whom he felt profound friendship and admiration. Fabian von Schlabrendorff was a Resistance hero who had tried to murder Hitler with bombs hidden in a package of brandy bottles and stowed aboard the *Führer's* plane. He had recruited Count von Stauffenberg into the anti-Hitler plot. In February 1945, he had been about to be sentenced to death by a Nazi court when bombs shattered the courtroom, killing the judge and incinerating his records. Someone of unquestionable bravery, von Schlabrendorff was reputed to have been the survivor most tortured by the Gestapo. A distinguished lawyer, he was among the Resistance figures aided by Eric in the rubble of 1945. Each year, Eric attended the Commemoration Day services in Berlin for veterans of the July 20, 1944, plot and kept in touch with von Schlabrendorff.

Now, in Eric's office, this Resistance hero represented a convicted war criminal. Apparently operating in good faith, he seemed sympathetic to the demands of the Claims Conference and he and Eric worked out a deal that he could take back to his boss.[12] It proved a deceptively easy start. When Schlabrendorff had a heart attack, it postponed negotiations for six months and after that he became noncommittal.[13]

To restart talks, the Claims Conference dredged up SS records documenting that concentration camp inmates had worked at Nobel. For an extended period, Eric dickered with von Schlabrendorff about the size of a settlement. Then Flick delegated the matter to his assistant, Dr. Wolfgang Pohle, who had joined the Nazi party in 1933 and defended him at Nuremberg. Occasionally Pohle intimated that a settlement was near, but nothing would ever happen after this bluff. Even as Flick engaged in such flagrantly dilatory tactics, Schlabrendorff insisted he would pay. In January 1967, when the Nobel board met to take up the question, Schlabrendorff assured Eric that "we have the contract in the bag."[14]

The outcome was a calculated insult. The Nobel board said they weren't liquid enough to pay anything, even though Flick's personal wealth had swollen to an estimated two billion deutsche marks. Despite the good offices of McCloy and Hermann Abs of Deutsche Bank, Eric could make no further headway. Later, he said, quite bitterly, that Flick could have paid from his vest pocket.[15] In January 1970, after nine years of cruelly abusing the hopes of thirty-five hundred Jewish victims, Flick informed McCloy that he had decided not to make any payments.[16] In 1972, an unrepentant Friedrich Flick died at age eighty-nine. Worth more than one billion dollars, he had not paid one penny to his Jewish victims.[17]

———

After moving back to Germany, Eric wanted to guarantee the employment of his E. M. Warburg & Co. staff in New York. A small firm of aging foreigners, it needed to be modernized, invigorated, Americanized. Through Eric's friendship with Freddy, the firm participated in Kuhn, Loeb syndicates and managed clients' portfolios, but found it hard to broaden its base beyond its original German clientele. To stimulate change, Donald Blinken introduced Eric to a tall, handsome young man named Lionel Pincus in 1965. Pincus's grandfather had migrated from Poland and his parents had a clothing and real estate business in Philadelphia. As a Ladenburg, Thalmann partner, he invested money in corporate ventures for wealthy families.

Though Eric was sixty-five and Pincus thirty-one years younger, their rapport was instantaneous, the sort of father-son relationship that never occurs between real fathers and sons. Like Eric, Pincus was genial, low-profile, and discreet. If Pincus thought Eric a banker of middling talents, he honored him as a human being. At first, Pincus didn't realize he had stumbled into the tangled, maddening web of Warburg relationships. Never having been to Germany, he was naïve about this brilliant, perpetually warring clan. Over time he would learn the lesson that wherever the Warburgs were concerned, nothing was ever simple.

Taking down atlas and annals, Eric laid out for Pincus the long, colorful chronicle of the Warburgs and urged his new surrogate son to learn German (Pincus never did). They had long talks about Eric's decision to return to Germany, Eric saying how his aristocratic friends had urged him to return and that the sons shouldn't be punished for their fathers' sins. It was all alien to Pincus, but pleasantly so. Although everybody at E. M. Warburg & Co. spoke German, as soon as Pincus entered the room, they all switched in unison to English. In January 1966 Pincus acquired a 50 percent stake in E. M. Warburg & Co. and Eric and his group kept 50 percent.

On their first trip to Germany together in 1967, Pincus admired Eric's diplomatic arts and pondered the awkward position of a Jewish banker in postwar Germany. The day they arrived in Hamburg, newspapers carried front-page photos of a desecrated Jewish cemetery. Eric and Pincus visited companies, including soap and chemical concerns, that had made a tidy profit in the Holocaust. Whether from genuine contrition, guilt, or patent self-interest, German executives rushed to do business with Eric. Pincus came to appreciate Eric's philosophy that one had to accept life in its terribly impure complexity, rather than sit back and wait for ideal situations.

In taking over E. M. Warburg, Pincus didn't know that he had signed on for a package that included the formidable, tempestuous Siegmund. Eric always complained about Siegmund's meddling, yet encouraged his involvement. As Eric told Siegmund in 1961, "I am most anxious that we should work very closely together not only in Hamburg but everywhere."[18] If there were wounds, there was also resilience in their relationship. Like old punch-drunk prizefighters, they could fight, make peace, and live to fight again. Once, in the early 1960s, Siegmund—to general amazement—kept Eric waiting the entire day in his London office.[19] Eric, in turn, was the one of the few who dared to twit the sensitive Siegmund. However much Siegmund scorned Eric, he was the only Warburg he stayed in touch with. He still saw Eric as weak, vain, and prone to grandiose statements. He would say dismissively, "Oh, he's not serious."[20] Eric, in turn, saw Siegmund as conniving, completely insincere, and power-hungry. Yet lashed together by the Warburg name, they still trudged along together.

Siegmund's colleagues believe that by the 1960s Eric was terribly envious of what Siegmund had done in London, while his own firm had fizzled in New York. Loosely speaking, Siegmund had a dual agenda with Eric: to erase the E. M. Warburg name on Wall Street and clear the way for the S. G. Warburg name. At the same time, he wanted Eric to restore the M. M. Warburg name in Hamburg, undoubtedly as a prelude to S. G. Warburg & Co. taking over afterward. As with all Eric-Siegmund dealings, their battle over the Warburg name in New York became convoluted, theatrical, byzantine, producing hurt feelings. Once again, the name debate was a proxy for the deeper and more delicate question of who was rightful heir to the Warburg throne.

As early as 1961, Siegmund was firing salvoes at Eric to drop the Warburg name in New York, saying he didn't see how Eric could surrender voting control and still allow his name to be associated with a firm. "It would seem to me a sort of prostitution of the name," said Siegmund, pointing out that he had voting control in London through Warburg Continuation Limited.[21] After the fuss over the Warburg name in London and Hamburg, Siegmund was appalled that Eric might sell it in New York. Yet this is precisely what Eric did, to Lionel Pincus.

Eric was in a bind. The major value of E. M. Warburg was its name. Lionel Pincus knew full well that he was purchasing classy, old-money cachet. On the other hand, Eric had promised Siegmund to withdraw his name from E. M. Warburg & Co. Complicating matters was that Siegmund thought Pincus the wrong kind of Jew—of Eastern European ancestry, with a garment-district background. Professionally, he thought Pincus well below *haute banque* stature in the venture capital world. At that point, the Pincus résumé wasn't likely to impress Siegmund.

Contending that Eric was cheapening the Warburg name (not to mention thwarting his own Wall Street plans), Siegmund directed a steady stream of letters and emissaries to Eric and Pincus. For Siegmund, the persistence of the E. M. Warburg name was an intolerable irritant. Each year, he would photocopy a page of the Manhattan telephone directory and send it to Eric, circling the E. M. Warburg name and asking why it remained. Outwardly Pincus found Siegmund and Eric correct with each other, if disgusted underneath. After a deftly orchestrated campaign of hints, bluffs, and demands, Siegmund finally got the name changed in January 1970 to E. M. Warburg, Pincus & Company to differentiate it from S. G. Warburg & Company. But for several years, Siegmund and Pincus didn't speak.

In the end, Lionel Pincus had the last laugh on Siegmund. He expanded Eric's tiny firm into a gigantic, thriving business, with three and a half billion dollars in venture capital partnerships. He became a philanthropist and Park Avenue socialite into the bargain. Despite his own, superior contribution to the firm, Pincus never dropped the Warburg name and always proudly displayed a painting of Eric in his reception area. He knew the meaning of gratitude and he had learned to value the Warburg name.

—

The Hamburg crusade to restore the M. M. Warburg name bound not only Siegmund and Eric, but the entire Warburg family. For their first three years, Brinckmann and Eric tactfully avoided the subject. Then, in June 1960, they sat down again to thrash the matter out. For forty years before, Eric said, they had been like brothers, but the three years of silence about the name change had introduced insincerity. Eric noted the irony that Hamburg now had a street named for the Warburgs, "but in the Ferdinandstrasse that wasn't the case and the situation has become unbearable for me."[22] When Eric suggested M. M. Warburg, Brinckmann & Co., Brinckmann refused. He was a prickly foe and Eric didn't relish confrontation. Whenever Eric broached the name issue, Brinckmann always said it was an inappropriate time. Stingy and moody, Brinckmann had a rigid style; employees who wished to see him about a loan had to make appointments two weeks in advance. Relations between Eric and Brinckmann steadily worsened.

Unable to talk to his own partner, Eric, in desperation, wrote to Brinckmann that autumn while the latter vacationed in Sicily. He noted that his son, Max, age twelve, was now in school in Germany, which made it far more likely that he would someday enter the bank as a sixth-generation Warburg. Eric no longer hedged his words: "Should the name extinguished by the Nazis really remain blotted out? But that can't be your answer. . . . To put up with that further would be an impiety that I couldn't justify to my entire family, and above all someday to my son."[23] He asked Brinckmann for his *Stellungnahme*—his opinion. The hot-tempered Brinckmann blamed Eric for spoiling his vacation and objected to the legalistic tone of the term *Stellungnahme*.[24] His position was now hardening by the day and he demanded that the firm, if renamed, should be called Brinckmann, Warburg & Co.[25]

It fell to Siegmund to step up pressure. In 1960, enraged by Brinckmann's arrogance, he began a systematic campaign to force the name change. When he met with Brinckmann, he might begin with highfalutin talk about Nietzsche or a solemn discourse about the Hamlet enigma. Then, in his inimitable way, he would graciously, but firmly, steer the discussion around to the name change. In "Dear Brinckie!" letters, he artfully mixed flattery and threats. In a March 1960 letter, Siegmund graciously said that nobody was a better friend of the Jews than Brinckie. Then he noted, in a tone of deep regret, that every week somebody asked him why—now that Eric had returned—the original name hadn't been revived. Finally, slipping off the velvet gloves, Siegmund said bluntly that "some people" suggested that Brinckmann hesitated for fear of offending latent Nazi sentiment.[26] The fat was in the fire.

When Brinckmann suggested that the name be changed to Brinckmann, Wirtz–M. M. Warburg & Co., Siegmund hit the roof. Fearing compromise, he warned Eric that only two names—M. M. Warburg & Co. or M. M. Warburg,

Brinckmann, & Co.—were acceptable. "If one flouts the conventions for reasons of expediency or tactics, one exposes the firm in question to just the kind of ridicule and undignified comment which one wants to counteract."[27] At bottom, Siegmund wanted plain M. M. Warburg & Co. Eric thought that desirable but unattainable and was prepared to compromise on M. M. Warburg, Brinckmann & Co.[28]

In the summer of 1960, Siegmund visited Hamburg to engage in verbal duels with Brinckmann. Brinckmann noted that he had urged Eric to move back after the war and restore the name, but that Eric had refused. In matters of honor, Siegmund rejoined, no statute of limitations applied. When Brinckmann pointed out that the Warburgs had failed to exercise their option to increase their stake to 50 percent by 1953, Siegmund refreshed his memory about Schilling's savage opposition to Eric.[29]

On that or another trip to Hamburg, Siegmund received a surprise invitation from Dr. Hjalmar Schacht, who had set up a financial boutique in Hamburg. It must have been with philosophic curiosity that Siegmund, now the lord of the London financial world, went to see the quondam wizard of the Nazi economy. Siegmund listened politely while a nervous Schacht prattled on about a proposal for a financial operation in the Philippines. Groveling before Siegmund, he kept interrupting his own long-winded speech to say apologetically, "In short," as if he were taking up too much of a great man's time. Siegmund promised to think over the proposal but never did.[30]

When Brinckmann proposed making his son, Christian, a bank partner, it confirmed Siegmund's fear that Brinckmann had delusions about initiating his own banking dynasty.[31] The Warburgs thought Christian a mediocre banker and Siegmund, to slow the move, suggested that Christian first become a holder of the power of attorney. To Siegmund's mind, they had coddled Brinckmann for too long. For fifteen years, he told Eric, Brinckmann had "been surrounded by yes-men" and was "inclined to take the attitude that anybody who does not agree with him is unfriendly, or '*treulos*,' or lacking in kindness."[32] It grated on Siegmund when Brinckmann said he had inherited the shell of a bank in 1938, whereas Siegmund believed he had taken over a firm with a superlative name and excellent earning power. Siegmund pointed out to him that more than two thirds of Brinckmann, Wirtz's reserves dated from the old firm—the bank building, plus stakes in Beiersdorf and Karstadt.[33] In letters to Eric, Siegmund described Brinckmann as vicious, senile, ruthless, and bullying.[34] Brinckmann, in turn, dropped all pretense of civility, muttering to visitors that the Warburgs should be grateful to him, not vice versa.[35]

Both Siegmund and Eric probably underrated the stubborn cunning and resourcefulness of their old retainer. At a dramatic board meeting in March

1961, Siegmund and Eric watched as key members, heavily lobbied by Brinckmann, voted a partnership for Christian.[36] The Warburgs somewhat offset this by arguing for a second junior partner, Dr. Hans Wuttke, a smart car-industry veteran from Daimler–Benz, who believed that the Warburg name would open doors overseas.[37] A handsome, charming character, known as Prince Benz, Wuttke would serve as Siegmund's man in Germany. Eric, in time, would come to regard him as Siegmund's spy.

All this jockeying led to an angry stalemate between Eric and Brinckmann, and they simply stopped talking to each other. At the morning meeting of senior people, they saw each other for fifteen minutes, then withdrew to their offices and didn't speak for the rest of the day. A credulous business press swallowed the public relations line that all was well between the Brinckmann and Warburg families. As the *Financial Times* said of Brinckmann in 1966, he "regarded himself as more of a custodian than the Nazis would have liked, and relations with the Warburgs have been fairly warm since the war."[38]

Among the Warburgs, the name issue never died. Lola and Rudo thought the idea of Brinckmann, Warburg & Co. a terrible slap in the face.[39] Many notables in the German banking world, including Hermann Abs, considered the Brinckmann, Wirtz name a scandal.[40] Eric even recruited Fabian von Schlabrendorff to reason with Brinckmann. One day in February 1963, Jakob Wallenberg stopped by to lunch with Eric and commiserated over the name, pointing out that Pferdemenges & Co. had reverted to Sal. Oppenheim Jr. & Company in 1947. Dr. Robert Pferdemenges, a gentile employe, had taken over the Cologne bank in 1938, but had written to all of the bank's clients in 1947, informing them that the original name had been restored. Brinckmann had the misfortune to stop by at that moment and say hello to Wallenberg. "Do you know, Dr. Brinckmann," said Wallenberg, "I was a little boy when my father first took me along to this house in the year 1913. And you know, the name of the firm was then M. M. Warburg & Co. and not, as today, Brinckmann, Wirtz & Co."[41] Fortified by such loyalty, Eric began to champion the unadulterated name, M. M. Warburg & Co.[42]

Despairing of appeals to Brinckmann's honor, Siegmund decided to argue the name question on purely practical grounds: the Warburg name was better for business.[43] In July 1963, strolling with Brinckmann by the Alster Lake, Siegmund reminded him that the Warburg name had existed for 143 years, the Brinckmann name for only 22 years. Moreover, the Warburg name would aid the bank overseas and get it into syndicates of the sort Siegmund was now assembling in London.[44] The Brinckmann family saw history quite differently. Christian told Eric that his father, not the Warburgs, had built up almost all of the bank's foreign connections.[45] In 1964, in a last-ditch effort, the Warburgs tried in vain to get Brinckmann to retire at age seventy-five. By this point, Siegmund said he could scarcely stand to be in the same room with him.[46]

Aside from matters of honor, Brinckmann's peevish obstinacy was also foiling Siegmund's master plan for a London-based financial empire, with major subsidiaries in New York and Hamburg. Siegmund boldly decided to open another front in Germany. In July 1964, without consulting his Hamburg partners, Siegmund announced that he had taken a majority interest in the private Frankfurt bank of Hans. W. Petersen. It was run by a bluff, easy-going man named Richard Daus who had been in the wartime tanks corps. Siegmund renamed the firm S. G. Warburg & Co. Suddenly, for the first time since Hitler, the Warburg name had returned to Germany—but in Frankfurt instead of Hamburg.

Since Siegmund sat on the Brinckmann, Wirtz finance committee, this news hit the bank like a thunderclap. While Eric defended Siegmund, Christian Brinckmann spied a secret strategy at work. He thought Siegmund would use the Frankfurt firm as a beachhead to conquer the Hamburg bank.[47] Indeed, Siegmund viewed Hans W. Petersen as an instrument to dominate M. M. Warburg, with the long-term aim of possibly folding it and the Hamburg firm into a major German bank named M. M. Warburg & Co.[48]

Soon after his bombshell announcement, Siegmund invited the Hamburg firm to take a stake in Frankfurt. Some Hamburg partners suspected a trap but Eric and Dr. Hans Wuttke belatedly became partners in the Frankfurt bank in 1966. In their lifelong minuet, this foreshadowed closer ties between Siegmund and Eric. As the *Financial Times* said, "For Siegmund Warburg the Hamburg-Frankfurt *entente* is part of a plan inspired as much by family feeling as by bankerly ambition—he would like the House of Warburg once again to be the power in Germany it was before the war."[49]

In January 1970, two events altered the German landscape for the Warburgs. Siegmund merged the tiny Hans W. Petersen with another acquisition, the Deutsche Effecten und Wechsel Bank in Frankfurt, which was ten times its size. The new entity was christened Effectenbank–Warburg AG, with a stake reserved for Brinckmann, Wirtz. It was controlled by a holding company in which Siegmund's London firm had a 51 percent stake and Eric's Hamburg firm a 25 percent stake. But Siegmund, characteristically, negotiated a deal by which he kept the voting rights. Still hoping to forge a Warburg colossus, Siegmund drafted Eric and Hans Wuttke onto the board of his London firm, giving him German strength unmatched by any other London banker. Richard Daus of Hans W. Petersen didn't want to be merged, so he left to form his own firm. Though Daus had been extremely proud to be part of the Warburg empire, Siegmund dismissed him as a lightweight and cast him off.

Despite his bold move in Frankfurt, Siegmund retained a sentimental at-tachment to the Hamburg bank. The city's largest private bank and the third largest in Germany, the ancestral bank on the Ferdinandstrasse remained a great prize. In January 1970, the long-running struggle waged by Eric and Siegmund paid off. Now eighty-one, quite deaf and weakened by age, Brinck-mann caved in on the name issue after being subjected to enormous pressure. He agreed to rename the firm M. M. Warburg–Brinckmann, Wirtz & Co. When the name was formally changed on January 5, 1970, Eric made a little speech and cited his father's farewell speech of May 1938. Even as the Warburgs rejoiced, *The Times* of London noted, "The Brinckmann family, headed by octogenarian Dr. Rudolf Brinckmann, did not welcome a change in the name of the Hamburg bank."[50] Elated by victory, Eric and Siegmund tightened their links, the Hamburg bank taking a 22 percent interest in S. G. Warburg & Co. International Holdings.

By this point, Eric was seventy-one, but the feud between the Warburgs and the Brinckmanns never faded. In the early 1970s, Eric commissioned Dr. Eduard Rosenbaum and A. Joshua Sherman to write a history of the Warburg bank from 1798 to 1938. Brinckmann resented the insinuation that history had somehow ended in 1938. When Rosenbaum and Sherman lunched at the bank, Brinckmann sat, indignant and alone, at the other end of the long mahogany table, while Eric, in his good-natured way, tried to smooth things over.[51] The Warburgs and Brinckmanns kept up the facade of harmony. In January 1973, when the firm celebrated its 175th birthday, a press release thanked Brinckmann for guiding the bank during the war and early postwar years.[52]

On the last day of 1973, Rudolf Brinckmann, age eighty-four, ended fifty-four eventful years with the bank and formally resigned. He planned a vale-dictory address to the staff on January 3, 1974. On January 2, Eric suggested that Brinckmann and he attend together one last reception at the Hamburg branch of the Bundesbank. It was a fine, conciliatory gesture, designed to show they had parted on friendly terms. So on a cold, crisp day, Eric and Rio, who had shared such a long and curious history, set off on foot together for the noon reception a few blocks away. As they crossed the plaza before the Town Hall, Rudolf Brinckmann had a sudden heart attack, collapsed, and died in the embrace of his ancient adversary, Eric Warburg.

Of all the acts of forgiveness that Eric had carried out over the years, few could have been as hard as paying tribute to the gruff, testy Brinckmann. On January 15, Eric gathered the four hundred bank employees in the same canteen in which his father had handed over the reins to Brinckmann thirty-six years before. If there was some vanity in Eric's nature, there was no pettiness, and he gave Brinckmann his due. "The trust that those forced to emigrate placed in him with the handing over of the firm, he more than fulfilled." Eric alluded to "the years of reconstruction, where he truly had to begin from scratch."[53] Those who knew the whole story knew how much anguish Eric had to repress. In death he praised Brinckmann more robustly than he ever had been able to in life.

CHAPTER 46

The European

Siegmund Warburg had joined Kuhn, Loeb in a junior status, then his stature had risen in an almost vertical line in London. Nonetheless, his celebrated triumph with British Aluminium drew yawns from many self-satisfied Kuhn, Loeb partners. Relaxing at his Virginia horse farm, Freddy Warburg heard grousing from London friends and said Siegmund should have compromised. John Schiff, who avoided controversy, said the financial world hadn't seen such bitterness since Jacob Schiff and Pierpont Morgan vied for the Northern Pacific Railroad in 1901.[1]

In the early 1950s, Kuhn, Loeb had seemed a wondrous asset to Siegmund. After British Aluminium, he didn't need it so desperately. With his firm soaring into the stratosphere in London, he couldn't afford to spend so much time on Wall Street. His new London eminence also persuaded the paranoid camp at Kuhn, Loeb that he intended to dominate them. Constant friction frayed relations between S. G. Warburg and Kuhn, Loeb as the two firms couldn't decide whether to compete or cooperate. Since they were only engaged, not married, the temptation to cheat was always strong. Each side claimed to bring more business to the party than the other and wished to be rewarded accordingly.

To arbitrate disputes, the two firms agreed to hold twice-yearly summit meetings. In 1961 Siegmund also proposed that they exchange small holdings in each other—before he was the sole link—to bridge the differences between them.[2] This arrangement didn't quiet the churning waters and in 1962 Siegmund suggested an end to it.[3] It was an artificial, jerry-built structure and destined to collapse.

The rickety structure took a mortal drubbing during the summer of 1962 when the U.S. Treasury secretary, Douglas Dillon, told an international banking conference in Rome that America wanted to staunch the flow of its gold reserves abroad. To this end President John F. Kennedy enacted an Interest Equalization Tax (IET) in 1963. By making it prohibitively expensive for foreigners to raise money on Wall Street, the tax pushed business to London and other European capitals—in other words, to Siegmund's home turf. Many Kuhn, Loeb partners feared that Siegmund would exploit the situation. Their fears seemed to be confirmed; reports filtered back to Wall Street that bright young S. G. Warburg executives were telling Kuhn, Loeb clients that S. G. Warburg & Co. would serve them and save them. Even some Kuhn, Loeb partners sympathetic to Siegmund became disillusioned, for they believed they were quite capable of placing issues abroad.[4]

Even before the IET, there had been personality clashes between Kuhn, Loeb and S. G. Warburg people. One irritant was Ronnie Grierson, a young protégé of Siegmund's and probably the first of his surrogate sons. Born as Griessmann to a Jewish family in Nuremberg, he had been educated in France and Britain. After joining the British Army during the war, he changed his Germanic name and served with distinction. At the start of the war he was interned by the British then imprisoned by the Germans at the end. This very Warburgian character became a British citizen in 1946 while keeping his German passport. "I happen to be a German who is loyal to Britain," he would say.[5]

Bright, witty, fluent in several languages, Grierson was Siegmund's court jester and a foil to the dour uncles. A social butterfly, he knew all the lords and ladies and made the social rounds shunned by Siegmund. Siegmund loved Grierson's hilarious accounts of his nocturnal escapades. If you wanted to know the gossip, he would say, just ask Ronnie Grierson. Grierson treated Siegmund with just the right blend of flattery and respect.

Touched by Grierson's devotion to his refugee German mother, Siegmund defended him against critics. For Siegmund, his adopted son could do no wrong. Yet Grierson's swaggering flamboyance rubbed many people the wrong way. To critics, he seemed too loud and self-promoting, too quick to flaunt his connections or drop names. A strong, rather theatrical personality, he could be whimsical one moment and explosive the next and he tended to

Siegmund and Eva Warburg with their son-in-law,
Dov Biegun, and granddaughter, Batya, in Roccamare, Italy, 1966.
(Private collection)

make friends and enemies very quickly. When Grierson lost his temper with the Kuhn, Loeb partners, generating tension, Siegmund stuck by him, telling one Kuhn, Loeb partner, "I will destroy anybody who criticizes Ronnie Grierson."

After the IET, Siegmund's foes at Kuhn, Loeb argued that the two firms had an inescapable conflict of interest since Kuhn, Loeb's American clients would now seek financing in Siegmund's backyard. They predicted that Siegmund would steer business to his London firm ahead of Kuhn, Loeb. Pretty soon the arrangement began to unravel. Seeing an end to his dream of restoring Kuhn, Loeb's glory, Siegmund was heartbroken. He had devoted years to the firm of Paul and Felix Warburg, introducing many foreign clients, and hiring many young associates. Siegmund grew so despondent about the divorce that Henry Grunfeld flew secretly to New York to confer with John Schiff at his huge Oyster Bay estate. They talked from five one afternoon until three in the morning, trying to salvage something. While sympathetic to Siegmund, Schiff explained that he couldn't flout his own people. The situation could only be saved, he said, if Siegmund moved to New York and worked full time at Kuhn, Loeb. That was as impossible as it had been in the early 1950s when Schiff first proposed it.

Trying to strike a brave note, Siegmund said that Kuhn, Loeb and S. G. Warburg could now go their separate ways with greater freedom. As Freddy said to Eric, "Between you and me and the lamp-post, I agree with him."[6] By the end of 1964, the two firms had formally parted. The following July Siegmund opened a subsidiary office in New York and hired David Mitchell, son of a former J. P. Morgan & Co. partner, to run it. Siegmund knew the Morgan bank's anti-Semitic history and it must have tickled him to hire the offspring of a partner.

The lesson of the Kuhn, Loeb debacle seemed to be that Siegmund could serve as a king but not as a prince. In London, he worked with German and Austrian refugees who implicitly shared his values, were schooled in his ways, and deferred to his leadership. His challenging ideas didn't please rich American partners, who preferred the status quo to the intense team effort sought by Siegmund.

Far from cooling his ambition, Siegmund's failure at Kuhn, Loeb heightened his need for success in America. He had some nagging sense of inferiority beside such Wall Street barons as André Meyer and Robert Lehman. New York was a formidable place to penetrate, and Siegmund overestimated the mystique of the Warburg name. Through shrewd legerdemain, he tried to project an aura of great power, and David Mitchell would talk of peddling "bottled mystique."[7] Siegmund lacked the enormous capital needed to make headway in New York. Once again, he wanted to harness other fortunes and manage them under his own name and leadership.

In November 1963, Siegmund had lunch in New York with J. Richardson Dilworth, who now managed the Rockefeller family money, and George Love, the chairman of Chrysler and Consolidation Coal. In a prophetic vein, he conjured up a potential business union of American and European talent. He dreamed of taking pools of transatlantic money, leveraging them, and taking stakes in companies. The corporate executives would contribute "financial engineering"—a phrase Siegmund relished—to revamp the laggard companies.

The three men agreed on an action plan. Dilworth would approach David Rockefeller, Love would pursue the Mellon and Hanna families, and Siegmund would scour Europe for investors. The lunch became grimly memorable when the maître d' came over to announce, "Gentlemen, you should know the President has been shot."[8]

Five years later, Siegmund's inspiration was realized in a venture called American European Associates (AEA). It was run by a genial young man named Carl Hess, who liked the way Siegmund blended imagination and down-to-earth practicality. However, he disliked Siegmund's German sense of hierarchy and the air of grandeur he sometimes wore.

After taking five million dollars from Kommerzbank and five million from the Rockefellers, then adding Du Pont and Harriman money, Siegmund established AEA in the same building at 640 Fifth Avenue that housed his New York office. The two operating partners were S. G. Warburg and Laird & Co., each contributing one million dollars. As if Siegmund suffered from some jinx in New York, AEA at once ran into serious trouble. Laird went bankrupt, tying up money in court proceedings. And when AEA made its first investment in a Los Angeles recreational equipment maker, The Leisure Group, the company promptly reported an embarrassing loss.[9]

With so much pride and frustrated ambition invested in his Wall Street comeback, Siegmund couldn't bear another setback and he took out his anger on Hess, whom he saw as ruining his splendid concept. Hess hadn't exactly covered himself in glory with AEA, yet he felt that Siegmund's punishment was excessive. Though Siegmund wanted to fire him, Hess had an ironclad employment contract, which Siegmund took home nightly and scrutinized for loopholes.[10] When that approach failed, Siegmund turned up the heat. One day, Hess was shocked to learn that the London headquarters had ordered a stairway built between the AEA offices on the 15th floor and the S. G. Warburg office on the 16th. When Hess wouldn't accept this back-door maneuver, Siegmund ordered him to London with another executive, insisting they take separate planes.

In London, Siegmund said flatly that he wanted to merge his New York office and AEA. Referring to the stairway, Hess said he had no desire to be subordinated to S. G. Warburg's New York office. Siegmund couldn't brook such defiance, got extremely upset, and started wagging his finger in Hess's face. "We have the power to compel this," he said. "We have the power to make you do this. We have the power to destroy Carl Hess in the financial community." Hess shrugged and said coolly, "Everybody has to die someday, Siegmund."[11]

Withdrawing the Rockefeller and Kommerzbank money from AEA, Siegmund sent Eric Roll to New York to announce that the experiment was being wound up. Hess had lined up a powerful ally in Chrysler chairman George Love, who said to Roll, "Tell Siegmund that he owes one to this bald-headed man."[12] Because Chrysler was a major client, Siegmund couldn't afford to antagonize Love. So AEA bought out the S. G. Warburg stake at ten cents a share. Having badly bungled his maiden venture, Hess soon hit his stride. By the late 1980s the AEA shares had zoomed to $150, as it evolved into a billion-dollar club for retired Fortune 500 CEOs who invested their money to restructure companies. With his usual flair for innovation, Siegmund had devised a marvelous idea. Had he stuck with it, he might have gratified his Wall Street aspirations. Instead, he let a vision of transatlantic cooperation fall victim to a power struggle.

———

Starting with his early days at M. M. Warburg & Co., Siegmund had specialized in international securities issues. In postwar London he had been hampered by capital controls. Now, in the early 1960s, Siegmund would help to rejuvenate London as a world financial center, lavishly repaying Britain for its hospitality. In creating the Euromarkets, Siegmund would again inject tremendous dynamism into a lethargic London scene.

The Euromarkets would give Siegmund a chance to reverse many earlier disappointments. After the war, he had vainly urged Britain to join the Common Market, lobbying Jean Monnet and Konrad Adenauer for a central British role. "They would have gone down on their hands and knees and would have thanked the British in the first five postwar years if they would have agreed to lead a united Europe and to make London its capital city," Siegmund recalled.[13]

Now, through the private markets, he was about to accomplish something that would bring closer his vision of an integrated Europe. With the pending imposition of the Interest Equalization Tax in America, Siegmund consulted both the Bank of England and the Bundesbank about creating a new global market in London to supplant New York. This new market would issue Eurobonds, using three billion surplus dollars that had circulated in Europe since the war. While British investors would supply a small portion of the money, this new, extraterritorial market would float, like a small, foreign island, in a sea of domestic business. When the British and German central banks expressed support for such a move, Siegmund quickly formed an in-house team to explore ways to accomplish it.

The new business played to S. G. Warburg strengths. As Sir David Scholey recalled, "The development of the Eurobond market was fascinating because there were people in our firm, such as Siegmund and Gert Whitman and Eric Korner and Henry Grunfeld, who had been active participants in the international bond market of the '20s and '30s."[14] While other firms saw the new market as transient and experimental, the S. G. Warburg people correctly guessed that it represented an enduring revolution. Siegmund lacked the capital or distribution networks for these securities, but he knew how to offset his weakness by forming strong syndicates. He would sit day and night at the phone, dialing the world over until an issue was fully placed. Having done foreign issues at Kuhn, Loeb in the 1950s, he knew that as much as 90 percent of those issues had been placed with European banks and so when he made his telephone calls, he had the best black book in the world.

In January 1963, S. G. Warburg and Deutsche Bank were ready to launch the inaugural Eurobond issue for the European Coal and Steel Community. When the ECSC decided to postpone the issue, Siegmund launched the market instead with a fifteen-million-dollar, six-year loan for the Autostrade Italiane, which built and maintained the Italian highways. The historic deal was signed on July 1, 1963. (The real recipient of the money was the steel-making company Finsider, a sister subsidiary of the Autostrade in the state-owned IRI conglomerate.) It was the first foreign industrial loan issued in London in a generation and in several ways was a landmark. To eliminate a 4 percent stamp tax on the transaction, Siegmund had the bonds listed in Luxembourg. This imaginative issue was therefore signed in Holland, under English law, for an Italian borrower, with the loan quoted in Luxembourg, and paid in American dollars.[15] It didn't sell particularly well—Italy wasn't a special favorite of investors—but for a self-styled world citizen who had inveighed against nationalism since Hitler, this new borderless world of finance was a refreshing tonic to the spirit.

In developing the new market, Siegmund wanted to avoid dogma or conventional thinking. After his Autostrade coup, he followed with issues for the ECSC and the city of Oslo. (Oslo—a Kuhn, Loeb client—gave the business to Warburgs on the mistaken assumption that it was still tied to Kuhn, Loeb.)[16] Then Siegmund asked: Why must payment be made in dollars or any single currency? Why couldn't investors have the option of choosing among different payment methods? After getting the go-ahead from the Bank of England and the Bundesbank, Siegmund issued a bond for the Communist city of Turin in which payment could be taken in sterling or deutsche marks. He followed with option loans for Mobil Oil and the governments of New Zealand and Ireland. Though the Euromarkets didn't account for more than 10 to 15 percent of S. G. Warburg revenues, Siegmund used them to feed clients to his merger team, giving his firm irresistible momentum. The Euromarkets also brought great renown to Siegmund who had transported the City back to its Edwardian days, when London served as banker to the world.

Siegmund kept trying to broaden the insular world of London finance. In 1962, he and other bankers visited Japan under the aegis of the Bank of England, and their hosts included the chairman of Nomura Securities. The bustling Japanese captivated Siegmund who praised their "unique mixture of utter discipline and infinite self-criticism."[17] The Japanese, in turn, liked Siegmund's exquisite manners. By urging German friends to invest 10 percent of their money in Japan, Siegmund recaptured the goodwill that Max Warburg and Jacob Schiff had enjoyed in Tokyo when they financed Japan in the Russo-Japanese War.

In launching the Euromarkets, Siegmund suffered from one critical deficiency: He lacked a fingertip feel for markets. He therefore relied upon Eric Korner and, even more, upon a man named Gert Whitman. Many people believe that Siegmund never gave adequate credit to Gert in the development of the Euromarkets. Like Siegmund, Gert came from a prominent German family, and the two men had been friends in Germany. Gert's father, Robert Weismann, was a distinguished state secretary for Prussia, while his heiress mother was a baptized Jew. The Weismanns lived on the Wilhelmstrasse in Berlin in a massive stone mansion adorned with Chinese art later stolen by the Nazis. In the early 1930s, Siegmund and Eva attended balls at the Weismann home. Through his father, Gert had become a private secretary to Dr. Schacht in 1924, attending the Young Conference with him in Paris.

In the 1930s, Gert had emigrated to America. After his gilded upbringing in Berlin, exile came as a rude shock, and he grew very depressed. He worked for Lee, Higginson and Harris, Upham and, hoping to improve his prospects, changed his name from Weismann to Whitman. After the war, he worked on the American High Commission in Germany under John McCloy and collaborated with Monnet, Schuman, and Adenauer in creating the European Coal and Steel Community.

Siegmund often showed flashes of ambivalence toward people from privileged background and Gert was destined to bring out both his admiration and scorn. In the 1950s, Gert helped Kuhn, Loeb with its European work and married a gentile woman from Hamburg named Gretchen. Siegmund coaxed him into coming to London to perform Kuhn, Loeb work from the S. G. Warburg office. After a time, Gert shifted to the Warburg payroll. Unlike Siegmund, Gert was thrilled by fast-moving markets. Endowed with a visionary streak, he frequently expounded his forward-looking plan for a single European currency called the "Eurodukat."

A short, witty man with a pink, bald head and blue eyes, Gert was genial and sophisticated. Always well groomed and natty, he traveled first-class, drove a fancy car, and lived opposite Siegmund on Eaton Square. He could also be cynical in his comments and played office politics. For a time, Siegmund was enamored of Gert. Every Sunday morning, they strolled together through the Eaton Square gardens. The Whitmans and the Warburgs often met for dinner and bridge and Gretchen and Eva attended exhibitions and fashion shows together.

Siegmund had many gripes about Gert: He went to too many parties, was vain and self-important, and wasn't dedicated enough to the firm. Siegmund disapproved of Gert's smoking and Gert of Siegmund's pedantic paperwork. When the uncles flicked on a light outside their office to indicate meetings in progress, Gert used his to steal cat naps. So the potential for trouble always existed, but was offset by Gert's evident utility.

In the Euromarkets, Siegmund and Gert were an ideal team. Siegmund had the strategic vision and salesmanship, as well as the clients to issue the bonds and the Continental bankers to absorb them. Gert knew the marketplace mechanics of currencies, interest rates, and syndicates—things remote from Siegmund's ken. With his fine intuition and broad experience, he could determine the appropriate price and maturity for a new issue.

However complementary in the Euromarkets, Siegmund and Gert began to grate on each other as personalities. Gert wouldn't play the servile courtier to Siegmund and trespassed on forbidden territory. Many bankers and chief executives liked to deal with Gert and this upset Siegmund, who jealously guarded his relationship turf from all intruders. As lead manager of issues, S. G. Warburg & Co. acquired tremendous power as banks around the world jockeyed to participate. Gert felt entitled to offer opinions about participants, which constituted *lèse-majesté* in Siegmund's eyes. As Gert asserted himself about Euromarket decisions, he fell irrevocably from favor.

Siegmund criticized self-promotion, yet always manipulated the press like a maestro. As he took credit in the press for the rise of the Euromarkets, Gert came to believe that Siegmund not only envied him but deliberately slighted his contribution. He tested his intuition. Whenever he suggested an idea, Siegmund branded it ridiculous. But if he had Peter Spira present it as his own, Siegmund lauded it to the skies.[18] This demotion was a crushing blow to Gert, who had been devoted to Siegmund. When Siegmund began to ignore him, Gert started coming home from work very despondent. His position soon became intolerable and he left the firm.

Gert had been on the board of S. G. Warburg and Company Frankfurt along with Richard Daus and Hans Petersen. Gert had annoyed Siegmund by defending Daus when the latter lost favor with Siegmund. When Daus left to form his own firm, Gert joined him in March 1970 without bothering to consult Siegmund. Siegmund construed this as a slap in the face and an act of unpardonable disloyalty.

Many S. G. Warburg executives thought the firm owed Gert a retirement dinner, but Siegmund adamantly rejected this. Ian Fraser, the former Reuters correspondent, said, "Sir Siegmund, I think you may have to reconsider that decision."[19] He and others felt strongly that Gert deserved recognition for his Euromarket work. In the end, after much prodding, Siegmund grudgingly acceded to the farewell dinner. But he devised an unexpected way to punish Gert and defy his colleagues.[20] When Siegmund rose to make the farewell speech, he talked of many things. Then he sat down without having made a single reference to Gert. An uncomfortable silence descended upon the room.

While working in Frankfurt with Daus, Gert suffered a heart attack on October 17, 1970. He was rushed to the hospital, but it was too late. After his death, Gretchen went through a hellish period. In listing the cause of death, the doctors had, for some reason, placed a question mark after "heart attack." This meant a four-week delay while an obligatory autopsy was performed, prolonging Gretchen's suffering.

For two years, Gert had suffered from angina pectoris, ignoring warnings from doctors to quit smoking. Yet Gretchen was convinced that Siegmund's unfair treatment of her husband had contributed to his death. Neither Siegmund nor Eva ever contacted her afterward and S. G. Warburg sent no representative to the funeral. The firm only acknowledged Gert's death through a cold, impersonal telegram.[21] When Raymond Bonham Carter called to inform him of Gert's death, Siegmund said dismissively, "Oh, I thought he died yesterday."[22] Some months later, Gretchen ran into Eva on Bond Street and Eva, flustered, said, "Oh, Gretchen, I'm so sorry about Gert." When she reached out to her former friend, Gretchen recoiled from her touch.[23]

In an unsigned *Times* obituary on October 21, 1970, Ian Fraser had tried to give Gert the due denied by Warburgs. Among the 250 houses active in the Euromarkets, Fraser noted, nobody's judgment on new bond issues was more prized than that of Gert Whitman. After sketching in Gert's background, Fraser wrote, "He later became a full-time executive director of S. G. Warburg & Co. in London and, together with Sir Siegmund Warburg, was largely instrumental in advancing the firm to the position which it occupies in the Eurobond and Eurodollar market today."[24] When Siegmund read this appraisal, he grew enraged at having to share credit with Gert.

Most of Siegmund's colleagues believe that he fully deserved his title as

Father of the Euromarkets. Siegmund created the essential concepts while Gert was the man of a million details. Even those who adhere to this view, however, believe that Siegmund grew envious of Gert and tried to erase his substantial contribution. Increasingly as the 1960s progressed, Siegmund seemed like a king who demanded absolute fealty from his liege lords and was quick to strike down those who overreached themselves. Gert Whitman was such a casualty.

For S. G. Warburg & Co., an ironic by-product of the Euromarkets was that it wedded this firm founded by Jewish refugees more closely to Germany. Young Britons at the firm were both baffled and intrigued by the interplay between their Jewish bosses and German banks. In the 1960s, Siegmund probably spent half his time in Germany and sold many Eurobond issues through his Swiss and German friends, especially Paul Lichtenberg of Commerzbank and Hermann Abs of Deutsche Bank. Once again, German banks, as before the Third Reich, tapped Jewish financial power and connections. For Siegmund, the idea of returning in triumph to Germany always had profound emotional reverberations.

Siegmund especially revered Hermann Abs, head of all-powerful Deutsche Bank, who had advised Adenauer and was the godfather of postwar German finance. The Warburgs had known Abs since the 1920s, when he had discussed with Max a possible apprenticeship with the International Acceptance Bank in New York. That Siegmund glorified Abs was strange, since many Jews faulted Abs for having been a director during the war of many large German companies, including I. G. Farben, which had employed slave labor from Auschwitz. Whether a genuine belief or convenient rationalization, Siegmund would always lay great stress upon the fact that Abs never allowed his children to join the Hitler Youth.[25] Abs wouldn't entirely reciprocate Siegmund's worshipful attitude. It was said in the firm that Siegmund would try to address Abs by the familiar *"du"* only to have Abs put him in his place with the more formal *"sie."*[26]

Siegmund prospered as a guide to German businessmen and culture. He had a knack for harmonizing diverse national groups. In 1969, Mobil Oil wanted to buy a German oil-production company, Gelsenkirchener Bergwerk, then trying to ward off French suitors. A majority of its stock was held by Dresdner and Deutsche Bank. Siegmund agreed to represent Mobil, and his good relations with Hermann Abs proved indispensable to his success. When he brought together his American clients and German executives to negotiate, only two people in the room spoke German *and* English: Siegmund and his personal assistant, Tony Korner, Eric's son. Unbeknownst to the Germans, the Mobil Oil people were being crassly belligerent; unbeknownst to the Mobil people, the Gelsenkirchener crowd were being arrogant and supercilious. In a bravura performance as negotiator and translator, Siegmund subtly toned down the Germans' arrogance, while elevating the coarse language of the Mobil Oil cowboys, thus bringing the two sides together.[27]

Siegmund thought it undignified to set a fee in advance and would invoke the great merchant bankers he had met in the 1920s who had identified something beyond money as their objective. In this respect, Siegmund's style harked back to the mystery-shrouded manner of Jacob Schiff and Max Warburg. When he went to Mobil Oil to discuss his fee, he expected it to be at most five to six hundred thousand dollars. Nervous about broaching the subject, Siegmund circled around it evasively for a while. When the Mobil people asked if a million-dollar fee would be suitable, he almost fainted. "I was just enjoying myself," he protested.[28]

——

Besides inventing the Euromarkets, Siegmund Warburg left another enduring monument: the firm of S. G. Warburg & Co. itself. No man was more slavishly devoted to his mistress. As he had since 1946, he continued to insist upon diversification, and in 1964 Mercury Securities added the British Gallup Poll firm to its portfolio of investments. Siegmund found it hard to let go of his creation and he would stage the longest retirement drama in modern business annals. As early as 1959, he circulated a memo about the need to step aside and make room for younger people. He thought it his duty to retire on time and made friends promise to warn him if he stayed too long. But he also observed, prophetically, that they wouldn't do so when the time came because they would feel sorry for him. The firm, which now had 250 employees, was an extension of his personality and he could no more cut himself off from it than he could amputate a limb.

Siegmund often referred to his semiretirement, which became a standing joke at Warburgs. He managed to keep three full-time secretaries busy. *The Times* of London noted that the semiretired Siegmund seldom left the bank before seven o'clock.[29] In 1964, amid much fanfare, he yielded the chairmanship of Mercury Securities to Henry Grunfeld and became, at least on paper, a nonexecutive director. As he said that year, "Leaders of industry and commerce are often inclined not to step down before the decline of their powers becomes manifest, holding on too long to their positions and thus preventing the formation of a strong chain of successors."[30] Siegmund himself would be strikingly guilty of this sin and his 1964 "retirement" was more a matter of show than substance.

Despite his years in England, Siegmund remained Continental at heart. In the early 1960s, he and Eva built a lovely house called Roccamare near Grosseto on Italy's west coast. About two hours north of Rome, the summer and weekend house was equipped with telephone, telex, and secretary. It was a beautiful but sweltering place, shrill with the sound of crickets. Siegmund took working vacations there but never learned the art of casual recreation. Every day at noon, he and his family tramped over the dunes to bathe in the Mediterranean. Siegmund could swim, but he would only go up to his waist, bend at the knees, and flap his arms. Whenever Eva pulled out a camera to take pictures of Anna and her baby, Batya, Siegmund would, as always, protest. He feared that pictures of him in shorts or swim trunks would fall into the wrong hands and destroy his image.

Often alone, Eva felt terribly isolated at Roccamare. When she complained to Siegmund, he was perfectly mystified. Hadn't he recently purchased the complete twenty-volume works of Sigmund Freud? And wouldn't such reading nicely fill the time? Apparently not. Siegmund was himself driven wild by the inconvenience and the inefficient Italian telephones. So the Warburgs sold the house to the Ferragamo family.

Even as he felt the old magnetic pull of the Continent, Siegmund was drawn more deeply into British politics. He often lamented that his Swabian accent had prevented him from engaging in English statecraft or diplomacy. While he loved the stuff and feel of politics, he lacked any set ideology. Even in Weimar Germany, he had seen the alternation of parties in power as a salutary thing.[31] Colleagues viewed him as an unpredictable floating voter, a heterodox Tory who often voted Labour. Mostly Siegmund hated weak, equivocating politicians and admired fearless, uncompromising personalities of either party. For that reason, he went through periods of being entranced by both Richard Nixon and Margaret Thatcher. His most consistent belief was in European integration, and he was saddened to see the European Community weakened by protectionism and sectional interests in the 1960s.

Siegmund liked the fiery intellect of Prime Minister Harold Wilson, who turned to Siegmund as an unofficial financial adviser in the 1960s, particularly about currency matters. This was a rare honor from a Labour leader—after all, Siegmund was one of eighty-one British millionaires, according to 1963 tax returns—and Wilson took heat for the move. Now in his sixties, Siegmund still liked to tweak the establishment. He certainly had more sympathy for Labour than most Tory bankers in the City, but never reflexively adopted Labour positions. For instance, he opposed cheapening the pound to stimulate exports, calling such an expedient defeatism and favoring tough, unpopular measures to restore British competitiveness.[32] His lifelong contempt for bureaucracy posed limits to his public flirtation with Labour. Yet he was closely enough identified with Wilson's government that in 1966 he had to issue a disclaimer in *The Sunday Times:* "I am not a Socialist and I believe that private enterprise has just as important a role to play in our time . . . as during the First Industrial Revolution."[33]

Siegmund's association with Wilson made him a traitor in the City—a status he surely enjoyed. He enjoyed remarkable access to the prime minister. When Chrysler considered shutting down one of its Scottish plants, Siegmund shepherded company executives to Chequers, a meeting he arranged on just a few days' notice. After Rhodesia declared its independence, Wilson made Siegmund governor of the rump central bank. In line with his antiapartheid views, Siegmund was an early contributor to the jailed Nelson Mandela in South Africa.

In July 1966, undoubtedly in recognition of his services to Wilson, Siegmund Warburg was knighted. At first, as an avowed foe of vanity, he hesitated to accept it and only did so when Henry Grunfeld told him the distinction would benefit the firm. He was stunned and delighted by the knighthood, which was actually very important to him, for it validated his decision to live in England and conferred some ultimate certificate of success. The new Lady Warburg was terribly happy for him.

As Siegmund was flooded with handwritten congratulatory notes, the press speculated, correctly, that he was sending batches of them to Zurich to be analyzed by Mrs. Dreifuss.[34] It was a great windfall to have a sudden collection of so many famous handwritings. Once again Mrs. Dreifuss turned in a stellar performance. When Siegmund sent her an unidentified letter from Oxford scholar Isaiah Berlin, she commented on his minute, spiky penmanship: "This handwriting is that of the most brilliant man I've ever analyzed."[35]

The knighthood came at a time when Siegmund was trying to ease into a nonexecutive role at S. G. Warburg. Wanting to give Henry Grunfeld more room, Siegmund and Eva abruptly moved to Blonay in Switzerland, about an hour from Geneva. At the advice of lawyers, Siegmund transferred his assets to Switzerland so that he could enjoy greater freedom to set up charitable trusts and the like. At a time of severe foreign-exchange controls in England, the move required the permission of the Bank of England.

Coming upon the heels of the knighthood, the move irked some Britons, who felt it showed base ingratitude. Siegmund's great ally in the Aluminium War, Lionel Fraser, was disappointed. "Lionel thought it was a bit shabby to get a knighthood and then move to Switzerland," said his partner, Michael Verey. "Siegmund didn't enhance his reputation in the City."[36] Nobody knows for sure why Siegmund chose Switzerland. He was critical of tax exiles, yet many suspect he joined their ranks. "Siegmund went to Switzerland to escape the high socialist taxes at the time," said Dr. Goldman. "He thought they were too high."[37]

There were other compelling reasons. For a veteran traveler, it provided a central European location. It also wasn't far from Swabia and perhaps stirred some old memories; as late as 1980, Siegmund attended a reunion of his

Gymnasium. He had more Continental than British friends and sometimes vacationed in the Black Forest. By going to Switzerland, Siegmund also sought to gain a fresh perspective on events in London. Finally, with sunshine and fresh air at Blonay, Siegmund could dispense with the need to go away on holiday. Eva would have preferred staying in London but at Blonay they at least had as neighbors her old Swedish friends, Ruth and Carl Kjellberg. It seems fitting that Siegmund ended up in Blonay. He was at home in the rich no-man's land along Lake Geneva. As a crossroads of the European business and social elite, it was an appropriate place for a world citizen and international banker.

With telephone lines, a corner telex, and a secretary often present, Siegmund now ruled at Gresham Street by remote control and was no less omnipresent *in absentia.* For two hours each morning, he dialed around the office. When slouching people suddenly sat bolt upright, everybody knew Sir Siegmund was on the other end. He endlessly plied people with questions and had an elephantine memory for answers. Sir Eric Roll, who became chairman in 1974, wrote that to know what was happening in the office, "the quickest and surest way was to telephone [Siegmund] at Blonay."[38]

Some visitors saw the Swiss house as a camouflaged office. Every day dense packets of material arrived from London and Siegmund's colleagues mocked his inability to retire. Siegmund always loved the delightful in-house satirical skits written in Evelyn Waugh style by one of the uncles, Charles Sharp. In one sketch called "Gloom," Sharp depicted Siegmund "in his villa in Blonay, amidst the theoretical beauty of the Lake of Geneva which cannot be seen from the window of the villa's telex-room where SGW spends his time when he is there for one of his 24 to 48 hour holidays."[39]

In January 1970, in yet another step in his protracted retirement pageant, Siegmund became president of S. G. Warburg & Co. and Mercury Securities and surrendered his directorships in both.

Ostensibly Siegmund had withdrawn to Blonay to give room to his successors. Yet his personality was no less forceful when filtered through a long-distance telephone. It was simply not in his nature to let his creation out of his grasp, and nobody at S. G. Warburg & Co. was particularly shocked that the sovereign continued to issue decrees in exile from his distant castle on Lake Geneva.

Siegmund Warburg and an "adopted son," Peter Spira,
signing a Eurobond issue for Bank Leumi, 1967.
(Courtesy of Peter Spira)

CHAPTER 47

Fathers and Sons

A painting of Siegmund Warburg from the early 1970s captures him in a characteristic pose. He slouches in a chair, brooding, lugubrious, with a languidly passive air. He looks slightly gaunt, the lines etched deep in his face. Yet upon closer inspection, the first impression fades. He is poised and watchful, ready for action, his tremendous drive concealed beneath a cloak of relaxed urbanity. The dark, piercing eyes are deeply ringed, keenly alive and alert, but also hard and disappointed. Now in his seventies, Sir Siegmund still betrays something of the coiled tiger, conserving his energies for the next spring. Staring from hooded eyes and a well-tended facade, he seems tired but restless within.

For all his career satisfaction in London, he was, in many ways, a frustrated man. Despite his great charm and curiosity about people, there was something, in the end, distantly cerebral about Siegmund. Sadness had settled over him, as in the later years of other Warburgs. He frequently quoted from *The Magic Mountain* how it was unthinkable "to have great joys on one side of the scale unless on the other side of the scale the pain and the suffering are just as high."[1] The melancholy was partly the dejection of the perfectionist who could never make peace with a slipshod world. It was also the weariness of a man still gripped by a relentless ambition, who couldn't sit back and enjoy his achievement. He saw the world edged in black. When Ernest Thalmann died in 1962, Siegmund spoke eloquently in a funeral oration of "the fog and mist of our daily doings and the long trails of dark clouds among which we have to find our way."[2]

At Blonay, his monkish side grew pronounced. He slept on an extremely hard bed with hard pillows, drank sparingly, ate simply, and, except for the news, seldom watched television. He said "the older I am, the more I feel possessions are a burden rather than an asset. To make one's life simple is for me a supreme urge."[3] Contemptuous of money-grubbing, he displayed no desire for a great fortune and showed scant interest in his personal finances. In 1970, he took fifteen thousand pounds in salary from his firm—less than many subordinates. Somebody else managed his money and he never followed the prices of his stocks. Charles Sharp, who oversaw his investments for several years, recalled, "I was always nervous to talk to Siegmund about details and these seemed to bore him tremendously."[4]

Siegmund could be astonishingly casual about money. When he telephoned the office one Saturday morning in the late 1960s, a new recruit named Geoffrey Elliott answered and Siegmund asked him to open a large envelope stamped "Strictly personal and confidential." The envelope contained Siegmund's tax returns. In a notable gesture of trust, he asked this stranger and newcomer to read him the results.[5] For his seventieth birthday in 1972, his colleagues gave him what he really loved most: specially bound volumes of Goethe and a bronze statue of Mercury.

At directors' meetings, Siegmund made a point of eating a minute piece of chicken and a small lettuce salad. His frugality was matched by the uncles, who still worked ten-hour days. Even as they grew rich, they didn't squander money. In one Charles Sharp sketch, a fictitious Henry Grunfeld chides him for writing and distributing his plays. "Do you know how much a page of foolscap-paper costs?" he asks.[6]

Siegmund's main indulgence continued to be doctors. Suffering from bronchitis and chest pains, he often stopped at consulting rooms en route to work. A notorious hypochondriac, he complained of so many maladies that Grunfeld and Geoffrey Seligman would nod and whisper to each other, "Psychosomatic." He suffered from back problems that probably weren't improved by toting his heavy black suitcase. His neck often stiffened from tension. Though he took oral medicine for diabetes, he disobeyed the strict diet and grew arteriosclerotic. When he suffered from anginal chest pains, he grew extremely worried. As the colossal energy began to ebb away, Dr. Goldman brought Siegmund back to life with vitamin shots before major meetings. Sometimes he still had the stamina of a much younger man. His main secretary, Doris Wasserman, would recall chasing him across Rockefeller Center, taking down rapid dictation as she struggled to keep up beside him.

Siegmund must have felt his father's darkness creeping over him as he endured fearsome headaches, sometimes two per week. Like his father, he got headaches when he was upset, and few dared to defy him in these black moods. After the tempest passed, he was tranquil again and acted as if nothing had happened. He scapegoated people for his headaches, and Eva always feared that she might inadvertently set one off. When Siegmund consulted Dr. Paul Sherwood about his headaches, the doctor diagnosed the problem as a spinal injury. After a time, Dr. Sherwood said, "In my opinion, you're all right," and Siegmund thundered back, "*I'll* tell you when I'm all right."[7] Even with physicians, Siegmund had to run the show.

S. G. Warburg was shedding the Jewish refugee character of early days. Sometimes the uncles themselves seemed to forget their antecedents. One day, Charles Sharp came back to the office after a reception for a Japanese company at the Dorchester. Amid general amusement, he boasted, in his heavy German accent, "There were hundreds of people there. I vas the only Englishman in the place."[8]

By 1970, more than a quarter of S. G. Warburg's executive directors were younger than forty and the vast majority were now British. In 1967, Siegmund recruited the Austrian-born civil servant, Sir Eric Roll, whom he had met when Roll was in the Ministry of Agriculture. Having grown up on a farm, Siegmund stopped by to talk about agricultural policy. The son of a provincial bank manager, the erudite, multilingual Roll had written a history of economic thought, headed the Department of Economic Affairs, and represented Britain at the IMF/World Bank. He helped Edward Heath to negotiate Britain's entry into the Common Market. Despite Roll's illustrious résumé, Siegmund made him submit to a graphology test. In 1974, Roll became chairman of S. G. Warburg & Co., succeeding Henry Grunfeld.

As a civil servant without a banking background, Roll's appointment provoked dissent at S. G. Warburg. Some thought that Siegmund had picked a passive figurehead so he could secretly pull the strings. At first, people snickered at Roll, naming him Sir Echo, since his views frequently reflected what Siegmund thought. Sometimes Siegmund seemed to delight in teasing Roll by unexpectedly changing his opinion and leaving Roll stranded. But over time, Roll made believers of many skeptics. In the 1970s, as Warburgs specialized in advising Third World governments on their debt, Roll's extensive contacts in foreign ministries helped to establish Warburg as preeminent in the field.

Roll was an honorary uncle by background, who looked and sounded awfully British. By the 1960s, Siegmund devoted a lot of time to grooming a brilliant, heterodox group of young Englishmen to succeed the uncles. "The capital of the place goes away in the elevator every night," he would say. S. G. Warburg was always the youngest merchant bank in the City, the quickest to promote ambitious recruits. Siegmund retained a pedagogical fascination with youth. "He revered people and enjoyed being revered," said his cousin, Ruth Fleck.[9] As a rule, he got more of that reverence from the young than from his peers, many of whom became more cynical about him with time.

Unlike other bosses, Siegmund hired good people as they were spotted, not as needed. He gambled on offbeat types, preferring mavericks steeped in history and literature. Distrusting "popular" people, he preferred outspoken nonconformists in his own mold. "As a rule those with whom I am close in my firm are people with whom I can also talk about books, about music, about human beings, human problems."[10] This made the firm a mecca for smart young people. It also guaranteed that the firm got people who had not been tutored in somebody else's style. The second generation was known as the "sons"—the nomenclature again reflecting the unfulfilled family cravings of these refugees.

For the sons, Siegmund could be a stern taskmaster who succumbed to ungovernable sulks and rages. Yet he could also be the soul of benevolence. He could take people by the elbow, warmly slip his arm around them, and stroll down the hallway with them. He spurred disciples to new levels of achievement because of his personal interest. "People regarded him with enormous awe and respect," said Dietrich Weismann, Gert Whitman's nephew. "He was almost like a god. There was a sense that he had a perspective that went beyond the normal."[11] Their first encounter with Siegmund often left recruits euphoric. It was heady stuff for young people to receive the undivided attention of this tycoon.

By the 1960s, S. G. Warburg was top-heavy with young talent. Like a fickle king, Siegmund wanted young courtiers to compete for his pleasure. Never a man of the middle ground, he was either thrilled with people's performance or aghast. Siegmund and Grunfeld had no scruples about pushing aside people who disappointed them and employees talked about being on the "up" or "down" escalator. If he saw an out-of-favor person approaching as he prowled the Gresham Street corridor, Siegmund would turn and stare away or slip into a office. Sometimes, he played the "Walking Enigma." One day, he shuffled into the investment department, jingled coins in his pocket, and said, "Good morning," to Charles Sharp and Peter Darling. After he left, a perplexed Sharp said, "But when Mr. Warburg said 'Good morning,' what did he really mean?"

With Siegmund, the craving for the lost father was converted into a yearning for the lost son. To become a surrogate son was risky business. A new favorite could be golden boy one moment, then cast into outer darkness the next. Siegmund had a widespread reputation for using up sons and throwing them away. If people stood up to him often and didn't give way, he would villainize them and blow up peccadilloes into major gaffes. One Wall Street executive remembers walking through Hanover Square when Siegmund suddenly clapped his hand on his shoulder and called him "My son." Afraid of the sequel, the man stopped calling Siegmund on subsequent trips to London. With his exaggerated expectations, people always disappointed Siegmund in the end. He converted the world into a test of how people treated him. To succeed required infinite tact and finesse, a constant catering to his smallest whims. One misstep could destroy the hard work of many years. This was more than just a tyrant's vanity. Siegmund was extremely sensitive and disappointments tapped into some deep well of loneliness, producing almost unbearable pain.

Almost all of Siegmund's friends and associates went through a banishment phase. They would do something that upset him and then he was suddenly unavailable when they called. The ostracism might last for months, even years. Then one day, the telephone would ring and Siegmund would be saying sweetly on the other end, "My dear so-and-so, how are you? It has been so long since I heard from you. Why don't you come round and have a cup of tea?" If the person mentioned the cold-shoulder treatment, Siegmund might admit it or profess astonishment. This behavior had its advantages for Siegmund: It made people extremely reluctant to cross him, for once out of favor, it was hard to reenter his good graces.

In the 1960s, the foremost son and heir apparent was Peter Spira, who was referred to Siegmund by the chairman of the *Financial Times*. Spira trained as a chartered accountant, joining the firm in 1957. Spira was a nonobservant Jew with a Jewish wife. Since Siegmund fretted that there weren't more promising Jewish employees, this augured well for Spira. Also, he excelled in Siegmund's favorite areas of corporate finance and international securities issues.

Spira didn't fathom how sensitive Siegmund could be, as became clear when he was named a director in 1964. Siegmund was afraid that Spira, with four children, might be distracted by financial worries. So he magnanimously gave him a large block of Mercury shares from his personal holding. Very grateful, Spira also knew that he would be liable for a large death-duty bill if Siegmund died within seven years. So he asked Siegmund if he could take out an insurance policy on his life, which meant that Siegmund would have to take a medical examination. Because the Mercury shares had a tiny dividend, Spira also asked if he could switch them into higher-yielding gilts. Siegmund acceded to both requests, but inwardly seethed. For years he nursed this wound in silence and only told Spira at a 1980 lunch how hurt he had been.[12]

Spira's error precipitated a fall from grace. It didn't help that Imperial Chemical Industries was so pleased with him that they wanted him to handle their account—the sort of thing that always aroused Siegmund's paranoia. Gradually Siegmund's adoration began to turn into anger, especially when Spira openly differed with him at meetings. In job interviews, Siegmund stressed that he wanted people who would stand up to him, but he preferred such courage in the abstract. "On minor issues, Siegmund liked disagreement," said Spira. "But if it were a major matter, he absolutely loathed it."[13] Everybody noticed Spira's exclusion from Siegmund's affection. One day, Eric Korner said to him, "Spira, you are still under a cloud, but it is no longer raining."[14] In fact, it never really stopped raining. By 1974 Siegmund no longer spoke to Spira, who resigned as an executive vice-chairman and became financial director of Sotheby's. It was shocking treatment of a person often touted as a possible successor to Siegmund.

Another son was the handsome, precocious John Craven. Educated in South Africa and trained as a chartered accountant, he had a remarkable instinct for snaring new business. Two years after joining Warburgs as a trainee in 1967, he was made a director while still in his twenties. By 1972, this young hotshot ran much of the international side. He cooperated on many Eurobond issues with White Weld, which offered him a lucrative deal to handle its London operations. When Craven presented his decision to defect to the rival firm as a *fait accompli*, Henry Grunfeld told him to clear out at once. Grunfeld's reaction typified the inbred Warburg culture, which demanded loyalty unto death. Even after they left, people were supposed to refrain from chasing Warburg clients. Craven briefly returned to the firm in the late 1970s but couldn't get used to being in a subordinate role again and left.

Peter Spira steered to Siegmund the real heir to the throne, David Scholey. The son of a partner at Guinness Mahon, he was a young man of eclectic musical, literary and artistic tastes, who enjoyed hunting and golf. After a year at Oxford (where he ran an illegal roulette game) he worked at Lloyd's and at Guinness Mahon. He also did a stint in Canada and married the daughter of the former leader of the Conservative party there, George Drew.

After joining S. G. Warburg in 1965, this future chairman was placed in the high-pressure room between Siegmund and Grunfeld. "It was known as either the nutcracker suite or the fall-out shelter," he said.[15] "Working for Siegmund was electrifying, enthralling—nothing was new yet everything was fresh."[16] In 1977, Scholey was named deputy chairman, then chairman in 1980. He won out for several reasons. Urbane and charming on the outside, he was very tough underneath. Patient, hardworking, he had a broad background in traditional banking and an encyclopedic memory for facts. Most of all, he was a deft diplomat who never committed major blunders or offended the sensibilities of superiors. He had extraordinary self-control in a place where an unguarded moment could be costly. In the end, he was the last survivor left on a battlefield of bloody corpses.

Besides rivalry among the sons, there was also generational friction at S. G. Warburg. The often aristocratic young Britons were more vocal and free-wheeling than the secretive gerontocracy at the top. Some thought Siegmund misjudged the British. Ian Fraser wrote, "Hating inefficiency and complacence, he often mistook English informality for sloppiness and English reticence for self-satisfaction. Consequently some of his judgments on British businessmen and politics were flawed."[17] Inevitably, his young turks grew restless. "A number of us found that when we were in our mid-forties, although one might be in a senior position, one began to find that the seventy-year-olds were beginning to look immortal," said Peter Spira.[18] London firms would be seeded with Siegmund's disciples. Ian Fraser would head Lazard Brothers and John Craven Morgan Grenfell. Except for Scholey, the sons all left and would look back on their mentor with a mixture of pain and affection.

In a 1980 interview with *Institutional Investor*, Siegmund called David Scholey and Ira Wender his adopted sons. Siegmund was extremely careful in choosing words and the expression seemed needlessly cruel to his real son, George. Scholey privately expressed profound discomfort with it. In his later years, Siegmund and Eva were dining at a hotel outside Frankfurt with another adopted son, James Wolfensohn, and his wife. Wolfensohn was a young Australian Jewish financier and lawyer whom Siegmund tried to hire in the 1960s. From the blue, Siegmund suggested that he might legally adopt Wolfensohn. Silence fell over the dinner since Wolfensohn didn't think Siegmund was joking. He changed the subject and they never discussed it again.[19]

Siegmund always wanted to repair relations with George, who had formed his own firm in 1963. Far from feeling dismayed by the "adopted sons," George was relieved that these other young men gave his father pleasure and relieved him of some paternal pressure. In late 1969, Milo Cripps—the nephew of Sir Stafford Cripps, former chancellor of the exchequer—defected to team up with George. A multifaceted S. G. Warburg executive, Cripps had run the investment side, and Siegmund didn't like losing him. The two defectors set up a small merchant bank called C. W. Capital Ltd. They had excellent ideas. They floated investment trusts to invest in small American companies and also acted as agents for regional American banks in the Euromarkets. Their profits and staff grew as George thrived away from the uncomfortably large presence of his father.

In January 1973, the two young men decided to capitalize on their famous names and rename the place Cripps Warburg. After browbeating Eric for not removing the Warburg name in New York, Siegmund was mildly shocked by George's step. Yet, for once, he was forbearing. In cooler moments, he acknowledged that he was an extremely strong father and that it might be a good idea for George to strike out on his own. To George's surprise, Siegmund raised no objection to his using the name. In a gracious gesture, S. G. Warburg even took a small symbolic stake in the new firm, thus giving it the seal of approval.

It all ended badly when Cripps Warburg got into difficulty. It never exactly went bust since its main shareholder, Williams and Glyn's Bank, came to its aid. What pained Siegmund was *why* the firm ran into trouble. The ever-cautious Siegmund had largely refrained from risky property or shipping loans, unless combined with long-term financing from an insurance company. Right before the real estate bust that rocked London in the early 1970s, George and Milo had poured thirteen million pounds into unsalable real estate loans. With his inordinate pride in the Warburg name, Siegmund was devastated by this failure, which became a taboo topic at Gresham Street.

Having gotten Siegmund's support, the two young men felt guilty and ashamed, as if they had let Siegmund down. With a tiny stake of less than 5 percent in the new firm, Siegmund didn't think it proper for S. G. Warburg & Co. to save George. A foe of nepotism, he wasn't a saintly Paul Warburg rescuing Max in 1931. As he later said, "I grew up in a family firm . . . as a result of these experiences I was always against nepotism of any kind. . . ."[20] Justly or not, many in the City and on Wall Street were stunned that Siegmund would let a firm bearing the Warburg name and associated with his own son come to an ignominious end.

A crestfallen George got on the telephone and helped to find jobs for all seventy of his employees. Twice Siegmund offered to bring his son back into the firm: in 1975, when Cripps Warburg folded, and in 1978 when George and his family moved to America and he took a job in a Connecticut bank. Having never gone to college, George took courses at Yale after his retirement. In Siegmund's last years, his relationship with George improved somewhat, to the immense relief of both. Although Siegmund had applied for a permit for Anna to come and live in Switzerland, she decided to stay in Israel. Both George and Anna loved their father, but they evidently found it easier to feel that love at a great distance.

—

Never an observant Jew—he thought Yom Kippur always fell on Saturdays—Siegmund displayed a Warburgian ambivalence toward religion. He was proud of being Jewish. Even in the early New Trading days, Chaim Weizmann had come for lunch at Felix's behest. Siegmund reviled those who denied their heritage. Early in his career, Robert Maxwell came for a disastrous lunch at Warburgs. Afterward, Siegmund sent around a blistering memo that Maxwell was a Jew who pretended not to be a Jew and who exploited Jews. He barred S. G. Warburg & Co. from doing business with him. Hence, the Warburg bank was later spared the fallout of Maxwell's collapse. And Siegmund could be so touchy about anti-Semitism that at one point he thought all Canadians were anti-Semitic except his own representative there.[21]

Yet Siegmund kept apart from Judaism. George, for instance, was never bar mitzvahed. When one Orthodox Jewish client came for lunch, he was surprised that he couldn't get kosher food, so the kitchen staff hastily whipped up scrambled eggs. The bank often held its annual general meetings on Jewish holidays. In the firm it was often said that Siegmund was tougher on Jews. Siegmund and the uncles so distanced themselves from Judaism that some employees felt free to voice anti-Semitic sentiments. George was once shocked when his boss, Frank Smith, made a statement hostile to Jews. He asked how he could say such a thing at a firm largely run by Jews. "But, George," Smith replied, "you don't understand. Your father and the uncles—*they* are not Jews."

Never a Zionist, Siegmund believed that the Jewish spirit flourished in the Diaspora and worried about the corrosive effect of a sectarian Jewish state. Like many wealthy German Jews, he had idealized Israel as a spiritual Eden and had hoped it would serve as "an exemplary community built on justice and humanity," as he phrased it.[22]

Siegmund developed an emotional investment in Israel's success. On his first visit in 1959, he was moved by his experience of a kibbutz. During the Six-Day War in 1967, Siegmund took up a collection among Jewish bankers on the proviso that afterward they reform Israeli finances. At a 1968 economic summit in Jerusalem, Siegmund emerged as the guiding spirit behind the Israel Corporation, which was to funnel foreign capital into Israel's nascent industry. During the next few years, S. G. Warburg & Co. was involved in diverse Israeli ventures and worked closely with Bank Leumi, the foremost Israeli bank.

When the Yom Kippur War broke out in 1973, young non-Jewish directors at Warburgs wanted to express their solidarity with the uncles. Speaking for these directors, Bernard Kelly went to Eric Korner and proposed that the firm make a one-hundred-thousand-pound gift to Israel. Siegmund and the uncles were touched by the gesture. Like Uncle Aby, Siegmund always heard the dark rustle of the bankruptcy vultures. Of the Arab oil embargo, he said, "this crisis will be of much longer duration than the one that started in 1929, but I do think it will be resolved eventually. Meanwhile, even if the crisis lasts 10 years, what is 10 years? As Arnold Toynbee says, it is only a minute in world history."[23]

Like all German Jews, Siegmund rediscovered his religious roots under attack. When S. G. Warburg & Co. appeared on the Arab blacklist, he was loath at first to admit it was even happening. His attitude changed when it became obvious that Warburgs and N. M. Rothschild *were* being blackballed from some Eurobond syndicates that included Arab banks. Firms that had obsequiously courted Siegmund to enter the Euromarkets now cast him aside to appease the Arabs.

As a refugee from Hitler, Siegmund felt that bullying must be resisted, and he confronted bankers who caved in to pressure, saying, "I hear you seem to be giving in to this blackmail of the Arabs. . . . Shall I interpret that as meaning you sympathize with anti-Semitism?"[24] When a Kommerzbank director came for lunch, Siegmund berated him for yielding to pressure. Afterward, he told Bernard Kelly, who had invited the German, "Please, Bernard, only invite people who are my friends!" Any bank that cooperated with the blacklist had a sternly worded letter from Siegmund on the chairman's desk the next morning. He was especially disgusted by the cowardice and timidity of the British Foreign Office and noted approvingly the tougher line of the U.S. State Department.[25]

As a wave of terrorist bombings and kidnappings hit Europe, S. G. Warburg posted police officers with machine guns in the reception area. Siegmund sent a confidential note to senior executives, saying that if he were kidnapped, the firm should refrain from paying ransom money, since such capitulation would only encourage terrorism. By 1976, the Arab pressure eased and within a few years S. G. Warburg was off the boycott list. Through channels, Siegmund had notified the Arabs that he wasn't a Zionist and was now retired from his firm anyway.

It was typical of Siegmund's headstrong, unpredictable nature that after the Arab problem disappeared, he became a vocal critic of Israel. When the Labour coalition gave way to Menachem Begin's nationalistic Likud bloc in 1977, Siegmund castigated the government for colonizing the West Bank. He supported the plan of his friend, Nahum Goldmann, to make peace with the Arabs. Opposed to dogma and fanaticism, Siegmund associated Begin with the Irgun and Yitzhak Shamir with the Stern Gang and tended to view the new Israeli leadership as so many former thugs and terrorists.

Irate over Begin's intransigence toward the Arabs, Siegmund refused to set foot in Israel. Like Jimmy Warburg, he wouldn't donate to the United Jewish Appeal. He aroused the ire of Britain's Jewish community by criticizing Israel in *The Times* of London in 1978. "Safety in this world can never be guaranteed by more barbed wire," he wrote. "Many Jews inside as well as outside

Israel who share the views put forward in this letter are reluctant to speak out publicly because they are afraid that this might be interpreted as lack of loyalty to the cause of Israel. However, loyalty to sound principles and moral precepts must override any other loyalties."[26] Siegmund tried to coax three or four prominent London Jews into joining him, but he ended up signing this letter alone. He was terribly distressed by their refusal to come clean with their private qualms.

In 1978, Siegmund met in Paris with President Anwar Sadat of Egypt and lobbied Begin to respond to his peace overtures. He denounced Israeli occupation of the West Bank and Gaza Strip as "petty nationalism" that diminished Israeli security. Siegmund's commitment to Israel clashed with his internationalism and he tended to dismiss Zionism as another brand of nationalism. "I don't believe in German chauvinism, never did," he said in 1980. "I don't believe in British chauvinism, I don't believe in American chauvinism and I don't believe in Israeli chauvinism."[27] After the Camp David accords, Siegmund and David Rockefeller made a secret trip to see Sadat in Cairo. Siegmund also cooperated with the French Socialist government to get peace talks going with the Palestine Liberation Organization. For Siegmund, Israel was like a backward child that he could never train, but could never entirely abandon. His concern for Israel showed how deeply he cared about the Jewish people yet how conflicted he felt at the same time.

Eva and Siegmund Warburg.
(St. Paul's Girls' School)

CHAPTER 48

Forgotten Gravestone

A t moments in the 1970s, Siegmund must have worried that his world of small, intimate merchant banks was dying. He often drew an analogy between bankers and physicians. "You listen to your patients, advise them well and strive to understand not just their special ailments, but the whole fellow."[1] The doctor, he thought, should deliver stern truths, not just flattery. If patients steadily flouted the doctor's advice, they should part company. Sometimes Siegmund dismissed people by saying, "Oh, my dear fellow, but he's not a banker." By that he meant that the person was a technician, not a rounded financial person with a broad view of events.

By the 1970s, world finance had evolved in a way that threatened the old-fashioned banker. With the rise of institutional investors, it became important to commit capital to trading, distribution, and portfolio management. Yet Siegmund had patronized brokers, traders, and money managers as an inferior breed. He seldom visited his own investment department. When he slipped in, a hush fell over the room as this infrequent visitor surveyed the premises. Wanting to control things, Siegmund loathed the stock market as a bedlam impervious to reason. Portfolio management struck him as a fool-proof way to alienate top clients. People assumed that this storied tycoon possessed hot stock tips. In fact, he was an abysmal stock picker who didn't care about market fads. Each year, he issued the same dreadful recommendation to buy Shell Oil at the annual investment meeting.

When Peter Stormonth Darling became chairman of Warburg Investment Management in 1979, Siegmund instructed him, "Now, Peter, you are the chairman of this business. Your first job is to get rid of it." Though the division managed about one billion pounds in assets, Siegmund waved it away as worthless. He and Darling lunched with two senior people at Robert Fleming to see if they could unload the investment division. They failed to do so because the Fleming people didn't comprehend that Siegmund wanted to give away the business *free*. Since nobody would take this intolerable burden off his hands, Siegmund instructed Darling to fix it. And he did. By the early 1990s, under the Mercury Asset Management rubric, S. G. Warburg would oversee the largest investment group in Britain, possibly in all of Europe, handling an astronomical forty billion pounds.

Anxious about the future of small merchant banks and afraid that S. G. Warburg was vulnerable to a takeover, Siegmund began to court larger, stronger partners. He pursued a liaison with Deutsche Bank, but was rebuffed. Then in 1973, amid a chorus of grumbling at Gresham Street, S. G. Warburg & Co. swapped shares with Paribas, a venerable French *banque d'affaires*. Siegmund made the deal complicated enough to hide the sizable imbalance between S. G. Warburg and its bigger bride. Siegmund nursed the relationship along, attending several meetings each year at the Ritz in Paris. With its branch network in the Persian Gulf, Paribas tapped its contacts to help to delete S. G. Warburg from the Arab blacklist.

Siegmund pursued Paribas knowing that its strong-willed president, Jacques de Fouchier, would soon retire. He had formed a close friendship with the more malleable Pierre Moussa, president after 1978, and wooed Moussa with gourmet meals, fine wines, and stimulating table talk. The two mulled over a possible merger of their firms, with Warburgs handling the British, American, and international side, and Paribas contributing its European, Mideast, and Latin American operations. This was another attempt by Siegmund to leverage his slender capital by merging with a larger partner. It also reflected a genuinely visionary desire to form a new species of European bank transcending national borders. Moussa admired Siegmund, with reservations, and spotted the striking contradictions of the man. He perceived that Siegmund was extremely cultured and self-possessed, but "very authoritarian and even hard."[2]

In the Paribas deal, Siegmund saw a last chance to make a major breakthrough on Wall Street after the modest success of his New York office under David Mitchell. Paul Judy was the brassy, aggressive head of a Chicago securities firm called A. G. Becker that dated from the late nineteenth century. In need of capital, he was intrigued by the Warburg-Paribas match. A medium-sized firm strong in commercial paper, Becker seemed an unlikely partner for such hallowed European names as Warburg and Paribas. Yet Judy managed to convince Paribas to form a triple alliance. Reluctant to upset his Parisian bride, Siegmund overrode his London colleagues and turned into a passionate advocate of the triangular merger with Becker.

During one Paris dinner with executives from Warburgs and Paribas, Peter Spira openly questioned the wisdom of such a link. Having just won Imperial Chemical Industries as a Warburg client he couldn't imagine referring his blue-ribbon conquest to the plebeian Becker. "Don't be ridiculous," Siegmund retorted. "Becker can do anything that Morgan Stanley can do." Slamming his fist on the table, he sent a bowl of chocolate-covered strawberries flying into the air. The king's prerogative had been challenged and Siegmund resorted to hyperbole. "Not only can Becker do anything that Morgan Stanley can do—but they can do it better."[3] Once again, Siegmund displayed a faulty sense of American corporate culture. He believed Becker could grab Midwestern business from New York firms and break into the august special bracket of underwriters. Indeed, Spira's warning proved correct, for many of S. G. Warburg's European clients would turn to an investment bank other than Becker on Wall Street.

To nobody's surprise, Siegmund insisted that the Warburg name appear first in the new corporate entity, even though S. G. Warburg and Paribas held equal stakes. In everyday speech, Siegmund knew that people, for the sake of speed, resorted to the shorthand of the first name. So the new American operation was christened Warburg Paribas Becker. Enriched by twenty-five million dollars in fresh capital from London and Paris—Warburg and Paribas each had a 20 percent stake while Becker employees held the remainder—the new operation started life in 1974 in sparkling new headquarters at 55 Water Street in lower Manhattan.

Even as Siegmund struggled to overcome the legacy of Kuhn, Loeb, his old Wall Street firm floated in a strategic limbo. In the late 1960s, Siegmund had made overtures to buy the house. Now he summoned up one last burst of energy to fuse Becker with Kuhn, Loeb. The talks dissolved in confusion when it became plain that both the Kuhn, Loeb and the Becker people believed they would run the show after any merger. The Kuhn, Loeb people also feared that Siegmund would impose tight restrictions on their more unconstrained style. So in 1977 an enfeebled Kuhn, Loeb was taken over by Lehman Brothers, which then vanished into the voracious maw of Shearson Lehman American Express. One of Wall Street's most distinguished names had disappeared because of the myopia of its partners. Of the Lehman Brothers merger, Siegmund said ruefully, "You know, I had proposed such a merger years ago. When I proposed it, Kuhn, Loeb would have been the dominant partner. That would have been different."[4]

Siegmund's talks with Kuhn, Loeb foundered at the same time as serious problems surfaced at Becker. The brash, abrupt style of Paul Judy, an ex-Marine, didn't sit well with the S. G. Warburg people, who never understood the gung-ho, money-driven mentality of Wall Street. Fatigued by clashes with his European bosses, Judy bowed out in 1977 and was replaced the next year by the soft-spoken, intellectual Ira Wender, a lawyer at Baker & McKenzie. A man who preferred literature to sports, Wender would be the last of the ill-fated "adopted sons." At first, Siegmund doted on Wender, thinking he had found a young Henry Grunfeld who could master reams of facts. The relationship ended in disillusionment.

For Siegmund, the new operation would represent another agonizingly visible New York failure. With his exaggerated sense of the Warburg mystique, he fooled himself into thinking that the new firm could be another Lazard Frères, serving an elite corporate clientele. He misread the strength of the ties that bound blue-chip companies to their traditional Wall Street houses. The schizoid Becker had to please two masters and never knew whether to steer clients to Warburg or Paribas for European business. Though the caliber of Becker people never matched that of their London and Paris superiors, they had managed to negotiate staggering compensation packages for themselves. Warburg people faulted Wender for being distracted by management and organizational matters to the neglect of corporate finance.[5] As we shall see, Wender would always regard this as the cover story for a far more serious political and personal drama unfolding behind the scenes.

—

At Blonay, Siegmund was never happier than when sitting in the sunshine beside a stack of heavy tomes. From the terrace, he could see snow-capped peaks across sparkling Lake Geneva. Following a long-cherished desire, he toyed with writing two books: *The Businessman's Book of Quotations* and *Education of the Adult*, the latter to expound the theme that education was a lifetime task.[6] The notion of being a teacher *manqué* was a seductive daydream for Siegmund, who could never admit he was a banker at heart. For all his intellectual aspirations, he never completed a single writing project. When asked to write an article by the London newspapers, he had an assistant draft it. Siegmund carried in his mind an ideal person he wanted to be. But there was always a discrepancy between that idealized being and the far more practical, fallible person he was at heart.

Though many publishers wanted the autobiography of this mysterious legend, he brushed aside all offers to write it. For a time in the 1970s, he had an intellectual infatuation with the Cambridge literary critic George Steiner, the son of an Austrian-Jewish banker. The bookish Steiner occupied a place in Siegmund's pantheon formerly occupied by Stefan Zweig. Siegmund cherished the epigrams that Steiner passed along—for instance, T. S. Eliot's dictum that "Mankind can bear only a little bit of reality"—and he sent many people copies of Steiner's books. For a time, they engaged in a collaborative book project, variously described as a Socratic dialogue and a biography of Siegmund. As always with Siegmund, the reverie ended in a feud and their relationship didn't survive this literary partnership. Steiner hotly denies that any such feud occurred.

In his reading, Siegmund had amassed two thousand quotations which he now arranged into a work tentatively entitled *An Anthology for Searchers*. This commonplace book—which has been erroneously described as a "secret diary"—sharply mirrors Siegmund's mind. He was quick to spot a kindred spirit and looked for quotes that certified his own beliefs. Certain themes recur in his choices: that happiness is a by-product of hard work and duty fulfilled, that human pleasure is fleeting, that great accomplishment is always intermixed with pain. When Henry Grunfeld later contemplated publishing Siegmund's anthology, he decided against it, fearing the quotes exhibited too bleak a view of human existence.

At Blonay, Siegmund would often invite young people for long, stimulating chats that lasted five or six hours and ran the gamut from great books to gossip. (He once defined banking as organized gossip.) By talking to people in semiconfessional style, he encouraged them to voice their own inmost thoughts. One young companion was Carey Reich, managing editor of *Institutional Investor* magazine. "Siegmund was the most facile and scintillating conversationalist I'd ever met in my life," Reich recalled.[7] In 1979, Siegmund agreed to a rare, extended interview with Reich on the condition that he review the transcript before publication. He spent as much time quibbling with Reich over punctuation and editing as in answering his questions in the first place.

In the interview, Siegmund sounded like an Old Testament prophet, bewailing modern societies that gorged themselves on superfluous consumer goods. He chided the sterile bureaucracies of modern business, the corporate obsession with ever-rising profits.[8] Deploring Britain's laziness, he saw a country in decline from creditor to debtor nation and he responded to Margaret Thatcher's appeal for a more entrepreneurial spirit.

If Siegmund sounded like that Spenglerian youth of Weimar Germany, he also embodied a fading world of elegance. He was ultramodern and old hat at once. One day in the 1970s, he had a busy day in New York. To avoid running into some Wall Street people at lunch, he suggested to his companions that they eat further uptown. They stopped at a MacDonald's in Greenwich Village where Sir Siegmund Warburg, in his seventies, tasted his first hamburger. He was fascinated that this strange brown thing on a bun had been named after his family's hometown. After eating it, he beamed with amazement and said he was impressed by this three-dollar meal, which he thought represented excellent value.

Yet his strong sense of tradition never deserted him. In 1978, he went to Japan to receive the First Class Order of the Sacred Treasure from Prime Minister Takeo Fukuda. The honor, awarded in the prime minister's residence, was signed by Emperor Hirohito. It pleased Siegmund greatly that he had restored the link cherished by Jacob Schiff and Uncle Max.

He softened with age—somewhat. He still had violent fits and shouted at the top of his lungs, but his anger didn't flare so readily. He and Eva recaptured some old closeness and struck visitors as a courtly, old-fashioned couple. But Siegmund often felt alone in Switzerland, burdened by the beautiful house. To Grunfeld, he sighed, "We become the slaves of our possessions." Increasingly detached from earthly things, he delighted in travel and felt at home in sleeping cars. As a practical man, he talked about moving into a hotel where he and Eva would each have a bedroom and share a sitting room. It was as if Siegmund were searching for some past simplicity—maybe some lost piece of his Swabian boyhood with Lucie—that he could never find again. It seemed emblematic of the Warburg saga that Sir Siegmund Warburg, the most successful of the clan, was also the saddest and most frustrated.

At moments, he betrayed a wish to erase his footprints from the sand and even expunge his name from his extraordinary creation, S. G. Warburg & Company. Trying to run the London office from Blonay, he sometimes sparred with Messrs. Grunfeld, Roll, and Seligman. Even in his late seventies, he was still so busy that Doris Wasserman set up appointments for his weekend telephone calls. He never stopped brooding about his firm or worrying about its runaway growth. At one point, he grew so upset about the way certain expenses were accounted for that he considered having the firm drop his name after his death. With his usual theatrics, he threw a mock tantrum and flung his glasses. Then he settled down and scrapped the idea when told of the legal problems involved.

In some ways, Siegmund now found his firm alien. "I think that with some of the people in charge there I would have very little chance to be hired. People would say, 'This fellow is much too nonconformist, much too eccentric.' "[9] He was too Jewish to be hired, he said. He experienced the founder's nightmare that his firm would become unrecognizable after his demise. To colleagues, he predicted that within five years of his death, they would join the establishment, grow larger, have glossy reports, change the Mercury

Securities name to S. G. Warburg & Co., and print brochures with photos. Virtually all of the prophecies would come true, confirming Siegmund's reputation for clairvoyance.

Siegmund didn't face death with equanimity. He evaded funerals and hated to visit sick people, as if they might be contagious. With age his face grew gaunt, making him appear ill, and his head sank deeper into his chest. He seemed smaller and wider. Frail, with a weak heart, he didn't like walking with a cane and camouflaged his weakness with an umbrella. But his eyes still sparkled with their old preternatural gleam from his thin, yellowish face.

—

Siegmund's success had been spectacular but lopsided. He had established the Warburg name in Britain, but had stumbled elsewhere. It haunted him that the Warburg name might not survive in Germany and America, where the family had made such an enormous contribution. Fate allowed him no surcease from his dream of restoring Warburg honor. In Germany, he had a big deal brewing. And Becker and Paribas gave him one last chance to reverse the Wall Street verdict. It seemed that, at the last moment, he might yet sweep the board.

Then fresh complications fractured his relationship with Paribas. In September 1981, the French Socialists announced plans to nationalize the Paris-based bank. Moussa warned the new government that this move would damage Paribas's international accords with Warburgs and Becker. He brought Siegmund to Paris, hoping he would convince the French government that Paribas was a global institution and that nationalization would irreparably tarnish France's image in world financial markets.

However sympathetic to Moussa's travails, Siegmund soon developed his own, quite different, agenda. Taking the French Socialists' rhetoric at face value, he believed they would engineer a far-reaching revolution, charting a middle path between capitalism and communism. As a matter of policy, Siegmund liked to stay on good terms with governments. Instead of following Moussa's lead, he decided to court the Socialists to get fair compensation for Warburg's Paribas stake or to have a special role in any nationalized firm. To this end, he not only met French president François Mitterand, but charmed and cultivated his receptive special assistant, Jacques Attali.

Moussa came up with a controversial plan to shield Paribas's Swiss assets from the grasp of the French government. He planned to transfer these assets to a holding company called Pargesa. It was a perfectly legal, if politically incendiary, idea. Moussa wanted S. G. Warburg & Co. and Becker to show their solidarity and to participate in an underwriting for the expanded Pargesa. From loyalty to Moussa, Ira Wender gave him his word that he would take part. But Siegmund, eager to exploit Paribas's weakness, shifted course and stayed aloof from the Pargesa underwriting. He applied tremendous pressure on Wender to back out, dispatching David Scholey, Eric Roll, and other high-level emissaries to convince him that it was unwise to provoke the French government. Wender didn't budge.

In the end, Moussa never stopped admiring Siegmund, but he revolted against his constant need to rule. As he wrote in his diary at the time, "Above all, Siegmund wants to be obeyed. He wants to reign, by sweetness and persuasion, but totally."[10] Some Warburg people surmise that Moussa had always planned to gain closer control of S. G. Warburg after Siegmund's death. The question became moot when Moussa was hounded from his job over the Pargesa affair. By ingratiating himself with the French government, Siegmund emerged with an enhanced role in the nationalized Paribas, confirming Moussa's suspicions.[11]

The repercussions of all this maneuvering were enormous at Becker. Siegmund wanted to push aside the weakened Paribas and buy out the 60 percent of Becker owned by Becker employees. Convinced of his fiduciary obligation to these employees, Wender again defied Siegmund's wishes. In this recession year of 1982, Becker was bleeding money, reporting millions in losses.[12] S. G. Warburg & Co. hadn't instilled the same taut discipline there as in London. Seething over the Pargesa affair, Siegmund blamed his "adopted son" Wender for Becker's failure and turned on him with a vengeance. David Scholey flew to New York to negotiate a bitter end to the relationship. Another adopted son had been sacrificed.

Time was running out for Siegmund. After S. G. Warburg and Paribas bought out the employee stake in Becker, Siegmund made a secret trip to New York in July 1982. To avoid press reports, he met with its new management at a hotel near Kennedy Airport. Siegmund was already so weak and sick that Henry Grunfeld warned him not to go. Arriving amid muggy summer weather, Siegmund let it be known that failure to attend would be tantamount to resignation. Despite his fragility, he spent six hours delivering the pep talk of his life, inspiring the troops with bold visions, chastening them with trenchant criticisms. He made one last show of unity with the French. The next day, he visited George in Connecticut, his first time at his son's new home, and felt triumphant, like an old trooper who had pulled off one last feat.

Paribas and S. G. Warburg subsequently traded back their stakes in each other, and the Becker operation was sold to the French after Siegmund's death. In the end, S. G. Warburg decided to create a Wall Street outpost from the ground up, which would prove to be the winning formula that had evaded Siegmund.

In his last months, Siegmund strained to bring off one last triumph in

Germany. He masterminded a scheme to merge the Effectenbank-Warburg in Frankfurt with two private banks owned by Munich's Bayerische Vereinsbank: the Bethmann Bank in Frankfurt and the Simon Bank in Düsseldorf. In September 1982, Siegmund flew to Munich to shake hands on the deal. He thought a prior agreement had been reached by which Peter Reimpell—a friend of Siegmund's and a Bayerische Vereinsbank executive—would chair the new entity. Then the chairman of the Bayerische Vereinsbank, Dr. Hackl, told Siegmund categorically that he had heard of no such deal to release Reimpell from his duties. Flabbergasted, irate, embarrassed, Siegmund left the meeting. At Siegmund's hotel, Grunfeld found his old ally packing his bags to return to Switzerland. Looking tired and very worried, Siegmund again bemoaned that S. G. Warburg & Co. was becoming too large and complacent.

Still fuming, Siegmund flew back to Geneva where a car met him at the airport. En route to Blonay, he had a severe stroke and by the time he reached the house, he lay unconscious in the back seat, with one arm paralyzed. (According to another version, the stroke occurred after he arrived home.) Siegmund was rushed to a general ward of a Lausanne hospital and Dr. Goldman flew out to treat him. Having failed in his grand finale, Siegmund remained feverish, determined to outwit fate. He couldn't bear the failure, as if he still wanted to rewrite the Warburg script torn up by the Nazis. To Grunfeld's astonishment, Siegmund called two days later from Switzerland and began talking about how to revive the aborted Bavarian deal while Grunfeld urged him to rest.

Teary-eyed, Siegmund begged Dr. Goldman to take him by ambulance plane to London and Dr. Goldman reluctantly acceded. Instead of resting, Siegmund was often angry and agitated in London. At times he babbled deliriously and offered to set up Dr. Goldman for life. Dr. Goldman couldn't get Siegmund to stop telephoning David Scholey and issuing instructions on business. One day, Siegmund had a conversation with the office that so upset him that he had a massive stroke afterward and never spoke again.[13] According to another version of events, Siegmund arrived semi-conscious at the London clinic and was unable to make telephone calls.

Several parties had been planned to celebrate Siegmund's eightieth birthday, and at first guests were informed that Siegmund had a cold. Now the festivities were canceled outright. Three weeks after the Munich meeting, on October 18, 1982, Sir Siegmund Warburg died, a deeply unhappy man devoured by a dream.

With his usual thoroughness, leaving nothing to chance, Siegmund had written up instructions in 1980 for how to handle his death. He didn't want a funeral service. "I believe in the old precept that it is better to give flowers to the living than wreaths to the dead," he wrote. He wanted to donate his body for medical research. He was eager that his eyes be used for implantation, but was talked out of this by his secretary, Doris Wasserman. Instead he was cremated and a small family group attended the scattering of ashes. Though Siegmund had requested no memorial service, Grunfeld, Scholey, et al. did gather at the Guildhall a few months later to remember him.

A curious coincidence followed Siegmund's death. In his hometown of Urach, the children at the local school were studying the Nazi period and were shaken by their new knowledge. They wanted to show that Germany didn't simply forget injustice. So they decided to restore the neglected grave of Siegmund's father, Georges. Since 1923 the forest had closed in around the tall forgotten gravestone and the children now cleared space around it. Eva wrote a moving letter to the headmaster, thanking him and noting Siegmund's love for Urach and its surroundings.[14]

Eva felt she needed to be strong for Siegmund while he was sick. For many years, she had played her part selflessly. Those close to Eva hoped she would now blossom in her own right. Instead, though she tried to stay busy in the lonely house, her life seemed empty. The cancer she had battled for fifty years gained the upper hand. She decided to return to her doctors in London where she faced her illness with great bravery. Though she suffered from pain and severe shortness of breath, she never complained and was the strong, dignified Viking that Siegmund had loved. When her nurse said that she couldn't recall such an uncomplaining patient, Eva—sounding very much like Lucie—said, "Then perhaps you ought to think back a little harder."

A few days before her death, Eva told her children what a great relief and triumph it had been for her to outlive Siegmund, for she felt he would have been defenseless without her. When her youngest grandson visited, she put on makeup and got especially dressed to receive him. Despite her extreme frailty, she still had an indefinable radiance, making the shocked young man cry out, "Why, Granny, you look simply *fabulous!*" He was inconsolable the next morning when he learned that his grandmother had died during the night. Eva had survived Siegmund by a year.

No member of Siegmund's family was now left in England, so that his conquest seemed a rather lonely one. He put the Warburg name back on the map, but he hadn't revived the tight cohesion and shared purpose of the old family. He had brought forth an empire, not a dynasty. The all-important success in America and Germany had eluded him.

The story of Siegmund and the uncles demonstrated the indomitable spirit of the German Jews in the Diaspora. They had displayed the same energy that had made them so envied in Germany. They had enriched their adopted country with their drive, discipline, and zest for new ideas, carrying abroad the best of German culture even as the worst had triumphed at home.

Sir Siegmund Warburg was a very complicated human being. Almost anything you could say about him, you could also say the reverse. Of his influence upon the financial world, however, there was no doubt. After his death, the British press extravagantly praised him for reawakening the City from its slumber in the 1950s. "More than any other single person," said *The Times* "he was responsible for the change in the City's habits which made it ready to take advantage of the circumstances of the second half of the twentieth century."[15] The *Financial Times* said, "Sir Siegmund Warburg . . . was perhaps the most influential financier in the City of London in the post-war period."[16] Once again, as with the Rothschilds, a German-Jewish immigrant had renewed London's financial supremacy. Siegmund's feat was singular in financial annals, for he had constructed his empire *ex nihilo*, within a generation, against astronomical odds. He had bequeathed to Britain a merchant bank that could compete around the world.

After Siegmund's death, the City wondered whether his firm would decline. Instead, his hand-picked successor, Sir David Scholey, arose as London's foremost banker, perpetuating the discipline, teamwork, and discretion instilled by Siegmund. Of his mentor's death, he said, "I suppose, in family terms, it was like the death of a father, and in personal terms it was the loss of a second father."[17] Scholey became a member of the Court of the Bank of England and was frequently touted as a future governor. While the German Jews had mostly disappeared from S. G. Warburg—though Henry Grunfeld, in a very Siegmundian retirement, still reported to work each day—their legacy lasted. "Siegmund once said he considered me an honorary member of the Jewish community," said Scholey. "It was one of the greatest compliments I've ever been paid."[18]

As financial houses swelled into big, anonymous bureaucracies, Sir Siegmund's legend took on a new luster. He became an inspiration for young bankers who preached his philosophy of relationship banking and top-flight professional service. He had shown that finance could be a rich human experience, that a banker's life transcended budgets and balance sheets. These acolytes imitated Siegmund's methods, repeated his aphorisms, spread his gospel of excellence. They were everywhere in world finance and they gave him his real immortality.

Siegmund had always thought that quantity could be harmful to quality in banking. With the Big Bank deregulation of London financial markets in the 1980s, Sir David Scholey transformed the firm into a vast, integrated securities house. Warburgs snapped up Rowe and Pitman, the Queen's stockbroker; Akroyd and Smithers, a leading jobber; and Mullens, the government's official broker. Siegmund's aversion to stocks and risk-taking gave way to financial realities. The staff ballooned to five thousand people, operating in over thirty-eight countries. No longer the intimate adviser of Siegmund's dreams, S. G. Warburg expanded eightfold in the decade after his death.

With commendable finesse, Scholey managed to blend the four firms into a single culture, all imbued with the Warburg spirit. He knew Siegmund would have been uncomfortable with such changes, but believed his mentor would have recognized their need. By 1991, S. G. Warburg & Co. ranked as the biggest securities firm in Great Britain and the nineteenth largest world-wide. It claimed as corporate-finance clients half of the blue-chip firms in the Financial Times 100 index. It was a miraculous story of something imperishable created from the turmoil of central European history. Forty-five years before, S. G. Warburg & Co. had sheltered a handful of immigrants in a strange land. They had talked a foreign tongue and wondered whether they would survive. Now their firm had become the emblem of the City of London.

A Town of Strangers

Eric never lost the irrepressible vivacity that had withstood the Third Reich. He tried to resurrect his father's world, right down to the fresh flower in his buttonhole. Like Max, he rose early to swim or walk in the Kösterberg park. Each September, he attended the annual IMF/World Bank meeting and made courtesy calls to David Rockefeller and other Wall Street worthies. He kept several secretaries busy in his corner office that had an Alster Lake view. On weekends, he painted delicate watercolors of maritime scenes. With his mischievous blue eyes and bow ties, he never lost his roving eye for pretty women. How had the shadowy history of German Jewry produced this sunny personality?

Confronted with problems, Eric would ask, "What can be done?" A tenacious fund-raiser, he would tell businesses how much they should contribute to a charity. If he thought a donor stingy, he returned the check. As the carrier of family tradition, he strove to redress past injustices. In 1979, he went to see the antique collection of the Munich Glyptothek, which had six glass cabinets filled with Jim Loeb's exquisite Greek figures. Eric persuaded the museum to post Jim's picture and a short biography at the room's entrance. He enjoyed the sudden vogue for Uncle Aby, as the Hamburg Senate voted to award a thirty-thousand-mark Aby Warburg Prize every four years.

Eric clung to his Judaism by the most tenuous of threads. As the years passed, he felt more German than Jewish, and his odyssey suggests what might have happened to the Warburgs if the Nazis had never come along. The family would have retained a real but attenuated Jewish identity that might have vanished in time. Where most Jews carried a ghostly map of Germany in their minds, flagged with prisons and death camps, Eric was able to screen out the past and simply pick up where he had left off in the 1920s.

Thankful for the sanctuary he had found in America, Eric always tried to strengthen the German-American partnership. Along with John McCloy, he was a driving force behind the *Atlantik-Brücke* and its counterpart, the American Council on Germany. Studiously low profile, Eric seldom appeared in the German press, and reporters groused that it was easier to secure access to the Kremlin than to Eric. In 1979, he sailed to Denmark and Poland on the Warburg schooner, *Atalanta,* with his fellow Hamburger, Chancellor Helmut Schmidt. After one Bonn summit, Schmidt borrowed the ship for a two-day trip with French president Valéry Giscard d'Estaing. When Schmidt visited the White House in the 1980s, Eric stood by unobtrusively on the White House lawn as the Reagans greeted the chancellor. As the forgiving scion of a German-Jewish banking family, he was the ideal person to represent a chastened, responsible West Germany.

In commenting on German anti-Semitism, Eric struck a concerned but cautious note. Never strident or militant, he also never let the issue fade and lectured newspaper editors who were insensitive on Jewish subjects. He would tell reporters that German youth couldn't be blamed for the Third Reich. Then he would add—slyly quoting Kurt Hahn—that they had the privilege to blush at what happened.

As Eric blended into the German milieu, some Warburgs found it commendable, while others found it bizarre and inexplicable. Eric was a thoughtful, good-natured relative, even if often twitted about his infatuation with German aristocrats. When he published his memoirs, Bettina teased him that he only seemed to know famous people.[1] In 1970, on his seventieth birthday, Eric threw a big Kösterberg bash, inviting relatives from around the world. The Warburgs packed the fancy *Vier Jahreszeiten* hotel on the lake. For many, it represented their first return to Germany since the 1930s. It was a happy but uneasy time, for Hamburg inspired a hundred emotions of loss and anguish, nostalgia and bitterness. Outwardly the city resembled their birthplace, but one eerily depopulated of the people who had made it *their* city.

Gabriele Schiff, Louise's daughter, was mystified by Eric's attachment to Germany and wondered in amazement, "How can he raise three children in Germany?"[2] A short, plucky woman of considerable charm and intelligence, she had the Warburgian ethic of public service. Feeling guilty at having spent

Eric Warburg.
(Courtesy of Anita Warburg)

the war safely in America, she had returned to postwar Europe as a psychiatric social worker under the Joint's auspices. She worked at a tuberculosis sanatorium in northern Italy and dealt with skeletal survivors from Bergen-Belsen. Then she was transferred to two rehabilitation centers in Germany crammed with masses of homeless Jews who clamored to leave a Germany that seemed accursed. During this first postwar return to Germany, she could not bring herself to visit Hamburg.

Gaby couldn't conceive of forsaking America for Germany. "What I am—good or bad—I owe to this country," she said of her adopted American home. "It would have been unthinkable to accept German nationality again."[3] In the 1950s, she took her husband, David Schiff (no relation to Frieda), to Hamburg to show him where she had lived. As she set eyes again on the Alster, she experienced a nostalgic twinge. But these echoes of the past only made her feel more keenly the loss and displacement of her generation of German Jews. By the second day, she had grown ill and had to leave. "A town in which you know nobody in the telephone book is no longer your hometown," she said of Hamburg. "It's an interesting, beautiful city, one of the most beautiful cities I know. But it's no longer the city in which I was born."[4] Gaby's mother, Louise—unlike twin brother, Fritz—had seldom returned to Germany from England, although she requested that her ashes be flown back for burial beside Dr. Derenberg.

Eric's youngest sister, Gisela, often pondered the baffling enigma of Germany. For her, a visit to Hamburg produced terribly confused feelings. Walking the Hamburg streets, she needed to remind herself that most pedestrians had not been alive in the 1930s or were only children then. Gisi had put up with much heartbreak. This avid organizer for Youth Aliyah never moved to Israel, as she had hoped. Yet she served on the national board of Hadassah, the Women's Zionist Organization of America. Often she was disappointed with Israel, especially its treatment of West Bank Arabs. Dismayed to see Jews acting like conquerors, she cooperated with an interfaith group called Fellowship in Israel for Arab-Jewish Youth.

An admirer of America, Gisi loved being in an immigrant country where every second person seemed to speak with an accent. She often visited Hamburg and sailed to Scandinavia with Eric as they had before the war. She never stopped thinking about the spectacularly rich and terrible history of the Jews in Germany. As she tried to locate the cause of anti-Semitism, she traced it to the church; to Jewish success; and to Jewish customs, such as eating kosher and not intermarrying, which had acted to keep Jews apart. If she sometimes wondered how Holocaust survivors could still pray to God, she never wavered in her own faith.[5]

Of the four sisters, Gisi was most disconcerted by Eric's return. She felt he was too quick to make excuses when Germany misbehaved, whereas any such intolerance merely confirmed her worst suspicions.[6] In the 1950s, she traveled to Europe with her two children and stopped at Kösterberg. She watched her children climbing the same beech tree she had clambered up as a child and saw the old slow-motion passage of ships slipping by on the Elbe. It unnerved Gisi how much her children enjoyed Germany; it was like something that ran in the Warburg blood. When they got back to Boston, her son went around telling everybody that Germany had been his favorite place in Europe. When a thunderstruck Gisi confronted him, he explained, "Mother, the boys I played with know as little of Hitler as I do."[7] This was hard for Gisi to take because she herself had once loved Germany so much. "There are wounds that never heal," she said of her feelings toward Germany. "So many frightful things happened. The feeling is as if a friend had betrayed you, and you never knew again, whether you could trust him one hundred percent."[8]

The murderous negation of Judaism by the Nazis had only deepened and enriched its meaning in Gisi's mind. For her it was far more than just a religion. It was a land, a speech, a people. German Jews, she felt, had forgotten all this until they were so ruthlessly reminded by their enemies. "I sometimes think that perhaps Hitler, the mortal enemy of the Jews, also did something for the Jews. He forced them to recognize again, what history had taught them, but that they had forgotten in Germany: Judaism doesn't mean only a community of faith, but also a community of struggle and a community of destiny."[9]

Like her sister, Anita was resilient and active in myriad organizations. She hadn't stumbled into self-pity, but had gamely started over again, even if she often acted now as a fund-raiser instead of a donor in her charity work. She brought artists to America for the Institute of International Education, introduced UNICEF Christmas cards in Scandinavia, served on the board of the Mannes College of Music, and worked for numberless causes. Like Gisi, she felt the permanent scar of disenchantment with Germany. Whenever she visited Eric, she savored the beauty of Kösterberg, but felt incongruous, a specter from the past. Her home was on the Upper East Side of Manhattan, in a pretty apartment decorated with Japanese screens that the finance minister, Korekiyo Takahashi, had given her father long ago.

Lola was less bothered by Eric's return to Hamburg. "I can't hate," she said and never bore a grudge against Germany.[10] Her Jewish identity was clear to her. Even on Eaton Square, she kept a kosher kitchen, attended synagogue on High Holy Days, and was dismayed when her two children married non-Jews. Though she visited Israel and raised money for Youth Aliyah, she too was critical of Israeli fundamentalism, especially after the invasion of Lebanon. She saw an erosion of the idealism embodied by Weizmann and the early Zionist leaders.

With a good deal of the *grande dame* about her, Lola sometimes seemed like an aging movie star or an exiled queen. When she visited poor relations, she brought along a bottle of her own expensive gin. With age, the delicate face had grown lined and parchment-dry and her eyes stood out big and haunted, like a sibyl's. Her voice steadily deepened from smoking unfiltered cigarettes. With her shaking hands, she scattered ashes everywhere, prompting fears that she would set the house ablaze. The old hand trembles got worse so that she had to command visitors, "Feed me, darling."[11]

Lola combined the fiery passion of Joan of Arc with the meddlesome curiosity of a Jewish mother. She had a touch of Siegmund's imperious quality. In fact, there was mutual admiration—if also distrust—between these monarchs of Eaton Square. (Siegmund always gave to Lola's charities, admiring her pluck.) Lola's egoism never abated. Once sitting in the back of a lecture hall, she was asked by a friend if she didn't care to move up to the front row. Lola drew herself up. "Where I sit *is* the front row," she declared.[12]

At age seventy-five, Lola still sped about town in a dark blue Triumph sports car. Because her hands shook, she was a menace to other motorists, yet she roared ahead. Making no concessions to age, she remained an incorrigible flirt with a magnetic allure for young men. Once, in her seventies, Lola was driving along an Israeli highway with a niece when she spotted a handsome young Israeli soldier hitchhiking. Abruptly she braked to a halt and started flirting with the young man, much to her niece's amazement. It was a vintage Lola performance.[13]

Lola and Rudolf maintained an air of marital amity. They would appear together socially and she provided a setting for his business entertaining. At the same time, Lola openly had her share of boyfriends. The strange *ménage à trois* with Kurt Hahn never ended. Lola and Rudo bought a house in Scotland called Burnside that wasn't far from Kurt's school, Gordonstoun. Kurt had his own room there. Lola ran Burnside with an iron hand, even assigning duties to amazed guests, and she organized Kurt's life. When she visited Salem, Kurt invented tasks to keep the hyperactive Lola busy, lest he be worn down by her surplus energy. Right before she arrived, he would tilt every picture in the building to keep her employed. When Kurt had a nervous breakdown and grew paranoid, it was Lola who nursed him in her flat.

Through Kurt, Lola became acquainted with the royal family. Prince Philip was one of Kurt's favorite ex-pupils and sent his sons to Gordonstoun. Despite her liberal politics, Lola played shamelessly on her royal connection. One year, for her annual holiday cards, she reproduced a photo of Burnside with a swank car parked out front. The license plate clearly showed the royal chariot.

In many ways, Lola metamorphosed into her father. Willful and charming, she had an exaggerated need for control. Her grandchildren couldn't join her formal, candlelit dinners until age fifteen. She divided her elaborate social life into hermetically sealed compartments, because she didn't want certain people to meet. Once she slammed the door in her granddaughter's face when she had arrived ten minutes early for a visit.[14] She liked to run people's lives and would grill young men who wanted to marry her granddaughters. In fact, Lola grilled everyone, pumping even taxi drivers for their life stories. "Even in the hospital after major surgery, when she couldn't speak above a whisper, she was still issuing orders like a sergeant major," said a friend.[15]

Thanks to Lola's tenacity and his own willpower, her son Oscar lived a full life despite his polio. He went to Gordonstoun and Cambridge, then entered Rudo's business, BKL Alloys. Funny and likable and a marvelous raconteur—if with a touch of Lola's arrogance—he was involved in many activities from race relations to the Shakespeare Festival in Stratford-upon-Avon. Over the years, Lola's motherly doting grew intrusive. At parties, she would sidle up to one of Oscar's bachelor colleagues and ask, "Tell me candidly, does Oscar do a good job in the firm?"[16] It was a fantastic blow to her when Oscar died. At once, with her highly developed organizational instincts, she began to plan his funeral arrangements, knowing that she had to stay active or she would fall apart.

Notwithstanding Lola's efforts to stop it, her daughter, Benita, married an Italian naval officer, Admiral Egidio Marco Cioppa. The bossy Lola didn't beat around the bush with the admiral. "I beg you, don't have a dozen children at once."[17] While Benita remained Jewish, the six children were brought up Catholic. In the end, the marriage to Admiral Cioppa was a long and happy one.

Fritz's daughter, Ingrid, also wrestled with her relationship to postwar Germany. In 1980, at Eric's urging, she took her son, Oliviero, to the town of Warburg and other spots in Germany. Only among old friends and Resistance fighters could she find isolated traces of *her* homeland. For Ingrid, West Germany seemed a self-absorbed consumer society, overly preoccupied with order and security. After she and Oliviero stopped to see Eric at the bank, they dined on the Kösterberg terrace and gazed over the beech trees at the extraordinary river scene. The beauty of this mountaintop eyrie tugged at her with its old charm, its timeless grace. As she wrote, "When I think back to Kösterberg, to the view of the river from my window and the ships going by, traveling all over the world, including to my relatives in England and America, then this place strikes me even today as an island, a steady, secure frame of reference amid all confusion, like a little piece of eternity."[18] But her life was no longer there. The past had contracted into a handful of bittersweet memories.

Even Jimmy Warburg, in his self-imposed exile from family matters, felt a subterranean pull from the distant past. He had never convinced Stevenson to join his solitary crusade to neutralize and reunify Germany. For Jimmy, postwar denazification had been a farce that allowed Germans to evade responsibility. He still found the Germans too passive, too reverential toward authority, and he was never especially impressed by German leaders. Of a 1954 visit to Germany, he wrote, "At several sessions of the Bundestag, I had an opportunity to observe the autocratic contempt with which the Chancellor treated the parliament. I made no attempt to see Dr. Adenauer, because I had known and learned to distrust him in my banking days when, as mayor of Cologne, he had tried to float an American bond issue."[19]

As ever, Jimmy was in headlong flight from his Jewish past. Jimmy's third wife, Joan, came from a devout Congregationalist family and they sent their four children to a Christian Sunday school. Never a believer in organized religion, Jimmy told his children, "I do not object to your becoming Christians, if you become good Christians."[20] Already fifty-four when Joan had their first child, he felt he had been a father too early and too late in life.[21]

Throughout the 1950s, Jimmy produced numerous books designed to steer the Democratic party in a more liberal direction and he often discussed policy with such figures as George Kennan, John Kenneth Galbraith, and Arthur Schlesinger. After John F. Kennedy's election in 1960 and a sudden progressive upsurge, it looked as if Jimmy's moment had at last arrived. He was a hero to young idealists who swarmed down to Washington. After the election, Stevenson gave John F. Kennedy one of Jimmy's foreign-policy memos for his inaugural address, saying, "Jim Warburg is very anxious for you to see this *personally* and has asked me to be the conduit. I am glad to do so, because I have found that whatever he says is arresting and often prescient."[22]

In April 1961, John J. McCloy asked Jimmy to become an economic-disarmament consultant for the State Department. For the first time in almost three decades, he was invited to become a government wise man again. The historical turnabout, alas, had come too late. That year, Jimmy underwent radical treatment for carcinoma of the tongue, surgeons removing glands on the right side of his head and neck and half his tongue. Suddenly weak and suffering from impaired speech that made him self-conscious, the articulate Jimmy had to curtail his lecture schedule.

He began to winter with Joan in Deerfield Beach, Florida, where they lived a simple life without servants and did their own cooking. They had a pretty banyan tree and Jimmy also planted white hibiscus bushes, mimosa trees, and Norfolk Island pine. He designed a restaurant and built luxurious high-rise buildings, making yet another fortune. As with many Warburgs, he had a golden business touch that he held of little account. He cared passionately about politics, ideas, and the arts. He chaired the board of the Juilliard School of Music and was a director of the New York Philharmonic Society.

While Jimmy welcomed Eric's efforts to restore the Warburg name, he hadn't placed much stress on such family matters in thirty years. Eric championed West German integration into NATO and Jimmy held a diametrically opposed view. Eric found Jimmy extreme and dogmatic in his views and said arguing against him was like tilting with windmills.[23] So Eric was absolutely stunned in 1963 when Jimmy suddenly wrote out of the blue and proposed a sentimental journey to Germany. Not only did he want to visit Kösterberg and the Hamburg bank with twelve-year-old Jimmy Jr., but he wanted to go with Eric and his teenage son, Max, for a tour of the ancestral town of Warburg. "I have in recent years missed some of the warmth and intimacy of a family hearth wider than one's own immediate circle of wife and children," Jimmy wrote.[24] Hence, Eric, Jimmy, and their sons journeyed to Warburg where the mayor led them to the ancient Jewish cemetery, the *Judengasse*, and other shrines. Jimmy completed this pilgrimage despite a torn ligament in his foot that forced him to hobble about with his leg in a cast.

The rapprochement with Eric was brief. A year later, when Jimmy published his memoirs, the reticent Eric was appalled at the indiscretions and complained that Jimmy was still the "dangerously ill boy" he had always been.[25] Jimmy never ceased to scandalize his more conventional Warburg relatives. In 1963, this offspring of a conservative banking family became a major donor to the new leftish Institute for Policy Studies. Five years later, he supported the insurgent candidacy of Senator Eugene McCarthy and was a vocal critic of the Vietnam War. He remained a brilliant, uncompromising iconoclast until the end. In 1969, at age seventy-two, Jimmy Warburg had a stroke and died in a Greenwich, Connecticut, hospital. He joined his parents in the Sleepy Hollow Cemetery.

———

Eric had taken an enormous gamble in returning to Hamburg. He had gambled that he would regain control of the bank from the Brinckmanns and vindicate the family's honor. He had gambled that his reluctant family would follow him. He had gambled that his story wouldn't recapitulate the sorry saga of the Warburgs in Germany. Most of all, he had gambled that his lone son, Max, would enter the bank and sustain the tradition that he had so laboriously revived. His older daughter, Marie, had become an internist at Beth Israel Hospital in Boston and Erica a landscape architect in Germany. Eric's unending battle with Brinckmann only made sense if he were preparing the way for young Max. The central question was: Could he coax his son into taking upon his shoulders the weighty, complex burden of Warburg history?

Almost fifty years younger than his father, Max had a different approach to things. As an Old World merchant banker, Eric possessed infinite layers of mystery and discretion. Max had his good looks, humor, and charm, but he was very American in his straightforward, outspoken style. He had a lot of his grandfather's bright energy and dash and was sometimes too impetuous for the finer points of diplomacy in which Eric specialized. As a student at Heidelberg in the late 1960s, he wrote radical tracts against multinational companies. Only gradually did he awaken to the mighty tradition that fate had bequeathed to him.

However eager Eric was to see Max enter the bank as a sixth-generation Warburg, he knew his son was very independent and that any heavy-handed tactics would backfire. He cleverly used various devices to lure him into banking. When Max was a teenager, Eric sometimes brought him to the bank when money was being transported by armed guards in an armored truck—the sort of thing to excite a boy's imagination. He ensured that Max was exposed to the elite of the banking world. "Eric used to trot young Max around like a pet monkey on a leash to meet the Rothschilds and other such types," said Eddie Warburg.[26] Whenever Max slouched at the table or showed bad table manners, Eric would both rally and reproach him by saying, "Think of how the Rothschilds would do it!" Having fathered his son at age forty-eight, Eric was eager to have Max go through a speedy apprenticeship and enter the bank. He constantly feared that he would die before Max could succeed him as a partner.

Despite this often uncomfortable parental impatience, Max insisted upon securing a better, if more leisurely, education. Becoming a German citizen in 1970, Max studied law and economics then received a first-rate banking education at Chase Manhattan and E. M. Warburg, Pincus in New York. He also apprenticed with Siegmund in London. Early on, Siegmund saw that Max was able and enterprising and it must have irked him that Eric had the son with banking in his veins. Siegmund knew one way to take over the Hamburg bank was to take over Max. So he closely studied the young man. Even when Max was a student, Siegmund would send him handwritten notes in the knowledge that German etiquette demanded a handwritten reply. Aware that Siegmund wanted to analyze his handwriting and probe the inner recesses of his psyche, Max would always borrow a typewriter to reply.

While acknowledging his father's capacity for acquiring clients, Max made no bones about his shortcomings as a banker. Yet he adored his father and it grated on him that Siegmund would bad-mouth and belittle his father in front of him. Finally, he had to protest in exasperation, "Please, Siegmund, you're talking about my father. I will not accept this."[27] Knowing the cargo of dreams that Max carried for Eric, Siegmund had tried to seduce him with tempting offers to become a managing director of S. G. Warburg & Company. Max came to see Siegmund as an extraordinary banker but his father as the man of superior character.[28]

The late 1970s witnessed no less than five separate merger negotiations to unite M. M. Warburg-Brinckmann, Wirtz & Co. with Siegmund's Effecten-bank-Warburg in Frankfurt. Despite his turbulent, mixed-up history with Siegmund, Eric strongly endorsed the proposed merger, which would have created the largest private merchant bank in Germany. He thought Frankfurt would emerge as the German money center and that it made little sense to vie with Siegmund there. He also believed their two operations had matching strengths.

Siegmund had little patience with the Brinckmanns and two other Ham-burg partners and they played a constant game of one-upmanship. When Eric suggested meeting in Hamburg or Frankfurt to discuss a merger, Christian Brinckmann insisted upon the neutral territory of Cassel. The official explana-tion for these failed talks was that the two sides differed about the concept. The real reason was that the Brinckmanns and their allies thought Siegmund would dominate the new entity. Eric disputed this, citing the diverse share-holder group that would control the bank. But even he had soured on the deal by the end.

After the collapse of these talks, Max went to visit Siegmund at Blonay one day. The two had grown somewhat closer. When Siegmund started groaning about the Hamburg partners and wondering why he held on to his stake there, Max stunned him by asking if he could buy his stake. He said the time had come for the Mittelweg and Alsterufer Warburgs to get out of each other's way and be friends again. On the spot, Siegmund agreed.

On January 1, 1982, Eric retired and Max became a partner with Sieg-mund's small stake. Thus ended Siegmund's dream of controlling a great Warburg bank in Germany. By that point, Siegmund had little fellow feeling for the Hamburg bank, which he sneered at as second-rate. He and Eric would see each other once or twice a year and talk on the telephone, but the relationship had cooled. In 1985, S. G. Warburg sold the Effectenbank, which had never flourished in corporate finance and whose credit business didn't square with the parent company's strategic vision.

Eric's battle with Siegmund may have ended, but not the internal one against the Brinckmanns. Segmented into separate baronies, the firm was paralyzed by the ancient feud. With a 23 percent stake and veto power over major decisions, Dr. Christian Brinckmann lacked an ambitious agenda for the bank. In 1986, Max brought in Dr. Christian Olearius, a managing director of the Norddeutsche Landesbank in Hannover. Olearius shared Max's vision and complemented his talents: Max thrived in investment banking and rapidly changing markets, Olearius in commercial banking. They had a stal-wart ally in Hans-Dieter Sandweg, but faced opposition from Dr. Christian Brinckmann and Dr. Hans Stracke. In 1987, Eric had a massive heart attack at the bank and stopped working that day. Henceforth, Max and Olearius carried the brunt of the battle.

After lengthy negotiations, the perplexing stalemate of many decades gave way to a stunning, almost magical, series of upheavals. First came the tremor of late 1988 when Stracke left the firm, followed by the full-scale earthquake of June 1989, when the Brinckmanns withdrew. Then the ailing Sandweg left and the Industriekreditbank (IKB) sold its 20 percent stake. This dramatic exodus left Max, age forty-one, and Dr. Olearius in charge. Through a leveraged buyout, they bought the nearly 45 percent share of the Brinckmanns and the IKB. Boosting their own stakes, they also resold portions to a group of friendly local investors, including cigarette heiress Gertrud Reemtsma, publisher John Jahr, and Hildegard Thoennes of the Voss margarine family. For the first time since 1938, the Warburgs, along with Dr. Olearius, had recaptured full managerial control of Hamburg's largest private bank and one of the largest in Germany, with more than five hundred employees. There were no more institutional owners. "We are again a purebred private bank," Max exulted to the press.

The bank began to thaw out from the deep freeze of the partnership struggle.[29] Max and Olearius mapped out an audacious strategy for a more universal bank. They started to create a stock-research department, to expand into major financial capitals, to issue interest and currency options, to push hard on mergers and other corporate-finance activities, to advise on real estate, and to expand trading and money-management operations.

These changes amazed and delighted Eric, who had been tossed on the waves of the twentieth century. "I was like a fish in a stormy sea," he once said, "now on the crests of the waves, now in their troughs."[30] During the Hitler period, the Warburgs had been stripped of their worldly goods. Eric had lived to enjoy a hero's return to Hamburg and to see the dread events of 1938 reversed. Where he and his family had been persecuted, he was now honored. In January 1988, the *Atlantik-Brücke* awarded to Eric himself its first Eric M. Warburg Prize for advancing German-American friendship. Because Eric was now infirm, the West German president, Richard von Weizsäcker, came to Kösterberg to award the prize. The son of a Third Reich official convicted at Nuremberg, Weizsäcker acutely (although he had not escaped criticism for his postwar defense of his father) felt the solemn obligation of the German people to make amends to the Jews. Dorothea Warburg, who had agonized over the move to Germany almost thirty years before, accepted the award in a small ceremony on the ground floor. Then Weizsäcker tiptoed up the old, squeaky stairs and spent several minutes alone with Eric, who lay in bed.

Toward the end, Eric's mind wandered and he often didn't recognize people. But he would suddenly become lucid on selected topics. When the Berlin Wall fell, he exclaimed, "It's unbelievable! I never would have thought it would happen. And, you know, what impresses me most—it's being done with such dignity."[31] After German reunification, Hamburg regained the Elbe hinterland that had accounted for much of its early maritime importance. Once again it was Gateway to the World and Germany resumed its place as the preeminent Continental power.

However clouded, Eric's mind was wont to clear on any matters pertaining to the bank or the name change. On his ninetieth birthday in 1990, Max brought him two and a half pounds of caviar—what Eric had termed the "black vegetable" as a boy. At this celebration, Max thanked his father for moving back to Germany. Then one day, about to go off sailing in Scandinavia, Max had the unutterable pleasure of informing his father that the bank had dropped "Brinckmann, Wirtz & Co." from the name. Starting on October 1, 1991, it would be called M. M. Warburg Bank on its logo and the pristine M. M. Warburg & Co. on the registry books—just as it had been from 1798 to 1938. Eric fully comprehended and it seemed nothing short of a miracle, a last-minute present from the gods. Dwarfed by the great joint-stock banks such as Deutsche Bank, M. M. Warburg was not the great prize it had been before the war. The role of the private banker was much more circumscribed in the modern world. But destiny had granted the Warburgs a chance to amend a terrible wrong.

On July 9, 1990, Eric died of cardiac arrest at age ninety in the old wooden hilltop house and former country inn that Moritz had purchased a century before. Even in death, Eric evinced the conflicted emotions toward Judaism that had distinguished his family's history and that of German Jewry. He had asked to be buried in the *non*-Jewish side of the cemetery, near a large stone marker that commemorated the baptized Altona Warburgs who had died in the concentration camps. In this way, Eric both held aloof from his fellow Jews and expressed his solidarity at once. A characteristic last act.

Despite his charitable work, the local Jewish community wouldn't perform burial rites in the non-Jewish side of the cemetery—as Eric must have known. About a thousand people, including many reporters, wanted to attend the funeral, yet Eric's family knew he would have favored his usual discretion. So a small knot of friends and family members stood by an open grave at eight o'clock one morning. Eric was the first Warburg banker buried on German soil since the Holocaust. Max read aloud prayers and speeches in German and English, but not in Hebrew. He wanted to conduct the ceremony in a way that seemed appropriate to his father.

Germany had regained the status quo ante of the pre-Hitler days by the time of Eric's death, but it conspicuously lacked one feature. The Jewish population of a unified Germany numbered somewhere between forty and fifty thousand people—about one tenth the pre-1933 number. Most were descendants of *Ostjuden* who had survived the concentration camps. Even as a fresh wave of Jews poured in from the Soviet Union, it was still unclear to what extent Germany had eradicated its long-standing anti-Semitism. A recrudescence of neo-Nazi activity, marked by more than two thousand attacks on foreigners and the desecration of many Jewish cemeteries and synagogues in 1992, posed the momentous question of whether Germany had genuinely fathomed the lessons of its troubled past. Had its postwar atonement been merely an exercise in public-relations piety?

As German Jews, the Warburgs didn't regard this question as an abstract matter, for they were ready to write a new chapter of the story. In 1992, Max, forty-four, married a tall, slim, quite striking twenty-four-year-old journalist named Alexa Chrambach, who was one-quarter Jewish; they spent their honeymoon in Israel. No less eager than his father to right past wrongs, Max joined efforts to establish a new Warburg Institute in Aby's old library building at 116 Heilwigstrasse. It was supposed to supplement, not supplant, the London institute. For the first time since the 1920s it seemed that meetings and seminars might be held in the famous elliptical reading room. Supporters of the project hoped to accomplish this by 1994 as a way of marking the seventy-fifth anniversary of the University of Hamburg that Aby had helped to found. And, indeed, in July 1993 the city of Hamburg completed negotiations to purchase the Heilwigstrasse house. The rediscovery of Aby and his forgotten world now seemed complete.

Like a Brahms symphony, the Warburg saga had been long and melancholic, sad but touched with hope, brave and strangely inspiring all at once. As German Jews, the family had known the sweetest rapture, the deepest torment, the most exquisite vindication. Fate had pommeled them many times yet they had survived, endured, and prospered anew. But as the generations changed in Hamburg, a tacit question disturbed the air. Was the germ of anti-Semitism finally dead in Germany? Or was it only dormant and waiting to flare up again? Had the Warburgs come back in vain?

APPENDIX

Thinking it time to turn the tables on him, I asked a distinguished American graphologist to analyze the handwriting of Sir Siegmund Warburg. Thea Stein Lewinson spent
eighteen years working for the Central Intelligence Agency and has coauthored a book
called *Handwriting Analysis*. When I contacted her, I disclosed the subject's name. She
was vaguely aware that Siegmund Warburg was a banker and knew that his firm
employed handwriting analysis. Otherwise she betrayed no special knowledge of him
and wasn't even aware that he had died ten years earlier. I furnished her with two
specimens of Sir Siegmund's handwriting—a long business letter written in the 1950s
and a shorter, more personal note written toward the end of his life. Ms. Lewinson
inquired only about his educational background, nationality, and age at the time he
wrote the letters. Below, I reproduce verbatim the remarkable report she sent me.

January 21, 1993.

Handwriting Assessment Report: S. W., Banker.

Subject appears to be a very bright and strong individual who handles his affairs in
a competent and effective manner.

His intelligence is considerably above the average; he is cultured and effective in
whatever he may be doing. He would not start an undertaking without having himself
thoroughly informed about all its details, He is alert, open to suggestions which seem
to fit into his program and willing to integrate them into his own activities. He will
discard them as soon as he considers them unsuitable. He learns quickly and has a
great capacity for distinguishing the essential from the unessential. His way of thinking is clear, logical and adaptable. He will understand other people's viewpoints, but

he is not likely to give up his own opinions. He is a mixture of flexibility and steadfastness which may not always be easy to understand and to cope with. He discards superfluous matters and tries to deal with the essentials as far as possible. He seems to have an understanding for the fact that most people are not as brilliant as he, and that he owes others explanations for his words and deeds. He possesses analyzing and particularly well developed synthesizing faculties and is particularly gifted for drawing the correct conclusions from the facts he finds. His gift of observation is well developed. He notices the smallest of details which could be important for him at the moment and fits them properly into the larger picture to which they belong. He has a rare capability: he is detail oriented in a very rational manner while at the same time, he is strongly intuitive; he senses instinctively the meaning and potential of facts. He may not be quite aware of this giftedness, but he uses it all the time, in a very useful manner. His rational sense of proportion is well developed. He possesses common sense and a good sense of proportion, and he can be systematic and methodical in his approach to a plan or project. Having a balanced judgment in the field of his knowledge and experience, he can be very critical and almost dissecting in his statements. He tries to be objective in his criticism, and while he may be harsh, he tries to be just. Most likely, due to his mental superiority, he has a clear picture of the larger and smaller aspects of a plan or a situation.

While subject's mental faculties are well developed, there is also emphasis on his practical and concrete tendencies and interests. However, there seems to be always a constructive balance between his intellectual and practical spheres. He is able to handle numbers and calculations, on a large scale, and usually seems to be rather conservative in using them. He has administrative abilities and should be a good organizer. Everything and everyone should have its proper place. If his arrangement is disturbed, he can become quite distressed. He is orderly and conscientious and demands the same from his co-workers. He is resourceful and possesses originality, and is enterprising and likes challenging assignments. Though possibly with some speculative aspects in his work, he is basically conservative and does not like to take uncalculated risks. He likes to make the best possible use of the material at his disposal, and he can become annoyed and possibly impatient with people who do not function according to his standards. Mechanical and routine work, he leaves to people who are temperamentally best suited for it. His gift of observation is well developed. He possesses analyzing as well as synthesizing faculties. He can dissect a problem into its elements, rearranging them into the proper order, from which he can draw new and unusual conclusions. He knows the limits of his competence and he is very consistent in working toward his goals, while he avoids being hasty. He possesses ease and fluency in expressing himself verbally as well as in writing. He can be pointed, clear and convincing in his statements. He is not likely to exaggerate, but he makes his ideas very clear. His ability to sell should be exceptional.

Emotionally, subject is quite well balanced. He has some problems, but he seems to cope with them quite well. His appearance is decided and sure, but not overbearing. Being exceptionally competent and in many respects a superior personality, may make people of less competence feel uneasy, without intending to do so. His feeling of self-confidence is not particularly strong, but he seems to check himself constantly and manages to show a self-confident appearance. He apparently does not want to appear overbearing. However, being as superior as he is in so many respects, he cannot help but demonstrating his competence. He has his feelings under a strict rational control and avoids being carried away by them. He likes being surrounded by people, but he does not like personal involvement. Basically, he is a private person who is quite secretive about his personal affairs. He is most selective as to the people in whom he confides. While he knows how to preserve secrecy, he may be rather open and direct in voicing his criticism in matters related to work. No matter how careful he may be, the criticized individuals may feel hurt and think that he wants to show his superiority. Basically, he is well-meaning and not very self-centered. He lives by fundamental ethical principles which he does not like to see violated. Except for usual customary social deceptions, he seems to be honest and sincere. It would require an unusually pressured situation for him to commit any major trespasses. This does not exclude the fact, that probably in his business dealings, this man has had to develop and use a certain shrewdness. There are indications that he is ambitious, however, he seems to be more ambitious for the work or works in which he is involved than for himself.

This man is sensuous and evidently enjoys the comforts and pleasures of life. Apparently, he has some aesthetic inclinations and probably, when his time allows, can enjoy cultural pleasures in the areas wherever he may find himself. He appears to be a cosmopolitan person who is able to learn from and enjoy a variety of cultures, but he will always preserve his individuality and cultural values. He is a very conscientious individual who is exact in the execution of his duties in the small details as well as in the larger aspects, and he expects his co-workers to do the same. He is a diligent worker, and he overcomes all possible obstacles, in order to complete the tasks which he considers his duty. He has administrative abilities and he likes to organize on a large scale, but he will not overlook the smallest detail which could be of importance, in the general framework of his work. He sets very high standards and expects the people with whom he is dealing to respect them and to live by them also, which may cause occasional difficulties.

Summarizing one could say that subject is an unusually gifted individual who could function as a competent business organizer and administrator on a large scale, but who also preserved the human qualities of warmth and decency in his personal relationships. There is also the possibility that some individuals will misjudge him, because they do not have the understanding for a personality of such an unusually magnitudinal scope.

Thea Stein Lewinson
(Thea S. Hall.)

ACKNOWLEDGMENTS

For decades, the Warburgs have hesitated to tell their story or open up their archives. Such reticence is understandable in a family once hounded and vilified by Nazi polemicists. When I began this independent book, several Warburgs expressed misgivings about my timing. They pointed to a worldwide resurgence of anti-Semitism, most notably in Germany and Eastern Europe, and the rebirth of old canards about Jewish bankers. They feared that any book, willy-nilly, would provide grist to malicious propaganda mills. I took the view that hocus-pocus thrives on fantasy, gossip, and speculation. Might not a meticulous account of a Jewish banking family, based on extensive interviews and original documents, help to dispel at least a particle of the ignorance? It seemed an appropriate time to introduce sunlight and disinfectant into the cobwebby netherworld of Jewish banker mythology.

In the end, I enlisted the cooperation of virtually the entire Warburg family. In addition to submitting to hours of interviews, many family members dredged up documents from drawers, closets, and vaults. Almost every page of this book has been enriched by materials unavailable to prior researchers. I am humbled by the courtesy and generosity shown by the Warburg family and hope that my book repays their effort.

With so many people to thank, I am powerfully tempted to list family members and colleagues in alphabetical order and leave it at that. Yet the singular contribution of several people demands separate acknowledgement. Above all, I am grateful to Max Warburg, who showed such exceptional trust in making me the first historian granted unconditional access to the M. M. Warburg papers in Hamburg. This remarkable trove of historical records was diligently gathered by his father, Eric, who tended to shield them from public view. I undertook my research just as records scattered in several places were reunited at the Hamburg bank, making this the first time that an authoritative Warburg history could have been written. It is astonishing that so many papers survived dislocation, exile, Hitler, and the Allied bombing of Hamburg.

Other people also made a signal contribution to rounding out the documentary record. I must thank Katharine and Nicholas Fox Weber for making available the Bettina Warburg papers; Maria Christina Warburg (Mills) for providing access to the papers of her father, Max Adolph Warburg; Marie Warburg, Alice Auerbach, and Gabriele Schiff for unearthing so much family memorabilia; Eddy Lachman for providing the papers of his grandfather, Aby S., and other Alsterufer Warburgs; and Lucie Kaye and Eva Mitchell for sharing their research into Lola Hahn-Warburg. Anita Warburg was an especially loyal and generous supporter of this project. No less important was the cooperation of Henry Grunfeld, Sir David Scholey, and other S. G. Warburg & Company executives who conquered their legendary corporate reticence and sat through extensive interviews about Sir Siegmund Warburg. Since they spoke on a background basis, my footnotes do not reflect their substantial contribution to the book. (Sharing their dismay over the unreliable biography of Siegmund Warburg by Jacques Attali, I decided to dispense with it entirely as a source.) Jacqueline Childs was kind enough to escort me through Siegmund Warburg's books at the St. Paul's Girls' School. The assistance of Doris Wasserman was particularly helpful in reconstructing Siegmund's life. I am also indebted to David T. Schiff, J. Richardson Dilworth, Anthony Griffin, Raymond Bonham Carter, and many others who gave me a glimpse of their private correspondence with Sir Siegmund. A. Joshua Sherman played an important strategic role throughout the research. Finally I must thank Madame Alexandra Danilova for breaking a fifty-five-year silence and sharing an intimate moment in her life.

In writing a book based on unpublished sources, I have required the courtesy of many archives. I would like to thank the staffs of the American Jewish Archives in Cincinnati; the Baker Library at the Harvard Business School; the Columbia University Oral History Collection; the *Forschungsstelle für die Geschichte des Nationalsozialismus* in Hamburg; the John F. Kennedy Library in Boston; the Leo Baeck Institute in New York; the Seeley G. Mudd Manuscript Library at Princeton; the Sterling Memorial Library at Yale; the Warburg Institute in London; and the YIVO Institute for Jewish Research in New York. Vanessa Drucker scrupulously checked my translations from the German. Nicola Clark assisted in compiling quotations for legal permissions. And in Germany, Dorothea Hauser brought many fascinating documents to my attention that might otherwise have escaped notice.

Many of the people listed below sat gamely through hours of relentless questioning that must have taxed their patience and stamina. I appreciate their candor, insight, and generosity.

Warburg Family: Jill Cartter, Benita Cioppa, Marco Cioppa, Ruth Domela, Phyllis Farley, Peter Fleck, Ruth Fleck, Alison Hahn, Margaret Hahn, Andrea S. Kaufman, Madeleine Marx, the late Felix Mitchell, Carol Noyes, Tamar Nussey, the late Elsbeth Oppenheimer, Adolf Prag, Frede Prag, Felicia Warburg Rogan, Walter N. Rothschild, Jr., Jeremy Warburg Russo, Esther Shalmon, Alice Speyer, the late Bettina Warburg, Dorothea Warburg, the late Edward M. M. Warburg, Joan Melber Warburg, Mary Warburg, the late Wilma Warburg, Dr. Renée E. Watkins, the late Gisela Wyzanski, and Geraldine Zetzel.

Friends, Business Associates, and Scholars: Hermann Abs, John Adams, Margaret

Anderson, Fred Baerwald, Nicholas Bolton, Hannah Borowitz, Marianne Breslauer, Dr. Ursula Büttner, Lawrence Buttenwieser, Ernst Cramer, John Craven, Joan Lewisohn Crowell, Peter Stormonth Darling, Countess Marion Dönhoff, Henry Eisenberg, Geoffrey Elliott, Pauline Baerwald Falk, Sir Ian Fraser, Alvin Friedman, Dr. Carl Heinz Goldman, Sir Ernst Gombrich, Martin Gordon, Harry Green, Sir Ronald Grierson, Fred Grubel, Sir Kenelm Lee Guinness, Charles E. A. Hambro, Carl Hess, Yves Istel, Robin Jessel, Bernard Kelly, Charles Kindleberger, Edgar Koerner, Anthony Korner, William Koshland, Harvey M. Krueger, Stephen S. Lash, Oscar Lewisohn, John K. Libby, Kurt Lipstein, Ralph Loewenberg, Richard Lutyens, Joseph McConnell, Vincent A. Mai, Dr. Nicholas Mann, R. W. Manners, Frank Mecklenberg, Edith Meisner, H. Nicolaas Millward, David Mitchell, Pierre Moussa, Edward F. Norton, Dr. Christian Olearius, Veronica Petersen, Lord Parmoor (Milo Cripps), Dr. Abraham Peck, Lionel Pincus, Renata Propper, Carey Reich, Werra Rittmeister, Wolfgang Rittmeister, Sir Eric Roll, Alan Root, Thomas W. Ryley, Geoffrey Samuels, Nathaniel Samuels, Hans-Dieter Sandweg, Peter Karl Schumann, George Schwab, Geoffrey Seligman, Michael Seligman, Charles Sharp, Andrew Smithers, Peter Spira, Jerome Sternstein, Katja Tenenbaum, Lewis Ufland, Ronald Utiger, Michael Verey, John Wehncke, Adelaide Weismann, Dietrich Weismann, John Whitehead, Gretchen Whitman, the late Arthur Winspear, Margot Wittkower, James D. Wolfensohn, Norbert Wollheim, and Ezra Zilkha.

I am no less indebted to those family members and friends who preferred anonymity.

I was able to write this book free of the cares that often cloud a writer's mind. For this I must thank my exceptionally fine team at Random House—my excellent editor, Ann Godoff, as well as Harry Evans and Alberto Vitale—who provided such enthusiastic and generous support. Andy Carpenter and J. K. Lambert performed exquisite design work on the book, while Carsten Fries ably supervised the production editing. My British editor, Jonathan Burnham of Chatto and Windus, and my British agent, Deborah Rogers, warmly supported the project. I am very grateful to Morgan Entrekin of Atlantic Monthly Press for a valuable early discussion of the book's focus. As always, Melanie Jackson proved the ideal agent, a true and steadfast business partner. She exhibited a cheerful efficiency that would have left even Sir Siegmund Warburg breathless with admiration. My parents were again models of wisdom and serenity. But all debts pale beside the one I owe to my wife, Valerie, who tolerated this second marathon in obsessional thinking with such patience, kindness, and love. Someday I plan to use my royalties to erect a statue to her in a busy public square so that the world may gaze with wonder.

BIBLIOGRAPHY

BOOKS.

Abramson, Rudy. *Spanning the Century: The Life of W. Averell Harriman. 1891–1986.* New York: William Morrow and Company, Inc., 1992.

Adler, Cyrus. *Jacob H. Schiff: His Life and Letters.* 2 Vols. Garden City, N.Y.: Doubleday, Doran and Company, 1928.

Agar, Herbert. *The Saving Remnant: An Account of Jewish Survival.* New York: The Viking Press, 1960.

Alsberg, Henry G., trans. and ed. *Stefan and Friderike Zweig. Their Correspondence 1912–1942.* New York: Hastings House, 1954.

Baden, Prince Max of. *The Memoirs of Prince Max of Baden,* trans. W. M. Calder and C. W. Sutton. New York: Charles Scribner's Sons, 1928.

Baden, Prince Max von. *Erinnerungen und Dokumente.* Stuttgart, Berlin, and Leipzig: Deutsche Verlags-Anstalt, 1927.

Baker, Ray Stannard. *Woodrow Wilson: Life and Letters.* Vol. 4. Garden City, N.Y.: Doubleday, Doran & Company, Inc. 1931.

Barkai, Avraham. *From Boycott to Annihilation: The Economic Struggle of German Jews, 1933–1943,* trans. William Templer. Hanover and London: Brandeis University Press, 1989.

Barnard, Harry. *The Forging of an American Jew: The Life and Times of Judge Julian W. Mack.* New York: Herzl Press, 1974.

Bauer, Yehuda. *American Jewry and the Holocaust: The American Jewish Joint Distribution Committee 1939–1945.* Detroit: Wayne State University Press, 1981.

———. *My Brother's Keeper: A History of the American Jewish Joint Distribution Committee 1929–1939.* Philadelphia: The Jewish Publication Society of America, 1974.

Bentwich, Norman. *For Zion's Sake: A Biography of Judah L. Magnes.* Philadelphia: The Jewish Publication Society of America, 1954.

Berkefeld, Henning, ed. *Hamburg in alten und neuen Reisebeschreibungen.* Düsseldorf: Droste Verlag, 1990.

Biegun, Dov. *David's Castle.* London: Poets and Painters Press, 1982. (Privately printed.)

Bielenberg, Christabel. *Ride out the Dark.* New York: W. W. Norton & Company, Inc., 1971.

Bird, Kai. *The Chairman: John J. McCloy: The Making of the American Establishment.* New York: Simon & Schuster, 1992.

Birmingham, Stephen. *"Our Crowd": The Great Jewish Families of New York.* New York, Evanston, and London: Harper & Row, 1967.

Black, Edwin. *The Transfer Agreement: The Untold Story of the Secret Agreement Between the Third Reich and Jewish Palestine.* New York: Macmillan Publishing Co., 1984.

Blumenfeld, Hans. *Life begins at 65.* Montreal: Harvest House, 1987.

Brandeis, Louis D. *Letters of Louis D. Brandeis.* Vols. III, IV, and VI. Ed. Melvin I. Urofsky and David W. Levy. Albany, N.Y.: State University of New York Press, 1975.

Bredekamp, Horst, Diers, Michael, and Charlotte Schoell-Glass, eds. *Aby Warburg: Akten des internationalen Symposions Hamburg 1990.* Weinheim: VCH Acta humaniora, 1991.

Broesamle, John J. *William Gibbs McAdoo: A Passion for Change 1863–1917.* Port Washington, N.Y.: Kennikat Press, 1973.

Brook, Stephen. *The Club: The Jews of Modern Britain.* London: Constable, 1989.

Bruhns, Maike. *Hier war doch alles nicht so schlimm.* Hamburg: VSA-Verlag, 1984.

Bullock, Alan. *Hitler: A Study in Tyranny.* New York: Harper Torchbooks, Revised Edition, 1964.

Burney, Christopher. *The Dungeon Democracy.* New York: Duell, Sloan and Pearce, 1946.

Büttner, Ursula. *Hamburg in der Staats-und-Wirtschaftskrise 1928–31.* Hamburg: Hans Christian Verlag, 1982.

Carl Melchior: Ein Buch des Gedenkens und der Freundschaft. Tübingen: J.C.B. Mohr, 1967.

Carroll, Wallace. *Persuade or Perish.* Boston: Houghton Mifflin Company, 1948.

Cassirer, Toni. *Mein Leben mit Ernst Cassirer.* Hildesheim: Gerstenberg Verlag, 1981.

Cecil, Lamar. *Albert Ballin: Business and Politics in Imperial Germany 1888–1918.* Princeton, N.J.: Princeton University Press, 1967.

Chandler, Lester V. *Benjamin Strong, Central Banker.* Washington, D.C.: The Brookings Institution, 1958.

Colvin, Ian. *Flight 777.* London: Evans Brothers Limited, 1957.

Clark, Kenneth. *Another Part of the Wood: A Self-Portrait.* New York: Harper & Row, 1974.

Cohen, Naomi W. *Not Free to Desist: The American Jewish Committee 1906–1966.* Philadelphia: The Jewish Publication Society of America, 1972.

Comfort, Richard A. *Revolutionary Hamburg: Labor Politics in the Early Weimar Republic.* Stanford, Calif.: Stanford University Press, 1966.

Craig, Gordon. *The Germans.* Reprint. New York: Penguin Books, 1991.

Dayer, Roberta Allbert. *Finance and Empire: Sir Charles Addis, 1861–1945.* Hampshire and London: Macmillan Press, 1988.

The Dearborn Independent. *The International Jew: The World's Foremost Problem.* Reprints from *The Dearborn Independent* of 1920 and 1921.

Diers, Michael. *Warburg aus Briefen.* Weinheim: VCH Acta humaniora, 1991.

Dodd, William E., Jr., and Martha Dodd, eds. *Ambassador Dodd's Diary, 1933–1938.* New York: Harcourt, Brace and Company, 1941.

Duckesz, Eduard, and Otto Hintze, eds. *Geschichte des Geschlechts Warburg.* 1928/9. Typescript in Leo Baeck Institute, New York.

Ehrlich, Judith Ramsey, and Barry J. Rehfeld. *The New Crowd: The Changing of the Jewish Guard on Wall Street.* Boston, Toronto, and London: Little, Brown and Company, 1989.

Farrer, David. *The Warburgs: The Story of a Family.* New York: Stein and Day, 1974.

Feder, Ernst. *Heute sprach ich mit . . . Tagebücher eines Berliner Publizisten 1926–1932.* Edited by Cécile Lowenthal-Hensel and Arnold Pauker. Stuttgart: Deutsche Verlags-Anstalt, 1971.

Feilchenfeld, Werner; Michaelis, Dolf; and Ludwig Pinner. *Haavara-Transfer Nach Palästina und Einwanderung Deutscher Juden 1933–1939.* Tübingen: J.C.B. Mohr, 1972.

Feis, Herbert. *1933: Characters in Crisis.* Boston, Toronto: Little, Brown and Company, 1966.

Feldstein, Stanley. *The Land That I Show You: Three Centuries of Jewish Life in America.* Garden City, N.Y.: Anchor Press/Doubleday, 1978.

Ferencz, Benjamin B. *Lohn des Grauens: Die verweigerte Entschädigung für jüdische Zwangsarbeiter.* Frankfurt, New York: Campus Verlag, 1979.

Ferretti, Silvia. *Cassirer, Panofsky, and Warburg: Symbol, Art, and History.* Translated by Richard Pierce. New Haven and London: Yale University Press, 1989.

Freimark, Peter. *Juden in Preussen—Juden in Hamburg.* Hamburg: Hans Christian Verlag, 1983.

Friedman, Thomas L. *From Beirut to Jerusalem.* Reprint. New York: Anchor Books, Doubleday, 1989.

Fritsch, Theodor. *Mein Streit mit dem Hause Warburg: Eine Episode aus dem Kampfe gegen das Weltkapital.* Leipzig: Hammer Verlag, 1925.

Füssel, Stephan, ed. *Mnemosyne. Beiträge zum 50. Todestag von Aby M. Warburg.* Göttingen: Gratia-Verlag, 1979.

Gay, Peter. *Weimar Culture: The Outsider as Insider.* New York: Harper & Row, 1970.

Gay, Ruth. *The Jews of Germany: A Historical Portrait.* New Haven and London: Yale University Press, 1992.

Genschel, Helmut. *Die Verdrängung der Juden aus der Wirtschaft im Dritten Reich.* Göttingen: Musterschmidt-Verlag, 1966.

Glouchevitch, Philip. *Juggernaut: The German Way of Business.* New York, Simon & Schuster, 1992.

Gombrich, E. H. *Aby Warburg: An Intellectual Biography.* London: The Warburg Institute, University of London, 1970.

Gordon, D. J., editor. *Fritz Saxl 1890–1948. A Volume of Memorial Essays from his friends in England*. London: Thomas Nelson and Sons Ltd., 1957.

Goren, Arthur A., ed. *Dissenter in Zion: From the Writings of Judah L. Magnes*. Cambridge, Mass., and London: Harvard University Press, 1982.

Hayes, Peter. *Industry and Ideology: I. G. Farben in the Nazi Era*. Cambridge: Cambridge University Press, 1987.

Helfferich, Emil. *Tatsachen: 1932–1946*. Jever: C. L. Mettcker & Söhne, 1969.

Herzig, Arno, and Saskia Rohde, eds. *Die Juden in Hamburg 1590 bis 1990*. Hamburg: Dölling und Galitz Verlag, 1992.

———. *Vierhundert Jahre Juden in Hamburg. Eine Ausstellung des Museums für Hamburgische Geschichte vom 8. November 1991 bis 29. März 1992.*

Hexter, Maurice. *Life Size: An Autobiography*. West Kennebunk, Maine: Phoenix Publishing, 1990.

Hochmuth, Ursel, and Gertrud Meyer. *Streiflichter aus dem Hamburger Widerstand 1933–1945*. Frankfurt am Main: Röderberg-Verlag, 1980.

Hoffman, Paul. *The Dealmakers: Inside the World of Investment Banking*. Garden City, New York: Doubleday & Company, Inc., 1984.

Hoffmann, Paul Th. *Die Elbchaussee*. Hamburg: Broschek Verlag, 1982.

Howe, Irving. *World of Our Fathers: The Journey of the East European Jews to America and the Life They Found and Made*. Reprint. New York: Shocken Books, 1983.

Institutional Investor. *The Way It Was: An Oral History of Finance: 1967–1987*. New York: William Morrow and Company, Inc., 1988.

Jablonski, Edward. *Gershwin: A Biography:*. New York: Doubleday, 1987.

Jochmann, Werner. *Als Hamburg unter den Nazis Lebte*. Hamburg: Rasch und Röhring Verlag, 1986.

Johnson, Paul. *A History of the Jews*. New York: Harper & Row, 1987.

Kerr, Ian M. *A History of the Eurobond Market. The First 21 Years*. London: Euromoney Publications, Ltd., 1984.

Keynes, John Maynard. *Two Memoirs: Dr. Melchior: A Defeated Enemy and My Early Beliefs*. New York: August M. Kelley, 1949.

Kimball, Robert, and Alfred Simon. *The Gershwins*. New York: Atheneum, 1973.

Kisch, Lt.-Colonel F. H. *Palestine Diary*. London: Victor Gollancz Ltd., 1938.

Klingaman, William K. *1929: The Year of the Great Crash*. New York: Harper & Row, 1989.

Kobler, John. *Otto the Magnificent: The Life of Otto Kahn*. New York: Charles Scribner's Sons, 1988.

Koelbl, Herlinde. *Jüdische Portraits: Photographien und Interviews*. Frankfurt am Main: S. Fischer Verlag, 1989.

Kolko, Gabriel. *The Triumph of Conservatism. A Reinterpretation of American History, 1900–1916*. New York: The Free Press, 1963.

Kopper, Christopher. *Nationalsozialistische Bankenpolitik am Beispiel des Bankhauses M.M. Warburg & Co. in Hamburg*. Unpublished dissertation. Bochum, 1988.

Krebs, Hans. *Otto Warburg: Cell Physiologist, Biochemist and Eccentric*, Trans. Hans Krebs and Anne Martin. Oxford: Clarendon Press, 1981.

Krohn, Helga. *Die Juden in Hamburg*. 2 Vols. Hamburg: Hans Christian Verlag, 1974.

Lachmann, Olga geb. Warburg. *Damals: Erinnerungen von Olga Lachmann geb. Warburg.* (Courtesy of Eddy Lachman.)

———. *Draft Memoirs*. 1961–62. (Courtesy of Eddy Lachman.)

Lindemann, Mary. *140 Jahre Israelitisches Krankenhaus in Hamburg*. Privately printed. Hamburg, 1981.

Lippmann, Leo. *Mein Leben und Meine Amtliche Tätigkeit*. Hamburg: Hans Christian Verlag, 1964.

Lorenz, Ina. *Die Juden in Hamburg zur Zeit der Weimarer Republik*. 2 Vols. Hamburg: Hans Christian Verlag, 1987.

McAdoo, William G. *Crowded Years: The Reminiscences of William G. McAdoo*. Port Washington, N.Y.: Kennikat Press, 1931.

McDonald, James G. *My Mission in Israel: 1948–1951*. New York: Simon & Schuster, 1951.

MacDonogh, Giles. *A Good German: Adam von Trott zu Solz*. London, New York: Quartet Books, 1989.

Marquis, Alice Goldfarb. *Alfred H. Barr Jr.: Missionary for the Modern*. Chicago: Contemporary Books, 1989.

Mason, Francis. *I Remember Balanchine: Recollections of the Ballet Master by Those Who Knew Him*. New York: Doubleday, 1991.

Massie, Robert K. *Dreadnought: Britain, Germany, and the Coming of the Great War*. New York: Random House, 1991.

Mayer, Gustav. *Erinnerungen: Vom Journalisten zum Historiker der deutschen Arbeiterbewegung*. Munich: Verlag der Zwölf, 1949.

Melchior, Elsa Warburg. *Random Memories*. Private typescript. (Courtesy of Elsbeth Oppenheimer.)

Morrissey, Evelyn. *Jewish Workers and Farmers in the Crimea and Ukraine*. Privately printed. New York, 1937.

Moussa, Pierre. *La Roue de la Fortune: Souvenirs d'un financier*. Paris: Fayard, 1989.

Müller-Hill, Benno. *Murderous Science: Elimination by Scientific Selection of Jews, Gypsies, and Others, Germany 1933–1945*. Trans. George R. Fraser. Oxford, New York: Oxford University Press, 1980.

Mürmann, Franz, ed. *Die Stadt Warburg: Beiträge zur Geschichte einer Stadt*. Warburg: Hermann Hermes Verlag, 1986.

Neumeyer, Alfred. *Lichter und Schatten: Eine Jugend in Deutschland*. Munich: Prestel-Verlag, 1967.

Nevins, Allan. *Herbert H. Lehman and His Era*. New York: Charles Scribner's Sons, 1963.

Ogger, Günter. *Friedrich Flick der Grosse*. Bern, Munich, Vienna: Scherz, 1971.

Parzen, Herbert. *The Hebrew University 1925–1935*. New York: Ktav Publishing House, Inc., 1974.

Peterson, Edward Norman. *Hjalmar Schacht: For and Against Hitler*. Boston: The Christopher Publishing House, 1954.

Peukert, Detlev J. K. *The Weimar Republic: The Crisis of Classical Modernity*. Translated by Richard Deveson. New York: Hill and Wang, 1992.

Pick, F.W. *Searchlight on German Africa: The Diaries and Papers of Dr. W. Ch. Regendanz*. London: George Allen & Unwin Ltd., 1939.

Potter, Jeffrey. *Men, Money & Magic. The Story of Dorothy Schiff*. New York: Coward, McCann & Geoghegan, Inc., 1976.

Rathenau, Walther. *Ein Preussischer Europäer: Briefe*. Berlin: Käthe Vogt Verlag, 1955.

Redmond, George F. *Financial Giants of America*. Vol. 1. Boston, Mass.: The Stratford Company, 1922.

Reznikoff, Charles, ed. *Louis Marshall: Champion of Liberty. Selected Papers and Addresses*. Philadelphia: The Jewish Publication Society of America, 1957.

Robinow, Hermann. *Aus dem Leben eines Hamburger Kaufmanns*. Leo Baeck Institute, New York.

Role. *Dr. Ley: Der Führer der Deutschen Arbeitsfront*. Berlin: Verlag Deutsche Kultur-Wacht, 1934.

Roll, Eric. *Crowded Hours*. London, Boston: Faber and Faber, 1985.

Rose, Norman. *Chaim Weizmann*. Reprint. New York: Penguin Books, 1989.

Rosenbaum, E., and A. J. Sherman. *M.M. Warburg & Co., 1798–1938: Merchant Bankers of Hamburg*. London: C. Hurst & Company, 1979.

Rosenstock, Morton. *Louis Marshall: Defender of Jewish Rights*. Detroit: Wayne State University Press, 1965.

Rothschild, Carola Warburg. *Sharing and Caring*. Privately printed, 1982.

Ruppin, Arthur. *Briefe, Tagebücher, Erinnerungen*. Edited by Schlomo Krolik. Königstein: Jüdischer Verlag Athenäum, 1985.

Schacht, Hjalmar Horace Greeley. *Confessions of 'The Old Wizard.'* Boston: Houghton Mifflin Company, 1956.

Schlabrendorff, Fabian von. *Begegnungen in fünf Jahrzehnten*. Tübingen: Verlag Wunderlich, 1979.

Schuker, Stephen A. *American "Reparations" to Germany, 1919–33: Implications for the Third-World Debt Crisis*. Princeton, N.J.: International Finance Section, Department of Economics, Princeton University, 1988.

Schwartz, Charles. *Gershwin. His Life and Music*. Indianapolis, New York: The Bobbs-Merrill Company, Inc., 1973.

Shepherd, Naomi. *Wilfrid Israel: German Jewry's Secret Ambassador*. London: Weidenfeld and Nicolson, 1984.

Sherman, A.J. *Island Refuge: Britain and Refugees from the Third Reich 1933–1939*. London: Paul Elek, 1973.

Simpson, Amos E. *Hjalmar Schacht in Perspective*. The Hague: Mouton & Co., N.V., 1969.

Soley, Lawrence C. *Radio Warfare: OSS and CIA Subversive Propaganda*. New York: Praeger, 1989.

Spinelli, Ingrid Warburg. *Erinnerungen, 1910–1989*. Hamburg: Dölling und Galitz Verlag, 1990.

Spring-Rice, Sir Cecil. *The Letters and Friendships of Sir Cecil Spring-Rice*. Vol. II. Edited by Stephen Gwynn. Boston and New York: Houghton Mifflin Company, 1929.

Stephan, Rolf. *Hamburg: ehemals, gestern und heute.* Stuttgart; J. F. Steinkopf Verlag, 1985.

Stephenson, Nathaniel Wright. *Nelson W. Aldrich: A Leader in American Politics.* Port Washington, N.Y.: Kennikat Press, reissued 1971.

Stern, Fritz. *Gold and Iron: Bismarck, Bleichröder, and the Building of the German Empire.* Reprint. New York: Vintage Books, Random House, 1979.

Stockhausen, Tilmann von. *Die Kulturwissenschaftliche Bibliothek Warburg: Architektur, Einrichtung und Organisation.* Hamburg: Dölling und Galitz, 1992.

Strauss, Lewis L. *Men and Decisions.* Garden City, N.Y.: Doubleday & Company, Inc. 1962.

Strum, Philippa. *Louis D. Brandeis: Justice for the People.* Reprint. New York: Schocken Books, 1984.

Stürmer, Michael; Teichmann, Gabriele; and Wilhelm Treue. *Wägen und Wagen. Sal. Oppenheim jr. & Cie. Geschichte einer Bank und einer Familie.* Munich, Zurich: Piper, 1989.

Teveth, Shabtai. *Ben-Gurion. The Burning Ground 1886–1948.* Boston: Houghton Mifflin Company, 1987.

Turner, Barry. *And the Policeman Smiled.* London: Bloomsbury Publishing Limited, 1991.

Turner, Henry Ashby, Jr. *German Big Business and the Rise of Hitler.* New York, Oxford: Oxford University Press, 1985.

Turner, Henry Ashby, Jr., ed. *Hitler—Memoirs of a Confidant,* trans. Ruth Hein. New Haven and London: Yale University Press, 1985.

Ueckert-Hilbert, Charlotte, ed. *Fremd in der Eigenen Stadt. Erinnerungen jüdischer Emigranten aus Hamburg.* Hamburg: Junius Verlag, 1989.

Verein für Hamburgische Geschichte. *Aby M. Warburg Preis: Vorträge und Aufsätze.* Hamburg: Hans Christian Verlag, 1981.

Voss, Carl Hermann, ed. *Stephen S. Wise: Servant of the People. Selected Letters.* Philadelphia, The Jewish Publication Society of America, 1969.

Waldman, Morris D. *Nor By Power.* New York: International Universities Press, Inc., 1953.

Wandel, Eckhard. *Hans Schäffer: Steuermann in wirtschaftlichen und politischen Krisen.* Stuttgart: Deutsche Verlags-Anstalt, 1974.

Warburg, Aby M. *Ausgewählte Schriften und Würdigungen.* Edited by Dieter Wuttke. Baden-Baden: Verlag Valentin Koerner, 1992.

———. *Fundstücke aus dem Warburg-Archiv.* From the Art History Department, University of Hamburg.

Warburg, Aby S. *Familie Anekdoten.* (Courtesy of Eddy Lachman.)

Warburg, Charlotte. *Sammelband.* (Extracts from the diary of Charlotte Warburg.) Hamburg, 1927. (Courtesy of Gabriele Schiff.)

Warburg, Edward M.M. *As I Recall: Some Memoirs.* Clifton, N.J.: Privately printed, 1979.

Warburg, Eric. *Zeiten und Gezeiten: Erinnerungen von Eric M. Warburg.* Hamburg: Privately printed, 1982.

Warburg, Felix M. *Letters to His Sons.* Privately printed, 1941.

Warburg, Fredric. *An Occupation for Gentlemen.* Boston: Houghton Mifflin Company, 1960.

Warburg, Frieda Schiff. *Reminiscences of a Long Life.* New York: Privately printed, 1956.

Warburg, James P. *A Book for Jimmy, Jennifer and Philip.* Greenwich, Conn.: Privately published, 1956.

———. *Germany—Bridge or Battleground?* New York: Harcourt, Brace and Company, 1946, 1947.

———. *Germany: Key to Peace.* Cambridge, Mass.: Harvard University Press, 1953.

———. *Hell Bent for Election.* Garden City, N.Y.: Doubleday, Doran & Company, Inc., 1935.

———. *The Long Road Home: The Autobiography of a Maverick.* Garden City, N.Y.: Doubleday & Company, Inc., 1964.

———. *Still Hell Bent.* Garden City, N.Y.: Doubleday, Doran & Company, Inc., 1936.

Warburg, Max M. *Aus Meinen Aufzeichnungen.* Privately printed, 1952.

Warburg, Paul M. *The Federal Reserve System: Its Origin and Growth.* Two Vols. New York: The Macmillan Company, 1930.

Warburg, Phyllis P. *New Deal Noodles.* Garden City, N.Y.: Doubleday, Doran & Co. Inc., 1936.

Warburg, Siegmund G. *An Anthology for Searchers.* Private typescript.

Weber, Nicholas Fox. *Patron Saints: Five Rebels Who Opened America to a New Art 1928–1943.* New York: Alfred A. Knopf, 1992.

Wechsberg, Joseph. *The Merchant Bankers.* Boston and Toronto: Little, Brown and Company, 1966.

Weizmann, Chaim. *The Letters and Papers of Chaim Weizmann,* ed. Barnet Litvinoff and Meyer Weisgal. Vols. I, II, and X–XVIII. Rutgers University: Transaction Books, 1979.

———. *Trial and Error: The Autobiography of Chaim Weizmann.* Two Vols. Philadelphia: The Jewish Publication Society of America, 1949.

Weizmann, Vera. *The Impossible Takes Longer.* As told to David Tutaev. London: Hamish Hamilton, 1967.

Welsh, Frank. *Uneasy City: An Insider's View of the City of London.* London: Weidenfeld & Nicolson, 1986.

Wenzel, Gertrud. *Broken Star: The Warburgs of Altona.* Smithtown, N.Y.: Exposition Press, 1981.

Yahil, Leni. *The Holocaust: The Fate of European Jewry.* Translated by Ina Friedman and Haya Galai. New York and Oxford: Oxford University Press, 1990.

Zweig, Stefan, and Friderike Zweig. *Briefwechsel 1912–1942.* Bern: Alfred Scherz Verlag, 1951.

ARTICLES, SPEECHES, TRIBUTES, AND PLAYS.

Adler, Cyrus. "Felix M. Warburg." *The American Jewish Year Book,* 5699 Vol. 40. September 26, 1938, and September 13, 1939, pp. 23–40.

————. *Jacob Henry Schiff: A Biographical Sketch.* New York: The American Jewish Committee, 1921.

Ahrens, Gerhard. "Werner von Melle und Die Hamburgische Universität." Zeitschrift des Vereins für Hamburgische Geschichte, Band 66, 1980. pp. 63–93.

"Alice Warburg née Magnus, 1873–1960." Privately printed.

American Jewish Committee. "The Jews in Nazi Germany." New York, 1933.

The American Scholar. A. M. Meyer. "Aby Warburg in His Early Correspondence." Summer 1988, Vol. 57, No. 3.

Barkai, Avraham. "German Interests in the Haavara-Transfer Agreement 1933–1939." *Leo Baeck Institute Year Book,* XXXV, 1990, pp. 245–266.

Bing, Dr. Gertrud. "A. M. Warburg." *Journal of the Warburg and Courtauld Institutes.* Vol. 28 (1965), pp. 299–313.

————. "Aby M. Warburg. Vortrag anlässlich der feierlichen Aufstellung von Aby Warburgs Büste in der Hamburger Kunsthalle am 31. Oktober 1958."

Brinckmann, Wirtz & Co. "Max M. Warburg: Gedenkfeier seines 100-jährigen Geburtstages am 5 June 1967." Privately printed.

————. "Worte zum Gedächtnis an Fritz M. Warburg." November 3, 1964. Privately printed.

Büttner, Ursula. "Not nach der Befreiung: Die Situation der deutschen Juden in der Britischen Besatzungszone, 1945–1948." Der Unrechtsstaat Bd. 2—Christians.

Cohn, Norman. "The Myth of the Jewish World-Conspiracy," *Commentary,* June 1966.

Diers, Michael. "Kreuzlinger Passion" in *Kritische Berichte.* 1979, Vol. 415, pp. 5–14.

Freimark, Peter. "Die Warburgs." In *Industriekultur in Hamburg.* Munich: Verlag C. H. Beck, 1984.

Glick, David. "Some Were Rescued." *Harvard Law School Bulletin,* December 1960.

Gombrich, Ernst H. "Aby Warburg Zum Gedenken." A commemorative speech on June 13, 1966, at Hamburg University in memory of Aby Warburg's 100th birthday.

Gordon, Martin. "Siegmund Warburg 1902–1982: A personal perspective from 1992." Private typescript.

Grunfeld, Henry. "Self-interview CFT questions." September 1, 1987.

Halpern, Dr. Georg. Interview in Jerusalem, February 9, 1956, and March 5, 1956. Leo Baeck Institute, New York.

Heise, Carl Georg. "Persönliche Erinnerungen am Aby Warburg." Gesellschaft der Bücherfreunde zu Hamburg, 1959.

Hilfe und Aufbau in Hamburg, Januar 1936 bis Dezember 1936. Privately printed. In Leo Baeck Institute, New York.

Jacobson, J. Letter on Max Warburg. *Leo Baeck Institute Year Book,* 1963, No. VIII. pp. 266–267.

Kahn, Dr. Bernhard. "Tribute to Max M. Warburg at the Annual Meeting of the Joint Distribution Committee, January 11, 1947." (Courtesy of Anita Warburg.)

Koonz, Claudia. "Courage and Choice Among German-Jewish Women and Men" in *The Jews in Nazi Germany 1933–1943.* Tübingen: J.C.B. Mohr, 1986.

"Kuhn, Loeb & Company: A Century of Investment Banking." New York: Kuhn, Loeb & Company, privately printed, 1967.

Landes, David S. "The Bleichröder Bank: An Interim Report." *Leo Baeck Institute Year Book,* V, 1960, pp. 201–220.

Levine, Herbert S. "A Jewish Collaborator in Nazi Germany: The Strange Career of Georg Kareski, 1933–37," *Central European History,* Volume VIII, September 1975, pp. 251–281.

Richarz, Monika. "Juden in der Bundesrepublik Deutschland und in der Demokratischen Republik seit 1945," pp. 13–30. in *Jüdisches Leben in Deutschland seit 1945.* Micha Brumlik et al., eds. Frankfurt, 1988.

Liebeschütz, Hans. "Aby Warburg (1866–1929) as Interpreter of Civilization," *Leo Baeck Institute Year Book,* Vol. XVI, 1971, pp. 225–236.

Roberts, Priscilla M. "A Conflict of Loyalties in Kuhn, Loeb and Company and the First World War, 1914–1917" in *Studies in the American Jewish Experience,* ed. Jacob R. Marcus and Abraham J. Peck. New York: University Press of America, 1984.

Rosenbaum, Eduard. "Albert Ballin: A Note on the Style of His Economic and Political Activities," *Leo Baeck Institute Year Book,* III, 1958, 257–299.

———. "A Postscript to the Essay on Albert Ballin," *Leo Baeck Institute Year Book,* IV, 1959.

———. "M.M. Warburg & Company, Merchant Bankers of Hamburg. A Survey of the First 140 Years 1798 to 1938." *Leo Baeck Institute Year Book,* 1962, VII, 121–149.

Rothfels, Hans. "The German Resistance in Its International Aspects," in *Studies in Diplomatic History and Historiography.* London: Longmans, Green & Co. Ltd., 1961.

Saxl, Fritz. Biographical Essay on Aby Warburg. Typescript, Warburg Institute.

Schiff, Gabriele. "The Legacy of Displaced Persons—A Personal Chronicle." Presented at a Meeting on the Holocaust, Hunter College, New York, October 22, 1979.

Sharp, Charles. Plays:

———. "Parsnip and Pickles" (1968)

———. "Repercussions" (1968)

———. "Lunch at 30 Gresham Street" (undated)

———. "The Party" (1977)

———. "Gloom" (1974). Courtesy of Doris Wasserman.

Sherman, A. Joshua. "Eine jüdische Bank in der Ära Schacht: M.M. Warburg & Co., 1933–1938" in *Die Juden im Nationalsozialistischen Deutschland,* pp. 167–172.

Szajkowski, Zosa. "Jewish Relief in Eastern Europe, 1914–1917." *Leo Baeck Institute Year Book,* X, 1965, pp. 24–56.

Tramer, Hans. "Die Hamburger Kaiserjuden." *Leo Baeck Institute Bulletin,* 1960, pp. 177–189.

Turner, Henry Ashby, Jr. "Emil Kirdorf and the Nazi Party," *Central European History,* Vol. 1, December 1968, pp. 324–344.

Tyrell, Albrecht. "Führergedanke und Gauleiterwechsel." *Vierteljahrshefte für Zeitgeschichte,* January 23, 1975. No. 4, pp. 341–374.

Vagts, Alfred. "M.M. Warburg & Co.: Ein Bankhaus in der deutschen Weltpolitik

1905–1933." *Vierteljahrschrift für Sozial-und Wirtschaftsgeschichte.* Wiesbaden: Franz Steiner Verlag, 1958.

Warburg Institute. "Chronik des Neubaues der Kulturwissenschaftlichen Bibliothek Warburg." Privately printed.

Warburg, Aby M. "A Lecture on Serpent Ritual." Translated by W. F. Mainland. *The Journal of the Warburg Institute* II, 1938–39, pp. 277–292.

Warburg, Edward M. M. " '1109': The Warburg House. An Informal Guided Tour." New York: The Jewish Museum, 1984.

Warburg, Eric M. "Max M. Warburg 1867–1946." Privately printed.

———. "Some Personal Experiences, 1942–1945." (Courtesy of Max Warburg.)

Warburg, James P. "Byrnes and the German Economic Problem." Broadcast over CBS Network—September 12, 1946.

———. "Israel and the American Jewish Community." The Current Affairs Press, 1960.

Warburg, Max M. et al. "Ansprachen gehalten anlässlich Umwandlung von M.M. Warburg & Co. in M.M. Warburg & Co. Kommanditgesellschaft, Hamburg, am 30 Mai 1938." Microfilm in Leo Beck Institute, New York.

Warburg, Max M. "Die Hamburgische Universität." Privately printed, 1913.

———. "Diese Reden Sollte Jeder Deutsche Lesen." Delivered in Hamburg March 12, 1919. Privately printed.

———. "Finanzielle Kriegslehren," Speech of August 1, 1915. In Leo Baeck Institute, New York.

———. "Begrüssungsworte zur Einweihung des Jüdischen Gemeinschaftshauses in Hamburg am 9. January 1938." In Leo Baeck Institute, New York.

M.M. Warburg & Co. *In Memoriam Rudolf Brinckmann Dr. jr.* Privately printed, 1974.

S. G. Warburg & Company. "A gathering of the members of S. G. Warburg & Co. to commemorate Sir Siegmund G. Warburg 1902–1982." The Guildhall in London, January 12, 1983. Private typescript.

Warburg, Siegmund G. "Address given at funeral of Ernest Thalmann on 22nd August, 1962." Private typescript.

———. "Lucie L. Warburg: 13 März 1866–25 Oktober 1955." Private typescript.

———. "Speech at the Funeral Service for Marc Rosenberg in Baden-Baden, September 9, 1930." Private typescript.

———. "Stefan Zweig." Private typescript.

Whitman, Gert. "Der Internationale Kapitalmarkt Insbesondere der Euro-Bondmarkt in U.S. Dollars und Anderen Währungsformen." Speech given in Baden-Baden, March 29, 1968. (Courtesy of Gretchen Whitman.)

Wolffsohn, Michael. "Banken, Bankiers und Arbeitsbeschaffung im Übergang von der Weimarer Republik zum Dritten Reich." *Zeitschrift zur Bankengeschichte,* May 1977, pp. 54–70.

GOVERNMENT DOCUMENTS.

Trials of War Criminals Before the Nuremberg Military Tribunals Volume VI. "The Flick Case." Washington, D.C.: United States Government Printing Office, 1952.

NOTES

ABBREVIATIONS

AD—Allen W. Dulles Papers, Seeley G. Mudd Manuscript Library, Princeton University, Princeton, New Jersey

AW—Aby M. Warburg Papers, The Warburg Institute, London

BW—Bettina Warburg Papers, courtesy of Katharine and Nicholas Fox Weber

CUOH—Columbia University Oral History Collection, New York

CUOH-BB—Columbia University Oral History Collection, Benjamin Buttenwieser

CUOH-GR—Columbia University Oral History Collection, George Rublee

CUOH-JG—Columbia University Oral History Collection, Jonah Goldstein

CUOH-JW—Columbia University Oral History Collection, James P. Warburg

DS—David Schiff Papers, courtesy of David Schiff

EH—Edward M. House Papers, Sterling Memorial Library, Yale University, New Haven, Connecticut

EL—Eddy Lachman Papers, courtesy of Eddy Lachman

FW—Felix M. Warburg Papers, American Jewish Archives, Cincinnati, Ohio

JFD—John Foster Dulles Papers, Seeley G. Mudd Manuscript Library, Princeton University, Princeton, New Jersey

JRD—J. Richardson Dilworth Papers, courtesy of J. Richardson Dilworth

JS—Jacob H. Schiff Papers, American Jewish Archives, Cincinnati, Ohio

JW—James P. Warburg Papers, John F. Kennedy Library, Boston, Massachusetts

JVF—James V. Forrestal Papers, Seeley G. Mudd Manuscript Library, Princeton University, Princeton, New Jersey

LBI—Leo Baeck Institute, New York

LBI-AP—Leo Baeck Institute, Arthur Prinz Papers

LBI-HS—Leo Baeck Institute, Hans Schäffer Papers

LBI—RDJ—Leo Baeck Institute, Reichsvertretung der Deutschen Juden Papers
LBI-SGW-SZ—Leo Baeck Institute, Correspondence of Siegmund G. Warburg and Stefan Zweig
LBI-WF—Leo Baeck Institute, Warburg Family Papers
MAW—Max Adolph Warburg Papers, courtesy of Maria Christina Warburg (Mills)
ML—Morris Lazaron Papers, American Jewish Archives, Cincinnati, Ohio
MMW—Private Archives of M. M. Warburg & Co., Hamburg
    Files starting with the letter:

    A   denotes the Aby M. Warburg or Warburg Library papers
    E   the Eric M. Warburg papers
    Frz the Fritz M. Warburg papers
    J   the James P. Warburg papers
    K   the Karl S. (Charles) Warburg papers
    Ma the Max M. Warburg papers

PW—Paul M. Warburg Papers, Sterling Memorial Library, Yale University, New Haven, Connecticut
SF-LB—Sigmund Freud-Ludwig Binswanger Correspondence, Sigmund Freud Copyrights, Wivenhoe, Colchester, England
TWL—Thomas W. Lamont Papers, Baker Library, Harvard Business School, Cambridge, Massachusetts
WW—Sir William Wiseman Papers, Sterling Memorial Library, Yale University, New Haven, Connecticut
YIVO—YIVO Institute for Jewish Research, New York
YIVO-AJC—YIVO Institute, American Jewish Committee Papers
YIVO-JR—YIVO Institute, Joseph Rosen papers
YIVO-LW-DM—YIVO Institute, Lucien Wolf and David Mowshowitch Papers
YIVO-MW—YIVO Institute, Morris Waldman Papers

CHAPTER 1

1. Duckesz, *Geschichte des Geschlechts Warburg*, p. 216.
2. Warburg, *A Book for Jimmy, Jennifer and Philip*, p. 25.
3. Lachmann, *Draft Memoirs*, III, p. 3A.
4. Duckesz, *Geschichte des Geschlechts Warburg*, p. 222.
5. Ibid, p. 80.
6. Tramer, *"Die Hamburger Kaiserjuden,"* p. 224.
7. Duckesz, *Geschichte des Geschlechts Warburg*, p. 222.
8. Blumenfeld, *Life begins at 65*, p. 12.
9. Warburg, *A Book for Jimmy, Jennifer and Philip*, p. 23.
10. Lachmann, *Draft Memoirs*, II, p. 5.
11. Duckesz, *Geschichte des Geschlechts Warburg*, p. 224.
12. MMW Ma XI, p. 2.

13. Warburg, *Aus meinen Aufzeichnungen,* pp. 2–3.
14. Lachmann, *Damals . . . Erinnerungen von Olga Lachmann,* p. 12a.
15. Melchior, *Random Memories,* p. 71.
16. *The New Yorker,* April 9, 1966.
17. Warburg, *A Book for Jimmy, Jennifer and Philip,* p. 24.
18. Rosenbaum and Sherman, *M.M. Warburg & Co.,* p. 34.
19. Ibid. p. 44.
20. Birmingham, *"Our Crowd,"* p. 210.
21. Rosenbaum and Sherman, *M.M. Warburg & Co.,* p. 50.
22. MMW Ma XIV, p. 528.
23. Duckesz, *Geschichte des Geschlechts Warburg,* p. 84.
24. Ibid, p. 85.
25. Farrer, *The Warburgs,* p. 176.
26. Warburg, *The Long Road Home,* p. 100.
27. *The American Scholar,* Summer 1988, p. 449.
28. Warburg, *The Long Road Home,* p. 5.
29. Rosenbaum and Sherman, *M.M. Warburg & Co.,* p. 97.
30. Mayer, *Erinnerungen,* p. 151.
31. Rosenbaum and Sherman, *M.M. Warburg & Co.,* pp. 48–49.
32. Duckesz, *Geschichte des Geschlechts Warburg,* p. 109.
33. MMW Frz I *Aufzeichnungen* (2nd series), p. 4.
34. Farrer, *The Warburgs,* pp. 26–27.

CHAPTER 2

1. Melchior, *Random Memories,* p. 54.
2. Lachmann, *"Damals . . . Erinnerungen von Olga Lachmann,"* p. 5.
3. Eddy Lachman, letter to the author, April 19, 1992.
4. Rosenbaum and Sherman, *M. M. Warburg & Co.,* p. 77.
5. Wechsberg, *Merchant Bankers,* p. 181.
6. Rosenbaum and Sherman, *M. M. Warburg & Co.,* p. 79.
7. Lachmann, *Draft Memoirs,* III, p. 3.
8. Stern, *Gold and Iron,* p. 511.
9. MMW Ma XV.
10. Gombrich, *Aby Warburg,* p. 21.
11. Ibid, p. 21.
12. Warburg, *Aus Meinen Aufzeichnungen,* p. 2.
13. Spinelli, *Erinnerungen,* p. 43.
14. Farrer, *The Warburgs,* p. 30.
15. Ibid, p. 31.
16. Warburg, *A Book for Jimmy, Jennifer and Philip,* p. 27.
17. Frieda Schiff Warburg, *Reminiscences,* p. 37.
18. Warburg, *A Book for Jimmy, Jennifer and Philip,* p. 32.
19. Gombrich, *Aby Warburg,* p. 22.

20. Melchior, *Random Memories*, p. 77.
21. Ibid, p. 102.
22. Ibid, p. 45.
23. Eddy Lachman, letter to the author, April 19, 1992.
24. Farrer, *The Warburgs*, pp. 27–28.
25. Melchior, *Random Memories*, p. 23.
26. MMW Frz I *Aufzeichnungen* (2nd series), p. 5.
27. Warburg, *Aus Meinen Aufzeichnungen*, p. 2.
28. Melchior, *Random Memories*, p. 154.

CHAPTER 3

1. Massie, *Dreadnought*, p. 102.
2. MMW Ma XI, 1, p. 6.
3. Lachmann, *Draft Memoirs*, III, p. 5.
4. MMW Ma XV.
5. MMW Ma XI, 1 p. 8.
6. MMW Ma V, letter from Max to Charlotte Warburg, March 25, 1889.
7. MMW Ma XI, p. 8.
8. Warburg, *Aus Meinen Aufzeichnungen*, p. 12.
9. Ibid, p. 12.
10. Ibid, p. 14.
11. MMW JW I, letter from Max to James Warburg, April 8, 1929.
12. Bettina Warburg, interview with author.
13. Frieda Schiff Warburg, *Reminiscences*, p. 34.
14. Eddy Lachman, letter to author, April 19, 1992.
15. MMW Frz I *Aufzeichnungen* (3rd series), p. 2.
16. Eddy Lachman, letter to author, November 2, 1992.
17. Dr. Renée Watkins, letter to author, December 1, 1991.
18. FW, Box 1163, "Farrer Corrections," ch. 3, p. 23.
19. MMW Ma XV.
20. Rosenbaum and Sherman, *M. M. Warburg & Co.*, pp. 99–100.
21. Weizmann, *Trial and Error*, Vol. 1, p. 31.

CHAPTER 4

1. Farrer, *The Warburgs*, p. 34.
2. Felix Warburg, *Letters to His Sons*, letter to Gerald F. Warburg, July 24, 1924.
3. FW, B343, F6, Juilliard Commencement Address, May 28, 1937.
4. Ibid.
5. Johnson, *History of the Jews*, p. 394.
6. Birmingham, *"Our Crowd,"* p. 148.
7. Frieda Schiff Warburg, *Reminiscences*, p. 61.
8. Potter, *Men, Money & Magic*, p. 22.

9. Ibid.

10. Birmingham, *"Our Crowd,"* p. 196.

11. Frieda Schiff Warburg, *Reminiscences*, p. 87.

12. Ibid., p. 88.

13. Rothschild, *Sharing and Caring*, p. 34.

14. Frieda Schiff Warburg, *Reminiscences*, p. 89.

15. Birmingham, *"Our Crowd,"* p. 420.

16. Frieda Schiff Warburg, *Reminiscences*, p. 89.

17. FW, Box 1163, "Farrer Corrections." Insert for ch. 3, pp. 26–27.

18. Frieda Schiff Warburg, *Reminiscences*, p. 52.

19. Ibid, p. 94.

20. Birmingham, *"Our Crowd,"* pp. 217–18.

21. Frieda Schiff Warburg, *Reminiscences*, p. 95.

22. BW.

23. Warburg, *A Book for Jimmy, Jennifer and Philip*, p. 62.

24. *The New Yorker*, June 11, 1955.

25. MMW Frz I *Aufzeichnungen* (3rd series), p. 3.

26. Birmingham, *"Our Crowd,"* p. 181.

27. Frieda Schiff Warburg, *Reminiscences*, p. 85.

28. Bettina Warburg, interview with author.

CHAPTER 5

1. MMW Ab MI5.

2. MAW.

3. MAW. "Speech at the Warburg Institute after the death of Gertrud Bing."

4. MMW Ab MI5.

5. Clark, *Another Part of the Wood*, p. 189.

6. Melchior, *Random Memories*, p. 189.

7. Ibid, p. 52.

8. MMW Ma XV.

9. Frieda Schiff Warburg, *Reminiscences*, p. 23.

10. Gombrich, *Aby Warburg*, p. 22.

11. MMW Frz I *Aufzeichnungen* (2nd series), p. 1.

12. AW Kopierbuch 6 26(7) Hamburg transcript, letter to Frau Lore, July 1, 1917.

13. AW. Family Correspondence 1887–1900, letter from unnamed *Kamerad*, June 20, 1894.

14. *The American Scholar*, Summer 1988, p. 447.

15. Ibid.

16. AW. Family Correspondence 1887–1900, letter to Charlotte Warburg, November 25, 1889.

17. AW. Family Correspondence 1887–1900, letter from Moritz Warburg, November 29, 1889.

18. Gombrich, *Aby Warburg*, p. 44.

19. Ibid, p. 53.
20. *The American Scholar*, Summer 1988, p. 447.
21. Warburg, *Aus Meinen Aufzeichnungen*, p. v.
22. Frieda Schiff Warburg, *Reminiscences*, p. 94.
23. Warburg, "A Lecture on Serpent Ritual," p. 288.
24. Ibid, p. 285.
25. Ibid, p. 286.
26. *The American Scholar*, Summer 1988, p. 450.
27. Warburg, *Zeiten und Gezeiten*, p. 41.
28. MAW. "Speech at the Warburg Institute after the death of Gertrud Bing."
29. MMW Ab MI.
30. AW. Family Correspondence 1887–1900, letter from Mary Hertz, May 19, 1897.
31. AW. Family Correspondence 1887–1900, letter to John Hertz May, 1897.
32. Ibid.
33. AW. Family Correspondence 1887–1900, letter from Charlotte Warburg, July 5, 1897.
34. AW. Family Correspondence 1887–1900, letter to Moritz Warburg, July 7, 1899.
35. AW. Family Correspondence 1887–1900, letter from Moritz Warburg, July 9, 1897.

CHAPTER 6

1. Warburg, *Zeiten und Gezeiten*, p. 26.
2. Warburg, *Gedenkfeier*, p. 9.
3. Warburg, *Aus Meinen Aufzeichnungen*.
4. Warburg, *Zeiten und Gezeiten*, p. 16.
5. MMW Ma XV.
6. Frieda Schiff Warburg, *Reminiscences*, p. 29.
7. *Leo Baeck Institute Year Book XVI—1971*, p. 225.
8. Lucie Kaye, interview with author.
9. Frieda Schiff Warburg, *Reminiscences*, p. 33.
10. Lucie Kaye, interview with author.
11. Anita Warburg, interview with author.
12. Ibid.
13. Warburg, *Zeiten und Gezeiten*, pp. 19–20.
14. Marie Warburg, letter to the author, October 31, 1991.
15. Warburg, *Zeiten und Gezeiten*, p. 26.
16. Ibid.
17. Anita Warburg, interview with author.
18. Lucie Kaye, interview with author.
19. MMW Ma XV.
20. Birmingham, *"Our Crowd,"* pp. 277–279.
21. Melchior, *Random Memories*, p. 184.

22. BW. "Nina L. Warburg."
23. BW. Letter from Nina to Jim Loeb—April 16, 1898.
24. MMW F47.
25. MMW Frz I *Aufzeichnungen* (3rd series), p. 3.
26. Ibid.
27. Spinelli, *Erinnerungen*, p. 48.
28. Ibid, p. 52.
29. Gabriele Schiff, interview with author.

CHAPTER 7

1. Frieda Schiff Warburg, *Reminiscences*.
2. Ibid.
3. CUOH-JW, p. 7.
4. MMW Ma XV.
5. Stern, *Gold and Iron*, p. 543.
6. Bettina Warburg, interview with author.
7. Adler, *Jacob H. Schiff*, Vol. I, p. 19.
8. Warburg, *The Federal Reserve System*, Vol. 1, p. 171.
9. *The Century* magazine, May 1915.
10. Warburg, *The Federal Reserve System*, Vol. 1, p. 18.
11. Bird, *The Chairman*, p. 72.
12. CUOH-JW, p. 18.
13. Ibid, p. 46.
14. Birmingham, *"Our Crowd,"* p. 318.
15. CUOH-JW, pp. 47–8.
16. CUOH-JW, p. 46.
17. Birmingham, *"Our Crowd,"* p. 402.
18. FW, Box 1163.
19. FW, Box 1163, "Farrer Corrections," ch. 14, p. 241.
20. *The American Jewish Year Book 5699 Vol. 40*, September 26, 1938–September 13, 1939, p. 37.
21. Kobler, *Otto the Magnificent*, pp. 29–30.
22. FW, "Personal Recollections," by Alice R. Emanuel.
23. Frieda Schiff Warburg, *Reminiscences*, p. 130.
24. Birmingham, *"Our Crowd,"* pp. 314–15.
25. Ibid, p. 314.
26. Ibid.
27. *The New York Times*, August 11, 1991.
28. Farrer, *The Warburgs*, p. 69.
29. Rothschild, *Sharing and Caring*, p. 29.
30. Farrer, *The Warburgs*, p. 68.
31. Rothschild, *Sharing and Caring*, p. 22.
32. Warburg, *As I Recall*, p. 3.

33. Frieda Schiff Warburg, *Reminiscences*, p. 121.
34. Weber, *Patron Saints*, p. 184.
35. Birmingham, *"Our Crowd,"* pp. 312–13.
36. Warburg, *Letters to His Sons*, letter to Frederick Warburg, December 4, 1913.
37. Birmingham, *"Our Crowd,"* p. 323.
38. Warburg, *As I Recall*, p. 20.
39. Rothschild, *Sharing and Caring*, introduction.
40. *The American Hebrew*, February 10, 1922.
41. Howe, *World of Our Fathers*, p. 133.
42. *The American Banker*, February 10, 1922.
43. *The Jewish Daily Bulletin*, June 9, 1930.
44. FW B 343 F1. "Eddie Cantor Address to delegates of Philadelphia AJJDC conference," November 22, 1937.
45. MMW Ma XV.
46. Waldman, *Nor by Power*, p. 232.
47. Adler, *Jacob H. Schiff*, Vol. II, p. 122.
48. Weizmann, *Trial and Error*, Vol. I, p. 62.
49. Adler, "Jacob H. Schiff," p. 55.

CHAPTER 8

1. *Hamburger Abendblatt*, August 14, 1982.
2. MMW MW 11, letter from Max Warburg to Herr Huldermann, December 28, 1921.
3. Cecil, *Albert Ballin*, pp. 33–34.
4. *Hamburger Abendblatt*, August 14, 1982.
5. MMW, Ma XI, 1.
6. Stern, *Gold and Iron*, p. 544.
7. *Nationaldemokrat*, April 1, 1912.
8. MMW Ma XV.
9. *Leo Baeck Institute Year Book III*, 1958, p. 270.
10. Massie, *Dreadnought*, p. 799.
11. *Hamburger Abendblatt*, November 24, 1976.
12. Warburg, *Zeiten und Gezeiten*, p. 14.
13. MMW Ma V, letter from Max Warburg to M.M. Warburg & Co., February 28, 1925.
14. Warburg, *Aus Meinen Aufzeichnungen*, p. 30.
15. Ibid.
16. Ibid.
17. Ibid, p. 31.
18. Ibid.
19. Weizmann, *Trial and Error*, Vol. I, p. 143.
20. Warburg, *Aus Meinen Aufzeichnungen*, p. 32.
21. Cecil, *Albert Ballin*, p. 101.

22. MMW MW II, letter from Max Warburg to Herr Huldermann—28 December 1921.

23. Cecil, *Albert Ballin*, p. 120.

24. MMW Ma XIV, p. 530.

25. Rosenbaum and Sherman, *M.M. Warburg & Co.*, p. 101.

26. MMW Ma VI, letter from Korekiyo Takahashi to Max Warburg, March 23, 1935.

27. MMW Ma XI, 1.

28. Warburg, *Aus Meinen Aufzeichnungen*, p. 20.

29. *Leo Baeck Institute Year Book*, 1962, p. 133.

CHAPTER 9

1. Warburg, *A Book for Jimmy, Jennifer and Philip*, p. 29.

2. *Mnemosyne*, p. 26.

3. MMW Ma XV.

4. Farrer, *The Warburgs*, p. 127.

5. AW. Family Correspondence 1887–1900. Report of female visitor to Florence.

6. Adolf Prag, interview with author.

7. Frieda Schiff Warburg, *Reminiscences*, p. 27.

8. *Mnemosyne*, p. 39.

9. Bing, "Aby M. Warburg," p. 18.

10. Gombrich, *Aby Warburg*, p. 117.

11. AW, Kopierbuch II 26(3) Hamburg Transcript, letter to Max Warburg, January 20, 1909.

12. Gombrich, *Aby Warburg*, p. 130.

13. Ibid., p. 325.

14. Ibid, p. 137.

15. *The American Scholar*, Summer 1988, p. 450.

16. *Leo Baeck Institute Year Book*, 1962, p. 133.

17. Warburg, *Aus Meinen Aufzeichnungen*, p. 6.

18. AW Kopierbuch 3 26(5), letter to Max Warburg, November 24, 1909.

19. AW Kopierbuch I Hamburg Transcript, p. 181, letter to Max Warburg, February 1, 1906.

20. AW 26(2) Kopierbuch I Hamburg Transcript, letter to Dr. O. Wulff, February 7, 1907.

21. AW. Family Correspondence, letter to Mary Warburg, March 26, 1907.

22. AW. Kopierbuch III, letter of July 27, 1909 to Dwelshauers, July 27, 1909.

23. AW. Kopierbuch 3 26(s), letter to Felix Warburg, December 12, 1909.

24. *Mnemosyne*, p. 43.

25. MAW. "Speech at the Warburg Institute after the death of Gertrud Bing."

26. AW. Kopierbuch II 26(3), Hamburg Transcript, letter to Herr Waetzoldt, February 28, 1909.

27. AW. Kopierbuch IV 25(6), letter to Dr. Sonderling, February 28, 1912.

28. AW. Kopierbuch III, letter to "Lieber Schwedeler," July 15, 1909.

29. *The American Scholar,* Summer 1988, p. 451.
30. AW, Family Correspondence, 1887–1900, letter to Charlotte Warburg, November 24, 1898.
31. Ruppin, *Briefe, Tagebücher, Erinnerungen,* p. 139.
32. Gisela Wyzanski, interview with author.
33. AW. Kopierbuch II 26(3), Hamburg Transcript.
34. *The American Scholar,* Summer 1988, pp. 451–52.
35. Ibid.
36. AW. Kopierbuch III 26(5), letter to Max Warburg, February 19, 1910.
37. Heise, *Persönliche Erinnerungen,* p. 33.
38. *Mnemosyne,* p. 52.
39. Heise, *Persönliche Erinnerungen,* p. 32.
40. Gombrich, *Aby Warburg,* p. 328.
41. Heise, *Persönliche Erinnerungen,* p. 18.
42. Ibid, p. 35.
43. Ibid., p. 37.
44. AW. Kopierbuch IV 25(6), letter to Max Warburg, July 23, 1912.
45. AW. Kopierbuch 5 26(7), Hamburg Transcript, letter to Fritz Warburg, December 2, 1913.

CHAPTER 10

1. Warburg, *A Book for Jimmy, Jennifer and Philip,* p. 6.
2. *Redmond's Financial Weekly,* October 19, 1923.
3. *Leo Baeck Institute Year Book,* 1962, p. 134.
4. *The Century* magazine, May 1915.
5. Warburg. *The Federal Reserve System,* Vol. I, p. 8.
6. Adler, *Jacob H. Schiff,* Vol. I, p. 279.
7. *The Century* magazine, May 1915.
8. Warburg, *The Federal Reserve System,* Vol. I, p. 19.
9. Ibid, Vol. II, p. 29.
10. Ibid, Vol. I, pp. 58–59.
11. Stephenson, *Nelson W. Aldrich,* p. 334.
12. Ibid.
13. Warburg, *The Federal Reserve System,* Vol. I, pp. 56–57.
14. Ibid, Vol. I, p. 60.
15. Stephenson, *Nelson W. Aldrich,* pp. 378–79.
16. *Philadelphia North American,* April 12, 1911.
17. Warburg, *The Federal Reserve System,* Vol. I, p. 76.
18. Ibid., Vol. I, p. 78.
19. CUOH—JW, p. 7.
20. Warburg, *The Federal Reserve System,* Vol. I, p. 91.
21. Ibid., Vol. I, p. 410.
22. Baker, *Woodrow Wilson,* Vol. 4, p. 147.

23. Warburg, *The Federal Reserve System*, Vol. I, pp. 98–99.
24. EH. SI B144a F 4015, letter from Paul Warburg, July 22, 1913.
25. Broesamle, *William Gibbs McAdoo*, p. 124.
26. Warburg, *The Federal Reserve System*, Vol. I, p. 421.
27. Farrer, *The Warburgs*, p. 90.
28. Warburg, *The Federal Reserve System*, Vol. II, p. 3.
29. Ibid., Vol. I, p. 407.
30. CUOH-JW, p. 17.
31. Warburg, *The Federal Reserve System*, Vol. I, p. 125.
32. Ibid., Vol. I, p. 140.
33. Ibid., Vol. I, p. 143.
34. *New York American*, May 18, 1914.
35. *Redmond's Financial Weekly*, October 19, 1923.
36. *Philadelphia North American*, July 10, 1914.
37. *The New York Times*, May 13, 1914.
38. Broesamle, *William Gibbs McAdoo*, p. 122.
39. *Philadelphia Inquirer*, July 12, 1914.
40. Warburg, *The Federal Reserve System*, Vol. I, p. 147.
41. PW. SI B2 F21, letter to Woodrow Wilson, July 3, 1914.
42. *The Wall Street Journal*, July 29, 1914.
43. PW. SI B2 F21, letter from Woodrow Wilson, July 25, 1914.
44. PW. SI B2 F21, letter to Woodrow Wilson, July 29, 1914.
45. New York Sun, August 13, 1914.
46. *Financial American*, August 13, 1914.
47. PW. SI B2 F22, letter to Colonel E. M. House, August 11, 1914.

CHAPTER 11

1. *Leo Baeck Institute Bulletin*, 1960, p. 182.
2. MMW Ma XI, 1.
3. Warburg, *Aus Meinen Aufzeichnungen*, p. 24.
4. MMW Ma XVI, 2.
5. Rosenbaum and Sherman, *M.M. Warburg & Co.*, p. 105.
6. Pick, *Searchlight on German Africa*, p. 5.
7. Vagts, "*M.M. Warburg & Co.*," p. 323.
8. Pick, *Searchlight on German Africa*, p. 9.
9. Ibid., p. 15.
10. Ibid., p. 14.
11. Ibid., p. 18.
12. Massie, *Dreadnought*, p. 726.
13. Vagts, "*M.M. Warburg & Co.*," p. 321.
14. Pick, *Searchlight on German Africa*, p. 23.
15. Ibid., p. 42.
16. Cecil, *Albert Ballin*, p. 179.

17. Warburg, *Aus Meinen Aufzeichnungen*, p. 25.
18. MMW Ma XI, 1.
29. Warburg, *The Long Road Home*, p. 17.
20. MMW Ma XI, 1 p. 4.
21. Ibid.
22. Rosenbaum and Sherman, *M.M. Warburg & Co.*, p. 100.
23. *Leo Baeck Institute Year Book*, 1962, p. 138.
24. *Leo Baeck Institute Year Book III*, 1958, p. 296.
25. MMW. "Albert Ballin File, November, 1912—December, 1914." Letter from Max Warburg to Jacob Schiff, April 30, 1913.
26. Rosenbaum and Sherman, *M.M. Warburg & Co.*, pp. 111–112.
27. Prince von Bülow, *Memoirs*, Vol. III. p. 198.
28. Rosenbaum and Sherman, *M.M. Warburg & Co.*, p. 112.
29. MMW Ma XIV, p. 647.
30. Mayer, *Erinnerungen*, p. 153.
31. Warburg, *Aus Meinen Aufzeichnungen*, p. 50.
32. Rosenbaum and Sherman, *M.M. Warburg & Co.*, p. 113.
33. Cecil, *Albert Ballin*, p. 213.
34. Ibid.
35. MMW. "Eric Warburg extracts for memoir."
36. Warburg, *Aus Meinen Aufzeichnungen*, pp. 35, 36.
37. Ibid., p. 36.
38. Spinelli, *Erinnerungen*, p. 54.
39. Rosenbaum and Sherman, *M.M. Warburg & Co.*, p. 114.
40. EL. Undated memo about Max Warburg trip to Belgium.
41. Warburg, *Aus Meinen Aufzeichnungen*, p. 37.
42. MMW Ma XII, p. 75.
43. Warburg, *Aus Meinen Aufzeichnungen*, p. 42.
44. Ibid., p. 43.

CHAPTER 12

1. Frieda Schiff Warburg, *Reminiscences*, p. 76.
2. Gay, *Weimar Culture*, p. 1.
3. Potter, *Men, Money & Magic*, pp. 44–45.
4. *The New York Times*, August 18, 1918.
5. Chandler, *Benjamin Strong*, p. 17.
6. PW. SI B3 F33. Speech of May 3, 1916.
7. Warburg, *The Federal Reserve System*, Vol. I, p. 151.
8. Warburg, *Germany: Key to Peace*, p. xii.
9. CUOH-JW, p. 36.
10. Ibid. p. 44.
11. Bettina Warburg, interview with author.
12. Ibid.

13. MMW. F47, letter from Paul Warburg to Max Warburg, December 19, 1922.
14. PW. SI B3 F42, memo of February 8, 1917.
15. *The New York Times*, August 18, 1918.
16. Spring Rice, *The Letters and Friendships*, p. 245.
17. Ibid., p. 243.
18. *The New York Times*, January 9, 1936.
19. Dayer, *Finance and Empire*, pp. 89–90.
20. Frieda Schiff Warburg, *Reminiscences*, p. 140.
21. FW. B171 F8, letter to Jacob Schiff, March 21, 1916.
22. Ibid.
23. Nevins, *Herbert H. Lehman*, pp. 68–69.
24. DS. Letter from Jacob Schiff to Max Warburg, February 25, 1916.
25. Birmingham, *"Our Crowd,"* pp. 323–24.
26. Bentwich, *For Zion's Sake*, p. 99.
27. Agar, *The Saving Remnant*, p. 19.
28. JS. B440 F8, letter to Max Warburg, January 5, 1915.
29. Kobler, *Otto the Magnificent*, p. 87.
30. JS. B440 F8, letter from Max Warburg, December 22, 1914.
31. JS. B440 F8, letter from Max Warburg, November 11, 1914.
32. MMW Ma 36.
33. JS. B440 F7, letter from Max Warburg, 4 January 1915.
34. Warburg, "Finanzielle Kriegslehren," p. 23.
35. Ibid.
36. JS. B440 F8, letter from Max Warburg, May 15, 1915.
37. Birmingham, *"Our Crowd,"* p. 345.
38. JS. B440 F8, letter to Max Warburg, September 22, 1915.
39. JS. Letter from Max Warburg, September 22, 1915.
40. Adler, *Jacob H. Schiff*, Vol. II, p. 252.
41. Birmingham, *"Our Crowd,"* p. 345.
42. JS. B440 F7, letter to Max Warburg, November 5, 1915.
43. JS. B440 F7, letter from Max Warburg, November 24, 1915.
44. Roberts, "A Conflict of Loyalties," p. 21.

CHAPTER 13

1. James W. Gerard, *Face to Face with Kaiserism*. p. 112.
2. EL. "Notiz für die Akte Antisemitismus über das Gespräch mit dem Kriegsminister von Stein." March 2, 1917.
3. Spinelli, *Erinnerungen*, p. 46.
4. MMW MW 56.
5. Lorenz, *Die Juden in Hamburg*, Vol. I, p. 46; and Krohn, *Die Juden in Hamburg*, Vol. I, p. 202.
6. *Hamburger Echo*, December 8, 1914.
7. *Leo Baeck Institute Year Book*, 1962, p. 141.

8. Ibid.

9. Roberts, "A Conflict of Loyalties," pp. 21–22.

10. *Leo Baeck Institute Year Book, 1965*, p. 54.

11. Ibid., p. 55.

12. Ibid., p. 31.

13. Rosenbaum and Sherman, *M.M. Warburg & Co.*, p. 117.

14. Warburg, *Aus Meinen Aufzeichnungen*, p. 46.

15. MMW Ma V. 1917 Annual Report of M.M. Warburg & Co.

16. Bing, "Aby M. Warburg," p. 31.

17. AW Kopierbuch 6 26(7) Hamburg Transcript, letter to Onkel Empel, August 9, 1914.

18. AW Kopierbuch 5 26(7) Hamburg Transcript, letter to Veth, September 2, 1914.

19. Blumenfeld, *Life begins at 65*, p. 47.

20. AW Kopierbuch 26(7) Hamburg Transcript, letters to Paul Warburg, August 28, 1914, and May 4, 1915.

21. BW. Letter from Jim Loeb to Paul and Nina Warburg, August 26, 1915.

22. AW Kopierbuch 6 26(7) Hamburg Transcript, letter to unnamed person, June 27, 1915.

23. AW Kopierbuch 6 26(7) Hamburg Transcript, letter to editor of *Frankfurter Zeitung*, February 2, 1915.

24. AW Kopierbuch 6 26(7) Hamburg Transcript, letter to Hübner, May 21, 1915.

25. AW Kopierbuch 6 26(7) Hamburg Transcript, letter to Paul Warburg, May 27, 1915.

26. AW Kopierbuch 6 26(7) Hamburg Transcript, letter to editors of *Simplicissimus*, August 29, 1915.

27. AW Kopierbuch 6 26(7) Hamburg Transcript, letter to Herr Hornbostel, August 18, 1915.

28. AW Kopierbuch 6 26(7) Hamburg Transcript, letter to Paul Davidsohn, April 16, 1915.

29. BW. Letter from Jim Loeb to Nina and Paul Warburg, July 27, 1915.

30. MMW Frz I, p. 35.

31. Spinelli, *Erinnerungen*, p. 56.

32. MMW Frz II, letter from Fritz Warburg to Herr von Trobe, December 15, 1919.

33. MMW Frz II, undated memo of Max Warburg.

34. MMW Frz II. "Eine Unterhaltung in Paxopolis." Also letter from Dr. Fritz Warburg to Lucius von Stödten, July 3, 1923.

35. MMW Frz II. Letter from Herr von Jagow to Dr. Fritz Warburg, November 18, 1919.

36. Fritsch, *Mein Streit mit dem Hause Warburg*, p. 77.

37. Warburg, *Aus Meinen Aufzeichnungen*, p. 45.

38. EL, letter from Paul to Max Warburg, December 1916.

39. Warburg, *Aus Meinen Aufzeichnungen*, p. 54.

40. FW. B171 F24, letter to Nina Warburg, April 10, 1916.

41. Warburg, *Aus Meinen Aufzeichnungen*, p. 7.

42. Adler, *Jacob H. Schiff*, Vol. II, p. 201.
43. Ibid, Vol. II, p. 204.
44. Roberts, "A Conflict of Loyalties," p. 28.
45. Warburg, *Letters to His Sons*, letter to Gerald Warburg, February 7, 1917.
46. Warburg, *Germany: Key to Peace*, p. xiii.
47. PW. SI B4 F57, letter to Colonel House, August 4, 1917.
48. Brandeis, *Letters*, Vol. IV, p. 317.
49. CUOH-JW, p. 4.
50. Warburg, *Germany—Bridge or Battleground?*, p. 136.
51. Warburg, *The Long Road Home*, p. 31.
52. CUOH-JW, p. 10.
53. Warburg, *The Long Road Home*, p. 38.
54. FW. "Corrections for Farrer book."
55. CUOH-JW, p. 21.
56. Warburg, *Germany: Key to Peace*, p. xiii.
57. Katharine Weber, interview with author.
58. BW, letter from Paul Warburg, February 16, 1920.
59. Warburg, *The Long Road Home*, p. 50.
60. Ibid., p. 49.
61. FW, B179 F33, letter to John Warburg, March 27, 1918.
62. Warburg, *Letters to His Sons*, letter to Frederick Warburg, July 10, 1917.
63. Ibid., letter to Gerald Warburg, August 5, 1918.
64. Warburg, *The Federal Reserve System*, Vol. I, p. 453.
65. Ibid., Vol. I, p. 447.
66. PW. SII B7 F92. Unpublished chapter on Federal Reserve Board.
67. Ibid.
68. Ibid.
69. *The Evening Sun*, March 14, 1918.
70. EH. SI B144 F4019, letter from Paul Warburg to Treasury Secretary McAdoo, April 7, 1918.
71. Ibid.
72. Warburg, *The Federal Reserve System*, Vol. II, p. 803.
73. *The New York Times*, August 12, 1918.
74. Ibid., August 18, 1918.
75. PW. SI B4 F57, letter to Colonel House, October 17, 1918.
76. Ibid.

CHAPTER 14

1. Letter from Eric Warburg to James Warburg, February 9, 1917. (Courtesy of Marie Warburg.)
2. Warburg, *Zeiten und Gezeiten*, p. 42.
3. Videotape of Eric Warburg interview. (Courtesy of Marie Warburg.)
4. Koelbl, *Jüdische Portraits*, p. 252.

5. AW Kopierbuch 6 26(7) Hamburg Transcript, letter to Wilhelm Hertz, October 1, 1916.

6. BW, letter from Jim Loeb to Nina Warburg, March 26, 1916.

7. *Mnemosyne*, p. 44.

8. Gombrich, *Aby Warburg*, p. 207.

9. AW Kopierbuch 6 26(7) Hamburg Transcript, letter to Anna Warburg, November 18, 1917.

10. AW Kopierbuch 6 26(7) Hamburg Transcript, letter to Aby S. Warburg, July 22, 1915.

11. AW Kopierbuch 6 26(7) Hamburg Transcript, letter to Bode, January 12, 1917.

12. AW Kopierbuch 6 26(7) Hamburg Transcript, letter to Dr. Orbaan, April 5, 1917.

13. AW Kopierbuch 6 26(7) Hamburg Transcript, letter to Percy Schramm, October 4, 1917.

14. AW Kopierbuch 6 26(7) Hamburg Transcript, letter to Herr du Bois, September 21, 1916.

15. Gustav Hillard, *Herren und Narren der Welt*, p. 285.

16. Warburg, *Aus Meinen Aufzeichnungen*, p. 57.

17. MMW Ma XII, p. 117.

18. Warburg, *Aus Meinen Aufzeichnungen*, p. 62.

19. Ibid. p. 64.

20. Ibid.

21. Warburg, *Zeiten und Gezeiten*, p. 54.

22. Prince Max of Baden, *Memoirs*, Vol. II, p. 9.

23. John W. Wheeler-Bennett, *Hindenburg—The Wooden Titan*, p. 165.

24. Prince Max of Baden, *Memoirs*, Vol. II., p. 13.

25. Ibid.

26. Warburg, *Aus Meinen Aufzeichnungen*, p. 67.

27. *Leo Baeck Institute Year Book III*, 1958, p. 298.

28. *Hamburger Abendblatt*, June 22, 1976.

29. EH. SI B114a F4014, letter from Max Warburg, June 9, 1921.

30. MMW Ma V. Letter from Max Warburg to M.M. Warburg & Co., February 28, 1925.

31. *Leo Baeck Institute Year Book III*, 1958, p. 298.

32. Warburg, *Aus Meinen Aufzeichnungen*, p. 68.

33. Ibid.

34. AW Kopierbuch 6 26(7) Hamburg Transcript, letter to Eric Warburg, July 15, 1918.

35. Bing, "Aby M. Warburg," p. 30.

36. Heise, *Persönliche Erinnerungen*, p. 51.

37. Ibid.

38. Ibid.

39. AW Kopierbuch 6 26(7) Hamburg Transcript, letter to Wilhelm Hertz, July 3, 1918.

40. AW Kopierbuch 6 26(7) Hamburg Transcript, letter to Max Warburg, May 19, 1918.
41. Birmingham, *"Our Crowd,"* p. 372.
42. MAW. "Speech at the Warburg Institute after the death of Gertrud Bing."
43. Ibid.
44. AW Kopierbuch 6 26(7) Hamburg Transcript, letter to Herr Professor, October 7, 1918.
45. Gombrich, *Aby Warburg*, p. 215.
46. Maria Christina Warburg (Mills), interview with author.
47. MAW. "Speech at the Warburg Institute after the death of Gertrud Bing."
48. Maria Christina Warburg (Mills), interview with author.
49. Staatsarchiv Hamburg, Percy Schramm Papers. "Aby Warburg 1866–1929."
50. Melchior, *Random Memories*, p. 191.
51. Warburg, *Zeiten und Gezeiten*, p. 34.

CHAPTER 15

1. Anita Warburg, interview with author.
2. MMW EW. "Memoir Extracts." Letter from Eric Warburg to Max Warburg, January 27, 1919.
3. MMW EW. "Memoir Extracts." Letter from Eric Warburg to his parents, December 25, 1918.
4. Warburg, *Aus Meinen Aufzeichnungen*, p. 71.
5. Ibid.
6. Ibid, pp. 50–51.
7. Ruth Fleck, interview with author.
8. MMW Ma XIV, p. 648.
9. MMW MW. Letter from Max Warburg to Albert Ballin, September 2, 1916.
10. Krohn, *Die Juden in Hamburg*, Vol. I, p. 106.
11. Keynes, *Two Memoirs*, p. 33.
12. Ibid., pp. 32–33.
13. Ibid., p. 48.
14. Ibid., p. 50.
15. Blumenfeld, *Life begins at 65*, p. 114.
16. Warburg, *Letters to his Sons*, letter to Gerald Warburg, March 17, 1919.
17. MMW Ma XIV, p. 577. Letter from Max to Alice Warburg, April 7, 1919.
18. TWL. B171 F27. "Memorandum as to Meeting at Chateau Villette Today," April 16, 1919.
19. TWL. B171 F27, Max Warburg memo of April 16, 1919.
20. TWL. B171 F27, letter from Thomas W. Lamont to Bernard Baruch, April 18, 1919.
21. MMW Ma XIV, p. 592.
22. Warburg, *Aus Meinen Aufzeichnungen*, p. 77.
23. Farrer, *The Warburgs*, p. 77.

24. MMW Ma XIV, p. 584.
25. Farrer, *The Warburgs*, pp. 78–79.
26. Warburg, *Aus Meinen Aufzeichnungen*, p. 98.
27. Ibid., p. 98.
28. Ibid., p. 86.
29. Krohn, *Die Juden in Hamburg*, Vol. I, p. 204.
30. MMW Ma XIV, p. 592. Letter from Max to Alice Warburg, June 23, 1919.
31. Rathenau, *Briefe*, p. 460.

CHAPTER 16

1. Letter from Charlotte Warburg to unnamed gentleman, June 16, 1919. (Courtesy of Anita Warburg.)
2. Adler, *Jacob H. Schiff*, Vol. II, p. 209. Letter from Jacob Schiff to Max Warburg, August 26, 1919.
3. MMW PM I. Letter from Paul to Alice Warburg, July 10, 1919.
4. BW. Letter from Paul Warburg, December 7, 1919.
5. BW. Letter from Paul Warburg, January 1920.
6. PW. SI B4 F57, letter to Colonel House, October 17, 1918.
7. PW. SI B4 F58, letter to Mortimer Schiff, March 21, 1919.
8. PW. SI B4 F58, letter from Mortimer Schiff, March 24, 1919.
9. MMW PM I. Letter from Paul Warburg to Alice Warburg, July 10, 1919.
10. Warburg, *The Federal Reserve System*, Vol. II, p. 647.
11. PW. SII B7 F93. Minutes of meeting in home of Dr. G. Vissering, October 13, 1919.
12. PW. SI B5 F59, letter to John W. Davis, November 17, 1919.
13. Keynes, *Two Memoirs*, p. 71.
14. Warburg, *The Federal Reserve System*, Vol. II, p. 55.
15. Ibid., Vol. II, p. 719.
16. Ibid., Vol. II., p. 654.
17. PW, *Evening Post* of New York, January 25, 1932.
18. Turner, *German Big Business*, pp. 47–48.
19. Krohn, *Die Juden in Hamburg*, Vol. I, pp. 202–3.
20. Rosenbaum and Sherman, *M.M. Warburg & Co.*, p. 125.
21. MMW MW 11. Letter from Max Warburg to Alice Warburg, June 7, 1921.
22. MMW MW 10. Letter from Max Warburg to Dr. Johann Becker, August 12, 1921.
23. EH. SI B114a F4014. Letter from Max Warburg, June 9, 1921.
24. Rosenbaum and Sherman, *M.M. Warburg & Co.*, p. 128.
25. Weizmann, *Trial and Error*, Vol. II, p. 288.
26. Gay, *Weimar Culture*, p. 153.
27. MMW Ma XII, p. 202.
28. MMW Ma XIII, p. 228.
29. MMW Ma XIII, p. 229.

30. Warburg, *Aus Meinen Aufzeichnungen*, p. 108.
31. Ibid.
32. *Leo Baeck Year Book VIII*, 1963, p. 267.
33. FW. B266 F11, letter to Louis Wiley, June 30, 1922.
34. Ibid.
35. Warburg, *Letters to His Sons*, letter to Gerald Warburg, October 16, 1922.
36. TWL. B136 F12, letter from Paul Warburg, November 14, 1922.
37. PW. SII B7 F91. "The Rehabilitation of Europe."
38. Warburg, *Letters to His Sons*, letter to Gerald Warburg, November 6, 1922.
39. Fritsch, *Mein Streit mit dem Hause Warburg*, p. 71.
40. JFD. B21. Excerpt from MW Autobiography.
41. Rosenbaum and Sherman, *M.M. Warburg & Co.*, p. 130.
42. MMW Ma XIII, p. 252.
43. MMW F47.
44. Warburg, *Zeiten und Gezeiten*, p. 71.
45. Vagts, "M.M. Warburg & Co.," pp. 381–82.
46. Peukert, *Weimar Republic*, p. 160.
47. MMW Ma XIII, p. 313.
48. Warburg, *The Long Road Home*, p. 85.
49. *The International Jew*, Vol. III, p. 235.
50. Cohen, *Not Free to Desist*, p. 131.
51. FW. B213 F21, letter to Ludwig Vogelstein, February 1, 1923.
52. Turner, *German Big Business*, p. 62.
53. MMW Ma XIII, p. 265.

CHAPTER 17

1. DS. Letter from Jacob Schiff to Max Warburg, January 19, 1920.
2. Potter, *Men, Money & Magic*, p. 19.
3. Warburg, *Letters to His Sons*, letter to Frederick Warburg, December 22, 1920.
4. Warburg, *As I Recall*, p. 5.
5. Warburg, *Letters to His Sons*.
6. Walter Rothschild, Jr., interview with author.
7. FW. B171 F19, letter from Walter Rothschild to Mr. Paul, May 15, 1916.
8. Rothschild, *Sharing and Caring*, p. 20.
9. FW. B213 F6, letter to Judah Magnes, January 22, 1923.
10. FW, letter of January 22, 1923.
11. Ibid.
12. Warburg, *Letters to His Sons*, letter to Frederick Warburg, July 30, 1920.
13. CUOH-JG, pp. 402–403.
14. Ibid., p. 404.
15. Bettina Warburg, interview with author.
16. Weber, *Patron Saints*, p. 83.
17. Warburg, *As I Recall*, p. 9.

18. Warburg, *Letters to His Sons*, letter to Gerald F. Warburg, January 19, 1925.
19. Geraldine Zetzel, interview with author.
20. Warburg, *As I Recall*, p. 9.
21. Katharine Weber, interview with author.
22. Warburg, *Letters to His Sons*, letter to Gerald Warburg, December 18, 1922.
23. MMW Ma XV.
24. DS. Letter from Jacob Schiff to Max Warburg, August 26, 1919.
25. MMW Ma XIV, p. 517.
26. Frieda Schiff Warburg, *Reminiscences*, p. 112.
27. Adler, "Felix M. Warburg," p. 39.
28. FW. "Personal Recollections," by Alice R. Emanuel.
29. Johnson, *History of the Jews*, p. 430.
30. Adler, *Jacob H. Schiff*, Vol. II, p. 165.
31. Feder, *Heute Sprach ich mit . . .*, p. 115.
32. Ruppin, *Briefe, Tagebücher, Erinnerungen*, p. 212.
33. FW. B213 F6, letter to Judah Magnes, January 22, 1923.
34. Weizmann, *Trial and Error*, Vol. II, pp. 309–10. Joshua Freundlich, editor of Volume XII of the Letters and Papers of Chaim Weizmann, says that the meeting with Felix that Weizmann said in *Trail and Error* took place in spring of 1923 may have been in December 1923.
35. Ibid., Vol. II, p. 310.
36. Ibid.
37. Ibid.
38. Ibid
39. Weizmann, *Letters and Papers*, Vol. XI, p. 316.
40. Ibid., p. 318. Letter from Chaim Weizmann to Berthold Feiwel, May 21, 1923.
41. FW. "A Prologue," by Carola Rothschild.
42. Weizmann, *Letters and Papers*, Vol. XIII, p. 134. Letter from Chaim to Vera Weizmann, November 17, 1926.
43. Weizmann, *The Impossible Takes Longer*, p. 106.
44. Frieda Schiff Warburg, *Reminiscences*, p. 148.
45. Weizmann, *Letters and Papers*, Vol. XII, pp. 55–56.
46. *The New Palestine News Bulletin*, May 27, 1932.
47. Ibid.
48. Ibid.
49. Kisch, *Palestine Diary*, p. 107.
50. Weizmann, *The Impossible Takes Longer*, pp. 105–6.
51. Weizmann, *Trial and Error*, Vol. II., p. 310.
52. Ibid., Vol. II, p. 311.
53. Weizmann, *Letters and Papers*, Vol. XIII, p. 142.
54. Cohen, *Not Free to Desist*, p. 143.
55. FW. B1163 chapter 10.
56. Farrer, *The Warburgs*, p. 69.
57. Parzen, *Hebrew University*, p. 16.

58. Ibid.
59. Ibid., p. 13.
60. Goren, *Dissenter in Zion*, p. 183.
61. Ibid.

CHAPTER 18

1. Farrer, *The Warburgs*, p. 127.
2. Bing, "A.M. Warburg," p. 302.
3. MAW. "Speech at the Warburg Institute after the death of Gertrud Bing."
4. *Mnemosyne*, p. 16.
5. Gay, *Weimar Culture*, p. 31.
6. Cassirer, *Mein Leben mit Ernst Cassirer*, p. 126.
7. Diers, "Kreuzlinger Passion," p. 5.
8. Heise, *Persönliche Erinnerungen*, p. 52.
9. Frieda Schiff Warburg, *Reminiscences*, p. 28.
10. Gisela Wyzanski, interview with author.
11. Ibid.
12. Gordon, *Fritz Saxl*, p. 15.
13. Bredekamp et al., *Aby Warburg*, p. 68, letter from Max Warburg to Ludwig Binswanger, November 3, 1928.
14. SF-LB. Letter from Binswanger to Freud, January 7, 1920.
15. Ibid.
16. Margot Wittkower, interview with author.
17. Bredekamp *et al.*, *Aby Warburg*, p. 68, letter from Ludwig Binswanger to Mary Warburg, December 18, 1929.
18. Ibid, p. 3.
19. SF-LB, letter from Freud to Binswanger, November 3, 1921.
20. Heise, *Persönliche Erinnerungen*, p. 51.
21. SF-LB, letter from Binswanger to Freud, November 8, 1921.
22. Gombrich, *Aby Warburg*, p. 303.
23. Bredekamp et al., *Aby Warburg*, p. 285.
24. Ferretti, *Cassirer, Panofsky, and Warburg*, p. 71.
25. Warburg, "A Lecture on Serpent Ritual," p. 292.
26. MAW. "Speech at the Warburg Institute after the death of Gertrud Bing."
27. Gombrich, *Aby Warburg*, pp. 226–27.
28. Cassirer, *Mein Leben mit Ernst Cassirer*, p. 151.
29. MAW. "Speech at the Warburg Institute after the death of Gertrud Bing."
30. Gombrich, *Aby Warburg*, p. 335.
31. Bredekamp et al., *Aby Warburg*, p. 7. Letter from Aby Warburg to Ludwig Binswanger, March 30, 1925.
32. Gay, *Weimar Culture*, pp. 62, 81.
33. Liebeschütz, "Aby Warburg," p. 227.
34. Bredekamp et al., *Aby Warburg*, p. 55.

35. Bredekamp et al., *Aby Warburg*, p. 58. Letter from Max Warburg to Ludwig Binswanger, April 25, 1925.
36. Ibid., p. 59. Letter from Mary Warburg to Ludwig Binswanger, April 28, 1925.
37. Heise, *Persönliche Erinnerungen*, p. 31.
38. Ibid.
39. *Mnemosyne*, p. 55.
40. Gisela Wyzanski, interview with author.

CHAPTER 19

1. MMW Ma XIII, p. 324.
2. Ibid.
3. Lorenz, *Die Juden in Hamburg*, Vol. II, p. 1019.
4. Fritsch, *Mein Streit mit dem Hause Warburg*, p. 8.
5. Ibid., p. 23.
6. Ibid., p. 24.
7. Ibid.
8. Ibid., p. 63.
9. Ibid.
10. Ibid., p. 65.
11. Ibid., p. 47.
12. Ibid., p. 84.
13. Lorenz, *Die Juden in Hamburg*, Vol. II., p. 1464.
14. Report of the International Acceptance Bank, Inc., January 20, 1925.
15. Rosenbaum and Sherman, *M.M. Warburg & Co.*, p. 134.
16. American Jewish Committee, "The Jews in Nazi Germany," p. 52.
17. CUOH-JW, pp. 50–51.
18. Lippmann, *Mein Leben*, p. 653.
19. MMW Ma XIII, p. 334.
20. Schacht, *Confessions of 'The Old Wizard,'* p. 408.
21. Tyrell, "Führergedanke und Gauleiterwechsel," pp. 360–61.
22. Role, *Hitlers Stabsleiter*, p. 22.
23. Turner, *German Big Business*, p. 247.
24. Lorenz, *Die Juden in Hamburg*, Vol. II, p. 1169.

CHAPTER 20

1. Spinelli, *Erinnerungen*, p. 53.
2. Heise, *Persönliche Erinnerungen*, p. 57.
3. MAW. "Speech at the Warburg Institute after the death of Gertrud Bing."
4. Ibid.
5. Cassirer, *Mein Leben mit Ernst Cassirer*, p. 151.
6. *Mnemosyne*, pp. 52–53.
7. Warburg, *As I Recall*, p. 32.

8. *Mnemosyne*, p. 49.
9. LBI-HS. B19. Letter to Eric Warburg, June 14, 1947.
10. AW. Family Correspondence, letter from Albert Einstein, September 10, 1928.
11. *Mnemosyne*, p. 24.
12. Clark, *Another Part of the Wood*, p. 190.
13. MAW. "Speech at the Warburg Institute after the death of Gertrud Bing." Also, Sir Ernst Gombrich, interview with author.
14. AW. Family Correspondence Folder 1928–1929, letter to Mary Warburg, December 21, 1928.
15. AW. Family Correspondence Folder 1928–1929, letter to Mary, Saxl, Wind, December 29, 1928.
16. Gombrich, "Aby Warburg Zum Gedenken," p. 25.
17. Clark, *Another Part of the Wood*, p. 189.
18. AW. Family Correspondence Folder 1928–1929, letter to Mary Warburg, February 19, 1929.
19. Weber, *Patron Saints*, p. 335.
20. Exhibition at Hamburg Kunsthalle. Letter from Aby Warburg to Gustav Pauli, May 25, 1929.
21. Warburg, *The Long Road Home*, p. 7.
22. Margot Wittkower, interview with author.
23. Liebeschütz, "Aby Warburg," p. 236.
24. Bredekamp et al., *Aby Warburg*, p. 71.
25. Bing, "Aby M. Warburg," p. 10.
26. Krebs, *Otto Warburg*, p. 77.
27. *The New Yorker*, February 2, 1987.
28. *The New York Times*, June 30, 1978.

CHAPTER 21

1. Warburg, *Letters to His Sons*, letter to Paul Felix and Edward Warburg, August 3, 1920.
2. YIVO-JR. Folder 17. "Minutes of the Meeting of the Committee of Seven," June 17, 1924.
3. Ibid.
4. Ibid.
5. Morrissey, *Jewish Workers and Farmers*, p. xii.
6. YIVO-JR. Folder 26. Letter from Joseph Rosen to Jacob Newman, June 8, 1928.
7. Rose, *Chaim Weizmann*, p. 241.
8. Marshall, *Champion of Liberty*, Vol. II, p. 755.
9. FW. "Personal Recollections," Alice R. Emanuel.
10. Ibid.
11. YIVO-JR. Folder 24. "From Mr. Warburg's Report on Conditions in Palestine, Russia and Poland."
12. FW. Nearprint File Paper, "May 15, 1927."

13. Voss, *Servant of the People*, p. 155.
14. Bauer, *My Brother's Keeper*, p. 102.
15. YIVO-JR. Folder 29. Cable from Joint Distribution Committee, Berlin, to Agro-Joint, New York, January 1, 1930.
16. FW. B266 F11, letter from Max Warburg, June 15, 1930.
17. Morrissey, *Jewish Workers and Farmers*, p. 41.
18. Shepherd, *Wilfrid Israel*, p. 213.
19. Weizmann, *Letters and Papers*, Vol. XIII, p. 524.
20. FW. Letter from Chaim Weizmann to Frieda Warburg, March 3, 1949.
21. Gisela Wyzanski, interview with author.
22. Ibid.
23. Ibid.
24. Lucie Kaye, interview with author.
25. Ibid.
26. Eva Mitchell, interview with author.
27. Weizmann, *Letters and Papers*, Vol. XIII, p. 524. Letter from Chaim Weizmann to Felix Warburg, December 28, 1928.
28. Anita Warburg, interview with author.
29. AW. Family Correspondence. Letter from Gisela Warburg, May 11, 1929.
30. FW. B277 F1. Statement of June 26, 1929. "Why the German Jews Entered the Jewish Agency."
31. Weizmann, *Letters and Papers*, Vol. XIII, p. 177.
32. Ibid., p. 557.
33. Marshall, *Champion of Liberty*, Vol. II, p. 702.
34. FW. B277 F1. Statement of June 26, 1929.
35. Rose, *Chaim Weizmann*, p. 243.
36. Rothschild, *Sharing and Caring*, p. 9.
37. Hexter, *Life Size*, p. 60.
38. Ibid., p. 64.
39. Ibid., p. 89.
40. Shepherd, *Wilfrid Israel*, p. 61.
41. Edward M.M. Warburg, interview with author.
42. FW. B252 F4, letter from Max Warburg, August 29, 1929.
43. FW. B252 F1, letter to Aby S. Warburg, October 30, 1929.
44. Hexter, *Life Size*, p. 96.
45. Ibid., p. 82.
46. *The New York Times*, October 23, 1930.
47. FW. B251 F3, letter to Judah Magnes, October 9, 1929.

CHAPTER 22

1. Birmingham, *"Our Crowd,"* p. 384.
2. CUOH-BB, p. 275.
3. Warburg, *A Book for Jimmy, Jennifer and Philip*, p. 62.

4. BW. Letter from Paul Warburg, February 12, 1927.
5. BW. Letter from Paul Warburg, November 21, 1926.
6. BW. Letter from Paul Warburg, August 27, 1926.
7. BW. Letter from Paul Warburg, October 22, 1927.
8. Warburg, *The Long Road Home*, p. 29.
9. CUOH-JW, p. 16.
10. Warburg, *The Federal Reserve System*, Vol. I, p. 513.
11. PW. SI B5 F65, letter to Ogden Mills, March 6, 1929.
12. Warburg, *The Federal Reserve System*, Vol. I, p. 824.
13. Klingaman, *1929*, p. 150.
14. Bird, *The Chairman*, p. 72.
15. MMW. Box 509 Warburg Family Akten. Letter from James to Eric Warburg, May 23, 1964.
16. BW. "Bettina W. Grimson Will" folder.
17. Ibid.
18. Warburg, *A Book for Jimmy, Jennifer and Philip*, p. 94.
19. Warburg, *The Long Road Home*, pp. 19–20.
20. Warburg, *As I Recall*, p. 7.
21. CUOH-JW, p. 33.
22. Ibid., p. 43.
23. Warburg, *The Long Road Home*, p. 58.
24. Warburg, *A Book for Jimmy, Jennifer and Philip*, p. 60.
25. Andrea Kaufman, interview with author.
26. Schwartz, *Gershwin*, p. 188. (Edward Jablonski dates this from the March 1926 party.)
27. Kimball and Simon, *Gershwin*, p. 64.
28. Schwartz, *Gershwin*, p. 190.
29. Warburg, *The Long Road Home*, p. 64.
30. Ibid.

CHAPTER 23

1. CUOH-JW, p. 53.
2. *Wanderer Between Two Worlds* by Norman Bentwich (Kegan Paul, Trench, Trubner & Co. Ltd, London, 1941), pp. 186–87.
3. FW. B252 F4, letter from Max Warburg, June 26, 1929.
4. Agar, *Saving Remnant*, p. 75.
5. Peukert, *Weimar Republic*, p. 196.
6. American Jewish Committee, "The Jews in Nazi Germany," p. 53.
7. MMW Ma XIX, p. 420.
8. Bullock, *Hitler*, p. 167.
9. CUOH-JW, p. 54.
10. Ibid.
11. Cohen, *Not Free to Desist*, pp. 157–58.

12. MMW Ma XIV, p. 424.
13. FW. B266 FII, letter from Max Warburg, September 21, 1930.
14. Warburg, *Zeiten und Gezeiten*, p. 110.
15. MMW Ma XIV, p. 452.
16. Max Warburg, interview with author.
17. Warburg, *Zeiten und Gezeiten*, p. 102.
18. MMW Ma XIV, p. 436.
19. JW. Box 1 Folder "Personal Affairs—6/16/31–6/19/31." Letter to Paul Warburg, June 17, 1931.
20. Warburg, *The Long Road Home*, p. 98.
21. JW. Box 1, Folder "Personal Affairs—6/8/31–6/15/31." Letter to Paul Warburg, June 10, 1931.
22. JW. Box 1, Folder "Personal Affairs—6/16/31–6/19/31." Letter from Paul Warburg, June 16, 1931.
23. JW. Box 1, Folder "Personal Affairs—6/8/31–6/15/31." Letter from James Warburg, June 15, 1931.
24. Warburg, *The Long Road Home*, p. 98.
25. JW. Box 2, Folder "Personal Affairs—8/18/31–8/20/31." Undated letter from James Warburg to Goldschmidt.
26. Warburg, *The Long Road Home*, p. 93.
27. JW. Box 2, Folder "German Banking Crisis of 1931—8/27/31–8/28/31." Letter to Paul Warburg, August 27, 1931.
28. Bullock, *Hitler*, p. 247.
29. Warburg, *Germany: Key to Peace*, p. xv; and Warburg, *The Long Road Home*, p. 94.
30. *The Nation*, February 3, 1932.
31. Warburg, *The Long Road Home*, p. 98.
32. Ibid., p. 309.
33. MMW. Box 509 Warburg Family Akten. Letter from James Warburg to Renate Lady Calder, May 14, 1964.
34. Bettina Warburg, interview with author.
35. BW. Letter from Paul Warburg, June 28, 1929.
36. Carol Noyes, interview with author.
37. Warburg, *A Book for Jimmy, Jennifer and Philip*, p. 63.
38. JW. Box 2, Folder "Personal Affairs—5/1/32–5/11/32." Letter to Felix Warburg, May 1, 1932.
39. JW. Box 1, Folder "Personal Affairs—3/21/32–4/13/32." Letter to Felix Warburg, April 13, 1932.
40. JW. Box 2, Folder "Personal Affairs—5/1/32–5/11/32."
41. Warburg, *The Long Road Home*, p. 102.
42. JW. Box 1, Folder "Personal Affairs—7/17/31–12/10/31."
43. Warburg, *The Long Road Home*, pp. 71–72.
44. Schwartz, *Gershwin*, p. 191.
45. Joan Melber Warburg, interview with author.

46. Katharine Weber, interview with author.
47. *The Independent*, February 3, 1993.

CHAPTER 24

1. Frieda Schiff Warburg, *Reminiscences*, p. 152.
2. Birmingham, *"Our Crowd,"* p. 420.
3. Ibid., p. 415.
4. Walter Rothschild, Jr., interview with author.
5. Warburg, *As I Recall*, p. 10.
6. Phyllis Farley, interview with author.
7. Jeremy Warburg Russo, interview with author.
8. Geraldine Zetzel, interview with author.
9. Jeremy Warburg Russo, interview with author.
10. *New York World Telegram*, February 19, 1941.
11. Frieda Schiff Warburg, *Reminiscences*, p. 136.
12. Warburg, *As I Recall*, p. 35.
13. Weber, *Patron Saints*, p. 39.
14. Warburg, *As I Recall*, p. 33.
15. Ibid.
16. Warburg, *Letters to His Sons*, letter to Edward M.M. Warburg, November 27, 1928.
17. Birmingham, *"Our Crowd,"* pp. 415–16.
18. Warburg, *As I Recall*, p. 51.
19. Weber, *Patron Saints*, p. 208.
20. Mason, *I Remember Balanchine*, p. 124.
21. Weber, *Patron Saints*, p. 244.
22. Mason, *I Remember Balanchine*, p. 126.
23. Edward M.M. Warburg, interview with author.
24. Weber, *Patron Saints*, p. 209.
25. Edward M.M. Warburg, interview with author.
26. Susan Quinn, *A Mind of Her Own*, p. 342.
27. Edward M.M. Warburg, interview with author.
28. Katharine Weber, interview with author.
29. Andrea Kaufman, interview with author.

CHAPTER 25

1. Anita Warburg, interview with author.
2. Carol Noyes, interview with author.
3. Farrer, *The Warburgs*, p. 187.
4. Melchior, *Random Memories*, p. 166.
5. Ibid., p. 175.
6. Warburg, "Lucie L. Warburg," p. 4.

7. Ibid., p. 2.
8. *Institutional Investor*, March 1980.
9. Wechsberg, *Merchant Bankers*, p. 193.
10. Ibid., p. 192.
11. Warburg, "Lucie L. Warburg."
12. *Institutional Investor*, March 1980.
13. Ibid.
14. Eddy Lachman, letter to the author, August 20, 1992.
15. MMW Ka IV, letter from Siegmund to Karl Warburg, November 2, 1923.
16. Frede Prag, interview with author.
17. Bettina Warburg, interview with author.
18. MMW Ka IV, letter from Siegmund to Karl Warburg, December 5, 1924.
19. Doris Wasserman, interview with author.
20. *Institutional Investor*, March 1980.
21. MMW Ka IV, letter from Siegmund to Karl Warburg, January 3, 1928.
22. Elsbeth Oppenheimer, interview with author.
23. Warburg, "Marc Rosenberg," p. 6.
24. Ibid.
25. MMW Ka IV, letter from Siegmund to Karl Warburg, April 7, 1930.
26. Wechsberg, *Merchant Bankers*, p. 210.
27. *Institutional Investor*, March 1980.
28. LBI-WF. Extracts from Alfred Vagts Tagebücher, February 5, 1934.
29. MMW Ka IV, letter from Siegmund to Karl Warburg, December 14, 1930.
30. Ibid.
31. JW. Box 3, Folder "Berliner Handels-Gesellschaft Merger Negotiations—12/9/31–12/24/31," letter from Siegmund Warburg, December 23, 1931.

CHAPTER 26

1. Hayes, *Industry and Ideology*, p. 66.
2. Borkin, *The Crime and Punishment of I. G. Farben*, p. 54.
3. MMW. MW 49, letter from Max Warburg to Heinrich von Gleichen, May 28, 1931.
4. MMW. MW 49, letter from Max Warburg to Hans Meyer, October 22, 1931.
5. Yahil, *Holocaust*, p. 22.
6. Warburg, *Zeiten und Gezeiten*, pp. 110–111.
7. Lorenz, *Die Juden in Hamburg*, Vol. II, p. 1059.
8. Bielenberg, *Ride Out the Dark*, p. 18.
9. MMW. JW II, letter from Max to James Warburg, April 9, 1932.
10. JW. Box 5 "Archive File—4/17/32–6/30/32."
11. MMW. MW F168 1932, letter from Max to James Warburg, June 12, 1932.
12. MMW. MW F168 1932.
13. *Leo Baeck Institute Bulletin*, 1960, p. 189.
14. Rosenbaum and Sherman, *M.M. Warburg & Co.*, p. 153.

15. JW. Box 5, "Archive File 9/32." Cable from Siegmund Warburg, September 14, 1932.
16. MMW. MW F168 1932, letter from Max to Felix Warburg, December 12, 1932.
17. Wolffsohn, "Banken, Bankiers und Arbeitsbeschaffung," p. 57.
18. MMW. "Gespräch am Mittagessen am 10 November 1982," p. 26.
19. Rosenbaum and Sherman, M.M. Warburg & Co., p. 157.
20. Gisela Wyzanski, interview with author.
21. Cohen, Not Free to Desist, p. 156.
22. Helfferich, Tatsachen, p. 47.
23. MW Ma XIV, p. 476.
24. Kopper, "Nationalsozialistische Bankenpolitik," p. 68.
25. Rosenbaum and Sherman, M.M. Warburg & Co., p. 158.
26. MMW. JW II, letter from Max to Jimmy Warburg, March 19, 1933.
27. Warburg, Zeiten und Gezeiten, pp. 113–114.
28. Adler, "Felix M. Warburg," p. 40.
29. FW. B294 F8, letter to Chaim Weizmann, April 6, 1933.
30. Yahil, Holocaust, p. 60.
31. Black, Transfer Agreement, p. 49.
32. Ibid.
33. FW. Letter to Gertrud Norman, April 18, 1933.
34. Black, Transfer Agreement, p. 50.
35. YIVO-LW-DM. Folder 95. "Notes of Conversation with Dr. Kahn on Afternoon of Saturday, March 31st, 1933."
36. MW Ma XIV, p. 488.
37. FW. B287 F12, letter to Margarete Dessoff, June 12, 1933.
38. Kopper, "Nationalsozialistische Bankenpolitik," p. 50.
39. Gisela Wyzanski, interview with author.
40. Turner, Hitler, p. 261.
41. Peterson, Hjalmar Schacht, p. 128.
42. Turner, German Big Business, p. 331.
43. Schacht, Confessions of 'The Old Wizard,' p. 274.
44. MMW. JW II, letter from Max to James Warburg, March 19, 1933.
45. MMW. JW II, letter from Max to James Warburg, June 4, 1933.
46. CUOH-JW, p. 687.
47. Schuker, Reparations, p. 74.
48. Helfferich, Tatsachen, p. 14.
49. Warburg, Zeiten und Gezeiten, pp. 119–120.
50. Rosenbaum and Sherman, M.M. Warburg & Co., p. 161.
51. MW Ma XIV, p. 479.
52. Kopper, "Nationalsozialistische Bankenpolitik," pp. 72–73.
53. Warburg, Zeiten und Gezeiten, p. 117.
54. Ibid.
55. Ibid., pp. 117–118.
56. FW. B295 F4, letter to Henry Wollman, November 30, 1934.

57. FW. B291 F5, letter to Paul Baerwald, June 14, 1933.
58. Kopper, "Nationalsozialistische Bankenpolitik," p. 73.

CHAPTER 27

1. Feis, *1933*, p. 152.
2. Warburg, *A Book for Jimmy, Jennifer and Philip*, p. 53.
3. JW. Box 3, "Berliner Handels-Gesellschaft Merger Negotiations 1/1/32–1/7/32," letter to Siegmund Warburg, January 2, 1932.
4. *The New York Times*, January 25, 1932.
5. Warburg, *The Long Road Home*, p. 107.
6. Ibid.
7. Abramson, *Spanning the Century*, p. 239.
8. CUOH-JW, p. 177.
9. *The New Yorker*, September 13, 1969.
10. Warburg, *The Long Road Home*, p. 112.
11. CUOH-JW, p. 247.
12. Ibid., p. 504.
13. Ibid. pp. 497–98.
14. Ibid., p. 504.
15. Brandeis, *Letters*, Vol. V., p. 516. Letter to Stephen S. Wise, May 18, 1933.
16. Voss, *Servant of the People*, p. 208.
17. CUOH-JW, p. 199.
18. JW. Box 7, "Personal 1933," letter to Frederick Warburg, April 24, 1933.
19. CUOH-JW, p. 644.
20. Feis, *1933*, p. 137.
21. CUOH-JW, p. 630.
22. Vagts, "M.M. Warburg & Co.," p. 387.
23. Dodd, *Ambassador Dodd's Diary*, p. 9.
24. FW. Box 291 F11, letter to Lewis Strauss, October 26, 1933.
25. McDonald, *My Mission in Israel*, p. 252.
26. Ibid., p. 253.
27. Bauer, *My Brother's Keeper*, p. 145.
28. Feis, *1933*, p. 158.
29. CUOH-JW, p. 655.
30. CUOH-JW, p. 681.
31. Warburg, *The Long Road Home*, p. 124.
32. CUOH-JW, p. 679.
33. MMW JW II, letter from Max to James Warburg, June 4, 1933.
34. YIVO-MW. Exo-29. Box 15. Folder "Germany Hitlerism." Confidential report of June 25, 1933.
35. FW. B287 F1.
36. CUOH-JW, p. 975.
37. Feis, *1933*, p. 191.

38. *The New Yorker*, September 13, 1969.
39. Feis, *1933*, p. 191 and CUOH-JW, p. 538.
40. Warburg, *The Long Road Home*, pp. 133–134.
41. Ibid., pp. 135–36.
42. CUOH-JW, p. 1123.
43. Warburg, *The Long Road Home*, pp. 135–136.
44. *The New Yorker*, September 13, 1969.
45. CUOH-JW, p. 1188.
46. CUOH-JW, p. 1193.
47. *The New Yorker*, September 13, 1969.
48. Warburg, *The Long Road Home*, p. 147.
49. CUOH-JW, p. 654.
50. Ibid., pp. 156–57.
51. Warburg, *Hell Bent for Election*, p. 70.
52. Ibid., p. xiv.
53. CUOH-JW, p. 1628.
54. Warburg, *New Deal Noodles*, p. 17.
55. Ibid., p. 39.
56. Warburg, *Still Hell Bent*, p. 1.
57. Warburg, *The Long Road Home*, p. 167.

CHAPTER 28

1. MMW Ma VI, letter from Max Warburg to Martin Buber, October 1, 1933.
2. *The New York Times*, August 22, 1934.
3. Rose, *Chaim Weizmann*, p. 301.
4. LBI-RDJ, letter from 3 Cologne Jews to Max Warburg, August 24, 1933.
5. Bauer, *My Brother's Keeper*, p. 259.
6. MMW Ma XIV, p. 653.
7. MMW Ma XIV, p. 654.
8. MMW. JW II, letter from Max to James Warburg. March 19, 1933.
9. YIVO-LW-DM. Folder 95, "Interview with Dr. Karl Melchior and Dr. Tietz," June 11, 1933.
10. Warburg, *Aus Meinen Aufzeichnungen*, p. 52.
11. MMW. Fritz M. Warburg Akten, Paket 3, "Charles Warburg" Folder, letter from Charles to Fritz Warburg, April 26, 1948.
12. Ahrens, "Werner von Melle," p. 89.
13. Gordon, *Fritz Saxl*, p. 22.
14. FW. B288 F6, letter to Abraham Flexner, August 9, 1933.
15. FW. B294 F7, memo to Max Warburg, November 27, 1933.
16. *The Warburg Institute Annual Report, 1952–1953*.
17. FW. B318 F6, letter from Dr. von Kleinschmit, December 11, 1933.
18. *Manchester Guardian*, December 13, 1944.
19. *Mnemosyne*, p. 45.

20. FW. B318 F6, letter to Max Warburg, November 2, 1934.

21. FW. B318 F6, memorandum "Re: Warburg Library."

22. MMW. AW Bibliothek Warburg 1935. MMW memo of September 16, 1935.

23. Ibid.

24. MMW. AW Bibliothek Warburg 1935, letter from Gertrud Bing to Eric Warburg, December 16, 1935.

25. FW. B318 F6, letter from Max Warburg, November 16, 1935.

26. FW. B318 F6, "Memo for Mr. Erich Warburg," October 1936.

27. BW, letter from American Consular Service, Department of State, Hamburg, to Eric Warburg, June 5, 1936.

28. Veronica Petersen, interview with author.

29. MMW. Fritz Akten, Paket 4, letter from Otto Sauter to Siegmund Warburg, July 17, 1932.

30. Warburg, "Lucie L. Warburg," p. 10.

31. MMW. Fritz Akten, Paket 4, letter from Dr. Peters to Siegmund Warburg, May 11, 1933.

32. Wechsberg, *Merchant Bankers*, p. 199.

33. Ibid.

34. Ibid.

35. Ibid.

36. Ibid., pp. 199–200.

37. Ibid.

38. Ibid.

39. Ibid., pp. 199–201.

40. CUOH-JW, p. 723.

41. CUOH-JW, p. 722–23.

42. MMW Ma XIV, p. 504.

43. MMW. Box 513 "Dutch International Corporation," letter from Hans Fürstenberg to Siegmund Warburg, June 19, 1934.

44. Hans Fürstenberg, *Mein Weg als Bankier*, p. 162.

45. FW. B194 F7, letter from Max Warburg, October 9, 1933.

46. MMW. Box 513, "Dutch International Corporation," letter from Max to Siegmund Warburg, August 26, 1933.

47. MMW Ma XIV, p. 560.

48. *Institutional Investor*, March 1980.

49. *The New Yorker*, April 9, 1966.

50. Raymond Bonham Carter, interview with author.

51. Arthur Winspear, interview with author.

52. MMW. Box 513, "Dutch International Corporation," letter from Max Warburg to Hans Fürstenberg, February 16, 1935.

53. MMW. Box 513, "Dutch International Corporation," letter from Ernst Spiegelberg to Max Warburg, August 21, 1934.

54. Ibid.

55. Raymond Bonham Carter, interview with author.

56. Ibid.
57. LBI-SGW-SZ. Letter from Stefan Zweig to Siegmund G. Warburg, December 14, 1934.
58. LBI-SGW-SZ. Letter from Siegmund G. Warburg to Stefan Zweig, July 20, 1935.
59. LBI-SGW-SZ. Letter from Siegmund G. Warburg to Stefan Zweig, September 1, 1937.

CHAPTER 29

1. Frieda Schiff Warburg, *Reminiscences*, p. 32.
2. Lucie Kaye, interview with author.
3. Benita Cioppa, letter to author, February 28, 1992.
4. Lucie Kaye, interview with author.
5. Esther Shalmon, interview with author.
6. Benita Cioppa, letter to author, February 28, 1992.
7. Weizmann, *Letters and Papers*, Vol. XVI, pp. 276–77. Letter to Lola Hahn-Warburg, April 22, 1934.
8. Ibid., letter to Lola Hahn-Warburg, January 20, 1935.
9. Ibid., letter to Lola Hahn-Warburg, April 22, 1934.
10. Interview with close friend of Lola Hahn-Warburg.
11. Gisela Wyzanski, interview with author.
12. *New York Herald Tribune*, May 1, 1942.
13. Gisela Wyzanski, interview with author.
14. Ibid.
15. Ibid.
16. FW. B294 F16, letter from Dr. Walter Derenberg, August 20, 1933.
17. Esther Shalmon, interview with author.
18. Ibid.
19. Spinelli, *Erinnerungen*, p. 42.
20. Ueckert-Hilbert, *Fremd in der Eigenen Stadt*, p. 109.
21. Ibid., p. 110.
22. Ibid., p. 109.
23. Spinelli, *Erinnerungen*, p. 114.
24. MacDonogh, *A Good German*, p. 61.
25. Ueckert-Hilbert, *Fremd in der Eigenen Stadt*, p. 110.
26. Ibid.
27. Ibid., p. 112.
28. Ibid.

CHAPTER 30

1. *Der Stürmer*, September 1934.
2. MMW Ma VI.
3. FW. B297 F3, letter to Paul Baerwald, October 27, 1934.

4. FW. B307, letter to *The Daily Worker*, December 11, 1935.
5. *Freiheit*, October 9, 1935.
6. FW. B307 F10, letter to Samuel Untermyer, June 4, 1935.
7. Anita Warburg, interview with author.
8. FW. B315 F1, letter from Dr. Bernhard Kahn, May 11, 1935.
9. Koonz, "Courage and Choice," p. 286.
10. FW. B328 F5, letter from Rabbi Morris S. Lazaron, May 13, 1935.
11. Ueckert-Hilbert, *Fremd in der Eigenen Stadt*, p. 111.
12. Felix Mitchell, interview with author.
13. Ibid.
14. MMW Ma XIV, p. 492.
15. Barkai, *From Boycott to Annihilation*, pp. 76–77.
16. Schacht, *Confessions of "The Old Wizard,"* p. 293.
17. FW. B315 F2, cable from Dr. Bernhard Kahn to Paul Baerwald, March 30, 1935.
18. Dodd, *Ambassador Dodd's Diary*, p. 218.
19. *Hamburger Abendblatt*, September 28, 1989.
20. MMW Ma XIV, p. 492.
21. MMW Ma XIV, p. 506 and MW 55. Memo by Hans Meyer of Max Warburg meeting with Hjalmar Schacht, September 18, 1935.
22. MMW. MW 55. "Auf zum Kampf zum wahren Frieden!" by Max Warburg.
23. FW. B315 F4, letter from James G. McDonald, November 7, 1935.
24. Weizmann, *Letters and Papers*, Vol. XVII, letter to Israel M. Sieff, December 25, 1935.
25. Ibid., p. 121.
26. Ibid., pp. 87–88. Letter to Simon Marks, December 15, 1935.
27. Bauer, *My Brother's Keeper*, p. 154.
28. *The New York Times*, January 6, 1936.
29. Ibid.
30. Shepherd, *Wilfrid Israel*, p. 111.
31. FW. B326 F8, letter to Dr. Bernhard Kahn, March 5, 1936.
32. Dodd, *Ambassador Dodd's Diary*, p. 280.
33. Kopper, "Nationalsozialistische Bankenpolitik," p. 103.
34. FW. B326 F9, letter from Bernhard Kahn, March 25, 1936.
35. FW. B326 F9, letter from Bernhard Kahn to Sir Osmond d'Avigdor Goldsmid, March 16, 1936.
36. FW. B326 F9, letter from Bernhard Kahn, March 26, 1936.
37. FW. Box 332 F10, cable to Siegmund Warburg, March 18, 1936. Letter from Siegmund Warburg, May 26, 1936.
38. FW. B318 F13, letter to Hans Fürstenberg, June 1, 1936.
39. BW. "Kara Corporation" Folder.
40. Glick, "Some Were Rescued," p. 7.
41. Ibid.
42. Kopper, "Nationalsozialistische Bankenpolitik," pp. 98–99.
43. *AJR Information*, June 1977. Hans Liebeschütz, "The Warburg Banking House."

44. Ueckert-Hilbert, *Fremd in der Eigenen Stadt*, p. 46.
45. MMW. MW 57. "Hilfsverein Speech, April 1936."
46. Hochmuth and Meyer, *Streiflichter aus dem Hamburger Widerstand*, p. 208.
47. FW. B326 F3, letter to Sidney E. Pritz, June 15, 1936.
48. *American Jewish World*, November 1936.
49. FW. B332 F10, letter from Siegmund Warburg, July 23, 1936.
50. FW. B332 F10, letter from Siegmund Warburg, March 1, 1936.
51. Kopper, "Nationalsozialistische Bankenpolitik," p. 99.
52. MMW. Ma XIV, p. 514–515.
53. Max Warburg, interview with author.

CHAPTER 31

1. Frieda Schiff Warburg, *Reminiscences*, p. 100.
2. *Der Stürmer*, March 1937.
3. FW. B336 F13. "Address at Briarcliff Lodge," September 25, 1937.
4. FW. B328 F5, letter from Governor Herbert H. Lehman to Franklin D. Roosevelt, November 1, 1935.
5. Johnson, *History of the Jews*, p. 460.
6. Voss, *Servant of the People*, p. 208.
7. Waldman, *Nor by Power*, p. 327.
8. Raymond Teichman of FDR Library, letter to author, August 25, 1992. The library cannot categorically rule out the possibility that such a letter exists somewhere in its collections.
9. Weizmann, *Letters and Papers*, Vol. XVII, p. 158.
10. Shepherd, *Wilfrid Israel*, p. 109.
11. FW. B341 F2, memo to Dr. Cyrus Adler, January 28, 1937.
12. FW. B318 F7, letter to Chaim Weizmann, October 10, 1935.
13. Weizmann, *Trial and Error*, Vol. II, pp. 381–82.
14. FW. B332 F11, letter to Chaim Weizmann, August 18, 1936.
15. FW. B332 F11, letter from Chaim Weizmann, January 24, 1936.
16. FW. B328 F17, letter to Simon Marks, August 26, 1936.
17. FW. B321 F3, letter to Sir Herbert Samuel, June 1, 1936.
18. Weizmann, *Letters and Papers*, Vol. XVII, p. 14.
19. LBI-AP. Box 2, letter from Max Warburg, May 26, 1937.
20. FW. B341 F2, memo for Dr. Cyrus Adler, January 28, 1937.
21. *The Jewish Forum*, June 1938.
22. Weizmann, *Letters and Papers*, Vol. XVIII, pp. 48–49. Letter to Lola Hahn-Warburg, March 4, 1937.
23. Ibid., p. 66, letter to Lola Hahn-Warburg, March 20, 1937.
24. FW. B341 F5, memo of March 24, 1937 meeting.
25. *The Jewish Forum*, June 1938.
26. FW. B341 F5, memo of March 24, 1937 meeting.
27. FW. Box 341 F4, letter to Max Warburg, July 16, 1937.

28. FW. B343 F8, letter to Dr. Morris Lazaron, July 28, 1937.
29. *Congress Journal*, Official Organ of the Twentieth Zionist Congress, Zurich, August 18, 1937.
30. Goren, *Dissenter in Zion*, p. 331.
31. FW. "Farrer Book Criticisms." Warburg Family Box 1163. Letter from Maurice B. Hexter to Edward M.M. Warburg, December 10, 1974.
32. Hexter, *Life Size*, p. 112.
33. Teveth, *Ben-Gurion*, pp. 624–25.
34. FW. B340 F3, letter to Maurice Hexter, September 28, 1937.
35. Teveth, *Ben-Gurion*, p. 619.
36. Shepherd, *Wilfrid Israel*, p. 109.
37. FW. B336 F13. "Address at Briarcliff Lodge," September 25, 1937.
38. Edward M.M. Warburg, interview with author.
39. Ibid.
40. Ibid.
41. Ibid.
42. MMW. 1937 Annual Report.
43. *The New York Times*, October 21, 1937.
44. Warburg, *As I Recall*, p. 67.
45. Mary Warburg, interview with author.
46. BW. "For Mary and Edward Warburg on their Marriage—December 6, 1939."
47. Weizmann, *Letters and Papers*, Vol. XVIII, p. 354.
48. Phyllis Farley, interview with author.
49. ML. B8 F29, letter from Frieda Warburg, March 14, 1938.

CHAPTER 32

1. MMW Ma XIV, p. 516.
2. Warburg, "Begrüssungsworte zur Einweihung," p. 1.
3. Ibid., p. 6.
4. MMW. "Gespräch Beim Mittagessen am 20 November 1982," p. 36.
5. FW. B343 F5, minutes of April 29, 1937, meeting of Joint Distribution Committee.
6. MMW Ma XIV, p. 518.
7. Warburg, *Aus Meinen Aufzeichnungen*, p. 154.
8. Farrer, *The Warburgs*, p. 117.
9. MMW. 1937 Annual Report.
10. Ogger, *Friedrich Flick*, p. 173.
11. Ibid., p. 165.
12. Ibid.
13. Ibid.
14. Genschel, *Die Verdrängung der Juden*, p. 226.
15. Ogger, *Friedrich Flick*, pp. 171–72.
16. Ibid., p. 172.

17. Trials of War Criminals, "The Flick Case," p. 46.
18. Anita Warburg, interview with author.
19. Lucie Kaye, interview with author.
20. Ogger, *Friedrich Flick*, pp. 171–72.
21. Kopper, "Nationalsozialistische Bankenpolitik," p. 122.
22. MMW Ma XIV, p. 518.
23. LBI-HS. Box 5, letter from Siegmund Warburg, January 27, 1938.
24. Kopper, "Nationalsozialistische Bankenpolitik," p. 123.
25. Ibid., p. 125.
26. Duckesz, *Geschichte des Geschlechts Warburg*, p. 154.
27. JW. Box 2, "M.M. Warburg & Co. 8/20/31–8/21/31."
28. MMW. MW 57, letter from Deutsche Effecten und Wechsel Bank—May 3, 1938.
29. Gisela Wyzanski, interview with author.
30. Rosenbaum and Sherman, *M.M. Warburg & Co.*, p. 168.
31. JW. Box 2, "M.M. Warburg & Co. 8/20/31–8/21/31." Speech of Dr. Rudolf Brinckmann, May 30, 1938.
32. Ibid. Speech of Max Warburg, May 30, 1938.
33. *The Times* of London, June 1, 1938.
34. MMW Ma XXVII. Tagebuch, Bertha Ehrenberg, July 15, 1938.

CHAPTER 33

1. MMW Ma VI, letter from Edward M.M. Warburg to Max Warburg, June 21, 1938.
2. Warburg, *Zeiten und Gezeiten*, p. 46.
3. Warburg, *Aus Meinen Aufzeichnungen*, p. 152.
4. LBI-HS. Box 19, Dr. Fritz Warburg, "Reminiscences of Max Warburg," 1947.
5. Gisela Wyzanski, interview with author.
6. *Der Stürmer*, September 1938.
7. Gisela Wyzanski, interview with author.
8. Frieda Schiff Warburg, *Reminiscences*, p. 31.
9. Warburg, *Zeiten und Gezeiten*, p. 130.
10. Gisela Wyzanski, interview with author.
11. FW. Warburg Family Box 1163. "A Copy of the Warburgs by David Farrer, with corrections." Memo by Dr. Wegener, 1975.
12. Spinelli, *Erinnerungen*, p. 153.
13. Ibid., p. 356.
14. Gisela Wyzanski, interview with author.
15. Turner, *And the Policeman Smiled*, pp. 230–31.
16. Ibid., p. 232.
17. CUOH-GR, p. 284.
18. Shepherd, *Wilfrid Israel*, p. 137.
19. Peterson, *Hjalmar Schacht*, pp. 248–49.
20. Schacht, *Confessions of "The Old Wizard,"* p. 351.

21. Sherman, *Island Refuge*, p. 200.
22. LBI-JS. Siegmund G. Warburg Correspondence 1938–1949. Letter from Siegmund G. Warburg, November 18, 1939.
23. Ibid. Letter from Siegmund G. Warburg, February 9, 1939.
24. Alexandra Danilova, interview with author.
25. Ibid.
26. Ibid.
27. Ibid.
28. Ibid.
29. Ruth Fleck, interview with author.
30. Wechsberg, *Merchant Bankers*, p. 180.
31. LBI-HS. Box 5. Private Correspondence. Letter from Siegmund G. Warburg, March 23, 1938.
32. LBI-HS. Siegmund G. Warburg Correspondence 1938–1949. Letter from Siegmund G. Warburg, November 22, 1938.
33. Ibid., letter from Siegmund G. Warburg, November 18, 1938.
34. Ibid.
35. Ibid., letter from Siegmund G. Warburg, December 12, 1938.
36. Bullock, *Hitler*, p. 490.
37. Shepherd, *Wilfrid Israel*, p. 161.
38. LBI-HS. Siegmund G. Warburg Correspondence 1938–1949. Letter from Siegmund G. Warburg, April 3, 1939.
39. Ibid., letter from Siegmund G. Warburg, July 20, 1939.
40. LBI-SGW-SZ, letter from Siegmund Warburg to Stefan Zweig, September 21, 1939.
41. Ibid., letter from Siegmund Warburg to Stefan Zweig, November 24, 1939.
42. Fabian von Schlabrendorff, *Begegnungen in fünf Jahrzenten*, p. 330.

CHAPTER 34

1. Warburg, *Zeiten und Gezeiten*, p. 157.
2. Warburg, *The Long Road Home*, p. 175.
3. Ibid., pp. 179–80.
4. Ibid., p. 183.
5. Ibid.
6. *The New York Times*, January 29, 1941.
7. *New York Herald Tribune*, April 25, 1941.
8. JW. Box 16, "Harry G. Green 5/41," letter to Senator Bennett C. Clark, May 8, 1941.
9. JW. Box 16, "Harry G. Green 5/41," letter from James Warburg to Senator Bennett C. Clark, May 8, 1941.
10. JVF, Box 55, letter from James Warburg, May 29, 1941.
11. JW. Box 16, "Harry G. Green 5/41," unsigned letter addressed to "Jew Warburg, New York, N.Y."

12. JW. Box 16, "Harry G. Green 5/41," undated letter from "An American Mother," May 26, 1941.
13. Spinelli, *Erinnerungen*, p. 125.
14. Ibid., p. 150.
15. Ibid., p. 129.
16. Ibid.
17. Ibid., p. 137.
18. Phyllis Farley, interview with author.
19. Spinelli, *Erinnerungen*, p. 282.
20. Ibid., p. 117.
21. Ibid., p. 116.
22. Ibid., p. 432.
23. Ibid., p. 202.
24. Ibid., p. 219.
25. Ibid., p. 220.
26. Ibid.
27. Ibid.

CHAPTER 35

1. MMW. EX. Letter from Siegmund Warburg to Rudolf Brinckmann, August 1963. (No precise date.)
2. Kopper, "Nationalsozialistische Bankenpolitik," p. 127.
3. MMW. "Gespräch beim Mittagessen am 10 November 1982," p. 40.
4. Ibid., pp. 14–15.
5. Ibid. Fraulein Martha Beyer testimony.
6. Ibid. Herr Brauer testimony.
7. MMW. Box 512. "Adolf van Biema, Berlin."
8. Kopper, "Nationalsozialistische Bankenpolitik," p. 128.
9. MMW. Robert Solmitz, "Das Sekretariat Warburg."
10. Ibid.
11. Ibid., pp. 7–8.
12. Wenzel, *Broken Star*, p. 97.
13. Ibid., p. 98.
14. Kopper, "Nationalsozialistische Bankenpolitik," p. 126.
15. MMW. Kara Corp. 1938 "Agreement between Kara Corp. and the European Warburgs."
16. MMW. Kara Corp. 1938–1946. Letter from Liebmann to Dr. E. Spiegelberg and Hans Meyer, December 6, 1938.
17. MMW. Affidavit of Ernst Spiegelberg, March 2, 1955.
18. MMW. "Gespräch beim Mittagessen am 10 November, 1982," p. 6.
19. Felix Mitchell, interview with author.
20. Bauer, *American Jewry and the Holocaust*, p. 275.
21. Peter Fleck, interview with author.

22. MAW. Letter from Josi Warburg, July 22, 1945.

23. Ibid.

24. Maria Christina Warburg (Mills), interview with author.

25. MAW. *The Eerde Herald.* Vol. VIII No. 2.

26. Maria Christina Warburg (Mills), interview with author.

27. MAW. Letter from Josi Warburg, July 22, 1945.

28. Maria Christina Warburg (Mills), interview with author.

29. MAW. Application filled out on February 4, 1956.

CHAPTER 36

1. *New York World Telegram,* February 19, 1941.

2. MMW Ma VI, letter from Max to Edward M.M. Warburg, July 13, 1939.

3. ML. Box 8F31, letter from Max Warburg, August 31, 1942.

4. Warburg, *As I Recall,* p. 70.

5. Edward M.M. Warburg, interview with author.

6. Warburg, *Aus Meinen Aufzeichnungen,* p. x.

7. Letter from Max to Anita Warburg, November 30, 1941. (Courtesy of Anita Warburg.)

8. MMW. Kara Corp, 1938–1946.

9. MMW Ma VI, letter from Hans J. Meyer to Gisela Wyzanski, April 6, 1945.

10. Warburg, *Aus Meinen Aufzeichnungen,* p. 146.

11. MMW Ma VI, letter from Jimmy to Max Warburg, April 3, 1945.

12. MMW MW 57 "Conclusions." Undated memo.

13. TWL. B136 F12, memo from Max Warburg, April, 3, 1942.

14. ML. B8 F31, letter from Max Warburg to Sol M. Stroock, June 28, 1942.

15. MMW. MW 57 "Conclusions."

16. Andrea Kaufman, interview with author.

17. Lucie Kaye, interview with author.

18. MMW. Fritz Akten. Paket 3. SGW Folder, letter from Siegmund to Fritz Warburg, December 27, 1947.

19. MMW. Fritz M. Warburg Akten. Paket 3. SGW Folder, letter from Siegmund to Fritz Warburg, June 7, 1947.

20. Spinelli, *Erinnerungen,* p. 121.

21. Ibid., p. 117.

22. Soley, *Radio Warfare,* p. 101.

23. Videotape of Eric Warburg interview. (Courtesy of Marie Warburg.)

24. Raymond Bonham Carter, interview with author.

25. MMW. EV, letter from Eric to Alice Warburg, September 7, 1942.

26. Warburg, *Zeiten und Gezeiten,* p. 166.

27. *Die Welt,* January 23, 1988.

28. Warburg, *Zeiten und Gezeiten,* p. 186.

29. Ibid., p. 188.

30. Videotape of Eric Warburg Interview. (Courtesy of Marie Warburg.)

31. Warburg, *Zeiten und Gezeiten*, p. 190.
32. Ibid., p. 158.
33. Ibid., p. 203.
34. Gordon, *Fritz Saxl*, p. 36.
35. Farrer, *The Warburgs*, p. 189.
36. MMW. Eric Warburg memoir extracts. "Air Force P/W Interrogation."
37. MMW. EW VIII, p. 1.
38. MMW. Eric Warburg memoir extracts. June 1, 1945. Hermann Göring report.
39. Warburg, *Zeiten und Gezeiten*, p. 240.
40. Ibid., p. 227.
41. MMW. Eric Warburg memoir extracts. June 1, 1945. Hermann Göring report.
42. Warburg, *Zeiten und Gezeiten*, p. 232.
43. Ibid.
44. Ibid.
45. MMW. Eric Warburg memoir extracts. June 1, 1945. Hermann Göring report.
46. Warburg, *Zeiten und Gezeiten*, p. 233.
47. MMW. EV, 1, letter from Eric to Freddy Warburg, May 31, 1945.

CHAPTER 37

1. MMW. EV, 1, letter from Eric Warburg to his parents, October 18, 1944.
2. MMW. Ibid.
3. MMW. EV, 1, letter from Eric to Bettina and Nina Warburg, June 13, 1945.
4. Warburg, *Zeiten und Gezeiten*, p. 244.
5. MMW. EV, 1, letter from Eric to Bettina and Nina Warburg, June 13, 1945.
6. Gisela Wyzanski, interview with author.
7. MMW. "Gespräch beim Mittagessen am 10 November 1982," pp. 26, 30. Herr Sellin statement.
8. MMW. Ibid., p. 22. Brauer statement.
9. MMW. Fritz Akten. Paket 3. SGW Folder, letter from Siegmund G. Warburg to Hans Meyer, January 24, 1948.
10. Warburg, *Zeiten und Gezeiten*, p. 245. Also MMW "Gespräch beim Mittagessen am 10 November 1982," p. 17.
11. MMW. "Gespräch beim Mittagessen am 10 November 1982," p. 18.
12. Warburg, *Zeiten und Gezeiten*, pp. 301–2.
13. MMW. EX, letter from Ernst Spiegelberg to Dorothea Warburg, November 15, 1960.
14. Warburg, *Aus Meinen Aufzeichnungen*, p. 157.
15. MMW. EV, letter from Eric to Max Warburg, June 21, 1945.
16. Warburg, *Zeiten und Gezeiten*, p. 207.
17. MMW. EV, letter from Eric to Alice Warburg, July 2, 1945.
18. MMW. EV, letter from Eric Warburg to his parents, July 23, 1945.
19. MMW. EV, letter from Eric to Freddy Warburg, June 2, 1945.
20. MMW. EV, 1, letter from Eric to Nina Warburg, September 16, 1945.
21. MMW. EV, letter from Eric Warburg to his parents, May 2, 1945.

22. MMW. EV.
23. Gay, *Jews of Germany*, p. 257.
24. Warburg, *Zeiten und Gezeiten*, p. 218.
25. MMW. EV, undated 1945 letter from Eric Warburg to his parents.
26. MMW. EV, 1, undated Eric Warburg memo, summer 1945.
27. Warburg, *Zeiten und Gezeiten*, p. 215.
28. Ibid., p. 147.
29. Ibid., p. 143.
30. Krebs, *Otto Warburg*, p. 59.
31. Farrer, *The Warburgs*, p. 152.
32. Warburg, *Zeiten und Gezeiten*, p. 145.
33. Ibid.
34. Farrer, *The Warburgs*, p. 152.
35. Videotape of Eric Warburg interview. (Courtesy of Marie Warburg.)
36. MMW. EV, 1, letter from Eric to Bettina and Nina Warburg, June 13, 1945.
37. George Schwab, interview with author.

CHAPTER 38

1. LBI-SGW-SZ. Letter from Siegmund G. Warburg to Stefan Zweig, May 14, 1941.
2. LBI-HS. Siegmund G. Warburg Correspondence, 1938–1949. Letter from Siegmund G. Warburg, September 11, 1944.
3. Ibid., letter from Siegmund G. Warburg, September, 11, 1944.
4. LBI-SGW-SZ. Letter from Siegmund G. Warburg to Stefan Zweig, July 3, 1941.
5. *The New Yorker*, April 9, 1966.
6. Henry Grunfeld, speech of June 1984.
7. Ibid.
8. Edgar Koerner, interview with author.
9. Andrew Smithers, interview with author.
10. Peter Spira, Robin Jessel, interviews with author.
11. Anthony Korner, interview with author.
12. Margaret Anderson, interview with author.
13. Raymond Bonham Carter, interview with author.
14. Ibid.
15. Margaret Anderson, interview with author.
16. LBI-HS. Siegmund G. Warburg Correspondence, 1938–1949. Letter from Siegmund G. Warburg, September 11, 1944.
17. Ibid.
18. Margaret Anderson, interview with author.
19. Warburg, *An Occupation for Gentlemen*, p. 241.
20. *Business Week*, March 14, 1977.
21. Alice Speyer, interview with author.
22. Ibid.
23. Alice Auerbach, interview with author.

24. Ibid.
25. Madeleine Marx, interview with author.
26. MMW. EV, letter from Eric to Max Warburg, April 18, 1943.
27. Farrer, *The Warburgs*, p. 225.
28. A former colleague of Paul Kohn-Speyer, interview with author.
29. Bettina Warburg, interview with author.
30. MMW. Fritz M. Warburg Akten. Paket 3. Letter from Fritz Warburg to Ernst Spiegelberg, May 6, 1952.
31. MMW. Fritz Akten. Paket 3. SGW Folder. Letter from Ernst Spiegelberg to Fritz Warburg, June 2, 1952.
32. Dorothea Warburg, interview with author.
33. MMW. EV, letter from Eric Warburg to his parents, December 13, 1943.
34. LBI-HS. Box 11. Private Correspondence. Letter from Dr. Fritz Warburg, September 20, 1944.
35. MMW. EV, letter from Eric to Max Warburg, September 30, 1944.
36. Ruth Fleck, interview with author.
37. *Institutional Investor*, March 1980.
38. MMW. EV, letter from Eric Warburg to Max Warburg, September 4, 1945. Fritz Akten. Paket 3. SGW Folder. Letter from Fritz to Siegmund G. Warburg, September 25, 1947. Also Ernst Spiegelberg Folder. Letter from Fritz Warburg to Ernst Spiegelberg, February 23, 1955.
39. Warburg, *Zeiten und Gezeiten*, p. 258.
40. MMW. Ka IV, letter from Siegmund to Charles Warburg, November 19, 1945.
41. MMW. Ka IV, letter from Siegmund to Charles Warburg, January 14, 1946.
42. *Institutional Investor*, March 1980.
43. *The Times* of London, January 29, 1946.
44. *Institutional Investor*, March 1980.
45. MMW. EV, letter from Max to Eric Warburg, January 30, 1945.
46. MMW. Ab MI, letter from Max Warburg to Professor Saxl, December 11, 1944.
47. MMW. Fritz M. Warburg Akten. Paket 3. Letter from Fritz Warburg to Ernst Spiegelberg, January 22, 1947.

CHAPTER 39

1. Farrer, *The Warburgs*, p. 186.
2. Dorothea Warburg, interview with author.
3. Ibid.
4. Ibid.
5. MMW. EX, letter from Kurt Hahn to Rudolf Brinckmann. September, 19, 1956.
6. MMW. Fritz M. Warburg Akten. Paket 3. "Siegmund G. Warburg Folder." Letter from Siegmund to Fritz Warburg, June 7, 1947.
7. Ibid., letter from Eric Warburg to Department of State, March 8, 1949.
8. Ibid., letter from Siegmund to Eric Warburg, March 29, 1947.
9. Ibid.

10. MMW. EX, letter from Ernst Spiegelberg to Dorothea Warburg, November 15, 1960.
11. MMW. Fritz M. Warburg Akten. Paket 3. "Ernst Spiegelberg" folder. Letter from Ernst Spiegelberg to Fritz Warburg, October 26, 1947.
12. MMW. Fritz M. Warburg Akten. Paket 3. "Ernst Spiegelberg" folder. Letter from Ernst Spiegelberg to Fritz Warburg, May 17, 1950.
13. AD. Box 27, letter from Eric Warburg, October 3, 1946.
14. MMW. "Gespräch beim Mittagessen am 10 November 1982," p. 44.
15. MMW. Fritz M. Warburg Akten. Paket 3. Letter from Fritz to Siegmund G. Warburg, January 6, 1948.
16. Ibid., letter from Siegmund G. Warburg to Hans Meyer, January 24, 1948.
17. MMW. Fritz Warburg Akten. Paket 4. Agreement between Eric Warburg and Brinckmann, Wirtz & Co., August 18, 1949.
18. MMW. "Gespräch beim Mittagessen am 10 November 1982," p. 29.
19. Warburg, *Zeiten und Gezeiten*, p. 269.
20. MMW. Fritz M. Warburg Akten. Paket 3. "Ernst Spiegelberg" folder. Memo by Ernst Spiegelberg, July 13, 1949. Letter from Ernst Spiegelberg to Fritz Warburg, August 20, 1949.
21. Charles Sharp, letter to the author, November 24, 1992.
22. *Institutional Investor*, March 1980.
23. Wechsberg, *Merchant Bankers*, p. 191.
24. LBI-HS. Siegmund G. Warburg Correspondence, 1938–1949, letter from Siegmund G. Warburg, October 1, 1949.
25. Dr. Carl H. Goldman, interview with author.
26. MMW. Fritz Warburg Akten. Paket 3, letter from Siegmund Warburg to Fritz Warburg, December 12, 1949.
27. Ibid.
28. Anita Warburg, interview with author.
29. Koelbl, *Jüdische Portraits*, p. 276.
30. Gisela Wyzanski, interview with author.
31. AD. Box 42. Undated 1949 memo by Eric Warburg.
32. Bird, *The Chairman*, p. 285.
33. Ibid., p. 315.
34. Warburg, *Zeiten und Gezeiten*, p. 265.
35. MMW. EV, 1, letter from Eric Warburg to John J. McCloy, August 27, 1949.
36. Marion Dönhoff, interview with author.
37. Johnson, *History of the Jews*, p. 513.
38. MMW. EW Ma-Mc, letter from Eric Warburg to John J. McCloy, March 1, 1985.

CHAPTER 40

1. JW. Box 32, Joseph Barnes 1953–68, letter to Joseph Barnes, September, 11, 1956.
2. JW. Box 21, Stevenson folder 1947–52, letter to Adlai Stevenson, March 17, 1952.

3. JW. Box 21, Stevenson September 1960–May 1965, letter from Adlai Stevenson to Dr. Jerome Davis, October 30, 1962.

4. BW.

5. Warburg, *The Long Road Home*, p. 227.

6. Ibid.

7. Warburg, *Germany: Key to Peace*, p. 9.

8. Warburg, *Germany—Bridge or Battleground?*, p. 177.

9. Warburg, *Germany: Key to Peace*, p. 173.

10. JW. Box 15, Dwight D. Eisenhower 1948–March 1953, undated letter to Milton E. Eisenhower.

11. MMW. Fritz Akten. Paket 3. "Siegmund G. Warburg Folder." Letter from Siegmund to Eric Warburg, July 16, 1952.

12. MMW. Fritz Akten. Paket 4, letter from Franz Schütte to Rudolf Brinckmann, November 24, 1952.

13. Ibid., letter from Eric Warburg to Rudolf Brinckmann, December 1, 1952.

14. Ibid.

15. Ibid.

16. Ibid.

17. MMW. Fritz Akten. Paket 4, letter from Eric to Fritz Warburg, November 21, 1952.

18. Ibid., memo of Rudolf Brinckmann, November 16, 1952.

19. Ibid.

20. Ibid., letter from Fritz Warburg to Hermann Schilling, November 12, 1952.

21. Ibid., memo of Rudolf Brinckmann, November 16, 1952.

22. Ibid.

23. Ibid.

24. Ibid., letter from Eric to Fritz Warburg, February 9, 1953.

25. MMW. Fritz M. Warburg Akten. Paket 3. "Ernst Spiegelberg Folder." Letter from Ernst Spiegelberg to Fritz Warburg, January 8, 1953.

26. Ibid., letter from Ernst Spiegelberg to Fritz Warburg, April 29, 1953.

27. *Time*, April 29, 1966.

28. MMW. Fritz Warburg Akten. Paket 4, letter from Siegmund to Fritz Warburg, November 24, 1952.

29. Ibid., letter from Eric Warburg to Rudolf Brinckmann, November 21, 1952.

30. Ibid., letter from Hans Meyer to Fritz Warburg, May 26, 1953.

31. MMW. Fritz Warburg Akten. Paket 3. "Siegmund G. Warburg Folder," letter from Siegmund to Fritz Warburg, June 24, 1953.

32. MMW. EX, letter from Siegmund to Eric Warburg, July 8, 1953.

33. Ibid., letter from Siegmund to Eric Warburg, February 6, 1954.

34. Ibid.

35. Ibid., letter from Siegmund to Eric Warburg, June 11, 1957.

36. MMW. Ernst Spiegelberg Files, letter from Ernst Spiegelberg to Siegmund G. Warburg, April 15, 1955.

37. MMW. EX, letter from Ernst Spiegelberg to Eric Warburg, December 1, 1960.

38. Hans-Dieter Sandweg, interview with author.
39. MMW. EX, letter from Eric to Siegmund Warburg, August 12, 1963.
40. Ibid., Siegmund Warburg memo of September 3, 1960.
41. Max Warburg interview.
42. MMW. EX, letter from Kurt Hahn to Eric Warburg, December 11, 1959.
43. Ibid., letter from Kurt Hahn to Eric Warburg, December 11, 1959.
44. Warburg, *Zeiten und Gezeiten*, p. 270.
45. *The New Yorker*, June 11, 1955.
46. MMW. EX, letter from Eric Warburg to Rudolf Brinckmann, December 21, 1956.
47. Marie Warburg, letter to the author, January 8, 1993.
48. Ibid.
49. Dr. Ursula Büttner, interview with author.
50. Richarz, "Juden in der Bundesrepublik Deutschland," pp. 21–22.
51. Dorothea Warburg, interview with author.
52. Ibid.
53. Bing, "Aby M. Warburg," p. 7.
54. *Jüdische Wochenzeitung*, July 19, 1990.
55. MMW. EV, letter from Eric to Max Warburg, January 27, 1943.
56. *Hamburger Abendblatt*, July 11, 1990.
57. YIVO-AJC. Alpha File, General 12, Box 190, letter from Zachariah Shuster to Dr. John Slawson, September 2, 1953.
58. *Das Freie Wort*, July 25, 1953.
59. BW. Eric Warburg File. July 15, 1949, statement of James P. Warburg.
60. *Die Welt*, August 2, 1956.
61. Warburg, *Germany: Key to Peace*, p. 242.
62. YIVO-AJC. Alpha File, General 12, Box 190, letter from Eric Warburg to Eugene Hevesi, June 6, 1957.
63. Ibid., letter from Eric Warburg to Eugene Hevesi, September 2, 1957.
64. MMW. Z II 7b letter from Eric Warburg to Henri Nannen about October 24, 1959, letter in *Stern*.

CHAPTER 41

1. Warburg, *As I Recall*, p. 71.
2. Frieda Schiff Warburg, *Reminiscences*, p. 185.
3. Felicia Warburg Rogan, interview with author.
4. Frieda Schiff Warburg, *Reminiscences*, p. 198.
5. Warburg, *Zeiten und Gezeiten*, p. 259.
6. MMW. Box 509. Warburg Family Akten. Eric Warburg reminiscence of Alice Warburg, July 6, 1957.
7. Ibid.
8. Warburg, *As I Recall*, p. 73.
9. Rothschild, *Sharing and Caring*, p. 37.
10. Weizmann, *Trial and Error*, Vol. II, pp. 456–67.

11. CUOH-JW, pp. 47–48.
12. Ibid., p. 48.
13. *Jewish Newsletter*, June 16, 1958.
14. Warburg, "Israel and the American Jewish Community," p. 7.
15. *The New York Times*, November 29, 1959.
16. FW. B336 F13. "Address at Briarcliff Lodge," September 25, 1937.
17. *Jewish Newsletter*, January 25, 1960.
18. Warburg, "Israel and the American Jewish Community," p. 9.
19. Marie Warburg, interview with author.
20. MMW. Fritz M. Warburg Akten. Paket 3, letter from Fritz Warburg to Hermann Bruck, August 24, 1942.
21. Ibid., letter from Ernest Minden to Ingrid Warburg Spinelli, August 19, 1952.
22. MMW. Box 509. Warburg Family Akten, letter from Eric to Frederick Warburg, December 15, 1961.

CHAPTER 42

1. MMW. Fritz M. Warburg Akten. Paket 3. Siegmund G. Warburg Folder. Letter from Siegmund to Fritz Warburg, June 7, 1947.
2. Ibid., letter from Siegmund to Fritz Warburg, February 21, 1951.
3. JRD. Letter from Siegmund Warburg, September 1, 1955.
4. MMW. Fritz Akten. Paket 3. Siegmund G. Warburg Folder, letter from Siegmund to Fritz Warburg, January 12, 1950.
5. Ibid., letter from Siegmund to Fritz Warburg, June 24, 1953.
6. Margaret Anderson, interview with author.
7. *Institutional Investor*, March 1980.
8. *The Way It Was*, p. 502.
9. DS. Memo of Siegmund G. Warburg, November 1, 1954.
10. JRD. Siegmund G. Warburg, "Coordination Plan," November 30, 1953.
11. DS. Letter from Siegmund G. Warburg to John Schiff, December 9, 1954.
12. Ibid., memo by Siegmund G. Warburg, November 2, 1954.
13. Ibid., letter from Siegmund G. Warburg to John Schiff, December 9, 1954.
14. Alvin Friedman, interview with author.
15. Cited in *The Times* of London, September 21, 1992.
16. Charles Sharp, letter to the author, November 24, 1992.
17. MMW. Box 509. Warburg Family Akten, letter from Frederick to Eric Warburg, July 31, 1958.
18. WW. Series II. B19 F145. Letter to Siegmund G. Warburg, March 9, 1959.
19. David Schiff, interview with author.
20. Ibid.
21. Warburg, *As I Recall*, p. 8.
22. Wilma Warburg, interview with author.
23. Alvin Friedman, interview with author.
24. J. Richardson Dilworth, interview with author.

25. Anthony Griffin, interview with author.
26. David Schiff, interview with author.
27. MMW. EX, letter from Frederick M. Warburg to Eric Warburg, October 16, 1957.
28. Edward M.M. Warburg, interview with author.
29. MMW. EX, letters from Siegmund to Eric Warburg, October 16 and 28, 1963.
30. MMW. Karton 511. Eric Warburg correspondence, letter from Siegmund to Eric Warburg, February 9, 1958.
31. Ibid.
32. WW. Series III. B19 F138. Letter from Siegmund G. Warburg, May 17, 1957.
33. J. Richardson Dilworth, interview with author.
34. DS. Letter from Siegmund Warburg to John Schiff, April 20, 1958.
35. Ibid.
36. DS. Letter from William Wiseman to John Schiff, December 22, 1958.

CHAPTER 43

1. Warburg, "Lucie L. Warburg," p. 13.
2. Ibid., p. 19.
3. Elsbeth Oppenheimer, interview with author.
4. Stephen Lash, interview with author.
5. *Institutional Investor*, March 1980.
6. Dr. Carl Heinz Goldman, interview with author.
7. John Adams, interview with author.
8. LBI-HS. Siegmund G. Warburg Correspondence, 1938–1949. Letter from Siegmund G. Warburg, September 11, 1944.
9. Harry Green, interview with author.
10. Andrew Smithers, interview with author.
11. Nathaniel Samuels and Alvin Friedman, interviews with author.
12. Alvin Friedman, interview with author.
13. Eddy Lachman, letter to the author, November 15, 1992.
14. *Institutional Investor*, March 1980.
15. Ibid.
16. Ibid.
17. Gordon, "Siegmund Warburg," p. 3.
18. *Institutional Investor*, March 1980.
19. Wechsberg, *Merchant Bankers*, pp. 180–81.
20. Carey Reich, interview with author.
21. *Euromoney*, September 1987.
22. MMW. Fritz Akten. Paket 3. Siegmund G. Warburg Folder, letter from Siegmund to Fritz Warburg, January 18, 1950.
23. Robin Jessel, interview with author.
24. Stephen Lash, interview with author.
25. Anthony Griffin, interview with author.
26. Bernard Kelly, interview with author.

27. Burney, *Dungeon Democracy*, p. 109.
28. John Libby, interview with author.
29. Roll, *Crowded Hours*, p. 195.
30. *The New Yorker*, April 9, 1966.
31. *Sunday Telegraph*, January 25, 1970.
32. Wechsberg, *Merchant Bankers*, pp. 178–79.
33. Dr. Carl Heinz Goldman, interview with author.
34. MMW Ma XV.

CHAPTER 44

1. Peter Spira, interview with author.
2. Sir Ian Fraser, interview with author.
3. Robin Jessel, interview with author.
4. Eddy Lachman, letter to author, November 15, 1992.
5. *Time*, April 29, 1966.
6. Edgar Koerner, interview with author.
7. David Mitchell, interview with author.
8. Arthur Winspear, interview with author.
9. *Institutional Investor*, March 1980.
10. Peter Spira, interview with author.
11. Edgar Koerner, interview with author.
12. Richard Lutyens, interview with author.
13. *The Economist*, December 5, 1987.
14. James Wolfensohn, interview with author.
15. Alvin Friedman, interview with author.
16. Dr. Carl Heinz Goldman, interview with author.
17. WW. Series III. B19 F139. Letter to Siegmund G. Warburg, August 29, 1957.
18. Sir William Wiseman Papers. Series III. B19. F143. Note for Sir William Wiseman et al. from Siegmund G. Warburg, September 20, 1958; and letter from Siegmund Warburg to Sir William Wiseman, September 25, 1958.
19. Michael Verey, interview with author.
20. *Institutional Investor*, March 1980.
21. *International Management Digest*, March 19, 1959.
22. Joseph McConnell, interview with author.
23. WW. Series III. B17 F104. 1959 Kuhn, Loeb memo about the Aluminium battle.
24. *The Economist*, January 10, 1959.
25. *The New Statesman*, January 10, 1959.
26. Joseph McConnell, interview with author.
27. WW. Series III. B19 F145. Letter from Siegmund Warburg, January 17, 1959.
28. Ibid.
29. Cited in *Financial Times*, January 8, 1959.
30. Roll, "A Gathering of the members . . ." p. 10.
31. *Business Week*, January 17, 1959.

32. *News Chronicle*, January 19, 1959.
33. *Financial Times*, January 8, 1959.
34. Michael Verey, interview with author.
35. *Institutional Investor*, March 1980.
36. John Libby, interview with author.
37. Michael Verey, interview with author.
38. Ronald Utiger, interview with author.
39. *Institutional Investor*, March 1980.
40. *Sunday Telegraph*, January 25, 1970.

CHAPTER 45

1. Warburg, *Zeiten und Gezeiten*, pp. 200–201.
2. *The Gazette* (Montreal), January 19, 1980.
3. Bird, *The Chairman*, p. 480.
4. Ibid., p. 481. Also Ferencz, *Lohn des Grauens*, pp. 113–14.
5. Bird, *The Chairman*, p. 481.
6. Ferencz, *Lohn des Grauens*, p. 154.
7. Ibid., pp. 155–56.
8. Ibid., p. 156.
9. Ibid., p. 198.
10. Ibid., p. 199.
11. Johnson, *History of the Jews*, p. 515.
12. Ferencz, *Lohn des Grauens*, p. 200.
13. Ibid., p. 201.
14. Ibid., p. 204.
15. Ibid., p. 205.
16. Ibid., p. 210.
17. Ibid., p. 212.
18. MMW. EX, letter from Eric to Siegmund Warburg, September 7, 1961.
19. Alvin Friedman, interview with author.
20. David Mitchell, interview with author.
21. MMW. EX, letter from Siegmund to Eric Warburg, September 4, 1961.
22. Ibid., memo of conversation between Eric Warburg and Rudolf Brinckmann, June 20, 1960.
23. Ibid., letter from Eric Warburg to Rudolf Brinckmann, October 18, 1960.
24. Ibid., letter from Rudolf Brinckmann to Eric Warburg, November 3, 1960.
25. Ibid., memo by Eric Warburg of October 11, 1960, meeting with Rudolf Brinckmann.
26. Ibid., letter from Siegmund Warburg to Rudolf Brinckmann, March 21, 1960.
27. Ibid., letter from Siegmund to Eric Warburg, May 30, 1960.
28. Ibid., letter from Eric to Siegmund Warburg, October 19, 1960.
29. Ibid., memo by Siegmund Warburg, September 3, 1960.
30. Edgar Koerner, interview with author.

31. MMW. EX, letter from Siegmund to Eric Warburg, July 25, 1960.

32. Ibid., letter from Siegmund to Eric Warburg, January 5, 1961.

33. Ibid., sketch of a letter from Siegmund Warburg to Rudolf Brinckmann, December 14, 1964.

34. Ibid., letter from Siegmund to Eric Warburg, January 5, 1961.

35. Ibid., letter from Siegmund to Eric Warburg, March 29, 1961.

36. Ibid., memo of meeting of March 20, 1961.

37. Ibid., Hans Wuttke memo, November 26, 1963.

38. *Financial Times*, January 3, 1966.

39. MMW. EX, letter from Lola Hahn-Warburg to Eric Warburg, November 10, 1960.

40. Ibid., letter from Siegmund to Eric Warburg, October 7, 1961.

41. Ibid., memo by Eric Warburg, February 20, 1963.

42. Ibid., letter from Eric to Siegmund Warburg, July 9, 1963.

43. Ibid., third draft of letter from Siegmund Warburg to Rudolf Brinckmann and letter from Siegmund to Eric Warburg, July 4, 1963.

44. Ibid., third draft of a letter from Siegmund G. Warburg to Rudolf Brinckmann, August 4, 1963.

45. Ibid., letter from Eric to Siegmund Warburg, August 23, 1963.

46. Ibid., letter from Siegmund to Eric Warburg, November 30, 1964.

47. Ibid., "Aktennotiz" of November 23, 1964, meeting of Brinckmann, Wirtz & Co. partners.

48. Alvin Friedman, et al., interviews with author.

49. *Financial Times*, January 3, 1966.

50. *The Times* of London, January 7, 1970.

51. A. Joshua Sherman, interview with author.

52. MMW. M.M. Warburg press release of December 20, 1972.

53. "In Memoriam Rudolf Brinckmann."

CHAPTER 46

1. WW. Series III. B18 F107, letter from John Schiff, January 13, 1959.

2. DS. Letter from Siegmund G. Warburg to John Schiff, December 11, 1959.

3. DS. Memo from Siegmund G. Warburg, June 4, 1962.

4. Nathaniel Samuels, interview with author.

5. *Financial Times*, December 12, 1992.

6. MMW. EX, letter from Frederick to Eric Warburg, December 3, 1964.

7. David Mitchell, interview with author.

8. Carl Hess, interview with author.

9. John Adams, interview with author.

10. Ibid.

11. Carl Hess, interview with author.

12. Ibid.

13. *Institutional Investor*, March 1980.

14. *The Way It Was*, p. 496.
15. Welsh, *Uneasy City*, p. 44.
16. Raymond Bonham Carter, interview with author.
17. *Institutional Investor*, March 1980.
18. Peter Spira, interview with author.
19. John Adams, interview with author.
20. Alvin Friedman, interview with author.
21. Gretchen Whitman, interview with author.
22. Raymond Bonham Carter, interview with author.
23. Gretchen Whitman, interview with author.
24. *The Times* of London, October 1970.
25. Nathaniel Samuels, interview with author.
26. Peter Spira, interview with author.
27. Anthony Korner, interview with author.
28. David Mitchell, interview with author.
29. *The Times* of London, January 1, 1970.
30. *The Statist*, July 17, 1964.
31. MMW Ka IV, letter from Siegmund to Karl Warburg, August 25, 1930.
32. *The Times* of London, November 21, 1964.
33. *The Sunday Times* of London, October 2, 1966.
34. *Sunday Telegraph*, November 18, 1973.
35. John Adams, interview with author.
36. Michael Verey, interview with author.
37. Dr. Carl Heinz Goldman, interview with author.
38. Roll, "A gathering of the members . . ." p. 11.
39. Sharp, "Gloom," February 1974.

CHAPTER 47

1. *Institutional Investor*, March 1980.
2. Warburg, "Address given at funeral of Ernest G. Thalmann," p. 2.
3. *Institutional Investor*, March 1980.
4. Charles Sharp, letter to the author, October 28, 1992.
5. Geoffrey Elliott, interview with author.
6. Sharp, "Gloom," February 1974.
7. Michael Seligman, interview with author.
8. Anthony Griffin, interview with author.
9. Ruth Fleck, interview with author.
10. *Institutional Investor*, March 1980.
11. Dietrich Weismann, interview with author.
12. Peter Spira, interview with author.
13. Ibid.
14. Ibid.
15. *Sunday Telegraph*, February 24, 1991.

16. Ibid.

17. *The Dictionary of National Biography, 1981–1985*, p. 410.

18. Peter Spira, interview with author.

19. James Wolfensohn, interview with author.

20. *Institutional Investor*, March 1980.

21. Anthony Griffin, interview with author.

22. *Institutional Investor*, March 1980.

23. *Business Week*, November 23, 1974.

24. *Institutional Investor*, March 1980.

25. Ibid.

26. *The Times* of London, February 18, 1978.

27. *Institutional Investor*, March 1980.

CHAPTER 48

1. *Institutional Investor*, March 1980.

2. Moussa, *La Roue de la Fortune*, p. 176.

3. Peter Spira, interview with author.

4. Alvin Friedman, interview with author.

5. *The Way It Was*, p. 500.

6. Wechsberg, *Merchant Bankers*, pp. 168–69.

7. Carey Reich, interview with author.

8. *Institutional Investor*, March 1980.

9. Ibid.

10. Moussa, *La Roue de la Fortune*, p. 229.

11. Ibid.

12. *The Times* of London, July 3, 1982.

13. Dr. Carl Heinz Goldman, interview with author.

14. MMW. Georges Warburg File, letter from Eva Warburg, April 12, 1983.

15. *The Times* of London, October 19, 1982.

16. *Financial Times*, October 20, 1982.

17. *The Way It Was*, p. 501.

18. *Sunday Telegraph*, February 24, 1991.

CHAPTER 49

1. BW. "Eric Warburg Folder," letter to Eric Warburg, February 1, 1983.

2. Gabriele Schiff, interview with author.

3. Ibid.

4. Ueckert-Hilbert, *Fremd in der Eigenen Stadt*, p. 127.

5. Koelbl, *Jüdische Portraits*, p. 277.

6. Farrer, *The Warburgs*, p. 193.

7. Ibid.

8. Koelbl, *Jüdische Portraits*, p. 274.

9. Ibid., p. 278.
10. Lucie Kaye, interview with author.
11. Eva Mitchell, interview with author.
12. Ibid.
13. Marie Warburg, interview with author.
14. Alison Hahn, interview with author.
15. Eva Mitchell, interview with author.
16. Anita Warburg, interview with author.
17. Ibid.
18. Spinelli, *Erinnerungen*, p. 42.
19. Warburg, *The Long Road Home*, p. 277.
20. Warburg, *A Book for Jimmy, Jennifer and Philip*, p. 100.
21. Joan Melber Warburg, interview with author.
22. JW. Box 21. Stevenson, September 1960–May 1965, letter from Adlai Stevenson to John F. Kennedy, December 30, 1960.
23. MMW. Warburg Family Akten. Box 509, letter from Eric Warburg to Hans Meyer, June 16, 1964.
24. MMW. EX, letter from Jimmy Warburg to Eric Warburg, July 4, 1963.
25. MMW. Warburg Family Akten. Box 509, letter from Eric Warburg to Hans Meyer, June 16, 1964.
26. Edward M.M. Warburg, interview with author.
27. Max Warburg, interview with author.
28. Ibid.
29. *Manager Magazin* (Hamburg), January 1990.
30. *Hamburger Abendblatt*, July 11, 1990.
31. Marie Warburg, interview with author.

INDEX

Page numbers in *italics* refer to illustrations.

Aachen, 531

Abs, Hermann, 358, 584, 615, 660, 665, 679

Accepting Houses Committee, 646

"Account X," 329

Acheson, Dean, 491, 577, 580, 581

Adams, Franklin P., 316

Adenauer, Konrad, 577, 581, 600, 616, 656, 674, 716

Adler, Cyrus, 101, 246, 373, 453

AEG, 224, 227

Afrika Korps, 523–24

Agar, Herbert, 165

Aid Society of German Jews, 106, 173, 174, 277, 402, 433

Aid Society of Jews in Germany, 433, 436, 442

Albers, Josef, 404

Alcoa, 648–51, 653

Aldrich, Nelson W., 132–35

Aldrich Plan, 134–35, 137, 308

Aldrich-Vreeland Currency Bill, 132

Algeciras pact, 144

Allenby, Edmund, 247

All Nations Volunteer League, 478

Alma Mater (ballet), 345

Almenröder, Lieutenant, 656

Alsace-Lorraine, 22, 182, 215, 486

Alsterufer Warburgs, 110, 351–64, 543–722
  establishment of, 14–16
  Mittelweg competition with, 20, 22, 24, 30–31, 41, 45, 356–57, 359, 559–62, 719
  see also specific individuals

Altona, 5, 277, 532, 536

Altona Warburgs, 5, 73, 505–6

Aluminium War, 647–54

American and Continental Corporation, 274, 351

American Ballet, 344–46

American Committee to Aid Survivors of the German Resistance, 575

American European Associates (AEA), 610, 673–74

American Federation of Jews from Central Europe, 514

American Jewish Committee (AJC), 100, 101, 164, 235, 236, 272, 301, 372–73, 391, 448, 452, 594–95

American Jewish Joint Agricultural Corporation (Agro-Joint), 292–96

American Jewish Joint Distribution Committee, 164–65, 173, 174, 246–47, 253, 289–90, 292, 373, 388, 389, 402, 403, 434, 439–40, 446, 448, 456, 461, 472, 474, 504–5, 513, 526, 542, 576, 602–3

American Jews, 101, 182, 437–38, 601–5
  Nazis and, 324, 325, 372–73, 388–89, 436, 480
  see also New York Jews

American Metal Climax, 647, 648

American Museum of Natural History, 163, 618

American Psychoanalytic Association, 439

American Society for Jewish Farm
    Settlements in Russia, Inc., 295
Anglo-German treaty, 151–52
Anglo-Palestine Bank, 400, 402, 693
Angola, 152
Anschluss, 466, 478, 484, 567
Anti-Semitic League, 25
Anti-Semitic Party, German, 40
anti-Semitism, 3–7, 22, 36, 37, 121,
    204, 205, 233–36, 248, 290,
    322, 408, 556, 584, 593–95,
    655, 710, 712
  Ballin and, 105, 106
  cemetery desecrations and, 368, 536,
    567–68, 721–22
  in clubs, 76, 95
  education and, 60, 252, 258
  first use of term, 25
  in German military, 37–38
  German nationalism and, 7, 11, 40
  idealism and, 121–22
  Kaiser-Juden and, 108–9
  of Luther, 194–95
  pogroms and, 97, 100–101, 106,
    110, 172, 173, 233, 246, 247,
    402, 474–75
  in Reichstag, 40, 43, 172
  ritual murders and, 11, 122, 268
  tokenism and, 76, 335, 341
  Versailles Treaty and, 210, 211,
    217–18
  Weizmann's views on, 43–44
  World War I and, 161–62, 163,
    171–72, 197
  see also concentration camps;
    Holocaust; *specific countries*
Arab Higher Committee, 450
Arabs, 604, 693–95, 712
  in Palestine, 247, 250, 301, 302–3,
    402, 449–50, 452–53
Armitage, Brigadier General, 534–35
Army Air Force Intelligence, U.S.,
    522–30, 583
Aryanizations, 462–70, 501–3, 506,
    549, 568, 569, 585
Asch, Sholem, 247, 426
Asquith, Herbert H., 415
Astor, Michael, 601
Atalanta (schooner), 572, 710
Atlantic Monthly, 315
Augusta Victoria, Kaiserin of Germany,
    107
Austria, 12, 21, 223, 245, 326, 466,
    486, 567, 615

Austria-Hungary, 151, 153
Austrian Jews, 246, 466, 479, 480,
    485, 489
Austro-Hungarian Jews, 163
Autostrade Italiane, 675

Baden, Prince Max von, 197–99, 217
Baden-Baden, 127, 194, 303, 322,
    431
Badoglio, Pietro, 521
Baeck, Leo, 403, 435, 537
Baer family, 503, 505
Baerwald, Paul, 387, 438, 440, 446,
    456
Baker, George F., 617
Balanchine, George, 344–45, 481, 483
Baldwin, Stanley, 414, 626
Balfour, Lord Arthur, 252
Balfour Declaration, 204, 247, 300,
    303
Ballin, Albert, 74, 76, 126, 146, 147,
    200–201, 380, 381
  Max and, 103–9, 112, 150–51, 153,
    201, 202, 211
  World War I and, 153, 154, 155,
    166, 173, 197
Balzac, Honoré de, 28
Bamberger, Ludwig, 24
B&O Railroad, 339
Bank for International Settlements,
    323, 403, 583
Bank für Deutsche Industrie Obligationen,
    468
Bank Leumi, 400, 402, 693
Bank of England, 132, 644, 646,
    674–76, 682
Bank of the Manhattan Company, 309,
    328, 339, 384, 385, 394, 397
Banque de France, 132
Banque Impériale Ottomane, 38
Banque Russe pour le Commerce
    Étranger, 40
Barclays Bank, 404
Baring family, 412, 413
Barings, Rothschilds, and Kleinworts,
    650
Barnes, Joseph, 582
Baruch, Bernard, 50, 137, 214, 217,
    271, 391
Bauer, Yehuda, 403
Bayerische Vereinsbank, 705
Bayerlein, Fritz, 656
Bayer pharmaceuticals, 275–76,
    615–16

Bearsted, Lord, 413, 437, 438, 479, 484
Beck, Ludwig, 479
Becker, James, 294
A. G. Becker, 699, 700, 703, 704
Beckmann, Heinz, 368
Begin, Menachem, 604, 694
Beitz, Berthold, 658–59
Belgium, 152, 155, 175, 214, 231, 528
August Belmont & Co., 140
Ben-Gurion, David, 449, 454, 455, 602
Benjamin, Adolph, 98
Benson, Rex, 550
Bentwich, Norman, 322, 437
Berenberg-Gossler, Baron Cornelius von, 476
Berenson, Bernard, 62, 77, 285
Berger, Klaus, 282
Berlin, 81, 83, 117, 151, 210, 298, 481, 536, 549
  anti-Semitism in, 11, 106, 110, 233, 435
  Jewish community in, 11, 25–26
  Nazis in, 368, 369, 409, 410, 435
  Siegmund's move to, 361–62, 363, 409
Berlin, Isaiah, 426
Berliner Handels-Gesellschaft, 332, 361–62, 393, 404, 412, 468
Berlin University, 217
Bethmann Bank, 705
Bethmann Hollweg, Theobald von, 145–46, 152
Bevin, Ernest, 573
Beyer, Martha, 502
Beyond Good and Evil (Nietzsche), 362
Biegun, Anna Warburg, 361, 480, 482, 628–29, 631, 681, 692
Biegun, Batya, 671, 681
Biegun, Dov, 629, 671
Bielenberg, Christabel, 368
Bielenberg, Peter, 426
Biema, Adolf van, 502
Biermann-Ratjen, Hans, 593
Bing, Gertrud, 116, 204, 255, 256, 259, 283–87, 405, 407, 408, 511
Bingham, Theodore, 98
Binswanger, Ludwig, 206, 259–60, 263–64, 284, 374
Binswanger, Otto, 80, 259
Binswanger, Robert, 259
Birmingham, Stephen, 46, 48, 50, 77

Bismarck, Otto von, 21–22, 24, 25, 36, 43, 109, 142, 573
Blankenese, 70, 72
Bleichröder, Gerson von, 22, 37, 106, 109
Blinken, Donald, 660
Blohm, Beatrice, 351
Blohm & Voss, 106, 575
Blonay, 682–83, 686, 700–701, 702, 705, 719
Blue Boy (Picasso), 343
Blum, Léon, 300
Blumenfeld, Hans, 212
Bolshevik Revolution, 179, 181, 182, 234, 235, 248, 272, 290, 442, 474, 594
Bolton, Sir George, 650
Bonn University, 60–61, 119
Botticelli, Sandro, 63
Bovenizer, George, 163
Braden, Marietta Warburg, 114, 116, 120–21, 205, 206, 536
Braden, Peter, 512, 536
Brahms, Johannes, 46, 73, 405, 505
Brandeis, Goldschmidt, 78, 81, 350, 413, 554–58, 619–20, 645
Brandeis, Louis, 173, 182, 387
Brändström, Elsa, 178, 575
Brauchitsch, Walther von, 528
Brauer, Max, 592
Braun, Wernher von, 539
Brettauer brothers, 415
Bridgeman, Lord, 646
Brinckmann, Christian, 587, 664–65, 666, 719
Brinckmann, Rudolf, 381, 441, 461, 467–68, 469, 501–3, 507–8, 534–36, 562, 564, 566–71, 583–89, 663–68, 717
Brinckmann, Wirtz & Co., 535, 568, 572, 573, 574, 583–87, 619–20, 663–68
Bristow, Joseph, 139
British Aluminium (BA), 622, 647–54, 669
British Jews, 437, 439, 480, 694–95
British Museum, 527
Brockdorff-Rantzau, Count, 211, 215
Brodetsky, Selig, 253
Brown, David, 301
Brownell, George A., 523, 530
Brüning, Heinrich, 323–24, 329, 368, 400

Bryn Mawr, 344
Buber, Martin, 399, 426
Bücher, Hermann, 276
Bullitt, William, 394
Bülow, Bernhard von, 36, 108, 153, 176
Bundesbank, 674, 675
Burckhardt, Carl, 524
Burckhardt, Jakob, 121, 258
Burney, Christopher, 636
Burnside, 714
Business Week, 652
Butler, Samuel, 633
Buttenwieser, Benjamin, 306
Bydale, 316, 333

Calder, Alexander, 343
Calder, Sir William, 423
Cantor, Eddie, 99
Capital Issues Committee, 187
Cardozo, Benjamin, 160
Carter, Raymond Bonham, 678
Carter, Violet Bonham, 415
Caruso, Enrico, 92
Casablanca declaration, 519
Cassel, Simon von, 3–4, 539
Cassel, Sir Ernest, 51–52, 88, 110, 136, 150–51, 153
Cassirer, Ernst, 256, 258, 262, 263, 264, 405
Cassirer, Toni, 258, 281
Central Association of German Citizens of Jewish Faith (*Centralverein*), 277, 370
Central British Fund, 436
Central Committee for Help and Reconstruction, 402–3
Central Wagon Company, 610
Century, 130
Century Group, 491
Chamberlain, Neville, 479, 480, 484, 485, 495, 626
Chamber of Commerce, Hamburg, 180, 200, 379
Chamber of Commerce, U.S., 131
Charles, Prince of Wales, 420
Chasen, Dave, 307
Chicago & Northwestern Railroad, 48
Chicago Tribune, 492–93
Children's Transport movement, 478
China, 142, 144, 166, 416
Chrysler, 674, 682
Churchill, Winston, 392, 519, 524, 546, 576

Cioppa, Benita Hahn, 419, 420, 421, 715
Cioppa, Egidio Marco, 715
Circle of Young Hamburgers, 366, 368
Civil War, U.S., 48, 97
Clark, Bennett C., 492–93
Clark, Kenneth, 58, 283, 285, 406
Clark-Darlan agreement, 520–21
Clemenceau, Georges, 215
Cobbold, C. F., 646, 648, 651
Cohen, Ben, 490
Coke, Gerald, 415
Colonial Institute, 142
Colonial Office, German, 144, 151
Commerzbank, 679
Commerz- und Disconto Bank, 24
Common Ground (Lazaron), 457
Common Market, 674, 681, 687
Communists, communism, 164, 232, 290, 324, 370, 418, 594
  Nazi fights with, 368, 369
concentration camps, 466, 470, 474, 505, 533
Conference on Jewish Material Claims Against Germany, 656, 658–60
Congress, U.S., 132–33, 135, 290, 492
  see also Senate, U.S.
Constable, W. G., 406
Control Commission for Germany, 538
Cook, Joe, 307, 318
Coughlin, Father Charles, 389, 394
Council for German Jewry, 438
Courtauld, Samuel, 406–8, 643
Court Jews, 4, 109, 267, 352–53
Cox, James M., 382, 392
Craven, John, 690, 691
Credit-Anstalt, 12, 326, 363
Creek Club, 341
Crimea, 289, 292, 294
Crimean War, 12, 15
Cripps, Milo, 691–92
Cripps Warburg, 692
Cunliffe, Geoffrey, 648
Cuno, Wilhelm, 230–32, 270, 325
C. W. Capital Ltd., 691

Dagset, Eric, 525
Daily Mirror (London), 653
Daily Worker, 430
Daimler-Benz, 615
Daimler Motors, 224
Daitz, Werner, 464
Daladier, Édouard, 479

Dall, Anna Roosevelt, 384
Dall, Curtis, 384
Damrosch, Frank, 77
Damrosch, Walter, 49, 317, 340, 447
Dan, Takuma, 111
Danat Bank, 326, 328–29
Daniels, Josephus, 184
Danilova, Alexandra, 473, 481–83,
    619
Darlan, J. F., 520–21
Darling, Peter Stormonth, 688, 698
Daus, Richard, 666, 678
Davis, Elmer, 520
Davis, John W., 223
Davison, Henry, 134, 158
Dawes, Charles, 273
Dawes Plan, 273–74
Dearborn Independent, 234–35
"Defects and Needs of Our Banking
    System" (Paul Warburg), 131
Defense Department, U.S., 524, 530
de Gaulle, Charles, 521
"Degenerate Art" exhibition, 460
Derenberg, Carl, 83
Derenberg, Gabriele, *see* Schiff, Gabriele
    Warburg
Derenberg, Julius, 83–84, 358, 712
Derenberg, Louise Warburg, 26, 27,
    29, 30, 79, 81, 83–84, 358, 424,
    477, 607–8, 712
Derenberg, Walter, 83, 424
Dernburg, Bernhard, 142, 144
Deutsche Bank, 46, 142, 152, 587,
    675, 679, 698
Deutsche Effecten und Wechsel Bank,
    666
Deutsche Volkspartei (DVP; German
    People's Party), 218, 225, 366,
    430
Dillon, Clarence, 618
Dillon, Douglas, 670
Dilworth, J. Richardson, 621, 673
Dimitriev, Vladimir, 345
Discount Bank of Israel, 616
Dodd, William E., 388, 389, 408, 434
Domela, César, 424, 477
Domela, Ruth Derenberg, 83, 424, 477
Dönhoff, Countess Marion, 488, 575,
    577
Donovan, William J., 520
Douglas, Lewis, 387, 491
Dreifuss, Theodora, 638–39
Dresdner Bank, 329

I. Dreyfus, 37
Dreyfus affair, 122, 324
Dubinsky, David, 290
Dulles, Allen, 491, 528, 538, 570, 575
Dulles, John Foster, 231, 350, 490–91
Dungeon Democracy, The (Burney), 636
Dutch East Indies, 568
Dutch International Corporation, 412,
    414

Eagle, Joe, 138
Eastman Kodak, 445
East Prussia, 215
Ebert, Friedrich, 196, 197, 202, 209,
    216, 275, 322
Economic Consequences of the Peace, The
    (Keynes), 223
Economics Ministry, German, 434, 438,
    460, 462, 466, 470, 485, 503,
    507
Eden, Anthony, 573
Educational Alliance, 99, 100
Edward VII, King of England, 88, 110,
    151
King Edward VII Foundation, 151
Eerde school, 425, 509–11
Effectenbank-Warburg, 705, 718–20
Egypt, 695
Ehrenberg, Bertha, 470
Einstein, Albert, 217, 252, 253, 283,
    300, 302, 387, 405, 448, 582
Eisenhower, Dwight D., 523, 535
Eisenhower, Milton, 582
Eliot, Charles, 166, 181
Elliott, Geoffrey, 686
Emanuel, Alice R., 293
Embden, Heinrich, 286
Emergency Rescue Committee (ERC),
    497–98
Emigré Charitable Fund, 389
Enskilda Bank, 358, 467
Erhard, Ludwig, 570
Erzberger, Matthias, 226
Ethiopia, Italy's attack on, 433
Euromarkets, 622, 674–80
European Coal and Steel Community
    (ECSC), 616, 675–76
Export-Import Bank, 490

Falkenhausen, Alexander von, 528
I. G. Farben, 275, 276, 365, 576,
    658
Fascism, Italian, 285, 442

Fascista Regime, 442
Feder, Ernst, 248
Feder, Gottfried, 236
Federal Bureau of Investigation (FBI), 496
Federal Reserve Act (1913), 135–37, 308
Federal Reserve Board, 135–40, 158, 160, 161–62, 186–89, 235, 271, 308–11, 384, 385, 474, 594
Federal Reserve System, 90, 135–40, 182, 220
Federation of Jewish Philanthropies, 165, 339, 618
Feis, Herbert, 383
Felix (Rothschild butler), 525–26
Fenthol, Fritz, 441, 507–8
Ferencz, Benjamin B., 658
Feuchtwanger, Leon, 556
Field, Marshall, 318
Fight for Freedom Committee, 492
Finance Ministry, German, 210
Financial Times (London), 665, 666, 707
Fine & Dandy (James and Swift), 318
Finkelstein, Louis, 598
Finland, 490
Finnish-American Trading Corporation, 490
First National Bank of Portland, 351
Fleck, Ruth, 560, 688
Flick, Friedrich, 463–66, 549, 572, 576, 659–60
Flight Capital Tax, 463, 467, 549
Florence, 62–63, 64, 68, 82, 113–14
Fogg Art Museum, 343
Folks, Homer, 100
Fontenay, 96
Ford, Henry, 234–36, 272
"Foreign Criminals in New York" (Bingham), 98
Foreign Office, British, 479, 694
Foreign Office, German, 110, 141, 142, 152, 226, 479, 495, 496
  Morocco and, 144–47
  World War I and, 153, 166, 173, 174, 178, 179, 180, 196
Forrestal, James V., 493
Fouchier, Jacques de, 698
France, 24, 151, 152, 226
  colonialism and, 142, 144–47, 151
  German reparations and, 216, 225, 230–31

Hamburg occupied by, 6–7, 10
  Ruhr and, 225, 231, 273
  World War I and, 153, 162, 167–69, 178, 179, 181, 202, 212, 214
  World War II and, 490, 491, 496, 520–21, 525
Franchetti, Alice Hallgarten, 79
Franco-Prussian War, 22, 24
Fränkel, Louis, 43, 112
Frankfurt, 4, 24, 37, 45–46
Frankfurter, Felix, 388, 496
Frankfurt University, 374
Franz Josef I, Emperor of Austria-Hungary, 12
Fraser, Ian, 635, 678, 691
Fraser, Lionel, 648–49, 682
Frederick III, Kaiser of Germany, 35
Freier, Recha, 421–22
Freiheit, 430
Freikorps, 209–10
French Jews, 498, 526
French Revolution, 5, 6
Freud, Sigmund, 259, 260, 405
Fritsch, Theodor, 179, 235–36, 268, 270–72, 391
Fry, Varian, 497–98
Fuhlsbüttel prison, 475–76, 532
Fukuda, Takeo, 702
Fürstenberg, Carl, 236
Fürstenberg, Hans, 412, 414, 434, 439
Fürstenberg family, 332, 412, 414, 415
Furtwängler, Wilhelm, 446

Gaevernitz, Gero von Schultz, 485–86, 552
Galbraith, John Kenneth, 598
Gay, Peter, ix, 157, 263
Geist, Raymond H., 440
Gelsenkirchener Bergwerk, 679–80
General Management Company, 535
George Gershwin's Song Book, 333
Gerard, James W., 172
German Atlantic Telegraph Company, 379
German Institute for Psychiatric Research, 80
German Jews, xv–xvii, 3, 5, 13, 36, 106, 141, 218, 324, 417–30, 551, 602
  assimilation of, 37, 43, 60, 61, 147, 172, 432, 589

German Jews (*cont'd*)
  emancipation of, 6, 14, 18, 21, 25,
    62, 121, 435
  identity of, xvi-xvii, 14, 322, 335,
    366
  intermarriage of, 14, 43, 62, 66–68,
    335, 366
  modernization and, 24, 25
  Nazi takeover as viewed by, 369–72
  in New York, 46, 48–56, 88–101,
    157–69, 182; *see also* New York
    Jews
  Nuremberg Laws and, 435, 443–44
  as refugees, 388–89, 400, 402–3,
    411, 412–13, 432, 436–37, 440,
    446, 448–51, 465–66, 472, 474,
    476–80, 484, 485, 489
  return of, 589–95
  Wilhelm II's relations with, 107–9
  World War I and, 171–74, 202
  Zionism and, 296–301, 322, 399,
    402, 417–18, 440
German Labor Front, 276
German People's Party (Deutsche
  Volkspartei; DVP), 218, 225, 366,
  430
German Southwest Africa, 152
Germany:
  colonialism of, 110, 141–42,
    144–47, 150, 151–52
  culture of, 36, 157–58, 176–77, 195
  economy of, 34, 142, 273–75, 368,
    375–78, 400, 402, 434–38,
    570–71; *see also* Germany,
    Weimar, inflation in
  Euromarkets and, 674–75, 679
  Franco-Prussian War and, 22, 24
  post–World War II, 531–39, 541–42,
    572–77, 581–95, 607, 615, 661,
    710, 712–13, 717–22
  stock market crash (1873) in, 24–25
  unification of, 21
  in World War I, 152–58, 160–69,
    171–83, 191–92, 195–204, 214
Germany, Nazi, xv, xvii, 179, 224,
    225, 248, 268, 270–77, 287–88,
    321–25, 329, 363–64, 368–81,
    391, 402–13, 417–23, 429–46,
    540–41, 545, 582, 592
  anti-Semitism of, 227–30, 233, 236,
    267, 270–75, 322, 324, 325,
    328, 363–66, 368–74, 378–81,
    390, 392–93, 400, 402–5, 410,
    425, 427, 428, 433–36, 439–40,
    459, 462–70, 472, 474–75,
    501–3, 506; *see also* concentration
    camps; Holocaust
  artists and intellectuals in, 404–5
  Aryanizations in, 462–70, 501–3,
    506, 549, 568, 569, 585
  boycott of Jewish business in, 372,
    400, 402
  economy of, 375–78, 400, 402,
    434–38
  foreign boycott of, 372–73, 429,
    436
  Nuremberg trials and, 465, 538–39,
    577
  World War II and, 485, 486,
    490–99, 519–32, 588
Germany, Weimar, 209–36, 263–88,
    321–32, 365, 410
  anti-Semitism in, 210, 211, 217–18,
    225, 227–30, 233, 236, 267,
    268, 270–75, 322, 324, 325,
    328, 363–66
  Depression and, 311, 323–24
  economic revival in, 273–75
  inflation in, 225, 226, 230, 231–32,
    236, 256, 271, 279, 505–6
  reparations of, 210, 216, 223, 225,
    226–27, 229, 230–31, 323, 331
Gershwin, George, 317–19, 333–34,
    345, 346
Gershwin, Ira, 317
Gestapo, 404, 420, 422, 430, 435,
    439–41, 465, 470, 472, 475,
    476, 496, 498, 503–5, 549, 582,
    617
Gibson, C. S., 406
Gilbert, Cass, 220
Gilbert, Charles P. H., 92, 93
Gilbert, S. Parker, 274
Giscard d'Estaing, Valéry, 710
Glass, Carter, 135–37, 308
Glick, David, 440
Glick, Peter, 440
Godowsky, Leopold, 445
Goebbels, Josef, 277, 324, 372, 373,
    375, 407, 438, 460, 519, 526
Goethe, Johann Wolfgang von, 282
Gold Discount Bank, 274
Goldman, Carl Heinz, 573, 627,
    637–38, 639, 682, 686, 705
Goldmann, Nahum, 694
Goldschmidt, Adolph, 60

Goldschmidt, Cecil, 556
Goldschmidt, Ernest, 78
Goldschmidt, Malchen Warburg, 8, 60, 72, 73
Goldschmidt, Markus, 18
Goldsmid, Sir Osmond d'Avigdor, 438, 439
Goldstein, Jonah A., 242
Gollancz, Victor, 554
Gombrich, E. H., 205
Good Hope Steel Company, 468
Gordon, Martin, 633
Gordonstoun school, 420, 465
Göring, Hermann, 232, 325, 372, 373, 376, 461, 462, 464, 466, 479, 485, 505, 515, 526, 528–30, 540
Great Britain, 152, 222, 303, 330, 387, 402, 450–52
    anti-Semitism in, 555
    Balfour Declaration and, 204, 247, 300, 303
    colonialism and, 142, 150, 151–52
    Euromarkets and, 674–76
    German naval program and, 150, 151
    Germany occupied by, 568, 570
    Jewish refugees in, 411, 477–78
    Warburg Library in, 406–8
    World War I and, 153, 154, 161, 162, 165, 166–69, 176–79, 181, 408
    World War II and, 485, 486, 490, 491–92, 496, 523, 524, 525, 531, 545, 551
Great Depression, 308–11, 323–30, 384–87, 405, 580
Grenfell, Edward C., 162
Grey, Sir Edward, 153, 161
Grierson, Ronnie, 670, 672
Griffin, Tony, 636
Grimson, Bettina Warburg, 56, 69, 96, 128, 160, 161, 170, 182–85, 220, 306, 312–13, 351, 357, 383, 408, 439, 580, 581, 605–6, 710
    father's death and, 330, 331
    as psychiatrist, 312, 313, 333, 347, 439, 555, 606
    religious background of, 90–91
Grimson, Samuel, 605–6
Grunfeld, Henry, 415, 548–51, 553, 554, 557, 558, 561, 572, 573,

636, 642–45, 648, 652, 653, 672, 675, 680, 682, 686, 688, 690, 700–706
Guinness, Sir Kenelm Lee, 414
Gunzburg, Baron de, 181–82
Gunzburg, Baroness Anna de, 15
Gunzburg, Baroness Rosa de, 181
Gunzburg, Baron Horace de, 15
Gunzburg family, 39
Gutmann, Eugen, 24

Haas, Irwin, 540
Haavara agreement, 400, 402, 436, 437, 439
Habimah theater troupe, 298
Haeften, Hans von, 199
Hagenbeck, Carl, 179–80
Hahn, Benita, *see* Cioppa, Benita Hahn
Hahn, Kurt, 196, 198, 298, 418, 420, 421, 463, 465, 588–89, 590, 710, 714
Hahn, Oscar, 367, 419, 420–21, 715
Hahn, Rudolf, 298, 418, 420, 421, 463, 465–66, 536, 665, 714
Hahn-Warburg, Lola, 74, 76, 226, 228, 367, 417–22, 419, 424, 425, 451, 458, 465–66, 511, 518, 524, 536, 568, 600, 665, 713–15
    Jewish children and, 477–78
    Weizmann and, 297–98, 300, 303, 418, 421, 713
Hahn Works, 463–65
Haldane, Lord, 151, 153
Halder, Franz, 528
Halifax, Lord, 480, 495
Hambro, Olaf, 648, 651, 652
Hambro family, 413, 545, 650
Hamburg, 5–20, 22, 24–32, 39–43, 66–68, 103–7, 116–24, 180, 200, 225–26, 228–33, 356–61, 459, 524–25
    anti-Nazi groups in, 366, 368, 370
    anti-Semitism in, 7, 43, 61, 172, 258, 368–71, 373–74, 404–5, 505
    Bürgerschaft of, 85–86, 109–10, 123, 172–73, 370, 430
    cholera epidemic (1892) in, 39–40, 58
    culture in, 117–18, 125, 126, 127, 285

Hamburg (*cont'd*)
  Japanese in, 111
  Max's security problems in, 228–29,
    233, 272
  Nazis in, 229, 277, 321–22, 325,
    368–71, 404–5, 426–27
  as port, 10–11, 35–36, 39
  postwar, 531–32, 534–36, 565,
    575, 577, 583, 587–95, 710, 712
  restitution law in, 570
  revolution in, 199–203
  riots and martial law in, 213, 217,
    232
  stock exchange of, 12, 13, 24–25,
    154
  university movement in, 118, 125,
    195, 197, 203, 206
  Warburg Library in, 264–66
  World War I and, 154–55, 179–80
Hamburg-American Line (HAPAG),
    103–7, 126, 151, 200–201, 274,
    569
  "Aryanization" of, 380–81
  China cartel and, 142, 144
Hamburg Bank of 1914, 155
Hamburg Bank of 1923, 231
Hamburg City Council, 202, 203, 206
Hamburg Economic Service, 379
Hamburg Metal Exchange, 81, 178
Hamburg Morocco Society, 144, 145
Hamburg National Club, 325
Hamburg Plan, 504
Hamburg Senate, 125, 154, 172–73,
    174, 200, 202, 203, 218, 229,
    568, 709
Hamburg University, 206, 256, 258,
    263–64, 285, 405, 426, 427–28,
    512
Harriman, Averell, 184, 318, 336,
    339, 379, 385–86, 397
Harriman, Edward H., 48, 88, 130,
    138
Harris, Jean, 599
Harris, Sir Arthur (Bomber), 524
Harvard *Crimson*, 183
Harvard Society for Contemporary Art,
    342–43
Harvard University, 618
Haselbacher, Karl, 440
Havenstein, Rudolf, 233
Heath, Edward, 687
Hebrew Technical Institute, 101
Hebrew University, 251, 252–53, 297,
    299, 448–49

Hecht, Levis and Kahn, 645
Heemskerk, L. Bysterus, 508, 509
Hegel, Georg Wilhelm Friedrich, 362
Heine, Heinrich, 8, 172, 405
Heise, Carl Georg, 123, 125, 175, 204,
    258, 280, 404–5, 562
Helbert, Wagg, 648, 653
Held, John, Jr., 345
Helfferich, Emil, 370–71, 378, 379,
    381
Helfferich, Karl, 180, 233
Hell Bent for Election (James Warburg),
    396
Hellman, Geoffrey, 54
Help & Reconstruction, 514, 518
Henriques, Otto R., 43
Henry Street Settlement, 99
"Hep Hep" riots, 7
Hertling, Georg von, 196, 197
Hertz, John, 62, 67–68
Hertz, Mary, *see* Warburg, Mary
    Hertz
Hertz, Wilhelm, 62, 204
Herzl, Theodor, 247, 299–300
Hess, Carl, 673–74
Hess, Rudolf, 321, 418, 420
Hessian Jews, 427
Heuss, Theodor, 573
Hexter, Maurice, 302, 303, 454
Heydrich, Reinhard, 440–41, 476
High Commission for Refugees from
    Germany, 389
Hilfsverein der Deutschen Juden, see Aid
    Society of German Jews
Hill, James J., 48
Hillard, Gustav, 196
Hillman, Sidney, 521
Himmler, Heinrich, 429, 439–41, 460,
    463, 503, 504, 549
Hindenburg, Oskar von, 329
Hindenburg, Paul von, 198, 217, 275,
    362, 369, 377, 410
Hirsch, Baron Maurice de, 292
Hirsch, Otto, 403, 435
Hitchcock, Gilbert M., 139
Hitler, Adolf, 217, 225, 275–77, 321,
    324, 329, 363, 365–66, 368–70,
    372–79, 387–91, 400, 409, 416,
    418, 427, 433, 466, 468, 526,
    528, 529, 536, 540, 565–66,
    575, 594
  assassination attempts and, 471,
    497, 519–20
  Beer Hall Putsch and, 232–33

Schacht and, 325, 376–78, 434–35, 460–62, 479, 484, 520
World War II and, 485, 486, 490, 496, 519
Zionism and, 449–50
Hoare, Sir Samuel, 477
Hoechst, 616
Hoffa, Else, 149, 472
Hoffman, Malvina, 331, 605
Holland, 405, 506–11, 675
Holman, Libby, 318
Holmes, Oliver Wendell, 160
Holocaust, 366, 463, 476, 505, 529, 535, 537, 559, 572, 589, 602, 656, 658
see also concentration camps
Holtzendorff, Arndt von, 180
Holtzendorff, Henning von, 156
Homage to Catalonia (Orwell), 554
Hoover, Herbert, 155, 223, 230, 290, 292, 314–15, 329
Hoover, J. Edgar, 496
Hopi Indians, 65–66
Hornbostel, Helene von, 73
House, Colonel, 136, 140, 161, 182, 188, 189, 213–14, 216, 220, 226
House of Representatives, U.S., 135
Houston, David, 160
Hübner, P., 121
Hughes, Charles Evans, 230
Hull, Cordell, 390, 392, 397, 486
Hungarian Jews, 246, 540
Hylan, John, 238

Illinois Central, 86
Imperator, 126, 147–48, 150
Imperial Chemical Industries, 690, 699
Imperial Purchasing Company, 173
Industriekreditbank, 468, 502
Institute of Musical Art, 77
Institutional Investor, 691
Interest Equalization Tax (IET), 670, 672, 674
Inter-Governmental Committee on Political Refugees, 479
Interior Ministry, German, 540
International Acceptance Bank (IAB), 224, 231, 274, 309, 310, 315, 328, 330, 332, 339, 350
International Art History Congress (1909), 121
International Jew, The (Ford), 236, 272

International Manhattan Company, 309, 384
International Trade and Investment Agency (Altreu), 439
Iran, 606
Iranian Jews, 591, 593
Isherwood, Christopher, 421
Israel, 602, 604, 607, 629, 656, 658, 693–95, 712, 713
Israel, Wilfrid, 298, 421–22, 498
Israel Corporation, 693
Italy, 285, 405–6, 433, 442
World War I and, 176, 177
World War II and, 499, 521
It's Up to Us (James Warburg), 396

Jahns, Franziska, 27, 28, 30
Jahr, John, 720
James, Paul, *see* Warburg, James, Sr.
Japan, 166, 442, 522, 528, 676, 702
Schiff's financing of, 110–11, 235
Javits, Jacob, 605
Jefferson, Thomas, 242
Jekyll Island talks, 133–34
Jessel, Dick, 414
Jessel, Robin, 635
Jewish Agency, 252, 300–301, 303, 400, 421, 449, 451–54, 457, 518, 542
Jewish Community Center, 459–60
Jewish Culture League, 459
Jewish Hospital, 122, 226, 279, 475, 476, 593
Jewish Museum, 93, 597–98
Jewish Orphanage, 148
Jewish Refugee Committee, 424
Jewish Theological Seminary, 101, 597
Jewish War Veterans, 391
Johnson, Philip, 344
Joint Distribution Committee, *see* American Jewish Joint Distribution Committee
Joly, Maurice, 234
Jones, Jesse, 394
Jones, Thomas D., 139
Joseph, Maxwell, 647
Joseph and His Brothers (Mann), 282
Josephson, Erland, 82
Joyce, William, 545
Judy, Paul, 698–99, 700
Juilliard School of Music, 77, 306, 716
Jung, C. G., 259

Kahn, Bernhard, 294, 373, 432, 438, 440
Kahn, Otto, 88, 92, 158, 168–69, 243, 309
Kapp, Wolfgang, 225
Kara Corporation, 328, 439, 506–7, 516
Karpf, Maurice J., 451, 452
Rudolf Karstadt department store, 325–26, 411, 412, 517
Kaufmann, Karl, 594
Kaulla, Albert, 361
Kaulla, Lilly Warburg, 352, 361
Kaulla, Lucie, *see* Warburg, Lucie Kaulla
Kaulla, Otto, 352, 361, 409
"Keep the Gate Open," 366, 368
Kelly, Bernard, 636, 693, 694
Kennedy, John F., 670, 673, 716
Kennedy, Joseph P., 336, 391
Keppler, Wilhelm, 378, 379
Kerensky, Alexander, 181, 182, 235
Keynes, John Maynard, 212, 216, 222–23, 386, 393, 575
Kiel Canal, 107, 524
Kiel Institute for Seafaring and World Economics, 380
Kiel uprising, 199
Kiel Week, 107, 108
Kindersley, Lord, 648, 649, 652
King, Cecil, 653
King, Georgiana Goddard, 344
Kingdon, Frank, 497
Kirstein, Lincoln, 342, 344, 345–46
Kisch, Frederick H., 250, 251, 299
Kishinev pogrom, 100
Kissinger, Henry, 628
Klausner, Margot, 298
Kleinschmit, W. von, 406, 408
Klinggräff, Cäcilie von, 472
Kneisel, Franz, 244
Knigge, Baroness Louise Sophie, 574–75
Knopf, Alfred A., 318, 394–95
Kohn-Speyer, Alfred, 78, 79
Kohn-Speyer, Alice, 555
Kohn-Speyer, Anna Leo-Wolf, 79, 555, 556
Kohn-Speyer, Edmund, 79, 555–58, 620
Kohn-Speyer, Paul, 39, 71, 78–79, 81, 350, 412, 413, 561
Kokoschka, Oskar, 73, 490, 523

Korda, Alexander, 415
Korner, Eric, 550–51, 572, 616–17, 675, 676, 690, 693
Korner, Tony, 679
Köster, H. J., 72
Kösterberg, 72, 79, 86, 90, 96, 147–49, 227, 228, 240, 269, 322, 351, 399, 425, 427, 441, 443–44, 470, 472, 490, 493, 503, 516, 533, 534–35, 540, 541–42, 558, 574–75, 590, 591, 713, 715
Krebs, Hans, 540
Kreisau Circle, 495, 496
Kristallnacht, 474–75, 477, 479–80, 483–84, 593, 602
Krogmann, Carl Vincent, 370–71, 378, 380
Krupp, Alfried, 576, 658–59
Krupp, Gustav, 576
Friedrich Krupp A. G., 110, 224, 443, 502, 576, 577, 658
Kuhn, Abraham, 48, 55
Kuhn, Loeb, 46, 48, 51, 65, 134, 189, 224, 238, 309, 397, 442, 474, 485, 594, 631
    Felix and, 52, 53, 85, 86, 92, 93, 97, 241, 246, 360, 445, 456, 612
    Freddy and, 243, 338, 612, 617–20, 660
    HAPAG shares purchased by, 105
    Jim Loeb and, 77, 80
    Jimmy and, 183–84, 309, 332–33
    Paul and, 86, 88, 89, 129, 132, 138, 139–40, 142, 612
    Siegmund and, 360–61, 583, 612–22, 647–48, 669–70, 672, 699–700
    M. M. Warburg & Co. and, 51, 56, 86, 110–11
    World War I and, 161, 165–69, 181
Kuhn, Regina Loeb, 55
Ku Klux Klan, 235
Kummerfeld, Louise, 75

Labor Front, German, 374, 501
Lachaise, Gaston, 344
Lachman, Eddy, 509, 632, 642
Lachmann, Grace, 509
Laird & Co., 673
Lamont, Thomas W., 213–14, 490, 518, 594

Land, Edwin H., 397–98, 579
Landon, Alfred M., 397
Lane, Franklin, 160
Langmaack, Gerhard, 264
Langwerth, Baron, 145
Lateran Treaty, 285
Laufenburg, Heinrich, 200, 203
Lazard Brothers, 648–51, 691
Lazaron, Morris, 432, 457
League of Nations, 214, 222, 247, 275, 288–89, 486, 518
Leclerc, Philippe, 525
Lederer, Hugo, 118
Lee, Lord, 406
Lehman, Herbert, 252, 290, 446, 448
Lehman, Irving, 388, 453
Lehman, Robert, 672
Lehman Brothers, 615, 699–700
Leisure Group, 673
Lend-Lease, 492
Levant, Oscar, 334
Levin, Shmaryahu, 101
Lewisohn, Margaret, 185
Lewisohn, Samuel, 77
Ley, Robert, 275–76, 374, 501, 538
Libby, John, 636
Liberia, 142
Liberty Bonds, 182, 186–87, 220
Lichtenberg, Paul, 679
Liebeschütz, Hans, 121, 441
Liebeschütz, Rahel, 441
Liebknecht, Karl, 209, 210
Lindbergh, Charles, 492
Lippmann, Leo, 371
Liquidation Bank, 436–38
List, Friedrich, 211–12
Lloyd George, David, 146
Lloyd's of London, 424, 481
Locarno Treaty, 275
Lodge, Henry Cabot, 187
Loeb, Betty Gallenberg, 54–55, 85, 90, 99
Loeb, Fanny Kuhn, 55
Loeb, Guta, 55, 77
Loeb, James, 55, 65, 77–80, 176, 177, 194, 312, 314, 374, 536, 709
Loeb, Marie Antonie Hambüchen (Toni), 80, 374
Loeb, Morris, 55, 77, 95
Loeb, Nina, *see* Warburg, Nina Loeb
Loeb, Regina, 55
Loeb, Solomon, 46, 47, 48, 54–55, 77, 85, 536

Loeb, Therese, *see* Schiff, Therese Loeb
Loeb Classical Library, 80, 306
London Rubber Company, 550
London Stock Exchange, 616
London University, 406–8, 527
Love, George, 673–74
Lovett, Bob, 394
Low, Seth, 99
Lowell, A. Lawrence, 183, 302
Lowenstein, Harriet B., 164
Lübeck, 524
Lübeck Blast Furnace, 463–65, 572
Lucas, Harry, 414, 485, 547, 635
Lucius, Baron von, 178
Ludendorff, Erich, 196, 197, 199, 232, 362
Ludendorff, Mathilde, 594
Luftwaffe, 523–27, 529
Lüneburg, 537–38
Lusitania, 150, 156, 167, 183
Luther, Hans, 323, 326, 329, 377, 390
Luther, Martin, 194–95
Lutyens, Richard, 645
Luxembourg, 675
Luxemburg, Rosa, 209, 210
Lybrand Ross Brothers & Montgomery, 360

McAdoo, William G., 139, 161–62, 186–88
McCarthy, Eugene, 717
McCloy, Ellen, 577
McCloy, John J., 455, 491, 528, 535, 538, 575–77, 581, 592, 619, 658–60, 710, 716
McConnell, Joe, 650
McDonald, James G., 388–89, 390, 436, 446, 602
MacDonald, Ramsay, 301, 303–4, 392, 420
McFadyean, Sir Andrew, 414, 485
Macmillan, Harold, 650
Madison Square Garden, 372, 373
Magic Mountain, The (Mann), 263, 685
Magnes, Judah, 90, 165, 250–53, 302, 303, 314, 453, 457
Magnus, Alice, *see* Warburg, Alice Magnus
Magnus, Dora, 192
Magnus, Hermann, 73
Magnus, Lola, 73
Mahler, Alma, 497

Manchester Guardian, 427, 436, 495, 527
Mandela, Nelson, 682
Mann, Thomas, 75, 203, 263, 282, 349, 405, 497, 685
Mannes, Leopold, 445
Mannesmann Brothers, 144, 465
Marc, Franz, 126
Marks, Simon, 436–38, 450
Marr, Wilhelm, 25
Marshall, Louis, 164, 249, 252, 272, 293, 300, 301
Marshall, Warner, 522, 524
Marx, Karl, 442
Massera, Giuseppe, 482
Max, Prince of Baden, 418
Maxwell, Robert, 693
Meadow Farm, 598, 599
Meier, Hans, 527
Mein Kampf (Hitler), 233, 321
Melchett, Lord, 300, 301, 303
Melchior, Carl, 86, 111, 144, 153, 155, 173, 208, 222, 223, 225, 226–27, 230, 273, 275, 322–24, 358, 377
    Fritsch and, 270, 271
    Nazis and, 363, 368, 402, 403–4
    Versailles Treaty and, 211–13, 215–16
Melchior, Elsa Warburg, 31, 58, 78, 205, 206, 211
Melle, Werner von, 203
Mellon, Andrew W., 230, 310
Memoirs (von Bülow), 153
Mendelssohn, Franz, 109
Mendelssohn & Co., 375, 461
Merchants and General Investment Corporation, 412
Mercury Asset Management, 698
Mercury Securities, 610, 680, 683, 689, 702–3
Messersmith, George S., 405, 440
Metropolitan Life, 616
Metropolitan Opera, 92, 244, 345–46
Meyer, André, 554, 616, 634, 649, 672
Meyer, Felix, 433
Meyer, Hans, 216, 361, 506, 516
Middlesex School, 313–14
Military Government in Germany, U.S., 581
Mills, Ogden, 310
Milner, Lord, 151

Mitchell, David, 672, 698
Mitsui, Baron, 60, 111
Mittelweg 17, 500, 503
Mittelweg Warburgs, 26–486, 543–722
    Alsterufer competition with, 20, 22, 24, 30–31, 41, 45, 356–57, 359, 559–62, 719
    establishment of, 18–20
    see also specific individuals
Mnemosyne, 284
Mobil Oil, 679–80
Molènes, Marie de, 404
Moley, Raymond, 384, 385, 386, 392
Moltke, Helmuth von, 495
Money Muddle, The (James Warburg), 395
Monnet, Jean, 616, 674
Samuel Montagu, 30, 40, 437, 651
Monticello, 242
Morawetz, Victor, 133
Morgan, J. Pierpont, 48, 88, 107, 131, 273
Morgan, J. Pierpont, Jr., 167, 223
J. P. Morgan & Co., 86, 88, 165, 167–68, 273, 594, 672
Morgan Grenfell, 651, 652, 691
Morgan Stanley, 699
Morgenthau, Henry, 135, 163, 394, 496
Morgenthau Plan, 575, 576, 581
Morocco, 144–47, 151
Morocco-Mannesmann, 144
Morrissey, Evelyn, 296
Mountbatten, Edwina, 601
Mountbatten, Lord, 601
Moussa, Pierre, 698, 703–4
Mozambique, 152
Munch, Edvard, 460
Munich, 117, 121, 374, 460
Munich Beer Hall Putsch, 232–33
Murder Exploding Detachment, 228
Murphy, Robert, 523
Murrow, Edward R., 581
Museum of Modern Art (MOMA), 342, 344
Mussolini, Benito, 285, 394, 433, 521
My Fight with the House of Warburg (Fritsch), 391

Napoleon I, Emperor of France, 6
Napoleon III, Emperor of France, 234

Napoleonic Wars, 6, 10
Nast, Condé, 340, 456
National Bank and Trust Company, 301
National Citizens' League for the Promotion of a Sound Banking System, 134
National City Bank, 88, 89
National Monetary Commission, U.S., 132
National Reserve Association, 134
Native Americans, 28, 59, 64–66
NATO, 577, 582, 717
Naumann, Friedrich, 150
Necarsulmer, Henry, 621
neo-Nazi movement, 594
Neu Beginnen, 496
Neues Deutschland, 391
Neuengamme, 532
Neurath, Konstantin von, 284, 410–11, 412
Nevins, Allan, 164
New Deal, 384–87, 580
New Deal Noodles (James and Phyllis Warburg), 396–97
New Republic, 388
New Statesman, 650
New Trading Company, 412–15, 485, 545, 547–53, 559–61, 572, 620
  see also S. G. Warburg & Company
New York, N.Y., 88–101, 131
  anti-Semitism in, 93, 98
  Board of Education of, 99–100
  Paul's move to, 85–86, 88–90
New York City Ballet, 346
New Yorker, 385, 413, 589
New York Federal Reserve Bank, 158
New York Jews, 46, 48–56, 88–101, 246
  intermarriage of, 184–85, 238, 314, 456–57, 599
  on Lower East Side, 97–99, 163, 238, 248
  Siegmund's views on, 360
  World War I and, 157–69
  see also specific individuals
New York Philharmonic Symphony Orchestra, 245, 340
New York Psychoanalytic Institute, 346
New York State Probation Commission, 100
New York Stock Exchange, 162, 613

New York Times, 101, 131, 138, 158, 161, 189, 230, 238, 331, 385, 437, 455–56, 508, 580
Nicholas II, Czar of Russia, 15, 179, 181
Niebuhr, Reinhold, 575
Niederlandische Bank, 37
Nietzsche, Friedrich, 63, 119, 120, 281, 362
"Night of the Long Knives, The," 429, 444, 549
Nixon, Richard M., 681
Noah's Ark, 72, 351, 575, 591
Noble, John, 547
Norman, Montagu, 413
Norske Creditbank, 460
Northern Pacific railroad, 88
North German Confederation, 21–22
North German Wool, 326
North Sea Fisheries, 443
Norton, Charles Eliot, 65
Norway, World War II and, 490, 520
Nuremberg, 11, 276, 442
Nuremberg Laws, 435, 443–44
Nuremberg trials, 465, 538–39, 577
Nyasa Consolidated Ltd., 152
Nyasaland, 152

Odhams Press, 653
Office for Raw and Synthetic Materials, German, 461
Office of Strategic Services, U.S., 538
Office of War Information (OWI), U.S., 520–21
Olearius, Christian, 719, 720
Olympic Games (1936), 442
On Jews and Their Lies (Luther), 195
Operation Torch, 520–21
Oppenheim, Charlotte, *see* Warburg, Charlotte Oppenheim
Oppenheim, Käthie, 374–75
Oppenheim, Moritz, 374–75
Oppenheim, Nathan, 18–19, 45–46
Oppenheim, Paul, 375
Sal. Oppenheim, Jr., 665
N. M. Oppenheim & Company, 45–46
Oppenheimer, Elsbeth, 624
Oppenheimer, Sir Ernest, 594
Ortega y Gasset, José, 606
Orwell, George, 554
Ostjuden, 172–74, 233, 238
  see also Polish Jews; Russian Jews
Our Crowd (Birmingham), 46

Our War and Our Peace (James Warburg), 492
Overseas Study Syndicate, 152
Owen, Robert L., 136, 187
Oxford University, 426

"P." (Max's protector), 228–29
Pale of Settlement, 103, 290, 402
Palestine, 101, 122, 247–53, 292, 293, 296–304, 421, 518, 602
   Balfour Declaration and, 204, 247, 300, 303
   Jewish immigration to, 247, 299, 303, 389, 400, 402, 422, 436–37, 448–55, 465, 477, 604
   World War I and, 163, 165
Palestine Economic Corporation, 252, 389, 448
Palestine Emergency Fund, 301
Palestine Foundation Fund, 252
Palestine Liberation Organization, 695
Palestine Trading Society, 122
Palestine Trust Company (Paltreu), 400, 402, 434, 439, 443
Paley, William F., 339
Panofsky, Erwin, 256, 258, 263, 265, 405, 407, 408
Papen, Franz von, 368, 429
Paraná Project, 432
Pargesa, 703–4
Paribas, 698–700, 703
Passfield, Sidney Webb, Lord, 303
Pearl Assurance, 415
Pecora, Ferdinand, 386
Peel Commission, 452
Pennemünde, 539
Pennsylvania Railroad, 48, 88
Pétain, Philippe, 520, 529
Petersen, Hans W., 666, 678
Pferdemenges, Robert, 665
Philadelphia American, 134
Philadelphia North American, 138
Philby, Harry St. John, 302
Philipson, Eva Maria, *see* Warburg, Eva Maria Philipson
Philipson, Mauritz, 358, 359, 360, 411
Picasso, Pablo, 343
Pincus, Lionel, 660–62
Plaut, Max, 503–4
Pohle, Wolfgang, 660
Poland, 165, 173, 179, 485, 491, 504
Polaroid Corporation, 397–98, 579

Polish Jews, 98, 173, 174, 238, 246, 247, 253, 474, 603
Polk, Frank, 491
Popitz, Johannes von, 570
Portal, Lord, 648–51
Portugal, colonialism of, 151–52
Prag, Adolf, 512
Prag, Frede Warburg, 114, 116, 120–21, 205, 357, 512
Priess, Friedrich, 588
Project Hope, 339
Prokofiev, Sergei, 319
Propaganda Ministry, German, 407
Protocols of the Elders of Zion, The, 228, 234–35, 272, 442
Protopopov, Alexander, 178–79, 236, 272
Proust, Marcel, 405
Prudential insurance company, 415
Prussia, 21–22
Pueblo Indians, 59, 65–66, 261

Quinn, Susan, 346

Random House, 333
Rath, Ernst vom, 474–75
Rathenau, Walther, 225–30, 272, 362
Rawack & Grünfeld, 463–65, 549
Reading, Lord, 167, 169
Red Cross, 522, 524, 527, 574, 575
Redmond, George F., 129
Reemtsma, Gertrud, 720
Reform Jews, 16, 18, 46, 48
Refugee Children's Movement, 478
Refugee Economic Corporation, 389, 448
Regendanz, Wilhelm Charles, 144–47, 151, 152
Reich, Carey, 701
Reich Loan Consortium, 86, 378, 461–62, 466
Reich Representation of German Jews, 403, 433, 435, 438
Reichsbank, 25, 43, 130, 132, 169, 174, 178, 218, 233, 273, 274, 323, 326, 376, 377, 390, 434, 451, 479, 484, 503
Reichstag, 196, 197, 268, 270, 272, 273, 324, 329, 368, 369, 424
   anti-Semitism in, 40, 43, 172
Reid, Sir Edward, 650
Reimpell, Peter, 705
Reinhardt, Severin, 594

"Reminiscences from a Journey to the Pueblo Indians" (Aby M. Warburg), 261–62
Resistance, German, 426, 427, 471, 486, 494–97, 519–20, 528, 538, 570, 589, 590, 659
Resources of National Socialism (Schoup), 391
Resseguier, Count, 374, 536
Resseguier, Countess, 374, 536
Reusch, Paul, 472
Reynolds, Richard, 647, 648
Reynolds Metals, 647–51, 653
Rheinmetall, 658
Rhineland, 416, 490
Rhodesia, 682
Ribbentrop, Joachim von, 479
Richman, Julia, 99
Rickenbacker, Eddie, 619
Riga, 505
Rio Tinto, 556, 585, 587
Rittmeister, John, 591
Rittmeister, Wolfgang, 351, 572, 591
Rivera, Diego, 346
Roccamare, 680–81
Rockefeller, David, 673, 695, 709
Rockefeller, John D., Jr., 292, 295
Rockefeller, Mrs. Nelson, 339
Rockefeller, Nelson, 344, 602
Rockefeller, William, 88
Rockefeller Foundation, 540
Rödern, Count, 380–81
Rodgers, Dick, 317
Rogers, James Harvey, 393
Rohde, Alfred, 464, 572
Röhm, Ernst, 429
Roll, Sir Eric, 636, 651, 674, 683, 687–88
Romania, 151, 173
Romanian Jews, 174, 246
Rome, Aby M. in, 119, 125, 284, 285
Roosevelt, Anna, 384
Roosevelt, Archie, 183
Roosevelt, Eleanor, 160, 384, 495, 496, 497, 607
Roosevelt, Franklin, Jr., 601
Roosevelt, Franklin D., 160, 384–97, 446, 448, 478–79, 480
    World War II and, 486, 490, 491–92, 496, 519, 524
Roosevelt, James, Jr., 384
Roosevelt, Sara Delano, 393

Roosevelt, Theodore, 89, 100, 134–35, 140, 183
Rosanoff, Marie, 317
Rosen, Joseph, 289–90, 292, 294, 295–96
Rosenbacher, Richard, 466
Rosenbaum, Eduard, 667
Rosenberg, Alfred, 236
Rosenberg, James N., 292
Rosenberg, Marc, 362, 363
Rosenberg, Théophilie, *see* Warburg, Théophilie Rosenberg
Rosenwald, Julius, 165, 292, 295
Ross, Harold, 316
Ross, Sir Denison, 406
Rostropovich, Mstislav, 342
Rothkirch, Count Edwin von, 528, 655–56
Rothschild, Alain de, 472, 526–27
Rothschild, Anthony de, 326, 479, 480
Rothschild, Baron Alfred de, 32, 38
Rothschild, Baron Edmond de, 247, 252, 450
Rothschild, Baron Lionel de, 100, 350, 389, 412, 436, 480, 526
Rothschild, Baron Louis von, 326, 466
Rothschild, Baron Robert de, 489–90, 525–26
Rothschild, Carola Warburg, 91, 94–95, 149, 219, 240–43, 300, 301, 337, 338, 454, 455, 574, 601
Rothschild, Eliede, 526
Rothschild, Eric, 526
Rothschild, Meier Carl, 10
Rothschild, Walter, 219, 240, 326, 338, 342, 601
Rothschild, Willy, 10
N. M. Rothschild & Sons, 38, 350, 358, 413, 550, 584, 694
Rothschild family, 10, 38, 100, 412, 413, 437, 545, 645
    Warburg family compared with, xvi, 7, 56
Royal Air Force, 523, 524
Royal Navy, 151
Rublee, George, 479, 480, 485, 507
Ruhr, 225, 231, 273, 616
Ruppin, Arthur, 249
Russell, John, 287
Russia, Imperial, 108, 152
    Pale of Settlement in, 103, 290, 402

Russia, Imperial (cont'd)
  pogroms in, 97, 100–101, 106, 110,
    172, 173, 402
  World War I and, 153, 154, 166,
    173, 178–79
  see also Bolshevik Revolution
Russian Jews, 43, 164, 174, 238, 251,
    289–90, 603
  anti-Semitism and, 97, 100–101,
    106, 110, 167, 181, 290, 402
  U.S. immigration of, 97–98, 100
Russo-Japanese war, 110
Rykov, Alexei, 294, 295, 439

Sachs, Paul, 343
Sachsenhausen, 539
Sadat, Anwar, 695
St. Petersburg, Gunzburg bank in, 39
Salem school, 418, 420, 465, 590
Samson, Hermann, 429–30
Samson, Mattanja, 423
Samson, Renate Warburg, see Calder,
    Renate Warburg
Samson, Richard, 423
Samuel, Sir Herbert, 300, 437, 438, 450
Sander, Gottschalk, 17, 58
Sanders, August, 11–12
Sandweg, Hans-Dieter, 719, 720
Sarnoff, Robert, 601
Sassetti, Francesco, 116
Sauter, Otto, 409
Saxl, Fritz, 123–24, 175, 195, 206,
    255–56, 258–60, 262, 264, 283,
    287, 405, 406, 407, 511, 527
Schacht, Hjalmar, 274, 275, 276,
    322–23, 325, 366, 371, 403,
    485–86, 520, 538–39, 547, 664,
    676
  Max and, 155, 233–34, 323,
    376–78, 402, 430, 434–36, 438,
    439, 460–62
  refugee plan and, 479–80, 484
  U.S. visit of, 389–91
Schiff, David, 712
Schiff, Dorothy, 598, 617
Schiff, Edith Baker, 617
Schiff, Frieda, see Warburg, Frieda
    Schiff
Schiff, Gabriele Warburg, 83, 358, 424,
    710, 712
Schiff, Helene, 260
Schiff, Jacob, 46, 47, 48–54, 77,
    91–101, 112, 130, 132, 138,

    144, 181, 343, 474, 594, 598,
      614
    central bank and, 89, 134
    death of, 237–38
    disinheritance policy of, 185, 238,
      338
    Felix's relationship with, 53, 88, 91,
      93, 246
    Japanese link of, 110–11
    philanthropy of, 49, 98–101, 158
    religiosity of, 91, 238, 242, 314
    Roosevelt and, 89, 100
    World War I and, 157, 162–69,
      173–74, 181, 219–20
    Zionism and, 101, 248
Schiff, John, 394, 612–14, 617, 619,
    620, 621, 631, 669, 672
Schiff, Mortimer, 50, 168–69, 222,
    237, 238, 241, 309, 336, 457,
    617
Schiff, Otto, 50, 51
Schiff, Paul, 12, 260
Schiff, Therese Loeb, 46, 48, 50, 51,
    52, 54, 237, 241–42, 336, 341
Schilling, Hermann, 535, 570, 571,
    584–88, 664
Schinckel, Max von, 380
Schlabrendorff, Fabian von, 659–60
Schleicher, Kurt von, 368
Schlotterer, Gustab, 466
Schmidt, Helmut, 572, 655, 710
Scholey, Sir David, 645, 675, 690–91,
    704–8
Schoup, J. G., 391
Schramm, Percy, 116, 206
Schröder, Baron von, 371
Schröder, Rudolph von, 380
Schumacher, Fritz (architect), 120,
    194, 264
Schumacher, Fritz (economist), 426
Schuman, Robert, 616
Schutzhaftbefehle, 410
Schutzjuden, 4
Schutz-und-Trutz Bündnis, 217
Schutzvertrag, 4
Schwärz, Kathi, 444, 541, 591
Secker, Martin, 554
Secker & Warburg, 554
"Secret Kaiser, The" (Fritsch), 268,
    270
Seligman, Edwin R. A., 131, 137
Seligman, Geoffrey, 646–47, 686
Seligman, Guta Loeb, 55, 77

Seligman, Isaac Newton, 77
Seligman, Reginald, 646
Seligman, Spencer, 646
Seligman Brothers, 646, 647
Senate, U.S., 138–40, 187, 308, 386
Serenade (ballet), 345
Serkin, Rudolf, 405
Sharp, Charles, 572–73, 617, 683, 686, 687, 688
Shaw, George Bernard, 633
Sherman, A. Joshua, 667
Sherwood, Paul, 687
Shirer, William, 440
Sieff, Israel, 448
Sieff Institute, 448–49
Siemens, 468, 658
Siemens Bauunion, 659
Sieveking, Kurt, 404, 461, 475, 502, 592
Silver Train, 12
Simon Bank, 705
Siqueiros, David, 346
Six-Day War, 656, 693
Smith, Al, 238
Smith, Frank, 630, 653, 693
Sobibor, 506
Social Democrats, German, 198, 201, 209, 225, 270, 273, 370, 429–30
Solmitz, Robert, 503–5
South Africa, 70, 682
Soviet Jews, 289–90, 292–96, 366, 721
Soviet Union, 213, 363, 439, 553, 575, 582–83, 609
  Germany occupied by, 524–25, 535, 537, 538, 539
  World War II and, 485, 524–25, 547
  see also Bolshevik Revolution
Spa conference (1920), 225
Spanish Summer (Reinhardt), 594
Spartacists, 209–10, 218
Spengler, Oswald, 362
Spiegel, 594
Spiegelberg, Ernst, 309, 361, 414, 464–65, 469, 570, 571, 572, 585, 587, 610, 630
Spinelli, Ingrid Warburg, 83, 331, 425–28, 465, 493–99, 607, 715
  Trott and, 426, 427, 432, 493, 495–97, 520
Spinelli, Oliviero, 715
Spinelli, Veniero, 498–99, 519, 607

Spira, Peter, 644, 677, 684, 689–90, 691, 699
Spring-Rice, Sir Cecil, 161
Stalin, Joseph, 295–96, 439, 485, 490, 524
Stalingrad, battle of, 519
Standstill Agreement, 329
Stanislavsky, Konstantin, 298
State Department, U.S., 246, 292, 296, 388, 408, 446, 496, 694, 716
Stauffenberg, Claus Schenk von, 519–20, 659
Stedeford, Sir Ivan, 648, 649
Stein, General von, 172
Steinbrinck, Otto, 466
Steiner, George, 287, 701
Steinmetz, Hermine, 53
Sterling, Sir Louis, 415
Stern, Fritz, 22
Stern, 595
Stevenson, Adlai, 580, 582, 604, 716
Still Hell Bent (James Warburg), 397
Stillman, James A., 89–90, 131
Stinnes, Edmund, 409, 411, 414, 560
Stinnes, Hugo, Jr., 409
Stinnes, Hugo, Sr., 225, 227, 409
Stockholms Enskilda Bank, 112
Stockholms Handelsbank, 43, 112
Stoecker, Adolf, 25
Stracke, Hans, 719–20
Strasbourg, anti-Semitism in, 61
Straus, Florence, 317
Strauss, Lewis, 490
Strauss, Renate Warburg, *see* Calder, Renate Warburg
Strauss, Walter, 423
Stravinsky, Igor, 346
Streicher, Julius, 273
"Strength Through Joy," 374
Stresemann, Gustav, 218, 232, 275, 282, 284, 311, 322, 362
Strong, Ben, 158
Strousberg, Bethel Henry, 25
Stürmer, 273, 375, 429, 443, 446, 474, 501, 584
Sullivan & Cromwell, 350
Sunday Telegraph (London), 637
Sunday Times (London), 653, 681
Svenska Handelsbanken, 358, 411
Swatland, Donald C., 490, 616
Sweden, 178, 411, 542
Swift, Ellen, 185

Swift, Katharine Faulkner, see Warburg, Katharine Faulkner Swift
Switzerland, 682–83, 686, 700–701, 702, 705, 719
Swope, Herbert Bayard, 316
Szold, Henrietta, 422, 477

Taft, Robert A., 490
Taft, William Howard, 144, 223
Takahashi, Korekiyo, 110, 111, 442
Takahashi, Wakiko, 111, 166
Talmud Torah School, 122, 148
Tarnower, Herman, 599
Taussig, Charles, 384
Taylor, Telford, 465, 576
Teheran summit, 524
"Terraces, The," 95
Thalmann, Ernest, 572, 641–42, 686
Thatcher, Margaret, 681, 701
Theresienstadt, 505, 529, 537
3rd Bavarian Light Cavalry Regiment, 37–38
Thoennes, Hildegard, 720
Thomas amendment, 386–87
Thomson, Roy, 653
Thorsch, Dorothea, see Warburg, Dorothea Thorsch
Thorsch, Eva, 567
Thyssen, Fritz, 366, 616
August Thyssen steelworks, 577, 616
Tiefenbacher, Clarita, 496
Time, 586
Times (London), 235, 470, 561, 650, 651, 667, 678, 680, 694–95
Tirpitz, Alfred von, 107, 151
Tonio Kröger (Mann), 75
Toscanini, Arturo, 92
Trading with the Enemy Act, 568
Trading with the Enemy Department, British, 534, 571
Treasury, British, 161, 162
Treasury, German, 210
Treasury Department, U.S., 161, 162, 182, 223
Tropical Hygiene Institute, 142
Trotsky, Leon, 235
Trott zu Solz, Adam von, 426, 427, 432, 493, 495–97, 519–20
Truman, Harry S, 582, 602, 607
Tube Investments Ltd. (TI), 648–51
Tugwell, Rexford, 384, 396–97

Tumulty, Joe, 188
Turkey, 163, 165, 247

Ukraine, 247, 289, 292, 294
Union Pacific, 48
United Jewish Appeal (UJA), 602–5, 694
United Palestine Appeal (UPA), 602
United States, 144, 224, 389
  anti-German sentiment in, 156, 157, 158, 160, 181
  anti-Semitism in, 93, 98, 234–35, 242, 272, 492–93, 494, 513–14
  banking crisis in, 384, 385
  central bank of, 86, 88–90; see also Federal Reserve Board; Federal Reserve System
  gold standard abandoned by, 386–87
  World War I and, 156, 157, 160, 162, 167, 173, 180–83, 195
  World War II and, 490–93, 520–32
  see also American Jews; New York Jews
Unser Kreis, 46
Untermyer, Samuel, 430, 435–36
Utiger, Ronald, 653

Vagts, Alfred, 363
Vanderlip, Frank, 134
Venice, 125
Verey, Michael, 649, 653, 682
Versailles Treaty, 167, 199, 209–18, 220, 225, 228, 232, 235, 247, 271, 326, 391, 490, 575
Veth, Jan, 19–20
Vinci, Leonardo da, 64, 113
Visiting Nurse Service, 99, 246
Vissering, Gerard, 222
Vogel, Hugo, 126
Vogt, Emil, 25
Völkischer Beobachter, 236, 407
Volkswagen, 571
Vossiche Zeitung, 233
Vuyk, Pieter, 152

Waetzoldt, Wilhelm, 123
Wagner, Richard, 46
Wainside, 631
Wald, Lillian, 55, 99, 100, 246
Waldpark Sanatorium, 127, 194
Walker, John, III, 342
Wallenberg, Knut, 178
Wallenberg family, 412, 467
Wall Street Journal, 139
Wall Street Money Trust, 134

Warburg, 3–5, 532
Warburg, Aby M., 26–30, 45, 57–58,
    60–68, 82, 113–27, 193, 257,
    258–66, *278*, 279–88, *320*, 362,
    404–8, 562, 593, 709, 722
  as ambivalent Jew, 60, 61, 121–22,
    123, 194–95, 204–5
  in American Southwest, 59, 64–66,
    261
  anti-Semitism experienced by, 61,
    122, 204
  as art historian, 60–64, 113, 116,
    119, 121, 125, 126, 204–5, 258,
    265, 281, 282–85, 287, 343
  astrology studies of, 120, 195, 264,
    282
  autocratic behavior of, 123, 125–26,
    256, 282
  banking partnership rejected by,
    29–30, 60
  book collecting and library of, 30,
    63–64, 117, 120–25, 175–76,
    194, 195, 206, 256, 263–66; *see
    also* Warburg Library
  death of, 286–88, 311, 608
  diary of, 114, 123, 261, 287
  as father, 114, 116, 120–21,
    280–81
  father's death and, 123
  financial dependency of, 62–63, 117,
    118, 125–26, 194, 205
  health of, 28, 30, 58, 119, 284–85
  lectures of, 118, 119, 124–25,
    260–64, 282, 284–85
  marriage of, 62, 66–68, 113–14,
    115
  mental instability and depression of,
    65, 114, 120–21, 126–27,
    174–77, 194, 203–6, 255, 256,
    258–63, 312, 512
  Paul compared with, 40, 131
  perfectionism of, 118–19, 125, 255
  practical jokes of, 58, 60
  publications of, 119, 287
  spiritual autobiography of, 119–20
  temper of, 28, 58, 116, 120–21
  typhoid fever of, 28, 30, 58
  World War I and, 174–77, 192,
    194–96, 203–6, 408
Warburg, Aby S., 16, 30, 31, 82, 154,
    172, 195, 231, 368, 404
  in M. M. Warburg & Co., 32, 41–42,
    110, 150, 329, 356

Warburg, Aby Samuel (Sarah's
    husband), 7–12, 536
Warburg, Albert, 505–6
Warburg, Alexa Chrambach, 722
Warburg, Alice Magnus, 73–76, 83,
    105, 114, 143, 148, 151, 192,
    202, 227, 258, 297, 299,
    324–25, 432, 485
  assassination plot and, 228, 229
  Eric's marriage and, 566–67
  Max's correspondence with, 213,
    215
  as mother, 74–76, 351, 424
  Nazis and, 371, 392–93
  in U.S., 472, 474, 475, 513, 514,
    518–19, 562, 574, 596, 599–600
Warburg, Andrea, 317, 333, 395, 396
Warburg, Anita, *see* Wolf, Anita
    Warburg
Warburg, Anna, *see* Biegun, Anna
    Warburg
Warburg, Anna Beata, 82–83, 178,
    279–80, 359, 425, 426, 470,
    474, 476, 499, 562, 580, 607–8
Warburg, April, 317, 333, 395
Warburg, Bettina, *see* Grimson, Bettina
    Warburg
Warburg, Betty, 506
Warburg, Carola, *see* Rothschild, Carola
    Warburg
Warburg, Charles (Karl), 42
Warburg, Charlotte Esther (Noni), 83,
    425, 607
Warburg, Charlotte Oppenheim, 15,
    18–20, 23, 26–31, 45, 50, 61,
    72, 83, 111, 536
  Aby M.'s correspondence with, 127,
    175
  children's marriages and, 52, 53, 62,
    68
  death of, 219, 279
  husband's death and, 123, 149
  memoirs of, 23, 122
  as mother, 26–30, 123
  nationalism of, 22, 24
  Olga's suicide and, 79, 149
  typhus of, 28–29, 58, 64
  Wilson's letter from, 180–81
Warburg (Astor), Daphne, 601
Warburg, Dorothea Thorsch, 566–67,
    583, 589–93, 720
Warburg, Edward, 91, 93–97, 238,
    280, 282, 335–36, 339–47, 384,

Warburg, Edward (cont'd)
  408, 455, 471, 514, 600–601,
  605, 718
  American Ballet and, 344–46
  art world and, 342–44, 404, 456
  Joint and, 456, 513, 526, 576,
    602–3
  marriage of, 456–57
  psychoanalysis of, 346–47
  World War II and, 522, 525, 526
Warburg, Elias Simon, 7, 8
Warburg, Ellen Josephson, 82
Warburg, Ellie Bozyan, 630–31
Warburg, Elly Simon, 41, 42
Warburg, Elsa, *see* Melchior, Elsa
  Warburg
Warburg, Emil, 539
Warburg, Eric, 74–76, 111, 286, 309,
  331, 349–52, 367, 412, 425,
  435, 485, *488*, 489–90, 508,
  517, 534–42, 559–62, 564,
  566–77, 582–95, 599–600,
  606, 607, 618, 655–68, 656,
  711
  father's correspondence with, 108,
    214
  Jewish refugees and, 439, 489
  Nazis and, 232, 366, 368, 369, 371,
    379, 387, 444, 471–72, 490,
    522, 538
  personality of, 192, 350–51
  postwar attitudes of, 518, 587–89
  in postwar Germany, 531–32,
    534–39, 587–95, 709–12,
    717–21
  Siegmund's rivalry with, 357–58,
    359–62, 568–69, 583, 586–87,
    619–20, 661–64
  as U.S. resident, 350, 371, 471, 474,
    475
  at M. M. Warburg & Co., 351–52,
    357–58, 361, 469
  Warburg Library and, 406, 407–8,
    592–93
  World War I and, 154, 191–92,
    199, 201
  World War II and, 485, 490, 515,
    522–30, 566
Warburg, Erica, 567, 590–91, 717
Warburg, Eva, 83, 425, 607
Warburg, Eva Maria Philipson,
  358–61, 401, 409, 476–77,
  480–84, 545, 546, 610, 623–34,

  624, 642, 647, 671, 676, 677,
    678, 680–83, 696, 702
  cancer of, 361, 411, 627, 706
  marriage of, *348*, 359–60
Warburg (Sarnoff/Roosevelt), Felicia,
  601
Warburg, Felix M., 26–29, 32, 47, 64,
  74, 90–101, 125, 147, 189, 194,
  212, 219, 224, 239, 240–47,
  258, 268, 269, 285, 286, 287,
  291, 311, 320, 368, 384, 387,
  431, 438–40, 445–57, 494,
  506–7, 514
  Aby M.'s correspondence with,
    122–23
  bank partnership of, 162, 181, 325,
    327, 328, 331, 332
  buoyant spirit of, 45, 91, 240
  Eddie's art interests and, 343–44
  as father, 94, 95, 240, 241–42,
    244–45, 336, 338–42, 346
  intermarriage and, 185, 340–41
  Jacob Schiff's relationship with, 53,
    88, 91, 93, 246
  Jewish refugees and, 388–89, 402,
    446, 448–55
  Joint Distribution Committee and,
    159, 164–65, 174, 440, 446,
    448, 461
  as Kuhn, Loeb partner, 52, 53, 85,
    86, 92, 93, 97, 241, 246, 360,
    445, 456, 612
  lifestyle of, 90–96, 240, 241
  marriage of, 46, 49–53, 56, 57
  Max's reunion with, 229–30
  mistresses of, 243, 455
  musical interests of, 46, 92, 244–45,
    389, 447
  Nazis and, 236, 324, 325, 369,
    371–72, 373, 375, 388, 405,
    430, 442, 446, 474
  Paul compared with, 54, 90, 220, 305
  in pearl and diamond business,
    45–46
  philanthropy of, 49, 90, 97–100,
    162–65, 238, 245–47, 249–53,
    256, 289–90, 292–96, 446, 456,
    597–98
  Schiff connection of, 46–53
  U.S. citizenship of, 86
  Warburg Library and, 407–8
  World War I and, 162–65, 169,
    182, 186, 195

Zionism and, 247, 249–53,
  296–304, 448–55, 604–5
Warburg, Frede, *see* Prag, Frede
  Warburg
Warburg, Frederick, 47, 91, 94–96,
  186, 241–43, 314, 332, 384,
  388, 456, 457, 522, 528, 583,
  597, 669
  fragmented identity of, 335–36, 338,
  618
  marriage of, 240, 338, 599
Warburg, Fredric, 553–54
Warburg, Frieda Schiff, 40, 46, 49–54,
  90–96, 157, 162, 230, 237, 239,
  240–43, 258, 268, 285, 293,
  327, 330, 344, 384, 449, 489,
  494, 496, 498, 518, 520, 566,
  567, 596, 619
  charity of, 90, 98, 99, 238, 246,
  338, 597–98, 600, 602
  deafness of, 92, 94, 242
  husband's death and, 455–57, 514,
  597
  intermarriage and, 185, 340–41,
  456–57, 599
  Jewish refugees and, 388–89
  last years and death of, 590, 597–600
  as mother, 74, 94–95, 96, 241–42,
  243, 245, 313, 339–42, 417
  wedding and honeymoon of, 52–53,
  64
  Zionism and, 250, 251, 296, 299,
  301, 457
Warburg, Fritz M., 26–30, 32, 80–83,
  127, 256, 265, 279–80, 286, 309,
  320, 359, 412, 424–26, 470,
  472, 474, 499, 558, 562, 573–74,
  575, 580, 585, 586, 609, 610
  as bank partner, 30, 81–82, 150,
  279, 467, 469
  emigration of, 476–77
  as father, 83, 493
  Jewish community role of, 81, 279,
  476
  Karstadt and, 325–26
  last years and death of, 606–8
  Nazis and, 179, 290, 321, 427,
  475–77
  Protopopov talks and, 178–79, 236,
  272
Warburg, George S., 360, 361, 413,
  480, 482, 544, 545, 551,
  628–32, 691–92, 693, 704
Warburg, Georges, 30–31, 352–54,
  356–57, 706
Warburg, Gerald, 91, 94–95, 240,
  243–45, 339–42, 456, 574
  fragmented identity of, 335–36, 338
  musical passion of, 244–45, 340,
  341–42
Warburg, Geraldine, 341
Warburg, Gerson, 5–7, 12
Warburg, Gerta, 506
Warburg, Gisela, *see* Wyzanski, Gisela
  Warburg
Warburg, Gumprich Marcus, 5, 6
Warburg, Heilwig, 510, 511
Warburg, Ingrid, *see* Spinelli, Ingrid
  Warburg
Warburg, Iris, 510, 511
Warburg, Jacob Simon, 4
Warburg, James, Jr., 717
Warburg, James, Sr., 69, 78, 96, 148,
  170, 182–85, 274, 285–86, 307,
  308, 311–19, 328, 360, 383–98,
  412, 516, 517, 518, 561, 578,
  579–82, 594, 603–6, 652,
  715–17
  bank jobs of, 314, 315, 326–33,
  383–84, 397, 506–7
  father's death and, 330, 331
  Hoover offer turned down by,
  314–15
  Kuhn, Loeb and, 183–84, 309,
  332–33
  marriages of, 184–85, 314, 316–19,
  333–34, 395–96, 580–81, 603
  Nazis and, 321, 324, 325, 363, 369,
  371, 379, 387–93, 411, 490–93,
  519
  New Deal work of, 385–87
  poetry writing of, 306, 315–16, 331
  psychoanalysis of, 333, 334, 397,
  637
  religious background of, 90–91, 314,
  603, 604
  Schacht and, 234, 389–91
  World Economic Conference and,
  382, 384, 391–92
  World War I and, 160, 182–85,
  191–92, 492–93
  World War II and, 490–93, 519,
  520–21
  Zionism and, 603–5
Warburg, Jean Stettheimer, 339
Warburg, Jenny, 8

Warburg, Joan Melber, 580–81, 716
Warburg, Josepha Spiero (Josi), 510–11
Warburg, Juspa-Joseph, 5
Warburg, Karl (Charles), 357, 363,
    404, 560, 561
Warburg, Katharine Faulkner Swift
    (Kay), 184–85, 244, 280, 307,
    315–19, 328, 345, 395
  Gershwin's affair with, 317–19, 333,
    334
  psychoanalysis of, 333–34, 346, 347
Warburg, Kay, 317, 333, 395, 396
Warburg, Lilly, 352, 361
Warburg, Lola, see Hahn-Warburg, Lola
Warburg, Louise, see Derenberg, Louise
    Warburg
Warburg, Lucie Kaulla, 352–57, 359,
    409–10, 483–84, 545, 546,
    623–24, 631, 645
Warburg, Lux, 510
Warburg, Malchen, see Goldschmidt,
    Malchen Warburg
Warburg, Marianne, 8, 9–10, 31, 79
Warburg, Marie, 567, 590–91, 717
Warburg, Marietta, see Braden,
    Marietta Warburg
Warburg, Marion Bab, 245, 340
Warburg, Mary Hertz, 120, 176, 204,
    205, 264, 283–87, 405, 407
  marriage of, 62, 66–68, 113–14,
    115
  as mother, 116, 258, 280
Warburg, Mary Whelan Currier,
    456–57
Warburg, Max (Eric's son), 567,
    590–91, 663, 717–22
Warburg, Max Adolph, 114, 116,
    120–21, 193, 205, 408, 425,
    509–12
  father's breakdown and, 205–6, 262,
    280–81
  psychological problems of, 206,
    511–12
Warburg, Max M., 9, 26–30, 37–40,
    45, 51, 52, 63, 68–70, 74, 77,
    78, 86, 102, 103–12, 114,
    117–19, 140–56, 143, 196, 221,
    222, 224–37, 245, 246, 256,
    269, 286, 296, 309, 311, 320,
    321–32, 349–52, 431, 432, 455,
    458, 485, 499, 506–7, 508,
    516–19, 536, 553, 559–63,
    566–70, 585, 638

  on Aby M., 60, 264
  Aby M.'s book collecting and, 30,
    117
  anti-Semitism experienced by, 106,
    110, 267, 268, 270–71, 365–66,
    378–81, 443
  assassination plot and threats
    against, 228–30, 233, 272
  Ballin and, 103–9, 112, 150–51,
    153, 201, 202, 211
  as bank partner, 30, 32, 38, 40,
    42–43, 56, 69–70, 112, 141–42,
    144–47, 149–50, 152, 226, 231,
    325–29, 332, 356, 361–62,
    375–79, 411–14, 433, 466–70,
    535
  in cavalry, 34, 37–38
  Eric's relationship with, 192, 471,
    521–22
  as father, 75, 76, 297–98, 303,
    424
  Fritsch lawsuit of, 235–36, 268,
    270–71
  German patriotism of, 106, 141–42,
    150, 213–14, 219–20, 297, 322,
    371, 399, 417, 424–25, 432–33
  as Jewish leader, 29, 43, 73–74,
    148, 267, 322, 399–400, 402–3,
    429–30, 432, 433, 436–42,
    459–60
  Jewish observance and, 74, 122,
    123, 399
  Jewish refugees and, 399–400,
    402–3, 436–37, 441, 472, 474,
    477, 480
  Kösterberg and, 72, 147–49, 399,
    516
  marriage of, 72–73
  memoirs of, 443, 516–18, 537, 593
  Nazis and, 216, 217, 236, 267, 290,
    363, 365–66, 368–81, 387, 388,
    392–93, 400, 411–14, 416, 422,
    429–30, 432–39, 448, 460–63,
    466–70, 474, 475, 514, 516–18
  Paul compared with, 42, 70, 190,
    275
  Schacht and, 155, 233–34, 323,
    376–78, 402, 430, 434–36, 438,
    439, 460–62
  Siegmund's relationship with, 356,
    361–62, 412–13, 559–60
  U.S. trips of, 166, 229–30, 404, 430,
    472, 474, 475

Versailles Treaty and, 167, 199,
210–18, 235, 391, 429
Warburg Library and, 265, 406–8
Weimar economic revival and,
274–75
Wilhelm II and, 106–9, 145,
152–53, 197
World War I and, 152–56, 160–61,
166–69, 171–74, 178–82,
196–203
World War II and, 485, 513–14,
516
Zionism and, 248, 297–99, 300,
303, 322, 399, 422, 436–37,
518
Warburg, Moritz, 8, 12–20, 23, 24,
26–30, 37–43, 45, 69, 74, 86,
105, 121, 150, 356, 474, 536,
638
Aby M. and, 61, 62, 67–68
country house of, 70, 72, 148
death of, 123, 147
Jacob Schiff and, 50–51, 52
Jewish observance and, 16, 17–18,
27, 67–68, 122
philanthropy of, 43, 122
Warburg, Moses Marcus, 5–8, 12
Warburg (Nast), Natica, 340–42
Warburg, Nina Loeb, 52–56, 69, 73,
77, 78, 80, 90, 96, 160, 170,
184, 189, 268, 306, 308, 327,
383, 498–99, 514, 516, 518,
537, 580, 596
as ambivalent Jew, 90, 314
death of, 598
in Hamburg, 53–54, 69, 85, 86
handicap of, 55–56, 69, 96
husband's death and, 330, 331
in Kösterberg, 72, 90
marriage of, 53–54, 56
as mother, 312–13, 385
son's marriage and, 184–85
Warburg (Kohn-Speyer), Olga, 26, 29,
52, 68, 71, 76–79, 81, 149, 350,
555
Warburg (Lachmann), Olga, 41, 509,
632
Warburg, Olga Lucie Leonine, 41
Warburg (Calder), Olga Renate, 74, 75,
76, 79, 297, 356, 417, 423, 424,
568, 600
Warburg, Otto (biochemist), 539–41
Warburg, Otto (botanist), 252, 539

Warburg, Paul Felix (Piggy), 91,
94–95, 240, 241–42, 332,
335–36, 338–39, 343, 350, 519,
619
philanthropy of, 339, 456
World War II and, 522, 523, 526
Warburg, Paul M., 26–29, 32, 40–43,
45, 52–54, 69–70, 72, 73, 87,
88, 96, 125, 128, 129–40, 144,
147, 170, 194, 222–24, 235,
249, 268, 271, 273, 286, 305–6,
320, 325–32, 350, 351, 390,
391, 408, 429, 506–7
in *Bürgerschaft*, 85–86, 109
central bank crusade of, 86, 88–90,
130–40
estate of, 385, 405
as father, 306, 308, 312–16
Federal Reserve Board and, 137–40,
158, 160, 161–62, 186–89, 235,
271, 308–11, 384, 385, 474, 594
Felix compared with, 54, 90, 220,
305
German sentimentality of, 158, 160,
220, 222
IAB and, 224, 231, 274, 309, 310,
315, 360
in Kuhn, Loeb, 86, 88, 89, 129,
132, 138, 139–40, 142, 612
marriage of, 53–54, 56, 57, 64, 65
Max compared with, 42, 70, 190,
275
Nazis and, 236, 324, 325, 474
philanthropy of, 77, 129–30, 256,
306
prophetic gifts of, 131, 223–24,
308–11, 385
son's relationship with, 182–85,
187, 314–16
U.S. citizenship of, 86, 134, 138,
158, 160
in M. M. Warburg & Co., 40, 41, 45,
69, 70, 86, 138, 150, 325,
327–28, 356
World War I and, 156, 158,
160–62, 167, 175, 180–90, 195
Warburg, Phyllis Baldwin, 395–97,
580
Warburg, Pius, 73
Warburg, Renate, *see* Calder, Renate
Warburg
Warburg, Rosa, 7
Warburg (Schiff), Rosa, 8, 12, 41, 260

Warburg, Sara, 2, 7–14, 16–17,
    18–19, 25, 31–32, 356, 536
Warburg, Siegmund, 8, 10–20, 22, 24,
    25, 26, 32, 58, 384, 356, 547
Warburg, Siegmund George, 232, 329,
    332, 349, 351–64, 368, 401,
    409–16, 480–86, 506, 518–19,
    545–54, 556–61, 568–74,
    583–87, 609–54, 611, 625, 640,
    661–67, 669–708, 671, 684, 696,
    714, 718–19, 723–25
  Danilova and, 481–83, 619
  emigration of, 410–13
  Eric's rivalry with, 357–58, 559–62,
    568–69, 583, 586–87, 619–20,
    661–64
  as father, 628–32, 691–92
  intellectualism of, 356, 362–63,
    632–33, 700–701
  Jewish refugees and, 438–39
  knighting of, 682
  Kuhn, Loeb and, 360–61, 583,
    612–22, 647–48, 669–70, 672,
    699–700
  marriage of, 348, 359–60
  Nazis and, 363–64, 369, 392,
    409–11, 415, 416, 442–43, 480,
    483–84
  New Trading and, 412–15, 545,
    547–53, 559–61, 620
  perfectionism of, 13, 354, 355–56,
    552, 626–27, 630, 641
  postwar attitudes of, 518, 589
  postwar Germany visited by, 572–74,
    664
  M. M. Warburg & Co. and, 351, 356,
    361, 413
  World War II and, 416, 485, 544,
    547
  Zionism and, 692–95
Warburg, Théophilie Rosenberg,
    14–16, 19, 22, 24, 30–31, 32, 41,
    45, 352
Warburg, Wilma Shannon, 338
Warburg & Company, 309, 325, 332,
    412, 415, 506–8
W. S. Warburg, 505
E. M. Warburg, Pincus & Company,
    662
E. M. Warburg & Co., 489, 509, 514,
    566–68, 571, 583, 660–62
M. M. Warburg & Co., 5–6, 8, 11–15,
    18, 24, 39, 41, 86, 155, 224,

    270, 273, 275, 277, 322, 359,
    400, 561, 661–65
  Aby S. in, 32, 41–42, 110, 150,
    329, 356
  Aryanization of, 466–70, 501–3,
    585
  bail-out attempt of, 325–29, 384
  board seats lost by, 378–81, 433,
    461
  board seats policy of, 105–6
  Bolsheviks and, 234–36
  colonialism and, 141–42, 144–47,
    152
  Depression and, 311, 325–29
  Eric at, 351–52, 357–58, 361, 469
  Felix and, 162, 181, 325, 327, 328,
    331, 332
  foreign investment companies of,
    233, 411–14
  Fritz and, 331–32
  inflation and, 231–32
  Jimmy's investigation of, 326–28
  Kuhn, Loeb and, 51, 56, 86,
    110–11
  Max as partner in, 30, 32, 38, 40,
    42–43, 56, 69–70, 112, 141–42,
    144–47, 149–50, 152, 226, 231,
    325–29, 332, 356, 361–62,
    375–79, 411–14, 433, 466–70,
    535
  Melchior as partner of, 211, 358
  in Nazi Germany, 3, 375–81, 393,
    404, 433, 442–43, 460–70,
    501–3, 506
  Paul in, 40, 41, 45, 69, 70, 86, 138,
    150, 325, 327–28, 356
  Rothschild connection with, 10, 11
  Sara's running of, 11–13
  Siegmund (grandfather) at, 12–14,
    22, 24, 356
  Siegmund (grandson) at, 351, 356,
    361, 413
  World War I and, 155, 156, 166,
    173, 174
S. G. Warburg & Company, 548,
    554–61, 571, 609–10, 613, 616,
    624, 630–36, 641–48, 650,
    661–62, 672–83, 689–91, 693,
    694, 697–700, 702–5, 707–8,
    719
  Euromarkets and, 622, 674–80
  Kuhn, Loeb's friction with, 669–70,
    672

M. M. Warburg-Brinckmann, Wirtz & Co., 718–20
Warburg Continuation, 610, 662
Warburg Institute, 722
Warburg Investment Management, 698
Warburg Library, 264–66, 282, 283, 285–87, 352, 405–8, 527, 592–93
Warburg Paribas Becker, 699–700
Warburg Secretariat, 500, 503–4, 505
War Finance Corporation, 187
War Metals Company, 178
War Ministry, German, 172
Warren, George, 393–94
Washington, Booker T., 306
Wasserman, Doris, 639, 687, 702, 705–6
Wassermann, Jakob, ix
Waugh, Evelyn, 683
Weber, Nicholas Fox, 342
Weimar Assembly, 218
Weinberg, Sidney, 455
Weismann, Dietrich, 688
Weismann, Robert, 676
Weiss, Bernhard, 369
Weizmann, Chaim, ix, 43–44, 108–9, 227, 239, 247–53, 292, 293, 296–300, 303, 372, 402, 418, 421, 436–37, 448–55, 457, 518, 598, 602, 692–93, 713
Weizmann, Vera, 239, 247, 249, 250, 298, 299, 303, 421, 449
Weizsäcker, Richard von, 720
Wender, Ira, 691, 700, 703–4
Wenzel, Gertrud, 506
Werfel, Franz, 497
Wertheim & Gomperz, 37
Wethling, Minna, 443–44
Wheeler, Burton K., 490
White Weld, 690
Whitman, Gert, 675–79
Whitman, Gretchen, 676, 677, 678
"Who Is Responsible for the Defeat?" (Fritsch), 270
Wiggin, Albert, 324
Wilhelm I, Kaiser of Germany, 21, 22, 35
Wilhelm II, Kaiser of Germany, 21, 35, 104, 142, 144–46, 210
  Anglo-German relations and, 150, 151, 197

Max's relationship with, 106–9, 145, 152–53, 197
  World War I and, 179, 180, 186, 188, 197, 201, 202
Kaiser Wilhelm Institute, 540
Wilkie, Wendell, 491
Williams and Glyn's Bank, 692
Wilson, Harold, 634, 681–82
Wilson, Woodrow, 135–36, 138, 139, 162, 186, 188–89, 213–14, 216, 223, 306
  World War I and, 165, 166, 167, 180–81, 198
Winchell, Walter, 388
Winsor, Robert, 313
Winspear, Arthur, 643
Winterton, Lord, 479, 480
Wirth, Josef, 226–27
Wirtz, Paul, 468, 469, 534–36, 562, 569
Wise, Stephen S., 293, 295, 387, 402, 438, 448
Wiseman, Sir William, 612–13, 618, 621, 647–48
Wissenschaftliche Stiftung, 118
Wohltat, Helmuth, 485, 507
Wolf, Anita Warburg, 74, 75, 76, 299, 350, 417, 423–24, 477, 478, 519, 524, 568, 574, 713
Wolf, Max, 424, 519, 574
Wolfensohn, James, 691
Wolff, Theodor, 228
Woodlands, 95–96, 99, 148, 230, 240, 241, 345, 350, 384, 494, 513, 567, 590, 600
Workers' and Soldiers' Council, 200, 202–3
World Economic Conference (1933), 382, 384, 391–92
World Jewish Organization, 449
World War I, 126, 127, 140, 152–204, 353–54, 408, 492–93
World War II, 416, 485–86, 489–99, 519–32, 550–51, 588, 623
World Zionist Organization, 247, 252
Wuttke, Hans, 665, 666
Wyzanski, Charles E., Jr., 519, 574
Wyzanski, Gisela Warburg, 74, 75, 258–59, 265, 417, 421–23, 468–69, 472, 475, 478, 516, 568, 574, 712–13
  education of, 76, 122, 297, 331, 426

Wyzanski, Gisela Warburg (*cont'd*)
　marriage of, 519
　Nazis and, 370, 375, 474
　Zionism and, 297, 299

Yom Kippur War, 693
Young Conference (1929), 322–23
Young Plan, 286, 323, 324, 363
Young Women's Hebrew Association,
　246
Youth Aliyah, 297, 422, 465, 468, 477

Zagury, Samuel, 9–10, 11, 31, 79
Ziegler, Paul, 634

Zilboorg, Gregory, 333–34, 346–47,
　396
Zimmermann, Arthur, 110, 145,
　180
Zionism, 101, 121, 122, 173, 174,
　204, 247–54, 293, 295–304, 399,
　421, 448–55, 594, 602–6,
　692–95
　German Jews and, 296–301, 322,
　399, 402, 417–18, 440
Zionist Congress (1909), 106
Zionist Organization, 451
Zweig, Stefan, 362–63, 415–16, 485,
　547